Footprint

Brazil Handbook

Ben Box, Jane Egginton and Mick Day

*Oh God, if there were a paradise on earth,
it wouldn't be far from here!*

Amerigo Vespucci

3rd edition

Brazil Highlights

1 Iguaçu Falls
These mighty falls lie in a scenic area on the border with Argentina

2 Praia do Forte
A charming village with just three sand streets, palm-fringed beaches and a turtle sanctuary

3 Salvador
Brazil's party city is a World Heritage Site with colonial architecture and African soul

4 The Amazon
The river and the jungle offer a once-in-a-lifetime experience

5 Morro de São Paulo
A pretty island with secluded beaches and lively nightlife

6 Santa Catarina
An island with a beach to suit everyone; a favourite spot for many visitors

7 Olinda
Colonial heritage and exquisite historic hotels; an atmospheric and relaxing highlight

8 Pantanal
The world's largest wetlands has bird and wildlife safaris by horse and by jeep

9 Dunes at Genipabu
A spectacular landscape of soaring sand dunes which can be 'surfed' or explored by camel

See colour maps at back of book

10 Petrópolis
A cool mountain retreat and South America's only Imperial city

11 Fernando do Noronha
Accessible only by plane, this island really is a diver's and beach lover's paradise

12 Paraty
Colourful colonial buildings, sailing trips around the bay and a trek along an ancient gold trail

13 Ouro Preto
Brazil's colonial capital has the best examples of baroque art and architecture

14 Chapada Diamantina
Biking, trekking and horse riding are the best ways to enjoy this national park

15 Chapada dos Guimarães
This ancient plateau studded with caves, canyons and waterfalls is little visited and great for bird-watching

16 Rio Grande do Sul
Gaúcho country, home to swaggering cowboys and enormous steaks

17 Pernambuco
Music and dance will permeate any trip to Brazil; join in the party at one of Pernambuco's distinctive festivals

Contents

The Amazon

Fortaleza & the
North Coast

Recife & the
Northeast Coast

Bahia

Brasília &
the Pantanal

Minas Gerais &
Espírito Santo

Rio de Janeiro
São Paulo

Iguaçu Falls
& the South

A foot in the door

The lights of Avenida Paulista (right) at dusk illuminate
the skyline of São Paulo, the largest city in South America
Ouro Preto (below). The riches of a gold mining past are
reflected in the colonial architecture and lavishly
decorated churches

Igreja do Rosária dos Pretos (above), at the
bottom of Largo do Pelourinho, in Salvador, was
built by slaves brought from Africa
Modern cathedral in Brasília (right). Angels
hang from the stained-glass ceiling
Copacabana Beach (previous page). A fruity
parade at the world's most famous carnival

Introducing Brazil

Brazil is a haven for hedonists and wherever you are the country will seduce you. Brazilians seem to move to a rhythm all of their own, whether swinging their hips to an impromptu samba session or simply smiling in the street. They know how to hold a party too, and the biggest of them all is Carnival. In fact the year doesn't really begin until after this ultimate outbreak of hedonism in February or March when people can indulge their fantasies and forget the reality of their daily lives.

The rainforests of the Amazon and the wetlands of the Pantanal – home to a wide variety of plants, animals and birds – provide memorable safaris. National parks in the rugged interior offer breathtaking views from mountain peaks as well as many opportunities for adventure sports. Deserted beaches and dunes on the seemingly endless coast can still be enjoyed in all the tranquillity of their natural state.

This giant of Latin America embraces diversity in its landscapes, people and culture, which goes way beyond the stereotypical images of samba, colonial churches, Copacabana and the concrete jungles. In the tourist capital, Rio de Janeiro, beautifully situated between the mountains and the sea, life revolves around the beach and the world's most famous carnival. In the Northeast, once the heart of the slave trade, the African legacy is still apparent today in the region's music, dance, cuisine, religion and festivals. In the North, the Amazon wilderness, some of the land's original inhabitants such as the Yanomami Indians still manage to cling precariously to their traditional way of life in demarcated reserves. The South, however, has a distinct European and Oriental flavour because of the large numbers of immigrants who arrived during the 19th century.

Music and passion

Origins of carnival Although the pre-Lent festivities have a long history, the present-day carnival tradition was brought to Brazil in the 18th century by settlers from the Azores. Mock battles were fought in the streets with revellers throwing water, ashes and even perfume over each other. Masked balls became popular in the 19th century but it wasn't until the 1920s that the colourful parades with imaginative costumes and floats became established.

Samba schools Community groups from the poorest neighbourhoods of Rio de Janeiro began to compete against each other for the honour of becoming carnival champion. The parades grew in sophistication and creativity, finally being moved from the main avenues to a purpose-built stadium. Every year the people's hard work and the designers' riotous imagination are displayed to the cheers of the crowd for one night only.

Street carnival Carnival in the streets still exists with *blocos* accompanied by bands playing popular music from the top of trucks. In Bahia and Pernambuco processions of *afoxes* and *maracatus* have maintained traditions brought from Africa. Costumed *bandas* often formed by transvestites can be found everywhere and represent defiance of authority and the overthrow of society's rules during the carnival period.

Music & dance These permeate daily life throughout the country. Bossa nova became internationally famous in the 1960s, but the country really is a musical treasure chest with widely different styles mainly unknown to foreign ears. The sensual *lambada* is still danced in Porto Seguro whilst *forró* accompanies the São João festivities of the Northeast.

Beach culture The beach is to Brazilians what the pub is to the English. It is also their gym, park and disco. Whether a sleepy river bank deep in the interior, or a busy urban beach, this is where most of life is lived out.

Football fervour Nothing is guaranteed to bring out the nation's infectious enthusiasm as much as football. The frenzied whistle-blowing and foot-stamping of Brazilian supporters is televised around the world during every World Cup. Once again, in 2002, it culminated in a dramatic World Cup win for Brazil – for the fifth time.

A beach hat vendor (left) passes Cariocas sunbathing on the beach
'Caretas' festival (below), in July, when people make their own scary masks
and parade through the streets of villages near Salvador de Bahia

Samba school (above). The energy during the
carnival must be maintained for the 1½ hours it
takes to parade the entire length of the
Sambódromo
Serra dos Órgãos National Park (left). The
natural beauty is a beacon for both walkers
and climbers
The cable-car up the Pão de Açúcar (next
page) provides an incredible bird's-eye view
over the city and beaches

Natural beauty

Rainbows & waterfalls The Iguaçu Falls are among the biggest and most spectacular in the world. Located on the Rio Iguaçu, dividing Brazil and Argentina, walkways lead to a viewpoint looking into the Devil's Throat. The subtropical rainforest around the falls is rich in flora and fauna such as coatis, often found near the visitors' centre, and many colourful butterflies.

Pantanal wildlife This vast wetland on Brazil's borders with Bolivia and Paraguay is one of the best places to see wildlife in the world. The fishing here is exceptional especially during the dry season from May to October. This is also the nesting and breeding season and the best time to view the animals and birds such as the jabiru stork and maned wolf.

The Great River Fed by many smaller rivers originating in the Andes, the mighty Amazon flows through northern Brazil to the Atlantic Ocean, passing many river communities – such as Santarém – on its way. At its mouth the force of the river meeting the sea causes a distinctive roar called Pororoca. River boats leave from Belém in the delta and are the main form of transport in the region.

Amazon rainforest Sometimes described as the 'Lungs of the World', this is the largest expanse of rainforest on the planet and is one of the last great wildernesses. Largely unaffected by human settlement, there is much to be explored in the depths of the tree canopy and along the many tributaries of the River Amazon.

Jungle tours The main centre for jungle tours is the once prosperous river city of Manaus. From here all kinds of wildlife can be seen on boat trips or stays in nearby jungle lodges. For the more adventurous, longer journeys to explore the region are also possible. Despite recent exploitation much of Amazônia remains unspoilt and is home to a wide variety of flora and fauna, such as the giant water lily and the jaguar. There are still many unknown species to be discovered and medicine is finding new remedies for many illnesses from research carried out in the rainforest.

Indian tribes Some of the continent's original inhabitants continue to live by hunting and gathering in forest reserves. Although it is very difficult to get permission to visit these areas the Indian heritage is expressed in the region's cuisine, handicrafts and festivals, such as the Festa do Boi of Parintins.

The scarlet macaw *(left) is one of Brazil's most beautiful birds*
Victoria Regia water lillies *(below) are to be found throughout the Amazon region*

Iguaçu Falls *(above). Rainbows form in the spray of these impressive falls near the triple border between Brazil, Argentina and Paraguay*
The River Amazon *(left) and its many tributaries divide the dense rainforest into channels, or igarapés*
Rio by night *(next page). A walk beside the famous Copacabana Beach towards the Sugar Loaf peak is a popular evening activity*

Essentials

Essentials

Planning your trip

Where to go

You have probably already realized that Brazil is a big place. It is actually the size of the whole of Western Europe or the United States; something to really bear in mind when planning a trip.

Brazil is usually divided into five regions. The **Southeast** is the industrial, mineral and agricultural heartland, with a strong tourist tradition. In the subtropical **South**, European immigration has had a strong influence; the **Northeast** is where Portuguese Brazil began, with a beautiful coast and an arid interior. The **North** has islands of development in the Amazon forest, and, where the Amazon meets the central plateau is the **Centre West**, frontier lands with the great wildlife reserve of the Pantanal wetlands. On this region's eastern edge is Brasília, the symbol of the nation's commitment to its empty centre.

The Southeast   So many journeys to Brazil begin and end in **Rio de Janeiro**. Both the state capital and the state itself offer a good mix of history and hedonism. The city's colonial history has largely been built over by successive regimes, but there are remnants of all the periods of Rio's time as a capital city. In the state there is an exceptionally fine example of a colonial Portuguese town in Paraty. Later periods are represented by the Imperial cities of Petrópolis and Teresópolis and the *fazendas* and towns which date from the coffee era.

On Brazil's Atlantic coast the Mata Atlântica coastal forest once covered the mountains of the seaboard, but very little is left. In Rio de Janeiro a few tiny pockets remain and national parks offer good opportunities to see natural habitats. The Serra da Bocaina contains Mata Atlântica, while the national parks of Serra dos Órgãos and Itatiaia preserve fine mountain landscapes. Within the city itself is the Tijuca Forest, one of the biggest urban forest parks anywhere in the world.

Southeast

Rio is, of course, one of the world's capitals of entertainment, with its famous annual carnival, its spirited and varied nightlife and the beach, which can be found the length of the Rio de Janeiro coast.

The city of Rio deserves at least three or four days. At one of the beach resorts like Búzios or Angra dos Reis you can spend a weekend (or the equivalent in midweek to avoid the crowds), and at least a couple of days in Paraty. Petrópolis and Teresópolis can just about be linked as a day trip, but an overnight stop is recommended, especially if you want to explore the Serra dos Órgãos. The same would apply to the former coffee zone of the Rio Paraíba do Sul and Itatiaia.

A visit to the city of **São Paulo** may just be long enough to know that you want to move on. But there are good museums and the cultural life and cuisine are some of the best in the country. All the São Paulo coast, with its varied resorts, is worth visiting too. In comparison with the Linha Verde which goes from Santos to Rio de Janeiro, the southern part of the coast is less developed and has more in the way of protected environments. Inland, there are excursions to hill resorts or colonial towns, either for a day or a weekend.

The state of **Minas Gerais** has everything except beaches. The modern capital, Belo Horizonte, makes a good starting point for the colonial cities which surround it and, if Portuguese colonial architecture, sculpture and painting is your thing, you can spend a good week in this area: Ouro Preto, Mariana, Sabará, São João del Rei, Tiradentes and Congonhas do Campo are all within a relatively short distance of each other. Further afield are Diamantina and Serro, which may be included on a route from Belo Horizonte to Bahia.

Other options in Minas include relaxing hydrothermal resorts, which could be visited en route between São Paulo and Belo Horizonte. Nature reserves like Caraça, Caparaó, Serra do Cipó and Ibitipoca offer beautiful scenery and opportunities for bird-watching. Minas Gerais is also a good place to buy gemstones because so many

South

are mined in the state. You could easily spend two weeks in the state and, even though it has no beaches, the sea is not far away in **Espírito Santo**, or Rio de Janeiro.

The South   Making the most of this region depends a bit on the time of year that you are visiting because the winters are more pronounced than further north. In addition, Santa Catarina's beaches can become very crowded in summer as they are popular with Argentine holidaymakers. This is a part of Brazil that has been heavily influenced by European immigration, and there is even an Oktoberfest in Blumenau (Santa Catarina).

The main attraction in the state of **Paraná** is Iguaçu, the magnificent series of waterfalls in the far west. Paraná also borders with Argentina and Paraguay, giving it an international feel. Although Paraná's coastline is short, there are beaches to enjoy, and the railway that runs from the state capital, Curitiba, to the sea at Paranaguá is one of the best on the continent.

The beaches of **Ilha Santa Catarina** are worth a visit, and April and May are ideal months if you want to avoid the crowds. There are other resorts, including Camboriú, Porto Belo and some smaller places. The coastal range in this state is high enough and far enough south to receive snow in winter, around the town of São Joaquim.

Rio Grande do Sul, the land of the Brazilian cowboy, the *gaúcho*, is also an immigrant area with a strong Italian influence, evident in the wine-growing region around Caxias do Sul. There is also a Bavarian feel to the towns of the Serra Gaúcha. The state capital, Porto Alegre, an important industrial city, gives access to yet more coastal areas, the beaches and the Lagoa dos Patos. In the far west (very little of interest seems

Northeast

to happen in the middle of these states), near the border with Argentina, are the Sete Missões, all that remains of the Jesuit missions which flourished in this region in the 17th and 18th centuries.

This part of Brazil is mainly known for colonial history, African influence and beaches. As elsewhere, though, a little delving yields rich rewards, for example in national parks, the *sertão* (see box, page 710) and culture.

The Northeast

Essentials

Bahia state has as its capital one of Brazil's most famous cities, Salvador. Like Iguaçu, it is one of the 'musts' of Brazil and more than likely will be included on any itinerary. Commonly referred to as Africa in Brazil, Salvador is one of Brazil's best-known colonial centres. The city also has a famous carnival, which many claim is better than Rio's. Salvador and the coast of Bahia are lined with beaches so it is easy to mix culture and leisure. Porto Seguro is a very popular holiday destination. Further south, offshore, is an accessible marine national park, Abrolhos.

The interior of Bahia is mostly a harsh land, but one town that attracts a great many visitors is Lençóis, a historical monument in an area where diamonds are found. The nearby Chapada Diamantina National Park is a great place for trekking, exploring caves and swimming in the rivers.

Sergipe and **Alagoas** are two small states which do not usually figure as major stops on itineraries. However, they have good beaches and, being in the zone which was first colonized by the Portuguese and which was intensively cultivated for sugar, they have historical associations which are also worth a look if you are in the area.

The capital of **Pernambuco** state, Recife, and the neighbouring former capital, Olinda, once again provide the colonial/beach combination. Recife is basically a modern city, while colonial Olinda boasts one of the greatest concentrations of Portuguese architecture in the country. Unspoilt Fernando de Noronha is a small archipelago which is particularly well known for its diving. Inland, Caruaru has a famous market and a strong tradition in ceramics.

Travelling North of Pernambuco means bathing and surfing, zooming up and down dunes in buggies, staying in sophisticated resorts or fishing villages. The beaches of Ceará, such as Jericoacoara, are a prime example and the state capital, Fortaleza, is a good base for exploring the coast. **Rio Grande do Norte**, **Ceará**, **Piauí** and **Maranhão**, despite being maritime states, all have distinct features, including national parks such as the caves of Ubajara, the strange rock formations of Sete Cidades and the beaches, lakes and dunes of Lençóis Maranhenses. The last city before the great Amazon Delta is São Luís, in whose centre the old houses are mostly covered in colonial tiles.

The North This section is dominated by the Amazon River and its tributaries. Boating up the Amazon is a memorable experience, but requires time. Belém-Santarém is two days; Santarém-Manaus two days; to continue from Manaus to the Colombia/Peru border is another eight days.

Belém is the major port of the state of **Pará**, associated with much of Brazil's history. The Ilha de Marajó, opposite, is a huge river island, whose links with Brazil's earliest inhabitants and present culture make it a special place.

Manaus is the city most people visit in the **Amazonas**, usually by air. The largest port on the river is also geared up for jungle tours of two or three days.

In **Rondônia** and **Acre**, Porto Velho and, further west, Rio Branco, are at the political frontier of Brazil and at the border between the jungle and the land invaders. Either city would provide an insight into the way of life of the cattle rancher, or the rubber tapper.

Tocantins, Brazil's newest state, contains areas which were previously home to many Indian tribes. The Ilha do Bananal, which disputes with Marajó the title of largest river island in the world, is where Brazilian and foreign fishers come to make the most of the fish-filled rivers.

The Centre Right in the middle of the country, **Brasília** is a long way from anywhere by road. But
West this remarkable 20th-century construction has good air connections. In **Goiás** state, Goiânia is another 20th-century, planned city like Brasília, but in the vicinity are old gold mining centres and colonial towns such as Goiás Velho and Pirenópolis. There are also some wonderful national parks such as Emas and Chapada dos Veadeiros, with impressive waterfalls and wildlife.

Centre West

The principal reason why most people go to the far western states of **Mato Grosso** and **Mato Grosso do Sul** is to see the wildlife in the Pantanal. The wetlands provide the opportunity to view a remarkable array of animal and birdlife at close quarters. You can visit Cuiabá and then go to the Chapada dos Guimarães, an immense geological formation with many interesting natural sites. Alternatively, you can come from the south to Corumbá on the border with Bolivia or Campo Grande, close to the delightful area around Bonito.

When to go

The best time for a visit is from April to June, and August to October. Business visitors should avoid from mid-December to the end of February, when it is hot and people are on holiday. In these months hotels, beaches and means of transport tend to be crowded. July is a school holiday month. If visiting tourist centres like Salvador, Rio and the colonial cities in Minas Gerais in the low season, be aware that some tourist sights may be closed for restoration.

In Rio de Janeiro conditions during the winter (May-September) are like those of a   Climate
North European summer (including periods of rain and overcast skies), with temperatures from 14°C to the high 20s. It is more like a North European autumn in São Paulo and the southern states and it can get very cold in the far south. In São Paulo, which is in the Highlands, warmer clothing is required in the winter and the climate can be treacherous with large temperature changes in a brief space of time. It can get surprisingly cold south and west of Rio, and on high ground anywhere in Brazil, at night; warm clothes are needed. The season of heavy rains is from November to March in Rio and São Paulo and from April to August around Recife (where irregular rainfall causes severe draughts). The rainy season in the north and Amazônia can begin in December and is heaviest March-May, but it is getting steadily shorter, possibly as a result of deforestation. It is only in rare cases that the rainfall can be described as either excessive or deficient. Few places get more than 2,000 mm – the coast north of Belém, some of the Amazon Basin, and a small area of the Serra do Mar between Santos and São Paulo, where the downpour has been harnessed to generate electricity.

Summer conditions all over the country are tropical, although temperatures rarely reach 40°C.

The average annual temperature increases steadily from south to north, but even on the Equator, in the Amazon Basin, the average temperature is not more than 27°C. The highest recorded was 42°C, in the dry northeastern states. From the latitude of Recife south to Rio, the mean temperature is from 23° to 27°C along the coast, and from 18° to 21°C in the Highlands. From a few degrees south of Rio to the boundary with Uruguay the mean temperature is from 17° to 19°C. Humidity is relatively high in Brazil, particularly along the coast. The luminosity is also very high, and sunglasses are advisable.

The most famous festival in Brazil is Carnival, particularly that of Rio de Janeiro   Festivals
although there are other cities that have traditions just as interesting. Carnival dates   *For Carnival dates,*
vary between February and early March. New Year's Eve is another popular party with   *see page 61*
beaches all over the country becoming packed with revellers. June is a busy month with São João festivities, especially in the Northeast, as well as the bull festival of Bumba-meu-Boi held in the North and Maranhão. Brazilians need little excuse to hold a party and there are always plenty of festivities year-round.

Tours and tour operators

See page 55 for an explanation of phone codes in Brazil

Austral Tours Ltd, 20 Upper Tachbrook St, London SW1V 1SH, T020-72335384, F020-72335385, www.latinamerica.co.uk *Condor Journeys and Adventures*, 2 Ferry Bank, Colintraive, Argyll PA22 3AR, UK, T01700-841318, F841398, www.condorjourneys-adventures.com *Cox & Kings Travel,* Gordon House, 10 Greencote Pl, London SW1P 1PH, T020-78735000, F76306038. *Encounter Overland* , 2001 Camp Green, Debenham, Stowmarket, Suffolk 1P14 6LA, UK, T01728-862222, F861127, www.encounter.co.uk *Explore Worldwide*, 1 Frederick St, Aldershot, Hants GU11 1LQ, UK, T01252-760000, F760001, www.exploreworldwide.com *Field Guides*, 9433 Bee Cave Rd, Building 1, Suite 150, Austin, Texas 78733, USA, T1-800-7284953, F1-512-2630117, www.fieldguides.com Specialists in bird-watching with regular tours to Brazil. *Focus Tours*, 103 Moya Rd, Santa Fe, NM87508, USA, T505-4664688, F505-4664689, www.focustours.com Specialists in bird-watching and environmentally responsible travel. *Hayes & Jarvis*, Sandrocks, Rocky Lane, Haywoods Heath, W Sussex RH16 4RH, UK, T0870-8989890, F0870-3331914, www.hayes-jarvis.com *Journey Latin America*, 12-13 Heathfield Terr, Chiswick, London W4 4JE, T020-87473108, F87421312, and 12 St Ann's Square (2nd floor), Manchester M3 7HW, T0161-8321441, F8321551, www.journeylatinamerica.co.uk Long-established company running escorted tours throughout the region. They also offer a wide range of flight options. *Ladatco Tours*, 3006 Aviation Av #4C, Coconut Grove, Florida 33133, USA, T1800-3276162, www.ladatco.com *Last Frontiers Ltd*, Fleet Marston Farm, Aylesbury, Bucks HP18 0QT, UK, T01296-653000, F658651, www.lastfrontiers.com *Scott Dunn Latin America* (*Passage to South America*), Fovant Mews, 12 Noyna Rd, London SW17 7PH, T020-86825030, www.scottdunn.com *Mila Tours*, 100 S Greenleaf Av, Gurnee, IL

Essentials

Essentials

60031-337, T847-2482111, T800-3877378 (USA and Canada), F847-2492722. *South American Experience*, 47 Causton St, Pimlico, London SW1P 4AT, T020-79765511, F79766908, www.southamericanexperience.co.uk *STA Travel*, 6 Wrights Lane, London W8 6TA, T0870-1600599, www.statravel.co.uk *Steppes Latin America*, 51 Castle St, Cirencester, Gloucestershire GL7 1QD, UK, T01285-651010, F01285-885888, www.steppeseast.co.uk *Tatur Turismo*, Av Tancredo Neves 274, Centro Empresarial Iguatemi, Sala 228, Bloco B, Salvador, 41820-020, Bahia, Brazil, T0XX71-4507216, F4507215, tatur@svn.com.br *Trailfinders*, 194 Kensington High St, London W8 7RG, T020-79383939, www.trailfinders.com

Finding out more

Tourist information
See also page 38

Tourist information can be obtained from Brazilian embassies and consulates (see box on page 33). Other sources of information are: *South American Explorers*, formerly the *South American Explorers Club*, 126 Indina Creek Rd, Ithaca, NY 14850, T607-2770488, F2776122, www.samexplo.org, a non-profit educational organization functioning primarily as an information network for South America. It is a useful organization for travellers to Brazil and the rest of the continent. The *Latin American Travel Advisor*, PO Box 17-17-908, Quito, Ecuador, F593-2562566, USA and Canada toll free F1-800-3273573, www.amerispan.com/lata/ is a complete travel information service offering up-to-date detailed and reliable information about Brazil and countries throughout South and Central America. Public safety, health, weather and natural phenomena, travel costs, economics and politics are highlighted for each nation. You can subscribe to the comprehensive quarterly newsletter (a free sample is available), obtain country reports by email or fax and choose from a wide selection of Latin American maps. Individual travel planning assistance is available.

Business travellers Specific information for UK exporters can be obtained from the Department of Trade and Industry's Brazil Desk, Bay 828, Kingsgate House, 66-74 Victoria St, London SW1E 6SW, T020-72154262, F72158247, www.trasdepartners.gov.uk

Brazil Report, published by Latin American Newsletters, has well written articles on recent political and economic news. They can be contacted at 61 Old St, London EC1V 9HW, T020-72510012, F72538193, www.latinnews.com

The American Chamber of Commerce in São Paulo is another good source of information on local markets, www.amcham.com.br

Useful websites
See also under individual sections in this chapter. For embassy websites, see page 33; newspaper and magazine websites, see page 56

www.atbrazil.com has a very useful currency converter, general country information and details of hotels with email/websites.

www.ipanema.com is a quirky, informative site on Ipanema and Rio.

www.spguia.com.br is dedicated to the city of São Paulo, in Portuguese only.

www.brazil-brasil.com is all in English and very wide ranging, with a chat room and information on cinema, etc.

www.brazilianmusic.com Good introductions to capoeira, various musical styles and CD and book recommendations. It also details 20 cases of torture during military rule for which no one has ever been punished.

www.maria-brazil.org A wonderfully personal introduction to Brazil, specifically Rio, featuring Maria's cookbook and little black book, features and reviews.

http://plasma.nationalgeographic.com/mapmachine for maps anywhere in the world, by satellite or by street, or even historically.

www.putumayo.com A world music site with information about Brazilian music and where to get hold of it

Language

See page 720 for a list of useful words and phrases

No quantity of dictionaries, phrase books or word lists will provide the same enjoyment of being able to converse directly with the people of Brazil. English is not widely spoken and it is definitely a good idea to learn some basic Portuguese before you go. As you travel you will pick up more of the language and the more you know, the more you will benefit from your stay. Efforts to speak Portuguese are greatly appreciated. Brazilians are very keen to communicate with foreigners and very patient generally. If you speak Spanish, you will probably be understood, but you will certainly have difficulty in understanding the answers. If you find yourself resorting to sign language, it might be useful to know that the 'ok' sign is actually an insult in Brazil and tugging your

ear means 'delicious'. There are many differences between the Portuguese of Portugal and Brazil (particularly in the pronunciation) and, if learning Portuguese before you go to Brazil, you may want to get lessons with a Brazilian, or from a language course which teaches Brazilian Portuguese. There are Brazilian tutors in most cities (in London, see *Time Out* and *Leros*, the Brazilian magazine, for advertisements). For information on centres offering Portuguese courses in Brazil, see Directory text of the relevant towns and cities.

Student travellers

If you are in full time education you will be entitled to an International Student Identity Card, which is distributed by student travel offices and travel agencies in 77 countries. The ISIC card gives you special prices on all forms of transport (air, sea, rail etc), and access to a variety of other concessions and services. If you need to find the location of your nearest ISIC office contact: The ISIC Association, Box 15857, 1001 NJ Amsterdam, Holland, T+45-33939303. ISIC cards can be obtained in Brazil from STB agencies throughout the country such as Av Brig Faria Lima 1713, São Paulo, T0XX11-8700555. Remember to take photographs when having a card issued.

In practice, however, the ISIC card is rarely recognized or accepted for discounts outside of the south and southeast of Brazil. It is nonetheless useful for obtaining half price entry to the cinema. Youth hostels will often accept it in lieu of a IYHA card or at least give a discount, and some university accommodation (and subsidized canteens) will allow very cheap short term stays to holders.

Disabled travellers

As in most Latin American countries, facilities for disabled travellers are severely lacking. Wheelchair ramps are a rare luxury and getting a wheelchair into a bathroom or toilet is practically impossible, except for some of the more modern hotels. Pavements are often in a poor state of repair or crowded with street vendors requiring passers-by to brave the passing traffic. Disabled Brazilians obviously have to cope with these problems mainly by relying on the help of others to get on and off public transport and generally move around.

But of course only a minority of disabled people are wheelchair-bound and it is now widely acknowledged that disabilities do not stop you from enjoying a great holiday. Some travel companies are beginning to specialize in exciting holidays, tailor-made for individuals depending on their level of disability. *A Global Access – Disabled Travel Network Site*, www.geocities.com/Paris/1502, provides travel information for 'disabled adventurers' and includes a number of reviews and tips from members of the public. You might also want to read *Nothing Ventured*, edited by Alison Walsh (Harper Collins), which gives personal accounts of world-wide journeys by disabled travellers, plus advice and listings.

Gay and lesbian travellers

Brazil is a good country for gay and lesbian travellers as attitudes are fairly liberal, especially in the big cities. Opinions in the interior and rural areas are far more conservative and it is wise to adapt to this. There is a well developed scene in Rio de Janeiro and São Paulo while Salvador is also a popular destination. Local information can be obtained from the *Rio Gay Guide*, www.riogayguide.com, and in Salvador from the *Centro Cultura*, Rua do Sodre, 45, close to the Museu de Arte Sacra da Bahia, which publishes a guide to the gay scene in the city for US$4.

Travelling with children

Travel with children can bring you into closer contact with Brazilian families and, generally, presents no special problems. In fact the path is often smoother for family groups. Officials tend to be more amenable where children are concerned and they are pleased if your child knows a little Spanish or Portuguese. Moreover, even thieves and pickpockets seem to have some of the traditional respect for families, and may leave you alone because of it!

People contemplating overland travel in Brazil with children should remember that a lot of time can be spent waiting for buses, trains, and especially for aeroplanes. On bus journeys, if the children are good at amusing themselves, or can readily sleep while travelling, the problems can be considerably lessened. If your child is of an early reading age, take reading material with you as it is difficult and expensive to find. The website, www.babygoes2.com, doesn't feature Brazil specifically and tends to focus on package holidays, but has good general advice for planning and packing, 'toy tips' and ideas for entertaining on journeys.

Food

This can be a problem if the children are not adaptable. It is easier to take snacks and drinks with you on longer trips than to rely on meal stops where the food may not be to their taste. Avocados are safe, easy to eat and nutritious and can be fed to babies as young as six months. A small immersion heater and jug for making hot drinks is invaluable, but remember that electric current varies. Try and get a dual-voltage one (110v and 220v).

Fares

On all long distance buses you pay for each seat, and there are no half-fares if the children occupy a seat each. For shorter trips it is cheaper, if less comfortable, to seat small children on your knee. Often there are spare seats which children can occupy after tickets have been collected. In city and local excursion buses, small children generally do not pay a fare, but are not entitled to a seat when paying customers are standing. On sightseeing tours you should *always* bargain for a family rate – often children can go free. (In trains, reductions for children are general, but not universal.)

On internal flights, airlines charge half for children under 12 (less for children under two), but some military services don't have half-fares, or have younger age limits. Note that a child travelling free on a long excursion is not always covered by the operator's travel insurance; it is advisable to pay a small premium to arrange cover.

Hotels

Try to negotiate family rates. If charges are per person, always insist that two children will occupy one bed only, therefore counting as one tariff. If rates are per bed, the same applies. In either case you can almost always get a reduced rate at cheaper hotels. Occasionally when travelling with a child you will be refused a room in a hotel that is 'unsuitable'. On river boat trips, unless you have very large hammocks, it may be more comfortable and cost effective to hire a two-berth cabin for two adults and a child. (In restaurants, you can normally buy children's helpings, or divide one full-size helping between two children.)

Working in Brazil

Volunteering

Contact RioVoluntário, which supports 450 voluntary organizations, from environmental to healthcare, T+5521-22621110, ask for Isadora or Fábio, www.riovoluntario.org.br In the UK, www.taskbrasil.org.uk, T020–7394 1177, welcomes donations and volunteers (in the UK or Brazil) for its programme to help Brazilian street children. Similarly, www.saomartinho.org.br, T21-2242 2238, and its sister company in England (Jubilee Action, www.jubileecampaign.co.uk), seeks volunteers in both Brazil and abroad to assist in its project for street children.

Essentials

Before you travel

Getting in

Documents
*See box on page 33
for a list of Brazilian
embassies worldwide*

Essentials

Visas are not required for stays of up to 90 days by tourists from Andorra, Argentina, Austria, Bahamas, Barbados, Belgium, Bolivia, Chile, Colombia, Costa Rica, Denmark, Ecuador, Finland, France, Germany, Greece, Iceland, Ireland, Italy, Liechtenstein, Luxembourg, Malaysia, Monaco, Morocco, Namibia, the Netherlands, Norway, Paraguay, Peru, Philippines, Portugal, San Marino, South Africa, Spain, Suriname, Sweden, Switzerland, Thailand, Trinidad and Tobago, United Kingdom, Uruguay, the Vatican and Venezuela. For them, only the following documents are required at the port of disembarkation: a passport valid for at least six months (or *cédula de identidad* for nationals of Argentina, Chile, Paraguay and Uruguay); and a return or onward ticket, or adequate proof that you can purchase your return fare, subject to no remuneration being received in Brazil and no legally binding or contractual documents being signed. Venezuelan passport holders can stay in Brazil for 60 days on filling in a form at the border.

Citizens of the United States, Canada, Australia, New Zealand and other countries not mentioned above, and anyone wanting to stay longer than 180 days, *must* get a visa before arrival, which may, if you ask, be granted for multiple entry. Visa fees vary from country to country, so apply to the Brazilian consulate in your home country. The consular fee in the USA is US$55. Students planning to study in Brazil or employees of foreign companies can apply for a one- or two-year visa. Two copies of the application form, two photos, a letter from the sponsoring company or educational institution in Brazil, a police form showing no criminal convictions and a fee of around US$80 is required.

Extensions Foreign tourists may stay a maximum of 180 days in any one year. Ninety-day renewals are easily obtainable, but only at least 15 days before the expiry of your 90-day permit, from the Polícia Federal. The procedure varies, but generally you have to do the following: fill out three copies of the tax form at the Polícia Federal, take them to a branch of *Banco do Brasil*, pay US$15 and bring two copies back. You will then be given the extension form to fill in and be asked for your passport to stamp in the extension. According to regulations (which should be on display) you need to show a return ticket, cash, cheques or a credit card, a personal reference and proof of an address of a person living in the same city as the office (in practice you simply write this in the space on the form). Some offices will only give you an extension within 10 days of the expiry of your permit.

Some points of entry such as the Colombian border refuse entry for longer than 30 days, renewals are then for the same period, insist if you want 90 days. For longer stays you must leave the country and return (not the same day) to get a new 90-day permit. If your visa has expired, getting a new visa can be costly (US$35 for a consultation, US$30 for the visa itself) and may take anything up to 45 days, depending on where you apply. If you overstay your visa, or extension, you will be fined US$7 per day, with no upper limit. After paying the fine to Polícia Federal, you will be issued with an exit visa and must leave within eight days. If you cannot pay the fine you must pay when you next return to Brazil.

Officially, if you leave Brazil within the 90-day permission to stay and then re-enter the country, you should only be allowed to stay until the 90-day permit expires. If, however, you are given another 90-day permit, this may lead to charges of overstaying if you apply for an extension.

Identification You must always carry identification when in Brazil. It is a good idea to take a photocopy of the personal details in your passport, plus your Brazilian immigration

Brazilian embassies and consulates

Argentina C Cerrito 1350, 1010 Buenos Aires, T005411-4515, F4515-2401, www.brasil.org.ar

Australia 19 Forster Cres, Yarralumla, Canberra ACT 2600, T00612-62732372, www.brazil.org.au

Austria Am Lugeck 1/5/15, A-1010 Wien, T00431-5120631, F5138374.

Belgium 350 Av Louise, 6ème Étage, Boîte 5-1050 Bruxelles, T00322-6402015, F6408134.

Bolivia C Capitán Ravelo 2334, Ed Metrobol, Sopocachi, La Paz, Casilla 429, T005912-8112233, F8112733.

Canada 450 Wilbrod St, Sandyhill, Ottawa, ON K1N 6M8, T001613-2371090, F2376144, www.brasembottawa.org

Chile C Alonso Ovalle 1665, Santiago, T00562-6982486, F6715961, www.brasembsantiago.cl

Colombia C 93, No 14-20, 8th floor, Aptdo Aéreo 90540, Bogotá 8, T00571-2180800, F2188393.

Denmark Ryvangs Alle, 24-2100 Kobenhavn Ø, T00453-9206478, F9273607.

France 34 Cours Albert I, 75008 Paris, T00331-45616300, F42890345, www.bresil.org

Germany Kennedyallee 74-53175 Bonn, T0049228-959230, F373696.

Ireland Harcourt Centre, Europa House, 5th Floor, 41-54 Harcourt St, Dublin 2, T003531-4756000, F4751341.

Israel Beit Yachin, 2 Kaplin St, 8th floor, Tel Aviv, T009723-6963934, F6916060.

Italy 14 Piazza Navona, 00186 Roma, T003906-683981, F6867858, www.ambasciatadelbrasile.it

Japan 2-11-12 Kita-Aoyama, Minato-Ku, Tokyo 107-8633, T00813-34045211, F34055846, www.braemb.or.jp

Netherlands Mauritskade 19-2514 HD, The Hague, T003170-3023959, F3023950.

New Zealand 19 Brandon St, level 9, Wellington 1, T00644-4733516, F4733517.

Norway Sigurd Syrs Gate 4, 1st floor, 0273 Oslo, T0047-22552029, F22443964.

Paraguay C Coronel Irrazábal esq, Av Mariscal López, 1521 Asunción, T0059521-214466, F212693, www.embajadabrasil.org.py

Peru Av José Pardo 850, Miraflores, Lima 100, T00511-4212759, F4452421.

Portugal Estrada das Laranjeiras, 1649-021 Lisboa, T003511-217248510, www.emb-brasil.pt

South Africa Hadefields, Block c, 1st floor, 1267 Pretorius St, Hatfield 0083, Pretoria, T002712-4269400, F4289494, www.brazil.co.za

Spain C Fernando El Santo, 6 DP 28010 Madrid, T00341-7004650, F7004660.

Sweden Sturgegatan 11, 2 Tr 114 36 Stockholm, T00468-234010, F234018.

Switzerland Monbijouster 68-3007 Berne, T004131-3718515, F3710525.

UK 32 Green St, London WIK 7AT, T020-7490877, F73999100, www.brazil.org.uk

USA 3006 Massachusetts Ave NW, Washington DC 20008-3699, T001202-2382700, F2382827, www.brasilemb.org

Uruguay Blvd Artigas, 1328, Montevideo, Aptdo Postal 16022, T005982-7072119, F7072086, www.brasmont.org.uy

Venezuela Centro Gerencial Mohedano, 6th floor, C Los Chaguaramos con Av Mohedano, La Castellana, 1060 Caracas, T00582-2616529, F2619601.

Essentials

stamp, and leave your passport in the hotel safe deposit. This photocopy, when authorized in a *Cartório*, US$1, is a legitimate copy of your documents. Be prepared, however, to present the originals when travelling in sensitive areas such as near the borders. Always keep an independent record of your passport details. It is also a good idea to register with your consulate to expedite document replacement if yours gets lost or stolen.

Warning Do not lose the emigration permit they give you when you enter Brazil. Leaving the country without it, you may have to pay up to US$100 per person. It is

Essentials

▶▶ **Insurance tips**

Insurance companies have tightened up considerably over recent years and it is now almost impossible to claim successfully if you have not followed procedures closely. The problem is that these often involve dealing with the country's red tape which can lead to some inconvenience at best and to some quite long delays at worst. There is no substitute for suitable precautions against petty crime.

The level of insurance is inevitably the highest if you go through the USA. Don't forget to obtain sports extensions if you are going to go diving, rafting, climbing, etc. Most policies do not cover very high levels of baggage/cash. Don't forget to check whether you can claim on your household insurance. They often have worldwide all risks extensions. Most policies exclude manual work whilst away, although working in bars or restaurants is usually alright.

Here are our tips: they apply to most types of policies but always check the details of your own policy before you leave.

1. Take the policy with you (a photocopy will do but make sure it is a complete one).

2. Do not travel against medical advice. It will invalidate the medical insurance part of the cover.

3. There is a 24-hour medical emergency service helpline associated with your insurance. You need to contact them if you require in-patient hospital treatment or you need to return home early. The telephone number is printed on the policy. Make sure you note the time of the call, the person you were talking to and get a reference number. Even better, get a receipt from the telephone company showing the number you called.

Should you need to be airlifted home, this is always arranged through the insurance company's representative and the hospital authorities. Ironically, this can lead to quite intense discussions which you will not be aware of: the local hospital is often quite keen to keep you!

4. If you have to cancel your trip for whatever reason, contact your travel agent, tour operator or airline without delay.

5. If your property is damaged by an airline, report it immediately and always within three days, and get a 'property irregularity report' from them.

6. Claims for baggage left unattended are very rarely settled unless they were left in a securely locked hotel room, apartment, etc; locked in the boot of a car and there is evidence of a forced entry; cash is carried on your person or is in a locked safe or security box.

7. All loss must be reported to the police and/or hotel authorities within 24 hours of discovery and a written report obtained.

8. If medical attention is received for injury or sickness, a medical certificate showing its nature must be obtained, although some companies waive this if only out-patient treatment is required. Keep all receipts in a safe place as they will be needed to substantiate the claim.

9. Check your policy carefully to see if there is a date before which claims must be submitted. This is often within 30 days of returning home. It is now usual for companies to want your policy document, proof that you actually travelled (airline ticket or travel agent's confirmation of booking), receipts and written reports (in the event of loss). Photocopies are not accepted.

suggested that you photocopy this form and have it authenticated at a *cartório*, US$1, in case of loss or theft.

Customs **Duty-free allowance** Clothing and personal articles are free of import duty. Articles such as cameras, camcorders, portable radios, tape recorders, typewriters and binoculars are also admitted free if there is not more than one of each. Tourists may also bring in, duty-free, 24 alcoholic drinks (no more than 12 of any one type), 400 cigarettes, 25 cigars, 280 g of perfume, up to 10 units of cosmetics, up to three each of any electronic item or watch, up to a total value of US$500 monthly. There is a limit of US$150 at land borders and a written declaration must be made to this effect. Duty-free goods may only be purchased in foreign currency.

You should be immunized against typhoid, polio, tetanus and hepatitis A. Visitors no longer require vaccination against smallpox. Poliomyelitis vaccination is required for children from three months to six years.

Vaccinations
See also page 67

Proof of vaccination against **yellow fever** is necessary if you are visiting Amazônia and the Centre West, or are coming from countries with Amazonian territories, eg Bolivia, Colombia, Ecuador, or Peru. It is strongly recommended that you have a yellow fever inoculation before visiting northern Brazil since anyone without a certificate will be inoculated on entering any of the northern and centre-western states. Although yellow fever vaccination is free it might be administered in unsanitary conditions.

Yellow fever and some other vaccinations can be obtained from the *Ministério da Saúde*, R Cais de Pharoux, Rio de Janeiro. Less common vaccinations can be obtained at *Saúde de Portos*, Praça 15 de Novembro, Rio de Janeiro.

What to take

Everybody has their own list. A **waterproof jacket** is recommended – it will probably rain several times on your trip. Take no more than two or three changes of clothes and one light sweater for chilly nights and overly air-conditioned buses. Light, natural fabrics are best in the heat. **Wax earplugs** (almost impossible to find outside large cities) and an airline-type **eye mask** can help you sleep in noisy and poorly curtained hotel rooms and on buses. Some people swear by inflatable **travel pillows** for long journeys. **Sports sandals** are much cooler than sweat-inducing trainers and can be worn in showers to avoid athlete's foot. A **sarong** or **sheet sleeping bag** is invaluable; for use as a towel, a bedsheet or beach towel. (Towels are provided at even the cheapest hotels, although not always at youth hostels.) A **hat** is necessary to protect against sunstroke.

When packing leave space in your bag; it makes it much quicker to re-pack and you will always accumulate more possessions on your way

Also useful are a **clothes line**, **nailbrush** (for scrubbing dirt off clothes as well as off oneself), a universal **plug** and a large **penknife**, preferably the famous Swiss Army knife. Possible extras include a **torch** (flashlight) – especially one that will clip on to a pocket or belt, and a **padlock** (combination lock is best) and **chain** for securing luggage to bed or bus/train seat.

It is wise to take a small **first aid kit**; useful medicaments are given in Health (see page 66). Also, lip salve with sun protection, and pre-moistened wipes. Major cities have a wide selection of products for **contact lens** wearers, so you don't need to take litres of lotions.

Money

The unit of currency is the *real*, R$ (plural *reais*) introduced on 1 July 1994 on a par with the US dollar, a link that was severed in 1999. In November 2002 the rate was R$3.715 = US$1. Any amount of foreign currency and 'a reasonable sum' in *reais* can be taken in, but sums over US$10,000 must be declared. Residents may only take out the equivalent of US$4,000. Notes in circulation are: 100, 50, 10, 5 and 1 *real*; coins: 1 *real*, 50, 25, 10, 5 and 1 centavo.

Currency
The exchange rate has been fairly volatile recently

ATMs, or cash machines, are common in Brazil. As well as being the most convenient way of withdrawing money, they frequently offer the best available rates of exchange. There are two international ATM acceptance systems, Plus and Cirrus. Many issuers of debit and credit cards are linked to one, or both (eg Visa is Plus, MasterCard is Cirrus). *Banco do Brasil* and *HSBC* are the two main banks offering this service. Look for the relevant symbol on an ATM (there is usually only one international machine per bank) and draw cash using your

ATMs

Essentials

Essentials

▶▶ Emergency numbers

Credicard: T0800-784411
Diners Club: T0800-784444
MasterCard: T000811-8870533
Visa: T000811-9335589
American Express: T011-2470966
Thomas Cook Visa: T000811-7840553
Thomas Cook refund service:
F+44-1733-502370

PIN. Red *Banco 24 Horas* kiosks advertise that they take a long list of credit cards in their ATMs, including MasterCard and Amex, but international cards cannot always be used.

Find out before you leave what ATM coverage there is and what international 'functionality' your card has. Check if your bank or credit card company imposes handling charges. Obviously you must ensure that the account to which your debit card refers contains sufficient funds. With a credit card, obtain a credit limit sufficient for your needs, or pay money in to put the account in credit. If travelling for a long time, consider a direct debit to clear your account regularly. Many major banks and credit card companies now have websites so you can monitor your account and even transfer funds and pay bills. Do not rely on one card, in case of loss. If you do lose a card, immediately contact the 24-hour helpline of the issuer in your home country (keep this number in a safe place).

Exchange Banks in major cities will change cash and travellers' cheques. If you keep the official exchange slips, you may convert back into foreign currency up to 50% of the amount you exchanged. The parallel market, found in travel agencies, exchange houses and among hotel staff, often offers marginally better rates than the banks. Many banks may only change US$300 minimum in cash, US$500 in travellers' cheques. Dollars cash (take US$5 or US$10 bills) are becoming more frequently used for tourist transactions and are useful for emergencies. Damaged dollar notes may be rejected. Parallel market and official rates are quoted in the papers and on TV news programmes.

Travellers' cheques Rates for cheques are usually lower than for cash, they are harder to change and commission may be charged. Tourists cannot change US dollar travellers' cheques into dollar notes, but US dollar travellers' cheques can be obtained on an American Express card (against official policy). It is a good idea to take two kinds of cheque: if large numbers of one kind have recently been forged or stolen, making people suspicious, it is unlikely to have happened simultaneously with the other kind.

Credit cards
See box on page 36 for a list of emergency telephone numbers to report card loss or theft

Credit cards are widely used; Diners Club, MasterCard, Visa and American Express are useful. MasterCard/Access is accepted by *Banco Real*. Overseas credit cards need authorization from São Paulo, which can occasionally take a while. MasterCard and Diners are equivalent to Credicard, and Eurocheques can be cashed at *Banco Alemão* (major cities only). Cash advances on credit cards will only be paid in *reais* at the tourist rate, incurring a 1.5% commission. Banks in small remote places may still refuse to give a cash advance: try asking for the manager (*gerente*).

Money transfers Money sent to Brazil is normally paid out in Brazilian currency, so do not have more money sent to Brazil than you need for your stay. A recommended method is, before leaving, to find out which local bank is correspondent to your bank at home, then when you need funds, telex your own bank and ask them to telex the money to the local bank (confirming by fax). Give exact information to your bank of the routing number of the receiving bank. Funds can be received within 48 banking hours.

In most large cities *Citibank* will hold US personal cheques for collection, paying the day's tourist dollar rate in *reais* with no charge. *Banco do Brasil* offers the same service with a small charge. From the UK the quickest method of having money sent is *Swift Air*.

To open a bank account in Brazil, you need to have a visa valid for more than one year.

As a very rough guide, prices are about a third of those in Western Europe and the Cost of travelling
United States. The devaluation of the *real* in 1999 has greatly reduced costs, but Brazil is
still more expensive than other countries in South America (including Argentina since
the collapse of its economy).

Accommodation is good value in every price range. Budget hotels with few frills
have rooms for as little as US$6, and you should have no difficulty finding a room cost-
ing US$10 wherever you are. Rooms are often pretty much the same price whether
one or two people are staying, so travelling alone pushes costs up. Eating is generally
inexpensive, especially in *comida a kilo* (pay by weight) restaurants, which offer a wide
range of food (salads, meat, pasta, vegetarian). Although bus travel is very reasonable,
because of the long distances, costs can soon mount up. Internal flights prices have
come down dramatically in the last couple of years and some routes work out cheaper
than taking a bus.

Essentials

Getting there

Air

International flights into Brazil 999 generally land at either Rio de Janeiro or São Paulo. *Regulations state that*
São Paulo has better domestic and international flight connections. Both cities are good *you cannot buy an*
points to enter Brazil and there are excellent transport connections between the two, *air ticket in Brazil for*
although tourists tend to choose Rio de Janeiro as their point of disembarkation. Prices *use abroad unless*
are more competitive during the low season and cheap flights can be very difficult to find *you first have a*
during the high season (generally between 15 December and 15 January, the Thursday *ticket out of Brazil*
before Carnival to the Saturday after Carnival and 15 June to 15 August). Flight frequency
changes regularly and you are advised to check current timetables.

If buying a ticket to another country but with a stopover in Brazil, check whether two
tickets are cheaper than one. Airline tickets are expensive in Brazil, buy internal tickets
with *reais* (you can pay by credit card). External tickets must be paid for in dollars.

Varig, T0845-6037601, www.varig.co.uk, also has an extensive 'Stopover'
programme which gives reduced rates on transfers and hotel rooms in many cities in
Brazil and throughout South America.

Rio de Janeiro and São Paulo are connected to the principal European cities direct by *From Europe*
Aerolíneas Argentinas (Amsterdam and Madrid), *Air France* (Paris), *Alitalia* (Rome), *Brit-
ish Airways* (London), *Iberia* (Barcelona and Madrid), *KLM* (Amsterdam), *LanChile*
(Frankfurt and Madrid), *Lufthansa* (Frankfurt), *Pluna* (Madrid), *Swissair* (Zurich),

Essentials

TAM (Paris), *TAP Air Portugal* (Lisbon), *Transbrasil* (Amsterdam, London and Vienna), *Varig* (Copenhagen, Frankfurt, London, Lisbon, Paris and Milan) and *Vasp* (Athens, Barcelona, Brussels, Frankfurt and Zurich).

Varig flies to Recife and Fortaleza from Milan and to Salvador from Rome. *TAP Air Portugal* flies to Fortaleza, Natal, Recife and Salvador from Lisbon. *Transbrasil* flies from Amsterdam and London to Recife and Salvador.

From the USA Rio de Janeiro and São Paulo are connected to the USA direct by *American Airlines* (Chi-
& Canada cago, Dallas, Miami), *Continental* (New York), *Delta* (Atlanta), *TAM* (Miami), *United Airlines* (Chicago, Miami), *Varig* (Los Angeles, Miami and New York) and *Vasp*. Other US gateways are Boston, Cincinnati, Denver, Detroit and San Francisco. The cheapest routes are probably from Miami.

American Airlines fly from Miami to Belo Horizonte. *Transbrasil* fly from New York, Orlando and Washington to Brasília. *Varig* fly from Miami to Belém, Fortaleza, Manaus and Recife. *Air Canada* flies direct to São Paulo from Toronto.

From Latin Most Latin American cities are connected by air to São Paulo and Rio de Janeiro. There
America are flights from Asunción with *American Airlines*, *TAM* and *Varig*; Bogotá with *Varig* and *Avianca*; Buenos Aires with *Aerolíneas Argentinas*, *TAM* and *Varig*; Caracas with *Varig*; Córdoba with *Varig*; Guayaquil with *Ecuatoriana* and *Vasp*; La Paz with *Varig*; Lima with *AeroMéxico*, *TAM* and *Varig*; Mexico City with *AeroMéxico* and *Varig*; Montevideo with *TAM*, *Pluna* and *Varig*; Santa Cruz with *LAB*, *TAM*, *Varig* and *Vasp*; San José, Costa Rica with *Lacsa*; Santiago with *LanChile*, *TAM* and *Varig*; Quito with *Ecuatoriana* and *Vasp*.

Penta fly from Cayenne to Belém and Macapá. *Pluna* fly from Montevideo to Porto Alegre. *Surinam Airways* fly from Paramaribo to Belém. *Varig* fly from Asunción to Curitiba, Florianópolis and Foz do Iguaçu; Buenos Aires to Porto Alegre; Mexico City to Manaus; Montevideo to Porto Alegre; Santiago to Porto Alegre.

From There are flights to São Paulo from Abidjan and Beirut with *Middle East Airlines*; Johan-
elsewhere nesburg with *South African Airways*; Nagoya, Japan with *Varig*; Osaka with *Vasp*; Tokyo with *JAL* and *Varig*.

Air passes *Aerolíneas Argentinas*, *Austral*, *Lan Chile*, *Lapa*, *Líneas Aéreas Paraguayas*, *Pluna*, *Transbrasil*, *Varig* and *Vasp* operate the **Mercosur Airpass**. Valid for a minimum of seven and a maximum of 30 days, the pass is for a maximum of eight flight coupons with no more than two stops allowed per country. At least two Mercosur member countries must be included; rerouting is not permitted. The air pass is available to all international return ticket holders travelling by air into the participating countries. Passes are price-banded according to mileage flown and fares range from US$225 to US$870. Children pay 67% whilst infants pay 10% of the adult fare and some of the carriers operate a blackout period between 17 December and 10 January.

LAB, *Ecuatoriana* and *Vasp* operate a **South American Airpass** valid for 90 days, available to non-residents of Brazil arriving in South America on long-haul flights. There is no child discount and infants pay 10% of the price which varies between US$560 for up to four flights and US$1,100 for the maximum of nine flights. Up to two transfers of less than five hours are permitted and coverage is from northern Argentina, Chile, Bolivia, Peru, Ecuador and Brazil.

Baggage Airlines will only allow a certain weight of luggage without a surcharge; this is normally
allowance 30 kg for first class and 20 kg for business and economy classes, but these limits are often not strictly enforced when it is known that the plane is not going to be full. On some flights from the UK, special outbound concessions are offered (by *Iberia*, *Air France*) of a two-piece allowance up to 32 kg, but you may need to request this.

Passengers seeking a larger baggage allowance can route via the USA, but with certain exceptions, the fares are slightly higher using this route. On the other hand, weight limits for internal flights are often lower; best to enquire beforehand.

1 Fares from Europe to Brazilian destinations vary from airline to airline, destination to destination and according to the time of year. Check with an agency for the best deal for when you wish to travel. There is a wide range of offers to choose from in a highly competitive environment in the UK.

2 Most airlines offer discounted fares of one sort or another on scheduled flights. These are not offered by the airlines direct to the public, but through agencies which specialize in this type of fare.

The very busy seasons are 7 December-15 January and 1 July-10 September. If you intend travelling during those times, book as far ahead as possible. Between February-May and September-November special offers may be available.

3 Other fares fall into three groups, and are all on scheduled services:

Excursion (return) fares (A) With restricted validity, eg 5-90 days, but with certain flexibility on payment of a fee.

Yearly fares (B) These may be bought on a one-way or return basis. Some airlines require a specified return date, changeable upon payment of a fee. To leave the return completely open is possible for an extra fee. You must fix the route (some of the cheapest flexible fares now have six months validity).

Student (or under 26) fares Some airlines are flexible on the age limit, others strict. One-way and returns available, or 'Open Jaws' (see below). Do not assume that student tickets are the cheapest; though they are often very flexible, they are usually more expensive than A or B above. On the other hand, there is a wider range of cheap one-way student fares originating in Latin America than can be bought outside the continent.

4 'Open Jaw' fares For people intending to travel a linear route and return from a different point from that which they entered, these fares are available on student, yearly, or excursion tickets.

5 Multi-stop itineraries Many fares require a change of plane at an intermediate point, and a stopover may be permitted, or even obligatory, depending on schedules. However, simply because a flight stops at a given airport does not mean you can break your journey there. If you want a multi-stop itinerary, you can save hundreds of pounds by dealing with a specialized agency.

6 Because of high local taxes, a one-way ticket from Latin America is more expensive than a one-way in the other direction, so it's usually best to buy a return (but see Student fares, above). Taxes are calculated as a percentage of the full IATA fare; on a discounted fare the tax can therefore make up as much as 30-50% of the price.

7 If you buy discounted air tickets always check the reservation with the airline concerned to make sure the flight still exists. Also remember the IATA airlines' schedules change in March and October each year, so if you're going to be away a long time it's best to reconfirm your flight well in advance or leave return flight coupons open.

8 Check whether you are entitled to any refund or re-issued ticket if you lose, or have stolen, a discounted air ticket. Some airlines require the repurchase of a ticket before you can apply for a refund, which will not be given until after the validity of the original ticket has expired. Travel insurance in some cases covers lost tickets.

9 Some South American carriers change departure times of short-haul or domestic flights at short notice and, in some instances, schedules shown in the computers of transatlantic carriers differ from those actually flown by smaller, local carriers.

Road

International
buses

There are good road connections between Argentina, Paraguay, Uruguay and the south of Brazil. Rio de Janeiro and São Paulo can easily be reached by international buses from Asunción, Buenos Aires, Santiago and Montevideo. Transport is not so easy in the north and west of the country, although a reasonable road now exists between Caracas and Manaus. Entry from Bolivia at Corumbá is fairly straightforward. Buses from here connect with the main Brazilian road system at Campo Grande. Other border crossings from French Guiana at Oiapoque and from Guyana at Bonfim require some effort to actually get to the Brazilian border. Once there bus services are frequent, although heavy rains may make for slow going or cause cancellations.

Driving

Foreign driving licences are acceptable in Brazil, although it may be worth taking an international licence as not all officials and rental companies are able to recognize foreign licences. If requested tourists driving in Brazil should be able to present their licence and a passport to the police. *Detran* in Rio de Janeiro is at Avenida Presidente Vargas 817, 2nd floor, T5509744.

There are agreements between Brazil and all South American countries (but check in the case of Bolivia) whereby a car can be taken into Brazil (or a Brazilian car out of Brazil) for a period of 90 days without any special documents; an extension of up to 90 days is granted by the Customs authorities on presentation of the paper received at the border, which must be retained; this may be done at most Customs posts and at the Serviço de Controle Aduaneiro, Ministério da Fazenda, Av Presidente Antônio Carlos, Sala 1129, Rio de Janeiro.

For cars registered in other countries, the requirements are proof of ownership and/or registration in the home country and valid driving licence (see above). A 90-day permit is given by Customs and procedure is very straightforward. Nevertheless, it is better to cross the border into Brazil when it is officially open because an official who knows all about the entry of cars is then present. You must specify which border station you intend to leave by, but application can be made to the Customs to change this.

Boat

There is an 8% tax on international shipping line tickets bought in Brazil

Voyages on passenger-carrying cargo vessels between Brazilian ports and Europe, the USA, or elsewhere, are listed here: the *Grimaldi Line* sails from Tilbury to Brazil (Vitória, Santos, Paranaguá, Rio) and Buenos Aires via Hamburg, Amsterdam and Antwerp, Le Havre, Southampton and Bilbao, round trip about 51 days, US$3,040-5,400, also from Genoa to Paranaguá, Santos and Rio for US$1,100-1,400 (round trip or southbound only, no northbound only passages). A number of German container ships sail the year round to the east coast of South America: Felixstowe, Hamburg, Antwerp, Bilbao or Algeciras, Santos, Buenos Aires, Montevideo, Rio Grande do Sul, Itajaí, Santos, Rio de Janeiro, Rotterdam, Felixstowe (about 45 days, £3,100-3,500 per person round trip). Four German vessels make a 49-day round trip: Tilbury, Hamburg, Antwerp, Le Havre, Suape, Rio de Janeiro, Santos, Buenos Aires, Montevideo, São Francisco do Sul, Paranaguá, Santos, Suape, Rotterdam, Tilbury. There are also German sailings from Genoa or Livorno (Italy), or Spain to the east coast of South America.

A cheaper option is Polish *Ocean Line*'s services to the east coast, Gdynia to Buenos Aires, Montevideo and Santos (2-2½ months).

From the USA, *Maritime Reederei* of Germany sails to Charleston, Miami, Puerto Cabello, Santos, Buenos Aires, Montevideo, Rio Grande do Sul, Santos, Puerto Cabello, Freeport, New York, from £3,540 per person on a 42-day round trip. A German consortium has a 48-day round trip to New York, Savannah, Miami, Rio, Santos, Buenos Aires, Montevideo, Rio Grande do Sul, Santos, Salvador, Fortaleza, Norfolk, Philadelphia, New York, £4,020 per person (one-way to Rio, 15 days £1,395).

The Name ◀◀

All the guide books will tell you that the name Brazil – Brasil in Portuguese – is derived from the tree, pau do brasil, so prized by the Europeans for its red dye that the east coast of South America became known as A Terra do Brasil *(the Land of Brazil wood).*

Pau do brasil *was called* ibira-pitanga *(red wood) by the local Indians. Its scientific name is* Caesalpina echinata*. It grows up to 30 m high, the trunk and boughs are covered in thorns, and it has yellow, aromatic flowers. The wood is hard, heavy and reddish-orange, turning darker as it ages. In the 16th century it was used in cabinet-making, musical instruments and the naval industry, but mainly as a dye. The wood contains a colourant,* brasilina*, which dissolves in water; on extraction it oxidizes, becoming* brasileína*, which was used for colouring fabrics and ink. In the 19th century, however, artificial dyes replaced pau do brasil and its main use now is in violin bows and as an ornamental tree. Not only the Portuguese, but also the Spanish and French, shipped large quantities of the wood out of Brazil.*

The name brasil *was not new in the 16th century. Brazil wood was known as a source of dye since at least the 10th century AD and the term was often applied to any tree that produced red dye. A Persian Geography of the World, dated 982, lists islands where brazil wood could be found. Marco Polo talks of the brazil crops in Sumatra. The island of Terceira in the Azores used to be called Insola de Braçil because the dyewood grew there (one of its volcanic peaks is still called Monte Brazil). Even though JH Parry calls it "a somewhat inferior red dye", its use had a long history before the Portuguese began to colonize their new territory.*

Inferior or not, brazil wood also lent its name to one of the more potent legends of the Middle Ages. It was believed that Brazil, or Hy-Brazil, was a perfectly circular island, divided in two by a channel, close to the west coast of Ireland. It was shrouded in fog and only appeared every seven years. Those who managed to reach its shores found it to be a pleasant, but enchanted place. Several documented reports of sightings and landings exist and the last sighting was in 1872. It remained on maps from 1325 until 1865 (by then no more than a rock). Its fame was such that mariners of the calibre of John Cabot set out to find it. (For more information on Hy-Brazil, and other mythical islands, see Donald S Johnson, Phantom Islands of the Atlantic. The Legends of Seven Islands that Never Were, London: Souvenir, 1997.)

Enquiries regarding passages should be made through agencies in your own country, or through John Alton of *Strand Voyages*, Charing Cross Shopping Concourse, The Strand, London WC2N 4HZ, T020-78366363, F74970078. *Strand Voyages* are booking agents for all the above. Advice can also be obtained from *Cargo Ship Voyages Ltd*, Hemley, Woodbridge, Suffolk IP12 4QF, T/F01473-736265. Also in London: *The Cruise People*, 88 York St W1H 1DP, T020-77232450 (reservations 0800-526313). In continental Europe, contact *Wagner Frachtschiffreisen*, Stadlerstrasse 48, CH-8404, Winterthur, Switzerland, T052-2421442, F2421487. In the USA, contact *Freighter World Cruises*, 180 South Lake Ave, Pasadena, CA 91101, T818-4493106, *Travltips Cruise and Freighter Travel Association*, 163-07 Depot Rd, PO Box 188, Flushing, NY 11358, T800-8728584, or *Maris Freighter Travel Inc*, 215 Main St, Westport, CT06880-3210, T1-800-9962747. It is not possible to get a passage on a non-passenger-carrying cargo ship to South America from a European port.

River

A popular entry point to the Amazon region is along the Rio Amazonas from Iquitos in Peru to Tabatinga in Brazil. Onward travel is then by river boat or air to Manaus. This border can also be crossed by land from Leticia in Colombia. Security is particularly tight on this triple border and there have been reports that Brazilian immigration often refuse to allow entry to Brazil for more than 30 days.

Touching down

Airport information

See also pages 76 and 189 for detailed airport information in Rio de Janeiro and São Paulo respectively

For most visitors the point of arrival will either be **Tom Jobim** international airport (also known as **Galeão**) on the Ilha do Governador, some 16 km from the centre of Rio de Janeiro, or **Cumbica** international airport at Guarulhos in São Paulo. Details of other entry airports are given in their respective sections. Make sure you arrive two hours before international flights and it is wise to reconfirm your flight as departure times may have changed.

Airport departure tax

The amount of tax depends on the class of airport. All airports charge R$69.50 (US$36) international departure tax. First class airports charge R$9.50 domestic tax; second class airports R$7; domestic rates are lower still in third and fourth class airports. Tax must be paid on checking in, in *reais* or US dollars. Tax is waived if you stay in Brazil less than 24 hours.

Tourist information

See page 55 for an explanation of phone codes in Brazil

Embratur, the Brazilian Tourist Board, is at Setor Comercial Norte, Quadra 02, Bloco G, Brasília, DF, CEP 70710-500, Brazil, T0XX61-3289100, F0XX61-3283517, www.embratur.gov.br *Embratur* also has an office in Rio de Janeiro at R Uruguaiana 174, 8 andar, Rio de Janeiro, RJ, CEP 20050-090, T0XX21-5096017, F0XX21-5097381, rio@embratur.gov.br See also Tours and tour operators (page 23) for a list of specialist agencies operating from both inside and outside of Brazil.

Details of state and municipal tourist offices are given in the Essentials section of the respective towns and cities. They are not usually too helpful regarding information on cheap hotels. It is also difficult to get information on neighbouring states.

National parks are run by *Ibama*, the Instituto Brasileiro do Meio Ambiente e dos Recursos Naturais Renováveis (Brazilian Institute of Environmental Protection): SAIN, Avenida L-4, bloco B, Térreo, Edifiço Sede de Ibama, CEP 70800-200, Brasília, DF, T0XX61-226 8221/9014, F0XX61-322 1058, www.ibama.gov.br The Institute is underfunded, often understaffed and visitors may find it difficult to obtain information. National parks are open to visitors, usually with a permit from Ibama. For further details, see individual parks in the text.

Local customs and laws

Clothing

In general, clothing requirements in Brazil are less formal than in the Hispanic countries. It is, however, advisable for men visiting restaurants to wear long trousers (women in shorts may also be refused entry) and jackets or pullovers in São Paulo. As a general rule, it is better not to wear shorts in official buildings, cinemas, interstate buses and on flights.

Conduct

Men should avoid arguments or insults (care is needed even when overtaking on the road); pride may be defended with a gun. Gay men, while still enjoying greater freedom than in many countries, should exercise reasonable discretion. It is normal to stare and comment on a woman's appearance, and if you happen to look different or to be travelling alone, you will undoubtedly attract attention. Be aware that Brazilian men can be extremely persistent, and very easily encouraged; it is safest to err on the side of caution until you are accustomed.

Touching down

Official time *Brazil has four time zones: Brazilian standard time is three hours behind GMT; the Amazon time zone (Pará west of the Rio Xingu, Amazonas, Roraima, Rondônia, Mato Grosso and Mato Grosso do Sul) is four hours behind GMT, the State of Acre is five hours behind GMT; the Fernando de Noronha archipelago is two hours behind GMT. Clocks move forward one hour in summer for approximately five months (usually between October and February or March), but times of change vary. This does not apply to Acre.*

IDD code *55.*
Business hours *Generally 0900-1800 Monday-Friday; closed for lunch some time between 1130 and 1400. **Shops** are open on Saturday till 1230 or 1300.*
Government offices: *1100-1800 Monday-Friday. **Banks**: 1000-1600 or 1630, closed on Saturday.*
Voltage *Generally 110 V 60 cycles AC, but in some cities and areas 220 V 60 cycles AC is used.*
Weights and measures *The metric system is used by all.*

Essentials

Colour

Racial discrimination is illegal in Brazil. There is, however, a complex class system which is informed both by heritage and by economic status. This effectively discriminates against the poor, who are chiefly (but by no means exclusively) black. There are very few black role models, television is dominated by white actors and the country has no visible black political movement. In Salvador, where 80% of the population is black, television coverage still manages to be limited to white participants. Black visitors to the country may encounter racial prejudice. A surprising number of Brazilians are unaware that black Europeans exist, so you could become the focus of some curiosity.

Time-keeping

Brazilians have a very 'relaxed' attitude towards time. It is quite normal for them to arrive an hour or so late even for business appointments. If you expect to meet someone more or less at an exact time, you can add *em punto* or *a hora inglesa* (English time) but be prepared to wait anyway.

Tipping

Tipping is usual, but less costly than in most other countries, except for porters. In restaurants, tip 10% of bill if no service charge is added, but give a small tip anyway if it is. Taxi drivers are not tipped. Give a small tip to cloakroom attendants; none to cinema usherettes; 10-15% to hairdressers; about US$0.50 per item for airport porters.

Prohibitions

Despite the wide distribution and use of drugs such as marijuana and cocaine, they are still illegal and you will face a heavy sentence if you are caught with them. Be especially aware when crossing borders and on no account bring coca leaves from Bolivia. A campaign against the exploitation of minors for sexual purposes gained wide publicity in 1997 (in Brazilian law a minor is considered to be under the age of 18). Although the local bikinis leave little to the imagination you will be prosecuted for nude bathing except on an official nudist beach of which there are very few. Never carry firearms; their possession could land you in serious trouble.

Responsible tourism
See also Ecotourism, page 63

Travel to the furthest corners of the globe is now commonplace and the mass movement of people for leisure and business is a major source of foreign exchange and economic development in many parts of South America.

The benefits of international travel are self-evident for both hosts and travellers – employment, increased understanding of different cultures, business and leisure opportunities. At the same time there is clearly a downside to the industry. Where visitor pressure is high and/or poorly regulated, adverse impacts on society and the natural environment may be apparent. Paradoxically, this is as true in undeveloped and

Essentials

▶▶ How big is your footprint?

Where possible choose a destination, tour operator or hotel with a proven ethical and environmental commitment – if in doubt ask.

Spend money on locally produced (rather than imported) goods and services and use common sense when bargaining – your few dollars saved may be a week's salary to others.

Use water and electricity carefully – travellers may receive preferential supply while the needs of local communities are overlooked.

Learn about local etiquette and culture – consider local norms and behaviour

and dress appropriately for local cultures and situations.

Protect wildlife and other natural resources – don't buy souvenirs or goods made from wildlife unless they are clearly sustainably produced and are not protected under CITES legislation (CITES controls trade in endangered species).

Always ask before taking photographs or videos of people.

Consider staying in local rather than foreign-owned accommodation – the economic benefits for host communities are far greater, as are the opportunities to learn about local culture.

pristine areas (where culture and the natural environment are less 'prepared' for even small numbers of visitors) as it is in major resort destinations.

The travel industry is growing rapidly and increasingly the impacts of this supposedly 'smokeless' industry are becoming apparent. These impacts can seem remote and unrelated to an individual trip or holiday (eg air travel is clearly implicated in global warming and damage to the ozone layer, resort location and construction can destroy natural habitats and restrict traditional rights and activities), but individual choice and awareness can make a difference in many instances (see box, page 44), and collectively, travellers are having a significant effect in shaping a more responsible and sustainable industry.

In an attempt to promote awareness of and credibility for responsible tourism, organizations such as **Green Globe** (greenglobe@compuserve.com, T020-79308333) and the **Center for Environmentally Sustainable Tourism** (CERT) (T01268-795772) in the UK now offer advice on destinations and sites that have achieved certain commitments to conservation and sustainable development. Generally these are larger mainstream destinations and resorts, but they are still a useful guide and increasingly aim to provide information on smaller operations.

Of course travel can also have beneficial impacts and this is something to which every traveller can contribute – many national parks are part funded by receipts from visitors. Similarly, travellers can promote patronage and protection of important archaeological sites and heritage through their interest and contributions via entrance fees. They can also support small-scale enterprises by staying in locally run hotels and hostels, eating in local restaurants and by purchasing local goods, supplies and arts and crafts.

In fact, since the Responsible Travel section was first introduced in the *South American Handbook* in 1992 there has been a phenomenal growth in *tourism that promotes and supports the conservation of natural environments and is also fair and equitable to local communities*. This ecotourism segment is probably the fastest-growing sector of the travel industry and provides a vast and growing range of destinations and activities in South America. For example, the Una Ecopark in Bahia offers visits and experiences in Brazil's Atlantic forest (one of the most endangered ecosystems in the world). A visit to the park provides opportunities to undertake walks in the forest canopy walkway suspended high above the forest floor (T/F0XX73-6341118, Vrisea@bitsnet.com.br). Other initiatives can be found in São Paulo state (amazonadv@aol.com).

While the authenticity of some ecotourism operators' claims need to be interpreted with care, there is clearly both a huge demand for this type of activity and also significant opportunities to support worthwhile conservation and social development initiatives.

Organizations such as **Conservation International** (T202-4295660, www.ecotour. org), the **Eco-Tourism Society** (T802-4472121, http://ecotourism.org), **Planeta** (www2.planeta.com/mader) and the UK-based **Tourism Concern** (T020-77533330, www.gn.apc.org/tourismconcern) have begun to develop and/or promote ecotourism projects and destinations and their websites are an excellent source of information and details for sites and initiatives throughout South America. Additionally, UK organizations such as **Earthwatch** (T01865-311601, www.earthwatch.org) and **Discovery International** (T020-72299881, www.discoveryinitiatives.com) offer opportunities to participate directly in scientific research and development projects throughout the region.

Essentials

Safety

Although Brazil's big cities suffer high rates of violent crime, this is mostly confined to the *favelas* where poverty and drugs are the main cause. Visitors should not enter *favelas* except when accompanied by workers for NGOs, tour groups or other people who know the local residents well and are accepted by the community. Visitors may be targets of theft, but if you don't take anything you aren't prepared to lose and insure yourself adequately, it should not ruin your trip. If the worst does happen and you are threatened, don't panic, and hand over your valuables. Do not resist, but report the crime to the local tourist police later. It is extremely rare for a tourist to be hurt during a robbery in Brazil. Being aware of the dangers, acting confidently and using your common sense, will reduce many of the risks.

Certain parts of the country are areas of drug cultivation and should be avoided. These are mentioned where appropriate in the travelling text. All border areas should be regarded with some caution because of smuggling activities. Violence over land ownership in parts of the interior have resulted in a 'Wild West' atmosphere in some towns which should therefore be passed through quickly. Red-light districts should also be given a wide berth as there are reports of drinks being drugged with a substance popularly known as 'Good night Cinderella'. This leaves the victim easily amenable to having their possessions stolen, or worse.

Apart from the obvious precautions of not wearing jewellery (wear a cheap, plastic *digital* watch), take local advice about safety and do not assume that daytime is safer than night. If walking after dark, walk in the road, not on the pavement/sidewalk and do not go on to the beach. Don't take valuables to the beach.

Protecting money & valuables

Photocopy your passport, air ticket and other documents, make a record of travellers' cheque and credit card numbers. Keep them separately from the originals and leave another set of records at home. Keep all documents secure; hide your main cash supply in different places or under your clothes. Extra pockets sewn inside shirts and trousers, moneybelts (best worn below the waist), neck or leg pouches and elasticated support bandages for keeping money above the elbow or below the knee have been repeatedly recommended (the last by John Hatt in *The Tropical Traveller*).

Avoiding con tricks

Never trust anyone telling sob stories or offering 'safe rooms', and when looking for a hotel, always choose the room yourself. Be wary of 'plainclothes policemen'; insist on seeing identification and on going to the police station by main roads. Do not hand over your identification (or money) until you are at the station. On no account take them directly back to your hotel. Be even more suspicious if they seek confirmation of their status from a passer-by.

Essentials

Hotel security

Hotel safe deposits are generally, but not always, secure. If you cannot get a receipt for valuables in a hotel safe, you can seal the contents in a plastic bag and sign across the seal. Always keep an inventory of what you have deposited. If you don't trust the hotel, lock everything in your pack and secure that in your room when you go out. If you lose valuables, report to the police and note details of the report for insurance purposes.

Public transport

When you have all your luggage with you at a bus or railway station, be especially careful and carry any shoulder bags in front of you. To be extra safe, take a taxi between airport/bus station/railway station and hotel, keep your bags with you and pay only when you and your luggage are outside; avoid night buses and arriving at your destination at night.

Rape

This can happen anywhere in the world. If you are the victim of a sexual assault, you are advised in the first instance to contact a doctor (this can be your home doctor if you prefer). You will need tests to determine whether you have contracted any sexually transmitted diseases; you may also need advice on post-coital contraception. You should also contact your embassy, where consular staff are very willing to help in cases of assault.

Women travellers

These additional hints have mainly been supplied by women, but most apply to any single traveller. When you set out, err on the side of caution until your instincts have adjusted to the customs of a new culture. Be prepared for the exceptional curiosity extended to visitors, especially women and try not to overreact. If, as a single woman, you can befriend a local woman, you will learn much more about the country you are visiting. There is a definite 'gringo trail' which you can follow which can be helpful when looking for safe accommodation, especially if arriving after dark (which is best avoided). Remember that for a single woman a taxi at night can be as dangerous as wandering around on your own. It is easier for men to take the friendliness of locals at face value; women may be subject to unwanted attention. Do not disclose to strangers where you are staying. By wearing a wedding ring and saying that your 'husband' is close at hand, you may dissuade an aspiring suitor. If politeness fails, do not feel bad about showing offence and departing. A good rule is always to act with confidence, as though you know where you are going, even if you do not. Someone who looks lost is more likely to attract unwanted attention.

Police

There are several types of police: Polícia Federal, civilian dressed, who handle all federal law duties, including immigration. A subdivision is the Polícia Federal Rodoviária, uniformed, who are the traffic police on federal highways. Polícia Militar are the uniformed, street police force, under the control of the state governor, handling all state laws. They are not the same as the Armed Forces' internal police. Polícia Civil, also state-controlled, handle local laws and investigations. They are usually in civilian dress, unless in the traffic division. In cities, the Prefeitura controls the Guarda Municipal, who handle security. Tourist police operate in places with a strong tourist presence. In case of difficulty, visitors should seek them out in the first instance.

Where to stay

Hotels

For a quick reference price guide to our hotel categories, see inside the front cover

Unless travelling in high season, always ask for a discount, especially if staying for more than one night. The best guide to hotels in Brazil is the *Guia Brasil Quatro Rodas*, with good maps of towns. Motels are specifically intended for very short-stay couples: there is no stigma attached and they usually offer good value (the rate for a full night is called the *pernoite*), though the decor can be a little unsettling. The type known as *hotel familiar*, to be found in the interior – large meals, communal washing, hammocks for

Hotel prices and facilities

◀◀

Prices include taxes and service charges, but are without meals unless otherwise stated. They are based on a double room, except in the **E** and **F** ranges where prices are almost always per person.

LL (over US$150) to **AL** (US$66-99) Hotels in these categories can be found in most of the large cities in Brazil, but especially in areas with a strong concentration of tourists or business travellers. They should offer pool, sauna, gym, jacuzzi, all business facilities (including email), several restaurants and bars. A safe box is usually provided in each room. In cities such as São Paulo and Rio de Janeiro the top hotels compare with the highest standards in the world, although service can sometimes still be very Brazilian.

A (US$46-65) and **B** (US$31-45) Hotels in these categories should provide more than the standard facilities and a fair degree of comfort. Most include a good breakfast and many offer extras such as colour TV, minibar, a/c and a swimming pool. They may also provide tourist information and their own transport for airport pick-ups. Service is generally good and most accept credit cards, although a lower rate for cash is often offered.

C (US$21-30) and **D** (US$12-20) Hotels in these categories range from very comfortable to functional and there are some real bargains to be had. You should expect your own bathroom, constant hot water, a towel, soap and toilet paper. There is sometimes a restaurant and a communal sitting area. In tropical regions rooms are usually equipped with a/c, although this may be rather old. Hotels used to catering for foreign tourists and backpackers often have luggage storage, money exchange and kitchen facilities.

E (US$7-11) and **F** (US$6 and under) Hotels in these categories are often extremely simple with bedside or ceiling fans, shared bathrooms and little in the way of furniture. Breakfast when included is very simple, usually no more than a bread roll and coffee. The best accommodation and facilities for under US$10 per night is generally found in the youth hostels (see below), although tourist areas with high quantities of bed spaces such as Porto Seguro often have good quality rooms at this price during low season.

Essentials

children – is much cheaper, but only for the enterprising. *Pousadas* are the equivalent of bed-and-breakfast, often small and family run, although some are very sophisticated and correspondingly priced. Usually hotel prices include breakfast; there is no reduction if you don't eat it. In the better hotels (our category A and upwards), the breakfast is well worth eating: rolls, ham, eggs, cheese, cakes, fruit. Normally the *apartamento* is a room with a bath; a *quarto* is a room without a bath. Leave rooms in good time so frigobar bills can be checked.

The star rating system for hotels (five-star hotels are not price controlled) is not the standard used in North America or Europe.

Business visitors are strongly recommended to book accommodation in advance, and this can easily be done for Rio or São Paulo hotels with representation abroad. *Varig* has a good hotel reservation service, with discounts of up to 50% for its passengers.

It's a good idea to book accommodation in advance in small towns which are popular at weekends with city dwellers (eg near São Paulo and Rio de Janeiro).

Roteiros de Charme In some 30 locations in the Southeast and Northeast, this is an association of hotels and *pousadas* which aims to give a high standard of accommodation in establishments which represent the town they are in. It is a private initiative. If you are travelling in the appropriate budget range (our A price range upwards), you can plan an itinerary which takes in these high-class hotels, with a reputation for comfort and good food, and some fine places of historical and leisure interest. *Roteiros de Charme* hotels are listed in the text and any one of them can provide information on the group. Alternatively, contact the office in the *Caesar Park Hotel* in Rio de Janeiro (Avenida Vieira Souto 460, Ipanema, F021-2871592, www.roteirosdecharme.com.br).

Advice &
suggestions

The service stations (*postos*) and hostels (*dormitórios*) along the main roads provide excellent value in room and food, akin to truck-driver type accommodation in Europe, for those on a tight budget.

The electric showers used in many hotels should be checked for obvious flaws in the wiring; try not to touch the rose while it is producing hot water.

Some taxi drivers will try to take you to the expensive hotels, who pay them commission for bringing in custom. Beware!

Cockroaches are ubiquitous and unpleasant, but not dangerous. Take some insecticide powder if staying in cheap hotels; *Baygon* (Bayer) has been recommended. Stuff toilet paper in any holes in walls that you may suspect of being parts of cockroach runs.

Away from the main commercial centres, many hotels, restaurants and bars have inadequate water supplies. Almost without exception, used toilet paper should not be flushed down the pan, but placed in the receptacle provided. This applies even in quite expensive hotels. Failing to observe this custom will block the pan or drain.

Youth hostels

For information about youth hostels contact **Federação Brasileira dos Albergues da Juventude**, R dos Andradas 1137, conj 214, Porto Alegre, Rio Grande do Sul, CEP 90.020-007, www.albergues.com.br; its annual book provides a full list of good value accommodation, with the addresses of the regional representatives. Also see the Internet Guide to Hostelling which has a list of Brazilian youth hostels: www.hostels.com/br.html

Low-budget travellers with student cards (photograph needed) can often use the **Casa dos Estudantes** (CEU) network.

Camping

Members of the **Camping Clube do Brasil** or those with an international campers' card pay only half the rate of a non-member, which is US$10-15 per person. The *Clube* has 43 sites in 13 states and 80,000 members. For enquiries, *Camping Clube do Brasil*, Divisão de Campings, R Senador Dantas 75, 29th floor, Centro, Rio de Janeiro, CEP 20037-900, T0XX21-2103171. It may be difficult to get into some *Camping Clube* campsites during the high season (January-February). Private campsites charge about US$8 per person. For those on a very low budget and in isolated areas where there is no campsite, service stations can be used as camping sites (Shell stations recommended); they have shower facilities, watchmen and food; some have dormitories; truck drivers are a mine of information. There are also various municipal sites. Campsites often tend to be some distance from public transport routes and are better suited to those with their own transport. Never camp at the side of a road; wild camping is generally not possible.

Good camping equipment may be purchased in Brazil and there are several rental companies. Camping gas cartridges are easy to buy in sizeable towns in the south, eg in HM shops. *Guia de Camping* is produced by Artpress, R Araçatuba 487, São Paulo 05058; it lists most sites and is available in bookshops in most cities. Quatro Rodas' *Guia Brasil* also lists main campsites.

Homestays

Experiment in International Living Ltd, 287 Worcester Rd, Malvern, Worcestershire WR14 1AB, T01684-562577, F562212, or **Friesdorferstrasse** 194A, 53175 Bonn 9, T0228-957220, F358282, can arrange stays with families from one to four weeks in Brazil; EIL has offices in 38 countries. This has been recommended as an excellent way to meet people and learn the language.

Getting around

Public transport in Brazil is very efficient, especially when compared to some other South American countries. The main issue is the great distances involved. Most visitors will find themselves travelling by buses and planes, except in the Amazon when often a river boat is the only way to get around. Train routes are practically non-existent, car hire is expensive and hitchhiking not widely accepted. Taxis are very reasonable and easy to come by.

Air

For addresses and telephone numbers of airline offices, see Directory of individual towns

Because of the size of the country, flying is often the most practical option and internal air services are highly developed. The larger cities are linked with each other several times a day and all national airlines offer excellent service. Internal flights used to be expensive, but recent deregulation of the airlines has reduced prices on some routes by about a third (although flights to and from the Amazon remain the most costly). In addition, no-frills airlines have been set up, offering fares that can be as cheap as travelling by bus. *Gol* is the main bargain airline; *BRA*, *Trip* and *ATA* are the three others. The largest airlines are *TAM*, *Varig* and *Vasp*. *Rio-Sul* and *Nordeste* (both allied to *Varig*), have extensive networks. Smaller airlines include *Penta*, who have recently built up a wide and cheap network throughout the Amazon region, and *Pantanal*, mainly operating flights between São Paulo state and Mato Grosso do Sul.

Double check all bookings and information given by ground staff. National toll-free numbers (except for *Gol*, which charges) for reservations and confirmations are detailed below. Most websites provide full information, including a booking service, although not all are in English.

Domestic air routes

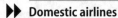

Essentials

▶▶ Domestic airlines

Gol *T0300 7892121 (US$0.10 per minute),*
English-speaking operators,
www.voegol.com.br, website in
Portuguese only
Nordeste *T0800-992004,*
www.nordeste.com
Pantanal *T0800-125833,*
www.pantanal-airlines.com.br

Rio-Sul *T0800-992004, www.rio-sul.com*
TAM *T0800-123100, www.tam.com.br*
Transbrasil *T0800-151151,*
www.transbrasil.com.br
Trip *T0800-7018747; www.voetrip.com.br*
Varig *T0800-997000, T0845-6037601*
(UK), www.varig.com.br,
Vasp *T0800-998277, www.vasp.com.br*

Airpasses *TAM, Transbrasil, Varig* and *Vasp* offer 21-day air passes for people resident outside of Brazil, but since deregulation they are not as good value as they used to be. They also offer limited flexibility; you must buy your airpass outside of Brazil in conjunction with an international scheduled flight and decide your itinerary at the time of purchase. There are no discounts for children and infants pay 10% of the price. The **Varig Airpass** is US$530 for five flights, with a maximum of four extra coupons available for US$100 each and valid for 21 days. Amendments may be made once prior to commencement of travel at US$30 per change. The *Varig* pass is only available to travellers arriving in Brazil with *Varig* or *British Airways*.

The **Transbrasil Airpass**, is valid for five flights and 30 days. It is available to individuals arriving on the services of other carriers as well as their own, but it costs US$440 if you have an international *Transbrasil* ticket, and US$600 if using another airline.

The **Vasp Airpass** is valid for 21 days and costs US$440 for five flights with a maximum of four extra coupons available for US$100 each which must be purchased with the airpass. It is available to anyone purchasing an international flight on any airline.

Like the *Vasp* airpass, the **TAM Airpass** allows you to arrive in Brazil on any airline. It costs US$530, is valid for 21 days and re-routing is permitted for US$50.

With airpasses, no journey may be repeated and none may be used on the Rio-São Paulo shuttle. Remember that domestic airport tax has to be paid at each departure. Hotels in the *Tropical* and *Othon* chains, and others, offer discounts of 10% to *Varig* airpass travellers. Promotions on certain destinations offer a free flight, hotel room, etc; enquire when buying the airpass. Converting the voucher can take some hours, do not plan an onward flight immediately, check at terminals that the airpass is still registered, faulty cancellations have been reported. Cost and restrictions on the airpass are subject to change.

Small scheduled domestic airlines operate Brazilian-built *Bandeirante* 16-seater prop-jets into virtually every city and town with any semblance of an airstrip. Internal flights often have many stops and are therefore quite slow. Most airports have left-luggage lockers (US$2 for 24 hours). Seats are often unallocated on internal flights; board in good time.

Road

Though the best paved highways are heavily concentrated in the southeast, those serving the interior are being improved to all-weather status and many are paved. Brazil has over 1,650, 000 km of highways, of which 150,000 km are paved, and several thousand more all-weather. Most main roads between principal cities are paved. Some are narrow and therefore dangerous and many are in poor condition.

Bus There are three standards of bus: *Comum*, or *Convencional* are quite slow, not very comfortable and fill up quickly; *Executivo* are more expensive, comfortable (many have reclining seats), and don't stop en route to pick up passengers so are safer. *Leito* (literally, bed) run at night between the main centres, offering reclining seats with leg rests, toilets, and sometimes refreshments, at double the normal fare. For journeys over 100 km, most buses have chemical toilets (bring toilet paper). Air conditioning can make buses cold at night, so take a blanket or sweater; on some services blankets are supplied.

Buses stop fairly frequently (every 2-4 hours) at *postos* for snacks. Bus stations for inter-state services and other long distance routes are usually called rodoviárias. They are frequently outside the city centres and offer snack bars, lavatories, left-luggage stores (*guarda volume*), local bus services and information centres. Buy bus tickets at rodoviárias (most now take credit cards), not from travel agents who add on surcharges. Reliable bus information is hard to come by, other than from companies themselves. Buses usually arrive and depart in very good time. Many town buses have turnstiles which can be inconvenient if you are carrying a large pack. Urban buses normally serve local airports.

Taxi Rates vary from city to city, but are consistent within each city. At the outset, make sure the meter is cleared and shows tariff 1, except (usually) 2300-0600, Sunday, and in December when 2 is permitted. Check that the meter is working; if not, fix the price in advance. The **radio taxi** service costs about 50% more but cheating is less likely. Taxis outside larger hotels usually cost twice as much. If you are seriously cheated note the number of the taxi and insist on a signed bill, threatening to go to the police; it can work. **Moto-taxis** are much more economical, but many are unlicensed and there have been a number of robberies of passengers.

Car Any foreigner with a passport can purchase a Brazilian car and travel outside Brazil. A letter in Spanish from your consul explaining your aims and that you will return the vehicle to Brazil can make life much easier at borders and check points. Foreigners do not need the CPF tax document (needed by Brazilians), and the official purchase receipt is accepted as proof of ownership. Don't buy an alcohol-driven car if you propose to drive outside Brazil. It is essential to have an external intake filter fitted, or dust can rapidly destroy an engine. VW Combi vans are cheapest in Brazil where they are made, they are equivalent to the pre-1979 model in Europe. If a lot of time is to be spent on dirt roads, the Ford Chevrolet pick-up is more robust.

Fuel It is virtually impossible to buy premium grades of petrol/gasoline anywhere. With alcohol fuel you need about 50% more alcohol than regular gasoline. Larger cars have a small extra tank for 'gasolina' to get the engine started; remember to keep this topped up. Fuel is only 85% octane (owing to high methanol content), so be prepared for bad consumption and poor performance and starting difficulties in non-Brazilian cars in winter. Diesel fuel is cheap and a diesel engine may provide fewer maintenance problems. Very few service stations open during Carnival week. Fuel prices vary from week to week and region to region: ordinary petrol, *gasolina comun*, is around US$1 per litre; *alcool comun* and diesel are cheaper. There is no unleaded fuel.

Preparation It's well worth installing extra heavy-duty shock-absorbers (such as Spax or Koni). Fit tubes on 'tubeless' tyres, since air plugs for tubeless tyres are hard to find, and if you bend the rim on a pothole, the tyre will not hold air. Take spare tubes, an extra spare tyre, spare plugs, fan-belts, radiator hoses and headlamp bulbs. Find out about your car's electrics and filters and what spares may be required. Similarly, know how to handle problems arising from dirty fuel. Take a 10-litre water container for self and vehicle. Note that in some areas gas stations are few and far between.

Security Spare no ingenuity in making your car secure. Try never to leave the car unattended except in a locked garage or guarded parking space. Remove all belongings and leave the empty glove compartment open. Also lock the clutch or accelerator to the steering wheel with a heavy, obvious chain or lock. Adult minders or street children will generally protect your car fiercely in exchange for a tip.

See Driving, page 40, for required documents

Essentials

Documents Be very careful to keep **all** the papers you are given when you enter, to produce when you leave.

Insurance against accident and theft is very expensive. If the car is stolen or written off you will be required to pay very high import duty on its value. The legally required minimum cover for third party insurance is not expensive. If anyone is hurt, do not pick them up as you may become liable.

Car hire Renting a car in Brazil is expensive: the cheapest rate for unlimited mileage for a small car is about US$50 per day. The minimum age is 21 and it is essential to have a credit card. Companies operate under the names *aluguel de automóveis* or *autolocadores*. Toll free numbers for nationwide firms are *Avis*, T0800-558066 and *Localiza*, T0800-992000 (www.localiza.com.br). Details of local companies are given in the text.

Car hire insurance Check exactly what the hirer's insurance policy covers. In many cases it will not apply to major accidents, or 'natural' damage (eg flooding). Ask if extra cover is available. Sometimes using a credit card automatically includes insurance. Beware of being billed for scratches which were on the vehicle before you hired it.

Motorcycling The machine you use should be off-road capable, eg the BMW R80/100/GS for its rugged and simple design and reliable shaft drive. A road bike can go most places an off-road bike can go at the cost of greater effort.

Preparations Many roads are rough. Fit heavy-duty front fork springs, the best quality rebuildable shock absorber you can afford (Ohlins, White Power) and lockable luggage such as Krausers (reinforce luggage frames). A large capacity fuel tank (Acerbis), +300 mile/480 km range is essential if going off the beaten track. A washable air filter is a good idea (K&N), also fuel filters and fueltap rubber seals, a good set of trails-type tyres, as well as a high mudguard. Get to know the bike before you go, ask the dealers in your country what goes wrong with it and arrange a link whereby you can get parts flown out to you. If using a fully enclosed chaincase on a chain-driven bike, an automatic chain oiler is a good idea. The Scott-Oiler (106 Clober Road, Milngavie, Glasgow G62 7SS, Scotland) has been recommended. Fill it with Sae 90 oil. A hefty bash plate/sump guard is invaluable.

A first-class tool kit is a must and if riding a bike with a chain then a spare set of sprockets and an 'o' ring chain should be carried. Parts are few and far between, but mechanics are skilled at making do and can usually repair things.

Security Try not to leave a fully laden bike on its own. An Abus D or chain will keep the bike secure. A cheap alarm can give you peace of mind. Look for hotels with a courtyard or secure parking and never leave luggage on the bike whilst unattended.

Documents Passport, International Driving Licence and bike registration document are necessary. Temporary import papers are given on entry, to be surrendered on leaving the country.

Cycling A mountain bike is strongly recommended. The good quality ones (and the cast-iron rule is never to skimp on quality) are incredibly tough, with low gear ratios for difficult terrain, wide tyres with plenty of tread for good road-holding, cantilever brakes, and a low centre of gravity for improved stability. Although touring bikes – and to a lesser extent mountain bikes – and spares are available in the larger cities, most locally manufactured goods are shoddy and rarely last. Buy everything you possibly can before you leave home.

Equipment A small but comprehensive tool kit (to include chain rivet and crank removers, a spoke key and possibly a block remover), a spare tyre and inner tubes, a puncture repair kit with plenty of extra patches and glue, a set of brake blocks, brake and gear cables and all types of nuts and bolts, at least 12 spokes (best taped to the chain stay), a light oil for the chain (eg Finish-Line Teflon Dry-Lube), tube of waterproof grease, a pump secured by a pump lock, a Blackburn parking block (a most invaluable accessory, cheap and virtually weightless), a cyclometer, a loud bell, and a secure lock and chain. *Richard's Bicycle Book* makes useful reading for even the most mechanically minded.

Strong and waterproof front and back panniers are a must. When packed these are likely to be heavy and should be carried on the strongest racks available. Poor quality racks have ruined many a journey for they take incredible strain on unpaved roads. A top bag cum rucksack (eg Carradice) makes a good addition for use on and off the bike. A Cannondale front bag is good for maps, camera, compass, etc. (Other recommended panniers are Ortlieb – front and back – which is waterpoof and almost 'sandproof', Mac-Pac, Madden and Karimoor.) 'Gaffa' tape is excellent for protecting vulnerable parts of panniers and for carrying out all manner of repairs. Pack equipment and clothes in plastic bags to give extra protection against dust and rain.

Useful tips Wind, not hills, is the enemy of the cyclist. Avoid dehydration by drinking regularly and carry an ample supply of water. Give your bicycle a thorough daily check for loose nuts or bolts or bearings. See that all parts run smoothly. A good chain should last 3,200 km but keep it as clean as possible – an old toothbrush is good for this – and to oil it lightly from time to time. Traffic on main roads can be a nightmare; it is usually far more rewarding to keep to the smaller roads or to paths if they exist. A rearview mirror has been frequently recommended to forewarn you of vehicles which are too close behind. Also, watch out for oncoming, overtaking vehicles, unstable loads on trucks, protruding loads, etc. Make yourself conspicuous by wearing bright clothing and a helmet. Most towns have a bicycle shop of some description, but in an emergency it is amazing how one can improvise with wire, string, dental floss, nuts and bolts, odd pieces of tin or electrical 'Gaffa' tape!

The Expedition Advisory Centre, administered by the Royal Geographical Society, 1, Kensington Gore, London SW7 2AR, has published a useful monograph entitled *Bicycle Expeditions*, by Paul Vickers. Published in March 1990, it is available direct from the Centre, price £6.50 (postage extra if outside the UK). (In the UK there is also the Cyclist's Touring Club, CTC, Cotterell House, 69 Meadrow, Godalming, Surrey GU7 3HS, T01483-417217, cycling@ctc.org.uk, for touring and technical information.)

Hitchhiking (*carona* in Portuguese) is difficult everywhere. This is partly because drivers are reluctant to give lifts because passengers are their responsibility. Try at the highway police check points on the main roads (but make sure your documents are in order) or at service stations (*postos*). **Hitchhiking**

Boat

The main areas where travel by boat is practical (and often necessary) are the Amazon region, along the São Francisco River and along the Atlantic coast. There are also some limited transport services through the Pantanal. *See also page 536 for details of river transport in the Amazon*

Train

There are 30,379 km of railways which are not combined into a unified system. Brazil has two gauges and there is little transfer between them. Two more gauges exist for the isolated Amapá Railway and the tourist-only São João del Rei line. There are still passenger services in the state of São Paulo, but most passenger services have been withdrawn. Full details are given in the text.

Maps and guide books

Essentials

Telephone yellow pages in most cities (but not Rio) contain good street maps which, together with the Quatro Rodas maps, are a great help for getting around

A recommended series of general maps is published by *International Travel Maps* (ITM), 345 West Broadway, Vancouver BC, V5Y 1P8, Canada, T604-8793621, F8794521, compiled with historical notes, by the late Kevin Healey. Available are *South America South*, *North East* and *North West* (1:4M), *Rio de Janeiro* (1:20,000). Also available is *New World Edition*, Bertelsmann, Neumarkter Strasse 18, 81673 München, Germany, *Mittelamerika*, *Südamerika Nord*, *Südamerika Sud*, *Brasilien* (all 1:4M). London's *Stanfords*, 12-14 Long Acre, Covent Garden, WC2E 9LP, UK, T020-78361321, F020-78360189, www.stanfords.co.uk also sells a wide variety of guides and maps.

Quatro Rodas, a motoring magazine, publishes an excellent series of maps and guides in Portuguese and English from about US$10. Its annual *Guia Brasil* is a type of Michelin Guide to hotels, restaurants (not the cheapest), sights, facilities and general information on hundreds of cities and towns in the country, including good country and street maps. These guides can be purchased from street newspaper vendors throughout the country and at Av das Nações Unidas 7221, 14 andar, Pinheiros, CEP 05425-902, T0XX11-30376004, F0XX11-30376270, www.publiabril.com.br *Quatro Rodas* guides may be bought in Europe from: 33, rue de Miromesnil, 75008 Paris, T00331-42663118, F00331-42661399, abrilparis@wanadoo.fr; and *Deltapress-Sociedade Distribuidora de Publica*ções, Capa Rota, Tapada Nova, Linhó, 2710 Sintra, Portugal, T003511-9249940, F9240429. In the USA: Lincoln Building, 60 East 42nd St, Suite 3403, New York, NY 10165/3403, T001212-5575990/3, F9830972, abril@walrus.com

Keeping in touch

Communications

Internet
The @ sign is known as ahoba in Brazil

For cybercafés see under Communications, in the Directory of individual towns

Brazil is said to be seventh in the world in terms of internet use. Public internet access is available in all towns and cities and anywhere popular with tourists. There is usually an hourly charge of around US$3, but you can almost always use partial hours at a reduced rate. More and more hotels offer an internet service to their guests, while some government programmes even offer free use (notably in Manaus and Cuiaba). In some more remote locations, such as Lençios in Bahia, connections are so slow as to be almost pointless. For a regularly updated list of locations around the world, check www.netcafeguide.com

To send a **standard letter** or **postcard** to the USA costs US$0.75, to Europe US$0.85, to Australia or South Africa US$1. Air mail should take about seven days to or from Britain or the US. Franked and registered (insured) letters are normally secure, but check that the amount franked is what you have paid, or the item will not arrive. Aerogrammes are most reliable. To avoid queues and obtain higher denomination stamps go to the stamp desk at the main post office.

The post office sells cardboard boxes for sending packages internally and abroad. They must be submitted open; string and official sellotape are provided. You pay by the kilo and fill in a list of contents. Courier services such as *DHL*, *Federal Express* and *UPS* (recommended) are useful, but they may not necessarily operate under those names.

Postes Restantes usually only hold letters for 30 days. Identification is required and it's a good idea to write your name on a piece of paper to help the attendant find your letters. Charge is usually minimal but often involves queuing at another counter to buy stamps which are attached to your letter and franked before it is given to you. Poste Restante for Amex customers is efficiently dealt with by the Amex agents in most large towns.

Important changes All ordinary phone numbers in Brazil are changing from seven-to eight-figure numbers. The process will last until 2005. Enquire locally for the new numbers as in many cases whole numbers will change while others will simply add an extra digit. Where confirmed, eight-digit numbers have been included in the text.

Telephone
For the area codes see under individual towns, the inside front cover, or look in the telephone directory

A trunk dialling system (DDD) links all parts of Brazil. Recent privatization of the telephone system has led to increased competition. The consumer must now choose a telephone company for all calls by inserting a two-digit code between the zero and the area code. Phone numbers are now printed in this way: 0XX21 (0 for a national call, XX for the code of the phone company chosen, 21 for Rio de Janeiro, for example), followed by the seven- or eight-digit number of the subscriber.

Nationwide and international telephone operators and their codes are:

Embratel, 21 (nationwide); *Telefônica*, 15 (state of São Paulo); *Telemar*, 31 (Alagoas, Amazonas, Amapá, Bahia, Ceará, Espírito Santo, Maranhão, most of Minas Gerais, Pará, Paraíba, Pernambuco, Piauí, Rio de Janeiro, Rio Grande do Norte, Roraima, Sergipe); *Tele Centro-Sul*, 14 (Acre, Goiás, Mato Grosso, Mato Grosso do Sul, Paraná, Rondônia, Santa Catarina, Tocantins and the cities of Brasília and Pelotas); *CTBC-Telecom*, 12 (some parts of Minas Gerais, Goiás, Mato Grosso do Sul and São Paulo state); *Intelig*, 23.

National calls Telephone boxes are easy to come by in towns and cities. Major cities have telephone kiosks, for both local and international calls (with an international calling card), in the shape of large orange shells, for which *fichas* can be bought from bars, cafés and newsvendors; in Rio they are known as *orelh*ões (big ears). Local phone calls and telegrams are quite cheap.

Phone cards are available from telephone offices, newstands, post offices and some chemists. They cost US$1.50 for 30 units and up to US$3 for 90 units. Public boxes for intercity calls are blue. To use the telephone office, tell the operator which city or country you wish to call, go to the booth whose number you are given; make your call and you will be billed on exit. Not all offices accept credit cards. Collect calls within Brazil can be made from any telephone – dial 9, followed by the number, and announce your name and city. Local calls from a private phone are normally free.

If you need to find a telephone number, you can dial 102 in any city (*auxílio à lista*) and the **operator** will connect you to a pre-recorded voice which will give the number. To find the number in a different city, dial the DDD code, followed by 121 (so, if you are in Salvador and want to know a Rio number, dial 021 121). If your Portuguese is not up to deciphering spoken numbers, ask a hotel receptionist, for example, to assist you.

International calls   Make sure you buy at least one 90-unit card or pay at the desk after making your call from a booth.The rate to Europe is US$1-2 per minute, to USA around US$1 depending on which operator you use. Between 2000 and 0600 and all day Sunday rates are normally reduced by about a fifth, although again this depends on which operator you use. *Embratel* offer a good service, covering most of the world, with very helpful English-speaking operators and international calls at less than a dollar a minute. *Embratel* cards are available from newsagents in large towns and cities, and have English instructions.

Brazil is linked to North America, Japan and most of Europe by trunk dialling (DDI). Codes are listed in the telephone directories. Home Country Direct is available from hotels, private phones or blue public phones to the following countries (prefix all numbers with 00080); Argentina 54, Australia 61, Belgium 03211, Bolivia 13, Canada 14, Chile 56 (*Entel*), 36 (*Chile Sat*), 37 (*CTC Mundo*), Colombia 57, Costa Rica 50, Denmark 45, France 33, Germany 49, Holland 31, Hong Kong 85212, Israel 97, Italy 39, Japan 81 (*KDD*), 83 (*ITJ*), 89 (*Super Japan*), Norway 47, Paraguay 18, Peru 51, Portugal 35, Singapore 65, Spain 34, Sweden 46, Switzerland 04112, UK 44 (*BT Direct*), USA 10 (*AT&T*), 12 (*MCI*), 16 (*Sprint*), 11 (*Worldcom*), Uruguay 59, Venezuela 58. For collect calls (*a cobrar*) from phone boxes, dial 107 and ask for the *telefonista internacional*. No collect calls are available to New Zealand.

Mobile phones have made a big impact in Brazil owing to past difficulties in getting fixed lines, especially outside the main towns. When using a *celular* telephone you do not drop the zero from the area code as you now have to when dialling from a fixed line. In Rio de Janeiro and São Paulo, mobile phones, or even a line for your own phone, can be hired. Pay-as-you-go phones are now available, which is another option for travellers. The systems in Brazil are mainly AMPS analog or TDMA digital.

Fax services operate in main post offices in major cities, at telephone offices, or from private lines. Rates are around US$1.50 per page within Brazil, US$5 to Europe and the USA. To receive a fax costs US$1.40.

Media

Newspapers & magazines   There is no national newspaper although the news magazines (see below) are distributed nationally. The main **Rio** papers are *Jornal do Brasil* (www.jb.com.br), *O Globo* (www.oglobo.com.br), *O Dia* (www.uol.com.br/odia) and *Jornal do Commércio* (www.jornaldocommercio.com.br). In **São Paulo** Morning: *O Estado de São Paulo* (www. estado.com.br), *Folha de São Paulo* (www.uol.com.br/fsp), *Gazeta Mercantil* (www.gazeta.com.br/) and *Diário de São Paulo*. Evening: *Jornal da Tarde*, *A Gazeta*, *Diário da Noite* and *Ultima Hora*. Around the country, the major cities have their own local press. Of particular note are *A Tarde* in **Salvador** (www.atarde.com.br), the *Diário de Pernambuco* in **Recife** (www.dpnet.com.br) and the *Estado de Minas* in **Belo Horizonte** (www.estaminas.com.br).

Foreign-language newspapers include *The Brazilian Post* and *Sunday News* in English, and *Deutsche Zeitung* in German. In Europe, the *Euro-Brasil Press* is available in most capitals; it prints Brazilian and some international news in Portuguese. London office 23 Kings Exchange, Tileyard Rd, London N7 9AH, T020-77004033, F77003540, eurobrasilpress@compuserve.com.

There are a number of good, informative weekly news magazines which are widely read: *Veja* (www.uol.com.br/veja), *Istoé* (www.uol.com.br/istoe), *Epoca* and *Exame*.

Television   Nationwide TV channels are *Globo* based in Rio de Janeiro and *SBT*, *Record*, *Bandeirantes* based in São Paulo. *Rede Amazônica* operates in the northern region. *TVE* is an educational channel showing documentaries and original-language films.

Programming revolves around light entertainment, soap operas, foreign films dubbed in Portuguese and football.

South America has more local and community radio stations than practically any-   **Radio**
where else in the world; a shortwave (world band) radio offers a practical means to brush up on the language, sample popular culture and absorb some of the richly varied regional music. International broadcasters such as the *BBC World Service*, the *Voice of America* and Boston (Mass)-based *Monitor Radio International* (operated by *Christian Science Monitor*) keep the traveller abreast of news and events, in English, Portuguese and Spanish.

There are English-language radio broadcasts daily at 15290 kHz, 19 m Short Wave (Rádio Bras, Caixa Postal 04/0340, DF-70 323 Brasília).

Compact or miniature portables are recommended, with digital tuning and a full range of shortwave bands, as well as FM, long and medium wave. Detailed advice on radio models (around US$240 for a decent one) and wavelengths can be found in the annual publication, *Passport to World Band Radio* (Box 300, Penn's Park, PA 18943, USA), £14.99. Details of local stations is listed in *World TV and Radio Handbook* (WTRH), PO Box 9027, 1006 AA Amsterdam, The Netherlands, £19.99. Both of these, free wavelength guides and selected radio sets are available from the *BBC World Service Bookshop*, Bush House Arcade, Bush House, Strand, London WC2B 4PH, UK, T020-75572576.

Essentials

Food and drink

The most common dish is *bife (ou frango) com arroz e feijão*, steak (or chicken) with rice   **Cuisine**
and the excellent Brazilian black beans. However, due to Brazil's rich cultural mix many other influences are found in the various regions. São Paulo is by far the best place for international and foreign cuisines.

Feijoada The most famous dish with beans is the *feijoada completa*: several meat ingredients (jerked beef, smoked sausage, smoked tongue, salt pork, along with spices, herbs and vegetables) are cooked with the beans. Manioc flour is sprinkled over it, and it is eaten with kale (*couve*) and slices of orange, and accompanied by glasses of *aguardente* (unmatured rum), usually known as *cachaça* (booze), though *pinga* (drop) is a politer term. Most restaurants serve the *feijoada completa* for Saturday lunch (up to about 1630).

Churrasco, a mixed grill, including excellent steak, served with roasted manioc flour is available throughout Brazil. Originating from the cattlemen of Rio Grande do Sul, it is normally served in restaurants known as *churrascarias* or *rodízios* (or *espeto corrido*). In *rodízios*, waiters ask you in advance what types of meat you want and then bring them round to you until you tell them to stop. Each one has its own variation on the red light/green light system for communicating to the staff. *Churrascarias* usually have a self-service salad bar. Both are good places for large appetites.

Minas Gerais has two delicious special dishes with pork, black beans, *farofa* and kale: *tutu á mineira* and *feijão tropeiro*. A white hard cheese (*queijo prata*) or a slightly softer one (*queijo Minas*) is often served for dessert with bananas, or guava or quince paste. *Comida mineira* is quite distinctive and very wholesome and you can often find restaurants serving this type of food in other parts of Brazil.

Bahia has some excellent fish dishes (see the note on page 378); some restaurants in most of the big cities specialize in them. *Vatapá* is a good dish in the north; it contains shrimp or fish in a sauce of palm oil or coconut milk. *Empadinhas de camarão*, shrimp patties, with olives and heart of palm, are worth trying.

There is fruit all the year round, ranging from banana and orange to mango, pawpaw,   **Desserts**
custard-apple (*fruta do conde*) and guava. Try *manga de Ubá*, a non-fibrous small   **& fruits**

Essentials

▶▶ Food and drink

Drinks Bebidas
beer cerveja
coffee café
fruit juice suco
hot chocolate chocolate quente
milk leite
mineral water água mineral
soft drink refrigerante
tea chá
tonic water água tónica
whisky uísque
wine vinho

Fruit Frutas
apple maçã
banana banana
coconut coco
grape uva
lime limão
mango manga
orange laranja
papaya mamão
passion fruit maracujá
pineapple abacaxi
strawberry morango
watermelon melancia

Meat Carne
beef bife
chicken frango/galinha
fish peixe
ham presunto
hot dog cachorro quente

kid cabrito
pork porco
**toasted cheese and ham
sandwich** misto quente
sausages salsichas
steak filé
turkey peru

Vegetables Legumes
carrot cenoura
lettuce alface
onion cebola
potato batata
rice arroz
salad salada
sweetcorn milho
tomato tomate

Others
bread pão
butter manteiga
cake bolo
cheese queijo
egg ovo
ice-cream sorvete
mustard mostarda
peanut amendoim
pepper pimenta
pie pastel
salt sal
sandwich sanduiche
sugar açúcar
yoghurt iogurte

---

mango. Also good are *amora*, a raspberry that looks like a strawberry, *jaboticaba*, a small black damson-like fruit, and *jaca* (jackfruit), a large yellow/green fruit. Don't miss the exotic flavours of Brazilian ice-creams.

Eating out
See also Useful words and phrases on page 720
Portions are usually for two and come with two plates. If you are on your own, you could ask for an *embalagem* (doggy bag) or get a takeaway called a *marmita* or *quentinha* and offer it to a person with no food (many Brazilians do). Many restaurants now serve *comida por kilo* where you serve yourself and pay for the weight of food on your plate. This is good news if your Portuguese is not up to much, if you want a cheap meal, and also if you don't want to spend time waiting for your food to be served.

The main meal is usually taken in the middle of the day; cheap restaurants tend not to be open in the evening. Always ask the price of a dish before ordering and, if travelling on a tight budget, ask for the *prato feito* or *sortido*, an excellent value set menu. The *prato comercial* is similar but rather better and a bit more expensive. *Lanchonetes* are cheap eating places where you generally pay before eating. *Salgados* (savoury pastries), *coxinha* (a pyramid of manioc filled with meat or fish and deep fried), *esfiha* (spicy hamburger inside an onion bread envelope), *empadão* (a filling – eg chicken – in sauce in a pastry case), *empadas* and *empadinhas* (smaller fritters of the same type), are the usual fare. *Pão de queijo* is a hot roll made with cheese. A *bauru* is a toasted sandwich which, in Porto Alegre, is filled with steak, while further north has tomato, ham and cheese filling. *Cocada* is a coconut and sugar biscuit.

Warning Avoid mussels, marsh crabs and other shellfish caught near large cities: they are likely to have lived in a highly polluted environment.

★

Five of the best: Brazilian drinks

- *Agua de coco* (coconut milk), good for rehydration, perfect for hangovers.
- *Caiprinha*, the national cocktail of firewater (*cachaça*) and fresh limes.
- *Suco*, fresh juice such as *acerola*, an Amazonian cherry. *Vitaminas* also contain *guarana*.
- *Batida*, vodka or *cachaça* with fresh juice (*maracuya*, passion fruit, is delicious).
- *Açai* (pronounced assayear), a fashionable Amazonian fruit drink.

Essentials

Drinks
If you don't want sugar in your coffee, suco, or even caipirinha, you must ask when you order it

The local firewater, *aguardente* (known as *cachaça* or *pinga*), made from sugar-cane, is cheap and strong; São Francisco, Praianinha, Nega Fulô, '51' and Pitu are some recommended makes. Mixed with fruit juice, sugar and crushed ice, *cachaça* becomes the principal element in a *batida*, a delicious and powerful drink. The most popular is a lime batida or *batida de limão*; a variant of which is the *caipirinha*, a *cachaça* with several slices of lime; a *caipiroska* is made with vodka. *Cachaça* with Coca-Cola is a *cuba*, while rum with Coca-Cola is a *cuba libre*.

Some genuine Scotch whisky brands are bottled in Brazil, which are very popular because of the high price of Scotch imported in the bottle. Teacher's is the most highly regarded brand. Locally made gin, vermouth and campari are very good.

Imported drinks are expensive, but there are some fair local wines. Among the better ones are Château d'Argent, Château Duvalier, Almadén, Dreher, Preciosa and Bernard Taillan. The red Marjolet from Cabernet grapes, and the Moselle-type white Zahringer, have been well spoken of. A new *adega* tends to start off well, but the quality gradually deteriorates with time; many vintners have switched to American Concorde grapes, producing a rougher wine. Greville Brut champagne-type is inexpensive and very drinkable. A white wine *Sangria*, containing tropical fruits such as pineapple and papaya, is worth looking out for. Chilean and Portuguese wines are sometimes available at little more than the cost of local wines.

The beers are good and there are plenty of brands: *Antarctica*, *Brahma*, *Bohemia*, *Cerpa*, *Skol* and *Xingu* black beer. Beers are cheaper by the bottle than on draught, which is known as *chope* or *chopp*, after the German Schoppen, and pronounced 'shoppi'.

There is an excellent range of non-alcoholic fruit juices, known as *sucos*. *Açai*, *acerola*, *caju* (cashew), *pitanga*, *goiaba* (guava), *genipapo*, *graviola* (*chirimoya*), *maracujá* (passion fruit), *sapoti* and *tamarindo* are recommended. *Vitaminas* are thick fruit or vegetable drinks with milk. *Caldo de cana* is sugar-cane juice, sometimes mixed with ice. *Água de côco* or *côco verde* (coconut water from chilled, fresh green coconut) should not be missed. The best known of many local soft drinks is *Guaraná*, which is a very popular carbonated fruit drink (see box, page 407), completely unrelated to the natural product from the Amazon.

Apart from the ubiquitous coffee, good tea is grown and sold.

Bars These can vary from basic neighbourhood bars open to the street, often known as *pé sujos* or *botequins*, to sophisticated places with waiter service. Food and snacks are often served and there is usually some form of music, whether a live band or the customers providing their own in an improvised samba session with guitars and drums.

Shopping

What to buy Gold, diamonds and gemstones are good buys throughout Brazil and there are innovative designs in jewellery. Buy at reputable dealers (the best value is in Minas Gerais), but cheap, fun pieces can be bought from street traders. There are interesting furnishings made with gemstones, and marble. Clay figurines from the Northeast, lace from Ceará, leatherwork, strange pottery from Amazônia, carvings in soapstone and in bone, tiles and other ceramic work, African-type pottery and basketwork from Bahia, are all worth seeking out. Brazilian cigars are excellent for those who like the mild flavours popular in Germany, the Netherlands and Switzerland. Recommended purchases are musical instruments, such as guitars, other stringed instruments and percussion instruments.

There are excellent textiles and good hammocks from the Northeast (ironmongers sell hooks – *ganchos pararede* – for hanging your hammock at home). Design in clothing is impressive, though unfortunately not equalled by manufacturing quality. Buy your beachwear in Brazil: it is matchless.

For those who know how to use them, medicinal herbs, barks and spices can be bought from street markets. Coconut oil and local skin and haircare products (fantastic conditioners) are better and cheaper than in Europe, but known brands of toiletries are exorbitant. Other bad buys are film, including processing, cameras and any electrical goods (including batteries). Sunscreen, sold in all department stores and large supermarkets, is expensive.

Prices & As a rule, shopping is easier, quality more reliable and prices higher in the shopping **bargaining** centres (mostly excellent) and in the wealthier suburbs. Prices are often confusingly displayed as 3X (figure) which means that customers can pay in three monthly installments, even for items like bikinis. Better prices are posted at the small shops and street traders. Shopping is most entertaining at markets and on the beach. Bargaining (with good humour) is expected in the latter.

Holidays and festivals

Festivals The major festival is **Carnaval**, which is held three days up to and including Ash **Carnival freephone** Wednesday and is celebrated all over Brazil. See boxes under Rio de Janeiro page 116, **number for tourists** São Paulo page 186, Salvador page 384 and Pernambuco page 442. **Semana Santa**, **for all Carnival** which ends on Easter Sunday, is celebrated with parades in many cities and towns. The **destinations** **Festas Juninhas** throughout the country and **Bumba-meu-boi** in Maranhão are held **T0800-701 1250,** throughout June, while the **Festa do Boi** is held in Parantins at the end of the month. **24 hrs, English,** Bahia has many festivals throughout the year but some of the most interesting are **Spanish, Portuguese** the **Lavagem do Bomfim** in January, the **Presente para Iemanjá** in February and the **Festa da Boa Morte** in August.

In the south the **Festa Nacional da Uva**, a grape and wine festival, is held in Caxias do Sul during February. São Paulo has the Brazilian Grand Prix at the end of March or beginning of April and the **Festa do Peão Boiadeiro in Barretos** during August.

In May the **Festa do Divino Espírito Santo** is celebrated throughout Brazil, but the parades in Pirenópolis are especially interesting.

Towards the end of the year in October the **Oktoberfest** is held in Blumenau, whilst the Círio de Nazaré festival takes place in Belém.

The festival year ends on 31 December with the hugely popular **Reveillon** festivities being held particularly on beaches.

National Aside from the festivals listed above, the main holidays are: 1 January, **New Year**; 21 April, **holidays** **Tiradentes**; 1 May, **Labour Day**; June, **Corpus Christi**; 7 September, **Independence Day**;

12 October, *Nossa Senhora Aparecida*; 2 November, *All Souls' Day*; 15 November, *Proclamation of the Republic*; and 25 December, *Christmas*. The local holidays in the main cities are given in the text. Other religious or traditional holidays (including Good Friday and, usually, 1 November, *All Saints' Day* and 24 December, *Christmas Eve*) must be fixed by the municipalities. Other holidays are usually celebrated on the Monday prior to the date.

Carnival dates

2003 1-5 March
2004 21-25 February
2005 5-9 February
2006 25-29 February

Sport and special interest travel

There are many sites where remains can be found of the continent's original inhabitants, whether human or other species such as dinosaurs. The best areas are probably in the central west and the northeast. Cave paintings are to be found in Serra do Roncador in Mato Grosso, Serra da Capivara in Piauí and near Xique-Xique in Bahia. Dinosaur tracks can be seen at Souza in the interior of Paraíba, whilst eggs have been found at Peirópolis in western Minas Gerais.

Archaeology & palaeontology

Brazil's large areas of unspoilt wilderness provide good opportunities for bird-watching. There are also popular and accessible tourist destinations such as Iguaçu Falls that are excellent for viewing many species. Some of the specialist tour agencies listed on page 24 such as *Focus Tours* and *Field Guides* offer packages to many good areas in all parts of Brazil.

Bird-watching
For more information on Flora and flora, see page 712

Details of the following key bird-watching sites are given in the main travelling text:

The Amazon Although probably not as good for viewing as the Pantanal, there are many interesting species such as the horned sungem which has the fastest wing beat yet discovered. Toucans and macaws are often seen, although probably the most common birds are vultures. Some birds can be seen in the Lago de Januari Reserve, only a short distance from Manaus, and there are plenty of jungle lodges further away from the city. The Rio Negro with its many islands is a good area, as are the Rio Tapajós near Santarém and the Rio Xingu which extends as far as Mato Grosso.

Minas Gerais This state is host to a large number of accessible national and state parks which are excellent for viewing a variety of different bird species. Recommended are the Parque Natural de Caraça, Parque Nacional da Serra do Cipó, Parque Florestal de Ibitipoca, Parque Florestal do Rio Doce and the Parque Nacional da Serra Canastra, among many other lesser known areas.

The Northeast The interior of Bahia, Pernambuco and Ceará is an excellent area for spotting many species such as blue macaws and cactus parakeets which make their homes in the arid *caatinga*. Many new species have recently been found in the Atlantic forests of Alagoas. The south of Bahia is also a good area for parrots and antbirds, as well as many other varieties of birds.

The Pantanal This large area of swampland on the Bolivian and Brazilian borders is home to more than 600 species of bird including the rhea, a tall ostrich-like bird. The best time to visit is probably between late June to early October which is the nesting and breeding season for many species such as cormorants, wood ibises and jabiru storks. Parakeets are a common sight especially at dusk and dawn. Other residents are egrets, kingfishers and spoonbills, as well as birds of prey such as the caracara. Nearby are the national parks of Chapada dos Guimarães in Mato Grosso and Emas in Goiás, which are both good areas with more undulating terrain.

The Serra do Mar This mountain range runs parallel to the coast from Rio Grande do Sul to Espírito Santo and still has some remains of the once mighty Atlantic rainforest. It is an excellent site for birds of prey including three types of eagles and the *acuuán* or laughing falcon. Turkey-like guans are frequently seen, as are humming-birds and parrots. Other common species are the pigeon-like *araponga* and the colour-ful varieties of *tanager*. Itatiaia National Park is a good starting point for this range but there are many others.

Canoeing   Canoeing is supervised by the *Confederação Brasileira de Canoagem* (R Fernando Abott 582/703, Estrela, CEP 95880-000, Rio Grande do Sul, T0XX51-7122600), founded in 1989. It covers all aspects of the sport, speed racing, slalom, downriver, surfing and ocean kayaking. For downriver canoeing, go to **Visconde de Mauá** (Rio de Janeiro state – see page 153 where the Rio Preto is famous for the sport); also the Rio Formoso at **Bonito** (Mato Grosso do Sul – see page 634). A recommended river for slalom is the Paranhana, **Três Coroas**, Rio Grande do Sul. For kayak surfing the best places are Rio, the Ilha de Santa Catarina and Ubatuba, while ocean kayaking is popular in Rio, Búzios and Santos (São Paulo).

Caving   There are some wonderful cave systems in Brazil, and Ibama (see National Parks, page 716) has a programme for the protection of the national speleological heritage. National parks such as **Ubajara** (see page 515) and **Chapada Diamantina** (page 395) and the state park of **PETAR** (page 213) have easy access for the casual visitor, but there are also many options for the keen potholer in the states of São Paulo, Paraná, Minas Gerais and the federal district of Brasília.

Cave diving   Cave diving can be practised in many of the 200 underwater grottoes such as **Bonito**, Mato Grosso do Sul, **Lapa de São Jorge**, 280 km from Brasília, in Chapada Diamantina and **Vale do Ribeira** located between São Paulo and Paraná. Gabriel Ganme, Diving College, R Dr Mello Alves 700, São Paulo, T011-8814723, and Rafael de Nicola, Divers University, are instructors in this specialized sport.

Climbing   As Brazil has no mountain ranges of Alpine or Andean proportions, the most popular form of climbing (*escalada*) is rock-face climbing. In the heart of Rio, you can see, or join, climbers scaling the rocks at the base of **Pão de Açúcar** and on the Sugar Loaf itself. Not too far away, the **Serra dos Órgãos** provides plenty of challenges, not least the **Dedo de Deus** (God's Finger – see page 146). In the state of São Paulo a good loca-tion for climbing is **Pedra do Báu** near São Bento do Sapucaí, and **Brotas** is popular for abseiling (*rappel*). **Pedra Branca** and the **Serra do Cipó** are recommended locations in Minas Gerais. Mato Grosso has the **Serra do Roncador** and there are other good areas in Paraná and Rio Grande do Sul.

Cultural   Several of the tour operators listed on page 24 offer customized packages for special
tourism   interest groups. Local operators offering these more specialized tours are listed in the text under the relevant location.

Diving   The Atlantic coast offers many possibilities for scuba diving (*mergulho*). The best site is the archipelago of **Fernando de Noronha** (Pernambuco), 345 km off the northeast coast in the open Atlantic. The underwater landscape is volcanic, with cliffs, caverns and some corals, but the marine life that shelters here is magnificent. There are sharks, a protected breeding ground for hawksbill and green turtles and, the greatest draw for divers, a bay which is the home for a pod of several hundred spinner dolphin (diving with the dolphins is not allowed). In the archipelago there are a number of dive sites including the wreck of the corvette *Ipiringa* at a depth of 53 m (*Atlantis* is an operator that specializes in deepwater diving). Average visibility is 30 m with an average depth of 22 m. The best time of year is January-February and July-October. Also in

Pernambuco, **Recife** (from where planes leave for Fernando de Noronha) is a diving centre, particularly for wrecks. The reef that protects the shore up to Recife provides sheltered swimming, natural pools and many, very rewarding diving spots. Full of marine life, with warm, clear, greenish-blue sea. Visiting sea anglers are, however, urged to respect local traditions: many species are in danger of extinction, as is the coral, which is threatened by any disturbance and all forms of pollution.

Moving south, Bahia's most popular dive sites are the marine park of **Abrolhos** and **Porto Seguro**. The best time to visit Abrolhos is July-November, when whales come from the Antarctic to breed, and January-February. Other attractions are Moray eels, Barracudas, a wide variety of corals and the wreck of the cargo ship *Rosalina* that sank in 1939. Visibility varies between 8 m and 20 m, with an average depth of 10 m in the archipelago.

In the Southeast, **Búzios**, **Arraial do Cabo**, visibility of 8 m to 15 m, depths of 7 m to 70 m, grottoes, ridges and the greatest number of wrecks in the country, and **Cabo Frio** are sites to the north of Rio. South of the state capital, the island-filled bay of **Angra dos Reis**, together with **Ilha Grande**, and **Paraty**, best from December-April with calm seas, visibility from 5 m to 20 m and an average depth of 15 m, are all recommended sites. **Ilhabela/São Sebastião** in São Paulo state, best visited January-May, offers good opportunities for wreck diving. Visibility is up to 12 m with depths from 6 m to 85 m. Other places in the state include **Ubatuba**, Laje de Santos, 22 km from the mainland with an anchor graveyard and rays has visibility up to 20 m and depths between 18 m to 40 m, and **Ilha de Alcatrazes**.

At Fernando de Noronha and Recife you can dive all year, although Recife (like anywhere on the coast) may be subject to strong currents. The further south you go, the lower the water temperatures become in winter (15-20°C). Visibility can also be affected by currents and weather. Many resorts have dive shops, some of which are listed in the Handbook. Whether you are already a qualified diver or a beginner seeking tuition, get local advice on which companies provide the level of expertise and knowledge of local waters that you need.

American/Brazilian Dive Club, 1645 SE 3 Road Court, Deerfield Bch, FL 33441, USA, T/F954-4200009. The club can be accessed through www.cris.com/apavan which has links to dive sites in Brazil. There is a diving magazine called *Mergulho*. *Océan* is a dive shop and tour operator based in Rio de Janeiro state (Rio, Angra dos Reis, Ilha Grande, Arraial do Cabo) which has a *Diving in Brasil* website, www.ocean.com.br (Portuguese only).

In some areas in Brazil, diving includes underwater sport fishing; for details, contact a company which specializes in fishing

There is a mingling of ecotourism and adventure tourism in Brazil. This is partly **Ecotourism** because the adventurous activities nearly always take place in unspoilt parts of the country, but also because the term 'ecotourism' is applied to almost any outdoor activity. Ecotourism is becoming very important as a form of sustainable development in the parts of Brazil most threatened by deforestation and as a way of alleviating local unemployment in a way that doesn't harm the environment. Many opportunities for visiting the rainforest are to be found in the North and efforts are being made to save what is left of the Atlantic forest cover in the Southeast.

The *Instituo Brasileiro de Ecoturismo* (IEB) is at R Minerva 156, Perdizes, São Paulo, T0XX11-36727571, F36735156, www.ecoturismo.org.br In Minas Gerais, *Amo-Te*, the Associação Mineira dos Organizadores do Turismo Ecológico, R Prof Morais 624, Apto 302, Savassi, Belo Horizonte, T0XX31-32815094, is helpful. *Terra Virgem* is a publishing house in São Paulo, R Galeno de Almeida 179, CEP 05410-030, T/F8837823, terravirgem@originet.com.br, which publishes guides in Portuguese and English for adventure tourism, accompanied by books of photographs.

Brazil has enormous potential for angling given the number and variety of its rivers, **Fishing** lakes and reservoirs. Add to this the scope for sea-angling along the Atlantic coast and it is not difficult to see why the sport is gaining in popularity (but see under Diving above). Officially, the country's fish stocks are under the control of *Ibama* (see National Parks, page 716) and a licence is required for fishing in any waters. The states of Mato Grosso and Mato Grosso do Sul require people fishing in their rivers to get the states' own fishing permit, which is not the same as an Ibama licence. All details on prices, duration and regulations concerning catches can be obtained from *Ibama*; the paperwork can be found at Ibama offices, some branches of the *Banco do Brasil* and some agencies which specialize in fishing. In Mato Grosso and Mato Grosso do Sul information is provided by *Sema*, the Special Environment Secretariat, and documents may be obtained at fishing agencies or Bamerindus in Mato Grosso do Sul.

Freshwater fishing can be practised in so many places that the best bet is to make local enquiries in the part of Brazil that you are visiting. You can then find out about the rivers, lakes and reservoirs, which fish you are likely to find and what types of angling are most suited to the conditions. Favoured rivers include tributaries of the **Amazon**, those in the **Pantanal** and the **Rio Araguaia**, but there are many others. Many agencies can arrange fishing trips and there are several local magazines on the subject. As an example, the best time to go fishing in the Araguaia and around the Ilha de Bananal is the dry season, May to October. In Aruanã, one of the towns which gives access to the river, the *Associação dos Barqueiros de Aruanã* (ABA), Praça Couto Magalhães, gives information about boat rentals and fishing tours. **Lages** in Santa Catarina is good for trout fishing, as is **Campos do Jordão** in São Paulo which also has good opportunities for salmon.

Information: *Pura Pesca Tour* operates tours in the Pantanal, Rio Araguaia and elsewhere, in São Paulo, T0XX11-5355880/5435901, F0XX11-55616447, or Cuiabá T0XX65-6241660, F0XX65-6249966. *Eldorado Pantaneiro* operates tours in fishing boats with a/c apartments, bar and all equipment, T0XX11-4340283, or Corumbá T067-2316369. *Fishing World's* website, www.fishingworld.com.br, is not exclusively about Brazil and in Portuguese, but is informative and also includes diving.

Hang gliding & paragliding These are both covered by the *Associação Brasileira de Vôo Livre* (ABVL – Brazilian Hanggliding Association, Rio de Janeiro, T0XX21-3220266). There are state associations affiliated with ABVL and there are a number of operators offering tandem flights for those without experience. Launch sites (called *rampas*) are growing in number. Among the best known are: Pedra Bonita at Gávea in **Rio**; Parque da Cidade in **Niterói**; in **São Paulo**, Pico do Urubu (Mogi das Cruzes), Serra de São Pedro, Pedra do Baú (Campos do Jordão), Pico Agudo (Santo Antônio do Pinhal), Pedra Grande (Atibaia); in **Espírito Santo**, Morro de Filette, Venda Nova do Imigrante; in **Minas Gerais**, Pico do Ibitiruna (Governador Valadares), Pico do Gavião (Andradas) and Serra de Santa Helena (Sete Lagoas); in **Paraná**, Morro do Picouto and Morro da Queixada at Foz do Iguaçu; **Santa Catarina**, Careca – Praia Brava (Itajaí), Pelado (Gaspar), Morro Azul, Morro da Turquia and Intermediário (all at Pomerode), Pico das Antenas (Jaraguá do Sul); in **Rio Grande do Sul**, Morro do Farrabraz (Sapiranga) and Ninho das Águias (Nova Petrópolis); in **Ceará**, Aratuba, Urucu (Meruoca) and Urucu (Queixada); Morro do Urucum, Corumbá, **Mato Grosso do Sul** (which offers views of the Pantanal); and the Vale do Paranã in **Brasília**.

Horse riding Some of the best trails for horse riding are the routes that used to be taken by the mule trains that transported goods between the coast and the interior. A company like *Tropa Serrana* in Belo Horizonte (T0XX31-33448986, tropaserrana@hotmail.com) is an excellent place to start because their tours, including overnight horse treks, explore many aspects of the Minas Gerais countryside that visitors do not normally see.

Mountain biking Brazil is well-suited to cycling, both on and off-road. On main roads it is important to obey the general advice of being on the look out for motor vehicles as cyclists are very much second-class citizens. Also note that when cycling on the coast you may encounter strong winds which will hamper your progress. There are endless roads and tracks suitable for mountain biking, and there are many clubs in major cities which organize group rides, activities and competitions. Serra da Canastra in Minas Gerais is a popular area. *Tamanduá* in São Roque de Minas offer personalized tours and equipment hire. (See also Getting around, page 45 .)

Brazil has a number of locations that have been claimed by seekers of hidden knowledge, or those interested in unusual sciences. Some of the best sites are to be found in the central west such as **Alto Paraíso de Goiás**, north of Brasília, and **Barra do Garças** in Mato Grosso. In these places 'new age' communities have formed dedicated to natural healing, alternative religions, or the search for UFOs and alien life-forms. In the south of Minas Gerais, a similar ambience is found at **São Tomé das Letras**, but there are many other examples across the country.

Mystical tourism

Whitewater rafting started in Brazil in 1992. There are companies offering trips in São Paulo state (eg on the rios **Juquiá**, **Jaguarí**, **do Peixe**, **Paraibuna**), in Rio de Janeiro (also on the Paraibuna, at **Três Rios** in the Serra dos Órgãos), Paraná (**Rio Ribeira**), Santa Catarina (**Rio Itajaí**) and Rio Grande do Sul (**Três Coroas**). Serra da Canastra in Minas Gerais is also popular for the local sport of *Bóia-cross* (rafting with rubber tubes).

Rafting

This can be enjoyed in just about every coastal state. It does not require permits; all you need is a board and the right type of wave. Brazilians took up surfing in the 1930s and have been practising ever since; in this beach-obsessed country, with 8,000 km of coastline, all shore and watersports are taken seriously. **Surfers Associations**: *Associação Brasileira de Surfe Profissional*, T0XX48-2231226; *Associação Brasileira de Bodyboard*, T0XX21-2590669.

Surfing

A favourite locale is **Fernando de Noronha**, a cluster of idyllic islands belonging to Pernambuco state, 345 km out in the Atlantic, but the best waves are found in the south, where long stretches of the Atlantic, often facing the swell head-on, give some excellent and varied breaks. The season is November-March in the archipelago, but it is an expensive place to surf. Many Brazilian surf spots are firmly on the international championship circuit: best known is **Saquarema**, in Rio de Janeiro state.

There are many other good surf spots in Rio de Janeiro state. Most of the coastline faces south, head-on to the powerful swell, and is freshened by an early morning north-northeast offshore wind blowing off the mountains which run parallel to the coast. It receives a consistent winter swell, although in summer it stays flat for long periods. The urban beaches have good surf, and are friendly, but beware of thieves. Don't leave your board unattended: get straight in the water. The beautiful, mountainous coast between Ubatuba and Rio de Janeiro has no surf except to the ocean side of Ilha Grande, which protects the mainland coast.

In the state of São Paulo, on the coast between Santos and Rio de Janeiro (Linha Verde) the best-known and the busiest beach near the city is **Pitangueiras** where professional and amateur championships are held at the spot known as Maluf, where the waves consistently break at 8 ft. São Sebastião has 21 good beaches and an adequate, but not over-developed tourist infrastructure. The many small islands offshore are very good for scuba diving; there is also sailing, fishing and canoeing. During high season, lively watersports events are held at **Marésias**, with excellent surfing.

One of the best states for surfing, **Santa Catarina** has a straight coastline with several islands offshore. Surfing is prohibited at some beaches from 15 May to 15 July, because of the *tainha* fish harvest. Ilha de Sta Catarina has more than 40 beaches, all different and all highly sought-after during the holiday season. The minute Carnival has ended, the smaller villages to the south of the island are deserted by holidaymaking city-dwellers, leaving the beaches relatively uncrowded.

Considered one of Brazil's finest surfing spots, **Silveira** is 3 km east of Garopaba, 96 km south of Florianópolis: follow the SC-434 for about 1 km and take a left turn. Swimming can be risky here because of the surf and sudden drops in the ocean floor. There is also excellent fishing.

Surfing in the northeast: the majority of beaches in **Salvador** are polluted, but south of the city there is surfing near **Itaparica**, **Itacaré** and **Ilhéus**. Beaches **north of Bahia** are protected by the reef which runs off the northeast shore up the coast to Recife, waves tend to be smaller and much less powerful than on the southern coasts. There are some interesting reef breaks, however, and a chain of palm-fringed, white sand beaches that beg to be visited even without your board. This coast is also good for Diving, see below.

At **Recife** surf is weak in the urban area, and banned at Boa Viagem because of shark attacks. **Porto de Galinhas** has pretty beaches and a variety of surf spots.

Rio Grande do Norte and **Ceará** also have surfing beaches, but not of the quality or quantity of further south.

Swimming   The extensive coastline means there are plenty of opportunities for good bathing. Do, however, observe local warnings as strong undertows and currents can make it extremely dangerous to swim in places. A number of people are drowned every year from recklessness on Rio de Janeiro's beaches. **Triathlon** has become a popular sport in the south and southeast of Brazil with many organized competitions.

Trekking   Trekking is very popular, especially in Rio de Janeiro, São Paulo, Minas Gerais, Paraná and Rio Grande do Sul. There are plenty of hiking shops and agencies which handle hiking tours. Trails are frequently graded according to difficulty; this is noticeably so in areas where *trilhas ecológicas* have been laid out in forests or other sites close to busy tourist areas. Many national parks and other protected areas provide good opportunities for trekking (eg the Chapada Diamantina in Bahia) and local information can easily be found to get you on the right track.

Yachting   A popular sport along Brazil's Atlantic coastline. **Angra dos Reis** and **Paraty** in Rio de Janeiro state as well as **Bahia** are good locations among many others.

Health

Local populations in Brazil are exposed to a range of health risks not encountered in other parts of the world. Many of the diseases are major problems for the local communities and the risk to travellers, although remote, cannot be ignored. Obviously five-star travel is going to carry less risk than back-packing on a minimal budget. The health care in the region is varied. There are many excellent private and government clinics/hospitals. As with all medical care, first impressions count. If a facility is grubby, staff wear grey coats instead of white ones then be wary of the general standard of medicine and hygiene. A good tip is to contact your embassy or consulate on arrival and ask where the recommendedclinics are (those used by diplomats). If you do get ill, you should also check with your medical insurer whether they are satisfied that the medical centre or hospital that you have been referred to is of a suitable standard.

Disease risk   The greater disease risk in Tropical Brazil is caused by the greater volume of insect disease carriers in the shape of mosquitoes and sandflies. The key **viral disease** is dengue fever, which is transmitted by a day biting mosquito. The disease is like a very nasty form of the flu with 2-3 days of illness, followed by a short period of recovery, then a second attack of illness. Westerners very rarely get the worst haemorrhagic form of the disease.

Bacterial diseases include tuberculosis (TB) and some causes of traveller's diarrhoea. The parasitic diseases are many, but the two key ones are malaria and South American trypanosomiasis (known as Chagas's Disease). The latter kills fit Brazilian footballers at a very young age.

Risk areas for malaria are in states of Acre, Rondonia, Amapa, Amazonas, Roraima, and Tocantins. Risk in parts of the states of Maranhao (western part), Mato Grosso (northern part), and Para (except Belem City). There is also transmission in urban areas, including large cities such as Porto Velho, Boa Vista, Macapa, Manaus, Santarem, and Maraba. The coastal states from the 'horn' south to the Uruguay border, including Iguaçu Falls, are not risk areas.

Before you go

Ideally see your GP or travel clinic at least six weeks before the departure for general advice on travel risks, malaria and vaccinations. Make sure you have adequate travel insurance; get a dental check; know your own blood group; and if you suffer a long-term condition such as diabetes or epilepsy make sure someone knows or that you have a Medic Alert bracelet/necklace with this information.

Vaccinations

Hepatitis A Recommended as the disease can be caught easily from food/water.
Polio Recommended if nil in last 10 years.
Rabies Recommended if travelling to jungle and/or remote areas.
Tetanus Recommended if nil in last 10 years (but after 5 doses you've had enough for life).
Typhoid Recommended if nil in last 3 years
Yellow fever Recommended if travelling around Brazil as it is needed for the Northern areas.

Malaria precautions

A for Awareness Brazil has areas with a risk of the deadly falciparum malaria. Always check with your doctor or travel clinic for the most up-to-date advice.
B for Bite avoidance Wear clothes that cover arms and legs and use effective insect repellents in areas with known risks of insect spread disease. Use a mosquito net dipped in permethrin as both a physical and chemical barrier at night in the same areas.
C for Chemoprophylaxis Depending on the type of malaria and your previous medical condition/psychological profile, take the right drug before, during and after your trip. Always check with your doctor or travel clinic for the most up-to-date advice.
D for Diagnosis Remember that up to a year after your return an illness could be caused by malaria. Be forceful about asking for a malaria test, even if the doctor says it is 'only flu.' The symptoms of malaria are wide ranging from fever, lethargy, headache, muscle pains, flu-like illness, to diarrhoea, convulsions. Malaria can lead to coma and death.

Further information

When you arrive in each country let the Embassy or Consulate know. The information can be useful if a friend/relative gets ill at home and there is a desperate search for you around the globe. You can also ask them about locally recommended medical facilities and do's and don'ts.

Websites

Foreign and Commonwealth Office (FCO), www.fco.gov.uk, is a key travel advice site, with useful information on the country, people, climate and lists the UK embassies/consulates. The site also promotes the concept of 'Know Before You Go'. And encourages travel insurance and appropriate travel health advice. It has links to the Department of Health travel advice site, listed below.
Department of Health Travel Advice (UK), www.doh.gov.uk/traveladvice, is an excellent site also available as a free booklet, the T6, from UK post offices. It lists the vaccine advice requirements for each country.

Essentials

Medic Alert (UK), **www.medicalalert.co.uk**, is the website of the foundation that produces bracelets and necklaces for those with existing medical problems. Once you have ordered your bracelet/necklace you write your key medical details on paper inside it, so that if you collapse, a medical person can identify you as someone with epilepsy, allergy to peanuts, etc.

Blood Care Foundation (UK), **www.bloodcare.org.uk**, is a Kent-based charity 'dedicated to the provision of screened blood and resuscitation fluids in countries where these are not readily available.' They will dispatch certified non-infected blood of the right type to your hospital/clinic. The blood is flown in from various centres around the world.

Public Health Laboratory Service (UK), **www.phls.org.uk**, has the 2001 malaria advice guidelines for travel around the world. It gives specific advice about the right drugs for each location. It also has useful information for those who are pregnant, suffering from epilepsy or planning to travel with children.

Communicable Disease Control (USA), **www.cdc.gov**, is a US Government site which gives excellent advice on travel health, has useful disease maps and has details of disease outbreaks.

World Health Organisation (WHO), **www.who.int**, has links to the WHO Yellow Book on travel advice. This lists the diseases in different regions of the world. It describes vaccination schedules and makes clear which countries have Yellow Fever Vaccination certificate requirements.

Tropical Medicine Bureau, **www.tmb.ie**, is an Irish-based site with a good collection of general travel health information and disease risks.

Fit for Travel, **www.fitfortravel.scot.nhs.uk**, from Scotland, provides a quick A-Z of vaccine and travel health advice requirements for each country.

British Travel Health Association (UK), **www.btha.org**, is the official website of an organization of travel health professionals.

NetDoctor (UK), **www.Netdoctor.co.uk**, is a general health advice site with a useful section on travel and an 'ask the expert' interactive chat forum.

Travel Screening Services (UK), **www.travelscreening.co.uk**, is the author's website. A private clinic dedicated to integrated travel health. The clinic gives vaccine, travel health advice, email and SMS text vaccine reminders and screens returned travellers for tropical diseases.

Books & leaflets

The Travellers Good Health Guide, Dr Ted Lankester (ISBN 0-85969-827-0).

Expedition Medicine (The Royal Geographic Society), Editors David Warrell and Sarah Anderson (ISBN 1 86197 040-4).

International Travel and Health, World Health Organisation Geneva (ISBN 92 4 158026 7).

The World's Most Dangerous Places, Robert Young Pelton, Coskun Aral and Wink Dulles (ISBN 1-566952-140-9).

The Travellers Guide to Health (T6) can be obtained by calling the Health Literature Line on T0800-555 777.

Advice for travellers on avoiding the risks of **HIV** and **AIDS** (Travel Safe) is available from Department of Health, PO Box 777, London Se1 6XH.

The Blood Care Foundation, order from PO Box 7, Sevenoaks, Kent TN13 2SZ, UK, T01732-742 427.

What to take

Antibiotics Ciproxin (*Ciprofloaxcin*) is a useful antibiotic for traveller's diarrhoea (which can affect up to 70% of travellers). You take one 500 mg tablet when the diarrhoea starts and if you do not feel better in 24 hours the diarrhoea is likely to have a non-bacterial cause and may be viral. Viral causes of diarrhoea will settle on their own. However, with all diarrhoeas try to keep hydrated by taking the right mixture of salt and water. This is available as Oral Dehydration Salts (ORS) in ready made sachets or can be made up by adding a teaspoon of sugar and a half teaspoon of salt to a litre of clean water. Flat carbonated drinks can also be used.

Anti-malarials   Specialist advice is required as to which type to take. General principles are that all except *Malarone* should be continued for four weeks after leaving the malarious area. *Malarone* needs to be continued for only seven days afterwards (if a tablet is missed or vomited seek specialist advice). The start times for the anti-malarials vary in that if you have never taken *Lariam* (Mefloquine) before it is advised to start it at least 2-3 weeks before the entry to a malarious zone (this is to help identify serious side effects early). *Chloroquine* and *Paludrine* are often started a week before the trip to establish a pattern, but *Doxycycline* and *Malarone* can be started only 1-2 days before entry to the malarious area. It is risky to buy medicinal tablets abroad because the doses may differ and there may be a trade in false drugs.

Diarrhoea treatment   *Immodium* is a great standby or those diarrhoeas that occur at awkward times, that is before a long coach/train journey or on a trek. It helps stop the flow of diarrhoea and in the author's view is of more benefit than harm. It was believed that letting the bacteria or viruses flow out had to be more beneficial. However, with *Immodium* they still come out, just in a more solid form. *Pepto-Bismol* is used a lot by Americans for diarrhoea. It certainly relieves symptoms but like *Immodium* it is not a cure for underlying disease. Be aware that it turns the stool black as well as making it more solid.
Sun block   The Australian's have a great campaign, which has reduced skin cancer. It is called Slip, Slap, Slop. Slip on a shirt, Slap on a hat, slop on sun screen.

First-aid kit   This should include water-sterilizing tablets, plasters/band-aids, antiseptic cream, etc. For longer trips involving jungle treks take a clean needle pack, clean dental pack and water filtration devices.

Insect bite relief   If you are prone to insects' bites or develop lumps quite soon after being bitten, carry an *Aspivenin* kit. This syringe suction device is available in the UK from *Boots* chemists and draws out some of the allergic materials and provides quick relief.

Painkillers   Paracetomol or a suitable painkiller can have multiple uses for symptoms but remember that more than eight paracetmol a day can lead to liver failure.

MedicAlert   These simple bracelets, or an equivalent, should be carried or worn by anyone with a significant medical condition.

Mosquito repellents   Remember that DEET (Di-ethyltoluamide) is the gold standard. Apply the repellent every 4-6 hours but more often if you are sweating heavily. If a non-DEET product is used check who tested it. Validated products (tested at the London School of Hygiene and Tropical Medicine) include *Mosiguard*, Non-DEET *Jungle Formula* and non-DEET *Autan*. If you want to use *Citronella* remember that it must be applied very frequently (ie hourly) to be effective.

Sun block   The Australians have a great campaign which has reduced skin cancer. It is called **Slip, Slap, Slop**: Slip on a shirt, Slap on a hat, Slop on sun screen.

Washing   Biodegradable soap for jungle areas or ordinary soap for emergencies. Washing your hands is the safest way of preventing unwanted muck-to-mouth transmission before you eat.

Health care A-Z

Essentials

Altitude sickness

Symptoms: This can creep up on you as just a mild headache with nausea or lethargy. The more serious disease is caused by fluid collecting in the brain in the enclosed space of the skull and can lead to coma and death. A lung disease with breathlessness and fluid infiltration of the lungs is also recognized.

Cures: The best cure is to descend as soon as possible.

Prevention: Get acclimatized. Do not try to reach the highest levels on your first few days of arrival. Try to avoid flying directly into the cities of highest altitude. Climbers like to take treatment drugs as protective measures but this can lead to macho idiocy and death. The peaks are still there and so are the trails, whether it takes you personally a bit longer than someone else does not matter as long as you come back down alive.

Chagas's Disease

Symptoms: The disease occurs throughout Brazil, affects locals more than travellers but travellers can be exposed by sleeping in mud-constructed huts where the bug that carries the parasite bites and defaecates on an exposed part of skin. You may notice nothing at all or a local swelling, with fever, tiredness and enlargement of lymph glands, spleen and liver. The seriousness of the parasite infection is caused by the long-term effects which include gross enlargement of the heart and/or guts.

Cures: Early treatment is required with toxic drugs.

Prevention: Sleep under a permethrin treated bed net and use insect repellents.

Dengue fever

Symptoms: This disease can be acquired throughout Brazil. In travellers this can cause a severe flu like illness with fever, lethargy, enlarged lymph glands and muscle pains. It starts suddenly, lasts for 2-3 days, seems to get better for 2-3 days and then kicks in again for another 2-3 days. It is usually all over in an unpleasant week. The local children are prone to the much nastier haemorrhagic form of the disease, which causes them to bleed from internal organs, mucous membranes and often leads to their death.

Cures: The traveller's disease is self-limiting and forces rest and recuperation on the sufferer.

Prevention: The mosquitoes that carry the dengue virus bite during the day unlike the malaria mosquitoes. Sadly this means that repellent and covered limbs are a 24-hour issue. Check your accommodation for flower pots and shallow pools of water since these are were the dengue-carrying mosquitoes breed.

Diarrhoea & intestinal upset

Summary: This is almost inevitable. One study showed that up to 70% of all travellers may suffer during their trip.

Symptoms: Diarrhoea can refer either to loose stools or an increased frequency; both of these can be a nuisance. It should be short lasting and persistence beyond two weeks, blood or pain all require specialist medical attention.

Cures: Ciproxin will cure many of the bacterial causes but none of the viral ones. Immodium and Pepto-Bismol provide symptomatic relief. Dehydration can be a key problem especially in hot climates and is best avoided by the early start of Oral Rehydration Salts (at least one large cup of drink for each loose stool).

Prevention: The standard advice is to be careful with water and ice for drinking. Ask yourself where the water came from. If you have any doubts then boil it or filter and treat it. There are many filter/treatment devices now available on the market. Food can also transmit disease. Be wary of salads (what were they washed in, who handled them), re-heated foods or food that has been left out in the sun having been cooked earlier in the day. There is a simple adage that says 'wash it, peel it, boil it or forget it'. Also be wary of unpasteurized dairy products these can transmit a range of dizeases from brucellosis (fevers and constipation), to listeria (meningitis) and tuberculosis of the gut (obstruction, constipation, fevers and weight loss).

Hepatitis

Symptoms: Hepatitis means inflammation of the liver. Viral causes of Hepatitis can be acquired anywhere in Brazil. The most obvious sign is if your skin or the whites of your eyes become yellow. However, prior to this all that you may notice is itching and tiredness.
Cures: Early on depending on the type of Hepatitis a vaccine or immunoglobulin may reduce the duration of the illness.
Prevention: Pre-travel Hepatitis A vaccine is the best bet. Hepatitis B is spread a different route by blood and unprotected sexual intercourse, both of these can be avoided. Unfortunately there is no vaccine for Hepatitis C or the increasing alphabetical list of other Hepatitis viruses.

Leishmaniasis

Symptoms: A skin form of this disease occurs in Brazil. If infected, you may notice a raised lump, which leads to a purplish discoloration on white skin and a possible ulcer. The parasite is transmitted by the bite of a sandfly. Sandflies do not fly very far and the greatest risk is at ground levels, so if you can avoid sleeping on the jungle floor do so.
Cures: Several weeks treatment is required under specialist supervision. The drugs themselves are toxic but if not taken in sufficient amounts recurrence of the disease is more likely.
Prevention: Sleep above ground, under a permethrin treated net, use insect repellent and get a specialist opinion on any unusual skin lesions soon after return.

Malaria & insect bite prevention

Symptoms: Malaria can cause death within 24 hours. It can start with something just resembling an attack of flu. You may feel tired, lethargic, headachy or worse develop fits, coma and then death. Have a low index of suspicion because it is very easy to write off vague symptoms, which may actually be malaria. Whilst abroad and on return get tested as soon as possible, the test could save your life.
Cures: Treatment is with drugs and may be oral or into a vein depending on the seriousness of the infection.
Prevention: Is best summarized by the B and C of the ABCD (see above). **Bite avoidance** and **Chemoprophylaxis**. Some would prefer to take test kits for malaria with them and have standby treatment available. However, the field test of the blood kits have had poor results, when you have malaria you do not perform well enough to do the tests correctly enough to make the right diagnosis. Standby treatment (treatment that you carry and take yourself for malaria) should still ideally be supervised by a doctor since the drugs themselves can be toxic if taken in correctly. The Royal Homeopathic Hospital does not advocate homeopathic options for malaria prevention or treatment.

Rabies

Symptoms Most of you will know when you have been bitten. It may take days or weeks before odd tingling sensations occur in the affected part, followed by a fear of drinking water and spasms which lead to death.
Cures There is no cure for rabies once it has hold of the Central Nervous System.
Prevention Avoid getting bitten. Dog lovers have to remember that this is a whole new ball game and you are the ball. A full course of rabies vaccine is 100% effective. If you get bitten you will need more vaccine and if you had no pre-exposure vaccine or an inadequate amount you will also need to be injected with something called immunoglobulin. It is always wise to wash the wound but animal bites should ideally not be stitched up in the early stages.

Sexual health

Unprotected sex can spread HIV, Hepatitis B and C, Gonorrhea (green discharge), chlamydia (nothing to see but may cause painful urination and later female infertility), painful recurrent herpes, syphilis and warts, just to name a few. You can cut down the risk by using condoms, a femidom or avoiding sex altogether.

Sun protection

Symptoms: White-skinned people who travel to hot countries and stay out longer without using adequate skin protection. This can lead to sunburn, which is painful and followed by flaking of skin. Aloe vera gel is a good pain reliever for sunburn. Long-term sun damage leads to a loss of elasticity of skin and the development of pre-cancerous lesions. Many years later a mild or a very malignant form of cancer may develop. The milder basal cell carcinoma, if detected early, can be treated by cutting it out or freezing it. The much nastier malignant melanoma may have already spread to bone and brain at the time that it is first noticed.

Prevention: Follow the Australians with their Slip, Slap, Slop campaign and use sun screen. **SPF** (Sunscreen Protection Factor) is measured by determining how long a given person takes to 'burn' with and without the sunscreen product on. If it takes 10 times longer with the sunscreen product then that product has an SPF of 10. If it only takes twice as long then that product has an SPF of 2. The higher the SPF the greater the protection. However, do not use higher factors just to stay out in the sun longer; 'flash frying' (desperate bursts of excessive exposure) is known to increase the risks of skin cancer.

Typhoid fever

Symptoms This a gut infection which can spread to the blood stream. You get it from someone else's muck getting into your mouth. A classic example would be the waiter who fails to wash his hands and then serves you a salad. The fever is an obvious feature, occasionally there is a mild red rash on the stomach and often you have a headache. Constipation or diarrhoea can occur. Gut pain and hearing problems may also feature.

Cures Antibiotics are required and you are probably best managed in hospital.

Prevention The vaccine is very effective and is best boosted every 3 years. Watch what you eat and the hygiene of the place or those serving your food.

Underwater health

Symptoms: If you go diving make sure that you are fit do so. The British Scuba Association (BSAC, Telford's Quay, South Pier Road, Ellesmere Port, Cheshire CH65 4FL, United Kingdom, T0151-350 6200, F0151-350 6215, www.bsac.com), can put you in touch with doctors who do medical examinations. Protect your feet from cuts, beach dog parasites (larva migrans) and sea urchins. The latter are almost impossible to remove but can be dissolved with lime or vinegar. Keep an eye out for secondary infection.

Cures: Antibiotics for secondary infections. Serious diving injuries may need time in a Decompression Chamber.

Prevention: Check that the dive company know what they are doing, have appropriate certification from BSAC or Professional Association of Diving Instructors (PADI) and that the equipment is well maintained.

Water purification

There are a number of ways of purifying water in order to make it safe to drink. Dirty water should first be strained through a filter bag (camping shops) and then boiled or treated. Bringing water to a rolling **boil** at sea level is sufficient to make the water safe for drinking, but at higher altitudes you have to boil the water for a few minutes longer to ensure that all the microbes are killed. There are **sterilizing** methods that can be used and there are proprietary preparations containing chlorine (for example *Puritabs*) or iodine compounds. Chlorine compounds generally do not kill protozoa (for example giardia). There are a number of water **filters** now on the market available in personal and expedition size. They work either on mechanical or chemical principles, or may do both. Make sure you take the spare parts or spare chemicals with you and do not believe everything the manufacturers say.

Rio de Janeiro

Introducing Rio de Janeiro

Rio, beautifully situated between jungle-covered mountains and an island-studded sea, is known the world over for being home to **Copacabana** beach, the legendary **Ipanema** girl and its spectacular **Carnival**. The city also has a fine artistic and architectural heritage from its time as capital of both Imperial and Republican Brazil and wonderful bird's-eye views from the **statue of Christ** and the **Pão de Açúcar** (Sugar Loaf). But mainly this is a city where hedonism always comes first, where days spent at the beach or playing soccer end with sipping caipirinhas and the sound of samba. Rio state is one of the country's prettiest, with lovely beach resorts and cool mountain retreats within easy reach of the capital. On the stunning 'Emerald Coast', historic **Paraty**, chic **Búzios** and the pirate lair of **Ilha Grande** are all definite highlights.

Travel inland, in the footsteps of the Imperial court who came to escape the summer heat, to find the Imperial palace at **Petrópolis** and lush green national parks near **Teresópolis** and at **Itatiaia**.

Things to do in the state of Rio

① Take a boat from Rio across Guanabara Bay to Niterói for spectacular views back to the city and to visit the Contemporary Art Museum designed by Oscar Niemeyer, one of the architectural wonders of the world.

② Jump in a jeep for a tour from Rio of Tijuca National Park, the largest urban forested national park anywhere on the planet.

③ Live it up in *fazenda* accommodation in the Imperial city of Petrópolis and see the glittering crown jewels at its Imperial palace.

④ Charter a fishing tug to take you out into the bay of Paraty and enjoy a freshly caught fish lunch or even oysters on an island restaurant.

⑤ Take a ferry to Ilha Grande, where there are 100 beaches, no cars and treks through tropical jungle to crystal clear waters.

Rio de Janeiro City

Phone code: 021
Colour map 4, grid C3
Population: 8 million

Brazilians say, "God made the world in six days; the seventh he devoted to Rio" (pronounced 'Heeoo' by locals). The city is certainly one of the world's most beautiful, boasting a magnificent setting which combines a dark blue sea, studded with rocky islands and tumbling wooded mountains. The best known of these rocky masses are the Pão de Açúcar (Sugar Loaf), the highest peak of a low chain of mountains on the fringe of the harbour, and the Corcovado (Hunchback), a jagged peak rising behind the city. There are other peaks, including Tijuca, the tallest point in the foreground, and 50 km away rise the strangely shaped Serra dos Órgãos.

Ins and outs

Getting there
See also Transport, page 124

Air Most international flights stop at the **Aeroporto Internacional Tom Jobim** (formerly Galaeão) on the Ilha do Governador. The air bridge from São Paulo ends at **Santos Dumont** airport in the city centre. Taxis from here are much cheaper than from the international airport. There are also frequent buses between the two airports, the bus station, city centre and Copacabana.

Buses International and from other parts of Brazil arrive at the **Rodoviária Novo Rio** near the docks.

Getting around
Because the city is a series of separate districts connected by urban highways and tunnels heavy with traffic, you will need to take public transport or taxis to get around. An underground railway, the Metrô, runs under some of the centre and the south. Buses run to all parts, but should be treated with caution at night when taxis are a better bet. There is a also a tram that runs from the Largo da Carioca to Dois Irmãos or Paula Mattos in Santa Teresa.

Tourist information
For best results, be specific as possible about your enquiry

Riotur, R da Assembléia 10, 9th floor, T22177575, F25311872, www.rio.rj.gov.br/riotur Information on the city, small, helpful information desk. The main office at Copacabana, Av Princesa Isabel 183, T25417522 (Mon-Fri 0900-1800), is helpful, with English anhd German spoken by some staff, has good city maps and a very useful free brochure *RIO* (in Portuguese and English). More information stands can be found at the international airport (0600-2400) and at the Novo Rio bus station (0800-2000), both, very friendly and helpful in finding accommodation. *Alo Rio* is a telephone service operating 0900-1800, T0800-7071808, 25428080. English information service, T22428000. *TurisRio*, R da Ajuda 5, 8th floor, T22150011, www.turisrio.rj.gov.br, for the state of Rio de Janeiro. Very helpful. *Embratur*, R Uruguaiana 174, 8th floor, Centro, T25096017, www.embratur.gov.br, for information on the whole country. *Touring Clube do Brasil*, Pres Antônio Carlos 130 and Av Brasil 4294 (out of town), publish maps, sold at newstands and in some hotels.

Guide books: *Trilhas do Rio*, by Pedro da Cunha e Meneses (Editora Salamandra, 2nd edition), US$22.50, describes walking trips around Rio. For a light-hearted approach to living in Rio, see *How to be a Carioca* by Priscilla Ann Goslin. Many hotels provide guests with the weekly *Itinerário (Rio This Month)*. Maps: *Guia Rex* street guide. *Guia Schaeffer Rio de Janeiro* is a good map. Maps are also available from Touring Clube do Brasil, news stands, touring agencies and hotels. The Geomapas tourist map is clear. Cia de Comunicaçao publishes a map of the city in perspective, which is good for orientation (US$2). Paulini, R Lélio Gama 75 (outside the entrance of the downtown tram station) sells topographical and other maps of Brazil and of South America. *Guia Quatro Rodas do Rio* in Portuguese and English (the *Guia Quatro Rodas*

24 hours in Rio

Start with a *suco* from one of the many juice bars in Copacabana. Join the body-conscious locals and order an energy-giving *guarana* or a fashionable *acai*, both fruits from the Amazon, together with cereal they are an atom bomb of energy. Then make your way down to the theatre that is the **beach**. This is where real life is lived out in Rio, and where locals are most at home, sunbathing, but also playing volleyball and mostly socializing. **Barra de Tijuca**, a 40-minute bus ride away, is a much cleaner, quieter beach where those in the know go. Later, you can take the scenic tram ride to Santa Teresa, Rio's hilltop artistic enclave with its cobbled streets and cooler climate. Have lunch at *Bar do Arnaudo*, one of Rio's best restaurants and shop for handicrafts and works by local artists at *La Vereda*. Head to Ipanema for a walk on the rocks and to watch the sunset over the water. Have a *chopp* (draught beer) and delicious appetizers at *A Garota de Ipanema*, the 'Girl from Ipanema' bar, where the famous song was written. For an altogether classier early-evening drink, step into the elegant 1920s oasis that is the *Copacabana Palace Hotel*. The poolside bar here cries out for a gin and tonic. Then enjoy a lakeside dinner at one of the restaurants lining Avenida Epitácio Pessoa on the eastern side of **Lagoa Rodrigo de Freitas**. *Bar Lagoa* has a terrace overlooking the water. Take a taxi to **Lapa** and visit some of its funky bars with live music and dancing. *Carioca da Gema* is a 'musical café', next door is *Sacrilegio*, a 'cultural café' with cutting-edge theatre. *Semente* is the venue for samba, choro and salsa. All are open until the early hours.

Rio de Janeiro

do Brasil, published annually in Nov, also has a good Rio section) has excellent maps.

Newspapers and magazines *Balcão*, an advertising newspaper, US$2, twice weekly, offers apartments in and around Rio, language lessons, discounted tickets, items for sale and advertises shops; similar advertisements in the classified sections of *O Globo* and *Jornal do Brasil*, daily. Both dailies have entertainments pages. *O Globo* has a travel section on Thurs; the *Jornal do Brasil*'s *Programa* on Fri is an essential 'what's-on' magazine, as is the *Rio* supplement to *Veja*, a weekly news magazine (*Veja* publishes similar supplements in other major cities). *Riotur's* fortnightly booklet listing main attractions; *Rio This Month* (less reliable), free from hotels. *TurisRio's* free magazine about the State of Rio de Janeiro is interesting; if your hotel does not have these publications, just ask at the reception of one of the larger establishments.

Climate Rio has one of the healthiest climates in the tropics. Trade winds cool the air. Jun, Jul and Aug are the coolest months with temperatures ranging from 22°C (18° in a cold spell) to 32°C on a sunny day at noon. Dec-Mar is hotter, from 32°C to 42°C. Humidity is high. Oct-Mar is the rainy season and the annual rainfall is about 1,120 mm. Carnival is something of a moveable feast, which runs for 5 riotous days from the Fri afternoon before Shrove Tue to the morning hangover of Ash Wed.

History

The coast of Rio de Janeiro was first settled about 5,000 years ago. When the Europeans arrived in the region, the indigenous inhabitants belonged to the Tupi or Tupi-Guarani, Puri, Botocudos and Maxacali linguistic groups. Tragically, no Indian people in what is now Rio de Janeiro state survived the European incursions.

The Portuguese navigator, Gonçalo Coelho, arrived at what is now Rio de Janeiro on 1 January 1502. Thinking that the Baía de Guanabara (the name

▶▶ **Arriving at night**

The airport is pretty safe, but watch your belongings. The excellent a/c bus doesn't run between 2300 and 0600, so if arriving in the early hours you will need to take a taxi or wait until morning – there is a 24-hour café in Terminal 1. Most hotels have someone on duty all night although they may not speak English.

the local Indians used) was the mouth of a great river, they called the place the January River.

But the bay wasn't settled until 1555 when the French, under the Huguenot Admiral Nicholas Durand de Villegagnon, occupied Lage Island. They later transferred to Seregipe Island (now Villegagnon), where they built the fort of Coligny. The fort has been demolished to make way for the Escola Naval (Naval College) and the island itself, since the narrow channel was filled up, has become a part of the mainland. Villegagnon set up a colony as the starting point for what he called Antarctic France.

In early 1559-60, Mem de Sá, third governor of Brazil, mounted an expedition from Salvador to attack the French, who were supported by Tamoio Indians. The Portuguese succeeded in capturing the French fort and putting an end to Antarctic France, but did not colonize the area until 1567 when they transferred their settlement to the Morro de São Januário. This is generally considered the date of the founding of the city of São Sebastião do Rio de Janeiro, so called in honour of the Portuguese prince who would soon assume the throne.

Though constantly attacked by Indians, the new city grew rapidly and when King Sebastião divided Brazil into two provinces, Rio was chosen capital of the southern captaincies. Salvador became sole capital again in 1576, but Rio again became the southern capital in 1608 and the seat of a bishopric. There was a further French incursion in 1710-11 as a result of the tension between France and Portugal during the war of Spanish Succession, and because of the flow of gold out of Minas Gerais through Rio.

Rio de Janeiro orientation

Safety in Rio

The majority of visitors enjoy Rio and all it has to offer without any problems. But Rio is one of the world's most densely populated cities and there are areas of extreme poverty; most robberies that occur are committed out of desperation. Overseas visitors are an obvious target. Many crimes against tourists are avoidable. Avoid wearing expensive clothes and jewellery and if you are carrying a camera, keep it out of view. Don't leave things unattended on the beach. You have the most to lose when carrying all your belongings and as you go in and out of banks, exchange houses and expensive shops, so take extra care then. At other times, put your passport, travellers' cheques, etc in the hotel safe. In other words, don't take too much out with you, have some sense and relax.

Certain parts of the city are best avoided: the city centre on Sunday when it is deserted; tunnels, quiet alleyways, jostling crowds and dark corners. Locals don't walk on the beaches at night: if you must, do not go out of sight of the pavement. The Tijuca forest is best explored with a group of six or more, except the stretch between Afonso Vizeu square and

Cascatinha which is well policed during the day; the tram to Santa Teresa (see page 95) attracts pickpockets; robberies sometimes happen on city buses, don't use them if guarding your property is essential (private frescão buses are more secure). The main bus station is patrolled inside, but uncomfortable outside. If you go to the Zona Norte at night, use a taxi; wandering around favelas alone at any time of day is ill-advised. The 'red light' districts of the Zona Sul are unlikely to offend anyone walking about at night, even children or unaccompanied women. Do, however, be suspicious of any club that you are invited into by a stranger (have your drink opened in front of you) and of anyone offering drugs. When ordering drinks in red-light bars, check prices first.

*The **Tourist Police**, Av Afrânio de Melo Franco, Leblon (in front of the Casa Grande theatre), T25115112, publish a sensible advice leaflet (available from hotels and consulates; consulates also issue safety guidelines). Tourist police officers are helpful, efficient and multilingual; they patrol all the main tourist areas and if you have any problems, contact them first.*

Rio de Janeiro was by now becoming the leading city in Brazil. Not only was it the port out of which gold was shipped, but it was also the focus of the export/import trade of the surrounding agricultural lands. On 27 January 1763, it became the seat of the Viceroy. After Independence, in 1834, it was declared capital of the Empire and remained the capital for 125 years.

When the Portuguese royal family fled to Brazil in 1808, the ideas that were brought over from Europe started a major transformation of the city. True, works to beautify and clean up the place had been undertaken when the city acquired viceregal status, but the remodelling which occurred in the early 19th century was on a different scale (see Fine art and Architecture on pages 700 and 703). The city also expanded beyond its historical boundaries. It grew north into São Cristóvão and Tijuca and south through Glória, Catete, Flamengo and Botafogo. The prosperous coffee barons and business class built their mansions and the Imperial court was the centre of the nation's attention. The decline of the coffee trade in Rio de Janeiro state and the proclamation of the Republic did not affect the city's dominance as political, economic and cultural heart of Brazil.

Growth continued into the 20th century and one of the most significant acts was the construction of a monumental new boulevard through the

The shaping of a city

middle of the commercial district. The 33-m wide Avenida Central, later renamed Avenida Rio Branco, was driven through the old city's narrow streets in 1904-05 as the principal means of access in Rio. Meanwhile, the city continued to expand outwards: north into industrial zones; south around the coast; and inland, up the hills, mainly in the form of the slums known as *favelas*.

When, in 1960, the nation's capital was moved to Brasília, Rio went into decline, especially the commercial centre, and began to suffer badly from poor urban planning decisions and too many high-rise buildings. However, in the late 1990s, the mayor of the city, Luiz Paulo Conde, embarked on a massive programme of regenerating the centre through remodelling and attracting residents to neglected districts. As an architect and urbanist he brought a social vision which encompasses the improvement of *favelas* and a plan to clean up the south of the city as far as Leblon.

In December 1997 a new 25-km expressway, the *Linha Amarela*, was opened from the Ilha do Fundão, near the international airport, to Barra de Tijuca, cutting by more than half the journey time to Barra.

Rio de Janeiro centre

Detailed
map
A Praça 15 de
Novembre,
page 83
Related maps
Rio de Janeiro
orientation,
page 78
A Rio west
of centre,
page 90
B Glória, Santa
Teresa, Catete,
Flamengo,
page 92

0 metres   200
0 yards   200

■ Sleeping
1 Itajubá

● Eating
1 Al-Kuwait

Sights

Central Rio

Known as 'Centro', this is the historical part of the city, which dates from 1567 when the Portuguese moved their settlement from the area now known as Urca to the Morro de São Januário. Today the centre stretches from the Mosteiro de São Bento to the Santos Dumont airport and inland as far as the Campo de Santana park.

The hill on which the original city was located was removed in the 1920s, so the historical centre effectively ends at the São José church. The 400 years following the founding of the city saw so many changes in architectural design and fashion that, today, the centre appears to be an incoherent collection of buildings, with the ultra-modern towering over the neoclassical, which in turn sits uneasily beside the colonial. Add to this the crowded streets and the constant traffic and it may seem a daunting place to explore. Don't give up! There is much to discover and your perseverance will be repaid.

Check opening times in advance of all churches, museums and public buildings; they change frequently. All museums and the Jardim Botânico close over Carnival

Rio de Janeiro

Rio de Janeiro

An example of the juxtaposition of so many elements in close surroundings is the **Travessa do Comércio**, which runs between the Praça 15 de Novembro and the Rua do Ouvidor. On the northwest side of Praça 15 de Novembro is the Arco do Teles, all that remains of an 18th-century construction, now incorporated into a modern building. Through the arch is the Travessa do Comércio, a narrow, twisting street with neoclassical houses and wrought-iron arches over the street lamps. This is how the whole city was in the 19th century. The Travessa, now dwarfed by 20th-century office blocks, leads to the church of Nossa Senhora da Lapa dos Mercadores, another 18th-century construction sandwiched between the concrete and glass. On Friday nights the Travessa is very lively; along it are several restaurants, including the *Arco Imperial*, where Carmen Miranda (see page 691) lived between 1925-30 (her mother kept a boarding house).

The city's main artery is the **Avenida Presidente Vargas**, 4½ km long and over 90 m wide. It starts at the waterfront, divides to embrace the famous Candelária church, then crosses the **Avenida Rio Branco** in a magnificent straight stretch past the Central do Brasil railway station, with its imposing clock tower, until finally it incorporates a palm-lined, canal-divided avenue. Most of the Avenida Rio Branco's ornate buildings have been replaced by modern blocks; a few remain by Cinelândia and the Biblioteca Nacional. Some of the finest modern architecture is to be found along the **Avenida República do Chile**, such as the Petrobrás, the Banco Nacional de Desenvolvimento Econômico and the former Banco Nacional de Habitação buildings and the new cathedral.

Around Praça 15 de Novembro   Originally an open space at the foot of the Morro do Castelo, the **Praça 15 de Novembro** (often called Praça XV) has always been one of the focal points in Rio de Janeiro. Today it has one of the greatest concentrations of historic buildings in the city. Having been through various phases of development in its history, it had major remodelling in the late 1990s. The last vestiges of the original harbour, at the seaward end of the Praça were restored. The steps no longer lead to the water and the Avenida Alfredo Agache now goes through an underpass, creating an open space between the praça and the seafront and giving easy access to the ferry dock for Niterói. The area is well illuminated and clean and the municipality has started to stage shows, music and dancing in the praça. At weekends an antiques, crafts, stamp and coin fair (Feirarte II) is held from 0900-1900.

On Rua 1 de Março, across from Praça 15 de Novembro, there are three buildings related to the Carmelite order. The convent of the **Ordem Terceira do Monte do Carmo**, started in 1611, is now used as the Faculdade Cândido Mendes. The Carmo church was appropriated by the royal family in the early 19th century as a residence for the queen, Dona Maria I (nicknamed A Louca because of her mental illness). Such buildings were called PR, that is, taken over by the Príncipe Regente (or, in popular terminology, *Prédio Roubado* – stolen building). To prevent the members of the Imperial family sullying their feet on streets used by all and sundry, a covered bridge was built between the ex-convento and the cathedral when the Rua 7 de Setembro was driven between them in 1857.

Between the former convent and the Igreja da Ordem Terceira do Carmo is the old cathedral, the **Igreja de Nossa Senhora do Carmo da Antiga Sé**, separated from the Carmo Church by a passageway. It was the chapel of the Convento do Carmo from 1590 until 1754. A new church was built in 1761, which became the Capela Real with the arrival of the Portuguese royal family in 1808 and subsequently the city's cathedral. In the crypt are the alleged remains of Pedro Alvares Cabral, the Portuguese explorer (though Santarém, Portugal, also claims to be his last resting place).

The order's present church, the **Igreja da Ordem Terceira do Carmo**, also in Rua Primeiro de Março, the other side of the old cathedral (see below) from the convent, was built in 1754, consecrated in 1770 and rebuilt between 1797 and 1826. It has strikingly beautiful portals by Mestre Valentim (see Fine Art and Sculpture, page 701), the son of a Portuguese nobleman and a slave girl. He also created the main altar of fine moulded silver, the throne and its chair and much else. ■ *Mon-Fri 0800-1400, Sat 0800-1200.* A fountain designed by Mestre Valentim stands in the praça: the Chafariz do Mestre Valentim, or Chafariz do Pirâmide.

At the rear of the old cathedral and the Carmo Church, on Rua do Carmo, is the **Oratório de Nossa Senhora do Cabo da Boa Esperança**, one of the few remaining public oratory from the colonial period in Rio.

The beautiful colonial **Paço Imperial** (former Royal Palace), on the southeast corner of the Praça 15 de Novembro, was built in 1743 as the residence of the governor of the Capitania. It later became the king's storehouse and armoury (Armazens), then the Casa da Moeda, before being made into the Paço Real when the Portuguese court moved to Brazil. After Independence it became the Imperial Palace. During the Republic it was used as the post and telegraph office and fell into decline. In the 1980s it was completely restored as a cultural centre. It has several exhibition spaces, one theatre, one cinema for art films, a library, a section showing the original construction, a superb model of the city and the *Bistro* and the *Atrium* restaurants (recommended). ■ *Tue-Sun 1100-1830, T25334407.*

Beside the Paço Imperial, across Rua da Assembléia, is the **Palácio Tiradentes**, built between 1922 and 1926. It is now the legislative assembly of

Praça 15 de Novembro

Teófilo Otóni

Praça Pio X

NS da Candelária

Av Pres Vargas

Centro Cultural Banco do Brasil

Casa França-Brasil

Espaço Cultural da Marinha

Av Alfredo Agache

Vist Itaboraí

Rua 1 de Março

Tinoco

Rua da Alfândega

Candelária

Espaço Cultural dos Correios

Nossa Senhora da Lapa dos Mercadores

Av Presidente Kubitschek

Rua Buenos Aires

Miguel Couto

Santa Cruz dos Militares

Rua do Mercado

Travessa do Comércio

Arco do Teles

Rua do Rosário

Rua da Quitanda

Rua do Carmo

Ordem Terceira do Monte do Carmo

Praça 15 de Novembro

Av Rio Branco

Rua do Ouvidor

Nossa Senhora do Carmo da Antiga Sé

Paço Imperial

Oratório de Nossa Senhora do Cabo da Boa Esperança

Convento do Carmo

Palácio Tiradentes

Museo Naval e Oceanográfico

Tr do Ouvidor

Gonçalves Dias

Riotur

Statue of Tiradentes

Rua da Assembléia

Av Carlos

Rua São José

Rua São José Manoel

Rua 7 de Setembro

São José

| 0 metres | 100 |
| 0 yards | 100 |

● Eating
1 Confeitaria Colombo 2 Rio Minho

Related map
Rio de Janeiro
centre, page 80

Rio de Janeiro

Rio de Janeiro

the State of Rio de Janeiro, but the building was closed twice in the 1930s as different administrations did not feel the need for a Chamber of Federal Deputies. The palace is in eclectic style (see Architecture, page 703), with a façade displaying heavy Greek influence. In front stands a statue of the Independence fighter, Tiradentes (see page 258), by Francisco de Andrade; the palace was given his name because it was on this spot, the site of the old prison, that the national hero was held prisoner while awaiting execution. ■ *Mon-Fri 1300-1900 by prior appointment, T25881000.*

In the next block southeast is the **Igreja de São José** (Rua São José e Avenida Presidente Antônio Carlos), considerably altered since its original construction in the 17th century. The current building dates from 1824 and was remodelled in 1969. ■ *Mon-Fri 0900-1200, 1400-1700, Sun 0900-1100.*

One block further northeast, at Rua Dom Manoel 15, is the **Museu Naval e Oceanográfico**. It had a collection of paintings and prints, as well as a display of weapons and figureheads, but most of the exhibits have been moved to the Espaço Cultural da Marinha.

Turning to the northwest side of Praça 15 de Novembro, you go through the Arco do Teles and the Travessa do Comércio (see above) to Rua do Ouvidor. The **Igreja Nossa Senhora da Lapa dos Mercadores** (Rua do Ouvidor 35) was consecrated in 1750, remodelled in 1869-72 and has been fully restored. ■ *Mon-Fri 0800-1400.* Across the street, with its entrance at Rua 1 de Março 36, is the church of **Santa Cruz dos Militares**, built 1780-1811. It is large, stately and beautiful and the inside has been well renovated in a 'light' baroque style.

Praça Marechal Âncora/Praça Rui Barbosa In the corner of the centre bounded by Praça 15 de Novembro and the Esplanada do Castelo is an area which has changed significantly since colonial times. Most alterations were made in the 20th century, first with the removal of the old municipal fish market, for health reasons, then with the levelling of the Morro do Castelo in the 1920s. There are two squares here, Praça Marechal Âncora, or Praça Rui Barbosa, and Praça do Expedicionário. The only remnant of the Morro do Castelo is a short stretch of the Ladeira da Misericórdia, at the foot of which is the church of Nossa Senhora de Bonsucesso, also known as the church of the Santa Casa da Misericórdia. The Santa Casa itself is behind the church. The colonial hospital made way for a neoclassical building in the mid-19th century. The main focus here is the **Museu Histórico Nacional**, which contains a collection of historical treasures, colonial sculpture and furniture, maps, paintings, arms and armour, silver and porcelain. The building was once the old War Arsenal of the Empire, part of which was built in 1762 (this part is called the Casa do Trem). Two years later the Pátio de Minerva was added and significant expansion was done in 1808. Further changes were made in 1922 when the museum was inaugurated. ■ *1000-1730 Tue-Fri, 1400-1800 Sat, Sun and holidays . US$1, T22409529.*

Museu da Imagem e do Som, also on Praça Rui Barbosa, has many photographs of Brazil and modern Brazilian paintings; also collections and recordings of Brazilian classical and popular music and a non-commercial cinema Friday-Sunday. ■ *1300-1800 Mon-Fri.*

Avenida Presidente Vargas The church of **Nossa Senhora da Candelária** (1775-1810), on Praça Pio X (Dez), at the city end of Avenida Presidente Vargas where it meets Rua 1 de Março, has beautiful ceiling decorations and romantic paintings. It is on the site of a chapel founded in 1610 by Antônio da Palma after he had survived a shipwreck, an event depicted by paintings inside the present dome. ■ *0730-1200, 1300-1630 Mon-Fri, 0800-1200 Sat, 0900-1300 Sun.*

In this part of the city a number of cultural centres have opened in recent years. The **Espaço Cultural dos Correios**, Rua Visconde de Itaboraí 20, holds temporary exhibitions and cultural events and a postage stamp fair on Saturdays. ■ *1300-1900 Tue-Sun, T25038770*. Opposite, with entrances on Avenida Presidente Vargas and Rua 1 de Março 66, is the **Centro Cultural Banco do Brasil (CCBB)**, highly recommended for good exhibitions, with a library, multimedia facilities, a cinema, concerts (US$6 at lunchtime) and a restaurant *(T38082000; 1230-1900, Tue-Sun)*. At the corner of Rua Visconde de Itaboraí (No 253) and Avenida Presidente Vargas is the **Casa França-Brasil**. This building holds temporary exhibitions and is dedicated to cultural exchanges between the two countries, but is much more important for its history. Its construction dates from the first French Artistic Mission to Brazil (see Architecture and Fine Art and Sculpture, pages 700 and 703 respectively) and it was the first neoclassical building in Rio. The interior is entirely neoclassical, although the pillars and mouldings are made of wood. The roof, though, is a hybrid between the colonial Brazilian style and the newly introduced European fashion. It was built as a customs house and the strong-room can still be seen. ■ *1200-2000 Tue-Sun, T22535366*. The newest cultural centre here is the **Espaço Cultural da Marinha**, on Avenida Alfredo Agache at Avenida Presidente Kubitschek. This former naval establishment now contains museums of underwater archaeology and navigation and the *Galeota*, the boat used by the Portuguese royal family for sailing around the Baía de Guanabara. Moored outside is the warship, *Bauru*. ■ *1200-1700 Tue-Sun.*

Offshore, but connected to the mainland by a causeway to Ilha das Cobras, is the **Ilha Fiscal**. It was built as a customs house at the emperor's request, but he deemed it too beautiful, so he said that it should be used only for official parties. Only one was ever held, five days before the Republic began. It is now a museum, linked with the Naval Cultural Centre. Boats leave Friday, Saturday and Sunday at 1300, 1430 and 1600 (30 minutes later October to March). T38706879. The island is passed by the ferry to Niterói.

The Praça Mauá marks the end of Centro and the beginning of the port zone. **Praça Mauá**
Many of the empty warehouses are used as workshops by the samba schools, where their beautiful floats are built.

Just north of Candelária, on a promontory overlooking the bay, is the World Heritage Site of **Mosteiro de São Bento**. The monastery's church, dedicated to Nossa Senhora de Monserrate (but usually referred to as the Igreja do Mosteiro de São Bento) contains much of what is best in the 17th- and 18th-century art of Brazil. Monks of the Benedictine order arrived in Rio de Janeiro in 1586, five years after their installation in Salvador.

São Bento is reached either by a narrow road from Rua Dom Gerardo 68, or by a lift whose entrance is at Rua Dom Gerardo 40 (taxi to the monastery from centre US$5). Both routes lead to a praça with tall trees, but stepping out of the lift into this oasis increases the sense of escape from the city below. The church's façade is in the mannerist style, plain and undecorated. You go through the *galilé*, the antechamber for the unbaptized with its fine tiles, and enter the main body of the church. *Corta ventos*, doors which keep out the draughts so that the candles inside are not extinguished, are the last obstacle to the sight of the interior. The carving and gilding is remarkable – not an inch is unadorned in gold and red – much of it by Frei Domingos da Conceição (see Fine Art and

Sculpture, page 700). The paintings, too, should be seen; 'O Salvador', the masterpiece of Brazil's first painter, Frei Ricardo do Pilar, hangs in the sacristy. The lamps (*lampadarios* – two of which are attributed to Mestre Valentim) are of solid silver which, coming from Peru and Bolivia, was of greater value than Brazil's own gold. See also the two *anjos tocheiros*, angels carrying torches, common in many baroque churches. On top of the main altar is a statue of Nossa Senhora de Monserrate, made by Frei Domingos da Conceição; the eyes of both the Virgin and her Child are made from painted birds eggs. The Chapels of the Immaculate Conception (Nossa Senhora da Conceição) and of the Most Holy Sacrament (Santíssimo Sacramento) are masterpieces of colonial art. The organ, dating from the end of the 18th century, is very interesting.

Every Sunday at 1000, mass is sung with Gregorian chant and music, which is free, but you should arrive an hour early to get a seat. On other days, mass is at 0715. At other times you may be lucky enough to hear the monks singing. The monastery is a few minutes' walk from Praça Mauá, turning left off Avenida Rio Branco; Rua Dom Gerardo 68 is behind the massive, new RBI building. ■ *0800-1230, 1400-1730 daily. Shorts not allowed.*

Also easily reached from Praça Mauá and requiring a climb is the **Morro da Conceição**, another hill from which the early Portuguese settlers could survey the bay. The first constructions on the hill were religious and a bishop's palace was built in 1702, the Palácio da Conceição. This and the subsequently built Fortaleza da Conceição are currently in the hands of the military. The Palácio has a small museum and the area is perfectly safe to visit as another remnant of colonial Rio. Above the door of the Fortaleza is another of the few remaining public oratories; it is lit at night.

Largo da Carioca   The Largo da Carioca, a remarkable ensemble of old and new plus the muddle of the street vendors who have occupied the praça beween Rua da Carioca and the Metrô station, is another good location for seeing a variety of sites within a small area.

See also box opposite   The second oldest convent in the city is the 17th-century **Convento de Santo Antônio**, on a hill off the Largo da Carioca, built between 1608 and 1615. Its church has a marvellous sacristy adorned with blue tiles and paintings illustrating the life of St Anthony. In the church itself, the baroque decoration is concentrated in the chancel, the main altar and the two lateral altars. Santo Antônio is a particular object of devotion for women who want to find husbands and many will be seen in the precincts.

Separated from this church only by some iron railings is the charming church of the Ordem Terceira de **São Francisco da Penitência**, built in 1773. Currently closed for renovation, it contains much more carving and gilding of walls and altar than its neighbour. The workmanship is superb. In the ceiling over the nave is a fine panel painted by José de Oliveira. There is a museum attached to the church.

Across Ruas da Carioca and 7 de Setembro is the church of **São Francisco de Paula**, at the upper end of the Rua do Ouvidor. The first stone was laid in 1759 and construction was completed in 1801. It contains some of Mestre Valentim's work – the carvings in the main chapel and the lovely Capela da Nossa Senhora da Vitória (Our Lady of Victory). The beautiful fountain at the back of the church plays only at night. ■ *0900-1300 Mon-Fri.*

One long block behind the Largo da Carioca and São Francisco de Paula is the **Praça Tiradentes**, old and shady, with a statue to Dom Pedro I. Erected in 1862, it is the work of Luís Rochet and shows the Emperor on horseback, declaring Independence. At the northeast corner of the praça is the **Teatro João Caetano**,

Wild Jock of Skelater

The crypt of Convento de Santo Antônio contains the tomb of a Scottish soldier of fortune known as 'Wild Jock of Skelater'. He was in the service of the Portuguese Government during the Napoleonic War, and had the distinction of being appointed the first Commander-in-Chief of the Army in Brazil. The statue of Santo Antônio was made *a captain in the Portuguese army after his help had been sought to drive out the French in 1710, and his salary paid to the monastery. In 1810 the statue became a major, in 1814 a lieutenant-colonel, and was granted the Grand Cross of the Order of Christ. He was retired without pay in 1914. The church and convent are open 1400-1700 Monday-Friday.*

named after a famous 19th-century actor. ■ *T22210305*. Shops in nearby streets specialize in selling goods for *umbanda*, the Afro-Brazilian religion.

South of the Largo da Carioca are the modern buildings on Avenida República do Chile mentioned above. The **New Cathedral**, the **Catedral Metropolitana**, was dedicated in November 1976. It is a cone-shaped building with an internal height of 68 m, diameter 104 m and external height 83 m; its capacity is 5,000 seated, 20,000 standing. The four enormous 60-m-high stained-glass windows are its most striking feature. It is still incomplete. ■ *0800-1800*.

Crossing Avenida República do Paraguai from the east side of the Catedral Metropolitana, you come to an open area with the Petrobrás building and the station, with museum, for the tram to Santa Teresa (entrance on Rua Senador Dantas – see below). Soon after leaving the station the tram traverses the **Arcos da Lapa**, which were built as an aqueduct to take water from the Rio Carioca to the Largo da Carioca.

Here are the last vestiges of the early 20th-century project of the grand **Avenida** Avenida Central. Facing Praça Marechal Floriano is the **Teatro Municipal**, **Rio Branco** one of the most magnificent buildings in Brazil in the so-called 'eclectic' style (see Architecture, page 703). It was built in 1905-09, in imitation of the Opéra in Paris. On either side of the colonnaded façade are rotundas, surmounted by cupolas. Above the columns are statues of two women, Poetry and Music. The decorative features inside and out represent many styles, all lavishly executed. ■ *For opera and orchestral performances, T25442900. To book a tour of the theatre (in English and Spanish, French or Portuguese), T22623501 in advance, 0900-1700 Mon-Fri, US$1.20 per person; the tour is worth it to see front and back stage, the decorations and the machine rooms. The box office is at the right-hand side of the building; ticket prices start at about US$10.*

Across the avenue is the **Biblioteca Nacional**, at Avenida Rio Branco 219. This building also dates from the first decade of the 20th century. The monumental staircase leads to a hall, off which lead the fine internal staircases of Carrara marble. The first national library was brought to Brazil by the Prince Regent, Dom João, in 1808. The original collection coming from the Ajuda Palace in Lisbon; today the library houses over nine million pieces, including the 15th-century *Book of Hours*, paintings donated by Pedro II and scores by Mozart. ■ *0900-1700 Mon-Fri, US$1, T22628255*.

The third major building in this group, opposite the Teatro Municipal, is the **Museu Nacional de Belas Artes**, Avenida Rio Branco 199. It was built between 1906 and 1908, also in 'eclectic' style. It has about 800 original paintings and sculptures and some thousand direct reproductions. There is a gallery dedicated to works by Brazilian artists from the 17th century onwards, including paintings by Frans Janszoon Post (Dutch 1612-80), who painted

Brazilian landscapes in classical Dutch style (see The Dutch in Brazil, page 436) and the Frenchmen Debret and Taunay (see Fine Art and Sculpture, page 700, for these and other painters represented). Another gallery charts the development of Brazilian art in 20th century, including works by Cândido Portinari, Alberto da Veiga Guignard and others. A third gallery contains work by foreign artists. There is also a hall for temporary exhibitions. ■ *1000-1800 Tue-Fri, 1400-1800 Sat, Sun and holidays. US$1. T22400068.*

Those interested in contemporary art should also visit the **Palácio Capanema**, the former Ministry of Education and Health building, then the Palácio da Cultura. It is on the Esplanada do Castelo, at the junction of Avenida Graça Aranha and Rua Araújo Porto Alegre, and dates from 1937-45 (Unesco has declared it an International Monument). A team of architects led by Lúcio Costa and under the guidance of Le Corbusier designed it; Oscar Niemeyer and Affonso Reidy were in the group (see Architecture, page 703). Inside are the great murals of Cândido Portinari, as well as other works by renowned artists. The gardens were laid out by Roberto Burle Marx (see page 106).

In the Rua de Santa Luzia, close by the Palácio Capanema and overwhelmed by tall office buildings, is the attractive little church of **Santa Luzia**. When built in 1752 it had only one tower; the other was added late in the 19th century. Feast day is 13 December, when devotees bathe their eyes with holy water, which is considered miraculous.

Cinelândia   **Praça Mahatma Gandhi**, at the end of Avenida Rio Branco, is flanked on one side by the old cinema and amusement centre of the city, known as Cinelândia. The cast-iron fountain in the ornamental garden was moved here from Praça 15 de Novembro.

Next to the praça is the **Passeio Público**, a garden planted in 1779-83 by the artist Mestre Valentim, whose bust is near the old former gateway. ■ *0900-1700 daily.*

Museu do Instituto Histórico e Geográfico, Avenida Augusto Severo 8 (10th floor), just off Avenida Beira Mar, is across the street from the Passeio Público. It has an interesting collection of historical objects, Brazilian products and artefacts. ■ *1200-1700 Mon-Fri* .

Praça da   **Campo de Santana**, Praça da República is an extensive and picturesque pub-
República   lic garden close to the Pedro II, or Central Railway station. The Parque Júlio Furtado in the middle of the square is populated by agoutis (or gophers), best seen at dusk; there is also an artificial grotto, with swans.

A plaque at Praça da República 197 marks the house of Marechal Deodoro da Fonseca, who proclaimed Brazil a republic in 1889. On the same side of the Praça is the Arquivo Nacional in the neoclassical former Casa da Moeda (Praça da República e Rua Azeredo Coutinho; closed for repairs, and the Faculdade de Direito, Rua Moncorvo Filho 8, in the Solar do Conde dos Arcos. On the opposite side of Avenida Presidente Vargas from the Praça are the Palácio and Panteão do Duque de Caxias.

Palácio do Itamaraty, Avenida Marechal Floriano 196, is in the next block east from the Palácio do Duque de Caxias. Built in neoclassical style in the 1850s for the coffee baron Francisco José da Rocha, it became the president's residence between 1889 and 1897 and then the Ministry of Foreign Affairs until the opening of Brasília. Now it houses the **Museu Histórico e Diplomático**. ■ *Free guided tours on Mon, Wed and Fri hourly between 1315 and 1615, T22532828. Recommended.*

Favelas, a numberless existence

Rio de Janeiro's favelas, the slums which creep up the city's hillsides and spread out across the flat lands, have been the source of much bad press for many years. They have been represented as no-go areas, where drug lords rule and fight for dominance, and out of which the city's criminals came. No sensible visitor would venture within their radius until favela tours were started in the mid-1990s. One such tour is to Vila Canoas and Rocinha, close to São Conrado. The tours are interesting and lead to a greater appreciation of Rio and its people. They have the same motivation as a major scheme, Favela-Bairro, designed to rehabilitate the favelas, to show that the favelados are hardworking, simple people, and that their communities deserve the same facilities and rights as other parts of the city. (It is unadvisable to visit the favelas unless on an organized tour.)

The name favela was first used at the end of the 19th century after soldiers on the Canudos campaign in Bahia set up their guns on a hill called the Morro das Favelas. The soldiers became known as favelados. When they returned to Rio after the campaign, the soldiers built their homes on the Morro da Providência, but the favela nickname stuck. In time, any temporary settlement acquired the name favela and, as urban and rural poor alike strove to make it in the city, many people stayed initially in the shanties before moving to better accommodation. Many, of course, were unable to better themselves. In the 1970s and 1980s, there were some attempts to improve conditions in the favelas and residents, given assurances that they would not be forcibly removed, began to make their dwellings more permanent. Electricity and water

supplies can be tapped into, usually illegally, but waste disposal and other basic facilities are rare. One of Rio's problems is that the favelas are in the middle of the city, not on the outskirts as in other metropolises. Almost a million people live in these conditions. The huge number of entries and exits make them difficult to police.

Since 1993, an ambitious project has been underway to upgrade the majority of the city's favelas by 2004. A US$350 m programme, aided by the Inter-American Development Bank, is providing the shanties with streets in place of alleys, sewerage, lighting, day-care centres, recreational areas, rubbish collection and transport. The favelas will be integrated with the surrounding neighbourhoods. The work also includes reforestation and the prevention of hill slides. Residents are given a say in how their district should be improved and no family will be rehoused in a part of the city which is alien to it. Having accepted that the favelas are permanent, not transitory, the city's authorities' task is to incorporate them into the whole, not leave them marginalized. An IADB special report on the project quoted O Globo: "Every citizen ought to have the right to live on or a street in a house with a number".

The Secretaria Municipal da Habitação and IplanRio, the Empresa Municipal de Informática e Planejamento, produce a magazine on Favela-Bairro, available from Avenida Afonso Cavalcanti 455, bloco B, 4 andar, CEP 20.211-110, Rio de Janeiro, T2732345, or R Gago Coutinho 52, Largo do Machado, CEP 22.221-070, Rio de Janeiro, T5563399. See Tour operators, page 122, for guides who can offer a safe, different and interesting experience.

Northern Rio

Over the Morro da Providência, which is between the Estação Dom Pedro II and the bay, is the **Cemitério dos Ingleses**, Rua da Gamboa 181. The cemetery, the oldest in Rio, was granted to the British community by Dom João, Regent of Portugal, in 1810. Catholics who could afford a burial were laid to rest inside their churches (see the numbers on the church floors, marking the graves), but the British in Rio, being non-Catholic, were not allowed to be buried in the religious establishments.

Rua da Gamboa

Rio de Janeiro

Maracanã Stadium Maracanã Stadium, officially called Estádio Mário Filho, is one of the largest sports centres in the world, with a capacity of 200,000. This is where Pelé scored his 1,000th goal in 1969. Matches are worth going to if only for the spectators' samba bands and the adrenalin-charged atmosphere. There are three types of ticket: *cadeiras* (individual chairs), the most expensive; *arquibancadas* (terraces), good for watching the game, but don't sit between two rival groups of fans; *geral* (standing), the cheapest, not recommended, not safe. Prices vary according to the game, but it's much more expensive to buy tickets from agencies than at the gate; it is cheaper to buy tickets from club sites on the day before the match.

Maracanã is now used only for major games; Rio teams play most matches at their home grounds (still a memorable experience). Hotels can arrange visits to football matches, a good idea on Sunday when the Metrô is closed and buses are very full. ■ *0900-1700 daily (0800-1100 on match days). A guided tour of the stadium (in Portuguese) from Gate 16 costs US$2 and of the museum, US$0.50, T25689962, highly recommended for football fans. Getting there: Maracanã Metrô station is on Linha 2, one stop beyond São Cristóvão. Buses: 238 and 239 from the centre; 434 and 464 from Glória, Flamengo and Botafogo; 455 from Copacabana; 433 and 464 from Ipanema and Leblon.*

Useful information Don't take valuables or wear a watch; take special care when entering and leaving the stadium. The rivalry between the local clubs Flamengo and Vasco da Gama is intense, often leading to violence, so it is advisable to avoid their encounters. Don't be tempted to buy a club shirt or favour on match day; if you find yourself in the wrong place, you could be in trouble.

Rio west of centre

Related maps
Rio de Janeiro orientation,
page 78
➡ *A Rio de Janeiro centre, page 80*

About 3 km west of the Praça da República (beyond the Sambódromo – see box on Carnival, page 116) is the Quinta da Boa Vista, formerly the emperor's private park, from 1809 to 1889. The palace in which the Imperial family lived now houses the Museu Nacional (see below). In recent years the Quinta da Boa Vista has had the problem of thieves operating by the park entrance and in the park itself. If you are comfortable in crowds, perhaps the best time to visit is Saturday, or better still, Sunday afternoon. There are more people and therefore more police because it is full of Cariocas looking for fun and relaxation. It is a good time for people watching (but don't take an expensive camera). The park becomes a noisy mixture of colours, smells of hot dogs and corn, people playing football, preachers warning of the end of the world and street sellers.

Quinta da Boa Vista

The **Museu Nacional** in the Quinta da Boa Vista has important collections which are poorly displayed. The building was the principal palace of the emperors of Brazil, but only the unfurnished Throne Room and Ambassadorial Reception Room on the second floor reflect past glories. In the Entrance Hall is the famous Bendegó meteorite, found in the State of Bahia in 1888; its original weight, before some of it was chipped, was 5,360 kg. Besides several foreign collections of note (for example, of Peruvian and Mexican archaeology, Graeco-Roman ceramics and Egyptian mummies), the museum contains collections of Brazilian Indian weapons, dresses, utensils, etc, of minerals and of historical documents. There are also collections of birds, beasts, fish and butterflies. Despite the need for conservation work, the museum is still worth visiting. ■ *1000-1600, closed Mon. US$2. Some of the collections are open to qualified research students only. Getting there: it is safest to take a taxi to the main door, but the museum can be reached by taking the Metrô to São Cristóvão, crossing the railway line and walking a few metres to the park. This is safer than taking a bus.*

Museu de Fauna, also in the Quinta da Boa Vista, contains a most interesting collection of Brazilian fauna. ■ *1200-1700 Tue-Sun.*

The church of **Nossa Senhora da Penha**, in the northern suburb of Penha, is on a bare rock in which 365 steps are cut. This staircase is ascended by pilgrims on their knees during the festival month of October; there is a funicular for those unable to do this. The church in its present form dates from the early 20th century, based on an early 18th-century chapel. The first religious building, a hermitage, was built in 1632. Its prominent position makes Nossa Senhora da Penha a major landmark and its balustrade provides fine views. ■ *Getting there: bus 497 from Copacabana, Nos 340 and 346 from centre.*

Glória, Catete and Flamengo

This commercial district ends where Avenida Rio Branco meets Avenida Beira Mar, with its royal palms, bougainvilleas and handsome buildings, coasting the Botafogo and Flamengo beaches.

Parque do Flamengo On the Glória and Flamengo waterfront, with a view of the Pão de Açúcar and Corcovado, is the Parque do Flamengo, designed by Burle Marx (see page 106), opened in 1965 during the 400th anniversary of the city's founding and landscaped on 100 ha reclaimed from the bay. The park (officially called

Glória, Santa Teresa, Catete & Flamengo

Related maps
Rio de Janeiro orientation, page 78
A Rio de Janeiro centre, page 80

Sleeping
1 Flórida D5
2 Glória C5
3 Imperial D4
4 Inglês D5
5 Monte Blanco D4
6 Novo Mundo D5
7 Paysandu F5
8 Regina D5
9 Rio Claro E4
10 Turístico C4
11 Unico E5
12 Venezuela F5
13 Vitória D4

0 metres 300
0 yards 300

Parque Brigadeiro Eduardo Gomes) runs from the *aterro* on which Santos Dumont airport stands to the Morro da Viúva and Botafogo beach. The area was reclaimed from the sea using 1.2 million metric tonnes of earth. Behind the War Memorial (see below) is the public yacht marina. In the park are many sports fields; there is a sailboat basin and model plane flying field, as well as night amusements, such as bandstands and areas for dancing. For children, there's a marionette theatre, a miniature village and a staffed nursery. Security in the park is in the hands of vigilante policemen and it is a popular recreation area. On Sunday and holidays between 0700 and 1800 the avenues through the park are closed to traffic.

At the city end of the Parque Flamengo is the **Museu de Arte Moderna**, a spectacular building at Avenida Infante Dom Henrique 85, near the War Memorial. It suffered a disastrous fire in 1978; the collection is now being rebuilt and several countries have donated works of art. There is also a non-commercial cinema. The collection of contemporary Brazilian art includes drawings by Cândido Portinari from the 1940s and 50s and drawings and etchings of everyday work scenes by Gregório Gruber, made in the 1970s. ■ *1200-1700 Tue-Sun (last entry 1630), US$2, T22404944, www.mamrio.com.br*

Praça Paris, built on reclaimed ground near the Largo da Glória, is much admired for the beauty of its formal gardens and illuminated fountains. Opposite Praça Paris, at Avenida Infante Dom Henrique 75, is the **Monumento aos Mortos da Segunda Guerra Mundial** (National War Memorial to Brazil's dead in the Second World War). The memorial takes the form of two slender columns supporting a slightly curved slab, representing two palms uplifted to heaven. In the crypt are the remains of the Brazilian soldiers killed in Italy in 1944-45. ■ *1000-1700 Tue-Sun (crypt and museum). Beach clothes and rubber-thonged sandals are not permitted.*

The beautiful little church on the Glória Hill, overlooking the Parque do Flamengo, is **Nossa Senhora da Glória do Outeiro**. It was the favourite church of the Imperial family;

● Eating

1 Adega do Pimenta *C2*
2 Alcaparra *E5*
3 Alho e Óleo *E5*
4 Amazônia *D4*
5 Bar do Arnaudo *C2*
6 Casa da Suíça *B4*
7 Galícia Grill *E4*
8 Sobrenatural *C2*

Dom Pedro II was baptized here. The building is polygonal, with a single tower. Construction began in 1735 and was completed in 1791. It contains some excellent examples of blue-faced Brazilian tiling. Its main altar, of wood, was carved by Mestre Valentim. ■ *1300-1700 weekdays 0800-1200 Sat-Sun. The adjacent Museum of Religious Art keeps the same hours, but is closed on Mon, T25566434. Getting there: bus 119 from the centre and 571 from Copacabana.*

Local museums **Museu da República**, on Rua do Catete 153, is the former palace of a coffee baron, the Barão de Nova Friburgo. The palace was built in 1858-66 and, in 1887, it was converted into the presidential seat, until the move to Brasília. The ground floor of this museum consists of the sumptuous rooms of the coffee baron's mansion. The first floor is devoted to the history of the Brazilian republic. You can also see the room where former president Getúlio Vargas shot himself. The museum is highly recommended. Behind the museum is the **Parque do Catete** with many birds and monkeys. ■ *1200-1700 Tue-Sun, US$2.50, T25573150. Getting there: bus 571 from Copacabana, or the Metrô to Catete station.*

Museu do Folclore Edison Carneiro, on Rua do Catete 181, houses a well selected and arranged collection of interesting objects which should not be missed. However, there are no explanations other than in a book in Portuguese which costs US$2.50. There is a collection of small ceramic figures representing everyday life in Brazil, some very funny, some scenes animated by electric motors. Many artists are represented and displays show the way of life in different parts of the country. There are fine Candomblé and Umbanda costumes, religious objects, ex-votos and sections on many of Brazil's festivals. It has a small, but excellent library, with friendly staff helpful for finding books on Brazilian culture, history and anthropology. ■ *1100-1800 Tue-Fri, 1500-1800 Sat-Sun. Free. T2850441. Photography is allowed, but without flash. Getting there: bus 571 from Copacabana, or Metrô to Catete station.*

Museu do Telefone, on Rua 2 de Dezembro 63, exhibits old telephones. On the top floor there is a semi-mechanical telephone exchange from the 1940s plus Getúlio Vargas' golden telephone and a replica of the telephone of Dom Pedro II. Recommended. ■ *0900-1900 Tue-Sun. T25563189.*

Santa Teresa

This hilly inner suburb southwest of the centre is well known as the coolest part of Rio. It has many colonial and 19th-century buildings, set in narrow, curving, tree-lined streets. Santa Teresa attracted well-to-do and foreign inhabitants not only because of its cooler climate, but also because it was free of the yellow fever which infested the lower parts of the city. Today, Santa Teresa's old houses are lived in by artists, intellectuals and makers of handicrafts. Many buildings between Largo do Guimarães and Largo das Neves are being restored.

Most visitors in the daytime will arrive on the tram (see Transport, page 125). If you continue to the end of the line, Largo das Neves, you will be able to appreciate the small-town feel of the place. There are several bars here, including *Goiabeira*, simple and charming with a nice view of the praça. Either on the way back, or on the way up from the centre, the essential stop is the **Largo do Guimarães**, which has some excellent eating places (see Eating, page 111) and a great atmosphere.

In 1624, Antônio Gomes do Desterro erected a hermitage dedicated to Nossa **History** Senhora do Desterro on the hill which was to become Santa Teresa. The name was changed from Morro do Desterro to Santa Teresa after the construction in 1750 of a convent in honour of two Carmelite sisters, Jacinta and Francisca. The Convento da Santa Teresa, at Joaquim Murtinho e Ladeira de Santa Teresa, can only be seen from the outside; the Carmelite nuns do not admit visitors. From the 17th to the mid-18th century, work was done in various stages to bring water from the Rio Carioca to the city. The final project was the Aqueduto dos Arcos (**Arcos da Lapa**), which carried water from Santa Teresa to the Chafariz da Carioca, with its 16 fountains, in the centre of the city. The aqueduct's use was changed at the end of the 19th century with the introduction of electric trams in Rio. The inaugural run along the tracks laid on top of the arches was on 1 September 1896. It has been a major task to preserve the Santa Teresa tram, called the *bondinho*, the last such service in Rio.

Some of the fine historical residences that can be seen include the Casa de **Sights** Valentim (a castle-like house in Vista Alegre), the tiled Chácara dos Viegas in Rua Monte Alegre and the Chalé Murtinho, Rua Murtinho Nobre 41. This was the house in which Dona Laurinda Santos Lobo held her famous artistic, political and intellectual salons at the turn of the 20th century. The house was in ruins until it was partially restored and turned into a cultural centre called **Parque das Ruínas**. It has superb views of the city, an exhibition space, an open-air stage (live music Thursday) and a snack bar. A bridge connects it to the Chácara do Céu (see below). ■ *1000-1700 daily*. Also in the district is the old hotel known as the *Hotel das Paineiras*. See also the Rua Aprazível and Largo de Guimarães.

The **Chácara do Céu**, or Fundação Raymundo Ottoni de Castro Maia, Rua Murtinho Nobre 93, has a wide range of art objects and works by modern painters, including Brazilian; exhibitions change through the year. ■ *1200-1700 daily except Tue. US$1. T22850891. Getting there: take the Santa Teresa tram to Curvelo station, walk along Rua Dias de Barros, following the signposts to Parque das Ruínas*. Castro Maia's former residence, **Museu Açude**, Estrada do Açude 764, Alto da Boa Vista, Floresta da Tijuca, is also a museum. ■ *Every Sun it has a 'brunch' with music, 1230-1700. T2380368.*

In recent years, visitors have been put off going to Santa Teresa because of a reputation **Security** for crime which has spilled over from neighbouring *favelas*. It would, however, be a great shame to miss this unique town-within-a-city. The crime rate has been reduced and normally a policeman rides each *bondinho*, but you are advised not to take valuables or look 'wealthy'. A T-shirt, shorts and enough money for a meal should be sufficient. Avoid long walks on streets that are far from the main centres of Largo das Neves and Largo do Guimarães. The area around the Hotel das Paineiras is well patrolled.

Santa Teresa is best visited on the traditional open-sided **tram**, the *bondinho*: take the **Transport** Metrô to Cinelândia, go to R Senador Dantas then walk along to R Profesor Lélio Gama (look for *Banco do Brasil* on the corner). The station is up this street. Take the Paula Mattos line (a second line is Dois Irmãos) and enjoy the trip as it passes over the **Arcos da Lapa** aqueduct, winding its way up to the district's historic streets. The journey ends at the round praça called Largo das Neves; here the tram turns round for the journey back to R Prof L Gama. The trams are open-sided; do not carry valuables. Fare US$0.40 one way. **Buses**: Nos 206 and 214 run from Avenida Rio Branco in the centre to Santa Teresa. At night, only take a **taxi** – about US$7.

Rio de Janeiro

Rio de Janeiro

Pão de Açúcar and Corcovado

The district of Botafogo sits roughly midway between the Pão de Açúcar and Corcovado, as the crow flies. On the ground, access to either peak from this part of the city is quite straightforward, but involves many more twists and turns than a bird would take. There are also plenty of other attractions at ground level.

Pão de Açúcar At 396 m, the Pão de Açúcar, or Sugar Loaf, is a massive granite cone at the entrance to Guanabara Bay. The bird's eye view of the city and beaches is very beautiful. There is a restaurant (excellent location, terrible food, closes 1900) and a playground for children on the Morro da Urca, halfway up, where there are also shows at night (consult the cultural sections in the newspapers). You can get refreshments at the top.

The sea level cable-car station is in a military area and is safe to visit. At Praia Vermelha, the beach to the south of the rock, is the *Círculo Militar da Praia Vermelha* restaurant, which is open to the public (no sign). It has wonderful views, but is not so good for food or service; stop there for a drink anyway. From Praia Vermelha, the **Pista Cláudio Coutinho** runs around the foot of the rock. It is a paved path for walking, or jogging, and for access to various climbing places. It is open until 1800, but you can stay on the path after that. Here you have mountain, forest and sea side-by-side, right in the heart of the city. You can also use the Pista Coutinho as a way of getting up the Pão de Açúcar more cheaply than the US$12.50 cable-car ride. About 350 m from the path entrance

Urca, Botafogo & Cosme Velho

Related map Rio de Janeiro orientation, page 78

Sleeping	**Eating**	
1 Argentina	1 Aurora	3 Círculo Militar de
2 Chave do Rio de Janeiro	2 Botequim	Praia Vermelha

is a track to the left which leads though the forest to Morro de Urca, from where the cable car can be taken for US$10 (you can come down this way, too, but if you take the cable-car from sea level you must pay full fare). You can save even more money, but use more energy, by climbing the Caminho da Costa, a path to the summit of the Pão de Açúcar. Only one stretch, of 10 m, requires climbing gear (even then, some say it is not necessary), but if you wait at the bottom of the path for a group going up, they will let you tag along. This way you can descend to Morro de Urca by cable-car for free and walk down from there.

There are 35 rock routes up the mountain, with various degrees of difficulty. The best months for climbing are April to August. See Sport, page 123, for climbing clubs; there is also a book on climbing routes. ■ *Getting there* **Buses**: *No 107 (from the centre, Catete or Flamengo) and 511 from Copacabana (512 to return) take you to the cable-car station, Av Pasteur 520, at the foot.* **Cable-car**: *Praia Vermelha to Morro de Urca: first car goes up at 0800, then every 30 mins (or when full), until the last comes down at 2200. From Urca to Sugar Loaf, the first connecting cable-car goes up at 0815 then every 30 mins (or when full), until the last leaves the summit at 2200; the return trip costs US$8 (US$6 to Morro da Urca, halfway up). The old cableway has been completely rebuilt. Termini are ample and efficient and the present Italian cable-cars carry 75 passengers. Even on the most crowded days there is little queuing.*

Urca The suburb of Urca was built in 1922 when an *aterro* was made at the base of the Pão de Açúcar on its north side. It is mostly residential. Note the small statue of São Pedro holding the keys to heaven on a rock in the sea in front of the church. From the esplanade there are lovely views of the sunset behind Corcovado.

Botafogo In the district is the Morro do Pasmado, which has fine views of the bay. Also in Botafogo is one of the city's main shopping malls, Rio Sul, a good place to go for entertainment, services, eating and, of course, shopping. It has been totally refurbished and is completely safe (more details are given under Shopping, page 120). As well as the Theatre Museum mentioned above (see Teatro Municipal, page 87), there are three important museums in Botafogo.

The **Museu do Índio**, Rua das Palmeiras 55, houses 12,000 objects from many Brazilian Indian groups, including basketry, ceramics, masks and weapons. There is also a small, well-displayed handicraft shop. It belongs to the Fundação Nacional do Índio (Funai) and was set up by Marechal Rondon. ■ *1000-1730 Mon-Fri, 1300-1700 Sat-Sun (shop closes for lunch 1200-1400). US$1.75,*

Rio de Janeiro

▶▶ Brazil's International Museum of Naive Art

MIAN, the Museu Internacional de Arte Naif do Brasil, grew out of the private collection of Lucien Finkelstein, a French jewellery designer who lives in Brazil and who, about 40 years ago, started to buy Naive paintings all over Brazil and abroad, on his frequent international trips. As the collection grew so large, he decided to create a foundation and in October 1995 the museum opened its doors to the public. The current director is Jaqueline Finkelstein. The museum is located in a huge, spacious old house surrounded by gardens and trees.

The museum's international section gathers together works from several countries, from the 17th century to today, including the world-famous paintings on glass from former Yugoslavia (Hlebine School) and impressive campesino paintings on leather from Ecuador.

The Brazilian section is remarkable for the vibrant tropical colours and the diversity of subjects. Among the most representative Brazilian Naive painters, the museum has several works by Antônio Poteiro, José Antônio da Silva, Rosina Becker do Vale, Lia Mittarakis and others (including our own Fábio Sombra). One of the most interesting works is an enormous painting (4 m by 7 m) by Lia Mittarakis, in the main hall, showing the city of Rio de Janeiro. This colourful work, full of funny details, is considered the biggest Naive painting in the world and took five years to complete.

T22868899. *Getting there: it's a 10-min walk from Botafogo Metrô; from Catete, bus 571 (Glória-Leblon) passes Ruas Bento Lisboa and São Clemente.* There is also a library of ethnology at the same location, which has friendly and helpful staff. ■ *Weekdays.*

Museu Villa-Lobos, Rua Sorocaba 200, houses a collection of personal objects belonging to the great composer, with instruments, scores, books and recordings. ■ *1000-1700 Mon-Fri, T22663845.*

Corcovado   To reach the statue of the **Cristo Redentor** at the summit of Corcovado, you have to go through Laranjeiras and Cosme Velho. The road through these districts heads west out of Catete. Near the station for the cog railway which climbs to the statue are two important cultural sites.

See also box above   The **Museu Internacional de Arte Naif do Brasil** (MIAN), Rua Cosme Velho 561, is one of the most comprehensive museums of Naive and folk paintings in the world. It is only 30 m uphill, on the same street as the station for Corcovado. There is a permanent collection of some 8,000 works by Naive artists from about 130 countries. The museum also hosts several thematic and temporary exhibitions through the year. Parts of its collection travel to other museums and exhibitions around the world. There is a coffee shop and a souvenir shop where you can buy small paintings by some of the artists on display, books, postcards and T-shirts. Courses and workshops on painting and related subjects are also offered. ■ *1000-1800 Tue-Fri, 1200-1800 Sat, Sun and holidays; closed on Mon. US$3.20, with discounts for groups, students and senior citizens. T22058612.*

Those who want to see what Rio was like in the early 19th century should go to the **Largo do Boticário**, Rua Cosme Velho 822, a charming small square in neo-colonial style. Much of the material used in creating the effect of the square came from old buildings demolished in the city centre. The four houses that front the square are painted different colours (white, pale blue, caramel and pink), each with different features picked out in decorative tiles, woodwork and stone. The square is close to the terminus for the Corcovado cog railway.

A hunch-backed peak 710 m high, Corcovado is surmounted by a 38-m high statue of **Cristo Redentor** (Christ the Redeemer), which was completed on 12 October 1931. There is a superb view from the top (sometimes obscured by mist), to which there are a cog railway and a road; both car and train put down their passengers behind the statue. The 3.8-km railway itself offers fine views. The railway was opened on 9 October 1884 by Emperor Dom Pedro II. Steam trains were used to begin with, but electric trains replaced them in 1910. The current rolling stock is Swiss and dates from 1979. Average speed is 15 kph on the way up and 12 kph on the way down. There is a new exhibition on the history of the railway with photos, videos, models and old wagons in the station; the coffee shop offers free coffee and mineral water. From the upper terminus there is a climb of 220 steps to the top (although an escalator is being installed), near which there is a café. Mass is held on Sunday in a small chapel in the statue pedestal. The floodlighting was designed in 1931 by Marconi and came into operation in the following year. ■ *0830-1900 daily. T/F5581329, www.corvocado.com.br The train runs every 20-30 mins according to demand between 0800 and 1830, journey time 10 mins (cost: US$8 return; single tickets available). Also, a 206 bus does the very attractive run from Praça Tiradentes (or a 407 from Largo do Machado) to Silvestre (the railway has no stop here now). An active 9-km walk will take you to the top and the road is shady. Take the narrow street to the right of the station, go through the gate used by people who live beside the tracks and continue to the national park entrance. Walkers are not usually charged entrance fees. Allow a minimum of 2 hrs (up to 4 depending on fitness) for the climb. If going by car to Corcovado, the entrance fee is US$2.20 for the vehicle, plus US$2.20 for each passenger. For safety reasons go in company, or at weekends when more people are about. Getting there: take a Cosme Velho bus to the cog railway station at Rua Cosme Velho 513: from the centre or Glória/Flamengo No 180; from Copacabana take No 583, from Botafogo or Ipanema/Leblon No 583 or 584; from Santa Teresa Microônibus Santa Teresa. Coach trips tend to be rather brief; taxis which wait in front of the station also offer tours of Corcovado and Mirante Dona Marta.*

To see the city by day and night go up at 1500 or 1600 and descend on the last train, approximately 1815

Rio de Janeiro

Copacabana, Ipanema and Leblon

Built on a narrow strip of land (only a little over 4 sq km) between mountain and sea, Copacabana has one of the highest population densities in the world: 62,000 per sq km, or 250,000 in all.

Copacabana began to develop when the Túnel Velho (Old Tunnel) was built in 1891 and an electric tram service reached it. Weekend villas and bungalows sprang up; all have now gone. In the 1930s the *Copacabana Palace Hotel* was the only tall building; it is now one of the lowest on the beach. The opening of the **Túnel Novo** (New Tunnel) in the 1940s led to an explosion of population which shows no sign of having spent its force. Unspoilt Art Deco blocks towards the Leme (city) end of Copacabana are now under preservation order.

There is almost everything in this 'city within a city'. The shops, mostly in Avenida Nossa Senhora de Copacabana and the Rua Barata Ribeiro, are excellent. Even more stylish shops are to be found in Ipanema and Leblon. It is at Copacabana and beyond, facing the open Atlantic Ocean, that Rio de Janeiro's true *praia* culture comes to the fore. The beach is divided into numbered *postos*, where the lifeguards are based. Different sections attract different types of people, whether young mothers, elderly card players or serious intellectuals. "Where do you go on the beach?" is the defining question for Cariocas.

A Carioca is said to be someone who goes to the beach before, after or instead of work

The safest places are in front of the major hotels which have their own security, for instance the *Meridien* on Copacabana beach or the *Caesar Park* on Ipanema. The *Caesar Park* also has 24-hour video surveillance during the summer season, which makes it probably the safest patch of sand in Rio. Also outside this hotel, Brazil's Olympic beach volley ball players practise. Sports of all types, however, can be seen or played all along the beaches: volley ball, football, aerobics, jogging and so on.

Copacabana
This celebrated curved beach backed by skyscraper apartments is a must for visitors

A fort at the far end of the beach, Forte de Copacabana, was an important part of Rio's defences and prevents a seashore connection with the Ipanema and Leblon beaches. Parts of the military area are now being handed over to civilian use, the first being the Parque Garota de Ipanema at Arpoador, the fashionable Copacabana end of the Ipanema beach. Tourist police patrol Copacabana beach until 1700.

Transport Buses to and from the city centre are plentiful and cost US$0.40. The buses to take are Nos 119, 154, 413, 415, 455 and 474 from Av Nossa Senhora de Copacabana. If you are going to the centre from Copacabana, look for 'Castelo', 'Praça 15', 'E Ferro' or 'Praça Mauá' on the sign by the front door. 'Aterro' means the expressway between Botafogo and downtown Rio (not open on Sun). From the centre to Copacabana is easier as all buses in that direction are clearly marked. The 'Aterro' bus does the journey in 15 mins.

Copacabana

Related maps
Rio de Janeiro orientation, page 78
A Urca, Botafoga, Cosme Velho, page 96

0 metres 200
0 yards 200

■ **Sleeping**	4 Castro Alves Othon	9 Lancaster Othon	14 Rio Roiss
1 Atlantis Copacabana	5 Copacabana Palace	10 Le Meridien	15 Sofitel Rio Palace
	6 Copacabana Praia	11 Ouro Verde	16 South American
2 Benidorm Palace	7 Copacabana Sol	12 Rio Atlântica	Copacabana
3 Biarritz	8 Debret	13 Rio Copa	17 Toledo

Beyond Copacabana are the beautiful seaside suburbs of Ipanema (a good place from which to watch the sunset) and Leblon. The two districts are divided by a canal from the Lagoa Rodrigo de Freitas to the sea, beside which is the Jardim de Alá. Ipanema and Leblon are a little less built-up than Copacabana and their beaches tend to be cleaner. Praia de Arpoadar at the Copacabana end of Ipanema is a peaceful spot to watch surfers, with the beautiful backdrop of Morro Dois Irmãos; excellent for walk on the rocks. There is now night-time illumination on these beaches. The seaward lane of the road running beside the beach is closed to traffic until 1800 on Sundays and holidays; this makes it popular for rollerskating and cycling (bicycles can be hired).

Backing Ipanema and Leblon is the middle-class residential area of **Lagoa Rodrigo de Freitas**, by a saltwater lagoon on which Rio's rowing and small-boat sailing clubs are active. The lake is too polluted for bathing, but the road which runs around its shores has pleasant views. On the western side of the lake is the **Hipódromo de Gávea**, the city's horse-racing track. By the track and the lake is the residential area known as Jardim Botânico, because of its proximity to the Botanical Gardens.

Well worth a visit is the **Jardim Botânico** (Botanical Garden), founded in 1808 by the king, Dom João VI, for acclimatizing plants on land in the Real Fazenda. When the electric tram line arrived in this part of the city, housing and industries soon followed, but the 137-ha gardens, then as now, remained a haven of peace. The most striking features are the transverse avenues of 30-m-high royal palms. Among the more than 7,000 varieties of plants from around the world are examples of the *pau-brasil* tree (see page 717), now endangered, and many other threatened species. Look for monkeys in the trees. There is a herbarium, an aquarium and a library, and a new pavilion contains sculptures by Mestre Valentim transferred from the centre. Visitors needing information in English should ask for Beatriz Heloisa Guimarães, of the Society of Friends of the Garden.

Bird-watchers should visit the Botanical Gardens, preferably early in the morning, as 140 species of bird have been recorded here: flycatchers are very prominent (the social flycatcher, great and boat-billed kiskadees, cattle tyrant); also tanagers (the sayaca and palm tanagers and the colourful green-headed tanager), and over 20,000 different kinds of hummingbird. Birds of prey include the roadside hawk, the laughing falcon and the American kestrel, and there are doves, cuckoos, parakeets, thrushes, woodpeckers and occasional flocks of toucans. ■ *0800-1700 daily, US$2. Getting there: The gardens are 8 km from the*

Ipanema & Leblon

Rio de Janeiro

Eating
1 A Marisquera
2 Aipo & Aipim
3 Cervantes
4 Chon Kou
5 Churrascaria Palace
6 Nino
7 Ponto de Encontro
8 Shirley
9 Siri Mole & Cia

Rio de Janeiro

centre; take bus No 170 from the centre, or any bus to Leblon, Gávea or São Conrado marked 'via Jóquei'; from Glória, Flamengo or Botafogo take No 571, or 172 from Flamengo; from Copacabana, Ipanema or Leblon take No 572 (584 back to Copacabana).

Parque Laje, near the Jardim Botânico at Rua Jardim Botânico 414, almost jungle-like, has small grottoes, an old tower and lakes, as well as the Escola de Artes Visuais (Visual Arts School) housed in the mansion. ■ *0900-1700, daily. Free.*

In Ipanema are the headquarters of two stores which have successfully adapted the Brazilian gemstone industry to the modern world. Both have exhibitions which you can visit without any pressurized selling attached (see Brazilian gems, page 687): **Amsterdam Sauer Museum**, Garcia d'Ávila 105 and Visconde de Pirajá, has reproductions of two Brazilian mines and a large exhibition of gemstones in both their rough state and cut into precious stones. ■ *1000-1700 Mon-Fri, 0930-1300 Sat. Free. T25121132.* **H Stern**, Garcia D'Ávila 113, has a self-guided exhibition which shows the complete process of turning an uncut stone into a piece of jewellery. As you walk around the display, you can see the experts at work in front of you. There is also a permanent exhibition of jewellery, including items which have won international prizes. ■ *0830-1800 Mon-Fri, 0830-1230 Sat. T22597442.*

The **Planetário** (Planetarium), on Padre Leonel Franco 240, Gávea, was inaugurated in 1979, with a sculpture of the Earth and Moon by Mario Agostinelli. ■ *Tours at 1400 and observations on Fri at 2000, Sat and Sun at 1630, 1800 and 1930. There are occasional chorinho concerts on Thu or Fri;*

Ipanema & Leblon

Related maps
Rio de Janeiro
orientation, page 78
A Copacabana,
page 100

	0 metres 500		0 yards 500

To Vidigal, São Conrado & Barra de Tijuca

■ **Sleeping**
1 Caesar Park
2 Ipanema Inn
3 Mar Ipanema
4 Marina Palace
5 Sol Ipanema

● **Eating**
1 Amarcord
2 Antiquarius
3 Alho e Óleo
4 Celeiro
5 Porção

check the press for details. T227400946. Getting there: buses 176 and 178 from the centre and Flamengo; 591 and 592 from Copacabana.

Transport Buses run from Botafogo Metrô terminal to Ipanema: some take integrated Metrô-Bus tickets; look for the blue signs on the windscreen. Many buses from Copacabana run to Ipanema and Leblon.

Leblon to Barra da Tijuca

The Pedra Dois Irmãos overlooks Leblon; on the slopes is Vidigal *favela*. From Leblon, two inland roads take traffic west to the outer seaside suburb of Barra da Tijuca.

Parque da Cidade, a pleasant park a short walk beyond the Gávea bus terminus, has a great many trees and lawns, with views over the ocean. However, the proximity of the Rocinha *favela* (see below) means that the park is not very safe. It is advisable to carry a copy of your passport here because of frequent police checks. ■ *0700-1700 daily. Free. Getting there: buses 170, 174, 546, 592 and 593 leave you just short of the entrance, but it should be OK to walk the last part if in a group. Similarly, do not walk the trails in the park alone.*

In the park is the **Museu Histórico da Cidade**, a former coffee *fazenda* with historical exhibits. Every third Sunday in the month it holds a gastronomic event with music from 1400. See the Capela de São João Bautista whose murals by Carlos Bastos so scandalized the patrons for their inclusion of famous people into the life of Christ that they were never finished (only open weekends). ■ *1100-1700 Tue-Sun, US$1.*

Beyond Leblon the coast is rocky. A third route to Barra da Tijuca is the Avenida Niemeyer, which skirts the cliffs on the journey past Vidigal, a small beach where the *Sheraton* is situated. Avenida Niemeyer carries on round the coast to São Conrado, with its Fashion Mall and the Gávea golf club; a very exclusive neighbourhood where few tourists stop. On the slopes of the Pedra da Gávea, through which the Avenida Niemeyer has two tunnels, is the Rocinha *favela*.

For favela tours, see box page 89

The flat-topped **Pedra da Gávea** can be climbed or scrambled up for magnificent views, but beware of snakes. Some say that the rock is sphinx-like and from the Tijuca Forest side there is clearly a conformation similar to a face with a beard. Claims have been made that Phoenician inscriptions have been found and many other legends surround the rock.

Behind the Pedra da Gávea is the Pedra Bonita. A road, the Estrada das Canoas, climbs up past these two rocks on its way to the Tijuca National Park. There is a spot on this road which is one of the chief hang-glider launch sites in the area (see Sports, page 121).

This rapidly developing residential area is also one of the principal recreation areas of Rio, with its 20-km sandy beach and good waves for surfing. At the westernmost end is the small beach of Recreio dos Bandeirantes, where the ocean can be very rough. The channels behind the Barra are popular with jetskiers. It gets very busy on Sundays. There are innumerable bars and restaurants, clustered at both ends, as well as campsites (see page 110), motels and hotels: budget accommodation tends to be self-catering. The facilities include Riocentro, a 600,000-sq m convention complex, and the huge Barra Shopping and Carrefour shopping centres.

Barra da Tijuca
Although buses do run as far as Barra, getting to and around here is best by car. A cycleway links Barra da Tijuca with the centre of the city

The **Bosque da Barra/Parque Arruda Câmara**, at the junction of Avenida das Américas and Avenida Ayrton Senna, preserves the vegetation of the

Rio de Janeiro

sandbanks which existed on this part of the coast before the city took over. ■ *0700-1700 daily.*

The **Autódromo** (motor racing track) is behind Barra and the Lagoa de Jacarepaguá, in the district of the same name. The Brazilian Grand Prix was held here during the 1980s before returning to Interlagos, São Paulo.

Terra Encantada, Avenida Ayrton Senna 2800, T24309800, is a 300,000 sq m theme park in Barra whose attractions are based on the different cultural heritages of Brazil: the indigenous, African and European. Among the attractions are roller coasters, river rapids, a cinema and shows. ■ *1000-2300 Thu-Sun. Rides close at 2200 and on the main street restaurants, bars and nightspots open.* www.terra-encantada.com.br

A bit further out is the **Museu Casa do Pontal**, Estrada do Pontal 3295, Recreio dos Bandeirantes. This is another collection of Brazilian folk art, put together by the French designer Jacques van de Beuque. Recommended. ■ *0900-1930 Tue-Sun.*

Transport Buses from the city centre to Barra are Nos 175, 176; from Botafogo, Glória or Flamengo take No 179; Nos 591 or 592 from Leme; and from Copacabana via Leblon No 523 (45 mins-1 hr). A taxi to Zona Sul costs US$15 (US$22.50 after midnight). A comfortable bus, *Pegasus*, goes along the coast from the Castelo bus terminal to Barra da Tijuca and continues to Campo Grande or Santa Cruz, or take the free 'Barra Shopping' bus. Bus 700 from Praça São Conrado (terminal of bus 553 from Copacabana) goes the full length of the beach to Recreio dos Bandeirantes.

Barra da Tijuca & National Park

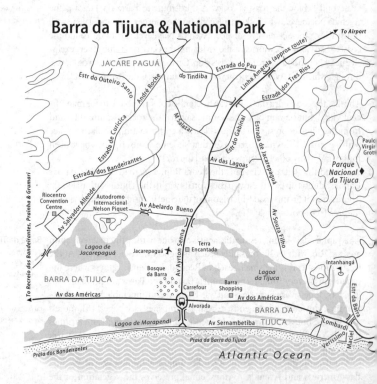

Tijuca National Park

The vegetation in the Parque Nacional da Tijuca, for all its abundance, is not primeval. Most of what is now the largest urban, forested national park in the world is reforested. The first Europeans in the area cut down trees for use in construction and as firewood. The lower areas were cleared to make way for sugar plantations. When coffee was introduced to Rio de Janeiro in 1760, the logical place to start cultivating it was on the hillsides surrounding the city. Huge tracts of the forest were cut down and coffee estates created. Conditions for the bushes were ideal, but for the city itself, it did not prove ideal. Although many people made lots of money, deforesting the hills disrupted the rainfall pattern and the water supply for the expanding city became insufficient. In 1861, therefore, the Imperial government decided that the whole area should be reforested. The job was given to Major Manuel Gomes Archer who, with just six slaves, completed the task in 13 years. They used saplings taken from neighbouring areas, but added to the native species many exotic varieties. The work was continued by Tomás de Gama. A national park of 3,300 ha, which united various different forests, was set up in 1961.

History

The **Pico da Tijuca** (1,022 m) gives a good idea of the tropical vegetation of the interior and a fine view of the bay and its shipping. A two- to three-hour walk leads to the summit: on entering the park at Alto da Boa Vista (■ *0600-2100*), follow the signposts (maps are displayed) to Bom Retiro, a good picnic place (1½ hours' walk). At Bom Retiro the road ends and there is another hour's walk up a fair footpath to the summit (take the path from the right of the Bom Retiro drinking fountain; not the more obvious steps from the left). The last part consists of steps carved out of the solid rock; look after children at the summit as there are several sheer drops, invisible because of bushes. The route is shady for almost its entire length. The main path to Bom Retiro passes the **Cascatinha Taunay** (a 30-m waterfall) and the **Mayrink Chapel** (built 1860). Panels painted in the Chapel by Cândido Portinari have been replaced by copies and the originals will probably be installed in the Museu de Arte Moderna. Beyond the Chapel is the restaurant *A Floresta* and Major Archer's house, now in ruins.

Exploring the park

Other places of interest not passed on the walk to the peak are the Paulo e Virginia Grotto, the Vista do Almirante and the Mesa do Imperador (viewpoints). Allow at least 5-6 hours for the excursion. Maps of the park are available. If hiking in the national park other than on the main paths, a guide may be useful if you do not want to get lost: *Sindicato de Guías*, T22674582.

■ Sleeping
1 Intercontinental

0 km 1
0 miles 1

Rio de Janeiro

Transport Bus No 221 from Praça 15 de Novembro, No 233 (which continues to Barra da Tijuca) or 234 from the rodoviária or from Praça Sáens Pena, Tijuca (the city suburb, not Barra – reached by Metrô), or No 454 from Copacabana to Alto da Boa Vista, for the park entrance. **Jeep tours** are run by *Atlantic Forest Jeep Tour* daily; T24959827, T9974 0218 (mob), or contact through travel agencies.

Western Rio

Almost half of the municipal area of Rio de Janeiro is in what is referred to as the Zona Oeste (the West Zone). On the coast, this stretches from Barra de Tijuca past the beaches at Prainha (a little cove, good for surfing) and Grumari (very attractive, rustic beach bars), neither accessible by public transport, but attracting heavy traffic at weekends. Further west still are the Barra de Guaratiba and Pedra de Guaratiba beaches and, finally, those at Sepetiba (on the bay, with calm sea, medicinal mud). This stunning coastal road (the start of the Costa Verde highway) is becoming obliterated by executive housing developments – visit soon, if you can.

Inland are suburbs such as Campo Grande and Santa Cruz, the Parque Estadual da Pedra Branca (T24453387) and sites such as the 19th-century Capela Magdalena (T24107183). The authorities are planning to develop the Zona Oeste. A Centro Cultural (NOPH), Praça Dom Romualdo 11, Santa Cruz, in the Igreja Matriz, can supply information, T3950260.

Two museums in the northwest of the city are well-established. **Capão do Bispo Estate**, Avenida Suburbana 4616, del Castilho, is an 18th-century estate house with an archaeological exhibition. ■ *1400-1700 Mon-Fri.* **Museu Aeroespacial**, Avenida Marechal Fontenele 2000, Campo dos Afonsos, has displays of early Brazilian civil and military aircraft, historic weapons and documents. ■ *0930-1500 Tue-Fri, 0930-1600 Sat, Sun and holidays*.

Sítio Roberto Burle Marx, Estrada da Barra de Guaratiba 2019, Barra de Guaratiba. From 1949 to 1994 this was the home of the great Roberto Burle Marx (1909-94), world famous as a landscape designer and artist. His projects achieved a rare harmony between nature, architecture and man-made landscapes. He created many schemes in Brazil and abroad; in Rio alone his work includes the Parque do Flamengo, the pavements of the Avenida Atlântica in Copacabana, Praça Júlio de Noronha in Leme, the remodelling of the Largo da Carioca, the gardens of the Museu Nacional de Belas Artes and of the Biblioteca Nacional and the complex at the Santa Teresa tram station near the Catedral Metropolitana.

Covering 350,000 sq m, the estate contains an estimated 3,500 species of plants, mostly Brazilian. It is run now by the Instituto do Patrimônio Histórico e Artístico Nacional and one of its main aims is to produce seedlings of the plants in its collection. Also on view are Burle Marx's collection of paintings, ceramics, sculptures and other objets d'art, plus examples of his own designs and paintings. The library houses 2,500 volumes on botany, architecture and landscape design. ■ *0930-1330 daily, by prior appointment only, T24101171.*

Ilha de Paquetá

Paquetá Island, the second largest in Guanabara Bay, is noted for its gigantic pebble-shaped rocks, butterflies and orchids. Its name means 'many shells' in Tupi, but it has also been called the Ilha dos Amores. The house of José Bonifácio, the opponent of slavery, may be seen. Another historical building is the **Solar D'El Rei**, which today houses the Biblioteca Popular de Paquetá and has recently been refurbished. At the southwest tip is the interesting **Parque Darke de Mattos**, with beautiful trees, lots of birds and a lookout on the Morro da Cruz. The island has several beaches, but ask about the state of the water before bathing. The only means of transport are bicycles and horse-drawn carriages (many have harnesses which cut into the horse's flesh). Neither is allowed into the Parque Darke de Mattos. A tour by *trenzinho*, a tractor pulling trailers, costs US$1.25, or just wander around on foot, quieter and free. Bicycles can be hired. The island is very crowded at weekends and on public holidays, but is usually quiet during the week. The prices of food and drink are reasonable.

Paquetá Island can be visited by ferry services that leave more or less every 2 hrs from Praça 15 de Novembro, where there is a general boat terminal; there are boats from 0515 (0710 on Sun and holidays) to 2300, T25337524, or hydrofoils between 1000 and 1600, Sat and Sun 0800-1630 hourly, T33970656 (fare US$1 by boat, 1 hr, US$4 by hydrofoil, 20 mins' journey, which more than doubles its price Sat, Sun and holidays). Buses to Praça 15 de Novembro: No 119 from Glória, Flamengo or Botafogo; Nos 154, 413, 455, 474 from Copacabana, or No 415 passing from Leblon via Ipanema.

Other boat trips: Several companies offer trips to Paquetá. There are day cruises, including lunch, to Jaguanum Island (see page 155, under Itacuruçá) and a sundown cruise around Guanabara Bay. *Saveiros Tour*, Rua Conde de Lages 44, Glória, T22246990, www.saveiros.com.br, offers tours in sailing schooners around the bay and down the coast, also 'Baía da Guanabara Histórica' historical tours.

Transport

Rio de Janeiro

Essentials

Sleeping

Economy hotels are found mainly in 3 districts of Rio: Flamengo/Botafogo (best), Lapa/Fátima and Saúde/Mauá. The city is noisy; an inside room is cheaper and much quieter.

Price codes: see inside front cover

LL-L *Copacabana Palace*, Av Atlântica 1702, T25487070, F22357330, www.copacabanapalace.com.br One of the best hotels in the world, dripping in 1920's elegance. Steeped in history, boasts many international celebrities as guests. It was here that Fred Astaire and Ginger Rogers first danced together, in *Flying Down to Rio* which was filmed here. Go for tea or cocktails if you can't afford to stay. **LL-L** *Le Meridien*, Av Atlântica 1020, T25460866, F25416447, sales@meridien-br.com World-renowned *Air France* hotel with pool, rooms quite small, good breakfast. **LL-L** *Sofitel Rio Palace*, Av Atlântica 4240, T25221232, F25220570, sofitelrio@accor.com.br Frequented by the likes of Michael Jackson and Madonna, all rooms locked by central system at 0130. **L** *Rio Atlântica*, Av Atlântica 2964, T25486332, F22556410, rioatlan@ netgate.com.br Stylishly designed, stunning rooftop pool and terrace. Swiss management, very high standards. Highly recommended.

L-A *Benidorm Palace*, R Barata Ribeiro 547, T25488880, F22566396, hotelbenidorm@zipmail.com.br Suites and double rooms, sauna. Recommended. **L-A** *Lancaster Othon*, Av Atlântica 1470, T/F25438300. Easy to change travellers' cheques, non-smoking rooms, balconies overlook the beach, helpful management, airline discount can cut price. Recommended. Next door is **L-A** *Ouro Verde*, Av Atlântica 1456, T25421887, F25424597. Good value, excellent all round, expensive restaurant. **L-A** *Rio Roiss*, R Aires Saldanha 48, T25221142, F5227719. Very good, restaurant. **L-A** *South American Copacabana*, R Francisco de Sá 90, T25220040, F22670748,

Copacabana
■ *on map, page 100*

The famous seaside residential and commercial area: many hotels on Av Atlântica charge about 30% more for a room with a seaview, but some town-side upper rooms have good views of the mountains

Rio de Janeiro

southamerican@uol.com.br Good location 2 blocks from the beach, safe area, front rooms noisy, helpful front desk staff, highly rated.

A *Castro Alves Othon*, Av Nossa Senhora de Copacabana 552, T/F25488815, srorio@othon.com.br Central, very comfortable and elegant. Recommended. **A** *Debret*, Av Atlântica 3564, T25220132, F25210899, sales@debret.com Good, helpful staff, some inner rooms dark. **A** *Rio Copa*, Av Princesa Isabel 370, T22756644, F22755545. Good value, 2 blocks back from beach. Very clean and friendly, English-speaking staff. Recommended.

A-B *Atlantis Copacabana*, Av Bulhões de Carvalho 61, T25211142, F22878896. Very good, swimming pool, Turkish bath, good breakfast, close to Ipanema and Copacabana beaches. **A-B** *Biarritz*, R Ayres Saldanha 54, T/F25221087, biarritz@hoteisgandara.com.br Very reasonable considering good position close to the beach. **A-B** *Copacabana Sol*, R Santa Clara 141, T22571840, F22550744, www.hpm.com.br/copacabanasol.html A/c, modern, safe, quiet, good breakfast, helpful. **A-B** *Toledo*, R Domingos Ferreira 71, a block from the beach, T22571991, F22571931. Good breakfast, single rooms are gloomy, but excellent value.

Ipanema & Leblon
■ *on map, page 102*

Outer seaside residential and commercial area

LL *Caesar Park*, Av Vieira Souto 460, T25252525, F25216000. One of Rio's finest hotels with an international reputation. High level of service includes beach patrol and child minding. Popular with business visitors. **L** *Mar Ipanema*, R Visconde de Pirajá 539, Ipanema, a block from the beach, T25129898, F25114038, maripa@domain.com.br Helpful, good buffet breakfast. **L** *Marina Palace*, Av Delfim Moreira 630, T22941794, F22941644, hotelmarina@callnet.com.br All rooms have sea view. Sauna, massage, pool. **L** *Sol Ipanema*, Av Vieira Souto, 320, T26252020, F22478484, hotel@solipanema.com.br Part of the British Best Western Chain. Recommended. **A** *Arpoador Inn*, Francisco Otaviano 177, T25230060, F25115094. Recommended. **A** *Ipanema Inn*, Maria Quitéria 27, behind *Caesar Park*, T25233092, F25115094. Good value and location. **B** *San Marco*, R Visconde de Pirajá 524, T2395032. Pleasant 2-star. Recommended. **D** *Harmonia*, R Barão da Torre 175, casa 18, T25234905, M98171331, hostelharmonia@hotmail.com 3 blocks from beach, doubles or dormitories, kitchen facilities, English, Spanish, German and Swedish spoken, good internet, very welcoming and helpful.

São Conrado
Spectacular settings, but isolated and far from centre

LL *Sheraton*, Av Niemeyer 121 (Vidigal), T22741122, res255sheraton@sheraton.com Several pricey restaurants located directly on beach front, 3 pools and full sports facilities, *Gray Line* travel agency and other services associated with 5-star hotel. **D** *The White House*, Estrada de Vidigal 605, T22494421. Clean hostel accommodation.

Flamengo & Catete
■ *on map, page 92*

Residential area between centre and Copacabana, with good bus and Metrô connections

L *Glória*, R do Russel 632, T25557572, www.hotelgloriario.com.br Stylish and elegant old building, 2 swimming pools. An old favourite. Highly recommended. **L** *Novo Mundo*, Praia Flamengo 20, T25574355, www.hotelnovomundo-rio.com.br Recommended but noisy. **AL** *Flórida*, Ferreira Viana, 71/81, T25565242, F22855777. Sauna, pool, safe, quiet. Good views, great breakfast. Recommended. **A** *Regina*, Ferreira Viana, 29, T25561647, F22852999, hotelregina@hotelregina.com.br Very safe, good breakfast.

B *Argentina*, Cruz Lima 30, T25587233, F25574447. Best rooms on 5th floor, cheapest on 1st. Recommended. **B** *Imperial*, R do Catete 186, T25565212, F25585815. A/c, TV, phone, pool, garage, smart. **B** *Paysandu*, opposite *Venezuela* at No 23, T22257270. Very clean, comfortable and good value, helpful staff, good location, organized tours available. **B** *Turístico*, Ladeira da Glória 30, T25577698. With breakfast, a/c, tourist information provided, mixed reports, some highly favourable.

C *Caxambu*, Ferreira Viana, Correia Dutra 22, T22659496. With bath, TV, popular cheap hotel. On Buarque de Macedo. **C** *Inglês*, R Silveira Martins, 20, T25583052, F25583447. A/c, TV, phone, reasonable breakfast. **C** *Unico*, Ferreira Viana, 54, T22059932, F22058149. TV, a/c, fridge. Recommended.

D *Monte Blanco*, R do Catete, 160, T22250121. Friendly staff and clean rooms. **D** *Opera*, Santa Amaro 75, T22423585. Convenient for metro. On the hillside is Ladeira da Glória. **D** *Rio Claro*, No 233, T25585180. Small rooms, breakfast, a/c, safe. Recommended. **D** *Rio Lisboa*, Artur Bernardes 29, T22659599. A/c (but staff will not always turn it on), a few cheaper single rooms **E**, safe, breakfast is just coffee, a roll and some crackers; family hotel in a quiet street (luck and patience are needed to get a room, no reservations either by phone or in person). **D** *Venezuela*, R Paissandu 34,T25577098. Very clean, a/c, TV, but rooms small and breakfast poor. **D** *Vitória*, R do Catete172, T22055397. With breakfast, hot water, a/c, friendly, mixed reports.

Near Cinelândia Metrô station are a lot of cheap hotels, but many are rented by the hour. This is not an area really recommended for tourists to stay as it is not very safe and the nearby sites of interest should only be visited in daylight. In Cinelândia is **B** *Itajubá*, R Álvaro Alvim 23, T22103163, F22407461, itahotel@openlink.com.br A little shabby, no English spoken but the staff are friendly, no credit cards accepted, convenient for the centre. **D** *Marajó*, in Lapa itself, near the Arches just beyond Passeio Público, R Joaquim Silva, 99, T22244134. With breakfast, varied rooms. **D** *Marialva*, Gomes Freire 430 (near New Cathedral, convenient for Av Rio Branco, buses, etc), 2-star, a/c, breakfast in room. Recommended. **D** *Pouso Real*, R Resende, 35, T22242757. Good, gay area. Recommended. **D** *Rio Hotel*, R Silva Jardim 3, Praça Tiradentes, T22821213. Noisy rooms on praça, quieter overlooking São Sebastião cathedral, with breakfast (only served in rooms). **E** *Love's House*, R Joaquim Silva 87, Praça Tiradentes, T25095655, ask for room with window, safe. Respectable, despite its name and good value.

Lapa & Fátima
Between Lapa and Praça Tiradentes is an inner residential area, less desirable than Flamengo. Parts of this area are deserted from 2200 onwards

Rio de Janeiro

D *Chave do Rio de Janeiro*, R Gen Dionísio 63, Botafogo, T22860303, F2865652. IYHA, cheaper for members, clean, laundry and cooking facilities. Superb breakfast. Noisy but frequently recommended. **D** *Copa Chalet*, R Henrique Oswald 103, T22360047, F22394528, www.copachalet.com.br Very friendly. Recommended. **E** per person *Copacabana Praia*, R Tte Marones de Gusmão 85, Bairro Peixoto, T22353817, F22375422, www.wcenter.com.br/cop-apraia Dormitory, apartments also available. **E** *Saint Roman*, R Saint Roman 48, Copacabana, T25527685, F25312234. Convenient, but dirty and not a safe area.

Associations: *ALBERJ* (for Rio), R da Assembleia 10, I 16, T25312234, F25311943. *Federação Brasileira* (Brazil), at *Chave do Rio de Janeiro* hostel, T22860303. If intending to stay between Christmas and Carnival, reserve youth hostels well in advance.

Youth hostels

A popular form of accommodation in Rio, available at all price levels: eg furnished apartments for short-term let, accommodating up to 6, cost US$300 per month in

Self-catering apartments

Maracanã, about US$400 per month in **Saúde**, **Cinelândia**, **Flamengo**. **Copacabana**, **Ipanema** and **Leblon** prices range from about US$25 a day for a simple studio, starting at US$500-600 a month up to US$2,000 a month for a luxurious residence sleeping 4-6. Heading south past **Barra da Tijuca**, virtually all the accommodation available is self-catering. Renting a small flat, or sharing a larger one, can be much better value than a hotel room. Blocks consisting entirely of short-let apartments can attract thieves, so check the (usually excellent) security arrangements; residential buildings are called *prédio familial*. Higher floors (*alto andar*) are considered quieter.

'Apart-Hotels' are listed in the *Guia 4 Rodas* and Riotur's booklet. Agents and private owners advertise under 'Apartamentos – Temporada' in publications like *Balcão* (twice weekly), *O Globo* or *Jornal do Brasil* (daily); advertisements are classified by district and size of apartment: 'vagas e quartos' means shared accommodation; 'conjugado' (or 'conj') is a studio with limited cooking facilities; '3 Quartos' is a 3-bedroom flat. There should always be a written agreement when renting.

The following rent apartments in residential blocks: *Paulo de Tarso*, Av Princesa Isabel, 236, Apto 102, T25425635, pauldetarso@ig.com.br Apartments near Copacabana beach from US$25 per person. Several languages spoken, very helpful. *Yvonne Reimann*, Av Atlântica 4066, Apto 605, T22270281. Rents apartments, all with phone, near beach, a/c, maid service, English, French, German spoken, all apartments owned by the agency, prices from US$50 per flat. *Fantastic Rio*, Av Atlântica 974, Suite 501, Copacabana, BR-22020-000, T/F25432667, hpcorr@hotmail.com, all types of furnished accommodation from US$20 per day. Owned by Peter Corr. Recommended. *Copacabana Holiday* at R Barata Ribeiro 90A, Copacabana, T25421525, www.copacabanaholiday.com.br Recommended, well-equipped small apartments from US$500 per month, minumum 30 days let. *Rio Residences*, Av Prado Júnior 44, apto 508, T25414568, F25416462. Swiss run, includes airport transfer.

Camping *Camping Clube do Brasil*, Av Sen Dantas 75, 29th floor, Centro, CEP 20037-900, T22103171, has 2 beach sites at Barra da Tijuca: Av Sernambetiba 3200, T24930628 (bus 233 from centre, 702 or 703 from the airport via Zona Sul, US$5 – a long way from the centre), sauna, pool, bar, café, US$12 (half price for members). During Jan and Feb this site is often full and sometimes restricted to members of the Camping Clube do Brasil; a simpler site at Estrada do Pontal 5900, T24378400, lighting, café, good surfing, US$6. Both have trailer plots. *Ostal*, Av Sernambetiba 18790, T24378350; and *Novo Rio*, at Km 17 on the Rio-Santos road, T24376518. If travelling by trailer, you can park at the Marina Glória car park, where there are showers and toilets, a small shop and snack bar. Pay the guards to look after your vehicle.

Eating

Cariocas usually have dinner at 1900 or 2000, occasionally later at weekends

You can eat well for an average US$5 per person, less if you choose the *prato feito* at lunchtime (US$1.50-6), or eat in a place that serves food by weight (starting at about US$0.65 per gram). You can expect to pay US$20-40 per person in the first-class places, more in the very best restaurants. While many of Rio's quality hotels offer world-class food and service, they may lack atmosphere and close at midnight. There are much livelier and cheaper places to eat if going out for an evening meal. In Rio, avoid mussels! There are many juice bars in Rio with a wide selection (eg the *Rei dos Sucos* chain). Most restaurants are closed on 24 and 25 Dec.

The guide *Restaurantes do Rio*, by Danusia Bárbara, published annually by Senac at around US$10 (in Portuguese only), is worth looking at for the latest ideas on where to eat in both the city and state of Rio. For the best traditional bars and eating places, see *Rio Botequim*, published annually by the Prefeitura da Cidade do Rio de Janeiro.

Expensive: *Republique*, Praça da República 63 (2nd floor), T25324000. Chic, designed by the architect Chicô Gouveia, good food. **Mid-range**: *Café do Teatro*, Rio Branco, Teatro Municipal. Traditional cuisine served in the grand manner, those wearing shorts or scruffy gear not admitted. Weekday lunch only. **Cheap**: *Albamar*, Praça Marechal Âncora 184-6, T22408428. Good, reasonably priced fish and seafood, with lovely views of the bay. Open 1130-1600 Mon, 1130-2200 Tue-Sat. *Al-kuwait*, Av Treze de Maio, T22401114. Charming Middle Eastern fan-cooled restaurant with wood panelling in unprepossessing alley off Treze de Maio. No English menu but helpful staff. Try a traditional *kofta* or the daily special. Open 1100-2300, closed Sat and Sun. *Bistro do Paço*, Praça 15 de Novembro 48 (Paço Imperial), T22623613. Excellent, good value food in attractive surroundings, Swiss-run. Recommended. Open 1130-2000 Mon-Fri, 1200-1830 Sat and Sun. *Fiorino*, Av Heitor Beltrão 126, Tijuca, T25674476. Delicious, home-cooked Italian food with indulgent deserts. Recommended. *Mala e Cuia*, R Candelária 92, T22534032. For *comida mineira*. Recommended. *Rio Minho*, R do Ouvidor 10, T25092338. For excellent seafood in historic building. **Seriously cheap**: Many *lanchonetes* offer good, cheap meals in the business sector. R Miguel Couto (opposite Santa Rita church) is called the *Beco das Sardinhas* because on Wed and Fri in particular is full of people eating sardines and drinking beer. There are several Arab restaurants on Av Senhor dos Passos, which are also open Sat and Sun. *Luciano*, R das Marrecas 44, a functional all-you-can-eat buffet, is one of several on this street.

Mid-range: One of the best restaurants in Rio is the *Bar do Arnaudo*, in the Largo do Guimarães, R Almte Alexandrino 316, T22527246. Open Tue-Sat 1200-2200, Sun 1200-1600, it is simple inside, decorated with handicrafts; the cuisine is from Northeast Brazil, prices are reasonable and portions huge; try the *caipirinhas*, the *carne do sol* (sun-dried beef, or jerky) with *feijão de corda* (brown beans and herbs), or the *queijo coalho* (a country cheese, grilled). Also in the Largo do Guimarães is *Adega do Pimenta*, R Almte Alexandrino 296. Open Mon, Wed-Fri 1130-2200, Sun 1100-1800. Very small German restaurant with excellent sausages, sauerkraut and cold beer. On the same praça *Sobrenatural*, R Almirante Alexandrino 432, T22241003, open daily 1200-2400 is a charming rustic restaurant serving fish caught daily on owner's boat, English menu. For a light lunch, order a mix of excellent appetisers. Recommended.

Mid-range: *Adega Flor de Coimbra*, R Teotônio Regadas 34, Lapa. Founded 1938, serving Portuguese food and wines, speciality *bacalhau* (dried cod). Very good. *Café Glória*, R do Russel 734, T22059647. Open daily for lunch and dinner. Beautiful Art Nouveau building, helpful staff, excellent food. *Casa da Suiça*, R Cândido Mendes 157, T22525182. Bar/restaurant with good atmosphere.

Mid-range/cheap: There are a lot of eating places on R do Catete: *Amazônia*, No 234B, downstairs, 1-price counter service, upstairs for good, reasonably priced evening meals. Recommended. *Catelandia*, No 204, excellent and cheap, pay by weight. *Catete Grill*, No 239, good. *Galícia Grill*, No 265, very good pizza, good service. At Largo do Machado, *Restaurante e Pizzeria Guanabara*, No 150, excellent value and selection. *O Bom Galeto*, R do Catete 282, for chicken and meats. Next door is *Trattoria Gambino*, recommended for pasta, pleasant on summer evenings. In the gallery at Largo de Machado 29 is *Rotisseria Sirio Libaneza*, lojas 32 and 33, very good-value Arabic food. *Parmê*, R do Catete 311, chain restaurant, pizzas, pastas and cakes. *Alcaparra*, Praia do Flamengo 144, elegant traditional Italian, reasonable. *Alho E Óleo*, R Buarque de Macedo 13. Fashionable, pleasant. Recommended. *Lamas*, Marquês de Abrantes 18A, excellent value, good food, great atmosphere, opens late, popular with Brazilian arts/media people. Recommended.

Centre
Many restaurants in this business district are open only for weekday lunch

Santa Teresa
● *on map, page 92*

Lapa & Glória
● *on map, page 92*

Flamengo & Catete
● *on map, page 92*

Rio de Janeiro

Botafogo   **Mid-range**: *Raajmahal*, R Gen Polidoro 29, one of the few restuarants offering authentic Indian food. In Baixo Botafogo, **R Visconde de Caravelas** has several interesting bars and restaurants, eg **Cheap**: *Aurora*, corner of R Capitão Salomão 43, and *Botequim*, No 184, varied menu, good food and value. *Cobal Humaitá*, a fruit market with many popular restaurants (Mexican tacos, pizzeria, etc). *Viena* (pay by weight). **Seriously cheap**: *Chez Michou*, 4th floor Rio Sul Shopping. Crêpes and *chopp*. *Habib's* Rio Sul Shopping, Arabic fast-food; there is a small delicatessen.

Copacabana   **Expensive**: The main hotels (see above); most expensive is *Le Saint Honoré* at the
& Leme   *Meridien*, Leme, good food and wonderful view. Near the *Meridien* is *Shirley*, R Gustavo
Beachfront   Sampaio 610, T22751398. Spanish, small, seafood, book in advance. **Mid-range**: *Chon*
restaurants usually   *Kou*, Av Atlântica 3880, T22873956, bizarrely (although not for Brazil) is a traditional
charge more. Go a   Chinese restaurant that also offers an extensive sushi menu. A/c with piped music; sit
block or two inland   upstairs for good views over Copacabana beach. A welcome change from most of the
for cheaper options   other options in this area. *Churrascaria Palace*, R Rodolfo Dantas 16B. Established nearly 50 years. 20 different kinds of meat, good food and value. *Mala e Cuia*, *comida mineira* at another of the restaurants in this recommended chain (see Centre, above and throughout Minas Gerais). *Nino*, Domingos Ferreira 242. Italian cuisine, Argentine beef, excellent dinner with wine for US$25 per person. **Cheap**: *Aipo and Aipim*, Av Nossa Senhora de Copacabana 391. Excellent food by weight at this popular chain with other branches on this road. *Cervantes*, Barata Ribeiro 07-B e Prado Júnior 335B. Stand-up bar or sit-down, a/c restaurant, open all night, queues after 2200. Said to serve the best sandwiches in town, a local institution. *A Marisquera*, Barata Ribeiro 232. Good seafood. *Maximix*, R Siqueira Campos 12, loja A. Buffet by weight, opens late, very popular, cheap. Recommended. *Ponto de Encontro* at No 750. Portuguese, try baked *bacalhau* (cod). *Siri Mole & Cia*, R Francisco Otaviano 90. Brazilian cuisine, don't miss coffee after the meal from an old-fashioned coffee machine. *Taberna do leme*, corner of Princesa Isabel and Av NS Copacabana. A simple, friendly bar/restaurant with helpful waiters with tables on pavement. Comprehehensive menu all in English includes delicious crab pancakes. Warmly recommended for eating as well as drinking. *La Tratoria*, Av Atlântica, opposite *Hotel Excelsior*. Italian. Good food and service very reasonable. Recommended. **Seriously cheap**: There are stand-up bars selling snacks all around this area. *Marakesh*, Av NS de Copacabana 599. Good quality and value, pay by weight.

Ipanema   Ipanema is quieter than Copacabana, many nice places round Praça Gen Osório.
● *on map, page 102*   **Expensive**: *Alho e Óleo*, next door. Fashionable, friendly. Recommended. *Amarcord*, R Maria Quitéria 136, T22870335. Recommended. *Barril 1800*, Av Vieira Souto 110, T25230085. Good, reasonably priced, Brazilian menu as well as banana splits and chocolate pave. Popular spot good for people-watching. Open 0900-0400 daily. *Il Capo*, Visconde de Pirajá 276. Recommended. *Porcão*, Barão de Torre 218. A very good *churrascaria*, US$25 per person. *La Mashera de Pulcinela*, R Farme de Amoedo 102. Italian. *Pax Delícia*, Praça Nossa Senhora de Paz, good food, lively crowd. **Mid-range**: *Grottamare*, R Gomes Carneiro 132, T25231596. One of the best seafood restaurants in the city. *Mostarda*, Av Epitácio Pessoa 980. Food excellent (often seasoned with mustard sauce), nightclub upstairs, entry fee can be avoided if you eat in the 1st floor restaurant before 2200-2300. Recommended. *Satyricon*, R Barão da Torre 192, T25210627. Upmarket establishment specializing in Mediterranean cuisine. *Yemenjá*, R Visconde de Pirajá 128. Brazilian food from the Bahia region. **Cheap**: *Casa da Feijoada*, Prudente de Morais 10. Serves an excellent *feijoada* all week. *La Frasca*, R Garcia d'Ávila 129. Good Italian, pleasant atmosphere. *Del Mare*, on the corner of Prudente de Morais and Vinícius de Morais. Recommended. **Seriously cheap**: *Amarelinho*, R Farme de Amoedo 62. Great corner *lanchonete* with tables outside,

fresh food, good value, friendly, open until 0300. Recommended. *Delicats*, Av Henrique Dumont 68. Good Jewish deli.

Expensive: *Antiquarius*, R Aristides Espínola 19. One of the best Portuguese restaurants in the city, serving seafood and international cuisine, open daily 1200-0200. **Mid-range**: *Ettore*, Av Ataulfo de Paiva 1321, loja A, T2595899. Excellent Italian. *Mediterráneo*, R Prudente de Morais 1810. Excellent fish. *Un, Deux, Trois*, R Bartolomeu Mitre 123. Very fashionable, restaurant, nightclub. **Cheap**: *Celeiro*, R Dias Ferreira 199. Some of the best salads in the city, and light food, pay by weight.

Leblon
● *on map, page 102*

Expensive: *Claude Troisgros*, R Custódio Serrão 62, T25378582. Elegant French restaurant. Recommended. *Enotria*, R Frei Leandro 20, T25279003. Excellent Italian food, service, atmosphere and prices. Recommended. **Mid-range**: *Mistura Fina*, Av Borges de Medeiros 3207, T25372844. Classy, popular, friendly nightclub upstairs.

Jardim Botânico & Lagoa

Expensive: *Caffe Milano*, R Rodolfo Amoedo 360, T24944671. Good Italian, no credit cards. **Seriously cheap**: *Amarelinho*, Av Ayrton Senna 3000. Warmly recommended *lanchonete*, see Ipanema above.

Barra

Grill or barbecue houses (*churrascarias*) are relatively cheap, especially by European standards. There are many at São Conrado and Joá, on the road out to Barra da Tijuca (see page 103). Look for the 'Churrascaria Rodízio', where you are served as much as you can eat. *McDonalds* and *Bob's* (similar) can be found at about 20 locations each. *Galetos* are lunch counters specializing in chicken and grilled meat, very reasonable. In the shopping centres there is usually a variety of restaurants and snack bars grouped around a central plaza where you can shop around for a good meal. Most less-expensive restaurants in Rio have basically the same type of food (based on steak, fried potatoes and rice) and serve large portions; those with small appetites, especially families with children, can ask for a spare plate and split helpings. *La Mole*, at 11 locations, serves good, cheap Italian food, very popular.

Fast food
There are plentiful hamburger stands and lunch counters all over the city

For those who like their teas served English style, the sedate *Confeitaria Colombo*, R Gonçalves Dias 32, near Carioca Metrô station, is highly recommended for atmosphere and the only one of its kind in Rio. Over 100 years old, it has the the original belle époque decor, open 0900-1800, lunch available, no service charge so tip the excellent waiters. More modern but similar establishments in some of the main hotels, eg *Copacabana Palace Hotel*, Av Atlântica 1702, Mon-Fri 1400-1700. Enjoy serenity and elegance in this historic, high-class hotel. Recommended. Also *Casarão*, Souza Lima 37A, Copacabana. *Traiteurs de France*, Av NS de Copacabana 386. Delicious tarts and pastries, not expensive.

Cafés

Bars and nightclubs

Rio nightlife is rich and infinitely varied, one of the main attractions for most visitors. If you are not in Rio for Carnival, it's worth seeing a samba show; entry is cheaper if you pay at the door.

See the book *O Guia dos Botequins do Rio de Janeiro*, which describes Rio's best, most traditional bars and their history, US$20.

A beer costs around US$1.50, but up to US$5 in expensive hotel bars. A cover charge of US$3-7 may be made for live music, or there might be a minimum consumption charge of around US$3; sometimes both. Snack food is always available. Copacabana, Ipanema and Leblon have many beach *barracas*, several open all night. The seafront bars on Av Atlántica are great for people-watching. The big hotels have good cocktail

Bars
Wherever you are, there's one near you

bars. *Copacabana Palace*, has an exquisite poolside terrace which just cries out for a gin and tonic. Recommended. There are only a handful of seafront bars, all of which are fairly low-key and double as restaurants, in *Ipanema*: *Barril 1800*, Av Vieira Souto 110. Nice place to watch the sunset. Highly recommended. *A Garota de Ipanema*, R Vinícius de Morais 49, is where the song 'Girl from Ipanema' was written, very lively; on the same street, No 39, 2nd floor, is *Vinícius*, live music and international cuisine from 1900. In Leblon is the *Academia da Cachaça*, R Conde de Bernadotte 26-G, with another branch at Av Armando Lombardi 800, Barra da Tijuca; *Pepe* at Posto 2, Barra da Tijuca beach, is very popular with young people (1997). Lots more bars are opening in districts to the south. *Bar Lagoa*, Av Epitácio Pessoa 1674, Lagoa. Recommended (arty crowd, evenings only). On weekday evenings, Cariocas congregate at the bars around Praça Santos Dumont, Gávea. British ex-pats meet at *Porão*, under the Anglican church hall, R Real Grandeza 99, Botafogo, Fri only.

Lapa bars Lapa, once a run-down area in the centre that was to be avoided at night, is now one of the trendiest districts to go for drinking and music. At the time of writing, those in the know were packing out the *Carioca da Gema*, a 'musical café' with a varied programme every night of the week, Av Mem de Sa 79, Centro, T22210043, open from 1800 Mon-Fri and 2100 Sat. Cover charge US$3.20 and minimum consumption US$3.20. Next door at No 81 is *Sacrilegio*, T25073898, a 'cultural café' open from 1900 every night for cutting-edge theatre and other events. *Semente*, R Joaquim Silva 138, T22425165, is popular for samba, choro and salsa from 2200 Mon-Sat, US$2.50 cover; minimum consumption US$2. Book a table at weekends. Great atmosphere both inside and in the streets outside. Recommended.

Nightclubs The usual system in nightclubs is to pay an entrance fee (about US$10) and then you are given a card onto which your drinks are entered. There is often a minimum consumption of US$10-15 on top of the entry charge. Do not lose your card or they may charge you more than you could possibly drink. Most places serve reasonable snack food.

Trendiest clubs (contemporary dance music) are *El Turf* (aka *Jockey Club*), opposite the Jardim Botânico, Praça Santos Dumont 31, opens at 2200, gets going at 2300, you may have to wait to get in at the weekend if you arrive after midnight, no T-shirts allowed, very much a singles and birthday party place; another branch in Rio Sul Shopping Centre. *Fun Club*, also in Shopping Centre Rio Sul, 4th floor. *Le Maxim's Club*, R Lauro Müller 119, Cobertura, T25419342, at the top of the Rio Sul tower. With a superb night view of Rio (single women and couples only). *Le Boy*, Raul Pompéia 94, Copacabana, gay. *Papillon*, Av Prefeito Mendes de Moraes 222, São Conrado, T33222200. *The Basement*, Av Nossa Senhora de Copacabana 1241, alternative. In Barra da Tijuca, *Rock 'n' Rio Café*, Barra Shopping. Good food, young crowd, a long way from the centre (taxis hard to find in the early morning). *Greenwich Village*, at Posto 6 on the beach front. Good reputation. There are dozens of other good clubs, most open Wed-Sun, action starts around midnight; lone women and male-only groups may have trouble getting in.

Gafieiras, for Samba dancing, including *Elite Club*, R Frei Caneca 4, 1st floor, Centro, also reggae. *Estudantina*, Praça Tiradentes 79, Thu-Sun. There are many cheaper *gafieiras*. All types of music and entertainment are represented: *Copa Show*, Av Nossa Senhora de Copacabana 435, has been recommended for *forró* and disco music (safe). *Reggae Rock Cafe*, Largo de São Conrado 20, T33224197. *Raizes*, Av Sernambetiba 1120, T33896240, for Afro-Brazilian beats.

Discoteca Fundição do Progresso, downtown, near Lapa/Centro. Very trendy disco. Copacabana is full of discos and bars where the girls are prostitutes Sleazier shows are concentrated around Leme, as are gay clubs; many gay clubs also around Lapa (Cinelândia), but good ones exist all over the city. *Stop-Night*, a disco bar at Av Atlântica (near *Copacabana Palace* hotel) is a popular gay pick-up joint: be careful.

Brazilian football – a beautiful game

The world's second favourite national team has done more than any other to elevate a sport involving 22 players and a round leather ball into an art form, more akin to ballet than the usual sweaty exertions of lesser nations.

It has been more than 100 years since Charles Miller, an English expatriate, returned to São Paulo from a trip to the UK and brought with him a couple of leather footballs and arranged a kickabout with some other Englishmen abroad. For the first decades of the 20th century Brazilian football was a white middle-class game. Then, in 1923, Vasco da Gama, with a team of black and poor white players, won the Rio championship in the first year of their promotion to the first division. Other local clubs responded by forming their own league and barring Vasco from joining.

Brazilian football has come a long way since then. Players now come from all walks of life, colours and creeds, and they become national heroes. When Garrincha, one of the heroes of the 1962 World Cup finals, died in 1983, millions of Brazilians mourned. The most famous Brazilian footballer remains Edson Arantes do Nascimento, better known as Pelé. He played for Brazil for the first time when he was 17 in 1958 when Brazil won its first World Cup and was still playing for the national squad when it claimed the Jules Rimet trophy, in Mexico 1970, for a third time, thus earning the right to keep it.

Such heady credentials have led to an impossibly hard-to-please, football-crazy population threatening revolution every time the national team falls even marginally below the superhuman standards set by the 1970 side. Brazilians not only expect their national team to win the World Cup, but to do so samba-style, with all the panache exhibited in 1970 and the early 1980s. The 1994 World Cup winning squad were criticized for not playing the jogo bonito, or 'beautiful game' and 'only' managed to squeeze past Sweden in the semi-finals and eventually win the tournament thanks to a woeful penalty miss in the final by Italy's Roberto Baggio.

But if that was bad, worse was to come in France 1998. It all started so well. Brazil were flowing, playing with an effortless abandon not seen for many a year. And there were new gods to worship, most notably the young Ronaldo, a buck-toothed genius who could embarrass opponents with his speed and skill and score seemingly at will. After blowing away Holland in the semis, Brazil met an improving but still less than impressive host side in the final. It should have been a classic Brazil victory but Ronaldo had suffered a mysterious fit the previous night and there were doubts over his inclusion. In the end, he played, but the Brazilians were clearly shell-shocked by what had happened to their talented talisman and were a shadow of their real selves. In a one-sided match France ran out 3-0 winners.

And so to 2002. For once Brazil were underdogs, having only just scraped through their South American qualifying group. With the team – and country – in disarray and still not fully recovered from the trauma of the previous World Cup, football pundits across the globe dismissed them. Ronaldo was back, true enough, but had barely kicked a ball in two years, due to a terrible injury. But what took place in the next four weeks was a revelation and, for the neutral observer, a joy to watch as the 'three R's' – Ronaldo, Rivaldo and the latest star, Ronaldinho – wreaked havoc on their opponents, including England, and swept majestically towards a record fifth win. In the process they have reaffirmed the world's faith in the 'beautiful game'.

Entertainment

Cinemas New American releases (with original soundtrack), plus Brazilian and worldwide films and classics are all shown. See the local press. The normal seat price is US$4, discounts on Wed and Thu (students pay half price any day of the week).

Rio de Janeiro

▶▶ Carnival

Carnival in Rio is spectacular. On the Friday before Shrove Tuesday, the mayor of Rio hands the keys of the city to Rei Momo, the Lord of Misrule, signifying the start of a five-day party. Imagination runs riot, social barriers are broken and the main avenues, full of people and children wearing fancy dress, are colourfully lit. Areas throughout the city such as the Terreirão de Samba in Praça Onze are used for shows, music and dancing. Bandas and blocos (organized carnival groups) seem to be everywhere, dancing, drumming and singing.

There are numerous samba schools in Rio divided into two leagues both of which parade in the Sambódromo. The 14 schools of the Grupo Especial parade on Sunday and Monday whilst the Grupos de Acesso A and B parade on Saturday and Friday respectively. There is also a mirins parade (younger members of the established schools) on Tuesday. The judging takes place on Wednesday afternoon and the winners of the various groups parade again on the following Saturday.

Every school presents 2,500-6,000 participants divided into alas (wings) each with a different costume and 5-9 carros alegóricos, beautifully designed floats.

Each school chooses an enredo (theme) and composes a samba (song) that is a poetic, rhythmic and catchy expression of the theme. The enredo is further developed through the design of the floats and costumes. A bateria (percussion wing) maintains a reverberating beat that must keep the entire school, and the audience, dancing throughout the parade. Each procession follows a set order with the first to appear being the comissão de frente, a choreographed group that presents the school and the theme to the public. Next comes the abre alas, a magnificent float usually bearing the name or symbol of the school. The alas and other floats follow as well as porta bandeiras and mestre salas, couples dressed in 18th-century costumes bearing the school's flag, and passistas, groups traditionally of mulata dancers. An ala of bahianas, elderly women with circular skirts that swirl as they dance is always included as is the velha guarda, distinguished members of the school who close the parade. Schools are given between 65 and 80 minutes and lose points for failing to keep within this time. Judges award points to each school for components of their procession, such as

Horse-racing *Jockey Club Racecourse*, by Jardim Botânico and Gávea, meetings on Mon and Thu evenings and Sat and Sun 1400, entrance US$1-2, long trousers required, a table may be booked. Take any bus marked 'via Jóquei'. Betting is by tote only.

Music Many young Cariocas congregate in Botafogo for live music. There are free concerts throughout the summer, along the Copacabana and Ipanema beaches, in Botafogo and at the parks: mostly samba, reggae, rock and MPB (Brazilian pop): there is no advance schedule, information is given in the local press (see below). *Centro Cultural Carioca* is an exciting new venue that combines music (mostly samba) and dance. R do Teatro, 37, T22429642, www.centroculturalcarioca.com, for advance information, 1830-early morning. This restored old house with wrap-around balconies and exposed brick walls is a dance school and music venue that attracts a lovely mix of people. Professional dancers perform with musicians; after a few tunes the audience joins in. Thu is impossibly crowded; Sat is calmer. Bar food available. US$3 cover charge. Highly recommended. For a taste of some purely local entertainment on Mon nights, make your way down to *Praia do Vermelha* at Urca. Residents bring musical intstruments and chairs onto the beach for an informal night of samba from around 2100-midnight. Free. Bus No 511 from Copacabana. *Canecão* is a big, inexpensive venue for live concerts, most nights, see press for listings: R Venceslau Brás 215, Botafogo, T22953044. Rio's famous jazz, in all its forms, is performed in lots of enjoyable venues, see the press.

costume, music and design, and make deductions for lack of energy, enthusiasm or discipline. The winners of the Grupos de Acesso are promoted to the next higher group while the losers, including those of the Grupo Especial, are relegated to the next lowest group. Competition is intense and the winners gain a monetary prize funded by the entrance fees.

The Carnival parades are the culmination of months of intense activity by community groups, mostly in the city's poorest districts. To understand the traditions of the schools, the meanings of the different parts of the parade, and carnival as a whole, visit the **Museu do Carnaval** in the Sambódromo; although small, it has lots of photographs and the English-speaking staff are very informative (entrance in R Frei Caneca, T5026996. Monday-Friday 1100-1700, free). The **Sambódromo**, a permanent site at R Marquês de Sapucai, Cidade Nova, is 600 m long with seating for 43,000 people. Designed by Oscar Niemeyer and built in 1983-84, it handles sporting events, conferences and concerts during the rest of the year.

Rio´s bailes (fancy-dress balls) range from the sophisticated to the wild. The majority of clubs and hotels host at least one. The Copacabana Palace hotel´s is elegant and expensive whilst the Scala club has licentious parties. It is not necessary to wear fancy dress; just join in, although you will feel more comfortable if you wear a minimum of clothing to the clubs (crowded, hot and rowdy). The most famous are the Red & Black Ball (Friday) and the Gay Ball (Tuesday) which are both televised.

Bandas and blocos can be found in all neighbourhoods and some of the most popular and entertaining are Cordão do Bola Preta (meets at 0900 on Saturday in Rua 13 de Maio 13, Centro), Simpatia é Quase Amor (meets at 1600 Sunday in Praça General Osório, Ipanema) and the transvestite Banda da Ipanema (meets at 1600 on Saturday and Tuesday in Praça General Osorio, Ipanema). It is necessary to join a bloco in advance to receive their distinctive T-shirts, but anyone can join in with the bandas.

The expensive hotels offer special Carnival breakfasts from 0530. Caesar Park is highly recommended for a wonderful meal and a top-floor view of the sunrise over the beach.

Theatre There are about 40 theatres in Rio, presenting a variety of classical and modern performances in Portuguese. Seat prices start at about US$15; some children's theatre is free.

Festivals

Carnival
See also box above

Tickets The Sambódromo parades start at 1900 and last about 12 hrs. Gates (which are not clearly marked) open at 1800. There are *cadeiras* (seats) at ground level, *arquibancadas* (terraces) and *camarotes* (boxes). The best boxes are reserved for tourists and VIPs and are very expensive or by invitation only. Seats are closest to the parade, but you may have to fight your way to the front. Seats and boxes reserved for tourists have the best view, sectors 4, 7 and 11 are preferred (they house the judging points); 6 and 13 are least favoured (being at the end when dancers might be tired) but have more space. The terraces, while uncomfortable, house the most fervent fans, tightly packed; this is the best place to soak up the atmosphere but it's too crowded to take pictures. Tickets start at US$40 for *arquibancadas* and are sold at travel agencies as well as the Maracanã Stadium box office. Tickets are usually sold out before Carnival weekend but touts outside can generally sell you tickets at inflated prices. Samba schools have an allocation of tickets which members sometimes sell, if you are offered one of these check its date. Tickets for the champions' parade on the Sat following Carnival are much cheaper. Taxis to the Sambódromo are negotiable and will find your

Rio de Janeiro

Samba across the globe

The samba, an utterly Brazilian art form, has, in recent years, become an irrepressible musical force across the world. Samba percussion is now regarded as the community art form par excellence. From Sweden to Japan, from France to Israel, professionals and aficionados have joined forces to recreate the collective abandon of the blocos and escolas.

In the UK alone there are more than 100 groups playing some form of samba, meeting regularly to beat out their rhythms on the surdo and tamborim, practise their dance steps and prepare for the local carnival parade.

Some are small percussion workshops, others form huge parades modelled on the classical forms of Rio, with 200-strong baterias and dancers of all types, Bahianas and Passistas all moving to the sound of a specially composed story-samba. In Helsinki, there is a carnival devoted entirely to samba where a select few of the hundreds of Scandinavian bands take to the streets. Street parades across the US are set alight by the American escolas; San Francisco alone boasts 10 or more samba groups. Mexicans, Italians, Austrians, Germans, Danes, all have fallen under the spell of the samba, getting together at regular encontros to share techniques, learn from Brazilian mestres and celebrate their particular brand of samba.

Many groups are striving to produce their own sound by incorporating such influences as jazz, Jamaican ragga and even Punjabi bhangra. The development of samba-jungle rhythms in London and beyond demonstrates that groups are often committed to innovation as well as celebration.

It's not hard to see why the samba school idea has proved so popular. Providing a focus for collective activity, the samba carnival is open to all who want to participate, a non-stop creative party. Whether struggling with the complex batucada rhythms, building carros alegóricos, sewing bahiana skirts or cooking a feijoada, making a parade involves a group effort where for one day in a year the streets of Tokyo, Brighton and Berlin ring to the irresistible rhythms of the samba.

You can find out about samba worldwide through the internet and email. The UK samba website is at http://www.farrie.demon.co.uk/samba/bands/htm. To subscribe to the UK samba email address, contact tardis.ed.ac.uk and send on sambistas@tardis.ed.ac.uk   The worldwide samba home page is at www.worldsamba.org/

gate, the nearest Metrô is Praça Onze and this can be an enjoyable ride in the company of costumed samba school members. You can follow the participants to the concentração, the assembly and formation on Avenida Presidente Vargas, and mingle with them while they queue to enter the Sambódromo. Ask if you can take photos.

Sleeping and security Visitors wishing to attend the Carnival are advised to reserve accommodation well in advance. Virtually all hotels raise their prices during Carnival, although it is usually possible to find a room. Your property should be safe inside the Sambódromo, but the crowds outside can attract pickpockets; as ever, don't brandish your camera, and only take the money you need for fares and refreshments (food and drink are sold in the Sambódromo.) It gets hot! Wear as little as possible (shorts and a T-shirt).

Taking part Most samba schools will accept a number of foreigners and you will be charged upwards of US$125 for your costume as your money helps to fund poorer members of the school. You should be in Rio for at least two weeks before carnival. It is essential to attend fittings and rehersals on time, to show respect for your section leaders and to enter into the competitive spirit of the event. For those with the energy and the dedication, it will be an unforgettable experience.

Rehearsals *Ensaios* are held at the schools' *quadras* from Oct onwards and are well worth seeing. It is wise to go by taxi, as most schools are based in poorer districts. Tour agents sell tickets for glitzy samba shows, which are nothing like the real thing. When buying a Carnival video, make sure the format is compatible (Brazilian format matches the USA; VHS PAL for most of Europe).

Samba schools *Acadêmicos de Salgueiro*, R Silva Teles 104, Andaraí, T22385564, www.salgueiro.com.br; *Beija Flor de Nilópolis*, Pracinha Wallace Paes Leme 1025, Nilópolis, T27912866, www.beija-flor.com.br; *Imperatriz Leopoldinense*, R Prof Lacê 235, Ramos, T22708037, www.love-rio.com/imperatriz/; *Mocidade Independente de Padre Miguel*, R Coronel Tamarindo 38, Padre Miguel, T33325823, www.mocidade. com; *Portela*, R Clara Nunes 81, Madureira, T33900471, www.gresportela.com.br; *Primeira Estação de Mangueira*, R Visconde de Niterói 1072, *Mangueira*, T25674637, www.mangueira.com.br; *Unidos da Viradouro*, Av do Contorno 16, Niterói, T27177540, www.databrasil.com/viradouro/

Useful information Carnival week comprises an enormous range of official and unofficial contests and events which reach a peak on the Tue. *Riotur's* guide booklet gives concise information on these in English. The entertainment sections of newspapers and magazines such as *O Globo, Jornal do Brasil, Manchete* and *Veja Rio* are worth checking. *Liga Independente das Escolas de Samba do Rio de Janeiro*, www.liesa.com.br Felipe Ferreira's *Rio Carnival Guide* has good explanations of the competition, rules, the schools, a map and other practical details.

Less hectic than Carnival, but very atmospheric, is the festival of **Yemanjá** (see Religion, page 684) on the night of **31 Dec**, when devotees of the *orixá* of the sea dress in white and gather on Copacabana, Ipanema and Leblon beaches, singing and dancing around open fires and making offerings. The elected Queen of the Sea is rowed along the seashore. At midnight small boats are launched as offerings to Yemanjá. The religious event is dwarfed, however, by a massive New Year's Eve party, called **Reveillon** at Copacabana. The beach is packed as thousands of revellers enjoy free outdoor concerts by big-name pop stars, topped with a lavish midnight firework display. It is most crowded in front of *Copacabana Palace Hotel*. Another good place to see the fireworks is in front of *Le Meridien*, famous for its fireworks waterfall at about 0010. Many followers of Yemanjá are now making their offerings on 29 or 30 Dec and at Barra da Tijuca or Recreio dos Bandeirantes to avoid the crowds and noise of Reveillon.

The festival of **São Sebastião**, patron saint of Rio, is celebrated by an evening procession on **20 Jan**, leaving Capuchinhos Church, Tijuca and arriving at the cathedral of São Sebastião. On the same evening, an **umbanda festival** is celebrated at the Caboclo Monument in Santa Teresa. Throughout Brazil, **Jun** is a month of festivals, the **Festas Juninas**. In Rio they start with the festival of **Santo Antônio** on **13 Jun**, whose main event is a Mass, followed by celebrations at the Convento do Santo Antônio and the Largo da Carioca. Throughout the state, the festival of **São João** is a major event, marked by huge bonfires on the night of **23-24 Jun**. It is traditional to dance the *quadrilha* and drink *quentão*, cachaça and sugar, spiced with ginger and cinnamon, served hot. The *Festas Juninas* close with the festival of **São Pedro** on **29 Jun**. Being the patron saint of fishermen, his feast is normally accompanied by processions of boats. **Oct** is the month of the feast of **Nossa Senhora da Penha** (see page 91).

Many people look for *umbanda* religious ceremonies. Those offered on the night tours sold at hotels are not genuine and are a disappointment. You need a local contact to see the real ones, which are usually held in *favelas* and are none too safe for unaccompanied tourists.

Other festivals

Rio de Janeiro

Shopping

Bookshops *Argumento*, R Dias Ferreira 417, Leblon, sells imported English books, including *Footprint*. *Da Vinci*, Av Rio Branco 185 lojas 2, 3 and 9, all types of foreign books, *Footprint Handbooks* available. *Kosmos*, R do Rosário 155, good shop (in the centre and Av Atlântica 1702, loja 5), and there are many others, eg *Livros Técnicos*, R Miguel Couto 35, wide selection; Branches of *Sodiler* at both airports and Barra Shopping, Rio Sul (2 branches), Via Parque, Iguatemi and Tijuca shopping centres and at R São José 35, loja V. *Siciliano*, Av Rio Branco 156, loja 26, European books, also at Nossa Senhora de Copacabana 830 and branches; French books at No 298. *Saraiva* has a megastore at R do Ouvidor 98, T25079500, a massive bookshop which also includes a music and video shop and a café; other branches in Shopping Iguatemi and Shopping Tijuca. *Unilivros*, Largo do Machado 29C, French and English bestsellers (7 branches); *Livraria Nova Galeria de Arte*, Av Copacabana 291D, international stock. *Eldorado*, Av das Américas 4666, loja 207. Second-hand books also at *Livraria São José*, R Carmo 61 (only a few in English); *Livraria Brasileira*, Av Rio Branco 156, sobreloja 229; Aimée Gilbert, R da Carioca 38 (some in English); *Livraria Antiquário*, 7 de Setembro 207 and in R Pedro I, all in centre. Also on Av Marechal Floriano, near Av Rio Branco, especially at No 63. On the south side of Praça Tiradentes, *Casa dos Artistas* trades in second-hand paperbacks. Second-hand English books at the Anglican church, R Real Grandeza 99, Botafogo. Also at Av NS de Copacabana 400, small selection, US$1 per book.

Camping equipment On R 1 de Março, north of Av Pres Vargas, are military shops which sell jungle equipment, such as hammocks, mosquito nets and clothing, eg *Casa do Militar*, No 145 and *London*, No 155; you can also buy the Brazilian flag in any size you want here. *Malamada*, R da Carioca 13, recommended for rucksacks.

Clothes *Saara* is a multitude of little shops along R Alfândega and R Senhor dos Passos (between the city centre and Campo Santana), where clothes bargains can be found (especially jeans and bikinis); it is known popularly as 'Shopping a Céu Aberto'. Little shops on Aires Saldanha, Copacabana (1 block back from beach), are good for bikinis and cheaper than in shopping centres.

Jewellery Buy precious and semi-precious stones from reputable dealers. *H Stern*, R Visconde de Pirajá 490/R Garcia D'vila 113, Ipanema, have 10 outlets, plus branches in major hotels throughout the city (as well as branches elsewhere in Brazil and worldwide); see page 102. *Amsterdam Sauer*, R Garcia D'Ávila 105, have 10 shops in Rio and others throughout Brazil, plus St Thomas (US Virgin Islands) and New York; they offer free taxi rides to their main shop; see page 102. *H Stern* is much the bigger of the two in terms of premises, shop space, tours, etc. There are several good jewellery shops at the Leme end of Av NS de Copacabana: For mineral specimens as against cut stones, try *Mineraux*, Av NS de Copacabana 195, Belgian owner.

Markets Northeastern market at Campo de São Cristóvão, with music and magic, on Sun 0800-2200 (bus 472 or 474 from Copacabana or centre). Sat antiques market on the waterfront near Praça 15 de Novembro, 1000-1700. Also in Praça 15 de Novembro is *Feirarte II*, Thu-Fri 0800-1800. *Feirarte I* is a Sun open-air handicrafts market (everyone calls it the *Feira Hippy*) at Praça Gen Osório, Ipanema, 0800-1800, touristy but fun: items from all over Brazil. *Babilônia Feira Hype* is held every other weekend at the Jockey Club 1400-2300. This lively and popular market has lots of stalls selling clothes and crafts, as well as massage and live music and dance performances. A *stamp and coin market* is held on Sun in the Passeio Público. Markets on Wed 0700-1300 on R Domingos Ferreira and on Thu, same hours, on Praça do Lido, both Copacabana (Praça do Lido also has a *Feirarte* on Sat-Sun 0800-1800). There is an *artesania* market nightly near the *Othon* hotel, near R Miguel Lemos: one part for paintings, one part for everything else. Sunday market on R da Glória, colourful, cheap fruit, vegetables and flowers; early-morning food market, 0600-1100, R Min Viveiros de Castro, Ipanema. Excellent food and household-goods markets at various places in the city and suburbs (see newspapers for times and places). *Feira do Livro* is a book market that moves around various locations (Largo do Machado, Cinelândia, Nossa Senhora da Paz – Ipanema), selling books at 20% discount.

Music

For a large selection of Brazilian music, jazz and classical, try *Modern Sound Música Equipamentos*, R Barata Ribeiro 502D, Copacabana. *Toca do Vinicius* R Vinícius de Moraes 129C, Ipanema. Speciliazies in Bossa Nova books, CDs and souvenirs, doubles as a performance space.

Photography
Kodachrome slide film is difficult to get in Rio

For processing, *Flash Studio*, R Visconde de Pirajá 156, expensive; *One Hour Foto*, in the Rio Sul and Barra shopping centres, is recommended; *Honório*, R Vinícius de Moraes 146E. Stocks lithium batteries. Nikon camera repairs, *T Tanaka Cia Ltda*, Av Franklin Roosevelt 39, of 516, T22201127. Also *Mecánica de Precisão*, R da Conceição 31, shop 202, good.

Shopping centres

The *Rio Sul*, at the Botafogo end of Túnel Novo, has almost everything the visitor may need. As mentioned above, it has been refurbished and is convenient and very safe. Some of the services in Rio Sul are: *Telemar* (phone office) for international calls at A10-A, Mon-Sat 1000-2200; next door is *Belle Tours Câmbio*, A10. There is a post office at G2. A good branch of *Livraria Sodiler* is at A03. Entertainment includes the *Fun Club* nightclub on the 4th floor, open all night, very young crowd (see under Entertainment above); live music at the *Terraço*; the *Ibeas Top Club* gym; and a cinema. Eating places include fast food restaurants, 2 branches of *Kotobuki* sushi bar (another branch on the road to Praia Vermelha, recommended) and *Chaika* for milkshakes, ice-creams and sandwiches (4th floor, original branch on Praça Nossa Senhora da Paz, Ipanema). A US$5 bus service runs as far as the *Sheraton* passing the main hotels, every 2 hrs between 1000 and 1800, then 2130.

Other shopping centres, which include a wide variety of shops and services, include: *Cassino* (Copacabana), *Norte Shopping* (Todos os Santos), *Plaza Shopping* (Niterói), *Barra* in Barra da Tijuca (see page 103). At São Conrado, *The Fashion Mall* is smaller and more stylish.

Sport

There are hundreds of excellent gyms and sports clubs; most will not grant temporary (less than 1 month) membership: big hotels may allow use of their facilities for a small deposit. *Paissandu Athletic Club*, Av Afrânio de Melo Franco 330, Leblon – tennis, bowls, swimming, Scottish dancing, Tue, Apr-Oct, 2000-2230, may admit non-members.

Cycling Tours (hire available) with *Rio Bikers*, R Domingos Ferreira 81, room 201, T22745872.

Diving *Squalo*, Av Armando Lombardi 949-D, Barra de Tijuca, T/F24933022, squalo1@hotmail.com Offers courses at all levels, NAUI and PDIC training facilities, also snorkelling and equipment rental.

Golf clubs There are both 18-hole and 9-hole courses at the Itanhangá Golf Club, Jacarepaguá, visiting cards from Av Rio Branco 26, 16th floor. The Gávea club, São Conrado, T33994141, and the Teresópolis Golf Club, Estr Imbuí (Várzea), both have 18 holes; 9 holes at Petrópolis Country Club, Nogueira.

Hang-gliding *Just Fly*, T/F 22680565, T 99857540 (mob), justfly@justfly.com.br, US$80 for tandem flights with Paulo Celani (licensed by Brazilian Hang-Gliding Association), pick-up and drop-off at hotel included, in-flight pictures US$15 extra, flights all year, best time of day 1000-1500 (5% discount for *South American* and *Brazil Handbook* readers on presentation of book at time of reservation). *Tandem Flight and Rio by Jeep*, T 96938800, www.riobyjeep.com Tandem flight tours above Rio from Pedro Bonita Mountain with instructors licensed by the Brazilian Hang-Gliding Association. Contact Ricardo Hamond. *Ultra Força Ltda*, Av Sernambetiba 8100, Barra da Tijuca, T 33993114; 15 mins. Rejane Reis, *Exotic Tours* (see Tour operators, below) also arranges hang-gliding, as well as paragliding, ultra light flights, walks and other activities.

Parachuting Tandem jumping (*Vôo duplo*); *Barra Jumping*, Aeroporto de Jacarepaguá, Av Ayrton Senna 2541, T33252494. Several other people offer tandem jumping; check that they are accredited with the *Associação Brasileira de Vôo Livre*.

Paragliding From Leblon beach with Sr Ruy Marra, Brazilian paragliding champion (US$75), T33222286, or find him at the beach.

Riding *Sociedade Hípico Brasileiro*, Av Borges de Medeiros 2448, T25278090, Jardim Botânico – riding.

Rock climbing and hill walking *ECA*, Av Erasmo Braga 217, room 305, T22426857, personal guide US$100 per day, owner Ralph speaks English; *Clube Excursionista Carioca*, also recommended for enthusiasts, R Hilário Gouveia 71, room 206, T22551348, meets Wed and Fri. *Paulo Miranda*, R Campos Sales 64/801, T/F22644501.

Sailing *Iate Clube do Rio de Janeiro*, Av Pasteur, Urca, T22954482 – yachting. Information: Federação Brasileira de Vela e Motor, R Alcindo Guanabara 15, sl 801, Centro, T22203738; Federação de Vela, Praça Mahatma Gandhi 2, 12th floor, T22208785.

Surfing For the state of the waves on the beaches in Rio de Janeiro and its environs, see Surfing, page 65. Various organizations you may wish to contact are: *Organização dos Surfistas Profissionais do Rio de Janeiro*, T24932472; *Federação de Surf do Estado do Rio de Janeiro*, T22872385; *Associação Brasileira de Bodyboard*, T22743614; and *Federação de Bodyboard do Estado do Rio de Janeiro*, T22565653.

Swimming On all Rio's beaches you should take a towel or mat to protect you against sandflies. In the water stay near groups of other swimmers. There is a strong undertow.

Tour operators

Blumar, R Visconde de Pirjajá 550, Subsolo 108/109, Ipanema, T25113636, F25113739, blumar@blumar.com.br, run extensive tours throughout Brazil as well as reservations for Rio. *Hamburg Imobiliária*, see Apartments above. Recommended. *Hanseatic*, R 7 de Setembro 111/20, T22246672. German-run (English, French, Portuguese spoken). Recommended. *Marlin Tours*, Av NS de Copacabana 605, office 1204, T25484433, F22352081, bbm.robin@openlink.com.br Recommended for hotel, flights and tours, Robin and Audrey speak English. *Metropol*, R São José 46, T25335010, F25337160, www.metropolturismo.com.br Eco, adventure and culture tours to all parts of Brazil. *Turismo Clássico*, Av NS de Copacabana 1059/805, T25233390, F25214636, classico@infolink.com.br Recommended.

Organized trips to **Samba shows** cost US$50 including dinner, good, but it's cheaper to go independently. *Fenician Tours*, Av NS de Copacabana 335, T22353843, are cheaper than some at US$30 including transport from/to hotel. Regular sightseeing tours are operated by *American Sightseeing*, T22363551, *Sul América*, T22574235, *Canbitur* (of Copacabana), *Passamar Turismo*, Av Rio Branco 25, T2338883, also at *Hotel Nacional*. *Adrianotour*, T22085103, for guided tours, reservations and commercial services (English, French, German and Spanish spoken). *Atlantic Forest Jeep Tour*, T24959827, T99740218 (mob). As well as running jeep tours to Tijuca National Park (see above), run trips to coffee *fazendas* in the Paraíba Valley, Angra dos Reis and offshore islands and the Serra dos Órgãos. *Dantur*, Largo do Machado 29 (Galeria Condor) loja 47, T25577144. Helena speaks English and is friendly and helpful. *Guanatur Turismo*, R Dias da Rocha 16A, Copacabana, T22353275, F22353664. Sells long-distance bus tickets.

Favela Tour, Estr das Canoas 722, Bl 2, apt 125, CEP 22610-210, T33222727, T99890074 (mob), www.favelatour.com.br Marcelo Armstrong is the first to offer guided tours of Rio's *favelas*; safe, different and interesting, US$20, 3 hrs. Also ask Marcelo about eco tours, river-rafting and other excursions. He speaks English, French, Spanish, Italian and can provide guides in German and Swedish. For the best attention and price call Marcelo direct rather than through a hotel desk. Rejane Reis, *Exotic Tours*, also has favela tours, 2½ hrs, US$30 (transport included) – tours are combined with a guide-training programme. English spoken. *Cultural Rio*, R Santa Clara 110/904, Copacabana, T33224872 or M99113829, www.culturalrio.com, tours escorted personally by Professor Carlos Roquette, English and French spoken, almost 200 options available. *Fábio Sombra* offers private and tailor-made guided tours focusing on the cultural aspects of Rio and Brazil, T22959220, M97295455, fabiosombra@hotmail.com

Helicopter sightseeing tours *Helisight*, R Visconde de Pirajá 580, loja 107, Térreo, Ipanema, T35112141, www.helisight.com.br Prices from US$43 per person for 6-7 mins from Morro de Urca over Sugar Loaf and Corcovado, to US$148 per person for 30 mins over the city.

Transport

Local
See also Ins and outs, page 226

Bus There are good services to all parts, but buses are very crowded and not for the aged and infirm during rush hours. Buses have turnstiles which are awkward if you are carrying luggage. Hang on tight, drivers live out Grand Prix fantasies. At busy times allow about 45 mins to get from Copacabana to the centre by bus. The fare on standard buses is US$0.40 and suburban bus fares are US$0.75. Bus stops are often not marked. The route is written on the side of the bus, which is hard to see until the bus has actually pulled up at the stop.

Private companies operate a/c *frescão* buses which can be flagged down practically anywhere: *Real*, *Pegaso*, *Anatur*. They run from all points in Rio Sul to the city centre, Rodoviária and the airports. Fares are US$1.50 (US$1.80 to the international airport).

City Rio is an a/c tourist bus service with security guards which runs between all the major parts of the city. Good maps show what sites of interest are close to each bus stop – marked by grey poles and found where there are concentrations of hotels. T0800-258060.

Driving Remember service stations are closed in many places on Sat and Sun. Road signs are notoriously misleading in Rio and you can end up in a *favela*. Take care if driving along the Estr da Gávea to São Conrado as it is possible to unwittingly enter Rocinha, Rio's biggest slum.

Car repairs *Kyoso Team Mecânico Siqueira Campos*, at the entrance to the old tunnel, T22550506, a good mechanic who enjoys the challenge of an unusual car. Recommended.

Metro The Metrô provides a good service; it is clean, a/c and fast. **Line 1** operates between the inner suburb of Tijuca (station Saens Peña) and Arcoverde (Copacabana), via the railway station (Central), Glória and Botafogo. **Line 2** runs from Pavuna, passing Engenho da Rainha and the Maracanã stadium, to Estácio. It operates 0600-2300, Sun 1400-2000; closed holidays. The fare is R$1 (US$0.50) single; multi-tickets and integrated bus/Metrô tickets are available. Substantial changes in bus operations are taking place because of the extended Metrô system; buses connecting with the Metrô have a blue-and-white symbol in the windscreen.

Taxi The fare between Copacabana and the centre is US$7. Between 2300 and 0600 and on Sun and holidays, 'tariff 2' is used. Taxis have red number plates with white digits (yellow for private cars, with black digits) and have meters. Smaller ones (mostly Volkswagen) are marked TAXI on the windscreen or roof. Make sure meters are cleared and on tariff 1, except at those times mentioned above. Only use taxis with an official identification sticker on the windscreen. Don't hesitate to argue if the route is too long or the fare too much. Radio Taxis are safer but almost twice as expensive, eg *Cootramo*, T25605442, *Coopertramo*, T22602022, *Centro de Táxi*, T25932598, *Transcoopass*, T25604888. Luxury cabs are allowed to charge higher rates. *Inácio de Oliveira*, T22254110, is a reliable taxi driver for excursions, he only speaks Portuguese. Recommended. *Grimalde*, T22679812, has been recommended for talkative daytime and evening tours, English and Italian spoken, negotiate a price.

Train There are suburban trains to Nova Iguaçu, Nilópolis, Campo Grande and elsewhere. Buses marked 'E Ferro' go to the railway station.

Tram The last remaining tram runs from near the Largo da Carioca (there is a museum open 0830-1700 Fri only) across the old aqueduct (Arcos) to Dois Irmãos or Paula Mattos in Santa Teresa – historical and interesting, US$0.40. For more details see above under Santa Teresa.

Rio de Janeiro Metrô

Rio de Janeiro

Long distance

See also Ins and outs, page 76

Air   Rio has 2 airports: Santos Dumont Airport on Guanabara Bay for domestic flights (see below) and the **Antônio Carlos Jobim International Airport**. The latter, previously called Galeão, is situated on Governador Island some 16 km from the centre of Rio. It is in 2 sections: international and domestic.

There are a/c taxis; *Cootramo* and *Transcopass* have fixed rates (US$19 Copacabana), buy a ticket at the counter near the arrivals gate before getting into the car. The hire is for the taxi, irrespective of the number of passengers. Make sure you keep the ticket, which carries the number to phone in case of difficulty. Ordinary taxis also operate with the normal meter reading (about US$12.50, but some may offer cheaper rates from Copacabana to the airport, US$7-8.50). Do not negotiate with a driver on arrival, unless you are a frequent visitor. Beware of pirate taxis which are unlicensed. It is better to pay extra for an official vehicle than run the risk of robbery.

The a/c *Real* bus runs very frequently from the first floor of the airport to Recreio dos Bandeirantes via the municipal rodoviária and city centre, Santos Dumont Airport, Flamengo, Copacabana, Ipanema and Leblon. Luggage is secured in the hold (receipted), passengers are given a ticket and fares are collected during the journey; to anywhere in Rio it costs US$3.50. The driver will stop at requested points (the bus runs along the seafront from Leme to Leblon), so it's worth checking a map beforehand so that you can specify your required junction. The bus returns by the same route. Town buses M94 and M95, *Bancários/Castelo*, take a circular route passing through the centre and the interstate bus station. They leave from the second floor of the airport.

There are *câmbios* in the departure hall of the airport. There is also a *câmbio* on the 1st floor of the international arrivals area, but it gives worse rates than the *Banco do Brasil*, 24-hr bank, 3rd floor, which has Visa ATMs and will give cash advances against Visa card.

Tourist packs are sold at the international airport are completely unnecessary

Duty-free shops are well stocked, but not especially cheap and are open to arrivals as well as departures. Only US dollars or credit cards are accepted on the air-side of the departure lounge. There is a wider choice of restaurants outside passport control.

Check at the *Riotur* counter before leaving, for folders, maps and advice, T33984073. They will give help in booking hotels if required.

The **Santos Dumont Airport** on Guanabara Bay, right in the city, is used for Rio-São Paulo shuttle flights (US$150 single, US$300 return), other domestic routes, air taxis and private planes. The shuttle services operate every 30 mins throughout the day from 0630-2230. Sit on the right-hand side for views to São Paulo, the other side coming back, book flights in advance.

Details of journey times and fares are given under destinations throughout the chapter

Bus   Rodoviária Novo Rio, Av Rodrigues Alves, corner with Av Francisco Bicalho, just past the docks, T22915151. Some travel agents sell interstate tickets, or will direct you to a bus ticket office in the centre. Agencies include *Dantur Passagens e Turismo*, Av Rio Branco 156, subsolo loja 134, T22623424/3624; *Itapemirim Turismo*, R Uruguaiana 10, loja 24, T25098543, both in the centre; *Guanatur*, R Dias da Rocha 16A, Copacabana, T22353275; and an agency at R Visconde de Pirajá 303, loja 114, Ipanema. They charge about US$1 for bookings. Buses run from Rio to all parts of the country; it is advisable to book tickets in advance.

The rodoviária has a Riotur information centre, which is very helpful. Left luggage costs US$3. There are *câmbios* for cash only. The local bus terminal is just outside the rodoviária: turn right as you leave and run the gauntlet of taxi drivers – best ignored. The bus station attracts thieves, so exercise caution. The a/c *Real* bus (opposite the exit) goes along the beach to São Conrado and will secure luggage. If you need a taxi collect a ticket, which ensures against overcharging, from the office inside the entrance (to Flamengo US$6).

International buses   Asunción, 1,511 km via Foz do Iguaçu, 30 hrs (*Pluma*), US$70; **Buenos Aires** (*Pluma*), via Porto Alegre and Santa Fe, 48 hrs, US$100 (book 2 days in advance); *Uruguaiana*, US$90, cheaper and quicker to get a through ticket; *Santiago de Chile*, (*Pluma*) US$135, or Gen Urquiza, about 70 hrs.

The main bus station is reached by buses M94 and M95, Bancários/Castelo, from the centre and the airport; 136, 172, Rodoviária/Glória/Flamengo/Botafogo; 127, 128, 136, Rodoviária/Copacabana; 170, Rodoviária/Gávea/São Conrado; 128, 172, Rodoviária/Ipanema/Leblon.

Car hire Many agencies on Av Princesa Isabel, Copacabana. A credit card is virtually essential for hiring a car. Recent reports suggest it is cheaper to hire outside Brazil, you may also obtain fuller insurance this way. *Avis*, Galeão international airport, T33985060, Santos Dumont airport, T38147378, Av Princesa Isabel 150A and B, Copacabana, T25438481; *Hertz*, international airport, T3984338, Av Princesa Isabel 273-A, Copacabana, T22757440; *Interlocadora*, international airport, T33983181; *Localiza*, international airport and Santos Dumont airport, T0800-992000, Av Princesa Isabel 150, Copacabana, T22753340; *Nobre*, Av Princesa Isabel 7, Copacabana, T25414646; *Telecar*, R Figueiredo Magalhães 701, Copacabana, T22356778.

Hitchhiking To hitch to **Belo Horizonte** or **Brasília**, take a C-3 bus from Av Pres Antônio Carlos to the railway station, cross through the station to a bus station and catch the Nova Iguaçu bus. Ask to be let off at the Belo Horizonte turn-off. For the motorway entrance north and south, take bus 392 or 393 from Praça São Francisco.

Distances and approximate journey times: Juiz de Fora, 184 km (2¾ hrs); **Belo Horizonte**, 434 km (7 hrs); **São Paulo**, 429 km (6 hrs); **Vitória**, 521 km (8 hrs); **Curitiba**, 852 km (12 hrs); **Brasília**, 1,148 km (20 hrs); **Florianópolis**, 1,144 km (20 hrs); **Foz do Iguaçu**, 1,500 km (21 hrs); **Porto Alegre**, 1,553 km (26 hrs); **Salvador**, 1,649 km (28 hrs); **Recife**, 2,338 km (38 hrs); **Fortaleza**, 2,805 km (48 hrs); **São Luís**, 3,015 km (50 hrs); **Belém**, 3,250 km (52 hrs).

Directory

Aerolíneas Argentinas, R São José 70, 8th floor, Centro, T22924131, airport T33983520. **Airline offices** *Air France*, Av Pres Antônio Carlos 58, 9th floor, T25323642, airport T33983488. *Alitalia*, Av Pres Wilson 231, 21st floor, T22924424, airport T33983143. *American*, Av Pres Wilson 165, 5th floor, T0800-7034000. *Avianca*, Av Pres Wilson 165, offices 801-03, T22404413, airport T33983778. *British Airways*, airport T33983889. *Iberia*, Av Pres Antônio Carlos 51, 8th and 9th floors, T22821336, airport T33983168. *Japan Airlines*, Av Rio Branco 156, office 2014, T22206414. *KLM*, Av Rio Branco 311A, T25427744, airport T33983700. *LAB*, Av Calógeras 30A, T22209548. *Lan Chile*, R da Assembléia 92, office 1301, T22209722/0800-5549000, airport T33983797. *Lufthansa*, Av Rio Branco 156D, T22176111, airport T33985855. *RioSul/Nordeste*, Av Rio Branco 85, 10th floor, T25074488 (has an advance check-in desk in Rio Sul Shopping). *Swissair*, Av Rio Branco 108, 10th floor, T22975177, airport T3398 4330. *TAP*, Av Rio Branco 311-B, T22101287, airport, T33983455. *United*, Av Pres Antônio Carlos 51, 5th floor, T0800-245532. *Varig*, Av Rio Branco 277G, T22203821, information, T0800-997000 bookings; airport T33982122. Most staff speak English. *Vasp*, R Santa Luzia 735, T0800-998277.

Lloyds Bank, R da Alfândega 332, 7th floor. *Banco Internacional* (*Bank of America* and **Banks** *Royal Bank of Canada*), R do Ouvidor 90. *Banco Holandês Unido*, R do Ouvidor 101. *Citibank*, R Assembléia 100, changes large US$ TCs into smaller ones, no commission. *Banco do Brasil*, there are only 2 branches in Rio which will change US$ TCs, Praia de Botafogo, 384A, 3rd floor (minimium US$200) and the central branch at R Sen Dantas 105, 4th floor (minimum US$500 – good rates). The international airport is probably the only place to change TCs at weekends. Visa cash withdrawals at *Banco do Brasil* (many ATMs at the R Sen Dantas branch, no queues) and *Bradesco* (personal service or machines). MasterCard, Visa and Cirrus cash machines at *HSBC* branches throughout the city. *Itaú*, on Av Atlântica (next to *Copacabana Palace*), R Visc onde de Pirajá, close to Praça Gen Osório (Ipanema) and other locations. Also at Santos Dumont airport.

Currency exchange *American Express*, Av Atlântica 1702, loja 1, T25482148 Mon-Fri 0900-1600, Av Pres Wilson 231, 18th floor, Centro, and at Galeão airport, T33984251 (VIP room 1st floor), good rates (T0800-785050 toll-free). Most large hotels and reputable travel agencies will change currency and TCs. Copacabana (where rates are generally worse than in the centre) abounds with *câmbios* and there are many also on Av Rio Branco. *Câmbio Belle Tours*, Rio Sul Shopping, ground floor, loja 101, parte A-10, Mon-Fri 1000-1800, Sat 1000-1700, changes cash. In the gallery at Largo do Machado 29 are *Câmbio Nick* at loja 22 and, next door but one, *Casa Franca*.

Communications   Internet: *@point*, Barra Shopping, Av das Americas 4666, Barra da Tijuca. Several places in Rio Sul Shopping, Botafogo. Many on Av NS de Copacabana and others on R Visconde de Pirajá, Ipanema. *Phone Serv*, Av N S de Copacabana 454, loja B. US$3 per hr internet, telephone service. *Tudo é Fácil*, 3 branches in Copacabana: R Xavier da Silveira, 19; Av Prado Júnior 78 and R Barata Ribeiro 396. Well-organized, with identification cards so once registered you can bypass the front desk, telephone booths and scanners, US$2 per hr, discounts for extended use. **Post office**: The Central Post Office is on R 1 de Março 64, at the corner of R do Rosário. Av N S de Copacabana 540 and many other locations. All handle international post. There is a post office at Galeão airport. **Poste Restante**: Correios, Av Nossa Senhora de Copacabana 540 and all large post offices (letters held for a month, recommended, US$0.10 per letter). Federal Express, Av Calógeras 23 (near Santa Luzia church) T22628565, is reliable. **Telephone** International calls can be made at Av NS de Copacabana 540, 2nd floor. Galeão international airport. Santos Dumont airport, mezzanine (0530-2300). Novo Rio rodoviária. R Dias da Cruz 192, Méier-4, 24 hrs, 7 days a week. Urca, near the Pão de Açúcar cable car. Praça Tiradentes 41, a few mins' walk from Metrô Carioca. R Visconde de Pirajá 111, Ipanema. R do Ouvidor 60, Centro. International telephone booths are blue. Larger *Embratel* offices have telex and fax, as do many larger *Correios*, eg Av NS de Copacabana 540. Telephone numbers often change in Rio de Janeiro and other Brazilian cities. If in doubt, phone 102, *Auxilio à Lista*, which is the current daily updated directory of telephone numbers. This number can be used all over the country, but if you want to find out a Rio phone number from outside Rio, dial the city code 021, then 121. If you do not understand Portuguese, you should seek assistance from a hotel receptionist or similar because the numbers are only spoken in Portuguese.

Cultural   *American Library*, União Cultural Brasil-Estados Unidos, R Col Oscar Porto 208. *Centro*
centres   *Brasileiro Britânico*, R Ferriera de Araújo 741, Pinheiros, T30390567. *Centro Cultural Fiesp*, Av Paulista 1313, open 0900-1900 Tue-Sun, has foreign newspapers and magazines. See under Entertainment for *Alliance Française Theatre*. *Goethe-Instituto*, R Lisboa 974 (open Mon-Thu 1400-2030).

Embassies &   *Argentina*, Praia de Botafogo 228, T25531646. Very helpful over visas, 1130-1600. *Aus-*
consulates   *tralia*, Av Presidente Wilson, T38244624. Mon-Fri 9000-1300, 1430-1800. *Austria*, Av Atlântica 3804, T25222286. *Canada*, R Lauro Müller 116, T25433004. *Denmark*, Praia do Flamengo, 66, T25586050. *France*, Av Pres Antônio Carlos, 58, T22101272. *Germany*, R Pres Carlos de Campos 417, T25536777. *Greece*, Praia do Flamengo 344, T25526799. *Israel*, Av NS de Copacabana 680, T25485432. *Netherlands*, Praia de Botafogo 242, 10th floor, T25529028. (Dutch newspapers here and at KLM office on Av Rio Branco.) *Paraguay*, same address, 2nd floor, T25532294. Visas US$5. *Sweden*, *Finland* and *Norway*,

Praia do Flamengo 344, 9th floor, T25535505. *Switzerland*, R Cândido Mendes 157, 11th floor, T22211867. *UK*, Praia do Flamengo 284, 2nd floor, T25533223 (consular section direct line), F25536850, consular section is open Mon-Fri 0900-1230 (the consulate's hrs are 0830-1700), Metrô Flamengo, or bus 170, the consulate issues a useful 'Guidance for Tourists' pamphlet. *Uruguay*, Praia de Botafogo 242, 6th floor, T25536030. *USA*, Av Pres Wilson 147, T22927117. Mon-Fri 0800-1100, passports 1330-1500.

Instituto Brasil-Estados Unidos, Av Copacabana 690, 5th floor, 8-week course, 3 classes a week, US$150, 5-week intensive course US$260. Good English library at same address. *IVM Português Prático*, R do Catete 310, sala 302, US$18 per hr for individual lessons, cheaper for groups. Helpful staff. Recommended. *Cursos da UNE* (União Nacional de Estudantes), R Catete 243, include cultural studies and Portuguese classes for foreigners. **Language courses**

Fénix, R do Catete 214, loja 20. *Laundromat* at Av NS de Copacabana 1216. In Rio Sul are self-service laundrettes such as *Lavelev*, about US$7 for a machine, including detergent and drying, 1 hr. Also at R Buarque de Macedo 43B, Catete, R Voluntários da Patria 248, Botafogo, Av Prado Júnior 63B, Copacabana. *Lavlev Flamengo*, RC de Baependi 78, or R das Laranjeiras 43, L28. **Laundry**

Vaccinations at *Saúde de Portos*, Praça Mcal Âncora, T22408628/8678, Mon-Fri 1000-1100, 1500-1800 (international vaccination book and ID required). *Policlínica*, Av Nilo Peçanha 38. Recommended for diagnosis and investigation. A good public hospital for minor injuries and ailments is *Hospital Municipal Rocha Maia*, R Gen Severiano 91, Botafogo, T22952295/2121, near Rio Sul Shopping Centre. Free, but there may be queues. *Hospital Miguel Couto*, Mário Ribeiro 117, Gávea, T22746050. Has a free casualty ward. **Dentist**: Amílcar Werneck de Carvalho Vianna, Av Pres Wilson 165, suite 811. English-speaking. Dr Mauro Suartz, R Visconde de Pirajá 414, room 509, T22876745. Speaks English and Hebrew, helpful. **Medical services**

Services other than in Portuguese: Christ Church, R Real Grandeza 99, Botafogo, T22262978 (Church of England/American Episcopalian). The proceeds of books sold here go to help the Boys' Town Charity for street kids. The British School, for children of 5-16, is nearby. Chapel of Our Lady of Mercy, R Visconde de Caravelas 48, Botafogo (Roman Catholic). *Union Church* (Protestant nondenominational), services held at R Parque da Lagoa de Marapendi, CP 37154, Barra da Tijuca. *International Baptist Church*, R Desembargador Alfredo Russel 146, Leblon. *First Church of Christ Scientist*, Av Mcal Câmara 271, room 301. *Masonic Temple*, in the British School at R da Matriz 76, Botafogo. Synagogues: *Associação Religiosa Israelita*, R Gen Severiano 170, Botafogo. *Beit Yaacov*, R Capelão Alvares da Silva 15, Copacabana. *Israelita Bet hel*, R Barata Ribeiro 469, Copacabana, includes kosher bakery. *Swedish Church*, Igreja Escandinava, Carlos Sampaio 251, Centro, open 1300-2200, Sun 1700-2100, will store luggage. **Places of worship**

Check out www.addresses.com.br/ for a comprehensive guide to addresses in the city. **Immigration**: Federal Police, Praça Mauá (passport section), entrance in Av Venezuela, T22912142. To renew a 90-day visa, US$12.50. **Students** Student Travel Bureau, Av Nilo Peçanha 50, SL 2417, Centro, T/F25442627, and R Visconde de Pirajá 550, lj 201, Ipanema, T25128577, www.stb.com.br (with offices throughout the country) has details of travel, discounts and cultural exchanges for ISIC holders. **Toilets** There are very few public toilets in Rio de Janeiro, but Shopping Centres, many bars and restaurants (eg *Macdonalds*) offer facilities. Just ask for the *banheiro*. **Useful addresses**

Rio de Janeiro

Rio de Janeiro State

Background

The state of Rio was associated with the development of and settlement along the roads. In the 16th century, the first established road became that which linked Paraty (see page 159) with the valley of the Rio Paraíba, continuing into southern Minas Gerais. This became a route for exporting gold in the 18th century and it was followed by the Caminho Novo, also from Minas Gerais, which ended on the shores of the Baía de Guanabara. Other gold routes were created, including one between Rio and São Paulo.

The demise of the Minas Gerais gold fields and the expansion of coffee growing in the Paraíba valley at the beginning of the 19th century opened up new routes between the interior and the coast. The crop was taken by mule train to new ports on the Baías de Guanabara, Sepetiba and Ilha Grande, and these roads were the main means of communication until the coming of the railways after 1855. At this point, Rio de Janeiro added to its political importance the trading dominance that came with the rail terminus, first from Petrópolis (see page 140), then from São Paulo and Minas Gerais. Industrialization soon followed.

In comparison with Rio de Janeiro city's steady growth, other centres rose and fell with the changing economic climate: Paraty was a major port while gold and, later, coffee were flowing through it, but fell almost into obscurity after the railways were built. Towns in the coffee zone, such as Vassouras (see page 149) and Valença, lost their importance as the coffee frontier moved.

Geography One of the main attractions of Rio de Janeiro state is its wonderfully varied geography. The coast has three large bays, intricately carved with inlets and dotted with islands. Where erosion has deposited soils at the foot of the coastal mountains, lowlands (*baixadas*) have formed a wide belt between the mountains and the sea. In these lowlands there are sand banks, salt marshes (*restingas*) and lakes. Another feature of the coast is the extraordinary number of beautiful beaches, some on the open sea and others, which are calmer, in the bays or on the lakes behind the sand bars.

Just inland from the Atlantic litoral is the Serra do Mar, a dramatic range of mountains which includes, among other features, the weird shapes of the Serra dos Órgãos. Further inland again is the Serra da Mantiqueira, which has the highest mountain in the state, Pico das Agulhas Negras (2,787 m). Between the two ranges runs the Rio Paraíba do Sul, the main valley of many in the state. Before the conquest of Brazil by the Portuguese, the entire region was covered in tropical forest, hardly any of which now remains.

Sights

Niterói

Phone code: 021
Colour map 4, grid C3
Population: 460,000

Just across Guanabara Bay is Niterói, the old capital of Rio de Janeiro state. *Cariocas* often joke that the best thing about Niterói is its views back to Rio, which are spectacular. It is also a pleasant excursion with some good beaches nearby and a star attraction in the futuristic Museu de Arte Contemporânea, designed by Oscar Niemeyer.

When the French under Villegagnon, with their Tamoio allies, established their colony on the western side of the mouth of the Baía de Guanabara, the Portuguese and the Temiminós set up camp on the eastern shore. The formal founding of a settlement here was in 1573 and once the Portuguese had established sovereignty, the area became a centre for sugar growing in the 17th century. It only really became important after Dom João VI's visit in 1816, when it was given the name of Vila Real da Praia Grande. In 1834 it was renamed Niterói ('hidden waters' in Tupi-Guarani) and was capital of the province (later state) of Rio de Janeiro until 1975 when the capital moved to Rio.

Many buildings associated with the city's period as state capital are grouped around the Praça da República (none is open to the public). The main avenue is Av Ernâni do Amaral Peixoto, with buildings similar to Avenida Presidente Vargas in Rio. At the end of the avenue is the dock for Rio, a statue of the Indian chief Araribóia and Bay Market shopping centre. The main green area in the centre is Campo de São Bento, which has many trees and handicraft stalls at weekends. **Tourist information** *Neltur*, Estrada Leopoldo Fróes 773, São Francisco, T27102727, open daily. A monthly newspaper, *Niterói, Esporte, Lazer, Turismo e Cultura*, is free.

Colonial churches include **São Lourenço dos Índios**, Praça General Rondon, which dates from at least 1627 and the **Capela da Boa Viagem** (1663), which stands on a fortified island, attached by a causeway to the mainland (open one day a month for mass). By Gragoatá beach in the city is the **Capela São Domingos** (1662) and the **Forte de Gragoatá**, from the same period (closed to the public).

The **Basílica de Nossa Senhora Auxiliadora**, Rua Santa Rosa 207, is an early 20th-century church. Its famous organ, made in Italy, was bought by the Salesian order during the Second World War and is one of the largest pipe organs in the world, certainly the largest in Latin America. ■ *0600-1100, 1500-2000 daily.*

The most important historical monument, however, is the 16th-century **Fortaleza Santa Cruz**, which is still a military establishment. It is situated on a promontory which commands a fine view of the entrance to the bay. Tours show the Capela de Santa Bárbara, whose statue was destined for Santa Cruz dos Militares in Rio. All attempts to move the saint were accompanied by great storms, which was taken as a sign to leave her at the fortress. Also shown are the dungeons, fortifications, execution sites and gun batteries. It is about 13 km from the centre of Niterói, on the Estrada General Eurico Gaspar Dutra, by Adão e Eva beach. ■ *0900-1600 daily. US$1.50. Tours have a compulsory guide, Portuguese only. T27107840.*

Museu de Arqueologia de Itaipu is in the ruins of the 18th-century Santa Teresa Convent and also covers the archaeological site of Duna Grande on Itaipu beach. It is 20 km from the city. ■ *1300-1800 Wed-Sun. T27094079.*

Museu de Arte Contemporânea, Mirante da Praia da Boa Viagem s/n, is an Oscar Niemeyer project and worth visiting for the building itself as much as for its exhibitions. It is best seen at night, expecially when the pond beneath the spaceship design is full of water. The exhibition inside changes. ■ *1100-1900 Tue-Sun, US$1, 1300-2100 Sat, free. T26202400. www.macnit.com.br*

The beaches closest to the city centre are unsuitable for bathing (Gragoatá, Vermelha, Boa Viagem, das Flechas). The next ones, also in the city and with polluted water have more in the way of restaurants, bars and nightlife (**Icaraí**, the smartest district, has good nightlife, **São Francisco** – for example Rua das Pedras, and Charitas – is even better). The road continues round the bay, past

Sights
The centre of Niterói is easily explored on foot

Museums

Beaches
To get to the ocean beaches, take a 38 or 52 bus from Praça Gen Gomes Carneiro

Rio de Janeiro

Preventório and Samanguaiá to **Jurujuba**, a fishing village at the end of the bus line (take Bus No 33 from the boat dock; sit on the right-hand side, it's a beautiful ride). About 2 km from Jurujuba along a narrow road are the attractive twin beaches of **Adão** and **Eva** beneath the Fortaleza da Santa Cruz, with lovely views of Rio across the bay.

Piratininga, **Camboinhas**, **Itaipu** (note the archaeology museum, above) and **Itacoatiara**, three fabulous stretches of sand, are the best in the area, about 40 minutes' ride through picturesque countryside. Buses leave from the street directly ahead of the ferry entrance, at right angles to the coast street. The undertow at Itacoatiara is dangerous, but the waves are popular with surfers and the beach itself is safe. Itaipu is also used by surfers.

Sleeping & eating **A** *Icaraí Praia*, R Belisário Augusto 21, T27102323, F27106142. **B** *Flat Icaraí*, R Col Moreira Cesar, 19, Icaraí, T27167176, F7167178. Facilities include bar, restaurant, pool and sauna. **Camping** *Piratininga*, Estr Frei Orlando Km 2, T26094581.

Mid-range: *Cantina Buonasera*, Estr Leopoldo Fróes 34, Icaraí, T26102762. Italian food with good view of the bay. *Bicho Papão*, Jurujuba, good seafood. **Cheap**: 3 good-value restaurants opposite the Ruínas de Estação da Cantareira (which has occasional shows and handicraft market): *Tio Cotó*, *Vila Real* and *Zia Amélia*.

Festivals Mar/Apr and May, *Festa do Divino*, a festival which traditionally begins on Easter Sun and continues for the next 40 days, in which the Bandeira (banner) do Divino is taken around the local municipalities. The festival ends at Pentecost with sacred and secular celebrations. **24 Jun**: *São João*. **22 Nov**: founding of the city.

Sport **Clubs** *Rio Cricket Associação Atlética* (RCA), R Fagundes Varela 637, T27175333. Bus 57 from ferry. *Rio Sailing Club* (late Clube de Niterói), Estr Leopoldo Fróes 418, lote 338, T26105810. Bus 33 marked 'via Fróes'.

Transport **Boats** Niterói, across Guanabara bay, is reached by ferry boats and launches crossing every 10 mins (15-20 mins, US$0.50) from the 'Barcas' at Praça 15 de Novembro (ferry museum at the terminal). There are also catamarans (*aerobarcas*) every 10 mins (about 3 mins, US$2.45; the fare is US$1.25 between 0700 and 1000 Rio-Niterói and after 1700 Niterói-Rio). The slow, cheaper ferry gives the best views. Ferries and catamarans to Rio de Janeiro leave from the terminal at Praça Araribóia.

Buses No 996 Gávea-Jurujuba, 998 Galeão-Charitas, 740-D and 741 Copacabana-Charitas, 730-D Castelo-Jurujuba, US$0.60-0.75.

Directory **Banks** *Banco 24 Horas*, Niterói Shopping, R da Conceição 188. *Bradesco*, R Gavião Peixoto 108. **Communications** Internet: *O Lido Cyber C@fé*, Av Rui Barbosa 29, lj 124, São Francisco. **Laundry** *Lavlev*, R Pres Backer 138. **Medical services** *Universitário Antônio Pedro*, Av Marques do Paraná, T26202828. **Voltage** 110 volts, AC, 60 cycles.

The Costa do Sol

To the east of Niterói lie a series of saltwater lagoons, the Lagos Fluminenses. Two small lakes lie behind the beaches of Piratininga, Itaipu and Itacoatiara, but they are polluted and ringed by mud. The next lakes, Maricá and Saquarema, are much larger. Although they are still muddy, the waters are relatively unpolluted and wildlife abounds in the scrub and bush around the lagoons. This is a prime example of the restinga *environment. The RJ-106 road runs behind the lakes en route to Cabo Frio and Búzios, but an unmade road goes along the coast between*

Itacoatiara and Cabo Frio, giving access to the many long, open beaches of Brazil's Costa do Sol. The whole area is perfect for camping.

The 36-km Itaipu-Açu, with many wild, lonely stretches, leads to Maricá, a sleepy fishing village with sand streets on its own lagoon. There is good walking in the Serra do Silvado, 14 km away on the road to Itaboraí. Between Maricá and Saquarema are Ponta Negra and Jaconé, both surfing beaches. The **tourist office** is at Av Ver Francisco Sabino da Costa 477.

Maricá
Phone code: 024
Population: 60,500

Sleeping and eating At Ponta Negra are **B** *Pousada Colonial*, T/F6481707. Suites and bungalows with breakfast and **B** *Solar Tabaúna*, T26481626. Pool. Both highly recommended. *Caranguejo e Cia*, Estr do Boqueirão (road to beach, car needed). Seafood served overlooking the lake. Warm service. Recommended.

Directory Banks: *Bradesco*, R Sen Macedo Soares 44.

Saquarema is a fishing and holiday village, known as the centre for surfing in Brazil. Its cold, open seas provide consistent, crashing waves of up to 3 m. Frequent national and international championships take place here. Beware of strong currents, though. The lovely white church of **Nossa Senhora de Nazaré** (1675) is on a green promontory jutting into the ocean. The local legend has it that on 8 September 1630, fishermen, saved from a terrible storm, found an image of the Virgem de Nazaré in the rocks. A chapel was founded on the spot and subsequent attempts to relocate the Virgin (as when the chapel was falling into disrepair) resulted in her miraculously returning to the original site.

Saquarema
Phone code: 024
Colour map 4, grid C3
Population: 44,000

Sleeping and eating B *Pousada Pedra d'Água Maasai*, Trav de Itaúna 17, T/F26511092. Seafood restaurant. **C** *Pousada do Holandês*, Av Vilamar 377, Itaúna beach. Recommended, many languages spoken by Dutch owner and his Brazilian wife. Good meals – follow the signs, or take a taxi, from Saquarema. **D** *Itaúna Surf*, R dos Robalos 17, Itaúna. **Youth hostel** *Ilhas Gregas*, R do Prado 671, Itaúna, T26511008. With pool, sauna, bar, restaurant. **Camping** *Itaúna's*, R dos Tatuís 999, access from Av Oceânica, T26511711. *Le Bistrô*, Av São Rafael 1134, Itaúna. Portuguese. *Tem Uma Né Chama Teré*, on the main square. Very good.

Festivals *Festa do Divino*, as above under Niterói; **8 May**, founding of the town; **29 Jun**, festival of São Pedro, at the end of the Festas Juninas; **7 Sep**, *Nossa Senhora de Nazaré*, the town's patron saint's day.

Transport Buses to Rio de Janeiro (*Mil e Um, 1001*), every 2 hrs 0730-1800, 2 hrs, US$3.40.

Directory Banks *Bradesco*, Rod Amaral Peixoto 83.

Araruama (220 sq km), is one of the largest lakes in Brazil and famous for its medicinal mud. The salinity is high, the waters calm and almost the entire lake is surrounded by sandy beaches, making it popular with families looking for unpolluted bathing. The constant breeze makes the lake perfect for windsurfing and sailing. The major industry of the area is salt, and all around are saltpans and wind pumps used to carry the water into the pans. The town itself is at the western end of the lake on the inland shore, 116 km from Rio.

Araruama
Phone code: 024
Colour map 4, grid C4
Population: 66,500

At the eastern end of the lake, also inland, is **São Pedro de Aldeia**, which has a population of 55,500, and which, despite intensive development, still retains much of its colonial charm. There is a lovely Jesuit church built in 1723, and a **tourist information office** on Avenida São Pedro.

Sleeping Araruama: **A** *Ver a Vista*, R São Sebastião 400, T/F26654721. **C** *Pousada do Peu*, RJ-132, Km 12, T26653614. **Camping** *Camping Clube do Brasil*, R República da Argentina 286. *Veneza*, Estr de Praia Seca Km 13, T26652667.

  São Pedro de Aldeia **A** *Enseada das Garças*, R José Costa 1088, Ponta da Areia, about 5 km from town, T/F26211924. A member of the Roteiros de Charme group. **B** *Pousada Pontal da Praia*, Praia do Sudoeste, T/F26212441. **Youth hostel** *Praia do Sudoeste*, R Pedro Américo, Lt 27, T26212763. Open high season only. **Camping** *da Colina*, RJ-106, Km 108, Praia da Teresa, T26211919.

Eating Araruama *Gigi*, RJ-106, Km 87. Seafood. **São Pedro de Aldeia** *Don Roberto*, Av Getúlio Vargas 272. Pizzas.

Festivals Like Saquarema, São Pedro celebrates the feast of *São Pedro* (the town's patron saint) on **29 Jun**, but also its founding on **16 May**.

Directory Banks: *Bradesco*, Av São Pedro 120, São Pedro de Aldeia.

Arraial do Cabo
Phone code: 024
Population: 21,500

The lake and the ocean are divided by the Restinga de Massambaba, mostly deserted except for the beaches of **Massambaba** and **Seca** at the western end and **Grande** in the east. Grande is the main beach for Arraial do Cabo, the town at the end of the Restinga de Massambaba, on the southern side of Cabo Frio. Arraial has lots of other small beaches on the bays and islands which form the cape, round which the line of the coast turns north. Excursions can be made by boat around the islets and by jeep or buggy over the sand dunes.

Praia do Farol, on Ilha do Cabo Frio, is considered one of Brazil's best beaches. It has dunes and crystal clear water. To get there you must obtain a free permit from the Navy (Marinha) office in Arraial do Cabo, then go to Praia dos Anjos from where fishermen will take you to Farol, about US$60 for nine people. You must arrange a pick-up time, take your own food and water and leave no rubbish behind. Included in the price can be a stop at the Gruta Azul, a cave carved in the rocks by the ocean. **Tourist information** is at Praça da Bandeira, T26205039. **Festivals** include 13 May, founding of the town and *Corpus Christi* in May/June.

Sleeping and eating A *Pousada Nautilus*, R Marcílio Dias 100, T26221611. Recommended. **B** *Orlamar*, Av Beiramar 111, Recanto da Prainha, T/F6222410. **B** *Pousada dos Atobás*, R José Pinto Macedo 270, T26222461. **Camping** *Camping Clube do Brasil*, Praia dos Anjos, T26221023. Crowded beach. For eating, try *Todos os Prazeres*, R José Pinto Macedo, T26222365.

Transport A very steep road connects the beaches of Itaipu and Itacoatiara with RJ-106 (and on to Bacaxá and Araruama) via the village of Itaipu-Açu. Most maps do not show a road beyond Itaipu-Açu; it is certainly too steep for buses. An alternative to the route from Niterói to Araruama through the lagoons is further inland than the RJ-106, via Manilha, Itaboraí and Rio Bonito on the BR-101 and RJ-124; this is a fruit-growing region. Bus Rio de Janeiro to Arraial do Cabo US$6.

Cabo Frio

This town, 168 km from Rio, is a popular holiday and weekend haunt of Cariocas because of its cool weather, white sand beaches and dunes, scenery, sailing and good underwater swimming (but mosquitoes are a problem).

Phone code: 024
Colour map 4, grid C4
Population: 127,000

History The navigator Americo Vespucci landed at Cabo Frio in 1503 and returned to Portugal with a boatload of *pau-brasil*. Since the wood in these parts was of better quality than that further north, the area became the target for loggers from France, the Netherlands and England. The Portuguese failed to capitalize on their colony here and it was the French who established the first defended settlement. Eventually the Portuguese took it by force but it was not until the second decade of the 17th century that they planned their own fortification, Forte São Mateus, which was started in 1616 on the foundations of the French fort. It is now a ruin at the mouth of the Canal de Itajuru.

Beaches The canal, which connects the Lagoa Araruama and the ocean, has a small headland at its mouth, which protects the nearest beach to the town, **Praia do Forte**. Backed by hotels, restaurants and bars, the water is calm and clear, the sand fine. The beach stretches south for about 7½ km to Arraial do Cabo, its name changing to **Praia das Dunas** and **Praia do Foguete**. These waters are much more suited to surfing. North of the canal entrance are the small, surfing **Praia Brava** (not too easy to get to, naturist beach) and the small, calm **Praia das Conchas**, which is ideal for watersports. Next is **Praia do Peró**, 7 km of sand on the open sea; it is used by surfers, fishermen and by sandboarders, who slide down the dunes on wooden boards. **Tourist information** Large orange building, Av Contorno 200, Praia do Forte, T26471689, www.cabofrio.tur.br

Sleeping **L** *La Plage*, R dos Badejos 40, Praia do Peró, T/F26435690. Close to the beach, with restaurant and pool. **A** *Pousada Portoveleiro*, Av dos Espadartes 129, T/F6473081. **B** *Pousada Suzy*, Av Júlia Kubitschek 48, conveniently located 100 m from the rodoviária, T26431742. **D** *Praia das Palmeiras*, Praia das Palmeiras 1, T/F26432866. **Youth hostel E** per person *Albergue da Juventude São Lucas*, R Goiás 266, Jardim Excelsior, 3 mins from the rodoviária, T26453037. IYHA. **Camping** *Camping Clube do Brasil*, Estr dos Passageiros 700, 2 km from town, T26433124; on the same road, at No 370 is *Camping da Estação*, T26431786. On Praia do Peró, *Dunas do Peró*, Estr do Guriri 1001, T26292323.

Reservations are necessary December-February

Eating **Mid-range**: *Picolino*, R Mcal FLoriano 319, T26432436. Serves good, local seafood with some international dishes in a pleasant setting. **Cheap**: *Do Zé*, on the canal quayside is a reliable option specializing in Brazilian food. In the centre, on Av Teixeira e Souza *Chico's* (No 30) and *Kilokura* (No 121) are a couple of self-service restaurants. **Seriously cheap**: Fast-food outlets can be found along the seafront (Av do Contorno) at Praia do Forte.

Festivals **29 Jun**: *São Pedro* (as above); **13 Nov**: founding of the town; **25 Dec**: patron saint's day, *Nossa Senhora da Assunção*.

Transport **Air** A new airport has opened linking the area with Belo Horizonte, Brasília, Rio de Janeiro, São Paulo. **Buses** The rodoviária is 2 km from the centre. Bus from Rio every 30 mins, 2½ hrs, US$8. To Búzios, from the local bus terminus in the town centre, every hr, US$1.

Directory **Banks** *Banco 24 Horas*, Av Assunção 925. *Bradesco*, Av Assunção 904. HSBC Av Assunção 793.

Rio de Janeiro

Búzios

Phone code: 024
Colour map 4, grid C4
Population: 18,000
(192 km to Rio
37 km to Arraial
do Cabo)

Some 25 km up the coast from Cabo Frio is the sophisticated yet informal Búzios. This charming seaside town (full name Armação de Búzios) is spread out with low-rise, attractive development. It is situated on a peninsula with more than enough beaches to choose from and is the perfect choice for those who want to enjoy the sun and the sea by day and, after dark, its internationally famous nightlife and gastronomy.

Originally a small fishing community, founded in 1740 when a trader called Braz de Pina started a whale fishery, Búzios remained virtually unknown until the 1950s when its natural beauty started to attract the Brazilian jet-set who turned the village into a fashionable summer resort. In 1964, Brigitte Bardot visited Búzios and the photos of her, walking barefoot along the beach, brought the focus of the world's press to this 'lost paradise in the tropics'. Soon many wealthy families, foreign tourists and the travel and leisure industry started to move to Búzios, building *pousadas* and restaurants as well as open-air cafés, bars, clubs, art galleries and boutiques. As many of these businesses are foreign-owned, English, French, German and Spanish are widely spoken (the resort is very popular with Argentinians).

Unless it is absolutely necessary, avoid visiting Búzios at Carnival, New Year's Eve and other main holidays. The city gets crowded, the price of food, accommodation and other services rises substantially and the long, stressful traffic jams on the roads will be an experience to be remembered forever.

During the daytime, the best option is to head for the beaches, of which there are 25. The most visited are **Geribá** (many bars and restaurants; popular with surfers), **Ferradura** (deep blue sea and calm waters), **Ossos** (the most famous and close to the centre), **Tartaruga** and **João Fernandes**. To help you to decide which beach suits you best, you can join one of the local two- or three-hour schooner trips which pass many of the beaches. These trips cost around US$10-15 and can be arranged through *Escuna Queen Lory*, T26231179.

Tourist offices *Manguinos*, T0800-249999, the main office (24-hour), on the western edge of the peninsula has lots of information and helpful staff, some of whom speak English. *Praça Santos Dumont*, T26232099, in the centre of town is more limited. For most of the hotels and services on the peninsula check **www.buzioturismo.com**

Sleeping

Prior reservations are needed in summer, during holidays such as Carnival and New Year's Eve, and at weekends. For cheaper options and better availability, try Cabo Frio

AL *Colonna Park*, Praia de João Fernandes, T26232245, colonna@colonna.com.br A high level of facilities, with a fantastic view of the sea, restaurant and pool. **AL** *Fazendinha Blancpain*, Estr Velha da Raza, T26236490, F26236420, a member of Roteiro de Charme group, see page 47. Lots of character and extras like horse riding and a nearby golf course. **AL** *La Mandrágora*, Av J B Ribeiro Dantas, Portal de Ferradura, T26231348. One of the most famous pousadas in Búzios, offering rooms or chalets. **A** *Pousada Hibiscus Beach*, R 1 No 22, Quadra C, Praia de João Fernandes, T26236221, www.hibiscusbeach.com.br A peaceful spot, run by its British owners, 15 pleasant bungalows, garden, pool, light meals available, help with car/buggy rentals and local excursions. **B** *Pousada dos Tangarás*, R dos Namorados 6, lote 4, Geribá, T26231275. Good. **B** *Pousada La Coloniale*, R das Pedras 52. Ideally located for nightlife, but you will hear all the noise of R das Pedras until the early hours. **B** *Saint Germain*, Altos do Humaitá 5, Praia da Armação, T2623 1044, www.buzioschannel.com.br/ saintgermain Includes breakfast, fully equipped, 150 m from beach, family run, English, Italian, Spanish and Scandinavian languages spoken, discount for *Handbook* owners. **D** *Brigitta's Guest House*, Rua das Pedras 131, T/F26236157, brigittas@mar.com.br Beautifully decorated little *pousada* with just 4 rooms on the main street of R das

Rio de Janeiro

Pedras. It's delightful restaurant, bar and tea house overlooking the water are worth a visit. **D** *Casa da Ruth*, R dos Gravatás, Geribá, T26232242. **D** *Pousada Axé*, R do Sossego 200, T2623 2008. Includes breakfast, a/c, TV, fridge, helpful, good value, pool. **Youth hostel E** *Praia dos Amores*, Av José Bento Ribeiro Dantas 92, T26232422. IYHA, not far from the bus station. Recommended. Several private houses rent rooms, especially in summer and holidays. Look for the signs: 'Alugo Quartos'.

Expensive: *Estância Don Juan*, R das Pedras, 178, Centro. Excellent grill and restaurant specializing in Argentinian steaks, popular with locals. *Moqueca Capixaba*, R Manoel de Carvalho 116, Centro. Brazilian seafood. **Mid-range**: *Chez Michou*, R das Pedras, 90, Centro. An open-air bar with videos and music, dozens of choices of pancakes accompanied by ice cold beer. Always crowded. *Satryicon*, Av J B Ribeiro Dantas 412, T26231595. Excellent Italian. **Cheap**: *Bob's*, R das Pedras opposite *Shopping One* for hamburgers and chips to take away from this national chain. *Skipper*, Av J B Ribeiro Dantas 392, Praia do Canto. Pizza House. **Seriously cheap**: A few places on *Praça Santos Dumont* off Rua das Pedras offer sandwiches and self-service food, including the homely *La Prima* on Av Manuel Turibo de Farias which doubles as a bakery. There's a small supermarket a couple of doors away.

Eating
Restaurants on R das Pedras tend to be expensive; explore the surrounding streets for cheaper options

A must in Búzios. All you have to do is walk along the R das Pedras (Stone St, as it is paved with irregular, huge blocks of stone). Here is the best choice of restaurants, cafés, art galleries and bars. Crowded at weekends and holidays, especially after 2300. Good options are: *Zapata Mexican Bar*, R das Pedras. A Mexican theme bar and restaurant that serves as the only disco in town. *Ta-ka-ta ka-ta*, R das Pedras 256. One of the craziest bars in Búzios; weird decoration, owned by a foreigner who obstinately refuses to say where he comes from, but who can speak fluent Portuguese, Spanish, English, German and Dutch, worth a visit.

Nightlife

Malizia, R das Pedras, T26232022. Money exchange, car hire and other tourist services. *Mister Tours*, R Germiniano J Luis, 3, Centro, T26232100.

Tour operators

Road By car via BR-106 takes about 2½ hrs from Rio. **Buses**: from Rio's Rodoviária Novo Rio, go to the 1001 counter T00XX21-25161001. Rio-Búzios US$8, 2½ hrs (be at the bus terminal 20 mins before departure). 4 departures daily 0815 from Rio a/c, 1300 from Búzios a/c. You can also take any busto Cabo Frio (many more during the day), from where it's 30 mins to Búzios and vice versa. Buying the ticket in advance is only recommended on major holidays. The Búzios rodoviária is a few blocks' walk from the

Transport

Rio de Janeiro (margin sidebar)

centre. Some *pousadas* are within 10 mins on foot, eg La Coloniale and Brigitta's, while others need a local bus (US$0.50) or taxi. The buses from Cabo Frio run the length of the peninsula and pass several *pousadas*.

Directory   **Banks** *Banco do Brasil*, R Manuel de Carvalho 70, Centro, T25232302. **Communications** Internet: *buzios@internet*, Av J B Ribeiro Dantas, 97, close to *Shopping One* US$1.20 per ½ hr. **Hospitals** Public: *Posto Municipal de Saúde de Manguinhos*, Av J B Ribeiro Dantas, Manguinhos, T192. Private: *Clínica Búzios*, Av J B Ribeiro Dantas 3000, Manguinhos, T26232465.

Macaé

Phone code: 024
Colour map 4, grid C4
Population: 120,500

Further north, is Barra de São João, **Rio das Ostras** and Macaé. These beaches are at the northern end of the Costa do Sol, all containing sheltered coves with good swimming and scuba diving.

Macaé is the supply centre for the offshore oil industry but is attempting to develop tourism as well. There are good views from the **Igreja de Santana** on Morro de Santana, 2 km away. Cavaleiros beach is good for surfing and has many bars and restaurants. **Tourist information** *Macaé Tur*, is on Av Rui Barbosa 780, 2nd floor, T27628456, www.macaetur.com

Sleeping   **Macaé A** *Colonial*, Av Elias Agostinho 140, Praia de Imbetiba, T/F27225155. Helpful, comfortable. **A** *Ouro Negro*, Av Pres Sodré 466, Praia do Forte, T27723305. **A** *Panorama*, Av Elias Agostinho 290, T/F27724455. **C** *Central*, R Rui Barbosa. Nice, good breakfast, secure parking. **Rio das Ostras A** *Pousada do Wagner*, R Nova Iguaçu 1199, Costa Azul, T27641889, F27641973. **B** *Hotel Mirante do Poeta*, T2641910. **Camping** *Costazul*, Av Heleno Nunes, Costa Azul, T27641389.

Eating   **Macaé Mid-range**: *Albatroz*, Av Atlântica 2374, Praia dos Cavaleiros. Seafood. **Cheap**: *Xandoca's Bar*, R Col José de Lima 365. Seafood. **Rio das Ostras Mid-range**: *Bar da Boca*, R Teresópolis 69, Praia Boca da Barra. Seafood.

Transport   **Macaé Air**: air taxis with *Líder*, T27723202, and *Aeróleo*, T27725995. **Bus**: Bus station, Av Ver Abreu Lima, T27724500. To **Rio de Janeiro** 2½-3 hrs, every 30 mins, *Mil e Um* or *Rápido Macaense*. To **Campos**, 1¾ hrs, US$4.

Directory   **Banks** *Bradesco*, Av Rui Barbosa 614, Macaé. **Medical services** *Casa de Caridade*, Praça Veríssimo de Melo 391, Macaé T27721005.

North to Espírito Santo

From Rio and Niterói, the BR-101 runs northeast past Campos and the border with Espírito Santo. There are many *fazenda* hotels in the area of **Rio Bonito**, 64 km from Niterói, including *Fazenda Pedras Negras* (**AL**), BR-101 Km 257, T/F27340425 and *Fazenda Serra dos Cambê* (**B**), BR101 Km 265, T27340027.

See also box opposite

At Km 222 is the **Biological Reserve of Poço das Antas**, the only natural habitat of the *mico-leão*, Golden Lion Tamarin (two hours' drive from Rio); it is not open to the general public. ■ *Contact Ibama, Av Pres Antônio Carlos 607-12°, CEP 20000, Rio de Janeiro.*

The golden lion tamarin

The tamarin, or mico-leão in Portuguese, is a small mammal, about the size of a squirrel, which lives off fruit, flowers, tender vegetation and insects. In Brazil there are three species of tamarin, all under threat of extinction: the golden lion tamarin; the black lion tamarin; and the golden-headed lion tamarin. The main problem for the tamarins is that their habitat, the mata atlântica of São Paulo, Rio de Janeiro, Espírito Santo and Bahia, has all but been destroyed and there has been further threat from predation by man.

These engaging creatures are quite beautiful, so much so that they were popular pets with European royalty in the 17th and 18th centuries. The golden lion tamarin, with its face surrounded by a bright, silky mane, was considered the most beautiful. It has been described as having a coat that "shines like gold dust in the light." And thereby hangs another of the animal's problems; its attractiveness made it a prize pet for non-royal collectors and demand in the trade soon contributed to the golden lion tamarin's dwindling numbers. By the 1970s it seemed a foregone conclusion that the golden lion tamarin and its Brazilian relatives were doomed to extinction.

Fortunately, the Golden Lion Tamarin Conservation Project, set up in 1983 at the Poço das Antas Biological Reserve (which was created in 1974), has been successful in breeding tamarins in captivity and returning them to the wild. Around the world, zoos have been helping with the
breeding programme. In 1997, a WWF estimate for the number of golden lion tamarins living in the wild in Poço das Antas was put at 800, but other figures suggest 550 (some even as low as 150). Whatever the number, the severest test for the survival of the species is the creation of more forest in which the tamarins can live. Corridors of suitable vegetation have to be set up so that the tamarins can move about safely and breed freely in their natural surroundings. This goal was undermined during the drought of 1997 which led to an increase in forest fires in Brazil (the majority started by man), posing a renewed threat to the tamarin's habitat. So the mico-leão-dourado's future is by no means secured; despite this, the animal has become a symbol of hope for forest conservation throughout Brazil. Many Brazilian and international agencies and specialist centres have contributed to its survival, but as with all such projects, the work never stops.

Besides the mico-leão-dourado *population at Poço das Antas, there is a conservation project for the* mico-leão-da cara-dourada *at Una in Bahia, and the* mico-leão-preto *can be seen near Praia do Forte, north of Salvador.*

Sources *WWF Update (World Wide Fund for Nature), Summer 1997, website www.wwf-uk.org; in the UK T01483 426444, F01483 426409, or contact your local office. Marya Rowan, 'Breeds Apart',* South American Explorer *(25 May 1990), pages 32-3.* Wildlife Fact File, *International Masters Publishers Ltd (London), #120.*

Rio de Janeiro

Campos

Campos (dos Goitacazes – after the Indian tribe which used to inhabit the area) is a busy industrial city, 276 km from Rio de Janeiro and 70 km from Macaé. It stands 56 km from the mouth of the Rio Paraíba, up which coffee planting originally spread to São Paulo state. Coffee is still grown near Campos, but the region has always been one of the largest sugar-producing zones in Brazil.

Phone code: 024
Colour map 4, grid C4
Population: 390,500

In the 1970s Brazil's answer to rocketing oil prices was the conversion of sugar into alcohol fuel for cars, where Campos became one of the major centres for this industry. Subsequently, important offshore oil and gas discoveries have been made nearby. On a historical note, this was the first Brazilian city to install electric lighting, inaugurated in 1883.

Beaches   The sea can be reached by road to São João da Barra (41 km), then a further 4 km to Atafona, at the mouth of the Rio Paraíba do Sul. The outflow of the river here pollutes the beach, but if you go further south to **Grussaí** or **Açu**, the sea is mostly OK. Further south still are beaches around **Farol de São Tomé**, **Barra do Furrado** and **Quissamã**. North of the Rio Paraíba are several beaches in the vicinity of **São Francisco** and **Itabapoana**.

Sleeping   **A** *Antares*, R Vig João Carlos 19, T27334055. **B** *Palace*, Av 15 de Novembro 143,
& eating   T27332277. **B** *Terrazo Tourist*, Joaquim Távora 22, T27331405. 2-star. **C** *Planície*, R 13 de Maio 56, T27234455. For eating, try *Kantão do Líbano*, Av Pelinca 101. Arabic. *Picanha Grill*, in Shopping Estrada, Av Nilo Peçanha 614. Churrasco.

Festivals   **28 Mar**: founding of the city; **May/Jun**: *Corpus Christi*; **29 Jun**: *São Pedro* (as above); **6 Aug**: patron saint's day, *Santíssimo Salvador*.

Transport   **Air**   Airport, BR-101, Km 5, T27330144. Flights to **Rio de Janeiro. Buses**   Bus station, BR 101, T27331001. To **Rio de Janeiro** (*Mil e Um, 1001*), hourly, 4 hrs, US$10.

Directory   **Banks**   *Banco 24 Horas*, Parque Centro Shopping, Av Pelinca 116. *Bradesco*, Blvd Francisco P. Carneiro 28. **Medical services**   *Beneficência Portuguesa*, R Barão de Miracema 142, T27330055.

Santo Antônio   As an alternative to taking the BR-101 to Vitória, one can take a detour inland,
de Pádua   going through São Fidélis, Cambiasca, Itoacara and on to Santo Antônio de
Phone code: 024   Pádua, 106 km from Campos, a pleasant town on the Rio Pomba. Canoeing is
Population: 36,000   popular in this area due to the large number of rapids. The **hydromineral spring** at Avenida Dr Themístocles de Almeida is unique for the chemical composition of its waters. ■ *0700-1100, 1300-1600 Mon-Fri, 0700-1100 Sat.* **Sleeping**   A short walk from the centre of Santo Antônio de Pádua is **C** *Hotel das Águas*, Rua Luís da Silva Magacho 170, T38510805. It is set in a park and associated with the health centre and bottling plant for the local mineral water. The bus station is at Rua José de Alencar Leite, T38510823.

Inland resorts

The three mountain resorts of Petrópolis, Teresópolis and Nova Friburgo are set high in the scenic Serra do Mar behind Rio. The Imperial city of Petrópolis boasts perhaps Brazil's finest museum and history on almost every corner. All three are lovely mountain retreats with accommodation in charming *fazendas*. This is a beautiful area that is becoming increasingly popular for walking, as well as horse riding and other activities.

These resorts became established originally because the cool mountain air offered an escape from the heat of Rio and meant a lack of yellow fever and other diseases which festered in the unhealthy port on the bay in the 19th century. Also, they provided the routes which brought first gold, then coffee from the interior to the coast.

Petrópolis

Phone code: 024   Standing at 809 m in the Serra da Estrela range of mountains in the Serra do
Colour map 4, grid C3   Mar, Petrópolis is reached by bus along a steep, scenic mountain road 68 km
Population: 290,000   north of Rio. For about 80 years this Imperial city was the 'summer capital' of

Brazil. Now it combines manufacturing industry (particularly textiles) and tourism with floral beauty and hill scenery. The town, with its distinctly European feel, is said by some to be one of the gastonomic centres of Brazil.

The pleasant **climate** which attracted the Imperial family has an average high temperature of 23°C and a low of 14°C. The warmest months are September to December. The wettest months are January-March, although it can start getting wet in November and rain can be expected at any time. It can get chilly at night all year round, but especially in winter. A unique climatic feature of the area is a dense fog, called *o ruço*, which usually forms in the late afternoon. While this can be atmospheric, it can also be dangerous for drivers as the fog can descend very quickly.

Tourist information *Petrotur*, in the Prefeitura de Petrópolis, at the rear of the Casa do Barão de Mauá, address: Praça da Confluência 03, T22433561, F2420639. It has a list of tourist sites and of hotels and a good, free coloured map of the city. Petrotur is open Monday-Friday 0900-1830, closed Saturday and Sunday. The tourist kiosk on Praça Dom Pedro II is open Monday-Saturday 0900-1800, Sunday and holidays 0900-1700.

History

Because the emperor Pedro I abdicated in 1831, he never realized his dream of building a summer palace in the Serra. Córrego Seco was rented out, lastly to Júlio Frederico Koeler, a German engineer who worked on the construction of a road to Minas Gerais. Koeler proposed the colonization of Córrego Seco by Germans. When the new emperor, Dom Pedro II, approved this plan in 1843, he stipulated that a summer palace should be built in addition to a town and the settlement scheme. Petrópolis dates its founding from 1843 and in little over a decade had become an important place. Once the Imperial palace was built, the emperor and his family began to spend six months of each year there (November-April). His court had to accompany him, so other fine residences sprang up in the city that Koeler had designed.

Petrópolis

To Pousada da Alcobaça, Orquidário Binot, Itaipava, Teresópolis & Minas Gerais

To Palácio de Quitandinha, Parque Cremerie, Museu das Armas & Rio de Janeiro

■ Sleeping	5 Comércio	● Eating
1 Bragança Palace	6 Margaridas	1 Cantina Bom Giovanni
2 Casablanca	7 Pousada dos	2 Casa d'Ângelo
3 Casablanca Center	Pássaros	3 Falconi
4 Casablanca Palace	8 York	

0 metres 200
0 yards 200

In April 1854, Brazil's first railway line was opened, from Porto Mauá on Guanabara Bay to Raiz da Serra, which greatly shortened the journey time between Rio and Petrópolis. By the 1880s the railway had crossed the mountains to Petrópolis itself. So by the time the Republic was proclaimed in 1889, Petrópolis was administrative capital of the country for half the year, an intellectual centre for the same months, had its own commercial importance and was directly connected to Brazil's rapidly growing transport links.

In the early 20th century it became the official summer seat of the president of the republic (the residence being the Palácio Rio Negro). In the 1940s it had a brief flirtation with gambling, when the *Hotel e Cassino Quitandinha* attracted Hollywood stars like Bing Crosby and other members of the international jet set until the banning of gaming in 1946. Since then, the city has thrived industrially and, most recently, in tourism.

Sights   Three rivers are dominant features in the design of Petrópolis: the Piabanha, Quitandinha and Palatino. In the historic centre (Centro Histórico), where most of the sites of tourist interest are to be found, the rivers have been channelled to run down the middle of the main avenues. Their banks, especially the Quitandinha, are planted with fine trees and flowers and the overall aspect is completely different from elsewhere in Brazil. You quickly get a sense that this was a city built with a specific purpose and at a specific time in Brazil's history.

The **Museu Imperial** (Imperial Palace) Brazil's most visited museum, is so well kept you might think the Imperial family had left the day before, rather than in 1889. The modest but elegant building, neoclassical in style, is fully furnished, but it's worth a visit just to see the Crown Jewels of both Pedro I and Pedro II. In the palace gardens is a pretty French-style tearoom, the *Petit Palais*. Descendants of the original family live in a house behind the palace. Horse-drawn carriages wait to be hired outside the gate (not all the horses are in good shape). ■ *1100 Tue-Sun, last entry 1700, US$2 (you pay at a small kiosk outside the entrance, then queue to deposit any bags and be admitted. On Sun during Easter and high season, expect long queues. R da Imperatriz 220, T22378000.*

The Gothic-style **Catedral de São Pedro de Alcântara**, completed in 1925, contains the tombs of the Emperor and Empress. The Imperial Chapel is to the right of the entrance. ■ *0800-1200, 1400-1800 Tue-Sat* .

The summer home of air pioneer **Alberto Santos Dumont** who was responsible for the first powered flight in Europe, is at Rua do Encanto 22. The small house was designed in 1918 as a mock Alpine-chalet. Santos Dumont called it 'the enchanted one', and it is a delightful example of an inventor's house. Steps to the roof lead to an observation point, a desk doubled as his bed and the alcohol-heated shower is said to be the first in Brazil. ■ *0900-1700 Tue-Sun. US$1.*

The **Palácio de Cristal** in Praça da Confluência was designed in the same style as several similar crystal palaces in Europe. This one was built in France in 1879, with the original intention of being an exhibition hall for local products, but became the Imperial ballroom, and is now sadly empty.

The exteriors of fine mansions built by the aristocracy of both the Imperial and republican eras can be seen on Avenida Koeler and Avenida Ipiranga. Among them are the neoclassical **Palácio Rio Negro** – the summer palace of the current President – and the **Palácio da Princesa Isabel** at Avenida Koeler 255 and 42 respectively and the Casa de Rui Barbosa, in the eclectic style, at Avenida Ipiranga 405. Another palace is the mid-19th-century Casa do Barão do Rio Branco, Avenida Barão do Rio Branco 279. It was here that the Treaty of Petrópolis was signed, settling with Bolivia the issue of the annexation of Acre (1903). None of these houses are open to the public, but **Casa de Petrópolis** –

Instituto de Cultura (Cultural Centre) R Ipiranga 716, T22372133, has recently thrown open its doors to visitors and is not to be missed. The completely original, over-the-top interior has been lovingly restored by family members and impressive art exhibitions and classical concerts take place. A charming restaurant in the old stables is worth a stop for coffee, if not for lunch. ■ *1100-1900 Tue-Sun, 1100-1300 Sat. US$2, US$1.20 when no exhibition.*

The twin praças of dos Expedicionários and Dom Pedro II (in which there is a tourist kiosk) are at the junction of Rua do Imperador and Rua da Imperatriz. A short distance up Rua da Imperatriz, on the same side as Praça Dom Pedro II, is the **Praça Visconde de Mauá**, in which is a statue of an eagle and a snake. On one side of the praça is the Palácio Amarelo (1850), now the Câmara Municipal, and on another the modern Palácio da Cultura. On Sundays in the square is a small antiques market. **Praça da Liberdade** (formerly known as Praça Rui Barbosa) is very busy on Sunday, with goat-drawn carriages for children and occasional open-air concerts.

Parks & praças

Southwest of the centre is the **Museu Casa do Colono**, Rua Cristóvão Colombo 1034, Castelânea, with exhibits on the way of life of the early German colonists. ■ *0930-1730 Tue-Sun. T22313011.* US$1.20. Also southwest is the **Parque Cremerie** and the **Palácio Quitandinha**, Avenida Estados Unidos 2, T421012. This vast, grandiose palace, built in 1944 as a casino and hotel, is now a tourist centre that holds events. ■ *0900-1700 Tue-Sun.* The lake in front of the building is in the shape of South America.

Excursions

    The Avenida Barão do Rio Branco, which heads north out of the city, passes the turning to the **Orquidário Binot**, Rua Fernandes Vieira 390. This has a huge collection of orchids from all over Brazil (plants may be purchased). ■ *0800-1100, 1315-1630 Mon-Fri, 0700-1100 Sat. T22420833. Take bus to Vila Isabel.* Continuing north, the road becomes the Estrada União-Indústria, going through Corrêas, the district in which is the Casa do Padre Correia (see History, above); it is not open to the public. Further out is **Itaipava**, about 20 km from Petrópolis, near where this road joins the BR-040 highway to Belo Horizonte and at the junction of the road to Teresópolis. This district is rapidly becoming a popular centre for eating, shopping and nightlife for Cariocas. There are outlets and boutiques for the local textile industry, a *feira* every Wednesday and Friday night and at weekends, a wide variety of good restaurants and several good, distinctly upmarket *pousadas*. For example, *Pousada Capim Santo*, a Roteiro de Charme hotel, 2 km on the road to Teresópolis.

In the Roteiros de Charme group (see page 47) is **L** *Pousada da Alcobaça*, R Agostinho Goulão 298, Correas, T22211240, F2223162. Delightful, family-run large country house set in flower-filled gardens leading down to a river, with pool and sauna. Worth stopping by for tea on the terrace, or for dinner at the restaurant. Recommended. **A** *Margaridas*, R Bispo Dom José Pereira Alves 235, Trono de Fátima, T22424686. A chalet-type hotel set in lovely gardens with a swimming pool, charming proprietors. **A** *Riverside Parque*, R Hermogéneo Silva 522, Retiro, 5 mins from the centre, with a helpful owner who can arrange tours in surrounding countryside, T0800-248011/ 22310730, F22432312. Of the 3 traditional, if somewhat faded *Casablanca* hotels **A** *Casablanca*, R da Imperatriz 286, T2426662, F2425946, is the most atmospheric and upmarket, conveniently situated next to the Museu Imperial, pool; **B** *Casablanca Center*, Gen Osório 28, T22422612, F22426298; and **B** *Casablanca Palace*, R 16 de Março 123, T22420162, F22425946. **B** *York*, R do Imperador 78, a short walk from the Rodoviária, T22433662, F22428220. Convenient, helpful, the fruit and milk at breakfast come from the owners' own farm.

Sleeping
■ *on map, page 141*
 Price codes:
see inside front cover

Good, budget accommodation is hard to come by, but bargaining is possible Monday-Friday

Rio de Janeiro

Recommended. **C** *Comércio*, R Dr Porciúncula 55, opposite Rodoviária, T22423500. One of the cheapest options. Very basic with shared bath.

On R Raul de Leoni (the continuation of R da Imperatriz) are: **A** *Pousada dos Pássaros* (**C** Mon-Fri); and almost opposite, at No 109, *Bragança Palace*, T22420434, F22435276.

Camping   *Associação Brasileira de Camping and YMCA*, Araras district. Space can be reserved through Rio YMCA, T021-2319860.

Eating
● *on map, page 141*

Mid-range: *Falconi*, R do Imperador 757, T22421252. A traditional restaurant with rustic elegance that has been serving Italian food since 1914. Good value, with pasta and pizza for US$3. Recommended. **Cheap**: *Cantina Bom Giovanni*, R do Imperador 729, T22425588. A 1st-floor simple, canteen-style Italian restaurant that is justifiably popular for self-service lunch and dinner. *Casa d'Ángelo*, R do Imperador 700, by Praça Dom Pedro II is a traditional, long-standing tea house with self service food that doubles as a bar at night. *Pavelka*, Rod Washington Luiz, T2242 7990, daily 0800-2100 (to 0200 Fri) (see below under Shopping). German, Austrian and Czech specialities, lovingly prepared on the premises. Recommended. **Seriously cheap**: Fast-food outlets, *pastel* shops and *lanchonetes* are all found around this square.

Pavelka, Rod Washington Luiz, T22427990, daily 0800-2100 (to 0200 Fri). On the mountain road from Rio, just before the entrance to the city, is this family-run café/deli. Locals in the know stock up with German, Austrian and Czech specialities such as sausages and trout smoked on the premises and tuck into the éclairs and mille-feuilles fresh from the bakery.

Tour operators

Coopetur offers horse riding, trekking (including a 3-day mountain trek to Teresópolis), whitewater rafting and a range of trips into the scenic mountain area as well as cultural tours around the city with enthusiastic, multi-lingual guides. Warmly recommended. R 16 de Março 155, Centro. T/F22318498, www.coopetur.com.br There are also possibilities for climbing and cycling in the vicinity.

Festivals

Petrópolis celebrates its foundation on **16 Mar**. Its patron saint's day, *São Pedro de Alcântara*, is **29 Jun**. Bohemia, Brazil's oldest beer, dates from 1853. It was originally brewed in the city, and although production has now been moved to Rio, the **Bohemia Beer Festival** is still held in Jun.

Shopping

R Teresa, southeast of the centre, is where the textile industry exhibits its wares. In common with Itaipava (see above), it draws buyers from all over the country and is a good place to find good quality knitwear and bargain clothes. Closed Mon morning and Sun.

Transport

Buses   From **Rio** every 15 mins throughout the day (US$3) with *Única Fácil*, Sun every hr, 1½ hrs, sit on the left hand side for best views. Return tickets are not available, so buy tickets for the return on arrival in Petrópolis. The ordinary buses leave from the rodoviária in Rio; a/c buses, hourly from 1100, from Av Nilo Peçanha, US$4. Bus to **Niterói**, US$4.50; to **Cabo Frio**, US$10. To **Teresópolis**, *Viação Teresópolis*, 8 a day, US$3. *Salutário* to **São Paulo** daily at 2330.

Directory

Banks   *Banco do Brasil*, R Paulo Barbosa 81. A *Banco 24 Horas* ATM is located by the Varig office at R Mcal Deodoro 98. Travel agencies with exchange: *BKR*, R Gen Osório 12, *Goldman*, R Barão de Amazonas 46 (between Praça da Liberdade and the Universidade) and *Vert Tur*, R 16 de Março 244, from 1000-1630. **Communications**   Internet: Compuland in R do Imperador opposite Praça Dr Sá Earo, US$1.50 per hr. Post office: R do Imperador 350 in the Palácio dos Correios. Telephones: R Mcal Deodoro, just above Praça Dr Nelson de Sá Earp, no fax.

Teresópolis

At 910 m this is the highest city in the state of Rio de Janeiro. It is named after Empress Teresa Cristina, for whom it was her favourite summer residence. Building in recent years has destroyed some of the city's character, but most visitors do not go only to see the town. Its location, at the foot of the Serra dos Órgãos, with the associated outdoor activities, is an essential part of its charm. **Tourist offices** *Secretaria de Turismo*, Praça Olímpica, T27423352, ext 2082; *Terminal Turístico Tancredo Neves*, Av Rotariana at the entrance to town from Rio, T27423352, ext 2106.

Phone code: 021
Colour map 4, grid C3
Population: 140,000

History

Because of its height above sea level and the relatively low temperatures, the area was not exploited by the early colonists since they could not grow the tropical crops which were in demand in Europe. The existence of *fazendas* in the region was first documented in the early-19th century, the best known being that belonging to an Englishman, George March. To accommodate a constant stream of visitors, March added lodgings to his farm and, not long after, other landowners followed suit. Before taking the name of the Empress, the parish was called Santo Antônio de Paquequer.

Sights

The **Colina dos Mirantes** hill is a 30-minute steep climb from Rua Jaguaribe (2 km from the centre; an inexpensive taxi ride), with sweeping views of the city and surroundings. Around the town are various attractions, such as the Sloper and Iaci lakes, the Imbui and Amores waterfalls and the Fonte Judith, which has mineral-rich water, access from Avenida Oliveira Botelho, 4 km southwest. Just off the road to Petrópolis is the **Orquidário Aranda**, Alameda Francisco Smolka, T27420628, 5 km from the centre.

The road to Nova Friburgo (see below) is known as the Vale das Hortaliças because it passes through a zone where vegetables and some flowers are cultivated. There is a rock formation called A Mulher de Pedra, 12 km out of Teresópolis on this road.

Sleeping

L *Fazenda Rosa dos Ventos*, Km 22 on the road to Nova Friburgo, T27428833. In the Roteiros de Charme group (see page 47). **A** *Alpina*, Av Pres Roosevelt 2500, Parque Imbui, on Petrópolis Rd, T/F27425252. **A** *Fazenda Montebello*, at Km 17 on the same road, T/F26446313. A modern hotel with pool, price includes 3 meals. Recommended. **C** *Várzea Palace*, R Sebastião Teixeira 41, T27420878. Highly recommended. Many cheap hotels in R Delfim Moreira, near the praça.

Youth hostel *Retiro da Inglesa*, 20 km on road to Nova Friburgo, Fazenda Boa Esperança, in the beautiful Vale dos Frades, T27423109. Book in advance in Jan-Feb, dormitory accommodation and family rooms, camping beside the hostel. **Camping** *Quinta de Barra*, R Antônio Maria 100, Km 3 on Petrópolis Rd, T26431050.

Eating

Expensive: *Da Irene*, R Tte Luís Meireles 1800, T27422901. Russian. Reservations necessary. **Mid-range**: *Taberna Alpina*, Duque de Caxias 131, German cuisine. *Bar Gota d'Água*, Praça Baltasar da Silveira 16, for trout or *feijoada* (small but recommended) and for *batidas*. **Cheap**: Cafetería in the *ABC supermarket*. Recommended.

Festivals

13 Jun, patron saint's day, *Santo Antônio*; 29 Jun, *São Pedro* is celebrated with fireworks. 7 Jul is the anniversary of the city's foundation. A 2nd saint's day is *Santa Terezinha*, 15 Oct. In May there is *Festa das Colônias*.

Rio de Janeiro

Transport **Buses Rio-Teresópolis**: buses leave every 30 mins from the Novo Rio rodoviária. Book the return journey as soon as you arrive at Teresópolis; rodoviária at R 1 de Maio 100. Fare US$3.60. From Teresópolis to Petropólis, 8 a day, US$3.

Directory **Banks** Cash or TCs at *Teretur*, Trav Portugal 46. English spoken. **Communications** Internet: *Cott@ge Cybercafe*, R Alfredo Rebello Filho 996, 2nd floor. US$3 per hr.

Serra dos Órgãos

Some 11,000 ha of the Serra dos Órgãos, so called because their strange shapes are said to recall organ-pipes, are a national park (created in 1939, the second oldest in the country). The main attraction is the precipitous peak Dedo de Deus ('God's Finger' – 1,692 m). The highest point is Pedra do Sino ('Bell Rock' – 2,263 m), up which winds a 14-km path, a climb of 3-4 hours. The west face of this mountain is one of the hardest climbing pitches in Brazil. Another well-known peak is the Pedra do Açu (2,245 m – the name is a Tupi word meaning 'large'). Many others have names evocative of their shape: for example, O Escalavrado ('The Scarred One'), O Dedo de Nossa Senhora ('Our Lady's Finger'), A Cabeça de Peixe ('Fish Head'), A Agulha do Diabo ('The Devil's Needle') and A Verruga do Frade ('The Friar's Wart'). Near the Sub-Sede (see below) is the **Von Martius** natural history museum, named after a German naturalist, Karl Friedrich Philipp Von Martius (1794-1868), who visited Brazil in 1817-20. ■ *0800-1700*.

Flora & fauna The park belongs to the Mata Atlântica ecosystem which, as frequently mentioned, is seriously threatened. There are 20-30 m high trees, such as paineiras (floss-silk tree), ipês and cedros, rising above palms, bamboos and other smaller trees. Flowers include begonias, bromeliads, orchids and quaresmeiras (glorybushes). The park is the home of the very rare and

Serra dos Órgãos

endemic grey-winged cotinga, as well as a number of other cotingas, berryeaters and other rare endemic birds. Less rare birds include hummingbirds, guans, araçaris and tinamous. Mammals include some species of monkey, wild cat, deer, armadillo, agouti and peccary. There are also a number of frogs and toads, including the *sapo-pulga* (the flea-toad, at 10 mm claimed by local literature to be the smallest amphibian in the world; although other sources say that the Cuban pygmy frog is the smallest).

The park has 2 dependencies, both accessible from the BR-116: the Sede (headquarters, T/F26421070) is closer to Teresópolis (from town take Avenida Rotariana), while the Sub-Sede is just outside the park proper, off the BR-116. By the Sede entrance is the Mirante do Soberbo, with views to the Baía de Guanabara. Anyone can enter the park and hike the trails from the Teresópolis gate, but if you intend to climb the Pedra do Sino, you must sign a register (those under 18 must be accompanied by an adult and have authorization from the park authorities). Entrance to the park is US$1, with an extra charge for the path to the top of the Pedra do Sino. For information from **Ibama** for the state of Rio de Janeiro, T0XX21-22311772.

Park essentials
A good way to see the park is to do the Rio-Teresópolis-Petrópolis-Rio circuit; a scenic day trip by car. It can also be hiked in two or three days (take a tent)

Ibama has some hostels, US$5 full board, or US$3 1st night, US$2 thereafter, a bit rough. At the Petrópolis side of the park, **A** *Campo de Aventuras Paraíso Açu*, Estr do Bonfim 3511, T0XX24-21426275, or T0XX21-29733618. Has various types of accommodation, from rooms to chalet, and specializes in adventure sports (credit cards not accepted); on the same road, at Km 3.5 and in the same price range, is *Cabanas Açu*, T0XX21-29835041, inside the Park, cabins, restaurant, sports include riding, canoeing and fishing (credit cards accepted). **Camping** 2 sites in the Sub-Sede part, 1 close to the Museum, the other not far from the natural swimming pool at Poço da Ponte Velha; 1 site in the Sede part. The Sede has a restaurant and the Sub-Sede a *lanchonete*.

Sleeping & eating

Swimming At both the Sede and Sub-Sede there are natural swimming pools, although between May and Oct the temperature may be a little too chilly for bathing. In the Sub-Sede they are called Poço Verde, Poço da Preguiça and Ponte Velha. It is possible to trek right through the park, from Teresópolis to Petrópolis, a distance of 42 km, but it is essential to take a guide; contact *Campo de Aventuras Paraíso Açu* (see Sleeping above).

Sport
The Serra dos Órgãos is considered Brazil's climbing capital and the park is also good for trekking

Tours of the park are offered by Francisco of *Lazer Tours*; T27427616, or find him at the grocery shop on R Sloper 1. Recommended. *Focus Tours* (see page 23) offer bird-watching tours.

Tour operators

Nova Friburgo

This town, standing at 846 m in a beautiful valley with excellent walking and riding, is a popular resort during the summer months. It was founded by Swiss settlers from Fribourg, the first families arriving in 1820. Apart from tourism, Nova Friburgo has an important textile industry, specializing in lingerie, and also produces cheeses, preserves, sweets and liqueurs. **Tourist information** *Centro de Turismo*, Praça Demerval Barbosa Moreira, T25238000, ext 236.

Phone code: 024
Colour map 4, grid C3
Population: 175,000

A cable car from Praça dos Suspiros goes 650 m up the **Morro da Cruz**, for a magnificent view of the rugged country (US$5). Most of the interesting sites are in the surrounding countryside, so a car may be necessary to see everything. About 10 km northeast are the **Furnas do Catete**, an area of forest,

Sights

Rio de Janeiro

caves, waterfalls and rock formations, one of which is called the Pedra do Cão Sentado ('The Seated Dog'); there is a small entry fee. Other natural attractions are the Pico da Caledônia (2,310 m) 15 km southwest, and the Véu de Noiva waterfall, 9 km north. The district of **Lumiar**, 34 km southeast, has beautiful scenery, waterfalls, natural swimming pools and good canoeing in the Rios Macaé and Bonito. These two rivers meet at a point called Poço do Alemão, or Poço Verde, 4½ km south of Lumiar.

Sleeping   **AL** *Bucsky*, 5 km out on the Niterói Rd, T25225052. With meals, tours and guided walks available. **AL** *Pousada do Riacho*, Estr Nova Friburgo Km 8, Cardinot, T25222823, riacho@openlink.com.br A Roteiro de Charme hotel (see page 47). **A** *Garlipp*, at Muri, 8 km south, Km 70.5 from Rio, T/F25421173. German-run, in chalets, with meals. **A** *Fazenda São João*, 11 km from *Garlipp* (under the same ownership) up a side road, T25421304. Riding, swimming, sauna, tennis, hummingbirds and orchids. The owner will meet guests in Nova Friburgo or even in Rio. **B** *Fabris*, Av Alberto Browne 148, T25222852. Central, TV, hot showers, plentiful breakfast buffet. **B** *Mount Everest*, R Manuel Ventura 75, T25227350. Comfortable, good breakfast. **C** *Maringá*, R Monsenhor Miranda 110, T25222309. **D** without bath. Good breakfast. Recommended. **Camping**: *Camping Clube do Brasil* has sites on the Niterói Rd, at Caledônia (7 km out, T25220169) and Muri (10 km out, T25422275). There is a private site at Fazenda Sanandu, 20 km out on the same road.

Eating   There are many options to choose from, several in European styles which reflect the background of the people who settled in the area. You can also find Brazilian food, pizzas and *confeitarias*. **Mid-range**: *Auberge Suisse*, R 10 de Outubro, T25411270. Swiss; *Chez Gigi*, Av Euterpe Friburguense 21, T25230107. French.

Festivals   In **May**, Nova Friburgo celebrates its founding (on the 16th) and throughout the month holds a festival (*Maifest*). 24 Jun, *São João Batista*, patron saint's day.

Transport   **Buses**   Bus station, Ponte da Suadade, T25220400. To **Rio** (every hr), 2 hrs, US$4.

Directory   **Banks**   *Bradesco*, Praça Demerval Barbosa Moreira.

Towns in the Coffee Zone

Although coffee no longer dominates this part of Brazil, as it did in the 19th century, there are still many reminders of the wealth of this trade. It can be seen in the towns of Vassouras and Valença, and especially in the fazendas which were the homes and production headquarters of the coffee barons. Today many of these plantations have been well and truly incorporated into a rural, cultural and historic tourist circuit, with some small towns in the Vale do Rio Paraíba do Sol such as Conservatória maintaining the seranading street tradition. Nearer to Rio, the train journey from Miguel Pereira has spectacular views of this mountainous terrain whilst the Museu da Cachaça at Pati doe Alferes is a shrine to this strong sugar cane spirit.

The coffee zone covered the valley of the Rio Paraíba do Sul and neighbouring hills and valleys. Before the coming of the railways in the second half of the 19th century, mule trains carried the coffee from the interior to the coast on roads such as the Estrada do Comércio from Minas Gerais, through Valença and Vassouras, to the town of Iguaçu on the river of the same name. At the end of the 19th century, the abolition of slavery, the exhaustion of the land and lower international prices for coffee caused the collapse of the coffee trade. The towns had to adapt to new economic activities or die, but many of the *fazendas* remain, and although not easy to get to, a visit is worth the effort. (*Fazendas: As Casas Grandes Rurais do Brasil*, by Fernando Tasso Frajoso Pires, Abbeville Press, is a beautiful book showing these magnificent houses.

This town, 113 km north of Rio de Janeiro, has an excellent mountain climate. In the mid-19th century the area was entirely given over to coffee; other industries were introduced when a railway branch line reached here in the late 19th century. The town was named after a doctor who, in the 1930s, promoted the region for holidays away from the coast. About 3 km from town on the road to Rio is the **Javari lake**, a popular recreational spot. Mountain roads through the Serra do Mar head east to Petrópolis (see above) and Vassouras (see below), but ask about their condition before using either of them. **Tourist Information**: *Setur*, Av Manuel Guilherme Barbosa 375, T24841616.

Miguel Pereira
Phone code: 024
Population: 24,0000

The **Miguel Pereira-Conrado railway**: a tourist train, also known as the *Trem Azul*, started operations in 1993 and affords beautiful views of mountains, rivers and waterfalls. The diesel train follows a meter gauge line constructed to take coffee to the port of Rio. Among the attractions of the journey is the Paulo de Frontin iron bridge, built in 1889 and said to be the only railway bridge built in a curve. The line is operated by *Montmar Turismo* of Angra dos Reis (see page 157). There is a museum at the railway station. ■ *The round trip of 56 km takes 4½ hrs, costs US$25 and leaves Miguel Pereira at 0930 on Sat, Sun and public holidays. The museum is open 1200-1700 Tue-Fri, 0900-1400 Sat-Sun, T24844877.*

Sleeping AL *Fazenda Javary*, Praça Frutuoso da Fonseca Fernandes 35, near town, T/F24843611 (or Rio T22409335), restaurant, pool, sports courts. **B** *Pousada Caçarola*, R Luís Marques 1204, 5 km from town, T24841499.

Vassouras

It is hard to believe that the small town of Vassouras was once one of the most important cities of the Brazilian Empire. During the coffee boom in the 19th century, it was surrounded by coffee farms whose owners became immensely rich. These coffee barons acquired noble titles and, as their power increased, they built enormous, opulent town houses in Vassouras. The majority of these buildings are still there, surrounding the beautiful main Praça Barão de Campo Belo. The Emperor Pedro II visited the city several times.

Phone code: 024
Colour map 4, grid C3
Population: 32,000

In 1875 the railway station was opened in Vassouras, allowing the local farmers to send their produce directly to Rio de Janeiro. But the town went into decline when the coffee boom ended. For many years it had almost no economic activity, except for some cattle ranching and small-scale agriculture. Nowadays, it has a university and is being rediscovered by the tourism industry. It still retains its small-town calm, but the reminders of its golden past mix with the student nightlife in the bars along a street called, unofficially, 'The Broadway'.

The best way to explore Vassouras is on foot. Starting at the rodoviária, walk as far as the **Estação Ferroviária**, the former railway station. Recently restored, it is now the headquarters of the Universidade de Vassouras. Carry straight on to the **Praça Barão de Campo Belo**, where you will find the most important old houses and public buildings, all dating from the 19th century.

Sights

Rio de Janeiro

Note the neoclassical influence. One of these old 'baronial' houses, at Rua Custódio Guimarães 65, on the lefthand side of the square as you enter, houses the **Casa da Cultura**, a municipal cultural centre which has tourist information and temporary exhibitions of local art and folklore. Ask if you can go upstairs and on the second floor, at the top of some of the internal walls, look for where the paint has peeled. You can see the 19th-century method of house construction, using clay over a frame of interwoven wood and bamboo.

At the top end of the praça is the church of **Nossa Senhora da Conceição**, the most important in the city, finished in 1853 in neoclassical style. Behind the church is the small Praça Sebastião Lacerda, surrounded by huge fig trees. The story goes that there is one fig tree for each of the rich coffee barons who lived in Vassouras in the last century. Keep on walking until you come to the cemetery. A visit is recommended; most of the wealthiest men of Brazil's second empire are buried here. Rich mausoleums decorated with Italian and Portuguese marble sculptures show the competition among the families. Two of the most important clans are represented: the Teixeira Leite family and the Correa e Castro family. On the grave of a catholic priest who died in 1866, Monsenhor Rios, a strange purple flower blooms every year in November on the 'Day of the Dead'. Its intense smell is reminiscent of rotting flesh. Scientists have studied it, but have reached no conclusion as to what it is. The flower vanishes after a few days and the small bush lives on until January or February. It is now protected by a small iron fence and miracles are reported to have occurred there.

Back at Praça Barão de Campo Belo, on Rua Barão de Vassouras, is the **Palacete do Barão do Ribeirão**, the former residence of a coffee baron, later converted into the town's court. Nowadays it is closed for restoration as it has been badly attacked by termites. Turn right and at the end of Rua Dr Fernandes Junior (No 160) you will find the fascinating **Casa da Hera** museum, an old country house covered with ivy, which belonged in the 19th century to one of the richest men in the town, Joaquim Teixeira Leite. After his death the house was inherited by his daughter, Eufrásia Teixeira Leite, who lost interest in the coffee business. She went to Paris, living a life of parties and luxury for many years. After her death in 1930, the house was made into a museum, according to her will. All the furniture, decoration and architecture is original, from the golden years of coffee. The wide variety of imported tapestries, pianos and porcelain contrasts with very rough building materials: a fantastic portrait of how life was in the 1850s. On some Sundays, depending on the number of visitors, they serve tea in a style that recreates the atmosphere of the old coffee *fazendas*. ∎ *1100-1700 Wed-Sun. T24712342.*

Because Vassouras is a university centre, it has more variety than in other towns of a similar size. The action is concentrated in Rua Expedicionário Oswaldo de Almeida Ramos, but you won't need to pronounce that: simply ask for the 'Broadway' and everybody will direct you to the right place. Here there are enough bars and open-air restaurants to suit all tastes and budgets.

Another possibility is a guided visit to the food technology centre at the **Senai**, close to the main praça. Here students learn how to process fruit, vegetables, meat and also how to work in a brewery. Most of the hotels can arrange a guided visit at weekends.

Excursions As yet, Vassouras lacks a well-developed tourist infrastructure. There is a lot to see around the city, especially the old *fazendas*, but they are only just starting to open to the public. The majority of them are privately owned and can only be visited with a prior appointment. The bigger hotels can arrange guided tours with transport at weekends. During the week, the only option is to go by car, as some of the *fazendas* are a long way away, down dirt roads. The best *fazendas* in the vicinity are: Fazenda Santa Mônica, Fazenda São Fernando, Fazenda Paraíso and Fazenda Oriente. More information can be obtained from the Casa da Cultura or from the Tourism Secretary, in the Municipalidade, Praça Barão de Campo Belo, T24711367.

AL *Santa Amália*, Av Sebastião Manoel Furtado 526, close to the rodoviária, **Sleeping** T/F24711897. Located in a very pleasant and quiet park, swimming pool, sauna, volleyball and soccer pitches, 1 of the best in town, try to negotiate in the low season (Mar-Jun and Aug-Nov) and during the week. **B** *Gramado da Serra*, R Aldo Cavalcanti 7, T/F24712314. Bar, restaurant, pool and sauna. **B** *Mara Palace*, R Chanceler Dr Raul Fernandes 121, T24711993. House built in 1870, fully and tastefully preserved, swimming pool, bar, sauna, sports, nice atmosphere and good service, owner (Gerson) can arrange visits to *fazendas*; also *Pousada Bougainville*, T24712451, and *Pousada Veredas*, T24712728.

The best restaurants are located in the centre, on R Expedicionário Oswaldo de **Eating** Almeida Ramos/'The Broadway'. Here, the most well known places (both in the **mid-range** category) are *Sputnik* and *Mafioso*; close neighbours, similar layouts and prices, with pasta, steak and pizzas. During the week they both offer meals 'by weight' at lunch time. On warm nights you can sit outside, but be sure to arrive before 2000 to avoid the crowds, especially at weekends.

Nightlife is found mostly in the bars and restaurants. University students often orga- **Bars &** nize parties at weekends; look for the advertisements posted on the walls or in other **nightclubs** public places. For people watching, stroll along 'The Broadway' on a Fri night.

Carnival (**Feb** or **Mar**) is one of the best in the region, with its own Samba schools and **Festivals** balls. In Jun, the days of *Santo Antônio*, *São Pedro* and *São João* are celebrated with traditional parties. **8 Dec**: the feast of *Nossa Senhora da Conceição*, the city's patron saint, with a mass and procession.

Country cheese and preserves made with local fruits are regional buys. **Shopping**

Buses Several buses daily from Rio de Janeiro's Rodoviária Novo Rio with *Normandy*. **Transport** Around 1½ hrs between departures 0615-2030, 2 hrs, US$6.50. More buses during summer and holidays.

Banks Change all the money you will need in Rio before departing. As a last resort, try **Directory** the local *Banco do Brasil*, R Caetano Furquim, in the centre. **Communications** Post office: R Irmã Maria Agostinha. Telephones: Telj between R Caetano Furquim and R Expedicionário Oswaldo de Almeida Ramos. **Medical services** *Hospital Eufrásia Teixeira Leite*, Praça Provedor Félix Machado 110, T24711796.

Valença and Conservatória

Like Vassouras, **Valença** is a historical monument and its history follows much the same pattern, with wealth from the coffee trade followed by some small-scale industry and agriculture. There are a number of *fazendas* nearby and in the town a Faculty of Medicine. *Secretaria de Turismo*, T24420102.

About 35 km from Valença is **Conservatória**, another town in the coffee zone. Although it did not become as wealthy as Vassouras or Valença, it still has some fine 19th-century houses and is much more peaceful. In

Rio de Janeiro

Conservatória, local farm produce can be bought, as well as blankets, macrame and crochet work. A local custom is the serenade through the streets; serenaders meet at the Museu da Seresta on Rua Osvaldo Fonseca on Friday and Saturday. This region can also be reached via the Japeri turn-off on the BR-116, a beautiful mountain drive. *Secretaria de Turismo*, T34381188.

Sleeping In and around Valença, Barra do Piraí and Conservatória, there are a number of *fazenda* hotels whose prices start in most cases in our **L** range. Besides lodging and food, most offer riding and other outdoor activities. Others offer day visits, usually guided tours only. Details should be obtained locally; phone Preservale T021-22407539 (*Quatro Rodas* publications list many of these establishments). **Youth hostel** At Barra do Piraí, *Na Toca*, Estr Mun Rui Pio Davi Gomes 1876, Dorândia, T0XX24-24425323.

West of Rio de Janeiro

Volta Redonda On a broad bend of the Rio Paraíba, 113 km west of Rio along the railway to
Phone code: 024 São Paulo, Volta Redonda has one of the largest steel works in Latin America.
Population: 243,000 The mills are on the river bank and the town spreads up the surrounding wooded and gardened slopes. To visit, apply for a permit from the Companhia Siderúrgica Nacional, Avenida Treze de Maio 13, Rio de Janeiro (10 days in advance), or locally from the *Bela Vista* hotel. Visits of 2½-3 hours start at 0900. On a hill overlooking town is *Bela Vista* (**A**), Alto de Boa Vista. On Avenida Alberto Pasqualini is *Sider Palace* (**A**), T/F33481032. Buses or minibuses from Rio de Janeiro take 2½ hours, US$5.

Resende Some 30 km west of Volta Redonda, in the town of Resende, is the Military
Phone code: 024 Academy of Agulhas Negras at Km 306 Rodovia Presidente Dutra. The
Population: 105,000 grounds, with captured German guns of the Second World War, are open to the public. There is a military museum. ■ *0800-1700*.

Sleeping **A** *Castel Plaza*, Av Mcal Castelo Branco 301, T33551091. **A** *River Park*, Av Nova Resende 262, T33353344.

Transport Buses: from Aparecida do Norte (see page 217), several daily, US$2.50; from Rio, frequent, 1¾ hrs, US$6, also from São Paulo and Volta Redonda. From Resende buses go to Barra Mansa (*Resendense*, 40 mins, US$2.50), where you can change for Belo Horizonte (*Útil* 1230, 8-9 hrs).

Penedo In the same region, 175 km from Rio, is the small town of Penedo which in the
Phone code: 024 1930s attracted Finnish settlers who brought the first saunas to Brazil. There is
Altitude: 600 m a Finnish museum, a cultural centre and Finnish dancing on Saturdays. This
Population: 8,000 popular weekend resort also provides horse riding and swimming in the Portinho River. There are five buses a day from Resende. **Tourist information** is at Avenida Casa das Pedras, T33511876.

Sleeping and eating A *da Cachoeira*, Estr das Três Cachoeiras, T33511262, F33511180. **B** *Bertell*, R Harry Bertell 47, T/F33511288. **B** *Pousada Penedo*, Av Finlândia, T33511309. Safe, pool. Recommended. **Camping** *Bandeirante*, Av Brasil 440, T33511071. For eating, try *Pequena Suécia*, R Toivo Suni, T33511275. Swedish.

Visconde de Mauá

About 33 km beyond Penedo (part of the road unpaved) is the charming small village of Visconde de Mauá in the **Serra da Mantiqueira**. In the early 20th century Swiss and German immigrants settled in the town which is popular with tourists today. The surrounding scenery is lovely, with green valleys, clear rivers, wild flowers and opportunities for good walks and other outdoor activities. Many places offer acupuncture, shiatsu massage and macrobiotic food and there is a hippy feel to the crafts on sale. Horses can be rented in Visconde de Mauá from Berto (almost opposite *Vendinha da Serra*), or Pedro (Lote 10) and many places in Maringá arrange riding. The Rio Preto is good for canoeing and there is an annual national event (dates change; check in advance). The tourist office, T33871283, is closed out of season.

Phone code: 024
Altitude: 1,200 m
Colour map 4, grid C3

Three other small hill towns are nearby: **Mirantão**, at 1,700 m, with semi-tropical vegetation; **Maringá**, just across the state border in Minas Gerais and a delightful two hours' walk; and **Maromba**. On the way to Maromba is the Mirante do Posto da Montanha, a lookout with a view of the Rio Preto, which runs through the region and is the border between Rio de Janeiro and Minas Gerais states. Also in Minas Gerais, 6 km up river from Maringá but on a different road, are the Santa Clara falls (turn off before Maromba). Between Visconde de Mauá and Maringá is a natural pool in the river (turn left before crossing the bridge). After Maromba follow the signs to Cachoeira e Escorrega, a small fall and waterslide with a cold natural swimming pool, a 2-km walk. A turning off this road leads to another waterfall, the Cachoeira Véu da Noiva.

LL *Fronteira*, Estr Visconde de Mauá-Campo Lindo, Km 4, T33871219. A Roteiro de Charme hotel (see page 47). **A** *Beira Rio*, T33541801; **A** *Pousada Vale das Hortênsias*, T33543030. Both in Maringá, both provide all meals. Recommended. ½ km on the road to Maringá is *Hotel Turístico*, with handicrafts and homemade food. Italian owner, Nino, and his Brazilian wife run excursions. Cheap lodgings are limited: enquire at *Vendinha da Serra*, an excellent natural food restaurant and store; next door is *Dona Mariana*, a recommended budget place to stay. **Camping** There are several sites, including *Barragen's*, in Maringá, T33871354.

Sleeping
There are many other fazendas, pousadas and chalés in the vicinity, but very little budget accommodation

Mid-range: *Gosto com Gosto*, R Wenceslau Brás. Mineiro. **Cheap**: *Bar do Jorge*, café. Everywhere in town shuts at about 2200.

Eating

Adega Bar, open till midnight, live music and dancing (Sat only). *Forró da Marieta* for forró dancing.

Bars & nightclubs

Buses To Visconde de Mauá from Resende, 1500 and 1630, 2 hrs, return 0900-0830, US$5. Direct bus Rio-Visconde de Mauá, Cidade de Aço, 0900 daily, plus 1 in evening, 3½ hrs, US$7.

Transport

Itatiaia National Park

Founded in 1937 on the Serra de Itatiaia in the Mantiqueira chain of mountains, the park was the first to be created in Brazil. Its entrance is a few kilometres north of the Via Dutra (Rio-São Paulo highway) by paved road. The town of Itatiaia is surrounded by picturesque mountain peaks and lovely waterfalls (tourist information T024-33521660). Worth seeing are the curious rock formations of Pedra de Taruga and Pedra de Maçã and the waterfalls Poranga and Véu de Noiva (many birds). Climbing is good, for instance on

The park is one of the most popular excursions in the state of Rio de Janeiro and is a good area for climbing, trekking and bird-watching

Rio de Janeiro

the Pico das Agulhas Negras (2,787 m) and the peaks in the Serra das Prateleiras (up to 2,540 m).

Flora & fauna The vegetation is determined by altitude, so that the plateau at 800-1,100 m is covered by forest, ferns and flowering plants (such as orchids, bromeliads, begonias), giving way on the higher escarpments to pines and bushes. Higher still, over 1,900 m, the distinctive rocky landscape has low bushes and grasses, isolated trees and many unique plants adapted to the high winds and strong sun. There is also a great variety of lichens.

The southern masked titi monkey is common, recognizable by its loud hee-haw-like call. There are also agoutis, sloths, peccaries and other rarer mammals. Sources vary on the number of bird species in the park, from 270 to 300 or even 400, but many species are endemic making it a top birding destination. Specialities include swallow-tailed, shrike-like and black-and-gold cotingas, white-bearded ant shrike, black-capped manakin, gilt-edged, brassy-breasted, brown and olive-green tanagers, and a number of hummingbirds. Needless to say, insects are plentiful, including some of the largest flies in the world, and there is a wide range of amphibians. There is a **Museu de História Natural** near the headquarters. ■ *1000-1600, closed Mon*. Also nearby is a wildlife trail, **Três Picos**, which starts near the *Hotel Simon* (see below).

Park essentials Information and maps can be obtained at the park office. The Administração do Parque Nacional de Itatiaia operates a refuge in the park which acts as a starting point for climbs and treks. Information can be obtained from **Ibama**, T024-33521461, for the local headquarters, or T021-32246463 for the Rio de Janeiro state department. Information on treks can be obtained from *Clube Excursionista Brasileira*, Av Almirante Barroso 2, 8th floor, Rio de Janeiro, T021-22203695. It is very difficult to visit the park without a car and some parts are only possible in a 4WD vehicle (it is 70 km from the *Hotel Simon* to the other side).

Sleeping Basic accommodation in cabins and dormitories is available in the park; you will need to book in season, say 30 days in advance, by writing to Administração do Parque Nacional de Itatiaia, Caixa Postal 83657, Itatiaia 27580-000, RJ, telephone as above. **A** *Hotel do Ypê*, on the road in the park, Km 14, T33521453. With meals. Recommended. **A** *Repouso Itatiaia*, Km 11 on the park road, T33521110. With meals. **A** *Simon*, Km 13 on the road in the park, T33521122. With meals, lovely views, beautifully set, helpful with advice on getting around the park. Recommended. **B** *Pousada do Elefante*, 15 mins' walk back down hill from *Hotel Simon*. Good food, swimming pool, lovely views, may allow camping; cheap lodging at R Maricá 255, T33521699. Possibility of pitching a tent on the premises, located close to the national park. **D** *Hotel Alsene*, at 2,100 m, 2 km from the side entrance to the park, take a bus to São Lourenço and Caxambu, get off at Registro, walk or hitch from there (12 km). Very popular with climbing and trekking clubs, dormitory or camping, chalets available, hot showers, fireplace, evening meal after everyone returns, drinks but no snacks. **Youth hostel** *Ipê Amarelo*, R João Maurício Macedo Costa 352, Campo Alegre, T/F0XX24-33521232. IYHA. **Camping** *Camping Clube do Brasil* site is entered at Km 148 on the Via Dutra.

Transport **Buses** A bus from Itatiaia, marked *Hotel Simon*, goes to the Park, 1200, returns 1700; coming from Resende this may be caught at the crossroads before Itatiaia. Through tickets to São Paulo are sold at a booth in the large bar in the middle of Itatiaia main street.

Further along the Dutra Highway (186 km from Rio) is the small town of **Engenheiro** Engenheiro Passos, from which a road (BR-354) leads to São Lourenço and **Passos** Caxambu in Minas Gerais (see page 273). By turning off this road at the *Phone code: 024* Registro pass (1,670 m) on the Rio-Minas border, you can reach the **Pico das** *Population: 3,500* **Agulhas Negras**. The mountain can be climbed from this side from the Abrigo Rebouças refuge at 2,350 m which is manned all year round. Take your own food, US$2.50 to stay. Around Engenheiro Passos there are many *fazenda* hotels: *Fazenda Villa Forte* (**L**), 1 km from town, T/F33571122, with meals, bar, sauna, massage, gym and other sports and *Fazenda Palmital* (**A**), Km 11 BR-354 towards Caxambu, T/F33571108.

The Costa Verde

The Rio de Janeiro-Santos section of the BR-101 is one of the world's most beautiful highways, hugging the forested and hilly Costa Verde southwest of Rio. The coast is littered with islands, beaches, colonial settlements and moun-tain fazendas.

The BR-101 is now complete through to Bertioga (see page 200), which has good links with Santos and São Paulo. Buses run from Rio to Angra dos Reis, Paraty, Ubatuba, Caraguatatuba and São Sebastião, where it may be necessary to change for Santos or São Paulo. Hotels and *pousadas* have sprung up all along the road, as have expensive housing developments, though these have not spoiled the views. The drive from Rio to Paraty should take four hours, but it would be better to break the journey and enjoy some of the attractions. The coast road has lots of twists and turns so, if prone to motion sickness, get a seat at the front of the bus to make the most of the views.

The BR-101 does not take the coastal route through Barra da Tijuca out of the **Itacuruçá** city, but goes around the north side, eventually hitting the coast at Coroa *Phone code: 021* Grande. This fishing village with summer houses and beach (the sea is pol- *Population: 3,500* luted), together with Itacuruçá and Mangaratiba, are all on the shore of the Baía de Sepetiba, which is protected from the open sea by a long sand spit, the Restinga da Marambaia. At the spit's western end is the Ilha da Marambaia, while the mouth of the bay is protected by Ilha Grande.

Itacuruçá, 91 km from Rio, is a delightful place, offering fine scenery, peace and quiet and islands off its coast. The sea in the town is too polluted for bath-ing, but you can walk along the railway to Castelo where the beach is cleaner. Separated from the town by a channel is the Ilha de Itacuruçá, the largest of a string of islands stretching into the bay. Further offshore is Ilha de Jaguanum, around which there are lovely walks. Both islands have beaches from which bathing is possible. *Saveiros* (schooners) sail around the bay and to the islands from Itacuruçá; *Passamar*, T99792429. Ilha de Itacuruçá can also be reached from **Muriqui**, a popular beach resort 9 km from Itacuruçá; bathing is also possible in the Véu de Noiva waterfall. The next beach along the coast is Praia Grande, then **Praia do Saí** which has the ruins of an old port.

Sleeping On Ilha de Itacuruçá are **AL** *Elias C*, Praia Cabeça do Boi, T22537444. Cha-lets, pool, restaurant, sports courts. **AL** *Hotel Pierre*, Praia da Bica, reached by boat from Coroa Grande on the mainland, 5 mins (boats also go from Itacuruçá), T/F6881560. Restaurant, bar, sports courts. For bookings in Rio, T22534102. **A** *Pousada Praia Grande*, Praia Grande, T99794882.

Rio de Janeiro

Mangaratiba
Phone code: 021
Population: 25,000

About 22 km down the coast, this fishing village is halfway from Rio to Angra dos Reis. It stands on a little bay within the Baia de Sepetiba and in the 18th century was a port for the export first of gold, later coffee and for the import of slaves. During the coffee era, it was the terminus for the Estrada São João Marcos from the Rio Paraíba do Sul. Mangaratiba's beaches are muddy, but the surroundings are pleasant and better beaches can be found outside town, for example Ibicuí (2 km) and Brava (between Ibicuí and Saí – see above) to the east, at the head of the bay Saco, Guiti and Cação, and further west São Brás.

Sleeping   D *Sítio Santo Antônio 12*, T27892192. Family-run. Recommended.

Transport Buses: from Rio Rodoviária with *Costa Verde*, several daily, US$4.25. **Ferries**: daily boats to Ilha Grande island (see below) at 0800, return 1730, US$30 return. This is a highly recommended trip. Ferry departures and destinations can be checked at the ferry station at Praça 15 de Novembro, Rio de Janeiro (see page 107).

Angra dos Reis

Phone code: 024
Colour map 4, grid C3
Population: 120,000

Said to have been founded on 6 January 1502 (O Dia dos Reis – The Day of Kings), Angra dos Reis is 151 km southwest of Rio by road. A small port with an important fishing and shipbuilding industry, it has several small coves with good bathing within easy reach and is situated on an enormous bay full of islands. It is one of the most sophisticated resorts on the Rio de Janeiro coast. **Tourist information** Largo da Lapa, opposite the bus station, T33651175, ext 2186. Very helpful.

History   Angra's past and present are bound to the sea, in earlier times through its importance as a port, today through tourism. Once a harbour had been established here, Angra became a stop on the sea route to São Vicente (Santos). In the 18th century it was used by the gold traders making their way to and from Minas Gerais. When coffee replaced gold as the boom product, it became the harbour for the exports carried down the Estrada do Caramujo. It was one of the most important ports in the country until the railway shifted the transport emphasis away from the old roads onto the direct route into Rio.

Sights   Several buildings remain from Angra's heyday. Of particular note are the church and convent of **Nossa Senhora do Carmo**, built in 1593 (Praça General Osório), the Igreja Matriz de **Nossa Senhora da Conceição** (1626) in the centre of town and the church and convent of **São Bernardino de Sena** (1758-63) on the Morro do Santo Antônio. On the Largo da Lapa is the church of **Nossa Senhora da Lapa da Boa Morte** (1752) and a museum of sacred art. ■ *1000-1200, 1400-1800 Thu-Sun.*

Excursions   On the Península de Angra, just west of the town, is the **Praia do Bonfim**, a popular beach and a little way offshore the island of the same name, on which is the hermitage of Senhor do Bonfim (1780). Some 15 km east are the ruins of the **Jacuecanga** seminary (1797).

   Boat trips around the bay are available, some with a stop for lunch on the island of Gipóia (five hours). Several boats run tours from the Cais de Santa Luzia and there are agencies for *saveiros* in town.

   The historic **Trem da Mata Atlântica** or **Trem Verde** has been reopened, making the coastal trip to Lidice. A steam locomotive and six carriages were renovated for the line, but the train may be pulled by a diesel engine. The six-hour round trip runs through beautiful countryside (hence the name 'Green Train'). It leaves Angra railway station at 1030 on Saturday, Sunday and public holidays and has a restaurant car; the fare is US$44. The operator is *Montmar Turismo*, Rua do Comércio 11.

In town A *Caribe*, R de Conceição 255, T33650033. Central. Recommended.

    Youth hostel *Rio Bracuí*, Estr Santa Rita 4, Bracuí, on the road to Santos at Km 115 (take any bus going beyond Angra to the bridge over the Rio Bracuí), T33631234, ajriobracui@quick.com.br Open all year.

Around Angra L *do Frade*, on the road to Ubatuba, Km 123 BR-101, 33 km from Angra, T33692244. Luxury hotel on the Praia do Frade with restaurants, bar, sauna, sports facilities on land and sea. **AL** *Porto Aquarius*, Saco de Itapirapuã, out of town access from Km 101 BR-101, 13 km, T33651642, F33651766. Lots of facilities, pleasant, helpful staff. **A** *Pousada Porto Marina Bracuhy*, Km 115 BR-101, 23 km from Angra dos Reis, T33651153, F33631122. Lots of facilities for watersports, nightly shows and dancing, restaurant.

Mid-range: *Taberna 33*, R Raul Pompéia 110. Italian, good, popular. *Tropicalitá*, Largo do Convento do Carmo.

In **Jan** there are several festivals: at New Year there is a *Festa do Mar*, with boat processions; on the 5th is the *Folia dos Reis*, the culmination of a religious festival that begins at Christmas; the 6th is the anniversary of the founding of the city. In **May** is the *Festa do Divino* and, on the 2nd Sun, the *Senhor do Bonfim* maritime procession. As elsewhere in the state, the *Festas Juninas* are celebrated in **Jun**. **8 Dec**: the festival of *Nossa Senhora da Conceição*.

Diving: *Aquamaster*, Praia da Enseada, take bus marked 'Retiro' from the port in Angra, T33652416. US$60 for 2 dives with drinks and food.

Buses At least hourly from Rio's rodoviária with *Costa Verde*, several direct, T22901484, accepts credit cards, new comfortable buses, several go through Copacabana, Ipanema and Barra then take the 'via litoral', sit on the left, US$5.75, 2½ hrs (you can flag the bus down in Flamengo, Copacabana, Ipanema, Barra de Tijuca, but it may well be full at weekends).

    Ferries To Ilha Grande 1½ hrs by boat, US$6.75, daily at 1530, return 1000. For day trips, go from **Mangaratiba**, see above. Fishing boats take passengers from Angra for about US$5.

Banks *Banco 24 Horas*, R do Comércio 250, *Bradesco*, R do Comércio 196. **Medical services** *Santa Casa*, R Dr Coutinho 84, T33650131.

Sleeping
There are many hotels around Angra

Eating

Festivals

Sport

Transport

Directory

Rio de Janeiro

Ilha Grande

A two-hour ferry makes a most attractive trip through the bay to **Vila do Abraão**, the main village on Ilha Grande. If you have a couple of days to spare, the island is definitely worth a visit because it encapsulates most of what the name 'Emerald Coast' suggests. It is mountainous, covered in Atlantic forest, surrounded by transparent green waters and largely unspoiled. The weather is best from March to June; it is best to avoid the peak summer months. In fact, visit the island soon, before it becomes overdeveloped. You willl see the very helpful **tourist office** as you get off the boat. It is run by Angela, who speaks some English and will act as a trekking guide.

Phone code: 021
Colour map 4, grid C3

History   Ilha Grande remained relatively untouched by the pressures of development because of what has been called 'a strange protection afforded by the forces of evil'. It was once an infamous lair for European pirates, then a landing stage for slaves. In the 19th century, it was the site of a leper colony and in the 20th century one of Brazil's larger high-security prisons deterred visitors. A famous inmate was the writer Graciliano Ramos (see Literature, page 696), whose *Memórias do cárcere* relate his experiences. The prison was closed in 1994 and is now overgrown rubble.

In the past, sugar cane and coffee were cultivated on parts of the island, but now most of it is a state park, including the **Reserva Biológica da Praia do Sul**. The main industry is fishing. Cars are not allowed on the island, so transport is either by boat, or on foot.

Beaches &   There are about 100 beaches around the island, about three dozen of which
excursions   are regular tourist spots. Those on the landward side are good for watersports, diving is good around most of the coast, there is fishing and some surfing. From Vila do Abraão there are trails to most of the beaches, but it is much less effort to go by boat. Even so, some parts of the island are a long journey.

Popular excursions include: the 20-minute walk from Abraão to the peaceful and clean beach at Abraãozinho. Another two hours in the same direction will take you to Palmas beach, which is also calm, and another 20 minutes to Lopes Mendes, good for surfing. This beach can be reached by boat, too, as can other lovely beaches: Lagoa Azul, with crystal clear water and excellent snorkelling, Freguesia de Santana and Saco do Céu.

To Provetá, at the eastern end, for instance, it takes 6½ hours by boat. You can ask in the port at Angra dos Reis for a fishing boat going to Provetá, where you can stay in boat sheds or, if lucky, with a fisherman. It is a beautiful village, from which you can walk through tropical forest over the mountain to Praia do Aventureiro (a day's leisurely walk each way), or go by boat. Take mosquito precautions when walking in the forest.

A couple of good treks are over the mountains to Dois Rios, where the old jail was situated. There is still a settlement of former prison guards here who have nowhere to go. The walk is about 13 km one way and takes about three hours; beautiful scenery and superb views. You can also hike to Pico do Papagaio (980 m) through forest; a stiff, three hours climb for which a guide is essential. The view from the top is breathtaking. Pico da Pedra d'Água (1,031 m) can also be climbed.

Sleeping   **A** *Fazenda Paraíso do Sol*, Praia Saco das Palmas (full board), 2 hrs' walk from Abraão, or 40 mins by boat, for reservations in Rio T22621226. Hotel reservations are necessary. Many *pousadas* in Abraão: eg, on R da Praia: **A** *Pousada do Canto*, 2 blocks from centre, T33615115. Quiet location, good value; *Água Viva*, No 26, T/F99862519, *Solar da Praia*, No 32, T99863396 and *Tropicana*, No 28, T33615047. French-run. Recommended, good open-air restaurant. **B** *Albatroz*, R das Flores 108, T26271730. Recommended. **B** *Beto's*, T27801202, central. Recommended. **B** *Hotel Ori*, R Prof Lima. Recommended. **B B** *Pousada da Vanda*, R Antônio Moreira 95, T22852429. In green surroundings. *Sonia/Tuti*, R Antônio Moreira 80, 5 mins from the beach, T654512. A small house with 2 rooms to let. Recommended. **C** *Pousada Cachoeira*, at the end of the village. Friendly, run by German-Brazilian couple, English spoken, bungalows in green surroundings, pleasant. **C** *Estalagem Costa Verde*, T0XX11-31047940. Pleasant surroundings near beach, ask for Márcia or Marly. **Youth hostel F** per person *Ilha Grande*, R Pres Vargas, T22646147. Alternatively, you can rent a room in Abraão.

Mid-range: *Casa da Sogra*, Trav do Beto. Recommended. *Minha Deusa*, R Prof Alice Coury 7, next to church. Brazilian, excellent food. **Eating**

Bicycles can be hired and tours arranged; ask at *pousadas*. **Boats** Boat trips cost **Transport** US$10 without food or drinks, but includes fruit. Recommended boats are *Victória Régia* (owned by Carlos, contact at *Pousada Tropicana*), *Papyk* or *André Maru* (owned by André). There is some good scuba diving around the coast; instructor Alexandre at *Bougainville* shop No 5. **Ferries** For boats to Ilha Grande, see above under Angra dos Reis and Mangaratiba. There are 5 ferries called *Isabel*, check which is going to the mainland destination you want.

Banks Only open at weekends. **Directory**

Paraty

The centre of this charming colonial town has been declared a national historic Phone code: 024 *monument in its entirety. In the pretty colonial buildings are a large number of* Colour map 4, grid C2 *art galleries, tourist shops and restaurants. The surrounding hills are covered in* Population: 30,000 *tropical forest, with treks to pristine waterfalls and along an historic Gold Trail. There are dozens of tiny beaches and islands in the glassy waters of the bay, with hundreds more within easy reach, best visited by boat. Paraty is Brazil's sailing capital and there are elegant schooners, whaling boats and tiny fishing tugs to choose from. Paraty is normally cooler than Rio de Janeiro.*

Ins and outs

The town centre is out of bounds for motor vehicles; heavy chains are strung across the **Getting around** entrance to the streets. Even though Paraty is easily accessible to tourists, they only come in great numbers at weekends and on holidays, so the rest of the time it keeps its small-town atmosphere.

The wettest times of year are Jan-Feb and Jun-Jul. In spring the roads are flooded, but **Climate** the houses are above the water level.

The tourist office is at *Centro de Informações Turísticas*, Av Roberto Silveira, near the **Tourist** entrance to the historical centre, T33371266 ext 218. Information here is limited and **information** they may try to sell you a basic map with lots of advertising for US$1.50. Instead pick up the *Welcome to Paraty* brochure, www.eco-paraty.com, which is well presented, in English and contains a compact map of the town. More information is available at www.paraty.com.br

History

Paraty was officially founded in the first half of the 17th century. Its name is usually said to derive from the indigenous word for a small fish common in these waters, called *paratii*, but others say it comes from language of the local tupi-guarani people in which it means 'gulf' or 'chasm'. Having a good harbour and a well-worn trail into the interior (used by the Guianas Indians before the Portuguese colonizers), Paraty was a natural choice for a port. Some parts of the old trail can still be walked; ask tour operators (see below). It became the chief port for the export of gold in the 17th century and thus grew rich. Most of its colonial churches date from this period, as do the fortresses which were built to prevent pirates and foreign ships stealing the valuable cargo (see the Forte do Defensor Perpétuo). Walls protected the landward side and the ruins of an old gate can be seen close to the football field at the entrance to town. Commerce prospered and farms around the city produced sugar and fine brands of *cachaça* (the name Paraty is still synonymous with *cachaça*). When a road was built to Rio de Janeiro from the mining regions at the beginning of the 18th century, shortening the journey by some 15 days, Paraty's importance declined.

It recovered in the 19th century as a coffee-exporting port for the *fazendas* of the valley of the Paraíba do Sul. At the same time, through its wharf came the imported European luxuries which furnished the barons' houses. It is now hard to imagine that slaves had to carry French furniture, pianos and fine porcelain over the hills through dense forest.

In the second half of the 19th century, the opening of the railway from the Paraíba Valley to Rio led to Paraty being effectively isolated again. The port being redundant, almost all its inhabitants left. Those that remained grew bananas, but the old sugar plantations were for the most part abandoned. Because so few people stayed in the town, there was no urge to modernize the buildings. In this way, Paraty has become an open-air museum.

Only in the 1950s was the town 'rediscovered' as a tourism and cultural centre. It was declared a national historic monument in 1966. Whereas in colonial times Paraty was dependent for its livelihood on the roads across the mountains, in the late 20th century the Rio-Santos road has brought a new prosperity.

Paraty

To Forte Do Defensor Perpétuo, Museum of Arts & Popular Traditions & Praia do Jabaquara

Sleeping	7 Pousada do Ouro	12 Solar dos Gerânios
1 Casa do Rio	8 Pousada do Sandi	
2 Da Matriz	9 Pousada Mercado	**Eating**
3 Marendaz	do Pouso	1 Café Paraty
4 Pardieiro	10 Pousada Porto	2 Candeeiro
5 Pousada Capitão	Paraty	3 Corto Maltese
6 Pousada do Corsário	11 Pouso Familiar	4 Hiltinho

5 Punto di Vinho	
6 Sabor da Terra	
7 Tailandês	
Bars	
8 Bar Coupé	
9 Bar Dinho	

Sights

In keeping with all Brazilian colonial towns, Paraty's churches were built according to social status and race. There are four churches in the town, one for the 'freed coloured men', one for the blacks and two for the whites. **Santa Rita** (1722), built by the 'freed coloured men' in elegant Brazilian baroque, faces the bay and the port. It is probably the most famous 'picture postcard' image of Paraty. It houses an interesting **Museum of Sacred Art**. ■ *0900-1200, 1300-1800 Wed-Sun. US$1*. **Nossa Senhora do Rosário e São Benedito** (1725, rebuilt 1757), Rua do Comércio, built by black slaves, is small and simple; the slaves were unable to raise the funds to construct an elaborate building. ■ *0900-1200 Tue*. **Nossa Senhora dos Remédios** is the town's parish church, the biggest in Paraty. In fact, the church was never completely finished. Started in 1787, but finished only in 1873, it was built on unstable ground, so the architects decided not to add weight to the structure by putting up the towers. The façade is leaning to the left, which is clear from the three doors: only the one on the right has a step. The church was built with donations from the whites and it is rumoured that a certain Dona Geralda Maria da Silva contributed with gold from a pirate's hoard found buried on the beach. ■ *0900-1200 Mon, Wed, Fri, Sat, 0900-1500 Sun*. **Capela de Nossa Senhora das Dores** (1800) is a small chapel facing the sea. It was used mainly by the wealthy whites in the 19th century. ■ *0900-1200 Thu*.

There is a great deal of distinguished colonial architecture in delightful settings. **Rua do Comércio** is the main street in the historical centre. It was here that the prominent traders lived, the two-storey houses having the commercial establishments on the ground floor and the residences above. Today the houses are occupied by restaurants, *pousadas* and tourist shops.

The **Casa da Cadeia**, close to Santa Rita church, is the former jail, complete with iron grilles in the windows and doors. It is now a public library and art gallery.

On the northern headland is a small fort, **Forte do Defensor Perpétuo**, built in 1822, of which the cannons and the ruins of the thick walls can be seen. From the fort there are good views of the sea and the roofs of the town. It's about 15 minutes' walk from the centre. To get there, cross the Rio Perequê Açu by the bridge at the end of the Rua do Comércio; climb the small hill, which has some nice *pousadas* and a cemetery, and follow the signs to 'Forte'. Also here is the **Museum of Arts and Popular Traditions** in a colonial-style building. It contains carved wooden canoes, musical instruments, fishing gear and other handmade items from local communities. ■ *Wed-Sun*. Also on the headland is the gunpowder store and, set in the grass, enormous hemispherical iron pans which were used for extracting whale oil to use in lamps and to mix with sand and cement for building.

Boat trips The most popular trip, and highly recommended, is a five-hour schooner tour around the bay with three stops at beaches for swimming and lunch on board, US$10, lunch (optional) extra. Smaller boats can be rented for around US$10 for an hour or US$20 for three. **Excursions**

Beaches Praia do Pontal is the town beach, five minutes' walk from the historic centre – cross the bridge and turn right along the river. The water and sand is not very clean but its handful of *barracas* under the trees are a nice place to hang out. **Praia do Jabaquara** is about 20 minutes on foot – cross the bridge and continue straight up the hill. The sand is cleaner and there are a few *barracas*, although the water tends to be muddy. There are other beaches further from town, many of which make worthwhile excursions. **Paraty Mirim**, a small town 17 km away with old buildings and nice beaches, is reached by four buses a day (three on Sunday). Once a hippy community, **Trinidade**, 27 km away, is the area's prettiest beach, as well as having a natural swimming pool reached by a short trail.

The Gold Trail This partly cobbled trail through the mountains was built by slaves in the 18th century to bring gold down from Ouro Preto before transporting it to Portugal. Recently restored, it can be visited, along with the ruins of a toll house, on foot or horse on a day trip. ■ *Tours leave Teatro Espaço, R Dona Geralda 327, T33711575 at 1000.*

There are several waterfalls (*cachoeiras*) in the area, such as the **Cachoeira da Penha**, near the church of the same name. It is 10 km from town on the road to Cunha; take a local bus from the rodoviária, US$1, there are good mountain views on the way. The tourist office and travel agencies (see below) can give details on trips to waterfalls and other hikes.

Fazenda Murycana, an old sugar estate and 17th-century *cachaça* distillery with original house and water-wheel, is a recommended excursion. You can taste and buy the different types of *cachaça*; some are aged in oak barrels for 12 years (try the *cachaça com cravo e canela*, with clove and cinnamon). There is an excellent restaurant and horse riding is available but English is not spoken by the employees. Mosquitoes can be a problem at the *fazenda*, take repellent and don't wear shorts. Take a Penha/Ponte Branca bus from the rodoviária, four a day; alight where it crosses a small white bridge and then walk 10 minutes along a signed, unpaved road. Returning to Paraty, there is also a good chance of hitching a lift. ■ *For information and organized tours, T33713930.*

Sleeping
■ *on map, page 160*
Price codes:
see inside front cover

Paraty is the ideal place for a splurge, although the hotels tend to get booked up at weekends

All the **AL** to **B**-range hotels are in the historic centre unless otherwise stated **AL** *Pousada do Ouro*, R Dr Pereira (or da Praia) 145, T/F3712221, ouro@contracthor.com.br Standard price rooms in annex; enormous suites in main building. Self-consciously chic, like its adjoining restaurant. **AL** *Pousada do Sandi*, Largo do Rosário 1, T33712100, sandi@paraty.com.br 18th-century building, charming, spacious rooms. Very comfortable and lovely adjoining restaurant. **AL** *Pousada Pardieiro*, R do Comércio 74, T33711370, F33711139, www.pousadapardieiro.com.br Tucked away in a quiet corner, with a calm, sophisticated atmosphere. Attractive colonial building with lovely gardens, delightful rooms facing internal patios, extremely pleasant, swimming pool. Always full at weekends, does not take children under 15.

A *Morro do Forte*, R Orlando Carpinelli, T/F3711211. Lovely garden, good breakfast, pool, German owner Peter Kallert offers trips on his yacht. Out of the centre. Recommended. **A** *Pousada do Portal*, Av Beira-Rio 100, T33712221. Charming, but some distance from the centre, relaxing. **A** *Pousada Porto Paraty*, R do Comércio, T33712105, F33712111. Good value. Highly recommended.

B *Pousada Capitão*, R Luiz do Rosário 18, T3711416, www.paraty.com.br/capitao.htm Charming, close to historical centre, swimming pool, English and Japanese spoken. **B** *Pousada do Corsário*, Beco do Lapeiro 26, T33711866, F33711319. New building in lovely, tranquil setting outside of historic centre. Pool, terrace and gardens overlook river and mountains. Very comfortable rooms, most with hammocks outside. Highly recommended. **B** *Pousada Mercado do Pouso*, Largo de Santa Rita 43, T/F33711114. Historic building in good position, close to the port and Santa Rita, with lovely views. Family atmosphere, no pool.

C *Pouso Familiar*, R José Vieira Ramos 262, near bus station, T33711475. Run by Belgian (Joseph Yserbyt) and his Brazilian wife (Lucia), laundry facilities, garage, rooms

around courtyard. English, French, German and Flemish spoken. Recommended.
C *Solar dos Gerânios*, Praça da Matriz, T/F33711550. Beautiful colonial family house on main square in traditional rustic style that is a welcome antidote to the more polished *pousadas*. Rooms have lovely wooden lattice balconies – ask for the corner one which has two. Very reasonably priced, English spoken. Warmly recommended.

D *Marendaz*, R Patitiba 9, close to the historical centre, T33711369. Family-run, simple, charming. **D** *Pousada Belmar*, Av Roberto Silveira 44, T33712363. Basic, includes breakfast. A range of rooms, some with TV, a/c and fridge. **D** *Pousada da Matriz*, R da Cadeia 334, close to corner of R do Comércio, in historic centre. Basic but clean rooms, with bath, without breakfast, friendly if a little noisy. **D** *Pousada Miramar*, Abel de Oliveira 19, T33712132. One room has its own kitchen, good value. Recommended.

Youth Hostel *Casa do Rio*, R Antônio Vidal 120, T33712223. Lovely, peaceful little house with riverside courtyard and hammock. Kitchen, price includes breakfast. Offers jeep and horse riding trips to waterfalls, mountains and beaches. Recommended.

Camping *Camping Beira-Rio*, just across the bridge, before the road to the fort. *Camping Club do Brasil*, Av Orlando Carpinelli, Praia do Pontal. Small, good, very crowded in Jan and Feb, US$8 per person, T33711877. Also at Praia Jabaquara, T33712180.

Restaurants in the historic centre tend to be expensive. As soon as you leave the cobbles, prices and pretensions drop. Watch out for hefty cover charges for live music which are often very discreetly displayed. The best dishes to try in Paraty are those with seafood, eg *peixe à Parati* – local fish cooked with herbs, green bananas and served with *pirão*, a mixture of manioc flour and the sauce that the fish was cooked in. Also popular is the *filé de peixe ao molho de camarão* – fried fish filet with a shrimp and tomato sauce. A recommended appetizer is *aipim frito*, fried pieces of manioc, which look like French fries. The *caipirinhas* in Paraty are among the best in Brazil because they include the excellent local *cachaça*.

Eating
● *on map, page 160*

Expensive: *do Hiltinho*, R Mcal Deodoro 233, historical centre, T/F3711432. Local dishes. Excellent seafood, good service, expensive but worth it. **Mid-range**: *Café Paraty*, R da Lapa and Comércio. Sandwiches, appetizers, light meals, also bar with live music nightly (cover charge). A local landmark. Open 0900-2400. *Corto Maltese*, R do Comércio 130. Italian, pasta. *Dona Ondina*, R do Comércio 2, by the river. Family restaurant, well-prepared simple food, good value (closed on Mon between Mar and Nov). *Punto Di Vino*, R Mcal Deodoro 129. Excellent Italian. *Restaurante Tailandês*, R Dona Geralda 345. Authentic Thai food served in a fairyland setting. In a lovely, quiet corner of the historic centre. *Candeeiro*, R da Lapa 335. Good local food. **Cheap**: The less expensive restaurants, those offering *comida a quilo* (pay by weight) and the fast food outlets are outside the historical centre, mainly on Av Roberto Silveira. *Sabor da Terra*, Av Roberto Silveira, next to *Banco do Brasil*. Reliable, if not bargain-priced self service food. Closes 2200.

Kontiki, Ilha Duas Irmãs, a tiny island 5 mins from the pier where a small speed boat runs a (free) shuttle service, T9999599, www.paraty.com.br/kontiki.htm Recommended for the wonderful setting, rather than the average food, main courses US$13.50-25. Open 1000-1500 daily and Fri and Sat for dinner (reservations recommended).

Bar Coupé, Matriz Square. A popular hang-out with outside seating. Good bar snacks and breakfast. *Bar Dinho*, Praça da Matriz at R da Matriz. Good bar with live music at weekends, sometimes mid-week. *Clube Bandeirantes*, for dancing (Fri Brazilian, Sat funk, Sun dance and disco music), an interesting place to meet local people, popular, entry US$3-5. *Umoya*, R Comendador José Luiz. Video bar and café, live music at weekends.

Bars & nightclubs

Theatre *Teatro Espaço*, *The Puppet Show*, R Dona Geralda 327, T33711575, F33711161, ecparati@ax.apc.org Wed, Sat 2100, US$12. This world-famous puppet show should not

Entertainment

be missed. The puppets tell stories, without words, which are funny, sad, even shocking, with incredible realism. The series of short pieces (lasting 1 hr) are works of pure imagination and emotion and a moving commentary on the human condition.

Festivals **Feb/Mar:** *Carnival*, hundreds of people cover their bodies in black mud and run through the streets yelling like prehistoric creatures (anyone can join in). **Mar/Apr:** *Semana Santa*, with religious processions and folk songs. **Mid-Jul:** *Semana de Santa Rita*, traditional foods, shows, exhibitions and dances. **Aug:** *Festival da Pinga*, the *cachaça* fair at which local distilleries display their products and there are plenty of opportunities to over-indulge. **Sep** (around the 8th): *Semana da Nossa Senhora dos Remédios*, processions and religious events. **Sep/Oct:** *Spring Festival of Music*, concerts in front of Santa Rita church. The city is decorated with lights for Christmas. **31 Dec:** *Reveillon*, a huge party with open-air concerts and fireworks (reserve accommodation in advance). As well as the Dança dos Velhos (see Music and dance, page 688), another common dance in these parts is the *ciranda*, in which everyone, young and old, dances in a circle to songs accompanied by guitars.

Shopping The town has plenty of handicraft and souvenir shops. The most interesting items are the small, wooden canoes and boats, oars carved in wood with peculiar designs and colourful T-shirts. You can find paintings and painted wall tiles. Don't forget to buy a bottle of *cachaça*; there are shops such as *Porto da Pinga*, R da Matriz, although if you are buying bottom of the range brands (around US$5), local supermarkets are cheaper. All the local brands (*Coqueiro*, *Corisco*, *Vamos Nessa*, etc) are good, but if you are visiting the distilleries, don't hesitate to buy there (see *Fazenda Murycana* above).

Tour operators *Antígona*, Praça da Bandeira 2, Centro Histórico, T/F33711165. Daily schooner tours, 5 hrs, bar and lunch on board. Recommended. *Fausto Goyos*, T99145506, offers off-road tours in an ex-US military jeep to rainforest, waterfalls, historical sites, also photo safaris, He also has highly professional horse riding tours and offers lodging in youth-hostel style rooms for US$5, or US$7.50 with 2 meals. *Paraty Tours*, Av Roberto Silveira 11, T/F3711327. English and Spanish spoken. *Soberana da Costa*, R Dona Geraldo 43, in *Pousada Mercado do Pouso*, T/F33711114, and others offer schooner trips in the bay. Recommended.

Transport
On holidays and in high season, the frequency of bus services usually increases. Taxis charge set rate of US$4 for historic centre

Buses Paraty has a new rodoviária at the corner of R Jango Padua and R da Floresta. Nine buses a day go to **Rio** (241 km, 3¾ hrs, US$8.10, *Costa Verde* – see under Angra dos Reis for details – only the 0630 from Rio and the 1730 from Paraty go through Barra da Tijuca); to **Angra dos Reis** (98 km, 1½ hrs, every 1 hr 40 mins, US$4); 3 a day to **Ubatuba** (75 km, just over 1 hr, *São José* company, US$4), **Taubaté** (170 km) and **Guaratinguetá** (210 km); 2 a day to **São Paulo**, 1100 and 2335 (304 km via São José dos Campos, 5½ hrs, US$8.50, *Reunidas*, booked up quickly, very busy at weekends), and **São Sebastião**.

Directory **Banks** *Banco do Brasil*, Av Roberto Silveira, just outside historic centre. ATM. Exchange 1100-1430, ask for the manager. **Communications** Internet: Internet connections are neither fast nor cheap in Paraty. *Paraty Cyber Café*, Av Roberto Silveira 17. Friendly, open 0900-2300, coffee and snacks served. US$3, 30 mins. Post office: R da Cadeia and Beco do Propósito, 0800-1700, Sun 0800-1200. Telephone: International calls, Praça Macedo Soares, opposite the tourist office. Local and long distance calls can be made from public phones; buy phone cards from the newspaper stand by the tourist information centre. **Laundry** *Paraty Wash* Shopping Martins, Loja 15, opposite bus station. **Medical services** *Hospital Municipal São Pedro de Alcântara* (Santa Casa), Av Dom Pedro de Alcântara, T33711623. **Voltage** 110 volts.

São Paulo

Introducing São Paulo

The state of São Paulo, with an area of 247,898 sq km, is about the same size as Great Britain and Northern Ireland. It is the industrial heart of Brazil as well as being strong in agricultural products. Its capital São Paulo is one of the largest cities in the world and Brazil's undisputed business and finance centre. It is also one of the most cosmopolitan, in both its large immigrant communities and in the varied cuisine of its fine restaurants. Sometimes described as a tropical New York it has excellent art collections and much else of cultural interest. Its fervent nightlife embraces all types of music from heavy metal to rave as well as more local rhythms. It is also home to the famous **Butantã Snake Farm** and the **Brazilian Grand Prix**.

Nearby Santos is the largest port in Latin America and a popular destination for cruise liners. There are many pretty beaches along the coast especially around **São Sebastião** and **Ilhabela**. Inland there are hill resorts such as **Campos do Jordão** and an important area of caves in the **Vale do Ribeiro** on the border with Paraná. In the interior of the state, the town of **Barretos** plays host to the largest rodeo in the world.

Things to do in São Paulo state

① Take a hike in Campos de Jordão; this mountain resort has good walking with scenic viewpoints.

② Surf the rolling waves and swim in the waters at Peruíbe, or bathe in the medicinal mud of its rivers.

③ Explore the Vale do Ribeiro, which has one of the largest cave systems in the world, some as vast as cathedrals.

④ Get lost in the seething cosmopolitan metropolis that is São Paulo. The city has enough culture and varied cuisine to keep you occupied for months.

São Paolo City

Ins and outs

Phone code: 011
Colour map 5, grid A5
Altitude: 850 m
Population: 18 million

São Paulo

Getting there **Air** Almost all international flights stop at Cumbica international airport at Guarulhos 30 km from the city. Some internal flights from Belo Horizonte and Vitória as well as the shuttle from Rio de Janeiro land at Congonhas airport a short taxi ride from the city centre.

From Guarulhos there are airport taxis which charge US$30 on a ticket system (go to the second booth on leaving the terminal and book a Co-op taxi at the Taxi Comum counter, the best value). *Emtu* bus service every 30 mins to Praça da República, US$6.50, 30-45 mins, 0500-0200, very comfortable (buy ticket at the booth in Domestic Arrivals); the same company runs services from Guarulhos to Tietê (every 45 mins, 0500-0200), Congonhas airport (hourly 0500-0200) and Av Paulista (0645-2315 every 45 mins, passing in front of, or near many major hotels on its route to the city: *Brasilton, Cá d'Oro, Caesar Park, Della Volpe, Crowne Plaza, Sheraton, Maksoud Plaza*). Inter-airport bus US$6.50.

Buses Most buses arrive at the Tietê rodoviária. There is a Metrô and buses to the centre. US$0.60. Buses cost US$0.80. Taxis to Praça da República cost US$5, US$9 at weekends. Buses from southern São Paulo state and many destinations in Paraná arrive at Barra Funda while buses from Minas Gerais arrive at Bresser bus terminals. Buses from Santos and the coast arrive at Jabaquara bus station. All are connected to the centre by Metrô.

Getting around São Paulo is vast, but for most visitors there are only a few parts of the city that are of interest: the centre, Av Paulista and the Jardins district, the Cidade Universitária and Butantã, possibly Morumbi and then the bus stations and airports.

See also Transport, page 188

Districts The shopping, hotel and restaurant centre embraces the districts of Av São Luís, the Praça da República, and Rua Barão de Itapetininga. The central commercial district, containing banks, offices and shops, is known as the Triângulo, bounded by Ruas Direita, 15 (Quinze) de Novembro, São Bento and Praça Antônio Prado, but it is rapidly spreading towards the Praça da República. A large part of the Triângulo and the area between it and Praça da República is mostly closed to cars.

Rua Augusta begins close to Av São Luís, extends as far as *Av Paulista*, and continues beyond into one of the most affluent areas, Jardins. Both sides of Rua Augusta have a variety of shops, snack bars and restaurants, but the Jardins side contains the more exclusive boutiques and fashion houses, while the part which leads to the centre is a rather curious but colourful mix of seedy bars, saunas and 5-star hotels. Av Paulista, once the home of coffee barons and São Paulo's wealthy citizens, is now Brazil's largest financial centre as well as housing the Museu de Arte de São Paulo. It has become a new downtown area, more dynamic, but considerably less colourful than the old centre. Set to replace Av Paulista as the main centre, is Av Faria Lima, at the southwest edge of Jardins 8 km from Praça da República. Newer still is the movement of offices to Av Luís Carlos Berrini, which is yet further southwest, parallel to the Av das Naçeõs Unidas and the Rio Pinheiros.

All the rodoviárias (bus stations) are on the Metrô (underground railway), but if travelling with luggage, take a taxi. Both airports can be reached by taxi and by the good bus service run by Emtu (full details are given in Transport, page 189).The centre is easily visited on foot but many other areas of interest are some way from here. The best and cheapest way to visit these is on the excellent Metrô system, which is clean, safe, cheap and efficient. Bus routes can be confusing for visitors and slow due to frequent traffic jams. Buses are normally crowded and rather slow, but clean. City bus fare is

24 hours in São Paulo

Start the day with a stroll along the 3-km **Avenida Paulista**, a cross between Oxford Street and Wall Street and home to designer boutiques and multinationals. It was once lined with the huge colonial mansions of the coffee barons. Few of these homes survive and some have been turned into offices; one has become perhaps the most beautiful *McDonalds* in the world.

On this avenue, don't miss **Museu de Arte de São Paulo** and you might want to take a look at *Shopping Ibirapuera*, one of the city's oldest and biggest shopping centres. For lunch, look for the *Praça da Alimentação*, found in most shopping centres, serving fast, good food.

At the very heart of the city **Praça da Sé** is a lively place. Here, the **Catedral Metropolitana** is an oasis in the mayhem. Visit the **Pátio Colégio**, a little to the north, in the old downtown part of São Paulo. This is where the Jesuits founded the original settlement, although what you see today is only a reconstruction. São Paolo is famous for its international **cuisine**, so spend the evening enjoying some of the gastronomic delights in the bohemian area of **Bixiga**, famous for its Italian restaurants and many bars, some with live music. The city has the best nightlife in Brazil; pick up a copy of *Veja* for weekly listings. São Paulo pretty much never sleeps so you could easily keep going until the early hours of the next day.

R$1.15 (or US$0.60). Maps of the bus and Metrô system are available at depots, eg Anhangabaú. Some city bus routes are run by trolley buses.

Tourist offices Information kiosks: **Praça da República**, T2312922, 0900-1800 daily very helpful; **Praça Dom José Gaspar**, on the corner of Av São Luís, T2573422, 0900-1800 Mon-Fri; **Av Paulista** at Parque Trianon, T2510970, 0900-1800 except Sat); and on **Av Brig Faria Lima**, opposite the Iguatemi Shopping Center, T2111277, 0900-1800 Mon-Fri. An excellent map is available free at all these offices (on newsstands it sells for US$4). **Head office**: Av Olavo Fontoura 1209, Parque Anhembi, T69715000. Tourist information for the state of São Paulo is given at the *Secretaria de Esportes e Turismo*, Antigo Prédio do Banco de São Paulo, entrances on Praça Antônio Prado 9, and R São Bento 380, 6th floor, T2390892, F2393604. There is not much literature available, but the office is helpful. **Tours of the city**: 3 types of tour leave the kiosk on Praça da República each Sun, costing US$2: 3 to places of 'green' interest, also historical and cultural, T69715000. Other tours leave R 15 de Novembro 347 Tue-Sun at 1000 and 1400, free. There are 2 different itineraries (2 hrs each). Tourist offices have free magazines in Portuguese and English: *Where* and *São Paulo This Month* (also available from most travel agencies and better hotels). Also recommended is Quatro Rodas' *Guia de São Paulo*. Newsstands sell a wide range of magazines and books which deal with tourism in the city and the state. *SPGUIA: O Guia Interativo Oficial da Cidade de São Paulo*, provide a lot of information at **www.spguia.com.br**

Maps A variety of maps and timetables are sold in newsstands. In addition to those already mentioned (Quatro Rodas, Mapograf, Cartoplam, and those given out by the tourist kiosks), *RGN Public* produces a map which distributed free and which is adapted to show its sponsors' locations (eg *Mappin*, *Pirelli*, *McDonalds*).

Safety **Tourist Police** *Deatur*, Av São Luís 91, T2140209 and R 15 de Novembro 347, T3107564/2. Radio Patrol, T190. At night you really need to know where you are going. It is best to go by taxi, but if you find yourself on foot be extra careful. The area under and around the Minhocão (the elevated expressway in the centre), west and south of

Praça da República, is used as a pick-up zone for sex and is best avoided. The areas around Luz station, Praça da República, Centro and the Jardins area below Alameda Lorena are not safe at night, and visitors should not enter *favelas*.

Climate The climate in São Paolo is tropical and rainfall is ample. Temperatures on the plateau are about 5°C lower than on the coast, but it is only south of the latitude of Sorocaba that frosts occur and then not frequently.

Visitors find the characteristic sharp changes of temperature troublesome and even Paulistanos seem to catch cold often. The amount of air pollution can be exasperating and thermal inversions, in which a blanket of warm air prevents the dispersal of the industrial and automobile pollutants, are common. In dry weather, eyes and nose are continually troubled.

São Paulo orientation

	2 Parque da Independência	9 Parque do Ibirapuera	3 Luz
	3 Jardim Botânico	10 Jóquei Clube	4 Sé
N	4 Jardim Zoológico & Simba Safári	11 Instituto Butantã	5 Paraíso
Not to scale	5 Parque do Estado	12 Ciudad Universitária	6 Vila Mariana
	6 Represa Billings	13 Campo de Marte	7 Jabaquara
Detailed maps	7 Autodromo de Interlagos	14 Parque Burle Marx	8 Barra Funda
A São Paulo centre detail, page 174	8 Represa de Guarapiranga	Ⓜ **Metro stations**	9 Bresser
B Jardins & Avenida Paulista, page 176	○ **Open spaces**	1 Tucuruvi	10 Corinthians-Itaquera
	1 Parque Ecológico do Tietê	2 Tietê	11 Clinicas
			12 Vila Madalena

Arriving at night

São Paulo's airport has 24-hour facilities (for food, banking and of course taxis) if you arrive late at night or in the early hours of the morning. It is a long drive from the airport to the city and the a/c bus to Praça da República does not operate between 0200 and 0500 and the service to Avenida Paulista does not run from 2315 to 0645.

History

The history of São Paulo state and São Paulo city were very much one and the same from the arrival of the Europeans until the coffee boom transformed the region's economic and political landscape. According to Hemming (*Red Gold*, see page 680), there were approximately 196,000 indigenous inhabitants living in what is now São Paulo state. Today there are none.

The first official settlement was São Vicente on the coast, near today's port of Santos. It was founded in 1532 by Martim Afonso de Sousa, who had been sent by King João III to drive the French from Brazilian waters, explore the coast and lay claim to all the lands apportioned to Portugal under the Treaty of Tordesillas.

In 1554 two Jesuit priests from São Vicente founded São Paulo as a *colégio*, a combined mission and school. The Jesuits chose to settle inland because they wished to distance themselves from the civil authority, which was based in Bahia, but was extending up and down the coast to form a defendable colony. Moreover, on the plateau there was much easier access to Indians to convert to Catholicism. In parallel with the Jesuit urge to win souls for the faith ran a drive to capture Indians to work on the Paulistas' own farms. Another stimulus for their journeys into the interior was the search for precious metals and gemstones. This long period of expeditions which pushed the frontiers of Portuguese territory further and further into Brazil was the era of the *bandeira* (see box, page 198).

In a sense, the *bandeirantes'* success in discovering gold led to a demise of São Paulo in the 18th century. Like everywhere else, the inhabitants rushed to the gold fields in the *sertão*, causing ruin at home and allowing São Paulo to fall under the influence of Rio de Janeiro. The relative backwardness of the region lasted until the second half of the 19th century when coffee spread west from Rio de Janeiro. Landowners became immensely rich. São Paulo changed from a little town into a financial and residential centre. Exports and imports flowed through Santos and the industrial powerhouse of the country was born. As the city boomed, industries and agriculture fanned outwards to the far reaches of the state.

Between 1885 and the end of the century the boom in coffee and the arrival of large numbers of Europeans transformed the state out of all recognition. By the end of the 1930s there had arrived in São Paulo state a million Italians, 500,000 each of Portuguese and immigrants from the rest of Brazil, nearly 400,000 Spaniards and nearly 200,000 Japanese. It is the world's largest Japanese community outside Japan and their main contribution to the economy of São Paulo has been in horticulture, raising poultry and in cotton farming, especially around cities such as Marília. Significant numbers of Syrian-Lebanese came too, adding an extra dimension to the cultural diversity of the city.

Much of the immigrant labour which flooded in during the early years of the 20th century was destined for the coffee *fazendas* and farms. Others went to work in the industries which were opening up in the city. By 1941 there were 14,000 factories and today the city covers more than 1,500 sq km – three times the size of Paris.

São Paulo

Sights

City centre

Since much of the centre of São Paulo is pedestrianized, there is no option other than to walk if you wish to explore it. This may seem a daunting prospect with the streets permanently crowded and the buildings towering above, but it is a challenge worth taking.

A focal point in the centre is the **Parque Anhangabaú**, an open space between the Triângulo and the streets which lead to Praça da República (Metrô Anhangabaú is at its southern end). Beneath Anhangabaú, north-south traffic is carried by a tunnel. Crossing it are two viaducts: **Viaduto do Chá**, which is open to traffic and links Rua Direita and Rua Barão de Itapetininga. Along its length sellers of potions, cures, fortunes and trinkets set up their booths, an incongruous sight in the middle of a district so dedicated to modern commerce. The **Viaduto Santa Ifigênia**, an iron bridge for pedestrians only, was constructed of 1,100 tonnes of Belgian iron in 1913. As a backdrop to the viaduct and its thousands of pedestrians is the massive frontage of the Sharp building.

Historical buildings in the centre The **Largo de São Bento** is a square in front of the Capela São Bento, which was built in 1598 on the site of the village of chief Tibiriça. Originally it was a public place where fish and vegetables were sold and where travelling circuses set up.

Facing the Largo is the **Igreja e Mosteiro de São Bento** (1910-22) on the site of the 1598 chapel mentioned above. In 1635 the building was enlarged and a new church and monastery was built in 1650, financed by the *bandeirante* Fernão Dias Paes Leme. It was demolished in 1907 to make way for the new church and college. On the main nave's ceiling are religious portraits and carved wooden pillars support the organ, which has 6,000 pipes. When the São Bento Metrô station was built, the church had to be reinforced and the Largo was remodelled; the station itself has an exhibition and concert space.

South of São Bento on the junction of Rua Líbero Badaró and Avenida São João is the **Martinelli building**, the city's first skyscraper, built in 1929 by Comendador Giuseppe Martinelli, a businessman. ■ *0900-1600 Mon-Sat. Entry to 26th floor, free.*

On Praça Antônio Prado stands the **Antigo Prédio do Banco do São Paulo**. This building, which is two interlinked office blocks, has some art nouveau elements and was constructed in the 1930s. The ground floor is now used for fairs and exhibitions. ■ *The building is open 0900-1800 Mon-Fri. From Praça Antônio Prado go down Rua 15 de Novembro to Praça Padre Manuel da Nóbrega.*

The **Pátio do Colégio**, just east of Praça Padre Manuel da Nóbrega, is the site of the founding of São Paulo. It houses the **Capela de Anchieta** and the **Museu Casa de Anchieta**. The original chapel collapsed in 1896; it is some of this building that has been preserved in the new complex. ■ *0730-1700 Mon-Fri. US$0.50.* The **Museu Casa de Anchieta**, houses items from the Jesuit era, including paintings and relics. It also has a model of Piratininga/São Paulo in the 16th-century museum. ■ *1300-1630 Tue-Sun. US$1.*

A short distance southeast of the Pátio do Colégio is the **Solar da Marquesa de Santos**, an 18th-century residential building, which now contains the **Museu da Cidade**. ■ *0900-1700 Tue-Sun. R Roberto Simonsen 136. T2304238.*

The **Praça da Sé** is a huge open space south of the Pátio do Colégio, dominated by the Catedral Metropolitana. The Praça has been, since colonial times, the heart of São Paulo. Around it were the cathedral and other churches; it was where religious processions started and finished. Over the years its aspect was altered, but most appreciably in 1911 when the whole area was remodelled into a monumental square. Today, with its avenue of palms, it is alive with stalls, music, hawkers, buses, fumes and people constantly on the move. Others sit on the steps or sleep on the grass.

Tietê to Liberdade

São Paulo

Sleeping ■
1 Aliança
2 Banri
3 Galeão
4 Hores Belgrano
5 Las Vegas
6 Linson
7 Ofir
8 Riviera
9 Uai

Detailed map
A São Paulo
centre detail,
page 174

Related maps
B Jardins &
Avenida
Paulista,
page 176

São Paulo

The **Catedral Metropolitana** was inaugurated during the 1954 festivities commemorating the fourth centenary of the city and was fully completed in 1970. This enormous building in neo-Gothic style has a capacity for 8,000 worshippers in its five naves. Its twin towers are 97 m high and the central, octagonal cupola is supported by 12 columns a staggering 30 m high. There are two gilt mosaic pictures in the trancepts: on the north side is the Virgin Mary (1952, by Gigotti) and on the south St Paul (1953, by M Avenali, Ravenna Gruppo Mosaicisti). The marble surround to the steps which lead up to the main altar is carved with biblical scenes.

West of the Praça da Sé, along Rua Benjamin Constant, is the Largo de São Francisco. Here is the **Igreja da Ordem Terceira de São Francisco**. The convent was inaugurated in 1647 and reformed in 1744. Note the blue-and-white tile decorations in the chancel and behind the font (up the lefthand passageway). To the right is the Igreja das Chagas do Seráphico Pai São Francisco (1787), painted like its neighbour in blue and gold. To the left is the Faculdade do Direito (Law Faculty) of São Paulo.

North is the Praça do Patriarca, on which stands the church of **Santo Antônio**, next to the *Hotel Othon*. Dating from 1717, the church has a

São Paulo centre detail

	Sleeping		4 Gran Corona	8 Plaza Marabá	● Eating
	1 Bourbon	5 Itamarati	9 San Juan	1 Almanara
	2 Central	6 Jaraguá	10 São Sebastião	2 Boi na Brasa
	3 Eldorado Boulevard	7 Othon Palace	11 Vila Rica	3 Delícia Natural & Sabor Natural

0 metres (approx) 200
0 yards (approx) 200

N

São Paulo

beautifully painted wooden ceiling. ■ *0600-1830 Mon-Fri.* Across the Viaduto do Chá on Praça Ramos de Azevedo is the **Teatro Municipal**, one of the few distinguished early 20th-century survivals that São Paulo can boast. Inaugurated in 1911, many famous international and national stars have played at the theatre. Viewing the interior may only be possible during a performance; as well as the full evening performances. Look out for midday, string quartet and *vesperais líricas* concerts (all free, usually once a week). ■ *T2233022.*

Praça da República

Praça da República is filled with tall trees and birds and is always busy. There are also lots of police. Nearby is the city's tallest building, the **Edifício Itália** on the corner of Avenida Ipiranga and Avenida São Luís. There is a restaurant on top, *Terraço Itália*, and a sightseeing balcony (see Eating, page 183). Also here is the curving Edifício Copan. Two blocks northwest of the Praça is the **Largo do Arouche**, by which is a large flower market, which is worth seeing.

North of the centre

About 10 minutes' walk from the centre of the city is the old **Mercado Municipal** covering 27,000 sq m at Rua Cantareira 306. ■ *0400-1600 Mon-Sat.* A new Mercado Municipal has been built in the outskirts.

Worth a visit is the **Parque da Luz** on Avenida Tiradentes. It was formerly a botanical garden. On the same avenue at No 141 is the **State Art Collection** (**Pinacoteca do Estado**). ■ *1000-1800 Tue-Sun. Free. T2299844.* Nearby, at No 676, the **Igreja e Convento Nossa Senhora da Luz** is one of the few colonial buildings left in São Paulo, although the chapel dates from 1579 and is an example of *taipa de pilão* construction (see Architecture, page 703). It houses the **Museu de Arte Sacra** which has a large collection of sacred objects from the 17th-20th centuries; not all are on show at one time. ■ *1300-1800 Tue-Sun. T2277694.*

Liberdade

Directly south of the Praça da Sé, **Liberdade** is the central Japanese district. An oriental market is held every Sunday (see Shopping, page 185) in the Praça da Liberdade Metrô station. Here you can buy traditional arts and crafts and sample all types of oriental foods, not just Japanese. On the streets of the quarter are Japanese stores, plenty of places to eat and street lights designed like oriental lanterns.

Museu da Imigração Japonesa, Rua São Joaquim 381, Liberdade, is excellent, with a nice roof garden; ask at the desk for an English translation of the exhibits. ■ *1330-1730 Tue-Sun. US$1.50. T2795465.*

4 Paddock
5 Saúde Sabor
6 Terraço Itália

- - ▶ - - Historic buildings walk

The next stop south on the Metrô is Vergueiro, near which is the **Centro Cultural São Paulo**, Rua Vergueiro 1000, which has art and photographic exhibitions, a library, music and dance shows (often regional) and films. ■ *Daily until 2200. T2773611.*

Avenida Paulista & the Jardins District Either Metrô station Vergueiro or Paraíso is convenient for the southeastern end of **Avenida Paulista**. This famous avenue was inaugurated in 1891 by the Uruguayan engineer Joaquim Eugênio de Lima, who wanted to construct an avenue similar to those found in European capitals. In no time, the wealthy built their elegant houses, many in the fashionable eclectic style (see Architecture, page 703), and transformed this into the grandest part of the city. The industrial explosion in the 1930s and 1940s brought a new role to the avenue as offices for commercial houses and service industries were put up. Land prices rose; residents relocated to other districts. In the 1970s the avenue was widened to cope with the ever increasing flow of traffic and in the 1980s the international finance companies, the banks and the multinationals erected the latest architectural towers that rise up on either side today.

The highlight of Avenida Paulista is **MASP**, or **Museu de Arte de São Paulo**. The present building was designed in 1957 and opened in 1968 by Queen

Jardins & Avenida Paulista

■ Sleeping	6 Pousada Dona Zilha	5 Fran's Café	12 Marcel
1 L'Hotel		6 Gero	13 Massimo
2 Mofarrej Sheraton	● Eating	7 Iti Fuji	14 Moraes
3 Monterey	1 Antiquarius	8 Le Bistingo	15 Shian-San
4 Pamplona Palace	2 Chamonix	9 Le Jardin Suisse	
5 Parthenon Crillon	3 Charlô	10 Lellis	● Bars
Plaza	4 Cheiro Verde	11 L'Osteria do Piero	16 Choperia Opçaõ

metres (approx) 0 — 500
yards (approx) 0 — 500

Elizabeth II. It is at Avenida Paulista 1578 (immediately above the 9 de Julho tunnel) and the nearest Metrô is Trianon-MASP. The building is a simple parallelepiped, but instead of resting on the ground it is suspended from two red, concrete arches so that the lowest floor spans a 74-m open space. The museum has major collections of European painters and sculptors, and some interesting work by Brazilian artists, including Portinari. Particularly interesting are the pictures of northeastern Brazil done by Dutch artists during the Dutch occupation (1630-54): the exotic tropical landscapes have been made to look incredibly temperate. Exhibitions vary, not all the artists above may be on view. Temporary exhibitions are also held and when a popular show is on, it can take up to an hour to get in. In this case, the later you go the better. ■ *1100-1800 Tue-Sun. US$8; first you must buy a ticket from the booth, then enter the building. T2515644. Bus 805A from Praça da República goes by MASP.*

On Sunday, an antiques fair is held in the open space beneath the museum, see Shopping, page 185. Opposite MASP is **Parque Tenente Siqueira Campos**, also known as Parque Trianon, covering two blocks on either side of Alameda Santos. It is a welcome, luxuriant, green area in the busiest part of the city. The vegetation includes native plants typical of the Mata Atlântica. ■ *0700-1830 daily. R Peixoto Gomide 949 and Av Paulista.* Next to the park is the smaller Praça Alexandre de Gusmão.

The **Museu da Imagem e do Som** (MIS), Avenida Europa 158, has photographic exhibitions, archives of Brazilian cinema, video and music, and a nice café on ground floor. ■ *1400-1800 Tue-Fri.*

At Avenida Europa 218 and Rua Alemanha 221, next door to MIS, the **Museu Brasiliero da Escultura** (MuBE) holds temporary exhibitions and offers courses in sculpture, painting, engraving and art history. ■ *Free to various temporary exhibitions and to recitals in the afternoons.*

Avenida Europa continues to Avenida Brigadeiro Faria Lima, on which is the **Casa Brasileira**, Avenida Faria Lima 774, a museum of Brazilian furniture. It also holds temporary exhibitions. ■ *1300-1800 Tue-Sun. T2102564.* A little further up the avenue is Shopping Iguatemi.

Memorial da América Latina, designed by Oscar Niemeyer, built in March 1989, at Avenida Mário de Andrade 664, next to Barra Funda Metrô station, has a relief map of Central and South America under a glass floor in the section which houses a permanent exhibition of handicrafts from all over Latin America; there is a photo library, books, magazines, newspapers and films shown on video. ■ *0900-2100 Tue-Fri, 0900-1800 Sat, 1000-1800 Sun. Free.* A few blocks west is **SESC Pompeia**, R Clélia 93, a sports and arts complex with a library, designed by Lina Bo Bardi in 1982-86. It is a vibrant place, with a theatre, exhibitions, workshops, restaurant and café, as well as areas for sunbathing and television watching.

Parque Água Branca, Avenida Francisco Matarazzo 455, not far west of Barra Funda, has beautiful gardens with specimens of tropical plants, Brazilian birds and wildlife. Pavilions house a well-stocked aquarium, a zoo, and exhibitions of food produce. It is also popular with children. ■ *0700-1800 daily.*

The Parque do Ibirapuera was designed by architect Oscar Niemeyer and landscape artist Roberto Burle Marx for the city's fourth centenary in 1954. The park is open daily 0600-1730 and the entrance is on Avenida Pedro Álvares Cabral. Bicycles can be hired. Within its 1.6 million sq m is the new architecturally impressive **Assembléia Legislativa**. There is also a **Planetarium** (■ *shows at 1530 and 1730 at weekends and on holidays, T5755206, US$5,*

Ibirapuera

half price for under 18s); a Japanese pavilion; a velodrome for cycle and motor-cycle racing; an all-aluminium covered stadium for indoor sports which seats 20,000 people; outdoor sports fields; children's play areas; and weekend concerts in the Praça da Paz.

In this park, too, is the **Museu de Arte Moderna** (MAM), with a collection of contemporary paintings, sculptures and photographs, a library specializing in Brazilian and international art and an exciting sculpture garden (look out for Nuno Ramos' *Craca* made of real fish, bones and shell. ■ *1200-1800 Tue, Wed, Fri, 1200-2200 Thu, 1000-1800 Sat-Sun. US$2, students half price, free all Tue and Fri after 1700. T5549 6688, www.mam.org.br* The recently refurbished and spectacular buildling now known as the **Oca** was designed by Niemeyer in the style of a simple Amazonian roundhouse. It houses temporary exhibitions. Bicycles can be hired from local character Maizena beside the city hall, Prodam (US$1.25 for a bike without gears, US$2 with gears, leave document as security). **Buses to Ibirapuera**, 574R from Paraíso Metrô station; 6364 from Praça da Bandeira; to Cidade Universitária 702U or 7181 from Praça da República.

Every even-numbered year the **Bienal Internacional de São Paulo** (São Paulo Biennial) at Ibirapuera has the most important show of modern art in Latin America, usually open from the beginning of September till November (next in 2004).

Cidade Universitária

Instituto Butantã/The Butantã Snake Farm and Museum, on the Cidade Universitária university campus, is one of the most popular tourist attractions in São Paulo. The snakes are milked for their poison six times a day but you may not witness this. The antidotes made from the venom have greatly reduced deaths from snakebite in Brazil. The centre also deals with spider and scorpion venom, has a small hospital and is a biomedical research institute. What visitors see is the museum of poisonous animals and public health, which is well-organized and educational, with explanations in Portuguese and English. ■ *0900-1700 Tue-Sun. US$1 (children and students half price). Av Dr Vital Brasil 1500, T8137222. Getting there: from Praça da República take bus marked 'Butantã' or 'Cidade Universitária' (Nos 701U or 792U) along Av Paulista, and ask to be let out at Instituto Butantã.*

The **Museu de Arte Contemporâneo** (MAC) with an important collection of Brazilian and European modern art is in the Prédio Novo da Reitoria. ■ *1200-1800 Tue-Sat, 1000-1800 Sun. Free. T3818 3039.* Also in the university is the **Museu de Arqueologia e Etnologia** (MAE), with a collection of Amazonian and ancient Mediterranean material. ■ *R Reitoria 1466, T3812 4001.*

Not far from the Butantã Institute, just inside the Cidade Universitária is the **Casa do Bandeirante**, the reconstructed home of a pioneer from 400 years ago. ■ *Praça Monteiro Lobato, T2110920.*

On the west bank of the Rio Pinheiros, just southeast of the campus, is the palatial **Jóquei Clube/Jockey Club** racecourse in the Cidade Jardim area on Avenida Lineu de Paula Machado 1263. ■ *Race meetings are held on Mon and Thu at 1930 and Sat and Sun at 1430. T8164011. Getting there: It is easily accessible by bus (Butantã from República, among others).* It has a **Museu do Turfe** on Avenida Lineu de Paula Machado 1263. ■ *Tue-Sun, but closed Sat and Sun mornings. T8164011.*

Morumbi

Morumbi is a smart residential district with some very imposing houses due south of the Cidade Universitária. In the area are the state government building, **Palácio dos Bandeirantes** (Avenida Morumbi 4500), the small, simple **Capela** de **Morumbi** (Avenida Morumbi 5387), and the **Parque Alfredo Volpi** (Rua Oscar Americano 480). This small park has native plants which are the last vestiges of the time when this was a farm, paths and a playground ■ *0600-2000. No public transport goes there.* Morumbi is most famous for the stadium of **São Paulo Football Club**, holding 100,000 people (it is known as Morumbi). Motor racing fans might like to visit the Morumbi cemetery, last resting place of Ayrton Senna. ■ *Getting there: take bus 6291 to R Profesor Benedito Montenegro.*

Museu da Fundação Maria Luisa e Oscar Americano, Avenida Morumbi 3700, Morumbi, close to the Palácio dos Bandeirantes, is a well-displayed, private collection of Brazilian and Portuguese art and furniture. The garden has fascinating plants, patios and native plants. ■ *1100-1830 Tue-Fri, 1000-1830 Sat-Sun.*

In the suburb of Ipiranga (a Tupi-Guarani word meaning 'red clay'), 5½ km southeast of the city centre, the **Parque da Independência** contains the famous **Monumento à Independência** to commemorate the declaration of Brazilian Independence; beneath the monument is the Imperial Chapel, with the tomb of the first emperor, Dom Pedro I, and Empress Leopoldina ■ *1300-1700 Tue-Sun.* The monument is the second to be built, in time for the centenary of Independence in 1922. The **Casa do Grito**, the little house in which Dom Pedro I spent the night before his famous Cry of Ipiranga – 'Independence or Death' – is preserved in the park. ■ *0930-1700 Tue-Sun.* When Independence was declared, Ipiranga was outside the city's boundaries, in an area where bricks were made, on the main trade route between Santos and São Paulo.

The **Museu Paulista** is housed in a huge palace at the top of the park. The original building, later altered, was the first Monument to Independence. The museum contains old maps, traditional furniture, collections of old coins and of religious art and rare documents, and a department of Indian ethnology. ■ *0900-1645 Tue-Sun. US$1.* Behind the museum is the **Horto Botânico/Ipiranga Botanical Garden** and the **Jardim Francês**, designed as a garden for plant study, now a recreational area. ■ *0900-1700 Tue-Sun. There is a light and sound show on Brazilian history in the park on Wed, Fri and Sat at 2030. Getting there: Take bus 478-P (Ipiranga-Pompéia for return) from Ana Rosa, or take bus 4612 from Praça da República.*

This large park is a long way south of the centre, at Água Funda (Avenida Miguel Estefano 3031-3687). It contains both the Botanical and Zoological Gardens and a game reserve called Simba Safári. The **Jardim Botânico** has a vast garden esplanade surrounded by magnificent stone porches, with lakes and trees and places for picnics, and a very fine orchid farm worth seeing during the flowering season, November-December. Over 19,000 different kinds of orchids are cultivated. There are orchid exhibitions in April and November. ■ *0900-1700 Wed-Sun. T55846300.* The astronomical observatory nearby is open to the public on Thursday afternoons. Take Metrô to São Judas on the Jabaquara line, then take a bus.

Burle Marx Park, Avenida Dona Helena Pereira de Moraes 200, was designed by famous landscape designer Burle Marx. It is the only place in the city where you can walk in trails in the Mata Atlântica (Atlantic rainforest). ■ *0700-1900 daily.*

Nearby, the wildlife park, **Simba Safári**, has over 200 animals roaming free. ■ *1000-1630 Tue-Fri, 0900-1630 Sat-Sun. Av do Cursino 6338, T9466249. Entry is by car only and price of admission depends on the number of people in the vehicle (eg US$25 for a car with 2 adults); children under 12 free.*

Parque da Independência

São Paulo

Parque do Estado (Jardim Botânico)

São Paulo

Excursions

Horto Florestal   In Tremembé, a little beyond Cantareira, 30 minutes north from the downtown area, is the Horto Florestal on Rua do Horto 931, in Parque Estadual Alberto Löfgren. The park contains examples of nearly every species of Brazilian woodland flora, 15 km of natural trails, museum with exhibits of regional flora and fauna and a view of São Paulo from Pedra Grande on the right of the entrance to the park. ■ *0600-1800 daily. T9528555.*

Pico de   This is the highest peak in the neighbourhood and, on a fine day, has good
Jaraguá   views of Greater São Paulo. Lots of hang-gliders fly here at weekends. It is
1,135 m   reached from Km 18 on the Campinas highway (Via Anhangüera) by a good road through Taipas and Pirituba.

Miraporanga   Situated in the foothills of the Serra do Mar, this is one hour's drive from São
Botanical &   Paulo city centre. It has a vast collection of orchids, carnivorous and aquatic
Wildlife   plants, waterlily pools, a lake and 20 glasshouses. It also contains armadillos,
Sanctuary   deer and other mammals, monitor lizards and a variety of hummingbirds. ■ *Contact Sr Samuel Jorge de Mello, T8160817, weekends T4766716, for information and prices.*

Santo Amaro   About 3 km from the centre of Santo Amaro suburb (a 30-minute bus ride
Dam (Old Lake)   from São Paulo) is this popular boating resort with several sailing clubs and
& Interlagos   many attractive cottages along the shore.
See box, page 187,   São Paulo's lake resort on the Santo Amaro Dam, **Avenida Interlagos**, has
for more on the   an 18-km motor-racing circuit. ■ *T5770522.* It can be reached from Santo
Brazilian Grand Prix   Amaro by bus. Close to the track, where the **Brazilian Grand Prix** takes place, is the 32-km long **Guarapiranga** artificial lake with good restaurants and several luxurious sailing and sports clubs. ■ *0600-1700 daily. Av Guarapiranga 575. There is a Camping Clube do Brasil site.* Guarapiranga is less polluted than the other artificial lake, **Billings**, which also has restaurants.

Embu   This colonial town has become a centre for artists and craftsmen. The town itself,
28 km to São Paulo   on a hill, is surrounded by industry and modern developments and the colonial centre is quite small. Many of the old houses are brightly coloured and most contain arts, furniture, souvenir or antiques shops. Good restaurants include *Orixa* and *Garimpo* on Rua Nossa Senhora do Rosário. The central Passeio das Artes, has been refurbished and signposts with maps have been erected, but these can be a bit confusing at times. On Sunday there is a large and popular arts and crafts fair (0900-1800), which is highly recommended for a visit. On Monday almost everything is closed. There is a **tourist office** on Rua Capelinha, which is on the Largo 21 de Abril, where the buses from São Paulo stop.
    The Jesuits founded the original settlement of Bohi, later M'Boy, meaning 'big snake', then Embu, in 1554. In 1690, they transferred the settlement to its present location, building the church of **Nossa Senhora do Rosário** and their residence in what is now known as the Largo dos Jesuítas. In this complex is the **Museu de Arte Sacra**. ■ *1200-1700 Sat-Sun.* The Jesuits and their Indian disciples are said to have inspired Embu's artistic tradition, particularly in the carving of saints, in painting and engraving. In the 20th century, this tradition gained full recognition after the first Arts Exhibition of 1964. Also in the 1960s, the Embu fair became popular, first as a hippy fair, then as a regular event in 1969. There is another chapel in the town centre, **São Lázaro**, which was built in the 1930s by local artists; it is on Rua da Matriz.

The **Festa de Santa Cruz** is held during the second half of May and **Folklore Week** is in August.

Transport Buses: from **São Paulo**, *Soamin* bus No 179 leaves from Av Cruzeiro do Sul between Tietê Rodoviária and Metrô station (it is marked 'Embu-Engenho Velho'); departures between 0610 and 2310, US$2, 1 hr 45 mins. The route passes Clínicas Metrô, goes down Av Francisco Morato, then through Taboão da Serra: you see a lot of southwest São Paulo, but it is a long ride. A quicker alternative is to take a SP-Pinheiros bus from Clínicas, which takes the main highway to Embu; 40 mins, it costs US$0.80. Get out at Largo 21 de Abril in Embu. To return to São Paulo, walk up R da Matriz from Lg 21 de Abril, turn left down Av Junior, then left again on R Solano Trindade to a junction where the buses stop.

Essentials

Sleeping

The best hotels are around Av Paulista and in Jardins (most of these offer discounts during the weekend). Near Praça da República there are some slightly cheaper, but very good hotels and cheaper hotels still can be found on the pedestrian streets between Praça da República and Anhangabaú. In the daytime, this area is OK, but at night you should be careful. Ask your hotel which streets should be avoided. The Japanese district of Liberdade, south of Praça da Sé, has some pleasant hotels and is quite a good place to stay.

■ *on maps, pages 173, 174 and 176 Price codes: see inside front cover*

LL *L'Hotel*, Av Campinas 266, T/F2830500, all suites. Part of the Roteiros de Charme group, see page 47. Recommended. **LL** *Mofarrej Sheraton*, Av Santos 1437, on the south side of Av Paulista, T2535544, F2898670. Recommended.

   A *Monterey*, Av Itu 265, T2856111, F2833247. Safe parking, comfortable accommodation. **A** *Parthenon Crillon Plaza*, R Haddock Lobo 807, T8818511, F30642155. Restaurant, pool, exercise room, one of a chain. Very few cheaper hotels in this area: try **A** *Pousada Dona Zilha*, Av Franca 1621, Jardim Paulista, T8521444, F8532483. With shower, nice patio, lounge. **B** *Pamplona Palace*, R Pamplona 851, T/F855301. Parking.

Around Av Paulista *See map page 176*

AL *Linson*, R Augusta 440, Consolação, T2566700, F2585371. Suites, TV security system, restaurant, pool. **B** *Hores Belgrano*, R Marquês de Paranaguá 88, T2580255, F2577803. Central, English spoken, special rates for long stays.

Consolação

AL *Bourbon*, Av Dr Vieira de Carvalho 99, T33372000, hbnsao@xpnet.com.br Very smart, pleasant, one of a local chain (others in Curitiba, Londrina and Foz do Iguaçu). **AL** *Eldorado Boulevard*, Av São Luís 234, T2141833, www.hoteiseldorado.com.br/hbouleva.htm Excellent. **AL** *Othon Palace*, R Líbero Badaró 190, T32326000, www.othon.com.br Only high-class hotel in the Triângulo, good. **A** *Gran Corona*, Basílio da Gama 101, T2140043, F2144503, in a small street. Comfortable, good services, good restaurant. Warmly recommended. **A** *Jaraguá*, R Maj Quedinho 44, near Praça Dom José Gaspar, T2566633, F2561377. **A** *San Juan*, R Aurora 909, just behind Emtu airport bus terminal, T/F3229100. Recommended. **B** *Itamarati*, Av Dr Vieira de Carvalho 150, T2224133, F2221878. Good location, safe. Highly recommended and very popular. **B** *Plaza Marabá*, Av Ipiranga 757, T2207811, F2207227. Recommended. **B** *Vila Rica*, Av Dr Vieira de Carvalho 167, T/F2207111. **D** *Central*, Av São João 288, T2223044. Good, helpful, central. **C** *São Sebastião*, R 7 de Abril 364, T2574988. TV, fridge, phone, laundry service.

Near Praça da República

São Paulo

Liberdade   **B** *Banri*, R Galvão Bueno 209, T2708877, F2789225. Good. Chinese owners. Recommended. **E** *Ikeda*, R dos Estudantes. With breakfast, shared bath, quiet. Both are near the Metrô station

Santa Ifigênia   Most of the cheaper hotels are in Santa Ifigênia between Av São João and Estação Luz. The area can be approached either from Metrô República or Luz. The red light district is in the blocks bounded by R Santa Ifigênia, R dos Andradas, R dos Gusmões and Av Ipiranga, and is definitely not recommended for women travelling alone. The whole area around Av Rio Branco is rather seedy and not entirely safe late at night.   **B** *Ofir*, R dos Timbiras 258, T2238822. Stores valuables but not money, big rooms, TV, well equipped, good value. **B** *Uai*, R Gen Osório 58, T2231370. Pleasant, rooms on street are good. Recommended. **C** *Riviera*, Av Barão de Limeira 117, T2218077. Excellent value. Highly recommended. **D** *Galeão*, R dos Gusmões 394, T2208211. Safe, helpful, hot showers. **D** *Las Vegas*, R Vitória 390, corner of Av Rio Branco, T2218144. Recommended. **E** *Aliança*, R Gen Osório 235, corner of R Santa Ifigênia, T2204244. Nice, with breakfast, good value.

Youth hostels   *Associação Paulista de Albergues da Juventude*, R 7 de Abril 386, Conj 22, T/F2580388, www.alberguesp.com.br   **E** *Praça da Árvore IYHA*, R Pageú 266, Saúde, T50715148, spalberg@internetcom.com.br   (**D** for non-members), kitchen, laundry, includes breakfast, internet service (US$4 per hr, overpriced). *Magdalena Tagliaferro IYHA*, Estr Turística do Jaguará 651, Km 18, Via Anhangüera, T2580388. Open all year, reservations necessary, take a Jaguará 8696 bus from Anhangabaú Metrô station to the Parque Estadual Jaguará, the hostel is 100 m from the entrance. An unaffiliated hostel is **E** *Primavera*, R Mariz e Barros 346, Vila Santa Eulália (bus 4491 from Parque Dom Pedro in the centre), T2153144, cooking and laundry facilities.

Eating

The main restaurant areas are Jardins, Pinheiros/Vila Madalena; Bixiga for Italian food; Liberdade and Pinheiros for Japanese. For fast food, go to the shopping centres

Apart from the international cuisine in the first-class hotels, here are a few recommendations out of many. The average price of a meal in 2002 was US$10-15 in trattorias, US$25-30 and up to US$75 in first-class places.

You can find restaurants catering for every taste and, given the huge influx of immigrants, a wide variety of nationalities. In addition to Brazilian *churrasco*, seafood and regional food and the more obvious choices such as French, German, Italian, Spanish, Japanese, Chinese, fast food and vegetarian, there are Arabic, Argentine, Greek, Hungarian, Indian, Korean, Mexican and Thai restaurants, to name but a few. Among the publications which give selections of restaurants in the city are the Quatro Rodas guides, the bi-monthly *Go Where?* (US$3), the monthlies *São Paulo Este Mês* and *Magazine Turismo e Hotelaria*.

Arabic   *Almanara*, a chain of reasonably priced restaurants serving Middle Eastern/Lebanese food, Oscar Freire 523 (Cerqueiro César), R Basilio da Gama 70 and Av Vieira de Carvalho 109/123 (either side of Praça da República) and in Shoppings Iguatemi, Morumbi amd Paulista. *Bambi*, Av Santos 59, Paraíso, T2844944. Mostly Arabic food, about US$20. *Rubayat*, Av Santos 86, T2896366. Excellent meat, fixed price meals.

Brazilian   *Bassi*, R 13 de Maio 666, T31042375, Bela Vista, for meat. *Boi na Brasa*, R Bento Freitas by Praça da República. Very good, reasonable prices. *Bolinha*, Av Cidade Jardim 53, Jardim Paulistano, T30612010. For *feijoadas* daily, and other dishes. *Dinho's Place*, Av Santos 45, Paraíso, T2845333. Fri seafood buffet, also meat, US$45, has daily bargains, also Av Morumbi 7976, T5364299. *Dom Place*, Largo do Arouche 246. Good food and very good value (US$7 plus drinks). *Moraes*, Av Santos 1105, Cerqueira César,

T2893347, and Praça Júlio de Mesquita 175, Vila Buarque (Centro), T2218066. Traditional meat dishes. *Oxalá*, Trav Maria Antônia 72, just off Consolação. Bahian specialities at modest prices. *Paddock*, R da Consolação 222, sobreloja, T2574768, and R Campo Verde 88, Jardim Paulistano, T8143582. Traditional fare, excellent *feijoada*. *Paulista Grill*, João Moura 257, Pinheiros, T8535426. Top-quality meat, popular. *Sujinho*, R da Consolação 2078, T2315207. Very popular *churrascaria*, with other branches on the same street.

La Casserole, Largo do Arouche 346, Centro, T2206283. Best known bistro in São Paulo, **French** closed Mon (US$30-50 per person). *Le Bistingo*, Av Franca 580, Cerqueira César, T2893010. *La Tambouille*, Av 9 de Julho 5925, Jardim Europa, T8836276. French and Italian, closed Mon, reserve in advance. *Marcel*, R da Consolação 3555, T30643089. Sensational soufflés.

Arnold's Naschbar, R Pereira Leite 98, Sumarezinho, T36725648. *Eisbein peruruca*. Rec- **German** ommended. *Bismarck*, Av Ibirapuera 3178, T2400313. Good food and excellent draught beer.

Massimo, Av Santos 1826, Cerqueira César, T2840311. Italian and international cuisine. **Italian** *Il Sogno di Anarello*, R Il Sogno di Anarello 58, Vila Mariana, T55754266. Open Mon-Fri 1900-0100 only, excellent, typical *cantina paulistana*. *Lellis*, R Bela Cintra 1849, T30833588. Very good but pricey, *salada Lellis* is a must, and fresh squid in batter. *L'Osteria do Piero*, Av Franca 1509, Cerqueira César, T8531082. Excellent. *Famiglia Mancini*, R Avanhandava 81, Bela Vista, T2564320. Excellent, salads and cold dishes, always queues between 2000-2400. *Gero*, R Haddock Lobo 1629, Jardins, T30640005. Good pasta. *Cantina Taberna do Julio*, R Conselheiro Carrão 392, Bela Vista. Inexpensive. *Gigetto*, Avanhandava 63, T2566530. For pasta at reasonable prices. *La Trattoria*, R Antônio Bicudo 50, Pinheiros, T2803572. Closed Mon, mid-week until 1900, Fri, Sat till 0100, reasonably priced food, *strozzapreti* a must. There are many Italian restaurants in the Bela Vista/Bixiga area, especially on R 13 de Maio. Recommended pizzerias are *Capuano*, R Conselheiro Carrão 416, T2881460, and *Margherita*, Av Tietê 255, T30862556.

Iti Fuji, Av Jaú 487, Cerquera César, T2851286. Typical Japanese. *Kar Wua*, R Mourato **Oriental** Coelho 30, Vila Beatriz, T8811581. Chinese, highly praised. *Komazushi*, R São Carlos do *Japanese tends to* Pinhal 241, loja 5, Bela Vista, T2871820. Renowned for its *sushi*, closed weekends. *be expensive* *Korea House*, R Galvão Bueno 43, Liberdade, T2783052. *Shian-San*, R Pamplona 1115, Jardins, T2876667. Inexpensive Chinese. *Sushi-Guen*, Av Brig Luís Antônio 2367, Lojas 13 and 14, Cerqueira César, T2895566. For *sushi* and *sashimi* but a bit overpriced, closed Sun. Many other Chinese and Japanese restaurants in Liberdade, the Japanese quarter, where there is a Japanese food market in the square by the Metrô station.

Antiquarius, Av Lorena 1884, Cerqueira César, T2823015. Portuguese. *Don Curro*, R **Seafood** Alves Guimarães 230, Pinheiros, T8524712. Especially paella, closed Mon.

Chamonix, R Pamplona 1446, T8533621, nice atmosphere, and *Le Jardin Suisse*, Av **Swiss** Franca 1467, T55053110. Both in Jardim Paulista, expensive, very good.

Charlô, R Barã de Capanema 440, Jardim Paulista. Mostly French but also Brazilian. **General** *Restaurante do MASP*, Av Paulista 1578. In the basement of the museum, reasonably priced, often has live music. *Terraço Itália*, on top of Edif Itália (Ipiranga 344 e São Luís), 41 floors up. Open 1130-0100, fixed price lunch and other meals, dancing with excellent band and superb view (minimum consumption charge of US$10 to be allowed to see the view), US$85 per person including wine in dancing part, US$65-70 otherwise, dress smartly.

São Paulo

São Paulo

Vegetarian   Almost always the cheapest option in São Paulo. 'Vida Integral' monthly newspaper has details of health food restaurants and stores. *O Arroz de Ouro*, Largo do Arouche 88. Shop as well, central. *Cheiro Verde*, Peixoto Gomilde 1413, Cerqueira César. More expensive than most. *Intergrão*, R Joaquim Antunes 377, Jardins. Macrobiotic. *Delícia Natural*, Av Rio Branco 211 (4th floor), corner of Av Ipiranga. Lunch only. *Sabor Natural*, same building, 1st floor. Lunch only. *Folhas e Raizes*, Líbero Bádaro 370, Centro. Good-value buffet lunch. *Saúde Sabor*, São Bento 500, Centro. Lunch only.

Fast food   *Comida por kilo* restaurants can be found all over the city; there are many on R Augusta, eg *Estoril*, No 2969, Jardim América, T30645458, charging US$1.25 per 100 g. Such places are very popular at lunchtime.
McDonalds and other chains can be found all over the city as well as many other not quite so fast, but infinitely more interesting alternatives. One recommended local chain is *Viena*. In most Shopping Centers there is a *Praça da Alimentação*, where various food counters are gathered together, fast and simple. The *Arabesco* chain (see Shopping) is good. *Frevinho Lanches*, R Augusta 1563. Famous for its *beirute* (speciality of São Paulo), as well as many other toasted sandwiches with pitta bread. *Baguette*, Consolação 2418, near Av Paulista, opposite Belas Artes cinema. For sandwiches, especially lively around midnight, also at R 13 de Maio 68. *Absolute*, Av Santos 843. Among the best hamburgers in town. *Rock Dreams*, Av Brigadeiro Faria Lima 743. For hamburgers and sandwiches. *Casa da Fogazza*, R Xavier de Toledo 328 and R 7 de Abril 60 (both close to Praça da República). *Calzone*, with different fillings, juices. Recommended.

Cafés   *Fran's Café*, open 24 hrs, Av Paulista 358, R Heitor Penteado 1326 (Sumaré), R Haddock Lobo 586, Av Lorena 1271 (Jardim Paulista), R Tamandaré 744 (Liberdade) and others. A recommended chain for a meal, day or night. *Café Paris*, Av Waldemar Ferreira 55, Butantã. Open every day of the year. There are several chains of bars selling *mate* and other teas and beverages, plus snacks and sandwiches, eg *Rei do Mate*, *Mister Mate*, *Uno e Due*.

Bars and nightclubs

Bars   *Café do Bexiga*, R 13 de Maio 76. Nice atmosphere, and lots of others in Bixiga/Bela Vista area with live music, eg *Café Piu Piu* (closed Mon) and *Café Pedaço*, at 13 de Maio 134 and 140. Bixiga is traditionally known as the 'Bohemian' area and bars here are usually cheaper than Jardins and Pinheiros areas. *Finnegan's Pub*, R Cristiano Viana 358, Pinheiros. Irish theme, specializes in hamburgers and whisky (not necessarily together). *Pé pra Fora*, Av Pompéia 2517, Sumarezinho. Closed Sun, open air. Recommended. *Choperia* Opçaõ, R Carlos Comenale 97, behind MASP. Popular open air bar. In **Itaim Bibi**   *Hard Rock Café*, R Brig Haroldo Veloso 707. Fake but still sells the T-shirts. *Blue Night Jazz Bar*, Av São Gabriel 558, T8849356, as the name describes.

Disco bars   *Cervejaria Continental*, packed, mixed music, Av Pres JK 373, Itaim Bibi, R dos
Entrance/cover   Pinheiros 1275 and R Haddock Lobo 1573. *Banana-Banana Café*, Av 9 de Júlio 5872,
charges US$10-20   Jardim Paulista. Closed Mon. *DaDo Bier*, Av Juscelino Kubitschek 1203, Itaim. Beer brewed on the premises, live music or disco. *HB Club*, R Cardeal Arcoverde 2958, Pinheiros. Closed Sun, bar, snooker, and informal dance lessons. Test your new skills at *Blen-Blen*, same address at weekends, live Latin bands.

B.A.S.E., Av Brig Luís Antônio 1137, Bela Vista. Techno and dance music. *Love Club & Lounge*, R Pequetita 189, Vila Olímpia. Trance, house, drum 'n' bass. *Columbia* upstairs, R Estados Unidos 1570. Lively. *Hell's Club* downstairs. Opens 0400, techno, wild. *Cha-Cha-Cha*, R Tabapuã 1236. Closed Mon, no Brazilian music, art on walls, candles, gay and straight. *Balafon*, R Sergipe 160. Wed-Sun, small, Afro-Brazilian. *Reggae Night*, Av Robert Kennedy 3880, Interlagos. Thu-Sun, outdoors on lakeside. *Limelight Industry*, R Franz Schubert 93. Pop hits, Japanese restaurant upstairs. 5 other nightspots on this street. *Plataforma 1*, Av Paulista 424. Dinner and folkloric show, very touristy but extremely popular.

Nightclubs

São Paulo is teeming with clubs catering to most preferences, entrance US$5-20 which may include a drink. We list a small section

Entertainment

See the *Guia da Folha* section of *Folha de São Paulo* and *Veja São Paulo* section of the weekly news magazine *Veja* for listings of concerts, theatre, museums, galleries, cinema, bars and restaurants.

Casa da Fazenda, Morumbi, exhibits in 19th-century house. *Espaço Cultural Ena Beçak*, R Oscar Freire 440. *Galeria São Paulo*, R Estados Unidos 1456.

Art galleries

In cinemas entrance is usually half price on Wed; normal seat price is US$3 in the centre, US$5-6 in R Augusta, Av Paulista and Jardins. There is no shortage of cinemas in the city. *Belas Artes*, R da Consolação 2423. Multiscreen. As well as those places showing the latest releases there are cine clubs, eg *Cine SESC*, R Augusta 2075; *Espaço Unibanco*, R Augusta 1470/1475 and cinemas at the *Museu da Imagem e do Som*, *Centro Cultural Itaú* and *Centro Cultural São Paulo*.

Cinema

See box page 187 for information on the Brazilian Grand Prix.

Motor racing

The Teatro Municipal (see Sights, page 175) is used by visiting theatrical and operatic groups, as well as the City Ballet Company and the Municipal Symphony Orchestra who give regular performances. There are several first-class theatres: *Aliança Francesa*, R Gen Jardim 182, Vila Buarque, T2590086. *Itália*, Av Ipiranga 344, T2579092. *Paiol*, R Amaral Gurgel 164, Santa Cecília, T2212462. Free concerts at *Teatro Popular do Sesi*, Av Paulista 1313, T2849787, at midday, under MASP (Mon-Sat). See also Museums above.

Theatre

Festivals

25 Jan, *Foundation of the City*; **Feb**, *Carnival* in *Escolas de samba* parade in the Anhembi Sambódromo, note that during carnival most museums and attractions are closed. In **Jun** there are the *Festas Juninas* and the *Festa de São Vito*, the patron saint of the Italian immigrants. There is a *Festa da Primavera* in **Sep**. In **Dec** there are various *Christmas* and *New Year* festivities. Throughout the year, though, there are countless anniversaries, religious feasts, international fairs and exhibitions, so it would be wise to look in the press or the monthly tourist magazines to see what is on while you are in town. See above for the São Paulo Biennial.

See also box on Carnival, page 186

Shopping

Livraria Cultura, Av Paulista 2073, loja 153, Conjunto Nacional. New books in English. *Livraria Freebook*, R da Consolação 1924. Ring bell for entry, wide collection of art books and imported books in English. *Livraria Triângulo*, R Barão de Itapetininga 255, loja 23, Centro. Sells books in English. *Livraria Kosmos*, Av São Luís 258, loja 6.

Bookshops

▶▶ Carnival in São Paulo

Carnival in São Paulo follows the lead of Rio de Janeiro and is improving in quality every year. The Samba Schools' parades take place in the Sambódromo, Avenida Olavo Fontoura 1209, Anhembi, T69715000. The Grupo 1 (Saturday), Grupo Especial (Sunday and Monday) and the Parade of the Champions on the following Saturday are the ones to watch. Tickets can be obtained from the Sambódromo, from the Saraiva chain of bookshops or on T8294559.

To take part or to visit a practice session at a quadra contact the Samba Schools directly: Gaviões da Fiel Torcida, Rua Cristina Tomás 183, Bom Retiro, T2212066 (Friday 2200); Mocidade Alegre, Avenida Casa Verde 3498, Bairro do Limão, T8577525 (Wednesday and Friday 2000); Rosas de Ouro, Avenida Coronel Euclides Machado 1066, near Ponte da Freguesia do Ó, T8574555 (Wednesday, Friday and Sunday 2030); Vai-Vai, Rua São Vicente 276, Bela Vista, T31058725 (Sunday 2100); X-9 Paulistana, Av Luiz Dumont Villares 324, Carandiru, T2677081 (Wednesday and Sunday 2000).

International stock. In various shopping malls *Livrarias Saraiva* and *Laselva* (also at airports) sell books in English. *Sodiler*, Shopping Market Place, Av Nações Unidas 13947, Brooklin, loja 121A, floor T. *Librairie Française*, R Barão de Itapetininga 275, ground floor. Wide selection, also at R Prof Atilio Innocenti 920, Jardins. *Letraviva*, Av Rebouças 1986. Mon-Fri 0900-1830, Sat 0900-1400, specializes in books and music in Spanish. *Book Centre*, R Gabus Mendes 29, between Basílio da Gama and 7 de Abril (Praça da Republica). Has books in English and German. *Duas Cidades*, R Bento Freitas 158, near República. Good selection of Brazilian and Spanish American literature. *Cinema Elétrico*, R Augusta 973, Centro, and *Sola Cinemateca*, R Fradique Coutinho 361. Sell postcards and books on cinema and art. A shop selling art books and CDs is *Gusto, Gôsto, Gusta*, R Augusta 2161.

Handicrafts Souvenirs *Casa dos Amazonas*, Av Jurupis 460. *Ceará Meu Amor*, R Pamplona 1551, loja 7. Good quality lace from the northeast. *Galeria Arte Brasileira*, Av Lorena 2163, galeria@dialdata.com.br Good value. There is a *Sutaco* handicrafts shop at República Metrô station; this promotes items from the State of São Paulo, open Tue-Fri 1000-1900, Sat 1000-1500; there is a showroom at R Augusta 435, 6th floor.

Jewellery There are many shops selling precious stones, including branches of *H Stern*, jewellers, at Praça da República 242, R Augusta 2340, R Oscar Freire 652 and at Iguatemi, Ibirapuera, Morumbi, Paulista and other shopping centres, hotels *Hilton, Sheraton* and *Maksoud Plaza*, and at the international airport. *Amsterdam Sauer* has outlets at Av São Luís 29, hotels *Maksoud Plaza* and *Sheraton*, shopping centres Iguatemi, Morumbi, and at the international airport. There are many other shops selling Brazilian stones.

Maps *Mapolândia*, 7 de Abril 125, shop 40. There are 2 private map publishers: *Geo Mapas*, R Gen Jardim 645, 3rd floor, Consolação, T2592166 (40% discount for volume purchases, excellent 1988 1:5,000,000 map of Brazil, town maps), and *Editorial Abril*, R do Cartume 585, Bl C, 3rd floor, Lapa, T8716004, F8716270.

Markets The *'hippy fair'* that used to take place in Praça da República was moved to Tiradentes Metrô station but is not nearly as lively or colourful. *Oriental fair*, Praça de Liberdade Sun 1000-1900, good for Japanese snacks, plants and some handicrafts, very picturesque, with remedies on sale, tightrope walking, gypsy fortune tellers, etc. Below the Museu de Arte de São Paulo, an **antiques** market takes place on Sun, 1000-1700.

The Brazilian Grand Prix

Motor racing has had a long and distinguished history in Brazil and the first race day for cars and motorcycles at Interlagos was held on 12 May 1940. The first Brazilian Grand Prix was held there in 1972 and Emerson Fittipaldi won in 1973 driving a Lotus in a time of one hour 43 minutes at an average speed of 183 kmph. He repeated this with an even faster time of one hour 24 minutes the following year in a McLaren and in 1975 another Brazilian José Carlos Pace (after whom the track is named) won in a Brabham. During the 1980s the race was held at the Jacarepaguá racetrack in Rio de Janeiro where the outspoken Nelson Piquet won twice in 1983 and 1986 with some of the fastest lap times seen on this track.

The race returned to the reformed Interlagos during the 1990s, and the legendary Aryton Senna was the last Brazilian driver to win here in 1991 and 1993. After his tragic death in 1994 as a result of mechanical failure, Brazilian viewing figures for motor racing fell drastically. Today, however, there are still many very capable Brazilians driving for the Formula One teams such as Pedro Paulo Diniz (Sauber), Ricardo Zonta (BAR) and Rubens Barrichello (Ferrari) who is probably only waiting for the right car to be up there with his fellow countrymen.

The Brazilian Grand Prix is usually the second of the year being held over a weekend at the end of March or the beginning of April. The race consists of 72 laps of the 4.292-km circuit for a total distance of 309.024 km. Approximately 55,000 people attend the race in addition to the millions watching around the world. The training session takes place on Friday morning; the time trial on Saturday morning and the race itself on Sunday afternoon with warm ups and the drivers' parade in the morning. Tickets can be bought from the racetrack during the whole week or by contacting ABN Amro Bank on T011-55072500 from abroad and T0800-170200 inside Brazil. Minimum ticket price is US$75 rising to US$350 depending on the viewing sector. Sectors A and G are uncovered and the cheapest, whilst sector D (S do Senna) is covered, provides a better view and is more expensive. Tickets for the training sessions are cheaper and can be bought from 0700 on the day from the box office at the circuit. VIP hospitality is readily available but at a high price.

Private cars are banned from the racetrack but park and ride facilities (US$5) are available on Saturday from Shopping SP Market, Avenida das Nações Unidas 22540, and on Sunday from Hipermercado, Avenida das Nações Unidas 4403 and Shopping Interlagos, Avenida Interlagos 2255. There are also buses (Saturday-Sunday) from Praça da República, between Rua do Arouche and Rua Marquês de Itu (295), from Praça Com Linneu Gomes at Congonhas airport and from Rua dos Jequitibás in front of the Jabaquara bus station (189). All buses have different coloured stickers to indicate which drop-off point they serve. Further general information about the Grand Prix in English can be obtained from www.gpbrasil.org.

Arts and handicrafts are also sold in Parque Tte Siqueira Campos/Trianon on Sun from 0900-1700. Av Lorena, which is one of the upmarket shopping streets off R Augusta in Jardins, has an open-air market on Sun selling fruits and juices. There are **flea markets** Sun in the main square of the Bixiga district (Praça Don Orione) and in Praça Benedito Calixto in Pinheiros. São Paulo is relatively cheap for film and clothes (especially shoes). The *Ceasa flower market* should not be missed, Av Doutor Gastão Vidigal 1946, Jaguaré, Tue and Fri 0700-1200.

For repairs to Canon and other makes: *Cine Camera Service*, R Conselheiro Crispiniano **Photography** 97, 2nd floor.

Shopping centres   Typical of modern development are the huge Iguatemi, Ibirapuera and Morumbi shopping centres. They include luxurious cinemas, snack bars and most of the best shops in São Paulo. Other malls include Paulista and Butantã. On a humbler level are the big supermarkets of *El Dorado* (Av Pamplona 1704) and *Pão de Açúcar* (Praça Roosevelt, near the *Hilton*); the latter is open 24 hrs a day (except Sun).

Sport

Football   The most popular local teams are *Corinthians*, *Palmeiras* and *São Paulo* who generally play in the Morumbi and Pacaembu stadiums. **Golf courses** (including outside the metropolitan area) about half an hour's drive from the centre there are 18-hole golf courses at the *São Paulo Golf Club*, Praça Dom Francisco Souza 635, in Santo Amaro, in beautiful surroundings. *Clube de Golf de Campinas*, Via Anhangüera, Km 108, Campinas. *Clube de Campo São Paulo* and *Guarapiranga Golf e Country*, both at Reprêsa Guarapiranga, Estr Paralheiros, Km 34. *São Fernando Golf Club*, Estr de Cotia, Km 29. There is a lakeside club at Km 50 on the Santos road. 9-hole courses at *São Francisco Club*, Estr de Osasco, Km 15. *Anglo Sports Center*, Barretos. *International golf club*, Via Dutra Km 232, Guaratinguetá. **Horse-racing** (Jockey Club) and **motor racing** (see Excursions, Interlagos) are mentioned above. For **nature trails**, etc, *Free Way*, R Leôncio de Carvalho 267, Paraíso, T2854767/2835983. **Yachting, sailing** and **rowing** take place on Santo Amaro reservoir (also see above).

Tour operators

Ambiental Viagens e Expedições, Av Prudente Morais 344, conj 5, T8148809. English and Spanish spoken, helpful. Recommended for trips to less well known places; *AmEx* office in *Hotel Sheraton Mofarrej*, Av Santos 1437, T2843515 (see Banks above). *Kontik-Franstur* (American Express representative), R Marconi 71, T2597566. *Lema Turismo*, Av Marquês de Itú 837, T231519. Personalized excursions, Marta Schneider speaks 8 languages, including Hungarian. *STB*, Av Brig Faria Lima 1713, T8700555. ISIC cards and student discounts. *Terra Expedições*, Osmar e Valdir, R Silva Jardim 429, Santa Terezinha, Santo André, T4463381, recommended for motocycle tours and information, Spanish and Italian spoken (English improving). Visits to coffee fazendas (May-Jun) and round trips into the surrounding country are organized by the travel agencies.

Transport

Local   **Driving**   The *rodízio* which curbs traffic pollution by restricting car use according to number plate may be extended beyond the winter months. Check.

See also Ins and outs, page 168

Metrô   The first metro in Brazil, it began operating in 1975 and has 2 main lines intersecting at Praça de Sé: north-south from Tucuruvi to Jabaquara; east-west from Corinthians Itaquera to Barra Funda (the interchange with Fepasa and RFFSA railways and site of the São Paulo and Paraná rodoviária); an extension east to Guaianases is to open soon. A 3rd line runs from Vila Madalena in the west, along Av Paulista, to Ana Rosa in the south, joining the Jabaquara line at Paraíso and Ana Rosa. A 4th line, Vila Sônia to Luz, is projected. The 2 main lines operate from 0500-2400, Vila Madalena to Ana Rosa 0600-2200. Stations are well-policed and safe. Fare US$0.75, US$6 for a book of 10 tickets; backpacks are allowed. Combined bus and Metrô ticket are available, US$1, eg to Congonhas airport.

Taxis   Taxis display cards of actual tariffs in the window (starting price US$3). There are ordinary taxis, which are hailed on the street, or at taxi stations such as Praça da

República, radio taxis and deluxe taxis. For Radio Taxis, which are more expensive but involve fewer hassles, **Central de Táxi**, T9740182; **Central Rádio Táxi**, T69146630; **Vermelho e Branco**,T2511733; **TeleTáxi**, T2331977, or look in the phone book for others; calls are not accepted from public phones.

Air **Cumbica international airport**: there are air services to all parts of the world from the international airport at Guarulhos, also known as Cumbica, Av Monteiro Lobato 1985, T64452945. *Varig* has its own, new terminal for international flights, adjoining the old terminal which all other airlines use. *Emtu* bus service every 30 mins to Guarulhos from Praça da República 343 (northwest side, corner of R Arouche) 0530-2300, and from Tietê rodoviária, US$6.50, 30-45 mins. Buses also run from Bresser bus station to Guarulhos and there are other buses from Jabaquara bus terminal to Guarulhos, without luggage space, usually crowded. Taxi fares from the city to the airport are between US$35-40 and vary from cab to cab. Rush hour traffic can easily turn this 30-min journey into an hour. There are plenty of banks and money changers in the arrivals hall open 0800-2200 daily. There is a post office on the 3rd floor of Asa A and tourist information is also available from the airport branch of *Secretaria de Esportes e Turismo* open 0800-2200, Sat-Sun and holidays 0900-2100.

Long distance

The domestic airport of **Congonhas**, 14 km from the city centre on Av Washington Luís, T50909000, is used for the Rio-São Paulo shuttle (about 400 flights a week US$100 one-way), some flights to Belo Horizonte and Vitória and private flights only. The airport at Campo de Marte, Av Santos Dumont 1979, T2902699 is used for charter flights and helicopters.

Buses There is a convenient Metrô connection to the main rodoviária at **Tietê**, T2350322, but the only way to the platforms is by stairs. This is very difficult for people with heavy luggage and, for the disabled, almost impossible. Tietê handles buses to the interior of São Paulo state, all state capitals (but see also under Barra Funda and

São Paulo

Sao Paulo metrô

To Railway Station, Rodoviária & Memorial da América Latina

Tucuruvi
Parada Inglesa
Jardim São Paulo
Santana
Carandiru
Tietê → To Rodoviária
Barra Funda
Marechal Deodoro
Santa Cecília
República
Anhangabaú
Armênia
Tiradentes
Luz
São Bento
Sé
Pedro II
Liberdade
São Joaquim
Verguiero
Ana Rosa
Vila Mariana
Santa Cruz → To Museu Lasar Segall (3 blocks)
Praça da Árvore
Saúde
São Judas
Conceição
Jabaquara

Vila Madalena
Sumaré
Clínicas
Consolação
Trianon-MASP
Brigadeiro
Paraíso

Brás
Bresser
Belém
Tatuapé
Carrão
Penha
Vila Matilde
Guilhermina-Esperança
Patriarca
Artur Alvim
Corinthians-Itaquera

To Rodoviária
To Museu da Imigração Japonesa (350m approx)
To Parque Ibirapuera (1.5 km approx)

North-South Line
East-West Line
Avenida Paulista Line

Bresser below) and international buses (see next paragraph). The left luggage charges US$0.80 per day per item. You can sleep in the bus station after 2200 when the guards have gone; tepid showers cost US$2.

Buses from Tietê: To **Rio**, 6 hrs, every 30 mins, US$12.50 (*leito*, 25), special section for this route in the rodoviária, request the coastal route via Santos ('via litoral') unless you wish to go the direct route. To **Florianópolis**, 11 hrs (US$23.75, *leito* 36.25). To **Porto Alegre**, 18 hrs, US$36.50 (*leito*, 60). To **Curitiba**, 6 hrs, US$10.25-12.50. To **Salvador**, 30 hrs, US$51 (executive, 64). To **Recife**, 40 hrs, US$60-70. To **Campo Grande**, 14 hrs, US$33. To **Cuiabá**, 24 hrs, US$42. To **Porto Velho**, 60 hrs (or more), US$75. To **Brasília**, 16 hrs, US$30 (*leito*, 60). To **Foz do Iguaçu**, 16 hrs, US$30. To **São Sebastião**, 4 hrs US$8.85 (say 'via Bertioga' if you want to go by the coast road, beautiful journey but few buses take this route).

International buses To **Montevideo**, via Porto Alegre, with *TTL*, departs Mon, Thu, Sat 2200, 31 hrs, US$100, cold a/c at night, plenty of meal stops, bus stops for border formalities, passengers disembark only to collect passport and tourist card on the Uruguayan side (also *EGA*, same price, US$67 to **Chuy**, Tue, Fri, Sun). To **Buenos Aires**, *Pluma*, 36 hrs, US$145. To **Santiago**, *Pluma* or *Chilebus*, 56 hrs, US$130, *Chile Bus*, poor meals, but otherwise good, beware overbooking. To **Asunción** (1,044 km), 18 hrs with *Pluma* (US$57, *leito* 112), *Brújula* (US$64) or *RYSA* (US$110), all stop at Ciudad del Este (US$43, 50 and 84 respectively, *Pluma leito* US$84). *Cometa del Amambay* runs to Pedro Juan Caballero and Concepción.

There are 3 other bus terminals, **Barra Funda**, T664682 (as described above), to cities in southern São Paulo state and many destinations in Paraná, including Foz do Iguaçu (check for special prices on buses to Ciudad del Este, which can be cheaper than buses to Foz). **Bresser** (Metrô Bresser), T66925191, for *Cometa* (T69677255) or *Transul* (T66938061) serving destinations in Minas Gerais. **Belo Horizonte**, 10 hrs, US$15.60, 11 a day (*leito* 31.20), 9 a day with *Gontijo*. *Translavras*, and *Util* also operate out of this station. Prices are given under destinations. **Jabaquara**, at the southern end of the Metrô line. Buses from here for **Santos**, US$3.60, leave every 15 mins, taking about 50 mins, last bus at 0100. Also serves destinations on the southern coast of São Paulo state.

Car hire *Avis*, Araújo 232 and at the airports, T0800-118066. *Budget*, R da Consolação 328, loja 1, and at Guarulhos, T2564355. *Hertz*, Araújo 216, 1st floor, and at the airports, T8837300 or T0800-147300. *Interlocadora*, several branches, São Luís T2555604, M Fontes T2573544, Guarulhos T64453838, Congonhas T2409287. *Localiza*, T0800-992000, or www.localiza.com.br, for all reservations, 8 branches in the city.

Hitchhiking To hitch to Rio, take the Metrô to Armênia, then a bus to Guarulhos, alighting where the bus turns off the Rio road for Guarulhos.

Trains Railways are being privatized and as a result many long distance passenger services have been withdrawn including services to Campo Grande, Corumbá and Brasília via Campinas. São Paulo has 4 stations: **Estação da Luz**, for commuter trains between the northwest and southeast of São Paulo state, on the former Santos a Jundiaí Railway. There is also a Metrô stop here. A train runs from Luz 8 times a day to connect with the **tourist train** from Paranapiaçaba to Rio Grande da Serra, US$0.50. **Barra Funda**, handles commuter destinations on the former Sorocabana and former Santos a Jundiaí railway lines. Services go to **São José do Rio Preto** (overnight), **Barretos**, **Ourinhos**, **Londrina**, **Maringá**, **Sorocaba** and **Ponta Grossa**. There is also a Metrô station and a rodoviária at Barra Funda. **Júlio Prestes** station, for commuter services to the west on the former Sorocabana metre-gauge railway; T0800-550121 for these 3 stations. **Roosevelt**, T9421132, for commuter trains to east on former Central do Brasil and Santos a Jundiaí railways.

Directory

Aerolíneas Argentinas, Araújo 216, 6th floor, T2590319 (Guarulhos T64453806). *Alitalia*, **Airline offices**
Av São Luís 50, cj 291, T2571922 (Guarulhos T64453791). *American Airlines*, Araújo 216,
1st floor, T568010. *Avianca*, R da Consolação 293, 10th floor T2576511 (Guarulhos
T64453798). *British Airways*, Av São Luís 50, 32nd floor, T2596144 (Guarulhos
T64452462). *Continental*, R da Consolação 247, 13th floor, T0800-554777 (Guarulhos
T64454187). *Delta*, R Marquês de Itu 61, T2585866. *Iberia*, Araújo 216, 3rd floor,
T25076711 (Guarulhos T64452060). *JAL*, Av Paulista 542, 2nd floor, T2515222 (Guarulhos
T64452040). *KLM*, Av São Luís 86, T2571363 (Guarulhos T64452011). *LanChile*, R da
Consolação 247, 12th floor, T259 2900 (Guarulhos T64452824). *Lufthansa*, R Gomes de
Carvalho 1356, 2nd floor, T30485868 (Guarulhos T64452220). *Rio-Sul*, R Bráulio Gomes
151, T55612161. *TAM*, R da Consolação 247, 3rd floor, T55828631 (Guarulhos
T64452220). *TAP*, Av São Luís 187, T255 5366 (Guarulhos T64452400). *United*, Av Paulista
777, 9-10th floor, T2532323 (Guarulhos T64453283). *Varig*, R da Consolação 362/372, Av
Paulista 1765, T50917000 (Guarulhos T64452825, Congonhas 535 0216). *Vasp*, Praça L
Gomes/Aurora 974, Av São Luís 72, T0800-998277.

Banco do Brasil will change cash and TCs and will advance cash against Visa. All trans- **Banks**
actions are done in the foreign exchange department of any main branch (eg Av São   *Banking hours are*
João 32, Centro), but queues are long. *Banespa*, eg at R Duque de Caxias 200, Centro,   *generally 1000-1600,*
or Praça da República 295, accepts Visa, TCs and cash. *Citibank*, Av Ipiranga 855, or Av   *although times differ*
Paulista 1111 (1100-1500). *MasterCard*, cash against card, R Campo Verde 61, 4th   *for foreign exchange*
floor, Jardim Paulistano.   *transactions (check at*
   Money changers There are many *câmbios* on or near Praça da República. Most   *individual branches)*
travel agents on Av São Luís change TCs and cash at good rates, but very few are open
on Sat. *Amoretur*, Praça da República 203, will change TCs. *Avencatur*, Av Nações
Unidas 1394, Morumbi, changes TCs, Deutschmarks, good rates. *Coraltur*, Praça da
República 95. *Interpax*, Praça da República 177, loja 13, changes cash (many currencies) and TCs, 0930-1800, Sat 0930-1300.

Internet At Av Paulista 1499, conj 1001 (Metrô Trianon), 1100-2200, English spoken, **Communica-**
second-hand books; *Kiosknet*, Shopping Light, 4th floor, R Cel Xavier de Toledo 23,   **tions**
opposite Teatro Municipal, T3151 3645, US$2.50 per hr; *O Porão*, R Tamandaré 1066,
near Vergueiro metro station. *Saraiva Megastore*, Shopping El Dorado, US$3.
   Post office Correio Central, Praça do Correio, corner of Av São João and Prestes
Máia, T8315222. Booth adjoining tourist office on Praça da República, weekdays only
1000-1200, 1300-1600, for letters and small packages only.
   Telephone *Embratel*, Av São Luís 50, and Av Ipiranga 344. For the international
operator dial 000111, for international collect calls dial 000107. Red phone boxes are
for national calls, blue ones for international phone calls.

Centro Brasileiro Britânico, R Ferriera de Araújo 741, Pinheiros, T3039 0567. *American* **Cultural**
Library, União Cultural Brasil-Estados Unidos, R Col Oscar Porto 208. *Goethe-Instituto*, R **centres**
Lisboa 974 (open Mon-Thu 1400-2030). *Centro Cultural Fiesp*, Av Paulista 1313, open
0900-1900 Tue-Sun, has foreign newspapers and magazines. See under Entertainment
for *Alliance Française* Theatre. If you are interested in cultural articles related São Paolo
and Brazil in general, check out the website of the *Instituto Cultural Itaú*, www.ici.org.br

Consulates *Argentina*, Av Paulista 1106, T2841355 (open 0900-1300, very easy to **Embassies &**
get a visa here). *Australia*, R Tenente Negrão 140, T38496281. *Austria*, R Augusta 2516, **consulates**
10th floor, T282 6223, Mon-Thu 0930-1130. *Bolivia*, R Honduras 1447, T30811688
(open 0900-1300). *Canada*, Av Nações Unidas 12901, T55094343, open 0900-1200,

São Paulo

1400-1700. *Denmark*, R Oscar Freire 379, T30613625, open 0900-1700, Fri until 1400 only. *France*, Av Paulista 1842, 14th floor, T2879522, open 0830-1200. *Germany*, Av Brigadeiro Faria Lima 2092, T38146644, open 0800-1130. *Ireland*, Av Paulista 2006, 5th floor, T2876362, open 1400-1700. T2842044. *Israel*, Av Brig Faria Lima 1713, T38157788. *Netherlands*, Av Brigadeiro Faria Lima 1779, T38130522, open 0900-1200. *New Zealand*, Av Campinas 579, T2880700. *Norway and Sweden*, R Oscar Freire 379, 3rd floor, T8833322 (Norway), T30611700 (Sweden) (Caixa Postal 51626), 0900-1300. *Paraguay*, R Bandeira Paulista 600, 15th floor, T38490455, open 0830-1600. *Peru*, R Votuverava 350, T38191793, open 0900-1300. *South Africa*, Av Paulista 1754, T2850433. *Switzerland*, Av Paulista 1754, 4th floor, Caixa Postal 30588, T2534951. *UK*, Av Paulista 37, 17th floor, T2877722, consulad@uol.com.br *Uruguay*, Av Santos 905, T2840998, open 1000-1600. *US*, R Padre João Manuel 933, T30816511, open 0800-1700. *Venezuela*, R Veneza 878, T38874583, open 0900-1130.

Language courses   The official *Universidade de São Paulo (USP)* is situated in the Cidade Universitária (buses from main bus station), beyond Pinheiros. There are a number of architecturally interesting buildings plus the museums mentioned above. They have courses available to foreigners, including a popular Portuguese course, registry is through the Comissão de Cooperação Internacional, R do Anfiteatro 181, Bloco das Colméias 05508, Cidade Universitária, São Paulo. Other universities include the Pontifical Catholic University, and the Mackenzie University.

Laundry   *Chuá Self Service*, R Augusta 728, T2584953, limited self-service, not cheap. *Di-Lelles*, R Atenas 409, T72983928, pricey.

Medical services   *Hospital das Clínicas*, Av Dr Enéias de Carvalho Aguiar 255, Jardins, T30696000. *Hospital Samaritano*, R Cons Brotero 1468, Higenópolis, T8240022. Recommended. Both have *pronto-socorro* (emergency services). Contact your consulate for names of doctors and dentists who speak your language

Useful addresses   Immigration: Federal Police, Av Prestes Maia 700, open 1000-1600 for visa extensions. **Emergency and ambulance**: T192. **Fire**: T193.

Voltage   110-220 volts AC, 60 cycles.

The Coast

The coast of São Paulo state, referred to as the Litoral Norte or Costa Linha Verde (North of Santos) and the Litoral or Costa Sul (South of Santos) is very popular with Paulistanos for weekends away from the city. In either direction there are many resorts to choose from. The central point is the port of Santos, but even here, the beach is close at hand and it is a good place from which to start exploring, especially if you don't want to waste time with the traffic in the state capital.

History

The coast around Santos is one of the sites which has yielded evidence of the *sambaqui* culture of c 5000 BC (see page 663). The Tupinikin were the people who lived in this region when the Portuguese arrived, but the first European settlements at São Vicente and Santos were under constant attack from the Tamoio (allies of the French), who lived further north. For a long time, it was touch-and-go whether the Portuguese settlements would survive. The colony on São Vicente island was founded in 1532 by Martim Afonso de Sousa and the port of Santos was founded soon after. By the 1580s it was reported that there were 400 houses in São Vicente and Santos.

The French and the Tamoio did not succeed in driving the Portuguese out of their captaincy of São Vicente and Santos became one of the most important ports on the Atlantic coast. The ascent of the Serra do Mar to the Paulista plateau, so treacherous in the early days because of both its steepness and Indian attacks, did not deter the harbour's growth. Sugar was grown on the levels at the foot of the mountains and on the plateau. This was the port's main commodity for shipping, but there was also the trade with São Paulo and, when coffee was introduced to the region, Santos was its outlet.

Up to the end of the 19th century, Santos had an evil reputation for its proneness to yellow fever. "Formerly whole ships' crews were stricken down with fever and died, and the ships being left without the slightest protection, ran ashore, and their skeletons are in evidence at the port at the present day". So wrote Frederick Alcock in 1907, who visited Santos "not without some slight feelings of fear". He was, in fact, pleasantly surprised by the place and, once measures been taken to eradicate the fever, Santos soon became a pleasure resort, in addition to its commercial activities.

The hinterland between the sea and mountains gained another reputation for horrors in the 20th century. A few kilometres inland from the city of Santos an important industrial area, including many chemical plants, built up round the steelworks, oil refinery and hydroelectric plant at Cubatão. At one time the pollution was so appalling that it was called 'The Valley of Death'. In the mid-1980s, it was claimed to be the most contaminated part of the planet, with so much toxic waste undermining the hills that the whole lot threatened to slip down into the sea. Such a tragedy has been averted and cleaning-up operations have taken place.

Santos

Although better known for its busy commercial port and football team (a museum dedicated to Peléhas has long been planned), the island has a long seafront with popular beaches especially during the weekend and holidays. Less than an hour away from São Paulo and its international airport, Santos makes a manageable, friendly base. Gonzaga is the centre of the city's leisure industry with cinemas, bars and restaurants. The centre has some interesting churches and other sights such as the imposing Bolsa Official de Café as well as good views from the summit of Monte Serrat.

Phone code: 013
Colour map 5, grid A6
Population: 418,000

The scenery on the routes crossing the Serra do Mar is superb and the roadway includes many bridges and tunnels. From Rio the direct highway, the Linha Verde (see pages 155 and 199) is also wonderful for scenery.

Situated 72 km southeast of São Paulo and 5 km from the open sea, Santos is the most important Brazilian port. By sea it is approached along the winding Santos Channel, at the mouth of which is an old fort (1709). A free-port zone for Paraguay, 1,930 km by rail or road, has been established. The island upon which the city stands can be circumnavigated by small boats.

The centre of the city is on the north side of the island. Due south, on the Baía de Santos, is **Gonzaga**, where hotels line the beachfront and the city's entertainment takes place. Between these two areas, the eastern end of the island curves round within the Santos Channel. At the eastern tip, a ferry crosses the estuary to give access to the beaches of the sophisticated resort of Guarujá. The city has

São Paulo

impressive modern buildings, wide, tree-lined avenues, and wealthy suburbs. There are **Tourist offices** at the rodoviária (limited information), Praía do Gonzaga on the seafront (in a disused tram, very helpful, lots of leaflets) and Orquidário Municipal (limited opening), T080-173887.

Security   Although poverty is apparent the city is generally safe but it is wise to exercise caution at night and near the port.

Sights   The streets around **Praça Mauá** are very busy in the daytime, with plenty of cheap shops. In the centre, an interesting building is the **Bolsa Oficial de Café**, the coffee exchange, at Rua 15 de Novembro 95, with a small coffee museum and café inside. Two restored churches in the centre are the 17th-century **Santo Antônio do Valongo**, which is by the railway station on Largo Monte Alegre, and the **Capela da Ordem Terceira de Nossa Senhora do Carmo** (1760), on Praça Barão do Rio Branco. A **Tourist Tram Line** runs from Mauá Square. ■ *1100-1700, Tue-Sun.*

Monte Serrat, just south of the city centre, has at its summit a semaphore station and look-out post which reports the arrival of all ships in Santos harbour. There is also a quaint old church, dedicated to Nossa Senhora da Monte Serrat, said to have performed many miracles. The top can be reached on foot or by funicular, which leaves every 30 minutes, US$6. Seven shrines have been built on the way up and annual pilgrimages are made by the local people. There are fine views.

There are many monuments: in Avenida Ana Costa to commemorate the brothers Andradas, who took a leading part in the movement for Independence; in the Praça Rui Barbosa to Bartolomeu de Gusmão, who has a claim to the world's first historically recorded airborne ascent in 1709; in the Praça da República to Brás Cubas, who founded the city in 1534; and in the Praça José Bonifácio to the soldiers of Santos who died in the Revolution of 1932.

Museu do Mar, Rua República do Equador 81, in the eastern part of the city, has a collection that includes several thousand shells. In the western district of José Menino is the **Orquidário Municipal**, Orchid Garden, in the Praça Washington (flowering October-February, orchid show in November). There is the opportunity here to wander among giant subtropical and tropical trees, amazing orchids and, when the aviary is open, to meet macaws,

São Paulo coast

toucans and parrots. The open-air cage also contains hummingbirds of 20 different species and the park is a sanctuary for other birds. ■ *Orquidário 0900-1700 Tue-Sun; bird enclosure 0800-1100, 1400-1700. US$0.50 (children and senior citizens free).*

Beaches

Santos' 8 km of beaches stretch round the Baía de Santos and lead into those of São Vicente at the western end. From east to west they are **Ponta da Praia**, below the sea wall and on the estuary, no good for bathing, but fine for watching the movements of the ships. Next come **Aparecida**, **Embaré**, **Boqueirão**, **Gonzaga** and **José Menino** (the original seaside resort for the merchants of Santos). São Vicente's beaches of **Itararé** and **Ilha Porchat** are on the island, while **Gonzaguinha** is on the mainland. The last beach is **Itaquitanduva**, which is in a military area, but may be visited with authorization. In all cases, check the cleanliness of the water before venturing in (a red flag means it is too polluted for bathing). See page 199 for Guarujá.

Excursions

Ilha Porchat This small island is reached by a bridge at the far end of Santos/São Vicente bay. It has beautiful views over rocky precipices, of the high seas on one side and of the city and bay on the other. At the summit is *Terraço Chopp*, a restaurant which has live music most evenings; the views from here are wonderful. On summer evenings the queues to get in can last up to four hours, but in winter, even if it may be a little chilly at night, the queues are non-existent. It is situated at Av Ary Barroso 274, Ilha Porchat, São Vicente.

Itatinga This village, 30 km from Santos in the Serra do Mar, offers the chance to see what is left of the Atlantic forest at close quarters and to trek through mangrove, sandbanks and hillside forest. The area is full of wildlife (lizards, toucans, butterflies), and thick with vegetation (bromeliads, orchids, eucalyptus). Each trail is graded according to difficulty. You travel to the village of Itatinga by boat on a three-hour trip down the Estuário and the Rio Itapanhaú and then by street car. Or take the BR-101 (Santos-Rio) road, a three-minute crossing by boat and then 7½ km by street car. Access is with one of the travel agencies officially permitted to lead groups: contact *Sictur* (the tourism department), Praça dos Expedicionários 10, 8th floor, T32224166.

São Paulo

São Paulo

Alto da Serra From here, the summit of the forest-clad mountain range, there are magnificent views. The return journey can be done in under two hours by road.

Sleeping
50% discounts often available in hotels during low season

A *Mendes Plaza*, Av Floriano Peixoto 42, T32894243, F32848253. 1 block from beach in shopping street. A/c, safe, TV, restaurant, sauna, massage, sports facilities. Afternoon tea served daily. The following 3 hotels are all on the seafront; rooms with a seaview are cheaper: **A** *Parque Balneário*, Av Ana Costa 555, T32895700, F32840475. Restaurant, rooftop pool, convention centre. **B** *Atlântico*, Av Pres Wilson 1, T32894500, www.atlantico-hotel.com.br A/c, TV, sauna, bar, restaurant. **B** *Avenida Palace*, Av Pres Wilson 10, T32893555, F32895961, www.avenidapalace.com.br Rather simple rooms, but pleasant. **D** *Independência*, Av Mcal Floriano Peixoto 206, T32376224. Friendly with small but bright airy rooms with a/c, radio and TV. Nice. **E** *Natal*, Av Mcal Floriano Peixoto 104, T32842732. Clean and friendly with good breakfast. **E** *Pousada do Marquês*, Av Floriano Peixoto 204, T32371951. Basic, small, family-run. Restaurant downstairs. **F** per person, shared bath. Recommended. There are many cheap hotels near the Orquidário Municipal a few blocks from the beach.

Eating

Mid-range: *Mare Mansi*, in *Hotel Avenida Palace*, Av Presidente Wilson, 9. Full menu, terrace overlooking beach. Seafaring theme, piped music, civilized. **Cheap**: *Dona*

Sleeping
1 Atlântico
2 Avenida Palace
3 Independência
4 Mendes Plaza
5 Natal
6 Parque Balneário
7 Pousada do Marquês

Eating
1 Dona Mineira
2 Point 44
3 Praia Gonzaga

The railway up the hill

The British-built Santos a Jundiaí up the hill to São Paulo is one of the railway wonders of the world; beyond São Paulo it carries on 60 km to Jundiaí. Having passed through Cubatão on the coastal plain, it runs on toothed tracks up the escarpment, going through interesting hill scenery.

Today, RFFSA, the national railway company, runs a tourist train at weekends between São Paulo and Santos (see *page 190 for the schedule).* *Today's timetable bears no relation to how the system operated in the line's heyday. Trains left São Paulo at 0600 in order to get the passengers to their businesses by 0800. At the top of the Serra, the engine was detached from the carriages which were attached to a wire rope. They were then allowed to go down the slope to the port by force of gravity, with another train coming up acting as a counterweight.*

São Paulo

Mineira, R Djalma Dutra 1, Gonzago. Self-service, pleasant wooden terrace, homely interior on 2 floors, excellent food. Recommended. *Point 44*, R Jorge Tibiriçá 44. Large, popular self service. Sports screen and live music from 2030, Tue-Sun. *Restaurante Praia Gonzaga*, Av Mal Floriano Peixoto, 104a, Gonzaga. Self-service with *churrasco*, lunch only. **Seriously cheap**: *Shopping Miramar*, Av Mal Floriano Peixoto 44, has a number of fast-food outlets, including *Bob's*.

Bars & nightclubs

Torto, Av Siquiera Campos 800, Boqueirão, Reggae, MPB. Rock Thu-Sun. *Bar do Três*, Av Washington Luís 422, Gonzaga. Bar with live music. *Disco Friday*, Mendes Convention Center, Av Francisco Gilcério 206, T32287575. A/c complex with 6 bars and dance floors. House and pop music. Minimum consumption US$10 for men, US$5 for women, plus US$2 entry. *Internetbar*, Av Mcal Floriano Peixoto 302, Pompéia. Popular, internet access R$5 per hr when eating or drinking.

Entertainment

Art galleries *Galeria de Arte Nélson Penteado de Andrade*, Praça dos Expedicionários 10, Gonzaga, T32354245. **Cinemas** Mainstream films at cinemas in Av Ana Costa, Gonzaga. *Cine Arte*, Posto 4, Av Vicente de Carvalho. Brazilian and foreign films. **Theatre** *Teatro Municipal Brás Cubas*, Av Sen Pinheiro Machado 48, Vila Mathias, T32336086.

Festivals

26 Jan, *Foundation of Santos*; *Good Friday*; *Corpus Christi*; *Festejos Juninos*. Throughout the summer there are many cultural, educational and sporting events. 8 Sep, *Nossa Senhora de Monte Serrat*.

Sport

Golf courses Two 9-hole courses: *Santos Golf Club*, Av Pérsio de Queiroz Filho, São Vicente. *Guarujá Golf Club* (see below).

Transport

Local It is easy to visit the centre on foot and the only real need to use buses or taxis is to connect between there and Gonzaga or to visit nearby beaches. **Buses**: in Santos, US$.60. To São Vicente, US$0.90. **Taxis**: all taxis have meters. The fare from Gonzaga to the bus station is about US$5. Cooper Rádio táxi, T32327177.

Long distance Plans for an airport have been put forward but for now the only access is by the Anchieta and Imigrantes highways from São Paulo and the coastal roads running north and south. Buses arrive from São Paulo at the main bus station in the centre as well as stops at Ponta da Praia and José Menino which are both nearer to the main hotel district in Gonzaga. Trains from São Paulo arrive at the station in the centre. Cruise liners anchor at the tourist terminal in the port close to the centre and are met by tour buses.

▶▶ The Bandeirantes

Reviled in some quarters for their appalling treatment of Indians, revered in others for their determination and willingness to withstand extreme hardship in the pursuit of their goals, the bandeirantes *are an indispensible element in the formation of Brazil.*

The Portuguese knew that South America held great riches; their Spanish rivals were shipping vast quantities back to Europe from Peru. They also knew soon after setting up their colonies on the Atlantic side of the continent that Brazil was not readily yielding equivalent wealth. Legends proliferated of mountains of precious stones, golden lakes and other marvels, also of terrifying places, all in the mysterious interior. Regardless of the number of expeditions sent into the sertão which returned empty-handed (or failed to return at all), there was always the promise of silver, emeralds or other jewels to lure the adventurous beyond the coast.

The one thing that Brazil had in abundance was Indians. Throughout the colony there was a demand for slaves to work the plantations and farms and the indigenous population satisfied the need for labour. This was especially true in the early 17th century when Portugal temporarily lost its African possession of Angola, from which it sent many slaves to Brazil.

The men who settled in São Paulo, both the Europeans and those of mixed parentage, the mamelucos, proved themselves expert at enslaving Indians. Without official sanction, and certainly not blessed by the Jesuits, these adventurers formed themselves into expeditions which would leave São Paulo, often for years at a time, to capture slaves for the internal market. The Guaraní Indians who had been organized into reducciones by the Jesuits around the Río Paraguay were the top prize and there developed an intense rivalry between the bandeirantes and the Jesuits. The priests regarded the Paulistas as murderous and inhumane; the slavers

felt they had some justification in attacking the missions because they were in Spanish territory and, in the 17th century, the entire western boundary of Brazil was in dispute.

This was one side of the coin. The other was that the bandeirantes were incredibly resourceful, trekking for thousands of kilometres, withstanding great hardships, travelling light, inspired not just by the desire to get rich, but also by a fierce patriotism. They certainly did show barbaric treatment to the Indians, but the enthusiasm that inspired the slave drives combined well with the desire to demystify the sertão, to uncover its riches. It was this which fuelled the prospecting expeditions after Angola had been recaptured in 1648. The bandeirantes trekked into Minas Gerais, Goiás and Mato Grosso looking for precious metals. Through their efforts, the Minas Gerais gold rush began. They were also enlisted by governors in the northeast to wage war on Indians and they were involved in the destruction of the quilombo at Palmares (see page 668).

The principal effect of the expansionist spirit of the bandeira movement was that the interior of Brazil was explored. In the bandeirantes' footsteps came settlers and cattle herders who took over the lands that had been emptied of their Indian population. Although Indians were exploited as labour and became a source of income for the Paulistas, they also intermarried with the Europeans. The mixed-race mamelucos and even Indians themselves took part in the bandeiras, hastening the miscegenation process which became so evident throughout Brazil. Portuguese control of territory was extended by the bandeirantes' journeys. In their later phase, these journeys also filled Portugal's coffers because much of the wealth derived from the discovery of gold was sent back to Europe.

Further reading John Hemming, Red Gold (chapters 12 and 13), and Richard M Morse (editor), The Bandeirantes.

São Paulo

Buses: rodoviaria, Praça dos Andrades, T32192194. For most suburbs buses start from Praça Mauá, in the centre of the city. There are buses to **São Paulo** (50 mins, US$3.60) at intervals of approximately 15 mins, from the rodoviária near the city centre, José Menino or Ponta da Praia (opposite the ferry to Guarujá). (The 2 highways between São Paulo and Santos are sometimes seriously crowded, especially at rush hours and weekends.) To **Guarulhos/Cumbica airport**, *Expresso Brasileiro* at 0600, 1330, 1830, return 0550, 0930, 1240, 1810, US$5, allow plenty of time as the bus goes through Guarulhos, 3 hrs. *TransLitoral* from Santos to **Congonhas airport** then to Guarulhos/Cumbica, 4 daily, US$7.25, 2 hrs. To **Rio** (*Normandy* company), several daily, 7½ hrs, US$22.50, to Rio along the coast road is via São Sebastião (US$7.25, change buses if necessary), Caraguatatuba and Ubatuba.

Banks Open 1000-1730. ATMs in Santos are very unreliable and often out of order. **Directory** Visa ATMs at *Banco do Brasil*, R 15 de Novembro 195, Centro and Av Ana Costa, Gonzaga. Many others. **Communications** Internet: *Viva Shop*, Shopping Parque Balneário. US$3 per hr. **Post office**: R Cidade de Toledo 41, Centro and at R Tolentino Filgueiras 70, Gonzaga. **Telephone**: R Galeão Carvalhal 45, Gonzaga. **Embassies and consulates** *Britain*, R Tuiuti 58, 2nd floor, T32196622. *Denmark*, R Frei Gaspar 22, 10th floor, 106, T32196455, open 1000-1100, 1500-1700. *France*, R General Câmara 12, sala 51, T32195161. *Germany*, R Frei Gaspar 22, 10th floor, 104, T32195092. **Laundry** Av Mcal Floriano Peixoto 120, Gonzaga, self-service, wash and dry US$5. **Medical services** *Ana Costa*, R Pedro Américo 42, Campo Grande, T2229000. *Santa Casa de Misericórdia*, Av Dr Cláudio Luiz da Costa 50, Jabaquara, T2347575. **Useful addresses** Immigration: Polícia Federal, Praça da República. For visa extensions. **Voltage** 220 Ac, 60 cycles.

The Litoral Norte

Guarujá

This sophisticated resort becomes very crowded in summer as holidaymakers come to take advantage of its fine beaches, hotels, restaurants and spas. There is a strong undertow on nearly all the Guarujá beaches; the Praia de Pernambuco (also called Jequiti-Mar) is the safest. The beaches in town are mostly built-up and can be polluted, while several of those further away have condominium developments which make public access difficult. If you have a car, try São Pedro beach, passing Praia de Pernambuco and Praia do Perequê with a fishing village beside it, where excellent seafood restaurants line the seafront. It was formerly a private beach, now open to the public, but be there as early as possible because only 150 cars are allowed: a beautiful spot. The tourist office is at R Quintino Bocaiúva 248, T33877199.

Phone code: 013
Colour map 5, grid A6
Population: 230,000

L *Casa Grande*, Av Miguel Stéfano 1087, T/F33552300. Luxury, in colonial style, with clean beach. **L** *Jequiti-Mar*, 8 km beyond Guarujá on the road to Bertioga, T/F33533111. Extremely attractive holiday complex with private beaches (excellent swimming and boating), fine fishing grounds, and chalet accommodation, excellent restaurant, 2 nightclubs open each weekend and every night from Dec to Mar. **AL** *Delphin*, Av Miguel Stéfano 1295, turn left in the centre of Guarujá and drive less than 1 km to the beginning of the long Praia da Enseada, T33862112, F33866844, delphin@tribuna.com.br *La Popote* restaurant. **AL** *Ferraretto Hotel*, R Mário Ribeiro 564, T33861112, F33875616. Facing sea, luxurious, nightclub, swimming pool. **B** *Canto da Enseada*, R São Paulo 132, Enseada, T/F33514819. Pool. **B** *Pousada Mira Mar*, R Antônio Marques 328, Tombo,

Sleeping & eating

T/F33541453. **Youth hostel E** per person *Guarujá*, R das Carmélias 10, Praia da Enseada, T33517779, IYHA. For eating, try *do Joca*, on the road to Bertioga, Km 12, T33051188. Seafood. There is a good *churrascaria* opposite the rodoviária.

Festivals   In **Aug** there is the *Procissão Marítima de Nossa Senhora dos Navegantes* and a *Festival de Folclore*.

Transport   The Guarujá vehicle ferry (every 10 mins, free for pedestrians) leaves from Ponta da Praia. The ferry is free from Santos, but back to Santos from Guarujá is US$2.80 on weekdays, US$4.20 Sat-Sun. On the other side proceed as far as Enseada das Tartarugas (Turtle Bay). During the season and weekends there is a long delay at the Ponta da Praia vehicle ferry; to avoid this take the ferry on foot and get the bus on the Guarujá side; motor boats also cross for US$0.50. A trolleybus runs from Praça Mauá in Santos to the ferry, then take one of the buses.

Directory   **Banks** *Banco 24 Horas*, in Pão de Açúcar supermarket, Av Dom Pedro I 195, Enseada. *Bradesco*, Av Dom Pedro I 1015, Praia da Enseada. **Medical services** *Ana Costa*, Via Santos Dumont 3651, T33868787.

Bertioga

Phone code: 013
Colour map 5, grid A6
Population: 17,000

There are good seafood restaurants on the road (SP-061) between Guarujá and Bertioga, the next major beach centre up the coast (one hour by bus). It, too, can be an overcrowded place in the summer. A ferry crosses the mouth of the Canal de Bertioga. The town is on the north bank of the canal and beyond is a long sweeping bay with seven beaches divided by a promontory, the Ponta da Selada. Going northeast, the beaches are **Praias de Bertioga** (Enseada, Vista Linda and Indaía), **Praia São Lourenço** (which has been developed as the Riviera de São Lourenço, with condos, hotels, green areas and sports facilities), **Praia Itaguaré**, **Praia Guaratuba** and **Praia Boracéia** (campsite, meals served). The hills behind Bertioga are covered in forest which is now being used for walking and appreciation of the Mata Atlântica by local agencies. **Tourist offices** *Departamento de Esportes e Turismo Municipal*, R Luiz Pereira de Campos 901, Vila Itapanhaú, T33171213, ext 2075.

Two forts, São Felipe and São João, were built to protect the coast from attack by the Tamoio Indians in the 16th century. São João, in Bertioga, can be visited and part of it houses the **João Ramalho Museum**, which contains a variety of historical objects. There is a *Festa da Primavera* in October.

Sleeping & eating   **B** *Balsa*, Av Tomé de Souza 3268, T/F33171226. Restaurant. **B** *Marazul 27*, Av Tomé de Souza 825, Enseada, T33171109. Good seafood restaurant.

Tour operators   *Suinã Turismo*, T33173667, offers 'eco-tours', including to Itatinga (see above, under Santos).

Directory   **Banks** *Bradesco*, in Shopping Riviera, Av da Riviera 1256. **Medical services** *Unidade Hospitalar Mista*, Praça Vicente Molinari, T3171593.

Camburi & Maresias
Phone code: 012

Beyond Boracéia are a number of beaches, including Barra do Una, Praia da Baleia and **Camburi**. The latter is surrounded by the Mata Atlântica. The sea is clean and good for bathing and watersports, including surfing (see Surfing, page 65, for this and other recommendations). There are a number of good hotels and restaurants in Camburi and at Praia de Boracéia, **B-C** *Chalés do*

Brasa, Rua E No 99, T43303149, family chalets, garden setting, close to beach. You can walk on the Estrada do Piavu into the Mata Atlântica to see streams, vegetation and wildlife (bathing in the streams is permitted, but use of shampoo and other chemicals is forbidden). About 5 km from Camburi is Praia Brava, 45 minutes' walk through the forest, camping is possible. The surf here is very heavy (hence the name).

The road carries on from Camburi, past beaches such as Boiçucanga to **Maresias**, a fashionable place for surfers. Its nickname is 'Copacabana without the buildings', although it is well supplied with bars, restaurants and accommodation.

Sleeping and eating Camburi: **A** *Canto da Praia*, R Amaragi 85, Praia de Juqueí, T/F34631294. Dinner. Recommended. **B** *Pousada da Rosa*, R das Rosas 139, T/F34651412, **C** in low season. Breakfast, pool. *Manacá*, R do Manacá 102, Camburizinho, T34651566. Fish. **Maresias**: **A** *Piccolo Albergue*, R Nova Iguaçu 1979, T34656227. Chalets and natural pool. *Ke Pantai*, Av Dr Francisco Loup 1555, T34656252, Thai cuisine. *Mr Harris Jazz Bar*. Recommended.

Transport 3 daily buses from **São Paulo** to Camburi, 160 km, en route to São Sebastião/Ilhabela, US$3.60.

São Sebastião

From Maresias it is 21 km to São Sebastião. In all there are 21 good beaches and an adequate, but not overdeveloped tourist infrastructure. The many small islands offshore are very good for scuba-diving. There is also sailing, fishing and canoeing.

Phone code: 012
Colour map 5, grid A6
Population: 59,000

São Sebastião is on a narrow strait which separates the mainland from the Ilha de São Sebastião, popularly called Ilhabela, Brazil's largest marine (as opposed to riverine) island. Since colonial times, this has been an important area. The island, which was called Ciribaí, island of peace, by the Indians, was reported by Amerigo Vespucci in 1502, who renamed it after the saint of the day of his discovery. São Sebastião was settled at the end of the 16th century. With good sugar-growing land on the mainland and the island it was both a port for sending the sugar back to Europe and another point of defence against the Tamoio. Gold was discovered in the vicinity in 1722 so this, too, and later coffee were shipped out. Slaves were also brought through here. The oil industry has subsequently taken advantage of the harbour by building a terminal here.

The natural attractions of the area include a large portion of the **Parque Estadual da Serra do Mar** on the mainland, with other areas under protection for their different ecosystems. Trails can be walked through the forests. There are also old sugar plantations. The Centro de Biologia Marinha da Univesidade de São Paulo is located here and, for divers, as well as the marine fauna, there are a large number of wrecks in the strait that can be explored.

Sights
For tourist information, contact Sectur, Av Dr Altino Arantes 174, T4521808, who are friendly and helpful except regarding Ilhabela

In São Sebastião the colonial centre is under the aegis of the Patrimônio Histórico e Artístico. A **Museu de Arte Sacra** is in the 17th-century chapel of São Gonçalo in the town centre (R Sebastião Neves 90 – closed for restoration in 1997). The town's parish church on Praça Major João Fernandes was built in the early 17th-century and rebuilt in 1819. There is a **Museu do Naufrágio** near the church exhibiting shipwrecks and natural history of the local area. ■ *Free*. Other colonial constructions are the Cadeia Pública (the prison), now

São Paulo

the military police HQ, on Praça Tobias de Aguiar, and the Casa Esperança at Avenida Altino Arantes 154. There is an internet café on the beachfront.

The beaches within 2 or 3 km of São Sebastião harbour are polluted; others to the south and north are clean and inviting. Ilhabela tends to be expensive in season, when it is cheaper to stay in São Sebastião.

Sleeping   **A** *Arrastão*, Av Manoel Hipólito do Rego 2097, direction Caraguatatuba, T/F4620099. Restaurant, pool. **B** *Roma*, on the main Praça, T4521016. Excellent. Warmly recommended. **C** *Bariloche*, R Três Bandeirantes 133. Basic but clean. About 6 km south of São Sebastião is *Camping do Barraqueçaba Bar de Mar de Lucas*. Hot showers, English spoken, cabins available. Recommended.

Festivals   **20 Jan**, festival of the patron saint, featuring *congadas*, a song and dance derived from slaves from the Congo; *Carnival* in **Feb**; *Festas Juninas* in **Jun**; folklore festival in **Aug**; *Mostrart*, a demonstration of arts and crafts, in **Dec**.

Transport   **Buses** 2 buses a day from **Rio** with *Normandy*, 0830 and 2300 (plus 1630 on Fri and Sun), to Rio 0600 and 2330, heavily booked in advance, US$12.50 (US$5 from Paraty); 4 a day from **Santos**, 4 hrs, US$7.60; 4 Litorânea buses a day also from **São Paulo**, US$8.85, which run inland via São José dos Campos, unless you ask for the service via Bertioga, only 2 a day. Free **ferry** to **Ilhabela** for foot passengers, see below.

Ilha de São Sebastião

The island of São Sebastião, known popularly as Ilhabela since the 1940s, is of volcanic origin, roughly 390 sq km in area. The four highest peaks are Morro de São Sebastião, 1,379 m above sea-level, Morro do Papagaio, 1,309 m, Ramalho, 1,285 m, and Pico Baepi, 1,025 m. All are often obscured by mist. Rainfall on the island is heavy, about 3,000 mm a year. The slopes are densely wooded and 80% of the forest is protected by the Parque Estadual de Ilhabela. This state park also encompasses the eight other islands in the archipelago, of which Ilhabela is the largest; only two other islands are inhabited, Vitória and Búzios.

Most of the flatter ground on Ilhabela is given over to sugar-cane. In the 19th-century illegal slave traders used the island. The only settled district lies on the coastal strip facing the mainland, the Atlantic side being practically uninhabited except by a few fisherfolk. The place abounds in tropical plants and flowers, and many fruits grow wild, whose juice mixed with *cachaça* and sugar makes as delicious a cocktail as can be imagined.

A 50-km return journey on foot over the hump of the island down towards the Atlantic, sometimes through dense tropical forest following the old slave trail, requires a local guide. There is a rough road to the Atlantic side, but it is very difficult to drive. The terraced **Cachoeira da Toca** waterfalls amid dense jungle close to the foot of the Baepi peak give cool freshwater bathing; lots of butterflies (entry, US$4, includes insect repellent). You can walk on a signed path, or go by car; it's a few kilometres from the ferry dock. The locals claim that there are over 300 waterfalls on the island, but only a few of them can be reached on foot. Those that can are worth the effort.

In all shady places, especially away from the sea, a species of midge known locally as *borrachudo* thrives. *Autan* repellent (sold locally) keeps them off for some time, but those allergic to insect bites should remain on the inhabited coastal strip. There is a small helpful hospital by the church in town.

Ilhabela

This town is very popular during summer weekends when it is very difficult to find space for a car on the ferry. It is, however, a nice place to relax on the beach, with good food and some good value accommodation. No alterations are allowed to the frontage of the main township, Ilhabela. The **tourist office** is *Secretaria de Turismo*, R Bartolomeu de Gusmão 140, Pequeá, T4721091.

Phone code: 012
Colour map 5, grid A6
Population: 21,000
(100,000 high season)

Sights The town's parish church, **Nossa Senhora da Ajuda e Bom Sucesso**, dates from the 17th century, but has been restored. Visit the old **Feiticeira** plantation, with underground dungeons. The road is along the coast, sometimes high above the sea, towards the south of the island (11 km from the town).

São Paulo

São Sebastião & Ilhabela

○ **Beaches**

1 Ponta das Canas	16 Perequê	31 Saco Grande	46 Cigarras
2 Armação	17 Cabras	32 Figueira	47 Olaria
3 Pinto	18 Pedra Miúda	33 Baía dos Castelhanos	48 Arrastão
4 Ponta Azeda	19 Portinho	34 Ponta da Cabeçuda	49 Pontal da Cruz
5 Pedra do Sino	20 Feiticeira	35 Eustáquio	50 Deserta
6 Arrozal	21 Julião	36 Guanxuma	51 Porto Grande
7 Siriúba	22 Grande	37 Caveira	52 Centro
8 Viana	23 Curral	38 Serraria	53 Preta
9 Mercedes	24 Veloso	39 Ponta Grossa	54 Grande
10 Saco do Indaiá	25 Ponta da Sela	40 Poço	55 Pitangueiras
11 Saco Grande	26 Ponta da Sepetiba	41 Ponta do Lobo	56 Timbó
12 Pequeá	27 Enchovas	42 Fome	57 Barraqueçaba
13 Engenho d'Água	28 Ponta do Diogo	43 Jabaquara	58 Guaecá
14 Itaguaçu	29 Ponta do Boi	44 Pacuíba	
15 Itaquanduba	30 Ponta da Pirabura	45 Enseada	

You can go by bus, taxi, or horse and buggy. A trail leads down from the *fazenda* to the beautiful beach of the same name. Another old *fazenda* is **Engenho d'Água**, which is nearer to the town, which gives its name to one of the busiest beaches (the *fazenda* is not open to the public).

Pedras do Sino (Bell Rocks) These curious seashore boulders, when struck with a piece of iron or stone, emit a loud bell-like note. There is a beach here, too, 4 km north of town. A campsite is nearby.

Beaches & watersports On the mainland side it is not recommended to bathe from the beaches 3 or 4 km either side of the town because of pollution. On this side of the island you should also look out for oil, sandflies and jellyfish on the sand and in the water. There are some three dozen beaches around Ilhabela, only about 12 of them away from the coast facing the mainland. **Praia dos Castelhanos**, reached by the rough road over the island to the Atlantic side (no buses), is recommended. Several of the ocean beaches can only be reached by boat. At **Saco do Sombrio**, a cove on the Atlantic coast, English, Dutch and French pirates sheltered in the 16th and 17th centuries. Needless to say, this has led to legends of hidden treasure, but the most potent story about the place is that of the Englishman, Thomas Cavendish. In 1592 he sacked Santos and set it on fire. He then sailed to Saco do Sombrio where his crew mutinied, hanged Cavendish, sank their boats and settled on the island.

On the south coast is the fishing village of **Bonete**, which has 500 m of beach and can be reached either by boat (1½ hours), or by driving to Borrifos at the end of the road, then walking along a trail for three hours.

The island is considered the **Capital da Vela** (capital of sailing) because its 150 km of coastline offers all types of conditions. The sheltered waters of the strait are where many sailors learn their skills and the bays around the coast provide safe anchorages. There are, however, numerous tales of shipwrecks because of the unpredictable winds, sudden mists and strange forces playing havoc with compasses, but these provide plenty of adventure for divers. There are over 30 wrecks that can be dived, the most notable being the *Príncipe de Asturias*, a transatlantic liner that went down off the Ponta de Pirabura in 1916.

Sleeping **AL** *Itapemar*, No 341, T4721329, F4722409. Windsurfing equipment rented. **AL** *Porto Pousada Saco da Capela*, R Itapema 167, T4722255, F4721052. **A** *Ilhabela*, Av Pedro Paulo de Morais 151, T/F4721083, hoibela@mandic.com.br Good breakfast. Recommended. **A** *Maison Joly*, R Antônio Lisboa Alves 272, Morro do Cantagalo, T4722364, F4721201. Good restaurant. **B** *Pousada dos Hibiscos*, Av Pedro Paulo de Morais 714, T4721375. Pool, good atmosphere. Recommended. Some less expensive hotels are found on the road to the left of the ferry.

Youth hostel **E** per person *Ilhabela*, Av Col José Vicente Faria Lima 1243, Perequê, T4728468, hostelling@iconet.com.br, IYHA. **Camping** In addition to Pedra do Sino, mentioned above, there are campsites at Perequê, near the ferry dock, and at Praia Grande, a further 11 km south.

Eating *Farol*, Av Princesa Isabel 1634, Perequê. Good, especially seafood. Recommended. *Perequê*, Av Princesa Isabel 337, reasonable. *Viana*, Av Leonardo Reale 1560, Praia da Viana, T4721089. Fish, best to make reservations.

Festivals Ilhabela is rich in folklore and legends. Its version of the *congada* (see above and Music, page 687) is famous, particularly at the festival of *São Benedito* in **May**. Other saints' days are *São Pedro*, **28 Jun**, with a maritime procession, and *Santa Verônica*, 1st week of **Jul** in Bonete. *Carnival* is held in **Feb**. The town's anniversary is in **Sep**. There are sailing weeks and fishing tournaments throughout the year; dates change annually.

Buses A bus runs along the coastal strip facing the mainland. *Litorânea* buses from **São Paulo** connect with a service right through to Ilhabela town; office in Ilhabela at R Dr Carvalho 136.

    Ferries At weekends and on holidays the 15-20-min ferry between São Sebastião and Perequê runs non-stop day and night. During the week it does not sail between 0130 and 0430 in the morning. Passengers pay nothing; the fare for cars is US$7 weekdays, US$10 at weekends. Reservations for cars can be made in advance at *Dersa*, R Iaiá 126, Itaim-Bibi, São Paulo, T011-8206655 (this service costs extra); office in São Sebastião, Av São Sebastião, T4521576.

Transport

Banks *Bradesco*, Praça Col Julião M Negrão 29.

Directory

On the Santos-Rio road is São Francisco da Praia, opposite the northern end of Ilhabela, beyond which begin the beaches of Caraguatatuba. In all there are 17 good beaches to the northeast and southwest, most divided between two sweeping bays. As well as watersports, Caraguatatuba is known for hang-gliding and, like so many places that are denominated 'capital' of something, is called the **Capital do Vôo Livre** (capital of hang gliding). It is a popular place at weekends and in the summer, with good hotels, restaurants, bars and campsites. For tourist information, contact the *Secretaria Municipal de Turismo*, R Luiz Passos 50, T4208142.

Caraguatatuba
Phone code: 012
Population: 69,000

    In common with other places on this coast, there are opportunities for walking in the forest behind the coastal strip. The road which goes inland, called the Rodovia dos Tamoios, climbs steeply into the densely wooded hills, with lots of hairpins. There are striking views of Caraguatatuba and the coast; one viewpoint is called O Mirante da Chegada, at Km 70. It takes about 25 minutes before the road levels out in the district of Paraibuna and crosses the high agricultural lands, running beside the bays of a huge artificial lake, the Represa de Paraibuna. The road joins the Dutra highway at São José dos Campos.

Sleeping AL *Pousada Tabatinga*, SP-55 Km 84, Praia da Tabatinga, T4241411, F4241544. Restaurant, pool. **C** *Guanabara*, R Santo Antônio 75, T4222533, F4226399. Pool. **Youth hostel E** *Recanto das Andorinhas*, R Eng João Fonseca 112, 1 street from the central bus terminal, 50 m from the beach, T4226181.

Transport Direct buses to Caraguatatuba from **Rio** (US$12, same schedule as for São Sebastião), **São Paulo**, **Santos** and **Ubatuba** (Local bus, every 30 mins, US$1); direct buses from São Paulo do not use the coast road, but go via São José dos Campos.

Further northeast from Caraguatatuba is **Lagoinha**, 34 km west of Ubatuba, with chalets and sailing boats for hire. There is exotic birdlife in the nearby forest and the ruins of an 18th-century *fazenda*, Engenho Bom Retiro. Boat trips can be made to beaches and islands.

Ubatuba

Phone code: 012
Colour map 5, grid A6
Population: 67,000

This is one of the most beautiful stretches of the São Paulo coast and has been recognized as such by the local tourist industry for many years. In all, there are 72 beautiful beaches, some large, some small, some in coves, some on islands. Surfing is the pastime of which it is said to be capital, but a whole range of watersports is on offer, including sailing to and around the offshore islands. The Tropic of Capricorn runs through Ubatuba (through the beach of Itaguá to be precise).

Ins and outs

The beaches are spread out over a wide area, so if you are staying in Ubatuba town, you need to use the buses which go to most of them. Either that, or hire a car. The area gets very crowded at carnival time as people from Rio come to escape the crowds in their city. Ubatuba, though, does celebrate carnival itself.

The commercial centre of Ubatuba is at the northern end of the bay, by the estuary which the fishing boats enter and leave. A bridge crosses the estuary, giving access to the coast north of town. A small jetty with a lighthouse at the end protects the river mouth and this is a nice place to watch the boats come and go. The seafront, stretching south from the jetty, is built up along its length, but there are hardly any high-rise blocks. In the commercial centre are shops, banks, services, lots of restaurants (most serving pizza and fish), but few hotels. These are on the beaches north and south and can be reached from the Costamar bus terminal. The **tourist office** is on the seafront on Av Iperoig opposite R Prof Thomaz Galhardo.

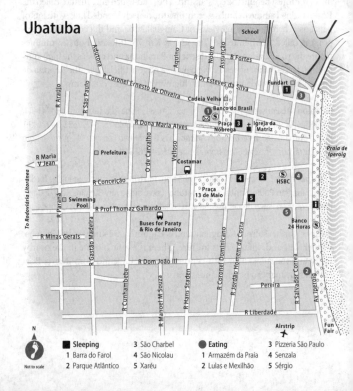

Ubatuba

Sleeping ■	3 São Charbel	Eating ●	3 Pizzeria São Paulo
1 Barra do Farol	4 São Nicolau	1 Armazém da Praia	4 Senzala
2 Parque Atlântico	5 Xaréu	2 Lulas e Mexilhão	5 Sérgio

São Paulo

History

This part of the coast was a hotly contested area between the local Indians and the Portuguese. The Jesuits José Anchieta and Manuel Nóbrega came to the village of Iperoig, as it was called in 1563, to put a stop to the fighting; the former was even taken hostage by the Indians during the negotiations. A cross on the Praia do Cruzeiro (or Iperoig) in the centre commemorates the peace which the town proudly claims to be the first peace treaty on the American continent. The colonists eventually prevailed and the town of Vila Nova da Exaltação da Santa Cruz do Salvador de Ubatuba (its next name) became an important port until Santos overtook it in the late 18th century. In the 20th century its development as a holiday resort was rapid, especially after 1948 when it became an Estância Balneária. The shortened name of Ubatuba derives from the Tupi-Guarani, meaning 'place of *ubas*', a type of tree used for making bows and canoes.

Sights

Ubatuba has a few historic buildings, such as the **Igreja da Matriz**, Praça da Matriz, which is 18th-19th century and has only one tower, the old 19th-century prison which now houses the small historical museum, **Cadeia Velha** on Praça Nóbrega, the 18th-century **Câmara Municipal** on Avenida Iperoig, and the **Sobrado do Porto**, the 19th-century customs house at Praça Anchieta 38, which contains **Fundart** (the Art and Culture Foundation). Mostly, though, it is a modern, functional town. In the surrounding countryside there are *fazendas* which are often incorporated into the *trilhas ecológicas* (nature trails) which are proliferating along the coast.

The **Projeto Tamar**, R Antonio Athanasio da Silva 273, Itaguá, T4326202, is a branch of the national project which studies and preserves marine turtles. The **Aquário de Ubatuba**, R Guarani 859 has well displayed Amazon and Pantanal species including caimans and piranhas. ■ *1000-2200 daily except Thu. T4321382.*

There is a small airport from which stunt fliers take off to wheel and dive over the bay. In summer 10-minute panaromic flights and helicopter rides over Ubatuba are on offer (US$15).

Beaches

The only beach where swimming is definitely not recommended is that part of the beach near the town's outflow between Praia do Cruzeiro and Praia Itaguá. The sand and water close to the jetty doesn't look too inviting either. The most popular are Praias Tenório, Grande and Toninhas (4½, 6 and 8 km south respectively). Condominiums, apartments, hotels and *pousadas* line these beaches on both sides of the coast road. Of the municipality's 72 beaches, those to the south are the more developed although the further you go from town in either direction, the less built up the beaches are. Boogie boards can be rented at many of the beaches, or you can buy your own in town for around US$5.

Saco da Ribeira, 13 km south, is a natural harbour which has been made into a yacht marina. Schooners leave from here for excursions to **Ilha Anchieta** (or dos Porcos), a popular four-hour trip (US$10, for agencies, see below). On the island are beaches, trails and a prison, which was in commission from 1908-52. The Costamar bus from Ubatuba to Saco da Ribeira (every 20 minutes, 30 minutes, US\$0.85) drops you at the turn-off by the *Restaurante Pizzeria Malibu*. It's a short walk to the docks and boatyards where an unmade road leads right, through the boatyards, to a track along the shore. It reaches the Praia da Ribeira which you can walk along to another track going round a headland. This leads to the beaches of Flamengo, Flamenguinho and Sete Fontes. It's a pleasant stroll (about one hour to Flamengo), but there is no shade and you need to take water. Note the sign before Flamengo on one of the private properties: "Propriedade particular. Cuidado c/o elefante!"

Essentials

Sleeping
■ *on map, page 206*
Price codes:
see inside front cover

Very cheap accommodation is hard to come by and at all holiday times no hotel charges less than US\$20

Beach hotels **L** *Recanto das Toninhas*, Praia das Toninhas, T4421410, F4420042, or São Paulo T2882022, F2882260, part of *Roteiros de Charme* group (see page 47). **AL** *Saveiros*, R Laranjeira 227, Praia do Lázaro, 14 km from town, T4420172. Pool, restaurant, English spoken. **A** *Solar das Águas Cantantes*, Estr Saco da Ribeira 253, Praia do Lázaro, 14 km, T4420178, F4420288. Reached by local bus, swimming pool, restaurant. At Baia Fortaleza, 25 km south of Ubatuba is **AL** *Refúgio do Corsário*, T4439148, F4439158. Full board, a clean quiet hotel on the waterfront, sailing and swimming, a good place to relax.

In town **B** *São Charbel*, Praça Nóbrega 280, T4321090, F4321080. Very helpful and comfortable, on busy main square, rooftop 'pool' is tiny plunge pool. **C** *São Nicolau*, R Conceição 213, T4325007, F4323310. Good, TV, fridge, good breakfast. **C** *Xaréu*, R Jordão Homem da Costa 413, T4321525, F4323060. Wrought-iron balconies, pleasant garden area. Good value, excellent breakfast. Recommended. (*São Nicolau* and *Xaréu* are both a 3-min walk from the bus station, convenient for the town beach, restaurants and services, and their prices rise to **B** in high season.) **D** *Barra do Farol*, R Dr Félix Guizard Filho 6, T4322019, **F** per person. Homely, motel-style, close to seafront.

Ubatuba coast

○ Beaches	10 Grande	20 Flamengo	30 Fortaleza
1 Vermelho do Norte	11 Toninhas	21 Flamenguinho	31 Cedro
2 Saco da Mãe	12 Fora	22 Sete	32 Deserta
3 Barra Seca	13 Presídio	23 Sununga	33 Grande do Bonete
4 Perequê-Açu	14 Leste	24 Lázaro	34 Bonete
5 Cruzeiro	15 Sul	25 Domingo Dias	35 Lagoinha
6 Itaguá	16 Enseada	26 Barra & Dura	36 Maranduba
7 Cedro	17 Santa Rita	27 Vermelha do Sul	37 Pulso
8 Vermelho do Centro	18 Lamberto	28 Costa	38 Cassandoca
9 Tenório	19 Ribeira	29 Brava	39 Cassandoquinha

São Paulo

North of town *Maurício*, Av Abreu Sodré 607, near Praia do Perequê-Açu. Has cheap rooms, clothes washing possible.

Youth hostels **E** pp *Cora Coralina*, Rod Oswaldo Cruz Km 89, near the Horto Florestal, T011-2580388. IYHA, open 0800-2300. **E** pp *JS Brandão*, R Nestor Fonseca 173, Jardim Sumaré, near the Tropic of Capricorn sign south of town, T4322337. IYHA, open 0700-2300.

Camping 2 *Camping Clube do Brasil* sites at Lagoinha (25 km from town), T4431536, and Praia Perequê-Açu, 2 km north, T4321682. There are about 8 other sites in the vicinity.

Expensive *Pizzeria São Paulo*, Praça da Paz de Iperoig 26. Undeniably chic gourmet pizzeria in beautifully restored building. Owned by a young lawyer who brings the authentic Italian ingredients for the gorgeous pizzas from São Paulo every weekend. **Mid-range**: *Arabí*, R Guarani 610, Itaguá. Popular, brightly lit, serving hot and cold Arabic food and desserts. *Giorgio*, Av Leovigildo Dias Vieira 248, Itaguá. Sophisticated Italian restaurant and American bar. On Av Iperoig, as far as the roundabout by the airport, there is a string of restaurants along the seafront, including *Lulas e Mexilhão*, No 600. Established 25 years, specializes in fish and *Senzala*, Italian, established 30 years, lovely atmosphere. Don't miss the seafood spaghetti. Recommended. **Cheap**: *Armazém da Praia*, R Cel Ernesto de Oliveira 149, opposite post office. Pretty, family-run self service, open for lunch only. *Sérgio*, R Prof Thomaz Galhardo 404. Serving ice-creams, pizzas and, at weekends, *feijoada*. Open for dinner weekends only.

Eating

Ubatuba is known for its handicrafts (carved wood, basketware) and it holds a *Festa da Cultura Popular* in **Sep**. Other festivals include *São Pedro* at the end of **Jun** and the *Festa do Divino Espírito Santo* in **Jul**. The town's anniversary is **28 Oct**. Surfing championships are also held.

Festivals

Agencies which run schooner trips to Ilha Anchieta and elsewhere: *Central de Passeios de Escuna*, Saco da Ribeira, T4411338. *Mykonos*, Av Leovigildo Dias Vieira 1052, Itaguá, T4322042, office also in Saco da Riberia. *Oceano Azul*, R Flamenguinho 277, Saco da Ribeira, T4420564. Companies which offer trekking: *Guaynumby*, T4322832, and *Terra Brasil*, T4351275. Trails are graded according to difficulty and last from 2 hrs to 2 days (to Pico do Corcovado). The *Guide Association*, T91413692, www.ubatuba.com.br/ecoturismo, have more information.

Tour operators

The road from São Sebastião is paved, so a journey from São Paulo along the coast is possible, 5 buses daily. Ubatuba is 70 km from Paraty (see page 159).

Buses There are 3 bus terminals: 1) Rodoviária Costamar, at R Hans Staden and R Conceição, which serves all local destinations; 2) Rodoviária at R Prof Thomaz Galhardo 513 for São José buses to **Paraty**, US$2.25, some Normandy services to **Rio de Janeiro**, US$9 and some Itapemirim buses; 3) Rodoviária Litorânea, the main bus station: go up Conceição for 8 blocks from Praça 13 de Maio, turn right on R Rio Grande do Sul, then left into R Dra Maria V Jean. Buses from here go to **São Paulo**, 3½ hrs, frequent, US$8, **São José dos Campos**, US$6, **Paraibuna**, US$5, **Caraguatatuba**, US$2.

Taxis In town can be a rip-off, eg US$6 from the town centre to T Tenório.

Transport

Banks There is a *Banco 24 Horas* next to the tourist office and an *HSBC* ATM at 85 R Conceição. The branch of *Banco do Brasil* in Praça Nóbrega does not have ATMs. **Communications** Internet: *Chat and Bar*, upper floor of *Ubatuba Shopping*. US$3 per hr, open Mon-Sat 1100-2000. **Post office**: R Dona Maria Alves between Hans Staden and R Col Dominicano. **Telephone**: on Galhardo, close to *Sérgio* restaurant.

Directory

São Paulo

Parque Nacional Serra da Bocaina

Straddling the border of São Paulo and Rio de Janeiro states is the Parque Nacional Serra da Bocaina, which rises from the coast to its highest point at Pico do Tira (or Chapéu) at 2,200 m, encompassing three strata of vegetation. Up to 1,000 m the forest is mainly made up of large trees such as *maçaranduba* (milk, or cow trees), *jatobá* (courbaril), cedar and *angelim* (angely). Between 1,000 and 2,000 m the predominant varieties are pines and myrtles. Higher than this, the landscape is more grassy and open, with bromeliads, orchids and lichens. The main river flowing through it is the Mambucaba, which cascades down the mountainsides in a series of waterfalls. Trails lead to some of the falls and an old gold trail leads through the park (a three or four-day hike).

Park essentials Permission to visit must be obtained in advance from Ibama, T0XX12-31172183/88 in São José do Barreiro, the nearest town; there are hotels and trekking agencies here, including *Vale dos Veados*, Estr da Bocaina, Km 42, T0XX12-5771194, F0XX12-5771303, part of the Roteiros de Charme hotel group, see page 47.

All the remaining patches of Mata Atlântica along the Linha Verde provide habitat for some of Brazil's rarer endemic birds. A book such as Nigel Wheatley's *Where to watch birds in South America* can give far greater detail than this guide has space for. Otherwise, contact specialists locally and, where necessary, ask permission to bird-watch on private land.

The Litoral Sul

The Litoral Sul between Santos and Cananéia is not continuously developed, unlike the Linha Verde. From São Vicente to Itanhaém, the whole coast is completely built up with holiday developments. Beyond Itanhaém, though, the road does not hug the shore, so that a large area has been untouched.

This zone and several others on the southern São Paulo coast add up to almost 80% of the region being under some form of environmental protection. An organization called *SOS Mata Atlântica* aims to help preserve what is left of the coastal vegetation, Rua Manoel da Nóbrega 456, São Paulo, CEP 04001-001, T011-88701195, F011-8851680, smata@ax.apc.org

São Vicente & Praia Grande
Phone code: 013
Population: 279,500 and 150,500 respectively

São Vicente was the first town founded in Brazil but there are few remains of this historic past. See the **Matriz São Vicente Mártir** (1542, rebuilt in 1757) in Praça do Mercado, João Pessoa and the Ponte Pênsil bridge (1914) on the road to Praia Grande. The beaches here have calmer waters and are good for watersports although not for bathing.

It is 8 km from São Vicente to **Praia Grande**, 22½ km of crowded beach. This is the beach most used by Paulistanos. The water is polluted but it is used by surfers. There are plenty of hotels, apartments, restaurants and lively nightlife, especially at Boqueirão in the middle.

Sleeping and eating São Vicente: **A** *Ilha Porchat*, Av Paulo Gonçalves 264, Ilha Porchat, T4683437, F4683735. Restaurant, pool. *Beni-Hama*, Av Newton Prado 271, near Ponte Pênsil, T4698039. Japanese. **Praia Grande B** *Ibérica's Praia*, R Pernambuco 177, Boqueirão, T/F4731178. *Nostra Casa*, R Guarapari 95, T4917245. Italian.

Directory Banks: *Banco 24 Horas*, in *Carrefour* supermarket, Av Pref Jose Monteiro 1045, São Vicente. *Bradesco*, Av Antônio Emmerich 772, São Vicente.

Some 61 km from Santos is Itanhaém. Its pretty colonial church of Sant'Ana (1761), Praça Narciso de Andrade, and the Convento da Nossa Senhora da Conceição (1699-1713, originally founded 1554), on the small hill of Morro de Itaguaçu, are reminders that all along this coast the Portuguese had settlements dedicated to the conversion of Indians to Catholicism. Also in the town is the Casa de Câmara e Cadeia, but the historic buildings are quite lost amid the modern development. The beaches here are attractive, but like those at Mongaguá and Praia Grande, several stretches are prone to pollution. Excursions can be made by boat up the Rio Itanhaém. Frequent buses run from Santos, an hour away. There are several good seafood restaurants along the beach, hotels and camping.

Itanhaém
Phone code: 013
Population: 72,000

Sleeping and eating B *Pollastrini*, Praça 22 de Abril 38, T/F4223222. *Taberna Baska*, Av Vicente de Carvalho 776, Praia do Sonho, T4224890. Spanish. *do Maneco*, Av Brasil 800, Praia de Cibratel II, T4251468. Seafood.

Peruíbe

There are more beaches 31 km south of Itanhaém at Peruíbe, but some fall within the jurisdiction of the Estação Ecológica Juréia-Itatins (see below). While the beach culture has been well developed here, with surfing, windsurfing, fishing and so on, a number of 'alternative' options have recently flourished. The climate is said to be unusually healthy owing to a high concentration of ozone in the air; this helps to filter out harmful ultraviolet rays from the sun. UFO watchers and other esoterics claim that it is a very mystical place. Local rivers have water and black mud which has been proven to contain medicinal properties. And the neighbouring ecological station is a major draw now that ecotourism has become big business in São Paulo state.

Phone code: 013
Colour map 5, grid A5
Population: 52,000

For **tourist information**, contact the *Secretaria de Turismo*, R Nilo Soares Ferreira 50, T4552070. You may have to ask permission in the *Departamento da Cultura*, Centro de Convenções, Av Sã João 545, T4552232 to visit Abarebebê and other sites. Also at this address is the *Secretaria Estadual do Meio Ambiente*, T4579243, for information on the Estação Ecológico Juréia-Itatins. There is a **Feira do Artesanato** on Saturday and Sunday on Av São João, 1400-0100 (2300 in winter).

Peruíbe's history dates back to 1530 when the village of Abarebebê was founded. About 9 km northeast, the ruins can be visited, with its church built of stone and shells.

A *Piero Al Mare*, R Indianópolis 20, Praia Orla dos Coqueiros, T4582603. Restaurant. **B** *Waldhaus*, R Gaviotas 1201, Praia do Guaraú, T4579170. Restaurant. **C** *Vila Real*, Av Anchieta 6625, T4582797. *Beira-Mar*, Av Beira-Mar 869, T4551701. Seafood.

Sleeping & eating

18 Feb, founding of the town; Jun, *Festival do Inverno*; Oct, *Mês das Missões*.

Festivals

Peruíbe marks the northernmost point of the Estação Ecológico Juréia-Itatins, 820 sq km of protected Mata Atlântica. The station was founded in 1986. The four main ecosystems are *restinga*, mangrove forest, Mata Atlântica and the vegetation at about 900 m on the Juréia range of mountains. Its wildlife includes many endangered species, including rare

Estação Ecológico Juréia-Itatins

São Paulo

flowers and other plants. There are deer, jaguar, monkeys, dolphins, alligators and birds, including the yellow-headed woodpecker and toucans. Human occupation of the area has included *sambaqui*, builders, *fazendeiros* and present-day fishing communities who preserve an isolated way of life.

Tourism in the ecological station is very carefully monitored and only certain areas are open to the public. These are: the **Núcleo Itinguçu**, 18 km from Peruíbe, which contains the Cachoeira do Paraíso (Paradise Falls) and other pools and waterfalls; **Vila Barra do Una**, a fishing village with a 2-km beach, camping and places to eat, 25 km from Peruíbe; and **Canto da Praia da Juréia** at the extreme southern end, 38 km from Iguape, with 7 km of beach and all the coastal ecosystems. Hikers can walk the 4-km **Trilha do Arpoador** and the 5-km **Trilha do Imperador**, but both need prior reservation and numbers are limited; similarly the Despraiado mountain bike trail. Trips can de made, again with authorization, up the **Rio Guaraú** (8 km from Peruíbe) and the **Rio Una do Prelado** (25 km from Peruíbe). Two other places of interest are **Vila do Prelado**, which used to be an overnight stop on the Imperial São Vicente-Iguape post route (electric light was only installed in 1995), and the **Casa da Farinha**, where manioc flour is made, 28 km from Iguape.

Park essentials Contact the Secretaria Estadual do Meio Ambiente, address above, or the Instituto Florestal (DRPE), Rua do Horto 931, CEP 02377, São Paulo, T011-9528555, for permission to visit the ecological station.

Iguape and Ilha Comprida

Phone code: 013
Colour map 5, grid A5
Population: 28,000

At the southern end of the ecological station is the town of Iguape founded in 1538. In the early days of its existence, ownership of the town was disputed between Spain and Portugal because it was close to the line drawn by the Pope marking Spanish and Portuguese territory in the 'New World'. Typical of Portuguese architecture, the small **Museu Histórico e Arqueológico** is

Estação Ecológica Juréia-Itatins

housed in the 17th-century Casa da Oficina Real de Fundição, Rua das Neves 45. ■ *0900-1730 Tue-Sun*. There is also a **Museu de Arte Sacra** in the former Igreja do Rosário, Praça Rotary. ■ *0900-1200, 1330-1700 Sat-Sun*. The main church, the **Basílica de Bom Jesus**, is a mid-19th-century construction. It has a market, hotels and restaurants. For **tourist information**, contact the *Prefeitura Municipal*, R 15 de Novembro 272, T8411626, F8411620.

Half a dozen beaches, but particularly yachting and fishing, bring tourists to the town. Excursions include the ruined *fazenda* of Itaguá. Handicraft specialities are items in wood and clay, basketware and musical instruments.

Opposite Iguape is the northern end of the **Ilha Comprida** with 86 km of beaches (some disappointing). This Área de Proteção Ambiental is not much higher than sea level and is divided from the mainland by the Canal do Mar Pequeno. The northern end is the busiest and on the island there are good restaurants, hotels, supermarket – fresh fish is excellent.

Sleeping & eating

B *Silvi*, R Ana Cândida Sandoval Trigo 515, T/F8411421, silvihotel@virtualway.com.br Good. **C** *Solar Colonial Pousada*, Praça da Basilica 30, T8411591, 19th-century house. *Veleiro*, Av Beira Mar 579, T8952407. Recommended. Others of varying quality. **Camping** There is a campsite at Praia da Barra da Ribeira, 20 km north, and wild camping is possible at Praia de Juréia, the gateway to the ecological station. *Panela Velha*, R 15 de Novembro 190, T8411869. Seafood restaurant.

Festivals

In **Jan** and **Feb** there is a summer festival in Iguape, while Ilha Comprida celebrates *Carnival* in Feb. *Semana Santa* and *Corpus Cristi*. **Aug** is the month of the pilgrimage of *Senhor Bom Jesus de Iguape*. **3 Dec** is Iguape's anniversary. Throughout the year there are other sporting and cultural events.

Transport

Buses To Iguape: from São Paulo, Santos, or Curitiba, changing at Registro (see below). **Ferries** A continuous ferry service runs from Iguape to Ilha Comprida (free but small charge for cars); buses run until 1900 from the ferry stop to the beaches. From Iguape it is possible to take a boat trip down the coast to Cananéia and Ariri (see below). Tickets and information from dpto Hidroviário do Estado, R Major Moutinho 198, Iguape, T8411122. It is a beautiful trip, passing between the island and the mainland.

Caverns of the Vale do Ribeiro

The caves are southwest of the state capital, west of the BR-116, in one of the largest concentrations of caverns in the world. Among the best known is the 8-km **Caverna do Diabo** (Devil's Cave), or **Gruta da Tapagem**. It has been described as huge 'as a cathedral' with well-lit rock formations in the 600 m open to the public. It is 40 km from **Eldorado Paulista**. ■ *0800-1100, 1200-1700 Mon-Fri, 0800-1700 Sat, Sun and holidays. US$2. Bar and toilets.*

Some 43 km from Caverna do Diabo is **Petar**, the Parque Estadual Turístico do Alto Ribeira. Here are three groups of caves: the Núcleo Santana, with the **Cavernas de Santana** (with 5.6 km of subterranean passages and three levels of galleries), Morro Preto and Água Suja, plus a 3.6-km ecological trail to the waterfalls in the Rio Bethary; and the Núcleo Ouro Grosso. This section of the park is 4 km from the town of **Iporanga**. Iporanga is the most convenient town for visiting all the caves; it is 64 km west of Eldorado Paulista, 42 km east of Apiaí, on the SP-165, 257 km southwest of São Paulo. The third Núcleo is Caboclos, near the town of Apiaí. Guided tours of Petar cost US$50 a day from the Associação Serrana Ambientalista, T015-5561188.

Sleeping   There are hotels in Iporanga, such as the **C** *Pousada das Cavernas*, T015-5561168 (or TXX011-5433082) and the **D** per person *Pousada Rancho da Serra*, T015-5561168 (or TXX011-5882011). **Camping** in Petar costs US$3 per person, 3 sites. There is a **youth hostel** near the Caverna do Diabo, *Província de Tokushima*, Parque Estadual da Caverna do Diabo, Km 43, SP-165, Eldorado Paulista, T0XX11-353077, open 0800-1800.

Transport   Bus: São Paulo-Apiaí, from Barra Funda rodoviária, US$22. If coming from Curitiba, change buses at Jacupiranga on the BR-116 for Eldorado Paulista.

Registro   A suitable stopping place for visiting the caves area is Registro on the BR-116, in
Phone code: 013   the heart of the tea-growing region, populated mainly by Japanese Brazilians.
Population: 49,000

Sleeping and eating   *Lito Palace* (**B**) is at Av Pref Jonas Banks Leite 615, T8211055, F8214470. Around the corner from the rodoviária is *Brasília* (**D**), R Brasília, with shower, clean, airy. For eating, try *Itatins*, BR-116 Km 444, for *churrasco*. There is a good *churrascaria* next to the bus station. **Transport**   The bus station is at R Neraldo Previb 835, T8211379.

Directory   Banks: *Bradesco*, Av Pref Jonas Banks Leite 520. **Communications**:   International calls can be made in the town centre. **Medical services**:   *São José*, Av Clara Gianotti de Sousa 420, T8216188.

Cananéia and Ilha do Cardoso

Phone code: 013   At the southern end of Ilha Comprida, across the channel, is Cananéia 270 km
Colour map 5, grid A5   from São Paulo. Another town with a long colonial history, it was one of
Population: 12,500   Martim Afonso de Souza's landfalls, it is now a peaceful place of gently decaying colonial charm. The colonial centre, around Praça Martim Afonso de Souza and neighbouring streets, contains the 17th-century church of **São João Batista** and the **Museu Municipal**. On 15 August, there is the Festa de Nossa Senhora dos Navegantes, with a procession of boats. To the south are a number of good beaches and the waterways are popular with fisherfolk.

For **tourist information**, contact the *Departamento de Esportes e Turismo*, Av Beira Mar 247, Cananéia, T8511473, ext 342. Guides Manoel Barroso, Av Independencia 65, T8511273, Portuguese only, recommended, or try the *Secretaria do Parque Estadual da Ilha do Cardoso*, Av Prof Besnard, near the port.

To reach the densely wooded **Ilha do Cardoso**, which is a Reserva Florestal e Biológica, take a ferry from the dock at Cananéia, four hours, three services daily (Rua Princesa Isabel, T8411122). Alternatively, drive 70 km along an unpaved road, impassable when wet, to **Ariri**, from where the island is 10 minutes by boat. The tiny village of Marujá, which has no electricity, has some very rustic *pousadas* and restaurants. Otherwise, the island is uninhabited. Camping is allowed at designated places. There are lots of idyllic beaches; best for surfing is Moretinho.

Sleeping   **A** *Cananéia Glória*, Av Luís Wilson Barbosa, T8511377, F8511378. Some chalets **B**, good
& eating   views. **C** *Villa São João Batista*, R Tristão Lobo 287, T8511587. Colonial-style 18th-century house, clean. *Naguissa do Silêncio*, Av Luís Wilson Barbosa 401, T8511341. Seafood.

The Interior

The interior of São Paulo state is diverse, with hill resorts and spa towns providing cool, peaceful alternatives to the beach. There are also towns with historical associations, industrial and agricultural centres.

About 13% of Brazil's population lives within 200 km of São Paulo city, a circle which includes 88 municipalities. Four of them – the big 'ABCD' towns – sharing a population of over a million – are Santo André, São Bernardo, São Caetano and Diadema, have many of the largest industrial plants.

The Northeast

Campos do Jordão

São Paulo

This mountain resort between Rio de Janeiro and São Paulo 1,628 m high in the Serra da Mantiqueira is prettily set in a long valley, with good walking. The climate is cold and dry in winter and cool in summer, a great relief from the coastal heat and humidity. *Minalba* mineral water is produced here and there are several mineral springs in the town. The **tourist office** is in the alpine-looking gateway to the city, the Portal da Cidade, T2622755, F2624100.

Phone code: 012
Colour map 5, grid A6
Population: 38,000

Campos do Jordão, named after a 19th-century landowner, is made up of three districts: Jaguaribe, the original nucleus, Abernéssia, founded by Scotsman Robert John Reid (the name he chose is a mixture of Aberdeen and Inverness), and Capivari, dating from the early 20th century. It was originally a *fazenda*, built in the 18th century by Inácio Caetano Vieira de Carvalho, on the gold route from Itajubá (Minas Gerais) across the Serra da Mantiqueira to the coast.

In April, there is the *Festa do Pinhão*; look out for classical music and dance festivals in June and July. There are plenty of chocolate shops, also jams and cheese for sale. Stalls on the main praça Thursday-Sunday sell local produce.

Palácio Boa Vista, 4 km from the centre of Abernéssia, was built in 1964 as a summer residence for the state governor. It was converted into a museum in 1970 and now houses works of art, furniture, sculpture and other items. ■ *1000-1200, 1400-1700, Wed, Thu, Sat and Sun. T2621122.* Other collections of art will be found in the **Museu Felícia Leirner**, an open-air museum with 85 sculptures in a park beside the Auditório Cláudio Santoro (Felícia Leirner herself was a sculptress); about 2 km from the Palácio Boa Vista. ■ *0900-1800 Tue-Sun. T2622324.* Also the **Casa da Xilogravura**, a museum specializing in woodcuts, founded by Antônio Fernando Costello, Avenida Eduardo Moreira da Cruz 295, Jaguaribe. ■ *1400-1700 Mon-Sat, 1000-1300 Sun. T2621832.*

Sights

Mineral springs within the town include the Fontes da Amizade, Renato and Simão. In Capivari is the **Morro do Elefante**, which has a road, path and chairlift to the belvedere at the top. About 12 km from Abernéssia is the **Pedra do Baú** (1,950 m), which has fine views from the summit. To get there take a bus to São Bento do Sapucaí at 0800 or 1500, then walk to Paiol Grande and then on an unmarked path to the Pedra. Return buses from São Bento at 0915 and 1615. Near Paiol Grande is the small waterfall of **Cachoeira dos Amores**. Also worth seeing is the **Gruta dos Crioulos**, 7½ km from Capivari. **Pico do**

São Paulo

Itapeva (2,030 m, 14 km southeast from Capivari) commands a beautiful view of the Paraíba valley. Also good for views is **Imbiri** (1,950 m). The nature reserve at **Horto Florestal** (15 km from Capivari) contains mostly pine forest in a 8,300-ha Parque Estadual. It ranges from 1,330m to 2,007 m above sea level and is very pretty – go in the morning to avoid crowds. There are lots of streams with bridges, waterfalls and lakes. Ornamental plants can be bought and various trails are laid out.

Campos do Jordão is a popular place for hikers; most of the roads leading off the main avenue lead to quiet areas with good views, for example up Avenida Dr Antônio Nicola Padula, turn left 500 m past *Refúgio na Serra* for waterfalls and Pico do Itapeva.

Estrada de Ferro Campos de Jordão   Railcars make round trips between Emílio Ribas station in Capivari (Campos do Jordão) and **Santo Antônio do Pinhal**, 16 km southwest. In season, the trains run six times a day, out of season (October-November, March-April) at 1310 only, a bit bumpy, but beautiful views (sit on the right on the way there, left coming back): hills, valleys, tight corners. The train is very crowded even though you are assigned a seat (buy your ticket in advance, and get a return immediately on arrival in San Antônio; watch your belongings on board). The whole trip takes about three hours: one hour each way on the train, 30 minutes-one hour in Santo Antônio. There is not much on offer in Santo Antônio: a few snack bars, handicraft shops, nice views, the viewpoint of Nossa Senhora Auxiliadora.

The **Emílio Ribas** station and **Recanto de São Cristóvão** are connected by a tram which runs every 40 minutes from 0630. The journey, which like the train runs the length of Campos do Jordão, takes one hour 10 minutes.

Sleeping & eating
Book accommodation in advance for June to July

LL *Toriba*, Av Ernesto Diederichsen 2962, T2621566, F2624211. Part of the Roteiros de Charme group, see page 47. **AL** *Refúgio Alpino*, Av Sen Roberto Simonsen 1461, T/F2631332, hralpino@iconet.com.br Full board. **B** *Refugio na Serra*, Av Dr Antônio Nicola Padula 275, T2631330. Comfortable, good breakfast, very helpful owners (some English spoken). Recommended. **Youth hostels E** per person *Recanto Tropical*, Estr Pindamonhangaba/Campos do Jordão 1650, T2422737, F2428312. IYHA. *Elis Regina II*, R Benigno Ribeiro 320, Recanto Feliz, T0XX11-353077. Open 0800-2300. **Camping** *Camping Clube do Brasil*, T2631130.

Sole Mio, Av Dr Emilio Lang 440. *Capivari*, Av Dr Emílio Ribas 814, on road to Horto Florestal, T2631429. Italian. *Baden Baden*, R Djalma Forjaz 93, Capivari, T2633610. German, good.

Transport   **Road** The road from Taubaté is 45 km, while that from São José dos Campos is 85 km. By car it takes about 3 hrs from São Paulo, 6-7 hrs from Rio. **Buses** Bus station, Av Dr Januário Miraglia, T2621996. From **São Paulo**, US$3.60, 3 hrs. From **Rio**, changing at São José dos Campos, US$5.75.

Directory   **Banks** *Bradesco*, Av Frei Orestes Girardi 1037. **Medical services** *São Paulo*, R Agripino Lopes de Morais 1100, T2621722.

The short road down to **Pindamonhangaba**, starting from the paved road 24 km southwest of Campos do Jordão, is paved (five buses daily, 50 minutes). A railcar runs to 'Pinda' out of season, leaving 1705 Monday-Thursday and weekends, from Pinda 0600 Tuesday-Friday, 0930 weekends (no service during the high season, when all cars are used on the Campos do Jordão-San Antônio route). There is a local railcar service within Pinda (very crowded but cheap). From Pinda buses run to **São Paulo** and to **Aparecida do Norte**, 1030, US$2.

Nearer to Rio than the Pindamonhangaba turn, just off the BR-116, is Brazil's chief place of pilgrimage and the seat of its patron saint, Nossa Senhora Aparecida. This small black image of the Virgin is said to have been taken by a fisherman from the nearby Río Paraíba, and quickly acquired a miraculous reputation. It is now housed in a huge modern basilica (1939) in Romanesque style on top of a hill, with the clean white-walled, red-roofed town below.

Aparecida do Norte
Population: 36,000

To Minas Gerais

This spa town in the Serra da Mantiqueira, 69 km from São Paulo calls itself the Brazilian Switzerland, with the second best climate in the world (after Switzerland itself). In the top climate stakes it is obviously competing with Peruíbe and Campos do Jordão. It also calls itself 'Cidade das Flores' (city of flowers) and the South American capital of strawberries – there is usually a flower and strawberry festival in September and a festival for strawberries alone in June. The Day of the Kings (*Reis Magos*), 6 January, is celebrated with *congadas* (see Music, page 687). Atibaia was founded in 1665 by the *bandeirante* Jerônimo de Camargo, on one of the roads to Minas Gerais.

Atibaia
Phone code: 011
Population: 98,000

A **Museu Ferroviário** on Avenida Jerónimo de Camargo preserves steam engines and rolling stock from the 19th century. It is in a park with a U-shaped railway line around a lake, with a station and turntable at each end. Latest reports indicate that no trains are running. ■ *T78710354*. About 14 km from town is *Recanto de Paz*, Av Jerônimo de Camargo (**L**), T78751369, which has chalets, restaurant, pool and horse riding. There are many other places to stay.

The Northwest

Campinas

The city is an industrial centre 88 km from São Paulo by the fine Via Anhangüera highway and important as a clearing point for coffee. Its university has an excellent reputation and there are many students in the town.

Phone code: 019
Colour map 4, grid C2
Population: 971,000

See the fine **Catedral Metropolitana Nossa Senhora da Conceição**, built in 1883 in neoclassical style with baroque elements (Praça José Bonifácio), and the **Mercado Municipal** (old market, 1908) on Avenida Benjamin Constant. There are several museums. **Museu Carlos Gomes**, Rua Bernardino de Campos 989, T32312567, has displays on art, literature and science; the city is the birthplace of the 19th-century Brazilian composer Carlos Gomes, his tomb is in Praça Bento Quirino. In the Bosque de Jequitibás are the **Museus de História Natural** and **do Folclore**. The arts centre in the **Centro de Convivência Cultural**, Praça Tom Jobim, T2525857, has a noted symphony orchestra. The modern Universidade Estadual de São Paulo, called Unicamp, is outside the city. Visits can be made to the **Instituto Agronômico** on Avenida Barão de Itapura 1481, Guanabara, to see all the aspects of coffee. ■ *0800-1100, 1300-1700 Mon-Fri. T2315330.*

Sights

At **Jaguariúna**, 25 km from Campinas, is a railway preservation group with steam engines and wagons. Every weekend and public holiday two **tourist trains** (three on Sunday) run between Jaguariúna and Campinas on a

São Paulo

two-hour trip. The route is along the old Mogiana Estrada de Ferro and is part of a tourism project based in Jaguariúna and the historic coffee-growing region. There are plans to restore the stations of Carlos Gomes, Tanquinho and Anhumas. You can either take an hourly bus from Campinas to Jaguariúna, or take the steam train itself from Campinas (station behind Carrefour, Anhumas, reached by town bus). ■ *For schedules and information, T2536067. The 2nd tourist train runs 1 Sat a month to Peruíbe, 0700, 6 hrs, run by Pettená-Tur. A tourist tram operates in Parque Taquaral.*

Sleeping **LL** with meals *Solar das Andorinhas*, 20 km outside the city on the Mogi-Mirim road, T32571411. A health farm with pool, sauna, horses, sports courts. **L** *Royal Palm Plaza*, R Com Dr José Cesar Gazi 200, outside town at the Trevo de Anhangüera, T37388000. **A** *Royal Palm Residence*, R Conceição 450, T32344766. Apartment hotel. **B** *Opala Avenida*, Av Dr Campos Salles 161, T32344115. Central. **B** *Savoy*, R Regente Feijó 1064, T32329444. **C** *Hotel IPE*, R Bernardino de Campos 1050, T32317746. Recommended. **C** *Parati Palácio*, R Bernardino de Campos 426, T32320395. German spoken. Recommended.

Eating **Mid-range**: *Bar Restaurante Barão*, Barão de Jaguará 1381 and *Churrascaria Gaúcha*, Av Dr Campos Salles 515, T2317449. Excellent for Brazilian food. **Cheap**: *Nutrir*, R Dr Quirino 1620. Vegetarian. **Seriously cheap**: *Sucão*, R Benjamin Constant 1108. Good variety of juices. *Pastelaria do Sr Júlio*, R de 13 Maio 143. Friendly, helpful, cheap. Recommended.

Entertainment Weekend nightlife is busy around the Centro de Convivência (see above), in the city centre. There are cinemas in the city centre and the Iguatemi and Galleria shopping centres.

Shopping **Bookshops** *Pontes Editores*, R Dr Quirino 1223, has English books. Second-hand at *Sebo Comércio*, R Bareto Leme 1265, and *O Livrão*, R Barão de Jaguará 936, loja 11.

Transport **Air** Viracopos international airport, Rod Santos Dumont Km 66, T7255000, is 11 km from Campinas, which also has its own airport. Flights to Belo Horizonte, Brasília, Curitiba, Joinville, Goiânia, Recife, Rio de Janeiro and São Paulo.
  Taxis *Central Geral de Taxi*, T2728313. *Disk Taxi*, T2420600.
  Trains A metre-gauge line, connecting with the broad-gauge former Paulista at Campinas, serves the northeastern part of the state. It goes through Ribeirão Preto to Uberlândia and Araguari in the Triângulo of Minas Gerais. Latest information suggests that no passenger services run on these lines.
  Buses Bus station, R Barão de Parnaíba 690, T2321355. To **São Paulo**, US$3, **Ribeirão Preto** and **Araguari**; to **Rio**, 7 hrs, US$12.

Directory **Airline offices** *TAM*, T2369022. *Varig*, T2316000. *Vasp*, T2322566. **Banks** *American Express*, R Irmã Serafina 863, 1st floor, conj 16, T2336797. **Medical services** *das Clínicas*, Cidade Universitária, T7887766. **Places of worship** Community church services in English at *School of Language and Orientation*, R Eduardo Lane 270.

Americana
Phone code: 019
Population: 182,000

This town, 42 km from Campinas, is situated in an area settled by Confederate refugees from the south of the US after the Civil War (see box, page 219). The town is now a centre for the textile industry and there are various factory outlets. In nearby **Santa Barbara d'Oeste** there is a **Museu de Imigração** explaining the history of the Confederates and other immigrants to this area. The bus station is on Rua Orlando Dei Santi, T4618077.

Confederados

At the end of the American Civil War, some 20,000 former Confederates were tempted to leave the United States and try their luck in Brazil. The emperor, Dom Pedro II, offered some very attractive incentives to the exiles, including subsidized passage, freedom of religion and land at 22 cents an acre. He was hoping that the Southerners would bring their expertise in cotton-growing to Brazil. They would certainly have been aware that slavery had not been banned in Brazil in the 1860s. First attempts at settlement were in the Amazon basin, but conditions there were too unhealthy and many of the original settlers soon returned to the US. Others settled further south and the only community which was successful was Villa Americana in São Paulo state. The Confederados, as they were known, cultivated cotton, watermelons, peaches and pecans. A few families still speak English at home.

There is a museum at Santa Bárbara d'Oeste, 12 km west, and a visit to the Confederados' cemetery nearby reveals an unusual number of English surnames.

Sleeping and eating A *Americana*, Av Cillos 1796, T4613579, F4612635. Restaurant. **A** *Florença Palace*, Av Cillos 820, T4616393, F4618575. Restaurant, pool. *Brüder*, Av Campos Sales 447. *Prima Pizza*, R 12 de Novembro 613.

Directory Banks *Banco 24 Horas*, Praça Com Müller 77, *Bradesco*, Av Campos Sales 720.

Spa towns

Four towns some 80-100 km northeast of Campinas are well known for the quality of their mineral waters. Hotels and parks have been established around the springs and the spas have become popular for conferences and conventions.

The region and its medicinal waters began to be settled after the *bandeirantes* (see box, page 198) and mule trains passed this way on their expeditions and trade routes into Minas Gerais and Goiás. The towns themselves were not created until the 19th century, the latest being Lindóia in 1898.

Serra Negra is a very pleasant spa town and summer holiday resort in the mountains, 78 km northeast of Campinas and 152 km from São Paulo. There are several springs, a *Balneário Municipal* with a convention centre and the longest chairlift in Brazil, to the Cristo Redentor on Pico do Fonseca. **Tourist information** is at Praça John F Kennedy, T8922131.

Phone code: 019
Population: 22,000

About 13 km from Serra Negra is the even better-known spa town of **Lindóia**, whose still waters are bottled and sent all over Brazil. The municipality is the largest producer of mineral water in Latin America. For tourist information, T8681211.

About 7 km away is a separate spa, **Águas de Lindóia**, with a *Balneário Municipal*, hotels and a wide range of conference facilities. The bus station is at Avenida das Nações Unidas 1179, T8241128. Nearby is **tourist information**, at Avenida das Nações Unidas 196, T8941126.

Some 22 km southeast of Lindóia is **Socorro** also with a *Balneário Municipal*. For tourist information, T8953000.

São Paulo

Sleeping & eating **Serra Negra**: **AL** *Rádio*, R Col Pedro Penteado 387, T8923311, F8921992, radiohotel@circuitodasaguas.com.br Restaurant, pool, sports courts, very nice indeed. **A** *Cordilheira*, Praça João Zelante 53, T8921552, F8921627. Pool. **Youth hostel D** per person *Estância Clube Veraneio*, Km 156 on the road to Águas de Lindóia, T8922155, F8322096. *Carlinhos*, Av Romeu de Campos Vergal 23. Churrasco restaurant. **Lindóia**: **B** *Flamingo's Chalés*, Av 31 de Março, T8981356. Pool, sports courts. **Águas de Lindóia**: **AL** *Vacance*, Av das Nações Unidas 1374, T/F8241191. Restaurant, pool, sports courts. **A** *das Fontes*, R Rio de Janeiro 267, T8241511, F8241872. Pool. *Spaghetti e Cia*, R Rio de Janeiro 403. Italian restaurant. **Socorro**: **A** *Best Western Grinberg's Village*, Estr da Pompéia 210, T/F8952909. **Youth hostel** *Paschoalino Sigolo*, R Antônio Leopoldino 215, in the centre. Restaurant. *Marchetti*, R 13 de Maio 43.

Directory **Banks** *Bradesco*, R Col Pedro Penteado 337, Serra Negra; Av Brasil 22, Águas de Lindóia; and R 13 de Maio 100, Socorro.

The North

Ribeirão Preto

Phone code: 016
Colour map 4, grid C1
Population: 505,000

The centre of a rich coffee-growing district, the town also has a steel industry. It is 319 km from São Paulo by the Via Anhangüera (four hours by bus). It also has an airport. **Tourist offices** For more details on the Roteiro Portinari, contact the *Departamanto de Cultura e Turismo* in Brodowski, Praça Martim Moreira, T6641666, or the *Secretaria da Cultura* in Ribeirão Preto, Praça Barão do Rio Branco, T6352424.

The **Museu do Café**, in the former Fazenda Monte Alegre on the campus of the Universidade de São Paulo, on the road to Sertãozinho, tells the history of coffee in the area. ■ *T6331986*. In the same location is a historical museum. The cathedral, **São Sebastião**, Praça da Bandeira, was built in gothic style and contains stained glass and frescos by Benedito Calixto. On the Morro de São Bento is the **Sete Capelas** sanctuary. *Feapam*, Feira Agropecuária da Alta Mogiana, agricultural show is held early August.

Excursions **The Roteiro Portinari** The artist Cândido Portinari was born in **Brodowski**, 30 km north of Ribeirão Preto. There is a museum at his house at Praça Cândido Portinari 298. In the garden of the house is the Capela da Nona, which Portinari built for his grandmother in 1941 when she was too ill to go to church. The walls are covered with beautiful murals of biblical figures. ■ *0900-1700 Tue-Sun. T6641284*.

Sleeping & eating **A** *Stream Palace*, R Gen Osório 850, T6100660, F6101007. **B** *Umuarama Recreio*, Praça dos Cafeeiros 140, T6373790. 6 km from centre, very pleasant, pool, gardens. *La Pyramide*, R Marcondes Salgado 1525, T6109121.

Transport **Air** Airport, T6263376. Flights to Brasília, São José do Rio Preto and São Paulo. **Buses** Bus station, Av Jerônimo Gonçalves, T6257386. *Rápido Ribeirão Preto* to São Paulo, 4-5 hrs, US$20.

Directory **Airline offices** *Interbrasil*, T6280909. *Passaredo*, T6281319. *Rio-Sul*, T6266848. *TAM*, T6282500. **Banks** *Banco 24 Horas*, R Gen Osório 432. *Banco do Brasil*, R Duque de Caxias 725.

São Paulo

The biggest rodeo in the world

The world's biggest annual rodeo, the Festa do Peão Boiadeiro, is held during the third week in August in Barretos, some 115 km northwest of Ribeirão Preto. The town is completely taken over as up to a million fans come to watch the horsemanship, enjoy the concerts, eat, drink and shop in what has become the epitome of Brazilian cowboy culture. There are over 1,000 rodeos a year in Brazil, but this is the ultimate. The stadium, which has a capacity for 35,000 people, was designed by Oscar Niemeyer so that the wind funnels through the middle, cooling the competitors and the spectators. Since the 1950s, when Barretos' rodeo began, the event grew slowly until the mid-1980s when it really took off.

Tours from the UK are run by Last Frontiers, Fleet Marston Farm, Aylesbury, Bucks HP18 0PZ, T01296-658650, F658651, www.lastfrontiers.co.uk

São Paulo

The West

The Rio Tietê was one of the principal routes used by the early explorers of the interior, either along its banks in the case of the bandeirantes, or as a waterway in the case of the monsoons (see page 651). Today, good paved highways travel in the same direction. The Caminho dos Bandeirantes, also called the Estrada dos Romeiros (the Pilgrims' Way), is the name given to about 130 km of road passing through a number of towns with historical associations.

The SP-300 is a picturesque paved road along the Tietê valley from São Paulo to Bauru. The first colonial town reached is **Santana do Parnaíba**, 41 km from the state capital; it was founded in 1580 and is known for its *cachaça*. The small town of **Pirapora de Bom Jesus** is a popular place of pilgrimage, in a most attractive setting on both sides of the river. The image of Bom Jesus, found in the river in 1725, is believed to be miraculous. A particularly important festival here is Corpus Christi. Next is **Cabreúva**, another producer of *cachaça*, and then **Itu**, 102 km from São Paulo. Itu was founded by the *bandeirantes* in the early 17th century and then became an important centre of sugar cultivation. Today, it contains a number of 18th and 19th-century churches, a museum of the Convenção Republicana da Provincia, one of the meetings which prompted the move towards the Brazilian Republic (Rua Barão do Itaim 67) and, in the surrounding countryside, colonial houses, old sugar estates and fine scenery. The beautiful falls of Salto de Itu, 8 km north, are flanked by a park and a textile mill. In and around the town are hotels; there are also nine campsites in the vicinity.

The Hidrovia Tietê-Paraná

The main rivers in the west of the state, the Tietê, the Grande, the Paranapanema and the Paraná are an enormous hydrological resource. Dams have formed great lakes, used for power, irrigation and, increasingly, tourism. The Tietê-Paraná system alone links 85 municipalities, accounting for just over 2½ million people.

Presidente Epitácio
Phone code: 018
Population: 39,000

This far southwest corner of São Paulo state is intensely farmed, but the authorities are trying to encourage 'ecoturismo' in the agricultural zone, with camping and hostelling, and on the Paraná and Paranapanema rivers, with marinas, resorts, watersports, fishing and condominiums.

Sleeping and eating **A** *Hotel Thermas e Fazenda de Presidente Epitácio*, 2½ km from Presidente Epitácio on the road to Campinal, T/F281253. Tourist complex on the Rio Paraná, with swimming pools, sauna, sporting facilities, shopping centre, etc. In town are hotels in our **A** range and a variety of restaurants, including some serving fish.

São Paulo

Minas Gerais and Espírito Santo

Introducing Minas Gerais and Espírito Santo

Diamonds, gold and other mineral riches were the driving force behind the settlement of this mountainous state. This abundant wealth has left behind a legacy of glorious colonial architecture and sculpture decorating its mining towns. The modern state capital **Belo Horizonte** is a good and interesting base for visiting **Ouro Preto** and the other historic cities. The *Mineiros* were the first to rebel against exploitation by Portugal and are still regarded today as independent and somewhat reserved. They are nonetheless very hospitable and have one of the best cuisines in Brazil. The rugged terrain of its national parks such as **Serra do Cipó** and **Caparaó** holds much of interest for trekkers and bird-watchers. There are some caves, the **Rio São Francisco** and a number of spas and hill resorts. The nearby state of Espírito Santo has a beautiful, mountainous and little-visited interior and 400 km of coastline dotted with pretty fishing villages and attractive beaches, including **Parque Estadual de Itaúnas** with its spectacular sand dunes.

Uberlândia

Araxá

Uberaba

Parque Nacional da Serra da Canastra

Três Corações

Poços de Caldas

Cambuquira

Lambari

Things to do in Minas Gerais and Espirito Santo

① Follow the trail of the Gold Rush and stop off to admire ornamental baroque architecture at colonial cities such as **Ouro Preto**.

② Visit the mysterious, mystical town of **São Tomé das Letras**, a hippie-hangout steeped in legend, with prehistoric rock carvings and maybe UFOs.

③ Take to the hills and explore dramatic mountain scenery dotted with national parks – on foot, horse or bicycle – or, if you're feeling more adventurous, you can try canyoning, caving or rafting.

④ Bathe in mineral-rich waters of hydro resorts in forest-covered hills, such as São Lourenço.

⑤ Visit the 'turtle beaches' of the **Reserva Biológica Comboios**, where mighty leatherbacks and other species haul themselves on the sands to lay their eggs.

Minas Gerais

The inland state of Minas Gerais was once described as having a heart of gold and a breast of iron. Half the mineral production of Brazil comes from the state, including most of the iron ore. Diamonds and gold are still found and Minas Gerais produces 95% of all Brazil's gemstones. The state is a little larger than France. The mountainous south rises to 2,787 m at the peak of Agulhas Negras in the Mantiqueira range (the peak itself is in Rio de Janeiro state). In the east, the Caparaó National Park contains the Pico da Bandeira (2,890 m). Both these areas of highland are part of the continuous chain of mountains which form the escarpment which cuts the state off from the coastal lowlands of the states of Rio de Janeiro and Espírito Santo.

Belo Horizonte

Phone code: 031
Colour map 4, grid B3
Population: 5 million

The capital of Minas Gerais is the third largest city in Brazil. Its soaring skyscrapers are circled by dramatic mountains. Together with Curitiba (Paraná), Belo Horizonte enjoys one of the best standards of living in the country.

It is one of Brazil's fastest-growing cities, now suffering from atmospheric pollution. It is in the process of introducing an integrated public transport system, like Curitiba's, to improve what is already a good bus network. The industrial area, apart from being the traditional centre of mining and agricultural industries (as well as diamond cutting and precious stones), has steelworks and an automobile industry.

Ins and outs

Getting there
See also Transport, page 234

International flights land at Confins airport, 39 km from Belo Horizonte. Shuttle services from several cities including Rio and São Paulo arrive at Pampulha airport closer to the city. Interstate buses arrive at the rodoviária next to Praça Rio Branco at the northwest end of Av Afonso Pena.

Getting around

The city has a good public transport system and some buses integrate with the regional, overground Metrô. Belo Horizonte is a hilly city with streets that rise and fall and trees lining many of the central avenues. The large Parque Municipal is in the heart of downtown Belo Horizonte and high-rise buildings dominate the centre. The broad main avenue of Afonso Pena, is constantly full of pedestrians and traffic, except on Sun morning when cars are banned from part of it which becomes a huge open-air market. The main commercial district on Av Afonso Pena and the surrounding streets is where activity is concentrated during the day (and is the best area to eat in at lunch time). At night the *movimento* shifts to Savassi, southwest of the centre, which is the best area for eating, drinking and entertainment.

Tourist information *Belotur*, the municipal information office at R Pernambuco 284 Funciários, T32779797, www.pbh.gov.br/belotur/index.htm, is very helpful, with lots of useful information and maps. The monthly *Guia Turístico* for events, opening times, etc, is freely available. *Belotur* has offices also at the southwest corner of Parque Municipal, at Confins and Pampulha airports, and at the rodoviária (particularly polyglot). *Turminas*, Praça Rio Branco 56, T32728573, F32725605, www.turminas.mg.gov.br/intminas.html The tourism authority for the state of Minas Gerais. It, too, is very helpful and its *Gerais Common Ways* booklet has a useful facts section. The daily newspaper, *Estado de Minas*, www.em.com.br, has interesting articles and information on the city and the state. **Other organizations**: *Ibama*, Av do Contorno 8121, Cidade Jardim, CEP 30110-120, Belo Horizonte, T33372624, F33359955. *Instituto Estadual de Florestas*, for information on state parks, etc, Maurício Luciano, T3307017. *Touring Club do Brasil*, Av Brasil 1505, T2616868. The daily newspaper, *Estado de Minas*, www.estaminas.com.br, has interesting articles and information on the city and the state.

As in any large city, watch out for sneak thieves in the centre and at the bus station. The **Safety** Parque Municipal is not too safe, so it is best not to enter alone.

Belo Horizonte enjoys an excellent climate (16-30°C) except for the rainy season **Climate** (Dec-Mar). The average annual temperature in is 21°C. The far north of the state where it borders Bahia, is semi-arid, but mountain resorts have been developed in the cooler heights of Minas Gerais.

Belo Horizonte orientation & Pampulha

0 km 2
0 miles 2

■ Sleeping
1 Ouro Minas

Detailed map
A Belo Horizonte
centre, page 229

Minas Gerais and Espírito Santo

Sights

The **Parque Municipal** is an oasis of green, right in the centre of the city. It has a small amusement park and playground and is closed at night and on Monday, except for a small section in the southwest corner, where a tourist office is located. The principal building in the park is the **Palácio das Artes**, Afonso Pena 1567, which contains the **Centro de Artesanato Mineiro** (with craft shop). ■ *1300-1800 Mon, 0900-2100 Tue-Fri, 0900-1300 Sat, 1000-1400 Sun. T2222400*. There is also an exhibition of the development of painting in Minas Gerais (all fairly derivative), a cinema, three theatres and temporary exhibitions. On the stretch of Avenida Afonso Pena outside the Parque Municipal an open-air market operates each Sunday morning. The avenue is transformed by thousands of coloured awnings covering stalls selling every conceivable type of local handicraft. It attracts thousands of shoppers. ■ *0800-1400*.

Praça Sete de Setembro (usually called Praça Sete) is at the busy junction of Avenida Afonso Pena and Avenida Amazonas, midway between the Parque Municipal and the Rodoviária. An obelisk commemorating Independence is the centre for political protests.

Six blocks up Avenida João Pinheiro from Avenida Afonso Pena is the **Praça da Liberdade**, which is surrounded by fine public buildings, some in eclectic, *fin-de-siècle* style, others more recent. These include the Secretaria da Fazenda, the Secretaria da Educação and the Casa Falci/Secretaria de Obras Públicas. At the end of the Praça is the **Palácio da Liberdade**. ■ *0900-1800 Sun only*. Among the new buildings are the Centro de Apoio Turístico Tancredo Neves (1991), which contains the offices of Turminas (see Tourist offices, above) and, not actually on the square, but visible from it, the Biblioteca Pública. The praça itself is very attractive, with trees, flowers, fountains which are lit at night and joggers and walkers making the most of the paths.

On the **Praça da Assembléia** are three fine modern buildings: the Legislative Assembly, a church and *Banco Central do Brasil*. At Rua da Bahia 1149, is a Gothic building near the Parque Municipal, which used to be the Museu da Mineralogia Professor Djalma Guimarães, remodelled as the **Centro Cultural de Belo Horizonte**.

As a modern city, Belo Horizonte has no **churches** to equal those of the colonial towns. In the centre are the **Catedral da Boa Viagem** (completed 1932), Rua Sergipe 175; **São José** (1906), the first church of the new city, Rua Tupis 164; and **Nossa Senhora de Lourdes** (begun 1923, consecrated 1958), Rua da Bahia 1596.

The **railway station**, with a museum on the second floor showing a model railway, is part of a complex which includes a number of buildings dating from the 1920s around the **Praça da Estação** (also called Praça Rui Barbosa). One of the earliest buildings on the Praça is now the Centro Cultural da Universidade Federal de Minas Gerais.

Museums **Museu Mineiro**, Avenida João Pinheiro 342, houses religious and other art in the old Senate building, close to the centre. There is a section dedicated specifically to religious art, six pictures attributed to Mestre Athayde (see under Ouro Preto), exhibitions of modern art, photographs and Naive painters. See also the wood carvings by Geraldo Teles de Oliveira (GTO). ■ *1230-1830 Tue-Fri, 1000-1600 Sat-Sun, T2711354*.

Museu Histórico Abílio Barreto, Rua Bernardo Mascarenhas, Cidade Jardim, in an old *fazenda* which is the last reminder of Belo Horizonte's predecessor, the village of **Arraial do Curral d'el Rey**, built by João Leite da Silva

Ortiz in the 18th century, houses most interesting historical exhibits.
■ *T2963896. Take bus 2902 from Av Afonso Pena.*

Museu de História Natural, in the Instituto Agronómico, Rua Gustavo da
Silveira 1035, Santa Inês, has a local geological, palaeontological and good
archaeological exhibits. ■ *0800-1130, 1300-1630 Mon-Thu, 0900-1600 Sat-Sun.
T4677723. Getting there: take bus 8001.* Also here is the **Jardim Botânico**.

Suburbs

Some 8 km northwest, this picturesque suburb is famous for its modern **Pampulha**
buildings and artificial lake, created in the 1930s and circled by the 18-km
Avenida Otacílio Negrão de Lima. The four main buildings on the lake shore,
designed by Oscar Niemeyer and landscaped by Roberto Burle Marx, are part
of a unified concept. The **Igreja São Francisco de Assis**, Avenida Otacílio
Negrão de Lima Km 12, was inaugurated in 1943. Its shape, one elongated
arch interlocking with the largest of four similar arches, and its separate bell-
tower, have become one of the most common symbols of Belo Horizonte. Its
exterior has beautiful blue and white tiles depicting St Francis' life and behind
the altar is a powerful composition, both by the painter Cândido Portinari.
The interior contains bronze panels by the sculptor Ceschiatti. ■ *0830-1200,
1330-1800 Mon-Fri, 0900-1800 Sat, Sun and holidays.*

Minas Gerais and Espírito Santo

Belo Horizonte centre

*Related map
Belo Horizonte
orientation &
Pampulha,
page 227*

■ **Sleeping**	**2** Esplanada	**4** Othon Palace	**6** Wembley Palace
1 Continental	**3** Magnata	**5** Sol Meliá	

On the opposite shore is the glass and marble **Museu de Arte de Pampulha** (MAP), at Avenida Octacílio Negrão de Lima 16585. It has a fine collection of modern art from Minas Gerais. It was originally a casino, set up by Juscelino Kubitschek, and was the first project in the complex to be designed and landscaped by the Niemeyer/Burle Marx team. People would dance in the **Casa do Baile**, take a boat across the lake for some gambling, and then dance again in what is now the Auditório in MAP (stand in the centre of the floor to hear the echo). The Casa do Baile is a perfect example of Niemeyer's fascination with the curved line, with its snaking canopy leading up to the main dance hall, which has windows all around to allow full views of the Burle Marx landscaping and the lake. ■ *0900-1900 Tue-Sun. Free. T2777946, www.comartevirtual.com.br Deals with art in general in Belo Horizonte and has a section on MAP*. The fourth building in the Pampulha architectural complex is the **Iate Tênis Clube**, the Yacht and Tennis Club. Take bus 2004 from Avenida Afonso Pena to the Lagoa da Pampulha.

Just 700 m south of the lake is the **Mineirão** stadium, the second largest in Brazil after the Maracanã stadium in Rio, seating 92,000. Seats cost between US$5 and US$10.

CEPEL, Centro de Preparação Equestre da Lagoa (The Lake Riding School), Avenida Antônio Francisco Lisboa 481, one of the largest equestrian centres in South America. ■ *0800-1700 Tue-Sun. T4410812.*

Mangabeiras About 3 km south of the centre, the **Parque de Mangabeiras** is on the Serra do Curral at between 1,000 m and 1,400 m above sea level. The recreation areas and public spaces were landscaped by Burle Marx in 1982. There are good views of the city, especially from the Mirante da Mata. Three forest trails have been laid out with picnic areas: the Roteiros do Sol (Sun Route), da Mata (Woods Route) and das Águas (Water Route). There are sports facilities and a café. ■ *0800-1800 Thu-Sun. Getting there: bus 2001 from Av Afonso Pena between Av Amazonas and Rua Tamóios.*

The natural amphitheatre of **Praça do Papa** where the Pope spoke in 1980 is on the way up to Parque Mangabeiras. Just below, Rua Professor Otávio Magalhães is nicknamed **Rua do Amendoim** (Peanut Street). Its fame rests in an optical illusion that makes it appear that cars in neutral run up the slope, rather than down. The same happens with cans, etc, but it is difficult to find the exact spot without local knowledge.

Excursions

Within easy reach of Belo Horizonte are several of the 400 caves and grottoes for which the state is famous

The **Gruta de Lapinha** is only 36 km north of the city. ■ *0900-1700 Tue-Sun. US$2 to enter the caves and small archaeological museum.*

About 10 km before Lapinha is the town of **Lagoa Santa**, a weekend resort for Belo Horizonte. The sandy beach on the lake (close to the town centre and bus station) is used for fishing, sun bathing and boating (do not swim, the water is infected with schistosomiasis). Along the beach are bars and restaurants, with more in the nearby main praça, which also has two small hotels and an interesting modernistic church.

Transport Buses (*Útil*) to the Gruta de Lapinha leave at 1015 and 1130 daily, returning 1600, also 1830 Mon only; 1¼ hrs, US$3.25 one-way. Half-hourly bus service Belo Horizonte-Lagoa Santa, US$2. Bus Lagoa Santa-Lapinha every 30 mins. The local bus stop for Lagoa Santa is 2 km downhill from the Lapinha caves.

Peter Lund and Lagoa Santa Man

Born in Copenhagen in 1801, Peter Wilhelm Lund came to be known as the father of Brazilian palaeontology. At the age of 24 he moved to Brazil for health reasons and settled in Nova Friburgo (now in Rio de Janeiro state). He collected material for the Danish Museum of Natural History, before sailing back to Hamburg in 1829. In 1833 he returned to Brazil and began to research the flora of Rio de Janeiro, São Paulo, Goiás and Mato Grosso, the results of which were published in Observações respeito da vegetação dos campos do interior do Brasil, especialmente fito históricas *(1835). His explorations then led him to Lagoa Santa, Minas Gerais, where he lived from 1840 to 1880, the year he died. He turned his attention to palaeontology and the caves in the area; the discoveries he made there were of enormous importance to the understanding of early peoples in Brazil.*

Lund found the fossils of humans who were dubbed Lagoa Santa Man. In the caves there were also the bones of mammals which, elsewhere on earth, had died out in the Pleistocene age (the first period of the quaternary era, before the Neolithic age). Until it was surmised that these mammals lived longer in South America than in other regions and until carbon dating confirmed that Lagoa Santa Man was not more than about 10,000 years old, Lund's discoveries predated by a long way any other humans found in Brazil. Regardless of the date of the human remains, the significance of Lagoa Santa Man lay in the fact that evidence of these people could be seen in a lasting form. Much of Brazilian palaeontology and archaeology was, and still is, hampered by the reliance of most early peoples on perishable materials (eg wood and natural fibres) for their houses and artefacts. Lagoa Santa Man also figured in the debate that raged after the publication of Charles Darwin's theories of evolution.

Near the town of Pedro Leopoldo, which is between Belo Horizonte and Sete Lagoas, is a village called Dr Lund. Beyond this village is a fazenda *which offers accommodation, riding, fishing, swimming and other country pursuits: Hotel Fazenda Tarumã, T031-3375379 Belo Horizonte, or T031-6611965, Pedro Leopoldo. For more details, contact Ametur in Belo Horizonte (see Tour operators).*

Some 80 km northwest of Belo Horizonte is the town of **Sete Lagoas**, near the **Gruta Rei do Mato** where prehistoric inscriptions and cave paintings have been found. ■ *0800-1700. T7730888.* Sete Lagoas, which has hotels, can be reached by *Expresso Setelagoano* bus from Belo Horizonte in 1½ hours.

The best and most famous of the caves is the **Gruta de Maquiné** with six chambers open to visitors. The caves are well lit, but hot at 26°C. ■ *US$5.* The restaurants nearby greet potential customers with a combined history and menu leaflet. The nearby town of **Cordisburgo** has a museum to the writer João Guimarães Rosa (see page 693). ■ *0800-1700 Tue-Sun. Av Padre João 744.*

Transport Several buses daily (*Irmãos Teixeira*), 2¼ hrs, US$8.

To the northeast of the city, the **Serra de Piedade** is a high peak giving spectacular views over the surrounding countryside, only accessible by car or special bus service. ■ *T4995679.* There is a telescope on the hill, a small chapel and a *churrascaria.* From the peak are views of the small town of Caeté (see page 239).

Minas Gerais and Espirito Santo

Essentials

Sleeping

■ *on map, page 229*
Price codes:
see inside front cover

You may only spend
the night in the
rodoviária if you have
an onward ticket
(police check at
midnight)

LL *Ouro Minas Palace*, Av Cristiano Machado 4001, T4294001 (toll free 0800-314000), omhmkt@br.homeshopping.com.br The most luxurious hotel in the city, palatial suites on the top floors, excellent service, not central but within easy reach of the centre and airports. **L** *Fazenda Boa Esperança*, in natural surroundings at about 900 m in the hills to the west of Belo Horizonte. It is part of the Roteiro de Charme group, see page 47. **L** *Othon Palace*, Av Afonso Pena 1050, T2733844. Deluxe, modern, glass-fronted, excellent, safe deposit boxes, good restaurant, pool on roof, helpful staff, right in the centre, opposite the Parque Municipal, rooms on lower floors can be noisy.

AL *Boulevard Plaza*, Av Getúlio Vargas 1640, Savassi district (chic shopping area), T2697000. Very nice. **AL** *Sol Meliá*, R da Bahia 1040, T/F2741344. Also in the heart of the city, comfortable, all facilities including pool and sauna.

A *Metrópole*, R da Bahia 1023, T2731544, F2225673. Central, convenient location. **A** *Wembley Palace*, R Espírito Santo 201, T2736866, F2249946. Excellent, central.

B *Ambassy*, R dos Caetés 633, near rodoviária, T2795000, F2712286. Helpful, English spoken, hot shower, TV, good restaurant. **B** *Esplanada*, Av Santos Dumont 304, T2735311. **D** without bath, good restaurant, own garage, good value. **B** *Estoril*, R dos Carijós 454, T/F2019322. Comfortable, pleasant.

C *Itatiaia*, Praça Rui Barbosa 187, near railway station, T2740003, F2744576. Central, a/c, good breakfast. **C** *Continental*, Av Paraná 241, T2017944. Central, quieter interior rooms recommended. **C** *Magnata*, R Guarani 124, T2015368. With breakfast, near rodoviária, good hot shower, safe deposit. Recommended. **C** *São Salvador*, R Espírito Santo 227, T2227731. Recommended.

D *Liz*, Av Olegário Maciel 95, T2011757. Basic. **D** *Madrid*, R Guarani 12, opposite the rodoviária, T2011088/6330. Recommended, but in a noisy location. **D** *São Cristovão*, Av Oiapoque 284, T2014860. Quiet, breakfast. Near the rodoviária and in R Curitiba many hotels are for very-short-stay couples.

Youth hostels E per person *Chalé Mineiro*, R Santa Luzia 288, Santa Efigênia, T4671576. IYHA, splash pool, attractive. Recommended. *Pousadinha Mineira*, R Araxá 514, Floresta, 15 mins from the rodoviária, T4462911, F4424448, pipe@gold.com.br IYHA, cheaper for members, popular with Brazilians. Bedding and towels can be hired, breakfast extra on request, very helpful. Recommended.

Eating

In all restaurants in
the centre, look for
lunchtime promotions

Local food *Comida mineira* is the local speciality; it is good, wholesome food, served in big black pots and earthenware dishes from which you help yourself. The hot dishes stand on a shelf above a wood-fired oven. There are a number of chicken recipes (such as *frango ao molho pardo*, chicken in a black sauce containing the bird's blood – delicious despite what it sounds like), dishes containing sausage, plenty of vegetables, beans, potatoes, rice and manioc. The other important local ingredient is cheese. In restaurants you usually pay after you have made your selection. Among those that serve *comida mineira* are *Chico Mineiro*, R Alagoas 626, corner of Av Brasil, T2613237. Good local chicken specialities; *Dona Lucinha*, R Sergipe 811, Savassi, T2615930. Recommended (also at R Padre Odorico 38, T2270562); *Emporium*, Av Afonso Pena 4034, Mangabeiras, T2811277; *Interior de Minas*, R Rio de Janeiro 1191, T2245549. Central, good for lunch, good value (also at Av Olegário Maciel 1781, Lourdes, T2925835); *Mala e Cuia*, a chain of restaurants serving good *comida mineira* at R Gonçalves Dias 874, Savassi, T2613059, Av Antônio Carlos 8305, Pampulha, T4412993, Av Raja Gabaglia 1617, São Bento, T3421421; *Xapuri*, R Mandacaru 260, Pampulha, T4966198. *Fazenda*, atmosphere, live music, very good food, expensive and a bit out of the way but recommended.

Other Brazilian *La Greppia*, R da Bahia 1204, Centro. Lunch only, good.

Seriously cheap   local food is served in the restaurants around the rodoviária, *prato feito* US$1. There are many bars and restaurants around Praça Raúl Soares; more on R Rio de Janeiro. *Flor de Líbano*, R Espírito Santo 234. Cheap and good.

International   *Santa Felicidade*, R Prof Morais 659, Savassi, T2215299. Pastas, fish, grill, buffet, open for lunch and in the evening.

Italian   *Buona Távola*, R Santa Rita Durão 309, Savassi, T2276155. Excellent. *Dona Derna*, R Tomé de Souza 1380, Savassi, T2236954. Highly recommended. *Pizzarela*, Av Olegário Maciel 2280, Lourdes, T2223000. Good for pizzas. *Vecchio Sogno*, R Martim de Carvalho 75 and R Dias Adorno, Santo Agostinho, under the Assembléia Legislativo, T2925251. Good food, top wine list, closed Sun evening.

French   *Taste Vin*, R Curitiba 2105, Lourdes, T2925423. Recommended.

German   *Alpino*, Av Contorno 5761, Savassi, T2219015. Good value and popular.

Oriental   *Kyoto*, R Montes Claros 323, Anchieta. Japanese. Recommended. *Yun Ton*, R Santa Catarina 946, T3372171, Chinese. Recommended.

Vegetarian   *Mandala*, R Inconfidentes 1006, T2617056.

Cafés   *Blue Mountain*, Av Cristóvão Colombo 536, Savassi, T2612296. *Café Belas Artes*, R Gonçalves Dias 1581, Lourdes, in the cinema foyer at Unibanco Belas Artes Liberdade. Popular. *Café Belas Artes Nazaré*, R Guajaras 37, near Av Afonso Pena, in the foyer of the Unibanco Nazaré Liberdade cinema. *Café Três Corações*, Praça Diego de Vasconcelos, Savassi. Coffees and snacks. *Casa Bonomi*, R Cláudio Manoel 460, Funcionários, T2613460. *Koyote Street Bar*, R Tomé de Souza 912. Street café. *Sabor e Saúde*, Av João Pinheiro 232. Vegetarian and meat snacks and meals, also sells *pão integral*. *Tia Clara*, R Antônio de Albuquerque 617. Tea room.

Bars   Recommended are *Alambique*, Av Raja Gabaglia 3200, Chalé 1D, specializes in *cachaça*, with *mineira* appetizers, designed like a country house; *Americana*, R Pernambuco 1025; *Bar Nacional*, Av Contorno 1076, Barro Preto, good value; *Heaven*, Av Getúlio Vargas 809.

Nightclubs   Recommended are *Ao Bar*, R Cláudio Manoel 572, Funcionários, T2617443; *L'Apogée*, R Antônio de Albuquerque 729, T2275133; *Máscaras*, R Santa Rita Durão 667, T2616050; *Partenon*, Rio Grande do Norte 1470, T2219856.

Bars & nightclubs

Cinema   Belo Horizonte is a good place to watch high quality Brazilian and foreign films beside the usual Hollywood fare. There are many art cinemas and cine clubs in the centre such as the Espaço Unibanco at R Guajaras 37.

Theatre   Belo Horizonte has at least a dozen theatres, eg the *Teatro da Cidade*, R da Bahia 1341, T2731050, *Teatro Alterosa*, Av Assis Chateaubriand 499, Floresta, T2376610, and *Teatro Marília*, Av Alfredo Balena 586, Centro, T2244445. The city prides itself on its theatre and dance companies (look out for the *Grupo Galpão*); don't expect to find many shows in any language other than Portuguese. The local press and tourist literature give details of shows and events.

Entertainment

Maundy Thursday; Corpus Christi; 15 Aug, *Assunção* (Assumption); 8 Dec, *Conceição* (Immaculate Conception).

Festivals

Bookshops   *Daniel Vaitsman*, R Espírito Santo 466, 17th floor, T2229071. For English language books. Foreign-language books at *Livraria Van Damme*, R das Guajaras 505, T2266492. Also good local and Portuguese selection; *Acaiaca*, R Tamóios 72. Good for dictionaries. Used foreign-language books at *Livraria Alfarrábio*, R Tamóios 320, T2713603.

Gem stones   *Manoel Bernardes*, Av Contorno 5417, Savassi, T2254200. Very reasonable.

Shopping

Minas Gerais and Espírito Santo

Market *Mercado Central*, Av Augusto de Lima 744, is large and clean, open every day until 1800. It sells produce, dry goods and crafts. See above for the Sun handicraft fair on Av Afonso Pena; hippies still sell their wares on R Rio de Janeiro, 600 block, each evening. A flower market is held at Av Bernardo Monteiro, near Av Brasil, every Fri from 1200 to 2000. Also here on Sat is a drinks and food market.

Music *Cogumelo*, Av Augusto de Lima 399, T2749915.

Shopping centres include *Bahia Shopping*, R da Bahia 1000 block, with a crashed helicopter built into its structure, and *Shopping Cidade*, R Tupis 337, both in the centre; *Minas Shopping*, Av Cristiano Machado 4000, near the *Hotel Ouro Minas*; *Shopping del Rey*, Av Pres Carlos Luz, Pampulha; and others. There are huge hypermarkets just outside the city on the highways to Rio and to São Paulo.

Sports **Caving** *Grupo Speleo* at the Universidade Federal de Minas Gerais; this group has the most experience in visiting out-of-the-way caves. **Ecotourism and adventure sports** *Amo-Te*, Associação Mineira dos Organizadores do Turismo Ecológico, R da Bahia 1340, Centro, CEP 30160-011, T/F2241930 or Caixa Postal 3059, Belo Horizonte, CEP 30130-140, T2854030, oversees ecotourism in the state of Minas Gerais. This includes trekking, riding, cycling, rafting, jeep tours, canyoning, visiting national parks, or *fazendas*. For companies which arrange these special interest tours, speak to *Amo-Te* first. **Horse riding** *Tropa Serrana*, Tullio Marques Lopes Filho, T3448986, Mobile 9832356. Recommended.

Tour operators *Master Turismo* (American Express representative), R da Bahia 2140, T33303655, www.masterturismo.com.br, at Sala VIP, Aeroporto de Confins and Av Afonso Pena 1967, T33303603. Very helpful. *Ouro Preto Turismo*, Av Afonso Pena 4133, Grupo 109, Serra, T32215005, and *Revetur*, R Espírito Santo 1892, 1st floor, Lourdes, T33372500, both recommended. *Ametur*, R Alvarengo Peixoto 295, loja 102, Lourdes, T/F32921976 has information on *fazendas* which welcome visitors and overnight guests. **Guides** A recommended nature guide is Regina Caldeira Ribeiro, R Herculano de Freitas 1246/202, CEP 30430-120, Belo Horizonte, T/FXX031-3342901, FocusTours@ aol.com; she is a representative for *Focus Tours* (see page 24). Tours in rural Minas and throughout Brazil can be arranged.

Transport **Local Buses**: red buses run on express routes and charge US$0.75; yellow buses have
See also Ins and outs, page 226
circular routes around the Contorno, US$0.50; blue buses run on diagonal routes charging US$0.65. Some buses link up with the regional, overground Metrô.

Taxis: plentiful but hard to find at peak hours. *BH Táxi*, T2158081, *Coopertáxi*, T4212424.

Long distance Air: Tancredo Neves International Airport is at Confins, near Lagoa Santa, 39 km from Belo Horizonte. A taxi to the centre costs US$50, co-operative taxis have fixed rates to different parts of the city. Airport bus, either *executivo* from the exit, US$11, or comfortable normal bus (*Unir*) from the far end of the car park hourly, US$2.20, both go to the rodoviária. Getting to the airport, buses from the rodoviária, *executivo*, US$10. Closer to the city, the domestic airport at **Pampulha**, has shuttle services to several cities including Rio and São Paulo. Transport from Pampulha airport is cheaper than from Confins. Blue bus 1202 to town leaves across the street from the airport, 25 mins, US$0.65, passing the rodoviária and the cheaper hotel district.

Buses: the rodoviária by Praça Rio Branco at the northwest end of Av Afonso Pena has toilets, post office, phones, left-luggage lockers (US$2.50, attended service 0700-2200), shops and is clean and well-organized.

To **Rio** with *Cometa*, T32015611 and *Util*, T32017744, 6½ hrs, US$12.75 (ordinary), *leito*, US$25.50. To **Vitória** with *São Geraldo*, T2711911, US$14.50 and *leito* US$29. To **Brasília** with *Itapemirim*, T2919991, and *Penha*, T32711027, 10 hrs, 6 a day including 2 *leitos*, only 1 leaves in daylight (0800), US$19.25, *leito* US$38.50. To **São Paulo** with *Cometa* and *Gontijo*, T32016130, 10 hrs, US$15.60. To **Foz do Iguaçu**, US$42, 22 hrs. To **Salvador** with *Gontijo*, US$40, 24 hrs, at 1900 daily, and *São Geraldo* at 1800. *São Geraldo* also goes to **Porto Seguro**, 17 hrs, direct, via Nanuque and Eunápolis, US$33. To **Recife** with *Gontijo*, 2000, US$41. To **Fortaleza**, US$63. To **Natal**, US$66. To **Belém** with *Itapemirim* at 2030, US$72. To **Campo Grande** with *Gontijo* (at 1930) and *Motta* (3 a day, T34640480), US$31-36, a good route to Bolivia, avoiding São Paulo. All major destinations served. For buses within Minas Gerais, see under each destination.

Car hire: *Interlocadora*, R dos Timbiras 2229, T2754090; *Localiza*, Av Bernardo Monteiro 1567, Pampulha and Confins airports, T2477957, or 0800-992000.

Hitchhiking to **Rio** or **Ouro Preto**, take a bus marked 'Shopping', to the *BH* shopping centre above Belo Horizonte on the Rio road.

Trains: to **Vitória**, daily 0700, tickets sold at 0530, US$17.50 *executivo*, US$11.50 1st class, US$7.80 2nd class, 14 hrs.

Airline offices *American*, R Guajajaras 557, T2733622, Confins T6892670. *TAM*, Pampulha T4435500. *United*, R Paraíba 1000, 10th floor, Funcionários, T2617777, Confins T6892736. *Varig/RioSul/Nordeste*, Av Olegário Maciel 2251, Lourdes, T2916444, Confins airport T6892305, Pampulha airport T4912466. *Vasp*, Av Olegário Maciel 2221, T0800-998277, Confins T6892411.

Banks *Banco do Brasil*, R Rio de Janeiro 750, Av Amazonas 303. Cash is given against credit cards at *Banco Itaú*, Av João Pinheiro 195. Visa ATM at Bradesco, R da Bahia 947. *Citibank*, R Espírito Santo 871. *Master Turismo*, Av Afonso Pena 1967, T3303603. American Express representative. Nascente Turismo, Rio de Janeiro 1314, no commission. Changing TCs is difficult, but hotels will change them for guests at a poor rate.

Communications **Internet**: Internet Café Club R Fernandes Tourinho 385, Plaza Savassi. US$5 per hr. **Post office**: Av Afonso Pena 1270. Poste restante is behind the main office at R de Goiás 77. The branch on R da Bahia is less slow. **Telephones**: Av Afonso Pena 1180, by the Correios. Open daily 0700-2200.

Embassies and consulates *Austria*, R José Américo Cançado Bahia 199, T33335363. *Denmark*, R Paraíba 1122, 5th floor, T32868626. *France*, R Pernambuco 712A, T32617805. *Germany*, R Timbiras 1200, 5th floor, T32131568. *Italy*, Av Afonso Pena 3130, 12th floor, T32814211. *Netherlands*, R Sergipe 1167, loja 5, T32275275. *UK*, R dos Inconfidentes 1075, sala 1302, Savassi, T32612072, F32610226, britcon.bhe@terra.com.br *USA*, R Timbiras 1200, 7th floor, T2131571.

Laundry *5 à Sec*, Av Prudente de Moraes 421, Cidade Jardim, T2967376. Dry cleaning.

Medical services *Mater Dei*, R Gonçalves Dias 2700, T3399000. Recommended.

Useful addresses Immigration: Polícia Federal, R Nascimento Gurgel 30, T2910005. For visa extensions. To get there take bus 7902 from the corner of R Curitiba and Av Amazonas and get off at the *Hospital Madre Teresa*.

Voltage 120-220 AC 60 cycles.

Directory

Minas Gerais and Espírito Santo

Nature reserves near Belo Horizonte

Parque Natural de Caraça This is a remarkable reserve about 120 km east of Belo Horizonte. It can be visited in a day, but you will get much more out of your trip if you stay overnight.

Caraça has been preserved so well because the land belongs to a seminary. The seminary buildings and the church with its tall spire stand at about 1,220 m above sea level, surrounded on three sides by mountains which rise to 2,070 m at their highest (Pico do Sol). The name means 'big face', so called because of a hill which is said to resemble the face of a giant who is looking at the sky. To appreciate the setting, climb up to the Cruzeiro, a cross which is close to the seminary.

The church, built in Gothic style in 1880, has a museum. Inside is a painting of the Last Supper attributed to Mestre Athayde (see below); Judas Iscariot's eyes follow you (he is the one holding the purse). In the altar is an effigy of São Pio Martir. The stained-glass windows at the east end were a gift from France. ■ *1300-1500 Sat, Sun and holidays (or for hotel guests on request).* Part of the seminary has been converted into a hotel, which is the only place to stay.

Habitat and wildlife The park extends from 720 m to 2,070 m. Its lower altitudes are covered in rich Atlantic forest while the heights are grassland and other mountain habitats. There are lakes, waterfalls and rivers. The rarest mammal is the maned wolf (the only wolf found in Brazil and endangered, partly because of loss of habitat, but also because of its insatiable appetite for chickens). Since the early 1980s, the monks have been leaving food for the wolves on the seminary steps in the evening; up to four may be seen. This is a popular tourist attraction, and the animals can be photographed. Another endangered mammal in the park is the southern masked titi monkey, of which family groups may be seen. Other primates include the black tufted-eared marmoset and the brown capuchin monkey.

Birdlife includes toucans, guans and hummingbirds (such as the Brazilian ruby and the white-throated), various tanagers, cotingas, antbirds, woodpeckers and the long-trained and scissor-tailed nightjars. Some of the bird species are endemic, others rare and endangered.

The trails for viewing the different landscapes and the wildlife are marked at their beginning and are quite easy to follow. A guide is a good idea for seeing the birds and animals.

Park essentials Park entrance US$5 per vehicle. The park is open 0700-2100; if staying overnight you cannot leave after 2100. The hotel has pleasant rooms; US$40-80 double, full board. Reservations, Santuário do Caraça, Caixa Postal 12, T35960000, Santa Bárbara, MG, T8372698. The restaurant serves good food from farms within the seminary's lands, lunch 1200-1330.

Transport Turn off the BR-262 (towards Vitória) at Km 73 and go via Barão de Cocais to Caraça (120 km). There is no public transport to the seminary. Buses go as far as Barão de Cocais, from where a taxi is US$12. Book the taxi to return for you, or hitch (which may not be easy). The park entrance is 10 km before the seminary. The alternative is to hire a guide from Belo Horizonte, about US$75 (including guiding, transport and meals).

It is possible to stay in **Santa Bárbara** (**D** *Hotel Karaibe*; **D** *Santa Inés*), 25 km away on the road to Mariana and hitchhike to Caraça. Santa Bárbara is served by 11 buses a day from Belo Horizonte (fewer on Saturday and Sunday).

There is also a bus service to Mariana, a beautiful route, via Catas Altas, which has an interesting church and a *pousada* belonging to the municipality of Santa Bárbara.

About 105 km northeast of Belo Horizonte, **Serra do Cipó**, 33,400 sq km of the Serra do Espinhaço, has scenic beauty and several endemic plants, insects and birds. In the last category, the Cipó Canestero is only found in one small area in the south of the park. There are also several carnivorous plants, many flowers, frogs, and black and orange grasshoppers. The predominant habitat is high mountain grassland, with rocky outcroppings; there are waterfalls, too. ■ *Full details from Ibama in Belo Horizonte. T2916588.*

Parque Nacional da Serra do Cipó

Park essentials The national park can be reached via road MG-010. This road continues unpaved to Serro (see Colonial cities, below); buses run on this route. Agencies offer excursions from the city to the park. It is recommended to take a guide because the trails are unmarked; ask locally. The nearest accommodation is in the municipalities of Santana do Riacho, a town northwest of the park, for example *Pousada Sempre Viva*, Km 99, MG-010, T6811327; *Fazenda Monjolos Pousada*, Km 100, MG-010, T2214253; *Camping Véu da Noiva*, Km 101, T2011166, or Jaboticatubas, *Cipó Veraneio*, Km 95, MG-010, T6511000. Further from the park, but in the municipality of Jaboticatubas, 50 km from Belo Horizonte, is a *Hotel Fazenda*, *O Canto da Siriema*, with full board, recreation, etc, T4636955, or contact *Ametur* in Belo Horizonte (address under Tour operators).

Colonial cities

The picturesque colonial cities described below fall roughly into four groups: east of Belo Horizonte (Sabará and Caeté); southeast (Ouro Preto and Mariana); south/southwest (Congonhas do Campo, São João del Rei and Tiradentes); north (Diamantina and Serro).

The most visited is without a doubt Ouro Preto; it can be done in a day trip from Belo Horizonte, but a day is nothing like enough. Mariana makes a good day trip from Ouro Preto. Sabará is an easy day trip from Belo Horizonte. The colonial monument in Congonhas do Campo requires only a few hours to visit and a couple of changes of bus to get there, but most regard it as well worth the effort. São João del Rei and Tiradentes make a logical combination and are perhaps best visited as an excursion from the Rio de Janeiro/Belo Horizonte route. Diamantina and Serro are in completely the other direction, on one of the routes to Bahia from Belo Horizonte; either stop off on that journey, or make an excursion from Belo Horizonte.

Sabará

East of the state capital by 23 km is the colonial gold-mining (and steel-making) town of Sabará. The town is strung along the narrow steep valleys of the Rio das Velhas and Rio Sabará. Since the late 17th century the Rio das Velhas was known as a gold-bearing river and a community soon grew up there. By 1702 it was the most populous in Minas Gerais. In 1711 the name Villa Real de Nossa Senhora da Conceição de Sabará was given to the parish and in 1838 it became the city of Sabará. **Tourist information** *Secretaria de Turismo*, R Pedro II 200, T6711522.

Phone code: 031
Colour map 4, grid B3
Population: 116,000

Minas Gerais and Espírito Santo

Sights   The old churches and fountains, rambling cobbled streets and simple houses with carved doors are of great interest. From the bus terminus, walk up Rua Clemente Faria to Praça Santa Rita, in which is a large *chafariz* (fountain). The square adjoins Rua Dom Pedro II, which is lined with beautiful 18th-century buildings. They include the **Solar do Padre Correa** (1773) at No 200, now the **Prefeitura**, a mansion with a rococo chapel and main reception room (*salão nobre*); the **Casa Azul** (also 1773), now the INSS building, No 215, with a chapel and a fine portal; and the **Teatro Municipal**, former Opera House, built in 1770 and the second oldest in Brazil. It has a superb interior, with three balconies, a carved wooden rail before the orchestra pit, wooden floors and *esteiro* (flattened, woven bamboo) ceilings.

At the top of Rua Dom Pedro II is the Praça Melo Viana, in the middle of which is **Nossa Senhora do Rosário dos Pretos** (left unfinished at the time of the slaves' emancipation). Behind the façade of the unfinished building are the chancel, sacristy (both 1780) and the first chapel (1713). There is a museum of religious art in the church. ■ *Church and museum are open 0800-1100, 1300-1700 Tue-Sun*. To the right of the church is the **Chafariz do Rosário**. Also on the Praça are the ornate Fórum Ministro Orozimbo Nonato and two schools. From the Praça Melo Viana, take Rua São Pedro to the church of **São Francisco** (1781); beyond the church is the **Chafariz Kaquende**.

In Rua da Intendência is the museum of 18th-century gold mining, the **Museu do Ouro**. It contains exhibits from all the stages of gold extraction, plus religious items and colonial furniture. The building itself is a fine example of colonial architecture. Sources disagree as to its date of construction, but the general consensus is that it was before 1730. Originally the foundry, it became the Casa da Intendência in 1735. For most of the 19th century it was abandoned and became the gold museum in 1945. ■ *1200-1730 Tue-Sun. US$1*.

Another fine example of civil colonial architecture is the **Casa Borba Gato**, Rua Borba Gato 71, so called because tradition has it that it belonged to the famous *bandeirante*, Manoel de Borba Gato, one of the first to settle on the Rio das Velhas, but exiled from the region after the murder of the king's representative, Rodrigo de Castel Blanco in 1682. The building currently belongs to the Museu do Ouro.

The church of **Nossa Senhora do Carmo** (1763-74), with doorway, pulpits and choirloft by Aleijadinho and paintings by Athayde, is on Rua do Carmo. From the ceilings, painted blue and grey and gold, religious figures look down surrounding the Virgin and Child and the Chariot of Fire. In the chancel, the Ten Commandments in blue work have a distinctly Moorish air, what with the tents and the night-time scenes. ■ *US$1; a leaflet about the town is given out*.

Similar in style externally is the **Capela de Nossa Senhora do Pilar**, which is beside the municipal cemetery and in front of a large building with blue gates and doors.

Nossa Senhora da Conceição (1720), on Praça Getúlio Vargas, has a lot of visible woodwork and a beautiful floor. The carvings have a great deal of gilding, there are painted panels and paintings by 23 Chinese artists brought from Macau. The clearest Chinese work is on the two red doors to the right and left of the chancel. ■ *Free*.

Nossa Senhora do Ó, built in 1717 and showing unmistakable Chinese influence (paintings much in need of restoration), is 2 km from the centre of the town at the Largo Nossa Senhora do Ó. ■ *Local bus marked Esplanada or Boca Grande*.

If you walk up the Morra da Cruz hill from the *Hotel do Ouro* to a small chapel, the Capela da Cruz, or Senhor Bom Jesus, you can get a wonderful view of the whole region. Look for beautiful quartz crystals while you are up there.

Passeio a Sabará, by Lúcia Machado de Almeida, with splendid illustrations by Guignard, is an excellent guide to the place.

A *Del Rio*, R São Francisco 345, T6713040. **B** *Solar das Sepúlvedas*, R da Intendência 371, behind the Museu do Ouro, T6712708. Grand, pool. **D** *Hotel do Ouro*, R Santa Cruz 237, Morro da Cruz, T6715622. With bath, hot water, clean, with breakfast, marvellous view, best value. For eating, try *314*, Comendador Viana 314, near Praça Santa Rita. *Cê Qui Sabe*, R Mestre Caetano 56. Recommended. **Sleeping & eating**

There are many festivals throughout the year. The most significant are the *Folia de Reis*, 25 Dec to 6 Jan; *Festas Juninas* and, also in Jun, a *Festival da Cachaça*; *Nossa Senhora do Rosário*, 2nd Sun in Oct. **Festivals** *The patron saint of Sabará is Nossa Senhora da Conceição*

Buses *Viação Cisne*, from **Belo Horizonte**, US$0.75, 30 mins, from separate part of Belo Horizonte rodoviária from main departure hall. **Routes** There is a road, mostly unpaved, that runs from Sabará to Ravena on the BR-381 Belo Horizonte-Vitória highway which crosses the hills and is a pleasant drive. **Transport**

Some 25 km from Sabará and 60 km from Belo Horizonte is Caeté. The town, originally called Vila Nova da Rainha, has several historical buildings and churches. On the Praça João Pinheiro are the **Prefeitura** and **Pelourinho** (both 1722), the **Igreja Matriz Nossa Senhora do Bom Sucesso** (1756 rebuilt 1790. ■ *1300-1800 daily*) and the **Chafariz da Matriz**. Also on the praça is the **tourist information office** in the Casa da Cultura, T6511855. Other churches are **Nossa Senhora do Rosário** (1750-68), with a ceiling attributed to Mestre Athayde, and **São Francisco de Assis**. The **Museu Regional**, in the house of the Barão de Catas Altas, or Casa Setecentista, Rua Israel Pinheiro 176, contains 18th- and 19th-century religious art and furniture. The house itself is a fine example of 18th-century civic architecture, with two floors and an interior patio. ■ *1200-1700 Tue-Sun*. **Caeté** *Phone code: 031* *Population: 37,000*

From Caeté you can go to the **Serra da Piedade**; see 231.

Set in eucalyptus forests 27 km southeast of Belo, Nova Lima's houses are grouped round the gold mine of Morro Velho, the deepest mine in the Americas. The shaft has followed a rich vein of gold down to 2,591 m (not open to tourists). There are interesting carvings by Aleijadinho, recovered from elsewhere, in the modern parish church. **Nova Lima** *Population: 52,500*

Ouro Preto

The famous former state capital founded in 1711 was declared a national monument in 1933. Built on rocky ground, its cobbled streets wind up and down steep hills crowned with 13 churches. Mansions, fountains, churches, vistas of terraced gardens, and towers shining with coloured tiles create a delightful 18th-century atmosphere. On 24 June of each year, Ouro Preto again becomes, for that day only, the capital of the state of Minas Gerais. From October-February the climate is wet, but the warmest month of the year is February (30°C on average). The coldest months are June, July and August, with lowest temperatures being in July (10°C). *Phone code: 031* *Altitude: 1,000 m* *Colour map 4, grid C3* *Population: 67,000*

The gold that was found in the streams and rivers was covered in a thin black layer of iron oxide, hence the name Ouro Preto: black gold. The first **History** encampments of prospectors were set up in the final years of the 17th century. By 1711 a number had become well established and were united under the name of Vila Rica de Albuquerque. The town had two parishes: Nossa Senhora da Conceição and Nossa Senhora do Pilar. As the town's wealth increased, so the lay brotherhoods within those parishes were able to lavish more and more money on their temples, creating the baroque and rococo splendours that are still visible in stone, gold, wood and painting.

It is hardly surprising that the production of gold created tensions between the miners and the Portuguese crown which demanded its share. From the founding of the Capitania of Minas Gerais in 1720, the citizens of Vila Rica

Ouro Preto

To Rodoviária & Belo Horizonte

Sleeping
1 Colonial
2 Grande
3 Luxor Pousada
4 Pousada dos Bandeirantes
5 Pousada do Mondego
6 Pousada Marília de Dirceu
7 Pousada Ouro Preto

N
Not to scale

were immediately up in arms. A revolt took place in that very year in protest against the *quinto*, the royal tax. Discontent and opulence continued side by side until the conspirators of the Inconfidência Mineira of 1789 attempted to find a way of resisting the demands from Portugal. Before any of their ideas could be put into practice, the leaders were betrayed and arrested. One, Joaquim José da Silva Xavier (Tiradentes), was hanged, the others exiled (see box, page 242). The exhaustion of the gold mines forced the Portuguese to lower their levy and, not long afterwards, the colony gave way to the empire when the Portuguese royal family fled from Europe. A year after their arrival in 1822, Vila Rica de Albuquerque became a city and was renamed A Cidade

			Eating
8 Pousada São Francisco de Paula	10 Pouso Chico Rei	1 Casa do Ouvidor
9 Pousada Tiradentes	11 Pouso da Ladeira	2 Ouro Grill
	12 Solar das Lajes	3 Tacho de Ouro

Tiradentes and the Inconfidência Mineira

In the last quarter of the 18th century, Vila Rica de Nossa Senhora do Pilar do Ouro Preto was a dynamic place. Gold had brought great wealth to the city and this was translated into fine religious and secular buildings. Much of the artistry that went into these constructions and their decoration was home-grown, such as the genius of O Aleijadinho (see page 251). In conjunction with this flowering of the arts an intellectual society developed. And yet all this went on under the heavy hand of the Portuguese crown, which demanded its fifth share (the quinto), imposed punitive taxes and forbade local industries to operate. While the artists and artisans could not travel and had to seek inspiration in what was around them, the intellectuals were often from families who sent their young to Europe to further their education. So, when the gold yields began to decline and the Portuguese demands became even more exorbitant, some members of society began to look to Europe and North America for ways to free Minas Gerais from the crown.

One side of the argument was the view of the governor, the Visconde de Barbacena, who refused to admit that the mines were exhausted and that poverty was beginning to affect the community. As far as he was concerned, there was no gold because it was being smuggled out of the captaincy and there was no economic problem, just a large unpaid debt to the Portuguese crown. On the other side was the idea, as expressed by the French poet Parny, that Brazil was a paradise on earth, with everything except liberty. The Jesuit Antônio Vieira, who lived in the previous century, put it thus: 'the cloud swells in Brazil and it rains on Portugal; the water is not picked up from the sea, but from the tears of the unfortunate and the sweat of the poor, and I do not know how their faith and constancy has lasted so long.'

In the late 1780s a group of people began to have secret discussions on how to resolve the intolerable situation. It included the poets Cláudio Manuel da Costa, Tomás Gonzaga and Ignacio de Alvarenga, the doctors Domingos Vidal Barbosa and José Alvares Maciel, Padres Toledo and Rolim and the military officers Domingos de Abreu Vieira, Francisco de Paula Freire de Andrade and José de Resende Costa. Into this group came Joaquim José da Silva Xavier, a junior officer (alferes), who was born at the Fazenda de Pombal near São João del Rei

---

Imperial de Ouro Preto, capital of the province of Minas Gerais. It lost that title in 1897 when Belo Horizonte was created. After that, the city's fame rested principally on its artistic merit, first gaining the accolade of National Monument (1933), then UNESCO Cultural Heritage site in 1980.

Sights

At least two days are needed to see everything. Photography is prohibited in all the churches and museums

The **tourist office** on Praça Tiradentes 41, T35512655 (opens 0800), has details of accommodation in *casas de família*, *repúblicas* and other places. It also has leaflets showing the opening times, which change frequently (very helpful but Portuguese only spoken). The *Secretaria de Turismo* is in the Casa de Gonzaga, R Cláudio Manoel 61, T35593282. It produces information including hotel and restaurant lists, a map and lists of local sites. Most of the churches now charge admission (conservation tax), between US$1.50 and US$5. In most churches and museums, bags and cameras are taken at the entrance and guarded in lockers (visitors keep their own key).

The best place to start exploring the city is the central **Praça Tiradentes**, where you'll see a statue of the leader of the **Inconfidentes**. Another Inconfidente, the poet Tomás Antônio Gonzaga (whose house at Rua Cláudio Manoel 61 is close to São Francisco de Assis church), was exiled to in about 1748. He was also a dentist and became known by the nickname Tiradentes – tooth-puller. Already dissatisfied with the way the army had treated him, by failing to promote him among other things, in 1788 he was suspended from active duty because of illness. The subsequent loss of pay roused him further. In trying to get reinstated he met Freire de Andrade and Alvares Maciel and later conversations prompted him to tell them of his idea of an uprising against the Portuguese. The Inconfidência grew out of these types of meeting, some planning action, others the future political and economic organization of a new, independent state.

The conspirators worked to gain support for their cause, but one soldier they approached, Coronel Joaquim Silverio dos Reis, used the information he had been given to betray the cause. The governor received reports from other sources and began to build up a picture of what was going on. Tiradentes was the first to be arrested, at the beginning of May 1789, in Rio de Janeiro. It seems that the plotters at this time still had no clear idea of what their ultimate aim was, nor of the importance of their attitudes. They never got the chance anyway because all were arrested soon after Tiradentes. They were imprisoned and kept incommunicado for two years while the case against them was prepared. Tiradentes was singled out as the most important member of the group and, under questioning, he did not disabuse his captors, taking full responsibility for everything. A defence for the Inconfidentes was prepared, but it almost totally ignored Tiradentes, as if he were being made a scapegoat. It made no difference, though, because the defence lost; 11 Inconfidentes were sentenced to death in November 1791. Soon afterwards the authorities in Brazil read out a surprising letter from the queen, Dona Maria I, commuting the death sentence for 10 of the conspirators to exile in Portugal or Africa. The 11th, Tiradentes, was not spared. On 21 April 1792 he was hanged and his body was quartered and his head cut off, the parts to de displayed as a warning against any similar attempts to undermine the crown. Even though Tiradentes would never have been freed, one of the astonishing things about the queen's letter was that it was dated 18 months before it was brought to light.

Africa. Most Brazilians know his poem based on his forbidden love affair with the girl he called Marília de Dirceu. Visitors are shown the bridge and decorative fountain where the lovers held their trysts (the house where she lived, on the Largo Marília de Dirceu, is now a school of that name).

On the north side of the Praça Tiradentes (at No 20) is a famous **Escola de Minas** (School of Mining), founded in 1876, in the fortress-like **Palácio dos Governadores** (1741-48); it has the interesting **Museu de Mineralogia e das Pedras**, a must. ■ 1200-1645 Mon, Wed-Fri, 0900-1300 Sat-Sun. US$1.50. On the south side of the Praça, No 139 next to Carmo Church, is the **Museu da Inconfidência**, a fine historical and art museum in the former **Casa de Câmara e Cadeia**, which has some drawings by Aleijadinho and the Sala Manoel da Costa Athayde, in an annex. ■ 0800-1800 Mon-Fri. US$1.50. In the Casa Capitular of NS do Carmo is **Museu do Oratório**, with many fascinating examples of oratories. ■ 0930-1220, 1330-1730 daily. T5515369, www.oratorio.com.br

Casa das Contas, Rua São José 12 (1787), is the Centro de Estudos do Ciclo de Ouro (Centre for Gold Cycle Studies) and a museum of money and finance, with manuscripts and coins; it also has a library. ■ 1230-1730 Tue-Sat, 0830-1330 Sun and holidays. US$0.50. The **Casa Guignard**, Rua

Conde de Bobadela 110, displays the paintings of Alberto da Veiga Guignard. ■ *1230-1730 Tue-Sat, 0830-1330 Sun and holidays. Free*. The **Teatro Municipal** in Rua Brigadeiro Musqueiro, is the oldest functioning theatre in Latin America. It was built in 1769. ■ *1230-1800 daily*.

The **Mina do Chico Rei**, Rua Dom Silvério, is not as impressive as some other mines in the area, but is 'fun to crawl about in'; restaurant attached. The Chico Rei is supposed to be an African king, called Francisco, who was enslaved but bought his freedom working in the mine. ■ *0800-1700. US$1.50*.

Close to Padre Faria church is **Mina Bem Querer**, a small mine through which clean water runs, filling a small swimming pool. ■ *US$0.50*.

Churches

These churches are all closed on Monday

São Francisco de Assis (1766-96), Largo de Coimbra, is considered to be one of the masterpieces of Brazilian baroque. Aleijadinho (see below) worked on the general design and the sculpture of the façade, the pulpits and many other features. The harmonious lines of the exterior and the beauty of the interior are exceptional. Mestre Athayde was responsible for the painted ceiling which depicts the Assumption of the Virgin Mary. She is in the centre of heaven, surrounded by cherubs and musicians. Pillars support the sky which is a celeste blue with realistic clouds. At the four corners stand saints Augustine, Hieronymous, Gregory and Ambrosius. Compare the brightness of the ceiling with the brown habits of the statues in the side altars. The blue scenes in the chancel show the life of Abraham. ■ *0830-1145, 1330-1640, US$1; the ticket also permits entry to NS da Conceição (keep your ticket for admission to the museum)*. In the Largo outside São Francisco is a handicraft market.

See also box, page 251

Nossa Senhora da Conceição (1722), the parish church of Antônio Dias (one of the original settlements that became Vila Rica de Albuquerque), is heavily gilded and contains Aleijadinho's tomb. It has a museum devoted to him, Aleijadinho Paróquia, which also exhibits work by others and religious objects. ■ *0830-1130, 1330-1645, Sun 1200-1645*.

Nossa Senhora das Mercês e Perdões (1740-72), Rua das Mercês, was rebuilt in the 19th century. Some sculpture by Aleijadinho can be seen in the main chapel. ■ *1000-1400*.

Santa Efigênia (1720-85), Ladeira Santa Efigênia e Padre Faria, has wonderful panoramic views of the city. Some say the church was decorated with gold dust washed out of slaves' hair, others that it was built by Chico Rei (see above). Manuel Francisco Lisboa (Aleijadinho's father) oversaw the construction and much of the carving is by Francisco Xavier de Brito (Aleijadinho's mentor). ■ *0800-1200*.

Nossa Senhora do Carmo, Rua Brigadeiro Mosqueira (1766-72), was planned by Manuel Francisco Lisboa and both his son and Mestre Athayde worked on the project. It was the favourite church of the aristocracy. There is a museum of sacred art with Aleijadinho sculptures. ■ *1300-1700. Entry is shared with NS do Pilar*. (1733). Nossa Senhora do Pilar has heavily gilded work by Francisco Xavier de Brito. This church also contains a religious art museum. ■ *1200-1700*.

Nossa Senhora do Rosário, Largo do Rosário, dates from 1785, when the present church replaced a chapel on the site. It has a curved façade, which is rare in Brazilian baroque. The interior is much simpler than the exterior, but there are interesting side altars.

Nossa Senhora das Mercês e Misericórdia (1773-93) is just north of the Praça Tiradentes; further west, on a neighbouring hill, is **São Francisco de Paula**, work on which started in 1804, making it the last colonial church in

Ouro Preto. ■ *0900-1700*. **São José**, Rua Teixeira Amaral, was begun in 1752, but not completed until 1811; some carving is by Aleijadinho.

There are a number of other churches and chapels. Also throughout the town are excellent examples of the public fountain (*chafariz*), oratories (*passos*) and stone bridges over the creeks and rivers.

Guides

Bandeira's *Guia de Ouro Preto* in Portuguese and English (US$3.50 with coloured map, US$1 with black and white one), is normally available at the tourist office. Also available is Lucia Machado de Almeida's *Passeio a Ouro Preto*, US$6 (in Portuguese, English and French). The tourist office sells a guide with maps to Ouro Preto and Mariana, *Guia Prática*, for US$5. Most churches and historic buildings open to the public have a selection of books for sale. A local guide for a day, *Associação de Guias de Turismo* (AGTOP), can be obtained through the tourist office (a recommended guide is Cássio Antunes), T35512655 at the tourist office, or 35511544 ext 269. Opposite the rodoviária is an office of the Guiding Association (T35512504, or 5511544 ext 205), which offers group tours of US$30 for 1 to 10 people, US$45 for more than 10. The guides also give advice to new arrivals. If taking a guide, check their accreditation. The map sold at either the tourist or the Guiding Association office costs US$2.50.

Excursions

The **Cachoeira das Andorinhas**, a waterfall north of town, is reached by taking a bus to Morro de Santana and then walking 25 minutes. To walk all the way takes 1½ hours. It is possible to visit the Zen Buddhist monastery near the waterfall, apply in advance: Mosteiro Zen Pico de Rajos, Morro de São Sebastião, Caixa Postal 101, 35400-000, Ouro Preto, T0XX31-9612484. Excursions of 2½ hours are arranged at 0830 and 1430 visiting many cultural and ecological sites of interest.

The town is dominated by a huge cross, easily reached from the road to Mariana. It affords lovely views of the sunset, but don't go alone as it's in a poor district.

Parque Estadual de Itacolomi and the **Estação Ecológica do Tripuí** are protected areas close to the city. The former (a three-hour walk from the centre, cars prohibited) includes the peak of Itacolomi, which the first gold prospectors used as a landmark, the source of the Rio Doce as well as endangered wildlife and splendid views. Tripuí is in the valley where the first gold was found; it protects a rare invertebrate, the Peripatus Acacioi. It can also be reached on foot, or the bus to Belo Horizonte will drop you near the entrance.

Sleeping
■ *on map, page 240*
Price codes:
see inside front cover
Prices indicated are
for high season;
many hotels will
negotiate lower prices
when things are quiet

Ask at the tourist office for reasonably priced accommodation in *casas de família*.

Avoid touts who greet you off buses and charge higher prices than those advertised in hotels; it is difficult to get hotel rooms at weekends and holiday periods.

AL *Pousada do Mondego*, Largo de Coimbra 38, T35512040, F5513094. Beautifully kept colonial house in a fine location by São Francisco church, room rates vary according to view, small restaurant, Scotch bar, popular with groups. Recommended (a Roteiro de Charme hotel, see page 47), the hotel runs a *jardineira* bus tour of the city, 2 hrs, minimum 10 passengers, US$10 for non-guests. **AL** *Pousada Solar de NS do Rosário*, Av Getúlio Vargas 270, T35514200, rosario@bis.com.br Fully restored historic building with a highly recommended restaurant, bar, sauna, all facilities in rooms. **A** *Luxor Pousada*, R Dr Alfredo Baeta 16, Praça Antônio Dias, T35512244. Converted colonial mansion, no twin beds, comfortable and clean but spartan, good views, restaurant good but service slow.

B *Pousada Casa Grande*, R Conselheiro Quintiliano, 96, T/F35514314. Including breakfast, safe, good views. Recommended. **C** *Colonial*, Trav Cônego Camilo Veloso

Minas Gerais and Espírito Santo

26, close to Praça Tiradentes, T35513133, colonial@ouropetro.feop.com.br With new rooms and older rooms refurbished, pleasant. **C** *Hospedária de Ouro Preto*, R Xavier da Veiga 1, T3552203. Restored colonial house. Recommended. **C** *Pousada Itacolomi*, R Antônio Pereira 167, T35512891. Small. Recommended. **C** *Pousada Marília de Dirceu*, R Conde de Bobadela 179/R Paraná 12, T35514327. **C** *Pousada Nello Nuno*, R Camilo de Brito 59, T35513375. Cheaper without bath, charming owner Annamélia speaks some French. Highly recommended. **C** *Pousada Ouro Preto*, Largo Musicista José dos Anjos Costa 72, T35513081. Small, laundry facilities, English spoken by owner, Gérson Luís Cotta (most helpful), noisy, good views. Recommended. **C** *Pousada Tiradentes*, Praça Tiradentes 70, T35512619. Comfortable, clean, TV, fridge, rooms a bit spartan and small, very convenient. **C** *Pouso Chico Rei*, R Brig Musqueira 90, T35511274. A fascinating old house with Portuguese colonial furnishings, very small and utterly delightful, book in advance (room No 6 has been described as a 'dream'). **C** *Solar das Lajes*, R Conselheiro Quintiliano 604, T/F35513388, www.solardaslajes.com.br A little way from centre, excellent view, pool, well run.

D *Pousada dos Bandeirantes*, R das Mercês 167, T35511996, behind São Francisco de Assis. Beautiful views, TV, fridge, very pleasant. **D** *Pousada Flávia Helena*, Padre Rolim 1273B, T35512069, 500 m from rodoviária. **D** *Pousada São Francisco de Paula*, Padre JM Pen 202, next to the São Francisco de Paula church, T35513456. In a garden, panoramic view, veranda with hammock, free use of kitchen, multilingual staff, trips organized to nearby villages, mountains, mines, waterfalls, 8 rooms including a dormitory, with or without a simple breakfast, private or communal bathroom, full breakfast and snacks available, 100 m from rodoviária. Recommended. **D** *Pouso da Ladeira*, R Camilo de Brito 50, T35513654. 100 m from Praça Tiradentes, colonial style, garden, views, owner speaks English and Spanish. **Youth hostel**: R Costa Sena 30-A, Largo de Coimbra, T/F3551 6705, http://users.task.com.br/albergue **F** per person *Brumas*, Ladeira São Francisco de Paula 68, 150 m downhill from rodoviária, just below São Francisco de Paula church, T3335 7809, brumasonline@hotmail.com Dormitory, kitchen, superb views. Don't walk down from bus station after dark.

Students may be able to stay, during holidays and weekends, at the self-governing student hostels, known as *repúblicas* (very welcoming, 'best if you like heavy metal music' and 'are prepared to enter into the spirit of the places'). The Prefeitura has a list of over 50 *repúblicas* with phone numbers, available at the *Secretaria de Turismo*. Many are closed between Christmas and Carnival.

Camping   *Camping Clube do Brasil*, Rodovia dos Inconfidentes Km 91, 2 km north, T35511799. Quite expensive but very nice.

Eating
● *on map, page 240*
Try the local licor de jaboticaba

Adega, R Teixeira Amaral 24. 1130-1530, vegetarian smorgasbord, US$5, all you can eat. Highly recommended. *Beijinho Doce*, R Direita 134A. Delicious pastries and cakes, try the truffles. *Café & Cia*, R São José 187. Closes 2300, very popular, comida por kilo at lunchtime, good salads, juices. *Casa do Ouvidor*, Conde de Bobadela 42, above Manoel Bernardis jewellery shop, good. *Casa Grande* and *Forno de Barro*, both on Praça Tiradentes (Nos 84 and 54 respectively). Good local dishes. On R São José, *Deguste*, next to Banco Itaú. Good value. *Ouro Grill*, R Sen Rocha Lagoa 61. Self-service at lunchtime, US$5, good value restaurant after 1600. *Pasteleria Lampião*, Praça Tiradentes. Good views at the back (better at lunchtime than in the evening). *Pizzeria Zebão*, R Paraná 43. *Restaurante e Chopparia Ouro Preto*, Praça Tiradentes 68. *Satélite*, R Conde de Bobadela 97. Restaurant and pizzeria, bar next door, good value. *Tacho de Ouro*, Conde de Bobadela 76. Good lunch buffet, popular. *Taverna do Chafariz*, R São José 167. Good local food. Recommended *Vide Gula*, R Sen Rocha Lagoa 79A. Food by weight, good, friendly atmosphere. Recommended.

Ouro Preto is famous for its *Holy Week* processions, which in fact begin on the Thu before Palm Sun and continue (but not every day) until Easter Sun. The most famous is that commemorating Christ's removal from the Cross, late on Good Fri. Attracting many Brazilians, Carnival here is also memorable.

Festivals
Many shops close during Holy Week and on winter weekends

In **Jun**, *Corpus Christi* and the *Festas Juninas* are celebrated. Every **Jul** the city holds the *Festival do Inverno da Universidade Federal de Minas Gerais (UFMG)*, the Winter Festival, about 3 weeks of arts, courses, shows, concerts and exhibitions. On **8 Jul**, is the anniversary of the city. **15 Aug**: *Nossa Senhora do Pilar*, patron saint of Ouro Preto. **12-18 Nov**, *Semana de Aleijadinho*, a week-long arts festival.

Shopping

Gems are not much cheaper from freelance sellers in Praça Tiradentes than from the shops. *Gemas de Minas* and *Manoel Bernardis*, Conde de Bobadela 63 and 48 respectively, are recommended. If buying gems on the street, ask for the seller's credentials. *Videmaju*, owned by Vicente Júlio de Paula, a professor at the School of Mines, sells stones at very good prices from his house at R Conselheiro Santana 175.

Buy soapstone carvings at roadside stalls and bus stops rather than in the cities; they are much cheaper. Many artisans sell soapstone carvings, jewellery and semi-precious stones in the Largo de Coimbra in front of São Francisco de Assis church. Also worth buying is traditional cookware in stone, copper or enamelled metal.

Sport

Yoga centre, Shiatsu and Kerala massage, down an alley between Nos 31 and 47 (Cine Teatro Vila Rica), Praça Alves de Brito, T35513337.

Transport

Buses The rodoviária is at R Padre Rolim 661, T5511081. A 'Circular' bus runs from the rodoviária to Praça Tiradentes, US$0.40; it is a long walk to the centre. Taxis charge exorbitant rates.

There are 11 buses a day from **Belo Horizonte** (2 hrs, *Pássaro Verde*), US$3.75, taxi US$30. Day trips are possible; book your return journey to Belo Horizonte early if returning in the evening; buses get crowded. Bus from **Rio**, *Útil* at 0830 or 2300 (US$15, 7½ hrs), return bus to Rio at 2330 (book in advance). There are also *Útil* buses to **Conselheiro Lafaiete**, 3-4 a day via Itabirito and Ouro Branco (see below), US$3.75, 2¾ hrs, for connections to **Congonhas do Campo**. Other *Útil* services to **Rio**, **Barbacena**, **Conselheiro Lafaiete** and **Congonhas** go via Belo Horizonte. Direct buses to **São Paulo**, 3 a day with *Cristo Rei*, 11 hrs, US$19.25. *Gontijo* go to Salvador via Belo Horizonte.

Directory

Banks Banco 24 Horas, Praça Alves de Brito, next to Correios. Banco do Brasil, R São José 189, good rates, also for TCs. Bradesco, on the corner of Sen Rocha Lagoa and Padre Rolim, opposite the Escola de Minas. **Communications** Internet: Point (language school and cultural centre), R Xavier da Veiga 501A. Post office: Praça Alves de Brito. **Voltage** 110 volts AC.

Minas de Passagem

Between Ouro Preto and Mariana is the Minas de Passagem gold mine, dating from 1719. A 20-minute guided tour visits the old mine workings and underground lake (take bathing suit), entrance US$7.50, visiting hours 0900-1800, Ouro Preto T5511068, Mariana T5571340. There is a waterfall, Cachoeira Serrinha, where swimming is possible, 30 minutes' walk from the bus stop to the mine. Initially you have to walk 100 m towards Mariana then ask for directions. Note that some signs say Mina de Ouro, omitting 'da Passagem'.

The nearest town to the Minas de Passagem is **Passagem de Mariana**. Where the bus stops at the edge of town is the *Pousada Solar dos Dois Sinos*, with a church behind it.

Mariana

Phone code: 031
Altitude: 697 m
Colour map 4, grid C3
Population: 47,000

Mariana, another old mining city, is the oldest town in Minas Gerais. It was first called Arraial de Nossa Senhora do Carmo, a settlement founded by the *bandeirantes* on 16 July 1696. In 1711 it became a town, Vila de Nossa Senhora do Carmo, and became the most important town, bishopric and administrative centre in the newly created Capitania de São Paulo e Minas do Ouro. In the mid-18th century, it was the only city in Minas Gerais, with the first town planning in the province. Its name was changed to Mariana in honour of the wife of Dom João V, Dona Maria Ana of Austria. Most of the fine colonial building was done in the second half of the 18th century. The artist Mestre Athayde was born here, as was the Inconfidente Cláudio Manuel da Costa.

Mariana was declared a national monument in 1945. Unlike Ouro Preto, in whose shadow the town tends to sit, it has remained a working mining centre. For many years the Companhia do Vale do Rio Doce (CVRD), the state mining company, had major operations here and provided a great deal of assistance for the restoration of the colonial heritage. Since CVRD's concentration on its new investments at Carajás and subsequent privatization, there have been doubts about its commitment to mining in Mariana and consequently to the town.

Tourist information *Terminal Turístico Manoel Costa Athayde*, Praça Tancredo Neves, houses the local guides' association (AGTURB, T35571158), who run tours for US$40. There is also a small tourist office; map US$1.50. A free monthly booklet, *Mariana Agenda Cultural*, has details of the historical sites, accommodation, restaurants, shopping, transport, etc, plus articles, poems and a calendar of events.

Sights The historical centre of the town slopes gently uphill from the river and the Praça Tancredo Neves, where buses from Ouro Preto stop. The first street parallel with the Praça Tancredo Neves is Rua Direita, which is lined with beautiful, two-storey 18th-century houses with tall colonial windows and balconies. At No 54 is the **Casa do Barão de Pontal** whose balconies are carved from soapstone, unique in Minas Gerais. The ground floor of the building is a museum of furniture. ■ *1400-1700 Tue*. At No 35 is the **Museu-Casa Afonso Guimarães** (or Alphonsus de Guimaraens), the former home of a symbolist poet: photographs and letters. ■ *Free*. No 31 is the office of *Mariana Turismo*. No 7 is the **Casa Setecentista**, another excellent example of 18th-century secular architecture which now belongs to the Patrimônio Histórico e Artístico Nacional. It has an enormous archive of documents from the colonial period, an exhibition hall and a multimedia centre.

Rua Direita leads to the Praça da Sé, on which stands the **Cathedral**, Basílica de Nossa Senhora da Assunção. Before Vila de Nossa Senhora do Carmo became a town, a chapel, started in 1703, stood on this spot. In various stages it was expanded and remodelled until its completion in 1760. The portal and the lavabo in the sacristy are by Aleijadinho and the painting in the beautiful interior and side altars is by Manoel Rabello de Sousa. Also in the cathedral is a wooden German organ (1701), made by Arp Schnitger, which was a gift to the first diocese of the Capitania de Minas do Ouro in 1747. It was restored in 1984 after some 50 years of silence. ■ *Organ concerts are given on Fri at 1100 and Sun at 1200 (US$7.50). Other concerts are held; see the local press for details.*

Turning up Rua Frei Durão, on the right is the **Museu Arquidiocesano**, which has fine church furniture, a gold and silver collection, Aleijadinho statues and an ivory cross. ■ *0900-1200, 1300-1700, closed Mon. US$1.50, R Frei Durão 49*. On the opposite side of the street is the **Casa da Intendência/Casa** de Cultura, No 84, which holds exhibitions and has a museum of music. The ceilings in the exhibition rooms are very fine; in other rooms there are *esteiro* (flattened bamboo) ceilings. ■ *0800-1130, 1330-1700*. At No 22 of the same street is the **Centro Cultural SESI Mariana**, with a theatre and occasional cinema presentations.

Praça Gomes Freire used to be where horses were tied up (there is an old drinking trough on one side) and where festivals were held. Now it has pleasant gardens. On the south side is the **Palácio Arquiepiscopal**, while on the north side is the **Casa do Conde de Assumar**, who was governor of the Capitania from 1717 to 1720; it later became the bishop's palace.

Praça Minas Gerais has one of the finest groups of colonial buildings in Brazil. In the middle is the **Pelourinho**, the stone monument to Justice, at which slaves used to be beaten. The fine **São Francisco** church (1762-94), has pulpits designed by Aleijadinho, paintings by Mestre Athayde, who is buried in tomb No 94, a fine sacristy and one side altar by Aleijadinho. The statue of São Roque is most important as he is the patron saint of the city (his day is 16 August). Among Athayde's paintings are the panels showing the life of St Francis on the ceiling of the right-hand chapel. The church is one of the most

Mariana

simple in Mariana, but in terms of art, one of the richest. There is a small exhibition of the restoration work funded by CVRD. ■ *0800-1700 daily.*

At right angles to São Francisco is **Nossa Senhora do Carmo** (1784), with steatite carvings, Athayde paintings, and chinoiserie panelling. Its exterior is considered the most beautiful in Mariana by some. Unfortunately this church was damaged by fire in early 1999. ■ *1400-1700 daily.* Across Rua Dom Silvério is the **Casa da Cámara e Cadéia** (1768), at one time the Prefeitura Municipal. It, too, is a superb example of civic colonial construction.

On Rua Dom Silvério the **Colégio Providência** at No 61 was the first college for boarding students in Minas Gerais (part of it is now a hotel, see below). Also on this street is the **Igreja da Arquiconfraria** and, nearing the top of the hill, the **Chafariz de São Pedro**. On the Largo de São Pedro is the church of **São Pedro dos Clérigos** (founded by Manuel da Cruz, first bishop of the town (1764), one of the few elliptical churches in Minas Gerais. It is unadorned, although there is a painting by Athayde of 'A Entrega do Menino Jesus a Santo Antônio'. The cedar altar was made by José Pedro Aroca. Look for the cockerel, carved in memory of the biblical verses about St Peter betraying Christ before the cock has crowed three times. Ask to see the view from the bell tower.

Capela de Santo Antônio, wonderfully simple and the oldest in town on Rua Rosário Velho is some distance from the centre. Overlooking the city from the north, with a good viewpoint, is the church of **Nossa Senhora do Rosário**, Rua do Rosário (1752), with work by Athayde and showing Moorish influence.

Outside the centre, to the west, but within easy walking distance, is the **Seminário Menor**, now the Instituto de Ciencias Históricas e Sociais of the Federal University.

South of the river, Avenida Getúlio Vargas leads to the new Prefeitura Municipal. It passes the Ginásio Poliesportivo and, across the avenue, the railway station. This is a romantic building with a clock tower, but it is rapidly falling into disrepair. No trains run on the line any more.

Excursions The small village of Antônio Pereira, 24 km north, is where the Imperial topaz is mined. Tours can be made of an interesting cave with stalactites: pay local children a small fee to show you round. ■ *3 buses a day from Mariana Mon-Fri, 0800, 1200, 1445, plus 1100, 1750 and 2100 on Sat.*

Sleeping **B** *Faísca*, R Antônio Olinto 48, T35571206. Also central, including breakfast. **B** *Pousada Solar dos Corrêa*, R Josefá Macedo 70 and R Direita, T/F35572080. Central, with breakfast, parking. **C** *Central*, R Frei Durão 8, T/F35571630. **D** without bath, on the attractive Praça Gomes Freire, pleasant, quiet. Recommended but avoid downstairs rooms. **C** *Pousada do Chafariz*, R Cônego Rego 149, T35571492. Parking, breakfast included, family atmosphere. Recommended. **C** *Providência*, R Dom Silvério 233, T35571444. Run by nuns, small rooms, pool, quiet. **D** *Müller*, Av Getúlio Vargas 34, T35571188, across the river from the Terminal Turístico. Recommended. The modern service station (*Posto Mariana*) on the highway above the town offers good clean rooms with hot showers.

Eating *Engenho Nôvo*, Praça da Sé 26. Bar at night, English spoken by the owners and clients. Recommended. *Mangiare della Mamma*, D Viçoso 27. Italian. Recommended. *Panela de Pedra* in the Terminal Turístico serves food by weight at lunchtime. *Tambaú*, R João Pinheiro 26. Regional food.

Festivals *Carnival* and *Holy Week* are celebrated in the town. **29 Jun** *São Pedro*. In **Jul**, Mariana shares some events of the *Festival do Inverno da UFMG* with Ouro Preto.

O Aleijadinho

Antônio Francisco Lisboa (1738-1814), the son of a Portuguese architect and a black slave woman, was known as O Aleijadinho (the little cripple) because in later life he developed a maiming disease (possibly leprosy) which compelled him to work in a kneeling (and ultimately a recumbent) position with his hammer and chisel strapped to his wrists. His finest work, which shows a strength not usually associated with the plastic arts in the 18th century, is probably the set of statues in the gardens and sanctuary of the great Bom Jesus church in Congonhas do Campo, but the main body of his work is in Ouro Preto, with some important pieces in Sabará, São João del Rei and Mariana.

Buses These leave **Ouro Preto** from beside the Escola de Minas, for Mariana, every 30 mins, US$0.60, all passing Minas de Passagem (buses also leave from Ouro Preto rodoviária). Ouro Preto buses stop at the new rodoviária, out of town on the main road, then at the *Posto Mariana*, before heading back to the centre of Mariana at Praça Tancredo Neves. Many buses seem to go only to the *posto* above the town, but it's a long walk from the centre. A bus from the rodoviária to the centre via the *posto* and Minas de Passagem costs US$0.40. Buses from Mariana to Ouro Preto can be caught by the bridge at the end of Rua do Catete.

    Bus from **Belo Horizonte** (via Ouro Preto), US$4.50, 2¼ hrs. Buses for **Santa Bárbara** (near Caraça) leave from the rodoviária.

Transport

Banks *Bemge* at *Ginásio Poliesportivo*, Av Getúlio Vargas, across the river from Praça Tancredo Neves. **Communications** Post office: corner of R Frei Durão and Praça Gomes Freire, also in *Ginásio Poliesportivo* (see above).

Directory

Congonhas do Campo

Most visitors spend little time in the town, but go straight to the Sanctuary of Bom Jesus de Matosinhos on a hill above the town. This masterpiece of colonial art can be visited in a day, but there are other things to see in the area should you decide to stay overnight.

Phone code: 031
Altitude: 866 m
Colour map 4, grid C3
Population: 42,000

    In the 18th century, Congonhas was a mining town. Today, in addition to the business brought by the tourists and pilgrims who come to the Sanctuary, its industries include mining and handicrafts.

    Tourist information *Fumcult*, in the Romarias, T37311300, ext 114, is very helpful.

O Santuário de Bom Jesus de Matosinhos, the great pilgrimage church, and its Via Sacra dominates the town. The idea of a sanctuary belonged to a prospector, Feliciano Mendes, who promised to erect a cross and chapel in thanks to Bom Jesus after he had been cured of a serious illness. The inspiration for his devotion came from two sources in Portugal, the cult of Bom Jesus at Braga (near where Mendes was born) and the church of Bom Jesus de Matozinhos, near Porto. Work began in 1757, funded by Mendes' own money and alms he raised. The church was finished in 1771, six years after Mendes' death, and the fame that the sanctuary had acquired led to its development by the most famous architects, artists and sculptors of the time as a Sacro Monte. This involved the construction of six linked chapels, or *pasos* (1802-18), which lead up to a terrace and courtyard before the church. On this terrace stand 12 prophets, sculpted by Aleijadinho between 1800 and 1805.

Sights
0700-1900 Tue-Sun

There is a wide view of the country from the church terrace, below which are six small chapels set in an attractive sloping area with grass, cobblestones and palms. Each chapel shows scenes with life-size Passion figures carved by Aleijadinho and his pupils in cedar wood. In order of ascent they are: the chapel of the Last Supper, the chapel of the Mount of Olives, the chapel of the taking, or betrayal of Christ, the chapel of the flagellation and the crowning with thorns, the chapel of Jesus carrying the Cross and the chapel of Christ being nailed to the Cross.

On the terrace stand the 12 prophets sculpted by Aleijadinho (thought of as his masterpieces). Carved in soapstone with dramatic sense of movement, they constitute one of the finest works of art of their period in the world. Note how Aleijadinho adapted the biblical characters to his own cultural references. All the prophets are sculpted wearing leather boots, as all important men in his time would have done. Daniel, who entered the lion's den, is represented with the artist's own conception of a lion, never having seen one himself: a large, maned cat with a face rather like a Brazilian monkey. Similarly, the whale which accompanies Jonah is an idiosyncratic interpretation. Each statue has a prophetic text carved with it. The statues 'combine in a kind of sacred ballet whose movements only seem uncoordinated; once these sculptures cease to be considered as isolated units, they take on full significance as part of a huge composition brought to life by an inspired genius.' (*Iberian-American Baroque*, edited by Henri Stierlin, page 178.) The beauty of the whole is enhanced by the combination of church, Via Sacra and wide landscape over which the prophets seem to preside.

Inside the church, there are paintings by Athayde and the heads of four sainted popes (Gregory, Jerome, Ambrose and Augustine) sculpted by Aleijadinho for the reliquaries on the high altar. Other artists involved were João Nepomuceno Correia e Castro, who painted the scenes of the life and passion of Christ in the nave and around the high altar, João Antunes de Carvalho, who carved

Santuário de Bom Jesus de Matosinhos

Adro dos Profetas detail

N
Not to scale

■ **Sleeping**
1 Colonial & Cova do Daniel Restaurant

○ **Prophets**
1 Abdias
2 Amós
3 Baruc
4 Daniel
5 Ezquiel
6 Habacuc
7 Isaías
8 Jeremias
9 Joel
10 Jonas
11 Naum
12 Oséias

the high altar, and Jerônimo Félix and Manuel Coelho, who carved the crossing altars of Santo Antônio and São Francisco de Paula. Despite the ornate carving, the overall effect of the paintwork is almost muted and naturalistic, with much use of blues, greys and pinks. Lamps are suspended on chains from the mouths of black dragons.

To the left of the church, as you face it, the third door in the building alongside the church is the Room of Miracles, which contains photographs and thanks for miracles performed. ■ *Getting there: A bus marked Basílica runs every 30 mins from the centre of the rodoviária to Bom Jesus, 5 km, US$0.45. A taxi from the rodoviária will cost US$5 1-way, US$10 return including the wait while you visit the sanctuary. The information desk at the bus station will guard luggage. In town, the bus stops in Praça JK. You can walk up from Praça JK via Praça Dr Mário Rodrigues Pereira, cross the little bridge, then go up Ruas Bom Jesus and Aleijadinho to the Praça da Basílica.*

On the hill are a tourist kiosk, souvenir shops, the *Colonial Hotel* and *Cova do Daniel* restaurant. There are public toilets on the Alameda das Palmeiras. From the hotel the Alameda das Palmeiras sweeps round to the **Romarias**, a large, almost oval area surrounded by buildings. This was the lodging where the pilgrims stayed. It now contains the Espaço Cultural, the headquarters of the local tourist office (*Fumcult*), workshops, the museums of mineralogy and religious art, the Memória da Cidade, the *Estalagem* restaurant and a *lanchonete*. A winter festival is held here for one week in July.

Other churches The oldest church here is **Nossa Senhora do Rosário**, Praça do Rosário, built by slaves at the end of the 17th century. The **Igreja Matriz de Nossa Senhora da Conceição**, in Praça 7 de Setembro, dates from 1749; the portal is attributed to Aleijadinho, while parts of the interior are by Manuel Francisco Lisboa. There are two 18th-century chapels, **Nossa Senhora da Ajuda**, in the district of Alto Maranhão, and the church at Lobo Leite, 10 km away.

Sleeping & eating **D** *Colonial*, Praça da Basílica 76, opposite Bom Jesus, T37311834. Good and comfortable but noisy, breakfast extra (cheaper without bath), fascinating restaurant (*Cova do Daniel*) downstairs is full of colonial handicrafts and good local food. **E** *Freitas*, R Marechal Floriano 69, T37311543. Basic, with breakfast, cheaper without bath. *Estalagem Romaria*, 2 mins from *Hotel Colonial* in the Romarias. Good restaurant and pizzeria, reasonable prices.

Festivals Congonhas is celebrated for its *Holy Week* processions, which have as their focus the Bom Jesus church. The most celebrated ceremonies are the meeting of Christ and the Virgin Mary on the Tue, and the dramatized Deposition from the Cross late on Good Friday. The *pilgrimage season*, first half of **Sep**, draws many thousands. **8 Dec**, *Nossa Senhora da Conceição*.

Transport **Buses** The Rodoviária is 1½ km outside town; bus to town centre US$0.40; for Basílica, see above. To/from **Belo Horizonte**, 1½ hrs, US$3, 8 times a day. To **São João del Rei**, 2 hrs, US$3.60, tickets are not sold until the bus comes in. To **Ouro Preto**, go via Belo Horizonte, Murtinho or Conselheiro Lafaiete. Whether going from Ouro Preto or Rio to Congonhas do Campo, there is no direct bus; you have to change at the town of **Conselheiro Lafaiete**. Frequent service Conselheiro Lafaiete-Congonhas do Campo, US$1.

Prados Just past Lagoa Dourada is the turning (12 km) for Prados, a pleasant town known for its musical and handicrafts traditions. It maintains its historical church music (see under São João del Rei, below), but the chief tradition is leatherwork, especially saddles (some say this dates back to the time when mule trains had to be equipped – Prados was one of the earliest places to produce gold). The forge produces the ironwork (bits, etc) and another workshop produces the frames for the saddles. In this and other shops animals are carved in wood. Excellent leather clothing can also be found, good prices from *Mara e Café*, Rua Magalhães Gomes 90. Other crafts include crochet and sisal carpets.

São João del Rei

Phone code: 032
Colour map 4, grid C3
Population: 79,000

The colonial city of São João del Rei lies at the foot of the Serra do Lenheiro, its streets paved with fossilized plants. It has a number of well preserved churches, several good museums and two renowned orchestras. A good view of the town and surroundings is from Alto da Boa Vista, where there is a Statue of Christ (Senhor dos Montes). **Tourist information** *Secretaria de Turismo*, in the house of Bárbara Heliodora, T33717833, 0900-1700, provides a free map.

History Before gold was discovered in this part of Minas, what is now São João del Rei was an important point on one of the main routes between the existing goldfields and the coast. Once gold was found here, the settlement of Arraial Novo de Nossa Senhora da Pilar was set up. In this neighbourhood one of the decisive actions of the Guerra dos Emboabas took place, in which the Paulistas were ambushed and murdered by the outsiders at the Capão da Traição (the Hedge of Treason). In another episode so many were killed that the river running between modern-day São João del Rei and Tiradentes was renamed the Rio das Mortes (River of Deaths). São João del Rei remained a commercial centre after the decline in gold mining and in 1833 it became a city. Two English travellers in the 19th century visited and wrote about this area (among others), Captain Richard Burton, *The Highlands of Brazil* (1869), and the Reverend J Walsh, *Notices of Brazil* (1830).

São João del Rei is known as the land of Tiradentes and Tancredo Neves. The former was born in the Fazenda de Pombal, about 15 km downstream from Tiradentes on the Rio das Mortes. After his execution, the *fazenda* was confiscated. It is now an experimental station owned by Ibama. Tancredo Neves, to whom there is a memorial in the town (see also below), was the man who would have become the first civilian president of Brazil after the military dictatorships of the mid-20th century, had he not died before taking office.

Sights The Corrego do Lenheiro, a stream with steep grassy banks, runs through the centre of town. Across it are two fine, stone bridges, A Ponte da Cadeia (1798) and A Ponte do Rosário (1800), as well as several other modern bridges. Both sides of the river have colonial monuments, which are interspersed with modern buildings. On the north side are many streets with pleasant houses, but in various states of repair. Rua Santo Antônio has many single-storey colonial houses which have been restored and painted. Rua Santo Elias has several buildings all in the same style. Behind the church of Nossa Senhora do Pilar (see below), the Largo da Câmara leads up to Mercês church, which has quite a good view. Throughout the city you will see locked portals with colonial porticos. These are *passinhos*, shrines that are opened in Holy Week. They can be seen for instance on Largo da Cruz and Largo do Rosário.

Many streets and squares seem to have more than one name, which can be a little confusing, but as the town centre is not large, it is hard to get lost. One such street crosses the Ponte da Cadeia from Rua Passos; it has three names: Rua da Intendência, Manoel Anselmo and Artur Bernardes.

In their book *Iberian-American Baroque*, Stierlin and Bottineau describe the design for the façade of **São Francisco de Assis** (1774), Praça Frei Orlando, as Aleijadinho's highest achievement, 'richly ornamented, yet, at the same time, simple and poetic in feeling'. The towers are circular, the doorway intricately carved and the greenish stone frames the white paint to beautiful effect. Inside are two sculptures by Aleijadinho, and others of his school. The six side altars are in wood; restoration has removed the plaster from the altars, revealing fine carving in sucupira wood. Their artistry is wonderful and the three pairs of altars mirror each other, each pair in a different style (note, for instance, the use of pillars and the different paintings which accompany each altar). The overall shape of the nave is elliptical, the gold altar has spiralling columns and an adoring St Francis kneels atop. ■ *0830-1200 and some afternoons. US$1.*

Basílica de Nossa Senhora do Pilar, the Cathedral on Rua Getúlio Vargas (formerly Rua Direita), was built in 1721, but has a 19th-century façade which replaced the 18th-century original. It has rich altars and a brightly painted ceiling (Madonna and Child in the middle, saints and bishops lining the sides). Note the androgynous gold heads and torsos within the eight columns set into the walls either side of the main altar. There is a profusion of cherubs and plants in the carving. This abundance and angelic innocence contrasts with the suffering of the Passion and the betrayal of the Last Supper (two

Churches
There are five 18th-century churches in the town, three of which are splendid examples of Brazilian colonial building

For concerts in the churches, see music page 257

Minas Gerais and Espírito Santo

São João del Rei

■ **Sleeping**
1 Aparecida
2 Brasil
3 Pousada Casarão

4 Lenheiro Palace
5 Porto Real
6 Quinta do Ouro
7 São Benedito

● **Eating**
1 Churrascaria Ramón
2 Tamandaré

Not to scale

pictures of which are before the altar), all common themes in Brazilian baroque. In the sacristy are portraits of the Evangelists. ■ *Open afternoons*.

Nossa Senhora do Carmo, Praça Dr Augusto Viegas (Largo do Carmo), all in white and gold, has been very well restored. Construction commenced in 1733. The façade is outlined in lights at night. ■ *Open afternoons*.

There are three other churches in town: the **Igreja do Rosário**, Largo do Rosário, in its present form dates from 1753, but the first chapel on the site was put up in 1719. It is all white, except for silver angels. ■ *Open afternoons*. The **Igreja de Santo Antônio**, Rua Santo Antônio, is a chapel built in the 1760s. The **Igreja das Mercês**, on the hill behind the Cathedral, is again a later construction than the original chapel. The present building is of 1853, just over 100 years younger than its predecessor.

Museums Almost opposite São Francisco is the house of **Bárbara Heliodora** (1759-1819), Rua Padre José Maria Xavier, which also contains the **Museu Municipal Tomé Portes del Rei**, with historical objects and curios. In the same building is the Instituto Histórico e Geográfico; downstairs is the **tourist office**. Next door is the Biblioteca Municipal and the Acadêmia das Letras.

Museu de Arte Sacra, Praça Gastão da Cunha 8, by Nossa Senhora do Pilar, is small but recommended; it has sculptures, vestments and a room full of silver. ■ *1100-1700 Tue-Sun. US$1*.

The **Memorial Tancredo Neves**, Rua Padre José Maria Xavier 7, is a homage to the man and his life. An eight-minute video on São João del Rei is shown. It also holds exhibitions and has a bookshop. ■ *1300-1800 Wed-Fri, 0900-1700 weekends and holidays. US$1*.

The **Museu de Arte Regional do Patrimônio Histórico**, in Praça Severiano de Resende, in a fine three-storey building (1859), has 18th- and 19th-century furniture and pictures and an archive of documents pertaining to the city. ■ *0800-1200, 1330-1730 Tue-Sun. US$1*.

The **Museu Ferroviário** (Railway Museum), Avenida Hermílio Alves 366, is well worth exploring. The museum traces the history of railways in general and in Brazil in brief. There is an informative display of the role of Irineu Evangelista de Souza, Barão de Mauá, who was a pioneer of both industry and the railways following his visit to England in 1840. The locomotive that ran on the first railway from Rio de Janeiro to the foot of the Serra do Mar was called *A Baronesa* after his wife. The railway to São João, the Estrada de Ferro Oeste de Minas was not a success, but it was instrumental in the development of the region.

In the museum is an 1880 Baldwin 4-4-0 locomotive from Philadelphia (No 5055) and a 1912-13 VIP carriage. Outside, at the end of the platforms are carriages and a small Orenstein and Koppel (Berlin) engine. You can walk along the tracks to the round house, in which are several working engines in superb condition, an engine shed and a steam-operated machine shop, still working. It is here that the engines get up steam before going to couple with the coaches for the run to Tiradentes. On days when the trains are running, you can get a good, close-up view of operations even if not taking the trip. Highly recommended. ■ *T3718004. US$0.50. See below for the train to Tiradentes*.

Sleeping **A** *Lenheiro Palace*, Av Pres Tancredo Neves 257, T/F33718155. Modern hotel with
■ *on map, page 255* good facilities, parking, cheaper in low season, teahouse, breakfast. **A** *Pousada Quinto do Ouro*, Praça Severiano de Resende 4, above the restaurant of the same name, T3712565. Cheaper in low season, fan. **B** *Porto Real*, Av Eduardo Magalhães 254, T/F33717000. Modern, comfortable, sizeable rooms, good restaurant. **C** *Aparecida*, Praça Dr Antônio Viegas 13, T33712540. Central, by the bus and taxi stop, has a

restaurant and *lanchonete*. **C** *Pousada Casarão*, Ribeiro Bastos 94, opposite São Francisco church, T33717447. Firm beds, pool, games room, in a converted mansion,
delightful. **D** *do Hespanhol*, R Mcal Deodoro 131, T33714677. Also central, price varies
according to room. **E** *Brasil*, Av Pres Tancredo Neves 395, T33712804. In an old house
full of character, on the opposite side of the river from the railway station, cheap. Recommended but basic, no breakfast. **E** per person *Pousada São Benedito*, R Mcal
Deodoro 254, T33717381. Shared rooms only, shared bath.

Quinto do Ouro, address as *pousada* above. Good regional food, reasonable prices. **Eating**
Also on Praça Severiano de Resende is *Churrascaria Ramón*, No 52. Good. *Portal del*   ● *on map, page 255*
Rey, Praça Severiano de Rezende 134. *Comida à kilo*, Minas and Arabic food, very good.
By the railway station is *Churrascaria e Pizzeria Chafariz*. For breakfast, go up Lopes
Bahia from Av Pres Tancredo Neves and on the corner opposite the BR filling station is
Tamandaré, with a *padaria* next door at No 9.

Apr, *Semana Santa*; 15-21 *Semana da Inconfidência*. May or Jun, *Corpus Christi*. First   **Festivals**
2 weeks of **Aug**, *Nossa Senhora da Boa Morte*, with baroque music (*novena barroca*).
Similarly, **12 Oct**, *Nossa Senhora do Pilar*, patron saint of the city. **8 Dec**, founding of
the city. FUNREI, the university (on R Padre José Maria Xavier), holds *Inverno Cultural* in
Jul each year.

São João del Rei has 2 famous orchestras which play baroque music. In colonial days,   **Music**
the music master not only had to provide the music for Mass, but also had to compose
new pieces for every festival. All the music has been kept and the **Riberio Bastos** and
Lira Sanjoanense preserve the tradition. Both have their headquarters, rehearsing
rooms and archives on Rua Santo Antônio (at Nos 54 and 45 respectively). The
Orquestra Ribeiro Bastos plays at Mass every Sun in São Francisco de Assis at 0915, as
well as at many religious ceremonies throughout the year (for example Holy Week).
The Orquestra Lira Sanjoanense plays at Massin Nossa Senhora do Pilar at 1900 every
Thu and on Sun in Nossa Senhora do Rosário at 0830 and Nossa Senhora das Mercês at
1000, as well as on other occasions. It is best to check at their offices for full details.
(There are similar orchestras in Prados – see above – and Tiradentes, but the latter is
not as well supported as those in São João.)

Worth a visit is the **pewter factory** (with exhibition and shop), Av Leite de Castro 1150,   **Shopping**
T33718000, 10 mins' walk from the rodoviária. Run by Englishman John Somers and his
son Gregory. Open 0900-1800. The nearby town of **Resende Costa** (30 km north) is
known for its textile handicrafts.

Buses The rodoviária, 2 km west of the centre, has a phone office, toilets, luggage store,   **Transport**
lanchonetes and a tourist information office. Buses to **Rio**, 5 daily with *Paraibuna* (3 on
Sat and Sun), 5 hrs, US$10-12. *Cristo Rei* to **São Paulo**, 8 hrs, 5 a day (also to Santos), and
Translavras, 4 a day (also to Campinas), US$12.50. **Belo Horizonte**, 3½ hrs, US$6.60. To
Juiz de Fora, US$5.40, at least 8 a day with *Transur*. Frequent service to **Tiradentes** with
Meier, 8 a day, 7 on Sat, Sun and holidays, US$0.65; on the return journey to São João, the
bus stops outside the railway station before proceeding to the rodoviária.

Banks *Bemge*, Av Pres Tancredo Neves 213. Has exchange, 1100-1600. **Communica-**   **Directory**
tions Telephone: Av Pres Tancredo Neves 119. 0700-2200.

Minas Gerais and Espírito Santo

Tiradentes

Phone code: 032
Colour map 4, grid C3
Population: 6,000

The centre of this charming little town, 15 km from São João, with its nine streets and eight churches, at the foot of the green Serra São José, at first glance hardly belongs to this century. Look behind the colonial façades, though, and you will see galleries, *ateliés*, antique shops, *pousadas* and restaurants. This is a mark of its popularity as a tourist centre, but in no way mars its attractiveness. The town is very busy during Holy Week, when there are numerous religious processions.

In 1938, Tiradentes' rich architectural and artistic heritage was recognized and it was declared a national monument. Since then it has been carefully restored.

History   Tiradentes stands on the site of yet another *bandeirante* encampment, the Arraial de Santo Antônio do Rio das Mortes. It prospered and was founded as an autonomous town with the name São José del Rei on 14 January 1718. During the 18th century its fortunes rested on mining and, as elsewhere, the wealthy lay orders spared no expense on their churches. After Independence, when the mines had become exhausted, São José fell into decay which not even the coming of the railway in 1881 could remedy. It was after the ousting of the emperor in 1889 that the town was renamed in honour of the Martyr of the Inconfidência, see page 242. Tiradentes was not the only Inconfidente associated with the place, though. Also resident was Carlos Correia de Toledo Pisa (Padre Toledo), a priest.

Sights   **Churches** The **Igreja Matriz de Santo Antônio**, first built in 1710 and enlarged in 1736, contains some of the finest gilded wood carvings in the country. The main church is predominantly white and gold. Lamps hang from the beaks of golden eagles. The symbols on the panels painted on the ceiling of the

The tourist office is in the Prefeitura, R Resende Costa 71

Tiradentes

■ Sleeping	4 Pousada do Largo	8 Pousada Três Portas
1 Ponto do Morro	5 Pousada do Laurito	9 Solar da Ponte
2 Porão Colonial	6 Pousada Mãe d'Água	10 Wellerson
3 Pousada do Alferes	7 Pousada Maria Barbosa	

nave are a mixture of Old Testament and medieval Christian symbolism (for instance the phoenix, and the pelican). A carved wooden balustrade separates the seating in the nave from richly carved side chapels and altars. The principal altar is also ornately decorated, as are the walls and ceiling around it. The church has a small but fine organ brought from Porto in the 1790s. The upper part of the reconstructed façade is said to follow a design by Aleijadinho. In front of the church, on the balustrade which overlooks the main street and the town, are also a cross and a sundial by him. ■ *0900-1700 daily.*

The charming **Nossa Senhora do Rosário** church, on a small square on Rua Direita, has fine statuary and ornate gilded altars. On its painted ceiling colonnades rise to heaven; two monks stand on a hill and the Virgin and Child are in the sky. Other ceiling panels depicting the life of Christ are in poor shape. The church contains statues of black saints, including São Benedito, patron saint of cooks; in one of the statues he is holding a squash. The church dates from 1727, but building by the Irmandade dos Pretos Cativos (black slave brotherhood) began as early as 1708. ■ *1200-1600 Thu-Mon. US$0.50.*

São João Evangelista is on the Largo do Sol, a lovely open space. It is a simple church, built by the Irmandade dos Homens Pardos (mulattos). It has paintings of the four evangelists and a cornice painted in an elaborate pattern in pink, blue and beige. ■ *0900-1700 Thu-Mon.*

Nossa Senhora das Mercês (18th century), Largo das Mercês, has an interesting painted ceiling and a notable statue of the Virgin. ■ *0900-1700 Sun.*

There are other churches and chapels in the town, including the **Igreja de Bom Jesus da Pobreza**, on the Largo das Forras. **Santuário da Santíssima Trindade**, on the road which leads up behind the Igreja Matriz de Santo Antônio is well worth seeing. The chapel itself is 18th century while the room of miracles associated with the annual Trinity Sunday pilgrimage is modern. On the grassy Morro de São Francisco is the small chapel of **São Francisco de Paula** (mid-18th century).

Secular buildings and a suggested tour From the main praça, Largo das Forras, take Rua Resende Costa up to the Largo do Sol (Igreja São João Evangelista – see above). Beside the church is the **Museu Padre Toledo**, the house of this leader of the Inconfidência Mineira. It exhibits some good pieces of furniture. See also the roof which depicts the Five Senses. The house belongs to the Fundação Rodrigo Mello Franco de Andrade, as does the **Casa de Cultura** in the row of 18th-century houses on Rua Padre Toledo, which leads from Largo do Sol to the Igreja Matriz de Santo Antônio. From this church you can make a detour to the chapel of Santíssima Trindade. From Santo Antônio, head down the Rua da Câmara, past the **Casa da Câmara e Antigo Fórum**. Here the road

Eating
1 Aluarte
2 Estalagem
3 Padre Toledo
4 Quinto do Ouro
5 Virados do Largo

--►-- Walking tour

R Silvio Vasconcelos

R de Mortes
R dos Inconfidentes
R Henrique Diniz
Antônio Carvalho
Rio Das Mortes
To Train Station & São João del Rei
Praça da Estação

divides, the left-hand street, Jogo de Bola, leading to the Largo do Ó (which rejoins the main street), while Rua da Câmara goes to the crossroads with Rua Direita. At this junction is the **Sobrado Ramalho**, said to be the oldest building in Tiradentes. It is believed to be where the gold was melted down and has a lot of soapstone carving inside. It has been beautifully restored as a cultural centre.

Before taking Rua Direita back to Largo das Forras, you can carry straight on to the river and cross the bridge to the magnificent **Chafariz de São José** (the public fountain), installed in 1749. The water is brought by a stone aqueduct from springs in the forest at the foot of Serra São José. It is still used for drinking, clothes washing and watering animals.

Rua Direita has some interesting old buildings. Opposite the Praça Padre Lourival, on which stands Nossa Senhora do Rosário, is the **Antiga Cadeia** (18th-19th century) which now contains the **Museu de Arta Sacra**. Rua Direita meets the Largo das Forras at the **Prefeitura Municipal**, a two-storey building with an extra room under the roof. It now houses the tourist, post and phone offices.

Excursions   The **train** on the line between São João del Rei and Tiradentes (13 km) has been in continuous operation since 1881, using the same locomotives and rolling stock, running on a 76-cm gauge track, all lovingly cared for. The maximum speed is 20 km per hour. ■ *The train runs on Fri, Sat, Sun and holidays, 1000 and 1415 from São João del Rei, returning from Tiradentes at 1300 and 1700. Tickets cost US$8.* To get to the railway station from the centre of the village you have to cross the river and head out of town on the Rua dos Inconfidentes. Follow this road until it becomes the Rua Antônio Teixeira Carvalho, which carries on to the bridge over the Rio das Mortes. On the opposite bank is a small park and the station. The railway museum at the railway station in São João del Rei is described above.

Walks   The forest on the Serra de São José is protected. Easiest access is from behind the Chafariz, where a black door in the wall is opened at 0730 (Wednesday-Sunday). In just five minutes you are in the forest, following the watercourse, and monkeys and birds can be seen.

From behind the Mercês church you can walk up into the Serra; ask for directions. It is recommended to take a guide if you wish to walk along the top of the Serra.

There is a good one- or two-hour walk from Tiradentes to the **Balneário de Águas Santas** which involves crossing the Serra. At the Balneário is a swimming pool, also a lake and a *churrascaria*, *Senzala*. A map can be obtained from the *Solar da Ponte*, or ask locally for directions (taxi US$15). On the way you pass **Parque Frei Mariano Vellozo**, which contains the Cachoeira do Mangue falls. It is busy at weekends and can be reached by car on the old road to São João.

Sleeping

■ on map, page 258
Price codes:
see inside front cover
Prices are generally
lower in the more
expensive hotels
between Sunday
and Thursday

AL *Solar da Ponte*, Praça das Mercês T33551255. www.roteirosdecharme/sol.htm   Has the atmosphere of a country house, run by John and Anna Maria Parsons, the price includes breakfast and afternoon tea, only 12 rooms, fresh flowers in rooms, bar, sauna, lovely gardens, swimming pool, light meals for residents only, for larger meals, the hotel recommends 5 local restaurants. Highly recommended (it is in the Roteiros de Charme group, see page 47). **A** *Candonga da Serra*, Estr Velha Tiradentes towards São João del Rei, T/F33551483. Out of town, calls itself 'ecológico', big rooms with firm beds but spartan, no TV, restaurant/bar, pool. **A** *Pousada Mãe D'Água*, Largo das Forras 50, T33551206. Including breakfast but not tax. Very nice. **A** *Pousada Três Portas*, R Direita 280A, T33551444. There are more expensive suites, has sauna, thermal pool, hydromassage, heating.

B *Hotel Wellerson*, R Foco Simbólico 218, T33551226. **B** *Pousada Maria Barbosa*, R Antônio Teixeira Carvalho 144, near the bridge that leads out of town, T/F33551227, www.idasbrasil.com.br Pool, very pleasant, at the weekend the price includes breakfast, lunch and evening snack. Not in the centre, but closer than *Maria Barbosa*. **B** *Porão Colonial*, R dos Inconfidentes 447, T3551251. Pleasant, with pool, sauna, parking. **B** *Hotel Ponto do Morro*, Largo das Forras 2, T33551342. With pool, sauna, also has 2 chalets, the hotel has a nice entry.

C *Pousada do Alferes*, R dos Inconfidentes 479, T33551303. **C** *Pousada do Largo*, Largo das Forras 48, T/F33551219. With TV, pool, sauna. **C** *Pousada do Laurito*, R Direita 187, T33551268.

Quartier Latin, R São Francisco de Paula 46, Praça da Rodoviária. French, cordon bleu chef, excellent but expensive. *Quinto de Ouro*, R Direita 159. Recommended. *Virados do Largo*, Largo do Ó. Good food and service. *Estalagem*, R Min Gabriel Passos 280. *Padre Toledo*, R Direita 202. *Aluarte*, Largo do Ó 1. Bar with live music in the evening, nice atmosphere, US$4 cover charge, garden, sells handicrafts. Recommended. There are many other restaurants, snack bars and lanchonetes in town and it is a small enough place to wander around and see what takes your fancy.

Eating
● *on map, page 258*

Art galleries *Fernando Pitta*, Beco da Chácara, T/F3551475, produces fascinating work, painting, mixed media and sculture, worth a visit. *Oscar Araripe*, R da Câmara, paints Tiradentes and other local scenes in bright colours, popular and commercial.

Entertainment

Buses Last bus back to **São João del Rei** is 1815, 2230 on Sun; fares are given above. **Taxis** to **São João del Rei** costs US$10. See Excursions above for the **train** between the 2 towns.

Around town there are pony-drawn taxis; ponies can be hired for US$5. For horse-riding treks, contact John Parsons at the *Solar da Ponte*.

Transport

Communications The combined post and telephone office is on the Largo das Forras in the Prefeitura Municipal, R Resende Costa 71. It closes at 1200 for lunch.

Directory

Diamantina

This friendly, beautiful town is situated deep in the interior, amid barren mountains. Once the centre of an active diamond industry, Diamantina has excellent colonial buildings. Its churches are difficult to get into, except for the modern Cathedral, and are not as grand as those of Ouro Preto. It is, however, possibly the least spoiled of all the colonial mining cities, with carved overhanging roofs and brackets.

Phone code: 038
Altitude: 1,120 m
Colour map 4, grid B3
Population: 48,000

Tourist information *Departamento de Turismo* in the Casa de Cultura in Praça Antônio Eulálio 53, 3rd floor, T35311636, F35311857. Pamphlets and a reliable map are available, also information about churches' opening times, friendly and helpful. The office will arrange a free tour of churches with guide who has access to keys (tip guide). One excellent guide is *Passeio a Diamantina*.

In 1720 diamonds were discovered at Arraial do Tijuco, the first settlement of gold prospectors who had come to the region. Within 14 years it had become important enough to be made the administrative capital of the Distrito de Diamantina. Since the Portuguese crown made the same impositions on diamond mining as on gold, there was a similar resentment among those people who saw no chance of improvement in their living conditions. One such was Padre José da Silva de Oliveira Rolim (Padre Rolim), who joined the Inconfidência Mineira. The town was one of the most wealthy in

History

Minas Gerais and Espírito Santo

18th-century Brazil and in 1838 it was elevated to the status of city and renamed Diamantina.

President Juscelino Kubitschek, the founder of Brasília, was born here. His house, Rua São Francisco 241, has been converted into a museum.

Sights **Churches** The oldest church in Diamantina is **Nossa Senhora do Rosário**, Largo Dom Joaquim, built by slaves in 1728. **Nossa Senhora do Carmo**, Rua do Carmo, dates from 1760-65 and was built by João Fernandes de Oliveira (see below) for the Carmélite Third Order. It is the richest church in the town, with fine decorations and paintings and a pipe organ, covered in gold leaf, made locally. Apparently, the tower is at the back of the church to please Chica da Silva (see below), who did not like to hear the sound of the bells.

São Francisco de Assis, Rua São Francisco, just off Praça JK, was built between 1766 and the turn of the 19th century. It is notable for its paintings. Other colonial churches are the **Capela Imperial do Amparo** (1758-76), **Nossa Senhora das Mercês** (1778-84) and **Nossa Senhora da Luz** (early 19th century), erected to fulfil the vow of a Portuguese lady, Dona Tereza de Jesus Perpétuo Corte Real, who survived the 1755 Lisbon earthquake.

The **Catedral Metropolitana de Santo Antônio** on Praça Correia Rabelo, was built in the 1930s in neo-colonial style to replace the original cathedral.

Secular buildings After repeated thefts, the diamonds of the **Museu do Diamante**, Rua Direita 14 in the house of Padre Rolim, have been removed to the *Banco do Brasil*. The museum does house an important collection of the materials used in the diamond industry, plus other items from the 18th and 19th centuries. ■ *US$1*. Diamonds are still sought; see traditional methods at Guinda, 7 km away. Other local industries are the making of Portuguese Arraiolos-style tapestry carpets by hand, at a cooperative in the centre, and etchings on leather.

Diamantina

Sleeping
1 Dália 2 Tijuco

At Rua Quitanda 48 is the **Biblioteca Antônio Torres**, also known as the **Casa Muxarabi**. This name derives from the enclosed balcony, of Moorish design, on one of the windows of this 18th-century house.

The **Casa de Chica da Silva**, is at Praça Lobo Mesquita 266. Chica da Silva was a slave in the house of Padre Rolim's father. She became the mistress of João Fernandes de Oliveira, a diamond contractor. They had 14 children and lived in luxury until Fernandes returned to Portugal in 1772 when his last contract ended. Chica, who died on 15 February 1796, has become a folk heroine among Brazilian blacks. ■ *Free.*

Behind the 18th-century building which now houses the **Prefeitura Municipal** (originally the diamonds administration building, Praça Conselheiro Matta 11), is the **Mercado Municipal** or **dos Tropeiros** (muleteers), Praça Barão de Guaicuí. It was built in 1835 as a residence and trading house before being expanded; it has wooden arches. The **Casa da Glória**, Rua da Glória 297, is in fact two houses on either side of the street connected by an enclosed bridge. Among its earlier inhabitants was the first bishop of Diamantina. It now contains the Instituto Eschwege de Geologia.

Excursions

Walk along the **Caminho dos Escravos**, the old road built by slaves between the mining area on Rio Jequitinhonha and Diamantina. A guide is essential and also cheap, ask at the Casa de Cultura (beware of snakes and thunderstorms).

About 9 km from town is the **Gruta de Salitre**, a big cave with a strange rock formation. There is no public transport, but it is a good walk and you can find some interesting minerals along the way. Ask the tourist office for directions. Alternatively, take a taxi. Closer to the town is the **Cachoeira da Toca**, a 15 m waterfall which is good for swimming.

Along the river bank it is 12 km on a dirt road to **Biribiri**, a pretty village with a well-preserved church and an abandoned textile factory. It also has a few bars and at weekends it is a popular, noisy place. About halfway there are swimming pools in the river; opposite them, on a cliff face, are red animal paintings whose age and origin are unknown. The plant life along the river is interesting and there are beautiful mountain views.

Sleeping

A *Pousada do Garimpo*, Av da Saudade 265, T/F35312523, pgarimpo@diamantina. uemg.br Upmarket option with pool and sauna although not too much character. **C** *Dália*, Praça JK (Jota-Ka) 25, T35311477. Fairly good. **C** *Tijuco*, R Macau do Melo 211, T/F35311022. Good food. **D** *JK*, opposite the rodoviária. With good breakfast, clean, friendly, hot showers. **E** *Pensão Comercial*, Praça M Neves 30. Basic. Wild camping is possible near the waterfall just outside town.

Eating

Capistrana, R Campos Carvalho 36, near Cathedral square. Recommended. *Santo Antônio* in the centre has a good self-service *churrasco* and salad for US$3 during the week.

Bars & nightclubs

Serestas (serenades) are sung on Fri and Sat nights. Many young people hang out in the bars in Beco da Mota. *Cavernas Bar*, Av Sílvio Felício dos Santos. Good for pagode on Sat and Sun from late afternoon. *Taverna de Gilmar* is recommended for a good mix of music, although it gets packed quickly.

Festivals

Carnival is said to be very good here and the town is trying to establish another festival in Sep. **12 Sep** is *O Dia das Serestas*, the Day of the Serenades, for which the town is famous; this is the birthday of President Juscelino Kubitschek, who was born here. Religious festivals: *Semana Santa*; *Corpus Christi* (**May-Jun**); *Santo Antônio* (**13 Jun**); *O Divino Espírito Santo* (50 days after Pentecost), a major 5-day feast; *Festa do Rosário* (first half of **Oct**).

Transport **Buses** There are 6 buses a day to **Belo Horizonte**, via Curvelo, with *Pássaro Verde*, 2½ hrs to **Curvelo**, US$3, to **Belo Horizonte**, US$10, 5½ hrs. There are daily *Gontijo* buses at 1600 to **São Paulo**, 16-17 hrs, US$19.25, but it is an uncomfortable journey; the journey ends at the Bresser terminal. It is better to go to Belo Horizonte and change buses there if you want to arrive at Tietê in São Paulo.

Routes If en route to Bahia, take the *Gontijo* Belo Horizonte-Salvador bus to **Araçuaí** and change there, the fare is US$11.50 but you have to check an hour or so beforehand to see if there is space in the bus. The bus passes Diamantina at about 1330-1400, or 0200. It's a very bumpy ride through Couto de Magalhães de Minas and Virgem da Lapa. At Araçuaí is **D** *Pousada Tropical*, opposite the rodoviária behind the policlínica, T37311765. With bath, clean and friendly. From there you can take a bus to Itaobim (US$2.65, 2 hrs, Rio Doce company) then make an onward connection to Vitória da Conquista (US$5.50, 4 hrs, same company – see page 276). The BR-116 passes interesting rock formations at Pedra Azul before crossing the border with Bahia.

Directory **Banks** *Banco do Brasil*, Praça Cons Mata 23. **Voltage**   110 AC.

Serro   This unspoiled colonial town on the Rio Jequitinhonha has six fine baroque
Phone code: 038   churches, a museum and many beautiful squares. It makes *queijo serrano*, one
Population: 22,000   of Brazil's best cheeses and is in the centre of a prosperous cattle region. The most conspicuous church is **Santa Rita**, on a hill in the centre of town, reached by a long line of steps. On the main Praça João Pinheiro, by the bottom of the steps, is **Nossa Senhora do Carmo**, arcaded, with original paintings on the ceiling and in the choir. The town has two large mansions. **Barão de Diamantina**, Praça Presidente Vargas is in ruins, but **Barão do Serro** across the river on Rua da Fundição is beautifully restored and used as the town hall and Casa de Cultura. ■ *Tue-Sat 1200-1700, Sun 0900-1200*. There are old mine entrances in the hillside behind the courtyard. The **Museu Regional Casa dos Ottoni**, Praça Cristiano Ottoni 72, is an 18th-century house now containing furniture and everyday objects from the region. The Ottoni brothers, who were born here, were prominent naval officers turned politicians in the 19th century. For **tourist information**, contact *Secretaria de Turismo*, Chácara do Barão do Serro, T35411368 ext 234.

Just by the Serro turn-off is the town of **Datas**, whose spacious church (1832) decorated in red and blue, contains a striking wooden image of Christ with the crown of thorns.

Sleeping **A** *Pousada Vila do Príncipe*, R Antônio Honório Pires 38, T/F35411485. Very clean, in an old mansion containing its own museum, the artist Mestre Valentim is said to have been born in the slave quarters. There are other cheaper hotels.

Eating *Itacolomi*, Praça João Pinheiro 20. Fair. *Churrascaria Vila do Príncipe*, Praça Dom Epaminondas 48.

Northern Minas Gerais

Rio São   Passenger services on the river have been discontinued but masters of cargo
Francisco   boats in the port may permit passage. The regular stops are at **Januária** (famous for Brazil's reputed best *cachaça*) and **Bom Jesus da Lapa** in Bahia (a pilgrimage centre with a church built in a grotto inside a mountain, but a very poor town; there are hotels and a choice of bars on the river beach).

Some 240 km northwest of Belo Horizonte is a lake five times as large in area as Rio de Janeiro bay, formed by the **Três Marias dam** on the upper reaches of the São Francisco River. The town is at the lake's northern end. To get there, take the *Sertaneja* bus from **Belo Horizonte** at 1615, US$9.

Tres Marias
Phone code: 038
Population: 26,000

North of Três Marias is the terminus for boat journeys on the Rio São Francisco (see also page 418). The cutting down of trees, in part as fuel for the boats, and the low rainfall in recent years, has greatly reduced the flow. The town itself is a tourist attraction because of the falls in the river which make for excellent fishing. The fishermen use punt-like canoes. The sandy river beaches are used for swimming. The riverboats' grotesque figureheads, *carrancas*, are made in the workshops of Lourdes Barroso, Rua Abaeté 390.

Pirapora
Phone code: 038
Population: 50,000

Sleeping and eating **B** *Canoeiras*, Av Salmeron 3, T7411933. Used by river-tour parties. **B** *Pirapora Palace*, Praça Melo Viana 61, 7 blocks west and 1 block south of the rodoviária, T7413851. Ask for a room on the garden, safe. **D** *Daila*, Praça JK 13. With breakfast but without bath. **D** *Grande*, R da Quitanda 70. With bath but without breakfast. *Lá em Casa*, 'meals by the kilo', huge caipirinhas, excellent value.

Between Pirapora and Januária is the colonial fishing town of São Francisco, with many attractive houses and a good handicraft market in the town hall. Of the two remaining wood-burning stern-wheel boats, allegedly built for Mississippi services in the 1860s and imported from the USA in 1922 to work on the Amazon, one, the *Gaiola*, was restored for services on the Rio São Francisco. The town is popular during Semana Santa, Festas Juninas and a carnival in July. **A** *Hotel Green Fish*, R Min Hermenegildo de Barros 560, T/F6311106.

São Francisco
Phone code: 038
Population: 50,000

Eastern Minas Gerais

This region is a centre of semi-precious stone processing and crystal carving, and also contains the Serra do Caparaó, where several of Brazil's highest mountains are found. The two principal towns, Governador Valadares and Teófilo Otôni, are both on the BR-116 inland Rio-Salvador road, and both have good connections with Belo Horizonte.

You can visit the private Caratinga Biological Station, 880 ha of mountainous, inland Atlantic forest which is home to four rare primates: the muriqui (formerly called the woolly spider monkey, the largest primate in the Americas and the largest mammal endemic to Brazil – also one of the world's most endangered primates), the black-capped capuchin, the brown howler monkey and the buffy-headed marmoset. Also at the station are brown-throated three-toed sloths and an incredible array of birds. The primates and many of the birds are not bothered by human presence. ■ *US$15 per person per day (payable only in reais). Tours can be arranged through* Focus Tours *(see Tour operators, page 23).*

Caratinga Biological Station

The **Parque Estadual do Rio Doce** is 248 km east of Belo Horizonte in the municipalities of Dionísio, Timóteo and Marliéria. Between 230 and 515 m above sea level and covering almost 36,000 ha, this is the largest tract of Mata Atlântica in southeast Brazil. As well as forest there are a number of lakes, on which boat trips are possible, besides swimming and fishing. The park is home to a great many birds and animals. There is an information centre, a campsite 6 km into the park and trails have been laid out for hiking. ■ *T8223006, or phone the Instituto*

Rio Doce

Minas Gerais and Espírito Santo

Estadual de Florestas T3307013/2951655. Access is by the roads BR-262 or 381, either of which you have to turn off onto dirt roads to get to the park.

Parque Nacional Caparaó

The park has rare Atlantic rainforest in its lower altitudes and Brazilian alpine on top; this is good walking country

In the park are the Pico da Bandeira (2,890 m), Pico do Cruzeiro (2,861 m) and the Pico do Cristal (2,798 m). From the park entrance (where a small fee has to be paid) it is 6 km on a poorly maintained road to the car park at the base of the waterfall. From the hotel (see below) jeeps (US$20 per jeep) run to the car park at 1,970 m (2½ hours' walk), then it's a 3-4 hour walk to the summit of the Pico da Bandeira, marked by yellow arrows; plenty of camping possibilities all the way up, the highest being at Terreirão (2,370 m). It is best to visit during the dry season (April-October). It can be quite crowded in July and during Carnival. ■ *Contact via Caixa Postal 17, alto Jequitibá, MG, CEP 36976-000, T255, via operator on 101-PS 1, Alto do Caparaó. Otherwise seek information from Ibama, T2916588, ext 119/122.*

Sleeping & eating

B *Caparaó Parque*, 2 km from the park entrance, 15 mins' walk from the town of Caparaó, nice, T7412559. Ask where **camping** is permitted in the park. In **Manhumirim**: **D** *São Luiz*, good value, but *Cids Bar*, next door, Trav 16 do Março, has better food.

Transport

Caparaó National Park is 49 km by paved road from Manhuaçu on the Belo Horizonte-Vitória road (BR-262). There are buses from Belo Horizonte (twice a day with Pássaro Verde), Ouro Preto or Vitória to **Manhumirim**, 15 km south of Manhuaçu. From Manhumirim, take a bus direct to Caparaó, 0930, 1630 US$1, or to Presidente Soares (several, 7 km), then hitch 11 km to Caparaó. By car from the BR-262, go through Manhumirim, Presidente Soares and Caparaó village, then 1 km further to the *Hotel Caparaó Parque*.

Teófilo Otôni

Phone code: 033
Population: 127,500

Situated 138 km from Governador Valadares, this is a popular buying spot for dealers of crystals and gemstones, with the best prices in the state. There are various hotels (**B**) and *Pousada Tio Miro* (**C**), R Dr Manoel Esteves 389, T35214343, which has a relaxed atmosphere. Recommended.

Transport Buses: from **Belo Horizonte** with *Gontijo*, US$15.50, *leito* US$29; to **Porto Seguro** via **Nanuque** (can break Belo Horizonte-Salvador journey here; **D** *Hotel Minas*, at the rodoviária, adequate, and others nearby).

Southern Minas Gerais

Juiz de Fora

Phone code: 032
Altitude: 695 m
117 km S of Barbacena
184 km N of Rio
Colour map 4, grid C3
Population: 424,500

This pleasant city lies on the Paraibuna river, in a deep valley between the Mar and Mantiqueira mountain chains. It is a good stopover on the route between Rio de Janeiro and the colonial cities or Belo Horizonte.

Tourist office *Secretaria de Desenvolvimento Econômico*, Avenida Rio Branco 3029, CEP 36010-012, T/F32155931, www.pjf.jfa.mg.gov.br

Juiz da Fora used to be known as the Manchester Mineira because it was the first city in Brazil to industrialize, principally through textiles. Another reason for the nickname was the widespread use of red brick as a building material. Nowadays there is no sign of the early industries nor of red brick and architecturally it is of little note. New industries like Mercedes Benz are being attracted to the city and Juiz is growing and changing fast.

The city centre is very busy commercially and the streets are a maze of shopping galleries. See especially the food shops selling sausages, fish and cheese. The main thoroughfare through the city centre is Avenida Barão do Rio Branco. Where this avenue meets Rua Halfeld is the Parque Halfeld. The junction is a major urban bus stop. Rua Halfeld is pedestrianized from Avenida Rio Branco to Avenida Getúlio Vargas; it is the banking as well as the main shopping street in the centre. The **Banco do Brasil** has a building close to the Rio Branco/Halfeld junction which was designed by Oscar Niemeyer (*Banco do Brasil* has another branch at the junction of Halfeld and Getúlio Vargas). Also on Rua Halfeld, at No 1179, is the **Teatro Municipal** (T32155255), opposite the Edifício São Joaquim.

Praça da Estação has good examples of Belle Epoque architecture, the station hall, the hotels *Príncipe* and *Renascença* and the Associação Comercial building. Also in this part of the city, at the railway end of Rua Halfeld, is the **Espaço Cultural Mascarenhas**, Avenida Getúlio Vargas 200 (T32297208). See the Portinari mural of tiles in the foyer of Edifício Clube Juiz de Fora, on Rua Halfeld.

On Avenida Rio Branco is the **Centro Cultural Pró-Música**, at No 2329, T32153951. It has a concert hall and art gallery. Each July, in conjunction with the Prefeitura and the business community, the centre promotes a festival of Música Colonial Brasileira, which is recommended. At No 3146 is the **Círculo Militar**, which is an interesting building. The **Centro de Estudos Murilo Mendes**, Avenida Rio Branco 3372, T32133931, is a small cultural centre which holds exhibitions, lectures, film shows, etc. It is part of the

Sights

Minas Gerais and Espírito Santo

Juiz da Fora

Sleeping		3 Hilton	6 Majestic	9 São Luiz	Eating
1 César Park		4 Imperial	7 Ritz Palace		1 Cantina do
2 Capri		5 Joalpa	8 São Jorge		Amigão

N

Not to scale

Universidade Federal de Juiz da Fora. It is dedicated to the work of the poet, Murilo Mendes, and has an exhibition on his links with famous painters (Picasso, Miró, Léger, Guignard, Portinari) and other poets (Cecília Meireles, Jorge de Lima). ■ *1300-1700 Mon-Fri.*

Museums The **Museu Mariano Procópio**, Rua Mariano Procópio, is in beautiful wooded grounds and has collections covering various stages of Brazilian history up to the New Republic. The room on Tiradentes, for example, has a huge painting by Pedro Américo de Figueiredo e Melo of his quartered body (1893). There are a great many objects and portraits from the Imperial period. It also houses some natural history, geology (including types of stones), paintings and sculpture. It is an enormous exhibition and a guide would be helpful to explain it all. In the grounds are a *cantina*, playground, lake, monkeys on an island and caged birds. ■ *Museum: 1200-1800 Tue-Sun. US$1. Grounds: 0800-1730 Tue-Sun. T32111145. The pedestrian entrance is on Rua Mariano Procópio, opposite the Mariano Procópio railway station. To get back to the centre, take any bus going to Av Rio Branco (for example No 606).*

There is a **railway museum** at Avenida Brasil 2001, next to the station. ■ *1300-1800 Tue-Fri, 1400-1800 Sat-Sun.* The Universidade Federal has a **Museu do Folklore** at Rua Santo Antônio 1112. ■ *1400-2100 Mon-Fri.*

Excursions An attractive train journey (25 km) from Estação Mariano Procópio (opposite the museum, Monday-Saturday), runs to South America's first hydro-electric power station at **Matias Barbosa** (return by bus, hourly).

Santos Dumont, 47 km north, is a town named after the aviator (see page 142). Some 17 km away is the *Fazenda Cabangu*, where he was born.

Mar de Espanha, 62 km east, is a charming 19th-century town with tame sloths in the trees. To get there, take a bus from Juiz da Fora rodoviária, one hour, six a day, US$4.50. **Rio Novo**, 48 km northeast, has colonial architecture and is renowned for its dairy produce.

Sleeping **AL** *César Park*, Av Getúlio Vargas 181, T/F32154898. Sauna, pool, parking, accepts credit cards. **A** *Joalpa*, R Afonso Pinto da Motta 29, between Av Rio Branco and Av Getúlio Vargas, T32156055. Sauna, pool, parking, credit cards accepted. **A** *Ritz Palace*, Av Barão do Rio Branco 2000, T32157300. Sauna, pool, parking, takes all credit cards except Amex. **B** *Imperial*, R Batista de Oliveira 605, T32157400. Popular business hotel in the centre, **C** without bath. **C** *São Luiz*, R Halfeld 360, T32151155. Art deco lobby, winter garden, TV, fridge, parking, good, helpful. **D** *Hilton*, Av Getúlio Vargas 483-99, near the junction with Batista de Oliveira, T32158112. Clean, polite. **D** *Majestic*, R Halfeld 284, T32155050. TV, cheaper without bath; also on this block of Halfeld are *São Jorge* and *Capri*. Many cheaper hotels on Av Getúlio Vargas, in **E** range, mostly short-stay.

Eating *Belas Artes*, Galeria Tte Belfort Arantes 26, entrance at Halfeld 631. Good. *Berttu's*, R Santo Antônio 572. Very good, mineira and international food. *Brasão*, Av Rio Branco 2262. Very smart. *Cantão Suíço*, R Santa Rita 557/59. Good self-service. *Cantina do Amigão*, R Santa Rita 552. Italian, good, including pizzas, T32152179 for home delivery. Others on same street and R São João Nepomuceno. *Le Beau Bistrot*, R Delfim Moreira 22. French bar/restaurant.

Bars & Best nightclub is *Clube Noturno Vila das Tochas*, R Roberto Stiegert 4, Bairro São
nightclubs Pedro. American bar, crêperie, dance floor. *Bar do Bené*, Pres Costa de Silva 2305, Bairro São Pedro. Friendly. *Prova Oral*, R A Braga 210. Highly recommended bar with live

music. For lots of bars, restaurants, pizzerias and nightlife, visit the Bairro São Mateus, bounded by Av Independência, R São Mateus, R Padre Café, R Monsenhor Gomes Freire with R Manoel Bernardino running down the middle.

Priscila Jóias, Galeria Solar, loja 228. Gold and silver workshop. Many interesting **Shopping** antique shops; plentiful regional foods.

Beijaflor, Shopping Santa Cruz, loja 1148, T32150249. French, Italian, some English **Tour operators** spoken. *Serra Branca*, R Aristóteles Braga 186, Cidade Universitária, T32311245. Local tours and to further afield in Minas Gerais. *Serra do Ibitipoca*, R Braz Bernardino 105, loja 212, Braz Shopping, T/F2163657, www.jfa.nutecnet.com.br/local/ibitipoca

Air Flights arrive at the small but modern airport, Av Guadalajara, T32331315. Flights **Transport** to **Belo Horizonte**, **Ipatinga** and **São Paulo**. Bus 520 on the hour to the centre.

Buses Local: town buses charge US$0.40. It is difficult to tell the routes because the route plaques are beside the back door entrance and cannot be seen as the bus approaches; you need to know the route numbers.

Long distance: the rodoviária is outside town on Av Brasil 4501, T32157696. Take bus 630 to town. Taxi to centre US$5. To/from **Rio**, many daily, *Útil*, US$5.50 *convencional*, US$6.75 *super* (a spectacular trip through mountains and tropical forest on an excellent, dualled highway); *Útil* to **Belo Horizonte**, frequent, US$9.15-11 (*Viaçao Útil*, T32153976, Rodoviária, or in town R Henrique Surerus 22, T32156759, Mon-Fri 0800-1800, Sat 0800-1200). To **São João del Rei** via Barbacena, 6 hrs, US$5; to **Conselheiro Lafaiete** (for Congonhas do Campo), US$5.75. To **Petrópolis**, 7 a day, 2 hrs, US$4.25. *Frota Nobre* to **Teresópolis** and **Nova Friburgo** once a day, US$4.80 and US$7.35 respectively. To **Foz do Iguaçu** with *Pluma*, US$40, via Londrina, Maringá and Cascavel, Tue, Thu, Sun 0800.

Airline offices *Nordeste/Rio Sul*, T32159184. *TAM*, T32331360. **Banks** *Banco 24* **Directory** *Horas*, Av Rio Branco 700. **Communications** Post office: at São João Nepomuceno 291. Telephone: Telemar, Av Rio Branco 2288. Another branch at R Halfeld 804. 0700-2200 Mon-Fri, 0700-1400 Sat. **Security** Take care if walking between Av Getúlio Vargas and the railway at night.

Parque Florestal de Ibitipoca

This park, 85 km from Juiz de Fora, contains quartzite caves, interesting rock *Altitude: 1,760 m* formations, many waterfalls, rivers, different types of vegetation, orchids, bromeliads, cactus and lots of lichens and flowers, such as purple *quaresmeiras*. Evidence suggests that it was under the sea at one time; more recently it was on the *bandeirantes'* trails (see box page 198). A little gold was found, but it was mostly micah that was taken out (there is quartzite everywhere you look).

Ibitipoca preserves birds and animals, including monkeys, which you will hear but not see. The French botanist Auguste St-Hilaire visited the area in 1822. To see all that the park has to offer takes four days. There are a number of trails of varying length; on the longest be prepared for stretches of up to eight hours (take water and protection against the sun). ■ *0800-1600, but you can stay overnight (see below). US$2.*

The nearest village, **Conceição de Ibitipoca**, is one of the oldest in Minas Gerais. Its church was built in 1768 and has original paintings on the ceiling. There is a statue of São Sebastião and a separate bell tower. The key for the church is at *Ibiti-Bike*. Mass is said once a month. Modern building in the village is giving it a messy look, but the park is definitely worth visiting.

Sleeping **Conceição**: there are various lodgings, including **C** per person *Estrela da Serra*, more expensive with TV and fridge, price includes breakfast and dinner; lunch costs US$10. A 4-star hotel is under construction outside the village. **Campsite** *Ibiti-Lua*, in the park itself is a campsite for 50 tents, with toilets, showers, restaurant/bar and car park. There are also various eating places. The local speciality is *pão de canela*. Also in the village, hand-dyed and woven bedspreads and handicrafts in wood are made.

Transport By unpaved road, 27 km, from Lima Duarte to Conceição de Ibitipoca. The road is rough and difficult in the wet, but in the dry season especially, ordinary cars can make it. From Conceição it is a 3 km walk (or hitchhike) to the park. Bus Frota Nobre from Juiz da Fora to Lima Duarte, 8 a day, US$2.10; bus Lima Duarte-Ibitipoca daily at 0700 and 1600. You can also take a tour from Juiz da Fora with the agency *Serra do Ibitipoca*, address above.

Towns and spas of southwestern Minas

Dec-Mar is the high season A group of popular spas are easily reached by road from Rio de Janeiro and São Paulo. Most of the hydro resorts lie south of the Dutra Highway (BR-381, Belo Horizonte-São Paulo). These are Cambuquirá, Lambari, São Lourenço and Caxambu, south of the town of Três Corações, which also gives access to the centre of São Tomé das Letras. Further west and north, on the Minas/São Paulo border is the much larger resort of Poços de Caldas. Some 240 km southwest of Belo is the huge lake formed by the Furnas Dam. It can be seen from the BR-381 road to São Paulo.

Tres Corações

Phone code: 035
Colour map 4, grid C2
Population: 64,000

The modern city of Tres Corações is a convenient place for making connections to the spas. It is the birthplace of Pelé, the legendary football star, to whom there is a statue in Praça Coronel José Martins.

The rodoviária is beside the old railway station where a steam engine is on show (the railway is used but there is no passenger traffic). On Avenida Getúlio Vargas is the Casa de Cultura Godofredo Rangel (Departamento de Turismo e Cultura and Library) at No 154. Praça Odilon Rua de Andrade has a post office and *Banco do Brasil* (no exchange facilities).

From Praça Martins Avenida Julião Arbex leads steeply uphill to a statue of Christ on top of a chapel on Praça Monsehnor Fonseca.

Sleeping **B** *Cantina Calabreza*, R Joaquim Bento de Carvalho 65, T/F32311183. Pool, sauna, has a reasonable restaurant (Italo-Brasileira), has a takeaway service. **D** *Capri*, Av Getúlio Vargas 111, not far from the bridge across the river, T32311427. With or without bath, simple but OK, TV in the more expensive rooms; nearer the bridge, at No 55, is the older *Avenida*. There are other, more basic hotels near the rodoviária.

Eating Opposite the *Cantina Calabreza* is the *Xodó*. *Quinta da Bock*, Av Getúlio Vargas, just up from *Hotel Capri*, open air restaurant and beer place. Opposite, above Bemge, is *Pizzeria Per Tutti*. Further up Av Getúlio Vargas, beyond the praça at No 363 is *Pizzeria Jardins*, cheap, good *executivo* menu and other dishes, popular, on 1st floor.

Transport There are 3 daily buses (2 on Sun) to **São Tomé das Letras**, US$1.65, 1½ hrs (the first 30 mins is on a paved road). To **Belo Horizonte**, *Gardénia*, 4 a day (3 on Sun), US$10.50,

5½ hrs, roadworks permitting. To **São Paulo**, *Transul*, 7 a day, US$8.10. *Beltour* runs buses to **Rio de Janeiro**; *Cristo Rei* to **Santos**.

São Tomé das Letras

São Tomé das Letras, 35 km from Três Corações, is a beautiful hilltop town which is very popular at weekends. At 1,291 m it is one of the five highest places in Brazil. The average maximum temperature is 26°C and the minimum is 14°C. The rainy season is October-March.

Phone code: 035
Colour map 4, grid C2
Population: 6,750

    Rock paintings found in caves have been dated to about 2000 BC. The inscriptions have lent the town a mystical reputation, attracting 'new age' visitors. Many believe it is a good vantage point for seeing UFOs (some claim that the inscriptions are extraterrestrial in origin) and that there are many places with special energies. The Carimbado cave is especially rich in myths and legends; its passages lead to an underground civilization; its powers form an energy source linked to Machu Picchu in Peru. Shangri-lá, which is a beautiful spot, is also called the Vale do Maytréia. The shops reflect this atmosphere and the hotels are classified by UFOs instead of stars! Whatever you think of it, São Paolo is certainly an unusual place. The **tourist office** is at R José Cristiano Alves 4.

A quarry town since the beginning of the 20th-century, there is evidence of the industry everywhere you look. Settlement in colonial times dates from the mid-to late-18th century when the *bandeirantes* from São Paulo moved into this area, displacing the indigenous Indians. Even before the 20th-century 'alternative' arrivals, the hill acquired a legend: at the end of the 18th century, an escaped slave hid in a cave for a long time. A finely dressed man appeared, asking him why he was living there. On hearing the slave's story, the man gave him a message on a piece a paper which, on presentation to his master, would earn the slave forgiveness. The slave duly did as the man said and the master, impressed by the writing and the paper, went to the cave to seek the mysterious man for himself. He found no one, but instead a statue of São Thomé (St Thomas). The master therefore built a chapel at the site, which was replaced by the Igreja Matriz in 1784, now standing beside the cave. The inscriptions, in red, can just about be seen in the cave; they are the 'Letras' of the town's name.

History

Minas Gerais and Espírito Santo

The spas of Minas Gerais & São Paulo

Sights The town is almost at the top of the hill. Behind it are rocky outcrops on which are the Pyramid House, the Cruzeiro (Cross, 1,430 m, with good 360° views), the Pedra da Bruxa and paths for walking or, in some parts, scrambling.

The bus stops at the main praça, on which is the frescoed 18th-century **Igreja Matriz** beside the fenced cave. A second church, the **Igreja das Pedras** (Nossa Senhora do Rosário, 18th century) is on a praça to the left as you enter town (Rua Ernestina Maria de Jesus Peixoto). It is constructed in the same style as many of the charming old-style buildings, with slabs of the local stone laid on top of each other without mortar.

Tours In the surrounding hills are many caves: Sobradinho, 12 km; Carimbado, 5 km; Gruta do Feijão, a short walk from town; Gruta da Bruxa, 6 km. Seven waterfalls are also close by, including: Cachoeira de Eubiose, 4 km; Véu de Noiva, 12 km; Paraíso, near Véu de Noiva; Vale das Borboletas; da Lua, 8 km; and do Flávio, 6 km. Also rapids such as Shangri-lá, 17 km, and Vale dos Gnomos, near the Vale das Borboletas. Some of these places make a good hike from the town, but you can also visit several in a day on an organized tour (car with four passengers): for example the waterfalls Flávio, Eubiose, Paraíso and Véu de Noiva, US$50; Shangri-lá, US$70; Vale das Borboletas, Gruta do Carimbado and Ladeira do Amendoim (a slope on which cars appear to run uphill when in neutral – like the one in Belo Horizonte), US$50. T32371283 or enquire at *Néctar* shop on Rua José Cristiano Alves. Tours run on weekends and holidays from the praça at 1000 and 1400 to waterfalls, caves, etc, T32371353 and ask for Jaime or Iraci.

Sleeping
There are lots of pousadas and rooms to let all over town.

Streets are hard to follow because their names can change from one block to the next; numbering is also chaotic

C *Pousada Arco-Iris*, R João Batista Neves 19, T/F32371212. Rooms and chalets, sauna, swimming pool. **D** per person *Sonhos II* (do Gê), Trav Nhá Chica 8, 32371235. Very nice, restaurant, swimming pool, sauna, television in rooms. Recommended. **E** per person *Hospedaria dos Sonhos I*, R Gabriel Luiz Alves. With bath, no TV, restaurant, shop, groups accommodated.

Clean accommodation, **D** per person, is available at the headquarters of the *Fundação Harmonia*, on the road to Sobradinho (4 km), Bairro do Canta Galo, São Tomé das Letras, CEP 37418-000, T32371280, or T0XX11-32043766 in São Paulo. The community emphasizes several disciplines and principles for a healthy lifestyle, for mind and body, 'new age', workshops, massage, excursions, vegetarian food (their shop is on the main praça. About 8 km on the road to Sobradinho is **B-D** *Rancho Paraíso*, T32371342. Lodging, campsite, restaurant, garden and trekking.

E per person *Mahã Mantra*, R Plínio Pedro Martins 48, T39895563. IYHA Youth hostel, open all year. Also **E** per person are *Pousada Baraunas*, R João Cristiano Alves 19, T33461330 and, next door, *Pousada Novo Horizonte*, at No 10.

Eating *O Alquimista*, R Capt Pedro Martins 7. *das Magas*, R Camilo Rosa. *Ximama*, Martins at the corner of G L Alves. Pizzas. *Veranda Pôr-do-Sol*, R Plínio Pedro Martins, comida caseira. Pizza. Two *Padarias Bom Dia*, 1 opposite the bus stop on the main Praça. There are many other restaurants and bars.

Transport If driving to the town, take care at the unsigned road junctions. After the pavement ends, at the next main junction, turn right. If going by bus, take the one that leaves Três Corações at dawn to see the mist in the valleys; schedule and fare are given under Três Corações.

Directory **Bank** *Bemge* in the main praça. **Communications** Post office: in the group of buildings at the top right of the praça, facing the Gruta São Tomé.

Hydro resorts

Some 20 km south of Três Corações by paved road, Cambuquirá's Parque das Águas is a hilly town with a pleasant atmosphere. Horse-drawn taxis ferry visitors around. Nearby *fazendas* sell *cachaça*.

Cambuquirá
Phone code: 035
Altitude: 946 m
Population: 13,000

Sleeping C *Santos Dumont*, Av Virgílio de Melo Franco 400, T32511466. **Transport** The São Paulo-Três Corações bus (*Gardênia*) passes through, US$8.10.

This is another hilly town, 27 km south of Cambuquirá. The Parque das Águas has seven mineral springs and mineral water swimming pools on Praça Conselheiro João Lisboa. ■ *0600-1800 daily*. There are boat trips on the Lago Guanabara and to Ilha dos Amores. The resort has a casino.

Lambari
Phone code: 035
Altitude: 900 m
Population: 19,000

Sleeping A *Parque Hotel*, R Américo Werneck 46, in the centre of town, T32712000 and B *Itaici*, R Dr Jos dos Santos 320, T/F32711366. **Transport** 4 buses a day run from Bresser station in São Paulo, US$8.10.

About 62 km southeast of Lambari, São Lourenço is easily accessible from Rio de Janeiro (5-6 hours by bus) or São Paulo (6-7 hours by bus). There is a splendid park, tennis, boating, swimming, a flying field, and fishing. Its rich mineral waters are used in the treatment of various medical complaints. The famous carbo-gaseous baths are unique in South America and can be found at **Parque das Águas**, Praça Brasil. ■ *0800-1700 daily*. There is a grand ride through fine scenery to the **Pico de Buqueré** at 1,500 m.

São Lourenço
Phone code: 035
Altitude: 850 m
Population: 35,000

Sleeping A *Emboabas*, Av Jorge Amado 350, T33324600. Restaurant. There are many others in all price ranges. **Camping** *Fazenda Recanto das Carvalhos*, BR-460 towards Pouso Alto, 10 km from town, T33322098.

The waters at Caxambu, 31 km northeast of São Lourenço, are used for treating stomach, kidney and bladder diseases, and are said to restore fertility (the Parque das Águas is closed on Monday). The waters seemed to work for Princess Isabel, daughter of Dom Pedro II, who produced three sons after a visit. The little church of Santa Isabel da Hungária (1868) stands on a hill as a thanks offering. The surrounding mountains and forests are very beautiful and there is a view over the city from Morro Caxambu, 1,010 m.

Caxambu
Phone code: 035
Altitude: 900 m
Population: 21,000

Sleeping About 3 km out of town is the charming B *Pousada Canto do Sabiá*, BR-354 towards Itamonte, T33413499. It has chalets and serves excellent breakfast. There are many other good hotels.

Poços de Caldas

The city is right on the São Paulo state border, some 150 km north of the hydro resorts around Lindóia. Sited at 1,180 m on the crater of an extinct volcano in a mountainous area, it has an excellent climate. The resort, a traditional honeymoon centre, has thermal establishments for the treatment of rheumatic, skin and intestinal diseases (you need a local doctor's certificate to use these facilities). Venetians from Murano settled here and established a crystal-glass industry.

Phone code: 035
Colour map 4, grid C2
(272 km to São Paulo
507 km to Rio
510 km to Belo
Horizonte)
Population: 124,000

Minas Gerais and Espírito Santo

Excursions These include the Véu das Noivas with its three waterfalls illuminated at night; the tall statue of Cristo Redentor at 1,678 m, which can be reached by cable car, hang gliders fly from here; Pedra Batão, an 80-m granite rock; and the Japanese teahouse at the Recanto Japonês. An arts and handicrafts fair is held every Saturday and Sunday in Praça Pedro Sanches.

Sleeping & eating
There are some 80 hotels and pensións

A *Novo Hotel Virgínia*, R Minas Gerais 506, T37222664. **A** *Palace*, Praça Pedro Sanches, T37223636. Old fashioned but well run, with sulphur baths. Good. Many others in this range, very few under US$50 a night (many more above it).

There are plenty of restaurants. All the good hotels have dining rooms. Local specialities are smoked cheese, sausages, sweets and jams (try squash-and-coconut).

Festivals *Carnival*; *São Benedito* 1-13 May; the *Festa UAI*, of popular *mineira* music and dance, foods and handicrafts is held in the second half of **Aug**.

Transport **Air** The town has an airport. A monorail runs down the main avenue, Av Francisco Sales, to the cable car station. **Buses** The rodoviária is 3 km from centre. **Rio**, 8 hrs, US$13.25; **São Paulo**, 4½ hrs, US$7.25.

Western Minas Gerais

Araxá
Phone code: 034
Altitude: 997 m
Population: 76,000

Situated in the Minas Triangle west of Belo Horizonte, Araxá has thorium and radioactive waters, sulphur and mud baths. The **L** *Grande Hotel Araxá* (where the springs and the ruins of the *Hotel do Rádio* are located) is 8 km from the town at **Estâncio do Barreiro**.

Sleeping *Grande Hotel Araxá*, Estâncio do Barreiro. Has been completely renovated while maintaining its 1940s-50s style and gardens designed by Burle Marx. It is now run by the Tropical chain (Av Paulista 1765, 1 andar, 01311-200, São Paulo, T/F0XX11-32532003, or T0XX34-36628001 for the thermal resort. **A** *Colombo*, Estâncio do Barreiro, T/F36624016. Pool, sports facilities. **A** *Virgilius Palace*, R Dr Franklin de Castro 545, T/F36625000. Restaurant. **C** *Imbiara*, Av Imbiara 356, T/F36612500.

Transport Bus from **Belo Horizonte**, *Gontijo*, US$12.65-23.50, depending on service. There is an airport.

Parque Nacional da Serra da Canastra

South of Araxá is the Serra da Canastra National Park, in which the Rio São Francisco rises. It is a cool region (temperatures in May and June average 18°C), comprising two ranges of hills, the Serra da Canastra and the Serra das Sete Voltas, with the Vale dos Cândidos between. The altitude ranges from 900 m to 1,496 m above sea level and the vegetation is mostly grassland, rising to high altitude plants on the uplands. Animals include the maned wolf, the great anteater, armadillos and deer. Birds that can seen in the park are rheas, owls, seriema, king vulture and the diving duck. There are also birds of prey, partridges and tinamous. Besides the source of the Rio São Francisco (6½ km from the São Roque park entrance), visitors can also see the two parts of the **Casca d'Anta waterfall**.
Park essentials Details on visiting the park can be obtained from Ibama in Belo Horizonte, Av do Contorno 8121, Cidade Jardim, CEP 30110-120, Belo Horizonte, T32916588, ext 119/122, or from Caixa Postal 01, CEP 37928-000 São Roque de Minas, T031-34331195. The park has a visitors' centre just inside the park, at the São Roque de Minas entrance. There are 3 other entrances, Casca d'Anta, São João Batista and Sacramento. All gates close at 1800.

Transport   The park is best reached from Piumhi, on the MG-050, 267 km southwest of Belo Horizonte (this road heads for Ribeirão Preto in São Paulo). From Piumhi you go to São Roque de Minas (60 km).

Uberaba

From Araxá the BR-262 heads 120 km west to Uberaba, also in the Minas Triangle on the Rio da Prata. It is an important road junction on the direct highway between São Paulo and Brasília and serves a large cattle-raising district. At the beginning of April each year the Rural Society of the Minas Triangle holds a famous cattle and agricultural exhibition at Uberaba.

Phone code: 034
485 km to São Paulo
Colour map 4, grid B1
Population: 240,500

Between Uberaba and Ponte Alta (31 km east on the BR-262) is **Peirópolis**, which is one of the world's most important palaeontological sites, with dinosaur remains, including eggs. The **Centro de Pesquisas Paleontológicas – Museu do Dinossauro** is 23 km east of Uberaba, at Km 784.5. ■ *0800-1800, 1100-1700 weekends. T9720023.*

Excursions

Sleeping **A** *Novotel*, Av Filomena Cartafina 150, off BR-050, 5 km from town, T33364288. Pool, restaurant. **A** *Pousada São Francisco*, on BR-330, 7 km from town, T33145553. Horse riding. **B** *Karajá*, Av Fernando Costa 146, T33361000. **C** *Porto Bello*, Av Barão do Rio Branco 1000, T/F33366701.

Transport   Bus from **Belo Horizonte**, US$15 (*leito* US$30), 7 hrs.

About 100 km north of Uberaba is Uberlândia, founded in 1888 as São Pedro do Uberabinha. It is a fast growing city with good communications by air and road. Several major bus routes (eg Campo Grande-Brasília) pass through here. There is a helpful **tourist information** kiosk in the rodoviária.

Uberlândia
Phone code: 034
Population: 439,000

Sleeping   **AL** *Plaza Inn Master*, R da Bandeira 400, T32398000, F2398100. Restaurant. **A** *Estância das Flores*, Km 166 BR-050, T32340120. Horse riding, fishing. **D** *Hotel Nacional*, Higino Guerra 273, opposite the rodoviária, T32354983. With view (cheaper without), shower and breakfast.

Transport   **Air**: Airport 8 km from town, T2125192. **Buses**: To **Brasília**, 6 hrs, US$9; To **Belo Horizonte**, 9 hrs, US$15; To **São Paulo**, US$18.

Directory   Airline offices   *Rio-Sul*, T32361414. *TAM*, T32531000.

Espírito Santo

Sandwiched between Rio de Janeiro, Minas Gerais and Bahia, the coastal state of Espírito Santo is relatively little known, except by mineiros *heading for the coast for their holidays. It has many beaches, but they are overshadowed by those of its northern and southern neighbours. There are a number of nature reserves and turtle breeding grounds in Espírito Santo, and European immigration has given the towns a distinctive atmosphere. The state capital, Vitória, is also the main industrial and commerical centre. People here are known as* Capixabas, *after a former Indian tribe.*

   Espírito Santo has a hot, damp seaboard with a more-or-less straight, low coastline and long beaches open to the Atlantic. In the south the vegetation is mainly of the restinga type, while the north is the broad coastal plain of the Rio Doce valley. In the far north of the state is an area of sand dunes. A mountainous interior in the south, the Serra da Chibata, gives way to the Rio Doce valley in the north.

Background Espírito Santo was one of the original captaincies created by the Portuguese in the 16th century, but their colony was very precarious in its early days. During the struggle for supremacy, the son of Mem de Sá (the governor in Bahia) was killed, but, as elsewhere, the invaders eventually prevailed. It was not as successful as some of the other captaincies because the Portuguese were unable to gain a foothold other than on the coastal plains. When the focus of attention moved away from the coast to the mines in Minas Gerais in the 18th and subsequent centuries, the state became strategically important. Initially it was not on the gold exporting route, but after iron mining began, a route from Belo Horizonte to Vitória was created. This remains one of the major economic corridors in the country.

Vitória

Phone code: 027
Colour map 4, grid C5
Population: 266,000

The town is beautifully set, its entrance second only to Rio's, its beaches are as attractive, but smaller, and the climate is less humid. Five bridges connect the island on which Vitória stands with the mainland.

Vitória dates from 1551 and takes its name from a battle won by the Portuguese over the Indians. There are a few colonial remnants, but it is largely a modern city and port. The upper, older part of town, reached by steep streets and steps, is much less hectic than the lower harbour area which suffers dreadful traffic problems. A rail connection westwards with Minas Gerais

Vitória

transports for export iron ore, coffee and timber. Port installations at Vitória and nearby Ponta do Tubarão have led to some beach and air pollution at places nearby. **Tourist information** *Cetur*, Avenida Princesa Isabel 54, T3228888, at airport T3278855 and at rodoviária (friendly, good free map). Also *Instituto Jones dos Santos Neves*, Av Marechal Campos 310, 3rd floor, Edif Vitória Center, CEP 29040-090, T3222033, ext 2215.

Sights

On Avenida República is the huge **Parque Moscoso**, an oasis of quiet, with a lake, playground and tiny zoo. Other parks are the **Morro da Fonte Grande**, a state park with good views from the 312-m summit, and the **Parque dos Namorados**, 6 km from the centre at Praia do Canto. Two islands reached by bridge from Praia do Canto are **Ilha do Frade** and **Ilha do Boi**.

Colonial buildings still to be seen in the city are the **Capela de Santa Luzia**, Rua José Marcelino in the upper city (1551), now an art gallery; the church of **São Gonçalo**, Rua Francisco Araújo (1766) and the ruins of the **Convento São Francisco** (1591), also in the upper city. In the **Palácio do Governo**, or **Anchieta**, Praça João Climaco (upper city) is the tomb of Padre Anchieta, the 16th-century Jesuit missionary and one of the founders of São Paulo. The **Catedral Metropolitana** was built in 1918 and stands in Praça Dom Luís Scortegagna. The **Teatro Carlos Gomes**, on Praça Costa Pereira, often presents plays, also jazz and folk festivals.

Vila Velha, reached by a bridge across the bay, has an excellent beach, but it is built up and noisy: take a bus from Vitória marked Vilha Velha. See the mostly ruined, fortified monastery of **Nossa Senhora da Penha**, on a high hill above Vila Velha; the views are superb. The Dutch attacked it in 1625 and 1640. There is also a pleasant ferry service to Vila Velha.

Beaches

Urban beaches such as **Camburi** can be affected by pollution (some parts of it are closed to bathers), but it is quite pleasant, with fair surf. South of the city is Vila Velha (see above), but for bigger waves go to **Barra do Jucu**, which is 10 km further south.

Excursions

The architecture and customs of the first German and Swiss settlers, who arrived in the 1840s, is preseved in the villages of **Santa Leopoldina** and **Domingos Martins**, both around 45 km from Vitória, less than an hour by bus (two companies run to the former, approximately every three hours). Domingos Martins (also known as Campinho) has a Casa de Cultura with some items of German settlement. (Hotels include **AL** *Pedra Azul*, BR-262 Km 88, T2481101, F2481201, which is part of the Roteiro de Charme hotel group, see page 47, and **B** *Imperador*, Praça Duque de Caxias 275, T/F2681115.) Santa

Morro da Fonte Grande

Altivo Viana

Pereira Pinto

Rua do Rosário

R Wilson Freitas

Itapemirim

G Dias

Av Governador Bley

Av Princesa Isabel

Praça Getúlio Vargas

P Blase

I Prado

A D Santos

Souza

Pinto Pacca

To Camburi, Tubarão & Airport

aça
io
XII

Av Marechal Mascarenhas de Moraes

B a í a   d e
V i t ó r i a

Minas Gerais and Espírito Santo

Leopoldina has an interesting museum covering the settlers' first years in the area. ■ *0900-1100 and 1300-1800 Tue-Sun.*

Population: 20,000

Santa Teresa is a charming hill town, a beautiful journey of 2½ hours, 90 km by bus, from Vitória (US$6). Among the hotels is **B** *Pierazzo*, Avenida Getúlio Vargas 115, T/F2591233, and there are many restaurants.

There is a unique hummingbird sanctuary at the **Museu Mello Leitâo**, Avenida José Ruschi 4, which is a library including the works of the hummingbird and orchid scientist, Augusto Ruschi. Hummingbird feeders are hung outside the library. ■ *0800-1200, 1300-1700. T2591182.* Also in the municipality is the **Dr Augusto Ruschi Biological Reserve** (formerly the Nova Lombardia National Biological Reserve), a forest rich in endemic bird species, including several endangered humming birds, Salvadori's antwren, cinnamon-vented Piha, russet-winged spadebill, Oustalet's tyrannulet, rufous-brown solitaire and hooded berryeater. Previous permission to visit must be obtained from *Ibama*, Avenida Marechal Mascarenhas de Moraes 2487, Caixa Postal 762, Vitória ES, CEP 29000.

Sleeping **AL** *Best Western Porto do Sol*, Av Dante Michelini 3957, Praia de Camburi, T3372244, F3372711. Overlooking the sea 7 km from the centre, with restaurant. **A** *Senac Ilha do Boi*, R Bráulio Macedo 417, Ilha do Boi, T3450111, F3450115. Government-run hotel school, luxurious, swimming pool, restaurant, on the ocean. **B** *Pousada da Praia*, Av Saturnino de Brito 1500, Praia do Canto, T/F2250233. Pool. **C** *Avenida*, Av Florentino Avidos 350, T2234317. With breakfast. Recommended. **C** *Vitória*, Cais de São Francisco 85, near Parque Moscoso. Excellent restaurant, changes money. Recommended. **D** *Europa*, 7 de Setembro, corner of Praça Costa Pereira. Noisy but cheap, good value restaurant (nearby is a good value vegetarian restaurant and a money changer, ask at the hotel). Adequate hotels can be found opposite the rodoviária. Other hotels are located in beach areas, Camburi to the north, Vila Velha to the south, both about 15 mins from city centre.

Youth hostels *Jardim da Penha*, R Hugo Viola 135, take Universitário bus, get off at the first University stop, T3240738. *Praia da Costa*, R São Paulo 1163, Praia da Costa, Vila Velha, T3293227. IYHA. *Príncipe Hotel*, Av Dario Lourenço de Souza 120, Ilha do Príncipe, T3222799, F2233392. IYHA.

Eating A local speciality is Moqueca capixaba, a seafood dish served in an earthenware pot. It is a variant of the moqueca which is typical of Bahia. *Lareira Portuguesa*, Av Saturnino de Brito 260, Praia do Canto, T3450329. Portuguese, expensive. *Mar e Terra*, opposite the rodoviária. Good food, live music at night. *Pirão*, R Joaquim Lírio 753, Praia do Canto. Regional food. *Lavacar* and many others at Praia Camburi offer food and live music.

Tour operators *Saytur*, Av Des Santos Neves 1425, T3251899, F3251391. American Express representative.

Transport **Air** Eurico Salles airport at Goiaberas, 11 km from the city, T3270811. There are flights to Belém, Belo Horizonte, Brasília, Guarapari, Maceió, Porto Alegre, Recife, Rio de Janeiro, Salvador and São Paulo.

The rodoviária is **Buses** **Rio**, 8 hrs, US$15 (*leito* 25). **Belo Horizonte**, US$14.50 (*leito* 29). **Salvador**,
15 mins' walk west 18 hrs, US$27; **Porto Seguro** direct 11 hrs with lots of stops, US$18 (also *leito* service);
of the centre alternatively, take a bus to Eunápolis, then change to buses which run every hour.

Car hire *Localiza*, Praça do Aeroporto, T3270211; at the airport T0800-992000; *Vila Velha*, Av Carlos Lindemberg 2707, T2004466.

Hitchhiking To hitch to **Salvador**, take a bus to Serra, which is 13 km beyond Carapina, itself 20 km north of Vitória; alight where the bus turns off to Serra.

Trains Daily passenger service to **Belo Horizonte**, 14 hrs, US$17.50 *executivo* (very comfortable), US$11.50 1st class, US$7.80 2nd.

Airline offices   *Rio Sul/Nordeste*, Av NS dos Navegantes 2091, conj 102, T2271588.   **Directory**
TAM, Av Fernando Ferrari 3055, Goiaberas, T3270868. *Transbrasil*, R José Teixeira 300,
Praia do Canto, T2253922, airport T3270308. *Varig*, Av Jerônimo Monteiro 1000, loja 3,
at airport T3270304. *Vasp*, R Desembargador Sampaio 40, T3241499, at airport,
T3270236. **Communications** Post office: Av Jerônimo Monteiro, between R
Gonçalves Ledo and R Quintino Bocaiúva. Telephone: Palácio do Café, Praça Costa
Pereira 52. **Embassies and consulates**   *Denmark*, R do Sol 141, Sala 210, T2224075,
open 0900-1300, 1500-1900. *Spain*, R Aristides Freire 22, Centro, T2232846. **Medical
services**   *Santa Casa*, R Dr Jones de Santos Neves 143, T3220074.

South of Vitória

Cachoeiro do Itapemirim a busy city on both banks of the fast-flowing Rio   **Cachoeiro do**
Itapemirim. **Cachoeira Alta** with a natural swimming pool is 38 km away on   **Itapemirim**
the road to Castelo.   *Population 150,000*

Sleeping and eating **A** *Mirante*, R Antônio Caetano Gonçalves 45, T/F5215588.
A *Rio Grande*, Av Beira-Rio 199, T/F5211980. **A** *San Karlo*, Av Beira-Rio 65, T5210755,
F5225737. Restaurant. For eating, try **Belas Artes**, Praça Jerônimon Monteiro 77.

Directory Banks: Banco do Brasil, Praça Jerônimon Monteiro 26. Bradesco, R Capt
Deslandes 68.

Some 54 km south of Vitória on the coast road is Guarapari whose beaches are   **Guarapari**
the closest to Minas Gerais, so they get very crowded at holiday times,   *Phone code: 027*
escpecially mid-December to the end of February. The beaches also attract   *Colour map 4, grid C4*
many people seeking cures for rheumatism, neuritis and other complaints   *Population: 74,000*
from the radioactive monazitic sands. Information about the sands can be
found at the Casa de Cultura (see below), the former seat of the prefeitura,
which was built in 1749 (open from 1300), and at the Antiga Matriz church on
the hill in the town centre, built in 1585 by Padre Anchieta. **Tourist information**: at Rua Davino Matos, Praça da Gratidão, T2612151. *Setuc*, in the Casa
de Cultura, Praça Jerônimo Monteiro, T2613058.

Sleeping **AL** *Flamboyant*, Km 38 Rod do Sol, T/F2290066. Fazenda hotel with fishing
and horse riding. **A** *Atlântico*, Av Edísio Cirne 332, Praia dos Namorados, T/F3611551,
atlantic@escelsa.com.br   Recommended. **A** *Best Western Porto do Sol*, Av Beira Mar 1,
Praia do Morro, T3611100, F2612929. Mediterranean-style village on a rocky point
overlooking a calm beach, pool, sauna. Recommended. **A** *Vieira*, R Joaquim da Silva
Lima 310, T3611122, F2611056. Recommended. **B** *Bom Jesus*, R Pedro Caetano 156,
T2611184. Breakfast, fan, simple, central, good. Recommended. **B** *Costa Sul*, R Getúlio
Vargas 101. Breakfast, loads of mosquitoes, otherwise recommended. **B** *do Angelo*, R
Pedro Caetano 254, T/F2610230. Restaurant. Recommended. **Youth hostel** IYHA
hostel at *Guara Camping*, R Antônio Guimarães s/n, quadra 40, Praia de Itapessu,
T2610475, F2610448: turn left out of the rodoviária, then right and right again, past
Pousada Lisboa, 2 blocks, across a dual carriageway (Av Jones de Santos Neves), 1
block to the campground, US$10 with good breakfast. Recommended.
   Camping   *Camping Clube do Brasil*, Setiba beach, 9 km from centre, T2621325.

Eating   *Guaramare*, Km 65 Rod do Sol, T2721300. Fish, expensive. Regional food at
Praia de Meaípe, 8 km south: *Cantinho do Curuca*, Av Santana 96 and *Gaeta*, Av
Santana 46.

Minas Gerais and Espírito Santo

Transport Buses: Alvorada has a separate rodoviária from Itapemirim/Penha, Sudeste, São Gerardo and others. They are close together, 15 mins' walk from the city centre or US$5 by taxi. Penha tickets are sold at *R-Tur Turismo*, in the centre at R Manoel Severo Simões and R Joaquim da Silva Lima where air tickets, free brochures, maps, and hotel addresses can also be obtained. To **Vitória**, 1 hr with *Sudeste*, US$2. To **Rio** with *Itapemirim*, 2 a day, US$12.

Directory Banks: Banco 24 Horas, Praça do Coronado, Praia da Areia. *Banco do Brasil*, R Joaquim da Silva Lima 550. *Bradesco*, R Henrique Coutinho 901.

Ubu   A little further south (20 km) is the fishing village of Ubu with calm waters and clear sand.

Sleeping and eating A *Pousada Aba Ubu*, R Manoel Miranda Garcia, T/F3450187, abaubu@tropical.com.br Restaurant, half board. **B** *Pontal de Ubu*, R Gen Oziel 1, T2613111. Good regional food at *Peixada do Garcia*, Av Magno Ribeiro Muqui and *Peixada do Menelau Garcia*, Av Mário Neves.

Anchieta   About 8 km further down the coast is Anchieta, with the **Igreja de Nossa Senhora da Assunão** (1569) and a museum. Nearby Praia de Castelhanos is 5 km east, on a peninsula. One of the attractions of Anchieta is to take a boat up the Rio Benaventes at dusk to see the egrets coming in to roost. The trip takes about 15 minutes and boatmen from the Colônia da Pesca charge about US$20 return.

Sleeping A *Pousada dos Castelhanos*, Rod do Sol 2679, T/F5361427. **A** *Thanharu Praia*, R Jovina Serafim dos Anjos, T/F5361246. Half-board, good. **B** *Porto Velho*, Av Carlos Lindenberg 183, T/F5361181.

Iriri & Piúma   Close by is Iriri, a small village in a beautiful setting with two beaches, Santa Helena and Inhaúma. There are a few hotels (**A-B**) at Praia Costa Azul. Lodging in private houses is possible. A regular bus runs from Guarapari.

The next spot down the coast, 5 km, is Piúma, a calm, little-visited place, renowned for its craftwork in shells. The skill has been passed down through generations of craftsmen and women. The name derives from the Indian word *pium*, meaning mosquito. About 3 km north of the village is Pau Grande beach, where you can surf.

Sleeping in Piúma B *Pousada Haras Monte Agha*, R das Castanheiras, T/F5201363. Fazenda hotel with horse riding. **B** *Solar de Brasília*, Av Eduardo Rodrigues 15, Praia Acaiaca, T/F5201521. **Campsite** *Mar a Mar*, Av Beira Mar 645, Praia da Piúma, T5201463.

Marataízes   The resort town of Marataízes, with good beaches, is 30 km south of Piúma
Colour map 4, grid C4   and just north of the Rio state border.

Sleeping A *Saveiros Palace*, Av Miramar 119, on the beach, T5321413, F5321285. **A** *Praia*, Av Atlântica 99, on the beach, T5322144, F5323515. **B** *Dona Judith*, Av Lacerda de Aguiar 353, T5321436, F5321305. **Camping** Municipal site on Praia do Siri, 9 km south of the centre, T3252202.

Directory Banks: Banco do Brasil, Av Lacerda de Aguiar 356.

North of Vitória

The ES-010 road follows the coast from Vitória north to the mouth of the Rio Doce. It passes beaches such as Manguinhos and Jacaraípe and the town of Nova Almeida before reaching Santa Cruz, 60 km north of the state capital. The town, at the mouth of the Rio Piraquê-Açu, depends economically on cellulose factories, which have been the subject of an international outcry over child labour. It is a simple place, with few facilities. The coast around Santa Cruz, called **Aracruz**, has several good beaches, mostly undeveloped, which are tranquil and uncrowded.

Santa Cruz

Sleeping **A** *Pousada dos Cocais*, Praia de Sauê, T/F2501515. Restaurant, pool. **B** *Coqueiral Praia Park*, Praia do Coqueiral, 6 km along the road to Barra do Riacho, T2501214. A/c, TV, restaurant, pool, pretty location. **C** *Pousada das Pedras*, Praia dos Padres, T2501716. There are pousadas at Praia Formosa, 3 km south of town, and campsites at Barra do Sahy, Praia do Putiry and Formosa beaches.

Turtle beaches

The **Reserva Biológica Comboios**, 44 km north of Santa Cruz, is designed to protect the marine turtles which frequent this coast. Three species use this long stretch of sand backed by *restinga* to lay their eggs, the leatherback, the green (*araunã*) and the *cabeçuda*, for which this is the prime nesting ground on the Brazilian seaboard. ■ *Contact Ibama, Av Marechal Mascarenhas 2487, Caixa Postal 762, CEP 29000, Vitória, or T2641452.*

Regência, at the mouth of the Rio Doce, 65 km north of Santa Cruz, is part of the reserve and has a regional base for **Tamar**, the national marine turtle protection project. On the north shore of the mouth of the Rio Doce is Povoação, which also has a Tamar office (Caixa Postal 105, CEP 29900-970, Lagoa do Monsorá, Povoação, Linhares, ES). Regência is popular with sailors, anglers, divers and surfers.

The town of Linhares, 143 km north of Vitória on the Rio Doce, has good hotels and restaurants. It is a convenient starting place for the turtle beaches. Besides those at the mouth of the Rio Doce, there is another Tamar site at **Ipiranga**, which is 40 km east of Linhares by an unmade road. ■ *For information on the turtles, also contact Tamar at Caixa Postal 105, CEP 29900-970, Linhares, ES.*

Linhares
Colour map 4, grid B5

Sleeping **B** *Linhatur*, R Augusto Pestana 1274, T3710300, F3711445. **B** *Pratti Park*, R Rufino de Carvalho 793, T/F3711866. Pool. **C** *Virgínia*, R Gov Santos Neves 919, T/F2641699. At **Pontal do Ipiringa**: **C** *Paraíso*, Av do Sol, T9843477. Pool

Linhares is close to two other nature reserves: the **Linhares Reserve** owned by CVRD (the former state-owned mining company, now privatized) is possibly the largest remaining lowland tract of Atlantic forest; permission from the reserve's director must be obtained to visit. There is very good bird-watching in the reserve; specialities include red-billed curassow, minute hermit, rufous-sided crake, blue-throated (ochre-cheeked) parakeet, black-billed scythebill and black-headed berryeater.

Linhares & Sooretama reserves

The **Sooretama Biological Reserve**, some 45 km north of Linhares and 65 km south of Conceição da Barra, on the BR-101, protects tropical Atlantic rain forest and its fauna and birds (it contains several bird species not found in the Linhares Reserve). Much of the wildlife is rare and endangered. Both Sooretama and Linhares have orchids apparently not found anywhere else. It was protected in 1969. With year-round tropical humidity, vegetation here is dense with ancient trees reaching over 40 m in height. Two rivers, the Barra Seca and the Cupido, cross the reserve and, together with Lagoa Macuco, provide marshlands which attract migratory birds as well as numerous resident flocks. ■ *The reserve is strictly monitored by Ibama and is not open to the public, but drivers and cyclists can cut across it by road. For authorization to visit, researchers should phone T3740016.*

São Mateus, 88 km north of Linhares, is a pleasant town. It is 13 km from good beaches at Guriri, which is another Tamar base (Caixa Postal 130.153, CEP 29930-000 São Mateus, T027-7611267).

Conceição da Barra
Phone code: 027
Colour map 4, grid B5
Population: 25,500

The most attractive beaches in the State, however, are around Conceição da Barra, 261 km north of Vitória. It is an organized town which welcomes visitors. Many come in summer and for Carnival, otherwise it is quiet. Viewed from its small port, the sunsets are always spectacular. Corpus Christi (early June) is celebrated with an evening procession for which the road is decorated with coloured wood chips.

Sleeping and eating There are pleasant beach hotels. **D** *Caravelas*, Av Dr Mário Vello Silvares 83, 1 block from the beach, T7621188. Basic, shared bathroom, light breakfast. Recommended. **E** *Pousada Pirámide*, next to rodoviária, T7621970. Owner Lisete Soares speaks English, good value, 100 m from beach. Recommended. *Camping Clube do Brasil* site with full facilities, Rod Adolfo Serra, Km 16, T7621346. *Tia Teresa*, R Dr Mário Vello Silvares 135. Brazilian food, self-service, good value.

Itaúnas
Itaúnas, 27 km north by road, is an interesting excursion (it has some *pousadas* and a small campsite). The small town has been swamped by sand dunes, 30 m high and has been moved to the opposite river bank. There is now a fantastic landscape of huge dunes and deserted beaches. From time to time, winds shift the sand dunes enough to reveal the buried church tower. The theory is that the sudden encroachment of the sands in the 1970s was caused by massive deforestation of the surrounding area. The coast here, too, is a protected turtle breeding ground (Tamar, Caixa Postal 53, Conceição da Barra, T7621124). Buses three to four times a day from Conceição da Barra.

Meleiras beach, 3 km south, is accessible only on foot or by boat (one of a number of pleasant trips). It is 12 km long and offers fabulous diving and fishing. **Guaxindiba**, 3 km north, is partially developed, with hotels and restaurants, but the natural vegetation is still intact.

Sleeping **A** *Barramar Praia*, Av Atlântica 3000, T7621311, F7621312. **A** *Praia da Barra*, Av Atlântica 350, T/F7621100. **B** *Pousada Gandia*, Av Atlântica 1054, T/F7621248. **B** *Pousada Mirante*, Av Atlântica 566, T/F7621311.

Transport **Buses**: bus from the *padaria* in Conceição da Barra at 0700, returns 1700.

Iguaçu Falls and the South

Introducing Iguaçu Falls and the South

The states of **Paraná**, **Santa Catarina** and **Rio Grande do Sul** form the subtropical south, where European immigration has had a strong influence. The Iguaçu Falls, one of Latin America's major natural attractions, is on most people's itinerary; nearby is the **Itaipu Dam**, one of the largest man-made constructions in the world. The scenic railway journey from **Curitiba to Paranaguá** runs through the beautiful coastal range of mountains and is also well worthwhile. The area around **Florianópolis** has some wonderful beaches, especially for surfers. Inland is the town of **Blumenau**, with its German architecture and lively **Oktoberfest**. The wine region of **Caxias do Sul** and the beautiful scenery around **Canela** are both popular. The pampas cowboy culture of the **Gaúchos** is strong around Port Alegre and the borders with Uruguay and Argentina. In the west there are the remains of the Jesuit missions long abandoned by their founders.

PARAGUAY

ARGENTINA

Uruguaiana

Barra do Quaraí

Bella Unión

Santana Do Livramento

Rivera

URUGUAY

Things to do in Iguaçu Falls and the South

① Charter a fishing boat to see the sea lions of Ilha dos Lobos during the winter months.

② Visit the tranquil sands of Praia da Rosa, the country's prime whale-watching site, where calving takes place between June and November.

③ Bring a blanket and spend the night at a beach party at Praia do Mole on the island of Santa Catarina.

④ Fish, hunt, shoot and ride or even work at one of the *fazendas* around Lages that provides rustic farm accommodation and rural activities.

⑤ At Monte Belo do Sol walk through the pretty vineyards, or take a steam train for a 'wine run' with a live band and local wine.

Paraná

Population: 9.5 million

Paraná has one of the premier tourist sites in South America, the Iguaçu Falls. No guidebook can do justice to the spectacle of the magnificent cataratas; they are a must on any itinerary to Brazil, or Argentina for that matter. The state has a short coastline and its main port, Paranaguá, is connected with the capital, Curitiba, by one of the best railways in South America. Curitiba itself is a pleasant, progressive city. The culture of Paraná has been heavily influenced by its large immigrant communities and its economy is principally agricultural.

The area of what is now Paraná was neglected by the Portuguese until the beginning of the 17th century when gold was discovered. The region fell under the control of São Paulo, but there was no great success in the extraction of gold, partly because Indian labour was unavailable to work the finds (they had all been sent elsewhere or had died of disease). As soon as the Minas Gerais gold was discovered, this aspect of Paraná's economy was abandoned. Instead, the colonists turned to agriculture and cattle-raising and, in the 18th and 19th centuries, *fazendeiros* and drovers were the dominant people of Paraná. Until 1853, the area was controlled from São Paulo. When the new province was created, cattle and *mate* growing were the most important activities, but to this was added timber at the end of the 19th century, with the coming of the railways.

When it was realized in the second half of the 19th century that the province of Paraná would not develop without a major increase in the population, an official immigration policy was launched. The Italians were the first, but later settlers came from Germany, Poland, the Ukraine, France, England, Holland, and, since the beginning of the 20th century, from Japan, Syria, the Lebanon and Jews.

Curitiba

Phone code: 041
Colour map 5, grid A4
Population: 1.6 million
Altitude: 908 m

Situated in the Serra do Mar, Curitiba is regarded as one of Brazil's model cities for quality of life. It has something of a European feel, with leafy squares and a street that is open 24 hours. It makes a pleasant base for exploring the coast and the surrounding mountains, and is the start of one of the world's most spectacular railway journeys.

Ins & outs
See also Transport, page 292

International and domestic flights usually arrive at Afonso Pena Airport. There are buses to the centre and bus station as well as taxis. International and interstate buses arrive at the Terminal Rodoviário on Av Afonso Camargo.

There is an integrated transport system with several types of bus route; pick up a map for details.

Tourist information

The Department of Tourism is at R da Glória 362, 3rd floor, T3528000, with an information kiosk at R 24 Horas, open 0800-2400 (closes 2200 weekends), T3247036. *Disque Turismo*, T1516 (for the state), T352 8000 (for the city). There are also booths at the Rodoferroviária and the airport (T3811153), helpful, English spoken, but no maps. *Paranatur*, R Deputado Mário de Barros 1290, 3rd floor, Centro Cívico, Edif Caetano Munhoz da Rocha, T2546933, www.pr.gov.br/turismo Free maps from R Ebano Pereira 187, 5th floor. Free weekly leaflet, *Bom Programa*, available in shops, cinemas, paper stands etc. *Guía Turística de Curitiba e Paraná*, annual, US$4, on sale at all kiosks, has been recommended.

Background

The state capital Curitiba was founded on 29 March 1693 in the spot which is now Praça Tiradentes, and was known as Vila Nossa Senhora da Luz dos Pinhais. For many years it was used as a stopping place for cattle herders travelling from Rio Grande do Sul to cattle fairs in São Paulo state and on to the mining towns of Minas Gerais. In 1842 it was elevated to the rank of city and given the name of Curitiba, and in 1853 it was made the state capital.

With the influx of European immigrants in the 19th and 20th centuries, Curitba is now a modern city on the plateau of the Serra do Mar. Prized as one of the three cleanest cities in Latin America, it has a rate of green area as high as 52 sq m per inhabitant. There is some exceptionally attractive modern architecture. The new opera house, Rua 24 Horas, the green house in the Botanical Garden and several of the larger 'tubo' bus stations all share the same semi-circular arch-steel-tube-and-glass style. Parks are well-manicured and the 'tubo' bus system, somewhat Metrô-like, trades a little in speed for more complete coverage of the entire city.

The city clearly benefits from the Itaipú hydroelectric plant in terms of spending on public works, but it has also benefited from integrated urban planning, which has made it one of the more pleasant Brazilian cities in which to live. In outlying areas, **Ruas da Cidadania**, 'citizenship streets', or malls, have been built next to bus stops to provide municipal services, shops, child care and leisure activities so that local people avoid the need to travel to the centre. These streets are of a colourful, vibrant design, the first of which was built at **Boqueirão**. Another, more central, is **Rua da Cidadania da Matriz**, which was inaugurated in 1997 next to the Praça Rui Barbosa transport terminal, with the added innovation of having 20 computer terminals for free access to the internet.

Sights

A panoramic view can be had from the glass observation deck of the telecommunications tower, **Torre Mercês**, built by Telepar and so also called the **Telepar Tower**, Rua Jacarezinho, on the corner with Rua Professor Lycio Veloso 191. The 109.5-m tower stands at an elevation of 940.5 m above sea level. There is a map of the city on the floor so that you can locate key sites. ■ *1230-2030, Tue-Fri, 1030-2030 Sat, Sun and holidays. US$1.50. T3228080.*

The commercial centre is the busy Rua 15 de Novembro, part of which is a pedestrian area called **Rua das Flores**. Since urban planning first began in 1720, the Rua das Flores has been a place for street happenings and is now well decorated with flowers and trees, with benches, cafés and restaurants, cinemas and shops. The **Boca Maldita** is a particularly lively part and a good meeting place. Another pedestrian area behind the cathedral, near Largo da Ordem, with a flower clock and old buildings, is very beautiful in the evening when the old lamps are lit – nightlife is concentrated here. There is an art market on Saturday morning in the **Praça Rui Barbosa**, and an even better one on Sunday morning in **Praça Garibáldi**, beside the attractive Rosário church.

The **Centro Cívico** is at the end of Avenida Dr Cândido de Abreu, 2 km from the centre: a monumental group of buildings dominated by the **Palácio Iguaçu**, headquarters of the state and municipal governments. In a patio behind it is a relief map to scale of Paraná. The **Bosque de João Paulo II**, behind the Civic Centre on Rua Mateus Leme, was created in December 1980 after the Pope's visit to Curitiba. It also contains the **Memorial da Imigração Polonesa no Paraná** (Polish immigrants memorial). In contrast to the Civic Centre is the old municipal government building in French Art Nouveau style, now housing the Museu Paranaense in Praça Generoso Marques.

All that remains of the magnificent old **Palácio Avenida**, on Travessa Oliveira Belo 11, T3216249, is the façade, which was retained during remodelling works in 1991. Nowadays it has a completely modern interior, with banks, offices, an auditorium for 250 people and various cultural activities. The **Solar do Barão** is another old building, built in 1880-83 as a home for the Baron of Serro Azul. Today it is used as a centre for art and leisure, with concerts in the auditorium, exhibitions and courses, Rua Presidente Carlos Cavalcanti 533, T3221525. The **Teatro Paiol**, south of the centre on Rua Coronel Zacarias next to Praça Guido Viaro, was built in 1906 as a depository for gunpowder, and its round construction has a defensive, military feel to it. It has been a theatre since 1971. ■ *T3221525*. In contrast, the **Teatro Guaíra** has always been a theatre. First built in 1884 as the Teatro São Teodoro, the present building dates from 1953 and has three auditoria of different sizes. ■ *R 15 de Novembro, T3222628.*

The **Ópera de Arame** and the **Pedreira Paulo Leminski** lie north of the centre on the site of an old stone quarry. The pit has been transformed into a site of major cultural importance where open air shows and concerts are held. It has a capacity to entertain up to 70,000 people and it was here that the tenor, José Carreras, gave his first performance in Brazil in March 1993, to celebrate

N
Not to scale

Sleeping		
1 Bourbon & Tower	4 Curitiba Palace	8 Lancaster
2 Cervantes	5 Del Rey	9 O'Hara
3 Costa Brava Palace	6 Estação Palace	10 Slaviero Palace
	7 Inca	11 Tibagi

Curitiba's 300th anniversary. The opera house itself is a beautiful tubular structure, circular, with a glass and metal dome, which radiates light when performances are held at night.

Another example of the use of tubular steel and glass is the arcade of **Rua 24 Horas**. The street's two clocks use the 24-hour system and the bars and cafes (all very similar) never close. The theme of light, glass and space is developed further in education. Attached to several schools are **Faroles de Saber**, lighthouses of knowledge, which are modular 5,000-book libraries with a lighthouse tower, a beacon on top and a guard.

The most popular public park is the **Passeio Público**, in the heart of the city **Parks** (closed Monday), with three lakes, each with an island, and a playground.

On the northeast edge of the city **Parque do Barigüi** (take bus 450 'São Braz' from Praça Tiradentes) contains an exhibition centre, amusement park, football, volleyball, churrascarias, a lake and lots of other entertainments. Near the shores of Lagoa Bacacheri, on the northern edge of the city (Rua Nicarágua 2453), is an unexpected Egyptian temple. Visits can be arranged to the Brazilian centre of the Rosicrucians; take Santa Cândida bus to Estação Boa Vista, then walk.

About 4 km east of the rodoferroviário, the **Jardim Botânico Fanchette Rischbieter** has a fine glass house, again with domes, curves and lots of steel, inspired by Crystal Palace in London. The gardens are in the French style and there is also a **Museu Botánico**, Rua Ostoja Roguski (Primeira Perimetral dos

Bairros), T3218646. It can be reached by the orange *Expreso* buses from Praça Rui Barbosa.

Other parks include: **Bosque João Carlos Hartley Gutierrez**, Rua Jacarezinho between Vista Alegre and Mercês, where there is a memorial to Chico Mendes; **Bosque de Portugal**, Rua Osório Duque Estrada, corner with Rua Fagundes Varela, with Portuguese architecture and some lovely hand painted tiles; **Bosque Alemão**, between Ruas Franz Schubert, Nicollo Paganini and Francisco Schaffer, where there is an Oratório Bach, used for concerts, and tile murals depicting the Hansel and Gretel fairy tale. **Parque Tingüi**, between Ruas Fredolin Wolf and José Valle, named after an Indian tribe who lived in the area, contains a **Memorial da Imigração Ucraniana**, in honour of one of the main sources of immigration to the city, and a replica of the church of São Miguel Arcanjo.

Iguaçu Falls and the South

12 Tourist Universo

● **Eating**
1 Happy Rango

2 Jangil
3 Saccy

● **Bars**
4 Fire Fox

Churches On Praça Tiradentes is the **Cathedral**. It was originally a small wooden chapel, which was elevated to the Primeira Igreja Matriz in 1715, but improvements in the colonial style of construction led to cracks appearing and in 1875 it had to be demolished. The present cathedral, built in neo-Gothic style and inaugurated in 1893, was restored in 1993 and promoted to Catedral Basílica Menor de Curitiba. ■ *Rua Barão do Serro Azul 31, T2221131.*

The oldest church in Curitiba is the **Igreja de Ordem Terceira de São Francisco das Chagas**, built in 1737 in Largo da Ordem. Its most recent renovation was in 1978-80. In its annex is the **Museu de Arte Sacra**. ■ *T2237545.* The **Igreja de Nossa Senhora do Rosário de São Benedito** was built in the Praça Garibáldi in 1737 by slaves and was the Igreja dos Pretos de São Benedito. It was demolished in 1931 and a new church was inaugurated in 1946. There is a mass for tourists, Missa do Turista, which is held on Sundays at 0800.

Museums **Museu Paranaense**, Praça Generoso Marques, was founded in 1876 by Agostinho Ermelino de Leão, although it has not always been at this location. The collection of exhibits includes documents, manuscripts, ethnological and historical material, stamps, works of art, photographs and archaeological pieces. ■ *0930-1730 Tue-Fri, 1300-1800 Sat-Mon, closed 1st Mon of each month. T3231411.* **Museu de Arte Contemporânea**, Rua Desembargador Westphalen 16, Praça Zacarias, displays Brazilian contemporary art in its many forms, with an emphasis on artists from Paraná. ■ *0900-1900 Tue-Fri, 1400-1900 Sat-Sun, T2225172.* **Casa Andersen**, Rua Mateus Leme 336, is the painter's house. ■ *0900-1200, 1400-1800 Mon-Fri.* **Museu de Arte do Paraná**, in the Palácio São Francisco, was built in the 1920s for the Garmatter family and used in 1938-53 as the Governor's palace. The museum dates from 1987 and exhibits the work of many of Paraná's artists. ■ *T2343172.* **Museu da Imagem e do Som**, Rua Barão do Rio Branco 395, was created with the aim of preserving audiovisual and photographic memories of Paraná. ■ *T2329113.* **Museo do Automóvel**, Avenida Cândido Hartmann 2300, has a collection of cars dating from as early as 1910 to the McLaren of Emerson Fittipaldi. ■ *1400-1800 Sat, 1000-1200, 1400-1800 Sun.* **Museu de História Natural**, Rua Benedito Conceição 407, is a natural history museum with lots of zoology and scientific collections of things like spiders, insects and parasites, which also has details on endangered species in the state. ■ *T3663133.*

Essentials

Sleeping **L** *Bourbon & Tower*, R Cândido Lopes 102, T3224001. Most luxurious in centre, grand
■ *on map, page 288* and enormous, with a distinctly old-fashioned air. **A** *Lancaster*, R Voluntários da Pátria
Price codes: 91, T/F3228953. Covered in wood-panelling, sedate and very comfortable, caters to
see inside front cover business clients as well as tourists. **A** *Slaviero Palace*, Sen Alencar Guimarães 50,
T3227271, F2222398. Central, conservatively decorated with cosy lobby bar.

There are some **B** *Costa Brava Palace*, R Francisco Torres 386, T2627172. Good restaurant. Recom-
incredibly good-value mended. **B** *Curitiba Palace*, R Ermelino de Leão 45, T3228081, F3223356,
hotels in the city in the curitibapalace@cwb.palm.com.br Central, polished and cosy with vast rooms, 24-hr
B and C categories restaurant, pool, good value. **B** *Del Rey*, R Ermelino de Leão 18, T/F3223242. In heart of
the city, on main R das Flores. Upmarket yet relaxed, large rooms, good restaurant. Fantastic value. Recommended. **B** *Tibagi*, R Carlos de Carvalho 9, T2233141, F2331811.
Central business hotel.

C *King's*, Av Silva Jardim 264, T3228444. Good apartment hotel, secure. Highly recommended. **C** *Nova Lisboa*, Av 7 de Setembro 1948, T2641944. With breakfast, bargain for cheaper rates without breakfast. Recommended. **C** *O'Hara*, R 15 de Novembro

770, T2326044. Good location, fan, excellent breakfast, parking. **C** *Paraty*, R Riachueto 30, T2231355. Central, apartments with kitchen, with breakfast, clean, spacious, good. **C** *Tourist Universo*, Praça Gen Osório 63, T3220099, F2235420. On one of the city's most attractive squares, in centre. Very smart for price, with sauna and pool. Intimate and excellent value. Recommended.

D *Cervantes*, R Alfredo Bufrem 66, T2229593. Central, small, but cosy. **D** *Estação Palace*, R Des Westphalen, 126, T3229840, F3245307. Excellent for price, 24-hr room service and internet, rather stark but immaculate. Recommended.

   E per person *Inca*, R João Negrão 370, T2238563. Breakfast OK, clean, friendly, safe, German spoken, good. **E** *Lusitano*, R João Negrão 420, T3232232. Basic, clean, front rooms noisy. **E** *Solar*, Jaime Reis 445. Basic but adequate.

   F *Pensão PP*, R Gen Carneiro 657, T2631169. Basic, no breakfast. There are good hotels southeast of the centre in the vicinity of the Rodoferroviária, but the cheaper ones are close to the wholesale market, which operates noisily throughout the night.

   Youth hostels E per person *AJ de Curitiba*, Av Padre Agostinho 645, Mercês, Curitiba PR, T2332746, F2332834, ajcwb@uol.com.br IYHA, youth hostel association for Paraná is located here. For those with ISIC student cards try **E** *Casa dos Estudantes*, Parque Passeio Público, north side. 4 nights or more. **E** *Casa do Estudante Luterano Universitario*, R Pr Cavalcanti, T3243313. Good.

   Camping *Camping Clube do Brasil*, BR-116, Km 84, 16 km in the direction of São Paulo, T3586634.

Expensive *99 Brasserie Cafe*, in upmarket *Bourbon Tower* hotel, see above, T3224001. Open daily for traditional *feijoada* lunch and buffet, 1200-1500. A/c and live music.   **Eating**

Mid-range *Baviera*, Alameda Augusto Stellfield, corner with Av Dr Murici. Intimate and atmospheric in style of beer cellar. Cantina, pizzeria and delivery service established over 30 years, open 1800-2300. *Jangil*, Praça Osório, 45, upper floor. Quirky place at top of stairwell, with balcony overlooking lovely main square. Go for a drink, tapas or dinner (pizza, pasta, fish and *churassco*) served by fatherly figures in white dinner jackets. *Saccy*, R São Francisco, 350, corner with Mateus Leme, 12. Pizza, tapas and lively bar with live music, see below. *Salmão* , R Emiliano Perneta, 924, T2252244. Restaurant in historic house, delicious fish and pizza, often special promotions, live music every night, open until 0100. Short taxi ride from centre.

Cheap *Kisco*, 7 de Setembro near Tibagi. Good, huge *prato do dia*, friendly. Cheap food also near the old railway station and good meals in the bus station. Close to the Rodoferroviária is the market, where there are a couple of *lanchonetes*. Hot sweet wine sold on the streets in winter helps keep out the cold. For addicts, there are *McDonald's*, and takeaway Chinese and pizzas.

Seriously cheap *Happy Rango*, Av Visconde de Nacar, 1350, near R 24 horas. Brightly lit, basic corner joint selling fast food and pizzas, open 24 hrs. *Mister Sheik*, Av Vicente Machado, 534. Arabic fast food in pitta with salad, popular for deliveries. Recommended.

A cluster of bars at the square of Largo da Ordem have tables and chairs on the pavement, music which tends to be rock, and bar food: *Fire Fox*, Av Jaime Reis, 46, flanked by *Tuba's* and *The Farm*. *London Pub*, São Francisco 350, São Francisco. Recommended. *Rua 24 Horas*, see above, an indoor street with very similar, fucntional bars and cafés, open 24 hrs. *Saccy*, R São Franscisco, 350, corner with Mateus Leme, 12. Pizza, tapas and lively bar with live music.   **Bars & nightclubs**

Iguaçu Falls and the South

Entertainment   **Cinema**   *Shopping Center Água Verde*, T2428741. *Shopping Crystal*, R Comendador Araújo 731, T3233061, and other places show films from all over the world. *Shopping Curitiba*, Praça Oswaldo Cruz 2698, T3261412. *Shopping Novo Batel*, T2222107. Tickets are usually US$4-5 Mon-Thu, and US$6-8 at weekends. Best to look in the newspaper for music and what's on in the bars, clubs and theatres. *Gazeta do Povo* has an arts and what's on section called *Caderno G.*

   Theatre   *Teatro Guaíra*, R 15 de Novembro, T3222628. Plays and revues (also has free events – get tickets early in the day). *Teatro Paiol*, in the old arsenal, R Col Zacarias, T3221525. *Ópera de Arame*, R João Gava, T2529637; *Opera house*. *Teatro Universitário de Curitiba* (TUC). *Teatro Novelas Curitibanas*, R Carlos Cavalcanti 1222, T2338552. *Teatro Fernanda Montenegro*, Shopping Novo Batel, T2244986.

Festivals   *Ash Wed* (half-day); *Maundy Thu* (half-day); **8 Sep** *Our Lady of Light.*

Shopping   Bookshop: *O Livro Técnico*, Shopping Itália, R João Negrão and Mcal Deodoro. Curitiba is a good place to buy **clothes and shoes**. **Jewellers** *H Stern* jewellers at Mueller Shopping Centre. **Souvenirs and handicrafts**   Try *Lojas Leve Curitiba*, at several locations, R 24 Horas, Afonso Pena airport, Ópera de Arame, Jardim Botânico, Memorial de Curitiba. *Lojas de Artesanato*, Casa de Artesanato Centro, R Mateus Leme 22, T3524021. *Lojas de Artesanato 'Feito Aqui'*, Dr Muricy 950, International Airport and Shopping Mueller. *Feira de Arte e Artesanato*, Praça Garibáldi, Sun 0900-1400.

Sport   **Golf**   *Graciosa Country Club*, Av Munhoz da Rocha 1146. 9 holes.

Tour operators   *BMP Turismo* (American Express), R Brig Franco, 1845, T2247560. *Stella Barros* (Thomas Cook), Av Visconde de Guarapuava 5170, T3424080, F3421266.

Transport   **Local**   **Buses**: there are several route types on the integrated transport system; pick up a map for full details. There are 25 transfer terminals along the exclusive busways and trunk routes, allowing integration between all the different routes. **Express** are red, often articulated, and connect the transfer terminals to the city centre, pre-paid access, they use the 'tubo' bus stops. **Feeder** orange conventional buses connect the terminals to the surrounding neighbourhoods. **Interdistrict** green conventional or articulated buses run on circular routes, connecting transfer terminals and city districts without passing through the centre. **Direct or speedy** silver grey buses use the 'tubo' stations (3 km apart on average), to link the main districts and connect the surrounding municipalities with Curitiba. **Conventional** yellow buses operate on the normal road network between the surrounding municipalities, the Integration Terminals and the city centre. **City circular** white mini buses, *Linha Turismo,* circle the major transport terminals and points of interest in the traditional city centre area. US$3.50 (multi-ticket booklets available), every 30 mins from 0900-1700, except on Mon. First leaves from R das Flores, narrow street in front of *McDonalds*. 3 stops allowed.

   Long distance   **Air**: there are 2 airports: Afonso Pena, 21 km away for international and national flights, T3811515, and Bacacheri for military and commercial flights, T2562121. There are buses to the centre and bus station as well as taxis. Bus 208 goes to Afonso Pena airport every 25 mins, US$0.60, 30 mins from hotels *Presidente* and *Araucária* with a stop near the bus terminal.

   Flights to **Campinas**, **Cascavel**, **Foz do Iguaçu**, **Joinville**, **Londrina**, **Maringá**, **Porto Alegre**, **Rio de Janeiro** and **São Paulo**.

   Buses: short-distance bus services within the metropolitan region (up to 40 km) begin at Terminal Guadalupe at R João Negrão, T3218611. The Terminal Rodoviário/Estação

Rodoferroviária is on Av Afonso Camargo, T3224344, for other cities in Paraná and other states. There are restaurants, banks, bookshops, shops, phones, post office, pharmacy, tourist agency, tourist office and other public services.

Frequent buses to **São Paulo** (6 hrs, US$10.25-12.50) and **Rio de Janeiro** (12 hrs, US$25). To **Foz do Iguaçu**, 10 a day, 10 hrs, US$15; **Porto Alegre**, 10 hrs; **Florianópolis**, every 2 hrs, 4½ hrs, US$12; **Blumenau** 4 hrs, US$6.50, 7 daily with *Penha/Catarinense*; good service to most destinations in Brazil. *Pluma* bus to **Buenos Aires** and to **Asunción**. *TTL* runs to **Montevideo**, 26 hrs, 0340 departure (*semi-cama*).

Car hire: *Localiza*, at the airport and Av Cândido de Abreu 336, T2530330. *Interlocadora*, at the airport, T3811370, F3324648.

Trains: Rodoferroviária, Av Afonso Camargo, T3229585, T3234007 (Serra Verde Express). Passenger trains to **Paranaguá**, see below.

Banks *Bradesco*, R 15 de Novembro, Visa ATM. Plus or Currus associated credit cards can be used at *Citibank*, R Mcal Deodoro 711, or at Buenos Aires 305 near Shopping Curitiba. *Credicard*, R Saldanha Marinho 1439, Bigorrillo. Cash with MasterCard. *Diplomata*, R Pres Faria 145 in the arcade. *Transoceânica*, R Mcal Deodoro 532, English and German spoken. *Triangle Turismo Travel*, Praça Gen Osório 213. Cash and TCs. **Directory**

Communications Internet: *Digitando o Futuro*, R 24 Horas. Open 24 hrs, free for 1 hr, government sponsored. Only 2 machines; T3506366 to book. *Monkey*, Av Vicente Machado, 534, corner with R Brigadeiro. Cool, modern with lots of computers and internet games. Open daily til 2400. **Post office**: Main Post office is at Mcal Deodoro 298. Branches at R 15 de Novembro and R Pres Faria. **Telephone**:Galeria Minerva, R 15 de Novembro. Information, T102.

Cultural centres *Instituto Goethe*, R Schaffenberg, near Military Museum, Mon-Thu 1500-1900, Library, Mon-Tue until 2130. *Sociedade Brasileira de Cultura Inglesa* (British Council), R Gen Carneiro 679, Caixa Postal 505.

Embassies and consulates *Austria*, R Cândido Hartmann 570, Edif Champagnat, 28th floor, T3361166. Mon-Fri 1000-1300. *Denmark*, R Prof Francisco Ribeiro 683, Caixa Postal 321, T8432211, F8431443. *Germany*, R Emiliano Perneta 297, 2nd floor, T2226920. Mon-Fri 0800-1200. *Netherlands*, Av Candido de Abreu 469, conj 1606, T2547846. Consul Tony Bruinjé, open 1400-1700, except emergencies. *Switzerland*, Av Mcal F Peixoto 228, Edif Banrisul, conj 1104/5, T2237553. *UK*, R Pres Faria 51, 2nd floor, T3221202, consulado.britanico@mais.sul.com.br Mon-Fri 0830-1200, 1400-1730. *Uruguay*, R Voluntários da Pátria 475, 18th floor.

Medical services Emergency, T192 or T100. *Cajuru Hospital*, Av São José 300, T3621100. *Evangélico*, Av Augusto Stellfeld 1908, T3224141. Both deal with emergencies.

Useful addresses Federal police, Dr Muricy 814, T3622313. For visa extensions 1000-1600.

Voltage 110 V 60 cycles.

Iguaçu Falls and the South

Curitiba to Paranaguá

The most spectacular railway journey in Brazil gives access to Parana's Atlantic coast. Popular expeditions during the summer are by paved road or rail to Paranaguá. There are numerous tunnels with sudden views of deep gorges and high peaks and waterfalls as the train rumbles over dizzy bridges and viaducts. Near Banhado station (Km 66) is the waterfall of Véu da Noiva, and from the station at Km 59, you can reach the Marumbi mountain range.

Train information Two trains run from Curitiba to Paranaguá. The *Litorina* is a modern a/c railcar with on-board service and bilingual staff, which stops at the viewpoint at the Santuário da Nossa Senhora do Cadeado and Morretes. Hand-luggage only. Tickets can be bought 2 days in advance; departs Sat and Sun 0900, returns 1500, US$28 one-way tourist class. The *Trem Classe Turística* stops at Marumbi and Morretes, buy tickets 2 days in advance, departs 0800 daily except Mon, returns 1600, *turístico* US$104. Schedules change frequently; check times in advance. For information and reservations, *Serra Verde Express*, T3234007. Tickets sold at the Rodoferroviária, Portão 8, Curitiba, 0800-1800. Sit on the left-hand side on the journey from Curitiba. On cloudy days there's little to see on the higher parts. The train is usually crowded on Sat and Sun. Many travellers recommend returning by bus (1½ hrs, buy ticket immediately on arrival, US$6.50), if you do not want to stay 4½ hrs. A tour bus meets the train and offers a tour of town and return to Curitiba.

Antonina and Morretes Colour map 5, grid A5
You can also visit the port of Antonina, which is not on the main train route, and Morretes, which is. These two sleepy colonial towns can be reached by bus on the old Graciosa road, which is almost as scenic as the railway. Some 14 km north of Morretes is the beautiful village of **São João de Graciosa**, 2 km beyond which is a flower reserve. The Graciosa road crosses the **Marumbi** range for 12 km, with six rest stops where there are fire grills, shelters and camping. Marumbi, a state park and area of special tourist interest, is very beautiful. You can also hike the original trail which follows the road and passes the rest stops. Take food, water and plenty of insect repellent.

Sleeping and eating in Morretes B *Porto Real Palace*, R Visc do Rio Branco 85, T4621344. Try *barreado*, beef cooked for 24 hrs. A highly recommended eating place is *Romanus*, R Visconde do Rio Branco 141, T4621500.

Around Curitiba

Sexual politics

◀◀

The world famous anti-impotency drug Viagra is big business in Brazil, but one wily mayor took it upon himself to distribute the pills free of charge in a desperate bid to boost his town's flagging population.

Elcio Berti, mayor of Bocaiuva do Sul in the southern state of Paraná, hoped to secure the city a bigger slice of federal cash, shared among municipalities according to their size.

"Enlarging the local population is the only way to get a larger chunk of the federal fund", the Brazilian daily newspaper O Globo *quoted Berti as saying.*

His plan was an improvement on an earlier attempt to increase the town's population, when he passed a municipal law banning the sale of condoms, a move quickly cancelled by a judge on the grounds of unconstitutionality.

Transport Buses from **Paranaguá** to Morretes at 1830, US$1, to Antonina, stopping en route at Morretes, 6 a day (US$1.50). 12 buses daily Morretes-Curitiba US$2; 11 buses a day Curitiba-Antonina.

Paranaguá

Chief port of the state of Paraná and one of the main coffee-exporting ports, Paranaguá was founded in 1585. It is on a lagoon 29 km from the open sea and is approached via the Baia de Paranaguá, dotted with picturesque islands. Paranaguá is also a free port for Paraguay.

Phone code: 041
(268 km S of Santos)
Colour map 5, grid A5
Population: 128,000

The fort of **Nossa Senhora dos Prazeres** was built in 1767 on a nearby island; one hour's boat trip. The former Colêgio dos Jesuitas, a fine baroque building, has been converted into a **Museu de Arqueologia e Artes Populares**. ■ *1200-1700 Tue-Sun. US$1.* Other attractions are a 17th-century fountain, the church of **São Benedito**, and the shrine of **Nossa Senhora do Rocio**, 2 km from town. **Tourist offices** are outside the railway station (1100-1700, free maps), and at the docks in front of the pier where boats leave for Ilha do Mel (T4226882, 0800-1900); boat schedules, toilet, and left-luggage available.

Sights

There are cruises on Paranaguá Bay by launch, daily from Cais do Mercado.

Matinhos, 40 km south, is a medium-sized Mediterranean-style resort, invaded by surfers in October for the Paraná surf competition. **B** *Praia e Sol*, Rua União 35, T4521922, has been recommended. There is the basic, cheap *Bolamar* and four campsites in the vicinity.

About 8 km south is **Caiobá**, at the mouth of a bay, the other side of which is **Guaratuba**, which is less built up than Caiobá. The ferry between the two towns is frequent and is a beautiful crossing, free for pedestrians, US$1.50 for cars. Both towns have a few hotels but most close in winter; there is also camping at Guaratuba. The *Sol Nascente* restaurant, Rua Vicente Machado 967, is superb.

Excursions

AL *Camboa*, R João Estevão, in the Centro Histórico, T/F4232121. **A** *Portofino*, Av Atlântica 4409, Balneário Porto Fino, T/F4581488. Very nice. **C** *Auana*, R Correia de Freitas 110, T4226531. Good value. Recommended. **D** *Litoral*, R Correia de Freitas 66. Without breakfast, comfortable. **E** *Karibe*, F Simas 86, T4221177. Good value, shared bath, with breakfast. **Camping** *Arco Iris*, Praia de Leste, on the beach, 29 km south of Paranaguá, T4582001.

Sleeping

Expensive *Aquárius*, Av Gabriel de Lara 40. Good but not cheap seafood. **Mid-range** *Bela Vista*, on the waterfront. Open in the evenings when many places

Eating

Iguaçu Falls and the South

shut, good, typical atmosphere, good food at reasonable prices. *Bobby's*, Faria Sobrinho 750. Highly recommended, especially for seafood. *Casa do Barreado*, R Antônio da Cruz 9. Good local food and drink. *Danúbio Azul*, 15 de Novembro 91. Good fish and view of river. **Cheap** There are cheap restaurants in the old market building, and near the markets on the waterfront.

Transport **Buses** All operated by *Graciosa*. To **Curitiba**, US$4, many, 1½ hrs (only the 1500 to Curitiba takes the old Graciosa road); direct to **Rio** at 1915, 15 hrs, US$23. 8 buses a day to **Guaratuba** (US$1, 2 hrs), **Caiobá** and **Matinhos**. The buses to Guaratuba go on the ferry, as do direct buses to Joinville, 0740, 1545. **Car hire** *Interlocadora*, T4234425, F3324648.

Directory **Banks** *Banco do Brasil*, Largo C Alcindino 27. *Bradesco*, R Faria Sobrinho 188. *Câmbio*, R Faria Sobrinho. For cash.

Ilha do Mel

Colour map 5, grid A5 The 'island of honey' is an ecological reserve (no cars permitted and visitors limited to 5,000 per day), but is well developed for tourism and is accessible by boat from Paranaguá or Pontal do Sul. There are beautiful beaches, caves, bays and hill walks; bicycles and kayaks can be hired.

History Ilha do Mel, at the mouth of the Baía de Paranaguá, was of strategic use in the 18th century. The Fortaleza da Barra was built in 1767 on the orders of King José I of Portugal, to defend what was one of the principal ports in the country. In 1850, a British warship captured three illegal slave trading ships, giving rise to a battle known as *Combate Cormorant*. The lighthouse, Farol das Conchas, was built in 1872 to guide shipping into the bay. The Gruta das Encantadas is surrounded with myths and legends about mermaids, enchanting all who came near them.

Ilha do Mel

The island's four villages, **Nova Brasilia**, **Praia das Encantadas**, **Praia da Fortaleza** and **Farol**, are linked by pathways. The hike to the fort is very rewarding. April-October are very rainy months here and there are very persistent *mutucas* (biting insects) in November, so December to March is the best time to visit. There are boats from Praia das Encantadas to Nova Brasília (US$10, or US$2 per person if more than five), or you can walk on a track (1½-2 hours) or follow the coast, walking in the sea. From Nova Brasília, a 20-minute walk leads to El Farol for good views.

Praia das Encantadas is more suitable for swimming than Nova Brasília. Praia Grande is a deserted, horse-shoe shaped beach on the east side with the best surfing. Fortaleza is one of the most popular beaches and can be crowded, with restaurants and *pousadas*. In between Praia de Fora and Praia das Encantadas, on the south point, is the Gruta das Encantadas, the rocky area of natural pools where mermaids are said to lurk (see above).

Sights & beaches

Praia do Farol B *Pousadinha*, Praia das Conchas, T973366. Good beds, fan, bath, mosquito nets, staff speak various languages, excellent breakfast, delightful rooms. **B** *Pousada Praia do Farol*, in front of the pier, T9783433. With breakfast. **C** *Estalagem Ancoradouro*. With breakfast.

Sleeping

   Praia Nova Brasília B *Pousada Pôr do Sol*, Praia do Limoeiro, T9781038. **C** *Estalagem Pirata*, wonderful house on the beach, music, easy atmosphere, run by Roberto and Darlene. *Pousada Portal*, T9783534. With breakfast. Good.
   Praia da Fortaleza B *Parque Hotel Ilha do Mel*, T9783322.
   Praia das Encantadas C *Pousada Estrela do Mar*, T9782010. **C** *Pousada Tia Maria*, in front of the pier, T9783352. You can rent a fisherman's house – ask for *Valentim's Bar*, or for Luchiano. Behind the bar is *Cabanas Dona Maria*, shared showers, cold water; food available if you ask in advance. Many *pousadas* and houses with rooms to rent (shared kitchen and living room). Shop around, prices from about US$10 double, low season, mid-week.
   Camping There are mini campsites with facilities at Encantadas, Farol and Brasília. Camping is possible on the more deserted beaches (good for surfing). If camping, watch out for the tide, watch possessions and beware of the *bicho de pé* which burrows into feet (remove with a needle and alcohol) and the *borrachudos* (discourage with Autan repellent).

Expensive *Forró do Zorro* (see below). **Mid-range** *Lanchonete Paraíso*, nice meeting place, good food and music. *Toca do Abutre*, Restaurant 1 km from Nova Brasília.

Eating

In summer and at holiday times the island is very crowded with an active nightlife and *Forró* dancing, whilst at other times it is very quiet. Bars *Barbeira* and *Forró do Zorro*, Praia das Encantadas. Dancing Thu-Sun, lively and popular.

Bars & nightclubs

There are 2 ways of getting to Ilha do Mel: by **ferry from Paranaguá**, Sat at 1000, Mon and Fri at 1500, 1 hr 40 mins, boats with a capacity of 40, 60 or 80 passengers leave from R Gen Carneiro (R da Praia) in front of the Tourist Information kiosk; by ferry from **Pontal do Paraná** (Pontal do Sul), daily from 0800 to 1800 (last boat from island to mainland) every hr at weekends, less frequently in the week. From **Paranaguá**, take the bus to Pontal do Sul (many daily, 1½ hrs, US$0.60), then wait for the ferry, US$3.25. At the ferry point are souvenir and handicraft stalls. The last bus back to Paranaguá leaves at 2200. Alternatively, go to the small harbour in Paranaguá and ask for a boat to Ilha do Mel, US$5 one-way (no shade). Make sure the ferry goes to your chosen destination (Nova Brasília or Encantadas are the most developed areas).

Transport

Iguaçu Falls and the South

Superagui National Park The island of Superagui is a national park and UNESCO World Heritage Site. With its neighbour Peças it forms one of the principal stations for research into Atlantic rainforest and its flora and fauna. Just north of Ilha do Mel, the park is reached by regular boat service from Guaraqueçaba, an interesting trip through the mangroves which separate the islands from the mainland, or from Paranaguá (negotiate a fare by fishing boat at the docks near the Mercado do Café). Many threatened and migratory species of birds are seen here – kingfishers, storks, herons and parrots among others – and animals such as the rare yellow-fronted alligator, otters, jaguars and black-faced monkeys. There is also an Indian village at the top of the island's hill; other inhabitants are mostly of European descent, living off fishing. There is a certain amount of resentment that the wildlife receives more help than the 1,200-strong community. Boat from Paranaguá Saturday 1000 arriving 1400, return Sunday 1530 (two stops en route), US$6 one way. Private boats from Ilha do Mel run if the weather is good. There is superb swimming from deserted beaches, but watch out for stinging jelly fish. Contact Ibama on the island, 2 km out of the village, for information. Commercially organized tours are available, T2520180.

Sleeping and eating There are some 10 *pousadas* on Superagui: most popular with foreigners is **E** per person *Carioca*, T99784213, cheaper without bath, breakfast, lots of information. Booking necessary at holiday times, Jan-Feb; can arrange rooms elsewhere if full. **E** per person *Bella Ilha*, T99982953, with breakfast. **F** per person *Golfinhos*, T99598852, with breakfast. **Camping** US$1.50. Take torch and mosquito repellent. The *Restaurante dos Golfinhos* (blue, on beach) can arrange boat trips for the Indian village, ask for Lurdinho or Nagibe, US$12 slow boat, US$15 motor boat, arrange pick-up time. Another restaurant is *Crepúsculo*. In both cases book lunch or dinner in advance. No dollars or credit cards accepted on the island.

Guaraqueçaba Guaraqueçaba is also an environmental protection area, preserving Atlantic coastal forest, a lagoon estuary complex, archaeological sites and traditional communities. For information, contact *Instituto Ambiental do Paraná*, T041-3225125. Guaraqueçaba is hard to reach by road. It is best to take a boat from Paranaguá, 1½ hours.

Vila Velha On the road to Ponta Grossa is Vila Velha, now a state park, 97 km from Curitiba, 10 km from Ponta Grossa. The sandstone rocks have been weathered into most fantastic shapes, although many have been defaced by thoughtless tourists. The **Lagoa Dourada**, surrounded by forests, is close by. Nearby are the **Furnas**, three waterholes, the deepest of which has a lift (US$1 – not always working) that descends almost to the level of the lake. ■ *Opens at 0800. US$1. The park office is 300 m from the highway and the park a further 1½ km. The entrance is also to the Furnas, so keep your ticket.* You can camp in the church grounds or put your tent up in a disused campground which is now overgrown with no facilities.

Transport Take a bus from **Curitiba** to the national park, not to the town 20 km away. Ask the bus driver where you should get off. *Princesa dos Campos* bus from Curitiba at 0730 and 0930, 1½ hrs, US$5.65 (return bus passes park entrance at 1600); it may be advisable to go to Ponta Grossa and return to Curitiba from there. Last bus from Vila Velha car park to Ponta Grossa at 1800. Bus from Vila Velha at 1310, 1610 and 1800, US$1, 4½ km to turn-off to Furnas (another 15-min walk) and Lagoa Dourada (it's not worth walking from Vila Velha to Furnas because it's mostly uphill along the main road). Allow all day if visiting all 3 sites (unless you hitch, or can time the buses well, it's a lot of walking).

Iguaçu Falls

As Cataratas do Iguaçu (Iguazú in Spanish) are the most overwhelming and spectacular waterfalls in South America. They are also one of the major natural attractions in Brazil. Situated on the Rio Iguaçu (in Guaraní guazú is big and I is for water), the border between Argentina and Brazil, they are made up of no less than 275 separate waterfalls. Bridges connect the Brazilian city of Foz do Iguaçu with the Argentine town of Puerto Iguazú and the Paraguayan city of Ciudad del Este.

The Caiagangue Indians originally inhabited the region, but the first European visitor to the falls was the Spaniard Alvaro Núñez Cabeza de Vaca in 1541. He nearly fell off one of the waterfalls on his search for a connection between the Brazilian coast and the Río de la Plata, and named them the Saltos de Santa María. Though the falls were well known to the Jesuit missionaries, they were forgotten, except by local inhabitants, until the area was explored by a Brazilian expedition sent out by the Paraguayan president, Solano López, in 1863.

The falls are 20 m higher than Niagara and about half as wide again

The most spectacular part is the *Garganta del Diablo* (Devil's Throat), visited from the Argentine side (see below). Downstream is a 28-km long gorge, stretching to the Río Alto Paraná and formed as the river has eroded its way back up the river.

Viewed from below, the tumbling water is majestically beautiful in its setting of begonias, orchids, ferns and palms. Toucans, flocks of parrots and cacique birds and great dusky swifts dodge in and out along with myriad butterflies (there are at least 500 different species). Above the impact of the water, upon basalt rock, hovers a perpetual 30 m high cloud of mist in which the sun creates blazing rainbows.

Around 80% of the falls lie in Argentina, but there are national parks on both sides: transport between the two parks is via the **Ponte Tancredo Neves**, as there is no crossing at the falls themselves. **Tourist facilities** on both sides are constantly being improved.

Ins & outs

Between October and February daylight saving dates change each year, Brazil is 1 hr ahead of Argentina and, from December, 2 hrs ahead of Paraguay

The **Brazilian park** offers a superb panoramic view of the whole falls and is best visited in the morning (4 hrs is enough for the highlights) when the light is better for photography. The **Argentine park** (which requires at least half a day) is incredible value, includes a boat trip in the entrance fee and offers closer views of the individual falls. It also provides an experience of the forest with its wildlife and butterflies, though to appreciate these properly you need to spend a full day and get well away from the visitors areas. Both parks can, if necessary, be visited in a day, starting at about 0700, but, in the heat, the brisk pace needed for a rapid tour is exhausting for the non-athletic .

Busiest times are holiday periods and on Sunday, when helicopter tours over the falls from the Brazilian side are particularly popular. Both parks have visitors' centres, though the information provided by the Argentine Centre is far superior to that in the Brazilian Centre.

Sunset from the Brazilian side is a worthwhile experience

There are many advantages in staying in Foz and commuting to the Argentine side (a bigger choice of hotels and restaurants, for example). Whichever side you decide to stay on, most establishments will accept *reais*, pesos or dollars. Cross-border transport usually accepts guaraníes as well.

A useful guidebook is *Iguazú, The Laws of the Jungle* (in Spanish, *Iguazú, las leyes de la selva*), by Santiago G de la Vega, Contacto Silvestre Ediciones (1999), available from the Visitors' Centre.

Parque Nacional Foz do Iguaçu (Brazil)

The Brazilian side of the falls is closed on Monday until 1300 for maintenance

The Brazilian National Park was founded in 1939 and designated a World Heritage Site by UNESCO in 1986. The park covers 170,086 ha, extending along the north bank of the Rio Iguaçu, then sweeping northwards to Santa Tereza do Oeste on the BR-277. The subtropical rainforest benefits from the added humidity in the proximity of the falls, creating an environment rich in vegetation and fauna. Given the massive popularity of the falls, the national parks on either side of the frontier are surprisingly little visited.

Fauna Coatis, which look very like racoons, get very close to humans, but should not be fed. Most frequently encountered are little and red brocket deer, South American coati, white-eared opossum, and a sub-species of the brown capuchin monkey. The following are also present, but much harder to see: jaguar, ocelot, jaguarundi, puma, margay, white-lipped peccary, bush dog and southern river otter. The endangered tegu lizard is common. Over 100 species of butterflies have been identified, among them the electric blue *Morpho*, the poisonous red and black *heliconius* and species of Papilionidae and Pieridae.

The birdlife is especially rewarding for bird-watchers. Five members of the toucan family can be seen: toco and red-breasted toucans, chestnut-eared araçari, saffron and spot-billed toucanets. In the bamboo stands you may see: spotted bamboo wren, grey-bellied spinetail, several antshrikes, short-tailed ant-thrush. In the forest: rufous-thighed kite, black-and-white hawk-eagle, black-fronted piping-guan, blue ground dove, dark-billed cuckoo, black-capped screech-owl, surucua trogon, rufous-winged antwren, black-crowned tityra, red-ruffed fruitcrow, white-winged swallow, plush-crested jay, cream-bellied gnatcatcher, black-goggled and magpie tanagers, green-chinned euphonia, black-throated and utlramarine grosbeaks, yellow-billed cardinal, red-crested finch. (Bird and mammal information supplied by Douglas Trent, *Focus Tours*; see Tours and tour operators, page 23.)

Iguaçu Falls orientation

■ **Sleeping**   ○ **Frontier markers**   **2** Brazilian
1 Das Catarates   **1** Argentine   **3** Paraguayan
Not to scale

Iguaçu Falls and the South

Unimpressed

In the 20th century, the falls have become recognized globally as a major attraction. This did not impress Malcolm Slesser in the 1960s, though: "Except for a night on the tiles in Rio de Janeiro, Brazil's greatest tourist attraction is the Iguaçu Falls where Argentina, Brazil and Paraguay meet. This huge cataract eclipses Niagara. These falls are a splendid frolic of 300 falls, 270-ft high, almost 3 miles wide, filling the place with spray. Here is a large government hotel, luxurious with absolutely nothing to do except eat, drink and lounge – and look at the falls. We did not go, on the principle that a waterfall was a waterfall." (Brazil: Land without Limit; London, George Allen and Unwin, 1969, pages 151-52).

Visitors' Centre All cars and public buses stop here. There are souvenir **The falls** shops, a *Banco do Brasil* ATM (cashpoint) and *câmbio* (1300-1700), a small café and car park here. If possible, visit on a weekday when the walks are less crowded. ■ *0800-1700 daily. 8 reais – US$3 – car parking fee, payable only in Brazilian currency; transfer made to free park shuttle bus.*

First stop with the shuttle bus is **Macuco Safari**, US$33, (bookable through most agencies, which may charge a premium for transfers). The safari takes one hour 45 minutes, leaving every 15 minutes and is highly recommended (see box).

Second stop with the bus is the *Cataratas Trail* (starting from the hotel of the same name, non-residents can eat at the hotel, midday and evening buffets). This 1½-km paved walk runs part of the way down the cliff near the rim of the falls, giving a stupendous view of the whole Argentine side of the falls. It ends up almost under the powerful Floriano Falls: from here an elevator carries visitors to the top of the Floriano Falls (from 0800; US$0.50) and to a path leading to Porto Canoa (if there is a queue, it is easy and quick to walk up). A catwalk at the foot of the Floriano Falls gives a good view of the Garganta do Diabo. There are toilets and a lanchonete on the path down and more toilets at the top of the elevator.

Helicopter tours over the falls leave from *Hotel das Cataratas*, US$60 per person, 10 minutes. Booked through any travel agency or direct with *Helisul*, T5231190. Apart from disturbing visitors, the helicopters are also reported to present a threat to some bird species which are laying thinner-shelled eggs: the altitude has been increased, making the flight less attractive.

The **Porto Canoas** complex, with its snack bar, souvenir shops and terraces with views of the falls, was completed in 2000 after some controversy. Its restaurant serves a delicious US$12 buffet. Highly recommended for a memorable lunch.

Transport Buses leave Foz do Iguaçu, from the *Terminal Urbana* on Av Juscelino Kubitschek, 1 block from the Infantry Barracks. The grey or red Transbalan service goes to the falls every 30 mins, 0530-2330, past the airport and *Hotel das Cataratas*. 40 mins, US$0.80 one-way, payable in *reais* only. Return buses 0800-1900. The bus terminates at the Visitor Centre, where you must pay the entrance fee (see above) and transfer to the free park shuttle bus, which leaves every 5 mins or so from 0830-1900. **Private cars** must be left in the visitor centre car park. **Taxis** charge US$7 or US$30 for return trip, including waiting (negotiate in advance). Many hotels organize tours to the falls: these have been recommended in preference to taxi rides.

Iguaçu Falls and the South

The Macuco Safari

Electric vehicles take visitors to the start of a short, steep trail (those with walking difficulties can be driven the whole way). After about 20 minutes' ride on the trailer, you get off and begin hiking your way down the side of the Iguaçu gorge to the Macuco Falls, which cascade into a deep dark plunge pool. Steps cut into the rock allow you to descend to the foot of the falls, but beware, they are slippery and steep (take stout walking shoes). The tour is taken at a relaxed pace and there is no pressure to rush back up those steps. After the falls, you descend to the banks of the river, where you take to water in inflatable rafts capable of carrying 20 people. The ride is bumpy, but make sure you look up

at the steep sides of the gorge. As the boat comes up to the edge of the falls, there is a deafening roar from above as the boat begins to turn and the spray is so powerful you have to shut your eyes. You will get very wet. Plastic raincoats are sold at the launch site and plastic bags are provided for cameras if you ask. The view of the falls is unbeatable. Once back on dry land, you are whisked up to the top of the canyon by jeep to rejoin the trailer to the entrance. From here, a free shuttle bus transfers you through the park to the top of the falls.

Guides speak Portuguese, English and Spanish; take insect repellent. Macuco Safari, Rodovia das Cataratas Km 22, T5296263, macucosafari@foznet.com.br

Parque Nacional Iguazú (Argentina)

Created in 1934, the park extends over an area of 67,620 ha, most of which is covered by the same subtropical rainforest as on the Brazilian side. It is crossed by Route 101, a dirt road which runs southeast to Bernardo de Yrigoyen on the Brazilian frontier. Buses operate along this route in dry weather, offering a view of the park.

Fauna You would have to be very lucky to see jaguars, tapirs, brown capuchin monkeys, collared anteaters and coatimundi. As in Brazil, very little of the fauna in the park can be seen around the falls: even on the nature trails described below you need to go in the early morning. Of the more than 400 species of birds, you are most likely to spot the following: black-crowned night heron, plumed kite, white-eyed parakeet, blue-winged parrolet, great dusky swift, scale throated hermit, suruca trogon, Amazon kingfisher, toco toucan, tropical kingbird, boat-billed flycatcher, red-rumped cacique, and the colourful purple-throated euphonia.

The falls A free train service completed in 2001 leaves every 20 minutes from the Visitors'
The catwalks and Centre, departing for the start of two sets of walkways, both taking about an
platform get very hour. The *Circuito Inferior*, Lower Trail, leads down very steep steps to the lower
crowded in falls and the start of the boat trip to Isla San Martin, see below. The *Circuito*
mid-morning after *Superior*, or Upper Trail, follows the top of the falls, giving panoramic views. (A
tour buses arrive path, the **Sendero Verde** taking about 20 mins, from near the Visitors' Centre
leads to the start of the Upper and Lower trails.) A second train route takes visitors to the start of the walkway to the **Garganta del Diablo** (Devil's Throat). A visit here is particularly recommended in the evening when the light is best and the swifts are returning to roost on the cliffs, some behind the water.

Below the falls, a free ferry leaving regularly, subject to demand, connects the Circuito Inferior with **Isla San Martín**. A path on the island leads to the top of the hill, where there are trails to some of the less visited falls and rocky pools (take bathing gear in summer).

Water features

The Iguaçu river basin extends over 62,000 sq km. The river rises in the Brazilian hills near Curitiba at an altitude of around 1,200 m. From here it flows for 1,300 km across the Paraná Plateau, a thick layer of very hard basalt lava formed as a result of a massive Triassic volcanic eruption over 100 million years ago. On its way it receives the waters of about 30 rivers before reaching the falls which lie at an altitude of 160 m at the edge of the plateau.

Above the main falls the river, sown with wooded islets, opens out to a width of 4 km. There are rapids for 3½ km above the falls: a 60-m precipice over which the water plunges in 275 falls over a frontage of 2.7 km at an average rate of 1,750 cu m a second.

Park essentials

Tours and activities A number of activities are offered, both from the Visitors' Centre and through agencies in Puerto Iguazú. *Aventura Náutica* is a journey by launch along the lower Río Iguazú, US$15. *Safari Náutico*, a 4-km journey by boat above the falls, US$15. *Gran Aventura*, an 8-km ride through the jungle, followed by a boat trip on the rapids to the Devil's Throat, US$33. *Full Day* combines *safari náutico* with *aventura náutica*, US$30 (5 hrs), or US$45 with *gran aventura* (7 hrs), lunch extra.

On clear nights the moon casts a blue halo over the falls. During the full moon, there are sometimes **night-time walking tours** between the *Hotel Sheraton* and the falls. **Mountain bikes** and **boats** can also be hired, US$3 per hr. For serious **bird-watching** and **nature walks** with an English-speaking guide, contact Daniel Samay (*Explorador* agency) or Miguel Castelino, Aptdo Postal 22, Puerto Iguazú (3370), Misiones, T420157, FocusTours@aol.com Highly recommended.

Clothing In the rainy season, when water levels are high, waterproof coats or swimming costumes are advisable for some of the lower catwalks and for boat trips. Cameras should be carried in a plastic bag. Wear shoes with good soles, as the rocks can be very slippery in places.

Services The park is open 0800-1900 every day. Entry US$5, payable in pesos, dollars or reais. Guests at *Hotel Sheraton* should pay and get tickets stamped at the hotel to avoid paying again. The Visitors' Centre includes a museum of local fauna and an auditorium for periodic slide shows (on request, minimum 8 people), no commentary, only music; it also sells a good guide book on Argentine birds. Food and drinks are available in the park but are expensive, so it is best to take your own. There is a Telecom kiosk at the bus stop. **Camping** Camping Puerto Canoas, 600 m from Puerto Canoas; tables, but no other facilities, nearest drinking water at park entrance.

Transport *Transportes El Práctico* buses run every hr from Puerto Iguazú bus terminal, stopping at the national park entrance for the purchase of entry tickets and continuing to Puerto Canoas. Fares US$5 return to Visitors' Centre (cars US$3), a further US$0.50 to Puerto Canoas, payable in pesos, dollars, guaraníes or reais. First bus 0740, last 1940, last return 2000, journey time 30 mins. These buses are sometimes erratic, especially when it is wet, even though the times are clearly indicated. There are fixed rates for taxis, US$15 one-way, up to 5 people. A tour from the bus terminal, taking in both sides of the falls, costs US$40. Hitchhiking to the falls is difficult, but you can hitch up to the Posadas intersection at Km 11, then it is only a 7-km walk. For transport between the Argentine and Brazilian sides see under Foz and Puerto Iguazú, below. Motorists can park overnight in the national park, free.

Iguaçu Falls and the South

Foz do Iguaçu

Phone code: 045
Colour map 5, grid A2
Population: 260,000

This is the third most visited city in Brazil, thanks to the falls, 28 km away. Although there are plenty of hotels nearer the main attraction, the town, despite having very little in the way of tourist attractions, has a wide range of restaurants, accommodation and good communications by air and road with the main cities of southern Brazil and Asunción in Paraguay. Avenida Juscelino Kubitschek and the streets south of it, towards the river, have a reputation of being unsafe at night.

Ins & outs   The **Secretaria Municipal de Turismo**, on R Rio Branco, open 0700-2300, is very helpful, as is 24-hr tourist help line, T0800-451516. Tourist information at rodoviária and airport open for all arriving flights, with free map and bus information. *Triplice Fronteira* is a local newspaper with street plans and tourist information.

Excursions   **Artificial beaches on Lake Itaipu** (see below for the Itaipu dam itself)   The closest to Foz de Iguaçu are at Bairro de Três Lagoas, at Km 723 on BR-277, and in the municipality of Santa Terezinha do Itaipu, 34 km from Foz. The leisure parks have grassed areas with kiosks, barbecue sites and offer fishing as well as bathing, US$2.50. It is also possible to take boat trips on the lake.

Foz do Iguaçu

■ Sleeping	7 Pousada	● Eating	7 Zaragoza
1 Athenas	de Laura	1 Bier Garten	
2 Baviera	8 Paudimar	2 Brasil & Brazil	● Bars
3 Bogarí	Centro IYHA	3 Bufalo Branco	8 Armazem
4 Foz do Iguaçu	9 Rafain Centro	4 City Caffé	9 BR3
5 Foz Presidente II	10 Tarobá	5 Marias e Maria	10 Capitão
6 Minas	11 Trento	6 Oficina do Sorvete	

The **Parque das Aves** bird park, entrance US$8, at Rodovia das Cataratas Km 16, Parque Nacional bus stops here, 100 m before the entrance to the falls, has received frequent good reports. It contains Brazilian and foreign birds in huge aviaries through which you can walk, with the birds flying and hopping around you. There is also a butterfly house. For a guided tour T5298282. The Parque is within walking distance of the *Hotel San Martin*; the *Paudimar* youth hostel (see below) offers a discount for its guests.

In a bid to get their commission, touts may say the hotel of your choice no longer exists, or offer you room rates below what is actually charged. In high season (eg Christmas-New Year) you will not find a room under US$15, but in low season there are many good deals.

Sleeping
Many hotels offer excursions to the falls

In Foz do Iguaçu **A** *Rafain Centro*, Mcal Deodoro 984, T/F5231213. Smart communal areas and attractive pool area, although rooms rather well worn. **B** *Baviera*, Av Jorge Schimmelpfeng, 697, T5235995, F5743566, hotelbavieraiguassu@foznet.com.br Chalet-style exterior, on main road, central for bars and restaurants, comfortable, if rather gloomy rooms. **B** *Suiça*, Av Felipe Wandscheer 3580, T5253232, F5253044. Swiss manager, helpful, pool. **C** *Bogarí*, Av Brasil 106, T/F5232243, www.bogarihotel.com.br Restful atmosphere, large pool with pleasant walled terrace, central, in shopping street. Opposite is **C** *Foz do Iguaçu*, Av Brasil 97, T5234455, F5741775, hotelfoz@purenet.com.br Newly, tastefully decorated, very serene, good value. Attractive, quiet pool area, smart breakfast room, English spoken. Recommended. **C** *Foz Plaza Hotel*, R Marechal Deodoro, 1819, T/F5231448, fozplaza@uol.com.br Serene and very nice. **C** *Foz Presidente*, R Xavier da Silva 1000, T/F5724450. Restaurant, pool, with breakfast, convenient for buses. Recommended. **C** *Foz Presidente II*, R Mcal Floriano Peixoto 1851, T5232318. Smaller but a little more expensive, also with pool, bar and restaurant. **C** *San Remo*, Kubitschek e Xavier da Silva 563, T5722956. A/c, good breakfast. Recommended.

D *Luz*, Av Costa e Silva Km 5, near Rodoviária, T5223535, F5222474. Recommended. **D** *Tarobá*, R Tarobá 1048, T5239722. Helpful, a/c, clean, small indoor pool, good value. Recommended. **E** *Pousada da Laura*, R Naipi 671, T/F5723374. Good breakfast, hot water, bathroom, central, friendly, secure, kitchen, laundry facilities, good place to meet other travellers, Spanish, English, Italian and French spoken, excellent. **F** *Athenas*, R Almte Barroso 2215 on corner with Rebouças, T5742563. Good value, special rates for backpackers, some rooms with shared bath, fan, breakfast extra, beers sold. **F** *Minas*, R Rebouças 809, T5745208. Basic, but fine for price and central position, a/c, hot water, safe, no breakfast, cheaper with fan. **F** *Pousada Evelina Navarrete*, R Irlan Kalichewski 171, Vila Yolanda, T/F5743817. Lots of tourist information, English, French, Italian, Polish and Spanish spoken, helpful, lots of information, good breakfast and location, near Chemin Supermarket, near Av Cataratas on the way to the falls. Warmly recommended. **F** *Trento*, R Rebouças 829, T5745111. Fan, with bath, without breakfast, noisy, but recommended.

Outside Foz do Iguaçu Options here tend to be very large, resort hotels. **L-AL** *Hotel das Cataratas*, also known as the *Tropical*, directly overlooking the falls, 28 km from Foz, T5217000, F5741688, 40% discount for holders of the Brazil Air Pass. Caters for lots of groups, attractive colonial-style building with pleasant gardens (where a lot of wildlife can be seen at night and early morning) and pool. Receipt of email for guests. Check the exchange rate if paying in dollars. Non-residents can eat here, midday and evening buffets (mixed reports); also *à la carte* dishes and dinner with show. **L** *Colonial*, Km 16, T5291777, F5297732, 1 km from the airport. Spacious and sophisticated, used by air crew. Fine location, price includes breakfast and mediocre dinner, no English spoken.

Youth hostel There are 2 branches of the *Paudimar* youth hostel, both **F** per person (in high season IYHA members only): *Paudimar Campestre*, Av das Cataratas Km 12.5, Remanso Grande, near airport, T/F5722430, paudimarcampestre@paudimar.com.br From airport or town take Parque Nacional bus (0525-0040) and get out at Remanso Grande bus stop, by *Hotel San Juan*, then take the free shuttle bus (0700-1900) to the hostel, or 1.2-km walk from main road. IYHA, camping as well, pool, soccer pitch, quiet, kitchen and communal meals, breakfast, very friendly. Highly recommended. For assistance, ask for owner, Gladis. *Paudimar Centro*, R Rui Barbosa 634, T/F5745503, paudimarcentro@paudimar.com.br Safe, laundry, kitchen, TV, central, convenient for buses to falls, also very friendly. Recommended. For assistance, ask for Lourdes. English, Spanish and Portuguese spoken. Hostel will pay half taxi fare from rodoviária or airport if staying more than 2 days. Both hostels have telephone, fax and internet for use of guests. You can stay at one hostel and use the facilities of the other; tours run to either side of the falls, US$8 to Argentine side 0830-1700, good value. *Paudimar* desk at rodoviária.

Camping Pretty cold and humid in winter. *Camping E Pousada Internacional*, R Manêncio Martins, 600 m from turn-off, T5233053. For vehicles and tents. *Camping Clube do Brasil*, by the national park entrance 17 km from Foz, T5238599, US$10 per person (half with International Camping Card), pool, clean. Park vehicle or put tent away from trees in winter in case of heavy rainstorms, no restaurants, food there is not very good, closes at 2300. Camping is not permitted by the *Hotel das Cataratas* and falls. Sleeping in your car inside the park is also prohibited.

Eating **Expensive** *Bufalo Branco*, R Rebouças 530. Superb all you can eat *churrasco*, includes filet mignon, bull's testicles, salad bar and desert. Sophisticated surroundings and attentive service. Highly recommended. *Cabeça de Boi*, Av Brasil 1325. Live music, buffet. Churrasco, but coffee and pastries also. *Rafain*, Av das Cataratas, Km 6.5, T5231177, closed Sun. Out of town, take a taxi or arrange with travel agency. Set price for excellent buffet with folkloric music and dancing (2100-2300) from throughout South America, touristy but very entertaining. Recommended. *Zaragoza*, R Quintino Bocaiúva 882, T5743084. Large and upmarket, for Spanish dishes and seafood. Recommended.

Mid-range *Bier Garten*, No 550. Pizzeria and choparia; beer garden in name only but some trees. *Boulevard*, Av das Cataratas, 1118, T5234245. Food court open daily from 1700, and all day Sun. *Brasil & Brazil*, Brasil 157. A handful of food stalls, with live music and dancing 2000-0200, bingo. *Tropicana*, Av Juscelino Kubitschek 228. All-you-can-eat pizza or *churrascaria* with salad bar, good value.

Cheap *Oficina do Sorvete*, Av Jorge Schimmelpfeng, 244, open daily 1100-0100. Excellent ice creams, a popular local hang-out. **Seriously cheap** *City Caffé*, Av Jorge Schimmelpfeng, 898. Stylish café open daily 0800-2330 for sandwiches, Arabic snacks and pastries. *Marias e Maria*, Av Brasil 50. Good *confeitaria*.

Bars & nightclubs Bars, all doubling as restaurants, concentrated on **Av Jorge Schimmelpfeng** for 2 blocks from Av Brasil to R Mal Floriano Peixoto. Wed-Sun are best nights; crowd tends to be young. *Alquimia*, No 334, T5723154. Popular. Nightclub, *Dancing*, attached, open 2400-0500, US$3. *BR3*, corner with Av Brasil. Modern, open until 2400. *Capitão Bar*, No 288 and Almte Barroso, T5721512. Large, loud and popular, nightclub attached. On R Edmundo de Barros, 446 *Armazém*, intimate and sophisticated, attracts discerning locals, good atmosphere, mellow live music, US$1 cover. Recommended. *Oba! Oba!*, Av das Cataratas 3700, T5742255/5724217 (Antigo Castelinho). Live samba show Mon-Sat 2315-0015, very popular, US$9 for show and 1 drink. *Rafain*, Av das Cataratas Km 6.5. With floor show and food, see Eating above.

Casinos Organized tours to casinos (illegal in Brazil) over the border in Paraguay and Argentina take 3 hrs. *Gran Casino Itaipu*, Av 11 de Septembre, 816, Cuidad del Este, Paraguay, T/F512294, restaurant, piano bar. *Casino Iguazú*, Ruta 12 Km, 1640, Puerto Iguazú, Misiones, Argentina, T3757-498000. Open weekdays 1800-0500, 24 hrs weekends, restaurant.

Entertainment

Cinema *Boulevard*, Av das Cataratas, 1118, T5234245. Large complex open from 1700 and all day Sun. Also bowling, games rooms and bingo.

Av Brasil is the main shopping street. *Kunda Livraria Universitária*, R Almte Barroso 1473, T5234606. Guides and maps of the area, books on the local wildlife, novels, etc in several languages, including French and English. *Tres Fronteiras*, Rodovia das Cataratas, Km11. Large shop on road to falls, frequent stop on tours. Chocolates, and huge selection of crafts and jewellery, some of it overpriced.

Shopping

Beware of overcharging for tours by touts at the bus terminal. Many travel agents on Av Brasil and in larger hotels. *Acquatur*, Av das Cataratas, 3175, T/F5299554, acquaturfoz@uol.com.br Offer full range of tours in executive cars with bilingual guides and airport transfers. *Caribe Tur* at the international airport and *Hotel das Cataratas*, T5231230, runs tours from the airport to the Argentine side and *Hotel das Cataratas*. *Jaha Iguassu Explorer*, T5231484, T91066985 (mob), 24 hrs, chilelindo7@ hotmail.com Provides useful bus information for all sights. Visits to rural Paraguay (full day, US$25), Argentinian falls (in mini-van, US$10, includes lunch but not guide or entrance fee), bike tours to Argentina, horse riding and overnight stays in national park. Recommended guides, *Wilson Engel*, T5741367, friendly, flexible. *Ruth Campo Silva*, STTC Turismo, *Hotel Bourbon*, Rodovia das Cataratas, T5743849, F5743557 (American Express). *Chiderly Batismo Pequeno*, R Almte Barroso 505, Foz, T5743367.

Tour operators

Local Taxis are only good value for short distances when you are carrying all your luggage.

Transport

Long distance Air Iguaçu international airport, 18 km south of town near the falls. In Arrivals is *Banco do Brasil* and *Caribe Tours* and *Câmbio*, car rental offices, tourist office and an official taxi stand, US$10 to town centre (US$11 from town to airport). *Transbalan* (Parque Nacional) town bus for US$0.50, first at 0530, does not permit large amounts of luggage but backpacks OK. Many hotels run minibus services for a small charge. Daily flights to **Rio**, **São Paulo**, **Curitiba** and other Brazilian cities.

Buses For transport to the falls, see above under Parque Nacional Foz do Iguaçu. Long distance terminal (*Rodoviária*), Av Costa e Silva, 4 km from centre on road to Curitiba, T5223633; bus to centre, any bus that says 'Rodoviária', US$0.65. Book departures as soon as possible. As well as the tourist office (see below), there is a Cetreme desk for tourists who have lost their documents, Guarda Municipal (police) and luggage store. To **Curitiba**, *Pluma, Sulamericana*, 9-10 hrs, 3 daily, paved road, US$15; to **Guaíra** via Cascavel only, 5 hrs, US$10; to **Florianópolis**, *Catarinense* and *Reunidas*, US$28, 14 hrs; *Reunidas* to **Porto Alegre**, US$30; to **São Paulo**, 16 hrs, *Pluma* US$30, *executivo* 6 a day, plus 1 *leito*; to **Rio** 22 hrs, several daily, US$38. To **Asunción**, *Pluma*, *RYSA* (direct at 1430), US$11.

Car hire *Avis*, airport, T5231510. *Localiza* at airport, T5296300, and Av Juscelino Kubitschek 2878, T5221608. *Unidas*, Av Santos Dumont, 1515, near airport, T/F3390880.

Airline offices *Rio Sul*, R Jorge Sanways 779, T5741680, freephone T0800-992994. *TAM*, R Rio Branco, 640, T5238500 (offers free transport to Ciudad del Este for its flights,

Directory

Iguaçu Falls and the South

all cross-border documentation dealt with). *Transbrasil*, Av Brasil 1225, T5743836. *Varig*, Av Juscelino Kubitschek 463, T5232111. *Vasp*, Av Brasil 845, T5232212.

Banks There are plenty of banks and travel agents on Av Brasil. *Banco do Brasil*, Av Brasil 1377 has ATM. High commission for TCs. *Bradesco*, Av Brasil 1202. Cash advance on Visa. *Banco 24 Horas* at Oklahoma petrol station. *HSBC*, Av Brasil, 1151, ATM.

Communications Internet: *Boulevard*, see *Cinema* above. *Café Internet*, R Rebouças 950, T/F5232122, US$1.50 per hr; also phone, fax and photocopying. Ask for fastest machine, open 0900-2300 and Sun afternoon. *Café Pizzanet*, R Rio Branco, 412, corner with Av Juscelino Kubitschek, US$2 per hr. Pizzeria, fax, phone, photocopier. *Zipfoz.com*, R Barão do Rio Branco, 412, corner with Av Juscelino Kubitschek. Smart, a/c, US$1.50 per hr. **Post office**: Praça Getúlio Vargas 72. **Telephone**: *Telepar* on Edmundo de Barros.

Embassies and consulates *Argentina*, Travessa Eduardo Bianchi 26, T5742969. Mon-Fri 1000-1430. *France*, R Federico Engels 48, Villa Yolanda, T5743693. *Paraguay*, Bartolomeu de Gusmão 480, T5232898.

Laundry *Londres Lavanderia*, R Reboucas, 711, only US$1.50 per kg, open Sat.

Medical services There is a free 24-hr clinic on Av Paraná, 1525, opposite Lions Club, T5731134. Few buses: take taxi or walk (about 25 mins).

Voltage 110 volts AC.

Border with Argentina This crossing via the Puente Tancredo Neves is straightforward. Even if crossing on a day visit, you must have your passport. If leaving to stay in Puerto Iguazú, you must visit Brazilian immigration to get your exit stamp. Then visit Argentine immigration on the Argentine side to get your entry stamp (if staying in Puerto Iguazú for only 24 hours, Argentine officials may not give you a stamp). Money exchange beside Argentine immigration.

Be sure you know when the last bus departs from Puerto Iguazú for Foz (usually 2000) and remember that in summer Argentina is an hour earlier than Brazil

Transport Buses: to Puerto Iguazú run every 20 mins from the Terminal Urbana, crossing the frontier bridge; 30 mins' journey, *Três Fronteiras*, US$1.50, or 2 *reais*. If you have to get out of the bus to get your passport stamped at immigration, the bus waits. To get to the Argentine side of the falls without going into Puerto Iguazú, get out of the bus from the frontier bridge at the first traffic lights and cross the road for the bus to the falls. To **Buenos Aires**, *Pluma* daily 1200, US$46. It is cheaper to go to **Posadas** via Paraguay. **Taxis**: Foz to the border, waiting for Brazilian immigration, US$10; Foz-Argentina US$35, US$45 to *Hotel Sheraton Iguazú*.

Itaipu

The **Itaipu Dam**, on the Río Paraná is the site of the largest single power station in the world built jointly by Brazil and Paraguay. Construction of this massive scheme began in 1975 and it came into operation in 1984. The main dam is 8 km long, creating a lake which covers 1,400 sq km. The height of the main dam is equivalent to a 65-storey building, the amount of concrete used in its construction is 15 times more than that used for the Channel Tunnel between England and France. The 18 turbines have an installed capacity of 12,600,000 Kw and produce about 75 billion Kwh a year, providing 80% of Paraguay's electricity and 25% of Brazil's. The Paraguayan side may be visited from Ciudad del Este. Both governments are proud to trumpet the accolade, 'one of the seven wonders of the modern world' (the only one in South America), which was given to it by the American Society of Civil Engineering in *Popular Mechanics* in 1995. Whatever your views on the need for huge hydroelectric projects, it is worth visiting Itaipu to gain a greater understanding of the scale and impact of such constructions.

The **Ecomuseu de Itaipu** (Av Tancredo Neves, Km 11, T5205813, 0900-1100, 1400-1700 Tue-Sat, 1400-1700 Mon) and Iguaçu Environmental

Education Centre are geared to inform about the preservation of the local culture and environment, or that part of it which isn't underwater. ■ *Free with guide. Recommended.* A massive reforestation project is underway, and over 14 million seedlings have already been planted. On the lake's shore, six biological refuges have been created.

Tours of Itaipu

Tours are free, but in groups only, Mon-Sat at 0800, 0900, 1000, 1400, 1530 (closed between 1100 and 1400). 'Technical' visits can be arranged. If it's sunny, go in the morning as the sun is behind the dam in the afternoon and you will get poor photographs. The Visitors' Centre, T5206999, www.itaipu.gov.br, has a short video presentation (ask for the English version) with stunning photography and amazing technical information, apparently available in English but usually only in Portuguese. The spillways are capable of discharging the equivalent of 40 times the average flow of the Iguaçu Falls. If you are lucky, the spillways will be open. After the film and a brief visit to the souvenir shop where an English guidebook is available, a coach will take you to the dam itself. As it crosses the top, you get a stomach-churning view of the spillways and really begin to appreciate the scale of the project. **Buses** The 'executive' bus and agency tours are an unnecessary expense. No 110 or 120 from Terminal Urbana (stand 50 Batalhão) go every 13 mins to the Public Relations office at the main entrance (US$0.40), 110, Conjunto C Porto Meira, 120 via Sul goes within 250 m.

Ciudad del Este

Iguaçu Falls and the South

Described as the biggest shopping centre in Latin America, Ciudad del Este attracts Brazilian and Argentine visitors in search of bargain prices for electrical goods, watches, perfumes, etc. Founded as Ciudad Presidente Stroessner in 1957, the city grew rapidly during the construction of the Itaipú hydroelectric project. Dirty, noisy, unfriendly and brashly commercial, it is worth a visit just for the people watching, but you should be careful with valuables and be particularly cautious after dark.

Phone code: 061
Population: 140,000

Excursions

The Paraguayan side of the **Itaipú** hydroelectric project can be visited. Buses run from Rodríguez y García, outside the terminal, to the Visitors' Centre. ■ *0730-1200, 1330-1700 Mon-Sat, 0800-1200, 1330-1630 Sun and holidays. Free conducted tours include a film show (in several languages) 45 mins before bus tours, which start at 0830, 0930, 1030, 1400, 1500, 1600, check times in advance. Take your passport.* On the way to Itaipú is **Flora y Fauna Itaipú Binacional**, with animals and plants rescued from the area when the dam was built. It is about 2 km from the visitors' centre on the road back to Cuidad del Este. ■ *0830-1030, 1330-1630.*

    Cascada de Monday (Monday Falls), where the Río Monday drops into the Paraná Gorge 10 km south of Ciudad del Este, is a worthwhile trip; there is good fishing below the falls. Return fare by taxi US$20.

Sleeping
Accommodation is generally expensive

A *Convair*, Adrián Jara y García, T500342. Comfortable, cheaper rooms without bath. **A** *Executive*, Adrián Jara y Curupayty, T500942/3. With breakfast – restaurant recommended. **A** *Residence de la Tour* at Paraná Country Club, 5 km from centre, T60316. Superb, Swiss-owned, excellent restaurant (US$12-16 per person), swimming pool, gardens, beautiful view. **B** *Catedral*, C A López 838, several blocks from commercial area, T500378. With breakfast, TV, a/c, large, modern with pool, restaurant. **B** *Gran Hotel Acaray*, 11 de Septiembre y Río Paraná, T/F511471/5. Pool, casino, nightclub, restaurant. **B** *San Rafael*, Abay y Adrián Jara, T68134. Large rooms, with breakfast, German and English spoken.

▶▶ Shop till you drop

Though hardly on every traveller's list of destinations, Ciudad del Este is worth a visit if you are in the area. As you enter the city across the bridge from Brazil you see hunched figures struggling back into Brazil, dwarfed by the massive bags strapped on their backs. Nearing the border control, many bundle their bags over the side of the bridge, jump down on to the riverbank after them and clamber back up the slope with their valuables, undoubtedly worth more than the US$150 allowed duty-free by the law, but unchecked by the customs officers who watch the spectacle with disinterest.

The streets of the city itself are narrow and congested. On every side you are bombarded by street vendors trying to convince you to buy steak knives, hair clippers, massaging hair brushes, sweatshirts..., the list is endless and is accompanied by a cacophony of shouting in Spanish, Portuguese, Guaraní and English. To get a more distant view of the action, try the Fleur de Lys bar on the main street: it accepts almost any currency, offers a good range of drinks and snacks and allows you to watch Ciudad del Este in action down below.

C *Itaipú*, Rodríguez y Nanawa, T500371. With breakfast, a/c. **C** *Munich*, Fernández y Miranda, T500347. With breakfast, a/c, garage. Recommended. **C** *Puerta del Sol*, Rodríguez y Boquerón, just off the main street, T500798. A/c. **C-D** *El Cid*, Recalde 425, T512221. With breakfast, a/c, cheaper with fan. **D** *Austria* (also known as *Viena*), Fernández 165, above restaurant, T500883. With good breakfast and a/c, Austrian family, good views from upper floors. Warmly recommended. **D** *Tripolis*, San Blas 331, T512450. A/c, poor restaurant, unhelpful, unsafe. **E** *Caribe*, Emiliano Fernández, opposite *Austria*. A/c, hot water, nice garden, helpful owner. Recommended.

Eating
Many restaurants close on Sunday

Coreio, San Blas 125. Good Korean food. *Hotel Austria/Viena*, good Austrian food, clean, good value. Cheaper restaurants can be found along García and in the market. *Mi Ranchero*, on Adrián Jara. Good food, service and prices, well known. *New Tokyo*, Adrián Jara 202. Authentic Japanese. *Osaka*, Adrián Jara. Good Japanese. *Seoul*, Curupayty y Adrián Jara. Good *parrillada*.

Shopping
Prices are decidedly high for North American and European visitors. The leather market is well worth a visit, be sure to bargain. Don't buy perfume at tempting prices on the street, it's only coloured water. Make sure that shops which package your goods pack what you actually bought. Also watch the exchange rates if you're a short term visitor from Argentina or Brazil.

Transport
Air To **Asunción**, *Arpa*, 3 flights Mon-Sat, 1 on Sun. Also *TAM* daily en route to São Paulo.

Buses The terminal is on the southern outskirts. No 4 bus from the centre goes there, US$0.50 (taxi US$3.50). Many buses (US$17.50 *rápido*, 4½ hrs, at night only; US$10 *común*, 6 hrs) to and from **Asunción**. *Nuestra Señora* and *Rysa* recommended. To **Encarnación** (for Posadas and Argentina), along a fully paved road, frequent, 3 hrs, US$7.50 (cheaper than via Foz do Iguaçu).

To Brazil International bus from outside the terminal to the new long-distance terminal (*Rodoviária*) outside Foz. Local buses from the terminal run along Av Adrián Jara and go to the city terminal (*terminal urbana*) in **Foz** every 15 mins, 0600-2000, US$0.65. Most buses do not wait at immigration, so disembark to get your exit stamp, walk across the bridge (10 mins) and obtain your entry stamp; keep your ticket and continue to Foz on the next bus free. Paraguayan taxis cross freely to Brazil (US$20), but it is cheaper to walk across the bridge and then take a taxi, bargain hard. You can pay in either currency.

To Argentina Direct buses to **Puerto Iguazú**, frequent service by several companies from outside the terminal, US$2, you need to get Argentine and Paraguayan stamps (not Brazilian); the bus does not wait so keep your ticket for the next bus.

Airline offices *TAM*, Edif SABA, Monseñor Rodríguez. **Banks** Local banks open Mon-Fri 0730-1100. Dollars can be changed into *reais* in town. *Banco Holandés Unido*, cash on MasterCard, 5% commission. Several exchange houses: *Cambio Guaraní*, Monseñor Rodríguez, changes TCs for US$0.50. Branch on Friendship Bridge has good rates for many currencies, including dollars and reais. *Tupi Cambios*, Adrián Jara 351. *Cambios Chaco*, Adrián Jara y Curupayty. *Casa de cambio* rates are better than street rates. Money changers (not recommended) operate at the bus terminal, but not at the Brazilian end of the Friendship Bridge. **Communications** Telecommunications: *Antelco*, Alejo García and Pai Pérez, near the centre on the road to the bus terminal. **Embassies and consulates** *Brazil*, C Pampliega 337, corner of Pai Perez, T561500984, F56163283.

Directory

Guaíra

In the far northwest of the state, also on the Rio Paraná, were the tremendous waterfalls known in Brazil as Sete Quedas (the Seven Falls), and in Spanish Latin America as the Salto de Guaíra; they were drowned by the filling of the lake behind the Itaipu dam in 1982. The 1978 *South American Handbook* described Sete Quedas thus: "The great river, nearly 5 km wide, hurls itself through the rocky gorges of the falls with a tremendous roar. Rocky islands between the falls are connected by wooden suspension bridges; the whole area can warrant a whole day. Many of the falls are from 30 to 40 m high. This is the most enormous volume of falling water in the world; it is double Niagara's."

Phone code: 044
Colour map 5, grid A2
Population: 29,000

Guaíra, about 130 km north of Iguaçu by air or road, has not been flooded, but much of its agricultural land and its clay beds have. The 4 km from Guaíra to the lake can be walked or done by car (US$2.50 one way, return taxi up to US$12). Entrance to the park is US$0.50. There is a small museum three blocks from Guaíra's rodoviária. ■ *0800-1100 and 1400-1700.*

A *Deville*, R Paraguai 1205, T/F6421617. Restaurant, pool. **C** *Palace Hotel*, Rui Barbosa 1190, near the rodoviária, T6421325. **D** *Majestic*, opposite rodoviária. With or without bath, with breakfast, good. **D** *Sete Quedas*, Otávio Tosta 385. With breakfast and sandwich lunch, not too clean. For eating, try *O Chopão*, Thomaz Luiz Zebalhos 427. Pleasant.

Sleeping & eating

Buses: to **Campo Grande**, buy a ticket (US$25) at the Guaíra rodoviária, take a ferry from the Porto da Paragem at the end of Av Almte Tamandaré to Porto Ilha Grande in Mato Grosso do Sul, then bus to Mondo Novo, change bus there for Campo Grande. Morning and night bus, 12 hrs in all. There is a bus service between **Curitiba** and Guaíra, US$15, 10 hrs. To **São Paulo**, US$30, 16 hrs. Other destinations include **Iguaçu** (bumpy, but interesting), 5 hrs, but may be cancelled in the wet, US$10.

Transport

Embassies & consulates *Brazil*, Av Pres Stroessner 259, T/F546305. *Paraguay*, T6421505.

Directory

Immigration and transport There is an hourly passenger ferry service from Porto de Lanchas and Porto Guaíra to Salto del Guayra on the Paraguayan side, US$0.50, and an hourly car ferry from Porto Guaíra (US$4 for car with 2 people). The car ferry runs until 1830 (Brazilian time). Customs and immigration for documentation close at 1700. There is a time change when you cross the Paraná. The area is intensively patrolled for contraband and stolen cars, ensure that all documentation is in order.

Border with Paraguay

Iguaçu Falls and the South

Santa Catarina

Population: 5.5 million

Today's mix of beach tourism, agriculture and industry give no indication of Santa Catarina's turbulent past. The old town of Laguna is especially interesting in this respect. Famous for its beaches and popular with Argentine and Paraguayan holidaymakers in high summer, this is one of the best beaches on the Brazilian coast for surfing. Immigrant communities, such as German, give a unique personality to many towns and districts and every year one million people visit the Oktoberfest in Blumenau. Rural tourism is increasingly important and the highlands just in from the coast are among the coldest in Brazil, giving winter landscapes reminiscent of Europe, or Brazil's southern neighbours. Except for the summer months of January and February, the beaches of Santa Catarina are pleasant and uncrowded. The best months to visit are April and May.

As well as each region having its own climate and scenery, Santa Catarina also has a distinctive culture depending on its immigrants. The Portuguese from the Azores settled along the coast, the Germans moved along the Itajaí Valley, the Italians headed for the south and into Rio Grande do Sul, while in the north there are Ukrainians, Japanese, Africans, Hispanics and Indians. Each group maintains its traditions and festivals, its architecture, food and language or accent. The vast majority of people today can trace their origin to these ethnic origins.

Florianópolis

Phone code: 048
Colour map 5, grid B5
Population: 345,000

Halfway along the coast of Santa Catarina is the state capital Florianópolis, founded in 1726 on the Ilha de Santa Catarina. The natural beauty of the island, beaches and bays make Florianópolis a magnet for holidaymakers in summer. The southern beaches are usually good for swimming, the east for surfing, but be careful of the undertow. 'Floripa' is accepted as a shortened version of Florianópolis, with the people known as 'Floripans', although they like to call themselves 'Ilhéus', or Islanders.

Ins & outs
See also Transport, page 316

Getting there International and domestic flights arrive at Hercílo Luz airport. Buses from international destinations and from other Brazilian cities arrive at the Rita Maia rodoviária on the island.

Getting around Florianópolis is a small city, quite hilly but easy and safe to walk around. To explore the island you need to use the good bus services; standard buses and more expensive yellow micro buses run to nearly every important point on the island.

Tourist information

The main office is in the Mercado Público, 3rd booth along from R Arcipreste Paiva, T2445822, open Mon-Fri 0800-1200 and 1330-1800, Sat and Sun 0800-1200. *Setur*, head office at Portal Turístico de Florianópolis, mainland end of the bridge, Av Eng Max de Souza 236, Coqueiros, T2445822, 0800-2000 (0800-1800 Sat/Sun). At rodoviária, Av Paulo Fontes, T2232777, and airport, 0700-1800 (0800-1800 Sat/Sun), maps available, free, www.guiafloripa.com.br Santur, Edif ARS, R Felipe Schmidt 249, 9th floor, T2246300, F2221145, helpful, www.ciasc.gov.br and www.sc.gov.br/santur A good series of bilingual books on all of southern Brazil is published by *Mares do Sul*, R Luiz Pasteur, Trindade, T/F3331544, www.maresdosul.com.br

Sights

The island is joined to the mainland by two bridges, one of which is Ponte Hercílio Luz, the longest steel suspension bridge in Brazil, now closed but beautifully lit up at night. The newer Colombo Machado Salles bridge has a pedestrian and cycle way beneath the roadway.

In the 1960s Florianópolis port was closed and the aspect of the city's southern shoreline was fundamentally changed, with land reclaimed from the bay. The two main remnants of the old port area are the late 19th-century **Alfândega** and **Mercado Público**, both on Rua Conselheiro Mafra, fully

Florianópolis

Iguaçu Falls and the South

■ **Sleeping**	4 Farol da Ilha	8 Portal da Ilha	● **Eating**	4 Lindacap
1 Castelmar	5 Felippe	9 Valerim Center	1 Box 32	5 Papparella
2 Central Sumaré	6 Florianópolis Palace	10 Valerim Plaza	2 Café das Artes	6 Vida
3 Faial	7 Mercure Diplomata		3 La Cucina	

restored and painted ochre. In the Alfândega is a handicraft market. ■ *0900-1900 Mon-Fri, 0900-1200 Sat. T2246082*. The market is divided into *stalls*, some are bars and restaurants, others shops. ■ *0600-1830 Mon-Fri, 0600-1300 Sat, a few fish stalls open on Sun, T2253200*. The **Cathedral** (1773) on Praça 15 de Novembro was built on the site of the first chapel erected by the founder of the city, Francisco Dias Velho. Inside is a life-size sculpture in wood of the flight into Egypt, originally from the Austrian Tyrol. **Forte Santana** (1763), beneath the Ponte Hercílio Luz, houses a **Museu de Armas Major Lara Ribas**, with a collection of guns and other items, mostly post Second World War. ■ *0830-1200, 1400-1800 Tue-Sun, 1400-1800 Mon. Free. T2296263*. There are four other museums. The **Museu Histórico**, in the 18th-century Palácio Cruz e Souza, on Praça 15 de Novembre, has a lavish interior with highly decorated ceilings and contains furniture, documents and objects belonging to governors of the state. ■ *1000-1800 Tue-Fri, 1000-1600 Sat, Sun and holidays. T2213504. US$1*. The **Museu de Antropologia**, at the Trindade University Campus, has a collection of stone and other archaeological remains from the cultures of the coastal Indians. ■ *0900-1200, 1300-1700 Mon-Fri. T3318821*. There is a look-out point at **Morro da Cruz** (take *Empresa Trindadense* bus, US$0.60, waits 15 minutes, or walk). On the north shore, outside the perimeter road, the mangroves of the **Mangue do Itacorubi** are being protected.

Essentials

Sleeping
■ *on map, page 313*

A *Baía Norte Palace*, Av Beira Mar Norte 220, T2253144, F2253227. On the main road, a/c, TV, safe, pool, business facilities, restaurant. **A** *Castelmar*, R Felipe Schmidt 1260, T2253228, www.iaccess.com.br/castelmar Pool, a/c, TV, laundry, restaurant. **A** *Faial*, R Felipe Schmidt 603, T2252766, F2250435. Comfortable and traditional with simple rooms. Good restaurant. **A** *Florianópolis Palace*, R Artista Bittencourt 14, T2249633, F2230300. Recommended. **A** *Mercure Diplomata*, Av Paulo Fontes 1210, T2244455, F2255082. Very good views, 4-star hotel but prices sometimes negotiable.

B *Baia Sul*, R Tiradentes 167, near Praça 15 de Novembro, T2232269, F2240810. With breakfast, a/c, safe, good. **B** *Farol da Ilha*, R Bento Gonçalves 163, T2252766, F2250435. New, a/c, TV, not far from rodoviária. **B** *Oscar*, Av Hercílio Luz 760, T2220099, F2220978. A/c, TV, safe, central. **B** *Porto da Ilha*, R Dom Jaime Câmara 84, T3220007, F3220144. Central, comfortable. Recommended. **B** *Valerim Plaza*, R Felipe Schmidt 705, T/F2253388. 3-star, more modern than *Valerim Center*, but rather bland, buffet restaurant open till 2300.

C *Pousada Recanto da Costa*, R 13 de Maio 41. With breakfast, hot water, laundry facilities, parking, 15 mins' walk from centre. **C** *Valerim Center*, R Felipe Schmidt 554, T2251100. Functional 2-star, large rooms, hot water, hard beds.

D *Central Sumaré*, R Felipe Schmidt 423, T2225359. Breakfast, clean and friendly, good value but rooms vary, **C** with bath; **F** for single. **D-E** *Felippe*, R João Pinto 132, 1 block from 15 de Novembro, by Terminal Urbano, T2224122. Small rooms, some with no windows, breakfast is just a cup of coffee, dirty bathrooms, **F** without bath.

Youth hostels **E** per person *Ilha de Santa Catarina*, R Duarte Schutel 227, T2253781, F2251692. IYHA, breakfast included, cooking facilities, clean, some traffic noise, very friendly, will store luggage. Recommended. Prices rise in Dec-Feb; more expensive for non-members. See under Canasvieiras, page 319.

Camping *Camping Clube do Brasil*, São Joã o do Rio Vermelho, north of Lagoa da Conceição, 21 km out of town; also at Lagoa da Conceição, Praia da Armação, Praia dos Ingleses, Praia Canasvieiras. 'Wild' camping allowed at Ponta de Sambaqui and Praias Brava, Aranhas, Galheta, Mole, Campeche, Campanhas and Naufragados; 4 km south of Florianópolis, camping site with bar at Praia do Sonho on the mainland, beautiful, deserted beach with an island fort nearby. 'Camping Gaz' cartridges from *Riachuelo Supermercado*, on R Alvim and R São Jorge.

Eating
● *on map, page 313*

Take a walk along Rua Bocaiúva, east of R Almte Lamego, to find the whole street filled with Italian restaurants, barbecue places and an exclusive fish restaurant, *Toca da Garoupa* (turn on to R Alves de Brito 178). A popular place to start a night out (after 2100) is the *Nouvelle Vague*, more commonly known as *A Creperia*, buzzing every weekend, wide selection of sweet and savoury pancakes. Shrimp dishes are good everywhere.

Expensive *Don Pepé Forno a Lenha* is a great place to go for a quiet romantic meal with a *serenador* (cover charge added to bill for singer).

Mid-range *Box 32*, see *bars* below. *Lindacap*, R Felipe Schmidt 1162 (closed Mon, Sun lunch only). Fish, chicken and meat *pratos* as well as seafood, smart, good views. Recommended. *Macarronada Italiana*, Av Beira Mar Norte 2458. Good, comfortable, upmarket Italian. Next door is *Pizza da Piedra*. *O Mercador*, Box 33/4 Mercado Público. Excellent self-service specializing in fish and seafood, tables outside on cobbled street. Recommended. *Papparella*, Almte Lamego 1416. Excellent giant pizzas. *Pirão*, Mercado Público, upper floor on main square. Elegant rustic style, with views over market, open 1100-1430. Self service. Recommended. *Trapiche*, Box 31, Mercado Público. Self service fish and seafood, tables on pavement.

Cheap *Café das Artes*, nice café at north end of R Esteves Junior, No 734. With excellent cakes. *Kayskidum*, Av Beira Mar Norte 2566. Lanchonete and crêperie, very popular. *Mirantes*, R Alvaro de Carvalho 246, Centro. Buffet self-service, good value. Recommended; also on R Vidal Ramos opposite Produtos Naturais. *Pim-Pão*, R Deodoro. Good cheap breakfast, lunches.

Seriously cheap For a wide selection of juices and snacks: *Cía Lanches*, Ten Silveira e R Trajano, downstairs, and, in Edif Dias Velho, Av R Felipe Schmidt 303, *Laranja Madura*, *Sabor e Sucos* and *Lanchonete Dias Velho*.

Vegetarian *La Cucina*, R Padre Roma 291. Buffet lunch, Mon-Sat, pay by weight, good, vegetarian choices. Recommended. *Vida*, R Visc de Ouro Preto 298, next to Alliance Française. Good.

Bars & nightclubs

The Mercado Público in the centre, which is alive with fish sellers and stalls during the day, has a different atmosphere at the end of the day when hard working locals turn up to unwind. However, this area is not particularly safe at night and most bars and restaurants are closed by 2200. The stall, *Box 32*, is good for seafood as well as a bar specializing in *cachaça*. *Restaurant Pirão* overlooks the market square with a quieter view and live Brazilian music on Tue, Thu and Fri. *Empórium*, Bocaiúva 79, is a shop by day and popular bar at night. Other clubs and bars may need a car: *Café Matisse*, Av Irineu Bornhausen 5000, inside the Centro Integrade de Cultura and the hotspots at the beaches. To find out about events and theme nights check the Beiramar centre for notices in shop windows, ask in surf shops or take a trip to the University of Santa Catarina in Trindade and check out the noticeboards. The news-paper *Diário Catarinense* gives details of bigger events, eg Oktoberfest.

Nightclubs *Ilhéu*, Av Prof Gama d'Eça e R Jaime Câmara, US$5. Bar open until early hours, tables spill outside, very popular with locals, fills up quickly, venue for live music rather than a disco (tiny dancefloor). *Café Cancun*, Av Beira Mar Norte, T2251029. Wed-Sun from 2000, US$5, bars, restaurant, dancing, sophisticated.

Iguaçu Falls and the South

Entertainment   **Cinema**   The 3-screen cinema at Shopping Centre Beiramar has international films with subtitles. **Music**   Free live music every Sat morning at the market place near the bus terminal.

Festivals   In **Dec** and **Jan** the whole island dances to the sound of the *Boi-de-Mamão*, a type of dance which incorporates the puppets of Bernunça, Maricota (the Goddess of Love, a puppet with long arms to embrace everyone) and Tião, the monkey. The Portuguese brought the tradition of the bull, which has great significance in Brazilian celebrations. Around **Easter** is the Festival of the Bull, *Farra de Boi*. It is only in the south that, controversially nowadays, the bull is killed on Easter Sunday. The festival arouses fierce local pride and there is much celebration around this time.

Shopping   *Shopping Centre Beiramar* is a famous shopping centre which attracts bus loads of eager shoppers from outside the state. There are many things on offer, from surfboards to fashion items. The 3-screen cinema is here. There are many smaller shopping malls dotted aroung the resorts. However, bargain hunters are better off bartering in the family-run businesses at the Mercado Público. Here, *Casa da Alfândega*, has a good selection of crafts and souvenirs.

Tour operators   *Ilhatur Turismo e Cambio*, R Jerónimo Coelho 185, T2246333, F2236921. Very popular boat trips can be made in the bay with *Scuna Sul*, T2221806, www.scunasul.com.br, from US$7.50.

Transport   **Local Buses**: there are 3 bus stations for routes on the island, or close by on the mainland: Terminal de Ônibus Interurbano between Av Paulo Fontes and R Francisco Tolentino, west of the Mercado Público; Terminal Urbano between Av Paulo Fontes and R Antônio Luz, east of Praça Fernando Machado; a terminal at R Silva Jardim and R José da Costa. Yellow micro buses (*Transporte Ejecutivo*), starting from the south end of Praça 15 de Novembro and other stops, charge US$0.75-US$1.45 depending on destination. Similarly, normal bus fares vary according to destination, from US$0.65.

Long distance Air: international and domestic flights arrive at Hercílio Luz airport, Av Deomício Freitas, 12 km from town, T2360879. Take *Ribeiroense* bus 'Corredor Sudoeste' from Terminal Urbano.

Buses: international and buses from other Brazilian cities arrive at the rodoviária Rita Maia on the island, at the east (island) end of the Ponte Colombo Machado Salles. Regular daily buses to **Porto Alegre** (US$16, 7 hrs), **São Paulo**, 9 hrs (US$23.75, *leito* US$36.25), **Rio**, 20 hrs (US$31 *convencional*, US$42 *executive*, 55 *leito*); to **Foz do Iguaçu** (US$22, continuing to **Asunción** US$30), to most other Brazilian cities. To **São Joaquim** at 1145, 1945 with *Reunidos*, 1815 with *Nevatur*, 5-6 hrs, US$9.30; to **Laguna** US$5.25. No direct bus to Corumbá, change at Campo Grande.

International buses: Montevideo, US$52, daily, by *TTL*. **Buenos Aires**, US$55, *Pluma*, buses very full in summer, book 1 week in advance.

Car hire: *Auto Locadora Coelho*, Felipe Schmidt 81, vehicles in good condition. *Localiza* at the airport, T2361244, and at Av Paulo Fontes 730, T2255558. *Interlocadora*, T2360179 at the airport, F2361370, rates from US$40 a day before supplements.

Directory   **Airline offices** *Aerolíneas Argentinas*, R Tte Silveira 200, 8th floor, T2247835, F2227267. *Gol*, T0300-7892121, www.voegol.com.br *Nordeste/Rio Sul*, Jerônimo Coelho 185, sala 601, T2247008, airport T2361779. *TAM*, at airport, T2361812. *Varig*, Av R Branco 796, T2247266, F2222725. *Vasp*, Av Osmar Cunha 105, T2241122, F2242970.

Banks *Banco do Brasil*, Praça 15 de Novembro, exchange upstairs, 1000-1500, huge commission on cash or TCs. Lots of ATMs downstairs, some say Visa/Plus. *HSBC*, ATM, R Felipe Schmidt 376, corner with R Álvaro de Carvalho. *Banco Estado de Santa Catarina* (BESC), câmbio, R Felip, Schmidt e Jerônimo Coelho, 1000-1600, no commission on TCs. *Lovetur*, Av Osmar Cunha 15, Ed Ceisa and *Centauro Turismo* at same address. *Açoriano Turismo*, Jaime Câmara 106, T2243939, takes Amex. Money changers on R Felipe Schmidt outside BESC. ATM for MasterCard/Cirrus at *Banco Itaú*, Shopping Centre Beiramar (not in the centre, bus Expresso).

Communications Internet: *Moncho*, Tiradentes 181. **Post office**: Praça 15 de Novembro 5. **Telephone**: Praça Pereira Oliveira 20.

Embassies and consulates *Austria*, R Luiz Delfino 66, Apto 501, T2225952, open 1500-1700 Mon-Fri, phone in advance. *Chile*, R Alvaro de Carvalho 267, 6th floor, Edif Mapil, T2233383. *France*, Alliance Française, T2227589, 0900-1200 Fri. *Spain*, R Almte Alvim 24, Casa 9, T2221821, F2241018. *Uruguay*, R Prof Walter de Bona Castela 26, T2344645, 0800-1200, 1400-1800.

Laundry *Lav e Lev*, R Felipe Schmidt 706, opposite *Valerim Plaza*.

Voltage 220 volts AC.

Ilha de Santa Catarina

The long, skinny island is scalloped by no less than 42 beaches; the only problem is choosing which one. The most popular are the surfers' beaches such as Praia Mole, Joaquina or Barra da Lagoa. For peace and quiet, try Campeche or the southern beaches; for sport, the Lagoa de Conceição has jet skis and windsurfing. You can walk in the forest reserves, hang glide or paraglide from the Morro da Lagoa, or sandboard in the dunes of Joaquina. Surfing is prohibited 30 April-30 July because of the migration of the island's largest fish, the *tainha*. Note that the temperature in the north can differ from the south of the island by several degrees. Almost all the beaches are easily reached by public buses (US$1), which run hourly. You need to ask at the Terminal Interurbano and the Terminal Urbano, or get a schedule from the Tourist Office.

Lagoa da Conceição is worth visiting for its beaches, sand dunes, fishing and the church of Nossa Senhora da Conceição (1730). It also has a market every Wednesday and Saturday. For tandem hang gliding, contact *Lift Sul Vôo Livre*, T2320543. From the Centro da Lagoa on the bridge there are daily boat trips to Costa da Lagoa which run until about 1830, check when you buy your ticket, US$4 return. The service is used mostly by the local people who live around the lake and have no other form of public transport. The ride is spectacular and there is a charming restaurant to greet you at the end of a thirsty journey. A recommended meal is the local fish, *tainha*, with salad, chips and an abundance of rice.

Across the island at **Barra da Lagoa** is a pleasant fishing village and beach, lively in the summer season, with plenty of good restaurants. You can walk across the wooden suspension bridge to one overlooking the bay, a spectacular setting for a meal. It is reached by *Transol* bus No 403, every 15 minutes from Terminal Urbano, 55 minutes, US$0.75. The same bus goes to beaches at **Mole**, which is a soft sand beach, good for walking. South of Mole is **Joaquina**, where surfing championships are held in January.

There is a pleasant fishing village at **Ponta das Canas**, walk 1 km to Praia Brava for good surfing, and the beach at **Canasvieiras** is good, with many watersports on offer (bus US$0.75). Also in the north of the island is **Praia dos Ingleses** (bus 602), which gets its name from an English ship that sank in 1700. Dunes separate it from **Santinho**, where Carijó inscriptions can be seen on the cliffs. Both are surfing beaches. Other northern beaches: Jureré, Daniela and Forte. **Forte São José da Ponta Grossa** is here, beautifully restored with a small museum of its history. ■ *US$1.50. Buses to Jureré and Daniela come here, 1 hr.*

On the west side, north of the city, you can visit the 'city of honey bees' with a Museo da Apicultura and the Church of Santo Antônio Lisboa. Take Trindadense bus 331 or any bus going north, to the turn-off, on the way to Sambaqui beach and fishing village (fare US$0.65).

In the south of the island are **Praia do Campeche**, 30 minutes by bus (Pantano do Sul or Costa de Dentro) from Florianópolis; offshore is an island with a beach which is good for diving. Just inland from **Praia da Armação** is **Lagoa do Peri**, a protected area. After Armação look for a bar by the roadside called *Lanchonette e Bar Surf*. Just before the bar there is a road to the left. Walk up a red clay path and after about 200 m you should see a path (unsignposted) on the left, leading up into the hills. A steady walk of up to two hours will lead you over two *montes* with a fabulous view from the top, down to **Praia da Lagoinha de Leste**. This is a beach rarely visited by the hoards and you can get away from the crowds even in the summer months. Camping is permitted. Further south is **Pantano do Sul**, an unspoilt and relaxed fishing village with a long, curved beach and lovely views across to the Três Irmãs islands. There are several *pousadas*, bars and restaurants, though not much nightlife. For **Praia dos Naufragados**, take bus to Caieira da Barra do Sul and walk for an hour through fine forests. **Forte Nossa Senhora da Conceição** is on a small island just offshore. It can be seen from the lighthouse near Praia dos Naufragados or take a boat trip with Scuna Sul from Florianópolis.

Sleeping **Lagoa da Conceição D** *Pousada Zilma*, R Geral da Praia da Joaquina 279, T2320161. Quiet, safe. Recommended. *Ricardo*, R Manoel S de Oliveira 8, CEP 88062, T2320107. Rents self-contained apartments, can arrange houses also. Recommended restaurant: *Oliveira*, R Henrique Veras. Excellent seafood dishes.

Barra da Lagoa A *Cabañas Verde Limão*, on the beach. Small cabins with bath, fan, fridge. **A** *Pousada 32*, on beach, T/F2323665. Comfortable apartments with kitchens, helpful. **C** *Pousada Floripaz*, Estrada Geral (across hanging bridge at bus station), T2323193. Book in advance, safe, family-run, helpful owners, will organize tours by boat and car on island. Highly recommended. **D** *Pousada-Lanchonete Sem Nome*, Praia do Moçambique. In 4-bunk rooms, bathrooms separate, kitchen, laundry. Recommended. **D** *Albergue do Mar*, basic, good for lone travellers. *Camping*

Ilha de Santa Catarina

1 Forte Nossa Senhora da Conceição
2 Forte São José da Ponta Grossa
3 Universidade Federal

0 km   5
0 miles   5

da Barra, T2323199. Beautiful site clean, helpful owner. Restaurant: *Meu Cantinha*, R Orlando Shaplin 89. Excellent seafood.

Joaquina   A *Hotel Cris*, T2325380. Luxurious. Recommended.

Ponta das Canas   A *Hotel Moçambique*, T/F2661172, in centre of village. Noisy at weekends; houses to let from Frederico Barthe, T2660897.

Canasvieiras   L *Lexus-Hotel*, RHG Pereira 745, T2660909, F2660919, on beach. Friendly, good breakfast, studio apartments. **Youth hostel**: *Albergue da Juventude Canasvieiras*, R Dr João de Oliveira 100, esq Av das Nações, T2662036, F2662220. IYHA, 2 blocks from sea, convenient, good, open from mid-Dec.

Praia dos Ingleses   A *Sol e Mar*, T2621271. Excellent. Recommended.

Praia de Campeche   A *Hotel São Sebastião da Praia*, Av Campeche 1373, T/F2374247. Resort hotel on splendid beach, offers special monthly rate Apr-Oct, excellent value. *Natur Campeche Hotel Residencial*, T2374011. 10 mins' walk from beach.

Near Pântano do Sul   B *Pousada dos Tucanos*, Estr Geral da Costa de Dentro 2776, T2375084, Caixa Postal 5016. English, French, Spanish spoken, spacious bungalows in garden setting. Excellent organic food. Very highly recommended. Take bus to Pântano do Sul, walk 6 km or telephone and arrange to be picked up by German owner. Hostelling International **F** *Albergue do Pirata*, Pântano do Sul, www.megasites.com.br/pirata With breakfast, natural surroundings, lots of trails.

Throughout the summer the beaches open their bars day and night; during the rest of the year the beginning of the week is very quiet. The beach huts of Praia Mole invite people to party all night (bring a blanket), while the *Club Seven* (in the Boulevard) and *L'Equinox* bar (Joaquina) are more for clubbers who don't mind 'sand in their shoes'. *Seven* offers theme nights and is very popular with surfers. Any bars are worth visiting in the Lagoon area (around the Boulevard and Barra da Lagoa) where the great Brazilian phrase *'cualquer lugar é lugar'* fits perfectly. This means whichever place is the place to be, reflecting the laid-back Brazilian mood at the beach. Other clubs and bars generally require a car: *Latitude 27*, near Praia Mole, *Ilhéus* bar (Canasvieras) and the popular *Ibiza* nightclub in Jureré.   **Bars & nightclubs**

The BR-282 heads west from the capital to Lages (see page 332). About 12 km along are the hot springs at **Caldas da Imperatriz** (41°C) and **Águas Mornas** (39°C). The latter are open to the public Monday-Friday morning only.   **Spas near Florianópolis**

There are 2 spa hotels at **Caldas da Imperatriz**: **AL** *Plaza Caldas da Imperatriz*, T2451333, has baths and swimming pools and is very well appointed. **A** *Caldas da Imperatriz*, T2451388, including meals and baths, was built in 1850 under the auspices of Empress Teresa Cristina and houses public baths. At **Águas Mornas**, **L** *Aguas Mornas Palace Hotel*, T2451315, is on the site of the springs.

The Parque Estadual da Serra do Tabuleiro, just south of the BR-282, is the largest protected area in Santa Catarina, covering 87,405 ha, or nearly 1% of the state. Apart from its varied and luxuriant flora which is home to many birds and animals, it is also important to Florianópolis for its water supply. There is a small reserve near the park headquarters (near Paulo Lopes, Km 252, BR-101), where animals and birds previously in captivity are rehabilitated before being released into the wild. ■ *0800-1700 daily.*   **Parque Estadual da Serra do Tabuleiro**

Iguaçu Falls and the South

North of Florianópolis

Porto Belo

Phone code: 047
Colour map 5, grid B5
Population: 10,500

The coast north of Florianópolis is dotted with resorts. They include Porto Belo, a fishing village on the north side of a peninsula settled in 1750 by Azores islanders, with a calm beach and a number of hotels and restaurants. Around the peninsula are wilder beaches reached by rough roads: Bombas, Bombinhas (both with the same sort of accommodation as Porto Belo), Quatro Ilhas (quieter, good surfing, 15 minutes' walk from Bombinhas), Mariscal, and, on the southern side, Zimbros (or Cantinho). Many of the stunning beaches around **Bombinhas** are untouched, accessible only on foot or by boat. Its clear waters are marvellous for diving.

Excursions Southwest of Porto Belo, reached by turning off the BR-101 at Tijucas and going west for 30 km, is **Nova Trento**, a small town in a valley first colonized by Italians and still showing heavy Italian influence. The local cuisine includes cheese, salami and wine such as you might find in Italy. There are several Italian restaurants and wine producers where you can buy *vinho artesanal*. A good view of the area, down the Tijucas valley and even as far as the sea (on a clear day), can be had from the top of Morro da Cruz, at 525 m.

Sleeping **B** *Baleia Branca*, Av Nena Trevisan 98, T3694011, F3694114. 3-star, with camping. **D** *Pousada Trapiche*, no breakfast. **Youth hostel** *Porto Belo*, R José Amâncio 246, T0XX47-3694483, F2431057. IYHA. Lots of apartments, mostly sleep 4-6, in **B** range, good value for a group.

West of Porto Belo is **Praia de Perequê**, with a handful of hotels: *Blumenauense*, Av Sen Atílio Fontana, T3694208. With bath and breakfast, on beach. *Perequê Praia*,

Porto Belo beaches

Sleeping
1 Baleia Branca
2 Blumenauense
3 Pousada Zimbros

0 km 2
0 miles 2

Italian Crosses and Saints   ◀◀

In 1889, Padre Jesuíta Luís Maria Rossi decided to commemorate the new century by erecting crosses on the highest hills above Nova Trento. Padre Alfredo Russel, a missionary, promised to put a statue of Nossa Senhora do Bom Socorro beside the highest cross, which eventually came to pass in 1901 on Morro da Cruz; a sanctuary was later built there.

Nova Trento's most famous inhabitant was Madre Paulina, who was beatified by the Pope in 1991. Born in

Trento, Italy, in 1865, the young Amabile Visintainer emigrated to Brazil with her family in 1875 and they were given land in Nova Trenta. Amabile cared for the sick and her charitable works led her to a religious calling and the founding of the Sisters of the Immaculate Conception. She took the name of her Sister Pauline, leading a humble life until her death in 1942. Since then several miracles have been claimed in her name, which led to her beatification.

R Ida Ceni Lorenzi 100, T3694279. **Zimbros B** *Pousada Zimbros*, R da Praia 527, T3693225. Cheaper off season, on beach, sumptuous breakfast, restaurant. Highly recommended. Spear fishing guide. **Camping** There are lots of campsites around the peninsula.

Buses Florianópolis to Porto Belo, several daily with *Rainha*, US$3, fewer at weekends, more frequent buses to **Tijucas**, **Itapema** and **Itajaí**, all on the BR-101 with connections. Buses from Porto Belo to the beaches on the peninsula.   **Transport**

Itapema, 60 km from Florianópolis, is another former fishing village on a wide sweep of sandy beach now dominated by tourism. In high season the town accommodates around 300,000 visitors. The *Plaza Itapema Resert e Spa*, all-inclusive, is the best such establishment on this part of the coast, T3682222. Around the headland there are several smaller and quieter beaches, Praia Grossa being one of the best, with good surf.

Some 80 km north of Florianópolis is Camboriú, once beautiful, but now the most concentrated urban development on Brazil's southern coast. From 15 December to late February it is very crowded and expensive and in low season it is popular with retired people. A few kilometres south, at Lojas Apple, there is Parque Cyro Gevaerd, a museum (archaeology, oceanography, fishing, local arts and crafts etc), zoo and aquarium; and Meia Praia, which is quieter and cleaner than Camboriú. A *teleférico* (cable car) has been built to Praia Laranjeiras, previously deserted; US$5 return from Barra Sul shopping centre to Laranjeiras via Mata Atlântica station. Between Itajaí and Camboriú is the beautiful, deserted (and rough) beach of Praia Brava. Note that from mid-July to mid-August it can be chilly.   **Camboriú**
Phone code: 047
Population: 42,000

Sleeping There are a huge number of modern hotels, 4-star and downwards, and aparthotels. From Mar-Nov it is easy to rent furnished apartments by the day or week. **Youth hostel E** per person *Alpino*, R Estados Unidos 180, Nacões, T/F3673332. IYHA.

Transport Buses: from **Florianópolis** (US$3.85), **Joinville** and **Blumenau**. *TTL* buses Montevideo-São Paulo stop here at about 1800, a good place to break the journey (US$68 from Montevideo).

Itajaí
Phone code: 047
Population: 135,000

Some 94 km up the coast from Florianópolis is the most important port in Santa Catarina at the mouth of the Rio Itajaí-Açu. It is the largest exporter of chicken in the country and the fourth largest container port. It has thriving fishing and shipbuilding industries and is the centre of a district largely colonized by Germans and Italians, although the town itself was founded by immigrants from the Azores.

Despite the port, tourism is heavily promoted and in summer the population triples. Itajaí celebrates a Marejada festival in October in honour of Portugal and the sea. It is held in the Centro de Promoções Itajaí Tur, where there are musical and folkloric festivities, a pavilion for dancing and shows, and a pavilion for food (with lots of different ways of preparing *bacalhau* and masses of seafood). For **tourist information**, contact the Centro de Promoções Itajaí Tur, T3481080.

The local beaches are Atalaia, Geremias and Cabeçudas (within walking distance, quiet and small), but within the municipality there is also Praia do Morcego which is considered a health resort because of the large amount of minerals in the water. There is also a cave here, the Caverna do Morcego, about which there are many myths and legends. About 50 km southwest of Itajaí is the **Caverna de Botuverá**, which you enter through a dripping tunnel which can flood in the wet season. The first gallery is like a cathedral, with stalactites and rock formations, one of which is called 'the organ', and the guide will play a sort of tune for you. There are several galleries, not all of which are fully explored. Pillars of 20 m have been found; each metre of rock taking 10,000 years to form. To get to Botuverá, take the road to Brusque off the BR-101, where there is tourist information and they can give you directions and other details.

Sleeping A *Grande*, R Felipe Schmidt 198, T3480968, F3482179. Good value. **B** *Marambaia Cabeçudas*, Praça Marcos Konder 46, Praia de Cabeçudas, 6 km out of town, T/F3487373, 3-star. **Bars and nightclubs** *Trudys*, on riverfront at end of main street. Good place for changing cash.

Penha
Population: 15,000

About 20 km north of Itajaí is Penha, another resort along the BR-101, with a broad, curved, sandy beach with rocky headlands at either end, offering smaller coves for swimming, surfing and fishing. The town was founded by Portuguese fishermen in the 18th century and fishing is still important as elsewhere along the coast. Tourism took off in the 1970s and during the high season the population rises to 100,000. Its major claim to fame is the **Beto Carrero World**, opened in 1991 on Praia de Armação, one of the largest theme park's in the world. Penha even offers themed shopping, at the Shopping Temático on Avenida Eugênio Krause, where you can visit different countries in different ages.

There are several **fiestas** and events in Penha, starting with a seafood festival in February, Carnival, the Festa do Divino (procession and crowning of the Emperor) in May or June, and the Festa de São João e São Pedro, 24-29 June (a tradition from the Azores). There are hotels, *pousadas* and camping.

Other resorts north of Itajaí include **Piçarras**, with sandy beaches interspersed with rocky headlands (ideal for fishing, several hotels), and **Barra Velha**, with a good, cheap hotel, *Hotel Mirante*, with a restaurant, and two more expensive hotels.

Blumenau

Blumenau is in a prosperous district settled mostly by Germans. A clean, orderly city with almost caricatured Germanic architecture, the German enxaimel design (exposed beams and brickwork) typifies some of the more famous buildings such as the Museum of the Colonial Family (1868), the Mayor's Residence and the Molemann Shopping, which resembles a medieval German castle. Blumenau offers a charming alternative to the less-organized Brazilian way of life.

Phone code: 047
Colour map 5, grid B4
Population: 262,000

The first Germans to arrive were the philosopher Herman Bruno Otto Blumenau and 16 other German explorers, who sailed up the river in 1850. Work soon began to build schools, houses and the first plantations, and the city soon became a notable textile centre. Today, high-tech and electronics industries are replacing textiles as the town's economic mainstay. The helpful **tourist office** is at Rua 15 de Novembro, on the corner of Rua Ângelo Dias.

See the **German Evangelical Church**, also the **Museu da Família Colonial**, German immigrant museum, on Avenida Duque de Caxias 78. ■ *0800-1130, 1330-1730 Mon-Fri, Sat morning only. US$0.15.* The houses, now **museums**, of **Dr Bruno Otto Blumenau** and of **Fritz Müller** are worth a visit. Müller, a collaborator of Darwin, bought the Blumenau estate in 1897 and founded the town. ■ *Both museums: 0800-1800.*

Sights

The **Parque Ecológico Spitzkopf** is a pleasant day trip for hiking, with very nice trails through the forest, passing waterfalls, natural pools, up to the Spitzkopf Peak at 936 m, 5½ km from the entrance, from where you get a wonderful view of the region. If you are not up to hiking up hills, there are paths around the lower slopes which will take you half a day. Get the 'Garcia' bus from Avenida 7 de Septembro via Rua São Paulo to Terminal Garcia, then change to 'Progresso' until the end of the paved road, US$0.60 each bus. Then 1½-km walk to the park entrance (US$1.50), German spoken, small zoo, cabins to rent, **D** *Pousada Ecológoca Spitzkopf*, R Bruno Schreiber 3777, T3365422, bar but no restaurant, pool, heating, beautiful, clean, extremely quiet.

Excursions

You can also visit Timbó and Pomerode (from the riverside road opposite the Prefeitura), by bus past rice fields and wooden houses set in beautiful gardens. At **Pomerode**, 33 km west of Blumenau, there is an interesting zoo, founded in 1932 and the oldest in the state. It can be found on Rua Hermann Weege 160, and houses over 600 animals of different species. The tourist office can be contacted on T3872627. Next door to the Prefeitura Municipal is the Associação dos Artistas e Artesãos de Pomerode, where you can find exhibitions of local arts and crafts and a shop. The north German dialect of Plattdeutsch is still spoken here and there are several folkloric groups keeping alive the music and dance of their ancestors: *Alpino Germánico, Pomerano, Edelweiss* and *Belgard*. Shooting and hunting is also traditional in the area and there are 16 *Clubes de Caça e Tiro* which are active at all festivities. The men compete for the title of Rei do Tiro Municipal in July and the women compete for the Rainha do Tiro Municipal in November. Other activities include parapenting (T3870803), a jeep club (T3872328), horse riding (T3872290) and swimming pools with waterslides. The **Museu Pomerano**, Rodovia SC 418, Km 3, tells the story of the colonial family. ■ *T3870477.* **Museu Ervin Kurt Theichmann**, Rua 15 de Novembro 791, has sculptures. ■ *T3870282.* The *Confeitaria Torten Paradies*, Rua 15 de Novembro 211, serves excellent German cakes.

Iguaçu Falls and the South

▶▶ Blumenau's Oktoberfest

In 1983, Blumenau suffered a great flood. After its destructive impact, the idea was born to introduce a German-style 'traditional' Oktoberfest beer-festival to motivate people to reconstruct the city. The festival celebrating German music, beer and the German way of life was started in 1984 here, and was expected to become the second largest in the world after Munich's (bands come from Germany for the event). It is the second largest street party in Brazil, after Carnival. It is set next to the São Francisco de Assis National Park and usually held in the first half of October. During the day the narrow streets are packed around the Molemann Centre, which is where many locals like to begin their festivities before the Oktoberfest Pavilion opens. The centre contains a mixture of bars, live music and, of course, Chopp. At 1900 the doors open and

you will find four decorated pavilions, each holding different events from drinking competitions to the 'sausage Olympics', all accompanied by non-stop traditional German music. The cultural pavilion holds traditional dress and cake-making competitions, as well as getting the audience involved in the singing, which grows steadily worse as the evening rolls on. There is also a fun fair and folk dancing shows. Food around the stalls is German and half a litre of Chopp will cost you around US$2. Brazilian popular bands are slowly being introduced, much to the disapproval of the older inhabitants. Visitors report it is worth attending on weekday evenings but weekends are too crowded. It is repeated, but called a 'summer festival', in the three weeks preceding Carnival.

Sleeping **C** *Schroeder*, R 15 de Novembro 514, T3870933. A/c, TV, phone, fridge, pool. **D** *Pousada Max*, R 15 de Novembro 257, T3870598. Apartment with satellite TV, fridge, a/c, parking.

Transport *Coletivos Volkmann* (T3871321), Blumenau-Pomerode, daily US$0.75, 1 hr, check schedule at tourist office. There are also buses from Pomerode to Jaraguá do Sul, Joinville, São Bento do Sul, Florianópolis, São Paulo, Curitiba and other local places with Rex (T3870387), *União*, *Reunidas* and *Penha/Itapemirim* (T3870387).

Half-day excursion to Gaspar (15 km) to visit the cathedral, Igreja Matriz São Pedro Apóstolo, set high above the river (*Verde Vale* bus company from stop outside the huge supermarket on Rua 7 de Setembro in the centre, office at Rua Angêlo Dias 220, sala 207, Blumenau, T3266179, www.braznet.com.br/~verdetur/index.html). There are two water parks in Gaspar with waterslides and other amusements: Parque Aquático Cascanéia, on Rua José Patrocínio dos Santos, T3390690, with chalets, parking, restaurants, and Cascata Carolina, Estrada Geral da Carolina-Belchior Alto, T3390779, with water coming straight from the rocks. *Fazenda Park Hotel* is new, with a swimming pool, fishing, walking and riding, on the Estrada Geral do Gasparinho 2499, T3265696.

Further west along the Rio Itajaí-Açu, around Ibirama, the river is good for whitewater rafting. You can take a break between rapids to bathe in the waterfalls.

Sleeping
Reservations essential during Oktoberfest

A *Garden Terrace*, R Padre Jacobs 15, T3263544, F3260366. **A** *Himmelblau Palace*, R 7 de Setembro 1415, T/F3265800. **A** *Plaza Hering*, R 7 de Setembro 818, T3261277, F3229409. 4-star. **C** *Blumenau Turist Hotel*, R Francisco Margarida 67, T3234640, 200 m from bus station. Helpful (all aforementioned hotels have heating in rooms). **C** *Glória*, R 7 de Setembro 954, T3261988, F3265370. German-run, excellent coffee shop. **D** *Central*, R 7 de Setembro 1036, T322057. Basic, **E** without bath, both without breakfast, clean. **D** *City*, R Ángelo Dias 263, T3222205. **D** *Herrmann*, central, Floriano Peixoto 213,

T3224370, F3260670. One of the oldest houses in Blumenau, clean, rooms with or without bath, excellent big breakfast, German spoken. Many cheap hotels do not include breakfast. **Youth hostel** *Pousada Albergue da Juventude Dusseldorf*, R São Paulo 2457, T3234332. **Camping** Municipal campsite, 3 km out on Rua Pastor Osvaldo Hesse; Paraíso dos Poneis, 9 km out on the Itajaí road, also Motel; Refúgio Gaspar Alto, 12 km out on Rua da Glória.

Good German food at *Frohsinn*, Morro Aipim (panoramic view) and *Cavalinho Branco*, Av **Eating**
Rio Branco 165. Huge meals. International eating at *Moinho do Vale*, Paraguai 66. *Amigo*, Peixoto 213. Huge cheap meals. *Caféhaus Glória*, in *Hotel Glória*. Excellent coffee shop. *Deutsches Eck*, R 7 de Septembro 432. Recommended, especially *carne pizzaiola*. *Gruta Azul*, Rodolfo Freygang 8. Good, popular, not cheap. *Internacional*, Nereu Ramos 61. Chinese, very good, moderate prices. *Chinês*, R 15 de Novembro 346, near tourist office. Good.

Theatre *Teatro Carlos Gomes*, 15 de Novembro between Kennedy and N Deeke; is **Entertainment**
also an exhibition centre; public library open 0800-1800.

German bookshops, *Librerias Alemãs*, at bus station and R 7 de Setembro (also stocks **Shopping**
English books), and 15 de Novembro. Craft shop, *Casa Meyer*, 15 de Novembro 401.

Buses Bus to the rodoviária (7 km out of town) from Av Pres Castelo-Branco (Beira **Transport**
Rio). There are good bus connections in all directions from Blumenau. To **Curitiba**
US$6.50, 4 hrs, 3 daily (*Penha* and *Catarinense*). Blumenau to **Caxias do Sul** at 1930
only, arrives 0400, US$9.50. **Car hire** *Localiza*, R 7 de Setembro 255, T3220843.

Banks At *Câmbios*/travel agencies: *Vale do Itajaí Turismo e Cambio*, Av Beira Rio 167. **Directory**
Very helpful, German spoken. *Tilotur Turismo*, Av Rio Branco e 15 de Novembro, 2nd
floor. **Communications** Telephones: corner of Av Brasil and República Argentina,
also a kiosk near the Prefeitura.

West of Blumenau

As an alternative to a direct bus, daily from Florianópolis and Itajaí to Iguaçu via **To Iguaçu**
Blumenau, you can travel through rich and interesting farming country in Santa
Catarina and Rio Grande do Sul, stopping at the following places. **Joaçaba** is a
town of German immigrants, in the centre of the Vale do Contestado (see box,
page 337). For information, T5223000. **Erexim** has a strong *gaúcho* influence.
Iraí is a town with thermal springs, situated in an Italian immigrant area. The
town is good for semi-precious stones. From any of these places you can go to
Pato Branco and Cascavel and thence to Foz do Iguaçu.

Two hours from Joaçaba is Treze Tílias, a village where 19th-century Tyrolean **Treze Tílias**
dialect is still spoken and the immigrant culture is perfectly preserved. It was set- *Phone code: 049*
tled in 1933 by a group led by Andreas Thaler, who had been the Austrian Min- *Population: 4,500*
ister of Agriculture. Dairy farming is the main economic activity and children
are taught German and Portuguese in school. The style of architecture has been
lifted straight from the Alps. The major festivity of the year is the four-day
Tirolerfest in October, celebrating the customs of the Tirol, with food, sculpture and art. Tourist information is at Praça Andreas Thaler 25, T/F5370176.

Sleeping **B** *Dreizhnlinden*, R Leoberto Leal 392, T5370297, F5370539. **B** *Tirol*, R São
Vicente de Paula III, T5370125. **C** *Alpenrose*, R Min João Cleophas 340, T5370273.
D *Áustria*, R Tirol 5, T5370132.

São Francisco do Sul

Phone code: 047
Population: 27,000

At the mouth of the Baia de Babitonga, São Francisco do Sul is the port for the town of Joinville, 45 km inland at the head of the Rio Cachoeira. It is the country's third oldest city (Binot Paulmier de Gonneville landed here in 1504), after Porto Seguro in Bahia and São Vicente in Rio de Janeiro. The colonial centre has over 150 historical sites and has been protected since 1987. An interesting **Museu Nacional do Mare** reflects Brazil's seafaring history. ■ *0900-1800 Tue-Fri, 1100-1800 Sat-Sun. US$1. Rua Manual Lourenço de Andrade, T4441868.* The **cathedral**, Nossa Senhora da Graça,(1719) still has its original walls made with sand, shells and whale oil. The **Museu Histórico de São Francisco do Sul** is on Rua Coronel Carvalho, in the 18th-century Cadeia Pública. There is a tourist information desk in the cinema behind the Prefeitura. Not far from the historical centre is the modern port. Petrobrás has an oil refinery here.

There are about 13 excellent **beaches** nearby, such as Ubatuba, Enseada, which has good nightlife, hotels, pensions and three campsites, Prainha (surf championships are held here) and Cápri. Quieter waters can be found at Ingleses, Figueiras, Paulas and Calixtos but, being in the bay, the sea is polluted. A ferry crosses the Baia de Babitonga from Bairro Laranjeiras, 8 km from the centre, to Estaleiro, 30 minutes. The historic town of Vila da Glória (6 km from Estaleiro) can be visited. See under Joinville for the *Príncipe de Joinville* boat trip. For schooner trips T9747266. Take mosquito repellent.

Sleeping **AL-A** *Zibamba*, R Fernandes Dias 27, T/F4442020. Central, pleasant, a/c, pool, good restaurant. **B** *Kontik*, Babitonga 211, T4442232. In historic centre, view of bay.

Transport Bus terminal is 1½ km from centre. Direct bus (*Penha*) daily to **Curitiba** at 0730, US$6, 3½ hrs.

Joinville

Phone code: 047
Colour map 5, grid B5
Population: 430,000

The state's largest city lies 2 km from the main coastal highway, BR-101, by which Curitiba and Florianópolis are less than two hours away. Joinville is known as the 'city of the princes' for its historical connections with royalty, although it is also nicknamed the 'city of flowers', and even 'Manchester Catarinense'. Although its industry does not spoil the character of the city and the large German population gives it a distinctly European feel, there is not much reason for visitors to stop here. **Tourist information** is at the corner of Praça Nereu Ramos with R do Príncipe, T4331511, F4331491, and at *Promotur*, Centreventos, Av José Vieira 315, sala 20, T4232633, www.promotur.com.br Also www.joinville.sc.gov.br

Sights

At **Expoville**, 4 km from the centre on BR-101 (continuation of 15 de Novembro), is an exhibition of Joinville's industry, although it is used for many other exhibitions and festivals as well. The new, multifunctional, **Centreventos Cau Hansen** has been built to house sporting activities, shows, festivals, conferences and other events. It has the first Bolshoi Ballet School outside Moscow. The tiled mural around the entrance, by Juarez Machado, depicts a circus. There are some 600 industries in the manufacturing park, many of which are substantial exporters.

Museums

Museu Nacional da Imigração e Colonização, in the Palácio dos Príncipes, Rua Rio Branco 229, has a collection of objects and tools from the original German settlement and other items of historical interest. ■ *0900-1800 Tue-Fri.* **Arquivo Histórico de Joinville**, Avenida Hermann August Lepper

65, houses a collection of documents dating from the town's foundation. ■ *0830-1200, 1330-2000 Mon-Fri. T4222154.* There is also the **Museu de Fundição**, Rua Helmuth Fallgatter 3345, with around 800 items, including books, documents, photographs, old equipment and tools, minerals and artistic items. ■ *0800-1200, 1330-1700 Mon-Fri. T4320133.* The interesting **Museu de Artes de Joinville** is in the old residence of Ottokar Doerfell, Rua 15 de Novembro 1400. It promotes temporary exhibitions by local and other Brazilian artists. ■ *0900-2100 Tue-Sun.* The **Casa da Cultura** (Galeria Municipal de Artes 'Vistor Kursansew'), Rua Dona Fransisca 800, also contains the School of Art 'Fritz Alt', the School of Music 'Vila Lobos' and the School of Ballet. ■ *0900-1800 Mon-Fri, 0900-1300 Sat.* **Casa Fritz Alt**, Rua Aubé, is the home of the sculptor, exhibiting his works of art and personal possessions; several of his monuments are on display in the town. ■ *0900-1200, 1400-1800, closed Mon.*

The **Museu Arqueológico do Sambaqui**, Rua Dona Francisca 600, has a collection dating back to 5000 BC, with an exhibition of Sambaqui man, his way

Joinville

Iguaçu Falls and the South

Sleeping	5 Mattes	9 Tannenhof	3 Pinheiro
1 Anthurium Parque	6 Novo Horizonte		4 Sopp Restaurante
2 Ideal	7 Novo Hotel Joinville	● **Eating**	e Choperia
3 Joinville Palace	8 Parthenon	1 Bierkeller	5 Trento Queijos e
4 Joinville Tourist	Prinz Suite	2 China	Vinhos

0 metres 200
0 yards 200

of life, funereal customs and sculpture. ■ *0900-1200, 1400-1800 Tue-Sun. T4330114*. There are also two archaeological reserves: **Sambaqui do Rio Comprido**, carbon dated to BC 2865, and **Sambaqui Morro do Ouro**.

The **Alameda Brustlein**, better known as the **Rua das Palmeiras**, is an impressive avenue of palm trees, leading to the **Palácio dos Príncipes**. The trees were planted in 1873 by Frederico Brustlein with seeds brought in 1867 by Louis Niemeyer. The **Railway Station** on Rua Leite Ribeiro, T4222550, dates from 1906 and is a fine example of the German style of architecture , and the **Mercado Municipal**, Praça Hercílio Luz, is in the enxaimel style. At the other end of the spectrum, the **Cathedral**, on Avenida Juscelino Kubitscheck with Rua do Príncipe, is futuristic with spectacular windows recounting the story of man. The **Cemitério dos Imigrantes**, on Rua 15 de Novembro 978, is interesting; the attached **Casa da Memória do Imigrante** has information on the town's history, with audiovisual and documentary displays. ■ *1400-1730 Mon-Fri*.

The **Parque Zoobotânico**, 15 minutes' walk in the direction of Mirante, on Rua Pastor Guilherme Rau 462, is a good zoo and park, with many local species of birds and animals and a children's park. ■ *0900-1800, closed Mon. T4331230*. From here it is another 25 minutes' walk to the **Mirante** for a beautiful view of the town and the bay. The tower on the top is at an altitude of 250 m and you can walk up a spiral staircase on the outside for a panoramic view. An **Orchid Farm** in Boa Vista is open to the public for sales or just to look around, on Rua Helmuth Fallgatter 2547, opposite the Terminal de Integração Tupy. ■ *0800-1200, 1330-1800*.

Excursions You can take a boat trip on the *Príncipe de Joinville III* at 1000 from Lagoa Saguaçú, Bairro Espinheiros (9 km from the centre), past several islands to São Franciso do Sul. Stops include the Museu Nacional do Mar, the port, lunch at a fish restaurant, Ilha da Rita and Ilha das Flores, getting back at 1600. ■ *US$10 per person. T4550824*.

Four daily buses go to **Ubatuba** beach, a weekend resort (see above under São Francisco do Sul).

Guaratuba (see page 295) by bus, 1¼ hours, US$2 (connections to Paranaguá).

The **festival of São João** in June can be seen best in Santa Catarina at **Campo Alegre**, the first town on the road inland to Mafra. There are bonfires, a lot of (German) folk dancing, and large quantities of *quentão* and *pinhões* (see under Gramado, Eating, below). It is a beautiful climb on the road from the BR-101 to Campo Alegre.

Sleeping
■ *on map, page 327*
Price codes:
see inside front cover

A *Anthurium Parque*, R São José 226, T/F4336299. Colonial building, once home to a bishop, good value, English spoken, pool, sauna, part of the Roteiro de Charme hotel group, see page 47. **A** *Parthenon Prinz Suite*, R Otto Boehm 525, T/F4339111. Pool, sauna, gym, squash, conference rooms, restaurant, café, bar. **A** *Tannenhof*, R Visc de Taunay 340, T/F4338011. 4-star, pool, gym, traffic noise, excellent breakfast, restaurant on 14th floor. **B** *Joinville Palace*, R do Príncipe 142, T4336111. A/c, heating, TV, Visa accepted. **B** *Joinville Tourist*, R 7 de Setembro 40, T4331288, F4331500. Pool, bar, restaurant. **B** *Novo Hotel Joinville*, R Abdon Batista 237, T/F4336112. A/c, TV. **D** *Ideal*, R Jerônimo Coelho 98, near Rodoviário Municipal, T4223660. **D** *Mattes*, 15 de Novembro 801, T4339886. Good facilities, big breakfast. **E** *Novo Horizonte*, at bus station. Basic, clean.

Eating
■ *on map, page 327*

Expensive *Pinheiro*, R Rio Branco 299, T4551254. Well worth a visit for excellent fish and shrimp dishes. *Tritão*, R Visc de Taunay 902, T4334816. Very good seafood.

Mid-range *Bierkeller*, R 15 de Novembro 497, T4221360, German cuisine; also *Sopp*, R Mcal Deodoro 640, on corner with R Jaraguá, T4223637. *China*, R Abdon Batista 131, opposite the Cathedral, T4223323. Eat in or home delivery service for oriental food. *Familiar*, R Dr João Colin 1872, T4271474. *O Fornão*, R Visc de Taunay 240, T4227866, and at No 299, T4338028. *Pizza rodízio*, good, very reasonable. *Rex (Baby Beef)*, Blumenau 3097, T4351722, churrasco. *Rudnick*, BR-101, Km 25, T4641122. *Trento Queijos e Vinhos*, R 15 de Novembro 2973, T4531796, traditional Italian. **Cheap** The Müeller Shopping has a good food hall.

There is an annual **flower festival** in **Nov** (mostly orchids, disappointing, US$1.50 entry) and a beer festival, *Fenachopp*, in **Oct**. Shooting is a favourite local past time and there are lots of competitions among the 2,000 or so members of the clubs, with an annual festival, *Fenatiro*, in **May**. In **Jul**, Joinville hosts one of the largest dance festivals in the world. Around 4,000 dancers stay for 12 days and put on shows and displays, ranging from jazz and folklore to classical ballet, seen by some 30,000 spectators in a variety of locations. **Festivals**

Air Airport 5 km from city, T4671000. **Buses** To **Blumenau**, US$3, 2¼ hrs. The rodoviária is 2½ km outside the town, south exit, T4332991 (regular bus service). **Car hire** *Localiza*, R Blumenau 1728, T4339393, or at the airport T4671020; *Interlocadora*, R do Príncipe 839, T4227888; *Olímpia*, R 9 de Março 734, T4331755. **Transport**

Airline offices *TAM*, T4332033. *Transbrasil*, R São Joaquim 70, *Hotel Colon* annex, T/F4226060, at airport T/F4671023. *Varig/Rio Sul*, R Alexandre Dohler 277, T4332800. **Communications** Internet: *Biernet Bar*, R Visconde de Taunay 456. **Medical services** 24-hr pharmacies: *Drogaria Catarinense*, Filial Boa Vista, in front of the Hospital Regional, T4372355, or Filial São João, Av Getúlio Vargas 1343, T4227691. *Farmacia Catarinense*, R 15 de Novembro 503, T4222318. **Directory**

South of Florianópolis

Two beaches south of Florianópolis which are worth a stop are **Pinheira** and **Guarda do Embaú**, which you get to by crossing a river in a canoe. The surfing is excellent here; Guarda in particular is a favourite spot of surfers from Rio and São Paulo (surfing is not permitted in the *tainha* fishing season, 15 May-15 July). **Garopaba**, 89 km south of Florianópolis, is a village of 11,000, which swells to 100,000 during the holiday season. Its Carijó Indian name 'Y-Gara-Paba' means 'much water, many fish and many hills'. There is a simple colonial church and a sandy coast. **B** *Pousada da Lagoa*, Rua Rosalina de Aguiar Lentz 325, T/F2543201. There is also a youth hostel, **E** per person, *Praia do Ferrugem*, Estr Gerals do Capão, T0XX48-2540035, IYHA.

Silveira, 3 km east, is considered one of Brazil's finest surfing spots. Swimming can be risky, though, because of the surf and sudden drops in the ocean floor. There is good fishing for *tainha*, lobster, anchovy and other varieties. **Praia da Rosa**, 18 km south, is a 3½-km beach with good swimming, fishing, diving and pleasant coastal walks. It is also one of Brazil's prime whale-watching sites, with right whales coming to the bay to calve between June and November. The headquarters of the Baleia Franca project is **L** *Pousada Vida Sol e Mar*, T3540041, www.vsmar.com.br; trips cost US$42 in a boat, US$20 on land. The *pousada* also has cabins for rent, with kitchen, TV, restaurant, sushi bar, tennis, surf school.

Sleeping Praia da Rosa: **A** *Caminho do Rei*, Caminho do Morro, T/F3556062. **A** *Morada do Bouganvilles*, Estr Geral do Morro, T3556100, F3556179. **B** *The Rosebud*, Estr Geral do Morro, T3556101.

Imbituba
Population: 33,000

At the port of Imbituba there is a carbo-chemical plant, from which air pollution is very bad. The rail link between Imbituba and Tubarão to the south was one of the busiest steam services in South America, but is now closed. Imbituba is now a popular resort with extensive beaches, lakes and lively surf. Just south of the town there are a few *pousadas* at **Vila Nova**, on the beach, further south along the BR-101 is *Quinta do Bucanero*, Estrada Geral do Rosa, T/F3556056, which is part of the Roteiro de Charme hotel group, see page 47; at **Itapirubá**, about 10 km further south, there is the four-star *Hotel Itapirubá*, on the beach, T/F6460294.

Laguna

Phone code: 048
Colour map 5, grid B4
(124 km S of Florianópolis)
Population: 48,000

The small fishing port of Laguna in southern Santa Catarina, founded in 1676, was a focal point of defence against Spanish invasions and still retains vestiges of its turbulent past. Now Laguna serves mainly as a holiday resort, perched between the ocean and a chain of three lakes. In 1839, Laguna was the capital of the Juliana Republic, a short-lived separatist movement led by Italian idealist Guiseppe Garibáldi. At that time he met a devoted lover, Ana Maria de Jesus Ribeiro, who followed him into battle, was taken prisoner, escaped and rejoined Garibáldi at Vacaria. Their first son, Menotti, was born in Rio Grande do Sul, but the family moved to Montevideo in 1841, where they lived in poverty. They later moved to Argentina and then to Italy, where they fought for the unification of the peninsula. Ana Maria (or Anita) died near Ravenna in 1849 while they were fleeing to Switzerland from the Austrian army. She became a heroine in both Brazil and Italy and there are monuments to her in Rome, Ravenna, Porto Alegre, Belo Horizonte, Florianópolis, Juiz da Fora, Tubarão and Laguna. At Laguna is the **Anita Garibáldi Museum**, containing documents, furniture, and her personal effects.

Laguna's beach, 2 km from the centre, is not very good, but 16 km away (by ferry and road) are beaches and dunes at **Cavo de Santa Marta**. Also from Laguna, take a *Lagunatur* or *Auto Viação São José* bus to **Farol** (four buses a day Monday-Friday, one on Saturday, US$1.50, beautiful ride). You have to cross the mouth of the Lagoa Santo Antônio by ferry (10 minutes) to get to Farol; look out for fishermen aided by dolphins (*botos*). Here is a fishing village with a lighthouse, the Farol de Santa Marta; the largest lighthouse in South America with the third largest view in the world. It was built by the French in 1890 of stone, sand and whale oil. Guided tours available (taxi, US$10, not including ferry toll). It may be possible to bargain with fishermen for a bed, or there are campsites at Santa Marta Pequena by the lighthouse, popular with surfers.

Sleeping
A *Laguna Tourist*, Praia do Gi, 4 km, T6470022, F6470123. 5-star, first-class. **B** *Hotel Farol de Santa Marta*, Farol, 18 km away, T9861257, F6441944. **C** *Turismar*, Av Rio Grande do Sul 207, T6470024, F6470279. 2-star, view over Mar Grosso beach, TV. **D** *Beiramar*, 100 m from *Recanto*, opposite *Angeloni Supermarket*, T6440260. No breakfast, clean, TV, rooms with view over lagoon. Also nearby, **D** *Farol Palace*, R Gustavo Richard. **D** *Recanto*, Av Colombo 17, close to bus terminal. With breakfast, modern but basic.

Buses To Porto Alegre, 5½ hrs, with *Santo Anjo Da Guarda*; same company goes to **Transport**
Florianópolis, 2 hrs, US$5.25, 6 daily; to Tubarão, every hr with *Alvorada*, US$2.75, 50 mins.

Some 75 km north of Araranguá is the coalfield town of Tubarão. Inland from **Tubarão**
the main road are the coalfields of Criciúma and Içara, with good beaches *Phone code: 048*
nearby. Tubarão has a railway museum with a large collection of steam *Population: 83,500*
engines used in South America. Trips are run once a month to Urussaga (see
below), April-October, and to Imbituba and Jaguaruna, November to
March. ■ *T9761257*. **Termos do Gravatal** can be visited from Tubarão for its
mineral pools. It is a quiet and peaceful area.

Sleeping Gravatal: **AL** *Gravatal Termas*, Av Pedro Zappelini 285, T6482122,
F6482056, 3-star. **AL** *Internacional do Gravatal*, Av Pedro Zappelini 882, T6482155,
F6482101, 4-star. **A** *Cabanas Termas*, Av Pedro Zappelini, T6482082, F6482147.

North of Gravatal are the towns of **Armazém**, settled by Germans, where agriculture and livestock are the main economic activities, and **São Martinho**,
with enxaimel architecture brought by German immigrants. West of Gravatal
is **São Ludgero**, also colonized by Germans and a major producer of cheese
and fruit. Along the same road and about 60 km inland from Tubarão is
Orleães, first colonized in 1883 by Italians, followed by the Germans, Portuguese and Polish. Its museum has an original water-powered workshop and
sawmill, complete with waterwheel. It dates from the original settlers, and is
still in working order. To get there get off the bus at the junction about 3 km
from the town. From here you can continue inland to the west through **Lauro
Müller** and up into the mountains, or south to **Urussanga**, where the Italian
influence is very strong, and down to Cruciúma and the coast.

Continuing down the coast on the BR-101, you come to Araranguá, 13 km **Araranguá**
from which is the beautiful beach of **Arroio do Silva**. Also reached from here *Phone code: 048*
is another beach resort, **Morro dos Conventos**, with hotels and campsites. *Population: 51,000*

Sleeping Arroio do Silva: **B** *Scaini Palace*, Av Mondardo 130, T/F5261266. Good
food. Recommended. **C** *Hotel Paulista*, R Dionizio Mondardo 58, T/F5261244.

Bars and nightclubs *Bar Nabar*, Av Getulio Vargas 970, close to beach. Cheap drinks,
English-speaking owners, live music. Recommended.

Just before you get to the border with Rio Grande do Sul (but not on the
BR-101) is **Praia Grande**, which has a hotel and a good, cheap *churrascaria* just
off the praça (see page 348 for access to Parque Nacional de Aparados da Serra).

São Joaquim

Buses from Tubarão go inland to Lauro Müller, then over the Serra do Rio do *Phone code: 049*
Rastro (beautiful views of the coast in clear weather, really spectacular). The *Colour map 5, grid B4*
road continues to São Joaquim. At 1,360 m, it is the highest town in Southern *Population: 23,000*
Brazil, with regular snowfalls in winter. About 11 km outside the town, on the
way to Bom Jardim da Serra, is the **Parque Ecológico Vale da Neve** (Snow
Valley). It is an easy hike and very beautiful, the entrance is on the main road,
US$3, and there is a restaurant. The owner is American and an English-speak-
ing guide will take you for a 1½-hour walk through the forest. From São
Joaquim, northeast over Pericó to Urubici is unpaved. These roads go around

Iguaçu Falls and the South

the **Parque Nacional de São Joaquim** (33,500 ha) in the Serra Geral, with canyons containing subtropical vegetation, and araucaria forest at higher levels. There is no bus (local *Ibama* office, T048-2226202, *Secretaria de Turismo de São Joaquim*, T2330258).

Sleeping **B** *Pousada Caminhos da Neve*, Av Irineu Bornhausen, T/F2330385. **C** *Incomel Park*, Av Ivo Silveira 340, 1 km from centre towards Lages, T2330980, F2330281. Heating, accepts Visa. **D** *Nevada*, R Manuel Joaquim Pinto 213, T/F2330259. Expensive meals. **E** *Maristela*, R Manoel Joaquim Pinto 220, 5 mins' walk from Rodoviária, T233007. French spoken, no heating so can be cold, friendly, helpful, good breakfast. **Camping** *Clube do Brasil* site.

Transport **Buses** To **Florianópolis** 0700 and 1700 via Bom Retiro (*Reunidos*) and 0800 via Tubarão (*Nevatur*), 5½ hrs, US$9. Several daily buses to **Criciúma**, **Tubarão**, **Cascavel** and **Foz do Iguaçu**.

Lages

Phone code: 049
Population: 160,000

West of Florianópolis, the area around Lages is particularly good for 'rural tourism', with lots of opportunities for hiking, horse riding, river bathing, working on a farm and other activities. The weather can get really cold in winter and even the waterfalls have been known to freeze. Many of the local *fazendas* are open for visitors and offer accommodation. This is *gaúcho* country and you will get gaúcho hospitality, culture and food.

Sleeping in Lages **A** *Grande*, R João de Castro 23, T/F2223522. Good. **B** *Presidente*, Av Pres Vargas 101, T/F2240014. One of the 3 hotels near the rodoviária is **D** *Rodeio*, T2232011, with or without bath, good breakfast. In the same building is a good *churrascaria*, open in the evening, US$7.50.

Sleeping in fazendas On average, prices are **A**, including all meals, all on working farms: *Fazenda Aza Verde*, Antiga BR-2, Soroptimista 13, T2220277. Horses, fishing, boats, games room, heating, pool. *Fazenda Ciclone*, BR-116, Km 276, localidade Vigia, T2223382. Horses, fishing, table tennis, billiards, river beach. *Fazenda do Barreiro*, Rod SC 438, Km 43, T2223031. Games room, library, horses, pool, fishing, boats, TV. *Fazenda Dourado Turismo Rural*, Estr Lages-Morrinhos Km 14, T2930360. *Fazenda Nossa Senhora de Lourdes*, R Aristiliano Ramos 565, T2220798. Pool, games room, library, horses, fishing, good walking. *Fazenda Pedras Brancas*, Rod SC 438, Km 10, Parque das Pedras Brancas, T2232073, 2222262. Horses, shooting, fishing, pool, sauna, heating, games room, river beach. *Fazenda Rancho do Boqueirão*, BR-282, Km 4, Saída São José do Cerrito, T2260354, F2260354. Heating, TV, library, games room, pool, horses, bicycles, good walking, fishing. *Fazenda Refúgio do Lago*, Rod SC 438, Km 10, Pedras Brancas, T2221416. Pool, games room, library, horses, shooting, fishing, boats, river beach.

Transport Bus station is 30 mins' walk southeast of the centre. Bus to the centre (Terminal Municipal), 'Rodoviária' runs Mon-Fri only, or 'Dom Pedro II' every 40 mins at weekends. To Florianópolis 6-8 buses daily on the direct road (BR282), 5 hrs, US$10; to Caxias do Sul, 3¾ hrs, US$5.60.

Rio Grande do Sul

Brazil's southernmost state stands out as utterly different from the rest of the country. A huge chunk of the population still retain the German or Italian appearance and values of their ancestors. This is gaúcho (cowboy) country and the herders are regularly seen in traditional garb. In restaurants, steaks the size of Texas are order of the day. The capital, Porto Alegre, is the most industrialized and cosmopolitan city in the south and tops the country's urban quality of life rankings. Nearby, there are good beaches, interesting coastal national parks and the stunning scenery of the Serra Gaúcha. On the border with Santa Catarina is the remarkable Aparados da Serra National Park where it can snow. In the far west are the remains of Jesuit missions. Look out for local specialities such as comida campeira, te colonial and quentão.

The Great Escarpment, in places over 1,000 m high, runs down the coastal area as far as Porto Alegre providing escape from the summer swelter. From the south of Santa Catarina to the borders of Uruguay, the green hills of Rio Grande do Sul are fringed along the coast by sand bars and lagoons, making one of the world's longest beaches. In southern Rio Grande do Sul, south and west of the Rio Jacuí, there are great grasslands stretching as far as Uruguay to the south and over 800 km westwards to Argentina. This is the distinctive land of the *gaúcho*, or cowboy (pronounced ga-oo-shoo in Brazil), of the flat black hat, *bombachas* (baggy trousers), poncho and *ximarão* (*mate* without sugar, also spelt *chimarrão*), the indispensable drink of southern cattlemen. There are many millions of cattle, sheep and pigs, rice production is on the increase, and some 75% of all Brazilian wine comes from the state. The *gaúcho* culture has developed a sense of distance from the African-influenced society further north. Many people will tell you they have more in common with Uruguayans or Argentines than Brazilians – apart from when it comes to football.

From Rio Grande do Sul there are various routes into Uruguay and Argentina

A lot of people from this region are strikingly beautiful: tall, with light brown skin and hair and intensely green eyes. Supermodel Gisele Bündchen comes from Horizontina, deep in the Serra Gaúcha. Folk dances, unchanged since early settlers brought them from Europe, are still practised, both privately and for the benefit of tourists.

A favourite all-purpose gaúcho exclamation, which means nothing but is used all the time, is 'Tchê'!

Since 1999, the state government has implemented a radical consultative scheme whereby people in all 497 municipalities jointly decide school, road and other infrastructure spending. The Participatory Budget, pioneered for over a dozen years in Porto Alegre, is widely supported and has attracted international acclaim. For more info log onto www.estado.rs.gov.br The state tourism website is: **www.turismo.rs.gov.br**

Porto Alegre

Sited at the meeting of five rivers and freshened by over a million trees, Porto Alegre is one of Brazil's more pleasant cities. Culturally rich, ethnically diverse and progressive, it is the capital of the southern frontier and the hub of trade with Argentina and Uruguay. It is a good base for exploring the rest of Rio Grande do Sul's natural beauty and historical sites.

Phone code: 051
Colour map 5, grid B3
Population: 1,361,000

Ins and outs

Getting there
See also Transport, page 341

International and domestic flights arrive at Salgado Filho airport. There are regular buses to the rodoviária and a Metrô service to the city centre. International and interstate buses arrive at the terminal at Largo Vespasiano Júlio Veppo, on Av Mauá with Garibáldi.

Getting around

First-class minibuses (*Lotação*), painted in a distinctive orange, blue and white pattern, stop on request. Safer and pleasanter than normal buses, fare about US$0.60. The Trensurb Metrô runs from the southern terminal at the Mercado Público (station beside the market), going as far north as Sapucaia do Sul. The 2nd station serves the

Porto Alegre

Rio Guaíba

Casa de Cultura Mário Quintana

Nossa Senhora das Dores

Noiva do Caí Boat Trips

Centro Cultural Usina do Gasômetro

Demetrio Ribeiro

Washington Luiz

Av Loureiro da Silva

Parque Maurício Sirotsky Sobrinho

N

0 metres 100
0 yards 100

■ **Sleeping**
1 Açores
2 Conceição Center
3 Continental
4 Embaixador
5 Everest
6 Lancaster

Iguaçu Falls and the South

rodoviária and the 5th the airport (10 mins), 0500-2300, single journey US$0.40.

Tourist offices *Tourist information*, T0800-517686, www.portoalegre.rs.gov.br/turismo *Central de Informações Turísticas*, R Vasco da Gama 253, Bom Fim, T3115289, open daily 0900-2100. *Setur*, Borges de Medeiros 1501, 10th floor, T32285400; also at Salgado Filho airport, friendly; interstate bus station, very helpful (free city maps); *Casa de Cultura Mário Quintana*, open 0900-2100 Tue-Fri, 1200-2100 Sat-Sun; *Usina do Gasômetro*, open 1000-1800 daily; *Mercado Público*, 0900-1600 Mon-Sat. On Sun there are guided walks from Praça da Alfândega and on Sat from Praça da Matriz, at 1500 or 1600, free, T0800-517686 or contact the tourist office at Vasco da Gama 153, or in the Mercado Público. *Touring Clube do Brasil*, Av João Pessoa 623.

Iguaçu Falls and the South

7 Palácio	9 Ritter	11 Uruguay
8 Plaza São Rafael	10 São Luiz	

● Eating
1 Atelier de Massas

Maps Army maps (1:50,000) of Rio Grande's trekking regions (Canela, Parque Nacional de Aparados da Serra) at *Junta Servicio Militar*, Prefeitura Municipal, R Prof E Castro 850, T32233611. Note these maps are not available in rural areas.

Climate Standing on a series of hills and valleys on the banks of Lake Guaíba, it has a temperate climate through most of the year, though the temperature at the height of summer can often exceed 40°C and drop below 10°C in winter.

The capital of Rio Grande do Sul is where cowboy culture meets the bright lights. Though it is the biggest commercial centre south of São Paulo, it is friendly and manageable on foot. Get a map out in downtown Porto Alegre and someone will try to help you (get a map out in downtown São Paulo and they will probably try to rob you). The freshwater port, one of the most up-to-date in the country, handles ocean-going vessels of up to 7,000 tonnes. It is one of the richest parts of Brazil; its population has a 97% literacy rate and life expectancy of 74 years for men, 79 for women. A stronghold of the leftist Workers Party (PT) for over a dozen years, Porto Alegre was holding the first three World Social Forums (2001-03) – giving over 50,000 participants opportunities to share successful economic and social initiatives from across the planet – and putting the city in a global spotlight.

Sights

The older residential part of the town is on a promontory, dominated previously by the **Palácio Piratini** (Governor's Palace) and the imposing 1920s metropolitan **cathedral** on the **Praça Marechal Deodoro** (or da Matriz). Also on, or near this square, are the neoclassical **Theatro São Pedro** (1858), the **Solar dos Câmara** (1818, now a historical and cultural centre) and the **Biblioteca Pública**, but all are dwarfed by the skyscraper of the **Assembléia Legislativa**. Down Rua General Câmara from Praça Marechal Deodoro is the **Praça da Alfândega**, with the old customs house, the Museu de Arte de Rio Grande do Sul (see below), the old post office and the Banco Meridional. A short walk east of this group, up Rua 7 de Setembro, is busy Praça 15 de Novembro, on which is the neoclassical **Mercado Público** selling everything from religious artefacts to spice and meat.

Do not miss the pedestrianized part of **Rua dos Andradas** (Rua da Praia). It is the city's principal outdoor meeting place, the main shopping area, and by around 1600 it is jammed full of people. Going west along Rua dos Andradas, you pass the pink **Casa Cultural Mário Quintana** in the converted Hotel Majestic (see Entertainment, below). A little further along is a wide stairway leading up to the two high white towers of the church of **Nossa Senhora das Dores,** the only National Heritage graded church in the city. Many tall buildings in this part of the city rise above the fine, sometimes dilapidated, old houses and the streets are famous for their steep gradients. On the banks of Lake Guaíba, the **Usina do Gasômetro** is Porto Alegre's answer to London's Tate Modern. Built 1926-28 as a thermoelectric station, it was abandoned in 1974 before being converted to showcase art, dance and film in 1992. Its 117-m chimney has become a symbol for the city. There is a café in the bottom of it. The sunset from the centre's balcony is stunning. In the **Cidade Baixa** quarter are the colonial **Travessa dos Venezianos** (between Ruas Lopo Gonçalves and Joaquim Nabuco) and the **house of Lopo Gonçalves**, Rua João Alfredo 582, which houses the **Museu de Porto Alegre Joaquim José Felizardo**, a collection on the history of the city. ■ *0900-1700 Tue-Sun. Free.*

Southern rebellions

In the 1830s a number of violent rebellions occurred in Brazil, largely as a reaction to the abdication of Dom Pedro I and the uncertain direction of the republic. There was the Cabanagem *in Pará (see page 545), the* Sabinada *in Bahia (1837-38) and the* Balaiada *in Maranhão (1838-42). A fourth revolt took place in Rio Grande do Sul between 1835-45. It was called the* Farroupilha *and involved estancieiros, the producers of* charque *(dried beef and hides), the local military and the forces of the central government. The leader was Bento Gonçalves, a landowner, mason and colonel, who favoured a federation between Rio Grande do Sul, the recently independent Uruguay and Argentina. There were strong links between the three regions, especially through the cattle trade. Whether all the rebels sought separation from Brazil is a debatable issue, but the declaration of the Independence of the province in 1836 was one of the catalysts of the war. It was during the conflict that the Italian Garibaldi lent his support with the formation of the Juliana Republic (see page 330). As far as the central government was concerned, Rio Grande do Sul was an important buffer against the volatile Río de la Plata region and a major supplier of taxes (on the cattle industry, on cross-border trade) and food for other parts of the country. The war dragged on for 10 years, causing a decline in the cattle economy. This, plus the fact that neither side was able to press for outright victory, led to the rebellion eventually petering out.*

Rio Grande do Sul also played an instrumental part in the 1930 Revolution, which brought the First Republic to an end. The political representatives of the state formed a large bloc in the Liberal Alliance with those of Minas Gerais and the Democrats of São Paulo; among their main aims was to shift power away from those states and politicians for whom coffee was the dominating interest. At the time, the governor of Rio Grande do Sul was Getúlio Vargas, who became the president of Brazil after the events of 1930 brought an end to the oligarchic system which had ruled the country for so many years (see History, page 672).

The South also had its own religious movement to rival the Canudos and Joazeiro revolts of the Northeast. This was the Contestado *movement (1911-16), led by José Maria de Santo Agostinho, who was declared a saint by his followers after his death early in the rebellion. The action took place in Paraná and Santa Catarina and the main participants, as well as the government forces intent upon its destruction, were rural workers, urban unemployed who had worked on a number of construction projects but had been abandoned at the end of their contract, and criminals. The townships which grew up during the movement stressed communal reward for labour, equality and support for the monarchy. The combination of religious belief and the organization of rural communities into an alternative way of life was perceived as a serious threat to the established elite. So, as at Canudos before it, the Contestado Movement was ruthlessly destroyed by the army.*

See Brazil, Empire and Republic 1822-1930 *(edited by Leslie Bethell)*, chapters 2 and 6; Modern Brazil, Elites and Masses in Historical Perspectives *(edited by Michael L Conniff and Frank D McCann).*

Museum Júlio de Castilhos, Duque de Caxias 1231, has an interesting histori-   **Museums** cal collection about the state of Rio Grande do Sul. ■ *0900-1700 Tue-Sun.* **Museu de Arte do Rio Grande do Sul**, Praça Senador Florêncio (Praça da Alfândega), is interesting. It specializes in art from Rio Grande do Sul, but also houses temporary exhibitions. ■ *1000-2100 Tue, 1000-1700 Wed-Sun. Free.* **Museu de Comunicação Social**, Rua dos Andradas 959, in the former *A Federação* newspaper building, deals with the development of the press in Brazil since the 1920s. ■ *1200-1900 Mon-Fri. T32244252.*

Iguaçu Falls and the South

Parks   Porto Alegre is well endowed with open spaces. Many of the trees are of the flowering varieties, such as jacarandas and flamboyants. There are seven parks and 700 squares in the city, of which the most traditional is the **Parque Farroupilha** (called Parque Redenção), a fine park near the city centre. It has a triangular area of 33 ha between Avenida Osvaldo Aranha, Avenida José Bonifácio and Avenida João Pessoa, and contains a lake, minizoo, amusement park, bicycle hire, the Araújo Viana auditorium and a monument to the *Expedicionário*. On Sundays there is a *feira* of antiques, handicrafts and all sorts at the José Bonifácio end, where locals walk, talk and drink *chimarrão*, the traditional gaúcho drink. **Parque Moinhos de Vento** is popular for jogging and you can see lots of fit people around who train in the gym of the same name nearby. There is a replica of a windmill in the middle of the park, but there used to be plenty of working mills, which gave the *bairro* its name. The riverside drive, Avenida Edvaldo Pereira Paiva, around Parque Maurício Sirotsky Sobrinho, is closed to traffic on Sunday, for cycling, skating, jogging and strolling. **Marinho do Brasil** is another large park between the centre and the *zona sul*, where there are lots of sporting activities. The **Jardim Botânico**, the **Botanic Garden** , is on Rua Salvador França 1427, zona leste (Bairro Jardim Botânico, bus 40 from Praça 15 de Novembro).

The 5-km wide **Lake Guaíba** lends itself to every form of boating and there are several sailing clubs. Two boats run trips around the islands in the estuary: *Cisne Branco*, from Cais do Porto, near Museu de Arte de Rio Grande do Sul, T32245222, several sailings on Sunday, fewer mid-week, one hour, US$5; and *Noiva do Caí*, from the Usina do Gasômetro, T2117662, several on Sunday, fewer mid-week, one hour, US$1.90 (check winter schedules). Jetskiers jump the wake of the tour boats. **Ipanema beach**, on the southern banks of the river, has spectacular sunsets. You can see a good view of the city, with glorious sunsets, from the **Morro de Santa Teresa** (take bus 95 from the top end of Rua Salgado Filho, marked 'Morro de Santa Teresa TV' or just 'TV').

Cervejaria Brahma, Avenida Cristovão Colombo 545, offers tours of its brewery (but not December-March).

Essentials

Sleeping   **L** *Plaza São Rafael*, Av Alberto Bins 514, T32227000, F32207001,
■ *on map, page 334*   www.plazahoteis.com.br Pool. **AL** *Continental*, Lg Vespasiano Júlio Veppo 77,
Price codes: T32112344, F32285024, www.hoteiscontinental.com.br High standards, pool, gym.
see inside front cover   Recommended. **A** (**B** Fri, Sat, Sun) *Embaixador*, R Jerônimo Coelho 354, T32156600,
F32285050, reservas@embaixador.com.br 4-star, comfortable, unexciting restaurant.
There are many   **A** (**B** Fri, Sat, Sun) *Everest*, R Duque de Caxias 1357, T32159500, F32284792,
good restaurants and   www.everest.com.br Business centre, good views. **A** *Porto Alegre Residence*, R Des
much of the tastiest   André da Rocha 131, T32258644, F32240366. Large rooms. Recommended. **B** *Açores*,
food can be found   R dos Andradas 885, T32217588, F32251007. Central, cramped but friendly. **B** (**C** Fri,
in street stalls and   Sat, Sun) *Alfred Executivo*, Av Otávio Rocha 270, T0800-7044849, F32262221,
cheap lancherias   www.alfredhoteis.com.br **B** *Conceição Center*, Av Sen Salgado Filho 201, T32257774,
F32256135, www.hoteisconceicao.bom.br Good. **B** *Lancaster*, Trav Acelino de
Carvalho 67, T32244737, F32244630. Central, quiet, a/c, restaurant. **B** *Ritter*, Lg
Vespasiano Júlio Veppo 55, opposite rodoviária, T32284044, F32281610,
www.ritterhoteis.com.br 4-star and 3-star wings, English, French, German spoken,
bar, small pool, sauna. Fine restaurant, good service. Recommended. **C** *Methropolitan
Centro*, R Andrade Neves 59, T/F32261800, www.methropolitan,com.br Sofas in
rooms, helpful, microwave, breakfast. **C** *Savoy*, Av Borges Medeiros 688, T32240511,
hotelsavoy@terra.com.br Garage, breakfast, good value. **D** *Conceição II*, R Garibáldi

165, T32243322. English spoken, friendly. **D** *Elevado*, Av Farrapos 65, T/F32245250, www.hotelelevado.cjb.net Big rooms, noisy at front, microwave and coffee, good value. **D** *Palácio*, Av Vigário José Inácio 644, T32253467. Central, hot water, family, safe. Recommended. **E** *América*, Av Farrapos 119, T/F32260062, www.hotelamerica.com.br Bright, friendly, large rooms with sofas, quiet rooms at back, garage. Highly recommended. **E** *Curitibano*, R Dr Barros Cassal 82, T32121761. Clean, plain, breakfast. **E** *Minuano*, Av Farrapos 31, T/F3226 3062. Small but immaculate rooms, parking. **E** *Uruguay*, Dr Flores 371. Simple but recommended. **F** *Conceição I*, Conceição 123, T32214559.

Hotels in the area around R Garibáldi and Voluntários da Patria between Av Farrapos and rodoviária are overpriced and used for short, ie 1-hr, stays.

Camping Praia do Guarujá, 16 km out on Av Guaíba.

Gaúcho cooking features large quantities of meat, while German cuisine is also a strong **Eating**
influence. Regional farm (*campeiro*) food, now a dying art, uses plenty of rice, vegetables, and interesting sauces. Vegetarians might try some of the *campeiro* soups and
casseroles and growing number of alternative or natural restaurants, otherwise stick to
Italian restaurants or *churrascaria* salad bars.

Churrasco *Galpão Crioulo*, Av Loureiro da Silva (Parque da Harmonia aka Maurício Sirotsky Sobrinho, Cidade Baixa), T32268194. Show and dancing, 1130-1600, 1900-0100. *Moinhos de Vento*, R Dona Laura 424, T33311847. Closed Sun afternoon. *Santo Antônio*, R Dr Timotéu 465, Floresta, T32223130, 1100-1430, 1900-2400. *Coqueiros*, R João Alfredo 208, T32271833. 1130-1430, 1930-2400, closed Sun and Mon evenings. Cheap and cheerful. Meat salty and a bit overdone.

General *Le Bon Gourmet*, Av Alberto Bins 514 (in *Plaza São Rafael* hotel), 1900-2300, closed Sun. Steaks, pasta and fine fish plates at mid-range prices. The 24-hr *514 Bar* is at back of hotel lobby. *Chalé da Praça 15*, Praça 15 de Novembro. Average Gaúcho food but recommended for early evening drinks and snacks. The Central Market along the Praça is lined with lancherias. *Komka*, Av Bahia 1275, San Geraldo, T32221881. 1130-1430, 1900-2300, closed Sun. Also do churrasco. Recommended.

German *Chopp Stübel*, R Quintino Bocaiúva 940, Moinhos de Vento, T33328895. Open 1800-0030, closed Sun. Recommended. *Wunderbar*, R Marquês do Herval 598, Moinhos de Vento, T32224967. Very busy. Open 1830 until the last diner leaves (about 0100). Good, welcoming. Mid-range. Recommended.

Italian *Al Dente*, R Mata Bacelar 210, Auxiliadora, T33431841. Expensive northern Italian cuisine. *Atelier de Massas*, R Riachuelo 1482, T32251125. Lunch and dinner, closed Sun. Fantastic pastas and 8-cm thick steaks, excellent value. Highly recommended.

Regional *Gambrinus*, Central Market ground level, Praça 15 de Novembro, T32266914. Lunch and dinner, closed Sun. Cheap. In *Casa de Cultura Mário Quintana*, R dos Andrades 736, *Café Dos Cataventos* in courtyard and *Restaurant Majestic* on roof. Both serve good drinks, snacks and meals. Fantastic rooftop sunsets. 1200-2300. The café in *Usina do Gasômetro* is also very good for sandwiches and speciality coffee. Cheap. *Lancheria Primavera*, Av Farrapos 187. Good breakfasts (toasties and juice) if staying nearby. 0630-1930 closed Sun. Cheap. Staff also run red metal shack round corner on R Dr Barros Cassal serving tasty German hotdogs and burgers.

Vegetarian *Ilha Natural*, R Gen Câmara 60, T32244738. Self-service, cheap, lunch only Mon-Fri. *Nova Vida Restaurant Alternativo*, Av Borges de Medeiros 1010, 1100-1500, closed Sun. Good lasagne. Also at Demetrio Ribeiro 1182. Cheap.

There are many classy bars, cafés and bistros in the pleasant Moinhos de Vento, the city's **Bars &**
richest suburb. Try the roads (like R Padre Chagas) around Moinhos de Vento shopping **nightclubs**
centre (a US$2 taxi ride from downtown). *Cía Sandwiches*, Getúlio Vargas 1430,
T32337414. 1800-0200, beer, sandwiches and music. *João de Barro*, R da República 546,

Iguaçu Falls and the South

Cidade Baixa. Good jazz. Don't miss a sunset drink at *Restaurant Majestic* on the roof of *Casa de Cultura Mário Quintana*, R dos Andradas 736. *Bar do Beto*, Av Venâncio Aires 876, Cidade Baixa, T33320063. 1700-0300, restaurant too. *Cult*, R Gen Lima e Silva 806, Cidade Baixa, T32216299. Open 1900-late, restaurant too. **Gay bars** include *Fly*, R Gonçalvo de Carvalho 189. Predominantly male, attractive bar with art exhibition, sophisticated, open 2100-0200, closed Tue. *Doce Vício*, R Vieira de Castro 32. 3 floors with games room, bar, restaurant, 1830-0230, closed Mon. *Kripton*, R Mariante 606, Rio Branco, T33316651. Popular music. *Bar do Goethe*, R 24 de Outubro 112, Moinhos de Vento, T2222043, www.compuserve.com.br/bardogoethe/ Reunion each Tue, 2030, for foreign-language speakers. *Bar do Nito*, Av Cel Lucas de Oliveira 105, Moinhos de Vento, T33334600. Popular music bar. *Trivial*, R Dona Laura 78, Rio Branco, T33467046, www.trivialbar.com.br Open from 2100. *Sargeant Peppers*, Dona Laura 329, T33313258. Live music Thu-Sat, closed Mon, live music. *Ossip*, Av Republica 677 (corner with João Afredo). Pleasant wine bar near *Dr Jekyll* nightclub (see below). On weekend nights, thousands spill out of the huge beer bars and clubs along Av Goethe between R Vasco de Gama and R Dona Laura in Rio Branco (a US$2 taxi ride from the centre).

Nightclubs: *Dr Jekyll*, Travessa do Carmo 76, Cidade Baixa, T32269404. Open from 2200, closed Sun. *Teatro de Elis*, Av Protásio Alves 1670, Petrópolis, T32863475. *Wanda Bar*, R Comendador Coruja 169, Floresta, T32244755. Gay, open from 2030.

Entertainment

Art galleries *Casa de Cultura Mário Quintana*, R dos Andradas 736, T32217147. A lively centre for the arts, with exhibitions, theatre etc, open 0900-2100 weekdays, 1200-2100 Sat-Sun. *Usina do Gasômetro*, Av Pres João Goulart 551, T32271387. Tue-Sun 1000-2200. Spunky displays by young artists. **Theatre** *São Pedro*, Praça Mcal Deodoro, T32275100. Free noon and late afternoon concerts Sat, Sun, art gallery, café.

Festivals

The main event is on **2 Feb** (a local holiday), with the festival of *Nossa Senhora dos Navegantes* (Iemanjá), whose image is taken by boat from the central quay in the port to the industrial district of Navegantes. *Semana Farroupilha* celebrates *gaúcho* traditions with parades in traditional style, its main day being on **20 Sep**. The Carnival parade takes place in Av A do Carvalho, renamed Av Carlos Alberto Barcelos (or Roxo) for these 3 days only, after a famous carnival designer.

Shopping

Bookshops *Idiomas*, Galeria Central Park, R Mostardeiro 333, Mon-Fri 0900-1200, 1400-1830, Sat 0930-1230, closed Sun. *Livraria Londres*, Av Osvaldo Aranha 1182. Used books in English, French and Spanish and old *Life* magazines. *Prosa i Verso*, Galeria Av Center, R Mostardeiro 120, T32222409. 0930-1800, closed Sun. *Saraiva Megastore*, in Shopping Praia de Belas. *Siciliano*, R dos Andradas 1273 and other branches. Each year a *Feira do Livro* is held in Praça da Alfândega, Oct-Nov. **Jewellers** *H Stern* jewellers at Shopping Center Iguatemi and international airport. **Markets** There is a street market (leather goods, basketware, etc) in the streets around the Central Post Office. Good leather goods are sold on the streets. Sun morning handicraft and bric-a-brac market (plus sideshows) Av José Bonifácio (next to Parque Farroupilha). There is a very good food market. **Shopping centre** The *Praia de Belas shopping centre*, among the largest in Latin America, is a US$1.50 taxi ride from town.

Sport

Gyms Weights and aerobics at *Academia do Parcão*, 24 de Outubro 684. **Golf** Porto Alegre Country Club, Av Líbero Badaró 524, Bela Vista, 18 holes, closed to non-members. Several 9-hole courses in nearby towns. **Swimming** Forbidden from the beaches near or in the city because of pollution, except for Praia do Lami, in the south of the city, which has been cleaned up. Beaches in Belém Novo and Ipanema are OK too. See Beaches, below.

Klift Tur, R Mcal Floriano 270, T32113255, F2287959. American Express. Several tour **Tour operators**
companies offer trips to Foz do Iguaçu and Ciudad del Este, overnight journey each
way (12 hrs in Paraguay). 3-day trips with 1 night's hotel accommodation, US$30
including sightseeing (time at the falls may be limited). See Turismo section in *Zero
Hora* classifieds (Tue) for tour companies' advertisements.

Air The international airport is on Av dos Estados, 8 km from the city, T33421082. A **Transport**
regular bus runs from the rodoviária, as well as a Metrô service from the centre. *See also Ins and outs, page 334*

Buses The rodoviária is on Lg Vespasiano Júlio Veppo, an easy walk from the city centre, T32868230, www.rodoviaria-poa.com.br (with links to bus companies running
inter-municipal, inter-state and international services which have timetable, fare and
availability information). There are good facilities, including a post office and long-distance telephone service until 2100. There are 2 sections to the terminal; the ticket
offices for interstate and international destinations are together in 1 block, beside the
municipal tourist office (very helpful). The intermunicipal (state) ticket offices are in
another block; for travel information within the state, ask at the very helpful booth on
the station concourse.

To **Rio**, US$60, 24 hrs (*Itapemirim* www.itapemirim.com.br); **São Paulo**
(*Itapemirim*), US$29.80 (*leito* 51), 18 hrs; **Brasília** (*Itapemirim*), US$60, 34 hrs;
Uruguaiana (*Pluma* www.pluma.com.br), US$17.50, 8 hrs; **Florianópolis**, US$16, 7 hrs
with *Santo Anjo* (take an *executivo* rather than a *convencional*, which is a much slower
service); **Curitiba** (*Itapemirim*), from US$21 *convencional* to US$17.50 (*leito* 28.50),
coastal and *serra* routes, 12 hrs; **Rio Grande**, US$9, every 2 hrs from 0600, 4 hrs. **Foz do
Iguaçu**, *convencional* US$26, 15 hrs, *executivo* US$30, 13 hrs (*leito* once a week 41).
Many other destinations. To **Cascavel** (Paraná) for connections to Campo Grande,
Cuiabá and Porto Velho: 4 daily with *Unesul*, US$27, 12 hrs. To **Jaguarão** on Uruguayan
border at 2400, US$10, 6 hrs.

International buses To **Montevideo**, with *TTL executivo* daily 2030 US$43 (*leito* *Take your passport
Fri only at 2100, US$43), alternatively take bus to border town of Chuí at 1200 and *and tourist card
2330 daily, US$12.60, 7 hrs, then bus to Montevideo (US$13). To **Asunción** with *when purchasing
Unesul* at 1900, Tue, Fri, 18 hrs via **Foz do Iguaçu**, US$18. **Santiago**, *Pluma* 0705, Tue *international bus
and Fri, US$79. *tickets*

There are bus services to **Buenos Aires** (Pluma), US$54, 19 hrs (depending on bor-
der) with *Pluma*, 1805 daily, route is Uruguaiana, Paso de los Libres, Entre Ríos and
Zárate. For **Misiones** (Argentina), take 2100 bus (not Sat) to Porto Xavier on the Río
Uruguay, 11 hrs, US$15, get exit stamp at police station, take a boat across to San
Javier, US$2, go to Argentine immigration at the port, then take a bus to Posadas (may
have to change in Leandro N Além).

Car hire *Allocar*, R 25 de Julho 102, T33371717, www.allocar.com.br *Bazzoni*,
T33252913, www.bazzoni.com.br *Hello Rent a Car*, T33422422, www.hellocar.com.br
At airport and delivers to hotels. *Milhas*, R Pereira Franco 400, T33372223. *Pontual*, Av
Pernanbuco 1700, São Geraldo, T33422282.

Roads Good roads radiate from Porto Alegre, and Highway BR-116 is paved to
Curitiba (746 km). To the south it is paved (mostly in good condition), to Chuí on the
Uruguayan frontier, 512 km. In summer visibility can be very poor at night owing to
mist, unfenced cows are a further hazard. The paved coastal road to Curitiba via Itajaí
(BR-101), of which the first 100 km is the 4-lane Estrada General Osório highway, is
much better than the BR-116 via Caxias and Lajes. The road to Uruguaiana is entirely
paved but bumpy.

Iguaçu Falls and the South

Directory **Banks** Exchange on Av Borges de Medeiros, good rate, cash only. *Platino Turismo*, R dos Andrades and Av Borges de Medeiros (only one to change TCs, Amex, but 6 less than cash). *Exprinter*, Sen Salgado Filho 247 (best for cash). *MasterCard*, cash against card, R 7 de Setembro 722, 8th floor, Centro. For other addresses consult tourist bureau brochure. *Lloyds Bank*, R Gen Câmara 249. 1000-1630. *Banco do Brasil*, Uruguai 185, 9th floor. 1000-1500, good rates for TCs. *Bradesco*, Praça Sen Florência, Visa machine. *Citibank*, R7 de Setembro 722, T32208619.

Communications Internet: *.Com Cyber Café*, Rua da Praia Shopping, S17, Rua dos Andradas 1001, T32864244, www.com-cybercafe.co.br US$3 per hr. *Ciber Café*, Câncio Gomes e C Colombo 778, T33463098. 0900-2300. *Livraria Saraiva Megastore*, Shopping Praia de Belas, T32316868, www.livrariasaraiva.com.br Mon-Sat 1000-2200. *PC2 Publicidad Café*, Duque de Caxias 1464, T32276853, pc2.com@terra.com.br US$2 per hr. *Portonet*, R Maracheal Floriano 185, T32274696. 0900-2100, US$2.50 per hr. **Post office**: R Siqueria Campos 1100, Centro. Mon-Fri 0800-1700, Sat 0800-1200. *UPS*, T3434972/3424602 (Alvaro). **Telephones**: R Siqueria de Campos 1245 and upstairs at rodoviária.

Cultural centres *Sociedade Brasileira da Cultura Inglesa*, Praça Mauricio Cardoso 49, Moinhos de Vento. *Instituto Goethe*, 24 de Outubro 122. Mon-Fri 0930-1230, 1430-2100, occasional concerts, bar recommended for German *Apfelkuchen*. See also Casa de Cultura Mário Quintana and Usina do Gasômetro, above.

Embassies and consulates *Argentina*, R Coronel Bordini 1033, Moinhos de Vento, T/F33211360. 0900-1600. *Germany*, R Prof Annes Dias 112, 11th floor, T32249255, F32264909. 0830-1130. *Italy*, Praça Marechal Deodoro 134, T32282055. 0900-1200. *Japan*, Av João Obino 467, Alto Petrópolis, T33341299, F33341742. 0900-1230, 1500-1700. *Portugal*, R Prof Annes Dias 112, 10th floor, T/F32245767. 0900-1500. *Spain*, R Eng Ildefonso Simões Lopez 85, Três Figueiras, T33381300, F33381444, 0830-1330. *Sweden*, Av Viena 279, São Geraldo, T32222322, F32222463. 1400-1745. *UK*, R Itapeva 110, Sala 505, Edif Montreal, Bairro Passo D'Areia, T/F33410720. 0900-1200, 1430-1800. *USA*, R Riachuelo 1257, 2nd Floor, T32263344. 1400-1700. *Uruguay*, Av Cristóvão Colombo 2999, Higienópolis, T33256200, F33256200. 0900-1500.

Language courses Portuguese and Spanish, Matilde Dias, R Pedro Chaves Barcelos 37, Apdo 104, T3331-8235, malilde@estadao.com.br US$9 per hr. ·

Laundry Several along Av Andre da Rocha including *Lavandería Lav-Dem*, No 225. US$1.50 per kg wash and dry.

Security The market area in Praça 15 de Novembro and the bus terminal can be a bit dodgy at night; thefts have been reported in Voluntários da Pátria and Praça Parcão.

Tap water is safe to drink in Porto Alegre.

Voltage 110-120 AC 50 cycles.

Beaches around Porto Alegre

Tramandaí
Phone code: 051
Population: 31,000

The main beach resorts of the area are to the east and north of the city. Heading east along the BR-290, 112 km from Porto Alegre is **Osório**, a pleasant lakeside town with a few hotels. From here it is 18 km southeast to the rather polluted and crowded beach resort of Tramandaí. The beaches here are very popular, with lots of hotels, bars, restaurants, and other standard seaside amenities. Extensive dunes and lakes in the region provide an interesting variety of wildlife and sporting opportunities. The beach resorts become less polluted the further north you travel, and the water is clean by the time you reach Torres (see below).

Sleeping Osório: **C** *Ibiama*, R Dr Mário Santo Dani 1161, T/F6632822. **Camping**: *Pinguela Parque*, BR-101, 22 km, T6288080. **Tramandaí**: **B** *Beira-Mar*, Av Emancipação 521, T6611234, F6611133. Thermal pool, sports facilities. **D** *São Jorge*, F Amaral 19,

T6611154. Quiet. Recommended. **Youth hostel: E** per person *Tramandaí*, R Belém 701, T2283802, F2265380. IYHA. **Camping**: *Lagoa e Mar*, RS-030, 5 km, T9882885.

Transport Bus: Porto Alegre-Tramandaí, 5 a day, US$3.50. Osório-Mostardas/ Tavares, 1600 daily, US$4.40.

The BR-101 heads north, just inland of the coast from Osório to Florianópolis and beyond. A series of lakes separates the road from the coastal belt and the beach resorts, but there is another road running all along the coast from Tramandaí to Torres and the border with Santa Catarina. Between the two towns are the resorts (heading south to north) of **Atlântida do Sul**, **Capão da Canoa**, **Arroio Teixeira** and **Arroio do Sal** (*Casa da Sogra*, good food). At **Capão da Canoa** there is surfing at Atlântida beach, while the Lagoa dos Quadros, inland, is used for windsurfing, sailing, water-skiing and jet-skiing.

Sleeping Capão da Canoa: **B** (**C** low season) *Napoli*, Av Paraguassu 3159, T/F6652231. **C** *Kolman*, R Sepé 1800, T6252022, T6252021. Pool. **Camping**: *Marina Park*, RS-389, 7 km, T3016150. **Arroio Teixeira** (18 km further north up the coast): **Camping**: *Alvorada*, on the beach, T6221242. Good facilities, café, only open Dec-Mar. *Camping Clube do Brasil*, RS-03, T6221209. Good, open year-round. *Parque*, Estr Interpraias 2222, T/F6221163. Dec-Mar only. At Arroio do Sal: **D** *Hotel D'Itália*, Av Assis Brasil 11, on beach. Highly recommended.

Porto Alegre coast

Torres

Torres is a well developed resort, with a number of beaches, several high class hotels, a wide range of restaurants, professional surfing competitions and entertainment. There is a lively club scene during the holidays. There is no lack of cheap accommodation, but from Christmas to Carnaval rooms are hard to find. Torres holds a ballooning festival in April. There is an annual Independence day celebration, when a cavalcade of horses arrives in town on 16 September from Uruguay.

Torres gets its name from the three huge rocks, or towers, on the town beach, Praia Grande. Some 2 km long, the beach is safe for swimming and there is surf near the breakwater. Fishing boats can be hired for a trip to **Ilha dos Lobos**, a rocky island 2 km out to sea, where sea lions spend the winter months. Dolphins visit Praia

Phone code: 051
Colour map 5, grid B4
Population: 30,900

Iguaçu Falls and the South

dos Molhes, north of the town, year round and whales en route to Santa Catarina can occasionally be seen in July. On the edge of Rio Mampituba, which marks the state boundary, this beach is good for net fishing and has restaurants. About 2 km south of Torres, past rocky little Prainha, is Cal (*Pradise Dunas* campsite, December-February only), popular with surfers. A further 2 km south, passing the Praia da Guarita leisure development, is Itapeva, with a campsite open year round. The water here is calm, OK for swimming and there is good dune trekking in the Parque da Guarita. There are bars and cafés.

Sleeping & eating
Hotels tend to be very full during the summer season

A (**B** low season) *Solar da Barra*, R Plínio Kroeff 465, Mampituba, T6641811, F6641090. Two pools, 1 of which is thermal, sauna, children's playground. **A** (**B** low season) *Dunas Praia*, Praça Marechal Deodoro 48, Praia Grande, T6641011, F6642080. Pool. **B** (**C** low season) *A Furninha*, R Joaquim Porto 281, T/F6641655. Good service. **B** (**C** low season) *Pousada Brisa do Mar*, R Júlio de Castilhos and R Borges de Medeiros, T6642019. Good breakfast. Recommended. **C** (**D** low season) *Grande Hotel Torres*, R Júlio de Castilhos 124, T6641887. Balcony and breakfast. **C** *Salth*, R Borges de Medeiros 209, T6641881. Good Dec-Feb. **D** *Hotel Costa Azul*, Av José Bonifácio 382, T/F6643291. Friendly, breakfast, close to rodoviária. Good. **D** *Central*, R Borges de Medeiros 296, T6642580. Good breakfast. **D** *Oceano Hotel*, Av Barão do Rio Branco 400, T6641154. Recommended. **Youth hostel E** per person *São Domingos*, R Júlio de Castilhos 875, T6641865, F6641022. IYHA, clean, closed out of season. **Camping** At Praia de Itapeva, 5 km, T6055112.

Bom Gosto, R Rio Branco 242. Churrasco. *Sol Macrobiótico*, R Júlio de Castilhos 746. Good cheap vegetarian with a cosy, personal atmosphere.

Transport
Bus Porto Alegre-Torres, 9 a day, US$6; Tramandaí 1300, 1700 daily, Osório 0630, 1100, 1300, 1830.

Directory
Banks *Banco do Brasil,* 15 de Novembro 236 and at Rodoviária. **Tourist information** R Rio Branco 315, T6641219/ 6261937. **Tours** Marcelo and Saraia Müller at Blue Beach Tur, Av Silva Jardim 257, T/F6643096, bluebeach@terra.com.br, offer boat trips up Rio Mampitumba, abseiling, trekking, and visits to Parque Nacional Aparados da Serra/ Geral. Recommended. During summer, Flamingo Turismo Náutico, run trips to Ilha dos Lobos, departing from Rio Mampitumba estuary.

Tramandaí to São José do Norte
There is a paved road running south from Tramandaí (mostly prohibited to trucks) along the coast to Quintão, giving access to many beaches. One such beach is **Cidreira**, 26 km south of Tramandaí. It is not very crowded and has *Hotel Farol* on the main street (**D** with bath). Bus from Porto Alegre US$3.40. A track continues to charming **Mostardas**, thence along the peninsula on the seaward side of the Lagoa dos Patos to São José do Norte, opposite Rio Grande (see below, Rio Grande Excursions). There is accommodation in **Palmares do Sul** (across the peninsula from Quintão) and Mostardas (**E** *Hotel Mostardense*, R Bento Conçalves 200, T6731368. Good). The latter also has a *Banco do Brasil* and good pizza at R Luís Araújo 941 (closed Mon). About 30 km south of Mostardas is **Tavares**, with a barely passable hotel (**F**) in the praça. Mostardas makes a good base for visiting the national park **Lagoa do Peixe**, one of South America's top spots for migrating birds. Flamingos and albatrosses are among the visitors. There is free access to the park, which has no infrastructure. From Mostardas you can hop off the bus (1045 daily) which passes through the northern end of the park on its way to the beach (where there are basic hotels and restaurants). The main lake (which has the highest bird concentration) is about 20 km from both Mostardas and

Tavares. Park info from Praça Luís Martins 30, Mostardas, T6731464. For local transport try José Carlos Martins Cassola, T6731186 or Itamar Velho Sessin, T6731431. There are three buses a week from Mostardas and Tavares to São José do Norte (130 km) via Bojuru (leaving Mostardas 0630 and Tavares 0700 Sunday, Wednesday, Friday, five hours, US$4.50). If travelling northwards from São José do Norte, the bus leaves 0800, Tuesday, Thursday, Saturday. There is also a daily bus from both Tavares and São José do Norte to Bojuru, where there is a basic hotel. The road south of Tavares is called the Estrada do Inferno. Car drivers should carry a shovel and rope. Four-wheel drive only after rains.

Another popular beach area is south of Porto Alegre, around Cassino, near Rio Grande (see page 333). Some 40 km to the south (towards Rio Grande) begins the Costa Doce of the Lagoa dos Patos; noted bathing points are Tapes, Barra do Ribeiro, Arambaré, São Lourenço do Sul and Laranjal. São Lourenço is a good place to enjoy the lake, the beaches, fish restaurants and watersports. The town hosts a popular four-day festival in March. Bus from Porto Alegre US$6.50, six a day.

São Lourenço do Sul
Phone code: 053
Colour map 5, grid C3
Population: 43,700

Sleeping **B** *Camussi*, R Dr Pio Ferreira 159, T/F2513180. **C** *Vilela*, R Almte Abreu 428, T2513335. Family hotel, clean, friendly. **Camping** At Lagoa dos Patos, T2513002, ext 221. Also at Reponte by the beach. Good facilities.

The Serra Gaúcha

Some of the Serra Gaúcha's most stunningly beautiful scenery is around the towns of Gramado and Canela, 130 km north of Porto Alegre. There is a distinctly Swiss/Bavarian flavour to many of the buildings in both towns. In spring and summer the flowers are a delight, and in winter there are frequently snow showers.

This is excellent walking and climbing country among hills, woods, lakes and waterfalls. The area is developing as an adventure tourism centre. For canoeists, the Rio Paranhana at Três Coroas is renowned, especially for slalom. It is 25 km south of Gramado. In both towns it is difficult to get rooms in the summer/Christmas. Local crafts include knitted woollens, leather, wickerwork and chocolate.

Gramado

At 850 m above sea level, Gramado provides a summer escape from the 40°C heat of the plains. The town lies on the edge of a plateau with fantastic views. It is clean and full of Alpine-style buildings making it feel either Swiss or like Disneyworld, depending on your point of view. Gramado lives almost entirely by tourism. Its main street, Avenida Borges de Medeiros, is full of kitsch artisan shops and fashion boutiques. In the summer, thousands of hydrangeas (*hortênsias*) bloom. Among its parks are **Parque Knorr** and **Lago Negro**, and **Minimundo**, a collection of miniature models such as European castles. ■ *1300-1700, closed Mon. T2861334.* About 1½ km along Avenida das Hortênsias heading towards Canela is the Prawer Chocolate Factory, Avenida das Hortênsias 4100, which offers free tours of the truffle-making process and free tasting. ■ *0830-1130 and 1330-1700, closed w/e. T2861580, www.prawer.com.br* Opposite is the incongruous but good **Hollywood**

Phone code: 054
Colour map 5, grid B4
Population: 28,600

Iguaçu Falls and the South

Dream Car Automobile Museum, which has an excellent collection of American gas guzzlers dating back to a 1929 Ford Model A and Harley Davidson motorbikes from 1926. ■ *0900-1900. US$2.10. Av das Hortênsias 4151, T2864515.* For a good walk/ bike ride into the valley, take the dirt road Turismo Rural 28, *Um Mergulho no Vale* (A Dive into the Valley), which starts at Avenida das Hortênsias immediately before Prawer chocolate factory. Each August, Gramado holds a festival of Latin American cinema. The **tourist information** offices are at Avenida das Hortênsias (Pórtico), T2861418, and Praça Maj Nicoletti/Avenida Borges de Medeiros 1674, T2861475, www.gramadosite.com.br

Sleeping **AL** *Serra Azul*, R Garibáldi 152, T2861082, F2863374. 2 pools, one of which is thermal, sauna, massage, tennis. **A** *Estalagem St Hubertus*, R da Carriere 974, Lago Negro, T/F2861273. Part of the *Roteiro de Charme* hotel group, see page 47. **A** *Gramado Parque*, R Leopoldo Rosenfeldt 818, T/F2862588. Bungalows, good breakfast, reasonable laundry service. **A** *Ritta Höppner*, R Pedro Candiago 305, T2861334, F2863129. Cabins with TV and fridge. Very good value, friendly, good breakfasts. German owners, pool and miniature trains in grounds, closed in May. **B** *Chalets do Vale*, R Arthur Reinheimer 161 (off Av das Hortênsias at about 4700), T2864151, chaletsdovale@via-rs.net 3 high-quality homely chalets in lovely wood setting, 2 double beds, kitchen, TV. Good deal for groups of 4/families. Recommended. **B** *Pequeno Bosque*, R Piratini 486, located in wood close to Véu da Noiva waterfall, T2861527, F2861771. Good breakfast. **B** *Pousada Zermatt*, R da Fé 187, Bavária, T/F2862426. Recommended. **C** *Luiz*, Sen Salgado Filho 432, T2861026. Good breakfast. **C** *Pousada Pertuti*, Av Borges de Medeiros 3571, T2862513. Good breakfast, use of kitchen, friendly. Recommended. **D** *Brisa Pousada*, R Tristão de Oliveira 252, T2866788. Another good cheap option. **D** *Dinda*, R Augusto Zatti 160, T2861588. One of the cheapest. **Youth hostel: E** *Albergue Internacional de Gramado*, Av das Hortênsias 3880, T2951020. 50 dormitory beds in new, cosy hostel.

Eating There's no lack of choice of decent, if a bit pricey, restaurants along Av Borges de Medeiros. Try also *Gasthof Edelweiss*, R da Carriere 1119, T2861861. Good German food. *Churrascaria Patrão Velho*, Av das Hortênsias 4759, T2860823. Good value, high quality meat in barn. Recommended. *Lancheria Tissot*, Av Borges de Medeiros 3283. Tasty, inexpensive lanches and meals in family-run lancheria.

Transport **Buses** Bus service to **Canela**, 10 mins, runs every 20 mins. Several daily buses from **Porto Alegre** US$3.85.

Directory **Banks** *Banco do Brasil*, R Garibáldi corner Madre Verónica. **Communications** Internet: *Cyber*, Av Borges de Medeiros 2016, T2869559. 1300-2300, US$2.80 per hr.

Canela

Phone code: 054
Colour map 5, grid B4
Population: 33,600

A few kilometres along the plateau rim, Canela has been spared the plastic make-over of its neighbour. The painted wooden buildings provide a certain downtown charm. Canela is surrounded by good parks and is developing as a centre of adventure tourism, with rafting, abseiling, trekking, etc on offer. The **tourist information** office is at Laga da Fama 227, T2822200, www.canela.com.br About 7 km from Canela is the **Parque Estadual do Caracol** which has a spectacular 130-m high waterfall. Emerging from thick forest, Rio Caracol tumbles like dry ice from an overhanging elliptical escarpment. East-facing, photos are best before noon. A 927-step metal staircase ("equivalent to a 45-storey building") leads to the plunge pool. If on bike, there is an 18-km circular route continuing on to Park Ferradura (along a 4-km spur) where there is a good view into the canyon of the Rio Cai. ■ *0830-1800. US$1.75. T2783035.* From the Ferradura junction, turn right to continue to the national forest **Floresta Nacional** run by IBAMA (the Brazilian Environment Ministry) with woodland walks. ■ *0800-1700. Free. T2822608.* From here, the dirt road continues round to Canela. Another good hike or bike option is the 4-km dirt track southeast of Canela past Parque das Sequóias to Morro Pelado. At over 600 m, there are spectacular views from the rim edge.

Maps Army 1:50,000 maps exist but are only available from military posts in Caxias do Sul and Porto Alegre. The urban department in Canela's Prefeitura Municipal, R Dona Carlinda, and the environmental lodge in Parque Estadual do Caracol have copies available for viewing only.

AL *Laje de Pedra*, Av Pres Kennedy Km 3, T2824300, F2824400. Restaurant, pool, thermal pool, sauna, tennis. **A** *Vila Suzana Parque*, R Col Theobaldo Fleck 15, T2822020, F2821793. Chalets, heated pool, attractive. **B** *Bela Vista*, Av Oswaldo Aranha 160, near rodoviária, T/F2821327. Good breakfasts. **C** *Canela*, Av Osvaldo Aranha, 223, T2822774. Breakfast, English-speaking staff. Recommended. **C** *Pousada das Sequóias*, R Godofrede Raymundo 1747, T2821373, www.sequoias.cjb.net Forest cabins. **D** *Central*, Av Júlio de Castilhos 146. Safe. Recommended. **D** *Pousada Schermer*, Travessa Romeu 30, T2821746. Friendly. Highly recommended. **Youth hostels** *Pousada do Viajante*, R Ernesto Urbani 132, behind rodoviária, T2822017. Kitchen facilities. Recommended. **Camping** *Camping Clube do Brasil*, 1 km from waterfall in Parque do Caracol, 1 km off main road (signposted), take bus for Parque Estadual do Caracol, 8 km from Canela, T282431. Excellent honey and chocolate for sale here. Highly recommended. *Sesi*, R Francisco Bertolucci 504, 2½ km outside Canela, T/F2821311. Cabins also available, restaurant, clean. Recommended. **Sleeping**

Bifão & Cia, Av Osvaldo Aranha 301, T2829156. *Café Canela*, Praça Joã Correa 7, T2823304. Good meat and cheese dishes, cheap. *Parati Lanches*, Praça Joã Correa 97. Traditional watering hole with pool tables, cheap, 0800-2400. **Eating**

Adventure sports *Atitude*, Av Osvaldo Aranha 391, T2826305, www.atitude.tur.br Rafting, waterfall abseiling, and trips to Aparados da Serra National Park. Recommended. *JM Turismo*, Av Osvaldo Aranha 1038, T2821542, www.jmrafting.com.br Class 3 and 4 rapids. **Sport**

Local Bike hire from *Pousada das Sequóias* or *Pousada Casa Rosa*, R Gov Flores da Cunha 150, T2822400. **Transport**

Long distance Bus Parque Estadual do Caracol, from outside *Parati Lanches*, Praça Joã Correa, 0800, 1200, 1730, US$0.30 (returning at 1220, 1800). Several daily Canela-**Caxias do Sul**, 2 hrs, US$2. Every 2 hrs to São Francisco de Paula, US$1.10. (Take 0800 for connection to Cambará for Parque Nacional de Aparados da Serra). From **Florianópolis**, it is quickest to go via Porto Alegre. Porto Alegre-Canela US$4.15.

Banks *Banco do Brasil*, Av Julio de Castilhos 465. **Communications** Internet: *Posto Telefônico*, Av Júlio de Castilhos 349, Sala 5, T2823305, 0800-2100, Sat 0900-2000, Sun 1000-1200/1400-1800. **Directory**

Iguaçu Falls and the South

Parque Nacional de Aparados da Serra   Some 88 km from São Francisco de Paula (138 km east of Canela, 117 km north of Porto Alegre) are the spectacular **Parque Nacional de Aparados da Serra** and **Parque Nacional da Serra Geral**. Formed 115-130 million years ago when the American and African plates were separating, the parks lie in a 250-km mountain range. Aparados da Serra's major attraction is the canyon Itaimbezinho, 7.8 km long and 720 m deep. Here, two waterfalls cascade 350 m into a stone circle at the bottom. For experienced hikers (and with a guide) there is a difficult path to the bottom of Itaimbezinho. Other easier hikes follow the upper rim of the canyon. You can then hike 20 km to Praia Grande in Santa Catarina (see page 331). **Parque Nacional da Serra Geral**, was opened in 1992. Its main attractions are the Malacara and Fortaleza canyons, the latter 1,170 m deep. From the top there are spectacular views to the coast. As well as the canyons, the parks and surrounding region have several bird specialities. Red-legged Seriema, a large conspicuous bird, can be seen on the way to the park, and there are two fox species.

Park essentials   There are tourist excursions, mostly at weekends, from São Francisco de Paula. At other times, take a bus (0945 and 1700, 1 hr 15 mins, US$2) to Cambará do Sul, get off at the crossroads (signposted Praia Grande), from where it is 18 km, unpaved, to the park entrance at Guarita Gralha Azul – bus (see below), walk or hitch-hike. Gralha Azul is 20 km by unpaved road from Praia Grande. There is a snack bar but no accommodation and camping is banned. From Cambará do Sul to the Fortaleza canyon is 23 km on an unmade road. Aparados da Serra is open Wed-Sun 0900-1700, entry US$2.10 plus US$1.75 for a car, T2511262. Serra Geral is open all year, daily, free. It has no infrastructure but does have a campground. The best time to visit is May to Aug. Rain is heaviest in Sep.

For more information, Ibama, R Miguel Teixeira 126, Cidade Baixa, Caixa Postal 280, Porto Alegre, CEP90050-250, T32252144, www.ibama.gov.br For guides in Cambará do Sul visit the Centro Cultural, R Adail Valim 39, T2511320 (which also has a 1:50,000 scale trekking map on view), or T2511265 and in Praia Grande T0XX48-5320330.

Sleeping   São Francisco de Paula: **A** *Veraneio Hampal*, RS-235 road to Canela, Km 73, T2441363. **C** *Pousada da Torre*, SV Estrada 669, T2443131. **E** *Hotel e Churrascarria Mirão*, B Constant 492, T2441273. Basic. There is a tourist information office on the southern entrance to the town. **Cambará do Sul**: **D** *Pousada Alvorada*, Av Getúlio Vargas 630, T2511284. **D** *Pousada dos Pinheiros*, Estrada Morro Agudo, T99672567. 12 km from Cambará, off road to Aparados da Serra and Praia Grande. Take right turn (signposted) and continue 2 km. Breakfast and dinner, rustic cabins at friendly, isolated farm amid stunning scenery. Recommended. **E** *Pousada Forteleza*, Av Getúlio Vargas 296, T2511248. Friendly, clean. **F** *Pousada Santos*, Av Getúlio Vargas 1175, T2511150.

Transport   Bus: Praia Grande (in Santa Catarina) 35 km, US$2, 1145 not Sun, passes national park entrance. Return at 1700 (passing park approx 1745). São Francisco de Paula 0630, US$2. Caixa do Sul daily.

Bank   Banrisul at Av Getúlio Vargas 1201.

Nova Petrópolis
Phone code: 054
Population: 16,900

About 24 km west of Gramado (bus US$1) is another city with strong German roots. Nova Petrópolis has a Parque do Imigrante, an open-air museum of German settlement. North of Nova Petrópolis is **Jammerthal**, a valley in the Serra Gaúcha with German farms, many of whose inhabitants still speak German; go to Joanette and walk from there.

Sleeping B *Petrópolis*, R Col Alfredo Steglich 33, T2811091, F2811644, www.hotelpetropolis.com.br Rooms and chalets, pool. **B** *Recanto Suiço*, Av 15 de Novembro 2195, on Parque dos Imigrantes, T/F2811229. Rooms, chalets or cabins, pool. **B** *Veraneio Schoeller*, RS-235, Km 8.5, T2811778. Pool, tennis, lake. **Youth hostel F** per person *Bom Pastor*, RS-235 Km 14, Linha Brasil, T2988066, F2811376. IYHA.

Caxias do Sul

Rio Grande do Sul's third largest city, 122 km from Porto Alegre, Caxias do Sul is the centre of the Brazilian wine industry. Caxias' population is principally of Italian descent. Vines were first brought to the region in 1840, but not until the end of the century and Italian immigration did the industry develop.

Phone code: 054
Colour map 5, grid B3
Population: 360,000

The church of **São Pelegrino** has paintings by Aldo Locatelli and 5-m high bronze doors sculptured by Augusto Murer. There is a good **Muséu Municipal** at Rua Visconde de Pelotas 586, with displays of artefacts of the Italian immigration. ■ *0830-1130, 1330-1700 Tue-Sat, 1400-1700 Sun. T2212423*. Italian roots are again on display in the **Parque de Exposições Centenário**, 5 km out on Rua Ludovico Cavinato, where a replica of Caxias do Sul in 1885 has been set up, with a light and sound show at 2000 about the migration from Italy. January and February is the best time to visit.

Sights

Caxias do Sul's festival of grapes is held in February and March. Many *adegas* accept visitors, but they do not always give free tastings. Good tour and tasting of six wines at *Adega Granja União*, Rua Os 18 de Forte 2346. Visit also the neighbouring towns and sample their wines.

Excursions

The town of **Farroupilha**, 20 km from Caxias do Sul, is a good place to buy shoes and jerseys direct from the factory.

A good *adega*, with free tasting, is *Cooperativa Viti Vinícola Emboaba Ltda*, in **Nova Milano**, 6 km away. ■ *Getting there: bus to Farroupilha, then change – day trip*.

At **Bento Gonçalves**, 40 km from Caxias do Sul, you can visit the *Adega Aurora*, Rua Olavo Bilac 500, T4514111, free, including tasting. There are about six others offering guided tours, tasting and sales. Approaching Bento Gonçalves, there is hardly a spot of land not covered with vines – though the results are variable. There is a **Museu do Imigrante**, Rua Erny Hugo Dreher 127, which documents the history of Italian immigration and life in the area. ■ *0800-1130, 1330-1730 Tue-Fri, Sat 0900-1700, Sun 0800-1200*. **Tourist information** at R Mal Deodoro 70, open 0800-1145, 1300-1900 Mon-Fri, 0900-1700 Sat, T4511088. About 13 km from Bento Gonçalves, at **Colônia São Pedro**, is the **Caminho de Pedra**, restored stone and wooden houses typical of the northern Italian style of architecture and artefacts and fabrics of the first wave of Italian colonization, very interesting and in beautiful landscape. There is no public transport so rent a car, or a bicycle. Other Italian colonial towns just over one hour from Bento Gonçalves, which can be reached by frequent buses, are **Veranópolis** and **Nova Prata**, both set in lovely countryside. A pleasant trip through vineyards is to **Monte Belo do Sul**, where you can find pleasant walks through the hills and vineyards; buses US$1.50, 45 minutes, **D** *Hotel Brasil* with bath, very quiet. Tourist information is in Bento Gonçalves at the town entrance at Pipa Pórtico and is very helpful. Currency exchange at *Banco do Brasil*, also travellers' cheques, US$15 commission.

Garibáldi has a dry ski slope and toboggan slope – equipment hire, US$5 per hour. Garibáldi is smaller than the other towns, but has more old colonial

Iguaçu Falls and the South

buildings than Bento Gonçalves and a nice atmosphere. There are some *adegas/vinícolas* in town which you can visit (*Adega Le Cantier, Cooperative Vinícola Garibáldi*, etc), and the town is known as the capital of Brazilian champagne with some other good wines as well.

A restored steam train leaves Bento Gonçalves Tuesday, Wednesday and Saturday at 1400 and 1500 for **Carlos Barbosa**; called '*a rota do vinho*' (the wine run), it goes through vineyards in the hills and terminates at a modern station outside town, rather than at the beautiful old railway station in the centre. US$25 round trip, including wines, with live band; reserve in advance through *Giordani Turismo*, R 13 de Maio 581, T4552788. It is often fully booked by groups, particularly on Saturday.

Another good excursion is to **Antônio Prado**, 1½ hours by *Caxiense Bus*. The town is now a World Heritage Site because of the large number of original buildings built by immigrants in the Italian style. Some to look out for are the **Casa de Neni** (1930) on Praça Garibáldi, **Farmácia Palombini** (1930) on Avenida Valdomiro Bocchese 439, and the **Prefeitura**, Praça Garibáldi. The **Museu Municipal** is also devoted to Italian immigration, Praça Garibáldi 77. There are two hotels on the main street. At *Restaurant Italia*, the *churrasco* lunch for US$6 is excellent.

Sleeping **A** *Alfred Palace*, R Sinimbu 2302, T/F2218655. **A** *Volpiano*, Ernesto Alves 1462, T2214744, F2214445. **B** *Samuara Alfred*, 10 km out on RS-122, road to Farroupilha, T2272222, F2271010. Lots of sporting facilities, tennis, football, pool etc. **C** *Alfred* at No 2266, same as Alfred Palace. **C** *Itália*, Av Júlio de Castilhos 3076, T/F2251177. **D** *Peccini*, R Pinheiro Machado 1939. Shared bath, good breakfast. **D** *Pérola*, corner Ernesto Alves and Marquês de Herval 237. Good value. Hotels fill up early in the afternoon.

Camping *Palermo*, 5 km out on BR-116 at Km 118, T2227255. *Recanto dos Pinhais*, on BR-453 towards Lajeado Grande at Km 23. At Garibáldi, Camping Clube do Brasil, estrada Gen Buarque de Macedo, 4 km.

Eating Good restaurants include *Cantina Honda*, R Francisco Paglioli 984, in Saint Etiene, T2222359. 1900-2300, closed Sun; Italian. *Dom Rafael*, Praça Rui Barbosa.

Transport **Bus** Rodoviária, R Ernesto Alves 1341, T2283000. 15-min walk from the main square, but many buses pass through the centre. Bus fare from Porto Alegre to both Caxias do Sul and Bento Gonçalves is US$5.25.

Directory **Banks** *Banco do Brasil*, exchange and TCs, US$20 charge. **Tourist information** Kiosk in Praça Rui Barbosa.

South of Porto Alegre

Pelotas

Phone code: 053
Colour map 5, grid C3
Population: 323,200

Pelotas, Rio Grande do Sul's second largest city, was founded in the early 19th century and grew rich on the *charque* (dried beef) trade. On the BR-116, 271 km south of Porto Alegre, it lies on the banks of Rio São Gonçalo which connects the Lagoa dos Patos with the Lagoa Mirim. Its heyday was 1860-90 and its early colonial architecture, among the usual flat-fronted buildings, enhances the city's air of being stuck in a time warp. It is sleepy yet prosperous, with much typically Brazilian charm. It has an array of shops, good for browsing, in the pedestrianized town centre, and pleasant parks with plenty of green. There is a 19th-century cathedral, **São Francisco de Paula**, and, as testament to British settlers of the time, the Anglican church **Igreja Episcopal do Redentor**, a couple of blocks from the main square on Rua XV de Novembro. The tree-lined boulevard Av Bento Gonçalves offers a pleasant escape from the summer heat. Pelotas is famous for its cakes and sweets; preserved fruits from the many small confectioners are worth trying.

Within a radius of 60 km (about an hour's drive), there are numerous excursions to the farms of settlers of German descent in the hilly countryside (for example Cerrito Alegre and Quilombo), where you can find simple and clean accommodation, with cheap, good and plentiful food.

    The **Lagoa dos Patos** is very shallow; at low tide it is possible to walk 1 km out from the shore. During heavy rain, saltwater entering the lake brings with it large numbers of crabs which are a local delicacy. Fishermen are generally happy to take tourists out on sightseeing or fishing trips for a small fee (best to go in a group). **Praia do Laranjal** is full of locals' beach houses and there are several friendly bars. **Barro Douro** is very green with no beach, but is the site of a big local festival for *Iemanjá* on 1-2 February, well worth visiting, campsite, *Ze3* buses (or taxi US$30) from Pelotas.

    South of Pelotas, on the BR-471, is the **Taim** water reserve on the Lagoa Mirim. The road cuts the reserve in two and capibaras, killed by passing traffic, are sadly a common sight along the route. Many protected species, including black-necked swans and the *quero-quero* bird, migrate to the Taim for the breeding season. There are no facilities. Visitors should stay in Rio Grande, 80 km away, or in Pelotas. About 5 km from Taim there is an ecological station with a small museum of regional animals; there is some accommodation for scientists or other interested visitors. ■ *Information from Ibama in Porto Alegre, T0XX51-2267211, www.ibama.gov.br*

Excursions

A *Manta*, R Gen Neto 1131, T2252411, F2259911. Pool. **B** *Estoril Hotel*, R Gen Osório 718. Run by same people as *Manta* (same phone). **C** *Plaza Ipiranga*, Av Fernando Osório 8079, on the BR-116 north, 12 km out of town, T/F2736677. Pool. **D** *Aleppo Hotel*, R Gen Osório 708, T/F2253950. Bright, clean and big rooms, breakfast. Recommended. **D** *Curi Hotel*, R Gen Osório 719, T/F2279955. **D** *Motel Mediterâneo*, Av Presidente João Goulont 5473, T2714746. About 150 m from Rodoviária. Recommended if arriving late.

Sleeping

El Paisano, R Mcal Deodoro 1093, T2271507. Legendary Uruguayan steak and style, mid-range, closed Mon, opening hours vary seasonally. *Lobão*, Av Bento Gonçalves 3460, T2256197. *Churrasco rodízio*. *Vila do Conde*, R Andrade Neves 1321, T2224612. 1100-1400, 1900-2300, closed Mon, Portuguese food. *Mama Pizza*, R Gen Osório 720. Good affordable pizza run by *Hotel Manta*. Lovely old-time *lancheria* at Mcal Deodoro 854. 1100-1500, 1900-0300.

Eating

Taxi Radio taxi *Princesa*. Recommended. T2258466. **Air** Mon-Fri flight to Porto Alegre (1530, US$60). **Bus** Rodoviária is far out of town, with a bus every 15 mins to the centre. Frequent daily buses to **Porto Alegre**, 244 km (US$7.50, 3-4 hrs, paved road); **Rio Grande** (US$1.80, 1 hr), Chuí (5 daily, US$6.15) *TTL* bus services (Montevideo-Porto Alegre) depart at 2400 daily, US$35. Bus service to Buenos Aires via Uruguaiana (0710, 2030, US$18). From Bagé, where there is a police post, the Uruguayan company Núñez runs buses 3 times a week to Melo, via Aceguá. Good direct road northwest to Iguaçu via **São Sepé**, which has a very friendly hotel (**C** *Trevo Parque Hotel*, with a/c), Santa Maria (see page 355) and São Miguel mission ruins (see below). Santa Maria (5 daily, US$8.80, 4 hrs) and Santa Ângelo (0805 daily, US$16, 8 hrs)

Transport

Iguaçu Falls and the South

Directory **Banks** *Banco do Brasil*, corner R Gen Osório and R Lobo da Costa. Also at R Anchieta 2122. Will change TCs. It is difficult to change money at weekends. **Tourist information** No official information but *Terrasul*, R Gen Neto 627, T2279973 has local maps and can organize good value city and regional tours. Recommended. Also *Cispella Viagens*, R Andrade Neves 1991, T2255944.

Rio Grande

Phone code: 053
Colour map 5, grid C3
Population: 186,500

At the entrance to the Lagoa dos Patos, 274 km south of Porto Alegre, is Rio Grande, founded in 1737. The city lies on a low, sandy peninsula, 16 km from the Atlantic Ocean. Today it is the distribution centre for the southern part of Rio Grande do Sul, with significant cattle and meat industries.

During the latter half of the 19th century, Rio Grande was an important centre. It has lost much of its importance but is still notable for the charm of its old buildings. The **Catedral de São Pedro** dates from 1755-75. **Museu Oceanográfico**, has an interesting collection of 125,000 molluscs. ■ *0900-1100, 1400-1700, daily. T2313496, 2 km centre on Av Perimetral; bus 59 or walk along waterfront.* At Praça Tamandaré is a small zoo.

Excursions **Cassino** is a popular seaside town with hotels and shops, 24 km from Rio Grande via a good road. There are several beaches within easy reach of Cassino, but they have no facilities. A wrecked ship remains on the shore where it was thrown by a storm in 1975; unfortunately the road is used as a roadway. Travelling south, the beaches in order are Querência (5 km), Stela Maris (9 km), Netuno (10 km), all with surf.

The breakwater (the Barra), 5 km south of Cassino, no bus connection, through which all vessels entering and leaving Rio Grande must pass, is a tourist attraction. Barra-Rio Grande buses, from the east side of Praça Ferreira, pass the Superporto. Very good fishing. The coastline is low and straight, lacking the bays to the north of Porto Alegre. One attraction is railway flat-cars powered by sail, settle the price in advance; the railway was built for the construction of the breakwater.

Across the inlet from Rio Grande, the little-visited settlement of **São José do Norte** makes a pleasant trip (see above, **Tramandaí to São José do Norte**). Founded in 1725 and still mostly intact, the village depends on agriculture and crab fishing. There are only three hotels, a good campsite, *Caturritas*, T2381476, in pine forests 5 km from the town, and several long beaches. Ferries (departing every half-hour, 30 minutes) link São José with Rio Grande; there are also three car ferries daily, T2321500. Tourist information from R General Osório 127.

Sleeping **A** *Atlântico Rio Grande*, R Duque de Caxias 55, T/F2313833. Good value. Recommended. **B** *Europa*, R Gen Neto 165, main square, T/F2313933. **D** *Paris*, R Mcal Floriano Peixoto 112. Old, charming. Recommended. **At Cassino**: **A** *Atlântico*, Av Rio Grande, 387, T2361350. Clean, refurbished, special rates for students. **B** *Marysol*, Av Atlântica 700, T2361240, near beach. Friendly. Private campsite on Av 33, on the way out to Rio Grande. Camping Clube do Brasil site near town.

Eating *Barrillada Don Lauro*, R Luís Loréa 369, T2332037. Uruguayan steak in nice restaurant, fairly cheap. *Blue Café*, R Luís Loréa 314. Expresso machine and good cake, 0830-1930 (2300 Fri, jazz/blues music), mid-range. *China Brasil*, R Luís Loréa 389. Chinese food. *Lancharia Benfica*, R Luís Loréa 351. Popular local place. *Rio's*, R Val Porto 393, T2311180. Vast but good *churrascaria*. *Tia Laura*, 29 km from town on, BR-392 north to Pelotas. Excellent, specializes in home cooking and *café colonial*.

The legend of Negrinho do Pastoreio

There used to be a cruel landowner in Rio Grande do Sul; greedy and evil-tempered, he treated the many slaves on his estância *very badly. Delimited only by natural boundaries, his property was enormous. Animals could roam more or less as they wished, but in those days it was normal to assign a slave to shepherd duties, keeping the livestock within reach of the farm.*

The slave assigned to the task on this property was known as Negrinho, because he was a little Negro. One day he lost an animal. Furious, the boss beat him until he bled, then tied him to a plank of wood and sent him out to find the animal. Barely able to walk, Negrinho searched all day. When night fell, he was sent out again. To light his way, his boss gave him a candle-end and an armful of cinders from the fire, still smoking.

Returning at dawn without the lost animal, Negrinho was tied once more to a plank. He was tied so tightly that he died – or he seemed dead. The boss sent his broken little body away, with instructions that it should be stuffed into the centre of a live ant hill.

Next day, the boss took a party to look at the ant hill. When they opened it up, there was Negrinho the shepherd, safe and well, with the lost animal by his side.

To this day, Negrinho do Pastoreio is the patron 'saint' of lost things. All he charges for his service is the stub of a candle, or some smoke. The most widespread of gaúcho *legends, the story is valued as a reminder of a shameful era in the region's history.*

Bus Pelotas every half hr, 60 mins, 56 km, US$1.75); **Bagé** 280 km, 0700 and 1400; **Transport**
Santa Vitória 220 km; **Porto Alegre** 5 a day, US$10, 4 hrs; **Itajaí**, 14 hrs, US$15. All buses to these destinations go through Pelotas. Road to Uruguayan border at **Chuí** is paved, but the surface is poor (5 hrs by bus, at 0700 and 1430). Bus tickets to **Punta del Este** or **Montevideo** (daily 2330) at rodoviária or *Benfica Turismo*, Av Silva Paes 373, T2321807. **Boats** Boat trip across mouth of Lagoa dos Patos, to pleasant village of São José do Norte, every hr from Porto Velho.

Communications Telephone: R Gen Neto 227. **Embassies and consulates** *Denmark*, R Mcal Floriano 122, T2337600. Open 0800-1200 and 1330-1800. *UK*, R Riachuelo 201, T2337700, F3211530. Open 0800-1200 and 1330-1730. **Tourist information** Kiosk at junction of R Duque de Caxias and R Gen Becaler. **Directory**

Western Rio Grande do Sul

Northwest of Porto Alegre by 328 km is Passo Fundo, regarded as 'the most **Passo Fundo**
gaúcho city in Rio Grande do Sul', so much so that the town's square boasts a *Phone code: 054*
statue of a maté gourd and bombilla. There is an international *rodeio* in *Population: 168,500*
December. The town has several hotels (**A-B**).

Jesuit Missions

West of here are the **Sete Povos das Missões Orientais**. Santo Ângelo is a **Santo Ângelo**
pleasant town with the best infrastructure for visiting the missions. It has a *Phone code: 055*
missionary **museum** in the main square where there is also a **cathedral** with *Population: 76,700*
a hideous fresco of missionaries indoctrinating the indigenous population.
The only considerable Jesuit remains in Brazilian territory are the very dramatic ones at **São Miguel das Missões**, some 50 km from Santo Ângelo. At São Miguel, now a World Heritage Site, there is a church, 1735-45, and

▶▶ The Jesuit aldeia

The typical plan of a Jesuit aldeia (also called a reduccão*) was rectangular, built around a large* praça de armas. *To the rear of the plaza stood the church. On one side of the church was the cemetery and on the other the* claustro, *where the Jesuits themselves lived and studied. Near this were the workshops (*ateliês*) in which the works of art etc were produced. Behind the church were the gardens. Around the other sides of the plaza were the houses in which the Indians lived. The streets between the buildings were at right angles to each other and the settlement could easily be expanded along this plan. Chapels were sometimes built on the sides of the plaza. Other buildings included the* cabildo, *the municipal building of the Indians, the* cotiguazu, *a house for widows, a prison, a hospital and an inn for visitors.*

(See Yves Bottineau and Henri Stierlin (ed), Iberian-American Baroque, *page 176; plan taken from* Folha de São Paulo, *30 June 1997.)*

1 Cemetery
2 Hospital
3 Inn (Alojamento)
4 Jesuits' residence (Claustro)
5 Prison
6 Workshops

small museum. ■ *0900-1800*. A *son et lumière* show in Portuguese is held daily, in winter at 2000, and later in summer, although all times rather depend on how many people there are. The show ends too late to return to Santo Ângelo. The *Hotel Barichello* (**C**), Av Borges do Canto 1567, T33811272, is nice, clean and quiet. It also has a restaurant, *Churrasco* for lunch. The **youth hostel** (**E**) next to the ruins, *Pousada das Missões*, T33811030, pousada.missoes@ terra.com.br, is very good. There is also the monstrous *Wilson Park Hotel* (**B**), R São Miguel 664, T33812000, www.wilsonparkhote.com.br, which has a vast and appalling restaurant. It is difficult to find a good place to eat in the evening; you could try a snack bar for hamburgers. *Gaúcho* festivals are often held some Sunday afternoons, in a field near the Mission (follow the music).

Sleeping and eating (Santo Ângelo) A *Maerkli*, Av Brasil 1000, T/F3122127. Recommended. **B** *Avenida*, Av Venâncio Aires 1671, T3133011. **D** *Brasil*, R Mal Fl Peixoto 1400, T33121299. **D-E** *Hotel Nova Esperança*, Trav Centenario 463, T33121173, behind bus station. No breakfast. **E** *Comércio*, Av Brasil 1178, T33122542. A bit run down but good for the price, clean, friendly. Hotel next door, also **E**, is more than basic. There are other cheap central hotels on or near Praça Rio Branco, fairly near old railway station. *Super Lanches*, corner of Av Mal Fl Peixoto and 25 de Julio, is good.

Tour operator *Caminho das Missões*, R Marquês do Herval 1061, T33129632, www.caminhodasmissoes.com.br, offers 3-, 5- and 7-day hikes ('pilgrimages' – 80, 130 and 180 km respectively) between the various ruins. US$77-150. Open to all beliefs.

Transport Bus Porto Alegre-Santo Ângelo, 5 *convencional* daily, 6 hrs, US$15, and *executivo* at 1830, US$19.50. São Miguel, 0715, 1100, 1530, 1700 (Sat 1000, 1330, Sun 0930, 1830), 1 hr, US$2. Foz do Iguaçu, via Cascavel, 1930, 13 hrs, US$21.

Directory Banks *Banco do Brasil* charges a commission of US$15 for TCs. Good rates for cash at the garage with red doors opposite *Hotel Maerkli* on Av Brasil.

You can continue into Argentina to see the mission ruins at San Ignacio Miní and Posadas by getting a bus from Santo Ângelo at 0615, 1300 or 1930 to the quiet border town of **Porto Xavier**, four hours, US$4, on the Rio Uruguay. Buses also to Porto Xavier, from Porto Alegre, one daily, and Santa Maria.

To the Argentine missions

Sleeping and eating D *Rotta*, Av Mal Fl Peixoto 757, T3541014, near the praça, with or without a/c, and/or TV, bath, breakfast, good restaurant closed Sat and Sun evening; good, cheap, *pizzeria* on the terrace on the main square. Recommended. The hotel is about 5 mins' walk from the ferry at the end of the main street. **Immigration** The Policia Federal post for the entry and exit stamps is about 100 m north of the ferry in a white building, friendly. **Transport Ferry** to Puerto Javier, on the Argentine side of Rio Uruguay, runs Mon-Fri 0800-1145 and 1400-1745, Sat 0900-0945 and 1500-1545. Closed Sun. US$1. From there, there are frequent **buses** to Posadas and, via connections at Alem and Santa Ana, to Iguaçu Falls.

Between November and April, the Rio Uruguay overflows along its east bank for over 1,800 m, making the world's longest waterfall. The 12 m-high Salto do Yucumâ is in the 17,000-ha Parque do Turvo. Its relative isolation (530 km northwest of Porto Alegre on the Argentine border) means not many tourists visit. Accordingly the park is a wildlife haven with over 220 bird species (including 10 under threat in Brazil) and 34 mammal species (12 threatened). The nearest town is **Derrumbadas**, 4 km from park, where there is an information point T35511558, ext 228. Lemon extract production is an important local industry.

Salto do Yucumâ

Sleeping D *Hotel Imperial*, Av Jn Castilhos 544, T35222135 and *Hotel Ideal*, Av Jn Castilhos 832, T35222339, are both in Três Passos, 28 km from park. F *Hotel Iucuma*, R Tapulas 271, T35511120 or F *Hotel Avenida*, beside petrol station, T35511859, both in Tenente Portela, 16 km from park. **Transport** There are 4 buses daily from **Três Passos** to Santo Ângelo. 2 daily **Tenente Portela**-Santo Ângelo.

Inland routes to Uruguay and Argentina

Rail and road to the west and southwest of Rio Grande do Sul go through Santa Maria. The town has a university and is an important commercial and farming centre. There is a Saturday morning fruit and veg market, R 13 de Maio. Nearby **Parque Balneário Oásis** on the BR-158 has nature trails, lakes and a minizoo.

Santa Maria
Population: 243,600
Phone code: 055

Sleeping and eating A *Itaimbé Palace*, R Venâncio Aires 2741, T2221144, F2212051. Good breakfast, pool. Recommended. D *Hotel Dom Rafael*, Av Rio Branco 192, T/F2231919. Recommended. E *Samara Hotel*, Av Rio Branco 135, T2235343. Clean. F *Popular*, R 7 de Setembro 987, T2215262. Clean but basic. *Restaurant Augusto*, R F Peixoto 1356. Traditional, chicken a speciality. Others included Vera Cruz in Av Medianeira; Frei Pança and Augusto, both in Av Mal Fl Peixoto.

Directory Laundry *Lave Só*, R F Peixoto 876.

In the extreme west are Uruguaiana, a cattle centre 772 km from Porto Alegre, and its twin Argentine town of Paso de los Libres with a casino. A 1,400-m bridge over the Rio Uruguai links the two cities.

Uruguaiana
Phone code: 055
Population: 127,000

Iguaçu Falls and the South

Brazilian immigration and customs At the end of the bridge, 5 blocks from the main praça. Exchange and information in the same building. Exchange rates are better in the town than at the border.

Sleeping B *Glória*, R Domingos de Almeida 1951, T4124422, F4124804. Good. **D** *Fares Turis*, Av Pres Vargas 2939, T4123358. May let you leave your bags while you look around town. **D** *Palace*, Praça Rio Branco. No breakfast.

Transport Taxi or bus across the bridge about US$3.50. Buses connect the bus stations and centres of each city every 30 mins. If you have to disembark for visa formalities, a following bus will pick you up without extra charge. There are bus services to **Porto Alegre**. *Planalto* buses run from Uruguaiana via Barra do Quaraí/Bella Unión (US$4.50) to Salto and Paysandú in Uruguay.

If wishing to break the journey between Uruguaiana and Porto Alegre, **Alegrete** (130 km east of the border) is a good place, with several hotels, eg **D** *Grandense*, near rodoviária, shared bath, TV, friendly. Good restaurant, *La Piazza*, on praça, excellent beef.

Directory **Banks**: If you arrive in Uruguaiana from Porto Alegre in the early hours of the morning and need money, cross the border with Pluma bus, wait in Paso de los Libres until opening time (0730) and then go to the Visa ATM in *Banco Francés* for cash.

The crossing furthest west is **Barra do Quaraí** to **Bella Unión**, via the Barra del Cuaraim bridge. This is near the confluence of the Rios Uruguai and Quaraí. Bella Unión has three hotels and a campsite in the Parque Fructuoso Rivera (T0642-2261). Brazilian Consulate, Calle Lirio Moraes 62, T/F7392054; buses to Salto and Montevideo.

Some 30 km east is another crossing from **Quaraí** to **Artigas**, in a cattle-raising and agricultural area. Brazilian consulate, Calle Lecueder 432, T86422504, F86424504. Artigas has hotels, a youth hostel and campsites. Buses also run to Salto and Montevideo.

There are two further crossings at **Aceguá**, 60 km south of Bagé, 59 km north of the Uruguayan town of Melo, and further east, **Jaguarão/Rio Branco**. The 1½-km long Mauá bridge across the Rio Jaguarão joins these two towns. The police post for passport checks is 3 km before the bridge; customs are at the bridge.

Border with Uruguay
For road traffic, Chuy is better than Río Branco or Aceguá

Before crossing into Uruguay, you must visit Brazilian Polícia Federal to get an exit stamp; if not, the Uruguayan authorities will send you back. **Brazilian consulates** are at Melo: R Del Pilar 786, T0462-2136. At Río Branco: Lavalleja and Palomeque. Exchange rates are usually better at Melo than at the frontier.

Santana do Livramento
Phone code: 055
Colour map 5, grid C2
Population: 91,100

The southern interior of the state is the region of the real *gaúcho*. Principal towns of this area include Santana do Livramento. Its twin Uruguayan city is Rivera (see below). All you need do is cross the main street, but by public transport this is not a straightforward route between Brazil and Uruguay. For motorists there are three customs offices in Santana do Livramento, about 30 minutes needed for formalities.

Sleeping C *Jandaia*, R Uruguai 1452, T2422288. Recommended. **C** *Portal*, Av Tamandaré 2076, T2423244. Parking, clean. Recommended. **C** *Uruguaiana*, close to bus station. **Youth hostel E** per person *Palace*, R Manduca Rodrigues 615, T2423340, F2423110. With breakfast, single rooms available.

Transport Bus Rodoviária is at Gen Salgado Filho and Gen Vasco Alves. To **Porto Alegre**, 2 daily, 7 hrs, US$20; 3 daily to **Urugaiana** (4 hrs, US$10), services also to **São Paulo** and other destinations.

Directory Banks *Banco do Brasil*, Av Sarandí. Best rates for Amex TCs at *Val de Marne*.

Santana do Livramento & Rivera

Uruguayan immigration is in the new Complejo Turístico at Sarandí y Viera, 14 blocks, 2 km, from the border (take bus along Agraciada). There is also a tourist office here. **Uruguayan customs** Luggage is inspected when boarding buses out of Rivera; there are also three check points on the road out of town.

Rivera has a park, the Plaza Internacional and the nearby Cañapirú Dam. There is also a casino and many duty-free shops.

Sleeping A *Casablanca*, Sarandí 484, T3221. With breakfast, comfortable, pleasant. **B** *Comercio*, Artigas 115. Comfortable, **C** without bath. **B** *Sarandí*, Sarandí 777, T3521. Fan, good, **C** without bath. **C** *Uruguay-Brasil*, Sarandí 440, T3068. A/c, breakfast. **D** *Ferrocarril*, Lavalleja and Uruguay, T3389. Without bath, basic, quiet. **Youth hostel** Uruguay and Brasil. **Camping** In Municipal site near AFE station, T3803, and in the Parque Gran Bretaña 7 km south along Route 27.

Transport Air: flights to **Montevideo**. **Train** Passenger service to **Tacuarembó**. **Bus** To **Montevideo** and other Uruguayan towns.

Directory Banks: there are plenty of exchange houses. **Embassies and consulates**: *Argentina*, Ituzaingó 524, T3257. *Brazil*, C Ceballos, 1159, T3278, F4470.

Uruguayan immigration
You must have a Brazilian exit stamp to enter Uruguay and a Uruguayan exit stamp to enter Brazil

Rivera
Phone code: 0622
Population: 55,500

Iguaçu Falls and the South

Coastal route to Uruguay

Chuí (Chuy)

Phone code: 053
Colour map 5, grid C2
Population: 5,200

From October to
February, Brazil is
one hour ahead of
Uruguay (GMT-2;
Uruguay GMT-3)

On the Brazilian side of the border is Chuí, a tranquil town, whilst on the Uruguayan side is Chuy. The BR-471 from Porto Alegre and Pelotas skirts the town and carries straight through to Uruguay, where it becomes Ruta 9. Each country's immigration is outside the town (see below); if you are staying in town you can walk anywhere as long as you do not go beyond the immigration posts. The main street is Avenida Internacional: on the Brazilian side it is called Avenida Uruguaí and on the Uruguayan side Avenida Brasil. Each side carries two-way traffic. On the Brazilian side the shops are mainly clothes, shoes and household goods, while the Uruguayan side has duty-free shops and a casino. São Miguel fort, built by the Portuguese in 1737, now reconstructed with period artefacts, is worth a visit. A lighthouse 10 km west marks the Barro do Chuí inlet, which has uncrowded beaches and is visited by sea lions.

Sleeping   **B** *Turis Firper*, Av Samuel Prilliac 629, T2651398, F2651068. A/c, TV, bar. **C** *Bertelli Chuí*, BR-471, 2 km from town, T2651266, F2651207. Comfortable with pool. **E** *Bianca*, Chile 1620, T2651500. With bath. **E** *Rivero*, Colômbia 163-A, T2651271. With bath, without breakfast. **E** *San Francisco*, Av Colômbia and R Chile. Restaurant, with bath.

Transport   Rodoviária on R Venezuela. Buses run from Chuí to **Pelotas** (6-7 daily, US$6.60, 4 hrs), **Rio Grande** (0700, 1400, 5 hrs, US$6.10) and **Porto Alegre** (1200, 2400, 7¾ hrs, US$13); also from Chuí to **Santa Vitória do Palmar** nearby, US$0.60, where there are a few hotels and rather quicker bus services to the main cities.

Directory   **Banks** *Cambios* on the Uruguayan side, see below. *Banco do Brasil*, Av Uruguaí, 3 blocks west of post office. Change all remaining Uruguayan pesos into *reais* before leaving Uruguay, since not even black marketeers in Brazil want them. **Communications** Post office: Av Uruguaí, between Colômbia and Argentina. **Telephone**: Corner of R Chile and Av Argentina.

Border with Brazil
Tourists may freely
cross the border in
either direction

Brazilian immigration Immigration is about 2½ km from the border, on BR-471, road to Pelotas. All buses, except those originating in Pelotas, stop at customs on both sides of the border; if coming from Pelotas, you must ask the bus to stop for exit formalities. International buses, for example *TTL* from Porto Alegre, make the crossing straightforward: the company holds passports; hand over your visitors card on leaving Brazil and get a Uruguayan one on entry. Have luggage available for inspection. Make sure you get your stamp, or you will have trouble leaving Brazil.

Uruguayan immigration Uruguayan passport control is 2½ km before the border on the road into Chuy, US$2.50 by taxi, officials are friendly and co-operative. If travelling by bus, make sure the driver knows you want to stop at Uruguayan immigration, it will not do so automatically. If you stay overnight in Chuy you cannot get your exit stamp in advance. You may only do so immediately prior to leaving the country.

Entering Brazil From Uruguay, on the Uruguayan side, the bus will stop if asked, and wait while you get your exit stamp (with bus conductor's help); on the Brazilian side, the appropriate form is completed by the rodoviária staff when you purchase your ticket into Brazil. The bus stops at Polícia Federal (BR-471) and the conductor completes formalities while you sit on the bus. Customs officials may ask you to open your luggage for inspection. Also, if entering by car, fill up with petrol in Brazil, where fuel is cheaper.

Iguaçu Falls and the South

Entering Uruguay To enter Uruguay, you must have a Brazilian exit stamp and a Uruguayan entry stamp, otherwise you will not be permitted to proceed. Those requiring a visa must have a medical examination before a visa can be issued in Chuí, cost about US$20 and US$10 respectively.

The Uruguayan town of **Chuy** is 340 km from Montevideo.

Into Uruguay
Phone code: 0474
Population: 9,000

Excursions On the Uruguyan side, on a promontory overlooking Laguna Merín and the gaúcho landscape of southern Brazil, stands the restored fortress of **San Miguel**, dating from 1752 and surrounded by a moat. It is set in a park in which many plants and animals are kept. (Bus from Chuy US$0.45, entry US$0.20, closed Monday.) The hotel nearby, **A** *Parador San Miguel*, is excellent, beautiful rooms, fine food and service, highly recommended. Tours (US$10 from Chuy) end for the season after 31 March.

Sleeping and eating **B** *Nuevo Hotel Plaza*, Gral Artigas y Arachanes, T/F0474-2309. On plaza, central, helpful, with breakfast, TV, *El Mesón de la Plaza* restaurant. **B-C** *Alerces*, Laguna de Castillos 578, T0474-2260. Heater, bath, TV, breakfast, nice. **C** *International*, Río San Luís 121, T0474-2055. TV, breakfast extra. **D** *Madrugada*, C S Priliac y India Muerta, T0474-2346. Clean, quiet. *Hospedaje El-Cort*, Lago de los Patos 287. With bath, parking. *Brisas*, Laguna Negra y Lago Castillos, T0474-2708. **Camping** From Chuy, buses run every 2 hrs to the Barra del Chuy campsite, Ruta 9 Km 331, turn right 13 km, T2425. Good bathing, many birds. *Cabañas* for up to 4 persons cost US$20 daily or less, depending on amenities. Most restaurants are on Av Brasil. A good one is *Parrillada Jesús* at the corner of L Olivera. Also *Parrillada/Pizzería Javier*, Arachanes 589, OK, and *Los Leños*, Av Gral Artigas, for meat and pizzas.

Transport Bus: to **Montevideo** (*COT*, *Cynsa*, both on Av Brasil between Olivera and Artigas, or *Rutas del Sol*, on L Oliveria) US$13, 5 hrs.

Directory Banks: several *cambios* on Av Brasil, eg *Cambio Gales*, Gral Artigas y Brasil, Mon-Fri 0830-1200, 1330-1800, Sat 0830-1200; in World Trade Center 1000-2200. Also *Los Aces* and *Val*, either side of Gales. All change TCs at US$1 per cheque and 1 commission and give similar rates, without commission, for cash (pesos, dollars and *reais*). On Sun, try the casino, or look for someone on the street outside the *cambios*. Brazilian currency can be bought here. *Banco de la República Oriental Uruguay*, Gral Artigas, changes TCs. **Communications**: Telephone: Antel, S Priliac, between C L Olivera and C Gen Artigas, 0700-2300. **Embassies and consulates**: *Brazil*, A Fossati, T0474-2049.

Iguaçu Falls and the South

Bahia

Introducing Bahia

This state, the size of France, was the heart of colonial Brazil and Salvador was its first capital. It is often dubbed '**Africa in exile**'. The slave trade brought cheap labour for the sugar plantations, as well as a culture that has endured over the years and is still evident in the religion, cuisine and racial mix today. The city's colonial architecture has been restored and the historic centre is a maze of bars, restaurants, workshops and music in the streets. There are fine beaches, particularly at **Morro de São Paulo** and in the south around **Porto Seguro**. Inland there is the **Chapada Diamantina National Park**, to be explored on foot or on horse. Colourful festivities and street carnivals are held throughout the year to the beat of the drummers of Olodum, Ilê Aiye and other African cultural groups.

Things to do in Bahia

① Attend a bewitching *Candomblé* (a kind of vodoo) ceremony in Salvador with dancing and trances and discover your own personal *Orixa*, or deity.

② Visit Salvador's *Mercado Modelo* to see displays of capoeira, a martial art that was once practised by African slaves.

③ Take a fishing tug to the one-time hippie island of Tinharé which still has a relaxed atmosphere and some untouched beaches.

④ Hire a horse to explore the wonderfully scenic hills of the Chapada Diamantina. This national park is dotted with pretty waterfalls, including Brazil's highest, Cachoeira da Fumaça at 384 m, and has a natural Jacuzzi at Serrano.

⑤ Go dancing in Porto Seguro, the birthplace of lambada. There is music for all tastes at local dance bars, as well as performances by major Brazilian bands at the beach clubs in summer.

Salvador

Phone code: 071
Colour map 4, grid A6
Population: 3.2 million

The capital of the State of Bahia, Salvador de Bahia, is often just called Bahia. Salvador is a definite highlight of Brazil, where many Brazilians choose to spend their holidays (and Carnival, now that Rio's has become so commercialized). It would be quite easy to spend a whole vacation here without leaving this heady mix of colonial buildings, beautiful beaches, African culture and pulsating musical rhythms.

Ins and outs

Getting there
See also Transport, page 386

Air Domestic and international flights arrive at the new Luís Eduardo Magalhães Airport (previously Dois de Julho), 32 km from the city centre, T2041244. An a/c bus service leaves every 30 to 40 mins between 0500 and 2200 weekdays and 0600 and 2200 weekends from the airport to the historic centre, US$1.20. This service stops at all the hotels along the coast road en route (a long way round if you are going to the centre). Also ordinary buses, US$0.50. 'Special' taxis to both Barra and centre (buy ticket at the airport desk next to tourist information booth), US$23; normal taxis (from outside airport), US$18, bus-taxi service, US$10. ATM machines are hidden around the corner on the ground floor to the right as you arrive. The tourist information booth (open 24 hrs, English spoken), has a list of hotels and useful map.

Buses Interstate buses arrive at the rodoviária near Iguatemi Shopping Centre. There are regular bus services to the centre (US$0.50); bus RI or RII 'Centro-Rodoviária-Circular' stops at the foot of the Lacerda lift (see below); buses also go to Campo Grande; the journey can take up to 1 hr, especially at peak periods. An executive bus (US$1.50, weekdays only) to Praça da Sé or the lower city (Comércio) via the coast road leaves from outside the shopping centre (reached from the bus station by a walkway but be careful at night). Taxi to the centre, US$10.

Getting around

The city is built on a broad peninsula and is at the mouth of the Bahia de Todos Os Santos. On the opposite side of the bay's entrance is the Ilha de Itaparica (see page 391). The commercial district of the city and its port are on the sheltered, western side of the peninsula; residential districts and beaches are on the open, Atlantic side. The point of the peninsula is called Barra, which is itself an important area.

The centre of the city is divided into 2 levels, the Upper City (or Cidade Alta) where the Historical Centre lies, and the Lower City (Cidade Baixa) which is the commercial and docks district. The 2 levels are connected by a series of steep hills called *ladeiras*. The easiest way to go from one level to the other is by the *Lacerda* lift, which connects Praça Municipal (Tomé de Sousa) in the Upper City with Praça Cairu and the famous Mercado Modelo (take care with belongings). There is also the Plano Inclinado Gonçalves, a funicular railway which leaves from behind the Cathedral going down to Comércio, the commercial district.

Most visitors limit themselves to the centre, Barra, the Atlantic suburbs and the Itapagipe peninsula, which is north of the centre. The roads and avenues between these areas are straightforward to follow and are well-served by public transport. Other parts of the city are not as easy to get around, but have less of a tourist interest. If going to these areas, a taxi may be advisable until you know your way around.

Tourist information *Bahiatursa*, R das Laranjeiras, 12, Historical Centre, T3212133, open daily 0830-2200; Rodoviária, T4503871, good, English spoken; airport, T2041244, open daily 0800-2245, friendly; in the Mercado Modelo, T2410242, 0900-1800 Mon-Sat; Sac Shopping Centre, Av Centenario 2992, T2644566. Useful information

The Bahians

Bahia is perceived in the south of the country as being a place where life moves at a different pace. The word pregiça *(laziness) will inevitably creep into a conversation with paulistas and cariocas when the topic is Salvador. This slightly malicious accusation from the southerners cannot take away the great infectious joy for life, so obvious in Bahians.*

Bahians have a great propensity for partying; there is even a popular carnival song that says that every day is party day in Bahia. The cycle of massive street festivals throughout the year is evidence of this.

There is no doubt that Bahians have a different slant on time keeping. For instance, the clock in the main bus station

is officially seven minutes fast as Bahians will almost always be late. The weekend and carnival are among the few events that start early: the former on Thursday night, the latter four days before anywhere else in the country. If you want someone to turn up for an appointment on time you will need to emphasize that you are expecting them at 'horário británico'. Another popular saying is that it takes nine months to leave the womb, so why hurry now! While this laid back attitude can be frustrating, Bahians are very open, warm, hospitable, endearing people to spend time with, willing to try to understand, either in words or gestures. People still have time to talk to one another in this town.

(often only available in Portuguese) includes *BahiaCultural*, the month's programme of events and leaflets with maps of themed points of interest. The offices also have details of travel throughout the State of Bahia, T131-06000030 for tourist information in English. Bahiatursa has lists of hotels and accommodation in private homes. Map, US$1.20, not all streets marked, but free, clear map of historic centre also available. Offices have noticeboards for messages. *Emtursa*, at airport, T3772262, 0800-2200 Mon-Sat, is helpful and has good maps.

Maps: from *Departamento de Geografia e Estadística*, Av Estados Unidos (opposite Banco do Brasil, Lower City): also from news-stands including the airport bookshop, US$1.50. A website with information of culture, tourism and history is www.bahiabeat.com.br

Climate It rains somewhat all the year, but the main rainy season is between May and Sep. The climate is pleasant and the sun is never far away. Temperatures range from 25°C to 32°C, never falling below 19°C in winter.

Safety Tourist Police: R Gregório de Matos 16, T2422885. Delegacia de Proteção ao Turista, R Gregório de Matos 1, T2423504. Be very careful of your money and valuables at all times and in all districts. At night, the area around and in the lifts and buses are unsafe. The civil police are reported to be very sympathetic and helpful and more resources have been put into policing the old part of the city and Barra, which are well lit at night. Police are little in evidence after 2300, however.

History

On 1 November 1501, All Saints Day, the navigator Amérigo Vespucci sailed into the bay. As the first European to see it, he named it after the day of his arrival. When Martim Afonso was sent by the Portuguese crown to set up a permanent colony in Brazil, he decided against the Bahia de Todos Os Santos in favour of São Vicente in present-day São Paulo, even though the bay was one of the finest anchorages on the coast and a favourite port of call for French, Spanish and Portuguese ships and a known export point for *pau brasil*.

Bahia

This strategic importance was finally recognized and it was chosen as the place from which the new colony of Brazil was to be governed when the first Governor General, Tomé de Sousa, arrived on 23 March 1549, to build a fortified city to protect Portugal's interest from constant threats of Dutch and French invasion. Salvador was formally founded on 1 November 1549 and remained the capital of Brazil until 1763. One short-lived disruption in the city's growth was its capture by the Dutch in 1624. The Portuguese, with the help of Spain, recaptured it a year later.

On the strength of the export of sugar and the import of African slaves to work the plantations, Salvador became a wealthy city. By the 18th century, it was the most important city in the Portuguese Empire after Lisbon, ideally situated in a safe, sheltered harbour along the trade routes of the 'New World'. Its fortunes were further boosted by the discovery of diamonds in the interior, but this could not compensate for the eventual decline in the sugar industry, which led to the loss of capital status and the rise of Rio de Janeiro as Brazil's principal city. Until the introduction of 20th-century industries such as tourism and petrochemicals, the local economy could not rival the gold and coffee booms of the Southeast, but the city always played an influential part in the political and cultural life of the country.

Salvador orientation

Detailed maps
A Salvador Centro Histórico, page 368
B Praça Castro Alves to Vitória, page 370
C Porto da Barra, page 372

Ochente!

The rest of Brazil tends to find the northeastern accent funny: in common with the poorest and oldest regions of many countries, it retains outmoded structures, expressions and pronunciations which, language historians claim, recall the Portuguese spoken by the earliest settlers. It is an attractive accent, with rising cadence that lends a sing-song quality to the language (considered downmarket in Southerners), and is easy for visitors to manage, since it is spoken comparatively slowly and clearly.

The minute you arrive in the northeast, you are likely to hear the local all-purpose exclamation: 'Ochente!', probably at maximum decibels. Meaning everything from "You don't say!" to the unprintable, it's a particularly satisfying yell, capable of a thousand inflections, and is almost impossible not to adopt. The short version, 'Oshh!', is reserved for situations where hushed tones are required, as in 'She didn't!'

African presence

The city's first wealth came from the cultivation of sugar cane and tobacco, the plantations' workforce coming from the west coast of Africa. For three centuries, Salvador was the site of a thriving slave trade. Even today, Salvador is described as the most African city in the Western hemisphere and the University of Bahia boasts the only chair in the Yoruba language in the Americas. The influence permeates the city: food sold on the street is the same as in Senegal and Nigeria, Bahian music is fused with pulsating African polyrhythms, men and women nonchalantly carry enormous loads on their heads, fishermen paddle dug-out canoes in the bay, and the pace of life is a little slower than elsewhere.

Modern Salvador

Salvador today is a city of 15 forts, 166 Catholic churches, 1,000 *candomblé* temples and a fascinating mixture of old and modern, rich and poor, African and European, religious and profane. It is still a major port, exporting tropical fruit, cocoa, sisal, soya beans and petrochemical products. Its most important industry, though, is tourism; after Rio it is the second largest tourist attraction in the country, being very popular with Brazilian tourists who see Bahia as an exotic destination. Local government has done much to improve the fortunes of this once rundown, poor and dirty city, and most visitors feel that the richness of its culture is compensation enough for any problems they may encounter.

Major investments are being made in infrastructure and public health areas. A new comprehensive sewage system has been installed throughout the city, with a view to improving living conditions and dealing with pollution.

The once forgotten Lower City, Ribeira and the Itapagipe Peninsula districts have received major facelifts. Bahia has become more industrialized, with major investments being made by multinational firms in the automotive and petrochemical industries, principally in the Camaçari complex, 40 km from the city. The Bahian economy is currently the fastest growing in the country.

Sights

Salvador stands on the magnificent Bahia de Todos os Santos, a sparkling bay dotted with 38 islands. The bay is the largest on the Brazilian coast covering an area of 1,100 sq km. Rising above the bay on its eastern side is a cliff which dominates the landscape and, perched on top, 71 m above sea level, are the older districts of Salvador, with buildings dating back to the 17th and 18th centuries.

Bahia

Centro Histórico

Most of the interesting sights are concentrated in the Upper City (see Getting around, page 364), particularly the Centro Histórico. From Praça Municipal to the Carmo area, 2 km north along the cliff, the Centro Histórico (Historical Centre), is a national monument and protected by UNESCO. It was in this area that the Portuguese built their fortified city and where today stand some of the most important examples of colonial architecture in the Americas. The historic centre has undergone a massive restoration programme. The colonial houses have been painted in pastel colours. Many of the bars have live music which spills out onto the street on every corner. Patios have been created in the open areas behind the houses, with open-air cafés and bars. Artist ateliers, antique and handicraft stores have brought new artistic blood to what was once the bohemian part of the city. Many popular traditional restaurants and bars from other parts of Salvador have opened new branches in the area.

Praça Municipal & Praça de Sé

Dominating the Praça Municipal is the old Casa de Câmara e Cadeia or **Paço Municipal** (Council Chamber – 1660), while alongside is the **Palácio Rio Branco** (1918), once the Governor's Palace and now the headquarters of Bahiatursa, the state tourist board. Leaving it with its panoramic view of the bay, Rua Misericôrdia goes north passing the **Santa Casa Misericôrdia** (1695 – see

Salvador Centro Histórico

N

0 metres 100
0 yards 100

Related maps
Salvador orientation, page 366
A Praça Castro Alves to Vitória, page 370

● Eating
1 Bahiacafé.com & Coffee Shop
2 Casa da Gamboa
3 Casa do Benin
4 Gramado
5 Jardim das Delicias
6 Pizzeria Michéluccio
7 Senac

■ Sleeping
1 Albergue das Laranjeiras
2 Paris
3 Pousada Praça
4 Solara

● Bars
8 Cantina da Lua
9 Casa do Olodum

✝ Churches
1 Conceição de Praia
2 Igreja do Desterro
3 Nossa Senhora da Ajuda
4 Nossa Senhora do Rosário dos Pretos
5 Ordem Terceira de São Domingos
6 Ordem Terceira de São Francisco
7 Palma
8 Santa Casa da Misericôrdia
9 Sant'Ana
10 São Francisco
11 São Pedro dos Clérigos

🏛 Museums
1 Abelardo Rodrigues
2 Afro-Brasileiro
3 Casa da Cultura Jorge Amado
4 Casa do Benin
5 Santa Casa

╫╫╫╫ Funicular Railway
■ ■ Lacerda Lift

the high altar and painted tiles, open by arrangement 0800-1700, T3227666) to **Praça da Sé**. This praça, with its mimosa and flamboyant trees, has a statue of Salvador's founder, Thomé da Souza and good views of the bay. On the platform is the Cruz Caido, by the sculptor Mario Cravo. It is dedicated to the old Igreja da Se, which was pulled down in 1933 and whose remaining foundations have been uncovered. One of the viewing pits displays the remains of slaves and mariners who were buried in the churches' grounds in the 16th century.

Terreiro de Jesus is a picturesque praça named after the church which dominates it. Built in 1692, the **church of the Jesuits** became the property of the Holy See in 1759 when the Jesuits were expelled from all Portuguese territories. The façade is one of the earliest examples of baroque in Brazil, an architectural style which was to dominate the churches built in the 17th and 18th centuries. Inside, the vast vaulted ceiling and 12 side altars in baroque and rococo frame the main altar completely leafed in gold. The tiles in blue, white and yellow in a tapestry pattern are also from Portugal. It houses the tomb of Mem de Sá. The church is now the city Cathedral (**Catedral Basílica**). ■ *0900-1100, 1400-1700 daily.* Across the square is the church of **São Pedro dos Clérigos**, which is beautifully renovated. ■ *0800-0930 Sun.* Alongside is the church of the **Ordem Terceira de São Domingos** (Dominican Third Order), which has a beautiful painted wooden ceiling. ■ *0800-1200, 1400-1700 Mon-Fri. US$0.25.*

Terreiro de Jesus

Facing Terreiro de Jesus is Praça Anchieta and the church of **São Francisco**. Its simple façade belies the treasure inside. The entrance leads to a sanctuary with a spectacular painting on the wooden ceiling, by local artist José Joaquim da Rocha (1777). The main body of the church is the most exuberant example of baroque in the country. The cedar wood carving and later gold leaf was completed after 28 years in 1748. The cloisters of the monastery are surrounded by a series of blue and white tiles from Portugal. ■ *0830–1700 (cloisters US$0.20, church free).* Next door is the church of the **Ordem Terceira de São Francisco** (Franciscan Third Order – 1703), with its façade intricately carved in sandstone. Inside is a quite remarkable Chapter House, with striking images of the Order's most celebrated saints. ■ *0800-1200 and 1300-1700. US$0.20.*

São Francisco

Bahia

Rua Alfredo Brito, a charming, narrow cobbled street lined with fine colonial houses painted in different pastel shades, leads to the **Largo do Pelourinho** (Praça José Alencar). Considered the finest complex of colonial architecture in Latin America, it was once the site of a slave market and a pillory where slaves were publicly punished and ridiculed. After complete renovation in 1993, new galleries, boutiques and restaurants have opened, and at night the Largo is lively, especially on Tuesday (see Nightlife below). **Nosso Senhor Do Rosário Dos Pretos** church, the 'Slave Church', dominates the square. It was built by former slaves, with what little financial resources they had, over a period of 100 years. The side altars honour black saints and the painted ceiling is very impressive. The overall effect is of tranquillity in contrast to the complexity of the Cathedral and São Francisco. ■ *Small entrance fee.*

Largo do Pelourinho

At the corner of Alfredo Brito and Largo do Pelourinho is a small museum dedicated to the work of local author Jorge Amado, **Casa da Cultura Jorge Amado**. Information is in Portuguese only, but the café walls are covered with colourful copies of his book jackets. ■ *Mon-Sat 0900-1900. Free.* A good way to get a feel of the city and its people is to read Jorge Amado's *Dona Flor e seus dois Maridos* (*Dona Flor and her two husbands*, 1966). The Carmo Hill is at the top of the street leading out of Largo do Pelourinho. The **Carmo** (Carmelite

Third Order) church (1709) houses one of the sacred art treasures of the city, a sculpture of Christ made in 1730 by a slave who had no formal training, Francisco Xavier das Chagas, known as O Cabra. One of the features of the piece is the blood made from whale oil, ox blood, banana resin and 2,000 rubies to represent the drops of blood. ■ *0800-1130, 1400-1730 Mon-Sat, 1000-1200 Sun. US$0.30.* **Museu do Carmo**, in the Convento do Carmo, has a collection of icons and colonial furniture. ■ *0800-1200, 1400-1800 Mon-Sat, 0800-1200 Sun. US$0.10.*

Praça Castro Alves to Vitória

Related map
Salvador orientation, page 366
A Salvador Centro Histórico, page 368
B Porto da Barra, page 372

0 metres 200
0 yards 200

■ **Sleeping**
1 Bahia do Sol
2 Caramuru
3 Tropical da Bahia

In the direction of the mouth of the bay is the more modern section of the city, with many skyscrapers. Rua Chile leads to **Praça Castro Alves**, with its monument to Castro Alves, who started the campaign which finally led to the Abolition of Slavery in 1888. Two streets lead out of this square, Avenida 7 de Setembro, busy with shops and street vendors selling everything imaginable, and, parallel to it, Rua Carlos Gomes. **São Bento** church (rebuilt after 1624, but with fine 17th-century furniture) is on Avenida 7 de Setembro. ■ *0630-1230 and 1600-1900 Mon-Sat, 0700-1130 and 1700-1900 Sun.*

South of the Praça Municipal

The best city beaches are in this area, which are busy at night with people playing football and volleyball and swimming. Many sidewalk restaurants and bars are open along the strip from Porto da Barra, as far as the Cristo at the end of the Farol da Barra beach. **Forte de Santo Antônio** is right at the mouth of the bay where Bahia de Todos Os Santos and the South Atlantic Ocean meet. On the upper floors, the **Museu Hidrográfico** has fine views of the bay and coast. Recommended. ■ *1300-1800 Tue-Sat. US$1.*

Barra

The promenade leads away from the fort and its famous lighthouse, following the coast to the beach suburbs of Ondina, Amaralina and Pituba. Confusingly the road is called both Avenida Oceânica and Avenida Presidente Vargas, but with different numbering. Beyond Pituba are the best ocean **beaches** at Jaguaripe, Piatã and Itapoã (take any bus from Praça da Sé marked Aeroporto or Itapoã, about one hour). En route the bus passes small fishing colonies at Amaralina and Pituba, where *jangadas* (small rafts peculiar to the northeast) can be seen. Near Itapoã is the **Lagoa do Abaeté**, a deep freshwater lake surrounded by brilliant, white sands. This is where local women traditionally come to wash their clothes and then lay them out to dry in the sun. The road leading up from the lake offers a panoramic view of the city in the distance and the white sands and freshwater less than 1 km from the sea and its golden beaches.

Near the lighthouse at **Itapoã** are two campsites on the beach. A little beyond them are the magnificent ocean beaches of Stella Maris and Flamengo, both quiet during the week but very busy at the weekends. Beware of strong undertow.

Atlantic beach suburbs

Avoid the more distant beaches out of season, when they are empty (eg Itapoã, Piatã, Placafor)

There have been reports of armed muggings on the sand dunes surrounding Lagoa do Abaeté. Don't visit them alone

See the famous church of **Nosso Senhor do Bonfim** on the Itapagipe peninsula in the suburbs north of the centre, whose construction began in 1745. It draws extraordinary numbers of supplicants (particularly on Friday and Sunday), making ex-voto offerings to the image of the Crucified Lord set over the high altar. ■ *0630-0800 Mon, 0600-1200 and 1400-2000 Tue-Sun.* The processions over the water to the church on the third Sunday in January are particularly interesting. Also on the Itapagipe peninsula is a colonial fort on **Monte Serrat** point, and at Ribeira the church of **Nossa Senhora da Penha** (1743). The beach here has many restaurants, but the sea is polluted (bus from Praça da Sé or Avenida França).

Bonfim & Itapagipe
See orientation map, page 366

The **Museu de Arte Moderna**, converted from an old estate house and outbuildings off Avenida Contorno, is only open for special exhibitions. But it has a good restaurant (*Solar do Unhão*), and the buildings are worth seeing for themselves (take a taxi there as access is dangerous). ■ *1300-2100 Tue-Fri, 1500-2100 Sat, 1400-1900 Sun. T3290660.*

Museums

Museu de Arte Sacra is in the 17th-century monastery and church of Santa Tereza, at the bottom of the steep Ladeira de Santa Tereza, at Rua do Sodré 276 (off Rua Carlos Gomes). Many of the 400 carvings are from Europe, but a number are local. Among the reliquaries of silver and gold is one of gilded

Bahia

wood by Aleijadinho (see page 700). ■ *1130-1730 Mon-Fri. US$1.50.* The collection of treasures which used to be in the Casa de Calmon, Avenida Joana Angêlica 198, are well worth a visit. Opposite is **Temporal**, a private museum of postcards, which is at Rua do Sodré 276. The proprietor is Antônio Marcelino do Nascimento. ■ *0900-1830, Tue-Fri 0900-1800 Sat-Sun.*

Museu Abelardo Rodrigues, Solar Ferrão, Pelourinho, is a religious art museum, with objects from the 17th, 18th and 19th centuries, mainly from Bahia, Pernambuco and Maranhão. ■ *1300-1900 daily except Mon. US$0.40.*

Museu Afro-Brasileiro is in the former Faculty of Medicine building on the Terreiro de Jesus. Its interesting displays (all in Portuguese) compare African and Bahian Orixás (deities) celebrations, beautiful murals and carvings. ■ *0900-1700 Mon-Fri. US$1.*

Museu Arqueológico e Etnográfico, in the basement of the same building, houses archaeological discoveries from Bahia, such as stone tools, clay urns, an exhibition on Indians from the Alto Rio Xingu area, including artefacts, tools, photos. Recommended. There is a museum of medicine in the same complex – **Memorial de Medicina**. ■ *0900-1700 Mon–Fri. US$0.40.*

Casa do Benin, below Nossa Senhora do Rosario dos Pretos, shows African crafts, photos, a video show on Benin and Angola. ■ *1000-1800 Mon-Fri.*

Bahia

Porto da Barra

Related map
Salvador orientation,
page 366

Sleeping	Eating
1 Porto da Barra	1 Marazul
2 San Marino	2 Oceânia
3 Villa Romana	

24 hours in Salvador

Start the day in Terreiro de Jesus, a lovely square at the heart of the historic centre. If you need breakfast, *Bahiacafe.com* around the corner at Praça da Se (No 20) is a funky, Belgian-run café with excellent food and atmosphere. Or, for just a caffeine hit, the Cuban-style *Coffee Shop*, a couple of doors along has great coffee and tea served in china cups.

On **Terreiro de Jesus**, the church which gives the praça its name is now a **cathedral** and just one of several examples of over-the-top baroque in this historic centre. In fact, Salvador has more than its fair share of historic churches. But if you go to just one, make it **São Francisco**, on the next square, Praça Anchieta, with its breathtaking interior almost completely covered in gold.

From here, wander down the ever so pretty cobbled street of **Avenida Brito**, with its pastel-painted buildings, craft and music shops, to the **Casa da Cultura Jorge Amado**, once home to one of Brazil's best-loved writers, with a café and bookshop. The house looks over the **Largo do Pelourinho**, where slaves were once sold, beaten and humiliated.

If by now you are ready for lunch, *Senac*, on Largo do Pelourinho, is the perfect spot, with a high-quality buffet at a really good price because all the food is prepared by catering students.

Walk back up João de Deus, parallel to Avenida Brito, an equally charming street with more small shops. You may want to stay and mooch around this area for a while; there always seems to be something to look at in the streets around here.

For something completely different, return to **Praça da Se** to pick up a bus for the beach of Barra. Get off at the **Forte de Santo Antônio**. Visit the museum on the top floor for sweeping views from the terrace of the bay below. Spend the afternoon on this breezy beach with good surf that seems to be busy day and night. Promenade down **Avenida Oceânica**, the seemingly endless beach road lined with cafés and restaurants. For fantastic sunset views out to sea, make a stop at *Barravento* for dinner or a just a drink. Return to the historical centre and sip caipirinhas while listening to African music outside one of the many casual bars. If you are here on Tuesday or Friday you'll witness the small scale **carnival** with drummers and dances on the cobbled streets. Also on Tuesdays you can watch the drumming troupe *Olodum*. Later, you can end up in *Cantina da Lua*, a popular hang-out that stays open until the early hours.

Museu da Cidade, Largo do Pelourinho, has exhibitions of arts and crafts and old photographs. From the higher floors of the museum you can get a good view of the Pelourinho. ■ *0930-1830 weekdays except Tue, 1300-1700 Sat, 0930-1300 Sun. Free.*

Museu Carlos Costa Pinto, Av 7 de Setembro 2490, Vitória, is a modern house with collections of crystal, porcelain, silver, furniture, etc. It also has the only collection of *balangandãs* (slave charms and jewellery). Highly recommended. ■ *1430-1900 weekdays except Tue, 1500-1800 Sat-Sun. US$2. www.guasar.com.br/mccp/mccp.htm*

Museu de Arte da Bahia, Av 7 de Setembro 2340, Vitória, has interesting paintings of Brazilian artists from the 18th to the early 20th century. ■ *1400-1900 Tue-Fri, 1430-1900 Sat-Sun. US$1.20.*

Bahia

▶▶ **Candomblé**

The pulse of the city is candomblé, a religion brought over by slaves from West Africa and syncretized with Catholicism and indigenous belief systems (see Religion, page 681). The pantheon of deities (orixás) worshipped in temples (terreiros) which can be elaborate, decorated halls, or simply someone's front room with tiny altars to the orixá. Ceremonies are divided into two distinct parts. The first is when the orixás are invoked through different rhythms, songs and dances. Once the dancers have been possessed by the orixá, they are led off in a trance-like state to be changed into sacred, often very elaborate costumes, and come back to the ceremonial area in a triumphant procession in which each one dances separately for their deity. Overseeing the proceedings are mães or pães de santo, priestesses or priests.

Candomblé ceremonies may be seen by tourists, usually on Sundays and religious holidays. The ceremonies can be very repetitive and usually last several hours, although you are not under pressure to remain for the duration. Appropriate, modest attire should be worn; visitors should not go in shorts, sleeveless vests or T-shirts. White clothing is preferred, black should not be worn especially if it is combined with red. Men and women are separated during the ceremonies, women always on the left, men on the right. No photography or sound recording is allowed. Most temples are closed during Lent, although each one has its own calendar. Bahiatursa often has information about forthcoming ceremonies, but accurate information on authentic festivals is not always easy to come by.

Excursions

From the lower city, a train (Trem do Leste) leaves Calçada for a 40-minute journey through the bayside suburbs of Lobato, Plataforma (canoes and motor boats for Ribeira on the Itapagipe peninsula), Escada (17th-century church), Praia Grande, Periperi and Paripe (take a bus for the 17th-century church at São Tomé de Paripe). The train runs Monday-Friday only; the same trip can be made by bus, less picturesquely, but much more comfortably. About 36 km from the city is the **Museu do Recôncavo** (Museu do Vanderlei do Pinho) in the old Freguesia Mill (1552), in which one can find artefacts and pictures of three centuries of the economic and social life of this region. The Casa Grande e Senzala (the home of the landowner and the combined dwelling and working area of the slaves) is still intact. It is a peaceful way to spend an afternoon, but difficult to get to by public transport; the museum is near the town of São Francisco do Conde, 7 km from the main highway. ■ *0900-1700 Tue, Thu and Sun.*

Essentials

Sleeping
■ *on map, page*

The historic centre is the ideal place to stay, particularly Santo Antônio

City centre B *Palace*, R Chile 20, T3221155, palace@e–net.com.br One of the few upper-range hotels in the centre, very traditional and a little past its best. **C** *Imperial*, Av 7 de Setembro 751, Rosário, T/F3293127. A/c, helpful, breakfast. Recommended. **C** *Pousada da Praça*, Rui Barbosa, 5, T3210642, gifc@zaz.com.br Simple, pretty old colonial house in quiet street with good security. Big breakfast, rooms with and without bath. Warmly recommended. **D** *Chile*, Rua Chile 7, T3210245. Dingy, but some rooms have harbour view. **D** *Internacional*, R Sen Costa Pinto 88, T3213514. Convenient, good value. **D** *Paris*, R Rui Barbosa 13, T3213922. A/c rooms more expensive, shared showers, breakfast, restaurant in same building. Recommended. **D** *São Bento*, Largo de São Bento 3, T2437511. Good cheap restaurant. Cheaper hotels on Av 7 de Setembro: **E** *São José*, No 847, T321492. Safe. **F** per person *Pousada*, No 2349.

Near the Praça da Sé The following have been recommended: **C** *Pelourinho*, R

Alfredo Brito 20, T2432324. Run down but central and charismatic. **D** *Solara*, R José Alencar 25, Largo do Pelourinho, T3264583. With shower, toilet, breakfast, laundry facilities. **D** *Themis*, Praça da Sé 398, Edif Themis, 7th floor, T3296955. Fan, wonderful views over bay and old city. Recommended restaurant with French chef. **E** *Ilhéus*, Ladeira da Praça 4, 1st floor, T3227240. Breakfast.

Santo Antônio is a quiet district just 5 mins' walk northeast of Pelourinho which has attracted Europeans who have set up *pousadas* in beautifully restored buildings over the last few years. Imaginatively designed and full of character, many have sweeping views of the bay. Most are mid-range, but there are cheaper options too. **A** *Pousada Redfish*, R Direita do Santo Antônio, T/F2438473, www.hotelredfish.com Incredibly stylish, modern design, English-owned, some rooms with terraces and open-air showers. Very special. Highly recommended. **B** *Pousada das Flores*, R Direita de Santo Antônio 442, near Santo Antônio fort, T/F2431836. Brazilian/French owners, excellent breakfast, beautiful old house. Recommended. **B** *Pousada do Boqueirão*, R Direita do Santo Antônio 48, T2412262, F2418064, www.pousadaboqueirao.com.br Family-run, beautiful house overlooking the bay, relaxed atmosphere, most European languages spoken, great food. **B** *Pousada Villa Carmo*, R do Carmo 58, T/F2413924. Italian/Brazilian owned, many European languages spoken, very comfortable, rooms with fan or a/c. **B-C** *Pousada Baluarte*, R Baluarte, 13, T3270367. Bohemian household, lovely owners. Just 5 rooms. Rooms without bath in cheaper category.

Campo Grande/Vitória L *Tropical Hotel da Bahia*, Praça 2 de Julho 2, Campo Grande, T2552000, F3369725. Well-run, owned by *Varig*, convenient for city centre. Rather dated; very much a business hotel. **A** *Bahia do Sol*, Av 7 de Setembro 2009, T3388800, F3367776. Comfortable, safe and frigobar in room, family run, good breakfast and restaurant, Bureau de change, but no pool. Recommended. **D** *Caramuru*, Av 7 de Setembro 2125, Vitória, T3369951. Cosy, with lounge and terrace, breakfast, safe parking. Recommended. **D** *Do Forte*, R Forte de São Pedro 30, Campo Grande, T/F3294080. Breakfast, bath. **D** *Santiago* at No 52, T2459293. Breakfast, bath.

A quiet, upmarket residential area, between Barra and city centre, convenient for museums

Barra Barra was once the focal point of nightlife in Salvador, but has fallen from grace a little in recent years. Unless you are desperate to be by the beach, it makes more sense to stay in the historic centre to enjoy its special nightlife and travel here by bus during the day if you want. Taxis are recommended after dark. Care should be taken on Sun when the beaches are extremely busy. **L** *Marazul*, Av 7 de Setembro 3937, Barra, T2648200, www.marazul.com.br 4-star, near Farol and Porto da Barra beaches, discounts for longer stays. **A** *Do Farol*, Av Oceânica 68, T3366611, F2454436. Good views, on seafront, a little noisy. **A** *San Marino*, Av Oceânica 889, Barra, T3364363. 3-star, on ocean. On Av 7 de Setembro: **B** *Barra Turismo*, No 3691, Porto da Barra, T2457433. Breakfast, a/c, fridge, on beach. Recommended. **C** *Porto da Barra*, No 3783, Porto da Barra, T2477711. Close to lighthouse, on beach. Some rooms very small. **B** *Pousada Hotel Ambar*, R Afonso Celso 485, T3321507. Good service, nicely decorated, excellent breakfast, convenient, run by Paulo and Christine (French, also speaks English). Recommended. **C** *Pousada Malu*, No 3801, T2644461. Small and homely, with breakfast, cooking facilities and laundry service. **C** *Villa Romana*, R Lemos Brito 14, T3366522, F2476748. Good location, pool, a/c. Highly recommended. **C** *Enseada Praia da Barra*, R Barão de Itapoã 60, Porto da Barra, T2359213. Breakfast, safe, money exchanged, accepts credit cards, laundry bills high, otherwise good value, near beach. **D** *Bella Barra*, R Afonso Celso 439, T2378401, F2354131. A/c. Recommended. **E** Rooms to let in private apartments: *Carmen Simões*, R 8 de Dezembro 326. Safe, helpful. *Gorette*, R 8 de Dezembro 522, Apt 002, Edif Ricardo das Neves, Graça, T2643016, gorete@e-net.com.br Recommended.

Most hotels in Barra are within a few blocks of the beach

Bahia

This modern suburban area runs along the coast from Ondina to Itapoã for 20 km towards the airport. Best beaches are after Pituba

Atlantic Suburbs A *Catharina Paraguaçu*, R João Gomes 128, Rio Vermelho, T2471488. Charming, small, colonial-style, tastefully decorated. Recommended. A *Mar A Vista*, R Helvécio Carneiro Ribeiro 1, Ondina, T/F2473866. With restaurant and bar. A *Ondina Plaza*, Av Pres Vargas 3033, Ondina, T2458158, F2477266. A/c, pool, good value, on beach. Recommended. A *Portobello Ondina Praia*, Av Oceânica 2275, Ondina, T3361033, F2453742, www.provider.com.br/portobelo Near beach. C *Mar*, R da Paciência 106, Rio Vermelho, T3312044, F2454440. Good nightlife in the area.

Patamares, 17 km from the city: A *Sol Bahia Atlântico*, R Manoel Antônio Galvão 100, T3709000, F3709001, near one of the best beaches in Salvador, set high on the hill with great views of the coastline.

Itapoã: L *Catussaba*, R Alameida da Praia, Itapoã, T3740555, F3741666, www.catussaba.com.br Elegant, Colonial–style interior. Beautiful gardens leading to beach, but beware of ocean currents when swimming. Convenient for airport. Recommended. A *Villa do Farol*, Praia do Pedra do Sol. Small Swiss-run *pousada*, pool, homely, great restaurant, 1 block from beach. Highly recommended. B *Grão de Areia*, R Arnaldo Santana 7, Piatã, T3754818. A/c, pool, near good beach. C *Europa*, R Genibaldo Figueiredo 53, T3759344. Breakfast. D *Pousada Glória*, R do Retiro 46, T/F3751503. No breakfast, near beach.

Near the bus station B *Portal Da Cidade*, Av Antônio Carlos Magalhães 4230, next to rodoviária, T3710099, F3711419. A/c, pool.

Self-contained apartments with fully equipped kitchen and a/c, with all the facilities of hotels, rented by the day. Standards are generally high

Apart hotels L *Ondina Apart Hotel*, Av Oceânica 2400, Ondina, T2038000. 5-star, self-contained apartments, on beach. Highly recommended. In A range: *Bahia Flat*, Av Oceânica 235, Barra, T3394140, F3394200, dflat@terra.com.br English spoken, on beach, pool, sauna. *Barra Apart Service*, R Marquês de Caravelas 237, Barra, T2647401. *Flat Jardim de Alá*, Av Otávio Mangabeira 3471, Armação, T3436014. Beautiful location by beach, pool, sauna. *Parthenon Farol da Barra Flat*, Av Oceânica 409, Barra. Pool, sauna, on beach. *Pituba Apart Hotel*, R Paraíba 250, Pituba, T2407077, F3458111. Pool, sauna. *Lucia Arleo*, R Miguel Bournier 59, Apto 203, 2372424. Specially furnished apartments near the beach.

Youth hostels *Albergues de Juventude*, **D-E** per person including breakfast, but sometimes cheaper if you have a IYHA membership card. Prices are higher and hostels very full at carnival. *Pelourinho*: *Albergue das Laranjeiras*, R Inácio Acciolli 13, T/F3211366, www.alaranj.com.br In a beautiful Colonial building in the heart of the historical district, can be noisy. Café downstairs, English spoken. Good for meeting other travellers. Warmly recommended. *Albergue Solar*, R Ribeiro dos Santos 45-47, T/F2410055. *Albergue do Peló*, same street No 5, T/F2428061. IYHA, laundry facilities. *Albergue do Passo*, No 3, T3261951, F3513285. Clean, safe, group rates available, English, French and Spanish spoken. Highly recommended. *Pousada Gloju*, R das Laranjeiras 34, T3218249. No breakfast but stunning views of Pelourinho, clean rooms, en suite bathrooms, warm showers. *Vagaus*, R Alfredo Brito 25, Pelourinho, T3216398, F3221179, vagaus@elitenet.com.br Independent youth hostel, all rooms collective with breakfast, internet access available. Recommended. **Carmo**: *Albergue do Carmo*, R do Carmo 06, www.albergue@bol.com.br Dormitories, safe, sea view, good staff, computers with free internet access. Recommended.

On the beaches: *Albergue do Porto*, R Barão de Sergy 197, T2646600, F2643131, albergue@e-net.com.br One block from beach, short bus ride or 20 mins on foot from historical centre. IYHA hostel in beautiful turn-of-the-20th-century house, breakfast, convenient, English spoken, double room with a/c and bath available, kitchen, laundry facilities, safe, TV lounge, games room, internet, courtyard. Highly recommended. *Casa Grande*, R Minas Gerais, 122, Pituba, T2480527, F2400074. IYHA, laundry and cooking facilities. *Pousada Azul*, R Praguer Fróis 97, Barra, T2649798, pousada@provider.com.br Youth hostel-style, near beach, airport transfers. *Pousada Marcos*, Av Oceânica 281, T2355117. Youth hostel-style, great location near the lighthouse, very busy, notices in Hebrew for potential travelling companions, efficient.

Pensionatos are places to stay in shared rooms (up to 4 persons per room); part or full board available. Houses or rooms can be rented for US$5-35 a day from Pierre Marbacher, R Carlos Coqueijo 68A, Itapoã, T2495754 (Caixa Postal 7458, 41600 Salvador), he is Swiss, owns a beach bar at Rua K and speaks English. At Carnival it's a good idea to rent a flat; the tourist office has a list of estate agents (eg José Mendez, T2371394/6). They can also arrange rooms in private houses; however, caution is advised as not all householders are honest.

Camping *Camping Clube do Brasil*, R Visconde do Rosario 409, Rosario, T2420482. *Camping de Pituaçu*, Av Prof Pinto de Aguiar, Jardim Pituaçu, T2317143. *Ecológica*, R Alameida da Praia, near the lighthouse at Itapoã, take bus from Praça da Sé direct to Itapoã, or to Campo Grande or Barra, change there for Itapoã, about 1 hr, then 30 mins walk, T3743506. Bar, restaurant, hot showers. Highly recommended. *Igloo Inn*, Terminal Turistico de Buraquinho, Praia Lauro de Freitas, T3792854.

Sea bathing is dangerous near the campsites

Eating

Pelourinho (historical centre) **Expensive**: *Bargaço*, R das Laranjeiras 26, T2426546. Traditional seafood restaurant, Bahian cuisine, open daily except Tue. *Casa do Benin*, Praça José Alencar 29. Afro-Bahian restaurant, great surroundings, try the shrimp in the cashew nut sauce, closed Mon, open 1200-1600, 1900-2300. *Maria Mata Mouro*, R Inácio Acciolli 8, T3213929. International menu, excellent service, relaxing atmosphere, a quiet corner in bustling Pelourinho. Closed Sun night. *Pizzeria Micheluccio*, R Alfredo Brito 31, T3230078. Best pizzas in Pelourinho, open daily 1200 till late. Does not accept visa. Recommended. *Uaua*, R Gregorio de Matos, 36, T3213089. Elegant, colonial restaurant and bar, typical Bahian cuisine. Open 1130-0200.

Mid-range: *Jardim das Delicias*, R Joao de Deus, 12, T3211449, is an elegant restaurant and antiques shop with an enchanting tropical garden. Incredibly reasonable for its setting. Classical or live music. Warmly recommended. *Senac*, Praça José Alencar 8, Largo do Pelourinho. State-run catering school, a selection of 40 local dishes, buffet, lunch 1130-1530, dinner 1830-2130, all you can eat for US$16, inconsistent quality but very popular, folkloric show Thu-Sat 2030, US$5. *Quilombo do Pelô*, R Alfredo Brito 13, T3224371. Rustic Jamaican restaurant, open daily 1100-2400, good food with relaxed, if not erratic service. One of the few places offering vegetarian options.

Cheap: *Bahiacafe.com*, Praça da Se, 20. Funky, Belgian-run internet café. Good breakfast menu, excellent food, English spoken. Highly recommended. *Coffee Shop*, Praça da Se. Cuban-style café serving sandwiches; main attraction is excellent coffee, and tea served in china cups. Doubles as cigar shop. Recommended.

Seriously cheap: *Gramado*, Praça da Se. One of few food by weight restaurants in area. Basic, lunch only.

Near the Carmo Church: *Axego*, R do Carmo 36. Good views. *Casa da Roça*, R Luís Viana 27. Pizzas, caipirinhas and live music at weekend.

Atelier Maria Adair, R J Castro Rabelo 2. Specializing in coffees and cocktails, owner Maria is a well-known artist whose highly original work is on display. Recommended. Good wholemeal snacks and juices at *Bar da Tereza*, No 16, open daily 0900-2330. Recommended. *Dona Chika-Ka*, No 10. 1100-1500 and 1900-0200, good local dishes. Open gates beside *Dona Chika-Ka* lead to an open square, Largo de Quincas Berro d'Água (known locally as Quadra 2M), with many bars and restaurants. Recommended here is *Quincas Berro D'Agua*, T3215472. Bahian cuisine, expensive. On the next block

Bahia

▶▶ Bahian cuisine

Bahian cooking is spiced and peppery. The main dish is moqueca, seafood cooked in a sauce made from coconut milk, tomatoes, red and green peppers, fresh coriander and dendê (palm oil). It is traditionally cooked in a wok-like earthenware dish and served piping hot at the table. Served with moqueca is farofa (manioc flour) and a hot pepper sauce which you add at your discretion, it's usually extremely hot so try a few drops before venturing further. The dendê is somewhat heavy and those with delicate stomachs are advised to try the ensopado, a sauce with the same ingredients as the moqueca, but without the palm oil.

Nearly every street corner has a Bahiana selling a wide variety of local snacks, the most famous of which is the acarajé, a kidney bean dumpling fried in palm oil which has its origins in West Africa. To this the Bahiana adds vatapá, a dried shrimp and coconut milk paté (also delicious on its own), fresh salad and hot sauce (pimenta). For those who prefer not to eat the palm oil, the abará is a good substitute. Abará is steamed and wrapped in banana leaves. Seek local advice on which are the most hygienic stalls to eat from.

Recommended Bahianas are Chica, at Ondina beach (in the street behind the Bahia Praia Hotel) and in Rio Vermelho, Dinha (who serves acarajé until midnight, extremely popular) and Regina at Largo da Santana (very lively in the late afternoon), and Cira in Largo da Mariquita. Bahians usually eat acarajé or abará with a chilled beer on the way home from work or the beach at sunset. Another popular dish with African origins is Xin-Xin de Galinha, chicken on the bone cooked in dendê, with dried shrimp, garlic and squash.

down is **Tempero da Dadá**, R Frei Vicente 5. Open daily 1130 till late, closed Tue, Bahian cuisine, owners Dadá and Paulo are genial hosts, extremely popular. Across the street is **Quereres**, a restaurant and bar with good live music. **Kilinho**, Ribeiro dos Santos 1. Fresh salads, popular with locals. Recommended. **Restaurante e lanchonete Xango**, Praça Cruzeiro de São Francisco. Good for fruit juices. **Carvalho**, R Conselheiro Cunha Lopez 33, Centro, T7413249. *Comida a kilo*, tasty, excellent fish, cheap. Recommended.

Uauá, R Gregório de Matos 36 (upstairs). 1130-1500 and 1900-2330, closed Tue, excellent northeastern cuisine, try the *carne de sol (sun-dried beef)*, very reasonably priced. Highly recommended. **Casa da Gamboa**, R João de Deus 32, 1st floor. 1200-1500 and 1900-2400, closed Mon; also at R Newton Prado 51 (Gamboa de Cima), beautifully located in old colonial house overlooking the bay, good reputation, open Mon-Sat 1200-1500 and 1900-2300, not cheap. Good *feijoada* at **Alaide do Feijão**, R Francisco Muniz Barreto 26. Open daily 1100-2400. Also at **da Dinha** on Praça José Alencar 5, Mon-Sat 0800-2000. **Encontro dos Artistas**, R das Laranjeiras 15, T3211721, Ribeiro do Santos 10. Passo – Pelourinho, cheap.

Between the Historical Centre and Barra Expensive: *Chez Bernard*, R Gamboa de Cima, 11. French cuisine, open daily except Sun. On Av Contorno, **Solar Do Unhão**, a beautiful manor house, formerly a sugar mill, on the edge of the bay, lunch and dinner with the best folklore show in town.

Mid-range: The best *churrascaria* in Salvador is **Baby Beef**, Av AC Magalhães, Iguatemi. Top class restaurant, excellent service, extremely popular, not expensive, open daily 1200-1500 and 1900-2300. Highly recommended. An excellent Japanese restaurant is **Beni-Gan**, Praça A Fernandes 29, Garcia, intimate atmosphere, Tue-Sun 1900-2400. **Casa D'Italia**, corner of Av 7 and Visconde de São Lourenço. Reasonable prices, good service. **Recanto das Coroas**, underneath the *Hotel Themis* (see above), looks uninviting but the food is excellent. **Ristorante d'Italia**, Av 7 de Setembro, 1238, Campo Grande has won awards. Very reasonable, with large portions. Closed Sun night. Music some evenings. At the bottom of the Lacerda Lift is Praça Cairu and the famous *Mercado Modelo*: on the upper floor of the market are 2 very good restaurants, *Camafeu De Oxossi* and *Maria De São Pedro*, both specializing in Bahian dishes, great atmosphere, good view of the port, daily 1130 till 2000, Sat lunchtime is particularly busy.

Cheap: There are some good snack bars on Av 7 de Setembro: *Nosso Cantinho*, near *Hotel Madrid*. Good value. *Kentefrio*, No 379. The best, clean, counter service only, closed Sun. *Grão de Bico*, No 737. Very good vegetarian. Opposite the Mercado Modelo, the *Paes Mendonça* supermarket self-service counter is good value, 1100-1500, 1st floor.

Barra Expensive: The best Bahian restaurant in the area is *Frutos Do Mar*, R Marquês de Leão 415. There are a number of restaurants specializing in crab, something of a tradition throughout coastal northeastern Brazil, along the seafront promenade. *Barravento*, has a wonderful position right next to the beach and a great view but food can vary in quality, good for sunset views. *Caranguejo do Farol*, Av Oceânica 231. Raised above the road, specializing in crab, extremely busy, young clientèle, you might have to wait for a table. A little further along is *Restaurante do Sergipe*, also very busy.

Mid-range: Near the lighthouse at the mouth of the bay (Farol Da Barra area) are a number of good places like *Micheluccio*, Av Oceânica 10. Good pizza, always busy. Next door is *Baitakão*, good hamburgers and sandwiches. *Mon Filet*, R Afonso Celso 152. Good steaks, pastas, open 1830-midnight. *Ban Zai*, Av 7 de Setembro 3244, Ladeira da Barra, T3364338, by the yacht club. Sushi bar, always busy, open daily except Mon. *Oceânia*, Av Oceânica. Street café, noisy, good people-watching, open every day until late. Almost next door is *Don Vitalone Pizzeria*, No 115. Excellent pizzas. *Don Vitalone Trattoria*, T2357274, is a block away. Part of the same chain, great Italian food, open daily for lunch and evening meal. On R Marques de Leão parallel to the promenade at No 77 is *Pizzeria Il Forno*, T2477287. Italian food at a good price, good service, open daily for lunch and evening meal. *Yan Ping*, on R Airova Galvão, T2456393. Good Chinese, open daily 1100-midnight, reasonably priced, very generous portions, clean.

Cheap: On R Afonso Celso, are a number of good, very reasonable restaurants, including *Pastaxutá*, pizza, pasta, and *Maná*, open 1100 till food runs out, different menu each day, closed Sun, popular, owner Frank speaks a little English. *Mediterrânio*, R Marques de Leão 262. Pay by weight, open daily. *Zobbi Ilê*, open for lunch, good pay by weight restaurant, good salads and cooked dishes, busy, cheap. Recommended. At R Afonso Celso 287, 2 blocks back from the seafront, *A Porteira*, T2355656. Open for lunch only, pay by weight northeastern Brazilian food. *Nan Hai*, same street No 3671. Good Chinese, lunch and dinner (Porto da Barra).

Seriously cheap: Good snacks at the Goethe Institute and the American Institute. *Unimar* supermarket, good cheap meals on 2nd floor. *Califa's* on the 1st floor of Shopping Barra is a basic Arabian place.

Ondina *Double Gula* in *Mar A Vista Hotel*. For excellent meat. Further along Av Oceânica, towards the Rio Vermelho district, is *Sukiyaki*, No 3562. Excellent Japanese, open 1200-1500, 1900-midnight, not cheap. *Extudo*, Largo Mesquita 4, T2374669. Good varied menu, lively bar at night, attracts interesting clientèle, open 1200-0200, closed Mon, not expensive. Recommended. *Manjericão*, R Fonte do Boi (the street leading to *Meridien Hotel*). Excellent wholefood menu, Mon-Sat 1100-1600. Highly recommended. *Marisco*, at Paciência Beach nearby. Good seafood, 1100-1500, 1800-2100, good value. *Margarida*, R Feira de Santana, Parque Cruz Aguiar. Open daily for lunch 1130-1500, original dishes, pasta, seafood, meat, imaginative salads, pay by weight, great desserts, very friendly owners, attracts interesting clientèle. Highly recommended. *Postudo*, R João Gomes 87, T2455030. Over a small shopping mall called *Free Shop* , open daily except Sun, reasonably priced good food in an interesting

▶▶ Moqueca de Peixe

There are as many recipes for this marinaded fish dish, as there are cooks in Brazil. Named after the main Indian method of barbecuing fish wrapped in banana leaves, developed in the great plantation houses of the sugar zone, the dish is now cooked on top of the stove in a pan. Many cooks add coconut milk, giving the sauce a Caribbean flavour typical of the Northeast. In this recipe, the fish flavour is fresh and sharp, balanced by coconut rice.

To serve 6

Marinade ingredients

1 kg fillets of mixed, fresh white fish
1 chopped medium onion
50 ml dendê (palm) oil or olive oil
2 fresh hot chillis, seeded and chopped
2 large peeled tomatoes, chopped

1 crushed clove of garlic
A handful of fresh coriander leaves
3 tbsp lime juice
Salt

Method

Crush the marinade ingredients to a purée in a mortar, or use a blender. Cut the fish into 5-cm pieces, mix with the purée in a non-metallic bowl and leave for one hour. Transfer to a saucepan. Add 75 ml water and half the oil. Cover and simmer until the fish is cooked (about 10 minutes). One minute before serving, add the rest of the oil and turn up the heat.

*Serve with hot pepper and lime sauce (see **Feijoada** recipe in Essentials, page 57) and coconut rice.*

---

setting, always busy. Across the street, at the base of the hill in Largo da Santana, is *Santana Sushi Bar*, T2375107. Open Tue-Sat, authentic.

There is an interesting fish market at Largo da Mariquita with a number of stalls serving food from noon until the small hours, clean, good atmosphere, popular with locals. A good kiosk is *Riso e Nega* (kiosk with green tables), friendly, good basic food. Nearby is *Brisa*, R Augusto Severo 4. Mon-Sat 1100-1500, excellent wholefood restaurant, small, simple, cheap, owner Nadia is very friendly. *Cantina Famiglia-Salvatore*, Largo da Mariquita 45. Delicious, authentic Italian pasta, 2 other branches. Recommended.

Further along Av Oceânica at Jardim Armação **Expensive**: *Bargaço*, open daily 1200-1600 and 1900-2400. Great selection of starters, oyster, lobster, freshwater shrimp, crab meat, etc, expensive but worth it. **Mid-range**: *Rodeio*, Jardim dos Namorados, Pituba, T2401762. Always busy, good value 'all you can eat' *churrascaria*, open daily from 1130-midnight. *Yemanjá*, Av Octavio Mangabeira 4655, T4619010, a 20-min taxi ride from the centre. Excellent Bahian seafood, open daily from 1130 till late, very typical, always busy, reasonably priced, good atmosphere.

Bars & nightclubs

Much of the nightlife is concentrated in the historical centre. The compact network of cobbled streets around R João de Deus is dotted with small, basic bars with plastic tables and chairs on the pavement. Busy nights in the Pelourinho are Tuesday and weekends

Pelourinho See box, page 384, for times and venues of the *bloco* rehearsals. The best time to hear and see artists and groups is during carnival, but they are also to be seen outside the carnival period.

There is free live music every night throughout the summer in the other squares of Pelourinho (Quincas Berro d'Água and Pedro Arcanjo). Sat nights are very busy, a popular band being the *Fred Dantas Orchestra* which plays a fusion of big band music and Latin rhythms. Monthly printed handouts can be found in most hotels or check with Bahiatursa.

Reggae hangs in the air of Pelourinho with many reggae bars such as *Bar do Reggae*, *Casa do Olodum* and *Bar do Olodum*, all within a short walk of each other. *Casa do Olodum*, R Gregorio de Matos, is a bar and dance floor where the band Olodum performs on Tue to packed crowds (hang out on the pavement outside if you don't want to pay the entrance fee); the rest of the week it's open to all. Almost directly opposite at No 15 is: *NR*, a great after-hours bar with live music (which is not always so great). There's a US$0.50 charge if you sit down.

Bahia

Good bars are *Cantina da Lua*, Terreiro De Jesus. Open daily, popular and a good spot on the square with outdoor seating, but gets crowded and the food isn't good. Many bars on the Largo de Quincas Berro d'Água (see above). Good café and great chocolate at *Cailleur*, R Gregório de Matos 17, open daily 0930-2100, bar service continues till 0100.

Barra *Mordomia Drinks*, Ladeira Da Barra. Enter through a narrow entrance to an open air bar with a spectacular view of the bay, very popular. Most Barra nightlife happens at the Farol da Barra (lighthouse). R Marquês de Leão is very busy, with lots of bars with tables on the pavement: *Habeas Copos*, R Marquês de Leão 172. Famous and traditional street side bar. *Barra Vento 600* is a popular open air bar on the beachfront. Bar in the ICBA (Goethe Institute), has good light snacks, attracts a young bohemian clientèle, closes 2300, very pleasant courtyard setting. Further along the coast at Ondina is the *Bahia Othon Palace Hotel* with a disco called *Kasullo Dancing Hall*, busy at weekends.

Rio Vermelho This district was once the bohemian section of town and it still has good nightlife. *Alambique* is a good dance bar (especially on Sat night US$10). *Chico* and *Rocco* are along the same strip. *Porto Seguro* at *Salvador Praia Hotel*, T2455033. *New Fred's*, Av Visconde de Itaboraí 125, T2484399 (middle-aged market, singles bar). *Bell's Beach* disco at Boca Do Rio. Open Tue-Sat 2200-0400, up-market, expensive.

Entertainment

The Fundação Cultural do Estado da Bahia edits *BahiaCultural*, a monthly brochure listing the main cultural events for the month. These can be found in most hotels and Bahiatursa information centres. Local newspapers *A Tarde* and *Correio da Bahia* have good cultural sections listing all events in the city.

Cinema The main shopping malls at Barra, Iguatemi, Itaigara and Brotas, and *Cineart* in Politeama (Centro), run more mainstream movies. The impressive Casa do Comércio building near Iguatemi houses the *Teatro do SESC* with a mixed programme of theatre, cinema and music Wed-Sun.

Theatre *Castro Alves*, at Campo Grande (Largo 2 de Julho), T3398000, seats 1400 and is considered one of the best in Latin America. It also has its own repertory theatre, the *Sala de Coro*, for more experimental productions. The theatre's *Concha Acústica* is an open-air venue used frequently in the summer, attracting the big names in Brazilian music. *Teatro Vila Velha* Passeio Publico, T3361384. Márcio Meirelles, the theatre's director works extensively with Grupo Teatro Olodum; although performed in Portuguese, productions here are very visual and worth investigating. *Instituto Cultural Brasil-Alemanha* (ICBA) and the *Associação Cultural Brasil Estados Unidos* (ACBEU), both on Corredor de Vitória, have a varied programme, the former with a cinema; *Teatro Santo Antônio*, part of the Escola de Teatro da Universidade Federal da Bahia; *Teatro de Arena*. The Universal English Course (UEC) also owns the 400-seat *Teatro Jorge Amado*, T3558620 in Pituba. In Pelourinho *Teatro XVIII*, R Frei Vicente, T3320018, an experimental theatre. *Teatro Gregorio de Matos* in Praça Castro Alves, T3222646 offers space to new productions and writers.

Festivals
See box, page 384, for Carnival information

6 Jan (Epiphany); **Ash Wed** and **Maundy Thu**, half-days; **2 Jul** (Independence of Bahia); **30 Oct**; **Christmas Eve**, half day. An important local holiday is the *Festa do Nosso Senhor do Bonfim*; it takes place on the 2nd Sun after Epiphany, but the washing or *lavagem* of the Bonfim church, with its colourful parade, takes place on the preceding Thu (usually mid-Jan). The *Festa da Ribeira* is on the following Mon. Another colourful festival is that of the fishermen of Rio Vermelho on **2 Feb**; gifts for Yemanjá, Goddess of the Sea, are taken out to sea in a procession of sailing boats to an accompaniment of *candomblé* instruments. The *Holy Week* processions among the old churches of the upper city are also interesting.

Bahia

▶▶ **Music in Bahia**

Walking the streets of the old town on busy nights is like surfing the wavebands of your radio. A short walk from one bar and you hear the music coming from the next. Grupo Cultural Olodum *began life in 1980 as a carnival option for the inhabitants of Pelourinho, then a much neglected area. Every Tuesday night* Banda Olodum, *a drumming troupe made famous by their innovative powerhouse percussion and involvement with Paul Simon, Michael Jackson and Branford Marsalis, rehearse in the Largo Teresa Batista (starts 1930, US$10) in front of packed crowds. They also rehearse free of charge in the Largo do Pelourinho on Sunday, T3215010.*

Ilê Aiyê is just as much revered for its socio-political profile as its musicality; it still maintains its original pure percussion format. Established in Liberdade, the largest suburb of the city, Ilê Aiyê *is a thriving cultural group dedicated to preserving African tradition, which under the guidance of its president Vovô is deeply committed to the fight against racism. Rehearsals take place mid-week at Boca do Rio and on Saturday nights on the street in front of their headquarters at Ladeira do Curuzu in Liberdade. You don't need to understand the words to be moved by the sheer joy in the air.*

Araketu hails from the sprawling Periperi suburb in the Lower City. Once a purely percussion band, Araketu *has travelled widely and borrowed on various musical forms (samba, candomblé, soukous etc) to become a major carnival attraction and one of the most successful bands in Bahia. Rehearsals take place on Wednesday nights on Avenida Contorno. These get very full and it is best to buy tickets in advance from Avenida Oceânica 683, Barra Centro Comercial, Sala 06, T2476784.*

Neguinho do Samba was the musical director of Olodum *until he founded* Didá, *an all-woman drumming group based along similar lines to Olodum. They rehearse on Friday nights in the Praça Teresa Batista, Pelourinho (starts 2000, US$10).*

Sport **Football** *Esporte Clube Bahia* and *Vitória* play at the Otávio Mangabeira Stadium, Trav Joaquim Maurício, Nazaré, T/F2423322. The stadium holds 90,000 and is better known as the Fonte Nova. It is 10 mins away from the Pelourinho, and the Barroquinha terminal.

Shopping The Barra and Iguatemi shopping centres are big and modern with a/c and major department stores. Quality *artesanato* at the 3 official FIEB-SESI shops: Av Tiradentes 299 (Bonfim); Av Borges dos Reis 9 (Rio Vermelho); Av 7 de Setembro 261 (Mercês).

Pelourinho The major carnival *afro blocos* have boutiques selling T-shirts and souvenirs: *Boutique Olodum*, on Praça José Alencar, *Ilê Aiyê*, on R Francisco Muniz Barreto 16, and *Muzenza* next door. On the same street is *Modaxé*, a retail outlet for clothes manufactured by street children under the auspices of the Projeto Axé, expensive, but these are the trendiest T-shirts in town. Also on this street at No 18 is *Brazilian Sound*, for the latest in Brazilian and Bahia music, CDs mainly. Another good music shop is *Mini Som* in the nearby Praça da Sé. The record shop at the Rodoviária is good for regional Bahian music.

Instituto Mauá, R Gregorio de Matos 27, open Tue-Sat 0900-1800, Sun 1000-1600, good-quality **Bahian handicrafts** at fair prices, better value and better quality for traditional crafts than the Mercado Modelo. A similar store is *Loja de Artesanato do SESC*, Largo Pelourinho (T3215502), Mon-Fri 0900-1800 (closed for lunch), Sat 0900-1300. *Rosa do Prado* , R Inacio Aciolly, 5. Cigar shop packed with every kind of Brazilian 'charuto' imaginable. Handmade traditional percussion instruments (and percussion lessons) at *Oficina de Investigação Musical*, Alfredo Brito 24 (T3222386), Mon-Fri, 0800-1200 and 1300-1600. US$15 per hr.

Bahia

Faithful to their traditions are Filhos de Gandhi, *the original African drumming group and the largest, formed by striking stevedores during the 1949 carnival. The hypnotic shuffling cadence of* Filhos de Gandhi's *afoxé rhythm is one of the most emotive of Bahia's carnival.*

Carlinhos Brown is a local hero. From humble beginnings he has become one of the most influential musical composers in Brazil today, mixing great lyrics, innovative rhythms and a powerful stage presence. He played percussion with many Bahian musicians, until he formed his own percussion group, Timbalada. *His first album,* Alfagamabetizado, *is perhaps the most successful fusion album in Brazilian music. Ever faithful to his background in the poor Candeal district, he has invested heavily in his old neighbourhood, both socially and culturally. He has created the Candy All Square, a centre for popular culture where the* Timbalada *rehearsals take place every Sunday night (1830, US$10) from September to March. Not to be missed.*

During the winter (July-September), ring the blocos to confirm that free rehearsals will take place.

Artists and bands using electronic instruments and who tend to play in the trios eléctricos draw heavily on the rich rhythms of the drumming groups, creating a new musical genre known as Axé. The most popular of such acts is Daniela Mercury, following the steps to international stardom of Caetano Veloso, Maria Bethânia, João Gilberto and Gilberto Gil. Other newer, interesting acts are Margareth Menezes, who has travelled extensively with David Byrne. Gerónimo was one of the first singer/songwriters to use the wealth of rhythms of the Candomblé in his music and his song 'E d'Oxum' is something of an anthem for the city. All of the above have albums released and you can find their records easily in most record stores. See Shopping, page 382. Also try Billbox in the Shopping Barra on the third floor.

Scala, Praça da Sé, T/F3218891. **Handmade jewellery** using locally mined gems (eg aquamarine, amythyst and emerald), workshop at back. Other jewellery stores are *Lasbonfim* (T2429854) and *Simon* (T2425218), both in the Terreiro de Jesus. They both have branches in the nearby Carmo district. *Casa Moreira* , Ladeira da Praça, just south of Praça da Sé. Exquisite jewellery and antiques. Most very expensive, but some affordable charms. Excellent handmade lace products at *Artesanato Santa Bárbara*, R Alfredo Brito 7. For local art the best stores are *Atelier Portal da Cor*, Ladeira do Carmo 31 (T2429466), run by a co-operative of local artists, Totonho, Calixto, Raimundo Santos, Jô, good prices. Recommended. Also across the street at *Casa do Índio*, Indian artefacts and art, restaurant and bar open here till late, good surroundings. Good wood carvings on R Alfredo Brito next to *Koisa Nossa* (No 45), by a cooperative of sculptors – Palito and Negão Barão being the most famous.

Bookshops *Livraria Brandão*, R Ruy Barbosa 104, Centre, T2435383. Second-hand English, French, Spanish and German books. *Livraria Civilização Brasileira*, Av 7 de Setembro 912, Mercês, and in the Barra, Iguatemi and *Ondina Apart Hotel* shopping centres have some English books. Also *Graúna*, Av 7 de Setembro 1448, and R Barão de Itapoã 175, Porto da Barra, many English titles. *Livraria Planeta*, Carlos Gomes 42, loja 1, sells used English books. The bookshop at the airport has English books and magazines.

Confectionery *Feitiço Baiano*, R Inácio Acioly 09, T2410775. Makes sweets and liqueurs from every tropical fruit imaginable. Recommended. *Marrom Marfim Chocolates*, R Gregório de Matos 17. Also make delicious sweets.

Markets The *Mercado Modelo*, at Praça Cairu, lower city, offers many tourist items such as wood carvings, silver-plated fruit, leather goods, local musical

▶▶ **Carnival in Bahia**

The **pre-Carnival festive season** begins towards the end of November with São Nicodemo de Cachimbo (penultimate Sunday of November), then comes Santa Bárbara (4 December), then the Festa da Conceição da Praia, centred on the church of that name (normally open 0700-1130) at the base of the Lacerda lift. (8 December is the last night – not for those who don't like crowds!) The last week of December is the Festa da Boa Viagem in the lower city; the beach will be packed all night on 31 December. On 1 January is the beautiful boat procession of Nosso Senhor dos Navegantes from Conceição da Praia to the church of Boa Viagem, on the beach of that name in the lower city. The leading boat, which carries the image of Christ and the archbishop, was built in 1892. You can follow in a sailing boat for about US$1; go early (0900) to the dock by the Mercado Modelo. A later festival is São Lázaro on the last Sunday in January.

Carnival officially starts on Thursday night at 2000 when the keys of the city are given to the Carnival King 'Rei Momo'. The unofficial opening though is on Wednesday with the Lavagem do Porto da Barra, when throngs of people dance on the beach. Later on in the evening is the Baile dos Atrizes, starting at around 2300 and going on until dawn, very bohemian, good fun. Check with Bahiatursa for details on venue, time etc (see under Rio for carnival dates).

Carnival in Bahia is the largest in the world and encourages active participation. It is said that there are 1½ million people dancing on the streets at any one time.

There are two distinct musical formats. The **Afro Blocos** are large drum based troupes (some with up to 200 drummers) who play on the streets, accompanied by singers atop mobile sound trucks. The first of these groups was the Filhos de Gandhi (founded in 1949), whose participation is one of the highlights of Carnival. Their 6,000 members dance through the streets on the Sunday and Tuesday of Carnival dressed in their traditional costumes, a river of white and blue in an ocean of multicoloured carnival revellers. The best known of the recent **Afro Blocos** are Ilê Aiye, Olodum, Muzenza and Malê Debalê. They all operate throughout the year in cultural, social and political areas. Not all of them are receptive to foreigners among their numbers for Carnival. The basis of the rhythm is the enormous surdo (deaf) drum with its bumbum bumbum bum anchorbeat, while the smaller repique, played with light twigs, provides a crack-like overlay. Ilê Aiye take to the streets around 2100 on Saturday night and their departure from their headquarters at Ladeira do Curuzu in the Liberdade district is not to be missed. The best way to get there is to take a taxi to Curuzu via Largo do Tanque, thereby avoiding traffic jams. The ride is a little longer but much quicker. A good landmark is the Paes Mendonça supermarket on the corner of the street, from where the bloco leaves. From there it's a short walk to the departure point.

The enormous **trios eléctricos**, 12-m sound trucks with powerful sound systems that defy most decibel counters, are the

instruments. Lace items for sale are often not handmade (despite labels), are heavily marked up, and are much better bought at their place of origin (eg Ilha de Maré, Pontal da Barra and Marechal Deodoro, see page 429). *Cosme e Damião*, musical instrument sellers on 1st floor, has been recommended, especially if you want to play the instruments. Bands and dancing, especially Sat (but very much for money from tourists taking photographs), closed at 1200 Sun. There is a photograph exhibition of the old market in the basement. (Many items are often cheaper on the Praça da Sé.) The largest and most authentic market is the *Feira de São Joaquim*, 5 km from Mercado Modelo along the seafront: barkers, trucks, *burros*, horses, boats, people, mud, all very smelly, every day (Sun till 1200 only), busiest on Sat morning; interesting African-style pottery and basketwork; very cheap. (The car ferry terminal for Itaparica is nearby.)

second format. These trucks, each with its town band of up to 10 musicians, play songs influenced by the **afro blocos** and move at a snail's pace through the streets, drawing huge crowds. Each **Afro Bloco** and **bloco de trio** has its own costume and its own security personnel, who cordon off the area around the sound truck. The **bloco** members can thus dance in comfort and safety.

The traditional Carnival route is from Campo Grande (by the Tropical Hotel da Bahia) to Praça Castro Alves near the old town. The **blocos** go along Avenida 7 de Setembro and return to Campo Grande via the parallel Rua Carlos Gomes. Many of the trios no longer go through the Praça Castro Alves, once the epicentre of Carnival. The best night at Praça Castro Alves is Tuesday (the last night of Carnival), when the famous 'Encontro dos Trios' (Meeting of the Trios) takes place. Trios jostle for position in the square and play in rotation until the dawn (or later!) on Ash Wednesday. It is not uncommon for major stars from the Bahian (and Brazilian) music world to make surprise appearances.

There are grandstand seats at Campo Grande throughout the event. Day tickets for these are available the week leading up to Carnival. Check with Bahiatursa for information on where the tickets are sold. Tickets are US$10 (or up to US$30 on the black market on the day). The blocos are judged as they pass the grandstand and are at their most frenetic at this point. There is little or no shade from the sun so

bring a hat and lots of water. Best days are Sunday to Tuesday. For those wishing to go it alone, just find a friendly barraca in the shade and watch the blocos go by. Avoid the Largo da Piedade and Relógio de São Pedro on Avenida 7 de Setembro: the street narrows here, creating human traffic jams.

The other major centre for Carnival is Barra to Ondina. The **blocos alternativos** ply this route. These are nearly always **trios eléctricos**, connected with the more traditional blocos who have expanded to this now very popular district. Not to be missed here is Timbalada, the drumming group formed by the internationally renowned percussionist Carlinhos Brown (see box, page 382).

Recommended Blocos Traditional Route (Campo Grande): Mel, T245-4333, Sunday, Monday, Tuesday; Cameleão, T336-6100, Sunday, Monday, Tuesday; Pinel, T336-0489, Sunday, Monday, Tuesday; Internacionais, T245-0800, Sunday, Monday, Tuesday; Cheiro de Amor, T336-6060, Sunday, Monday, Tuesday. **Afro Blocos**: Araketu: T237-0151, Sunday, Monday, Tuesday; Ilê Aiye, T388-4969, Saturday, Monday; Olodum, T321-5010, Friday, Sunday. **Blocos Alternativos**: Timbalada, T245-6999, Thursday, Friday, Saturday; Nana Banana, T245-1000, Friday, Saturday; Melomania, T245-4570, Friday, Saturday.

Prices range from US$180 to US$450. The quality of the **bloco** often depends on the act that plays on the **trio**. See box, page 382.

Bahia

Iguatemi Shopping Centre sells good handicraft items, it is run by the government so prices are fixed and reasonable; similarly at Instituto Mauá, Porto da Barra. Every Wed from 1700-2100 there is a **handicrafts fair** in the 17th-century fort of Santa Maria at the opposite end of Porto da Barra beach. On Fri from 1700-2100, there is an open air market of handicrafts and Bahian food in **Porto da Barra**, a popular event among the local young people. Mosquito nets from *Casa dos Mosquiteros*, R Pedro Sá 6F, Calçada, T2260715.

Photography *Pepe*, R da Ajuda, Ed Triúnfo, 1st floor, Centre. *Maxicolor*, R Estados Unidos (Mercado Modelo), for cut-price developing. *Fotocolor*, R da Misericórdia 3, a recommended place for slide film. *Gil Filmes*, R Chile 7, recommended for Fujichrome and Ektachrome (well priced).

Capoeira

Capoeira *is a sport developed from the traditional foot-fighting technique introduced from Angola by African slaves. The music is by drum, tambourine and berimbau; there are several different kinds of the sport. You can also see the experts outside the Mercado Modelo on most days, around 1100-1300, and at Campo Grande and Forte de Santo Antônio on Sunday afternoons (they often expect a contribution; negotiate a price before taking pictures or demands may be exorbitant).*

If you want to attempt capoeira, *the best school is* Academia de Mestre Bimba, *Rua das Laranjeiras, T3220639,* open 0900-1200, 1500-2100, basic course US$25 for 20 hours. Other schools are Filhos de Bimba, R Durval Fraga, 6, Nordeste, T3457329 and Escola de Mestre Pastinha, Rua Castro Rabelo, T321 6251. Classes on Monday, Wednesday and Friday 1900-2100, Saturday-Sunday 1500-1700. Classes are held in the evening (if you want to get the most out of it, knowledge of Portuguese is essential). There are two more schools in Forte de Santo Antônio behind Pelourinho. Exhibitions take place in the Largo do Pelourinho, very picturesque, in the upper city (US$2).

Tour operators Bus tours are available from several companies: *LR Turismo*, T2640999, also offers boat trips. *Itaparica Turismo*, T2483433. *Tours Bahia*, T3223676 and *Alameda Turismo*, T2482977, city tour US$15 per person. Bahiatours' Bahia by Night includes transport to the *Senac* restaurant, a show, dinner and a night-time walk around Pelourinho (US$15 per person). All-day boat trip on Bahia de Todos Os Santos, last from 0800-1700 including a visit to Ilha dos Frades, lunch on Itaparica (US$10 extra), US$15 per person. *Tatur Turismo*, Av Tancredo Neves 274, Centro Empresarial Iguatemi, Bloco B, Sala 228, Iguatemi, Salvador, T4507216, T9729322 (mob, urgent only), F4507215, tatur@svn.com.br, run by Irishman, Conor O'Sullivan, who specializes in Bahia, arranges private guided tours and can make any necessary travel, hotel and accommodation arrangements. Highly recommended. A recommended guide who speaks German, English and Portuguese is *Dieter Herzberg*, T3341200.

Transport
See also Ins and outs, page 364

Local Buses: US$0.70, a/c *executivos* US$1.40, US$1.5 or US$3 depending on the route. On buses and at the ticket sellers' booths, watch your change and beware pickpockets (one scam used by thieves is to descend from bus while you are climbing aboard). Take a 'Barra' bus from Praça da Sé for the nearest ocean beaches. The Aeroporto *frescão* (last 2130) leaves from R Chile, passing Barra, Ondina, Rio Vermelho, Amaralina, Pituba, Costa Azul, Armação, Boca do Rio, Jaguaripe, Patamares, Piatã and Itapoã, before turning inland to the airport. The glass-sided Jardineira bus goes to Flamengo beach (30 km from the city), following the coastal route; it passes all the best beaches; sit on the right-hand side for best views. It leaves from the Praça da Sé daily 0730-1930, every 40 mins, US$1.50. For beaches beyond Itapoã, take the *frescão* to Stella Maris and Flamengo beaches. These follow the same route as the Jardineira.

Taxis: meters start at US$0.50 for the 'flagdown' and US$0.10 per 100 m. They charge US$15 per hr within city limits, and 'agreed' rates outside. Taxi Barra-Centro US$3 daytime; US$4 at night. Watch the meter, especially at night; the night-time charge should be 30% higher than daytime charges. *Teletaxi* (24-hr service), T3219988.

Long distance Air: The new Luís Eduardo Magalhães Airport (previously Dois de Julho) is 32 km from Salvador. International flights to Amsterdam, London, Paris and Rome. Domestic flights to Aracaju, Barreiras, Belo Horizonte, Brasília, Ilhéus, Maceió, Paulo

The Sand Captains

In his earlier works, Bahia's most famous son, the internationally renowned author Jorge Amado (see page 698), campaigned for the oppressed. One of his own favourites is the novel Capitães de areia *(Sand Captains), which is about the daily life of a group of abandoned street children in Salvador. The problem of street children still exists in Salvador and their treatment at the hands of the authorities and vigilante groups sometimes makes international headlines.*

The Projeto Axé *(pronounced ash-ay, Yoruba for 'life source') was begun by Cesare Florio de la Rocca and an Italian NGO, Terra Nuova, to reach out to children and adolescents living on their wits in the streets of Salvador.*

Using a team of highly professional educators and sociologists, the project won the trust of the children who had hitherto seen any approach from adults as being potentially threatening. Once initial

contact had been made, the children would gain confidence and seek further contact with the project where they would be offered the opportunity to take part in activities such as capoeira, dance, percussion and circus skills. A number of local companies offer them work experience and training programmes monitored by the project. There is a paper recycling unit and a clothes manufacturing unit, where all stages, from design to the final finished product, are taught. Goods such as T-shirts and paper products can be purchased in the project's store in Rua Francisco Muniz Barreto das Laranjeiras. All proceeds go to the project. There is a visitor centre in Rua Professor Lemos Brito in Barra, where there is more information in English.

The Projeto Axé *is a shining example of a major social problem being dealt with in a non-patronizing way, laying real foundations in the future instead of the sands of the past.*

Bahia

Afonso, Petrolina, Porto Seguro, Recife, Rio de Janeiro, São Paulo and Vitória da Conquista. A/c buses leave from Praça da Sé via the coast road between 0630 and 2100, US$2, 1¼ hrs (1 hr from Barra). Ordinary buses 'Aeroporto' from same stop US$0.50. Taxis from the city to the airport are less restricted, but still can be expensive, US$20.

Buses: the Rodoviária is 5 km from the city with regular bus services, US$0.70, take bus RI or RII, 'Centro-Rodoviária-Circular', get on in the Lower City at the foot of the Lacerda lift (the journey can take up to 1 hr especially at peak periods). A quicker executive bus from Praça da Sé or Praça da Inglaterra (in front of McDonalds), Comércio, run to Iguatemi Shopping Centre, US$1.50, weekdays only, from where there is a walkway to the rodoviária (take care in the dark, or a taxi, US$10).

There are frequent services to the majority of destinations; a large panel in the main hall of the terminal lists destinations and the relevant ticket office

To **Belém**, US$48 *comercial* with *Itapemirim*. To **Recife**, US$18-25, 13 hrs, 2 a day and 1 *leito*, *Itapemerim*, T3580037. To **Rio** (28 hrs, US$45.50, *leito* US$91, *Itapemirim*, good stops, clean toilets, recommended). To **São Paulo** (30 hrs), US$51, *leito* US$64 (0815 with *Viação Nacional*, 2 in afternoon with *São Geraldo*, T3580188). To **Fortaleza**, 19 hrs, US$33 at 0900 with *Itapemerim*. To **Ilhéus**, 7 hrs, *Aguia Branca*, T3587044, *comercial* US$14.50, *leito* US$29, several. To **Lençóis** at 2200, 8 hrs, US$12 with *Real Expresso*, T3581591. To **Belo Horizonte**, *Gontijo*, T3587448, at 1700, US$40 *comercial*, US$50 *executivo*, *São Geraldo* at 1800. There are daily bus services to **Brasília** along the fully paved BR-242, via Barreiras, 3 daily, 23 hrs, *Paraíso*, T3581591, US$27.

Car hire: *Avis*, Av 7 de Setembro 1796, T2370155, also at airport, T3772276 (toll free 0800-118066). *Budget*, Av Pres Vargas 409, T2373396. *Hertz*, R Baependi, T2458364. *Interlocadora*, T3772550 (airport), T3774144 (centre). *Localiza*, T0800-992000 (airport) Oceânica 3869 (T3321999), and Av Otávia Mangabeira 29 (T3368377). *Unidas*, Av Oceânica 2456, Ondina, T3360717. If renting a car check whether credit card or cash is cheapest.

Hitchhiking: out of Salvador, take a 'Cidade Industrial' bus from the rodoviária at the port; it goes on to the highway.

Directory **Airline offices** *Aerolineas Argentinas*, R da Belgica 10, Loja D, T3410217. *Air France*, Edif Regente Feijo, R Portugal 17, T3516631. *Alitalia*, Av Tancredo Neves 3343, Sala 503, T3415831. *American Airlines*, Trav Marques de Leão 13, T2454077. *British Airways*, T0800-996926. *KLM*, Av Tancredo Neves 3323, Pituba, T3410217. *Lufthansa*, Av Tancredo Neves 805, Sala 601, Iguatemi, T3415100. *Nordeste/Rio-Sul*, R Almte das Espatodias 100, Caminho das Arvores, T0800992004. *TAM*, Praça Gago Coutinho, T0800 123100.*TAP*, Edif Ilheus, sala 401, Av Estados Unidos 137, T2436122. *Transbrasil*, R Almte Marques de Leão 465, Barra, T0800 151151. *Varig*, R Carlos Gomes 6, T0800 997000. *Vasp*, R Chile 27, T0800998277.

Banks Selected branches of major banks have ATMs (which accept Visa and Cirrus cards) and exchange facilities. Don't change money on the street (see below), especially in the Upper City where higher rates are usually offered. Changing at banks (open 1000-1600) can be bureaucratic and time-consuming. *Citibank*, R Miguel Calmon 555, Comércio, centre, changes TCs. Branch at R Almte Marquês de Leão 71, Barra, has ATM. *Banco Econômico*, R Miguel Calmon 285, Comércio is the American Express representative (also in Ondina, under *Ondina Apart Hotel*). Visa ATM at *Banco do Brasil*, Av Estados Unidos 561, Comércio, in the shopping centre opposite the Rodoviária (also a *câmbio* here), very high commission on TCs, at the airport on the 1st floor (open 0830-1530 and 1600-2100 Mon-Fri and 0900-1600 Sat, Sun and holidays); branches in Barra, R Miguel Bournier 4, in Shopping Barra and in Ondina. MasterCard at *Credicard*, 1st floor, *Citibank* building, R Miguel Calmon 555, Comércio. *Figueiredo*, opposite *Grande Hotel da Barra* on Ladeira da Barra, will exchange cash at good rates. *Shopping Tour* in Barra Shopping centre changes dollars, as will other tour agencies. If stuck, all the big hotels will exchange, but at poor rates.

Communications Internet: *Bahiacafe.com*, Praça da Se, historical centre (see Eating, above). US$1.20 for 30 mins. *Internetcafe.com*, Av 7 de Setembro, 3713, Porto da Barra and R Joao de Deus, 2, historical centre. US$2 per hr. Closed Sun. *Internet Access* , R Alfonso Celso, 447, Barra, T26641289. Only US$1.20 per hr. *Novo Tempo*, Ladeira do Carmo 16, Centro Histórico, T/F2431241. **Post office**: Main post office and poste restante is in Praça Inglaterra, in the Lower City, open Mon-Fri 0800-1700, Sat 0800-1200, F2439383 (US$1 to receive fax). Other offices are at Praça da Sé in Ed Associação Bahiana de Imprensa on R Guedes de Brito 1, T2406222; R Alfredo Brito 43, Mon-Sat 0800-1700, Sun 0800-1200, has a philatelic section; Rodoviária, Mon-Sat 0800-1800 (till 1200 on Sun); airport; Barra and Iguatemi Shopping Malls (Mon-Fri); Av Princesa Isabel, Barra, and R Marquês de Caravelas; in Ondina by the hotels there is a booth by the beach next to *Ondina Apart Hotel*. **Telephone**: *Embratel*, R do Carro 120. *Telemar* has branches at Campo da Pôlvora, on Trav Joaquim Mauricio (0630-midnight), airport (daily 0700-2200), Porto da Barra (1200-2200 daily) and Rodoviária (0700-2200 daily).

Cultural centres *Cultura Inglesa*, R Plínio Moscoso 357, Jardim Apipema. *Associação Cultural Brasil-Estados Unidos*, Av 7 de Setembro 1883, has a library and reading room with recent US magazines, open to all, free use of internet for 30 mins. At No 1809 on the same avenue is the German *Goethe Institut*, also with a library and reading room.

Embassies and consulates *Austria*, R Jardim Armacao, T3714611. *Belgium*, Av Trancredo Neves 274A, sala 301, Iguatemi, T6232454. *Denmark*, Av 7 de Setembro

3959, Barra, T3369861. Mon-Fri 0900-1200, 1400-1700. *France*, R Francisco Gonçalves 1, sala 805, Comércio, T2410168, Mon/Tue/Thu 1430-1700. *Germany*, R Lucaia 281, floor 2, Rio Vermelho, T3347106, Mon-Fri 0900-1200. *Holland*, Av Santa Luzia, 1136 Edif, Porto Empresarial Sala 302, T3410410, Mon-Fri 0800-1200. *Italy*, Av 7 de Setembro 1238, Centro, T3295338, Mon, Wed, Fri 1500-1800. *Norway* , Av Estados Unidos, 14, floor 8, T3268500, Mon-Fri 0900-1200, 1400-1600. *Portugal*, Largo Carmo, 4, Sto Antonio, T2411633. *Spain*, R Mcal Floriano 21, Canela, T3361937, Mon-Fri 0900-1400. *Sweden*, Av EUA 357, Edif Joaquim Barreto, sala 501, Comércio, T2424833. *Switzerland*, Av Tancredo Neves 3343, 5th floor, sala 506b, T3415827. *UK*, Av Estados Unidos 4, 18B, Comércio, T2437399, Mon-Thu, 0900-1100, 1400-1600, Fri 0900-1100. *USA*, R Pernambuco, 51 Pituba, T3451545, Mon-Fri, 0900-1130, 1430-1630.

Language courses *Casa do Brasil*, R Milton de Oliveira 231, Barra, T2645866, Portuguese for foreigners. *Superlearning Idiomas*, Av 7 de Setembro 3402, Ladeira da Barra, T3372824, www.allways.com.br/spl

Laundry *Kit Lavaderia*, Av Amaralina 829, Amaralina. *Laundromat*, R Oswaldo Cruz, Rio Vermelho. *Lav e Lev*, Av Manoel Dantas da Silva 2364, loja 7. *Unilave*, Av Magalhães Neto 18, Pituba.

Medical services Clinic: Barão de Loreto 21, Graça. *Dr Argemiro Júnior* speaks English and Spanish. 1st consultation US$40, 2nd free. **Health**: Yellow fever vaccinations free at *Delegação Federal de Saúde*, R Padre Feijó, Canela. *Sr Marcus*, T2475769, who speaks Hebrew, can also give medical (or other) advice .

Useful addresses **Immigration:** Polícia Federal, Av O Pontes 339, Aterro de Água de Meninos, Lower City, T3196082. Open 1000-1600. For extensions of entry permits show an outward ticket or sufficient funds for your stay, visa extension US$15.

Voltage 110-220 AC, 60 cycles.

Bahia

Islands in the bay

For tours of the bay, see page 392

Small boats go 25 km to **Ilha da Maré** between 0900 and 1100, connecting the island's villages of Itamoaba, Praia Grande and Santana (US$1.70); the boat returns next day from Santana at 0400-0500. The departure point is near the naval base; take a 'Base Naval/São Tomé' bus from the foot of the Lacerda Lift; follow a path that leads off from the left-hand side of the naval base gate. Santana is a centre for lace-making, Praia Grande for basket-weaving. None of the villages has a hotel, but there are restaurants and bars and camping is possible. From São Tomé de Paripe, near the naval base at Aratu, irregular boats go to **Ilha dos Frades**, sparsely populated, no electricity, one *pousada* (C *Ponta de Nossa Senhora de Guadalupe*, beachfront, T071-2458536). The beach is busy at lunchtimes with excursions from Salvador, but otherwise is quiet, with good snorkelling.

Itaparica

Phone code: 071
Colour map 4, grid A6

Across the bay from Salvador lies the island of Itaparica, 29 km long and 12 km wide. The town of Itaparica is very picturesque, with a fair beach in the town, and well worth a visit. Take a bus or kombi by the coast road (Beira Mar) which passes through the villages of Manguinhos, Amoureiras and Ponta de Areia. The beach at Ponta de Areia is one of the best on the island and is very popular. There are many *barracas* on the beach, the most lively is *Barraca Pai Xango*.

In Itaparica there are many fine residential buildings from the 19th century, plus the church of **São Lourenço**, one of the oldest in Brazil, a delightful walk through the old town. During the summer months the streets are ablaze with the blossoms of the beautiful flamboyant trees. There are many *pousadas* in Mar Grande and at the nearby beaches of Ilhota and Gamboa (both to the left as you disembark from the ferry). The beaches at Mar Grande are fair but can be dirty at times.

From Bom Despacho there are many buses to other towns such as Nazaré das Farinhas, Valença (see below) and also **Jaguaribe**, a small, picturesque colonial port. Both of these towns are on the mainland connected by a bridge on the southwest side of the island, turn off between Mar Grande and Cacha Pregos (bus company is Viazul). There are good beaches across the bay on the mainland, but a boat is needed to reach these (US$12).

Sleeping There is a popular **L-LL** *Club Med* on the island (Fazenda Boca do Rio, 44470 Vera Cruz, Bahia, T8807141, F2410100). A good simple *pousada* at Amoureiras is **C** *Pé na Praia*, T8311389, good-sized rooms, English and French spoken.

Ilha de Itaparica

Baía de Todos Os Santos

Itaparica · Ponta de Areia · Amoureiras · Manguinhos · Porto dos Santos · Bom Despacho

Beira Mar · BR 881 · Misericórdia · Gameleira · Mar Grande · Ilhota & Gamboa · Penha · Baiacu · Barra do Gil · Barra do Pote Coroa · Conceição · BR 001 · Ilha Matarandiba · Barra Grande · BR 001 · Atlantic Ocean · Tairu · Jiribatuba · Catu · Aratuba · Berlinque · Cacha Pregos · Cacha-Pregos · BR 882

To São Joaquim, Salvador · To Terminal Marítimo, Salvador · To Nazaré das Farinhas

N

Sleeping
1 Club Med

0 km 5
0 miles 5

Bahia

There are a few *pousadas* in the town. The best is **A** *Quinta Pitanga*, T8311554. Beautifully decorated by the owner Jim Valkus, 3 suites and 2 singles, beachfront property, a retreat, excellent restaurant, expensive but highly recommended, accepts day visitors. **D** *Icarai*, Praca da Piedade, T8311110. Charming, good location. **D** *Zula*, R Monsenhor Flaviano 3, near the fort, T/F8313119, taiike@hotmail.com With breakfast, laundry facilities, email available, manager Henrique speaks English and Spanish.

Mar Grande **A** *Pousada Arco Iris*, Estr da Gamboa 102, T8331130. Magnificent building and setting in mango orchard, expensive, good if slow restaurant, *Manga Rosa*. They have camping facilities next door, shady, not always clean. **D** *Lagoa e Mar*, R Parque das Dunas, 01-40, T/F8231573. Very good breakfast, spacious bungalows, swimming pool, 200 m to beach, restaurant, helpful. **D** *Pousada Estrela do Mar*, Av NS das Candeias 170, T8331108. Good rooms, fan or a/c. **D** *Pousada Scórpio*, R Aquárius, T8231036. Breakfast, beach, swimming pool, simple rooms, weekend restaurant. **D** *Pousada Sonho do Verão*, R São Bento 2, opposite *Pousada Arco Iris*. Chalets and apartments, cooking facilities, French and English spoken, T8331616. Like other *pousadas* they rent bicycles (US$3 per hr); they also rent horses (US$5 per hr). Near the church in the main praça is the **D** *Pousada Casarão da Ilha*, T8331106. Spacious rooms with a great view of Salvador across the bay, swimming pool, a/c. **E** *Pousada Samambaia*, Av NS das Candeias 61. Good breakfast, French spoken.

Aratuba **D** *Pousada Zimbo Tropical*, Estrada de Cacha Pregos, Km 3, R Yemanjá, T/F8381148. French/Brazilian run, good breakfast, evening meals available.

Cacha Pregos *Hotel Village Sonho Nosso*, T8371040 or 2261933. Very clean huts on clean beach, good service, collect you from anywhere on the island – also Bom Despacho Kombis stop in front of entrance, a 5-min walk. Recommended. **D** *Pousada Cacha Pregos*, next to the supermarket, T8371013. With fan, bath, no breakfast, good. Also **C** *Pousada Babalú*, T8371193. Spacious bungalows, frigobar, fan, good breakfast.

Good restaurants in Mar Grande are *Philippe's Bar and Restaurant*, Largo de São **Eating** Bento. French and local cuisine, information in English and French. *O Pacífico* is peaceful. *Restaurant Rafael* in the main praça for pizzas and snacks. Also pizzas at *Bem Me Quer*, opposite *Pousada Samambaia*, down an alley. There are many Bahianas selling *acarajé* in the late afternoon and early evening, in the main praça by the pier.

Ferries The island is reached from the main land by several ferry services. The main **Transport** passenger ferry leaves for Bom Despacho from São Joaquim (buses for Calçada, Ribeira stop across the road from the ferry terminal; the 'Sabino Silva-Ribeira' bus passes in front of the Shopping Barra). The first ferry from Salvador leaves at 0540 and, depending on demand, then at intervals of 45 mins until 2230. Returning to Salvador, the first ferry is at 0515 and the last one is at 2300. During the summer months the ferries are much more frequent. Enquiries at the Companhia de Navegação Bahiana (CNB), T3217100 from 0800 to 1700. A one-way ticket for foot passengers on Mon-Fri is US$1, Sat-Sun US$1.20. There is also a catamaran service departing for Bom Despacho twice daily, US$3.

Mar Grande can be reached by a smaller ferry (*lancha*) from the Terminal Marítimo, in front of the Mercado Modelo in Salvador. The ferries leave every 45 mins and the crossing takes 50 mins, US$1.80 return.

Road From Bom Despacho there are many buses, kombis and taxis to all parts of the island. The best beaches are at Ponta de Areia, Mar Grande (US$1 by kombi), Berlinque, Aratuba and Cacha Pregos. Kombi and taxis can be rented for trips around the island but be prepared to bargain, US$30 for a half-day tour.

Bahia

Nazaré das Farinhas
Phone code: 075
Population: 25,000

On the mainland some 60 km inland from Itaparica, Nazaré das Farinhas is reached over a bridge by bus from **Bom Despacho**. This 18th-century town is celebrated for its market, which specializes in the local ceramic figures, or *caxixis*. There is a large market in Holy Week, particularly on Holy Thursday and Good Friday. About 12 km from Nazaré (taxi US$4.25, also buses) is the village of **Maragojipinha**, which specializes in making the ceramic figures. Bus from Salvador, 1530, takes five hours.

Tours of the bay

Small boats for trips around the bay can be hired privately at the small port by the Mercado Modelo, called Rampa do Mercado. A pleasant trip out to the mouth of the bay should take 1½ hours as you sail along the bottom of the cliff. When arranging to hire any boat, ensure that the boat is licensed by the Port Authority (Capitânia dos Portos) and that life-jackets are on board. The Companhia de Navegação Bahiana, T3217100, sails five times a week to **Maragojipe** on the Rio Paraguaçu to the west (see page 394). The trip across the bay and up the valley of the river takes three hours. There are some very beautiful views along the way with two stops. A good trip would be to continue to Cachoeira by bus from Maragojipe and return to Salvador the following day. Departures from Salvador from the Terminal Turístico in front of the Mercado Modelo, Monday-Thursday 1430 (1530 in summer). Friday departure is at 1130. Departures from Maragojipe Monday-Thursday 0500 and Friday 0830, US$4.50.

American yachtsman Steve Lafferty is highly recommended for enjoyable sailing trips, for up to four people: Rua do Sodré 45, apt 301, T2410994.

The Recôncavo

The area around Salvador, known as the Recôncavo Baiano, was one of the chief centres of sugar and tobacco cultivation in the 16th century. The town of Cachoeira, with fine examples of colonial buildings and friendly inhabitants, is also famous for its many interesting festivals. There are small fishing villages on the bay such as Bom Jesus dos Pobres and the decaying ruins of the once productive engenhos (sugar refineries), which can be visited.

Leaving Salvador on the Feira road, at Km 33, fork left on the BR-324 to visit the **Museu do Recôncavo Vanderlei de Pinho** (see page 374). Further west, round the bay, is **São Francisco do Conde**, 54 km from Salvador, with a church and convent of 1636 and the ruins of Don Pedro II's agricultural school, said to be the first in Latin America.

Santo Amaro da Purificação

Phone code: 075
Colour map 4, grid A6
Population: 59,000

Some 73 km from Salvador Santo Amaro da Purificação is an old and sadly decaying sugar centre. It is noted for its churches, which are often closed because of robberies, municipal palace (1769), fine main praça and ruined mansions including Araújo Pinto, former residence of the Barão de Cotegipe. It is also the birthplace of the singers Caetano Veloso and his sister Maria Bethania. Other attractions include the splendid beaches of the bay, the falls of Vitória and the grotto of Bom Jesus dos Pobres. The festivals of **Santo Amaro**, 24 January to 2 February, and **Nossa Senhora da**

Purificação on 2 February itself, are interesting. There is also the **Bembé do Mercado** festival on 13 May. Craftwork is sold on the town's main bridge. There are no good hotels or restaurants.

About 3 km beyond Santo Amaro on BR-420, turn right onto BA-878 for **Bom Jesus dos Pobres**, a small, traditional fishing village with a 300-year history. There is one good hotel, *Água Viva* (**A**), T075-6991178, reservations T071-3591132, on the beach front, with chalets or apartments, air conditioning or fan, good breakfast and restaurant, on one of the oldest farms in the region, good beach. Recommended. Bus from Salvador rodoviária four a day (Camurjipe), US$3.

Cachoeira and São Félix

At 116 km from Salvador, and only 4 km from the BR-101 coastal road, are the towns of Cachoeira (Bahia's 'Ouro Preto'), and São Félix, on either side of the Rio Paraguaçu below the Cachoeira dam.

Phone code: 075
Colour map 4, grid A6

Set deep in the heart of some of the oldest farmland in Brazil, Cachoeira was once a thriving riverport that provided a vital supply link with the farming hinterland and Salvador to the east. The region was the centre of the sugar and tobacco booms which played such an important role in the early wealth of the colony. The majestic *saveiro*, a gaff-rigged boat, traditionally transported this produce down the Rio Paraguaçu to Salvador across the bay. These boats can still be seen on the river at Cachoeira. The town was twice capital of Bahia: once in 1624-25 during the Dutch invasion, and once in 1822-23 while Salvador was still held by the Portuguese.

History
The impressive colonial architecture, particularly its fine examples of baroque and rococo churches, have made Cachoeira a UNESCO heritage site

With the introduction of roads and the decline of river transport and steam, the town stopped in its tracks and thus maintains its special charm. As in Salvador, *candomblé* plays a very important part in town life (see box page 374). Easy access by river from Salvador allowed the more traditional *candomblé* temples to move in times of religious repression. Cachoeira was the birthplace of Ana Néri, known as 'Mother of the Brazilians', who organized nursing services during the Paraguayan War (1865-70).

Cachoeira's main buildings are the **Casa da Câmara e Cadeia** (1698-1712), the **Santa Casa de Misericórdia** (1734 – the hospital; someone may let you see the church), the 16th-century **Ajuda** chapel (now containing a fine collection of vestments) and the Convent of the **Ordem Terceira do Carmo**, whose church has a heavily gilded interior. Other churches are the **Matriz**, with 5-m high *azulejos*, and **Nossa Senhora da Conceição do Monte**. There are beautiful lace cloths on the church altars. All churches are either restored or in the process of restoration.

Sights

The **Museu Hansen Bahia**, on Rua Ana Néri, houses fine engravings by the German artist who made the Recôncavo his home in the 1950s, recommended. There is a great wood-carving tradition in Cachoeira and many of its artists can be seen at work in their studios. Best are Louco Filho, Fory, both in Rua Ana Néri, Doidão in front of the Igreja Matriz, and J Gonçalves on the main praça. A 300-m railway bridge built by the British in the 19th century spans the Rio Paraguaçu to São Felix, where the Danneman cigar factory can be visited to see hand-rolling in progress. A trail starting near the *Pousada do Convento* leads to some freshwater bathing pools above Cachoeira. There are beautiful views from above São Félix. The **tourist office** is in the Casa de Ana Néri, Cachoeira.

Bahia

The Sisters of Good Death

The Sisterhood of the Boa Morte (Good Death) was formed nearly two centuries ago in the senzalas (slave quarters), where slaves would gather to discuss abolition and pray for those killed in the struggle for emancipation. Once freed, ex-slaves would often form religious associations under the mantle of the Catholic church. The real purpose of these associations, however, was to free other slaves from captivity, help them to survive in the free world and preserve the traditions handed down orally from generation to generation. To this day they continue the tradition of only admitting women of African descent. Each August they parade through the streets of Cachoeira with the image of Nossa Senhora da Boa Morte. The sisterhood worships iyá's, the female spirits of the dead. The sisters were expelled from the Catholic Church for refusing to surrender their statue of Nossa Senhora to the Vatican. At one point they were reduced to only 25 members, but the sisterhood has managed to survive through the support of African American solidarity groups from Bahia and the USA, and through the

promotion of the ceremony as a tourist attraction by the state government. The sisters are a living document of the African Diaspora in the Americas.

The first procession takes place on the Friday after 15 August, on the Feast of the Assumption of the Virgin Mary, and is followed by a banquet. On the Saturday, after prayers, a funeral procession takes place, accompanied by a local brass band. On the Friday and Saturday, ceremonies begin at 1800. The following morning, after a night's vigil and a ceremony in the Casa da Irmandade at 1000, the sisters and novices parade through the town in their finery with the miraculously reborn Nossa Senhora carried aloft. Then the celebrations begin as the sisters dance Samba de Roda, a spinning samba danced in beautifully coloured skirts which create a kaleidoscope effect as the sisters twirl to the music. This form of samba originated in Cachoeira and is seldom seen anywhere else. During the festival weekend there are also displays of capoeira and top Brazilian reggae starsoften play to honour the sisterhood and the town.

Excursions About 6 km from Cachoeira, on the higher ground of the Planalto Baiano, is the small town of **Belém** (the turning is 2½ km on the road to Santo Amaro), a healthy spot where people from Salvador have summer homes. **Maragojipe**, a tobacco exporting port with a population of 39,000, is 22 km southeast of Cachoeira along a dirt road (BA-123); it can also be reached by boat from Salvador. See the old houses and the church of São Bartolomeu, with its museum. The main festival is **São Bartolomeu**, in August. Good ceramic craftwork is sold in the town. The tobacco centre of Cruz das Almas can also be visited, although transport is poor.

Sleeping **Cachoeira** A *Pousada do Convento de Cachoeira*, T7251716. In a newly restored 16th-century convent, good restaurant. *Pousada do Guerreiro*, 13 de Maio 14, T7251104. No restaurant. **D** *Pousada do Pai Tomaz*, R 25 de Junho 12, T7251288. **D** *Santo Antônio*, near the rodoviária, T7251402. Basic, safe, laundry facilities. Recommended. **E** *Pousada Tia Rosa*, near Casa Ana Neri, T7251692. With breakfast, very basic. **E**, **Youth hostel** at Av Parnamirim 417, T2684844.

São Félix **D** *Pousada Paraguassu*, Av Salvador Pinto 1, T7252550. Pretty riverside *pousada*, with breakfast.

Eating **Cachoeira** *Bahiana's Point*, good riverside bar, although open irregularly. *Cabana do Pai Thomaz*, 25 de Junho 12. Excellent Bahian food, good value, also a hotel, **C** with private bath and breakfast. *Casa do Licor*, R 13 Maio 25. Interesting bar, try the banana-flavoured spirit. *Do Nair*, R 13 de Maio. Delicious food and sometimes Seresta music. *Gruta Azul*, Praça Manoel Vitorino. Lunch only.

São Félix *Xang-hai*, good, cheap food, try the local dish, *maniçoba* (meat, manioc and peppers). Warmly recommended.

São João (**24 Jun**) 'Carnival of the Interior' celebrations include dangerous games with fireworks, well attended by tourists. The festival of *Nossa Sehora da Boa Morte* is held in **mid-Aug**, see box on page 394. A famous *candomblé* ceremony at the Fonte de Santa Bárbara is held on **4 Dec**. **Festivals**

Local tour guide *Claudio*, doesn't speak much English, but is friendly and knowledge-able, T9826080. **Tour operators**

Buses From **Salvador** (Camurjipe) every hr or so from 0530. To **Feira Santana**, 2 hrs, US$3. **Transport**

Banks *Bradesco*, in the main square, Cachoeira, ATM accepts Visa credit but not debit cards, open Mon-Fri 0830-1700. **Communications Post office**: in the main square, Cachoeira, open Mon-Fri 0900-1700. **Directory**

The Chapada Diamantina

The road from Salvador to Brasília passes through Feira de Santana, famous for its Micareta, an extremely popular out-of-season carnival, before arriving at Lençóis. This small colonial town, once a main centre for diamond prospectors, is now an excellent base for exploring the Chapada Diamantina National Park, with its many waterfalls and rock formations. *Colour map 4, grid A5*

Located 112 km northwest of Salvador, Feira de Santana is the centre of a great cattle breeding and trading area. Its Monday market, known as Feira do Couro (leather fair), is said to be the largest in Brazil and attracts great crowds to its colourful display of local products. The permanent Artesanato market in the centre, however, has a bigger selection, including leather, than the Monday market. The rodoviária has an interesting wall of painted tiles (made by Udo-Ceramista, whose workshop is in Brotas, Avenida Dom João VI 411, Salvador). The *Micareta* held in late April is the biggest out of season carnival in Bahia and attracts many popular *Axé* music groups from Salvador. Bus from Salvador every 20 minutes, 1½ hours, US$3. **Feira de Santana** *Phone code: 075* *Population: 450,500*

Sleeping and eating A *Feira Palace*, Av Maria Quitéria 1572, T2215011, F2215409. **A** *Luxor*, Km 437, BR-116 South, T2215922. **B** *Flecha*, Km 171, BR-101, 20 km away, T2215999. **B** *Senador*, R Sen Quintino 10, T/F6235111. Recommended. Several cheap hotels in Praça da Matriz and near the rodoviária (both are quite near the centre). *Panela de Barro*, R Sen Quintino 259. Good Bahian food.

Directory Banks: *Banco 24 Horas*, Av Senhor dos Passos 1332. *Banco do Brasil*, Av Getúlio Vargas 897.

Lençóis

This historical monument and a colonial gem was founded in 1844 to exploit the diamonds in the region; the tents assembled by the prospectors who first arrived there looked like sheets, *lençóis* in Portuguese, when seen from the hills, hence the *Phone code: 075* *Colour map 4, grid A5* *Population: 9,000* name. While there are still some *garimpeiros* (gold prospectors) left, it is not precious metals that draws most visitors, but the cool climate, the relaxed atmosphere and the wonderful trekking in the hills of the Chapada Diamantina. This is also a good place for buying handicrafts. **Tourist information** *Sectur*, on Praça Oscar Maciel, next to the church across the river from town, T3341327.

Sleeping **A** *Portal de Lencois*, R Chacara Grota, at the top of the town,T3341233. Luxury, fridge, pool, breakfast, tours arranged. **A** *Pousada de Lençóis*, R Altinha Alves 747, T/F3341102. With breakfast, swimming pool. Recommended. **A** *Recanto das Águas*, Av Senhor dos Passos, T/F3341154. Comfortable, good location, swimming pool, a/c or fan, good service. Recommended. **B** *Aguas Claras*, opposite tourist office, 100 m from the rodoviaria, T3341236. TV, fridge, pool, breakfast, excellent view. **B** *Fazenda Guaxo*, Estr da Granja, by first bridge before town, T3341356. Quiet. **C** *Estalagem de Alcino*, R Gen Vieira de Morais 139, T3341171. Shared bath, beautiful, restored 19th-century house, superb breakfast. Highly recommended. **C** *O Casarão*, Av 7 de Setembro 83, T3341198. Breakfast, fridge, a/c. Recommended. **C** *Pousada Village Lapão*, T3341117. 10 chalets of various size, quiet. **C** *Pousalegre*, R Boa Vista 95, T3341124. Dormitories only, good regional breakfast, safe, hot showers, good vegetarian restaurant.

Chapada Diamantina

D *Casa da Geleia*, R Gen Viveiros 187, T3341151. Two excellent chalets set in a huge garden at the entrance to the town, English spoken, good breakfast (Ze Carlos is a keen bird-watcher and an authority on the region, Lia makes excellent jams). **D** *Casa de Hélia*, R da Muritiba, T3341143. Attractive and homely. English and some Hebrew spoken, good facilities, legendary breakfast. Recommended. **D** *Tradição*, R José Florêncio, T3341137. TV, breakfast, fridge, mosquito net, pleasant. **E** *Pousada dos Duendes*, R do Pires, T/F3341229. Shared bath, with breakfast, run by Olivia Taylor, an Englishwoman whose agency *Saturno* on R Miguel Calmon arranges tours and treks from 1 to 11 days and more. **Camping** *Alquimia*, 2 km before Lençóis, T3341213, and **Camping** *Lumiar*, near Rosário church in the town centre, T3341241. Popular restaurant. Friendly, recommended. There are also houses to rent in the town. Most of these are basic, with cooking and washing facilities. Juanita on R do Rosário rents rooms with access to washing and cooking facilities, US$3.50 per person. Claudia and Isabel, R da Baderna 95, T3341229, rent a house on the main praça in front of the Correios, US$4 per person without breakfast.

Mid-range *Lajedo*, good food with good view of town, popular meeting place at night. *Via Terra*, R Silva Jardim 89. Creative menu, pastas. Recommended. *Picanha na Praça*, on main praça. Best steak in town. *Artistas da Massa*, R Miguel Calmon, Italian. **Cheap** *Goody*, R da Rodaviária, good simple cooking. **Very cheap** *Lanchonette Zacão*, on main praça, natural yoghurts, juices and *bolinhos de queijo*, fried balls of dough filled with melted cheese. Recommended.

Eating

The busiest spot at weekends is *Amigo da Onça*, R José Florêncio, near the municipal market. Lambada, forró and samba-reggae until the small hours, good fun. *Bar Lençóis* on the main praça. Recommended. *Clube Sete*, R das Pedras. Nightclub open Fri and Sat nights.

Bars & nightclubs

Artesanato Areias Coloridas, Rua das Pedras, owned by Taurino, is the best place for local sand paintings made in bottles. These are inexpensive and fascinating to see being done. For ceramic work, the most original is *Jota*, who has a workshop which can be visited. Take the steps to the left of the school near the *Pousada Lençóis*. The market on Mon and Fri mornings is recommended. There are Artesanato stalls in the main square, open every evening.

Shopping

Cirtur, R da Baderna 41, T3341133, cirtur@neth.com.br *Lentur*, Av 7 de Setembro 10, T/F3341271. Speak to Paulo and Eliane, open daily 0730-1200 and 1500-2200, organizes day trips to nearby caves and to see the sunset at Morro do Pai Inácio. *Pé de Trilha Turismo Aventura*, R Boa Vista 140, T3341124. Guiding, trekking, rents camping equipment etc, can make reservations for most of the *pousadas* in the Chapada Diamantina (see below), represented in Salvador by *Tatur Turismo* (T0XX71-4507216, F071-4507215).

There are many guides offering their services at most *pousadas*, about US$20-30 per trip; most of them are very young. Recommended are: *Trajano*, contact via Casa da Helia, T3341143, speaks English and some Hebrew, a good-humoured guide for treks to the bottom of the Cachoeira da Fumaça. *Edmilson* (known locally as Mil), R Domingos B Souza 70, T3341319, he knows the region extremely well and is very knowledgeable and reliable. *Roy Funch*, T/F3341305, royfunch@gd.com.br, the ex-director of the Chapada Diamantina National Park, is an excellent guide and has written a visitors' guide to the Chapada Diamantina, currently in translation into English. It is recommended as the best for information on the geography and trails of the Chapada. *Luiz Krug*, contact via *Pousada de Lençóis*, T3341102, an independent guide specializing in geology and espinology (the study of caves), speaks English. Christina, lives near the rodoviaria, T3341308, speaks French, English and Portuguese. *Índio*, contact at *Pousada Diangela*,

Tour operators & guides

R dos Minheiros 60, Centro Histórico. Specialist bird-watching guides are *Andre*, Alto do Bonfim, T3341340, and *Ereas*, R Jose Florencio 60, T3341155. Abseiling can be organized by Ze Americo and Ze Augusto, T3341314.

Transport **Air** Airport, Km 209, BR-242, T6256497. **Buses** *Real Expresso* from **Salvador** 3 times daily, US$17, *comercial*. Book in advance, especially at weekends and holidays. **Feira de Santana**, returns at 0900, 2100. Buses also from Recife, Ibotirama, Barreiras or Brasília, 16 hrs, US$33 (take irregular bus to Seabra, then 2 a day to Brasília).

Directory **Banks** It is difficult to change money in Lençóis. *Bank of Brazil*, 0900-1700 Mon-Fri, Visa ATM and changes TCs and US$ cash (high commission). There are no facilities for MasterCard. **Communications** Post office: on main square. Open 0900-1700 Mon-Fri. **Telephone**: open daily 0800-2200.

Parque Nacional da Chapada Diamantina

Palmeiras About 50 km from Lençóis is this headquarters of the Parque Nacional da Chapada Diamantina (founded 1985), which contains 1,500 sq km of mountainous country. There is an abundance of endemic plants, waterfalls, large caves (take care, and a strong torch, there are no signs and caves can be difficult to find without a guide), rivers with natural swimming pools and good walking tours. The park forms part of the Brazilian shield, like the Guayana Highlands, a geological remnant of when the world comprised only one land mass. ■ *Information, T075-3322175, or Ibama, Av Juracy Magalhães Junior 608, CEP 40295-140, Salvador, T071-2407322.*

Trekking The trails are often not on specially marked routes, and can involve a lot of clambering **equipment** over rocks and stepping stones. A reasonable level of physical fitness is advisable. Walking boots are preferable but good training shoes are adequate. Avoid using new shoes, which give less grip on rocks. The most essential item for any trek is a flashlight with strong beam. Some of the walking may be after nightfall, but guides take trouble to avoid this. Carry mosquito repellent as there are a lot of them around in the encampment areas. (For guides and tour operators, see under Lençóis, above.)

For overnight trips it is highly advisable to bring a sleeping bag and/or a blanket and a roll-up mattress as nights in the 'winter' months can be cold. Sometimes, guides can arrange these. A tent is useful but optional; many camps are beside reasonably hospitable caves. Matches and paper for kindling campfires, as well as a first aid kit, are necessary.

Around Near Lençóis, visit the **Serrano** with its wonderful natural pools in the **Lençóis** riverbed, which give a great hydro massage. A little further away is the **Salão de Areia**, where the coloured sands for the bottle paintings come from. **Ribeirão do Meio** is a 45-minute walk from town, here locals bathe in the river and slide down a long natural watershute into a big pool (it is best to be shown the way it is done and to take something to slide in). **Gruta do Lapão**, three hours from Lençóis, guide essential, is in quartz rock and therefore has no stalagmites. Some light rock climbing is required. **Cachoeira da Primavera**, two very pretty waterfalls close to town, recommended. **Cachoeira Sossego**, two hours from town, a 'picture postcard' waterfall, swimming in pool, recommended.

Morro de Pai Inácio, 30 km from Lençóis, has the best view of the Chapada, recommended at sunset (bus from Lençóis at 0815, 30 minutes, US$1). In the park is the **Cachoeira da Fumaça** (Smoke Waterfall, also called

Bahia

Glass), 384 m, the highest in Brazil. To see it, go by car to the village of **Capão** and walk 2½ hours. The view is astonishing; the updraft of the air currents often makes the water flow back up, creating the 'smoke' effect. Olivia Taylor at the *Pousada dos Duendes* offers a three-day trek seeing the falls from top and bottom, the village of Capão and Capivara and Palmital falls from US$45.

Other excursions are: **Lapa Doce**, a cave with fine stalagmites and stalactites, 70 km, **Andaraí**, 101 km, and the diamond ghost town of **Igatu**, a further 14 km on the other side of the Rio Paraguaçu. There is a bridge across the river. The town has a good *pousada*. A good day trip from Lençóis is to **Poço Encantado** (23 km southeast of the Chapada itself, 55 km from Andaraí), a mountain cave with a lake of crystal clear water, 60 m deep, which is spectacular. From April to August, the sunlight enters the cave from the mountain side, hits the water and is dispersed into the colours of the spectrum. A visit is recommended and can be followed by a trip to Igatu on the return to Lençóis. Southeast of the park is **Mucugé** (*Hotel Mucugé*, opposite the rodoviária, good food, basic, take mosquito coils), lovely walks among hills or along the Rio Paraguaçu. Buses from Mucugé to Seabra run Tuesday, Thursday, Saturday at 0500, frequent service from there to Lençóis and Palmeiras. Local guides can often arrange transport to the more remote excursions, certainly this is possible when groups are involved.

Sleeping Capão: **C** *Candombá*, good breakfast, excellent food, home-grown vegetables, run by Claude and Suzana (Claude speaks French and English and guides in the region), F075-3322176, or through *Tatur Turismo* in Salvador (address above). **D** *Pousada Verde*, at entrance to town, very good breakfast. Recommended. **E** *Pouso Riacho do Our*, friendly. Recommended. **E** *Tatu Feliz*, no breakfast.

The Southern Coast

This seemingly endless stretch of coast has one magnificent beach after another. Porto Seguro is a major draw for international tourists, and there are deserted beaches around pretty, tranquil Trancoso, unspoilt fishing villages and the island retreat of Tinharé.

Valença

This small, attractive town at the mouth of the Rio Una. Two old churches stand on rising ground; the views from Nossa Senhora do Amparo are recommended. The main attractions of Valença are the beaches on the mainland (Guabim, 14 km north) and on the island of Tinharé. The town is in the middle of an area producing black pepper, cloves and *piaçava* (used in making brushes and mats). Other industries include the building and repair of fishing boats (*saveiros*). The Rio Una enters an enormous region of mangrove swamps. Avoid touts at the rodoviária; it's better to visit the friendly **tourist office**, T7413311, opposite.

Phone code: 075
Colour map 4, grid A5
Population: 78,000

A *Portal Rio Una*, R Maestro Barrinha, T/F7415050. Pool. **B** *do Porto*, Av Maçônica 50, T7413066. Clean, helpful, safe, good breakfast, good restaurant. **B** *Guabim*, Praça da Independência, T7413408. Modest, good. **C** *Rafa*, T7411816. Large rooms. Recommended. **D** *Valença*, R Dr H Guedes Melo 15, T7411807. Comfortable, good breakfast. Recommended. For eating, try *Akuarius*, Praça da Independência. *Recanto do Luiz*, Km 43, BA-001, good seafood.

Sleeping & eating

Transport **Air** Several companies service the airport at Praia Guaibim, T3539227.

Buses Long-distance buses run from the new rodoviária, Av Maçônica, T7411280, while the old one is for local buses. Many buses a day to/from **Salvador**, 5 hrs, US$6, operated by several companies, including Aguia Branca T4504400. São Jorge to **Itabuna**, 5 hrs, US$5, very slow. For the shortest route to Valença, take the ferry from São Joaquim to Bom Despacho on Itaparica island, from where it is 130 km to Valença via Nazaré das Farinhas (see page 392). To/from **Bom Despacho** on Itaparica, *Camarujipe* and *Águia Branca* companies, 16 a day, 1 hr 45 mins, US$3.60.

Morro de São Paulo

Phone code: 075 **Tinharé** is a large island separated from the mainland by the estuary of the Rio Una and mangrove swamps, so that it is hard to tell which is land and which is water. The most popular beaches and *pousadas* are at Morro de São Paulo. 'Discovered' by hippies in the 1960s, it is now a fashionable destination for Brazilian holidaymakers, but still retains a mellow atmosphere. Immediately south is the island of **Boipeba**, separated from Tinharé by the Rio do Inferno. On this island, too, there are lovely beaches and a small fishing village, also called Boipeba.

Morro de São Paulo is situated on the headland at the northernmost tip of Tinharé, lush with ferns, palms and birds of paradise. The town is dominated by the lighthouse and the ruins of a colonial fort (1630), built as a defence against European raiders. This did not stop the Dutch and French using the waters around the island as hiding places for attacks on the Portuguese.

The village has a landing place on the sheltered landward side, dominated by the old gateway of the fortress. From the lighthouse a path leads to a ruined lookout with cannon, which has panoramic views. The fort is a good point to watch the sunset from. Dolphins can be seen in August. Fonte de Ceu waterfall is reached by walking along the beach to **Gamboa**, then inland. Watch the tide; it is best to take a guide. Alternatively, take a boat back to Morro (US$0.50-1). All roads are unmade and no motor vehicles are allowed on the island. The beaches are good and, at low tide, saltwater pools appear in which you can swim or watch fish. Fish to eat can be bought from the fishermen in summer, or borrow a pole and catch your own at sunset. On 7 September there is a big fiesta with live music on the beach.

The place is expensive December-March, but cheaper and more tranquil during the rest of the year. Morro de São Paulo gets very crowded during public holidays and with the influx of more tourists it is not the paradise it once was. Beware of prostitutes, drugs and theft at the busiest times. There is a port tax of US$1 payable at the *prefeitura* on leaving the island, which is resented by many.

Sleeping There are many cheap *pousadas* and rooms to rent near the fountain (Fonte Grande), but this part of town is very hot at night. **C** *Pousada Gaúcho*, huge breakfast, shared bath. A little further along and up some steep steps to the left is **B** *Pousada Colibri*, cool, always a breeze blowing, excellent views, only 6 apartments, Helmut, the owner, speaks English and German.

Beach hotels The beaches on Morro de São Paulo are at the bottom of the main street where one turns right on to the first beach (Primeira Praia). **A** *Pousada Vistabella*, T073-7831001. Owner Petruska is extremely welcoming, good rooms, those to the front have good views and are cooler, all have fans, hammocks. Recommended. **B** *Pousada Farol do Morro*, T4831036, F2434207. All rooms with sea view, cool. **C** *Pousada Ilha da Saudade*, good breakfast, simple. **C** *Pousada Ilha do Sol*, good views. Recommended. On the 2nd beach (Segunda Praia), which is the liveliest and can be noisy at night is **C** *Pousada Oxum*, on 3rd beach (Terceira Praia) **A** *Pousada*

Fazenda Caeira, T4411272, large grounds, private, well stocked library with snooker and other games,. Both of these are recommended. **A** *Hotel Ville Gaignon*, swimming pools, games rooms, convention rooms, etc. **D** *Pousada Aradhia*, balconies with ocean view. Highly recommended. *Albatroz*, T4831185. Managed by Johny, big rooms, good breakfast, good value. **E** *Pousada Govinda*, simple, good breakfast, other meals available, English and Spanish spoken. Recommended. On Quarta Praia (4th beach) is **A** *Pousada Catavento*, T/F4831052.

Boipeba A *Pousada Tassimirim*, T99812378 (R Com Madureira 40, 45400-000, Valença). Bungalows, bar, restaurant, includes breakfast and dinner, secluded. **D** per person *Pousada Tropical*, lunch available. **D** *Pousada Luar das Águas*, T99811012. Simple, good.

Mid-range *Bahiana*, on the main square, good food. Recommended. *Belladonna* on **Eating** the main street is a very good Italian restaurant with great music, a good meeting point, owner Guido speaks Italian, English and French, and is a willing source of information on the Morro, open daily from 1800 till the small hours. *Morena Bela*, good for *moqueca*. *Restaurant Gaúcho* for good, reasonably priced, typical regional cooking. **Cheap** *Casablanca* is a good simple restaurant, open daily till late, good breakfasts at *Comida Natural*, on the main street, *comida a kilo*, good juices.

Good pasta dishes at *Club do Balango* on 2nd beach, where many beach huts offering cool drinks and meals. *Barraca Caita* opens till late with good music at weekends. They have snorkelling equipment for hire, popular meeting point, potent cocktail parties every night! Another *barraca* is **Ponto da Ilha** alongside. There are many other *barracas* on the 3rd beach.

Ferries From **Salvador**, several companies operate a ferry (1 hr 30 mins) and catamaran **Transport** (30 mins) service from the Terminal Marítimo in front of the Mercado Modelo to Morro de São Paulo. Times vary according to the season and weather; check with the tourist office. Lancha Farol do Morro, T2417858 and Catamara Gamboa do Morro, T99756395. Part of the trip is on the open sea, which can be rough. There are also various water taxis.

Boats leave every day from **Valença** for Gamboa (1½ hrs) and Morro de São Paulo (1½ hrs) from the main bridge in Valença 5 times a day (signalled by a loud whistle). The fare is US$2.50. A *lancha rápida* taking 25 mins travels the route between Valença and Morro, US$8. Only buses between 0530 and 1100 from Salvador to Valença connect with ferries. If not stopping in Valença, get out of the bus by the main bridge in town, don't wait until you get to the rodoviária, which is a long way from the ferry. Private boat hire can be arranged if you miss the ferry schedule. A responsible local boatman is Jario, T75-7411681; he can be contacted to meet travellers arriving at the rodoviária for transfer to the Morro. He also offers excursions to other islands, especially Boipeba. Overnight excursions to the village are possible. There is a regular boat from Valença to Boipeba on weekdays 1000-1230 depending on tide, return 1500-1700, 3-4 hrs.

Ituberá, on a deep inlet, has a number of beaches best explored by boat. A further 27 km south is Camamu, where the 16th-century settlers took refuge from the Aimoré Indians (see Ilhéus, below). There are still some colonial buildings, such as the church of Nossa Senhora da Assunção (1631). Trips to beaches and around the bay can be made by boat. At the mouth of the bay is Ponta do Mutá, with fine beaches at Barra Grande. A dirt road runs up the peninsula to the point from **Ubaitaba**, on the north bank of the Rio de Contas.

**Ituberá &
Camumu**
Phone code: 073

The picturesque fishing village of Itacaré is at the mouth of the Rio de Contas. It is a beautiful area with a protected beach and crystal-clear water to the right of town; across the river there are beaches with good surfing. Other surfing

Itacaré
Phone code: 073

Bahia

beaches are Tiririca to the south and Farol at the rivermouth. A road built in the last few years has opened up the area to tourism. The **tourist office** is at *Secretaria de Turismo de Itacaré*, T2512134.

Sleeping C *Pousada Litoral*, R de Souza 81, 1 block from where buses stop. Owner João Cravo speaks English and can organize tours to remote beaches, hiring fishing boats. Recommended. C *Sage Point*, Cuban owner, Ana Cubana. Oceanfront *pousada* with wooden chalets showers, outings organized to nearby beaches. Recommended.

Transport Buses to Ilhéus, 1 hr 40 mins, US$7. To Salvador, change at Ubaitaba (3 hrs, US$3), Ubaitaba-Salvador, 6 hrs, US$12, several daily.

Ilhéus

Phone code: 073
Colour map 4, grid A5
Population: 242,500

Everyone is happy to point out that Ilhéus is the birthplace of Jorge Amado (1912) and the setting of one of his most famous novels, *Gabriela, cravo e canela* (*Gabriela, Clove and Cinnamon*, 1958; see box, page 698). Amado also chronicled life on the region's cocoa plantations in two novels, *Cacau* (1933) and the much better-known *Terras do Sem Fim* (*The Violent Lands*, 1942). A later novel, *São Jorge dos Ilhéus* (1944), continues the story. At the mouth of the Rio Cachoeira, Ilhéus' past stretches back to the earliest days of Portuguese colonization, when it was one of the captaincies created by King João III in 1534. Today the port serves a district which produces 65% of all Brazilian cocoa. Shipping lines call regularly. A bridge links the north bank of the river with Pontal, where the airport is located. The local beaches are splendid, but the central beach is polluted.

Sights The church of **São Jorge** (1556), the city's oldest, is on the Praça Rui Barbosa; it has a small museum. The cathedral of **São Sebastião**, on the Praça Dom Eduardo, near the seashore, is a huge, early 20th-century building. In Alto da Vitória is the 17th-century **Nossa Senhora da Vitória**, built to celebrate a victory over the Dutch. Ask in travel agencies for trips to Rio de Engenho to visit the church of Santana (see above). The **tourist information** office is on the beach opposite Praça Castro Alves (a few minutes' walk from the cathedral), friendly, maps US$2, recommended.

Ilhéus

Sleeping ■
1 Britânia
2 Ilhéus Praia
3 São Marino

North of Ilhéus, two good beaches are Marciano, with reefs offshore and good **Beaches** surfing, and Barra, 1 km further north at the mouth of the Rio Almada. South of the river, the beaches at Pontal can be reached by 'Barreira' bus; alight just after the *Hotel Jardim Atlântico* (the hotel, in our **AL** range, has sports facilities, restaurant, bar etc, T6322222). Between Ilhéus and **Olivença** are a number of fine beaches, for example Cururupe, Batuba (good surfing) and Cai n'Água in Olivença itself (also a surfers' beach). The Balneário de Tororomba, on the Rio Batuba, 19 km from Ilhéus, has hot, mineral baths. São Jorge or Canavieiras buses go there and frequent buses also go to Olivença. Youth hostel *Fazenda Tororomba* is in the centre of Olivença, Rua Luiz Eduardo Magalhães s/n, T2691139.

Buses run every 30 minutes to **Itabuna** (32 km), the trading centre of the rich **Excursions** cocoa zone (also many lumber mills). Ceplac installations at Km 8, on the Itabuna-Ilhéus road, show the whole processing of cocoa (T2143000, open Monday-Friday 0830-1230). Tours of cocoa plantations can be arranged through the *Ilhéus Praia* hotel. Also at Km 8, the Projeto Mico-Leão Baiano at the **Reserva Biológica del Una** is dedicated to the *mico-leão da cara dourada* (golden-faced tamarin); T2143024. This is the wettest part of Bahia (most notably in October). Visits to the reserve are not encouraged; information from Ibama in Salvador. Bus from Salvador, 6½ hours, US\$12. The paved BA-415 links Itabuna to Vitória da Conquista (275 km) on the BR-116.

A *Hotel Barravento*, on Malhado beach, R NS das Graças 276, T/F6343223. Ask for the **Sleeping** penthouse – usually no extra charge, includes breakfast and refrigerator. **A** *Ilhéus* ■ *on map, page 402* *Praia*, Praça Dom Eduardo (on beach), T6342533. Pool, helpful. Recommended. **A** *Pontal Praia*, Av Lomanto Júnior 1358, Praia do Pontal, T/F6343033. Swimming pool, outside city but frequent buses passing. **B** *Pousada Sol Atlântico*, Av Lomanto Júnior 1450, Pontal T2318059. Good view over bay, fan, TV, balcony. **B** *São Marino*, 28 de Junho 29, T2316511 and at No 16. **C** *Britânia*, T6341722. Plenty of cheap hotels near the municipal rodoviária in centre. Also **D** *Hotel Atlântico Sul*, R Bento Berilo 224, Centro, T2314668. Good bar/restaurant. Recommended.

    Camping *Estância das Fontes*, 19 km on road south to Olivença, T2122505. Cheap, shady. Recommended.

    Itabuna A *Itabuna Palace*, Av Cinqüentenário 1061, T/F6131233. The best in town, restaurant. **A** *Príncipe*, Av Amelia Amado 5, T6133272, F2113374. **B** *Imperial*, R Miguel Calmon 234, T2115764. **B** *Lord*, Quintino Bocaiúva 1017, T/F2111233.

Come Ben, near Praça Cairu. Cheap and good. *Nogar*, Av Bahia 377. Close to the sea, **Eating** good pizzas and pasta. *Os Velhos Marinheiros*, Av 2 de Julho, on the waterfront. Rec- *Local drink, coquinho,* ommended. *Vesúvio*, Praça Dom Eduardo. Next to the cathedral, made famous by *coconut filled with* Amado's novel (see above), now Swiss-owned, very good but pricey. *cachaça, only for the strongest heads*

Festa de São Sebastião, 17-20 Jan, *Carnival*, *Festa de São Jorge*, 23 Apr, *Foundation* **Festivals** *day* (*28 Jun*) and *Festa do Cacau* (throughout *Oct*).

Buses Rodoviária is 4 km from the centre on Itabuna Rd, but Itabuna-Olivença bus **Transport** goes through the centre of Ilhéus. Several daily to **Salvador**, 7 hrs, US\$14.40 (*leito* *Insist that taxi drivers* US\$29, Expresso São Jorge), 0620 bus goes via Itaparica, leaving passengers at Bom *have meters and* Despacho ferry station on the island – thence 50-min ferry to Salvador. To **Itacaré**, 4 *price charts* hrs, US\$5. To **Eunápolis**, 5 hrs, US\$5.40, this bus also leaves from the central bus terminal. Other destinations also served; local buses leave from Praça Cairu.

Travel Agency and Exchange *Empresa de Cambio e Turismo*, T6343900.

The paved coastal road continues south of Olivença, through Una, near the **Reserva Biologica de Una** (see above). The road ends at **Canavieiras**, a picturesque town which benefited from the cocoa boom. It has several beaches.

Porto Seguro

Phone code: 073
Colour map 4, grid B5
Population: 96,000

Pedro Álvares Cabral is credited with being the first European to lay eyes on Brazil, sighting land at Monte Pascoal south of Porto Seguro in 1500. The sea here was too open to offer a safe harbour, so Cabral sailed his fleet north, entering the mouth of the Rio Burnahém to find the harbour he later called

Porto Seguro

CIDADE HISTÓRICA

To Santa Cruz de Cabrália

To Airport

NS da Pena

Farol

NS da Misericórdia
Praça Pero Campos Tourinho

Monument to Mark Gonçalo Coelho's Landing

NS do Rosário

Praia do Cruzeiro

Av dos Navegantes

Av Beira Mar BR 367

R 15 de Novembro

R Mal Deodoro da Fonseca

R Lova da Moça

R da Faca

Banco do Brasil

R do Golfo

AV 22 de Abril

R do Cajueiro

2

Praça Inaiã

R Pero Vaz de Caminha

M Batista

R Antônio Osório

NS do Brasil

Praça Visconde de Porte Seguro

R 2 de Julho

Av Getúlio Vargas

R P Cabral

R Assis Chateaubriand

R São Pedro

Rio Buranhém

1

Praça da Bandeira

Ferry Terminal

Praça dos Pataxós

N

0 metres 100
0 yards 100

■ **Sleeping**
1 Pousada Aquarius
2 Pousada dos Navegantes

Bahia

'Porto Seguro' (safe port). On the road between Porto Seguro and Santa Cruz Cabrália a cross marks the spot where the first mass was celebrated. A tourist village, **Coroa Vermelha**, has sprouted at the site of Cabral's first landfall, 20 minutes by bus to the north of Porto Seguro. It has souvenir shops selling Pataxó-Tupi Indian items, beach bars, hotels and rental houses, all rather uncoordinated.

Today, the old town of Porto Seguro is a popular holiday resort with many charter companies flying in directly from Rio de Janeiro and São Paulo. It is now Bahia's second most popular tourist destination. Building is subject to controls on height and materials, in keeping with traditional Bahian styles (colonial or Indian). In the area are remains of original Atlantic coastal forest, with parrots, monkeys, marmosets and snakes.

There are borrachudos, little flies that bite feet and ankles in the heat of the day; coconut oil keeps them off; at night mosquitoes can be a problem (but there is no malaria, dengue or yellow fever)

From the roundabout at the entrance to Porto Seguro take a wide, steep, unmarked path uphill to the **Cidade Histórica** (historical city), three churches – **Nossa Senhora da Misericórdia** (1530), **Nossa Senhora do Rosário** (1534) and **Nossa Senhora da Pena** (1718) – the former jail and the stone monument marking the landfall of Gonçalo Coelho, a small, peaceful place with lovely gardens and panoramic views.

Guided tours of the area can be arranged with *BPS*, at the Shopping Centre, T2882373. *Companhia do Mar* (Praça dos Pataxós, T2882981) does daily trips by schooner to coral reefs off the coast. The most popular is to Recife de Fora, with good snorkelling; it leaves daily at 1000, returns at 1630, about US$18, US$3 extra for snorkelling gear. Dugout canoes fish on the Rio Burnahém and trips can be taken by canoe to explore the mangroves. The **tourist office** can be contacted at T2884124, turismo@portonet.com.br

Beaches

The best beaches are north of the town along the road to Santa Cruz de Cabrália (known as Avenida Beira Mar – BR-367). Most popular beaches are Itacimirim, Curuípe, Mundaí and Taperapuã. Regular buses (*Expresso Brasileiro*) run along this busy road from Praça dos Pataxós, with many stops on the seafront in the town. Porto Belo and Santa Cruz Cabrália buses go to the beaches frequently from the port. There are many *barracas* on these lively beaches. The biggest (and busiest) are *Barra Point*, *Toá Toa*, *Axé Moi*, *Vira Sol* and *Barramares*. Most of these have jet-ski and other watersports facilities for hire. Some cater mainly for coach groups from the larger charter companies, so expect crowds. For beaches south of the Rio Buranhém, see below under Arraial d'Ajuda and points further south.

The town beaches are not recommended

Sleeping
■ *on map, page 404*

Room capacity of the local hotel industry is greater than that of Salvador. Outside Dec-Feb, rooms with bath and hot water can be rented for about US$150 per month.

AL *Paradise Resort Hotel*, Praia do Apaga Fogo, T8751010, F8751016. 5-star luxury resort with all watersport facilities, 10 mins by free exclusive shuttle from Porto Seguro. **A** *Estalagem Porto Seguro*, R Mcal Deodoro 66, T2882095, F2883692. In an old colonial house, relaxing atmosphere, a/c, TV, pool, good breakfast. **A** *Pousada Alegrete*, Av dos Navegantes 567, T/F2881738. All facilities, very friendly. Recommended. **A** *Pousada Casa Azul*, 15 de Novembro 11, T/F2882180. TV, a/c, good pool and garden, quiet part of town. **A** *Pousada Gaivota*, Av dos Navegantes 333, Centro, T/F2882826. A/c, pool, sauna, parking facilities. **A** *Pousada Imperador*, Estr do Aeroporto, T2882759, F2882900. 4-star, all facilities, interesting architecture, above the city, great views from pool deck. **B** *Pousada dos Raizes* (**D** without breakfast), Praça dos Pataxós 196, T/F2884717. Clean, friendly. Recommended. **B** *Pousada Las Palmas*, Praça Antônio Carlos Magalhães 102, T/F2882643. A/c, TV, no pool. Highly recommended.

Prices rise steeply December-February and July. Off-season rates can drop by 50%, negotiate the rate for stays of more than 3 nights

Bahia

The Festival of Nossa Senhora da Pena

The cult of Nossa Senhora da Pena began in Leiria, Portugal, a century after the reconquest of the country from the Moors. It arrived in Porto Seguro in 1535 when a Portuguese noble, Donatário Pero do Campo Tourinho (a recipient of one of Brazil's 16th-century capitanias), brought with him a small image of Nossa Senhora da Pena (Our Lady of Suffering). He named his captaincy 'Villa de Nossa Senhora da Pena de Porto Seguro' and built a small church to house his favourite saint. The church was rebuilt in the 18th century.

Nossa Senhora da Pena is the patron saint of Art and Literature and her day is celebrated on 8 September in the historic city on the cliff, overlooking the beach hotels

of the modern resort of Porto Seguro. Devotees of the cult called romeiros travel great distances to her shrine and the surrounding area becomes a huge campsite of tents, caravans and tour buses.

The festival resembles a cross between a Brazilian street party and market, with cheap clothes, household goods, as well as the usual ice-cold beer and barbecued meat on sale. During the weekend there are displays of capoeira and nightly dances of pagôde and forró are held during the festival period. After prayers on the afternoon of the eighth, the festival is officially closed with a religious procession through the streets of this beautiful colonial town.

C *Pousada Alcantara*, R das Papagaias 70, T/F2881657. Fan, clean, central. **C** *Pousada Coral*, R Assis Chateaubriand 74, T/F2882630. A/c, TV, good location. **C** *Pousada da Orla*, Av Portugal 404, T/F2881131. Fan, good breakfast, great location. Highly recommended. **C** *Pousada do Francês*, Av 22 de Abril 180, T/F2882469. A/c, TV, breakfast. Recommended. **C** *Pousada dos Navegantes*, Av 22 de Abril 212, T2882390, F2882486, navegantes@portonet.com.br, www.portonet.com.br/navegantes A/c, with bathroom, TV, pool. **C** *Pousada Jandaias*, R das Jandaias 112, T2882611, F2882738. Fan, great breakfast, tranquil. Recommended. **C** *Pousada Mar e Sol*, Av Getúlio Vargas 223, T/F2882137. Fan in most apartments, a/c in a few, family run. **D** *Estalagem da Ivonne*, R Mcal Deodoro 298, T2881515. Some rooms with a/c. **D** *Pousada da Praia*, Av Getúlio Vargas 153, T/F2882908. A/c, TV, pool, breakfast, comfortable. **D** *Pousada Aquarius*, R Pedro Álvares Cabral 174, T/F2882738. No breakfast, clean, family run, friendly, central.

E *Porto Brasília*, Praça Antônio Carlos Magalhães 234. Fans, mosquito nets, with breakfast. **E** *Pousada Sapucaia*, Av Getúlio Vargas 397, T2882331. Without breakfast. **E** *Rio do Prado*, R Portugal 228, T2881019. **F** *Pousada Casa Grande*, Av dos Navegantes 107, Centro, T288 2003. Comfortable, multilingual, hearty breakfast.

Youth hostels D per person *Porto Seguro*, R Cova da Moça 720, T/F2881742. *Maracaia*, Coroa Vermelha, on road to Santa Cruz Cabrália, T8721155, F8721156. Both IYHA.

Camping *Camping da Gringa*, Praia do Cruzeiro, T2882076. Laundry, café, pool, excellent, US$5 per night. *Camping do Sítio*, R da Vala. Mosquitoes can be a problem here. *Camping dos Marajas*, Av Getúlio Vargas, central. *Camping Mundaí Praia*, T8792287. US$8 per night. *Tabapiri Country*, BR-367, Km 61.5, next to the Rodoviária on the road leading to the *Cidade Histórica*, T2882269.

Eating **Expensive** *Cruz de Malta*, R Getúlio Vargas 358. Good seafood. **Mid-range** *Anti-Caro*, R Assis Chateaubriand 26. Good. Recommended. Also antique shop, good atmosphere. *Les Agapornis*, Av dos Navegantes 180. Wide selection of crêpes and pizzas. *Prima Dona*, No 247. Italian, good. *Tres Vintens*, Av Portugal 246. Good imaginative seafood dishes. Recommended. *Vida Verde*, R Dois de Julho 92, T2882766. Vegetarian food, open 1100-2100 except Sun. **Cheap** Good breakfast at *Pau Brasil*, Praça dos Pataxós. *Preto*

Bahia

Night out in Porto Seguro

The night has always been one of the main attractions in Porto Seguro. It was here that the lambada craze boomed. Although now pretty much a thing of the past, it is still possible to see the lambada being danced and to try your hand, or feet, at learning the steps. Couples twist and swirl, glued together, at breakneck speed. They sometimes unglue when males fling their female partners about with wild abandon in a mesmerizing display of technique, swing and stamina. All important here is the ability to requebrar (from the word quebrar, to break) as you break to the left or right, and then break again (re-break) in the same direction. There is a lot of standing on locals' feet involved before the requebra is finally conquered and then the floor, and the night, is yours.

A night out will inevitably start at the Passarela do Álcool (roughly translated as Alcohol Broadway), a short section of Avenida Portugal, the seafront promenade, where most of the nightlife of Porto Seguro is centred. Houses from the last century have been transformed into a multitude of bars and restaurants. A long row of stalls (barracas) to one side sell a staggering array of lethal cocktails made from exotic tropical fruit. They do not taste like potent drinks but be warned. Most of these stalls specialize in capeta, a slang word for devil. The drink is made from vodka, cachaça or conhaque, condensed milk, guaraná and fruit of your choice. The result is devilish, the effect too. Each stall tries to outdo their competitors with wonderful fruit arrangements that would do Carmen Miranda proud. The most popular barraca is Barraca de Macelinho, halfway along the passarela, always busy.

The latest craze is lambaérobica, as the name would suggest, a mixture of the dance and aerobics. The essential energy for this is helped along with the assistance of a local liqueur called guaraxaça, a potent blend of the natural stimulant from the guaraná berry, and cachaça (sugar cane rum). This concoction is not to be underestimated though. It is also seen as something of an elixir. Potency, in all its forms, is claimed to be its main attribute. It can be bought from Thia Siessa, Avenida Passarela do Álcool, 228. No prescription required.

The night continues in the barracas of the Avenida Beira Mar towards Santa Cruz de Cabrália. Barra Point, Toá Toa, Axé Moi, Vira Sol and Barramares all have intense nightlife, the most popular being Barramares, Toá Toa and another, Jungle Bar, at Mundaí. During the low season each one of the above is open on a particular night, in the high season many open each night.

Monday: Axé Moi, Wednesday: Barramares, Thursday: Toá Toa, Friday: Jungle Bar, Saturday: Barra Point. It is good to check with locals though for any changes.

Velho, on Praça da Bandeira. Good value à la carte or self-service. On Praça Pataxós: da Japonêsa, No 38. Excellent value with varied menu, open 0800-2300. Recommended. Ponto do Encontro, No 106. Good simple food, owners rent rooms, open 0800-2400.

Porto Seguro is famous for the lambada (see box on page 407 and Music and Dance, page 687). A good bar for live music is Porto Prego on R Pedro Álvares Cabral, small cover charge. Sotton Bar, Praça de Bandeira, is lively, as are Pronto Socorro do Choppe, Doce Letal 50 and Studio Video Bar. There are bars and street cafés on Av Portugal. **Bars & nightclubs**

Diving Portomar Ltda, R Dois de Julho 178, equipment hire, also arranges diving and snorkelling trips to the coral reefs offshore, professional instructors. **Sport**

Brazil travel, Av 22 de Abril 200, T/F2881824 and braziltravel@braziltravel.tur.br Dutch-run travel agency, all types of trips organized. English, German, Dutch, French and Spanish spoken. Several agencies at the airport, including Grou Turismo, T2884155, Soletur, T2881736, and Viagens Costa, T2885288. **Tour operators**

Bahia

Transport **Long distance** **Air**: flights to Belo Horizonte, Rio de Janeiro, Salvador and São Paulo. Taxi to airport US$7. Airport, T2881877.

At Brazilian holiday **Buses**: the rodoviária has reliable luggage store and lounge on 3rd floor, on the road to
times, all transport Eunápolis, 2 km from the centre, regular bus service (30 mins) through the city to the
north or south should old rodoviária near the port. Local buses US$0.30. Taxis charge US$5 from the
be booked well in rodoviária to the town or ferry (negotiate at quiet times).
advance

To **Salvador** (*Águia Branca*), daily, 12 hrs, US$22.25. To **Vitória**, daily, 11 hrs, US$18. **Ilhéus**, daily 0730, 5½ hrs, US$11. To **Eunápolis**, 1 hr, US$2. For **Rio** direct buses (*São Geraldo*), leaving at 1745, US$35 (*leito* 70), 18 hrs, from Rio direct at 1600 (very cold a/c, take warm clothes), or take 1800 for Ilhéus and change at Eunápolis. To **Belo Horizonte** daily, direct, US$33 (*São Geraldo*). To **São Paulo** direct, 1045, 25 hrs, not advisable, very slow, much better to go to Rio then take Rio-São Paulo express. Other services via Eunápolis (those going north avoid Salvador) or Itabuna (5 hrs, US$9). (For the routes from Vitória see page 278 and from Belo Horizonte page 234.)

Car hire: Several companies located at the airport, including *Localiza*, T2881488 (and R Cova da Moça 620, T2881488) and *Nacional*, T2884291. Bicycles, *Oficina de Bicicleta*, Av Getúlio Vargas e R São Pedro, about US$10 for 24 hrs, also at Praça de Bandeira and at 2 de Julho 242.

Directory **Banks** *Agência do Descobrimento*, Av Getúlio Vargas, also arranges flight tickets and house rental. *Banco do Brasil*, Av Beira Mar open 1000-1500, changes TCs and US$ cash, also Visa ATMs. Also at airport. *Bradesco*, Av Getulio Vargas, Visa ATMs. *Deltur*, in the new shopping centre, near Banco do Brasil. **Communications** Post office: In the mini-shopping on the corner of R das Jandaias and Av dos Navegantes. **Telephone**: Shopping Av, open 0700-2300, corner of Av dos Navegantes and Av Beira Mar, also at Praça dos Pataxós, beside ferry terminal. Open daily 0700-2200, cheap rates after 2000, receives and holds faxes, F2883915. **Laundry** *New Porto*, Shopping Av, open 0900-2230, priced per item.

Santa Cruz Cabrália

Phone code: 073 About 10 minutes north of Coroa Vermelha, Santa Cruz Cabrália is a delightful
Colour map 4, grid B5 small town at the mouth of the Rio João de Tiba, with a lovely beach, river port, and a 450-year-old church with a fine view. It is believed to be the site of the first landing in Brazil by Portuguese explorer Pedro Álvares Cabral in 1500. A good trip from here is to **Coroa Alta**, a reef 50 minutes away by boat, passing along the tranquil river to the reef and its crystal waters and good snorkelling. There is a daily departure at 1000. A recommended boatman is Zezé (T/F2821152) on the square by the river's edge, who is helpful and knowledgeable. The trip costs around US$15 without lunch. The company next door is less helpful.

A 15-minute river crossing by ferry to a new road on the opposite bank gives easy access to the deserted beaches of **Santo André** and **Santo Antônio**. As yet few tourists make it to here, but the new road is certain to change this. There are two *pousadas*: *Victor Hugo*, T9855292 (mob), and *Tribo da Praia*, T2821002, with a helpful American owner. Hourly buses from Santa Cruz to Porto Seguro (23 km).

Sleeping **A** *Baía Cabrália*, R Sidrack de Carvalho 141, in the centre, T/F2821111. Sauna and gym.
& eating **C** *Pousada Coroa Alta*, T/F2821148. A/c, waterfront. **C** *Pousada do Mineiro*, T2821042. A/c, pool, sauna, friendly, also good *churrascaria*. Recommended.**C** *Pousada Estrela do Paz*, T2821258. On the hill overlooking the town: **C** *Pousada Atobá*, T/F2821131. A/c, pool, sauna.

Arraial da Ajuda

Across the Rio Buranhém, south from Porto Seguro, is the village of Arraial da Ajuda, the gateway to the idyllic beaches of the south coast. Set high on a cliff, there are great views of the coastline from behind the church of Nossa Senhora da Ajuda in the main square. Ajuda has become very popular with 'younger' tourists and there are many *pousadas*, from the very simple to the very sophisticated, restaurants, bars and small shops. There is also a *capoeira* institute; ask for directions. It has become known as a 'hippie' resort: drugs are said to be widely available, but easily avoided. Parties are held almost every night, on the beach or in the main street, called the *Broadway*. At Brazilian holiday times (especially New Year and Carnival) it is very crowded and, with the coastline up for sale, it may become overdeveloped in a few years.

Phone code: 073
Colour map 4, grid B5

The beaches, several protected by a coral reef, are splendid. The nearest is 15 minutes' walk away. During daylight hours those closest to town (take Rua da Praia out of town to the south) are extremely busy; excellent *barracas* sell good seafood, chilled drinks, and play plenty of music. The best beaches are Mucugê, Pitinga ('*bronzeamento irrestrito*' or nude sunbathing) and Taipé.

Each August there is a pilgrimage to the shrine of Nossa Senhora da Ajuda (1549). In the church is an interesting room full of ex-voto offerings. There are fine views from behind the church. Legend has it that a spring miraculously appeared during mass, aiding the construction of the Jesuit church. The spring can be seen at the foot of the steep hill leading up to the town.

Out of season, some *pousadas* change hands, so the following recommendations may change. *Pousada Canto d'Alvorada*, on road to Ajuda, T8751218. **C** out of season, Swiss-run, 7 cabins, restaurant, laundry facilities. **A** *Pousada Pitinga*, Praia Pitinga, T5751067. Bold architecture amid Atlantic forest, a hideaway, great food and pool, member of the *Roteiros de Charme* group, see page 47. Recommended. **B** *Pousada Arquipélago*, T/F8751123. Every room decorated differently, reading library, relaxed atmosphere. **A B** *Pousada Caminho do Mar*, Estr do Mucugê 246, T/F8751099. Owners helpful. **B** *Pousada do Robalo*, T8751053/1528, F8751078. Good grounds, welcoming, good pool. **B** *Ivy Marey*, near centre on road to beach, T8751106. 4 rooms and 2 bungalows, showers, nice decor, good bar, French/Brazilian owned. Nearby is **B** *Le Grand Bleu*, T8757272. Same owner, good *pizzeria*. **B** *Sole Mio*, T8751115, just off the beach road leading from the ferry to Arraial. French owners, English spoken, laid back, 4 chalets, excellent *pizzeria*.

C *Pousada Erva Doce*, Estr do Mucugê 200, T8751113. Good restaurant, well appointed chalets. Highly recommended. **C** *Pousada Natur*, T2882738. Run by a German environmentalist. Recommended, English spoken. **C** *Pousada Tubarão*, R Bela Vista, beyond the church on the right, T8751086. Good view of the coastline, cool, good restaurant. Recommended. **C** *Vila do Beco*, beautiful garden, good value. **C** *Pousada Mar Aberto*, Estr do Mucugê 554, T/F8751153, very near Mucugê beach, 400 m from the centre of the village. Set in lush gardens.

D *Pousada Flamboyant*, Estr Mucugê 89, T8751025. Pleasant, good breakfast. **D** *Pousada Flor*, on square, T8751143. Owner Florisbela Valiense takes good care of female guests. **D** *Pousada Gabriela*, Trav dos Pescadores, T8751237. With breakfast. Recommended. **D** *Pousada do Mel*, Praça São Bras, T8751309. Simple, clean, good breakfast. Recommended. On the way to the beach are: **D** *Pousada Corujão*, T/F8751508. Bungalows, cooking facilities, laundry, restaurant and book exchange. **D** *Pousada Nova Esperança*, nearby, without breakfast, bath. **D** *Pousada Tio Otto*, without breakfast, next to *Pousada Aconchego*, opposite Telebahia post.

Sleeping
At busy times such as New Year's Eve and Carnival, don't expect to find anything under US$15 per person in a shared room, for a minimum stay of 5-7 days

D-grade hotels tend to be at the uppermost end of that range

Bahia

Camping *Praia*, on Mucugê Beach. Good position and facilities. *Chão do Arraial*, 5 mins from Mucugê beach. Shady, good snack bar, also hire tents. Recommended. Generally, Arraial da Ajuda is better for camping than Porto Seguro.

Eating **Mid-range** *Los Corales*, Trav dos Pescadores 167. Spanish, *paella* a speciality. *Mão na Massa*, an excellent Italian restaurant, behind the church. Recommended. *São João*, near the church, is the best typical restaurant. **Cheap** *Paulinho Pescador*, open 1200-2200, excellent seafood, also chicken and meat, one price (US$5), English spoken, good service, *bobó de camarão* highly recommended, very popular, there are often queues for tables. Recommended *barracas* are *Tem Q Dá* and *Agito* on Mucugê beach, as well as *Barraca de Pitinga* and *Barraca do Genésio* on Pitinga.

Bars & nightclubs The *lambada* is danced at the *Jatobar* bar by the church on the main square (opens 2300 – *pensão* at the back is cheap, clean and friendly). *Gringo Louco* is a good bar as is *Duere*, great dance bar. Highly recommended. Many top Brazilian bands play at the beach clubs at Praia do Parracho during the summer, entry is about US$20. Entry to other beach parties is about US$10.

Tour operators *Arraialcen*, T8751555, various excursions. *Arrialtop*, T5751380.

Transport **Ferries** Rio Buranhém from Porto Seguro takes 15 mins to the south bank, US$0.60 for foot passengers, US$3.60 for cars, every 30 mins day and night. It is then a further 5 km to Arraial da Ajuda, US$0.50 by bus, kombis charge US$0.75 per person, taxis US$5.

Directory **Banks** There is a mobile *Banco do Brazil* in the main square during the high season periods. Several bars on Broadway change US$ cash, but rates are poor. Best to go to Porto Seguro for money. **Communications** Internet: *Ellisnet*, Shopping Ajuda, Caminho da Praia. Also long-distance calls. **Post office**: Praça São Bras. **Telephone**: Telemar on the main square, 0800-2200, number for receiving faxes is F8751309, US$1.

Trancoso

Phone code: 073
Colour map 4, grid B5

About 25 km to the south of Porto Seguro and 15 km from Ajuda is Trancoso. From Ajuda it is a three-hour walk along the beach, but watch out for the tides. This pretty, peaceful village, with its beautiful beaches (Praia dos Nativos is recommended, Pedra Grande is nudist), is popular with Brazilian tourists and many Europeans have built or bought houses there. There are good restaurants around the main square. From the end of Praça São João there is a fine coastal panorama. Trancoso has a historic church, São João Batista (1656). Between Ajuda and Trancoso is the village of Rio da Barra.

Sleeping **A** *Caipim Santo*, to the left of the main square, T6681122. Has the best restaurant in Trancoso. Recommended. **A** *Pousada Brasília*, Estr do Arraial, T6681128. **B** *Pousada Calypso*, Parque Municipal, T6681113. Good apartments, comfortable, rooms at lower price also available, good library, German and English spoken. Recommended. **B** *Pousada Terra do Sol*, on the main square, T/F8681036. Good. **C** *Gulab Mahal*, on the main square. Oriental style, lovely garden, vast breakfast. Highly recommended. **C** *Pousada Canto Verde*, T024-2437823. Restaurant only in high season. **C** *Pousada do Bosque*, on the way to the beach. English, German and Spanish spoken, with breakfast, camping facilities also available, good value. About 500 m inland, away from main square (known as the 'quadrado'), lies the newer part of Trancoso (known as the 'invasão'), with 2 good value *pousadas*: **D** *Pousada Quarto Crescente*, English, German, Dutch and Spanish spoken, cooking facilities, laundry, helpful owners, library. Highly recommended. About 15 mins from beach. **D** *Luna Pousa*, further along on the left. Well ventilated. Recommended. **E** *Pousada Beira Mar*, with bath, restaurant serving *prato feito*. There are many houses to rent, very good ones are rented by Clea who can be contacted at *Restaurant Abacaxi* on the main square on the right.

Urano, just before the main square. Good portions. *Rama* has also been recommended, as has *Silvana e Cia* in the historical centre. *Abacaxi* on the main square does good breakfasts, light snacks and very good crêpes. Good breakfast also at *Pé das Frutas*, *Maré Cheia* next door for good simple dishes, great *moqueca*. *Pacha* on the seafront does a good *prato feito*. Good ice-cream at *Tão Vez*. Apart from restaurants which serve breakfast, most others open at 1500 until 2200 or so. **Eating**

Buses Trancoso can be reached by bus (1 every hr, from 0800, last returns at 1800, US$1.25, 1 hr, more buses and colectivos in summer), colectivo, or by hitchhiking. Colectivos run hourly from Trancoso to Ajuda (US$1.15). **Transport**

Caraíva

This incredibly peaceful, atmsopheric town, 65 km south of Porto Seguro, is on the banks of the Rio Caraíva. There are no wheeled vehicles (the streets are sand), no electricity nor hot water, and this fishing village with marvellous beaches is a real escape from the more developed Trancoso and Porto Seguro. Despite the difficulty of getting there, it is becoming increasingly popular. *Phone code: 073* *Colour map 4, grid B5*

Good walks are north to Praia do Satu (Sr Satu provides an endless supply of coconut milk), or 6 km south to a rather sad Pataxó Indian village (watch the tides as you may get cut off). Horses can be hired from *Pousada Lagoa* or *Pizzeria Barra Velha*. Boats can be hired for US$40 per day from Zé Pará to Caruípe beach, snorkelling at Pedra de Tatuaçu reef and Corombau (take your own mask and fins) or for diving (best December-February). Prainha river beach, about 30 minutes away, and mangrove swamps can also be visited by canoe or launch. The high season is December-February and July; the wettest months are April-June and November. Use flip-flops for walking the sand streets and take a torch. There are no medical facilities and only rudimentary policing.

Around Porto Seguro

To Itabuna & Salvador
Guaiú
Santo Antônio
Santo André
Santa Cruz Cabrália
Coroa Vermelha
Ponta do Mutá
Eunápolis — BR 367
Recife de Fora
Rio Buranhém
Curuípe
Arraial de Ajuda — Porto Seguro
Mucugê
Itabela
Pitinga
Lagoa Azul
Rio dos Frades
Rio da Barra
Trancoso
Caraíva
Ponta do Corumbau
Parque Nacional de Monte Pascoal
Itamaraju
Barra do Caí
Curumuxatiba
Praia das Ostras
Atlantic Ocean
Prado
Guaratiba
Parque Nacional Marino de Abrolhos
Teixeira de Freitas
Rio Itanhém
Alcobaça
Barra de Caravelas
Caravelas
To Linhares & Vitória
BR 101
N
0 km   20
0 miles   20

D *Pousada Lagoa*, T/F99656662. Chalets and bungalows under cashew trees, good restaurant, own generator; the owner, Hermínia, speaks English, is very helpful and can arrange local trips and excursions. **D** *Pousada da Terra*, far end of the village near the Indian reserve. With breakfast. Recommended. Similar is *Pousada da Barra*. Simpler lodging: *Pousada da Canoa*, attached to *Bar do Pará*, by the river, which serves the best fish in the village, US$7-8 (try *sashimi* or *moqueca*). *Santuzzi*, 100 m from *Canaã* grocery store. *Oasis*, run by taxi driver Batista. Other **Sleeping & eating**

Bahia

good restaurants are *Natal* by *Bar do Pará*, and *Pizzeria Barra Velha*, by the canoe crossing. There is forró dancing 0100-0600 at *Pelé* and *Ouriços* on alternate nights in season.

Transport Caraíva can only be reached by canoe across the river. Access roads are poor and almost impossible after heavy rain. From Porto Seguro either go to Arraial da Ajuda and take the Rio Buranhém ferry crossing, or take the detour to the Eunápolis road then on to Trancoso, after which the road is bad, especially after the turn-off to Oteiro das Brisas, 13 km before Caraíva. *Aguia Azul* bus company takes this route from Porto Seguro at 1500. Taxis are unwilling to go from Porto Seguro or Arraial, so call Batista in Caraíva, who charges US$60. If arriving by bus from the south, change to *Aguia Azul* bus in Itabela, departs at 1500, or take a taxi, about 50 km.

Parque Nacional de Monte Pascoal The National Park was set up in 1961 to preserve the flora, fauna and birdlife of the coastal area in which Europeans made landfall in Brazil (Caixa Postal 076, CEP 45830-000 Itamaraju, T2812419). A Pataxó Indian reservation is located at Corombau village, on the ocean shore of the park, where a small luxury resort has been built. Corombau can be reached by schooner from Porto Seguro. From Caraíva there is a river crossing by boats which are always on hand. Buses run from Itamaraju 16 km to the south, at 0600, Friday-Monday only.

Curumuxatiba & Prado
Phone code: 073

From Itamaraju (93 km south of Eunápolis) are the coastal towns of Curumuxatiba and Prado. The latter has some 16th-century buildings and beautiful beaches north and south. It is 214 km south of Porto Seguro via Eunápolis.

Sleeping Curumuxatiba: **D** *Pousada Guainamby*, R Bela Vista, CEP 45983. German and Brazilian owned, small, clean, comfortable chalets, good views to long beach, good breakfast and fish and Italian meals. Recommended. Also reached from Itamaraju is the *Jacotoka* holiday village, which offers diving, surfing and riding in a tropical paradise, US$50 per day, reservations at 7 de Setembro 149, Porto Seguro, T2882291, F2882540, it can also be reached by boat from Porto Seguro. **Youth hostel**: *Praia de Cumuruxatiba*, Av Beira Mar s/n, T8731020, F8731004.

Prado: The proprietors of the *Casa de Maria*, R Seis, Novo Prado, T2981377, claim to serve the best breakfast in the region. **D** *Pousada Talipe* (1125 Central Av, 23rd St, Los Alamitos, T5556539, USA). Friendly, good breakfast. Recommended.

Caravelas
Phone code: 073

Further south still, 107 km from Itamaruju, is this charming little town, rapidly developing for tourism, which was a major trading town in the 17th and 18th centuries. Caravelas is in the mangroves; the beaches are about 10 km away at Barra de Caravelas (hourly buses), a fishing village. There is a helpful tourist information at *Ibama Centro de Visitantes*, Barão do Rio Branco 281.

Sleeping A *Marina Porto Abrulhos*, on the beach front. Very luxurious. **C** *Pousada Caravelense*, 50 m from the rodoviária, T2971182. TV, fridge, good breakfast, excellent restaurant. Recommended. **D** *Shangri-la*, Barão do Rio Branco 216. Bath, breakfast. **Barra de Caravelas**: **C** *Pousada das Sereias*, French-owned. **E** *Pousada Jaquita*, use of kitchen, big breakfast, bath, airy rooms, the owner is Secka who speaks English. There are some food shops, restaurants and bars.

Tour operators Teresa and Ernesto (from Austria) organize boat trips (US$40 per day), jeep and horse hire (turn left between the bridge and the small supermarket). 'Alternative' beach holidays (organic vegetarian food, yoga, meditation, other activities) with Beky and Eno on the unspoilt island of Coçumba, recommended, contact *Abrolhos Turismo*, Praça Dr Imbassahi 8, T2971149, also rent diving gear and arrange boat trips.

Transport Buses to Texeira de Freitas (4 a day), Salvador, Nanuque and Prado. Flights from Belo Horizonte, São Paulo and Salvador to Caravelas; otherwise fly to Porto Seguro. Rail connection to Minas Gerais.

Directory Banks: *Banco do Brasil*, Praça Dr Imbassahi, does not change money.

Parque Nacional Marinho dos Abrolhos

The Parque Nacional Marinho dos Abrolhos is 70 km east of Caravelas. Abrolhos is an abbreviation of Abre os olhos, 'Open your eyes', from Amérigo Vespucci's exclamation when he first sighted the reef in 1503. Established in 1983, the park consists of five small islands (Redonda, Siriba, Guarita, Sueste, Santa Bárbara), which are volcanic in origin, and several coral reefs. Darwin visited them in 1830 and Jacques Cousteau studied the marine environment here. The islands and surrounding reefs are home to goats, birds, whales, fish, turtles and giant fire corals. The warm current and shallow waters (8-15 m in depth) make a rich undersea life (with 160 species of fish) and good snorkelling. The park is best visited October-March, when underwater visibility reaches 30 m. The waters are warmest and calmest at this time too. Humpback whales breed and give birth from July to December. Diving is best December-February.

The archipelago is administered by Ibama and a navy detachment mans a lighthouse on Santa Bárbara, which is the only island that may be visited. Permission from Parque Nacional Marinho dos Abrolhos, Praia do Kitombo, Caravelas, Bahia 45900, T2971111, or Ibama, Av Juracy Magalhães Junior 608, CEP 40295-140, Salvador, T071-2407322. Visitors are not allowed to spend the night on the islands, but may stay overnight on schooners.

Transport The journey to the islands takes between 1 and 6 hrs, depending on the boat. Mestre Onofrio Frio in Alcobaça, Bahia, T2932195, is authorized by the Navy to take tourists. Tours also available from *Abrolhos Turismo*, see above, Caravelas (about US$170 for a slow 2½ day tour by *saveiro*). One-day tours can be made in a faster boat (US$100) from Abrolhos or the Marina Porto Abrolhos. 3-day, 2-night packages from São Paulo cost around US$700, including return flights.

The Northern Coast

Heading north from Salvador airport, the coast road (BA-099), or Estrada de Coco (Coconut Highway), passes many coconut plantations and 50 km of beautiful beaches. From south to north the best known are Ipitanga (famous for its reefs), Buraquinho, Jauá, Arembepe, Guarajuba, Itacimirim, Castelo Garcia D'Ávila, where there is a 16th-century fort, and Forte. North of Praia do Forte, the road is called the Linha Verde (Green Line) as it runs along another beautiful stretch of coast. Buses serve most of these destinations.

Arembepe
Phone code: 071
Colour map 4, grid A6

Some 45 km north of Salvador, this former fishing village is now a quiet resort. There is an 'alternative' village of palm huts, 30 minutes' walk along the beach, behind the sand dunes, with a café and swimming. The best beaches are 2 km north of town. A popular music festival is held the weekend after Carnaval. There is *Pousada da Fazenda* (**B**), on the beach, which has thatched huts and good but expensive seafood. At *Mar Aberto* (**D**), Lg de São Francisco 43, T8241257, English and French are spoken and it has very good food. Recommended. Try *pastel de banana* at *Verá's* restaurant. Bus from Terminal Francês, Salvador, every two hours, 1½ hours, US$2, last one back at 1700. Buses also run from Itapoã.

Bahia

Praia do Forte

Phone code: 071
Colour map 4, grid A6

About 80 km north of Salvador, is this charming, tranquil fishing village with sand streets and lovely beaches. There is a strong emphasis on preservation of the local flora and fauna. Inland from the coast is a *restinga* forest, which grows on sandy soil with a very delicate ecosystem. Near the village is a small *pantanal* (marshy area), which is host to a large number of birds, caymans and other animals. Bird-watching trips on the *pantanal* are rewarding.

The Tamar Project was set up to preserve the sea turtles which lay their eggs in the area. Address is Caixa Postal 2219, Rio Vermelho, Salvador, Bahia CEP 40210-990, T8761045, F8761067. Praia do Forte is the headquarters of the national turtle preservation programme and is funded by the Worldwide Fund for Nature. There is a visitors' centre at the project (US$1.50 to visit the turtle sanctuary). Praia do Forte is also ideal for windsurfing and sailing, owing to constant fresh Atlantic breezes.

History Praia do Forte takes its name from the castle built by a Portuguese settler, Garcia D'Ávila, in 1556, to warn the city to the south of enemy invasion. Garcia D'Ávila was given a huge area of land, from Praia do Forte to Maranhão, on which he made the first farm in Brazil. He brought the first head of cattle to the country, cleared the virgin Atlantic forest and brought the first coconut and mango trees to Brazil.

Sleeping **LL** *Praia do Forte EcoResort*, Av do Farol,
Prices rise steeply in the summer season. It can be difficult to find cheap accommodation
T6764000, F6761112, reservas@pfr.com.br Polynesian-inspired and deserving of its name. Spacious, beautiful beachfront grounds and full programme of activities. 5 pools. Recommended. **A** *Pousada Praia do Forte*, Av do Farol, T6761116, F8761033. Chalets in peaceful setting, in ideal position on beach. Recommended. **A** *Pousada Solar da Lagoa*, R do Forte, T6761271. Good location, spacious rooms. **A** *Sobrado da Vila*, Av do Sol, T/F6761152. In village, balcony, pleasant, good value restaurant. **A** *Solar dos Arcos*, on the beach. 2-bedroom apartments with pool, gardens, lawns. Warmly recommended. **B** *Pousada da Sereia*, R da Corvina, T6761032. Fan, good breakfast. **B** *Pousada João Sol*, R da Corvina, T6761054. Owner speaks English, Spanish and German, good. Recommended. Only 6 apartments, great breakfast. **B** *Pousada Sol Nascente*, on the street parallel to the main street. Good, bath, frigobar, fan, breakfast.

Linha Verde

B *Pousada Tatuapara*, T6761015. Friendly. **C** *Tia Helena*, Helena being the motherly proprietor who provides an excellent meal and enormous breakfast, nice rooms, price reduced for 3 day stays. Highly recommended. **Youth hostel D** *Albergue da Juventude Praia do Forte*, R da Aurora 3, T6761094, praiadoforte@albergue.com.br Private bathroom, fan, breakfast, kitchen and shop, more expensive for non-IYHA members.

Expensive *Praia do Forte EcoResort*, See above. Brazilian and international food in serene surroundings. Recommended. **Mid-range** *Bar Da Souza*, on the right as you enter the village. Best seafood in town, open daily, live music at weekends. Recommended. Reasonably priced. *Brasa Na Praia*, grilled seafood and meat, open daily, peaceful setting. Recommended. *Pernetas*, good value pizzeria. **Cheap** *La Crêperie*, excellent crêpes, Tue-Sun, good music, popular, owner Klever very friendly. *Pizzeria Le Gaston*, good pizza and pasta, also good home-made ice-creams, open daily. In a lively square just off R da Aurora are *BarForte Creperia* and *Mundo Blu*, Italian food. *Cafe Tango*, pleasant tea and coffee bar, family atmosphere, great pastries and cakes. **Seriously cheap** *Tutti-Frutti*, recommended ice-cream parlour. **Eating**

Afro-Bahia for good T-shirts. *Boutique Ogum Marinho* for excellent wood carvings. *Kennedy Bahia*, gallery run by a family of Irish-Brazilian artists. Recommended. **Shopping**

Bahia Adventure, T6761262, F6761018, baadventure@svn.com.br Eco-tourism, abseiling and Land Rover trips. *Odara Turismo*, in the *EcoResort Hotel*, T6761080, F6761018, imaginative tours to surrounding areas and outlying villages and beaches using 4WD vehicles, very friendly and informative, recommended; owners, Norbert and Papy, speak English and German. *Rentamar UK*, 338 M ilton Rd, Cambridge, CB4 1LW, T/F+44-1223-424244, Glauce.UK@tesco.net For whale- and turtle-watching packages. **Tour operators**

Buses To Praia do Forte from **Salvador**: Santa Maria/Catuense leaves 5 times daily from the rodoviária, 1½ hrs, US$2. **Transport**

To the Sergipe border

The **Linha Verde** runs for 142 km to the Sergipe state border; the road is more scenic than the BR-101, especially near Conde. There are very few hotels or *pousadas* in the more remote villages. Among the most picturesque are **Subaúma** (*pousada*) and **Baixio**, the latter, where the Rio Inhambupe meets the sea, is very beautiful.

About 14 km from Praia do Forte is the simple village of Imbassaí, which has a beach at the mouth of the Rio Barroso. Other nearby beaches are Praia de Santo Antônio, 4 km away, with sand dunes and a small fishing village, and **Porto Sauípe**, 22 km north, which has a hotel (**B**). **Imbassaí** *Phone code: 071*

Sleeping B *Pousada Caminho do Mar*, T/F8322499. Bungalows with a/c, restaurant, German-run. **B** *Pousada Imbassaí*, T/F8761313. Chalets and apartments. **C** *Pousada Lagoa da Pedra*, T2485914. Large grounds, some English spoken, friendly. **D** *Pousada Anzol de Ouro*, T3224422. Chalets, fan, pool.

Situated on the coast, 6 km from Conde, Sítio do Conde is a site for *Projeto Tamar* (the national project which studies and preserves marine turtles). The beaches are not very good but it's an ideal base to explore other beaches at Barra do Itariri, 12 km south, at the mouth of a river, which has fine sunsets. The road passes unspoilt beaches; the best are Corre Nu and Jacaré. You can also go to Seribinha, 13 km **Sítio do Conde** *Phone code: 075*

Bahia

north of Sítio do Conde. The road goes along the beach through coconut groves and mangroves; at Seribinha are beach huts serving cool drinks or food.

Sleeping and eating **A** *Hotel Praia do Conde*, T4291129, in Salvador T071-3212542. A/c, pool. **C** *Pousada Oasis*, T4212397. Simple. *Bar e Restaurante Zeca*, local dishes. **Transport** Bus from Salvador to Conde with *São Luís*, T071-3584582, 3 a day, 4 on Fri, US$7.25.

Mangue Seco The last stop on the Linha Verde is Mangue Seco. Access from Sergipe is by boat
Phone code: 075 or canoe on the Rio Real from Pontal (10-minute crossing). A steep hill rising behind the village to tall white sand dunes offers a superb view of the coastline. The encroaching dunes have caused the mangrove to dry up. The town was immortalized in Jorge Amado's book *Tieta*. On the left from the boat landing, 15 mins' walk, is **B** *Village Mangue Seco*, Praia do Rio Real, T079-2242965, with a pool. Seafood restaurants can be found at the boat landing.

The Sertão

Phone code: 075 *The harsh beauty of the Sertão and its hospitable people are the reward for those wanting to get off the beaten track. The region has been scarred by droughts and a violent history of bandits, rebellions and religious leaders. Euclides da Cunha and Canudos are good places to start to explore this history. The Raso da Catarina, once a hiding place for Lampião, and the natural beauty of the Falls of Paulo Afonso, can both be visited from the town of Paulo Afonso located on the Rio São Francisco. This important river continues through the Sertão, linking agricultural settlements such as Juazeiro, Ibotirama and Bom Jesus de Lapa before entering northern Minas Gerais. For those wanting to get off the Bahia tourist trail, the less-developed beaches of the northern coast along the Linha Verde are good options.*

Situated 250 km from Salvador, and surrounded by the dry Bahian *sertão*, are the spa towns of **Cipó**, on the banks of the Rio Itapicuru and nearby **Caldas do Jorro**. Both are popular for their thermal springs and have hotels: **C** *Grande Hotel Caldas de Cipó*, Praça Juraci Magalhães, T/F4351312, Cipó, and **A** *Caldas Palace*, Av José Carlos Arleo 210, T2561103, F2561134, Caldas do Jorro.

Euclides North of Feira da Santana, at Km 225 on the BR-116 road to Fortaleza, is
da Cunha Euclides da Cunha, a good base for exploring the Canudos area.

Sleeping **B** *do Conselheiro*, Av Mcal Juarez Tvora 187, T271814. *Lua*, T27111108, simple. *Varanda do Sertão*, T2711164. **C** *Grapiuna*, Praça Monsenhor Berenguer 401, T2751157. Cheaper without bath. Recommended. **Transport** The bus station is on the BR-116, T2711365.

Monte Santo About 38 km west is the famous hill shrine of Monte Santo in the Sertão, reached by 3½ km of steps cut into the rocks of the Serra do Picaraça. It takes about 45 minutes' walk each way, so set out early). This is the scene of pilgrimages and great religious devotion during Holy Week. The shrine was built by an Italian who had a vision of the cross on the mountain in 1765. One block north of the bottom of the stairs is the **Museu do Sertão**, with pictures from the 1897 Canudos rebellion.

Canudos Canudos itself is 100 km away. Religious rebels, led by Antônio Conselheiro, defeated three expeditions sent against them in 1897 before being overwhelmed. The Rio Vaza Barris, which runs through Canudos, has been dammed, and the town has been moved to Nova Canudos by the dam. Part of the old town is still located 10 km west in the Parque Estadual de Canudos, created in 1997. For **tourist information**, contact the *Prefeitura*, T8942165. There are direct buses to Canudos from Salvador. In Nova Canudos is **E** *Brasil*, with bath, fan, clean, simple, cheaper without breakfast.

Senhor do Bonfim is a busy market town with lots of life and a good place to buy leather goods. The **Catedral do Senhor do Bonfim** is in Praça Juracy Magalhães and there is a jewellery school specializing in emeralds 25 km from the town. Popular festivals are *Senhor do Bonfim* in January and *São João* in June. The bus station is at Km 124, BR-407, T8413839. About 25 km from town is *Rio das Pedras* (**B**), Praça Frei Lino, Campo Formosa, T/F8451307.

Senhor do Bonfim
Phone code: 074
Population: 84,500

Directory Banks: *Banco do Brasil*, Praça Dr José Gonçalaves 210. **Medical services**: *Regional*, Praça Duque de Caxias 172, T8414122.

Some 112 km from Senhor do Bonfim and 344 km from Salvador is the friendly and interesting agricultural town of Jacobina. Once a major mining centre, gold, diamonds and emeralds are still found in the surrounding hills. *Serra do Ouro* (**B**), Lg Monte Tabor, T6213325, is a hotel with air conditioning, good views of the city, pool and restaurant.

Jacobina
Phone code: 074

Paulo Afonso

Part of the northern border of Bahia is formed by the Rio São Francisco. From Salvador, the paved BR-110 runs 471 km north to the river at Paulo Afonso. The town was founded in 1913 during the construction of the dam and is some distance from the falls in the Parque Nacional de Paulo Afonso. Handicrafts (embroidery, fabrics) are available from *Núcleo de Produção Artesanal*, Av Apolônio Sales 1059. Nearby is the **Raso da Catarina**, a series of trails in the caatinga which was used as a hideout by the bandit Lampião; guides and a four-wheel drive vehicle are recommended due to the heat and lack of shade – for information, T2813347.

Phone code: 075
Colour map 2, grid C5
Population: 94,000

B *Belvedere*, Av Apolônio Sales 457, T2813314. A/c, pool. **B** *Palace*, Av Apolônio Sales (next door to Belvedere), T2814521. A/c, pool, 'best value in town'. *Da Parada*, Qd E1. Good regional food.

Sleeping & eating

Air Airport, 4 km from town. Flights to Recife and Salvador. **Buses** Bus station, Av Apolônio Sales, T2814769. To **Aracaju** with *Bonfim*. To **Maceió** via Palmeira dos Índios with *Real Alagoas*. To **Recife** with *Progresso*, 7 hrs, US$9.65. To **Rio** with *Itapemirim*. To **Salvador** with *Viazul*. To **São Paulo** with *São Geraldo*.

Transport

Airline offices *Rio-Sul*, T2813260. **Banks** *Banco do Brasil*, Av Landulfo Alves 46. **Tourist information** R Apolônio Sales, T2812757, guides available.

Directory

About 25 km northwest of Paulo Afonso is the Parque Nacional de Paulo Afonso. The Falls of Paulo Afonso, once one of the great cataracts of the world but now exploited for hydroelectric power, are 270 km from the mouth of the São Francisco river, which drains a valley three times the size of Great Britain. There are 2,575 km of river above the Falls to its source in Minas Gerais. The 19th-century British linguist and explorer, Sir Richard Burton, took an

Parque Nacional de Paulo Afonso

Bahia

expedition down the river and negotiated some of its treacherous rapids. Below the falls is a deep, rock gorge through which the water rushes. The national park is an oasis of trees and the lake amid a desert of brown scrub and cactus. The best time to visit the falls is in the rainy season (January-February); only then does much water pass over them, as almost all the flow now goes through the power plant. The best view is from the northern (Alagoas) bank.

■ *The falls are in a security area with admission from 0800-1100 only by car or taxi, accompanied by a guide from the tourist information office, T2821717, 2 hrs, US$6 per car.*

Sleeping **B** *Grande Hotel de Paulo Afonso*, T2811914, F2811915, which has a pool as well as a guesthouse (apply for room in advance) at the falls.

Rio São Francisco

The São Francisco River is navigable above the falls from above the twin towns (linked by a bridge) of Juazeiro, in Bahia, and Petrolina, in Pernambuco, thriving towns compared to many on the upper São Francisco. Navigation is possible as far as Pirapora in Minas Gerais, linked by road to the Belo Horizonte-Brasília highway (see page 264).

Juazeiro
Phone code: 074
Population: 172,500

Juazeiro is located at an important crossroads where the BR-407 meets the Rio São Francisco. For information on river transport, T075-8112465. On the opposite bank in Pernambuco is Petrolina (see page 457). The local economy revolves around agriculture and its exportation. There is a market on Friday and Saturday.

Sleeping and eating **A** *Grande Hotel*, R José Pititinga, T8117710. Also *União* (recommended) and *Oliveira* in R Conselheiro Saraiva. **B** *Pousada de Juazeiro*, 6 km south on BR-407, T8117820, F8116547. A/c, pool, restaurant, bar, pleasant. A unique restaurant known as the *Vaporzinho* is high and dry on the riverfront, a side-wheel paddle steamer (poor food), the *Saldanha Marinho*, built at Sabará in 1852.

Transport Bus to **Canudos**, 5 hrs, is crowded; buy ticket early to get a seat. The second half of the route is unpaved.

Xique-Xique
Phone code: 074

The next major town upriver is Xique-Xique, an agricultural town 587 km from Salvador. The remains of what may be a pre-Neanderthal man have been found in the nearby **Grotto of the Cosmos**, whose cave paintings suggest that it was used as an observatory. **Sleeping** **B** *Carranca Grande*, at Km 1, BA-052, T/F6611674, has a pool and restaurant.

Phone code: 077

The next town upriver, **Ibotirama**, 650 km from Salvador on the BR-242, is famous for its fishing especially for *Surubim* and *Pocomã*. There are a few hotels with restaurants (**B-C**).

Phone code: 077

An important stop on the Rio São Francisco and 148 km from Ibotirama on the BR-242 is **Bom Jesus de Lapa**. The **Igreja Nossa Senhora da Soledad** is situated within a grotto near to Praça da Bandeira. This sanctuary, discovered by a monk in the 17th century, is the centre of a *romaria* between July and September which brings thousands of visitors to the town. There are a few places to stay. The airport is at Av Manuel Novais, T4814519.

Directory **Airline offices**: *Abaeté*, T4814264. **Banks**: *Banco do Brasil*, R Avelino Bastos 264. **Medical services**: *Carmela Dutra*, Av Manuel Novais, T4814714.

Recife and the Northeast Coast

Introducing Recife and the Northeast Coast

Sergipe and Alagoas are the first states encountered on the coast road north. There are good beaches near their capitals **Aracaju** and **Maceió**, as well as historic **Penedo** on the mouth of the Rio São Francisco. **Pernambuco**, with the colonial city of **Olinda** near the state capital Recife, also has the Atlantic archipelago of **Fernando de Noronha**. Inland is the handicraft and market centre of **Caruaru**. Brazil's most easterly point is located near the pleasant city of **João Pessoa** in Paraíba, while **Campina Grande**, on the edge of the Sertão, is renowned for its São João festival, one of Brazil's liveliest.

PERNAMBUCO

Petrolina

N

0 km   50
0 miles   50

Things to do in Recife and the Northeast Coast

① Shop for hand-crafted ceramic figurines and leather goods, while being serenaded by folk musicians in Caruaru.

② Go diving in the hidden paradise of Fernando de Noronha. The archipelego, with its crystal clear water and colourful coral, is a haven for underwater activities.

③ Soak up the atmosphere of the World Heritage site of Olinda. Luxuriate in one of its historic hotels and explore its pretty, colonial churches.

④ Strip off at Tambaba, one of Brazil's few nudist beaches and one of the loveliest in the country.

⑤ Bathe in the warm salty pools at Porto de Galinhas, or take a traditional *jangada* fishing boat along this scenic stretch of coast.

Sergipe

This state has beautiful beaches around its capital Aracaju, as well as some interesting towns such as colonial São Cristóvão and Imperial Laranjeiras, making it worth at least a short stop en route along the coastal highway between Salvador and Recife. Most of the population of Sergipe lives near the coast. The Rio São Francisco forms the border with Alagoas to the north, whilst the Rio Real defines the southern border with Bahia. The area of sertão is quite small in this state compared with other parts of the northeast.

Aracaju

Phone code: 079
Colour map 2, grid C5
Population: 462,600

Founded in 1855, the state capital stands on the south bank of the Rio Sergipe, about 10 km from its mouth and 327 km north of Salvador.

In the centre is a group of linked, beautiful parks: **Praça Olímpio Campos**, in which stands the cathedral, **Praça Almirante Barroso**, with the Palácio do Governo, and praças **Fausto Cardoso** and **Camerino**. Across Avenida Rio Branco from these two is the river. The streets are clean and parts of Laranjeiras and João Pessoa in the centre are reserved for pedestrians. There is a handicraft centre, the **Centro do Turismo** in the restored Escola Normal, on Praça Olímpio Campos, Rua 24 Horas; the stalls are arranged by type (wood, leather, etc). ■ *0900-1300, 1400-1900.* The commercial area is on ruas Itabaianinha and João Pessoa, leading up to Rua Divina Pastora and Praça General Valadão. At Rua Itabaianinha 41 is the **Instituto Geográfico e Histórico de Sergipe**. ■ *0800-1200, 1400-1700 Mon-Fri.*

Tourist offices *Bureau de Informações Turísticas de Sergipe*, R 24 Horas, T2245168, are very friendly, helpful, and have abundant leaflets. *Emsetur*, Trav Baltazar Gois 86, Edif Estado de Sergipe, 11th-13th floors, T2228373, F2243403, emsetur@prodase.com.br, www.prodase.com.br/emsetur In the centre, go to *Aracatur*, R Maruim 100, Sala 10, T2241226, F2243537, which has leaflets and maps such as *Aracaju no bolso* and *Onde?*, helpful, English spoken.

Aracaju

Not to scale

■ **Sleeping**
1 Amado
2 Aperipê & Serigy
3 Brasília
4 Grande
5 Oásis
6 Palace de Aracaju

● **Eating**
1 Cacique Chá

A 16-km road leads to the fine **Atalaia** beach (although there are oil-drilling **Beaches** rigs offshore). Beaches continue south down the coast along the Rodovia Presidente José Sarney. This long stretch of sand is between the mouths of the rios Sergipe and Vaza Barris; the further you go from the Sergipe, the cleaner the water. There is an even better beach, **Nova Atalaia**, on Ilha de Santa Luzia across the river. It is 30 km long and is easily reached by boat from the Hidroviária (ferry station), which is across Avenida Rio Branco from Praça General Valadão. Boats cross the river to **Barra dos Coqueiros** every 15 minutes. Services are more frequent at weekends, when it is very lively. The river at Barra dos Coqueiros is busy with fishing and pleasure craft.

About 23 km northwest from Aracaju is **Laranjeiras**, a small pleasant town with **Excursions** a ruined church on a hill. It is reached by the São Pedro bus, from the old rodoviária in the centre of Aracaju, 30-60 minutes. It has several churches from the Imperial period, when it was an important sugar producer, although the town was originally founded in 1605. The 19th-century Capela de Sant'Aninha has a wooden altar inlaid with gold. There are three museums: **Museu Afro-Brasileiro** (■ *1000-1700 Tue-Fri, 1300-1700 weekends. R José do Prado Franco 70*); **Museu Sacro** (■ *1000-1700 Tue-Sun. Praça Dr H Diniz Gonçalves*); and the **Centro de Cultura**, on João Ribeiro. Its main festival is **São Benedito** in the first week of January. Hotels include **B** *Pousada Vale dos Outeiros*, Av José do Prado Franco 124, T2811027, 10 rooms, restaurant. Recommended.

Some 70 km west of Aracaju is **Itabaiana**, which has a famous gold market on Saturday. There are a few hotels in the centre (**D**). See below for São Cristóvão.

A *Palace de Aracaju*, Praça Gen Valadão, T2245000. 3-star, a/c, TV, fridge, central, res- **Sleeping** taurant, pool, parking. **A** *Grande*, R Itabaianinha 371, T/F2111383. A/c, TV, fridge, cen- tral, *Quartier Latin* restaurant. **A** *Aperipê*, R São Cristóvão 418, T2111880. Central, a/c, phone, fridge, restaurant. **A** *Serigy*, R Santo Amaro 269, T2111088. Same management and facilities, comfortable. **B** *Brasília*, R Laranjeiras 580, T2248022. Good value, good breakfast. Recommended. **B** *Oásis*, R São Cristóvão 466, T2242125. Good breakfast, hot water, fair, a bit tatty. **C** *Amado*, R Laranjeiras 532. A/c (less with fan), laundry facilities. **D** *Turista*, R Divina Pastora 411, noisy, mosquitoes, no hot water or breakfast, friendly.

Cacique Chá, in the cathedral square is a good bar and restaurant. Lively at weekends. **Eating** Also on Praça Olímpio Campos is *Rancho Gaúcho*, No 692. Quite good, very friendly. *Bar e Lanchonete Dom Qui Chopp*, Laranjeiras opposite *Telemar*. Popular. *Gonzaga*, R Santo Amaro 181. Lunch only, good value, very popular, excellent traditional dishes. **In Atalaia**; on Av Oceânica try *Chapéu de Couro*, No 128. Recommended. *Cantinha da Bahia*, No 180. Recommended for fresh crab.

Augustu's, T2432274. Nightclub, closed Mon. *Espaço Ernes*, Av Tancredo Neves 225, **Bars &** T2319138. Venue for live shows. *Gonzagao*, Av Heraclito Rollemberg. Live shows. **nightclubs**

Cinema Ten-screen *Cinemark*, in Shopping Jardins. **Entertainment**

On **8 Dec** there are both Catholic (Nossa Senhora da Conceição) and Umbanda (*Iemenjá*) **Festivals** religious festivals. Other festivals include the procession on the river on **1 Jan**, *Bom de Jesus dos Navegantes*; *Santos Reis*, on 1st weekend in Jan and the *Festas Juninas*, in Jun.

The *Artesanato* is interesting: pottery figures and lace particularly. See above for the **Shopping** *Centro de Turismo*. A fair is held in Praça Tobias Barreto every Sun afternoon. The municipal market is a block north of the Hidroviária.

Transport **Local Bus**: Look for route plates on the side of buses and at bus stations in town. The old bus terminal in town is at Santo Amaro and Divina Pastora, Praça João XXIII. Buses from here to Laranjeiras and São Cristóvão (45 mins, US$1.25).

Long distance Air: Santa Maria airport is 11 km from the centre, on Av Sen Júlio César Leite, Atalaia, T2431388. Flights to Maceió, Rio de Janeiro and Salvador.

Bus: Interstate buses arrive at the rodoviária, 4 km from the centre, linked by local buses from the adjacent terminal (buy a ticket before going on to the platform). Bus 004 'T Rod/L Batista' goes to the centre, US$0.50. Buses go from Praça João XXIII, the terminal near the Hidroviária and from Capela at the top of Praça Olímpio Campos.

To **Salvador**, 6-7 hrs, 11 a day with *Bonfim*, US$11, executive service at 1245, US$14, saves 1 hr. To **Maceió**, US$9 with *Bonfim*. Many coastal destinations served; also **Vitória** (US$26.50), **Rio** (US$51), **São Paulo**, **Belo Horizonte** (US$35). To **Estância**, US$2, 1½ hrs. To **Recife**, 7 hrs, US$12-14, 1200 and 2400.

Directory **Airline offices** *Transbrasil*, T2431155. *Varig*, T2433464. *Vasp*, T2432535. **Banks** Visa ATMs at Shopping centres, *Banco do Brasil*, Praça Gen Valadão and *Bradesco* in the city centre. MasterCard ATMs at *Banco 24 hours*, Av Francisco Porto and Av Geraldo Sobral, in the city centre close to the Shell gas station. **Communications** Post office: Laranjeiras and Itabaianinha. **Telephones**: Laranjeiras 296, national and international calls until 2200, also at rodoviária. **Embassies and consulates** *France*, T2248610. *Italy*, T2433814. *Portugal*, T2226662. **Medical services** *Clinica São Domingos Savio*, T2111344, casualty department. *São Lucas*, R Col Stanley Silveira 33, São Jose, T2111738. **Dental emergencies**: *Pronto Odonto*, Av Barão de Maruim, T2222927.

São Cristóvão

Phone code: 079
Colour map 2, grid C5
Population: 65,000

The old state capital of Sergipe, 17 km southwest of Aracaju on the road to Salvador, was founded in 1590 by Cristóvão de Barros. It is the fourth oldest town in Brazil. Built on top of a hill, its colonial centre is unspoiled, the majority of buildings painted white with green shutters and woodwork.

The **Museu de Arte Sacra e Histórico de Sergipe**, in the **Convento de São Francisco**, contains religious and other objects from the 17th-19th centuries. ■ *1000-1700 Tue-Fri, 1300-1700 Sat-Sun.* Also worth visiting (and keeping the same hours) is the **Museu de Sergipe** in the former **Palácio do Governo**; both are on Praça de São Francisco. On the same square are the churches of **Misericórdia** (1627) and the **Orfanato Imaculada Conceição** (1646, permission to visit required from the Sisters), and the **Convento de São Francisco**.

On Praça Senhor dos Passos are the churches of **Senhor dos Passos** and **Terceira Ordem do Carmo** (both 1739), while on the Praça Getúlio Vargas (formerly Praça Matriz) is the 17th-century **Igreja Matriz Nossa Senhora da Vitória**. ■ *All are open 1000-1700 Tue-Fri, 1500-1700 Sat-Sun.* Also worth seeing is the old **Assembléia Legislativa** on Rua Coronel Erundino Prado.

Sleeping & eating There are no hotels, but families rent rooms near the rodoviária at the bottom of the hill. *Senzala do Preto Velho*, R Messias Prado 84, recommended for Northeastern specialities.

Festivals *Senhor dos Passos* is held 15 days after Carnival and *Nossa Senhora de Vitória*, the patron saint's day, is on **8 Sep**. The town holds a *Festival de Arte*, usually in **Nov** but check the date as it sometimes falls in Oct.

Bus *São Pedro* buses depart from the old rodoviária in the centre of Aracaju, see above. **Train** A tourist train runs between Aracaju and São Cristóvão each Sat and Sun, 0900, 3½ hrs, T2113003 to check that it is running – a minimum of 15 passengers is needed.

Transport

Estância is 247 km north of Salvador, on the BR-101, almost midway between the Sergipe-Bahia border and Aracaju. It is one of the oldest towns in Brazil. Its colonial buildings are decorated with Portuguese tiles (none are open to the public). Its heyday was at the turn of the 20th century and it was one of the earliest places to get electricity and telephones. Estância is also called Cidade Jardim because of its parks. The month-long festival of São João in June is a major event.

Estância
Phone code: 079
Population: 57,000

Sleeping and eating **C** *Jardim*, Praça Joaquim Galazans 202, T5221638. Modern, a/c, huge buffet breakfast. Recommended. **C** *Turismo Estanciano*, Praça Barão do Rio Branco 176, T5221404. **D** *Dom Bosco*, bath and breakfast. **D** *Magnus*, T5222453. Breakfast, TV, fridge. **D** *Praia Abais*, T7510020. Breakfast, TV, pool. **D** *Sawana*, T9851570. With own restaurant. **Transport** Many buses stop at the rodoviária, on the main road. Bus from Salvador 4 hrs, US$12-14.

Alagoas

The state of Alagoas has a pleasant capital, Maceió, with many beaches. There is also the interesting river culture of Penedo at the mouth of the important Rio São Francisco, which flows from Minas Gerais through the arid interior to meet the Atlantic Ocean. It is one of the poorest and least developed states; most people live near the coastal strip and in the capital.

After the Portuguese had regained their territory from the Dutch invasion during the 17th century, Alagoas remained under the influence of the larger colonial centre Pernambuco until it was made a province and took on an identity of its own.

Maceió

The capital of the state of Alagoas is a friendly city with a low crime rate. It is mainly a sugar port, although there are also tobacco exports and a major petrochemical plant. A lighthouse (farol) stands in a residential area of town, about 1 km from the sea. The commercial centre stretches along the seafront to the main dock and climbs the hills behind.

Phone code: 082
Colour map 2, grid C6
Population: 780,000

Getting there Flights arrive at Campos dos Palmares airport, 20 km from the centre. Taxis to the centre charge about US$20. Interstate buses arrive at the rodoviária, 5 km from the centre. Luggage store is available. Take bus marked 'Ouro Preto p/centro' (taxi quicker, US$7) to Pajuçara.

Ins & outs
See also Transport, page 428

    Getting around The commercial centre is easy to walk around but you need to take a bus to the main hotel and beach area of t he city at Pajuçara. Frequent buses, confusingly marked, serve all parts of the city. Bus stops are not marked; it is best to ask where people look as if they are waiting. The ferroviária is in the centre, R Barão de Anádia 121. Train services are suburban.

Sights

Two of the city's old buildings, the **Palácio do Governo**, which also houses **Fundação Pierre Chalita** (Alagoan painting and religious art) and the church of **Bom Jesus dos Mártires** (1870 – covered in tiles), are particularly interesting. Both are on the Praça dos Martírios (or Floriano Peixoto). The **cathedral**, Nossa Senhora dos Prazeres (1840) is on Praça Dom Pedro II.

Instituto Histórico e Geográfico, Rua João Pessoa 382, T2237797, has a good small collection of Indian and Afro-Brazilian artefacts.

Lagoa do Mundaú, a lagoon, whose entrance is 2 km south at **Pontal da Barra**, limits the city to the south and west: excellent shrimp and fish are sold at its small restaurants and handicraft stalls; a nice place for a drink at sundown. Boats make excursions in the lagoon's channels, T2317334.

Beaches

For beaches beyond the city, see Excursions below

Beaches fronting the old city, between the Salgema terminal and the modern port area (Trapiche, Sobral), are too polluted for swimming. Beyond the city's main dock, the beachfront districts begin; within the city, the beaches are more exclusive the further from the centre you go. The first, going north, is Pajuçara where there is a nightly craft market. At weekends there are wandering musicians and entertainers and patrols by the cavalry on magnificent Manga Larga Marchador horses. There are periodic *candomblé* and *axé* nights and rituals to the goddess Iemanjá. Next is Ponta Verde, then Jatiúca, Cruz das Almas, Jacarecica (9 km from the centre), Guaxuma (12 km), Garça Torta (14 km), Riacho Doce (16 km), Pratagi (17 km) and Ipioca (23 km). Jatiúca, Cruz das Almas and Jacarecica are all good for surfing. The beaches, some of

Maceió

To Cruz das Almas, Jacarecica, Riacho Doce & Ipioca

Not to scale

■ **Sleeping**
1 Buongiorno
2 Casa Grande da Praia, Sete Coqueiros & Velamar
3 Enseada
4 Tambaqui Praia

🚌 **Buses**
1 Rodoviária

the finest and most popular in Brazil, have a protecting coral reef 1 km or so out. Bathing is much better three days before and after a full or new moon, because tides are higher and the water is more spectacular.

There is a natural swimming pool 2 km off Pajuçara beach (**Piscina Natural de Pajuçara**), at low tide you can stand on the sand and rock reef (beware of sunburn). You must check the tides, there is no point going at high tide. *Jangadas* cost US$5 per person per day (or about US$20 to have a *jangada* to yourself). On Sunday or local holidays in the high season it is overcrowded. At weekends lots of *jangadas* anchor at the reef, selling food and drink.

Tourist offices *Ematur* (*Empresa Alagoana de Turismo*), Av da Paz 2014, Centro, T2219465, F2218987, also at the airport and rodoviária. Helpful, has good maps and leaflets. The municipal tourist authority is *Emturma*, R Saldanha da Gama 71, Farol, T2234016; information post on Pajuçara beach, opposite *Hotel Solara*.

Essentials

AL *Enseada*, Av A Gouveia 171, T2314726, F2315394, enseada@vircom.com.br Recommended. **AL** *Sete Coqueiros*, Av A Gouveia 1335, T2318583, F2317467. 3-star, a/c, TV, phone, popular restaurant, pool. Next door is the smaller **A** *Velamar*, No 1359, T3275488, F2316849. A/c, TV, fridge, safes in rooms. **B** *Buongiorno*, No 1437, T2317577, F2312168. A/c, fridge, English-speaking owner, helpful. **C** *Casa Grande da Praia*, No 1528, T2313332. A/c, TV, cheaper without. Recommended. *Amazona*, No 1095. Great breakfast. **C** *Costa Verde*, No 429, T2314745. Bath, fan, good family atmosphere, English, German spoken, rooms on 1st floor are best. **C** *Pousada Shangri-La*, Antônio de Mendonça 1089, T2313773. Safe. **D** *Pousada Saveiro*, No 805. A/c, bath, TV, clean, simple, good value, cheaper without a/c. *Mandacaru*, Almte Maranenhas 85, 2 corners from the beach. Safe, good value.

Ponta Verde beach L *Tambaqui Praia*, R Eng Mário de Gusmão 176, T2310202. A/c, TV, phone, restaurant. **B** *Dos Corais*, R H Guimarães 80. Helpful. **B** *Hotel do Mar*, Av R Kennedy 1447, T2313171. Good. **C** *Baleia Azul*, Av Sandoval Arroxeias 822. A/c, fridge, TV. **C** *Sol de Verão*, R Eng Mário do Gusmão 153, **D** in small rooms without bath. **C** *Pousada Bela Vista*, Av Eng Mário de Gusmão 1260, T2318337. Well situated, excellent breakfast, a/c, TV. Recommended.

Further from the centre, **L** *Matsubara*, on Cruz das Almas beach, Av Brig Eduardo Gomes 1551, T2353000, F2351660. Pool, tennis, all facilities. Recommended. **C** *Hospedaria de Turismo Costa Azul*, Av João Davino and Manoel Gonçalves Filho 280, T2316281. Shower, fan, English spoken, discounts for stays over a week. **C** *Pousada Cavalo Marinho*, R da Praia 55, Riacho Doce (15 km from the centre), facing the sea, T/F2351247.

Sleeping
■ on map, page 426
Price codes:
see inside front cover

There are many hotels on Praia Pajuçara, mostly along Avenida Dr Antônio Gouveia and Rua Jangadeiros Alagoanos. It can be hard to find a room during the December-March holiday season, when prices go up

(map)

To Northern Beaches

Av Dr A Gomes de Barros
JATIÚCA
Av Dr J Marques Luz
Sgto Alberto
H Tradines
José Lages
Walfredo Otacílio
Alvaro Otacílio
Wilfredo Bandeira
Praia de Jatiúca
Sandoval Arrochelas
Vital Barbosa
J Sampaio Luz
Alagoanos
Ximena
Mário de Gusmão
Vasconcelos
Vasconcelos
deiros
Cenoifo
Av Robert Kennedy
Plech
PONTA VERDE
Praia Sete Coqueiros

2 To Marechal Deodoro & Praia do Francês   **3** To Riacho Doce

Recife and the Northeast Coast

Use of bicycle, canoes and body boards included, hot showers, German and English spoken, tropical breakfasts, Swiss owner. Very highly recommended (nearby is *Lua Cheia*, good food and live music at night).

Centre C *Pousada Sol e Mar*, Av Rosa da Fonseca, T2212615. Helpful owners, safe. Recommended. **D** *Golf*, R Prof Domingos Moeda 38A (near the Cathedral). Clean. Cheap hotels (mostly without windows) in R Barão de Atalaia.

Youth hostels *Nossa Casa*, R Pref Abdon Arroxelas 327, Ponta Verde, T2312246. IYHA. *Pajuçara*, R Quintino Bocaiúva 63, Pajuçara, T2310631. *Stella Maris*, Av Des Valente de Lima 209, Mangabeiras, T3252217. All require reservations Dec-Feb, Jul and Aug.

Camping There is a *Camping Clube do Brasil* site on Jacarecica beach, T2353600. A 15-min taxi drive from the town centre. *Camping Pajuçara*, Largo da Vitória 211, T2317561. Clean, safe, food for sale. Recommended.

Eating *Ao Lagostão*, Av Duque de Caxias 1348. Seafood, fixed price (expensive) menu. *Pizzeria Sorrisa*, Av Alagoana and J Pessoa Imperador. Very cheap and good food, popular with Brazilians. **Vegetarian**: *O Natural*, R Libertadora Alagoana (R da Praia) 112. *Nativa*, Osvaldo Sarmento 56. Good views. Many good bars and restaurants in Pajuçara: on Av Antônio Gouveia are: *Paraíso*, No 631, vegetarian, open late. *O Dragão*, No 21, Chinese. *Comes e Bebes*, No 981, Italian and Arabic, good, takeaway service. *Tempeiro Paulista*, No 1103, regional food, good service, cheap. *Massarella*, Jangadeiras Alagoanas 1255, Italian, small, good. *Mello's Bar*, R Epaminondas Gracindo 194, excellent food and value.

The beaches for 5 km, from the beginning of Pajuçara to Cruz das Almas in the north, are lined with *barracas* (thatched bars) providing music, snacks and meals until midnight (later at weekends). Vendors on the beach sell beer and food during the day; clean and safe. There are many other bars and *barracas* at Ponto da Barra, on the lagoon side of the city.

Local specialities include oysters, *pitu*, a crayfish (now becoming scarce), and *sururu*, a kind of cockle. Local ice-cream, *Shups*, is recommended.

Bars & nightclubs
These are relaxed and varied

Popular *barracas* are *Bar Lampião* (or *Tropical*) and *Ipaneminha* on Pajuçara (Brazilian pop), and *Fellini* on Ponta Verde (varies: good blues and jazz). There are nightclubs to suit most tastes. *Calabar*, in Pajuçara, for *forró* and *lambada*, *Lambadão* at Cruz das Almas (excellent *lambada*, weekends only). *Bar Chapéu de Couro*, José Carneiro 338, Ponto da Barra, is a popular music bar for young people.

Entertainment **Cinema** *Cinema São Luiz*, R do Comércio, in the centre. *Arte 1 and 2*, Pajuçara and Iguatemi shopping centres. **Theatre** *Teatro Deodoro*, Praça Mcal Deodoro, in the centre.

Festivals 27 Aug: *Nossa Senhora dos Prazeres*; 16 Sep: *Freedom of Alagoas*; 8 Dec: *Nossa Senhora da Conceição*; 15 Dec: *Maceiofest*, a great street party with *trios elétricos*; *Christmas Eve*; *New Year's Eve*, half-day.

Tour operators *Aeroturismo*, R Barão de Penedo 61, T3262020, F2214546, American Express representative.

Transport
See also Ins and outs, page 425

Local Bus: the 'Ponte Verde/Jacintinho' bus runs via Pajuçara from the centre to the rodoviária, also take 'Circular' bus (25 mins Pajuçara to rodoviária). Taxis from town go to all the northern beaches (for example 30 mins to Riacho Doce), but buses run as far as Ipioca. The Jangadeiras bus marked 'Jacarecica-Center, via Praias' runs past all the beaches as far as Jacarecica. From there you can change to 'Riacho Doce-Trapiche', 'Ipioca' or 'Mirante' buses for Riacho Doce and Ipioca. These last 3 can also be caught in the centre on the seafront avenue below the Praça Sinimbu (US$0.50 to Riacho Doce).

To return take any of these options, or take a bus marked 'Shopping Center' and change there for 'Jardim Vaticana' bus, which goes through Pajuçara.

Buses and kombis to Marechal Deodoro, Praia do Francês and Barra de São Miguel leave from R Barão de Anádia, outside the ferroviária, opposite *Lojas Americanas*: bus US$0.75, kombi US$1 to Marechal Deodoro, 30 mins, calling at Praia do Francês in each direction. Last bus back from Praia do Francês to Maceió at 1800.

Long distance Air: airport, BR-101, 20 km north, T3221300. Flights to Aracaju, Recife, Rio de Janeiro, Salvador and São Paulo. Taxi about US$25. Buses to airport from near *Hotel Beiriz*, R João Pessoa 290 or in front of the Ferroviária, signed 'Rio Largo'; alight at Tabuleiro dos Martins, then 7-8 mins' walk to the airport, bus fare US$0.75.

Bus: the rodoviária is on a hill with good views. Bus to **Recife**, 10 a day, 3½ hrs express (more scenic coastal route, 5 hrs), US$9. To **Aracaju**, US$9, 5 hrs (potholed road). To **Salvador**, 10 hrs, 4 a day, US$20 (*rápido* costs more).

Car hire: *Localiza*, Av Alvaro Otacilio 6445, Jatiuca, T3256565/6553. *Rotacar*, R Quintino Bocauiva 123, Pajucara, T3273388.

Banks Open 1000 to 1500. Good rates at *Banespa*. Cash against MasterCard at *Banorte*, R de Comércio, 306, Centro. **Communications Post office**: R João Pessoa 57, Centro, 0700-2200. **Telephones**: R do Comércio 508, almost opposite *Bandepe*. There is a small post on Pajuçara beach, opposite the *Othon* hotel. Also at the rodoviária. **Embassies and consulates** *France*, T2352830. *Portugal*, T3364564. *Spain*, T2412516. **Laundry** *Lave-Sim*, R Jangadas Alagoanas 962, Pajuçara. *Washouse*, R Jangadas Alagoanas 698, Pajuçara. **Medical services** *Unimed*, Av Antonio Brandao 395, Farol, T2211177, used to be São Sebastião hospital. *Pediatria 24 horas*, R Durval Guimaraes 519, Ponta Verde, T2317742/7702. **Dentist**: *Pronto Socorro Odontologico de Maceio*, Av Pio XV11, Jatiuca, T3257534. **Voltage** 220 volts AC, 60 cycles.

Directory

Excursions from Maceió

About 22 km south, by bus past Praia do Francês, is the attractive colonial town and former capital of Alagoas, Marechal Deodoro, which overlooks the Lagoa Manguaba. The 17th-century **Convento de São Francisco**, Praça João XXIII, has a fine church (Santa Maria Magdalena) with a superb baroque wooden altarpiece, which has been badly damaged by termites. You can climb the church's tower for views. Adjoining it is the **Museu de Arte Sacra**. ■ *0900-1300 Mon-Fri, US$0.30, guided tours available, payment at your discretion.* Also open to visitors is the **Igreja Matriz de Nossa Senhora da Conceição** (1783).

The town is the birthplace of Marechal Deodoro da Fonseca, founder of the Republic; the modest house where he was born is on the Rua Marechal Deodoro, close to the waterfront. ■ *0800-1700 Mon-Sat, 0800-1200 Sun, free.*

The *Restaurant São Roque* is simple but good. Good local lacework can be bought.

On a day's excursion, it is easy to visit the town, then spend some time at beautiful **Praia do Francês**. The northern half of the beach is protected by a reef, the southern half is open to the surf. Along the beach there are many *barracas* and bars selling drinks and seafood; try *agulhas fritas*.

Marechal Deodoro
Schistosomiasis is present in the lagoon

Sleeping and eating A *Cumaru*, T260-1110. 3-star, good. **A** *Pousada Le Baron*, Av Caravelas, T2601165. On the road from the beach to the highway, good. **B** *Pousada*

Bougainville e Restaurant Chez Patrick, T2601251. A/c, TV, pool, seafood and international cooking, very nice. **C** *O Pescador*, T2316959. Restaurant, beach huts, chalets with fridge, TV, 40 m from Praia do Francês beach, T2601306 for information. Eating places include *Panela Mágica*. Recommended.

Further out from Maceió is the beach of **Barra de São Miguel**, entirely protected by the reef. It gets crowded at weekends. You can make excursions to other beaches. Several good, cheap *barracas* serve food and drink (*da Amizade*, recommended). Carnival here has a good reputation. At the *Village Barra Hotel* (**A**), R Sen Arnon de Mello, T2721207, is a pool, restaurant, excursions run. The *Pousada da Barra* is good.

Penedo

Phone code: 082
Colour map 2, grid C5
Population: 57,000

A more interesting crossing into Alagoas can be made by frequent ferry crossings from **Neópolis** in Sergipe, to Penedo some 35 km from the mouth of the Rio São Francisco.

Penedo is a charming town, with a nice waterfront park, **Praça 12 de Abril**, with stone walkways and walls. Originally the site of the Dutch Fort Maurits (built 1637, razed to the ground by the Portuguese), the colonial town stands on a promontory above the river. Among the colonial buildings, modern structures such as the Associação Comercial and *Hotel São Francisco*, both on Avenida Floriano Peixoto, do not sit easily. **The tourist office is in Casa da Aposentadoria, Praça Barão de Penedo, T5512827, ext 23.**

On the Praça Barão de Penedo is the neoclassical **Igreja Matriz** (closed to visitors) and the 18th-century **Casa da Aposentadoria** (1782). East and a little below this square is the Praça Rui Barbosa, on which are the **Convento de São Francisco** (1783 and later) and the church of **Santa Maria dos Anjos** (1660). As you enter, the altar on the right depicts God's eyes on the world, surrounded by the three races (indigenous, black and white). The church has fine *trompe-l'oeil* ceilings (1784). The convent is still in use. ■ *Free guided tours*.The church of **Rosário dos Pretos** (1775-1816), on Praça Marechal Deodoro, is open to visitors as are **Nossa Senhora da Corrente** (1764), on Praça 12 de Abril, and **São Gonçalo Garcia** (1758-70) on Avenida Floriano Peixoto between 0800-1200, 1400-1700 weekdays only. Also on Avenida Floriano Peixoto is the pink **Teatro 7 de Setembro** (No 81) of 1884. ■ *0800-1200, 1400-1730 weekdays, Sat morning only, closed Sun*. Between it and the old covered market are fruit and vegetable stalls.

The **Casa de Penedo**, at Rua João Pessoa 126 (signs point the way up the hill from F Peixoto), displays photographs and books on, or by, local figures. ■ *0800-1800 Tue-Sun*. T5512516.

River traffic Very few of the long two-masted sailing vessels that used to cruise on the river can be seen now, although there are plenty of smaller craft. Beaches in Sergipe (for example, Arambipe) or Alagoas (for example, Peba) can be reached by boat; the latter also by road. Either side of the river mouth are turtle nesting grounds which are protected. For information contact the **Fundação Pró-Tamar**, Reserva Biológica de Santa Isabel, CEP 49190-000, Pirambu, SE, T079-2761201, F2761217.

Sleeping **A** *São Francisco*, Av Floriano Peixoto, T5512273, F5512274. Standard rooms have no a/c, others have a/c, TV, fridge. Recommended except for poor restaurant.

The slave state of Palmares

From the introduction of African slaves to northeast Brazil, fujões (runaways) would disappear into the interior and set up villages or mocambos. Between the 1630s and the end of 17th century the mocambos prospered – especially during times of crisis such as the Dutch invasion in 1630 – and together formed quilombos, free territories which accepted not only runaway slaves but also freed ones and whites who had fallen out with the re-established Portuguese colony. The most famous of these quilombos, established in what is now the state of Alagoas, was called Palmares after the large number of palm trees in the area. It consisted of 30,000 people living in several mocambos in an area of 17,000 square miles (44,000 sq km). According to reports from Bartholomeus Lintz, the leader of a Dutch expedition in 1640, the largest settlement in Palmares had 220 buildings, a church, four smithies and a meeting house.

The political and social structures were very similar to those found in West Africa, and although Catholicism was practised, so was polyandry, mainly due to the lack of women in the republic. The leader of Palmares was one Ganga-Zumba who

was revered like a king. But it appears he was killed by his followers in 1680 after making some concessions to the Portuguese two years earlier; he was succeeded by the republic's brave military commander, Zumbi. The existence of Palmares was a constant thorn in the side of Portuguese domination of Brazil and dozens of attempts were made to destroy it. However, Zumbi managed to defend the republic until it was finally smashed by the Portuguese with bandeirante help in 1695. Zumbi was killed and his decaptitated head was put on display in Recife to discourage other potential runaways and prove that he was not immortal as his followers believed. He is still remembered every year on 20 November, Brazil's Black Conciousness Day. He has also become a popular theme at Carnival time.

The site of the Palmares Republic is situated on the Serra da Barriga, close to modern União do Palmares in Alagoas state, reached by driving north out of Maceió on the BR-101, turning left after Messias and driving for 40 km along a paved road. There is one hotel, Parque Hotel dos Quilombos, T2811135, on the BR-104 towards Recife, TV, a/c, fridge, restaurant.

B *Pousada Colonial*, Praça 12 de Abril 21, T5512355, F5513099. *Luxo* and suite have phone, TV and fridge, suites have a/c, spacious, good cheap restaurant, front rooms with view of Rio São Francisco. **D** *Turista*, R Siqueira Campos 143, T5512237. With bath, fan, hot water. Recommended.

Eating

Forte da Rocheira, R da Rocheira (take either of the alleys running west off the hill between Praças Barão de Penedo and 12 de Abril, turn right), T5513273. Good food, including *ensopada de jacaré* (alligator stew). Continue along the cliff walkway to the riverside for *Churrascaria O Scala*, at the end of R 15 de Novembro.

Shopping

Daily market on streets off Av Floriano Peixoto, good hammocks. Ceramics for sale outside Bompreço supermarket on Av Duque de Caxias.

Transport

Bus **Salvador**, 451 km (US$12-14, 6 hrs, by daily bus at 0600, book in advance), at same time for **Aracaju** (US$6); buses south are more frequent from Neópolis, 6 a day (0630-1800) to Aracaju, 2 hrs, US$3.60. **Maceió**, 115 km, 5 buses a day in either direction, US$5.40-6.60, 3-4 hrs. The rodoviária is on Av Duque de Caxias, behind Bompreço.

Ferry Frequent launches for foot passengers and bicycles across the river to **Neópolis**, 25 mins, US$0.50. The dock in Penedo is on Av Duque de Caxias, below Bompreço. The ferry makes 3 stops in Neópolis, the second is closest to the rodoviária (which is near the Clube Vila Nova, opposite the Texaco station). There is also a half-hourly car ferry (US$3, take care when driving on and off).

Directory   **Banks** Open 0830-1300. *Banco do Nordeste do Brasil*, on Av Floriano Peixoto. *Banco do Brasil* and *Bradesco* on Av Duque de Caxias, opposite Bompreço supermarket. *Restaurant e Bar Lulu*, Praça 12 de Abril, will change cash if conditions suit the owner, fair rates. **Communications** Post office: Av Floriano Peixoto, opposite *Hotel Imperial*. Telephones: On Barão de Penedo.

North of Maceió

There are many interesting stopping points along the coast between Maceió and Recife. At **Paripueira**, 40 minutes' bus ride from Maceió (Rodoviária), the beach is busy only during high season. As at Pajuçara (see above), low tide leaves lots of natural swimming pools.

Barra de   Some 45 km north is this busy fishing village, with a palm fringed beach on a
Santo Antônio   narrow peninsula, a canoe ride away. The beaches nearby are beautiful: to the south, near the village of Santa Luzia, are Tabuba and Sonho Verde. To the north is Carro Quebrado, from which you can take a buggy to Pedra do Cebola, or further to Praia do Morro, just before the mouth of the Rio Camaragibe.

Sleeping and eating D *São Geraldo*, simple, very clean, restaurant. *Pousada Buongiorno* has 6 modest rooms to rent in a farmhouse, bathrooms but no electricity, many fruit trees (in Maceió T2317577, F2312168). Accommodation can be found through local people. *Peixada da Rita*, try prawns with coconut sauce. Recommended for local seafood. *Estrela Azul*, more expensive, good, popular with tourists.

Beyond Barra do Camaragibe, a coastal road, unpaved in parts, runs to the Pernambuco border and São José da Coroa Grande. The main highway, BR-101, heads inland from Maceió before crossing the state border to Palmares.

Pernambuco

Once producer of all the world's sugar, today the state of Pernambuco offers a variety of attractions from beaches, traditional culture, colonial cities and museums. Recife, the state capital, is the main industrial and commercial centre, while Olinda offers colonial elegance and imposing churches. Towns such as Caruaru in the agreste, the region between the coast and the Sertão, have distinctive regional fairs selling clay, straw and leather handicrafts. The archipelago of Fernando de Noronha, a marine national park, has fascinating wildlife and is great for diving and other watersports. Pernambuco is saturated in music, from the rustic forms of forró to the urban mixes of maracatu with modern pop which spawned bands that have influenced mainstream Brazilian music and fortified Northeastern pride. Carnival here is distinctive, a mixture of Latino party atmosphere and African cultural processions, all set to the backdrop of breathtaking colonial architecture.

Recife

Recife is a major city and the gateway to the Northeast. It is a popular tourist destination thanks to its beaches, historical monuments and its close neighbour Olinda. Spending carnival here is a good option.

Phone code: 081
Colour map 2, grid B6
Population: 1.2 million

Ins and outs

International and domestic flights arrive at Guararapes airport in the hotel district of Boa Viagem (airport taxis US$5 to the seafront) and 12 km from the city. Bus to airport, No 52, US$0.40. There is a bank desk before customs which gives much the same rate for dollars as the moneychangers in the lobby.

Unlike just about every other city, Recife's airport is central and its bus station is in the suburbs. Long-distance buses arrive at the Terminal Integrado dos Passageiros, or TIP (pronounced 'chippy'), 12 km outside the city. There is a 30-min Metrô connection to the central railway station. The train to the centre is much quicker than the bus.

Getting around
For more information, see Transport, page 443

The city centre consists of 3 sections: Recife proper, Santo Antônio and São José, and Boa Vista and Santo Amaro. The first 2 are on islands formed by the rivers Capibaribe, Beberibe and Pina, while the third is made into an island by the Canal Tacaruna, which separates it from the mainland. The centre is always very busy by day; the crowds and the narrow streets, especially in the Santo Antônio district, can make it a confusing city to walk around. Recife has the main dock area, with commercial buildings associated with it. South of the centre is the residential and beach district of Boa Viagem, reached by bridge across the Bacia do Pina. Olinda, the old capital, is only 7 km to the north (see page 446).

Tourist offices

Empetur, main office, Centro de Convenções, Complexo Rodoviário de Salgadinho, T34278000, F32419601, between Recife and Olinda, www.empetur.gove.br Branches at airport, T32242361 (24 hrs, cannot book hotels, helpful but few leaflets, English spoken), and Boa Viagem, T34633621 (English spoken, very helpful). Maps are available, or can be bought at newspaper stands in city; also sketch maps in monthly guides *Itinerário Pernambuco* and *Guia do Turista*. *Secretaria de Turismo do Recife*, T32247198. Hours of opening of museums, art galleries, churches, etc are published in the newspapers, *Diário de Pernambuco* and *Jornal do Comercio*.

Sights

About 285 km north of Maceió and 839 km north of Salvador, Recife was founded on reclaimed land by the Dutch prince Maurice of Nassau in 1637 after his troops had burnt Olinda, the original capital. **Forte do Brum** (built by the Dutch in 1629) is an army museum. ■ *0900-1600 Tue-Fri, 1400-1600 Sat-Sun, donation optional.* **Forte das Cinco Pontas** was built by the Dutch in 1630 and altered by the Portuguese in 1677. The two forts controlled access to the port at the northern and southern entrances respectively. Within Forte das Cinco Pontas is the **Museu da Cidade do Recife**, which houses a cartographic history of the settlement of Recife. ■ *0900-1800 Mon-Fri, 1300-1700 Sat-Sun. US$0.50 donation preferred.*

The first Brazilian printing press was installed in 1706 and Recife claims to publish the oldest daily newspaper in South America, *Diário de Pernambuco*, founded 1825 (but now accessible on the Internet). The distinctive lilac building is on the Praça da Independência.

Recife orientation

Detailed maps
A *Recife*, page 438
B *Boa Viagem*, page 440

The artists' and intellectuals' quarter is based on the **Pátio de São Pedro**, the square round São Pedro dos Clérigos. Sporadic folk music and poetry shows are given in the square during the evening from Wednesday to Sunday, and there are atmospheric bars and restaurants. ■ *For more information, T34262728.* The square is an excellent shopping centre for typical northeastern craftware; clay figurines are cheapest in Recife.

Not far away off Avenida Guararapes, two blocks from the central post office, is the **Praça do Sebo**, where the city's second-hand booksellers concentrate; this Mercado de Livros Usados is off the Rua da Roda, behind the Edifício Santo Albino, near the corner of Avenida Guararapes and Rua Dantas Barreto. You can also visit the city **markets** in the São José and Santa Rita sections.

The former municipal prison has now been made into the **Casa da Cultura**, with many cells converted into art or souvenir shops and with areas for exhibitions and shows (also public conveniences). ■ *0900-1900 Mon-Sat, 0900-1400 Sun.* Local dances such as the *ciranda, forró* and *bumba-meu-boi* are held as tourist attractions. ■ *1700 Mon, Wed and Fri. T32842850 to check in advance.*

Among other cultural centres are Recife's three traditional theatres: **Santa Isabel**, built in 1850 (■ *Praça da República, open to visitors 1300-1700 Mon-Fri*); the restored and beautiful **Parque** (■ *Rua do Hospício 81, Boa Vista, 0800-1200, 1400-1800*); and **Apolo** (■ *Rua do Apolo 121, 0800-1200, 1400-1700*).

The best are **Santo Antônio do Convento de São Francisco** (1606), which has beautiful Portuguese tiles, in R do Imperador, and adjoining it the finest sight of all, the **Capela Dourada**, or Golden Chapel (1697). ■ *US$0.25, no flash photography; entry through the Museu Franciscano de Arte Sacra, 0800-1130 and 1400-1700 Mon-Fri, 0800-1130 Sat. US$1.*

Churches
Often closed to visitors on Sunday because of services. Many are in need of repair

São Pedro dos Clérigos in São José district (1782) should be seen for its façade, its fine wood sculpture and a splendid *trompe-l'oeil* ceiling. ■ *0800-1130 and 1400-1600 daily.* **Nossa Senhora da Conceição dos Militares**, Rua Nova 309 (1771), has a grand ceiling and a large 18th-century primitive mural of the battle of Guararapes. There is a museum next door. ■ *0800-1700 Mon-Fri.*

Other important churches to be seen are **Santo Antônio** (1753-91), in Praça da Independência, rebuilt in 1864 (■ *0800-1200 daily and 1400-1800 Mon-Fri, 1700-1900 Sun*); **Nossa Senhora do Carmo** (1663), Praça do Carmo (■ *0800-1200, 1400-1900 Mon-Fri, 0700-1200 Sat-Sun*); **Madre de Deus** (1715), in the street of that name in the district of Recife, with a splendid high altar, and sacristy (■ *0800-1200, 1400-1600 Tue-Fri*); the **Divino Espírito Santo** (1689), the original church of the Jesuits, Praça 17 in Santo Antônio district (■ *0800-1630 Mon-Fri, 0800-1400 Sat, 1000-1200 Sun*).

About 14 km south of the city, a little beyond Boa Viagem and the airport, on Guararapes Hill, is the historic church of **Nossa Senhora dos Prazeres**. It was here, in 1648-49, that two Brazilian victories led to the end of the 30-year Dutch occupation of the Northeast in 1654. The church was built by the Brazilian commander in 1656 to fulfil a vow. ■ *0800-1200 and 1400-1700 Tue-Fri, 0800-1200 Sat, closed to tourists on Sun.*

The **Museu do Homem do Nordeste**, Avenida 17 de Agosto 2223, Casa Forte, comprises the **Museu de Arte Popular**, containing ceramic figurines (including some by Mestre Alino and Zé Caboclo); the **Museu do Açúcar**, on the history and technology of sugar production, with models of colonial mills, collections of antique sugar bowls and much else; the **Museu de**

Museums

Recife and the Northeast Coast

The Dutch in Brazil

At the beginning of the 17th century, the Dutch were looking for ways of expanding their influence on the western hemisphere. It seemed to them that controlling land in Brazil would be the ideal place to start. Not only would they obtain rich, sugar-producing territory, they would also have a good base from which to raid the treasure fleets of Spain and eventually attack the Spanish colonies of Peru and Mexico. Moreover, the Portuguese crown, nominal overlord of Brazil, was in the power of Spain, which itself was too busy protecting its own far-flung colonies to pay much attention to defending Brazil.

In 1624, the Dutch captured Bahia, but the next year they lost it. Five years later (1630) they turned their attention to Olinda and Recife, successfully took them and, by 1634, had control of a stretch of the coast from Rio Grande do Norte to Cabo de Santo Agostinho. The Dutch position was strengthened by the arrival in 1637 of Johan Maurits of Nassau-Siegen (1604-79) as governor. He fell in love with Brazil, and his desire to win the trust of the Indians and his tolerance towards Jews (and Catholics) was markedly different from that of most of the Portuguese colonists. Johan Maurits' job, however, was military. With Bahia still in Portuguese hands, there was constant tension with Pernambuco. He attacked Salvador in 1638, but failed. In the following year, a Spanish armada was sent to attack the Dutch, but the two sides did not engage until 1640, after

which the Spanish gave up all thought of attacking Recife.

When the Portuguese threw the Spanish out of Lisbon late in 1640, the Portuguese in Brazil were delighted. In the following year, the Portuguese and Dutch signed a truce, covering Europe, Africa, the East Indies and Brazil, but ratification was slow in coming, during which time the Dutch and Portuguese in Brazil were engaged in a bitter war. Johan Maurits extended Dutch control to São Luís do Maranhão in 1641, but he was not able to capitalize on the possession. In 1644 he returned to Holland, partly because his rule was economically unviable. The West India Company, which controlled a large part of the trade of Brazil, resented the cost of supporting Recife. Too much sugar was being cultivated (trade which was handled by free traders, not the Company), too little other produce was being grown to feed the city and Johan Maurits had failed to secure the countryside. A year after his departure, fighting intensified and, because the Dutch had no real power base outside their main cities, the Portuguese gradually won back their territory. Dutch supremacy at sea and their heavily defended forts meant that neither side could win outright victory and the war dragged on until 1654. By this time, the Dutch were also at war with England, which weakened their navy in Brazilian waters. They surrendered on 26 January 1654. The last real threat to Portuguese rule in Brazil was over.

Antropologia, the **Nabuco Museum** (at No 1865) and the modern museum of popular remedies, **Farmacopéia Popular**. ■ *1100-1700 Tue-Fri, 1300-1700 Sat-Sun, US$1, T34415500.*

You can take the 'Dois Irmãos' bus (check that it's the correct one, with 'Rui Barbosa' posted in window, as there are two) from outside the Banorte building near the post office on Guararapes, but it is much easier to get to the museum complex by taxi.

The **Museu do Estado**, Avenida Rui Barbosa 960, Graças, has excellent paintings by the 19th-century landscape painter, Teles Júnior. ■ *0900-1700 Tue-Fri, 1400-1700 Sat-Sun.* **Museu do Trem**, Praça Visconde de Mauá, is small but interesting, especially the Henschel locomotive. ■ *0900-1200, 1400-1700 Tue-Fri, 0900-1200 Sat, 1400-1700 Sun.* **Museu de Imagem e**

Som, on the Rua da Aurora 379, Boa Vista, has exhibitions of photographs, films and temporary shows. ■ *0900-1700 Mon-Fri.*

This is the main residential and hotel quarter, currently being developed at the northern end of town. The 8-km promenade lined with high-rise buildings commands a striking view of the Atlantic, but the beach is backed by a busy road, crowded at weekends and not very clean. During the January breeding season, sharks come close to the shore. You can go fishing on *jangadas* at Boa Viagem with a fisherman at low tide. The main praça has a good market at weekends.

Boa Viagem

Bus To get there by bus from the centre, take any marked 'Boa Viagem'; from Nossa Senhora do Carmo, take buses marked 'Piedade', 'Candeias' or 'Aeroporto' – they go on Av Domingos Ferreira, 2 blocks parallel to the beach, all the way to Praça Boa Viagem (at Av Boa Viagem 500). Back to the centre take buses marked 'CDU' or 'Setubal' from Av Domingos Ferreira.

Essentials

Boa Viagem is the main tourist district and the best area to stay. All hotels listed in this area are within a block or two of the beach, although none in any price range have much character. There is not much reason to be in the city centre, and accommodation here is of a pretty low standard. Hotels in the Santa Rita area are not recommended as this area is dangerous at night. Many hotels sell 5-day Carnival packages (at high prices), which you must take regardless of the length of time you wish to stay, although you may find regular priced accommodation at Boa Viagem. Shop around.

Sleeping
■ *on map*
Price codes:
see inside front cover

For Olinda hotels,
see page 448

Centre A *Recife Plaza*, R da Aurora 225, T32311200. Boa Vista, overlooking the Rio Capibaribe, every comfort, fine restaurant (very popular at lunchtime). **B** *4 de Outubro*, R Floriano Peixoto 141, Santo Antônio, T32244900, F34242598. 4 standards of room, hot water, TV, phone, a/c. **C** *Hotel Park 13 de Mayo*, T32317627 (not the same as *Hotel Parque* nearby, both opposite park), R do Hospicio. Safe, OK. **D** *América*, Praça Maciel Pinheiro 48, Boa Vista, T2211300. 2-star, with a/c (cheaper without), front rooms pleasanter, quiet. **D** *Interlaine*, R do Hospício 186, T4232941. Good value, in town centre.

Boa Viagem The main beachfront road is Av Boa Viagem; hotels here tend to be more expensive. **AL** *Mar*, near the beach at R Barão de Souza Leão 451, T4624444, F4624445. Enormous, anonymous and rather dated. **A** *Recife Monte*, corner of R Petrolina and R dos Navegantes 363, T34657422, F34658406. Very smart and good value for category, caters to business travellers. **B** *Aconchego*, Félix de Brito 382, T33262989, aconchego@novaera.com.br Motel style rooms around pleasant pool area, a/c, sitting room. English-speaking owner, will collect you from the airport. **B** *Do Sol*, Av Boa Viagem 978, T34656722, reservas@hsol.com.br Decent, if rather bland, business facilities. **B** *Praia*, Av Boa Viagem 9, T/F4653722. Large modern block with bar, restaurant and decent sized pool. **B** *Setúbal*, R Setúbal 932, T33414116. Helpful, good breakfast, comfortablee. **C** *Coqueiral*, R Petrolina, 43, T33265881. Dutch-owned (Dutch, English, French spoken), a/c, small and homely with pretty breakfast room. Recommended. **C** *Praia Mar*, Av Boa Viagem 1660, T34653759. Intimate and safe. Recommended. **C** *Uzi Praia*, Av Conselheiro Aguiar 942, T/F34669662. A/c, cosy, sister hotel across the road. **D** *Navegantes Praia* , R dos Navegantes, 1997, T33269609, F33262710. One block from beach, basic but a/c, TV and room service. Good value **D** *Pousada da Julieta*, R Prof Jose Brandao 135, T33267860, hjulieta@elogica.com.br Friendly and clean. One block from beach, very good value. Recommended. **D** *Pousada da Praia*, Alcides Carneiro Leal 66, T33267085. A/c, TV, safe, a/c, rooms vary (some tiny), very helpful, popular with Israelis. Roof-top breakfast room.

Praia de Piedade C *Casa da Praia*, Av Beira Mar 1168, T34611414. On a quiet street, with garden, good breakfast, owner speaks French. Recommended.

Youth hostels D *Albergue Mandacaru*, R Maria Carolina 75, T3261964. Stores luggage, English and German spoken, good breakfast. Recommended. **E** *Maracatus do Recife*, R Maria Carolina 185, T33261221, alberguemaracatus@yahoo.com *IYHA*, pool, simple, safe, cooking facilities, mosquitoes can be a problem, membership not needed,

Recife

Sleeping
1 4 de Outubro
2 América
3 Park 13 de Mayo
4 Recife Plaza

Eating
1 Galo d'Ouro
2 Gelattos
3 Leite

Churches
1 Capela Dourada
2 Espírito Santo
3 Madre de Deus
4 Matriz de Boa Vista
5 Nossa Senhora da Conceição dos Militares
6 Nossa Senhora do Carmo
7 Nossa Senhora do Livramento
8 Nossa Senhora do Rosário dos Pretos
9 Pilar
10 Santo Antônio
11 São José do Ribamar
12 São Pedro dos Clérigos
13 Santo Antônio do Convento de São Francisco

Buses
1 To Itamaracá & Igarassu
2 To Porto da Galinhas
3 To Boa Viagem

0 metres 200
0 yards 200

good breakfast. **E** *Albergue do Mar*, R dos Navegantes 81, T33262196. Good breakfast and atmosphere.

Camping *Paraíso Camping Clube*, Av Dantas Barreto 512, loja 503, T32243094. Can give information on camping throughout the state. There is no camping within the city.

Private accommodation During Carnival and for longer stays at other times, private individuals rent rooms and houses in Recife and Olinda; listings can be found in the classified ads of *Diário de Pernambuco*, or ask around the streets of Olinda. This accommodation is generally cheaper, safer and quieter than hotels.

Many of the restaurants in the city centre cater to office workers and are closed evenings and weekends. Be careful of eating the local small crabs, known as *guaiamum*; they live in the mangrove swamps which take the drainage from Recife's *mocambos* (shanty towns).

City centre Expensive: *Leite* (lunches only), Praça Joaquim Nabuco 147/53 near Casa de Cultura. Old and famous, good service, smart (another branch in Boa Viagem, at Prof José Brandão 409). *Lisboa á Noite*, R Geraldo Pires 503. Good, reasonable prices, open Sunday evenings (unlike many). *Tivoli*, R Matias de Albuquerque, Santo Antônio. Lunches downstairs, a/c restaurant upstairs, good value. **Mid-range**: *Galo D'Ouro*, Gamboa do Carmo 83. Well-established, international food. *Casa de Tia*. Gamboa do Carmo, 136. Lunch only, must arrive by 1215, try *cosido*, a meat and vegetable stew, enough for 2. *O Vegetal*, R Cleto Campelo and Av Guararapes (second floor) behind Central Post Office. Lunch only, closed Sat-Sun. **Cheap**: *Casa dos Frios*, da Palma 57, loja 5. Delicatessen/sandwich bar, salads, pastries, etc. *Buraquinho*, Pátio de São Pedro. Lunch only, all dishes good, generous servings of caipirinha, friendly. **Seriously cheap**: *Lanchonetes* abound in the city, catering to office workers, but tend to close in evening. *Gelattos*, Av Dantas Barreto, 230. Great *sucos* (try the delicious *guarana do amazonas* with nuts), hamburgers and sandwiches. Pay at counter. Recommended.

Boa Viagem Restaurants on the main beach road of Av Boa Viagem are, like the hotels here, pricier. Venture a block or two inland for cheaper deals.

Expensive: *Bargaço*, Av Boa Viagem 670. Typical northeastern menu specializing in seafood dishes. Sophisticated with small bar. *La Maison*, Av Boa Viagem, 618, T33251158. Fondue restaurant in low-lit basement with illicit feel. Appropriately cheesey and good fun, with rosé wine and peach melba on menu.

Mid-range: *Chica Pitanga*, R Petrolina, 19, T34652224. Upmarket, excellent food by weight. Be prepared to queue. Recommended. *Churrascaria Porcão*, Av Eng Domingos Ferreira 4215. Good for meat and salad eaters alike, very popular. *Ilha da Kosta*, R Pe Bernardino Pessoa, 50, T34662222. Self-service seafood, sushi, pizza and Brazilian cuisine. Nothing special, but open 1100 to last client and all afternoon. *La Capannina*, Av Cons. Aguiar, 538, T34659420. Italian pizzas, salad, pasta and sweet and savoury crepes. Delivers. Recommended. *Parraxaxa*, R Baltazar Pereira, 32, T91080242. Rustic-style, award-winning. Buffet of northeastern cuisine, including breakfast. Recommended. **Shopping Center Recife** (open 1000-2200, T34646000) in Boa Viagem has a range of options in this price category, eg *Sushimi*, T34636500. Classic, Japanese fast-food in suitably sterile surroundings.

Cheap: *Peng*, Av Domingos Ferreira, 1957. Self-service, some Chinese dishes. Bargain, rather than gourmet food, in area with few other restaurants. *TioDadá*, R Baltazar Pereira, 100. Loud, TV screens, good-value portions of beef.

Seriously cheap: *Gibi*, Av Cons Aguiar, 542. Basic but popular hamburger joint. *Real eza*, Av Boa Viagem, on corner with Av Atlântico. Beachfront location, hamburgers, snacks and pizza. *Romana*, R Setubal, 225. Deli/bakery with a few tables and chairs. Sells pastries, coffee, yoghurt for breakfast or snack. *Tempero Verde*, R S.H, Cardim, opposite *Chica Pitanga*. Where the locals go for a bargain meal of beans, meat and salad, US1.50. Simple, self-service, pavement tables.

Eating

There are many good restaurants, at all prices, in the city, and along the beach at Boa Viagem

Recife and the Northeast Coast

Boa Viagem

Boa Viagem detail

To Recife Centre

Atlantic Ocean

N

0 metres 200
0 yards 200

■ **Sleeping**
1 Aconchego
2 Albergue do Mar
3 Coqueiral
4 Do Sol
5 Mar
6 Maracatus do Recife
7 Navegantes Praia
8 Pousada da Julieta
9 Pousada da Praia
10 Praia
11 Recife Monte
12 Uzi Mar
13 Uzi Praia

● **Eating**
1 Bargaço
2 Chica Pitanga
3 Churrascaria Porção
4 Dunkin' Donuts
5 Ilha da Kosta
6 La Capannina
7 La Maison
8 Parraxaxa
9 Peng
10 Real eza
11 Romana
12 Tempero Verde
13 Tio Dadá

● **Bars**
14 Balthazar

Recife and the Northeast Coast

Cafés *Cafe Cordel*, R Domingos Jose Martins. Northeastern dishes, cordel literature, regional books (some in English), good CD collection with requests accepted. *Savoy*, Av Guararapes, open since 1944 and a haunt of Pernambucan intellectuals, Simone De Beauvoir and Jean Paul Sartre once ate here according to a book written on the bar, poetry all over the walls.

Most bars (often called 'pubs', but nothing like the English version) stay open until dawn. The historic centre of *Recife Antigo* has been restored and is now an excellent spot for nightlife. Bars around R do Bom Jesus such as **London Pub**, No 207 are the result of a scheme to renovate the dock area. *Calypso Club*, R do Bom Jesus, US$5, has live local bands playing anything from traditional music to rock. The 2 most popular nightclubs (both enormous, open 2300 to dawn) are **Downtown Pub**, R Vigário Tenório, disco, live music, US$5 and **Fashion Club**, Av Fernando Simões Barbosa, 266, Boa Viagem in front of *Shopping Centre Recife*, T33274040, US$8. Techno and rock bands. The Graças district, west of Boa Vista, on the Rio Capibaribe, is popular for bars and evening entertainment. Recommended bars are **Capibar**, Aflitos, on River Capibaribe. *Shoparia*, 2 doors from *Maxime* restaurant, good beer and atmosphere, live rock music after 2200. Discotheques tend to be expensive and sophisticated. Best times are around midnight on Fri or Sat, take a taxi.

The Pina zone, north of the beginning of Boa Viagem, is one of the city's major hang-out areas with lively bars, music and dancing. In Boa Viagem, **Baltazar**, R Baltazar Pereira 130, T33270475. Live music nightly, bar snacks, large and popular. Open 1600 to early hours.

Try to visit a northeastern *Forró* where couples dance to typical music, very lively especially on Fri and Sat, several good ones at Candeias. *Papillon Bar*, Av Beira Mar, 20, Riedade, T33417298. *Forró* Wed-Sat.

Bars & nightclubs

Look out for *Agenda Cultural*, a free booklet available from tourist offices, and some shops and theatres, which details the cultural events for the month, in Portuguese only.

Entertainment

Spectator sport Football Recife's 3 clubs are *Sport*, *Santa Cruz* and *Nautico*. Sport play at Ilha do Retiro, T32271213, take Torrões bus from Central Post Office on Av Guararapes. Santa Cruz play at Arruda, T34416811, take Casa Amarela bus from Central Post Office. Nautico play at Aflitos, T34238900, take Água Fria or Aflitos bus. Local derbies are sometimes full beyond safe capacities. Avoid 'Arquibancada' tickets for Santa Cruz-Sport games. For games at Arruda, dress down. **Racing** *Pernambucan Jockey Club*, T32274961.

Theatre Shows in the Recife/Olinda Convention Center, US$10, traditional dances in full costume.

1 Jan, *Universal Brotherhood*. **12-15 Mar**, parades to mark the city's foundation. **Mid-Apr**, *Pro-Rock Festival*, a week-long celebration of rock, hip-hop and manguebeat at Centro de Convenções, Complexo de Salgadinho and other venues. Check *Diário de Pernambuco* or *Jornal de Comércio* for details. **Jun**, *Festejos Juninos*, see box, page 442. **11-16 Jul**, *Nossa Senhora do Carmo*, patron saint of the city. **Aug** is the *Mes do Folclore*. **Oct**, *Recifolia*, a repetition of the carnival over a whole weekend; dates differ each year. **1-8 Dec** is the festival of *Iemanjá*, with typical foods and drinks, celebrations and offerings to the goddess; also **8 Dec**, *Nossa Senhora da Conceição*.

Festivals
For Carnival, see box on page 442

Diving Offshore are some 20 wrecks, including the remains of Portuguese galleons; the fauna is very rich. *Mergulhe Coma*, T35522355, M91026809, atlanticdivingasr@ hotmail.com English-speaking instructors for PADI courses. *Seagate*,

Sport

Carnival in Pernambuco

Carnival in Pernambuco encompasses trios eléctricos and samba schools as well as having its own distinctive dances and rhythms such as Maracatu and Frevo. Avenida Guararapes in Recife, Pina near Boa Viagem, Largo do Amparão and Mercado Eufrásio Barbosa (Varadouro) in Olinda are the main centres for the festivities.

There is a pre-carnavalesca week which starts with the 'Bloco da Parceria' in Boa Viagem bringing top Axé music acts from Bahia and the 'Virgens de Bairro Novo' in Olinda which features men in drag. These are followed by Carnival balls such as Baile dos Artistas (popular with the gay community) and the Bal Masque held at the Portuguese club, Rua Governador Agamenon Magalhães, T2315400. On the following Saturday morning the bloco Galo da Madrugada with close on a million participants officially opens carnival (wild and lively), see the local press for routes and times. The groups taking part are maracatu, caboclinhos, troças, tribos de índios, blocos, ursos, caboclos de lança, escolas de samba and frevo.

Usually they start from Rua Conde da Boa Vista and progress along Rua do Hospício, Rua da Imperatriz, Ponte da Boa Vista, Praça da Independência, Rua 1° de Março and Rua do Imperador. This is followed by the main days Sunday to Tuesday. During Carnival (and on a smaller scale throughout the year) the Casa de Cultura has frevo demonstrations where visitors can learn some steps of this unique dance of Pernambuco (check press for details of Frevioca truck and frevo orchestras during Carnival in the Pátio de São Pedro). The best place to see the groups is from the balconies of Hotel do Parque or Recife Palace Hotel. Seats in the stands and boxes can be booked up to a fortnight in advance at the central post office in Avenida Guararapes.

The Maracatu groups dance at the doors of all the churches they pass; they usually go to the Church of Nossa Senhora do Rosário dos Pretos, patron saint of the slaves (Rua Estreita do Rosário, Santo Antônio), before proceeding into the downtown areas. A small car at the head

T34261657/99729662, www.seagaterecife.com.br Daily departures and night dives. **Golf** *Caxangá Golf Clube*, Av Caxangá 5362, T32711422. 9 holes. **Yachting** *Recife Yacht Club*, T34652002. *Itamaraca Yacht Club*, T32212648.

Shopping **Bookshops** *Livraria Brandão*, R da Matriz 22 (used English books and some French and German), and bookstalls on the Rua do Infante Dom Henrique. *Livro 7*, a huge emporium with a very impressive stock, R Sete de Setembro 329. *Saraiva*, R Sete de Setembro 280, best selection of Brazilian literature in the city. *Sintese*, Riachuelo 202. *Almanque Livros*, Largo do Varadouro 418, loja 58, bohemian atmosphere, sells food and drink. *Sodiler* at Guararapes airport has books in English, newspapers, magazines; also in the *Shopping Center Recife*. *Livraria do Nordeste*, between cells 118 and 119, Ralo Leste, Casa da Cultura, for books in Portuguese on the Northeast. *Livraria Nordeste*, R Imperatriz 43, Boa Vista. A great local character, *Melquísidec Pastor de Nascimento*, second-hand bookseller, at R Bispo Cardoso Aires, 215; also has a second-hand stall at Praça do Sebo (see page 435).

Markets The permanent craft market is in the **Casa da Cultura** (see above); prices for ceramic figurines are lower than Caruaru (see below). *Mercado São José* (1875) for local products and handicrafts. *Hippy fair* at Praça Boa Viagem, on the sea front, lifesized wooden statues of saints, weekends only. Saturday craft fair at *Sítio Trindade*, Casa Amarela: during the feast days of 12-29 Jun, fireworks, music, dancing, local food. On 23 Apr, here and in the Pátio de São Pedro, one can see the *xangô* dance. Herbal remedies, barks and spices at Afogados market. *Cais de Alfândega* , Recife Barrio, bears the figure of some animal and is followed by the king and queen under a large, showy umbrella. The bahianas, who wear snowy-white embroidered skirts, dance in single file on either side of the king and queen. Next comes the dama do passo carrying a small doll, or calunga. After the dama comes the tirador de loas who chants to the group which replies in chorus, and last comes a band of local percussion instruments.

Still flourishing is the dance performance of the caboclinhos. The groups wear traditional Indian garb: bright feathers round their waists and ankles, colourful cockades, bead and animal teeth necklaces, a dazzle of medals on their red tunics. The dancers beat out the rhythm with bows and arrows; others of the group play primitive musical instruments, but the dance is the thing: spinning, leaping, and stooping with almost mathematical precision. Further information from Casa da Carnaval, office of Fundação da Cultura de Recife, Pátio de São Pedro, lojas 10-11. Galo da Madrugada, Rua da Concórdia,

Santo Antônio, T2242899.

Festejos Juninos In the June festas, the days of Santo Antônio (13 June), São João (24 June), São Pedro and São Paulo (29 June), form the nuclei of a month-long celebration whose roots go back to the Portuguese colony. Intermingled with the Catholic tradition are Indian and African elements. The annual cycle begins in fact on São José's day, 19 March, historically the first day of planting maize; the harvest in June then forms a central part of the **festejos juninos**. During the festivals the forró is danced. This dance, now popular throughout the Northeast, is believed to have originated when the British builders of the local railways held parties that were for all. This is one aspect of the festivities which makes Pernambuco's **festejos juninos** distinct from those that celebrated all over Brazil.

The Prefeitura and Secretaria de Turismo has published three booklets on História Junina, História de Carnaval and História do Folclore, all by Claudia Lina, which provide a good introduction to these topics.

market of local artisans work, 1st weekend of every month. *Domingo na Rua*, Sunday market in Recife Barrio, with stalls of local artesanato and performances.

Shopping malls *Shopping Center Recife* between Boa Viagem and the airport, one of the largest malls in South America, www.shopping-recife.com.br *Shopping Tacaruna*, in Santo Amaro, buses to/from Olinda pass it.

Jacaré e Cobra de Água Eco-Group, T34473452, M9687360, www.truenet.com.br Regular **Tour** excursions in Pernambuco. *Souto Costa Viagens e Turismo Ltda*, R Felix de Brito Melo 666, **operators** T34655000, and Aeroporto de Guararapes (American Express representative). *Stella Barros* (Thomas Cook), R Monsenhor Ambrosino Leite 93, Graças, T/F32315201. *Student Travel Bureau (STB)*, R Padre Bernardino Pessoa 266, T34654522, F34652636, stbmaster@ stb.com.br, ISIC accepted, discounts on international flights but not domestic Brazilian flights. *Trilhas*, T32226864, recommended for ecologically oriented excursions.

Local Bus City buses cost US$0.30-0.60; they are clearly marked and run frequently **Transport** until about 2230. Many central bus stops have boards showing routes. On buses, especially at night, look out for landmarks as street names are written small and are hard to see. Integrated bus-metrô (see Trains below) routes and tickets (US$1) are explained in a leaflet issued by CBTU Metrorec, T32515256. See below for buses to Olinda and other destinations outside the city. Trolleybuses run in the city centre. Taxis are plentiful; fares double on Sun, after 2100 and during holidays.

Train Commuter services, known as the **Metrô** but not underground, leave from the central station; they have been extended to serve the rodoviária (frequent trains,

▶▶ Recife's New Wave

If Bahia produced Brazil's musical innovations in the late 1980s and early 1990s, more recent steps forward have been taken by Pernambucans. It is again a case of outside influences mixing well with Brazilian rhythmic flair. As in Bahia, where Olodum took reggae and added it to 'afoxe' rhythms, a local band called Chico Science & Nacão Zumbi took Pernambucan popular music forms including maracatu, baião and ciranda, and welded them to modern dance forms such as hip-hop, electro and jungle. The fusion became known as Mangue-Beat, best translated as 'Mangroove', after a 1991 manifesto written by a local DJ, Renato Lins, summed up the local music scene and the local mangrove swamps with the same word: stagnant.

Chico Science was killed in February 1997, casting a shadow over the carnival of that year, but, in 1999, Nacão Zumbi

returned with a reshuffled line-up to prove, with devastating new material, that their intention was always to carry on Chico's work. Although there are also innovative and exciting rock bands like Eddie, River Raid and Supersoniques, the so-called 'Mangue -Beat' sees to it that talent scouts from Rio and Sao Paulo-based record companies still descend on Pernambuco regularly, in the hope of finding new stars.

Three major festivals take place each year which showcase new bands. February sees Carnival's Rec-Beat in Recife take over the Rua da Moeda in the renovated old town. In April, the Pro-Rock festival is to be found at the Pernambuco State Convention Centre between Recife and Olinda – Sepultura played in 1999 – and in July each year, Pe-No-Rock takes place at the Circo Maluco Beleza in the Aflitos district of Recife. At least there aren't any awkward dance steps to learn.

0500-2300, US$0.40 single). If going to Boa Viagem from the rodoviária, get off the Metrô at Central station (Joanna Bezerra station is unsafe) and take a bus or taxi (US$8) from there.

Long distance Air: Guararapes airport, conveniently located in the hotel distict of Boa Viagem, 12 km from the city centre. International flights to Lisbon and Milan. Domestic flights to Brasília, Campina Grande, Fernando de Noronha, Fortaleza, João Pessoa, Juazeiro do Norte, Maceió, Natal, Paulo Afonso, Petrolina, Rio de Janeiro, Salvador and São Paulo.

Bus: rodoviária, mainly for long distance buses, is 12 km outside the city at São Lourenço da Mata, T34521999/1163. There is a 30-min Metrô connection from the central railway station, entrance through Museu do Trem, opposite the Casa da Cultura, 2 lines leave the city, take train marked 'Rodoviária'. From Boa Viagem a taxi all the way costs US$20, or go to Central Metrô station and change there. Bus US$, 1 hr, from the centre or from Boa Viagem.

Bus tickets are sold at Cais de Santa Rita (opposite EMTU).

To **Salvador**, daily 1930, 12 hrs, US$18-25, 4 a day (all at night) (1 *leito*, 70). To **Fortaleza**, 12 hrs, US$20 *convencional*, US$30 *executivo*. To **Natal**, 4 hrs, US$9. To **Rio**, daily 2100, 44 hrs, US$58-65. To **São Paulo**, daily 1630, 50 hrs, US$60-70. To **Santos**, daily 1430, 52 hrs, US$60. To **Foz do Iguaçu**, Fri and Sun 1030, 55 hrs, US$90. To **Curitiba**, Fri and Sun, 52 hrs, US$76. To **Brasília**, daily 2130, 39 hrs, US$49-60. To **Belo Horizonte**, daily 2115, 34 hrs, US$41. To **São Luís**, 28 hrs, *Progresso* at 1430 and 1945, US$75. To **Belém**, 34 hrs (*Boa Esperança* bus recommended). To **João Pessoa**, every 30 mins, US$2.50. To **Caruaru**, every hr, 3 hrs, US$3. To **Maceió**, US$9, 3½ hrs (express), 6 hrs (slow), either by the main road or by the coast road daily via 'Litoral'.

Buses to the nearby destinations of **Igarassu** (every 15 mins) and **Itamaracá** (every 30 mins) leave from Av Martins de Barros, in front of *Grande Hotel*. To **Olinda**, see below; those to the beaches beyond Olinda from Av Dantas behind the post office. To **Cabo** (every 20 mins) and beaches south of Recife from Cais de Santa Rita.

Car hire: *Budget*, T33412505. 24 hrs, just outside Guararapes airport. *Localiza*, Av Visconde de Jequitinhonha, 1145, T33410287, and at Guararapes airport, T33412082, freephone, T0800-992000. *Hertz*, T4623552.

Airline offices *BRA*, T34217060, *Gol*, T34644793. *TAM*, reservations T3425011, at air-
port, T34624466. *TAP Air Portugal*, Av Conselheiro de Aguiar 1472, Boa Viagem T34658800, at airport T33410654. *Transbrasil*, Av Conde de Boa Vista 1546, T34232656, Av Conselheiro de Aguiar, Boa Viagem, T34650450, at airport, T34650333. *Nordeste/RioSul*, Av Domingos Ferreira 801, loja 103-5, T4656799 (*RioSul* T34656799), at airport, T3413187. *Trip*, 34644610. *United*, R Progreso 465/802, T34232444. *Varig*, R Conselheiro de Aguiar 456, Boa Viagem, T34644440, R J E Favre 719, T33392998, at air-port T33414411, cargo T34658989. *Vasp*, R da Palma 254, Santo Antônio, T34213088, R Dr Nilo Dornelas Câmara 90, Boa Viagem, T34213611, F33253434, at airport, T33417742.

Directory

Banks *Banco do Brasil*, R Barão da Souza Leão 440, Boa Viagem, Av Dantas Barreto, 541, Santo Antonio, exchange and credit/debit cards, TCs. *Bandepe*, Av Dantas Barreto 1110, Santo Antonio. MasterCard ATMs. *Bradesco*, Av Cons Aguiar 3236, Boa Viagem, T34653033. Av Conde de Boa Vista, Boa Vista, R da Concordia 148, Santo Antônio, 24-hr VISA ATMs, but no exchange. *Citibank*, Av Marquês de Olinda 126, T32161144, takes MasterCard. Av Cons Aguiar, 2024, ATM. *Lloyds Bank*, R A.L. Monte 96/1002. *MasterCard*, Av Conselheiro Aguiar 3924, Boa Viagem, cash against card. **Money changers:** *Anacor*, Shopping Center Recife, loja 52, also at Shopping Tacaruna, loja 173. *Monaco*, Praça Joaquim Nabuco, cambio, TCs and cash, all major currencies, no commission but poor rates. *Norte Cambio Turismo*, Av Boa Viagem 5000, also at Shopping Guararapes, Av Barreto de Menezes.

Open 1000-1600, hours for exchange vary between 1000 and 1400, sometimes later

Communications Internet: In Shopping Centre Recife, Boa Viagem. Also, *lidernet*, Shopping BoaVista, city centre. *popul@r.net*, R Barao de Souza Leao, near junction with Av Boa Viagem. Open daily 0900-2100. **Post office**: Poste Restante at Central Correios, Av Guararapes 250, next to Rio Capibaribe. Open 0900-1700, outgoing mail leaves at 1500 each day. Also has a philately centre. Another on R 24 de Maio 59. Poste Restante also with American Express representative *Souto Costa*, R Félix Brito de Melo 666, T4655000, also at Av Conselheiro Aguiar, Boa Viagem. **Telephones**: *Embratel*, Av Gov Agamenon Magalhães, 1114, Parque Amorim. Also at Praça da Independencia. International calls at phone centres on Av Cons Aguiar, Boa Viagem, Av Herculano Bandeira, 231, Pina and Av Conde da Boa Vista, open 0800-1800, phone cards sold, faulty cards replaced. The news-stand on the corner of Av Guararapes and Dantas Barreto is an official vending point. Also at R Diario de Pernambuco 38 and airport, 2nd floor.

Cultural centres *British Council*, Av Domingos Ferreira 4150, Boa Viagem, T34657744, F34657271, www.britcoun.org/br Open 0800-1500, reading room with current British newspapers, very helpful. *Alliance Française*, R Amaro Bezerra 466, Derby, T32220918.

Embassies and consulates *Denmark*, Av Marques de Olinda 85, Edif Alberto Fonseca 2nd floor, T32240311, F32240997, open 0800-1200, 1400-1800. *France*, Av Conselheiro Aguiar 2333, 6th floor, T34653290. *Germany*, Av Dantas Barreto 191, Edif Santo Antônio, 4th floor, T34253288. *Japan*, R Pe Carapuceiro, 733, 14th floor, T33277264. *Netherlands*, Av Conselheiro Aguiar 1313/3, Boa Viagem, T33268096. *Spain*, R Sirinhaem, 105, 2nd floor, T34650607. *Sweden*, Av Conde de Boa Vista 1450,

T32312581. *Switzerland*, Av Conselheiro Aguiar 4880, loja 32, Boa Viagem, T33263144. *UK*, Av Eng Domingos Ferreira 4150, Boa Viagem, T34657744, open 0800-1130. *USA*, R Gonçalves Maia 163, Boa Vista, T34212441, F32311906.

Laundry *AcquaClean*, Domingos Ferreira, 4023, Boa Viagem, T34660858, 0630-1900 Mon-Fri, 0800-1600 Sat.

Medical services Dengue has been resurgent in Recife. Previous sufferers should have good insurance as a second infection can lead to the haemorrhagic form, requiring hospitalization. *Hospital Santa Joana*, R Joaquim Nabuco 200, Graças, T34213666. *Unicordis*, Av.Conselheiro Aguiar 1980, Boa Viagem, T33265237 and Av Conselheiro Rosa de Silva 258, Aflitos, T34211000, equipped for cardiac emergencies. *Unimed*, Av Bernardo Vieira de Melo 1496, Guararapes, T34621955/34611530, general medical treatment, general practitioners. **Dental**: Artur Queroz, R Aldemar da Costa Almeida, 140, T34613835, T99657446 (mob). 24 hours.

Security Opportunistic theft is unfortunately common in the streets of Recife and Olinda (especially on the streets up to Alto da Sé). Keep hold of bags and cameras, and do not wear a watch. Prostitution is reportedly common in Boa Viagem, so choose nightclubs with care. **Tourist Police**, T33269603.

Voltage 220 volts AC, 60 cycles.

Olinda

Phone code: 081
Colour map 2, grid B6
Population: 350,000

About 7 km north of Recife is the old capital, founded in 1537 and named a World Heritage Site by UNESCO in 1982. The compact network of cobbled streets are steeped in history and invite wandering. This is a charming spot to spend a few relaxing days, and a much more appealing base than Recife. A programme of restoration, partly financed by the Netherlands government, was initiated in order to comply with the recently conferred title of National Monument, but many of the buildings are still in desperate need of repair.

Sights
Many of the historic buildings have irregular opening hours, but can be viewed from the outside

The city boasts an ornate church on almost every corner, but its 16th-century monastery and convent are worth seeking out. The tourist office can provide a complete list of all historic sites with a useful map, *Sítio Histórico*. **Basilica e Mosterio de São Bento**, R São Bento, was founded 1582 by the Benedictine monks, burnt by the Dutch in 1631 and restored in 1761. This is the site of Brazil's first law school and the first abolition of slavery. The magnificent gold altar was on loan to New York's Guggenheim Museum at the time of writing. ■ *0830-1130 and 1430-1700 Mon-Fri. Mass Sat 0630 and 1800; Sun 1000, with Gregorian chanting. Monastery closed except with written permission.* Despite its weathered exterior, the **Convento de São Francisco** (1585), Ladeira de São Francisco, has splendid woodcarving and paintings, superb gilded stucco, and *azulejos* in the Capela de São Roque within the church of **Nossa Senhora das Neves** in the same building. ■ *0700-1130 and 1400-1700 Tue-Fri, 0700-1200 Sat, US$0.40. Mass 1900 Tue, 1700 Sat and 0800 Sun.*

Make the short, but very steep, climb up to the **Alto da Sé** for memorable views of the city and the coastline stretching all the way to Recife. Here, the simple **Igreja da Sé** (1537), a cathedral since 1677, was the first church to be built in the city. ■ *0800-1200 and 1400-1700 Mon-Fri*. Nearby, the **Igreja da Misericórdia** (1540), R Bispo Coutinho has fine tiling and gold work but limited opening hours. ■ *1145-1230 and 1800-1830 daily*. On a small hill overlooking Praça do Carmo, the **Igreja do Carmo** church (1581) has been closed for several years due to planned restoration.

There are some 17th-century houses with latticed balconies, heavy doors and brightly painted stucco walls, including a house in Moorish style at Praça João Alfredo 7, housing the *Mourisco* restaurant and a handicrafts shop, Sobrado 7. The local colony of artists means excellent examples of regional art (mainly woodcarving and terracotta figurines) may be bought in the Alto da Sé, the square on top of the hill by the cathedral, or in the handicraft shops at the **Mercado da Ribeira**, Rua Bernardo Vieira de Melo (Vieira de Melo gave the first recorded call for Independence from Portugal, in Olinda in 1710). Handicrafts are also sold at good prices in the Mercado Eufrásio Barbosa, by the junction of Avenida Segismundo Gonçalves and Santos Dumont, Varadouro. There is a **Museu de Arte Sacra** in the former Palácio Episcopal (1696) at Alto da Sé 7. ■ *0900-1300 Tue-Fri*. At Rua 13 de Maio 157, in the 18th-century jail of the Inquisition, is the **Museu de Arte Contemporânea**. ■ *0900-1700 Tue-Fri, 1400-1700 Sat-Sun.* The **Museu Regional**, Rua do Amparo 128, is excellent (same hours). **Museu do Mamulengo**, Amparo 59, houses Pernambucan folk puppetry. ■ *0900-1800 weekdays, 1100-1800 Sat-Sun.* **Corredor Artístico do Amparo**, formally identified as the cultural and artistic zone, has artists workshops, while the **Casa dos Bonecos** houses papier mache giants; there are also many restaurants.

Tourist office *Secretaria de Turismo*, Praça do Carmo, T34299279, open daily 0900-2100. **Guides** with identification cards wait in Praça do Carmo.

Olinda

Recife and the Northeast Coast

N
Not to scale

Sleeping ■
1 7 Colinas
2 Albergue da Olinda
3 Pousada do Amparo
4 Pousada d'Olinda
5 Pousada dos Quatro Cantos
6 Pousada Peter
7 Pousada São Francisco

Eating ●
1 Goya
2 Maison do Bonfim
3 Marola
4 Mourisco
5 Oficina do Sabor

Bars ●
6 Farandola

They are former street children and half the fee for a full tour of the city (about US$12) goes to a home for street children. If you take a guide you will be safe from mugging which does, unfortunately, occur.

Beaches The beaches close to Olinda are polluted, but those further north, beyond Casa Caiada – at **Janga**, and **Pau Amarelo** – are beautiful, palm-fringed and usually deserted (although the latter can be dirty at low tide). Take either a 'Janga' or 'Pau Amarela' bus, Varodouro bus to return. At many simple cafés you can eat *sururu* (clam stew in coconut sauce), *agulha frita* (fried needle-fish), *miúdo de galinha* (chicken giblets in gravy), *casquinha de carangueijo* (seasoned crabmeat) and *farinha de dendê* (served in crabshells). Visit the Dutch fort on Pau Amarelo beach where there is a small craft fair on Saturday nights.

Sleeping All of the following, and even most of the cheaper hotels outside the old city, have a pool.
Prices at least triple during Carnival when five-night packages are sold. Rooms at regular prices can often be found in Boa Viagem during this time

Historic city Accommodation is mostly in converted mansions that are full of character. If you can afford it, staying in one of these *pousadas* is the ideal way to absorb Olinda's Colonial charm. **AL** *Pousada do Amparo*, R do Amparo 199, T34391749, www.pousadoamparo.com.br Undoubtably Olinda's best hotel. Gorgeous, 18th-century house, full of atmosphere. Very individual rooms with a/c and fridge, some with Jacuzzi. Flower-filled garden, sauna, good view, very helpful, English spoken, romantic restaurant, in the *Roteiros de Charme* group (see page 47). Highly recommended. **AL** *7 Colinas*, Ladeira de Sao Francisco 307, T/F34396055, 7colinas@hotel7 colinas.com.br Spacious, new hotel in beautiful grounds with large swimming pool. An oasis with full facilities. **B-C** *Pousada dos Quatro Cantos*, R Prudente de Morais 441, T34290220, F34291845, www.pousada4cantos.com.br Converted mansion with original furniture; full of character, yet homely. Garden, terraces and simple restaurant open til 2100. Highly recommended. **C** *Pousada d'Olinda*, P João Alfredo 178, T/F34942559. Nice pool area,sociable. Discount of 10% for owners of *Footprint Handbooks*, 2 communal rooms with good view (**E** category), restaurant, English, French, German and Spanish spoken. Warmly recommended. **C-D** *Pousada Peter*, R do Amparo 215, T/F34392171, www.pousadapeter.com.br With bath, a/c, clean, small pool, German owner, family atmosphere, good value. Rooms can viewed and booked on website.

Outside the historic centre Hotels on Rua do Sol and in Bairro Novo are below the old city and on the roads heading north. *Pousada São Francisco* and *Albergue da Olinda* on Rua do Sol are only a 5-min walk from the centre; the others are further out. **B** *Oh! Linda Pousada*, Av Ministro Marcos Freire 349, Bairro Novo, T34392116. Recommended. **C** *Pousada São Francisco*, R do Sol 127, T34292109. Comfortable, with very pleasant pool area. Recommended, modest restaurant, a/c. **C** *Cinco Sóis*, Av Ministro Marcos Freire 633, Bairro Novo, T/F34291347. A/c, fridge, hot shower, parking. **C** *Hospedaria do Turista*, Av Marcos Freire 989, Bairro Novo, T34291847, Mobile 9632961. Excellent. **C** *Olinda Bellomonte*, Av Beira Mar 1414, T34290409. **D** *São Pedro*, Praça Conselheiro João Alfredo 168, T34292935. Cosy, helpful, laundry, Danish run, English spoken. Recommended. **E** *Jangada*, R 15 de Novembro 98, T34294747.

Youth hostels **E** *Albergue da Olinda*, R do Sol 233, T34291592. Motel-style rooms with bath in **C** category, as well as communal bunk roomslaundry facilities and TV room. Large seating area with hammocks around pool. Highly recommended. **D** *Cheiro do Mar*, Av Min Marcos Freire 95, T34290101. IYHA, more expensive for non-members, very good small hostel with some double rooms (room No 1 is noisy from the disco), cooking facilities, ask driver of 'Rio Doce/Piedade' or 'Bairra de Jangada/Casa Caiada' bus (see below) to drop you at Albergue de Juventude on the sea front.

Camping *Olinda Camping*, R Bom Sucesso 262, Amparo, T34291365. US$5 per person, space for 30 tents, 5 trailers, small huts for rent, quiet, well-shaded, town buses pass outside. Recommended.

Expensive *Oficina do Sabor*, R do Amparo, 355, T34293331. Probably the city's best restaurant, consistently wins awards. Pleasant terrace overlooking city, food served in hollowed-out pumpkins and lots of vegetarian options. *Goya*, R do Amparo, 157, T34394875. Regional food, particularly seafood, beautifully presented.

    Mid-range *Maison do Bomfim*, R do Bonfim, 115, T34291674. Serene, fan-cooled, rustic-style restaurant. French cuisine, such as chicken chasseur and escargots, as well as Brazilian and Italian food. *Marola*, The perfect spot for a seafood supper. See under Entertainment below. *Samburá*, Av Min Marcos Freire 1551. With terrace, try *caldeirada* and *pitu* (crayfish), also lobster in coconut sauce or daily fish dishes, very good.

    Cheap *Grande Pequim*, Av Min Marcos Freire 1463, Bairro Novo. Good Chinese food. *Mourisco*, Praça João Alfredo 7, Excellent, good value food by weight in lovely, part-covered, garden. Delicious deserts. A real find. Warmly recommended.

    Seriously cheap Several *lanchonetes* and fast-food options along the seafront, such as *Mama Luise* and *Gibi*, on Av Min Marcos Freire, and *Leque Moleque* at Av Sigismundo Gonçalves 537.

    Local specialities The traditional Olinda drinks, *Pau do Índio* (which contains 32 herbs) and *Retetel*, are both manufactured on R do Amparo. In Olinda also try *tapioca*, a local dish made of manioc with coconut or cheese.

Eating

Cantinho da Sé, Ladeira da Sé 305, T34398815. Lively, good view of Recife, food served. *Farandola*, R Dom Pedro Roeser, 190, tucked away behind Igreja do Carmo church. Mellow bar with festival theme and 'big-top' style roof. Live mellow music nightly, plans for a circus next door. Drinks are cheap; try *bate bate de maracuja* (smooth blend of cachaça, passionfruit juice and honey) or *raspa raspa* fruit syrup. Warmly recommended. *Marola*, Trav. Dantas Barreto 66, T34292499. Funky wooden *barraca* on rocky shoreline specializing in seafood. Great *caiprifrutas* (frozen fruit drink with vodka – try the cashew). Can get crowded. Recommended. *Pernambucanamente*, Av Min Marcos Freire 734, Bairro Novo, T34291977. Live, local music every night.

    Beginning at dusk, but best after 2100, the Alto da Sé becomes the scene of a smallstreet fair, with arts, crafts, makeshift bars and barbecue stands, and impromptu traditional music; even more animated at Carnival. Every Friday night bands of wandering musicians walk the streets serenading passers-by. Each Sun from 1 January to Carnival there is a mini Carnival in the streets of the city, with music and dancing.

Entertainment

At Olinda's *Carnival* thousands of people dance through the narrow streets of the old city to the sound of the *frevo*, the brash energetic music which normally accompanies a lively dance performed with umbrellas. The local people decorate them with streamers and straw dolls, and form themselves into costumed groups (*blocos*) which you can join as they pass (take only essentials). Among the best-known *blocos*, which carry life-size dolls, are *O homem da meia-noite* (Midnight Man), *A Corda* (a pun on 'the rope' and 'acorda' – wake up!), which parades in the early hours, *Pitombeira* and *Elefantes*. Olinda's carnival continues on Ash Wednesday, but is much more low-key, *a quarta-feira do batata*" (Potato's Wednesday, named after a waiter who claimed his right to celebrate carnival after being on duty during the official celebrations). The streets are very crowded with people dancing and drinking non-stop. The local cocktail, *capeta* (guaraná powder, sweet skimmed milk and vodka) is designed to keep you going. *Foundation Day* is celebrated with 3 days of music and dancing, **12-15 Mar**, night-time only.

Festivals

Tour operators *Victor Turismo*, *Felitur*, Rua Getulio Vargas 1411, Bairro Novo, T/F4391477. *Viagens Sob O Sol*, Prudente de Moraes 424, T/F4293303, T9718102 (Mob), English spoken, transport offered to all parts and car hire. *Victor Turismo*, Av Santos Domont, 20, Loja 06, T34941467. Day and night trips to Recife.

Transport **Bus From Recife**: take any bus marked 'Rio Doce', No 981, which has a circular route around the city and beaches, or No 33 from Av Nossa Senhora do Carmo, US$0.60, or 'Jardim Atlântico' from the central post office at Siqueira Campos; from Boa Viagem, take bus marked 'Piedade/Rio Doce' or 'Barra de Jangada/Casa Caiada' (US$0.60, 30 mins). Change to either of these buses from the airport to Olinda: take 'Aeroporto' bus to Av Domingos Ferreira, Boa Viagem, and ask to be let off; and from the Recife Rodoviária: take the Metrô to Central station (Joana Bezerra is unsafe) and then change. In all cases, alight in Praça do Carmo. Taxi drivers between Olinda and Recife often try to put their meters onto rate 2 (only for Sun, holidays and after 2100), but should change it to 1 when queried. (taxi to Boa Viagem US$8, US$12 at night).

Directory **Banks** There are no facilities to change TCs, or ATMS, is the old city. *Banco do Brasil*, R Getulio Vargas 1470. *Bandepe*, Av Getulio Vargas, MasterCard ATMs. *Bradesco*, R Getulio Vargas 729, Visa ATMs. **Communications** Internet: Studyo Web, Praça do Carmo, US$1.20, 30 mins, a/c. Olind@.com:, 15, Av Beira Mar, $US1.50, 30 mins. **Post office**: Praça do Carmo, open 0900-1700. **Telephone**: Private booths and international phones in Praça do Carmo across the road from the bus stop, open Mon-Sat 0900-1800. **Laundry** *Cooplav*, Estr dos Bultrins, cost per weight of laundry, easily visible from main road, take Bultrins bus from Olinda. **Medical services** *Prontolinda*, R Jose Augusto Moreira 1191, T4321700, general, but also equipped for cardiac emergencies. **Security** Olinda has been severely afflicted by rapidly worsening poverty, the effects of which are perhaps more noticeable in this attractive and comparatively prosperous area. Please exercise caution, and sympathy.

Biological reserves Pernambuco's two reserves are **Saltinho**, in the south of the state, which preserves some of the last vestiges of Atlantic Forest in the Northeast, and **Serra Negra**, in the centre of the state, which has some of the last remaining forest at higher altitude in the interior. ■ *For information contact Ibama, Av 17 de Agosto 1057, Casa Forte, CEP 52060-590, T4415033, F4411380, Recife.*

The Southern Coast

About 30 km south of Recife, beyond Cabo, is the beautiful and quiet **Gaibu** beach, with scenic Cabo de Santo Agostinho on the point 5 km east of town. It has a ruined fort. In 1996 surfing in this area was banned owing to the danger of shark attacks. To get there, take bus 'Centro do Cabo' from the airport, then frequent buses – 20 minutes – from Cabo. Places to stay include *Pousada Beto Qualhado*, *Oliver y Daniel*, Av Laura Cavalcante 20, German, very relaxed, *Pousada Águas Marinhas* (**C**), Belgian-Brazilian owned, beautiful garden and location, highly recommended. There are cheap restaurants. About 1 km on foot from Gaibu is **Praia Calhetas**, which is very nice. **Itapuama** beach is even more empty, both reached by bus from Cabo. **Cabo**, Pernambuco's main industrial city, has interesting churches and forts and a **Museu da Abolição**, and at nearby **Suape** there are many 17th-century buildings and a biological reserve.

Porto de Galinhas
Phone code: 081
Brazilians rave about Porto Galinhas, with its sand streets, and beautiful beach. But because of a reef close to the shore, swimming is only possible at high tide (take heed of local warnings) and a rash of recently built upmarket

resorts is changing its rustic atmosphere. The name means 'port of chickens' because slaves were smuggled here in chicken crates. For **tourist information**, call T35521480; otherwise you can contact Roberto, T35521514, for information and assistance on all aspects of Porto Galinhas' attractions. He can also give lifts to Recife and Olinda. Alternatively, Sylvie, a well-known local French guide, speaks five languages and knows the area well.

Sleeping and eating A *Solar Porto de Galinhas*, on the beach, T/F35521211 or T33250772. Many facilities, a beautiful place. **B** *Pousada Beira Mar*, Av Beira Mar 12, T/F35521052, www.pousadabeiramar.com.br On beach, pleasant, comfortable. *Pousada Som das Ondas*, in Ipojuca, T/F35521454, somdasondas@ somdasondas.com.br Close to beach, pleasant pool area, hammocks. Run by Jean-Marc, 5 European languages spoken. **C** *Morada Azul*, Loteamento Recanto Porto de Galinhas, Lote 5, Ipojuca, T35521143. **C** *Maracatu*, ½ block from beach, cool, bath, TV, nice rooms and, next door, **D** *Meninão*, above bakery, includes breakfast and dinner. *Pousada do Dona Benedita*, in the street where the bus stops. Very basic, clean.

Sport For **diving** and **canoeing** trips, as well as excursions to Santo Aleixo island, contact *Porto Point Diving*, Praça Principal de Porto de Galinhas, T5521111. Also *AICA Diving*, Nossa Senhora do Ó, T/F5521290 or T9684876 (mob), run by Mida and Miguel. Porto de Galinhas is reached by bus from the far end of Av Dantas Barreto, 8 a day,7 on Sun, 0700-1700, US$1.25.

Further south (80 km from Recife) are the beaches of Barra do Sirinhaém, with some tourist development and three hotels including **D** *Dos Cataventos*. Fishermen make trips to offshore island (good views).

Barra do Sirinhaém

The Northern Coast

Some 39 km north of Recife on the road to João Pessoa, Igarassu has the first church built in Brazil (SS Cosme e Damião, built in 1535), the Livramento church nearby, and the convent of Santo Antônio with a small museum next door. The church of Sagrado Coração is said to have housed Brazil's first orphanage. Much of the town, which was founded in 1535, has been declared a National Monument; it is an attractive place, with a number of colonial houses and Brazil's first Masonic hall.

Igarassu
Phone code: 081
Colour map 2, grid B6
Population: 77,500

There is a hotel, *Fazenda Praia da Gavoa* (**A**), Estrada do Ramalho (Nova Cruz), T/F35431413. *Camping Clube do Brasil* has a site nearby at Engenho Monjope, an old sugar estate, now a historical monument (it is 5 km before Igarassu coming from Recife – bus US$1 – alight at the 'Camping' sign and walk 5-10 minutes, T35430528, US$5). Igarassu buses leave from Cais de Santa Rita, Recife, 45 minutes, US$1.

North of Igarassu you pass through coconut plantations to Itapissuma, where there is a bridge to **Itamaracá** island. According to the locals, this is where Adam and Eve spent their holidays (so does everyone else on Sunday now). It has the old Dutch **Forte Orange**, built in 1631; an interesting penal settlement with gift shops, built round the 1747 sugar estate buildings of Engenho São João, which still have much of the old machinery; charming villages and colonial churches, and fine, wide beaches. At one of them, **Praia do Forte Orange**, Ibama has a centre for the study and preservation of manatees (*Centro Nacional de Conservação e Manejo de Sirênios* or *Peixe-boi*). ■ *1000-1600 Tue-Sat.*

Itamaracá
Phone code: 081
Population: 14,000

There are pleasant trips by *jangada* from Praia do Forte Orange to **Ilha Coroa do Avião**, a recently formed sandy island (developing wildlife and migratory birds – for which there is a research station) with rustic beach bars. **Praias do Sossego** and **da Enseada** have some bars but are quiet and relatively undiscovered. The crossing is 3 km north of Itamaracá town, recommended for sun worshippers.

Further north again, two hours from Recife by bus, is **Pontas de Pedra**, an old fishing village, nice beach, fishing and diving expeditions, lots of bars.

Sleeping and eating **B** *Casa da Praia*, Av da Forte Orange, T35441255. With breakfast, pool, minibar, breakfast and optional dinner. **B** *Itamaracá Parque*, Estr do Forte, T35441030, F5441854. **C** *Pousada Itamaracá*, R Fernando Lopes 205/210, T35441152. Pool, some mins from the beach. **C** *Pousada Jaguaribe*, R Rios 355 (close to bus terminal) near the beach. Fans and mosquito nets in all rooms, kitchen, laundry facilities, swimming pool. Those with a car and above budget means should have lunch and a swim at charming *Vila Velha* (Call T9712962, ask for Newton Bezerra, dealer for artist Luis Jasmim. Visit them, and any purchase comes with an offer of lunch included in the deal), allow all afternoon. *Bar da Lia*, R do Jaguaribe, close to the Forte Orange, weekends feature Cirandas danced at the bar, led by the well known singer, Dona Lia, and her band.

Transport Buses from **Recife** (Av Martins de Barros opposite *Grande Hotel*, US$1.10, very crowded) and **Igarassu**.

Goiana
Phone code: 081
Population: 67,250

Situated on the Recife-João Pessoa road and founded in 1570, Goiana is an important town for ceramics. The **Carmelite church** and monastery, founded 1719, is impressive but poorly restored. **Matriz Nossa Senhora do Rosário dos Brancos** (17th century), on Rua Direita, is only open for 1800 mass. Also worth a visit are the **Convento da Soledade** (1735), on Rua da Soledade; **Nossa Senhora do Amparo dos Homens Pardos** (1681), Rua do Amparo, with a sacred art museum; and **dos Milagres da Misericórdia** church (1723), Rua da Misericórdia.

Visit the workshop of Zé do Carmo, opposite the *Buraco da Giá* restaurant (excellent seafood; owner has a tame crab which will offer you a drink), Rua Padre Batalha 100. *Hotel Dois Irmãos* (**D**) is in the town centre.

At the Pernambuco-Paraíba border, a 27-km dirt road goes to the fishing village of **Pitimbu**, with *jangadas*, lobster fishing, surf fishing, and lobster-pot making. There are no tourist facilities but camping is possible; food from *Bar do Jangadeiro*. Bus from Goiana, US$1.

West of Recife

Gravatá

Phone code: 081
Colour map 2, grid B6
Population: 62,000

Some 82 km west of Recife, by the paved BR-232 road that passes through the Serra dos Russos, is Gravatá, known as the Switzerland of Pernambuco for its scenery and good hill climate. On one of its hills is a replica of the Cristo Redentor of Rio de Janeiro. The former municipal prison on Rua Cleto Campelo has been made into a Casa da Cultura and historical centre. ■ *Mon-Fri.* **Tourist offices** *Secretaria de Turismo*, R Cleto Campelo, is open Mon-Fri.

L *Casa Grande Gravatá*, BR-232 Km 82, T34653011, F35330812. 4-star, very comfort-   **Sleeping**
able, restaurant serving regional food, excellent breakfast, swimming pool and
waterslides, English-speaking owner, splendid gardens, sauna, hydromassage. **A** *Por-*
tal de Gravatá, BR-232 Km 82, T32270345, F35330610. 3-star, comfortable, a/c, TV,
phone, restaurant with regional food, good breakfast, pool, large gardens, bar. **C-D** *da*
Serra, BR-232 Km 77, T35330014. The 1st hotel in Gravatá, 2-star, a/c, TV, phone, swimming pool, bar, garden, English-speaking owner. **C-D** *Petur-Hotel Centro Gravatá*,
BR-232 Km 77, T35330016, F35330075. 2-star, small, no bar or restaurant, a/c, TV,
phone, swimming pool.

There are many good restaurants with regional and international food; fondue is very   **Eating**
good in Gravatá. *Faisão Dourado*, BR-232 Km 82. Old and famous, Swiss architecture,
good service, international and regional food, T35330054, open Sat and Sun. *Taverna*
Suíça, BR-232 Km 78. Old, Swiss style, good service, international food (fondue a speciality), good wine list, English, French and Italian spoken by the owner, T35330299.
Picanha da Serra, R 15 de Novembro 1472, T9629960. Good service, regional food,
good value, closed Mon.

In Holy Week, *Semana Santa*, there is dancing, music and a *vaquejada* (rodeo) at Km   **Festivals**
78 on the BR-232, Haras da Serra. In **Jun**, the feast of *São João* is celebrated with fireworks, music, dancing and local food throughout the city. In **Oct** there is the *Straw-*
berry festival of the Northeast, with more typical food, drink, music and dancing.

Bus To **Recife** and **Caruaru** run every hr; the rodoviária is at Km 80 on the BR-232,   **Transport**
T35330691.

Banks *Banco do Brasil*, in the centre of town, open 1000-1600, very helpful, Eng-   **Directory**
lish-speaking manager, T5330388.

About 15 km further west on the BR-232 is Bezerros, on the Rio Ipojuca. It has   **Bezerros**
some old houses, fine praças and churches. Some, like the Igreja de Nossa   *Population: 52,000*
Senhora dos Homens Pretos, São José and the Capela de Nossa Senhora, date
from the 19th century. The former railway station has been converted into the
Estação da Cultura, with shows and other cultural performances. The city's
main attraction is handicrafts, which are found in the district of **Encruzilhada**
de São João; items in leather, clay, wood, papier maché and much more. The
best known artist and poet is J Borges (born 1935), whose work has been
exhibited internationally. Most typical are the Papangu masks, made of
painted papier maché (see below). The masks are used at carnival, as interior
decoration, even as key-holders. Wooden toys are also popular. About 10 km
from the centre of Bezerros, near the village of Serra Negra, a small ecotourism
park, **Serra Negra ecological tourism trail**, has been set up. Trails lead to
caves and springs; the flora is typical of the *agreste*.

Carnival here is famed throughout Brazil and is known as *Folia do*
Papangu. The Papangu characters wear masks that resemble a cross between a
bear and a devil and are covered from head to foot in a costume like a bear skin
(a variant is an all-covering white tunic). Other celebrations in the year are *São*
João in June, and Christmas.

For **tourist information** contact the *Departamento de Turismo*, Praça Duque
de Caxias 88, Centro, CEP 55660-000, T3281286, F37281316. *Associação dos*
Artesãos de Bezerros, the Artisans' Association, is at the same address.

Recife and the Northeast Coast

Caruaru

Phone code: 081
Altitude: 554 m
Colour map 2, grid B6
Population: 254,000

Situated 134 km west of Recife, the paved road there passes through rolling hills, with sugar cane and large cattle *fazendas*, before climbing an escarpment. As the road gets higher, the countryside becomes drier, browner and rockier. Caruaru itself is a busy, modern town, one of the most prosperous in the *agreste* in Pernambuco. It is also culturally very lively, with excellent local and theatre and folklore groups.

Worth a visit are the **Espaço Cultural Tancredo Neves** (known as the Forro Village), which has an exhibition space, **Museu do Barro e da Cerâmica**, which does contain works by Vitalino and other clay sculptors and **Museu da Fábrica de Caroá**, with an art gallery, music school and headquarters of the municipal tourist office. **Casa da Cultura José Condé**, in Parque 18 de Maio, contains the **Museu José Condé** and a **museum of Forró**, as well as an art gallery, the municipal library and a theatre.

The little clay figures (*figurinhas* or *bonecas de barro*) originated by Mestre Vitalino (1909-63), and very typical of the Northeast, are the local speciality; most of the local potters live at **Alto da Moura**, 6 km away, and you can visit a house – **Casa Museu Mestre Vitalino** – once owned by Vitalino, with personal objects and photographs, but no examples of his work. Unesco has

Caruaru

■ Sleeping
1 Centenário
2 Central
3 Grande São Vicente de Paulo

N
Not to scale

recognized the area as the largest centre of figurative art in the Americas. There is a bus, 30 minutes, bumpy, US$0.50.

A *Grande Hotel São Vicente de Paulo*, Av Rio Branco 365, T37215011, F37215290. Good, central, a/c, laundry, garage, bar, restaurant, pool, TV, houses the local cinema. **C** *Centenário*, 7 de Setembro 84, T37224011, F37211033. Also has more expensive suites, good breakfast, pool, in the town centre so not very quiet, otherwise recommended. **C** *Central*, R Vigario Freire 71, T37215880. Suites or rooms, all with a/c, TV, good breakfast, in the centre. Recommended.

Sleeping
■ *on map, page 454*
A large number of cheap hospedarias are around the central square, Praça Getúlio Vargas

Lots of cheap lunch restaurants (US$3-4) in the centre near *Banco do Brasil*. Recommended are *A Massa*, R Vidal de Negreiros. Excellent pizzas, reasonably priced. *Costela do Baiano*, close to Igreja do Rosário. Very good value. *Tia Teta*, Av Agamenon Magalhães. Good for dinner. For drinks, *Catracho's*, close to the São Sebastião hospital. Has a Caribbean feel and the Honduran owner mixes great cocktails with salsa. Alto da Moura is a real tourist spot so it gets very busy, but good places to eat are *Bode de Luciano*, on the left as you enter, barbecued goat. *Tengo Lengo*, 1 km up from Bode de Luciano, serves traditional Pernambucan dishes.

Eating

17 Dec-2 Jan, *Festas Natalinas*; *Semana Santa*, Holy Week, with lots of folklore and handicraft events. **18-22 May**, *city's anniversary*. **13 Jun**, *Santo Antônio* and **24 Jun** *São João*, the latter a particularly huge *forró* festival, are part of Caruaru's *Festas Juninas*. The whole town lights up with dancing, traditional foods, parties like the Sapadrilha, when the women dress as men, and the Gaydrilha, where the men dress as women, and there is even a Trem do Forró which runs from Recife to Caruaru, rocking the whole way to the rhythms. **Sep**, *Micaru*, a street carnival; also in Sep, *Vaquejada* (a Brazilian cross between rodeo and bull fighting), biggest in the Northeast.

Festivals

Caruaru is most famous for its markets which, combined, are responsible for about 70% of the city's income. The *Feira da Sulanca* is basically a clothes market supplied mostly by local manufacture, but also on sale are jewellery, souvenirs, food, flowers and anything else that can go for a good price; in one part, electronic goods are sold (this is called the *Feira de Paraguaí*, or the illegal import market). The most important day is Mon. There is also the *Feira Livre* or *do Troca-Troca* (free, or barter market). On the same site, Parque 18 de Maio, is the *Feira do Artesanato*, leather goods, ceramics, hammocks and basketware, all the popular crafts of the region; it is tourist-oriented but it is on a grand scale and is open daily 0800-1800.

Shopping

The rodoviária is 4 km from the town; buses from Recife stop in the town centre. Alight here and look for the *Livraria Estudantil* on the corner of Vigário Freire and R Anna de Albuquerque Galvão. Go down Galvão, turn right on R 15 de Novembro to the 1st junction, 13 de Maio; turn left, cross the river to the Feira do Artesanato. Bus from the centre, at the same place as Recife bus stop, to rodoviária, US$0.40. Many buses from TIP in **Recife**, 2 hrs express, US$3. Bus to **Maceió**, 0700, 5 hrs, US$9. Bus to **Fazenda Nova** 1030, 1 hr, US$2, returns for Caruaru 1330.

Transport

Banks *Banca Terceiro Mundo*, a magazine stall which exchanges dollars, in front of the new Cathedral, will tell you what's going on. **Cultural centres** *Cultura Inglesa*, Av Agamenon Magalhães 634, Maurício de Nassau, CEP 55000-000, T37214749, cultura@netstage.com.br, will help any visitors with information. **Useful information** The local *Vanguarda* newspaper, is weekly.

Directory

Recife and the Northeast Coast

São João and the Festas Juninas

As well as the Brazilian equivalent to Valentine's Day falling on 12 June, St John is one of the three saints homaged in the Festas Juninas (June Festivals). The first official party on the Brazilian calendar after Lent, these winter celebrations take up the month of June with the main celebration on the eve of St John's Day, 23 June. Potential visitors to Brazil with a fear of fireworks should take note: this is when the streets of northeastern cities fill with stalls offering their bangers, catherine wheels and rockets.

In June, the rural areas of Brazil provide the entertainment. The region's many maize-based recipes such as pamonha and canjica are traditionally eaten and washed down with a drink known as quentão, pinga heated with cloves and cinnamon. The cities of Caruaru, Pernambuco and Campina Grande, Paraíba have built up a reputation for staging the wildest parties, with a million people descending on Caruaru. The Pernambucan town possesses a 'Forró Village', a full mock-up of a Sertão town complete with a bank and a post office which are fully functional throughout the festivities. The most exciting way to arrive must surely be the 'forró trains' from Recife's central station to Caruaru, which promise live forró trios to entertain the passengers. Brazil's biggest forró bands and singers perform in all the major cities. The festival will always be the best setting to hear the music of Forró king, Luiz Gonzaga, who died in 1989 but whose classic São João song, 'Olha pro Céu' (Look to the Sky), is sung to this day. Gonzaga tells of falling for a girl at a São João party and, in the song, he tells her to look to the sky... purely for her to admire the fireworks, of course.

Fazenda Nova & Nova Jerusalém During Easter Week each year, various agencies run package tours to the little country town of Fazenda Nova, 23 km from Caruaru. Just outside the town is Nova Jerusalém, where, from the day before Palm Sunday up to Easter Saturday, an annual passion play, suggested by Oberammergau, is enacted. The site is one third the size of the historic quarter of Jerusalem, with nine permanent stages on which scenes of the Passion are presented; 50 actors and 500 extras re-enact the story. The latest sound and lighting effects are used in the performance. The audience moves from one stage to another as the story unfolds. Performances begin at 1800, lasting around three hours. Also in Fazenda Nova is a sculpture park, where gigantic figures carved from blocks of stone represent motifs of *Nordeste* culture.

Sleeping Fazenda Nova The best hotel is **E** *Grande*, Av Poeta Carlos Penha Filho, T7321137.

Garanhuns
Phone code: 081
Population: 110,000

Good roads via Caruaru or Palmares run to the city of Garanhuns, 209 km southwest of Recife. Its claims to be the best holiday resort in the Northeast are attributed to its cool climate – it stands at 890 m, and has an average temperature of 21°C – its mineral waters and its beautiful landscapes and parks.

Sleeping B *Tavares Correia*, Av Rui Barbosa 296, T37610900, F37611597. 4-star. **C** *D'Nyl*, Praça Dom Moura 302, T/F37610998. Telephone, TV, minibar, breakfast included, also serves optional dinner. **C** *Village*, Av Santo Antônio 149A, T37613624. Central, 15 mins' walk from rodoviária, good, bath, fridge, TV, fan (cheaper than a/c). **D** *Diplomata*, R Dr Jose Mariano 194. Telephone, shower, TV, minibar, breakfast included. **Camping** *Camping Treze*, BR-432, Km 105.

About 126 km west of Caruaru (bus 2½ hours, US$6) is Arcoverde, a market **Arcoverde**
town in the Sertão, with a market every Saturday; it is cool at night. There are
various hotels (**C-D**).

About 200 km west of Arcoverde, via Serra Talhada, is this delightful small **Triúnfo**
town in the Serra de Borborema. It has a good climate and a great variety of *Colour map 2, grid B5*
crops, flowers and fruits. There is a sugar mill, **Engenho Boa Esperança**, that *Phone code: 081*
can be visited, and waterfalls, for example at **Cachoeira do Pingas**, 6 km away *Population: 15,000*
(signposted); if there has been no rain the waterfalls may be dry, so ask before
setting off. You can also see the convent of **São Boaventura**, and the **Museu
do Cangaço**, which has exhibits on the lives and relics of the traditional bandits of the *Nordeste*.

Sleeping and eating **C** *Fazenda Calugi*, Estr Santa Tereza, T38461183. TV, pool,
minibar, breakfast. Recommended. **D** *Lar Santa Elizabeth*, opposite church on hill near
rodoviária, T38461236. The sisters offer lodging and profits support social work, good,
bath, fan, balcony, clean, patio. **D** *Pousada Baixa Verde*, R Manoel Paiva dos Santos
114, T/F38461103. Nice rooms, good breakfast.

Transport 2 *Progresso* buses daily to and from **Recife** (10 hrs). It is quicker to take a bus
from Recife to Serra Talhada, then a colectivo to Triunfo (US$2). In Truinfo colectivos
leave from the lakeside. To Triúnfo from **Caruaru**, 1 bus per day, 0830, US$10.

The Sertão

Beyond Serra Talhada the BR-232 continues to Salgueiro, where it meets the
BR-116 heading north to Fortaleza. The BR-232 becomes the BR-316 and
heads northwest to Araripina before entering Piauí. This part of Pernambuco
was the haunt of the bandit Lampião until his death in 1938. Even today the
area is still quite lawless and buses are often escorted by armed police. Also
cultivation of marijuana in the area between Salgueiro and Floresta means
that visitors are not generally welcome.

Located on the Rio São Francisco which forms the southern border of **Petrolina**
Pernambuco, Petrolina is best visited from Juazeiro in Bahia (see page 418). *Phone code: 081*
Like Pirapora, Petrolina is famous for the production of *carrancas* (boat fig- *Population: 173,500*
ureheads, mostly grotesque) of wood or ceramic. Petrolina has its own airport
and close to this is the small **Museu do Sertão**, with relics of rural life in the
Northeast and the age of the *coronéis* and the bandit Lampião (see page 488).

Sleeping **C** *Hotel Neuman*, Av Souza Filho 444, T9610595, overpriced, small room,
bath, a/c, clean). **D** *Pousada da Carranca*, BR-122, Km 4, T9613421. *Hotel Central* is
not recommended.

Fernando de Noronha

Sometimes called Fernando de Loronha, this small archipelago, 345 km off the *Phone code: 081*
northeast coast, was declared a Marine National Park in 1988. The only inhab-
ited island is dominated by a 321-m peak and has many unspoilt beaches and
interesting wildlife, especially in the waters that surround it. The scuba-diving
and snorkelling are both excellent.

Recife and the Northeast Coast

The islands were discovered in 1503 by Amérigo Vespucci and were for a time a pirate lair. In 1738 the Portuguese built the Forte dos Remédios (later used as a prison), and a church to strengthen their claim to the islands. Remains of the early fortifications still exist. One of the more famous prisoners in the 20th century was Luis Carlos Prestes, who led the famous long march, the Prestes Column, in 1925-27.

Vila dos Remédios, near the north coast, is where most people live and socialize. At the northeast end is Baía de Santo Antônio, which has a jetty. Some of the beaches on this side are Conceição, Boldró, Americano, Bode, Baía dos Porcos (a beautiful cove at the beginning of the marine park) and Baía do Sancho. Beyond is the Baía dos Golfinhos, with a lookout point for watching the spinner dolphins in the bay. On the south, or windward side, there are fewer beaches (for example Praia do Leão, Baía do Sueste, Atalaia), higher cliffs and the whole coastline and offshore islands are part of the marine park. As with dive sites, Ibama restricts bathing in low-tide pools and other sensitive areas to protect the environment.

Ibama has imposed rigorous rules to prevent damage to the nature reserve and everything, from development to cultivation of food crops to fishing, is strictly administered, if not forbidden. Many locals are now dependent on tourism and most food is brought from the mainland; prices are about double. Entry to the island has been limited to 100 tourists per day because of the serious problems of energy and water supply. A maximum of 420 tourists is allowed on the island at any one time. Moreover, there is a tax of US$13, payable per day for the first week of your stay. In the second week the tax increases each day. Take sufficient *reais* as dollars are heavily discounted. For information, contact the park office, Paranamar-FN, T6191210.

The rains are from February to July; the island turns green and the seawater becomes lovely and clear. The dry season is August to March, but the sun shines all year round. The time is one hour later than Brazilian Standard Time. Repellent is not available for the many mosquitoes.

Recife and the Northeast Coast

Fernando de Noronha

Essentials

L *Pousada Esmeralda*, T/F36191355. The only establishment classified as a hotel, rates **Sleeping** are full board, it is none too comfortable, its location used to be an airbase, packages from mainland travel agents usually place visitors in the *Esmeralda*. **B** *Estrela do Mar*, T36191366. With breakfast, excursions arranged. Independent travellers can go much cheaper as many local families rent out rooms with full board, from US$50 per person per day. The best known is that of Suzanna and Rocha, T36191227, rooms with fan and bathroom. Vanilda across the street has been highly recommended. There are plenty of others and the home owners have an association, *Associação das Hospedarias Domiciliares de Fernando de Noronha*, T36191142 for information.

There are 3 restaurants, *Anatalício*, *Ecológico* and *Miramar*. The speciality of the island **Eating** is shark (*tubarão*), which is served in bars and at the port (Noronha Pesca Oceânica). There aren't many bars, but a good one is *Mirante Bar*, near the hotel, with a spectacular view over Boldró beach, it has loud music and at night is an open-air disco.

Scuba-diving is organized by *Atlantis Divers*, T6191371, *Águas Claras*, T36191225, in **Sport** the hotel grounds, and *Noronha Divers*, T36191112. Diving costs between US$50-75 and equipment rental from US$50. This is the diving mecca for Brazilian divers with a great variety of sites to explore and fish to see. Further details will be found in the Adventure sports, page 61. Enquire in advance if it is possible to swim with the dolphins at the Baía dos Golfinhos. If it is not allowed they can be seen from the beach. Similarly, sharks and turtles can be seen without entering the water. For details on the turtles, contact Fundação Pró-Tamar, Caixa Postal 50, CEP 53990-000, Fernando de Noronha, T36191269, F6191386.

Boat trips and jeep tours around the island are available; it is also possible to hire a **Tour** beach buggy (US$100 a day without a driver, US$30 with driver) or a motorbike can be **operators** rented for US$80 a day. You can hitch everywhere as everyone stops. There are good hiking, horse riding and mountain biking possibilities, but you must either go with a guide or ranger in many parts.

Air Daily flights from Recife, with Nordeste and Transporte Regional do Interior **Transport** Paulista and with the latter from Natal, 1 hr 20 mins from Recife, 1 hr from Natal, US$400 and US$300 return respectively.

Paraíba

This state has a historic and pleasant capital with a rich cultural heritage. There are some wonderful beaches beside the turquoise waters of the Atlantic Ocean. The most easterly point in Brazil is to be found at Ponta das Seixas. Inland, the town of Campina Grande on the edge of the dry Sertão, is famous for its very lively São João celebrations in June.

The Portuguese did not gain a foothold on this part of the northeast coast until the very end of the 16th century. Their fort grew into the city of Filipéia (the third in Brazil), renamed Parahyba, then João Pessoa.

The dense tropical forest which once covered the coastal strip now only survives in patches. The seaboard is marked for much of its length by offshore reefs. Inland from the coastal plain the *Zona da Mata* is an abrupt line of hills

Recife and the Northeast Coast

and plateaus, a transitional region between the moist coast and the much drier interior. Most people live in this zone, especially in and around the state capital and a couple of other industrial centres.

João Pessoa

Phone code: 083
Colour map 2, grid B6
Population: 598,000

It is a bus ride of two hours through sugar plantations over a good road from Recife (126 km) to João Pessoa, the state capital, on the Rio Paraíba. It retains a small town atmosphere.

Sights

Founded in 1585 as Nossa Senhora das Neves, it became Friederikstaadt during the Dutch occupation (1634-54) and was only given its current name in 1930 in memory of a governor who was killed in Recife.

The well preserved **Centro Histórico** has several churches and monasteries which are worth seeing. The São Francisco Cultural Centre (Praça São Francisco 221), one of the most important baroque structures in Brazil, includes the beautiful 16th-century church of **São Francisco** and the Convento de Santo Antônio, which houses the **Museu Sacro e de Arte Popular**, with a magnificent collection of colonial and popular artefacts. ■ *0800-1100 Tue-Sat, 1400-1700 Tue-Sun, T2212840.* This is also the best point to see the sun set over the forest.

Other tourist points include the **Casa da Pólvora**, an old gunpowder store which has become the city museum, and **Museu Fotográfico Walfredo Rodríguez**, Ladeira de São Francisco. ■ *0800-1200 and 1330-1700 Mon-Fri.* The **Teatro Santa Roza** at Praça Pedro Américo, Varadouro, was built in 1886 with a wooden ceiling and walls. ■ *1400-1800 Mon-Fri, T2411230.* The **Espaço Cultural José Lins de Rego**, Rua Abdias Gomes de Almeida 800, Tambauzinho, a cultural centre named after the novelist (see Literature, page 693), includes an art gallery, history and science museums, several theatres, cinema and a planetarium. ■ *T2441360.* The **Fundação José Américo de Almeida**, Avenida Cabo Branco 3336, Cabo Branco, should be visited by those interested in modern literature and politics; it is in the former house of the novelist and sociologist.

João Pessoa prides itself in being a green city and is called **Cidade Verde**. Its parks include the 17-ha **Parque Arruda Câmara**, also known as Bica, located north of the centre in the neighbourhood of Roger; it has walking trails, an 18th-century fountain, an aviary and a small zoo. **Parque Solon de Lucena** or **Lagoa** is a lake surrounded by impressive palms in the centre of town, the city's main avenues and bus lines go around it. **Mata** or **Manancial do Bouraquinho** is a 471-ha nature reserve of native *mata atlântica*, one of the largest urban forest reserves in Brazil. It is located south of the centre and administered by Ibama (T2441626), which organizes guided walks; access is otherwise restricted.

Urban beaches

The beachfront stretches for some 30 km from Ponta do Seixas (south) to Cabedelo (north); the ocean is turquoise green and there is a backdrop of lush coastal vegetation. By the more populated urban areas the water is polluted, but there are also parts away from town which are reasonably clean, some spots are calm and suitable for swimming while others are best for surfing.

About 7 km from the city centre, following Avenida Presidente Epitáceo Pessoa, is the beach of **Tambaú**, which has many hotels, restaurants and the state tourism centre. The pier by *Hotel Tambaú* affords nice views (bus No 510 'Tambaú' from outside the rodoviária or the city centre, alight at *Hotel Tropical Tambaú*). South of Tambaú are Praia de Cabo Branco and Praia do Seixas and to the north are the beaches of Manaíra, Bessa, Intermares, Poço and Camboinha, before reaching the port of Cabedelo.

João Pessoa orientation

Recife and the Northeast Coast

0 km 1
0 miles 1

■ Sleeping
1 Tropical Tambaú

➤ To Airport, Campina Grande, Fortaleza & Recife

Detailed map A João Pessoa centre, page 462

The **tourist office** *PBTUR*, in Centro Turístico, Almte Tamandaré 100, Tambaú, T2470505. Also at rodoviária and airport (no telephone), all open 0800-2000. Little English spoken, basic maps.

Excursions

About 14 km from the centre, south down the coast, is the **Cabo Branco** lighthouse at Ponta do Seixas, the most easterly point of continental Brazil and South America (34° 46' 36"W) and thus the first place in the Americas where the sun rises; there is a panoramic view from the cliff top. **Cabo Branco** is much better for swimming than Tambaú. Take bus 507 'Cabo Branco' from outside the rodoviária to the end of the line; hike up to the lighthouse. At low tide you can walk from Tambaú to Ponta do Seixas in about two hours.

The port of **Cabedelo**, on a peninsula between the Rio Paraíba and the Atlantic Ocean, is 18 km north by road or rail. Here, Km 0 marks the beginning of the Transamazônica highway. At the tip of the peninsula are the impressive, but somewhat run down, walls of the 17th-century fortress of Santa Catarina, amid oil storage tanks and the commercial port. The **Mercado de Artesanato** is at Praça Getúlio Vergas, Centro.

The estuary of the Rio Paraíba has several islands; there is a regular boat service between Cabedelo and the fishing villages of **Costinha** and **Forte Velho** on the north bank; Costinha had a whaling station until the early 1980s.

The beaches between João Pessoa and Cabedelo have many bars and restaurants and are very popular with the locals on summer weekends. *Bar do Sumé*, Rua Beira Mar 171, Praia Ponta do Mato, Cabedelo, has good fish and seafood. Take bus marked Cabedelo-Poço for the beach as most Cabedelo buses go inland along the Transamazônica; taxi Tambaú-Cabedelo US$24.

At Km 3 of the Transamazônica, about 12 km from João Pessoa, is the access to **Jacaré**, a nice beach on the Rio Paraíba (take Cabedelo bus and walk

João Pessoa centre

Related map
João Pessoa
orientation, page 461

N
Not to scale

■ **Sleeping**
1 Aurora
2 Guarany
3 Pousada Fênix
4 Rio Verde

1½ km or take the train and walk 1 km, taxi from Tambaú US$10). There are several bars along the riverfront where people congregate to watch the lovely sunset to the sounds of Ravel's Bolero. Here you can hire a boat along the river to visit the mangroves or ride in an ultralight aircraft (Flaviano Gouveia, T9821604, US$19 for eight-minute ride or US$115 for an hour). Brian Ingram, originally from Kent, England, runs *Sea Tech* (PO Box 42, João Pessoa, 56001-970, T2451476, F2452302), a boat yard and frequent port of call for international yachtspeople plying the Brazilian coast.

From Tambaú tour boats leave for **Picãozinho**, a group of coral reefs about 700 m from the coast which at low tide turn into pools of crystalline water, suitable for snorkelling (US$20 per person). Further north, across from Praia de Camboinha (boats leave from here), is **Areia Vermelha**, a large sandbank surrounded by corals. This becomes exposed at low tide, around the time of the full and new moon, and is a popular bathing spot (US$20 per person tour, US$5 per person transport in a *jangada*). Floating bars are set up at both locations, travel agencies arrange trips.

Essentials

Centre **B** *Pousada dos Estrangeiros*, Alberto Falco 67 and Epitácio Pessoa, Miramar, T2264667, F2262787. Bath, a/c. **C** *Guarany*, R Almeida Barreto 181 and 13 de Maio, T/F2415005, guarany@bomguia.com.br (**D** without a/c and TV, cheaper still in low season). Pleasant, safe, extremely good value, own self service restaurant. Recommended. **D** *Aurora*, Praça João Pessoa 51, T2413238, a/c, cheaper with fan. On attractive square, pleasant enough. **D** *Ouro Preto*, Idaleto 162, T2215882, Varadouro near rodoviária. With bath, fan. Cheaper hotels can be found near the rodoviária. **G** *Pousada Fênix*, R 13 de Maio, 588, T2221193. 'Love hotel', rents rooms by hour, but very clean and a real bargain.

Tambaú **AL** *Caiçara*, Av Olinda 235, T/F2472040, caicara@zaitek.com.br Slick, business oriented, pleasant restaurant attached. **AL** *Tropical Tambaú*, Av Alm Tamandaré 229, T2473660, F2471070, reservas.tambau@tropicalhotel.com.br Enormous round building, looks like a rocket launching station and a local landmark. Motel style rooms around perimeter, comfortable, good service. Recommended. **A** *Victory Business Flat*, Av Tamandaré 310, T2451196, F2473100. Furnished apartments, pool, sauna, cheaper in low season. **A** *Royal Praia*, Coração de Jesus, T2473006, F2264346. A/c, fridge, pool. **A** *Sol-Mar*, Rui Carneiro 500, T2261350, F2263242. Pool, superb restaurant (reduced to **C** in low season). **B** *Costa Bela Praia*, Av Négo 131, T2261570. With bath, a/c, small. **B** *Tambia Praia* , R Carlos Alverga 36, T2474101. Centrally located and one block from beach, intimate, balconies with sea view. Recommended. **B** *Villa Mare Apartment Hotel*, Av Négo 707, T2262142. Apartments for 2 or 3 people, US$500-600 per month, helpful. Recommended. **E** *Pousada Mar Azul*, Av João Maurício 315, T2262660. Beachfront, clean, real bargain.

Manaíra **AL** *Ponto do Sol*, Av João Maurício 1861, T2463100, F2462782. A/c, pool, nice location (**A** low season). **A** *Gameleira*, Av João Maurício 157, T2261576, F2262360. Good breakfast, dirty, noisy at night, **C** with fan, cheaper in low season. **A** *Pousada Casa Grande*, Av Édson Ramalho 530, T2265622. A/c, fridge, pool.

Cabo Branco **L** *Littoral*, No 2172, T2471100, F2471166. Full service, luxury, low season discounts available. **AL** *Xênius*, No 1262, T2263535, F2265463. A/c, fridge (low season reductions). **A** *Veleiros*, No 3106, T/F2261332, F2261332. A/c, fridge. **B** *Escuna Praia*, No 1574, T2265611. A/c, fridge. **B** *Pouso das Águas*, No 2348, T/F2265103. Homely atmosphere, landscaped areas, pool. **B** *Pousada Casa Rosada*, No 1710, T2472470. With bath, fan, **C** with shared bath, family run. Accommodation can also be found in the outer beaches such as Camboinha and Seixas, and in Cabedelo.

Sleeping
The town's main attractions are its beaches, where most tourists stay. Hotels in the centre tend to cater to business clients

All are across from the beach, along Avenida Cabo Branco unless otherwise noted

Coconut rice with shellfish

Use condensed or dried coconut milk, or the solid concentrate available from Asian grocers. Make it up, according to the instructions, to a milky (not creamy) consistency. Quantity serves 6-8.

Ingredients:
350 g long-grain rice
50 ml olive oil
1 finely chopped medium onion
350 ml coconut milk
1 tomato, peeled, seeded and chopped
1 tbsp lime or lemon juice
2 handfuls fresh coriander, chopped
24 clams or mussels (fresh, canned or preserved in water)
Water to make the fish juice up to 350 ml

Method:
In a heavy saucepan, sauté the onion with the oil over a medium heat. When it is soft and transparent, add the rice. Stir for a few minutes until the rice is coated with oil, but not brown. Add the coconut milk with the fish water, the tomato, and some salt if needed. Bring to the boil, then reduce the heat and simmer until the rice is tender and the liquid all absorbed (about 30 minutes). Pour the lime juice over the shellfish. Five minutes before the rice has finished cooking, stir in the shellfish and herbs.

Youth hostels *Albergue de Juventude Cabo Branco*, R Padre José Tringuero 104, Cabo Branco, T2472221, F2263628, IYHA. *Albergue de Juventude Tambaú*, Bezerra Reis 83, Manaíra, T2265460. US$8 per person. Also at Av das Trincheiras, at Palácio dos Esportes, T2217220/1.

Camping *Camping Clube do Brasil*, Praia de Seixas, 13 km from the centre, T2472181.

Eating   **Centre** There are few eating options in this area. Locals eat in the stalls in Parque Solon de Lucena next to the lake, where there are a couple of simple restaurants.

Tambaú Expensive: *Adega do Alfredo*, Coração de Jesus. Excellent, popular, Portuguese. *Sagaranda*, Av Tamandaré near *Hotel Tambaú*. Very good *cozinha criativa* (similar to *nouvelle cuisine*). **Mid-range**: *Apetito Tratoria*, Osório Paes 35. Very good Italian, charming atmosphere. *Cheiro Verde*, R Carlos Alverga 43. Self service, well established, regional food. **Cheap**: Every evening on the beachfront stalls are set up selling all kinds of snacks as well as barbecued meats.

Cabo Branco *Sapore d'Italia*, Av Cabo Branco 1584, Italian, pizza. *Palhoça do Seixas*, Pescadores 43, Praia do Seixas, straw hut on the beach, past the Cabo Branco lighthouse. Seafood, meats, daytime only. *Olho de Lula*, Av Cabo Branco 2300, straw hut by the beach. Varied menu and cheap.

Bars &   There are many open bars on and across from the beach in Tambaú and Cabo Branco;
nightclubs the area known as *Feirinha de Tambaú*, on Av Tamandaré by the *Tambaú Hotel* and nearby streets, sees much movement on weekend nights, other beachfront neighbourhoods also have popular bars (see Excursions above). *Bahamas*, Av J Maurício, Tambaú, large beachfront *baracca* with live music every night. Food and music tends to be mediocre, but usually lively. *Acrópolis*, behind *Tropical Tambaú* and *Coffee33*, across the road from *Bahamas*, are the 2 liveliest nightclubs. Open 2200-0400. *Friends'*, Av J Maurício, Tambaú, has *forró* performances nightly and 4 dance floors In the centre, Praça Anthenor Navarro has been restored and is the setting for *Paraiba Cafe* , a bar with happy hour, and *Intoca*, a mix of music, entry US$2.

Festivals Pre-carnival celebrations in João Pessoa are renowned: the bloco *Acorde Miramar* opens the celebrations the Tue before *Carnival* and on Wed, known as *Quarta Feira de Fogo*, thousands join the *Muriçocas de Miramar*, forming a bloco second only to Recife's *Galo da Madrugada* with as many as 300,000 people taking part in the celebrations. The street celebrations for the patroness of the city, **Nossa Senhora das Neves**, take place for 10 days around **5 Aug**, to the rhythm of *frevo*.

Regional crafts, including lace-work, embroidery and ceramics, are available at the fol- **Shopping** lowing centres: **Mercado de Artesanato**, Centro de Turismo, Almte Tamandaré 100, Tambaú. Open daily 0800-1800. **Mercados de Artesanato Paraibano**, Av Rui Carneiro, Tambaú. Open daily 0900-1700. **Bosque dos Sonhos**, by the Cabo Branco lighthouse. Open weekends only.

Half-day city tours (US$6), day trips to Tambaba (US$8) and Recife/Oldina (US$12) **Tour operators** organized by **Vida Mansa**, T2261141. **Roger Turismo**, Av Tamandaré 229, T2471856, large agency with some English-speaking guides, range of tours. **Preocupação Zero Turismo**, Av Cabo Branco 2566, T2264859, F2264599, local and regional tours, floating bars. **Navegar**, Artur Monteiro de Paiva 97, Bessa, T/F2462191, buggy tours (US$25 to Jacumã). **Cabo Branco**, Des Souto Maior 186, Centro, T2215044, F2224023. **Comvitur**, Cecília Miranda 20, T2227200, T2411354, tours to Tambaba. **Stella Barros**, Av Epitácio Pessoa 1250, Tambauzinho, T2244989, F2251165, Thomas Cook representative.

Local Bus: all city buses stop at the rodoviária and most go by the Lagoa (Parque **Transport** Solon de Lucena). Take No 510 for Tambaú, No 507 for Cabo Branco.

Long distance Air: domestic flights arrive at Presidente Castro Pinto airport, 11 km from centre, T2321200. Flights to Recife and Rio de Janeiro. Taxi to centre costs US$8, to Tambaú US$12.

Bus: rodoviária is at R Francisco Londres, Varadouro, 10 mins from the centre, T2219611. Luggage store and PBTUR information booth, helpful. Taxi to the centre US$1.50, to Tambaú US$5.

To **Recife** with **Boa Vista** or **Bonfim**, every 30 mins, US$2.50, 2 hrs. To **Natal** with *Nordeste*, every 2 hrs, US$6*convencional*, US$7.50 *executivo*, 3 hrs. To **Fortaleza** with *Nordeste*, 2 daily, 10 hrs, US$18. To **Campina Grande** with *Real*, every 30 mins, US$4, 2 hrs. To **Juazeiro do Norte** with *Transparaíba*, 2 daily, 10 hrs, US$14. To **Salvador** with *Progresso*, 4 weekly, US$30, 14 hrs. To **Brasília** via Campina Grande, with *Planalto*, 2 weekly, US$57, 48 hrs. To **Rio de Janeiro** with *São Geraldo*, daily, US$67*convencional*, US$80 *executivo*, 42 hrs. To **São Paulo** with *Itapemirim*, daily, US$73 *convencional*, US$76 *executivo*, 47 hrs. To **Belém** with *Guanabara*, daily, US$46, 36 hrs.

Car hire: *Avis*, Av Nossa Senhora dos Navegantes, 402, T2473050. *Localiza*, Av Epitácio Pessoa 4910, T2474030, and at the airport, T0800-992000. *Tempo*, Almte Tamandaré 100, at the Centro de Turismo, T2471288.

Train: ferroviária at Av Sanhauá, Varadouro, T2214257. Regional service west to Bayeux and Santa Rita and Cabedelo to the north.

Airline offices *BRA*, Av Almirante Barroso 651, T2226222, T2442050. *TAM*, at airport, **Directory** T2322747, Av Senador Rui Carneiro 512, T2472400. *Transbrasil*, Gen Osório 177, Centro, T2412822, F2412829, freephone T080015151.*Varig*, Av Getúlio Vargas 183, Centro, T2211140, F2216580, freephone T0800-997000. *Vasp*, Parque Solon de Lucena 530, Centro, T2211140, F2223879, at airport,T2472400. **Banks** *Banco 24 horas* , Av Almirante Tamandaré, 100, in front of Centro de Turismo, Tambaú, ATM for Cirrus, Visa and MasterCard. *Banco do Brasil*, Praça 1817, 3rd floor, Centro, Isidro Gomes 14, Tambaú, behind Centro de Turismo, helpful but poor rates. *HSBC*, R Peregrino de Carvalho, 162, Centre, ATM for cirrus and visa. *Mondeo Tour*, Av Négo 46, Tambaú,

T2263100. Open 0900-1730, cash and TCs. *PB Câmbio Turismo*, Visconde de Pelotas 54C, Centro, T2214676, open Mon-Fri 1030-1630, cash and TCs. **Communications** Internet: *Cyberpointy Cafe*, Av Almirante Tamandaré, 100, in Centro Turístico Tambaú, open daily 0800-2100, US$1.60 per hr. **Post office**: main office is at Praça Pedro Américo, Varadouro; central office is at Parque Solon de Lucena 375; also by the beach at Av Rui Carneiro, behind the Centro de Turismo. **Telephones**: Calling stations at: Visconde de Pelotas and Miguel Couto, Centro; Centro de Turismo, Tambaú; Av Epitácio Pessoa 1487, Bairro dos Estados; rodoviária and Airport. **Voltage** 220 volts AC, 60 cycles.

The Paraíba Coast

The Paraíba coastline has 117 km of beautiful beaches and coves, surrounded by cliffs and coconut groves. These are among the least developed of the Northeast.

Tambaba

Colour map 2, grid B6 The best known beach of the state is Tambaba, the only official nudist beach of the Northeast and one of only two in Brazil. It is located 49 km south of João Pessoa in a lovely setting: the green ocean, warm water, natural pools for swimming formed by the rocks, cliffs up to 20 m high full of caves, palms and lush vegetation. Two coves make up this famous beach: in the first bathing-suits are optional, while the second one is only for nudists. Strict rules of conduct are enforced, unaccompanied men are not allowed in this area and any inappropriate behaviour is reason enough to be asked to leave. The only infrastructure is one bar (meals available).

Between Jacumã and Tambaba are several nice beaches such as **Tabatinga**, which has many summer homes built on the cliffs, and **Coqueirinho**, surrounded by nice vegetation, good for bathing, surfing and exploring caves.

Near the border with Pernambuco is the 10-km long beach of **Pitimbu**, see page 452.

Sleeping **B** *Pousada Corais de Carapebus*, Av Beira Mar, Carapebus, T2901179, a few kilometres
& eating south of Jacumã. With bath, pool, restaurant, nice breeze since it is located on a cliff across from the ocean. **B** *Chalé Suiço*, R Chalé Suiço 120, Tabatinga, T9812046. Small, shared bath, restaurant, upstairs rooms with balconies towards the ocean. **B** *Vivenda Ocean*, R Sidine C Dore 254, Carapebus, T2266017. Chalets for 5, restaurant. **C** *Vallhalla*, R Niterói, Jacumã, T2901015. Away from the beach, simple, fan, nice views, Swedish-run, restaurant with varied menu. *Solemar*, Jacumã, T2901032. **Camping** is possible in Tambaba with permission from the guards, also in Coqueirinho, no infrastructure in either.

Transport Access to Jacumã is via the BR-101, 20 km south from João Pessoa to where the PB-018 goes 3 km east to Conde and continues 11 km to the beach of Jacumã; from here a dirt road goes 12 km south to Tambaba. There are hourly buses from the João Pessoa rodoviária (0530-1900) to Jacumã; in the summer, dune buggies can be hired at Jacumã to go to Tambaba. Buggy from João Pessoa to Tambaba US$25 per person return (leave 0930, return 1730). Day trip in a taxi US$95.

Campina

The nicest beaches of northern Paraíba are in the vicinity of the fishing village of **Campina**; although there is little infrastructure in this area, the shore is worth a visit. Access is via a turnoff to the east at Km 73.5 of the BR-101, 42 km north of João Pessoa. It is 28 km along a dirt road (PB-025) to Praia Campina, with a wide beach of fine sand, palms and hills in the background. Nearly 3 km south is **Praia do Oiteiro**, in which the white sand stands out in contrast with the multicoloured cliffs and the calm blue ocean. About 2 km north of Campina is **Barra do Mamanguape**, where Ibama runs a centre for the preservation of the marine manatee.

Some 85 km from João Pessoa is **Baia da Traição**, a fishing village and access point for a number of beaches. Its name refers to a massacre of 500 residents of a sugar plantation in the 16th century. There is an Indian reserve near town where wood and string crafts are made. An annual festival, **Festa do Toré** (an Indian dance), takes place on 19 April. Inho, a fisherman, offers tours by sea to the more inaccessible beaches in the area (US$15 per person). **Barra de Camaratuba**, about 17 km north of Baia da Traição, is a popular surfing beach.

C *Pousada Ponto do Sol*, Dom Pedro II 537, Baia da Traição, T2961050. With bath, fridge, restaurant. On the same street are the simpler *pousadas Alvorada* and *2001*, T2961043. Several others in town. **Barra de Camaratuba C** *Pousada Porto das Ondas*, T2472054. Bath, fan, restaurant.

Sleeping & eating

The Sertão

The Transamazônica runs due west of João Pessoa as the BR-230, along the axis of the state of Paraíba and through the heart of the *sertão*.

Campina Grande

Located in the Serra da Borborema at 551 m above sea level and 130 km west of João Pessoa, the second city in Paraíba has a very pleasant climate. Known as the *porta do sertão*, it is an important centre for light industry and an outlet for goods from most of the Northeast. In the 1920s it was one of the most important cotton producing areas in the world; a decline in this industry brought a decrease in prosperity in the 1940s and 1950s and the diversification of industry to areas such as sisal and leather. The city's two universities have been instrumental in technological development and reactivation of the local economy.

Phone code: 083
Colour map 2, grid B6
Population: 340,500

Avenida Floriano Peixoto is the main street running east-west through the entire city, with Praça da Bandeira at its centre. The **Museu de Arte Assis Chateaubriand**, Parque do Açude Novo, has a collection of paintings and etchings by Brazilian artists and temporary exhibits. ■ *0900-1200 Mon-Fri, 1400-2200 Mon-Sun, T3413300.* **Museu Histórico de Campina Grande**, Avenida Floriano Peixoto 825, Centro, is the city museum housed in a 19th-century building, with a photo and artefact collection reflecting the cycles of prosperity and poverty in the region. ■ *0800-1130, 1300-1645 daily.* **Museu da História e Tecnologia do Algodão**, Centro Nacional de Produção do Algodão, Oswaldo Cruz 1143, Centenário, has machines and related equipment used in the cotton industry in the 16th and 17th centuries. ■ *0730-1130 and 1330-1730 Mon-Fri, 0800-1200 Sat-Sun, T3413608.* **Museu Regional de São João**, Largo da Estação Velha, Centro, houses a collection of objects and photographs pertaining to the June celebrations. ■ *0800-1300 daily, T3412000.*

Sights

Recife and the Northeast Coast

The **Teatro Municipal Severino Cabral**, Avenida Floreano Peixoto, is a modern theatre where there are regular performances. The main parks in town are: the **Parque do Açude Novo** (Evaldo Cruz), a green area with playgrounds, fountains and restaurants; the nearby **Parque do Povo** with its *forródromo*, where the main festivities of the city take place; and the **Açude Velho**, a park around a dam south of the centre. The **Mercado Central**, where a large roof has been built over several blocks of old buildings, has regional crafts and produce; interesting and worth a visit. The **tourist offices** are *PBTUR*, T156 for information and *DEMTUR* (Municipal), T3413993.

Excursions Some 35 km east of Campina Grande, off the road to João Pessoa, is Ingá, site of the **Pedra de Itacoatiara** archaeological centre, where inscriptions dated as 10,000 years old were found on a boulder 25 m long and 3 m high; a small museum at the site has fossils of a giant sloth and a tyrannosaurus. During the June festivities there is a train service to Itacoatiara.

The **Boqueirão** dam on the Rio Paraíba, 70 km southeast of town, is where locals flock on holidays for watersports; there is a hotel-*fazenda*, T3911233.

To the north, 46 km of Campina Grande, is **Areial**, main town of the *Brejo Paraibano*, a scenic region of green hills and valleys, with a pleasant climate, where colonial sugar *fazendas* have been transformed into hotels like *Bruxaxá* (**A**), Floriano Peixoto, T3622423, with a pool and restaurant. About 10 km north from Campina Grande is Lagoa Seca, where figures in wood and sacking are made and there is a **Museu do Índio**.

Sleeping **A** *Serrano*, Tavares Cavalcante 27, T3413131, F3210635. Luxury, pool, restaurant, dis-
Many hotels are counts for cash. **A** *Ouro Branco*, João Lourenço Porto 20, T3412929, F3225788.
clustered around Cheaper rooms available, discounts for cash. **B** *Souto Maior*, Floriano Peixoto 289,
Praça da Bandeira T3218043, F3212154. With bath, a/c, fridge. **B** *Mahatma Gandi*, Floriano Peixoto 338, T/F3215275. With bath, a/c (**C** with fan), fridge. **C** *Pérola*, Floriano Peixoto 258, T3415319. With bath, a/c, **D** with fan, parking, very good breakfast. **C** *Regente*, Barão do Abiaí 80, T3213843, F3213843. With bath, a/c (**D** with fan), fridge. **D** *Verona*, 13 de Maio 232, T3411926. With bath, fan, good value, friendly. **D** *Avenida*, Floriano Peixoto 378, T3411249. With fan, good value, cheaper with shared bath. **D** *Eliu's*, Maciel Pinheiro 31B, 1st floor, T3214115. Clean, friendly, a/c and bath (cheaper with fan, **E** without bath), good value, no breakfast. **E** *Aurora*, 7 de Setembro 120, T3214874. Shared bath, very basic, run down.

Eating R 13 de Maio by Rui Barbosa in the centre has several good restaurants including: *La Nostra Casa*, *Pizza & Cia* and *Pizzarella* for Italian; *Carne & Massa*, churrasco and by weight; *Possidônio*, varied menu; *Vila Antiga*, popular by weight, restaurant also at Maciel Pinheiro 305; *Manoel da Carne de Sol*, Félix de Araújo 263, regional specialties; *Lanchonette Casa das Frutas*, Marquês de Herval 54, good value meals, fruit juices and snacks; *La Suissa*, Dep João Tavares 663. Good savory and sweet snacks. Many bars near Parque do Povo, busy at weekends.

Festivals Campina Grande boasts the largest *São João* celebrations in Brazil; from the beginning of **Jun** into the 1st week of **Jul** the city attracts many visitors; there are bonfires and *quadrilhas* (square dance groups) in every neighbourhood; *forró* and invited artists at the Parque do Povo; *quentão*, *pomonha* and *canjica* are consumed everywhere. *Micarande*, the out-of-season Salvador-style carnival, takes place in **Apr**. In **Aug** there is an annual *Congresso de Violeiros*, which gathers singers and guitarists from all of the Nordeste.

Air Airport João Suassuna, 7 km south of centre on the road to Caruaru, T3311149. **Transport**
Daily flights to Recife with Nordeste. Taxi to airport US$7. City bus *Distrito Industrial*
from Praça Clementino Procópio, behind Cine Capitólio.

Bus Rodoviária is at Av Argemiro de Figueiredo, a 20-min ride from the centre,
T3215780. To **João Pessoa**, with *Real*, every 30 mins, US$3, 2 hrs. To **Souza** with
Transparaíba, 6 daily, US$7, 6 hrs. To **Juazeiro do Norte** with *Transparaíba*, 2 daily,
US$10, 9 hrs. To **Natal** with *Nordeste*, 0800 daily, US$6, 18 hrs. To **Rio** with *Itapemirim*,
1600 daily, US$65, 42 hrs. To **Brasília** with *Planalto*, 2 weekly, US$55, 46 hrs.

Car hire On R Tavares Cavalcante are *Intermezzo*, No 27, T3214790, F3210835.
Kelly's, No 301, T/F3224539. *Localiza*, R Dr Severino Cruz 625, T3414034, and at the airport, T3314594.

Banks *Banco do Brasil*, 7 de Setembro 52, cash and TCs at poor rates. *Mondeo* **Directory**
Tour, R Índios Cariris 308, T/F3216965, cash at good rates and TCs, Mon-Fri
1000-1600. **Communications Post office**: R Marquês do Herval, Praça da
Bandeira. **Telephone**: Floriano Peixoto 410 by Praça da Bandeira, in the industrial
district and at the rodoviária.

West of Campina Grande the landscape turns to vast, flat expanses, flanked by **Patos**
rolling hills and interesting rock formations; very scenic when green, but a sad *Population: 84,500*
sight during the prolongued *sertão* droughts. Situated 174 km from Campina
Grande is Patos, centre of a cattle ranching and cotton growing area, and an
access point for the Serra do Teixeira 28 km away, which includes Pico do
Jabre, the highest point in the state, at 1,130 m above sea level. There are various hotels and restaurants in Patos.

West of Patos by 130 km is this pleasant *sertão* town, with hot temperatures **Souza**
year-round, which is gaining fame for the nearby dinosaur tracks and prehis- *Phone code: 081*
toric rock carvings. The **Igreja do Rosário** at the Praça Matriz has paintings *Population: 59,000*
dating to the Dutch occupation of the area. It currently functions as a school.
About 3 km from the centre, atop a hill, is a statue to Frei Damião, an important religious leader of the northeast who died in 1997. Frei Damião was an
Italian friar who came to Brazil in the 1930s and stayed to become an inspiration for the faith of its most recent generation of dispossessed. He is seen very
much as belonging to the same tradition as O Conselheiro and Padre Cícero.

Fossilized dinosaur prints, of as many as 90 different species which inhabited the area between 110 and 80 million years ago, are found in a number of
sites in the Souza region. These were extensively studied by the Italian
Palaeontologist Giussepe Leonardi in the 1970s and 1980s. The **Vale dos
Dinossauros**, on the sedimentary river bed of the Rio do Peixe, is one of the
closest sites to Souza; it has some impressive Iguanodontus prints; access is
4 km from town along the road north to Uiraúna; the best time to visit is the
dry season, July to October. The area has no infrastructure and is best visited
with someone who can guide you. Contact Robson Marques of the
Movisaurio Association (Rua João Rocha 7, Souza, PB 58800-610,
T5221065), he worked with Leonardi and is very knowledgeable; or contact
the Prefeitura Municipal.

Sleeping and eating B *Gadelha Palace*, Trav Luciana Rocha 2, T5211416. With bath,
a/c, fridge, pool, restaurant. **B** *Santa Terezinha*, R Col Zé Vicente 101, T5211412. With
fan, bath, overpriced. **C** *Dormitório Sertanejo I*, R Col Zé Vicente. With bath, fan, clean,
no breakfast, good value. Recommended. **E** *Dormitório Aguiar*, R João Gualberto. Very
basic. Several restaurants on R Col Zé Vicente. *Diagonal*, Getúlio Vargas 2. Pizza.

Transport The rodoviária is 1 km from the centre, there are no city buses, walk (hot), take a moto-taxi (US$1) or a taxi (US$5). To **Campina Grande** with *Transparaíba*, 6 daily, US$7, 6 hrs. To **João Pessoa** with *Transparaíba*, 6 daily, US$10, 8 hrs. To **Juazeiro do Norte** with *Transparaíba* or *Boa Esperança*, 4 daily, US$4, 3½ hrs. To **Mossoró**, RN, with *Jardinense*, 4 daily, US$6, 4½ hrs.

Cajazeiras
Population: 51,000

Some 37 km west of Souza, the Transamazônica (BR-230) reaches Cajazeiras, centre of a cotton growing area, with an impressive looking tower on the main church and various hotels. This is an access point for the **Brejo das Freiras** thermal, mineral baths 32 km to the north, an oasis with natural springs in the middle of the *sertão, Estância Termal Brejo das Freiras.*

Sleeping **A** *Estância Termal Brejo das Freiras*, São João do Rio do Peixe, T5221515, rooms or chalets with bath, a/c, fridge, pool, restaurant. **C** *Regente*, in centre, 15 mins' walk from rodoviária, a/c, cheaper without, TV, bath. **E** *Cacique*, near rodoviária, cheaper without a/c. **Directory** There is no money exchange in Cajazeiras.

From Cajazeiras it is 17 km to the Ceará border; the Transamazônica continues west across the *sertãos* of Ceará and Piauí and on to Maranhão, Tocantins and Pará. Southwest of Cajazeiras it is 118 km to Juazeiro do Norte, an important pilgrimage centre, see page 512.

Introducing Fortaleza and the North Coast

The towering dunes around **Natal**, in Rio Grande do Norte, provide a spectacular backdrop to much of the coast as well as adrenaline-inducing buggy rides. Brazil's 'sun city' is fast becoming the North's holiday capital, with an increasing number of international visitors flocking to its beautiful beaches. Fine beaches are also to be found at **Fortaleza**, where traditional *jangadas* still sail, and at the isolated **Canoa Quebrada** and **Jericoacoara** on the coast of Ceará.

Inland lies the harsh and arid **Sertão** but there's much of cultural interest in towns such as **Juazeiro do Norte**. At Piauí there are archaeological remains in the **Capivara National Park** and the natural beauty of the **Parnaíba delta** leading to the **Lençóis Maranhenses** in Maranhão. This state, where the Northeast meets Amazônia, has historic **Alcântara** and **São Luís**, Brazil's reggae capital. The state interior also has superb mountain scenery and waterfalls around **Carolina**.

Things to do in Fortaleza

① Follow in the footsteps of the Portuguese who were enchanted by the 'beautiful bay' of Baía Formosa, a stunning 15-km stretch of sand surrounded by forest.

② Go sand skiing, tobogganing or buggy riding down sky-high sand dunes around Natal.

③ Make a pilgrimage to Juazeiro do Norte, a popular centre for religious tourism. In the Cariri region, you may witness the *bandas cabaçais ou de pífaros*, musicians and performers who join in the local traditional festivities.

④ Search for the stars at the planetarium in the state-of-the-art *Centro Cultural Dragão do Mar* in Fortaleza

⑤ Visit the prehistoric rock paintings in the UNESCO World Heritage Site of Parque Nacional de Sete Cidades. A staggering 30,000 have been found, some as much as 12,000 years old, as well as remains of extinct animals.

Rio Grande do Norte

This state is famous for its beaches and their dunes, especially around Natal. The coastline begins to change here, becoming gradually drier and less green, as it shifts from running north-south to east-west. The vast sugar cane plantations and a few remaining strands of mata atlântica (coastal forest) are replaced by the dry caatinga vegetation and caju orchards. The people are called 'Potiguares', after an Indian tribe that once resided in the state.

Like its neighbour to the south, Rio Grande do Norte was not taken into Portuguese possession until the end of the 16th century, but here the impediment was French and Indian resistance. Only after the construction of the Forte dos Reis Magos and a year-long struggle did the Portuguese prevail in 1599. The Dutch domination during 1630-50 saw the expansion of salt production, sugar cane and cattle rearing.

In the late 17th and early 18th centuries there was a rebellion by Indians against enslavement, the Confederação dos Cariris, but it was put down by troops led by *bandeirantes* (see page 198). In the mid-18th century, the Portuguese crown banned the export of salt and dried beef, which decimated the economy; it did not recover until Brazilian Independence removed the prohibition. Throughout its history, drought has been a determining factor in Rio Grande do Norte's fortunes.

Natal

Phone code: 084
Colour map 2, grid B6
Population: 713,000

The state capital, located on a peninsula between the Rio Potengi and the Atlantic Ocean is one of the most attractive cities of Brazil's northeast coast, as well as a popular destination for those seeking sun and good beaches. During World War II, the city was, somewhat bizarrely, the second largest US base outside the United States. As the most easterly point in the Americas, it was used for African airborne operations and was home to 8,000 American pilots.

Ins & outs
See also Transport, page 481

Getting there Flights arrive at Augusto Severo airport, 15 km south from centre. Taxi US$25 to centre, US$20 to Ponta Negra. Bus every 30 mins to the old rodoviária near the centre, US$0.65. Interstate buses arrive at the rodoviária, 6 km southwest of the centre. Buses from the south pass Ponta Negra first, where you can ask to be let off. Luggage store. City bus 'Cidade de Esperança Avenida 9', 'Areia Preta via Petrópolis' or 'Via Tirol' to centre. Taxi US$6 to centre, US$10 to Ponta Negra.

Getting around Unlike most Brazilian cities, in Natal you get on the bus in the front and get off at the back. The old rodoviária on Av Junqueira Aires, by Praça Augusto Severo, Ribeira, is a central point where many bus lines converge. Buses to some of the beaches near Natal also leave from here.

Tourist offices *Secretaria Estadual de Turismo (SETUR)*, Av Alfonso Pena, 1155, Tirol, T2322500. Information booths at *Centro de Turismo*, T2116149 (see Shopping, below), Av Pres Café Filho sem número, Praia dos Artistas (0800-2100 daily), Cajueiro de Pirangi, Parnamirim, T2382347 (see Excursions, below), rodoviária, T2054377 and airport, T6431811. For information T1516 or 2194216. SETUR publishes a list of prices for tourist services such as tours, taxi fares, food and drinks.

24 hours in Fortaleza

Take off to one of the city's many beaches which spread over 25 km. If you catch a bus to **Praia do Futuro** (marked 'Caça e Pesca') you will pass all the southeast beaches en route. 'Jardineira' buses leave from the centre and from Avenida Beira Mar. **Praia do Mucuripe**, is a good spot for a seaside lunch. The city's fishing is concentrated here, so as well as guaranteed fresher-than-fresh fish, you can enjoy the spectacle of the day's catch being brought in on traditional *jangada* rafts.

Visit **Praia de Iracema** for tradition of a different sort; this long-established beach resort has some historic buildings, including *Estoril*, a bar and restaurant, where you can have a drink or a snack before strolling down to the shore (**Ponte Metálica** and **Ponte dos Ingleses** are good points) to watch the sun disappear behind the water; if you are lucky, you'll see dolphins.

Head back to the city centre to join the locals in an early evening promenade when whole families walk, roller skate or cycle on **Avenida Beira Mar**, which winds along the scenic palm-fringed shore. Pause to drink in the scene with a cocktail on the beachfront and maybe stroll down to the craft fair in front of the *Imperial Othon Palace Hotel*. The *Centro Cultural Dragão do Mar* is the perfect spot for dinner and some live music; make your way to one of the beautifully restored restaurants. *Caros Amigos*, on R Dragão do Mar 22, has live music nightly at 2030.

Grab a beer at *Chopp do Bixiga*, a bustling corner bar with pavement seating, or pull up a stool on the street and order a cocktail from one of a number of makeshift carts.

Move on to one of the other many bars in this area, such as *Ritzy&Cafe*, a casual place with a mix of retro music, or try *Armazém* for a full-on nightclub with techno. For more traditional entertainment, seek out one of the *forró* establishments, home to the most popular dance). None of the city's nightspots close much before dawn, so you can watch the sunrise on the way home or even go straight back to the beach to start all over again.

Sights

No one comes to Natal for sightseeing, but the city is not without culture. The oldest part is the **Ribeira** along the riverfront where a process of renovation has been started. This can be seen on Rua Chile and in public buildings restored in vivid art-deco fashion, such as the **Teatro Alberto Maranhão** (built 1898-1904, Praça Agusto Severo, T/F2229935) and the **Prefeitura** (Rua Quintino Bocaiuva, Cidade Alta). The **Cidade Alta**, or Centro, is the main commercial centre and Avenida Rio Branco its principal artery. The main square is made up by the adjoining **praças: João Maria**, **André de Albuquerque**, **João Tibúrcio** and **7 de Setembro**. At Praça André de Albuquerque is the old cathedral (inaugurated 1599, restored 1996). The modern cathedral is on Avenida Deodoro, Cidade Alta. The church of **Santo Antônio**, Rua Santo Antônio 683, Cidade Alta, dates from 1766, and has a fine, carved wooden altar and a sacred art museum. ■ *0800-1700 Tue-Fri, 0800-1400 Sat.*

The **Museu Câmara Cascudo**, Avenida Hermes de Fonseca 1440, Tirol, has exhibits on archaeological digs, Umbanda rituals and the sugar, leather and petroleum industries. ■ *0800-1100, 1400-1600 Tue-Fri, 1000-1600 Sat. US$1.50, T2122795.*

The 16th-century **Forte dos Reis Magos** is at Praia do Forte, the tip of Natal's peninsula; between it and the city is a military installation. Walk along the beach to the fort (or to go on a tour, or by taxi), for good views. ■ *0800-1645 daily. US$1.50.*

Fortaleza and the North Coast

Museu do Mar, Avenida Dinarte Mariz (Via Costeira), Praia de Mãe Luiza, has aquariums with regional sea life and exhibits with preserved specimens. ■ *0800-1100, 1400-1700 Mon-Fri. T2154433.* At Mãe Luiza is a lighthouse with beautiful views of Natal and surrounding beaches (take a city bus marked 'Mãe Luiza' ■ *Get the key from the house next door.*

Natal

Natal orientation

To Forte dos Reis Magos

Genipabu

Rio Doce

Redinha

Igapó

Rio Potengi

Mãe Luiza

NATAL

NEÓPOLIS

Ponta Negra

Parnamirim

To Fortaleza BR 226

To Fortaleza BR 304

Rio Pirangi

To Pirangi & Búzios

To Recife BR101

Lagoa da Jiqui

Via Costeira

R Cel Flamínio

Av Praia do Forte

SANTOS REIS

Av Pres Café Filho

ROCAS

R Décio Fonseca

R Vietnam

Av Pres Café Filho

Atlantic Ocean

Port

R S João

Av Eng H Go

R Simões

Av Duque de Caxias

R S Jardim

RIBEIRA

F Gal Elicério

R Gen Gustavo Cordeiro de Farias

R Sachet

de Contorno

R V Barreto

São Tomé

Av Rio Branco

Ulisses Caldas

Praça André de Albuquerque

Santo Antônio

Cathedral

CIDADE ALTA

Padre Pinto

R S Antônio

João Pessoa

Av Princesa Isabel

R Gal Osório

R Apodi

To Alecrim

Av Deodoro

Mossoró

R Mipibu

R Traíri

Prudente de Morais

Av Hermes da Fonseca

Av Afonso Pena

To Tirol

To Airport

To Rodoviária

R do Areial

PRAIA DO MEIO

Praia do Meio

PRAIA DOS ARTISTAS

R do Motor

Dr Manoel Dantas

Av Nilo Peçanha

Getúlio Vargas

Av Hilário Peixoto

R Serido

Joaquim Fabrício

R Potengi

To Bruma Hotel & Via Costeira

To Areia Preta

To Mãe Luiza

Museu Câmara Cascudo

N

Not to scale

■ **Sleeping**   2 Natal   ● **Eating**   2 Raro Sabor
1 Casa Grande   3 Praia do Sol   1 A Macrobiótica

Fortaleza and the North Coast

Beaches

The urban beaches of Praia do Meio, Praia dos Artistas and Praia de Areia Preta have recently been cleaned up and there's a new beachside promenade. The **Via Costeira** runs south along the ocean beneath the towering sand dunes of **Parque das Dunas** (access restricted to protect the 9 km of dunes), joining the city to the neighbourhood and popular beach of **Ponta Negra**. A cycle path parallels this road and provides great views of the coastline.

Natal has excellent beaches, some of which are also the scene of the city's nightlife

East of the centre, from north to south are: Praia do Forte, do Meio, dos Artistas, de Areia Preta, Mãe Luzia, Barreira d'Água (across from Parque das Dunas) and Ponta Negra. The first two have reefs offshore, therefore little surf, and are appropiate for windsurfing. The others are urban beaches and local enquiries regarding pollution are recommended before bathing. Vibrant and pretty **Ponta Negra**, 12 km (20 minutes by bus) from the centre, is justifiably the most popular and has many hotels (see below). The northern end of the beach is good for surfing, while the southern end is calmer and suitable for swimming. At the south end of the beach **Morro do Careca** is a 120-m high dune with a sand-skiing slope surrounded by vegetation. It is crowded on weekends and holidays, but it is not safe to wander alone when deserted, as there are robberies.

Excursions

The beautiful beaches around Natal are good both for day trips and longer stays year-round. There are developed beaches with hotel and restaurant infrastructure, as well as pristine ones accessed only by foot. Those closer to Natal are built-up with beach homes and get busy during the summer holidays (December to Carnival), when dune-buggy traffic can become excessive. The coast north of the city is referred to as *Litoral Norte*, to the south is *Litoral Sul*; dune buggies are a popular way to travel here. Tours are available through travel agencies. See page 480 for details.

See also the Southern Coast and the Northern Coast, pages 482 and 484 respectively

Pirangi do Norte, 25 km south, or 30 minutes by bus from new rodoviária, is popular for watersports and has the world's largest cashew-nut tree (*cajueiro*), see page 482. A number of good beaches and attractive villages may be found along this coast. North of Natal are extensive cashew plantations. Land or boat tours of the Litoral Sul usually include a stop at Pirangi.

Boat tours on the Rio Potengi and along the nearby beaches of the Litoral Sul are available from *Albacora Azul* (T2392160, F2382204) or *Marina Badauê* (T2382066, F2382166); a two-hour tour includes hotel pick-up, a snack, and allows time for a swim, US$15 per person. Boat trips to Barra do Cunhaú, 86 km south of Natal, go through mangroves, visit an island and a salt mine (*Passeio Ecológico Cunhaú*, T2111123); see beaches below. **Fishing** for marlin, possible just 11 km from shore, is said by some to be the best in Brazil.

Ultralight flights over the Rio Potengi and sand dunes and beaches north of Natal are available for US$29 per person including hotel pick-up (Ultraleve, T9827348).

The **Centro de Lançamento da Barreira do Inferno**, launching centre for Brazil's space programme, is located 11 km south of Natal on the road to Pirangi; visits by appointment on Wednesday starting 1400, T2114799.

Fortaleza and the North Coast

Essentials

Sleeping The **Via Costeira** is a strip of enormous, upmarket beachfront hotels, which are very isolated, with no restaurants or shops within easy walking distance. **Ponta Negra** is the ideal place to stay, with its attractive beach and concentration of restaurants. Economical hotels are easier to find in the city proper but there is otherwise not much reason to stay there.

Via Costeira **L** *Ocean Paláce*, Km 11, near Ponta Negra, T2194144, F2193081. Luxury hotel, rooms and facilities of suitable standard, generally well designed with lovely ocean front pool and terrace; service very Brazilian. **AL** *Marsol* , No 1567, Km 7, Parque das Dunas, T/F2021300. 4-star (**A** in low season). **AL** *Imirá Plaza*, No 4077, T2114104, F2115722, **A** in low season. On beach, pool, tennis. Recommended.

Centre **L** *Maine*, Av Salgado Filho 1741, Lagoa Nova, T2065774, F2065707. Full service, 4-star, restaurant. **L** *Sol Potengi Natal*, Potengi 521, Petrópolis, T2113088, F2113006. Luxury suites, **AL** in low season, a/c, pool, restaurant. **A** *Natal Center*, R Santo Antônio 665, T2212355, F2212351. A/c, fridge. **B** *Casa Grande*, R Princesa Isabel 529, T2110555. 'Big house' built around family home, popular with business visitors. A/c, cheaper without bath (also low season discounts), good breakfast, pleasant, excellent value. Recommended. **B** *Oassis Swiss*, R Joaquim Fabrício 291, Casa 08, Petrópolis, T/F2022455. Swiss-owned, a/c, cheaper with fan (cheaper still in low season), pool, massive breakfasts, exceptional value. **C** *Pousada Ibérica*, R Fabrício Pedrosa 98, Petrópolis, T2022224. Fan, TV. **D** *Bom Jesús*, Av Rio Branco 384. Good value, popular. **D** *Fenícia*, Av Rio Branco 586, Centro, T2114378. (More with a/c), with breakfast and shower, English spoken, low season discount. **E** *Natal*, Av Rio Branco 740, Centro, T2222792, F2220232. Dark rooms, noisy street, a/c, cheaper with fan, basic. **E** *Pousada Marina*, at No 860, T2021677, F2023223, www.pousadamarina.com.br Simple, a/c, TV, fridge.

Near rodoviária are **B** *Pousada Esperança*, Av Capt Mor Gouveia 418, T2051955. With bath, a/c, cheaper with fan or without bath. **D** *Cidade do Sol*, Piancó 31, T2051893. With bath, a/c, cheaper with fan. **E** *Pousada Beth Shalom*, R Patos 45, T2051141. Fan, friendly.

Praia do Meio, **Praia dos Artistas** and **Praia de Areia Preta** The distinction between these first two beaches is often blurred. Most hotels here are on the beachfront Av Pres Café Filho, the numbering of which is illogical. **AL** *Porto Mirim*, Av Pres Café Filho, 68, T2024200. Large, smart, rooftop pool and deck, rooms reduced to **C** off season. **A** *Praia do Sol*, Av Pres Café Filho 750, Praia do Meio, T2114562, F2226571. Opposite beach, renovated, quiet, a/c, TV. Recommended. **A** *Reis Magos*, Av Café Filho 822, Praia do Meio, T2021991, F2023288, by the sea, **B** in low season. A/c, fridge, pool. **B** *Bruma*, No 1176, T/F2114308, www.hotelbruma@zaz.com.br Slick, intimate, beachfront balconies, pool, terrace. Recommended. **D** *Beira Mar*, Av Pres Café Filho, Praia do Meio, T2021470, motel-style, beach front, with breakfast, a/c, small pool, good value, popular. Recommended. **D** *Le Bateau*, Praia de Areia Preta, on beachfront. Helpful, good breakfast, English and French spoken. **D** *Pousada Terra do Sol*, Av Pres Café Filho, 11, Praia dos Artistas, T2114878. Noisy, arranges good Passeio de Buggy. *Papa Jerimum*, R Rodrigues Dias 445, Praia do Meio. English spoken. Recommended. **E** per person *Pousada Ponta do Morcego*, R Valentin de Almeida 10, Praia dos Artistas, T2022367. Dorm style. **F** *Pousada do Paxá*, Av Pres Café Filho, 11, T2022848, www.paxaturismo.hpg.com.br Clean, beachfront, breakfast extra, real bargain. Recommended.

Ponta Negra LL *Manary Praia*, R Francisco Gurgel 9067, T/F2192900, manary@digi.com.br Stylish, beachfront rooms and pool/terrace, member of the *Roteiro de Charme* group, see page 47. **AL** *Praia Azul Mar*, R Franscisco Gurgel, 92,

T2193555, F2194979, www.marazulpraiahotel.com.br Very nice, clients include Europeans on package holidays. **A** *Bella Napoli*, Av Erivan França 3188, T2192666. A/c (**B** in low season), fridge. **A** *Chalés Suíço*, R Luiz Esteves 2272, T2363090. Furnished cabins for up to 5 persons, **C** in low season. **A** *Hotel e Pousada O Tempo e o Vento*, R Elias Barros 66, T/F2192526, www.digicom.br/otempoeovento A/c (**B** in low season), fridge, cheaper with fan, pool, clean, *luxo* rooms are very comfortable. Recommended. **B** *Caminho do Mar*, R Des HH Gomes 365, near Ponta Negra beach, T2193363. **B** *Ingá Praia*, Av Erivan França, 17, T2193436, F2194431, www.ingapraiahotel.com.br Very comfortable, clean and cosy. Recommended. **B** *Maria Bonita 2*, Estrela do Mar 2143, T2362941, F2192726. With a/c, **C** with fan. **B** *Miramar*, Av da Praia 3398, T2362079. Family-run, very clean, Engish spoken. **B** *Ponta Negra Beach*, R Des João V da Costa 8896, T/F2193264. Pool. Recommended. **B** *Pousada do Mar*, T2362509. Pool. **C** *Pousada Porta do Sol*, R Francisco Gurgel 9057, T2362555, F2052208. TV, fridge, fan excellent breakfast, pool, beachfront, good value. Recommended. **D** *Pousada Maravista*, R da Praia, 223, T2364677, f2363402, marilymar@hotmail.com Good breakfast, English spokem, TV, fridge. **E** *Pousada Porto Seguro*, Av Pres Café Filho, 1174, T94121039. Very sociable, beachfront terrace, good rooms and good value. Warmly recommended.

Youth hostels D per person *Lua Cheia*, R Dr Manoel Augusto Bezerra de Araújo 500, Ponta Negra, T2363696, luacheia@digi.com.br, www.luacheia.com.br Outstanding, in 'castle' with 'medieval' *Taverna Pub* in basement (see *Bars and nightclubs* below). IYHA, includes breakfast. Highly recommended. *Verdes Mares*, R das Algas 2166, Conj Algamar, Ponta Negra, T2362872, F2362872. IYHA, includes breakfast, discount in low season. **E** *Ladeira do Sol*, R Valentin de Almeida 10, Praia dos Artistas, T2022647. *Meu Canto*, R Manoel Dantas 424 Petrópolis, T2113954. Highly recommended.

Camping *Camping Clube do Brasil* site at Sítio do Jiqui, Pirangi, T2172603. Expensive. Vale das Cascatas, Via Costeira Km 8.5, Ponta Negra beach. Little shade, swimming pool, leisure facilities.

Centre Expensive: *Doux France*, R Otâvio Lamartine, Petrópolis. Authentic French cuisine, outdoor seating. *Raro Sabor*, R Seridó 722, Petrópolis, T2021857. Exclusive bistro, Russian caviar on menu.

Mid-range: *Bella Napoli*, Av Hermes da Fonseca 960, Tirol. Good Italian food. *Camarões Express*, Av Sen Salgado Filho, 2234, Natal Shopping. Express prawns in 15 styles. Open for lunch only at weekends. *Thin-San*, Av Hermes da Fonseca 890, Tirol. Reasonable Chinese.

Cheap: *Bob's*, Av Sen Salgado Filho, 2234, Natal Shopping. Hamburger chain open daily 1000-2200. *A Macrobiótica*, Princesa Isabel 524, vegetarian, shop, lunch only. *Saint Antoine*, R Santo Antônio 651, Cidade Alta. Self-service by kg.

Expensive *Chaplin*, Av Pres Café Filho 27, Praia dos Artistas. Traditional, seaviews, good seafood, part of leisure complex with bar, English pub and nightclub. *Estação Trem de Minas*, Av Pres Café Filho, 197, Praia dos Artistas, T2022099. Charming rustic style, distinctly upmarket. 40 brands of *cachaça* live music nightly, terrace and cocktails. Self-service lunch and dinner. *Doux France*, R Otâvio Lamartine, Petrópolis. Very good French food.

Mid-range *Carne de Sol Benigna Lira*, R Dr José Augusto Bezerra de Medeiros 09, Praia do Meio. Traditional setting, regional cuisine. *Fiorentina*, 529, delivery T2020020, Italian pizzeria, huge range of seafood, try the lobster with spaghetti. Friendly service, 10% tax. Warmly recommended. *Peixada da Comadre*, R Dr José Augusto Bezerra de Medeiros 4, Praia dos Artistas. Specializes in seafood, popular with visitors.

Eating
Prawns feature heavily on menus here as Natal is the largest exporter of prawns in Brazil

Praia do Meio, Praia dos Artistas & Praia de Areia Preta

Fortaleza and the North Coast

Seriously cheap   For snacks, try the stalls along the beaches.

Ponta Negra   **Expensive** *Sobre Ondas*, No 14, T2194222. Seafood and international dishes, average
Street numbering is   food, underwater theme. *Tereré*, Estr de Pirangi 2316, T2194081. All-you-can-eat bar-
not logical, but all   becue, including Argentinian beef, ribs, as well as fish and salad.
restaurants are on Av
Erivan França, the
short beach road   **Mid-range** *Atlântico*, No 27, T2192762. Relaxed, warm service, semi-open air, beachfront. Portuguese-owned, Italian and Portugese dishes, fish and carne do sol.
Recommended. *Barraca do Caranguejo*, No 1180, T2195069. Live music nightly from
2100. 8 prawn dishes for US$8. *Camarões*, Av Eng Roberto Freire, 2610. Also at Natal
Shopping Centre. Touristy, but very good seafood. *Cipó Brasil*, jungle theme, 4 levels,
sand floors, lantern-lit, very atmospheric. Average food (pizzas and crepes), good for
cocktails, live music nightly after 2100. *Ponta Negra Grill*, No 20, T2193714. Large, several terraces, popular, lively. Steaks, seafood and cocktails.

Seriously cheap   Beach *baraccas* for snacks and fast food. *Ponta Negra Mall*, stalls sell
sandwiches and snacks.

Bars &   Ponta Negra beach is lively at night and the venue for a full-moon party, when there is live
nightclubs   music all night. *Aquamarina Praia*, Av Roberto Freire 22a, Ponta Negra, T2195546, pavement beachfront bar, attached to restaurant/hotel, large TV screen, open 24 hrs. *Baraonda*,
Av Erivan França, 44, Ponta Negra, T94813748. Live music nightly (closed Tue), including
swing and ambiente from 2300 to last customer. *Taverna Pub*, R Dr Maneol, A. B. de Araújo,
500, Ponta Negra, T2363696. Medieval-style pub in youth hostel basement. Eclectic (rock,
Brazilian pop, jazz, etc.) live music Tue-Sun from 2200, best night Wed. Recommended.
　　　Dance is an important pastime in Natal. The *Casa da Música Popular Brasileira* has
dancing on Fri and Sat night and Sun from 1700, very popular. Daily shows also at
Zás-Trás, R Apodi 500, Tirol, T2111444, closed Sun. The *Centro de Turismo* (see
Shopping below) has *Forró com Turista*, a chance for visitors to learn this fun dance, Thu
at 2200; many other enjoyable venues where visitors are encouraged to join in. In an
area in the centre known as Riberia, there are two popular bar/nightclubs in restored
historic buildings in Rua Chile: *Blackout B52*, No 25, T2211282, 1940s theme, best
night is 'Black Monday' and *Downtown Pub* , No 11, 4 bars, dancefloor, games area,
cybercafé, live bands Thu-Sat. *novakapital*, Av Presidente Café Filho, 872, Praia dos
Artistas, T2027111, *forró*, live music, especially rock, foam parties, US$4, from midnight.

Festivals   In **Jan** is the *Festa de Nossa Senhora dos Navegantes* when numerous vessels go to
sea from Praia da Redinha, north of town. In **mid-Oct** there is a country show, *Festa do
Boi*, bus marked Parnamirim to the exhibition centre, it gives a good insight into rural
life. **Mid-Dec** sees *Carnatal*, the Salvador-style out of season carnival, a lively 4-day
music festival with dancing in the streets.

Shopping   *Centro de Turismo*, R Aderbal de Figueiredo, 980, off R Gen Cordeiro, Petrópolis,
T2122267. A converted prison with a wide variety of handicraft shops, art gallery,
antique shop and tourist information booth, offers good view of the Rio Potengi and
the sea, open daily 0900-1900, Thu 2200. *Centro Municipal de Artesanato*, Av Pres
Café Filho, Praia dos Artistas. Daily 1000-2200. Sand-in-bottle pictures are very common in Natal. *Natal Shopping*, Av Senador Salgado Filho, 2234, between Ponta Negra
and Via Costeira. Large mall with restaurants, ATMS, cinemas and 140 shops. Free shuttle bus service to major hotels.

Tour operators   A city tour costs US$15; if it includes the northern beaches US$20-25, including southern
beaches US$30-35. Buggy tours are by far the most popular, US$35-90, depending on

the destination (3 options). *Manary Ecotours*, R Francisco Gurgel 9067, Ponta Negra, T/F2192900, manary@digi.com.br, tours to beaches and interior. *Nataltur*, Av Deodoro 424, Centro, T2110117, F2116325. *Marsol Turismo*, Av Senador Salgado Filho, 141, T2063308. *China's Turismo*, R Mossoro 574, T2221564, American Express representative.

Local Taxis are expensive compared to other cities (eg 4 times the price of Recife); US$8 for 10-min journey.

Long distance **Air**: Aeroporto Augusto Severo, Parnamirim, T6441000. Flights to Belém, Brasília, Fernando de Noronha, Fortaleza, Recife, Rio de Janeiro, Salvador and São Paulo.

Buses: rodoviária, Av Capitão Mor Gouveia 1237, Cidade da Esperança, T2054377. Regional tickets are sold on street level, interstate on the 2nd floor.

To **Recife** with *Napoles*, 5 daily, US$6.60 *convencional*, US$9 *executivo*, 4 hrs. With *Nordeste* to **Mossoró**, US$6 *convencional*, US$10 *executivo*, 4 hrs. To **Aracati**, US$7.50, 5½ hrs. To **Fortaleza**, US$11 *convencional*, US$15.50 *executivo*, US$25 *leito*, 8 hrs. To **João Pessoa**, every 2 hrs, US$4 *convencional*, US$5 *executivo*, 3 hrs. With *São Geraldo* to **Maceió**, buses both direct and via Recife, US$14 *convencional*, US$20 *executivo*, 10 hrs. To **Salvador**, US$32.50 *executivo*, 20 hrs. To **Rio de Janeiro**, US$69.65. To **São Paulo**, US$66 *convencional*, US$84 *executivo*, 46-49 hrs. With *Boa Esperança* to **Teresina**, US$26 *convencional*, US$31.25 *executivo*, 17-20 hrs. To **Belém**, US$45, 32 hrs.

Car hire: *Hertz*, airport, T6431660. *Dudu Locadora*, Av Rio Branco 420, Centro, T2117000, F2214694. *Buggy Mille*, Av Praia de Ponta Negra 8848, T2363373, F2362382. *Localiza*, Av Nascimento de Castro 1792, T2065296, or at airport, T0800-992000. *Avis*, at airport, T644 2500. Buggy tour of dunes US$, to Pipa US$115.

Airline offices *BRA*, Av Prudente de Morais, 507, Centro, T2211155, at airport, T6432068. *FLY*, Av Prudente de Morais, 3857, T2069070, at airport, T6432124. *Nordeste*, at airport, T2726814. *TAM*, Av Campos Sales, 500, Tirol, T2012020, at airport, T6431624, F2722624, freephone 0800 123100. *Transbrasil*, Av Deodoro 429, Petrópolis, T2211805, F2216025, at airportT6431135, freephone 0800 151151. *Trip*, T2341717, freephone 08002747. *Varig*, R Mossoro, 598, Centro, T2019339, F2211531, at airport,T7431100, freephone 0800 997000. *Vasp*, R João Pessoa 220, Centro, T2214453, F2213548, at airport, T6431441.

Banks Banco 24 horas, Natal Shopping, Cirrus, Visa, MasterCard and Plus. *Banco do Brasil*, Seafront ATM, Ponta Negra for Cirrus, Visa, MasterCard and Plus. Also, Av Rio Branco 510, Cidade Alta, US$ cash and TCs at poor rates, cash advances against Visa, Mon-Fri 1000-1600. *Banespa*, Av Rio Branco 704, Cidade Alta, US$ cash and TCs at *dolar turismo* rate, Mon-Fri 1000-1430. *Sunset Câmbio*, Av Hermes da Fonseca 628, Tirol, T2122552, cash and TCs, 0900-1700. *Dunas Câmbio*, Av Roberto Freire 1776, Loja B-11, Capim Macio (east of Parque das Dunas), T2193840, cash and TCs, 0900-1700.

Communications Internet: Sobre Ondas, Ponta Negra (also bar and restaurant, see above), open 0900-2400, 10 centavos 1 min. **Post office**: R Princesa Isabel 711, Centro; Av Rio Branco 538, Centro, Av Engenheiro Hildegrando de Góis 22, Ribeira, Av Praia de Ponta Negra 8920, Ponta Negra. **Poste restante** is in Ribeira, near the old rodoviária, at Av Rio Branco and Av General Gustavo Cordeiro de Farias, hard to find. **Telephone**: R Princesa Isabel 687 and R João Pessoa, Centro; Av Roberto Freire 3100, Ponta Negra, Shopping Cidade Jardim, Av Roberto Freire, Ponta Negra; and rodoviária.

Embassies and consulates *Canada*, Av Roberto Freire 2951, Bloco 01, Loja 09-CCAB Sul, Ponta Negra, T2192197. *Germany*, R Gov Sílvio Pedrosa 308, Areia Preta, T2223596. *Italy*, R Auta de Souza 275, Centro, T2226674. *Spain*, R Amintas Barros 4200, Lagoa Nova, T2065610.

Security Tourist police: *Delegacia do Turista*, T2363288, 24 hrs.

Voltage 220 volts AC, 60 cycles.

Transport
See also Ins and outs, page 474

Directory

Fortaleza and the North Coast

The Southern Coast

Rota do Sol

The *Rota do Sol/Litoral Sul* (RN-063) follows the coastline for some 55 km and is the access to beaches south of Ponta Negra (bus from Natal: Campos, in summer every 30 minutes, from both rodoviárias, US$1 to Pirangi, one hour; US$1.50 to Tabatinga, 1¼ hours). **Praia do Cotovelo**, 21 km from Natal, offers a view of the Barreira do Inferno rocket launching centre to the north. At its southern end it has some cliffs and coconut palms where camping is possible.

Pirangi do Norte, 25 km from Natal, has calm waters, is popular for watersports and offshore bathing (500 m out) when natural pools form between the reefs. Nearby is the world's largest cashew-nut tree (*cajueiro*); branches springing from a single trunk cover an area of some 7,300 sq m. From Natal (Viação Campos), US$0.60, five times a day from 0630 to 1815, three on Sunday, 0730, 0930, 1645; the snack bar by the tree has schedules of buses back to Natal. Pirangi has a lively Carnival. Lacemakers here offer good bargains for clothing and tableware.

Búzios, 35 km from Natal, has a pleasant setting with vegetation-covered dunes and coconut palms, the water is mostly calm and clear; making it good for bathing.

Barra de Tabatinga, 45 km from Natal, is surrounded by cliffs used for parasailing. Waves are strong here, making it a popular surfing beach. A new 'shark park' complete with resident biologist is its latest attraction.

Camurupim and **Barreta**, 46 and 55 km from Natal respectively, have reefs near the shore, where bathing pools form at low tide; this area has many restaurants specializing in shrimp dishes. Beyond Barreta is the long, pristine beach of **Malenbar** or **Guaraíra**, access walking or by 10-minute boat ride accross the Rio Tibau to the south end. Buggy tour from Natal US$100.

Sleeping **Cotovelo** A *Cotovelo Apart-hotel*, R Estrela D'Alva 34, T2372051. Kitchenette, pool. A *Colinas Chalés*, Estr de Pirangi, T2372168. Cabins, fridge, restaurant, pool. B *Portal do Kutuvelo*, Estr para Búzios, T2372121. Kitchen, pool. *Pousada do Francês*, R Belém do Pará, T/F2372161.

Pirangi do Norte *Chalés de Pirangi*, R Sebastião 56, T2382241, apart hotel. B *Pousada Esquina do Sol*, R Dom Bosco and Av Dep Márcio Marinho, T2382078, F2115637. Rooms and cabins for 4, no breakfast. *Posada Pirangi*, R Projetada 24. B *Pousada Vista do Atlântico*, R do Cajueiro 141, T23820778. Away from shore, upstairs rooms better ventilated, good views. Across the river in **Pirangi do Sul** B *Barreira do Sol*, Estr para Búzios, T2382230. With bath. *Enseada das Pedras*, R Pedra Grande 200, T2392240, F2392202.

Búzios B *Balneário Rio Doce*, pool, games. Highly recommended. B *Pousada da Lagosta*. Recommended. *Amaris Apart-hotel*, R Chico Mendes 10, T2068031. *Enseada de Pirambúzios*, R da Pedra Grande, T/F2116645. *Mar de Búzios*, Praia de Búzios, T2216939. B *Varandas de Búzios*, Estr Principal, T2392121. Cabins with fridge, pool, restaurant.

Camurupim *Pousada Pontal de Camurupim*, Estr de Tabatinga.

Tibau do Sul and around

Colour map 2, grid B6
Population 6,124

The lovely beaches circled by high cliffs, the lagoons, Atlantic forest and the dolphins are some of the attractions that make this one of the most visited stretches of the southern coast (it can get crowded during holiday periods and weekends).

Caju! ◀◀

CAJU! Although you may be tempted to respond "God bless you", this is not a sneeze, it is the Brazilian term for cashew. The northeastern states of Ceará and Rio Grande do Norte are the country's largest growers of this internationally prized delicacy and important export product. The municipality of Serra do Mel (RN) alone produces some 20 to 40 tonnes of cashews every year.

The cashew tree (Anacardium occidentalis) thrives in the dry soil and extreme heat of Brazil's northeast coast; being broad and bushy it provides much welcome shade. The flowers are small and unimpressive but the pungent, pepper shaped, fruits are quite remarkable in that a single large seed hangs off them, on the outside. In season, their characteristic aroma fills the warm night air.

The cashew fruit (without the seed) has an entirely unique flavour. Tangy, almost astringent, it is guaranteed to pucker even the most reserved of lips. It is commonly used to make excellent juices, ice-cream and sweets.

The cashew seed is the familiar crescent-shaped nut known throughout the world, but beware of trying some fresh off the tree, it is poisonous! Raw cashew nuts are impregnated with an irritating oil which can cause painful lesions of the mouth and lips, as well as a generalized skin reaction. The nuts are roasted to burn off this oil and kilns are scattered among the orchards. During the harvest season, their acrid black smoke may fill the air, making eyes water and everybody sneeze. CAJU!

The fishing town of Tibau do Sul is located atop a 38-m high cliff, overlooking the ocean and the scenic Lagoa Guaraíra where fishing boats are anchored; boat tours to the secluded Praia de Malenbar (see above) are available.

South of town there are fine, wide, white-sand beaches, separated by rocky headlands, set against high cliffs and coconut groves. **Praia do Madeiro** or **dos Golfinhos**, 5 km south of Tibau do Sul, has a few upmarket hotels in a very scenic setting at the top of the cliffs.

The ocean is calm and clear and dolphins can often be seen here, you have the best chance in early morning. Access to the shore is down the steps built by hotels or walking along the beach for an hour from Pipa at low tide. There are boat tours to see the dolphins from Pipa, US$5 per person.

Praia da Pipa, located 3 km further south (85 km from Natal), is popular with Brazilians and foreigners alike, for its beautiful beaches and charming restaurants. Just north of town, on a 70-m high dune, is the **Santuário Ecológico de Pipa**, a 60-ha park created in 1986 to conserve the *mata atlântica* forest; there are several trails and lookouts over the cliffs which afford an excellent view of the ocean and dolphins. ■ *0800-1600, US$3.* South of town is **Praia do Amor**, a good surfing beach, secluded by the cliffs.

Tibau do Sul A *Marinas Tibau Sul*, T/F5022323. Cabins for 4, pool, restaurant, watersports, horse riding, dock. **A** *Village Natureza*, Estr para Pipa Km 5, T/F5022325, has chalets overlooking the sea, a/c, pool, nice grounds, lovely views. **A** *Ponta do Madeiro*, Rua da Praira, Estr para Pipa Km 3, T/F5022377, has chalets with a/c, fridge, pool, restaurant, good views.

Praia da Pipa AL *Sombra e Água Fresca*, Praia do Amor, T2462376 (**A** in low season). A/c, fridge, pools, restaurant with beautiful view especially at sunset. **A** *Toca da Coruja*, T5022333. Comfortable chalets and rooms (cheaper in low season), with bath, hot water, a/c, fridge, member of the *Roteiros de Charme* group, see page 47. **A** *Hotel Pousada da Pipa*, Praia do Amor, T2462256. With bath, restaurant, pool.

Sleeping

In Pipa more than 30 pousadas and many private homes offer accommodation

Fortaleza and the North Coast

A *Marajoara*, T2462270. A/c, fridge, cheaper with fan, pool, nice views. **C** *Enseada dos Golfinhos*, R Principal s/n, T2462393. **D** *Vera-My house*, T2462295. With bath, US$5 per person in dormitory, use of kitchen, no breakfast. Good value, friendly. Recommended. **D** *Tropical*, T9832642. Good food. Recommended. **D** *Pousada da Pipa*, T2462217. Bath in room. **Camping** *Espaço Verde*, behind restaurant, T9885145, US$3 per person. Sandy lot with some shade.

Eating   **Pipa** Many restaurants along the main street. For seafood *Casarão* (good views), *Embarcação*, *O Jangadeiro* (also regional specialties), *Barraca do Ernandes* (shrimp specialities). For pizza *Caligula* and *Pipa Brasil*. *Espaço Verde*, self-service by kg. *Bocca Ratton* for soups.

Transport   **Buses** From **Natal** *Queiroz e Melo*, from new rodoviária, 0800 and 1515, to Tibau do Sul, US$3, 2 hrs. To Pipa, US$4, 2¼ hrs, return from Pipa 0500, 1600. Minivans also do this run. They are easiest to catch from the beach to Natal. Buggy tour Natal-Pipa US$115. **Bike** Rentals from *Blue Planet*, Pipa. US$5 ½ day, US$10 full day. **Buggy** Rentals, US$50 south to **Barra de Cunhaú**, US$100 to **Paraíba** border, US$80 north to **Barra de Tabatinga**.

Praia da Barra de Cunhaú   Praia da Barra de Cunhaú at the mouth of the Rio Curimataú is a 5-km wide beach with calm waters. There is a small beachcomber village by the river and some shrimp ponds. For boat tours from Natal, see Excursions above.

Sleeping **A** *Caribe Sul*, T5022624, with bath, pool and restaurant. **C** *Mirante*, T2412313, has chalets by the beach and a restaurant. There are seafood restaurants by the beach.

Baía Formosa   Pretty fishing villages dot the coast in southern Rio Grande do Norte and northern Paraíba, many of which are difficult to reach. One of the most popular is Baía Formosa, in a bay surrounded by forest. Its name 'beautiful bay' was given by the Portuguese who were charmed by the area. The 15-km long beach, interrupted periodically by reddish outcrops of rock, is popular with surfers. Bus from Natal: *Queiroz e Melo*, from the new rodoviária, US$3, 2½ hours.

South of Baía Formosa is **Sagi**, an isolated beach just before the state border, with coconut groves and small dunes, reached only by foot or dune buggy.

Sleeping and eating **B** *Pousada Sonho Meu*, R Dr Manuel Francisco de Melo 143, T9821704. With bath, a/c, fridge, restaurant. Several fish restaurants including *Elila* at Praça da Conceição.

The Northern Coast

The coast north of Natal is known for its many impressive, light-coloured sand dunes, some reaching a staggering 50 m in height. Fixed dunes are protected and should not be disturbed, but shifting dunes are popularly used for thrilling buggy rides, while those encroaching on the edge of a lake or the ocean are favourites for scenic tobogganing trips.

Redinha   A 25-minute ferry crossing on the Rio Potengi, or a 16-km drive along the *Rota*
Colour map 2, grid B6   *do Sol/Litoral Norte*, takes you from Natal to Redinha, an urban beach, with ocean and river bathing, and buggies to hire. The local delicacy is fried fish with tapioca, served at the market. About 5 km north of Redinha on a point is **Santa Rita**. From its high dunes there is a great view of the nearby coastline.

Sleeping and eating A *Atlântico Norte*, Av Litorânea, Redinha Nova, T2242002, F2242001. Luxury, a/c, fridge, pool, restaurant. **A** *Redinha Praia*, Av Litorânea, Redinha Nova, T2242130, F2242109. A/c, fridge, pool, safe, restaurant.

Transport Ferries: frequent ferry service for Redinha from Cais Tavares de Lira, Ribeira, weekdays 0530-1900, weekend and holidays 0800-1830, US$0.50 per person, US$3 for car. **Buses**: regular bus service from the old rodoviária, last bus back starting at Genipabu at 1830.

Genipabu

The best-known beach in the state, Genipabu is 30 km north of the city. Its major attractions are very scenic dunes and the Lagoa de Genipabu, a lake surrounded by cashew trees and dunes where tables are set up on a shoal in the water and drinks served. There are also many bars and restaurants on the sea shore. Buggy rental from Associação dos Bugueiros, T2252077, US$25 for dune tour, ultralight flights available.

A must for visitors to Natal

North of Genipabu, across the Rio Ceará Mirim, are several beaches with coconut groves and dunes. They have fishing villages combined with summer homes owned by people from Natal; access is via the town of Extremoz. One of these beaches, **Pitangui**, 35 km from Natal, is 6 km long and has a cristaline lake where colourful schools of fish can be seen in the water. **Jacumã**, 49 km from Natal, has a small waterfall and inland Lagoa de Jacumã, a lake surrounded by dunes where sand skiing is practised.

Muriú, 44 km from Natal, is known for its lovely green ocean where numerous small boats and *jangadas* anchor, the beach has nice palms (buggy tour from Natal, including shifting dunes US$100). About 5 km to the north is **Prainha** or **Coqueiro**, a beautiful cove with many coconut palms and strong waves.

Lovely beaches continue along the state's coastline; as you get further away from Natal the beaches are more distant from the main highways and access is more difficult. Some 83 km north of Natal, by **Touros**, centre of a coconut and lobster producing region, the coastline veers east-west.

Genipabu A *Genipabu*, Estr de Genipabu, s/n, 2 km from beach,T2252056. Marvellous views, isolated. A *Aldeia*, R Principal, Estr de Genipabu, T/F2252011. 5 luxury bungalows and a restaurant. Several *pousadas* on R da Igreja including **B** *Mar-Azul*, T2252065. With bath, fridge, restaurant. **B** *Casa de Genipabu*, on beach, T2252141. With bath, fridge, pool. **B** *Pousada Villa do Sol*, Loteamento Tabú, Quadra 09, T2252132, F2252037. With bath, restaurant, pool. **C** *Pousada do Coruja*, R Principal 100, T2252592. With fan. **C** *Tabuão*, R Principal, T2252134. Furnished bungalows, no breakfast. **E** *Pousada Porta Alberta*, on beach. Good breakfast. Several restaurants serving seafood and regional dishes on R da Igreja by the beach.

Sleeping & eating

　Pitangui **C** *Pousada Marruá*, Av Beira Mar 438, T2022404. Simple.

　Muriú *Bangalôs Muriú*, T/F2193731. Furnished chalets. Several self-service restaurants at the beach include *Guiomar* and *Marina's Muriú*.

　Touros A *Rio do Fogo*, Praia Rio do Fogo, 9 km south of town, T2215872. With bath, pool. **B** *do Gostoso*, Praia Ponta de Santo Cristo, 27 km west of town, T2214399. Chalets, restaurant. **B** *Barra do Punau*, Praia Zumbi, 27 km south of town at the mouth of the Rio Punau, T2312875. Chalets, restaurant. *Chalés de Touros*, Estr de Carnaubinha, T2113252.

Mossoró

Phone code: 084
Colour map 2, grid B6
Population: 206,000

About halfway between Natal (277 km) and Fortaleza (262 km) is the second city of Rio Grande do Norte, commercial centre for the largest salt and land-based petroleum-producing region in the country. The area also produces natural gas, cashew nuts, carnauba wax, fruits and minerals. With an average of 30°C, temperatures are high all year round.

Sights

The *Hotel Thermas Mossoró*, a resort with a hot, mineral water pool system, 10 pools, each on a terrace, with temperatures ranging from 54°C at the top to 30°C at the bottom, water-slide, spa, sports facilities, restaurant, is open to the public. ■ *0700-2300, US$14 per person.* While drilling for thermal water here in 1979 oil was struck, and this first derek in the area is still working and can be seen at the hotel.

The **Museu Histórico Lauro da Escossia**, Praça Antônio Gomes 514, Centro, has a small but interesting display, with the highlights of the region's history and an extensive photo collection relating to the *Cangaço* (see page 492). ■ *0700-1800 Tue-Fri, 0800-1100 and 1400-1700 Sat, Sun 0800-1100, free.* The Escola Superior de Agricultura de Mossoró (ESAM), which concentrates on agricultural and veterinary studies specific to semi-desert areas, runs a park, **Parque Zoobotânico Onélio Porto**, with species of the Sertão, T3215755.

Essentials

Sleeping **L** *Hotel Thermas Mossoró*, Av Lauro Monte 2001, by entrance to town from Fortaleza, T3181200, F3182344. Luxurious resort, a/c, fridge, friendly management (see above). **A** *Imperial*, R Santos Dumont 47, Centro, T3216351, F3173524. A/c, fridge, modern, very clean, restaurant. **B** *Ouro Negro*, Av do Contorno, on BR-304, near rodoviária, T/F3172070. With bath, a/c, fridge, modern, restaurant, parking, small pool. **B** *São Luiz Plaza*, R Dionísio Filgueira 125, Centro, T3216580. With bath, a/c. **B** *Scala*, R Dionísio Filgueira 220 (across from market), T3213034. With bath, a/c, **C** with fan. **D** *Zenilândia*, Praça Souza Machado 89, Centro, T3212949. With fan, bath, **E** with shared bath, breakfast not included.

Eating *Churrascaria A Gauchinha*, R Bezerra Mendes 99, Centro. Grill, closed Sun. *Drago*, Av Dix-Sept Rosado 190, Centro, Chinese. *O Severino*, R Felipe Camarão 2975 (road to Apodi, by airport). Regional specialities. *La Gôndola*, R Amaro Duarte 450, near rodoviária. Italian. *Flavio's*, Av Pres Dutra, Ilha de Santa Luzia. Varied. *Taberna D'Angelo*, R Wenceslau Braz 468, São José. Pizza.

Bars & nightclubs *Cheiro Nordestino*, R Wenceslau Braz 817, São José. Drinks and snacks, pleasant atmosphere, live music on weekends. *Acapulco's*, R Chico Linhares, quadra 7. Snacks and drinks, open Wed-Sun.

Festivals 3-13 Dec, *Santa Luzia*, 10 days of fairs and celebrations closed by a large procession; *Fest Verão* in Jan sees much movement during the local *Carnaval fora de época*.

Transport **Buses** The rodoviária is at Av do Contorno (BR-304); bus to centre 'Boa Vista' or 'Circular', US$0.50, taxi US$6. With *Nordeste* to **Natal**, US$6 *convencional*, US$10 *executivo*, 4 hrs. To **Fortaleza**, US$5, 4 daily, 4 hrs. To **Aracati**, US$2.50, 2 hrs, not all buses bound

Mossoró mix-up

It could not have been any hotter. The shimmer off the black ribbon of asphalt, known as highway BR-304, conjured up many a mirage but no relief. We were taking a bus on the long haul from Fortaleza to Recife and drinking water was in short supply. The air conditioning had failed and everybody's patience wore thin.

"Dez minutos", grumbled the driver as we lurched into the Mossoró rodoviária, still in a haze. Bathrooms ... a line-up ... a shop for água mineral ... tem não? ... another shop ... Oh my God, the bus has gone! We could see it pulling away, but our sprint and acrobatics attracted no-one's attention. Still well in sight, it accelerated along the endless BR with all our gear onboard. At the crowded Recife bus terminus it would quickly disappear.

What do we do now? A taxi, "Follow that bus!", and so we did, but the fusca (VW Beetle) was no match for the motor coach on the open highway. In an hour that seemed an eternity we managed to overtake it, only because it had made

another stop along the way. The bleary-eyed bus driver didn't even seem surprised to see us. We breathed a transient sigh of relief until the taxi driver presented us with the bill.

How much was an hour-long break-neck chase worth? How much was our luggage worth? Regardless, we didn't have enough at hand. The bus driver wanted to be on his way, the taxi driver wanted his money (or we were going back with him to visit the Mossoró jail) and we were feeling increasingly desperate when someone came forward, sweat dripping from his brow. "These estrangeiros are lost. We've passed the hat among the passengers and collected enough to pay for the cab. Let's get going!"

It would be many years before we understood the complex meaning of o jeitinho brasileiro, 'the Brazilian way' (out of any predicament), but we had certainly experienced it that day outside Mossoró, where the heat of the climate was only matched by the warmth of the people.

---

for Fortaleza will let you off at Aracati, enquire before. *Guanabara* to Recife. *São Geraldo* for main cities in the south. Several regional carriers for points in the interior.

Car hire *Yes*, Av Pres Dutra 2020, Alto de São Manoel, T3214526.

Directory **Banks** *Banco do Brasil*, Praça Dix-Sept Rosado. **Communications** Post office: Praça Rafael Fernandes. **Telephone**: Av Dix-Sept Rosado 56, Centro, national and international calls, 0730-1130 and 1330-1730.

Excursions from Mossoró

Grossos, 46 km to the north, is an Antarctic landscape in the tropical heat. As the centre of the important salt mining industry, white salt dunes extend into the horizon against the blue sky and turquoise ocean. They are very scenic and worth a visit. Official tours can be hired at *Hotel Thermas* or arranged with the different companies' headquarters in Mossoró (for example, Salina Maranhão, T3211290, Monday-Saturday); just walking around can be very interesting. Bus from Mossoró weekdays 0630 and 1330, US$1.50, leaves from near *Hotel Zenilândia*.

From Grossos a ferry crosses the Rio Mossoró (every 30 minutes, Monday-Friday 0730-1630, Saturday until 1700, Sunday until 1730, US$5 car, US$1 per person) to **Areia Branca**, the main port for salt exports and access to the Costa Branca, 42 km of beaches to the east. The area remains undeveloped for the time being, with pleasant coves and some fishermen's villages, but tourist development may not be far off. There are several places to stay in Areia Blanca.

Heroes or villains?

Were they subversives, common criminals or heroes? The debate rages on about the armed band led by Virgulino Ferreira da Silva, better known as Lampião. He is regarded by some as a Robin Hood of the Northeast, stealing from the coroneis (wealthy landowners with almost feudal powers) and urban gentry, to give to the ubiquitous poor of the Sertão. Others look on Lampião and his followers as nothing more than common criminals; looting, raping and killing as they terrorized towns in the Northeast during the 1920s and 1930s. This was the Cangaço, the reign of banditry, which inspired so much fear and fascination throughout Brazil and attracted worldwide attention.

The controversial religious leaders of the Sertão were also involved (see page 513). Lampião claimed the spiritual protection of Padre Cícero and the legacy of the Cangaço retains an unusual religious dimension. The tomb of Jararaca, for example, one of Lampião's lieutenants who was captured during the band's unsuccessful 1927 siege of Mossoró, and supposedly buried alive, is

attributed miraculous powers and has become a site of pilgrimage. Yet Jararaca is reputed to have been a ruthless killer.

There was even a middle eastern connection. Several early cinematographers from the US, Germany and France tried to film Lampião and his band, but only Lebanese-born Benjamin Abrahão was sufficiently taken into his confidence to do so. Abrahão spent almost seven months recording the day-to-day life of the cangaceiros. His footage was considered so subversive that he was subsequently murdered under mysterious circumstances and his film confiscated by the government of Getúlio Vargas. It languished in an official vault for 20 years, much of it destroyed by time and the elements.

Today the Sociedade Brasileira de Estudos do Cangaço is one of the organizations which collects data, anecdotes and artefacts from this important episode in the region's and the nation's history. It also carries on the unresolved debate as to whether the cangaceiros were really heroes or villains.

Fortaleza and the North Coast

Tibau The main beach resort for Mossoró is Tibau, 44 km to the north, just on the Ceará border, set in a lovely palm-fringed bay. A village of 5,000 inhabitants, its population swells to 35,000 during the peak vacation period between December and Carnival. The town is particularly lively in January during Mossoró's *Fest Verão* and during Carnival. The beach here is wide, with good waves and is popular for surfing. Beach homes continue to the east at Praia das Manoelas, beyond where access is by buggy to several beaches with good fishing. Ricardo Lopes, *Alibi Turismo*, T3262398, offers tours in this area and has very good photographs of the region. The local handicraft is coloured sand arrangements in bottles. Bus from Mossoró leaves near *Hotel Zenilândia*, 0630 and 1330, returns 1130 and 1630, US$1.60, 40 minutes.

Sleeping B *Dunas Praia*, Praia das Manoelas, T3262304, F3173185, is friendly and has chalets, fridge and restaurant. **B** *Leiria Mar*, Tibau, T3262541, a/c, fridge, pool, restaurant. **D** *Panorama*, Tibau, with bath, more with fan, restaurant. There are several other *pousadas* in town and many restaurants and bars along the beach.

The Sertão

The interior of Rio Grande do Norte, like that of its neighbours, is a combination of semi-desert sertão, with hilly areas covered in green vegetation and pleasant temperatures between 16°C and 25°C. The state is rich in archaeological sites and numerous caves with primitive paintings have been found.

In the mountainous south-central region of the state is **Acari**, with an 18th-century church of Nossa Senhora da Guia. It is the access point for the Serra do Bico de Arara and is 221 km from Natal and 224 km from Mossoró. South of town, in the **Seridó** area, are multicoloured cave paintings where human remains dating back 11,000 years have been discovered. About 5 km from Acari is **C** *Pousada do Gargallheiras*, Açude Marechal Dutra, with a restaurant. Some 27 km south of Acari is *Conceição Palace Hotel*, Rua Otávio Lamartine 432, Jardim do Seridó, T4722249 (one-star).

Population: 11,000

In the centre of the state, on the east shore of the Armando Rua Gonçalves dam, is **São Rafael**. The town is surrounded by granite mountains on top of which are natural waterholes of up to 3 m deep, containing countless fossils of giant fauna of the Pleistocene period. There are also rock paintings and engravings in boulders in this area.

Some 76 km southwest of Mossoró is **Apodi**, a town with colonial mansions, where people live from agriculture, ceramics and lime extraction. About 10 km from town is **Lajedo de Soledade**, a limestone shelf, 1 km wide and 2 km long which has been weathered into canyons, grottos and interesting formations. Paintings of animals and geometric figures, dated between 3,000 and 5,000 years, have been found in the caves. On the BR-405, Km 76, is *Passeio Hotel*, T3332031 (one-star). In Apodi is *Pousada Chapado*, Rua Dep Dauto Cunha 30, Apodi, T3332049, with air conditioning, fridge and a restaurant serving regional food.

Ceará

The state which has been dubbed terra da luz *(land of light) is known for its 573 km of coastline, with glorious beaches, scenic dunes and almost constant sunshine. The sophisticated city of Fortaleza is still home to traditional* jangadas, *while inland is the harsh* sertão *and several sites of natural and cultural interest such as Juazeiro de Norte.*

It was only during the period of Dutch rule that efforts were made to populate the interior of Ceará. Many Portuguese, fleeing the Dutch, moved into the *sertão* to raise cattle. Beef and leather came to typify the region. The Cearenses participated in the republican movements that flared up in the Northeast in the early 19th century, but real development did not begin until the second half of that century. Ceará was one of the foremost provinces in the drive to abolish slavery. It remains largely underdeveloped.

The ocean is warm with average temperatures of 29°C and a constant breeze makes the temperature pleasant. One third of the coast is east of Fortaleza in the *Litoral Leste* or *Costa Sol Nascente* (Sunrise Coast), which has a fair concentration of towns and fishing villages. Two thirds of the coastline is west of Fortaleza in the *Litoral Oeste* or *Costa Sol Poente* (Sunset Coast), which has some beautiful undeveloped stretches.

Fortaleza

Phone code: 085
Colour map 2, grid A5
Population: 2.1 million

The fifth largest city in Brazil and capital of the State of Ceará is a busy metropolis with many high-rise buildings, an important clothes manufacturing industry, lots of hotels and restaurants and a lively nightlife. Fishermen's jangadas *still dot the turquoise ocean across from the beach and transatlantic cruise ships call in for refuelling. The midday sun is oppressive, tempered somewhat by a constant breeze, evening temperatures can be more pleasant, especially by the sea.*

Ins & outs
See also Transport, page 498

Getting there International and domestic flights arrive at Pinto Martins airport, 6 km south of the centre. Bus 404 from the airport to Praça José de Alencar in the centre, US$0.90. Expresso Guanabara minibus runs to the rodoviária and Beira-Mar (US$1.50). Taxi to Praia de Iracema US$8 (watch out for unscrupulous drivers in both directions who claim a set fee, which will invariably be more than the metered fare). Interstate buses arrive at the rodoviária, 6 km south from the centre. No luggage store, only lockers.

Getting around The city is spread out, its main attractions are in the centre and along the seashore, transport from one to the other can take a long time. The city bus system is efficient if a little rough. Fare US$0.90; vans also charge US$0.90. The cheapest way to get to know the city is to take the *Circular 1* (anti-clockwise) or *Circular 2* (clockwise) buses which pass Av Beira-Mar, the Aldeota district, the University (UFC) and the city centre and cathedral; fare US$0.90. Alternatively, take the new *Top Bus* of Expresso Guanabara, a/c minibus starting at Av Abolição, US$1.50, T0800-991992.

Tourist offices *Setur* (*Secretaria do Turismo*), state tourism agency, main office at Centro Administrativo Virgílio Távora, Cambeba, T4883858, www.turismo.ce.gov.br,

Fortaleza

■ **Sleeping**	3 Chevalier	6 Esplanade Praia
1 Alfa Residence	4 Colonial Praia	7 Imperial Othon Palace
2 Caxambu	5 Dom Luis	8 Nordeste Palace

To Rodoviária & Airport   *BR 116 to the South & to East Coast*

N   Not to scale

freephone 0800 991516, information booths at Centro de Turismo, T4887411 in ex-municipal prison, helpful, has maps (sometimes), information about beach tours (0700-1800, Sun 0700-1200), rodoviária, T2564080 (0600-2100 daily), airport, T4771667 (24 hrs) and Museu de Fortaleza, old lighthouse, Mucuripe, T2631115 (0700-1730). *Fortur* municipal agency; main office at Av Santos Dumont 5335, Papicu, T2651177, F2653430, for information T2521444, information booths at Praça do Ferreira, Av Beira Mar (*calçado* at Praia do Meireles, very informative and friendly, several languages spoken) and at the airport, www.ceara.net

Security Tourists should avoid the Serviluz *favela* between the old lighthouse (Av Vicente de Castro), Mucuripe and Praia do Futuro; the *favela* behind the railway station; the Passeio Público at night; Av Abolição at its eastern (Nossa Senhora da Saúde church) and western ends. Generally, though, the city is safe for visitors.

Sights

Walking through the centre of Fortaleza, it is hard to ignore the city's history, which dates back to the 17th century. **Pedestrian walkways radiate from thePraça do Ferreira**, the heart of the commercial centre, and the whole area is dotted with shady green squares. **The Fortaleza Nossa Senhora da Assunção**, Avenida Alberto Nepomuceno, originally built in 1649 by the Dutch, gave the city its name. ■ *0800-1100, 1400-1700 daily. T2551600.* Near the fort, on Rua Dr João Moreira, is the 19th-century **Passeio Público** or Praça dos Mártires, a park with old trees and statues of Greek deities. West of here a neoclassical former prison (1866) houses a fine tourist centre, the **Centro de Turismo do Estado** (*Emcetur*), with museums, theatre and craft

Fortaleza and the North Coast

shops on Avenida Senador Pompeu 350, near the waterfront. ■ *Closed Sun. T0800 991516.* Further west along Rua Dr João Moreira, at **Praça Castro Carreira**, is the nicely refurbished train station **Estação João Felipe** (1880).

The **Teatro José de Alencar**, on the praça of the same name, was inaugurated in 1910. It is a magnificent iron structure imported from Scotland and decorated in neoclassical and art nouveau styles, and is worth visiting. It also houses a library and art gallery. ■ *0800-1700 Mon-Fri, hourly tours, some English-speaking guides. US$1, Wed free. T2291898.* The mausoleum of President Castelo Branco (1964-67) may be visited, it is part of the **Palácio da Abolição**, a former state government building on Avenida Barão de Studart 505. ■ *0800-1800 daily.* The **Praça dos Leões** or **Praça General Tibúrcio** on Rua Conde D'Eu has bronze lions imported from France. Around it stand the 18th-century **Palácio da Luz**, former seat of the state government, T2315699; the **Igreja Nossa Senhora do Rosário**, built by slaves in the 18th century; and the former provincial legislature, dating from 1871, which houses the Museu do Ceará (see below). The new **cathedral**, completed in 1978, in Gothic style but built in concrete, stands beside the new **Mercado Central**, with beautiful stained-glass windows on Praça da Sé, Avenida Alberto Nepomuceno.

Museums At the Centro de Turismo are the **Museu de Arte e Cultura Populares**, T2123566, which is the most interesting, and the **Museu de Minerais**. ■ *0800-1700 Mon-Fri, 0800-1400 Sat, US$0.50.*

Museu do Ceará, Rua São Paulo, next to Praça dos Leões, has displays on history and anthropology. ■ *0830-1730 Tue-Fri, 0830-1400 Sat. US$0.80. T2511502. Take bus marked 'Dom Luís'.*

Museu do Maracatu, Rufino de Alencar 231, at Teatro São José, has costumes of this ritual dance of African origin.

Museu Artur Ramos (Casa de José de Alencar), Avenida Perimetral, Messejana, 15 km from the centre, displays artefacts of African and indigenous origin collected by the anthropologist Artur Ramos, as well as documents from the writer José de Alencar, see below. ■ *0800-1200, 1400-1700 Tue-Sun, Mon 1400-1730. T2291898.*

Museu de Fortaleza, Avenida Vicente de Castro, Praia de Mucuripe, housed in a lighthouse, has photographs and artefacts relating to the city's history. There are good views of the coast and nearby beches from the top. ■ *0800-1700 Mon-Fri, 0800-1200 Sat-Sun. Free. T2631115.*

The ultra-modern **Centro Cultural Dragão do Mar**, R Dragão do Mar 81, Praia de Iracema, houses a contemporary art museum (Museu de Arte Contemporânea do Ceará), planetarium and a cultural memorial (Memorial da Cultura Cearense) with a highly recommended folk arts collection. There are also several temporary exhibitions and shows as well as cafés and bookshops. This area is very lively at night (see Entertainment below). ■ *1000-1730 Tue-Thu, 1400-2130 Fri-Sun. US$1 (free Sun). T4888600.*

Parks The main green area in the city is **Parque do Cocó**, a 446-ha park with forest and mangroves along the Rio Cocó, on Avenida Engenheiro Santana Jr and Rua Andrade Furtado, in the south of the city; there are sports fields, an amphitheatre and snack bars. Nearby on Avenida Pontes Vieira, Bairro Dionísio Torres, is **Parque Adahil Barreto**, where boat rides on the Rio Cocó can be arranged.

Urban beaches

Those beaches between Barra do Ceará (west) and Ponta do Mucuripe (east) are considered polluted and not suitable for swimming. *Jardineira* buses are a special transport service from the centre and from Avenida Beira Mar to the beaches (US$2). Various minibus day tours to beaches, $US4 and Jericoacoara, US$15; minibuses gather along seafront, also agency CPVTUR, Av Monsenhor Tabosa, 1001.

Fortaleza has 25 km of beaches, many of which are the scene of the city's nightlife

Just east of the centre is **Praia de Iracema**, one of the older beach suburbs, with some original turn-of-the-century houses. It is not much of a sunbathing beach as there is little shade or facilities and swimming is unsafe, but don't miss it at night. Of its many bars and restaurants, the *Estoril*, housed in one of the earliest buildings, has become a landmark. At the shore Ponte Metálica or Ponte dos Ingleses is a good place to see the sunset and view dolphins.

Eastern beaches

Buses to Praia do Futuro, marked 'Caça e Pesca', pass all southeast beaches en route

East of Iracema, the **Avenida Beira Mar** (Avenida Presidente Kennedy) connects Praia do Meireles (divided into Praia do Ideal, dos Diários and do Meireles proper) with Volta da Jurema and Praia do Mucuripe; it is lined with high-rise buildings and most luxury hotels are located here. A *calçado*, or walkway, following the palm-lined shore becomes a night-time playground as locals promenade on foot, roller skates, skate boards and bicycles (children ride mini-motorbikes, scooters or the 'happiness' train with its real life *Disney* characters). Take in the spectacle sipping a *agua de coco* or *caipirinha* on the beachfront where there are volleyball courts, bars, open air shows and a crafts fair in front of the *Imperial Othon Palace Hotel*.

Praia do Mucuripe, 5 km from the centre, is Fortaleza's main fishing centre, where *jangadas* (rafts with triangular sails) bring in the catch; there are many restaurants serving *peixada* and other fish specialities. The symbol of this beach is the statue of Iracema, the main character of the romance by José de Alencar (see Literature section, page 693); from the monument there is a good view of Mucuripe's port and bay. At Mucuripe Point is a lighthouse built by slaves in 1846, which houses the Museu de Fortaleza (see above). There is a lookout at the new lighthouse, good for viewing the *jangadas* which come in, in the late afternoon, and the sunset.

Praia do Futuro, 8 km southeast of the centre, is the most popular bathing beach. It is 8 km long, with strong waves, sand dunes and freshwater showers, but no natural shade. Many vendors and straw shacks serve local dishes. On Thursday nights it becomes the centre for the city's nightlife, with people enjoying live music, *forró* and crab. The south end of the beach is known as Caça e Pesca; water here is polluted because of the outflow of the Rio Cocó.

At **Praia de Sabiaguaba**, 20 km southeast of the centre, is a small fishing village known for its seafood; the area has mangroves and is good for fishing.

Some 29 km southeast of the centre is **Praia Porto das Dunas**, a pleasant beach popular for watersports including surfing. Buggies and ultralight tours can be arranged. The main attraction is **Beach Park**, the largest water park in South America, with pools, water toboggans, sports fields, restaurants. ■ *Admission US$20. Jardineira bus from centre or Av Beira Mar.*

Northwest of the centre is **Praia Barra do Ceará**, 8 km, where the Rio Ceará flows into the sea (take a Grande Circular 1 bus). Here are the ruins of the 1603 Forte de Nossa Senhora dos Prazeres, the first Portuguese settlement in the area, partially covered by dunes; with beautiful sunsets. The palm-fringed beaches west of the Rio Ceará are cleaner but have strong waves. A bridge

Western beaches

Fortaleza and the North Coast

across this river has been built, making the area more accessible and open to development, as at **Praia de Icaraí**, 22 km to the northwest, and **Tabuba**, 5 km further north.

Beyond Tabuba, **Cumbuco** is a lively beach (it can be dirty in high season) with palm trees and a number of bars. For the active, there are buggies, horse riding and jangadas as well as dunes which you can slide (known locally as *Skibunda*) down into a freshwater lake (Lagamar de Cauípe). You can also walk 5 km to Cauípe. Take the 'Jardineira' bus, US$1, 45 minutes, from Avenida Rui Barbosa next to *Ideal Clube*, Fortaleza, which passes Icaraí, Tabuba and Cambuco. Best to take 0815, 0900 or 1030 departures, returning at 1530, 1700 or 1745 (last bus), for information T2521402. The restaurant at the final bus stop has lockers, US$0.50 per day, and provides tours. Buggy tour, US$7 per person, is recommended.

Excursions

Sailing boat or yacht tours along the coast leave from Praia do Mucuripe (see Tour operators below). There are diving possibilities off the coast, including Pedra da Risca, off Mucuripe, rich in shoals of colourful fish and rays; shipwrecks across from Pecém northwest of the city and Portal de Maceió to the southeast. There are 14 dive sites along the state's coast; regular weekend outings, guides and equipment from *ASPA* or *Projeto Netuno* (see Sports below).

Train tours on the *Litorina*, a railcar, go on Saturday (0720) to **Praia da Lagoinha** to the northwest, 64 km by train to Croatá and 43 km by bus. This beach is very scenic, see page 506 for details (tour US$30).

Another train/bus combination tour on the *Litorina* goes on Sunday (0710) to the **Maciço de Baturité**, an attractive highland area with many waterfalls and much history. It is 103 km by rail to the town of Baturité, then by bus up the massif (tour, including lunch at Estância das Flores, Pacoti, US$40). Information from *Turistar* at the railway station, T2113090, F2122456, see Interior of Ceará below.

The **Serra de Maranguape** (altitude 890 m) with tropical growth and distant views back to the city, is 30 km inland from Fortaleza, with some resorts with swimming possibilities. The path to the top starts from *Pousada Serra Verde* (**B**, Sítio São José, green surroundings, nice views, at the end of a 5-km cobblestone road from the town centre). It's a two-hour walk and a rewarding climb. Frequent buses from rodoviária or from the centre, near the train station, US$3.

Another possible day trip is to the **Serra da Aratanha** (775 m) in Pacatuba, southeast of Maranguape. Passing a colonial church and *Pousada das Andreias* (**B**), it's a two-hour walk to the top through plantations of banana, mango and jack-fruit trees. There is a waterfall halfway (see the turbines from a 1980s plane crash). Near the top is a house with a pond where you should ask for permission or help to continue to the summit and the Pedra de Letreiro, with ancient inscriptions, views of metropolitan Fortaleza and a colony of vultures. Bus from rodoviária one hour, US$2.

Those interested in crafts should visit **Aquiraz**, 31 km southeast of Fortaleza, and the nearby beaches of **Prainha** (6 km north) and **Iguape** (18 km south), where craftspeople can be seen using the techniques of *bilro* and *labirinto* with amazing speed, to create beautiful lacework. Several hotels and restaurants in all these locations, see Eastern Coast below.

Essentials

LL *Ceasar Park*, Av Beira Mar 3980, Mucuripe, T2631133, F2631444. Full luxury hotel, 5-star, pool, Brazilian, French and Japanese restaurants, heliport. **L** *Imperial Othon Palace*, Av Beira Mar 2500, Meireles, T2429177, F2427777. 5-star, beach front location (recommended *feijoada* on Sat). **L** *Marina Park*, Av Pres C Branco 400, Jacarecanga, T2525253, F2531803. Huge 5-star luxury leisure complex with all facilities, modern mooring for yachts at reasonable prices, day rates available for non-residents. **L** *Seara Praia*, Av Beira Mar 3080, Meireles, T2429555, F2641666, reservas@ hotelseara.com.br Luxury 4-star, covered pool, restaurant. **AL** *Praiano Palace*, Av Beira Mar 2800, Meireles, T24293333, F2443333. 4-star, restaurant, pool. **AL** *Beira Mar*, Av Beira Mar 3130, Meireles, T2425000, F2615659. 4-star, swimming pool. **AL** *Novotel Magna*, Av Beira Mar 2380, Meireles, T2449122, F2612793. 4-star, pool, restaurant.

A *Esplanada Praia*, Av Beira Mar 200, Meireles, T2481000, F2488555, www.esplanadapraia@secrel.com.br Enormous, spacious, beachfront, somewhat isolated location, caters to business visitors. **A** *Samburá Praia*, Av Beira Mar 4530, Meireles, T2631999, F2632177. Cheaper than most beach hotels. **A** *Colonial Praia*, R Barão de Aracati 145, Iracema, T4559600, F21935011. 4-star, pleasant grounds and big pool, laundry service (10 mins' walk from Av Beira Mar). **A** *Ibis Praia*, Atualpa Barbosa de Lima 660, Iracema, T2192121, F2190000. A/c, fridge, restaurant, pool. **A** *Praia Mar*, Av Beira Mar 3190, Meireles, T/F2449455. A/c, fridge, restaurant. **A** *Pousada Jardim*, Ildefonso Albano 950, Aldeota, T2269711, F2263256, www.hoteljardim.com.br No sign outside, by Iracema beach, nice garden, excursions arranged, many languages spoken, 20% discount for owners of *Brazil Handbook*. Warmly recommended. **A** *Praia de Iracema*, Av Raimundo Giro 430, Iracema, T2542299, F2314356. A/c, fridge. **A** *Zen Praia*, Av Abolição 1894, Meireles, T2443213, F2612196. A/c, pool, restaurant. Recommended.

B *Apart-hotel Aquidabá*, Av Raimundo Girão 630, at beginning of Praia Iracema, T2319733, F2319697, 20 mins' walk from centre. With bath, pool and bar, quiet. **B** *Chevalier*, Av Duque de Caxias 465, T2314611. Fan, pleasant. **B** *Nordeste Palace*, R Assunção 99 in centre, T2211999, F2211999. Large rooms, good value. **B** *Ondas Verdes*, Av Beira Mar 934, Iracema, T2190871. Fan, TV. Recommended. **B** *Pousada Jangada da Praia*, Silva Paulet 155, Aldeota, T2612263. Near the beach, a/c, good breakfast. **C** *Abrolhos Praia*, Av Abolição, 2030, Meireles, T/F2481217, abrolhos@rotaceara.com.br Pleasant, 1 block from beach, Internet access. **C** *Alfa Residence*, Av Monsenhor Tabosa 1320, Meireles, T2482020, F2483417. 11 apartments, a/c, TV, fridge, sauna, pool. Also own apartments in 3 nearby blocks **C** *Nossa Pousada*, Av Abolição 2600, Meireles, T2614699. Without bath, near beach, helpful, has good value *churrasco*. **C** *Pousada Abril em Portugal*, Av Almte Barroso 1006, Iracema, T2199509. With bath, breakfast, fan, good value. Recommended. **C** *Pousada Central*, Av Dom Manuel 470, near Costa Barrios, T2525040, F2274640. Good value. **C** *Pousada da França D'Eloise*, Av Monsenhor Tabosa 2623, Meireles, T/F2274640. Cheaper without a/c, 5 mins from beach. **C** *Pousada da Praia*, Av Monsenhor Tabosa 1315, Iracema, 2 blocks from beach, T2485935, a/c, fridge, some rooms slightly damp, but OK. **C** *Pousada Jambo*, R Antonia Augusto 141, T2193873, T9929481 (mob). Very private, no sign, quiet street. Variety of rooms, some with kitchens at no extra cost, small pool. A/c, cheaper with fan, Swiss-run, very friendly, changes cash and travellers' cheques. Warmly recommended. **C** *Pousada Santa Maria*, Almte Barroso 617, T2444019. Laundry, kitchen, English-run. Recommended. **C** *Pousada Sol e Mar*, Av Beira Mar 3052, T2425636. Basic, family-run, above restaurant, good value for beachfront location. **C** *Pousada Vida da Praia*, José Vilar 252, in Aldeota district, T2610444, F2681243. Safe, helpful, English spoken. **C** *Pousada Village Mar e Sol*, R Idelfonso Albano 614, Praia Iracema, T2523206. With or without bath. Recommended. **C** *Villamaris* , Av Abolição, 2026, Meireles, T2483834, villamaris@fortalnet.com.br Cosy, security guard, TV, fridge, small rooftop pool, 1 block from beach.

Sleeping

■ *on map, page 490*
Price codes:
see inside front cover
Most hotels offer
reduced prices in
the low season

There is a wide range
of accommodation
and places to eat at all
the beaches closer to
the city and Cumbuco

Fortaleza and the North Coast

D *Dom Luís*, R Ildefonso Albano, 245, T/F2191321. Quiet street, small terrace/garden and bar, TV, a/c, fridge, laundry. Friendly, good value. Recommended. **D** *Pousada Kalahara*, R Raimundo Esteves 41, Praia do Futuro, T2623144, near beach. Big rooms, pool, friendly. Recommended. Several hotels along R Senador Pompeu, eg **D** *Universo*, at No 1152. Without breakfast, may rent by the bed (ie single sex clients 3 to a room), smokers not welcome, some rooms have mosquito nets. Try student houses on Av Universitários, cheap or even free.

Centre C *Big*, Gen Sampaio 485, in centre by train station, T2122066. With bath, fan, **D** with shared bath, clean, friendly, good value, caution recommended at night. **D** *Caxambu*, Gen Bezerril 22, T2262301. Central location opposite cathdral. A/c, smart for category. Good value. **D** *Passeio*, R Dr João Moreira 221, T2269640, F2536165. Opposite lovely park and Centro Turismo, homely, rooms with high ceilings, a/c or fan, good value. Recommended.

Youth hostel *Albergue de Fortaleza*, R Rocha Lima 1186, Aldeota, T2441850. Separate men and women dormitories, 1 room for couples, cheaper for members. *Coqueiro Verde*, R Frei Mansueto 531, 5 blocks from Beira-Mar, Meireles, T2671998. Dormitories, kitchen, laundry facilities.

Camping *Fortaleza Camping Club*, R Pedro Paulo Moreira 505, Parque Manibura, Água Fria, 10 km, T2732544. Many trees for shade, US$7 per person. *Barra Encantada*, Praia do Barro Preto, 42 km southeast, T2441916 (office Av Barão de Studart 2360, s 1607). US$9 per person, Camping Club members US$4 per person, see East Coast below. *Fazenda Lago das Dunas*, Uruaú (115 km southeast), T2442929. US$4 per person for Camping Club members, US$9 per person others, also rents rooms, see Beberibe, East Coast below.

Eating

At Praia de Iracema, good outdoor nightlife and a collection of cafés on the beach, serve good fast food and great coffee

Expensive Several good fish restaurants at Praia de Mucuripe, where the boats come ashore between 1300 and 1500. Recommended on Av Beira Mar, Meireles are: *Alfredo*, No 4616, and, next door, No 4632, *Peixada do Meio*. *Francés-Italiano*, Av Des Moreira 155. Good lobster. Good view of Fortaleza from *Restaurant Panorámico*, R Mirante, in Mucuripe district, near the lighthouse.

Mid-range *Amici's*, Rua Dragão do Mar, 80, T2195454, pasta, pizza and lively atmosphere in music-filled street. Evenings only. *Carneiro de Ordones*, R Azevedo Bolão 571, Parquelândia, near North Shopping. Crowded with locals at weekends for every kind of lamb dish (try *buchada*, a kind of haggis). *Caros Amigos*, R Dragão do Mar, 22, T226657, oysters and other dishes, live music. *Chopp do Bixiga* , T2197690, serves Sat *feijoada* with live Brazilian music, also a bar. *Estoril*, R dos Tabajaras 397, Iracema. Varied food, restaurant and school. *Hong Kong*, Av Beira Mar 4544, Meireles. *La Trattoria*, R dos Pacajus 125, Iracema. Good. *Mikado*, Av Barão de Studart 600, Aldeota. Japanese. *Parque Recreio*, Rui Barbosa 2727. For good *churrasco*.

Cheap *Churrascaria Picanha de Veras*, R Carlos Vasconcelos 660, Adoleta, good for chicken. *Dom Pastel*, R Carlos Vasconcelos 996, Adoleta, pay-by-weight. R Julo Ibiapina, this street in Meireles, 1 block behind beach has pizzerias, fast-food restaurants and sushi bars. *Tropical* ice-cream parlour, several branches, try *murici*, *cajá* and other northeast flavours.

Seriously cheap *Casa Nossa*, Barão de Aracati, adjacent to *Holiday Inn*, self-service (lunch only), part-covered courtyard, where the locals eat, excellent value. Recommended. *Habib*, Antônio Justa Abolição, corner with Av Barão de Studart. Bustling, modern middle-eastern fast-food restaurant, excellent service. Bargain set menus, eg *kibe* (meatball), chips and *suco*, US$1, pizza, *tabule*, good deserts. Highly recommended. One block east, *Ideal*, Antônio Justa Abolição, supermarket/lanchonette, sandwiches, breakfast.

Praia do Futuro *Sandras*, Av Engenheiro Luís Vieirra 555. Lobster has been recommended.

Centre Expensive: Emcetur restaurant, *Xadrez*, in the old prison, good atmosphere, overpriced, open to 2400, safe to 2100. **Cheap**: Several options around and in the railway station. *Alivita*, Barão do Rio Branco 1486. Good for fish and vegetarian, lunch only, Mon-Fri. *Fonte de Saúde*, R Pedro 339. Excellent vegetarian food, sold by weight, and a wide range of fruit juices.

Some of the best areas for entertainment, with many bars and restaurants are: the Av Beira Mar, Praia de Iracema, the hill above Praia de Mucuripe and Av Dom Luís. The streets around Centro Cultural Dragão do Mar on R Dragão do Mar are lively every night of the week. Brightly painted, historic buildings house restaurants where musicians play to customers on their terraces and the pavements are dotted with cocktail carts. The cultural centre hosts free concerts some nights, pick up a copy of the month's events. *Caros Amigos*, R Dragão do Mar, 22, T226657. Live music at 2030: Tue, Brazilian instrumental; Wed, Jazz; Thu, samba; Sun, Beatles covers, $US1. *Chopp do Bixiga* , T2197690 lively outdoor corner bar. Clubs here include *Armaz*ém, Av Almirante Barroso, 444, T2194322, techno, free entry; Fri and Sat US$4. *Ritzy&Cafe*, mix of retro music, US$2. Some recommended bars: *Mucuripe Club*, on Av Beira Mar, popular. *Espaço Cultural Diogo Fontenelle*, R Gustavo Sampaio 151, art gallery and bar with live music.

Bars & nightclubs
Fortaleza is renowned for its nightlife and prides itself with having the liveliest Monday night in the country

Forró is the most popular dance and there is a tradition to visit certain establishments on specific nights. **Monday** *Forró* is danced at the *Pirata Bar*, US$5, open-air theme bar, from 2300, and other establishments along R dos Tabajaras and its surroundings, at Praia de Iracema. **Tuesday** Music and comedy at *Subindo ao Céu*, Praia do Futuro. Live golden oldies at *Boate Oásis*, Av Santos Dumont 6061, Aldeota. **Wednesday** Regional music and samba-reggae at *Clube do Vaqueiro*, city bypass, Km 14, by BR-116 south and E-020, at 2230. **Thursday** Live music, shows and crab specialities at the beach shacks in Praia do Futuro, *Chico do Caranguejo*, lively bar. Recommended. **Friday** Singers and bands play regional music at *Parque do Vaqueiro*, BR-020, Km 10, past city bypass. **Saturday** *Forró* at *Parque Valeu Boi*, R Trezópolis, Cajueiro Torto, *Forró Três Amores*, Estrado Tapuio, Euzébio and *Cantinho do Céu*, CE-04, Km 8. **Sunday** *Forró* and *música sertaneja* at *Cajueiro Drinks*, BR-116, Km 20, Euzébio.

Cinema For information about cinema programming, T139. **Theatre** In the centre are *Teatro José de Alencar*, Praça José de Alencar (see Sights above), and *Teatro São José*, R Rufino de Alencar 363, T2315447, both with shows all year.

Entertainment

6 Jan, *Epiphany*; Ash Wednesday. 19 Mar, *São José*; Christmas Eve; New Year's Eve, half-day.

Festivals

A festival, the *Regata Dragão do Mar*, takes place at Praia de Mucuripe on the last Sun in **Jul**, during which the traditional *jangada* (raft) races take place. Also during the last week of Jul, the out-of-season Salvador-style carnival, *Fortal*, takes place along Av Almte Barroso, Av Raimundo Giro and Av Beira Mar.

In Caucaia, 12 km to the southeast, a *vaquejada*, traditional rodeo and country fair, takes place during the last weekend of **Jul**.

On **15 Aug**, the local Umbanda *terreiros* (churches) celebrate the *Festival of Iemanjá* on Praia do Futuro, taking over the entire beach from noon till dusk, when offerings are cast into the surf. Well worth attending (members of the public may 'pegar um passo' – enter into an inspired religious trance – at the hands of a *pai-de-santo*). Beware of pickpockets and purse-snatchers.

Diving Diving trips (see Excursions above), lessons and equipment rental from: *ASPA (Atividades Subaquáticas e Pesquisas Ambientais)*, R Eduardo Garcia 23, s 13, Aldeota,

Sport

T2682966/9874341; or *Projeto Netuno*, R do Mirante 165, Mucuripe, T/F2633009. **Golf** The *Ceará Golf Club* has 9 holes. **Surfing** Surfing is popular on a number of Ceará beaches, including those by the towns of Paracurú and Pecém to the west of Fortaleza and Porto das Dunas to the east. *Projeto Salva Surf*, a surfers rescue service operated by the fire department, may be reached by dialling 193. **Trekking** The Fortaleza chapter of the *Trekking Club do Brasil* has walks once a month to different natural areas, visitors are welcome to join, US$20 for transport and T-shirt, T2122456. **Windsurfing** Due to constant trade winds, a number of Ceará beaches are excellent for windsurfing. Equipment can be rented in some of the more popular beaches such as Porto das Dunas and in the city from *Windclub*, Av Beira Mar 2120, Praia dos Diários, T9825449. Lessons also available.

Shopping Fortaleza has an excellent selection of locally manufactured textiles, which are among the cheapest in Brazil, and a wide selection of regional handicrafts. The local craft specialities are lace (mostly hand-made) and embroidered textile goods; also hammocks (US$15 to over US$100), fine *alto-relievo* wood carvings of Northeast scenes, basketware, leatherwork and clay figures (*bonecas de barro*). Bargaining is OK at the **Mercado Central** near Praça da Sé (closed Sun), and the *Emcetur Centro de Turismo* in the old prison (more expensive). Leather, lacework and cashew nuts at the Mercado Central are excellent.

Crafts are also available in shops near the market (eg *Itaparica*, R Conde D'Eu 434). The *SINE* shop, at R Dr João Moreira 429, is part of a state government initiative to promote small independent producers. Every night (1800-2300), there are stalls along the beach at Praia Meireiles, lively, fair prices. *Ceart*, Av Santos Dumont 1589, Aldeota, is good but expensive. Crafts also available in the commercial area along Av Monsenhor Tabosa as it approaches the beach. Clothes boutiques along Monsenhor Tabosa are closer to the centre, between Sen Almino and João Cordeiro.

Tour operators City and beach tours are offered by most of the following: *Lavila*, Rui Barbosa 1055, T2614777.Recommended. *Eurotur*, Av Abolição 2686, very helpful, good tours to beaches for US$20. *Lafuente Turismo*, Av Sen Virgílio Tavora 496, T2421010. *Petrelli Turismo*, R Barbosa de Freitas 1440, T2611222, F2444335. *Planet Tur*, R Eduardo Garcia 23, loja 1, Aldeota, T2616011, F2610642. In the same building is *Duplatour*, loja 2, T2642810, F2612656. *Nettour*, Av Rui Barbossa, 780, Aldeota, T2683099, F2682724. Tours to Jericoacoara with *Pousada Ondas Verdes*, recommended, and *Duplatour*, see above. *Hippopotamus*, Av Abolição, 2950, Aldeota, T2449191, F2240043. *Magia Turismo*, R Dep Moreira Rocha 329, Meireles, T/F2522217. Boat tours with *Ceará Saveiro*, Av Beira Mar 4294, T2631085, sailboat and yacht trips, daily 1000-1200 and 1600-1800 from Praia de Mucuripe. *Martur*, Av Beira Mar 4260, T2631203, sailing boat and schooner trips, from Mucuripe, same schedule as above. *Marina Park Hotel*, T2525253, boat trips with minimum 30 passengers, daily 1600-1800. Tours to the interior by rail and bus with *Turistar*, Praça Castro Carreira at the railway station, T2123090/9824675, F2122456, helpful with general information (see Excursions above). *BIC Turismo*, Av Senador Virgicio Távora, 480, T2424599, American Express representative. *Stella Barros*, Av Dom Luís 55, Aldeota, T/F2445427, Thomas Cook representative.

Transport
See also Ins and outs, page 490
Air: Aeroporto Pinto Martins, Praça Eduardo Gomes, 6 km south of centre, T4771200, F2726166. International flights to Lisbon, Milan and Rome. Domestic flights to Belém, Natal, Juazeiro do Norte, Parnaíba, Recife, São Luís and Teresina.

Buses: rodoviária at Av Borges de Melo 1630, Fátima, 6 km south from centre, T186, many city buses (US$0.65) including 'Aguanambi' 1 or 2 which go from Av Gen Sampaio, 'Barra de Fátima-Rodoviária' from Praça Coração de Jesus. ATM outside left luggage office.

Nordeste to **Aracati**, many daily, US$4, 2 hrs; to **Mossoró**, 10 daily, US$7 *convencional*, US$9 *executivo*, 4 hrs; to **Natal**, 7 daily, US$15 *convencional*, US$18 *executivo*, US$29 *leito*, 8 hrs; to **João Pessoa**, 2 daily, US$15 *convencional*, 8 hrs. *Guanabara* to **Recife**, 5 daily, US$27 *convencional*, US$33 *executivo*, US$40 *leito*, 12 hrs, book early for weekend travel. *Itapemirim* to **Salvador**, US$33, 21 hrs. *Timbira* and *Boa Esperança* to **Teresina**, several daily, US$13.50, 10 hrs (or *Top Bus*, US$18, *leito* US$27); to **Belém**, 2 daily, US$35 *convencional*, US$40 *executivo*, 23 hrs (*Expresso Timbira* also sells Belém-Manaus boat tickets). *Piripiri*, to **Parque Nacional de Sete Cidades**, US$11, 9 hrs, a good stop en route to Belém. *Guanabara* to **São Luiz**, 3 daily, US$27, 18 hrs. *Rápido Juazeiro* to **Juazeiro do Norte**, 4 daily, US$13.50, 9 hrs. *Guanabara* to **Campina Grande**, US$19.50, 13 hrs.

Buses to beaches: *Redençao* to **Gijoca** and **Jericoacoara**, daily 0900, 2100, US$7.50 to Gijoca, US$8.50 to Jericoacoara, 7 hrs, book ahead in high season. For eastern beaches near Fortaleza (Prainha, Iguape, Barro Preto, Batoque) and towns such as Aquiraz, Eusébio or Pacajus, you must take *São Benedito* buses from Av Domingos Olímpio 184 (10 mins' walk from downtown), not from the rodoviária. At the rodoviária buses leave for Caponga and further on (Morro Branco, Aracate, etc). Details are given below.

Car hire: *HM*, R Vicente Leite 650, Aldeota, T2617799, cars and buggies. *Avis*, Av Barão de Studart 1425, Aldeota, T2616785. *Localiza*, Av Antônio Justa 2400, T2424255, or airport T0800-992000. *Loc Car*, Av Virgílio Távora 206, Aldeota, T2248594, cars and buggies. *Loca Buggy*, Av Beira Mar 2500, Meireles, T/F2426945.

Trains: Station at Praça Castro Carreira in the centre, T2114255. Commuter service southwest to Caucaia and south to Maracanaú. Tourist trains run on Sat to Croatá, plus bus trip to Praia da Lagoínha and on Sun to Baturité, plus bus to the mountains; see Excursions above.

Airline offices On Av Santos Dumont, Aldeota are: *BRA*, T4771470. *Fly*, at airport, T4771501. *Varig*, No 2727, T2668000, F2440500, freephone 0800 997000. *Vasp*, No 3060, sala 803, T2543434, F2723046, freephone T0800 998266. *Transbrasil*, No 2813, T2441477, F2441560. *TAM*, Av Santos Dumont, 2849, T2610916. *TAF* (*Transportes Aéreos Fortaleza*), T2727474, flights to Juazeiro do Norte and other places in the interior.

Directory

Banks *Banco do Nordeste*, R Major Facundo 372, a/c, helpful, recommended. *Banco Excel*, R Major Facundo 322, T2111834, sells TCs on Amex card. TCs exchanged and cash with Visa at *Banco do Brasil*, R Barão do Rio Branco 1500, also on Av Abolição. ATM for Cirrus, Visa and MasterCard outside cinema at Centro Cultural Dragão do Mar. Also at Av Antonio Sales and *Iguatemi Shopping*. *Banco Mercantil do Brasil*, R Mayor Facundo 484, Centro, Praça do Ferreira, cash against MasterCard. Exchange at *Tropical Viagens*, R Barão do Rio Branco 1233, T2213344, English spoken. *Libratur*, Av Abolição 2794, recommended. *ACCtur* has exchange booths for dollars (cash and TCs) throughout the city, main office Av Dom Luís 176, Aldeota, T2619955. *Rudy Constantino* has automatic exchange machines for several currencies, eg Av Virgílio Távora 150, Meireles, T2617288 and Av Desembargador Moreira 1155. *IJB Câmbio*, Av Dom Luís 655, Aldeota, T2617466.

Open 0900-1630

Communications Internet:*Abrolhos Praia*, Av Abolição, 2030, Meireles, part of hotel of same name, US$2.50 per hr, open daily, closes 1400 Sun. *Center Net*, Av Monsenhor Tabosa 1001, Meireles, T219 1909. **Post office**: Main branch at R Senador Alencar 38, Centro; Av Monsenhor Tabosa 1109, Iracema; at train station. Parcels must be taken to Receita Federal office at Barão de Aracati 909, Aldeota (take 'Dom Luiz' bus). **Telephone**: International calls from Emcetur hut on Iracema beach and from *Telemar* offices: R Floriano Peixoto 99, corner of R João Moreira, Centro; R José Vilar 375, Aldeota; Av Beira Mar 736, Iracema; Av Beira Mar 3821, Meireles; Av César Cals 1297, Praia do Futuro; at rodoviária and airport.

Fortaleza and the North Coast

Embassies and consulates *Belgium*, R Eduardo Garcia 609, Aldeota, T2641500. *Denmark*, R Inácio Capelo 50, Colônia, T2285055, open 0800-1800. *France*, R Bóris 90, Centro, T2542822. *Germany*, R Dr Lourenço, Meireles, 2244, T2462833. *Italy*, Miguel Dibe 80, cj Wash Soares, T2786352. *Portugal*, R Pedro Borges 33, Ed Palácio Progresso, Centro, T2542900. *Sweden* and *Norway*, R Leonardo Mota 501, Aldeota, T2420888. *Switzerland*, R Dona Leopoldina 697, Centro, T2269444. *UK*, Praça da Imprensa, Aldeota, T4668888 (consul is Annette, her secretary Eunice). *USA*, Nogueira Acioli 891, Centro, T2521539.

Laundry *Laundromat*, Av Abolição 3038, Meireles.

Medical services *Instituto Dr José Frota (IJF)*, R Barão do Rio Branco 1866, T2555000, recommended public hospital.

Voltage 220 volts AC, 60 cycles.

The Eastern Coast

The most prominent feature of the Eastern Coast is the impressive coloured-sand cliffs. There are also freshwater springs near the shore, along with palm groves and mangroves. Lobster fishing is one of the main activities.

Aquiraz

Phone code: 085
Colour map 2, grid A5
Population: 61,000

The first capital of Ceará conserves several colonial buildings and has a religious art museum. Some 31 km east of Fortaleza, it is also the access point for the following beaches:

Prainha, 6 km east, a fishing village and weekend resort with a 10-km long beach and dunes. The beach is clean and largely empty and the waves are good for surfing. You can see *jangadas* coming in daily in the late afternoon. The village is known for its lacework; the women using the *bilro* and *labirinto* techniques at the **Centro de Rendeiras**. In some of the small restaurants it is possible to see displays of the *Carimbó*, one of the North Brazilian dances. Just south of Prainha is **Praia do Presídio** with calm surf, dunes, palms and *cajueiros* (cashew trees).

About 18 km southeast of Aquiraz is **Praia Iguape**, another fishing and lacework village. The beach is a large, elbow-shaped sandbank, very scenic especially at Ponta do Iguape. Nearby are high sand dunes where skiing is popular. There is a lookout at Morro do Enxerga Tudo; trips on *jangadas* one hour for US$8.50. Lacework is sold at the **Centro de Rendeiras**. Locals are descendants of Dutch, Portuguese and Indians, some traditions such as the *coco-de-praia* folk dance are still practised. About 3 km south of Igape is **Praia Barro Preto**, a wide, tranquil beach, with sand dunes, palms and lagoons.

Sleeping & eating

Prainha L *New Life*, Alto da Prainha, T3621314. Weight reduction centre, with fridge, pool, restaurant. A *Aquiraz Praia e Escola de Hotelaria*, Estr da Prainha, Km 5, T3621006. With bath, fridge, pool, restaurant. B *Da Prainha*, R Berlim, Alto da Prainha, T3621122. With bath, rooms in top floor have more air, nice views. B *Prainha Solar*, R Principal, T3621355, F3621366. With fridge, restaurant, pool, comfortable. C *Pousada*, R Principal near rodoviária. No name and no breakfast, owner lives on the beach, noisy but clean; fishermen also rent space in their homes. Good fish restaurant, *O Leonção*, R Principal. There are several small, cheap and good restaurants along the beach (eg *Mar Aberto*, *Mar e Sol*) where crab, shrimp, lobster and fish figure prominently on the menu.

Praia do Presidio B *Do Sol*, T3701222. Large rooms with bath, a/c, a couple of chalets, pool, restaurant. B *Iguape Hotel de Turismo*, R 8, T3701444. Cabins, pool with springwater, restaurant. B *Jangadeiro Praia*, T3701039. With bath, fridge, restaurant, pool.

Iguape **B** *Sol Leste*, R São Pedro, T/F3701233. With bath, fridge, pool, restaurant, sports fields. Other hotels and *pousadas* also available. *Peixada do Iguape*, Av Stuart at the beach. Fish specialities. *O João do Camarão*, Av Stuart. Fish and seafood. *O Caldinho*, Estr do Iguape. Regional food.

Barro Preto **A** *Marina Barro Preto*, R Francisco das Chagas 10, T3701166. With bath, fridge, pool, restaurant. **B** *Chalés Barra Encantada*, R Francisco das Chagas 13, T3701466. Cabins for up to 6, fridge, pool, restaurant, large camping area with palms, US$9 per person, Camping Club members US$4 per person. **B** *Recanto da Fantasia*, R Francisco das Chagas, T2394943. Equipped cabins for up to 4, no breakfast.

Buses Daily service to all these beaches from the terminal at Av Domingos Olímpio **Transport** 184, **Fortaleza**. For information T2721999; **Prainha**, 11 daily, US$1; **Iguape**, hourly between 0600 and 1900, US$1.10.

Caponga and Águas Belas

Cascavel, 62 km southeast of Fortaleza, has a Saturday crafts fair by the market. It is the access point for the beaches of Caponga and Águas Belas, where traditional fishing villages coexist with fancy weekend homes and hotels.

Caponga, 15 km northeast of Cascavel, has a 2-km long beach which is *Phone code: 085* wide and lined with palms. *Jangadas* set sail in the early morning; arrangements can be made to accompany fishermen on overnight trips, 90-minute ride by beach, US$14 for up to five people. There is a fish market and crafts sales (ceramics, embroidery and lacework) on the beach.

A 30-minute walk south along the white-sand beach leads to **Águas Belas**, on the mouth of the Rio Mal Cozinhado, offering a combination of fresh and saltwater bathing (access also by road, 15 km from Cascavel, 4 km from Caponga). The scenery here, and 5 km further east at Barra Nova, changes with the variations of the tide. A walk north along the beach for 6 km takes you to the undeveloped Praia do Batoque, which is surrounded by cliffs and dunes.

It is possible to hike along much of the eastern coast. From Prainha to Águas Belas, for example, is seven hours (take plenty of water and sun protection). Where rivers have to be crossed, there is usually a boatman. Fishing villages have accommodation or hammock space.

Caponga **A** *Village Barra Mar*, T/F3351088. Chalets with a/c, fridge, restaurant, pool, **Sleeping** nice grounds, watersports. **B** *Summer House*, a/c, pool, restaurant. **B** *La France*, **& eating** T3351100, F3351016. Fridge, pool, restaurant. On R Laureano de Paula Santana are **B** *JS*, T3351006. With bath, restaurant. **C** *Fateixa*, No 555, T3351122. With bath, pool, garden. **C** *Coqueiral*, No 537, T3351073. With bath, porch with hammocks. **C** *Mon Kapitan*, R Pedro Moita on the square, T3351031. Large rooms with bath, very helpful, good restaurant. *Bybloss*, by beach, T3351045. Shared bath, horse and buggie rental, restaurant. **D** *Versailles*, R J Irineu Araujo, 1.5 km from the beach, T3351071. With small bath, breakfast extra. Snacks from *Gula-Gula*, Estr de Caponga. Varied menu at *Aqui Agora*, R Antonio Camilo and *Na Boca do Povo*, Av Henrique Rodrigues, Centro.

Águas Belas **B** *Praia Águas Belas*, T3351060. Room with bath and cabins, pool, restaurant. **B** *Le Paradis*, T3351050, F3351289. With bath, pool, restaurant. Fishermen offer housing in their homes. Cheaper seafood restaurants are available in the village. **Barra Nova** **D** *Encontro das Águas*, no sign, friendly.

Buses Direct *Pratius* bus to Caponga from **Fortaleza** rodoviária (hourly, fewer on Sun, **Transport** US$1.50) or take a bus to Cascavel from terminal at Av Domingos Olímpio 184 (not rodoviária, 80 mins) then a bus from Cascavel (20 mins); bus information in Fortaleza,

T2721999, in Caponga T3341485. Bus from Av Domingos Olímpio 184, Fortaleza, direct to Barra Nova, 0900, or go to Cascavel and change there.

Morro Branco and Praia das Fontes

Phone code: 085 **Beberibe**, 78 km from Fortaleza, is the access point for Morro Branco and Praia das Fontes, some of the better known beaches of the east coast.

About 4 km from Beberibe is Morro Branco, with a spectacular beach, coloured craggy cliffs and beautiful views. *Jangadas* leave the beach at 0500, returning at 1400-1500, lobster is the main catch in this area. The coloured sands of the dunes are bottled into beautiful designs and sold along with other crafts such as lacework, embroidery and straw goods. *Jangadas* may be hired for sailing (one hour for up to six people US$30). Beach buggies (full day US$100) and taxis are also for hire. There are summer homes along the beach which can get very crowded at holiday times.

South of Morro Branco and 6 km from Beberibe is Praia das Fontes, which also has coloured cliffs with freshwater springs; there is a fishing village and at the south end a lagoon. Near the shore is a cave, known as Mãe de Água, visible during low tide. Buggies and ultralight aircraft can be hired on the beach. A luxury resort complex has been built here, making the area expensive.

South of Praia das Fontes are several less developed beaches including **Praia Uruaú** or **Marambaia**, about 6 km from Praia das Fontes along the beach or 21 km by road from Beberibe, via Sucatinga on a loose sand road. The beach is at the base of coloured dunes; there is a fishing village with some accommodation. Just inland is Lagoa do Uruaú, the largest in the state and a popular place for watersports. Buggy from Morro Branco US$45 for four.

About 50 km southeast of Beberibe is **Fortim**, access point to **Pontal de Maceió**, a reddish sand point on the mouth of the Rio Jaguaribe, from where there is a good view of a large section of the eastern coast. In the winter the river is high and shrimp is fished, while in the summer it dries up, forming islands and freshwater beaches; boats go to the islands from Fortim. A fishing village is about 1 km from the ocean; there are bars, restaurants and small *pousadas*.

Sleeping **Morro Branco** B *Recanto Praiano*, T2247118. Good breakfast. Recommended.
& eating B *Pousada dos Ventos*, T3301137. Chalets, pool, restaurant. B *Cabana do Morro*, Av Beira Mar, T3300140. Mosquitoes, fan, shower, restaurant, pool, porch with hammocks. B *Pousada do Morro Branco*, T3301040. Fridge, pool, restaurant. C *Pousada Sereia*, on the beach, T3301144. Good breakfast. Highly recommended. D *Rosalias'*, T3301131. With use of kitchen, 50 m from bus stop, somewhat run down. You can rent fishermen's houses. Meals can also be arranged at beach front bars (try *O Jangadeiro*). Double room at D *Bar São Francisco*, or 7-room house for rent.

Praia das Fontes L *Praia das Fontes*, Av A Teixeira 1, T3381179, F3381087. Luxurious resort, watersports, horses, racket games, spa. Recommended. B *Das Falésias*, T3381018, F3011117, clean, German owner, fridge, pool, restaurant.

Camping *Lago das Dunas*, access 9 km south of Beberibe on CE-004, then east from Sucatinga 5 km on a poor dirt road; large area with grass and palms for shade, pool, restaurant, sports fields, it is 1 km through dunes to Praia Marambaia or Uruaú, US$4 per person Camping Club members, US$9 per person non members; also rents rooms with shared bath (US$45 room for 4, US$55 room for 6).

Transport **Buses** *São Benedito* bus from **Fortaleza** to Morro Branco, US$2.15; 2½ hrs, 5 a day; information in Fortaleza, T2721999. To get to **Natal**, take 0600 bus to Beberibe, then 0800 bus (only one) to Aracati, US$0.60, then on to Natal.

Life's a beach

With almost 7,500 km of Atlantic coastline, it is little wonder that beaches are an integral part not only of Brazil's geography but also of its mentality. For many Brazilians, the term férias (vacation) is synonymous with praia (beach). Those unfortunate souls who live deep inland must get by finding a river, lake or dam to which to flock at weekends and holidays. And if that is not good enough, places like Manaus' five-star Hotel Tropical have built a wave-pool; an artificial beach within sight of the Amazon.

While the seashore is attractive throughout almost all of its length, the beaches of the northeast are among the country's most famous, and justifiably so. Their towering sand dunes, turquoise lagoons, coloured sand cliffs, coconut palms, quiet fishing villages and lively resorts attract countless Brazilians and foreigners alike.

With so many to choose from, how do you go about selecting a beach? There is something for almost every taste: Jericoacoara (CE), with its famous sand dunes and sunsets, Canoa Quebrada (CE), the ultimate party beach, Tambada (PB)

and its strictly controlled nudist colony, havens for surfers, sailors and divers; as well as thousands of others that have yet to be 'discovered'. Even the big city beaches can have their charm, sports or cultural events and nightlife, although they are frequently too polluted for bathing.

Brazil's beaches also call for appropriate precautions. Sun protection is vital (some reports suggest that ultraviolet radiation may have increased by as much as 45% between 1996 and 1997). Always enquire locally about tides, the strength of the surf, currents and undertows before swimming. Don't go wandering off on your own amid sand dunes, it is easy to get lost. Always protect your valuables, especially on crowded urban beaches.

A general description of the better beaches is provided throughout this Handbook. Hard-core beach bums may wish to obtain the 4-Rodas Guia de Praias, published annually and available at most news-stands (US$15), with detailed descriptions and satellite photos of each and every beach in Brazil. Surely no other country has such a publication!

Situated on the shores of the Rio Jaguaribe, Aracati is the access point to the southeastern-most beaches of Ceará. The city is best known for its Carnival, the liveliest in the state, and for its colonial architecture, including several 18th-century churches and mansions with Portuguese tile façades. There is a religious art museum (closed lunch time and Sunday afternoon) and a Saturday morning crafts fair on Avenida Coronel Alexandrino. On the same street is **B** *Pousada Litorânea*, R Col Alexandrino 1251, T4211001, with air conditioning, **D** with fan, near rodoviária. **C** *Beira Rio* is on Trav Senhor do Bonfim, T4211881, with bath and fan.

Aracati
Phone code: 088
Population: 62,000

Transport Bus Natal-Aracati via Mossoró, 6 hrs, US$7.50; from Mossoró US$2.50, 2 hrs; Fortaleza-Aracati, São Benedito, Guanabara or Nordeste many daily, US$4, 2 hrs; Aracati-Canoa Quebrada from General Pompeu e João Paulo, US$0.60; taxi US$3.60.

Canoa Quebrada

Canoa Quebrada stands on a sand dune 10 km from Aracati. An isolated fishing village until 1982, when a road was built, it is now a very popular resort known for its easygoing party atmosphere (there have been reports of drug problems here), many bars, restaurants and *forró* establishments. The village is also famous for its *labirinto* lacework and coloured sand sculpture, for sand-skiing on its dunes and for its beaches. Fishermen have their homes in

Phone code: 088
Colour map 2, grid A5

Esteves, a separate village also on top of the cliff; they still live off the sea and rides on *jangadas* can be arranged at the beach. To avoid biting insects (*bicho do pé*) it is best to wear shoes or sandals. There is nowhere to change money except *Banco do Brasil* in Aracati. In the second half of July the *Canoarte* festival takes place, which includes a *jangada* regatta and music festival.

Excursions   South of Canoa Quebrada, **Majorlândia** is a very nice village, with many-coloured sand dunes (used in bottle pictures and cord crafts) and a wide beach with strong waves, good for surfing. The arrival of the fishing fleet in the evening is an important daily event; lobster is the main catch. It is a popular weekend destination with beach homes for rent and Carnival here is quite lively. About 5 km south along the beach is the village of **Quixaba** on a beach surrounded by coloured cliffs, with reefs offshore and good fishing (*Pousada Lúcia*, T4211576). At low tide you can reach Lagoa do Mato, some 4 km south. Between Canoa Quebrada and Majorlândia is **Porto Canoa**, a resort town (opened 1996), fashioned after the Greek islands. It includes beach homes and apartments, shopping areas, restaurants and hotels, and there are facilities for watersports, horse riding, ultralight flights, buggy and *jangada* outings.

Buggy rentals are available at Canoa Quebrada beach; a popular destination going through the dunes is **Lagoa do Mato**, about 12 km southeast, a pristine beach, surrounded by dunes, cliffs and palms (buggy US$30 for four). There is a hotel with a restaurant. **Ponta Grossa**, about 30 km southeast, is another beautiful beach, where there is a natural lookout on the cliffs (buggy US$75 for four, four hours). The fishing community here has many inhabitants of Dutch origin, following a shipwreck in the 19th century. To the south are the beaches of **Redonda** and **Barreiras**, good for surfing, with a hotel.

Sleeping   **Canoa Quebrada**   **A** *Tranqüilândia*, T339. Fridge, restaurant. **B** *Pousada Latitude*, R Dragão do Mar, T323. A/c, fridge, cheaper with fan, restaurant. **B** *Pousada Lua Estrela*, R Nascer do Sol 106, T333, F2347472. IYHA affiliated. Fan, fridge, hot shower. **B** *Pousada Logus*, at entrance to town, T9641416. A/c, fridge, quiet. **C** *Pousada do Rei*, R Nascer do Sol 112, T316. Fan, fridge. Recommended. **C** *Pousada Alternativa*, R Francisco Caraço, T335. With or without bath, central. Recommended. **C** *Pousada Via Láctea*, off the main street (so quieter), beautiful view of beach which is 50 m away. Some rooms with hot shower, fridge, fan, good breakfast, safe parking, horse and buggy tours, English spoken. Highly recommended. **C** *Tenda do Cumbe*, at end of the road on cliff, T4211761. Thatched huts, restaurant. Warmly recommended. **D** *Pousada 3 de Junho*, L Bezerra with access to beach, T2136510. No breakfast. **D** *Pousada Novo Horizonte*, R Dragão do Mar, T322, above souvenir shops. With bath, breakfast extra, restaurant. **D** *Beco's*, R José Melancia 2300, T328. With bath, inner courtyard with porch and hammocks. **D** *Pousada do Holandês*, R Nascer do Sol, rooms without bath (**E**). No breakfast, use of kitchen. Villagers will let you sling your hammock or put you up cheaply. Verónica is recommended, European books exchanged. Sr Miguel rents good clean houses for US$10 a day.

Majorlândia   **C** *Pousada Esquina das Flores*, T188. Nice. **C** *Pousada Dunas Praia*, T4211846. With bath, restaurant. **D** *Pousada do Gaúcho*, R do Jangadeiro 323, T195. With bath, restaurant, friendly. **D** *Apartamentos Beira Mar*, on beach, T134. Furnished apartments, no breakfast. **D** *Pousada e Restaurante Requinte*, 100 m before beach on main road. Airy rooms, use of kitchen, rooms with or without bath. Recommended. **D** *Pousada a Sereia*, T130. With bath, fridge, restaurant. *Pousada Beira Mar*, T134. With bath, fridge. *Restaurant O Gilberto*, for fish.

Redonda   **D** *Pousada O Pescador*, T0XX88-4321127, and 2 others.

Bars and restaurants, vegetarian food in *Espácio Cultural*, cheap seafood (don't drink the water). *Casaverde*, R Dragão do Mar. Good food – Chinese, Mexican and typical Brazilian – good atmosphere, cards and darts available, good music. Home cooking at *Estrela do Mar*, R Dragão do Mar, *Bom Apetite* and *Rasgo de Lua*, both on R José Melancia. Several shacks along the descents to the beach serving *peixe na telha*, the local fish speciality.

Eating

Buses Fortaleza-Canoa Quebrada, *São Benedito*, 3 daily, US$4.25. Fortaleza-Majorlândia, *São Benedito*, 4 daily, US$4.25. Bus information in Fortaleza, T2270385, 2721999. To **Redonda**: no direct bus, but 4 daily from Fortaleza to Icapuí (US$8), ask the driver to stop about 6 km before the town at a *jangada* which serves as a roadsign at the access road, unpaved, to Redonda, 5 km.

Transport

The Western Coast

The coast northwest of Fortaleza has many wide beaches, near fixed or shifting dunes, surrounded by swathes of coconut groves. The main roads are some distance from the shore, making access to the beaches somewhat more difficult than on the eastern coast. This means the fishing villages retain a traditional lifestyle and responsible travel is especially important.

Some 58 km northwest of Fortaleza, Pecém is a village set by a cove with a wide beach, dunes, inland lagoons. There is a strong surf, here and in Taíba, a 14-km long beach to the north (19 km by road), and surfing and fishing championships. By Taíba, a long point filled with palms extends into the sea. Nearby is **Siupé**, a village that maintains colonial characteristics, where embroidered hammocks, a trademark of Ceará, are made.

Pecém & Taíba
Phone code: 085
Population: 5,500
(Pecém)

Sleeping and eating **Pecém B** *Pecém Praia*, R São Luís, T189. Fridge, pool. *Pousada Isca do Sol*, Colônia de Férias, T112. Chalets or rooms with bath, pool, restaurant with Swiss specialties. *Pousada do Gaúcho*, Colônia de Férias, T173. With bath, fan. Restaurant. *O Manoel*, R São Luís. Fish dishes. At the Colônia de Férias are several beach shacks including *Joselito*, seafood specialities. *Porto Alegre*, meat, pizza, snacks.

Town's calling centre: T3441064 and T3401328, 3-digit numbers indicated are extensions on these central lines

   Taíba **E** *Pousada Vitória*, T2235715, good value. *Le Petit Resto Bar*, lobster, shrimp, fish. *O Barão*, regional specialities, *carne de sol*, lamb.

Transport From **Fortaleza** rodoviária, to Pecém 11 daily, US$1.75. To Taíba 4 daily, US$3, information T2521402.

Some 106 km northwest of Fortaleza is Paracuru, a fishing port which has the most important Carnival in the northwest coast, including street dancing and parades, decorated boat parades, sports championships and a beauty contest. It has some lovely deserted white sand beaches with good bathing and surfing, and the people are very friendly. There are several *pousadas* in the centre. Restaurant *Ronco do Mar* has good fish dishes. *Boca do Poço* bar has *forró* at weekends. There are eight buses daily from Fortaleza rodoviária, US$3, information in Fortaleza, T2724483.

Paracuru & Lagoinha
Phone code: 085
Population: 28,000
(Paracuru)

   West of Paracuru and 12 km from the town of Paraipaba, is Lagoinha, a very scenic beach with hills, dunes and palms by the shore; a fishing village is on one of the hills. Nearby are some small but pleasant waterfalls and 3 km west of town Lagoa da Barra, a lake surrounded by dunes. Local legend says that one of the hills, Morro do Cascudo, has hidden treasure, left by French pirates.

Fortaleza and the North Coast

Lagoinha's calling
centre: T3631232,
3-digit numbers
indicated are
extensions on this
central line

Sleeping and eating Lagoinha: C *O Milton*, T102. Cabins, outdoor restaurant. **C** *Ondas do Mar*, T146. With bath, porch with hammocks, restaurant. **C** *Sol e Mar*, small rooms with bath, restaurant, large portions. **C** *Monalisa*, T126. Large rooms with bath. Beach shacks serve fish.

Transport Bus service from **Fortaleza** rodoviária to Lagoinha, 3 daily, US$3.15, information T2724483, train tours from Fortaleza on Sat, see Excursions, page 494.

Fleixeiras

Phone code: 085
Colour map 2, grid A4

Further northwest, some 135 km from Fortaleza, is **Trairi**, access point to a series of beaches which conserve a natural beauty and, until the mid-1990s, were untouched by tourism. North of Trairi, 15 km by road, is Fleixeiras, where at low tide pools, good for snorkelling, form near the beach. There are strong waves for surfing and wind for windsurfing as well as dunes by the wide beach. In the village there is a *jangada* repair shop, a good place to learn about these crafts, and a needlework workshop, where lacework and embroidered clothing and linen are made.

About 5 km west is **Imboaca**, a scenic beach with interesting rock formations and shifting dunes. Further west, at the mouth of the Rio Mundaú, is **Mundaú**, another nice beach, with palms, dunes and an old working lighthouse. A common sport here is fishing for *camurupim*, a large fish, good for eating. Access roads from Imboaca and Cana to the south are often impassable because of shifting dunes; at low tide it is possible to reach it along the beach from Fleixeiras. A fishing village is near the beach; there are some *pousadas* and restaurants. From Fortaleza to Fleixeiras there are three buses daily, US$3.85, information T2724128.

You can cross the Rio Mundaú and walk 8 km to Baleia, a developing beach resort with plenty of *pousadas* (**C** *Maresia*, Swiss-run; **C** *Som das Águas*, OK). There is one daily bus from Fortaleza, 1300, five hours, US$10. For another 40 km there are beautiful dune landscapes and fishing villages, how Canoa Quebrada and Jericocoara must have been 30 years ago. Icaraí de Amontada is in a windy bay, good windsurfing, simple accommodation (**D**). There is one daily bus from Fortaleza, 0900, six 'horrible' hours, US$12.

Sleeping
& eating
Calling centres:
Fleixeras, T511184,
Mundaú, T3511210;
3-digit numbers
indicated are
extensions on
this central line

Fleixeiras A *Solar das Fleixeiras*, T136. With bath, pool, restaurant. On R São Pedro are **C** *Da Célia*, T105. With bath, no breakfast. **C** *O Coqueiro*, T125. With bath. On Av Beira Mar are several restaurants including *O Edmar*, varied menu and *São Pedro*, seafood.

Mundaú A *Mundaú Dunas*, T3511020, x197. Fridge, pool, restaurant. **B** *Sombra dos Coqueiros*, T200. With bath, restaurant. **D** *Brisa do Mar*, small rooms with bath, breakfast extra. **E** *Casa de Retiro Estrela do Mar*, T3511220, ext 154. Priest's retreat home, must reserve ahead, rooms with hammocks, some with bath, use of kitchen.

Almofala

Colour map 2, grid A4

The sleepy fishing village of Almofala, 230 km from Fortaleza, is home of the Tremembés Indians who live off the sea and some agriculture. There is electricity, but no hotels or restaurants, although locals rent hammock space and cook meals. Bathing is better elsewhere, but the area is surrounded by dunes and is excellent for hiking along the coast to explore beaches and lobster-fishing communities. In Almofala, the church, with much of the town, was covered by shifting sands and remained covered for 50 years, reappearing in the

1940s; it has since been restored. From Fortaleza there are buses at 0700 and 1530 daily, US$6, information on Fortaleza, T2722728.

Jijoca de Jericoacoara

Jijoca de Jericoacoara (alternative spelling: Gijoca), near the south shore of scenic Lagoa Paraíso (or Lagoa Jijoca), is the access point for Jericoacoara, one of the most famous beaches of Ceará and all Brazil. Lagoa Paraíso is turquoise and a good place for swimming and watersports; there are some nice hotels by the lake, from town it is 1 km along the shore when the lake is low, or 3 km along the road with high water, taxi (pick-up truck) US$5.

Phone code: 088
Colour map 2, grid A4

On the lakeshore are **B** *Jardim do Paraíso*, small, with bath, restaurant, windsurfing equipment. **C** *Capitão Tomaz*, rooms and chalets, sports equipment, boat trips. **C** *Pousada do Paulo*, 4 km from town, nice chalets, pleasant, restaurant. **C** *Paraíso da Lagoa*, chalets, area for camping. In town are **C** *Pousada da Lagoa*, with bath. **D** *Pousada dos Corsos*, T6691144, friendly, excellent, Corsican food. **E** *Pousada São Sebstião*, R Vicente Paulo 146, shared bath, basic. There are a couple more *pousadas*. **Restaurante Central** is recommended.

Sleeping & eating
Town's calling centre: T6114244, for hotel reservations

A *jardineira* (open-sided 4WD truck) does the 23 km, 1½ hrs, trip from Jijoca to Jericoacoara. A rough but very pretty ride through sand dunes and hills, sadly criss-crossed by vehicle tracks which have damaged the fragile *caatinga* vegetation (4WD and high clearance are necessary on this road).

Transport

Banks *Banco do Brasil* does not change foreign currency in Jijoca.

Directory

Jericoacoara

Nestled in the dunes is the fishing community of Jericoacoara, or Jerí as the locals call it. It is popular with both Brazilian and international travellers, crowded at weekends mid-December to mid-February, in July and during Brazilian holidays. Despite the large influx of visitors, it remains a tranquil and safe town. Visitors are rewarded with towering sand dunes, deserted beaches with little shade, cactus-covered cliffs rising from the sea, interesting rock formations and a pleasant atmosphere. Watching the sunset from the top of the large dune just west of town, followed by a display of capoeira on the beach, is a tradition among visitors. There is nightly forró in high season; Wednesday and Saturday at other times.

Phone code: 088
Colour map 2, grid A4

Jericoacoara is part of an environmental protection area which includes a large coconut grove, lakes, dunes and hills covered in *caatinga* vegetation. A youth group publishes *Força Jovem Jericoacoara*, a monthly newspaper with information for visitors and general issues of environmental protection in the area. There are several possibilities for walks, horse riding (US$2-3 per hour) and dune-buggy trips (many for hire, ask for recommendations as some drivers are considered unsafe). Take water and sun protection, it gets very hot and there is no shade; several hotels offer tours.

Going west along the beach takes you through a succession of sand dunes and coconut groves; the views are beautiful. In 2 km you reach the beach of **Mangue Seco**, and 2 km beyond an arm of the ocean which separates it from **Guriú** (bridge across), where there is a village atop a fixed dune. Some of the

Excursions

Fortaleza and the North Coast (vertical sidebar text)

best scenery in the area is by **Nova Tatajuba** (see below), about 35 km west of Jerí. It is reached by land from Camocim, or along the beach by dune-buggy including a river crossing on a barge (US$20 per person, minimum four) or by sea, three hours (US$100); there are basic *pousadas*, see details below.

A 45-minute walk to the east takes you to the *pedra fourada*, a stone arch sculpted by the sea, one of the symbols of Jerí, accessible only at low tide (check the tide tables at *Casa do Turismo*). In the same direction, but just inland, is *Serrote*, a large hill with a lighthouse on top; it is well worth walking up for the magnificent views.

About 15 km east along the shore (43 km by road via Jijoca and Caiçara) is **Praia do Preá**, with light sand and blue ocean (**D** *Pousada Azul do Mar*, T6601238, with bath, no electricity), and 10 km beyond (62 km by road) is the beach of **Barrinha**, access to the scenic *Lagoa Azul*.

About 10 km inland through the dunes (20 km along the road), to *Lagoa Paraíso* or *Jijoca*, is a turquoise, freshwater lake, great for bathing (buggy US$10 per person).

Essentials

Sleeping

Town's calling centre: T88-6210544; you can leave a message for most hotels through this number

Around half of the hotels close out of season when hotel prices go down some 30%. **A** *Avalon*, R Principal, T2245677 (Fortaleza). Nice rooms with fan, pleasant, restaurant; **A** *Hippopotamus*, R do Forró, T085-2449191 (Fortaleza). Nice, with pool, light, fan, restaurant, tours. **A** *Matusa*, R São Francisco. Pool, restaurant and bar. **B** *Capitão Tomáz*, on east end of beach, T6691185. Good. Recommended apart from breakfast. **C** *Acoara de Jerico*, R Principal, by beach. Gas lamps, restaurant. **C** *Casa Nostra*, R das Dunas. Nice rooms, good breakfast, can pay with US$ or German marks, money change, Italian spoken. Recommended. **C** *Casa do Turismo*, R das Dunas, T088-6210211, jericoacoara@secrel.com.br Nice cabins, information, tours, horse rental, bus tickets, telephone calls, post office, exchange, friendly. **C** *Isabel*, R do Forró by beach. Light and shower. Recommended. **C** *Papagaio*, Beco do Forró, T/F2682722 (Fortaleza). With bath, recommended, tours. **C** *Pousada Renata*, patio with hammocks, breakfast, English, Italian and German spoken. **D** *Calanda*, R das Dunas, T6211144. With bath, solar energy, Swiss run, good rooms, good breakfast, good views, helpful, German, English and Spanish spoken, full moon party every month. Warmly recommended. **D** *do Coqueiro*, R Principal. **D** *Pousada do Véio*, R Principal. With and without bath (**E**), **camping** in shady area US$3 per tent, tours. **E** *Por do Sol*, Bairro Novo Jerí, 1 street west of R das Dunas, behind main dune. Basic, good value. **Camping** in grounds of *Senzala* restaurant, see below.

Eating

There are several restaurants serving vegetarian and fish dishes: *Alexandre*, *Isabel*, both on the beach, good seafood, pricey. *Acoara do Jerico*, R Principal by the beach, reasonable. *Avalon*, R Principal. Crêpes a speciality, good. Also on R Principal: *Samambaia*, good value; *Catavento*, good; *Espaço Aberto*, also recommended for breakfast; *Sorrisa de Natureza*, cheap, tasty food. Recommended. Italian food and pizza at: *Pizza Banana*, R Principal. Good. *Senzala*, same street. Nice, pleasant atmosphere (allows camping in its grounds). *Cantinho da Masa*, R do Forró. Good. *Casinha da Barra*. Several shops sell basic provisions, so camping is possible.

Bars & nightclubs

There are frequent parties to which visitors are welcome. About once a week in high season there is a folk dance show which includes *capoeira*. *Forró* nightly in high season at R do Forró, Wed and Sat in low season, starts about 2200. Action moves to the bars when *forró* has stopped about 0200. *Bar Barriga da Lua* and *Pizza Reggae*, opposite *forró*.

Pau de Arara

Pau de Arara, *a parrot's perch. This very descriptive term refers to an unusual vehicle which has become part of the culture of the Northeast. A large flat-bed truck, with narrow wooden slats for seats, it may have a tattered tarpaulin stretched overhead for shade. Lurching over the rutted back-roads of the* Sertão, *passengers impregnated with dust from head to toe, they were for decades the staple of rural public transport throughout the region. They were also the only affordable conveyance for legions of drought-stricken* nordestinos, *fleeing to the industrialized south. Today, better roads and improved fleets of buses mean the* pau de arara *are increasingly rare, but custom remains more important than comfort in some places. Hence the anachronistic sight of the latest-model truck, complete with a sophisticated sound system and air conditioning for the cab, but fitted with the traditional narrow wooden slats of a* pau de arara *at the back.*

A *jardineira* (open-sided 4WD truck) meets *Redenção* bus from/to **Fortaleza**, at Jijoca: 1½ hrs, US$1.05, from Jijoca at 1400, 0200, from Jericoacoara at 0600, 2200, from R das Dunas by *Casa do Turismo*. At other times pick-ups can be hired in Jijoca, US$6 per person. For a direct connection take the *Redenção* bus leaving Fortaleza at 0900 (arrive Jerí 1600) or 2100 (arrive Jerí 0330); the 0600 bus from Jerí arrives in Fortaleza 1430, the 2200 bus arrives between 0430 and 0600, from the rodoviária it goes to Praia Iracema; night buses are direct, while daytime ones make many stops; Fortaleza-Jericoacoara US$8.50. 2 or 3-day tours from Fortaleza are available, book through travel agencies. You can also get there by **boat**, 'seasickness guaranteed'. If coming from Belém or other points north and west, go via Sobral (from Belém US$28.25, 20 hrs), where you change for Cruz (Sobral-Cruz: Mon-Sat at 1200; Cruz-Sobral: Mon/Wed/Fri at 0400, Tue/Thu/Sat at 0330; US$7.25; 3-4 hrs), several *pousadas* (see below) continue to Jijoca the next day (Cruz-Jijoca, daily about 1400, US$1.25, meets Jardineira for Jerí, Cruz-Jericoacoara, US$2.20).

An alternative from the west, especially if going through Parnaíba, is by bus from **Camocim** approximately 45 km west along the beach (see below); a private bus goes most days Jijoca-Camocim, about 0230, return Camocim-Jijoca at 1130, US$4.25; pickups also do the run for US$4.25-7.75 per person, depending on demand; alternatively you can go through Sobral, a much longer trip, or hire a buggy along the beach, beautiful scenery, Jericoacoara-Camocim US$72.50 for 4; from Camocim there is a regular bus service to Parnaíba. If you are looking for more adventure, take a truck from Camocim to **Guriú** where hammock space can be found. The village musician sings his own songs in the bar. Walk 4 hrs, or take a boat across the bay to **Jericoacoara**.

Some 40 km east of Jijoca is Cruz, an obligatory stop if travelling by bus from Sobral to Jericoacoara. It is a pleasant small town, surrounded by a *carnauba* palm forest (used in making brooms). At the south end is a large wooden cross dating from 1825, nearby is a statue to São Francisco. There is a lively market on Sunday when, at dawn, *pau d'arara* trucks, mule carts and bicycles converge on the town. There are two very basic hotels (**F**) with shared bath, *Hotel Magalhães*, R Teixeira Pinto 390, friendly, meals available and *Hospedaria*, R 6 de Abril 314, as well as *Pousada Ideal*, R Teixeira Pinto. *Churrascaria Casa do Sol Nascente* is near the cross at the south entrance to town. The bus to Jijoca goes through about 1400, US$2 or US$3.50 to Jericoacoara, wait for the bus by 1330.

Transport
If on a motorcycle, it is not possible to ride from Jijoca to Jericoacoara (unless you are an expert in desert conditions). Safe parking for bikes in Jijoca is not a problem

Cruz

Fortaleza and the North Coast

Camocim
Phone code: 088
Population: 51,500

This regional centre with some industry is an important fishing port and crafts centre. In the area there are many lagoons and unspoilt beaches such as Maceió, 28 km west, and Nova Tatajuba, 40 km east, access requires a vehicle with good traction. **Nova Tatajuba** has magnificent scenery, it is on the west margin of the outflow of Lagoa Grande; the beach is wide, dunes follow the shore, the ocean is clear and calm and there is a fishing village with a few basic *pousadas*. The town was built to replace old Tatajuba which was buried by the shifting sands. For transport see Jericoacoara above; bus information in Fortaleza, T2272999.

Sleeping and eating Camocim: **C** *Hotel Municipal*, Av Beira Mar, T6210274. With bath, pool. **D** *Hotel Lusitania*. *Dimas Restaurant*, Av Beira Mar, 2 km from centre. Varied menu. **Nova Tatajuba**: **B** *Tatajuba*, basic, rooms with and without bath, no electricity, meals served in proprietor's home included in the price. **D** *Verde Folha*, adapted fisherman's home, 1 room with bath, 2 shared bath (**E**), restaurant, breakfast extra.

The Sertão

Two types of area characterize the interior of Ceará, the serras, highlands and tablelands with a pleasant climate and green scenery, and the sertões, *arid expanses of semi-desert. The interior is not high on any visitor's list as a place to visit, especially when compared with the coast. However, there are some very scenic and interesting sites, particularly religious ones such as important shrines and pilgrimage sites.*

Baturité

Colour map 2, grid A5
Phone code: 085
Population: 32,000
Altitude: 171 m

The town of Baturité is surrounded by hills and waterfalls, with some colonial buildings and a historical museum. It is home of the *Pingo de Ouro* distillery which can be visited and there are hotels and restaurants. You can also stay in the Jesuit Seminary where a few monks still work in the local community and tend the cloister garden (**E** per person full board, ask for 'Jesuitas' if taking a taxi, or walk up; T3470362 in advance, Irmão João Batista). Baturité is the largest town in the **Maciço de Baturité**, an irregular massif with beautiful scenery. About 19 km northwest of Baturité and at 365 m above sea level is **Guaramiranga**, centre of a fruit and flower growing area, home of the *Festival Nordestino de Teatro*, held in September. In the area is a remnant of native forest, now a nature reserve. Nearby is Pico Alto (1,115 m above sea level), which offers special views and sunsets. About 7 km further north is **Pacoti**, with large botanical gardens (*horto forestal*), trails and several waterfalls; good for a dip and for viewing the highland flora.

Sleeping **A** *Estância Vale das Flores*, Sítio São Francisco, Pacoti, T3251233. Chalets and rooms, price includes lunch, fridge, restaurant, pool, sauna, lake, horses. **B** *Remanso Hotel da Serra*, 5 km north of Guaramiranga, T3251222. Bath, restaurant, pool, lake, sports fields. **B** *Hotel Escola de Guaramiranga*, in Guaramiranga, T/F3211106. Bath, fridge, hot water, restaurant, pool, atop a hill in an 8-hut estate which includes forest, orchards and an old convent, it doubles as a tourism school, run by the state agency SETUR.

Transport *Redenção* bus from Fortaleza rodoviária, mornings only, 3 hrs. Also a tourist train round trip, Sun (US$22 including museum, bus to Guaramiranga and lunch at *Hotel da Serra*).

The pilgrimage centre of Canindé, 108 km southwest of Fortaleza, is located **Canindé**
in the Sertão Central of Ceará. A large modern church stands on a hill; it has
carved baptistry doors and many *ex votos*. It receives hundreds of thousands
of pilgrims from all over the northeast between 26 September and 3 October;
devotees of São Francisco das Chagas, '*O pobrezinho de Asis*', many of them
dressed like Franciscan priests. The pilgrims flock to town on foot, by bus and
mostly on *pau de arara* trucks (see box). There is a regional museum with
artefacts representative of northeast culture and several restaurants. There is a
daily bus service from Fortaleza rodoviária with *Viação Nova Esperança*, three
hours, and interesting dry-land vegetation along route.

Quixadá is on the **Serra do Estevão**, with its rocky dry hills representative of **Quixadá**
the central *sertão*. The town has a dam built during the empire by order of *Phone code: 088*
Dom Pedro II, following the terrible drought of 1877-79. The scenery around *Population: 64,500*
the dam has interesting rock formations including the *galhina choca* (brood-
ing hen). The area is popular for sports such as hang gilding and there is a historical museum. About 21 km from town is Gruta do Pajé, a complex of
religious buildings dating from the early 1900s, which includes the **A** *Casa de
Reposo São José*, today a popular hotel run by nuns (T8120155, with bath).

Quixeramobim is an important regional centre, with nearby archaeological sites with ancient inscriptions on boulders (contact Sr Simão, R Mons
Salviano Pinio 233, T6380000). The regional dam has been used for irrigation
with good results. In August it has an important musical event, the *Festival de
Violas e Violeiros*, drawing participants from far and near, and in September
the *Grande Vaquejada de Quixeramobim* (a typical *sertão* rodeo). *Redenção*
bus from Fortaleza rodoviária to Quixadá, three hours, US$4.50. Same com-
pany to Quixeramobim, 0900, four hours, US$7.

Because of the Rio Jaguaribe, 20% of the agricultural land of the state is con- **Vale do**
centrated in the east, in the region known as the **Vale do Jaguaribe**. Using **Jaguaribe**
irrigation, the *sertão* becomes quite fertile, with rice and beans as the main
crops here. Among the towns are **Morada Nova**, 161 km from Fortaleza and
Limoeiro do Norte, 201 km from Fortaleza; just south of Limoeiro is
Tabuleiro do Norte, where an important religious pilgrimage takes place in
honour of Nossa Senhora da Saúde, 11-15 August. Festivities include processions, musical shows and much *forró*. The area is rich in crafts made with *carnauba* palm thatch, including fine basketry and hats. The town of
Jaguaruana, 185 km from Fortaleza, is an important producer of hammocks.
A deeply rooted tradition in this area is the *vaquejada* (rodeo), accompanied
by country *violeiros* (guitar music) and regional food.

South of the Vale do Jaguaribe is the area known as the **Sertões do Salgado**,
in the Rio Salgado valley. The most prominent feature here is the **Orós** dam,
with a capacity of 2.1 billion cubic meters; the reservoir has 300 islands and is
used for watersports. Some of the towns in the area are **Orós** (403 km from
Fortaleza), **Icó** (372 km from Fortaleza) and **Iguatu** (378 km from Fortaleza),
all historical cities with well preserved colonial structures; and **Lavras de
Mangabeira** (432 km from Fortaleza), surrounded by rocks, caves and a canyon formed by the Rio Salgado, 4 km from town.

Fortaleza and the North Coast

Juazeiro do Norte

Phone code: 088
Colour map 2, grid B4
Population: 200,000

The south of the state is known as the Cariri region, the name of an indigenous Indian group which lived in the interior and resisted Portuguese colonization for a long time. The main centre in this area is Juazeiro do Norte, the second city in Ceará. Along with its two satellites, Crato and Barbalha, 10 km to the west and south respectively, they form an oasis of green in the dry sertão.

Juazeiro do Norte was the home of Padre Cícero Romão Batista, a controversial and very popular priest who advocated the interests of the city and its most dispossessed inhabitants from the 1870s to the 1930s (see box, page 513). Even before his death, Padre Cícero had become a legend and Juazeiro do Norte an important pilgrimage site, drawing the faithful from throughout the northeast and increasingly nationwide. Today it is the most important pilgrimage centre of the region; there are six main annual pilgrimages but visitors arrive all year round. Religious tourism is the principal source of income in this otherwise poor area; prices rise during pilgrimages and there are many beggars at all times. Another cultural manifestation seen throughout the Cariri region is the *bandas cabaçais ou de pífaros*, musical groups which participate in all celebrations. As well as playing instruments, they dance, imitating animals, and perform games or fights.

Sights

Memorial Padre Cícero, Praça do Cinquentenário, is a museum featuring photographs and religious artefacts; a good selection of books is on sale. ■ *0730-1130 and 1330-1730 Mon-Fri, 0800-1200 Sat-Sun. Free.* Nearby is the **Chapel of Nossa Senhora do Perpétuo Socorro**, which houses Padre Cícero's tomb. A 27-m high statue to him stands in the Logradouro do Horto, a park overlooking the town; either take the pilgrim trail up the hill (one hour, start early because of the heat) or take the Horto city bus. Also worth seeing is

Juazeiro do Norte

Padre Cícero

◀◀

Padre Cícero Romão Batista came to Juazeiro in 1872 as a young priest where he worked for many years, gaining respect in his pastoral duties and caring for the poor. However, his life was dramatically changed with the occurrence on 1 March 1889 of a miracle during a communion service at which he was presiding. One of the congregation, Maria de Araújo, received the host and immediately collapsed, as it turned to blood which dripped on to the communion cloth and down to the floor. This event was repeated several times over the next few months and Padre Cícero was confused as to what was happening. He contacted the bishop in Fortaleza, Dom Joaquim, who initially ignored what was going on in the hope that it would go away, but after a doctor published an article saying that it was impossible to find a scientific explanation for the host turning to blood, the bishop sent two priests to investigate. It is probable that Dom Joaquim hoped that they would uncover a fraud being perpetrated in this poor and backward part of the state, but they returned agreeing that the events were miraculous. Only the Vatican claimed that the miracles were a sham and put it down to local superstition, but by that time the ball had started to roll and Padre Cícero's name was spreading far and wide. Brazilians were convinced that miracles were happening in the town and that Padre Cícero was a living saint.

Pilgrims started arriving to ask his blessing. He cared for the poor and the dispossessed, using the money donated by pilgrims to invest in schools and orphanages. His ability to attract large numbers of workers drew him to the attention of political bosses, with whom he reached an understanding (unlike Antônio Conselheiro at Canudos). Most of the pilgrims were, and still are, poor farmers and workers from nearby states such as Pernambuco and Alagoas. Some spend days travelling through the arid sertão before reaching the green valley of Juazeiro: a geographical and spiritual oasis. Before he died aged 90 in 1934, he contributed further to the mysticism surrounding him by saying, "I am not going to die. I am going on a journey. I will come back in a while".

Although the Church still regards prayers to Padre Cícero as superstitious and refuses to beatify him, his popularity remains undimmed and appeals to Brazilians' strong spiritual and syncretic traditions. Today's pilgrims are still convinced of his miracles, believing that he restores people to health and is the cause of unexplained recoveries. Many come to Juazeiro to carry out promessas, promises made to Padre Cícero in their prayers that if they survived an illness, or overcame a problem, they would make a pilgrimage to give thanks. In the museum dedicated to him, the walls are lined with photographs and messages from grateful people, while in the next room there are piles of ex-votos, carvings of limbs in wood or wax, representing the parts of the body which prayers to Padre Cícero have cured.

the **Church of Nossa Senhora das Dores** with the adjacent pilgrimage grounds, roughly fashioned after St Peter's Square in Rome.

Excursions

The **Chapada do Araripe**, a tableland about 850 m high, is south of Juazeiro do Norte and extends from east to west for 220 km. The area is believed to have been uplifted and numerous fossilized plants and animals including giant sloths have been found. It has one of the main native forest reserves in the state, the **Floresta Nacional do Araripe**, 20 km from Crato, with grottos, palaeontological sites, springs and cloud forest with ferns and orchids. Some 22 km south of Juazeiro do Norte, within the Chapada, is *Balneário do Caldas*, a pool fed with natural springwater (0700-1700), access through Barbalha; here is **A** *Hotel das Fontes*, T5321060, with bath, fridge, restaurant.

In the area of **Jardim**, 34 km south of Barbalha, there are several natural springs, while by **Missão Velha**, 22 km east of Barbalha, are the rapids on the Rio Salgado and a nice waterfall. Another access to the Chapada is through **Santana do Cariri**, 60 km west of Juazeiro do Norte. Its main attraction is the **Nascente dos Azedos**, a natural spring good for bathing. There is also a palae-ontology museum, one basic hotel; transport with *Pernambucana*, daily at 1430, returning 0600, US$2.50, two hours.

Population: 90,360

Crato is an older city which lost its limelight in the region, owing to the increased importance of Juazeiro do Norte. It has several nice *praças* and a small **Museu de Fósseis**, Praça da Sé 105, housing an impressive collection of fossils from the Cretaceous period gathered in the Chapada do Araripe. ■ *0800-1200 and 1400-1800 Mon-Fri. Free.* **Sleeping** The friendly **B** *Crato*, Rua Bárbara de Alencar 668 near Praça Cristo Rei, T5212824, with bath, a/c, **D** with fan, restaurant. There are also two other simpler hotels in town.

Essentials

Sleeping
You can expect prices to be higher during pilgrimages

A *Verde Vales Lazer*, Av P A Castelo, 3 km from town on the road to Barbalha, T/F5712544. Pool, restaurant. **B** *Panorama*, Santo Agostinho 58, T5213100, F5123110. Pool, restaurant, good value. **C** *Viana Palace*, São Pedro 746, T5112585, F5112476. With bath, a/c, fridge, **D** with fan. **C** *Municipal*, São Francisco 220, Praça Padre Cícero, T5122899. Comfortable large rooms, good value, cheaper with fan. Recommended. **C** *Plaza*, Padre Cícero 148, T5110493. With bath, a/c, **D** with fan and cheaper still with shared bath. **D** *Aristocrata*, São Francisco 402, T5111889. With bath, fan, cheaper without bath, basic, family run, restaurant. **D** *Maceió*, São José 208, T5112930. With bath, fan, cheaper with shared bath. restaurant. **D** *Pousada Cariri*, São José 218, T5122079. With bath, **E** without breakfast, basic, friendly, family run, good restaurant. Many basic hotels and *hospedarias* for pilgrims on R São José and around Nossa Senhora das Dores Basilica.

Eating
Cheiro Verde, S Cândido 72, varied menu. Several restaurants around Praça Padre Cícero, more economical ones on R São José; *Pousada*, good food.

Festivals
The following pilgrimage dates are listed in decreasing order of importance: **1-2 Nov**, *Finados*, the city receives some 600,000 visitors for the *All Saints' Day* pilgrimages; **10-15 Sep**, *Nossa Senhora das Dores*, the city's patron saint; **2 Feb**, *Candeias*(Candelmas), *Nossa Senhora da Luz*; **20 Jul**, *Padre Cícero's death*; **24 Mar**, *Padre Cícero's birth*; **6 Jan**, *Reis Magos* (Epiphany).

Transport
Air Airport is 7 km from the centre along Av Virgílio Távora, T5112118. Flights to Fortaleza, Petrolina and Recife. Taxi from centre US$5.75, motorcycle taxi US$3; taxi from rodoviária US$8.40.

Buses Rodoviária, Av Dalmiro Gouveia, on the road to Crato, T5112868. Taxi from the centre US$3, motorcycle taxi US$0.60. To **Fortaleza** with *Rio Negro*, 2 daily, US$13.50 *convencional*, US$17.50 *executivo*, 8 hrs. To **Picos** with *Boa Esperança*, 2 daily, US$5.75, 5 hrs. To **Teresina** with *Boa Esperança*, *Progresso* or *Aparecida*, 3 daily, US$11-12, 11 hrs. To **São Luís** with *Progresso*, US$20, 16 hrs. To **Belém** with *Boa Esperança*, 1 daily (often full), US$30, 25 hrs. To **Campina Grande** with *Transparaiba*, 2 daily, US$9, 9 hrs. To **João Pessoa** with *Braga*, 1 daily, US$12, 10 hrs. To **Recife** with *Braga*, 1 daily, US$14, 11 hrs. To **Salvador** with *Itapermirim*, 2 weekly, US$17.50, 14 hrs. To **São Paulo** with Itapemirim, 1 daily, US$63, 40 hrs.

Car hire *Unidas*, Av Padre Cícero, Km 2 on road to Crato, T5711226, F5711855. *IBM*, Santo Agostinho 58, T5110542. *Localiza*, Airport and Av Padre Cícero Km 03, No 3375, T5712668.

Airline offices *TAF* (*Táxi Aéreo Fortaleza*), T5110699. **Banks** *Banco do Brasil*, R São Francisco, near Praça Pradre Cícero, poor rates, Mon-Fri 1100-1600. No *câmbios* in town. **Communications Post office**: R Conceição 354 and at rodoviária. **Telephone**: R São Pedro 204, half a block from Praça Padre Cícero and at rodoviária.   **Directory**

Western Ceará

Sobral

Sobral, 238 km west of Fortaleza, is the principal town in western Ceará and the access point to beaches in the west of the state. The city has a handful of well-preserved colonial buildings including the Catedral da Sé, Teatro São João and a mansion on the Praça da Sé. There is a **Museu Diocesano** at Praça São João, a Cristo Redentor Statue and a monument to the 1919 solar eclipse. Near town is the Parque Ecológico Lagoa da Fazenda.   *Phone code: 088*
Colour map 2, grid A4
Population: 145,000

A *Beira Rio*, R Conselheiro Rodrigues 400 across from the rodoviária, T6131040. A/c, with fan, fridge. **A** *Visconde*, Av Lúcia Saboia 473, 10 mins from the rodoviária, T6114222, F6114197. Friendly, a/c, cheaper with fan, good breakfast. **B** *Cisne*, Trav do Xerez 215, T/F6110171. A/c, cheaper with fan, friendly. **B** *Vitória*, Praça Gen Tibúrcio 120, T6131566. Bath, a/c, cheaper with fan, some rooms without bath (**C**), restaurant. **D** *Francinet's*, R Col Joaquim Ribeiro 294. With fan, bath, cheaper with shared bath. *Casa Grande o Louro*, R Tabelo Idelfonso Cavalcante 611. Good meat. *Hotel Vitória*, good lunch buffet. Recommended. *Churrascaria Gaúcho*, Av Dom José, meat. *Chico 1000* and *2000*, varied menu. *Lataro*, self-service.   **Sleeping & eating**

Chapada de Ibiapaba

In the Chapada de Ibiapaba, an area of tablelands, caves, rock formations, rivers and waterfalls, is **Tianguá**. The town is surrounded by waterfalls; 3 km to the north is Cachoeira de São Gonçalo, a good place for bathing; 5 km from town are natural pools at the meeting place of seven waterfalls. About 16 km from town on the edge of the BR-222 is Cana Verde, a 30-m high waterfall surrounded by monoliths and thick vegetation. About 2 km from town is **A** *Serra Grande* hotel, BR-222 Km 311, T6711818, F6711477, all amenities, good. In Tianguá is **D** *Hotel Gean*, on the central praça. Bus from Fortaleza US$10, from Belém US$30.

Some 30 km north of Tianguá is **Viçosa do Ceará**, a colonial town also within the Chapada, known for its ceramics. The Igreja de Nossa Senhora das Vitórias, a stone church on top of the 820-m high Morro do Céu, is reached walking up 360 steps. There is an excellent view of the town, the surrounding highlands and the *sertão* beyond. Near the town are interesting rock formations such as the 100-m wide **Pedra de Itagurussu** with a natural spring. There is good walking in the area.

Parque Nacional Ubajara

About 18 km south of Tianguá is **Ubajara**, which has an interesting Sunday morning market selling produce of the *sertão*; buses to Fortaleza.   *Colour map 2, grid A4*

About 3 km from town is Ubajara National Park, the smallest of Brazil's national parks, with 563 ha of native highland (similar to that found in the *planalto central*) and *caatinga* brush. The park's main attraction is the Ubajara cave on the side of an escarpment. Some 15 chambers totalling 1,120 m have been mapped, of which 400 m are open to visitors, well worth seeing.

Access is along a footpath and steps (2-3 hours, take water) or with the *bondinha*, a cablecar which descends the cliff to the cave entrance, 0830-1630, US$4. Lighting has been installed in nine caverns of the complex, but a torch and spare batteries may be useful. An Ibama guide leads visitors in the cave; the Ibama office at the park entrance, 5 km from the caves, is not always helpful and not always open, T6341388. The views of the *sertão* from the upper cablecar platform are superb; beautiful walks among forest and waterfalls and old sugar-mills are scattered around the plateau. To walk all the way up to the top of the plateau takes 14 hours, if you want to do this take plenty of water.

Sleeping **Near the park** **B** *Pousada da Neblina*, Estr do Teleférico, 2 km from town, T6341270, in
& eating beautiful cloud forest. Swimming pool, with breakfast and private shower (**C** without breakfast), restaurant open 1100-2000, meals recommended, campsite (US$15 per tent). Opposite is **C** *Pousada Gruta da Ubajara* rustic, restaurant. Recommended. **D** *Sítio do Alemão*, take Estr do Teleférico 2 km from town, after the *Pousada da Neblina* turn right, 1 km to Sítio Santana, in the coffee plantation of *Herbert Klein*, on which there are three small chalets. Warmly recommended, with full facilities, excursions, walking maps, bicycle hire offered, homemade jams, if chalets are full the Kleins accommodate visitors at their house.

Ubajara town **C** *Le Village*, on Ibiapina road 4 km south from town, T6341364. Restaurant, pool, sauna, good value. **D** *Ubajara*, R Juvêncio Luís Pereira 370, T6341261. Small restaurant.

The Chapada de Ibiapaba continues south from Ubajara for some 70 km. Other towns along the highlands are: **Ibiapina**, with the nearby Cachoeira da Ladeira, reached by a steep trail, a good place for bathing; **São Benedito**, known for its straw and ceramic crafts (**B** *Pousada de Inhuçu*, R Gonçalo de Freitas 454, T6261173, pool, restaurant); **Carnaubal**, with waterfalls and a bathing resort; and **Ipu**, with a 180-m high waterfall, site of the legendary love affair between the Indian, Iracema, and the founder of Fortaleza (**E** *Hotel Ipu*, in upper town, basic, friendly; there is a *pousada* at the waterfall).

Monsenhor Tabosa, in the centre of the state, has the highest peak in Ceará. This remote town is very friendly, with three hotels: *dos Viajantes* and *São Sebastião*, both contactable through the phone exchange, 0XX88-8261150, and *Márcia's Buffet*, T0XX88-8261213, ask for Márcia or Honório Júnior. Honório will draw rough walking maps and, if asked, can arrange for the *forró* band to play. It can get very wet in the rainy season (around March). The easiest way to get there is by car or Horizonte bus on the CE032 from Canindé, but there are roads from Nova Russas, south of Ipu, and the BR-020 from Boa Viagem (very rough).

Continuing south, the greenery of the Chapada de Ibiapaba eventually gives way to the dry **Sertão dos Inhamuns**. One of the main towns in this area is **Crateús**, about 210 km south of Sobral, a remote town with rich folkloric traditions seen during festivals in August (*Mergulho Folclórico*) and September (*Festival de Repentistas*); nearby are archaeological sites with rock inscriptions. There is the very reasonable and clean **D** *Crateús Palace Hotel*, with breakfast, good restaurant. *Churrascaria Pequena Cabana* is at the back of the hotel. There is a regular bus service on the paved road to Fortaleza (347 km). Bus service from Crateús over a very bad road to Teresina, every two days.

Piauí

Piauí is possibly the poorest state in Brazil. Its population is about 2.7 million, but many leave to seek work elsewhere. The economy is almost completely dependent upon agriculture and livestock, both of which in turn depend on how much rain, if any, falls.

The history of Piauí springs from cattle farmers who moved into the interior from Bahia, beginning in the 17th century. Until the early 19th century, though, the state was under the control of Maranhão. At Independence, there was bitter fighting between the Portuguese supporters of the colony and the Brazilians who sought their freedom.

Teresina

About 435 km up the Rio Parnaíba is the state capital. There are paved road and rail connections (freight only) with the neighbouring state capitals. The city itself is reputed to be the hottest after Manaus, with temperatures up to 42°C.

Phone code: 086
Colour map 2, grid A3
Population: 716,000

Ins and outs

There are **Piemtur** tourist offices at R Álvaro Mendes 2003, Caixa Postal 36, and at R Magalhães Filho (next to 55 N, English spoken); also at R Acre, Convention Centre, T2217100, and kiosks at the rodoviária and airport. The **Singtur** (Sindicato dos Guías de Turismo de Piauí) office, R Paissandu 1276, T2212175, has information booths at the Centro de Artesanato, Praça Dom Pedro II (helpful, friendly), the Encontro das Águas, Poty Velho and on the shores of the Rio Poty. **Ana Turismo** is at R Álvaro Mendes 1961, Centro, T/F2233970.

Tourist information

Sights

The **Palácio de Karnak** (the old governor's palace), just west of Praça Frei Serafim, contains lithographs of the Middle East in 1839 by David Roberts RA. ■ *1530-1730 Mon-Fri.* Also see the **Museu do Piauí**, Praça Marechal Deodoro. ■ *0800-1730 Tue-Fri, 0800-1200 Sat-Sun. US$0.60.*

There is an interesting open market by the Praça Marechal Deodoro and the river is picturesque, with washing laid out to dry along its banks. The market is a good place to buy hammocks, but bargain hard. Every morning along the river bank there is the **troca-troca**, where people buy, sell and swap. An undercover complex, **Mercado Central do Artesanato**, has been built at Rua Paissandu 1276, Praça Dom Pedro II. ■ *0800-2200 Mon-Fri.* Most of the year the river is low, leaving sandbanks known as *coroas* (crowns).

Essentials

L *Rio Poty*, Av Mcal Castelo Branco 555, Ilhota, T2231500, F2226671. 5-star. Recommended. **A** *Real Pálace*, R Lizandro Nogueira 1208, T2212768, F2217740. A/c, pool, restaurant. **A** *São José*, João Cabral 340, T2232176, F2232223. Reasonable restaurant. **B** *Royal Pálace*, R 13 de Maio 233N, T/F2217707. A/c, restaurant. **B** *Sambaíba*, R Gabriel Ferreira 230-N, T2226711. 2-star, central, good. **D** *Fortaleza*, Felix Pacheco

Sleeping
■ on map

1101, Praça Saraiva, T2222984. Fan, basic. Recommended. **D** *Santa Terezinha*, Av Getúlio Vargas 2885, opposite rodoviária, T2195918. With a/c, cheaper with fan, clean, friendly. Many other cheap hotels and *dormitórios* around Praça Saraiva. **D** *Grande*, Firmino Pires 73. Very friendly and clean. Many cheap ones in R São Pedro and in R Alvaro Mendes. **D** *Glória*, at 823 (clean, best), blocks 800 and 900 on each street.

Eating
Many places for all budgets in Praça Dom Pedro II

For fish dishes, *Pesqueirinho*, R Domingos Jorge Velho 6889, in Poty Velho district. *Camarão do Elias*, Av Pedro Almeida 457, T2325025. Good seafood. *Sabores Rotisserie*, R Simplício Mendes 78, Centro. By kg, good quality and variety.

Festivals
Teresina is proud of its *Carnival*, which is then followed by *Micarina*, a local carnival in **Mar**. There is much music and dancing in **Jul** and **Aug**, when there is a Bumba-meu-Boi, the Teresina dance festival, *Festidanças*, and a convention of itinerant guitarists.

Shopping
Teresina is an excellent and cheap source of northeastern *artesanato*, for which Piauí is renowned throughout Brazil. Panels of carved and painted hardwood, either representing stylized country scenes or of religious significance, are a good buy, as are clay or wooden models of traditional rural characters. Many of these eccentric figures come from the region's rich fund of myths and legends. Hammocks, straw and basket ware are also varied, interesting and well made here. Other local handicrafts include leather and clothes. Supermarket, Praça Mcal Deodoro 937, clean, good, fresh food.

Teresina

Sleeping
1 Real Pálace
2 Royal Pálace
3 Sambaíba
4 São José

Cabeça-de-Cuia

Crispim was a fisherman who lived at the confluence of the rivers Poti and Parnaíba, in Teresina. One day, returning home after a hard day's fishing with no catch whatsoever, he discovered that there was no food in the house. Infuriated, he grabbed a large bone which was lying nearby and beat his mother to death. Her dying curse was that Crispim should live out his days as a hideous monster with an enormous head.

A young and single man, Crispim was driven to despair by his now terrifying appearance. He drowned himself in the Parnaíba. Legend has it that Crispim will be restored to life, and his good looks, when he has managed to eat seven virgins named Maria. Young laundresses, when they go to the river, are still afraid of him.

Cabeça-de-Cuia means 'head of a gourd'. Carvings of this strange figure are a common sight in Teresina.

Air: flights to Fortaleza, Brasília, Rio de Janeiro, São Paulo, Goiânia, São Luís. Buses from outside the airport run straight into town and to the rodoviária. **Transport**

Buses: the bus trip to Fortaleza is scenic and takes 9 hrs (US$13.50). There are direct buses to **Belém** (13 hrs, US$23.40), **Recife** (16 hrs, US$27) and **São Luís** (7 hrs, US$12).

Banks Banks with ATMs *Banco do Brasil* and *Unibanco*, Av Nossa Senhora de Fátima, in front of Caixa Econômica Federal. *Itaú*, in same avenue at P Center Shopping. *Bradesco*, Av Frei Serafim, at corner of 1 de Maio. *Mirante Câmbio*, Av Frei Serafim 2150, T2233633. *Alda Tur*, R A de Abreu 1226. **Directory**

Parque Nacional de Sete Cidades

Some 190 km northeast of Teresina, this interesting park has strange eroded rock formations which from the ground look like a medley of weird monuments. The inscriptions on some of the rocks have never been deciphered; one theory suggests links with the Phoenicians, and the Argentine Professor Jacques de Mahieu considers them to be Nordic runes left by the Vikings. Within the 20 sq km of the park, there is plenty of birdlife and iguanas, which descend from their trees in the afternoon. If hiking in the park, beware of rattlesnakes. Ibama provides a free bus (see below). *Colour map 2, grid A3*

Ibama, Av Homero Castelo Branco 2240, Teresina, CEP 64048-400, T2321142. Small booklet with sketch map (not really good enough for walking), entrance US$3. Local food is limited and monotonous: bring a few delicacies, and especially fruit. Some 50 km away, **Pedro Segundo** is a good place to buy opals. **Park essentials**

Situated 6 km from the park entrance is **B** *Hotel Sete Cidades*, Km 63 on BR-222, T086-2762222. Chalets with private bath, swimming pool, good restaurant and bicycle or horse transport; also has a free pick-up to the park (and a most unpleasant zoo). In the park is an Ibama hostel, T3431342, **E** per person. Rooms with bath, pleasant, good restaurant, natural pool nearby, camping. Recommended. **Sleeping**

Piripiri Located 26 km from the park; several good ones, including **E** *Novo Hotel Central*, in the centre. With fan, bath, breakfast and safe parking, friendly. Recommended. Also **D** per person *Martins*, T2761273. Others can be found near bus offices and behind the church. Exchange at the bank only. *Piripiri is a cheap place to break the Belém-Fortaleza journey, 26 km from the park*

Fortaleza and the North Coast

Transport   A free bus service leaves the Praça da Bandeira in Piripiri (in front of Telemar office), at 0700, passing *Hotel Fazenda Sete Cidades* at 0800, reaching the park 10 mins later; return at 1630, or hitchhike. Taxi from Piripiri, US$15, or from Piracuruca, US$20. Bus Teresina-Piripiri and return, throughout the day 2½ hrs, US$4. Bus São Luís-Piripiri, 1200, 1630, 2130, 10 hrs, US$15. Several daily buses Piripiri-Fortaleza, 9 hrs, US$11. Bus Piripiri-Ubajara (see above), marked 'São Benedito', or 'Crateús', 2½ hrs; US$4, first at 0700 (a beautiful trip).

Parnaíba

Phone code: 086
Colour map 2, grid A3
Population: 133,000

Between the states of Maranhão and Piauí runs the Rio Parnaíba. Near the river mouth is the anchorage of Luís Correia, where ships unload for final delivery by tugs and lighters at Parnaíba; 15 km upriver, the collecting and distributing centre for the trade of Piauí: tropical products and cattle. It is partly encircled by shifting sands in white dunes up to 30 m high. The town is a relaxed, friendly place. If crossing the delta, buy all provisions here. There is a regular connection here to Tutóia, for boats across the Parnaíba delta (see page 529); a tour in the delta costs US$20 per person.

Beaches   There are beaches at Luís Correia, 14 km from Parnaíba, with radioactive sands (**A** *Rio Poty Praia*, Av dos Magistrados 2350, T/F3671277, bar, restaurant, pool). About 18 km from Parnaíba is Pedra do Sal, with dark blue lagoons and palm trees. At Lagoa de Portinho, 12 km from Parnaíba, there are bungalows, a bar and restaurant, and it is possible to camp; canoes for hire. Praia do Coqueiro is a small fishing village with natural pools formed at low tide (**A** *Aimberê Resort*, T3661144, F3661204. *Alô Brasil* and *Bar da Cota* for seafood).

Sleeping   **L** *Cívico*, Av Gov Chagas Rodrigues 474, T3222470, F3222028. Restaurant, pool, good breakfast. Recommended. **A** *Pousada dos Ventos*, Av São Sebastião 2586, Universidade, T3222177, F3224880. Pool. Recommended. **D** *Rodoviária*, and other basic hotels in the centre.

Eating   *Recanto Gaúcho*, Trav Costa Fernandes, next to university, churrasco. *Renatinho*, Av das Nações Unidas, Beira Rio. Crab and seafood. *Sorveteria Araújo*, R Pires Ferreira 615. Good ice-cream from local fruits.

Bars &   *Centro Cultural Porto das Barcas*, a pleasant shopping and entertainment complex
nightclubs   with several good restaurants and a large open-air bar on the riverside.

Shopping   *Artesanato de Parnaíba*, R Dom Pedro II 1140 and *Cooperativa Artesanal Mista de Parnaíba*, R Alcenor Candeira, for local handicrafts.

Directory   **Banks** *Banco do Brasil*, Praça da Graça 340. *Bradesco*, Av Pres Getúlio Vargas 403. **Communications** Post office: Praça da Graça. **Telephone**: Av Pres Getúlio Vargas 390. **Medical services** *Pró-Médica*, Av Pres Vargas 799, T3223645. 24-hr emergency ward. **Tourist offices** *Piemtur*, T3211532, and *Secretaria de Turismo e Meio Ambiente*, T3231715, both at Porto das Barcas (see above).

Southern Piauí

Oeiras is the old capital of Piauí, where the state government is restoring some of the old buildings, such as the bishop's palace and the church of Nossa Senhora da Vitória.

The BR-407 is reported unsafe near the border with Pernambuco due to robberies of vehicles travelling this route

Parque Nacional Serra da Capivara

About 500 km south of Teresina is this 130,000-ha park, on the UNESCO World Heritage list. Some 30,000 prehistoric rock paintings on limestone have been found, dating to between 6,000 and 12,000 years ago. The paintings are of daily life, festivities and celebrations, as well as hunting and sex scenes. Excavations by Brazilian and French archaeologists have uncovered fossilized remains of extinct animals such as the sabre-toothed tiger, giant sloths larger than elephants and armadillos the size of a car.

Colour map 2, grid B3

Nearly 400 archaeological sites have been identified in the park since research began in 1970. About 22 of those sites have been set up to receive tourists. Roads and all-weather paths allow visitors to view the site with ease. Specially trained guides are available. The area is good for hiking in the *caatinga*, with its canyons and mesas. It is also possible to see much of the *caatinga* wildlife, in particular the birds.

Much investment has gone into the park, not just for visitors' facilities, but also in educating the local population about protecting the paintings and establishing a beekeeping project to provide income in times of drought. The main organization is the **Fundação do Homem Americano** (Fumdham), Rua Abdias Neves 551, CEP 64770-000, São Raimundo Nonato, Piauí, T5821612/1389, F5821656, which has a museum for scientists. For further information on the park and reservations in local hotels, contact Dr Niéde Guidon, Fumdham Parque Nacional, at the address above.

Access is from São Raimundo Nonato on the BR-324, or from Petrolina in Pernambuco (the nearest airport, 290 km away). Taxi from Petrolina airport will cost about US$200 one way, or there are buses.

Transport

In the far southwest of the state, near **São Gonçalo do Piauí**, is one of the best places for seeing hyacinth macaws. The Hyacinth Site is on private land, 20 km from São Gonçalo, in a region of *cerrado* with red sandstone cliffs where the macaws nest. This used to be an area in which the illegal bird trade flourished, but the local people now guard the site, which is supported by the Kaytee Avian Foundation (USA) and others. Many other *cerrado* birds may be seen, together with black-and-gold howlers and, less commonly, maned wolf and giant anteaters. Accommodation is in very simple huts with mosquito nets, sand floors and shared bathrooms. Meals are served at the site. Access is via the airport at Barreiras in Western Bahia, 340 km south, five or six hours' drive away. Tours are only possible through *Focus Tours*, see Tours and tour operators, page 24.

Hyacinth Site

Fortaleza and the North Coast

Maranhão

Population: 5.8 million *The colonial centre of São Luís, with its use of ceramic tiles as exterior decoration, has been restored and is now part of UNESCO's list of sites of worldwide cultural importance. The coast to the east, stretching to the Parnaíba delta, contains an area of sand dunes and freshwater lakes, the Lençóis Maranhenses, which deserves a visit for its beauty and remoteness. The area around Carolina, south of Imperatriz, is renowned for its mountain scenery and spectacular waterfalls. As for culture, the Bumba-Meu-Boi is typical of the region and the African influence harks back to the days when slaves were imported into the city, which is also considered Brazil's reggae capital.*

Initially, the Portuguese did not show much interest in this part of the Northeast, so the French were the first to bring in colonists. By the end of the 16th century, the Portuguese took over, but this was interrupted by a brief period of Dutch dominance in the early 1640s. The Companhia Geral do Comércio do Maranhão e Grão-Pará, 1685-1777, was the major influence in the area, but after its demise, there was unrest until Maranhão finally bowed to the Independence movement.

Maranhão state is about the size of Italy, with flat and low-lying land and highlands to the south. The Atlantic coastline – a mass of sandbanks and creeks and sandy islands on one of which stands São Luís – is 480 km long. The wet season lasts from January to March and the temperature is generally between 24 and 34°C throughout the year.

São Luís

Colour map 2, grid A2
Phone code: 098
Population: 870,000
1,080 km west
of Fortaleza
830 km southeast
of Belém

The capital and port of Maranhão state, founded in 1612 by the French and named after St Louis of France, stands upon São Luís island between the bays of São Marcos and São José. The urban area extends to São Francisco island, connected with São Luís by three bridges. The historic centre is being restored with UNESCO support and the splendid results (eg the part known as the Reviver) rival the Pelourinho in Salvador. An old slaving port, the city has a large black population and has retained much African culture. It is located in a region of heavy tropical rains, but the surrounding deep forest has been cut down to be replaced by babaçu palms, the nuts and oils of which are the state's most important products.

Sights The old part of the city, on very hilly ground with many steep streets, is still almost pure colonial. The damp climate stimulated the use of ceramic tiles for exterior walls, and São Luís shows a greater variety of such tiles than anywhere else in Brazil; in Portuguese, French and Dutch styles. The commercial quarter (Rua Portugal, also called Rua Trapiche) is still much as it was in the 17th century; the best shopping area is Rua de Santana near Praça João Lisboa. The **tourist offices** (*Fumtur*) are at Praça Benedito Leite, T2225281, and at the airport. *Maratur* is at Praça João Lisboa 66, opposite the post office, T2312000, maratur@geplan.ma.gov.br

The **Palácio dos Leões** (Governor's Palace), Avenida Dom Pedro II, has beautiful floors of dark wood (*jacarandá*) and light (*cerejeira*). There are marvellous views from the terrace. ■ *1500-1800 Mon, Wed and Fri.* The restored **Fortaleza de Santo Antônio**, built originally by the French in 1614, is on the bank of the Rio Anil at Ponta d'Areia.

The **Fábrica Canhamo**, Rua São Pantaleão 1232, Madre de Deus, near Praia Grande, is a restored factory and houses an arts and crafts centre. ■ *0900-1900 Mon-Fri, T2322187*. The **Centro da Creatividade Odylo Costa Filho**, Rua da Alfândego 200, Praia Grande, is an arts centre with theatre, cinema, music, etc, with a bar and café; a good meeting place. ■ *0800-2200 Mon-Fri, T2314058*.

Churches The best colonial churches in town are the **cathedral** (1629) on Praça Dom Pedro II, and the churches of **Carmo** (1627), Praça João Lisboa, **São João Batista** (1665), Largo São João, **Nossa Senhora do Rosário** (1717 on Rua do Egito), and the 18th-century **Santana**, Rua de Santana. On Largo do Desterro is the church of **São José do Desterro**, which was finished in 1863, but has much older parts.

Museums The **Cafua das Mercês**, Rua Jacinto Maia 43, is a museum housed in the old slave market. It is well worth the effort to find it: a small building opposite the Quartel Militar. ■ *1330-1700 Mon-Fri*. Also worth a visit is the **Casa dos Negros** next door. The **Museu Histórico e Artístico do Estado**, in a fine early 19th-century mansion (complete with slave quarters) at Rua do Sol 302. Also on the Rua do Sol is the **Teatro Artur Azevedo** (1816). **Museu de Artes Visuais**, Avenida Portugal 289, shows ceramics and post-war art. ■ *0800-1300, 1600-1800 Mon-Fri*.

Excursions **Calhau** is a huge beach, 10 km away. **Ponta D'Areia** is nearer to São Luís but more crowded. **Raposa**, a fishing village built on stilts, is a good place to buy

São Luís

N

Not to scale

■ Sleeping
1 Vila Rica

handicrafts. There are a few places to stay on Av Principal. It is an hour's bus ride with *Viação Santa Maria*, every 30 minutes from the Mercado Central, São Luís. Another fishing village is **São José de Ribamar**, whose church dedicated to the patron saint is a centre for *romeiros* in September. There is *Hotel Sol e Mar*, Av Gonçalves Dias 320, with a restaurant; many bars on the seafront serve local specialities such as fried stonefish. It is a 30-minute bus ride with *Maranhense* from in front of the market, São Luís.

Sleeping **AL** *La Ravadière*, Av Mcal Castelo Branco 375, São Francisco, T2352255, F2352217. Pool, restaurant, sauna. **AL-A** *Praia Mar*, Av São Marcos, Ponta d'Areia, on the beach, T2352328. **B** *Deodoro*, R de Santaninha 535, T2315811. A/c, parking, good. **B** *Ponta D'Areia*, Av dos Holandeses, Ponta D'Areia, T2353232, F2272892. Pool. **B** *Pousada Colonial*, R Afonso Pena 112, T2322834. In a beautiful restored, tiled house. Recommended. **B** *São Marcos*, R da Saúde 178, T2323768, F2317777. Restored colonial house, a/c, family-run. Recommended. **B** *Vila Rica*, Praça Dom Pedro II 299, T2323535, F2327245, www.hotelvilarica.com.br Central, pool, business centre with internet connection. Recommended. **C** *Lord*, R de Nazaré 258, facing Praça Benedito Leite, T/F2214655. A/c, comfortable, good value, good breakfast. Recommended. **D** *Pousada Solar dos Nobres*, R 13 de Maio 82, Centro, T2325705. Bright, welcoming, superb breakfast, very good. **D** *Pousada Turismo Jansen Müller*, R Jansen Müller 270, T2310997. With breakfast and bath. **D** *Hotel Casa Grande*, R Isaac Martins 94, Centro, T2322432. Clean, basic, single, double or triple rooms. Recommended. Many cheap hotels can be found in R das Palmas, very central, and R Formosa. eg **G** *Pousada Ilha Bela*, safe, R Formosa. **Youth hostels (E-F):** *Dois Continentes*, R 28 de Julho 129, Praia Grande, T/F222 6286, family run, and *Solar das Pedras*, R da Palma 127, T/F232 6694.

Eating
Bases are good for home cooking in simple surroundings, although most are found away from the centre and beaches

Typical dishes are *arroz de cuxá* and *torta de camarão*. Desserts and liquors are made from local fruits. Try the local soft drink called *Jesús* or *Jenève*. *Base do Edilson*, R Joao Damasceno 21, Ponta do Farol. Excellent for prawns. *Base do Germano*, Av Venceslau Brás, Camboa. Excellent *caldeirada de camarão* (shrimp stew). *Beiruth 2*, Av Mcal Castelo Branco 751B. Recommended. *Naturalista Alimentos*, R do Sol 517. Very good, natural food shops and restaurants, open till 1900. *Base da Lenoca*, Av Dom Pedro II 181. Good view, big portions. *Senac*, R Nazaré 242, next to hotel *Lord*. Tourism school restaurant, good food in a beautifully restored mansion. *Tia Maria*, Av Nina Rodrigues 1, Ponta d'Areia. Recommended for fried fish with *castanha* and *caju*.

Bars & nightclubs Many bars in Praia Grande such as *Antigamente* with live music from Thu-Sat. *Poeme-Sei*, R João Gualberto 52, Praia Grande is a bar/gallery open in the evening, good atmosphere, no food. Piano bar in *Senac* (see above) from Thu-Sat. Reggae is extremely popular. Good places are *Tombo da Ladeira*, Praia Grande on Wed, and *Coqueiro Bar*, Av dos Holandeses, Praia da Ponta D'Areia on Thu. A good nightclub is *Extravagance*, Av Conselheiro Hilton Rodrigues, Calhau.

Entertainment **Cinema** *Colossal*, Av Mcal Castelo Branco 92, São Francisco. *Passeio*, R Oswaldo Cruz 806. **Theatre** *Teatro Artur Azevedo*, see Sights above. *Teatro Viriato Correa*, Av Getúlio Vargas, Monte Castelo, T2189019.

Festivals On **24 Jun** (São João) is the *Bumba-Meu-Boi*, see box, above. For several days before the festival street bands parade, particularly in front of the São João and São Benedito churches. There are dances somewhere in the city almost every night in Jun. In **Aug**, *São Benedito*, at the Rosário church. Festival in **Oct**, with dancing, at Vila Palmeira suburb (take bus of same name).

Bumba-Meu-Boi

Throughout the month of June the streets of São Luís are alive to the sound of tambores *and dancers recreating the legend of Catirina, Pai Francisco and his master's bull. Although this mixture of African, indigenous and Portuguese traditions exists throughout the North it is in Maranhão that it is most developed with around 100 groups in São Luís alone. Here there are various styles called* sotaques, *which have different costumes, dances, instruments and* toadas. *These are* Boi de Matraca da Ilha *and* Boi de Pindaré, *both accompanied by small percussion instruments called* matracas, Boi de Zabumba *marked by the use of a type of drum, and* Boi de Orquestra *accompanied by string and wind instruments. Although there are presentations throughout June the highpoints are the 24th (São João) and the*

29th (São Pedro) with the closing ceremony lasting throughout the 30th (São Marçal), particularly in the bairro *João Paulo. The shows take place in an* arraial, *which are found all over the city, with the ones at* Projeto Reviver *and* Ceprama *being more geared towards tourists (however be aware that a livelier more authentic atmosphere is to be found elsewhere in other* bairros, *such as Madre Deus). The Centro de Cultura Popular Domingos Vieira Filho at Rua do Giz 221, Praia Grande is the place to learn more about these variations as well as many other local festivals and traditions such as Tambor de Crioula or Cacuriá, both sensual dances derived from Africa. A good location to see these dances and capoeira practised is* Labouarte, *Rua Jansen Muller, Centro (Cacuriá de Dona Tetê is particularly recommended with participation encouraged).*

The *Parque do Bom Menino*, Av Jaime Tavares, has a running track and sports courts. **Sport** **Gyms** *Vida e Sade*, R Rio Branco 174. *São Francisco*, Av Mcal Castelo Branco 120.

Ceprama, R de São Pantaleão 1232, Madre Deus, handicraft shops in an old colonial house. **Shopping**

Taguatur, R do Sol 141, loja 15, T2320906, F2321814. *Babaçu Viagens*, Av Dom Pedro II **Tour** 258, lojas A/B/C, T/F2314747, good. **operators**

Air Marechal Cunha Machado airport, 15 km from centre, Av Santos Dumont, **Transport** T2451688. Flights to Belém, Fortaleza, Imperatriz, Parnaíba and Teresina. *São Cristovão* buses to city until midnight, US$0.75. Taxi to city US$12.50.

Buses Rodoviária is 12 km from the centre on the airport road, 'Rodoviária via Alemanha' bus to centre (Praça João Lisboa), US$0.50. To **Fortaleza**, US$270, 4 a day, 18 hrs. To **Belém**, 13 hrs, US$20, *Transbrasiliana* at 1900 and 2000 (no *leito*). Also to **Recife**, US$45, 25 hrs, all other major cities and local towns.

Ferries These cross the bay daily from Porto do Itaqui to Porto do Cujupe. T2228431 for times. US$3 foot passenger, US$15 car.

Trains 3 trains a week on the Carajás railway to Parauapebas, 13½ hrs, 890 km, leave São Luís 0800, Mon, Wed, Fri, return 0800, Tue, Thu, Sat (crowded, take your own food). For the station take 'Vila Nova' or 'Anjo da Guarda' bus.

Airline offices *TAM*, T2440461. *Transbrasil*, Praça João Lisboa 432, T2321414. **Directory** *Varig/Nordeste*, Av Dom Pedro II 267, T2315066. *Vasp*, R do Sol 43, T2314422. **Banks** *Banco do Brasil*, Praça Deodoro, for TCs and Visa ATMs. *HSBC*, off Praça João Lisboa. Accepts MasterCard/Cirrus/Maestro. *Agetur*, R do Sol 33A. **Communications** Internet: *HCG*, R Paparaúbas 11, São Francisco. **Post office**: Praça João Lisboa 292. **Telephone**: *Embratel*, Av Dom Pedro II 190. **Embassies and consulates** *Denmark*, Av Colares Moreira 444, Monumental Shopping, Sala 220, T2357033. *France*, R Santo Antônio

259, T2314459. *Germany*, Praça Gonçalves Dias 301, T2327766. *Italy*, R do Genipapeiro, Jardim São Francisco, T2270270. *Spain*, Praça Duque de Caxias 3, João Paulo, T2232846. *USA*, Av Daniel de La Touche, Jardim Buriti, T2481769. **Language courses** *Senhora Amin Castro*, T2271527, for Portuguese lessons. Recommended. **Laundry** *Nova China*, R da Paz 518. **Libraries** *Arquivo Púúblico*, R de Nazaré 218, rare documents on local history. **Medical services** *Clínica São Marcelo*, R do Passeio 546, English-speaking doctor. *Hospital Monte Sinai*, R Rio Branco 156, T2323260, 24 hrs.

Alcântara

Phone code: 098
Colour map 2, grid A2
Population: 22,000

Some 22 km away by boat is Alcântara, the former state capital, on the mainland bay of São Marcos. Construction of the city began at the beginning of the 17th century and it is now a historical monument. There are many old churches (for example, the ruined **Matriz de São Matias**, 1648) and colonial mansions (see the **Casa**, and **Segunda Casa, do Imperador**, also the old cotton barons' mansions with their blue, Portuguese tiled façades). In the Praça da Matriz is the **Pelourinho** (1648), the traditional pillory, and a small museum. ■ *0900-1330. US$0.75*. You can also see the **Forte de São Sebastião** (1663), now in ruins, and the **Fonte de Mirititiua** (1747).

Canoe trips go to **Ilha do Livramento**, where there are good beaches and walking around the coast (can be muddy after rain). Watch out for mosquitoes after dark. A rocket launching site has been built nearby!

Alcântara

Sleeping
1 Pousada do Mordomo Régio
2 Pousada Pelourinho

Not to scale

B *Pousada dos Guarás*, Praia da Baronesa, T3371339. Bungalows with bath, good res-   Sleeping
taurant, canoe hire. **C** *Pousada do Mordomo Régio*, R Grande 134, T3371197. TV,   **& eating**
fridge, good restaurant. **D** *Pousada Pelourinho*, Praça da Matriz 55, T3371257. Breakfast, good restaurant, shared bathroom. Recommended. *Pousada do Imperador*, Beco
Escuro. *Pousada da Josefa*, R Direita, T3371109. Restaurant. Ask for hammock space or
rooms in private houses, friendly but no great comfort, provide your own mineral
water. *Bar do Lobato*, Praça da Matriz. Pleasant with good, simple food, fried shrimps
highly recommended. In R Direita, *Copos e Bocas* and *Pôr do Sol*.

Festa do Divino, at Pentecost (Whitsun); **29 Jun**, *São Pedro*; early **Aug**, *São Benedito*.   Festivals

Boats Lancha Diamantina leaves São Luís dock at about 0700 and 0930, returning   Transport
from Alcântara about 0815 and 1615: check time and buy the ticket at the *hidroviária*,
west end of R Portugal, T2320692, the day before as departure depends on the tides.
The journey takes 90 mins, return US$15. The sea can be very rough between Sep and
Dec. Old wooden boats, the *Newton Bello* and *Mensageiro da Fé*, leave São Luís at 0630
and 1600, returning at 0730 (1½ hrs, US$5 return). There are sometimes catamaran
tours bookable through tour operators in São Luís, meals not included.

Banks *Banco do Estado do Maranhão*, R Grande 76, exchanges US$ cash and TCs.   Directory
Communications Post office: R Direita off Praça da Matriz. **Telephone:** *Telemar*, R
Grande, 0700-2200 daily.

Parque Nacional Lençóis Maranhenses

To the east of São Luís, on the Atlantic Coast, is the **Parque Nacional Lençóis**   *Phone code: 098*
Maranhenses, 155,000 ha of beaches, lakes and dunes, with very little vegeta-   *Colour map 2, grid A3*
tion and largely unstudied wildlife.

Despite its remoteness, Lençóis Maranhenses (which means 'sheets of
Maranhão') is not too difficult to visit. Travellers with a few days to spare are
rewarded as much by the amazing panorama of watery dunes, reaching from
horizon to horizon, as by deserted beaches, boat rides on the aptly named Rio
Preguiça (Lazy River) and tiny, quiet hamlets where strangers are still a nov-
elty. Interest in the region among Brazilian holidaymakers – and developers –
is growing fast, so explorers would be well advised to go there soon.

A strange landscape of shifting white dunes, stretching about 140 km along
the coast between **Tutóia** and Primeira Cruz, west of **Barreirinhas**, has created a unique and delicate ecosystem which has been protected since 1981.
The sand, which extends from the coast up to 50 km inland, is advancing by as
much as 200 m a year in some places. Dumped by the sea and blown by the
wind, it forms ridges 50 m high in long flowing patterns which change constantly. The best time to visit is during the rainy season (June-September),
when the dune valleys fill with water. Reflections of the sky make the water
appear vivid blue, a spectacular contrast against brilliant white sand.

Barely visited until recently, Lençóis Maranhenses provides a refuge for
severely endangered species: giant turtles come here to lay their eggs; among
the mammals are *paca*, some deer and sea cow; and there are almost-extinct
varieties of fish such as the *camurupim*, which likes both salt and freshwater.
The dunes are a breeding ground for migratory birds and recent studies have
shown the sparse vegetation to include grasses unknown elsewhere. Excavations were begun in 1995 on the supposed site of a Jesuit settlement which,
according to persistent local rumour, was buried intact by a sandstorm.

Fortaleza and the North Coast

Traversing Lençóis Maranhenses The area to the west of Rio Preguiça is the park proper. The dunes east of the river form a 'protected area' which is easier to travel through, and has several small, friendly settlements.

Along the coast from Barreirinhas to Tutóia in either direction, allow about three days on foot. Camping is permitted, but you must take all supplies with you including water, since some dune lakes are salty. Because of the hot and sandy conditions, this is a punitive trek, only for the very hardy. Do not try the treacherous hike inland across the dunes. By horse: contact Ibama, see below. Allow two days by jeep, staying overnight at Paulino Neves (US$20). From Tutóia, José Neves Rodrigues, known as 'O Anjo' (the Angel), does the trip for around US$40 per passenger. By boat: a regular river-boat service plies between Tutóia and Paulino Neves/Rio Novo; another from there goes to Barreirinhas (both four hours, US$10). It is also possible to hire a speedboat, or get a ride from a fisherman. A very bad road passing inland links Tutóia and Barreirinhas: hardy drivers could stop at Rio Novo and explore the dunes from there.

Sleeping & eating **Tutóia** *Tutóia Palace Hotel*, Av Paulino Neves 1100, T4791115, F4791247. Attractive. **D** *Pousada Em-Bar-Cação*, R Magalhães de Almeida 1064, T4791219, on the beach. Breakfast US$3, friendly, recommended for good food and *tiquira*, a drink made of manioc. There are *pousadas* and restaurants at Rio Novo and Paulino Neves.

Barreirinhas **D** *Pousada Lins*, Av Joaquim Soeiro de Carvalho, T3491203. Restaurant, good, but shop around before taking their tours. **D** *Pousada do Baiano*, R Col Godinho, T3491110. Many others.

Tour operators *Ribamar* at Ibama, Avenida Jaime Tavares 25, São Luís, T2223066/3006, is helpful on walks and horse rides along lesser routes; other Ibama address, Avenida Alexandre Mowa 25, Centro, T2313010, F2314332, or T2212063/3070. Agencies in São Luís are *Nasaturismo*, T2354429; *Baluz Turismo*, T2226658; *Jaguarema*, T2224764; *Sunset Turismo* at the airport; *Maratur*, T2211231. At Barreirinhas, *Pousada Lins* (but see below); *Parna Lençóis Maranhenses*, director Sr Edson; *Pocof Barreirinhas*, director José de Ribamar Santos Silva, both at Rua Cazuza Ramos 3, T3491155. Barreirinhas residents are generally keen to help tourists out.

Transport **Buses** Parnaíba-Tutóia: bus, 4 hrs, US$6; river boat up the Parnaíba delta, 8 hrs, US$6. Recommended. Private boat hire is also possible. São Luís-Barreirinhas: bus, 8 hrs on an awful road, US$12; private tour buses, US$24, are more comfortable but cannot improve the road, organized bus tours cost US$72.50; plane (single propeller), 1 hr, US$75. Recommended. A fabulous experience, giving panoramic views of the dunes, pilot Amirton, T2252882. Agencies charge about US$200 for a tour with flight.

Boats Excursions from/to Barreirinhas: regular boat service between Barreirinhas and Atins (7 hrs return, US$5): boat along Rio Preguiça, 4 hrs then 1 hr's walk to the dunes, US$12. Highly recommended. **Speedboats**, about US$100 for 5 people, from Cláudio, T5491183, or Sr Carlos, T3491203. They also have a Kombi, US$150 for up to 15 people. The only forms of transport that can get across the dunes right into the park are a **jeep** or a **horse**, both about US$15. It is a 2-3 hr walk from Barreirinhas to the park; you will need at least another 2 hrs in the dunes. At Mandacuru, a popular stop on tours of the area, the lighthouse gives a very impressive view.

The Parnaíba delta

The extensive Parnaíba delta, its 70 islets variously covered in forest, palms or dunes, is the only seawater delta in the Americas: river and saltwater flow side by side through its channels. Catch a boat on the riverside in Parnaíba, hook up your hammock, and pass a few desultory hours watching herons nesting in the trees, fishermen asleep in their rowing boats and admiring the daily crab harvest.

When you arrive at the delta mouth you have the choice between stopping at **Ilha do Caju**, which gets its name from the hundreds of cashew trees that grow there (www.ilhadocaju.com.br), or continuing to **Tutóia**, where millions of birds populate freshwater lakes, formed by rain collecting between massive white dunes. Both are protected areas of outstanding natural beauty. Good food and accommodation are available on the island and in Tutóia, but many people in this region live as they have done for generations, in adobe houses, on a diet of fish cooked in baked-earth ovens. Illiteracy is the norm. Travel is by jeep, or, more commonly, by horse. There is no mains electricity and the nearest shopping is at Parnaíba.

See box on page 529 for Ilha do Caju

Transport Crossing the Parnaíba delta, which separates Piauí from Maranhão, is possible by boat, arriving in **Tutóia**; an interesting trip through swamps sheltering many birds. Trucks from Tutóia go to Barreirinhas, gateway to the **Parque Nacional dos Lençóis Maranhenses**, a vast protected area of sand dunes with rare birds and other wildlife (see above).

Virtually unchanged for four centuries, Ilha do Caju has an astonishing variety of terrain, with lakes, forest, marshes and an expanse of white dunes to the northwest. Much of the water, including the sea, is salobre – a mixture of fresh and salty. Swimming is from a vast, shimmering beach, through alternating currents of sea and river water, a heartily recommend experience.

There are lakes, caused by flooding, in which trees killed by the brine content stand, bleached and knotted, an unnerving image of lifelessness surrounded by vigorous vegetation. Another lake is full of nesting herons and peregrines, which take off in clouds of flashing green feathers as you pass. Tiny, long-legged cafézinho birds hop from leaf to leaf on the water lilies. Walking in the forest that surrounds the lake, myriad butterflies hover around your head. Many of the islanders still live in rustic adobe houses where the stove is made of baked earth. The whole island is environmentally protected and no chemical pesticides are used.

Ilha do Caju
Population: 70

Sleeping AL *Pousada Ecológica Ilha do Caju*, contact address: Av Presidente Vargas 235, Centro, 64-200-200, Parnaíba, Piauí, T086-3222380, F3211308, helpful, welcoming staff; the owner, Ingrid, and senior staff speak English. Children must be aged 12 or over.

The *pousada* is an attractive converted farmhouse with thatched guesthouses in the grounds; each has its own hammock outside, but inside there is a huge bed, hand-made by the same craftsmen who made much of the *pousada's* highly individual furniture.

The main road from Teresina passes through the Maranhense town of Caxias, a battle site during the Balaiada rebellion in 1838. It has a good churrascaria, *Selva do Braz*, Avenida Central 601, with live music in the evening. About 3 km from the town on the Buriti Bravo road is a spring for medicinal bathing, with a restaurant serving regional food.

Caxias
Population: 149,500

Fortaleza and the North Coast

Southern Maranhão

Imperatriz

Phone code: 098
Colour map 2, grid A1
Population: 295,000

On the Eastern bank of the Rio Tocantins, at Maranhão's western border with Tocantins, is Imperatriz, a city serving a large cattle region. Founded in 1851, the **Igreja de Santa Tereza D'Ávila** in Rua 15 de Novembro is dedicated to the city's patron saint. River beaches appear between July and October when the river is low.

Sleeping
& eating
There are many cheap hotels near the rodoviária

A *Posseidon*, R Paraíba 740, T7232323. Central, best, pool. Recommended. A *Imperatriz Park*, BR-010, Km 1347, opposite rodoviária, T7232950. Pool. *Fogão Mineiro*, Av Getúlio Vargas 2234. *Rafaello Grill*, in Imperatriz Shopping, Av Dorgival Pinheiro Sousa 1400. Self-service. *Fly Back Disco Club*, Beira Rio, north of the ferry crossing. Two dance floors, one fast, one slow (for couples only), good.

Transport

Air Airport, T7224666. Flights to Altamira, Araguaína, Belém, Brasília and São Luís. Air Taxi: *Heringer*, at airport, T7223009.

Bus Lying on the BR-010 **Belém-Brasília** highway, Imperatriz has bus connections with both cities; there is a slow, crowded bus service to **Teresina**. To get to **Marabá** on the Transamazônica, you can either take a Transbrasiliana bus direct, 7-10 hrs (starting on the Belém highway, the bus then turns west along a poorer road, passing finally through destroyed forest, new *fazendas* and unplanned cities), or a faster route, involving taking a ferry across the river in the early morning (0600-0700) to catch a pick-up on the other side, takes about 5 hrs, but is more expensive. To get to the ferry across the river, go along R Luís Domingues, which runs parallel to Av Getúlio Vargas.

Car hire *Interlocadora*, Av Dorgival Pinheiro de Souza 990, T7223050. *Localiza*, BR-010, Setor Rodoviária, T7214507, and at airport, T7218611.

Train Station, T7232260. Trains to Pará and other towns in Maranhão.

Directory

Airline offices *Penta*, R Luís Domingues 1420, T7231073. *TAM*, R Ceará 678, T7223148. *Varig/RioSul*, R Luís Domingues 1471, T7232155. **Banks** *Banco do Brasil*, Av Getúlio Vargas 1935. **Communications** Telephone: R Rio Grande do Norte 740, a side street off Av Getúlio Vargas, near *Hotel Posseidon*, 0630-2400. **Medical services** *Santa Mônica*, R Piauí, T7223415, 24 hrs emergency ward. **Security** The town can be quite a rough place and it is wise to exercise caution, especially at night.

Carolina

Phone code: 098
Population: 26,000

South of Imperatriz, also on the Rio Toncantins, is Carolina, set in an area of spectacular waterfalls and mountain scenery. Near to the **Cachoeira da Prata**, on the Rio Farinha, is **Morro das Figuras**, which has rock inscriptions. Access is by unmade road from the BR-230, requiring a four-wheel drive. Some 35 km south of Carolina, on the road to Estreito, is **Cachoeria de Pedra Caída**.

Sleeping and eating *Pousada Pedra Caída*, BR-010 Km 30, T7311318. Chalets with fan, restaurant, natural pool and 3 waterfalls. *Pousada do Rio Lages*, BR-230 Km 2, T7311499. Chalets with a/c. *Cafuné*, BR-230 Km 2. Local food.

Transport Bus station, R Lias Barros, Nova Carolina, T7311195.

Directory **Banks**: *Banco do Brasil*, A Mascarenhas 159. **Communications**: Telephone: Av E Barros, open 0730-2230. **Medical services**: *FNS*, R Benedito Leite 57, T7311271. **Tourist offices**: *Secretaria de Turismo*, R Duque de Caxias 522, T7311613, Mon-Fri 0800-1300.

Introducing The Amazon

The mighty Amazon stretches from the Atlantic to the Peruvian and Colombian borders. The river, its tributaries and the forests through which they flow, make up over half of Brazil's national territory. In this vast area there are only a few centres for visiting Amazônia. At the river's mouth is **Belém**, the capital of Pará. It's a good place to begin or end a river journey, with a fascinating market, historical associations and famous festival of candles. Riverboats ply the route from here to **Manaus** in Amazonas via Santarém.

On the north bank of the delta is **Macapá**, the capital of Amapá. **Santarém**, near the confluence of the Tapajós and Amazon rivers, makes an ideal stopping place on the long haul from the coast to Manaus, 1,600 km inland. This city grew rich in the rubber boom and is an excellent starting point for tours into the jungle. North of Manaus, on the Venezuelan border, is the state of Roraima and its capital **Boa Vista**. In the far southwest of Amazônia, towards the Bolivian border, is the state of Acre and its capital Rio Branco. **Porto Velho**, capital of Rondônia, is the crossroads of river and road connections from Amazônia and the Centre West of Brazil. A legendary railway, the **Madeira-Mamoré**, is an attraction in the west of the state. The new state of Tocantins, with its modern capital, includes the **Ilha de Bananal**, a huge river island with good opportunities for fishing. Indian culture remains strong in the region and is expressed in the **Festa de Boi**, held on Parantins island. Many types of rare animals, birds and plants can be encountered on trips into the rainforest.

The Amazon

Things to do in the Amazon

① Fish for piranha in the Amazon River and eat the catch with lime and chilli.
② One of the surprises of the Amazon is its blinding white-sand beaches. Join the locals on Sundays for a family day out with beer, barbecues and music.
③ Visit the extraordinarily opulent Opera House in Manaus.
④ Take a trip to Roraima, the possible inspiration for Sir Conan Doyle's *Lost World*.
⑤ Go shopping for the natural aphrodisiac of Guarana, or drink it fresh in a juice.
⑥ Explore the jungle-covered islands and deserted beaches of the Arquipélago de Anavilhanas, the second largest river archipelago in the world.

The Amazon

Background

History
A Spanish conquistador was the first person to travel across the region. In 1541 Francisco de Orellana successfully journeyed from Quito to the island of Marajó, close to the mouth of the Amazon. The river and its environs were called the 'Land of the Amazons' after the chronicler for the journey, Gaspar de Carvajal, described how the party had come across warlike women who resembled in temperament the Amazons of Greek mythology. In the 16th and 17th centuries the 'Green Hell' of the Amazon became the most likely site of the mythical 'El Dorado' and a number of expeditions were launched there by fortune-seeking Europeans, including Sir Walter Raleigh. In the 17th century the Portuguese consolidated their hold of the Amazon by establishing a fort at Belém in 1616 and one at Barra, the site of Manaus, in 1669.

During the 18th and 19th centuries the Amazon attracted the gaze of European scientists, botanists and philosophers who debunked the myth of the warrior women, but discovered more than enough realities to inspire further exploration and settlement. The British botanists Alfred Russel Wallace and Henry Walter Bates spent years in the Amazon Basin collecting species for the Natural History Museum which would help to provide evidence for the theory of evolution. During his travels of the Amazon Basin, Charles Marie de la Condamine described how the natives used the resin of the 'heve' tree to make balls, syringes and pumps and to waterproof their canoes. The inventions of the vulcanization process and the pneumatic tyre in Europe meant that the race for rubber was on.

Saving the rainforest?
Successive modern Brazilian governments have made strenuous efforts to develop Amazônia. Roads have been built parallel to the Amazon to the south (the Transamazônica), from Cuiabá in Mato Grosso, northwards to Santarém in Pará, and northeast from Porto Velho through Humaitá to the river bank opposite Manaus. Some maps show a road north of the Amazon, marked Perimetro (or Perimetral) Norte; this road does not exist, never has and probably never will. Unsuccessful attempts were made to establish agricultural settlements along these roads; major energy and mining projects for bauxite and iron ore are bringing rapid change.

More environmental damage has been caused to the region by gold prospectors (*garimpeiros*), especially by their indiscriminate use of mercury, than by organized mining carried out by large state and private companies using modern extraction methods. The most important cause of destruction, however, has been large-scale deforestation to make way for cattle ranching and to provide hardwoods for the Asian markets.

It is estimated that 600,000 sq km, an area the size of France, has now been shed of its forest cover, with more destruction occurring in the last three decades than in the last four centuries. To make a more regional comparison, an area the size of the state of Sergipe is lost every year to the chainsaw and match. A lot of the destruction occurred in the 1980s. It slowed down in the early 1990s, but with the recovery of the Brazilian economy and very dry weather in the mid-1990s the destruction sped up again.

There is a gradually growing awareness among many Brazilians that their northern hinterland is a unique treasure and requires some form of protection, and recently some encouraging moves have been made. At the end of 1997 the **Amanã Sustainable Development Reserve** (SDR) was set up, linking two other reserves to form the world's largest protected rainforest area. The Amanã SDR surrounds Lake Amanã north of Tefé and covers

The enchanted river dolphin

The Brazilian Amazon is no doubt one of the richest repositories of folklore in the world. Ancient Indian legends have mingled with the myths that were brought to the region by foreigners and the results are often amazing.

One of the most fascinating myths is the Enchanted River Dolphin, a story that exists throughout the entire Amazon region of South America. The people who live on the Amazon firmly believe that a certain species of river dolphin, the boto cor-de-rosa (Inia geoffrensis), has strange, magical powers. It is said that these pink, freshwater mammals can temporarily become human beings at night, leaving the river to socialize with us. Normally they assume the shape of a handsome young man, wearing a white suit and always sporting a hat. This covers the blow-hole at the top of his head (the only visible sign that he really is a dolphin). He loves parties and knows how to dance, sing and play the guitar and, above all, his favourite occupation is seducing pretty young girls, be they single or married.

The enchanted dolphin is reputed to be an extremely creative and ardent lover, at least for one night, because after sleeping with the girl he loses interest and, next morning, simply takes his normal shape and dives back into the nearest river, never to return. Most women get pregnant in these relationships and in the Amazon region people call any child of a single mother, or of an unknown father, filho de boto (dolphin's child).

23,500 sq km. It is sandwiched between the Jaú National Park to the east and the Mamiraua SDR to the west, forming a 640-km long corridor. It is hoped that whole ecosystems will be preserved and that local inhabitants will be able to find sustainable work in the reserve's management.

Much attention has been focused on ecotourism as a potentially non-destructive source of income for the region. But these are early days. It has been estimated that less than 5% of the earnings from Brazil's billion dollar tourist industry comes from 'ecotourism' in the Pantanal and the Amazon. The high cost of internal flights has meant that less than 1% of Brazil's foreign tourists visit Manaus.

Anyone interested in the Amazonian development programme and its ecological, social, economic and political effects should read Richard Bourne's masterly *Assault on the Amazon* (London, Gollancz, 1978), *Dreams of Amazonia*, by Roger D Stone (Penguin, 1986), or *Amazon*, by Brian Kelly and Mark London (Harcourt Brace Jovanovich, New York, 1983). *The Fate of the Forest*, by Suzanne Hecht and Alexander Cockburn (Penguin, 1991), has also been recommended.

Geography & climate The area is drained by the Amazon, which in size, volume of water – 12 times that of the Mississippi – and number of tributaries has no equal in the world. Between 80 and 90 million years ago the world supercontinent Gondwanaland split and South America, then a massive island, drifted away from Africa. At this time, Amazônia's only outlet to the sea was towards the Pacific. The Andes had not yet formed and the Guiana and Brazilian Highlands were joined together in the east, barring access to the Atlantic. In *Amazon – The Flooded Forest* (BBC Books 1989), Michael Goulding states that the ancestors of the stingrays that are found today in the turbid waters of the Amazon came from the Pacific, not the Atlantic. About 15 million years ago the South American continental plate crashed into the Nazca plate, forming the Andes. The Amazon became a huge swamp. During the Pliocene period 10 million years ago, the Amazon eventually found a course to the Atlantic between the

The Amazon

Guiana and Brazilian highlands. Nowadays at the base of the Andes, far to the west, the Amazonian plain is 1,300 km in width, but east of the confluences of the Madeira and Negro rivers with the Amazon, the highlands close in upon it until there is no more than 80 km of floodplain between them. Towards the river's mouth – about 320 km wide – the plain widens once more, and extends along the coast southeastwards into the state of Maranhão and northwards into the Guianas.

Brazilian Amazônia, much of it still covered with tropical forest, is 56% of the national area. Its jungle is the world's largest and densest rain forest, with more diverse plants and animals than any other jungle in the world. It has only 8% of Brazil's population, and most of this is concentrated around Belém (in Pará), and in Manaus, 1,600 km up the river. The population is sparse because other areas are easier to develop.

The rainfall is heavy, but varies throughout the region; close to the Andes, up to 4,000 mm fall annually, at Manaus it's under 2,000 mm. Rains occur throughout the year, but the wettest season is between December and May; the driest month is October. The humidity can be extremely high and the temperature averages 26°C. There can be cold snaps in December in the western reaches of the Amazon basin. The soil, as in all tropical forest, is poor.

River transport

Although air services are widespread throughout the region and road transport is gradually increasing, rivers remain the arteries of Amazônia for the transport of both passengers and merchandise. The two great ports of the region are Belém, at the mouth of the Amazon, and Manaus at the confluence of the Rio Negro and Rio Solimões. Manaus is the hub of river transport, with regular shipping services east to Santarém and Belém along the lower Amazon, south to Porto Velho along the Rio Madeira, west to Tabatinga (the border with Colombia and Peru) along the Rio Solimões, northwest to São Gabriel da Cachoeira along the Rio Negro, and more sporadically north to Caracaraí (for Boa Vista) along the Rio Branco. There is also a regular service connecting Belém and Macapá (on the northern shore of the Amazon delta), Santarém and Macapá, as well as Santarém and Itaituba, south along the Rio Tapajós. All of the above services call at many intermediate ports and virtually every village has some form of river boat service.

The size and quality of vessels varies greatly, with the largest and most comfortable ships generally operating on the Manaus-Belém route. Hygiene, food and service are reasonable on most vessels, but overcrowding can be a problem. Most boats have some sort of rooftop bar serving expensive drinks and snacks.

Types of tickets Many of the larger ships offer a/c berths with bunkbeds and, for a higher price, 'suites', with a private bathroom (in some cases, this may also mean a double bed instead of the standard bunkbed). The cheapest way to travel is 'hammock class'; on some routes first class (upper deck) and second class (lower deck) hammock space is available, but on many routes this distinction does not apply. Although the idea of swinging in a hammock may sound romantic, the reality is you will probably be squeezed in with other passengers, possibly next to the toilets, have difficulty sleeping due to noise and end up with an aching back.

River boat travel is no substitute for visiting the jungle. Except for a few birds and the occasional dolphin, little wildlife is seen. However, it does offer an insight into the vastness of Amazônia and a chance to meet some of its people, making a very pleasant experience.

The vessels operate on a particular route and their schedules are frequently changing; it is generally not possible to book far in advance. Extensive local inquiry and some flexibility in your schedule are indispensable for river travel.

Choosing a river boat
Refer to the appropriate city sections for details of port facilities in each

Agencies on shore can inform you of the arrival and departure dates for several different ships, as well as the official (highest) prices for each; they are sometimes amenable to bargaining. Whenever possible, however, see the vessel yourself (it may mean a journey out of town) and have a chat with the captain or business manager to confirm departure date and time, length of voyage, ports of call, price, etc. Inspect cleanliness in the kitchen, toilets and showers. All boats are cleaned up when in port, but if a vessel is reasonably clean upon arrival then chances are that it has been kept that way throughout the voyage. You can generally arrange to sleep on board a day or two before departure and after arrival, but be sure to secure carefully your belongings when in port. If you take a berth, lock it and keep the key even if you will not be moving in right away. If you are travelling hammock class, board ship at least 6-8 hrs before sailing in order to secure a good spot (away from the toilets and the engine and check for leaks in the deck above you). Be firm but considerate of your neighbours as they will be your intimate companions for the duration of the voyage. Always keep your gear locked. Take some light warm clothing, it can get very chilly at night.

Compare fares for different ships and remember that prices may fluctuate with supply and demand. As a general rule of thumb they will be about one-third of the prevailing 1-way airfare, including all meals, but not drinks. Most ships sail in the evening and the first night's supper may not be provided. Empty cabins are sometimes offered to foreigners at reduced rates once boats have embarked. Payment is usually in advance. Insist on a signed ticket indicating date, vessel, class of passage, and berth number if applicable.

All ships carry cargo as well as passengers, and the amount of cargo will affect the length of the voyage because of weight (especially when travelling upstream) and loading/unloading at intermediate ports. All but the smallest boats will transport vehicles, but these are often damaged by rough handling. Insist on the use of proper ramps and check for adequate clearance. Vehicles can also be transported aboard cargo barges. These are usually cheaper and passengers may be allowed to accompany their car, but check about food, sanitation, where you will sleep (usually in a hammock slung beneath a truck), and adequate shade.

The following are the major shipping routes in Amazônia, giving a selection of vessels and indicating intermediate ports, average trip durations, and fares. Prices vary depending on the vessel; generally it is not a good idea to go with the cheapest fare you are quoted. Not all ships stop at all intermediate ports. There are many other routes and vessels providing extensive local service. All fares shown are 1-way only and include all meals unless otherwise stated. Prices for berths and suites are for 2 people, hammock space is per person. Information is generally identical for the respective reverse voyages (except Belém-Manaus, Manaus-Belém).

Belém-Manaus via Breves, Almeirim, Prainha, Monte Alegre, Curua-Uná, Santarém, Alenquer, Óbidos, Juruti and Parintins on the lower Amazon. 5 days upriver, 4 days downriver, including 18-hr stop in Santarém, suite US$350 upriver, US$250 down, double berth US$180 upriver, US$150 down, hammock space US$75 upriver, US$65 down. Vehicles: small car US$250, combi US$320 usually including driver, other passengers extra, 4WD US$450 with 2 passengers; motorcycle US$80. *Nélio Correa* is best on this route. *Defard Vieira*, very good and clean, US$75. *São Francisco* is largest, new and modern, but toilets smelly. *Cisne Branco* of similar quality. *Cidade de Bairreirinha* is the newest on the route, a/c berths. *Lider II* has good food and pleasant atmosphere. *Santarém* is clean, well organized and recommended. *João Pessoa Lopes* is also recommended. The Belém-Manaus route is very busy. Try to get a cabin if you can.

Routes in Amazônia

The Amazon

Bates on the Amazon

"The birds were astir, the cicadas had begun their music, and the Urania Leilus, a strange and beautiful tailed and gilded moth, whose habits are those of a butterfly, commenced to fly in flocks over the tree-tops. Raimundo exclaimed 'Clareia o dia!' – 'The day brightens!' The change was rapid: the sky in the east assumed suddenly the loveliest azure colour, across which streaks of thin white clouds were painted. It is at such moments as this that one feels how beautiful our world truly is! The channel on whose waters our little boat was floating was about 200 yards wide; others branched off right and left, surrounding the group of lonely islands which terminate the land of Carnopijó. The forest on all sides formed a lofty hedge without a break: below, it was fringed with mangrove bushes, whose small foliage contrasted with the large glossy leaves of the taller trees, or the feather and fan-shaped fronds of the palms."

Henry Walter Bates, The Naturalist on the River Amazon, 1863. (This extract is taken from Abroad. A Miscellany of English Travel Writing 1700-1914, compiled by Alan Wykes, London: Macdonald & Jane's, 1973.)

Belém-Santarém, same intermediate stops as above. 2½ days upriver, 1½ days downriver, fares suite US$150, berth US$135, hammock US$45 upriver, US$38 down. All vessels sailing Belém-Manaus will call in Santarém.

Santarém-Manaus, same intermediate stops as above. Two days upriver, 1½ days downriver, fares berth US$85, hammock US$30. All vessels sailing Belém-Manaus will call in Santarém and there are others operating only the Santarém-Manaus route, including: *Cidade de Terezinha III* and *IV*, good. *Miranda Dias*, family-run and friendly. Speedboats (*lanchas*) are sometimes available on this route, 16 hrs sitting, no hammock space, US$35.

Belém-Macapá (Porto Santana) non-stop, 8 hrs on fast catamaran, *Atlântica*, US$30, 3 days a week, or 24 hrs on large ships, double berth US$110, hammock space US$30 per person, meals not included but can be purchased onboard (expensive), vehicle US$90, driver not included. *Silja e Souza* (Wed) is best. *Comandante Solon* (Sat) is state run, slightly cheaper, crowded and not as nice. Same voyage via Breves, 36 to 48 hrs on smaller river boats, hammock space US$25 per person including meals. *ENAL* (Sat); *Macamazônia* (every day except Thu), slower and more basic; *Bartolomeu I* of Enavi, food and sanitary conditions OK, 30 hrs; *Rodrigues Alves* has been recommended. *Golfinho do Mar* is said to be the fastest.

Macapá (Porto Santana)-Santarém via Vida Nova, Boca do Jari, Almeirim, Prainha, and Monte Alegre on the lower Amazon (does not call in Belém), 2 days upriver, 1½ days downriver, berth US$130, hammock US$40. Boats include *Viageiro V* (nice), *São Francisco de Paula*.

Santarém-Itaituba along the Rio Tapajós, 24 hrs (bus service on this route is making this river trip less common).

Manaus-Porto Velho via Borba, Manicoré, and Humaitá on the Rio Madeira. 4 days upriver, 3½ days downriver (up to 7 days when the river is low), double berth US$180, hammock space US$65 per person. Recommended boats are *Almirante Moreira II*, clean, friendly owner; *Lord Scania*, friendly; *Ana Maria VIII*, modern. The *Eclipse II* is a very nice boat which sails Manaus-Manicoré (2 days, US$80 double berth, US$20 hammock). Many passengers go only as far as Humaitá and take a bus from there to Porto Velho, much faster.

Manaus-Tefé via Codajás and Coari, 24 to 36 hrs, double berth US$70, first class hammock space US$20 per person, second class hammock space US$20 per person. *Capitão Nunes* is good. *Jean Filho* also OK. Note that it is difficult to continue west from Tefé to Tabatinga without first returning to Manaus.

Manaus-Tabatinga via Fonte Boa, Foz do Mamaria, Tonantins, Santo Antônio do Iça, Amataura, Monte Cristo, São Paulo de Olivença and Benjamin Constant along the Rio Solimões. Up to 8 days upriver (depending on cargo), 3 days downriver, double berth US$220, hammock space US$65 per person (can be cheaper downriver). When going from Peru into Brazil, there is a thorough police check some 5 hrs into Brazil. *Voyagers*, *Voyagers II* and *III* (T2363782) recommended; *Almirante Monteiro*, *Avelino Leal* and *Capitão Nunes VIII* all acceptable; *Dom Manoel*, cheaper, acceptable but overcrowded.

Manaus-Caracaraí (for Boa Vista) along the Rio Branco, 4 days upriver, 2 days downriver, many sandbars, impassable during the dry season. Now that the BR-174 (Manaus-Boa Vista) has been paved, it is almost impossible to get a passage on a boat. The only tourist boat is erratic.

Manaus-São Gabriel da Cachoeira via Novo Airão, Moura, Carvoeiro, Barcelos, and Santa Isabel do Rio Negro along the Rio Negro. Berth US$180, hammock US$60, most locals prefer to travel by road. Boats on this route: *Almirante Martins I* and *II*, *Capricho de Deus*, *Manoel Rodrigues*, *Tanaka Netto* departing from São Raimundo dock, north of main port.

A hammock is essential on all but the most expensive boats; it is often too hot to lie down in a cabin during the day. Light cotton hammocks seem to be the best solution. Buy a wide one on which you can lie diagonally; lying straight along it leaves you hump-backed. A climbing carabiner clip is useful for fastening hammocks to runner bars of boats. It is also useful for securing baggage, making it harder to steal.

Health
See also Essentials, page 66

There is a danger of malaria in Amazônia. Mosquito nets are not required when in motion as boats travel away from the banks and are too fast for mosquitoes to settle, though repellent is a boon for night stops. From April to October, when the river is high, the mosquitoes can be repelled by Super Repelex spray or K13. A yellow fever inoculation is strongly advised; it is compulsory in some areas and may be administered on the spot with a pressurized needle gun. The larger ships must have an infirmary and carry a health officer. Drinking water is generally taken on in port (ie city tap water), but taking your own mineral water is a good idea.

Food

This is ample but monotonous, better food is sometimes available to cabin passengers. Meal times can be chaotic. Fresh fruit is a welcome addition; also take plain biscuits, tea bags, seasonings, sauces and jam. Fresh coffee is available; most boats have a bar of sorts. Plates and cutlery may not be provided. Bring your own plastic mug as drinks are served in plastic beakers which are jettisoned into the river. A strong fishing line and a variety of hooks can be an asset for supplementing one's diet; with some meat for bait, *piranhas* are the easiest fish to catch. Negotiate with the cook over cooking your fish. The sight of you fishing will bring a small crowd of new friends, assistants, and lots of advice – some of it useful.

Local specialities Inevitably fish dishes are very common, including many fish with Indian names, eg *pirarucu*, *tucunaré* and *tambaqui*, which are worth trying. Also shrimp and crab dishes (more expensive). Specialities of Pará include duck, often served in a yellow soup made from the juice of the root of the manioc (*tucupi*) with a green vegetable (*jambu*); this dish is the famous *pato no tucupi*, highly recommended. Also *tacaca* (shrimps served in *tucupi*), *vatapá* (shrimps served in a thick sauce, highly filling, simpler than the variety found in Salvador), *maniçoba* (made with the poisonous leaves of the bitter cassava, simmered for 8 days to render it safe – tasty). *Caldeirada*, a fish and vegetable soup, served with *pirão* (manioc puree), is a speciality of Amazonas. There is also an enormous variety of tropical and jungle fruits, many unique to the region. Try them fresh, or in ice-creams or juices. Avoid food from street vendors.

Banks

Exchange Facilities are sparse in Amazônia: banks and exchange can be found in Belém, Macapá, Santarém and Manaus. Small amounts of US dollars cash can usually be exchanged in many other towns, but some boat captains will not take US dollars.

The Amazon

Amapá

Sometimes called the Brazilian Guyana, this isolated frontier state once exploited for its natural resources is now making efforts towards sustainable development. Located near the European Union territory of Guyane with its cheap air link to Paris, it is another good port of entry into Northern Brazil. Tourist infrastructure outside the capital Macapá is negligible, but for the adventurous there are opportunities for ecotourism such as the Cabo Orange National Park.

The state, a quarter the size of France, has a population of just under half a million. The Rio Oiapoque forms the border with Guyane. The northern channel of the Rio Amazonas and the Rio Jari define the borders with Pará, while the Atlantic Ocean washes the eastern coast. In the northwest is the Serra do Tumucumaque, reaching 500 m in parts. The wet season lasts from December to June, followed by the hot dry season for the rest of the year, with temperatures between 25 and 30°C. The state still retains some 70% of its forest coverage. Malaria is rampant in the interior, especially in the areas mined by gold prospectors.

Macapá

Phone code: 096
Colour map 1, grid A5
Population: 284,000

The capital of Amapá is a pleasant city on the banks of the northern channel of the Amazon Delta. It has an impressive fortress as well as a monument to the equator that divides the city. There is a museum detailing the research being carried out in the rainforest and nearby Curiaú, a village originally formed by escaped slaves.

Macapá

■ Sleeping	3 Frota Palace	6 Mercúrio	● Eating
1 Açai Palace	4 Glória	7 Santo Antônio	1 Chalé
2 Ekinox	5 Macapá		2 Sorveteria Macapá

The Amazon

The town was founded around the first Forte de São José do Macapá, built in 1688. In 1751 more settlers from the Azores arrived to defend the region from Dutch, English and French invasions and the aldea became a Vila in 1758. Many slaves were later brought from Africa for the construction of the Fortaleza.

Getting there Flights arrive at the airport close to the city. There are also international connections from Cayenne and Paramaribo. The centre is a short taxi ride from the airport. There are also buses. Boats from Belém and Santarém arrive at nearby Porto Santana, which is linked to Macapá by bus or taxi. Buses from Oiapoque pass through the centre of Macapá after a long and uncomfortable journey over mainly unsurfaced roads. This journey can take even longer during the rainy season from Jan-May.

Ins & outs
See also Transport, page 542

Getting around There is an air taxi service to some towns. Towns are linked by trucks, community minibuses and the main bus companies leaving from the new rodoviária on the BR-156 around 3 km north of the centre. The centre and the waterfront are easily explored on foot. Buses to other parts of the city leave from a bus station near the Fortaleza.

Tourist offices *Detur*, Av Raimundo Álvares da Costa 18, Centro, CEP 68906-020, T2230627, F2230567, mcp10009@zaz.com.br Branch at airport.

Sights

Each brick of the **Fortaleza de São José do Macapá**, built between 1764 and 1782, was brought from Portugal as ballast. Fifty iron cannons still remain and there is a museum. The Fortaleza is used for concerts, exhibits and colourful festivities on the anniversary of the city's founding on 4 February. **São José Cathedral**, inaugurated by the Jesuits in 1761, is the city's oldest landmark. The **Centro de Cultura Negra**, in Rua General Rondon, has a museum and holds frequent events. The **Museu do Desenvolvimento Sustentável**, in Avenida Feliciano Coelho 1509, exhibits research on sustainable development and traditional community life in Amazônia. ■ *0830-1200, 1500-1800 Tue-Fri, 1500-1800 Mon and Sat.*

The riverfront has been landscaped with trees, lawns and paths and is a very pleasant place for an evening stroll. The **Complexo Beira Rio** has food and drink kiosks and a nice lively atmosphere. The recently rebuilt pier (*trapiche*) is a lovely spot for savouring the cool of the evening breeze, or watching the sunrise over the Amazon.

There is a monument to the equator, **Marco Zero** (take Fazendinha bus from Avenida Mendonça Furtado). The equator also divides the nearby enormous (capacity 9,000) football stadium in half, aptly named O Zerão. The Sambódromo is located nearby. South of here, on Rodovia Juscelino Kubitschek, Km 12, are the **Botanical Gardens**. ■ *0900-1700 Tue-Sun.*

Excursions

Some 16 km from the centre, **Fazendinha** is a popular local beach, which is very busy on Sunday, with many seafood restaurants. **Curiaú**, 8 km from Macapá, is inhabited by the descendants of African slaves who have maintained many of the customs of their ancestors. They are analogous to the Bush Negroes of Suriname, but apparently the only such village in Brazil. Popular at weekends for dancing and swimming, the surrounding area is an environmental reserve with many water buffalo.

The Amazon

Essentials

Sleeping **A** *Atalanta*, Av Coaracy Nunes 1148, T/F2331612. Laundry service, bar. **A** *Ekinox*, R Jovino Dinoá 1693, T2224378, F2237554, jef@brasnet.online.com.br Library, French spoken, helpful, excellent restaurant. Recommended. **A** *Frota Palace*, Av Tiradentes 1104, T2233999, F2224488. Airport pick-up. **A** *Macapá*, Av Azarias Neto 17, on water-front, T2231144, F2231115. Pool, tennis courts, sauna, restaurant, convention centre. **A** *Marabaixo*, R Cândido Mendes 340, T2237853, F2232157. Apartment hotel, meals available. **B** *Açai Palace*, Av Antônio Coelho de Carvalho 1399, T2234899, 20 mins from centre. Cheaper without a/c. **B** *Gloria*, Leopoldo Machado 2085, T2220984. **B** *Mara*, R São José 2390, T2220859, F2234905. A/c, TV, fridge, good. **C** *Santo Antônio*, Av Coriolano Jucá 485, T2220226, **D** in dormitory, near main praça. Fan, good breakfast extra. **D** *Mercúrio*, R Cândido Mendes 1300, 2nd floor, T2231699, close to Praça São José (where bus from Porto Santana stops).

Eating **Expensive** *Chalé*, Av Pres Vargas 499. Good food and nice atmosphere. *Le Chateau*, Av 13 de Setembro 2022, corner of Barão de Mauá, T2422481. Small and intimate but a long way from the centre. **Mid-range** South of the Fortaleza, *Cantino Bahiano*, Av Beira-Rio 1, and *Martinho's Peixaria*, Av Beira-Rio 810, are good fish restaurants. *Soho*, Av Capt Pedro Baião, 2201. Chinese. *Zero Grau*, R Leopoldo Machado 2405. Pizzas. **Cheap** *Bom Paladar Kilo's*, Av Pres Vargas 456. Pay by weight buffet. Excellent ice-cream made from local fruits, try *cupuaçu*, *Sorveteria Jesus de Nazare*, R Leopoldo Machado 737. *Sorveteria Macapá*, R São José 1676.

Bars & *Rithimus*, R Odilardo Silva 1489, T2222354. Good for local rhythm *Brega*. *Arena*, R Ham-
nightclubs ilton Silva. Food and drink kiosks in *Complexo Beira Rio* have live music most evenings.

Entertainment **Art galleries** *Cândido Portinari*, corner of R Cândido Mendes and Av Raimundo Álvares da Costa. Exhibits of local art. **Cinemas** In *Macapá Shopping*, R Leopoldo Machado 2334. **Theatre** *Teatro das Bacabeiras*, R Cândido Mendes. Concerts, poetry and plays.

Festivals *Marabaixo* is the traditional music and dance festival held for **40 days after Easter**. **14 Aug**, *Festa de São Joaquim* held in Curiaú. The Sambódromo has parades of Escolas de Samba at *Carnival* and Quadrilhas during *São João* in **Jun**.

Shopping Macapá and Porto Santana were declared a customs-free zone in 1992. There are now many cheap imported goods available from shops in the centre. In the handicraft complex *Casa do Artesão*, Av Azárias Neto, Mon-Sat 0800-1900, craftsmen produce their wares onsite. A feature is pottery decorated with local manganese ore, also woodcarvings and leatherwork.

Tour operators *Amapá Turismo*, in *Hotel Macapá*, T2232667. *Fénix*, R Cândido Mendes 374, T/F2238200, and R Jovino Dinoá 1489, T2235353.

Transport **Air** Airport, 4 km from centre, T2232323. International flights to Cayenne and Paramaribo.
See also Ins & outs,
page 541 Domestic flights to Belém, Belo Horizonte, Boa Vista, Brasília, Breves, Manaus, Oiapoque, Rio de Janeiro, Santarém and São Paulo. Air taxi service with *Rio Norte*.

Boats To **Belém**, *Atlântica*, fast catamaran 8 hrs, 3 times a week, US$30, reservations at *Martinica*, Jovino Dinoá 2010, T2235777, F2223569. Slower but slightly cheaper boats are *Bom Jesus*, *Comandante Solon*, *São Francisco de Paulo*, *Silja e Souza* of Souzamar, Cláudio Lúcio Monteiro 1375, Santana, T2811946, car ferry with *Silnave*, T2234011. Purchase tickets from offices 2 days in advance (*Agencia Sonave*, R São José

The Amazon

2145, T2239090, sells tickets for all boats). Also smaller boats to **Breves** as well as a regular direct service to **Santarém** (see River transport, page 536).

Buses New rodoviária on BR-156, north of Macapá. *Estrela de Ouro*, office on the main square, in front of the cathedral, leaves daily at 2000, and *Cattani*, office on Nunes between São José and Cándido Mendes, leaves daily at 0630 to **Amapá** (US$20), **Calçoene** (US$25, 7 hrs) and **Oiapoque** (12 hrs – dry season – with several rest stops, 14-24 hrs in rainy season, US$35). The Oiapoque bus does not go into Amapá or Calçoene and it is therefore very inconvenient to break the trip at these places.

Pick-up trucks run daily to various locations throughout Amapá, crowded on narrow benches in the back, or pay more to ride in the cab. Despite posted schedules, they leave when full. To **Oiapoque** at 0800, 10-12 hrs, US$35 cab, US$15 in back, to **Lourenço** at 0900.

Car hire *Localiza*, R Independência 30, T2232799, and airport T2242336. *Sila Rent a Car*, Av Procópio Rola 1346, T2241443.

Train Limited services from Porto Santana to Serra do Navio.

Directory **Airline offices** *META*, Av Mendonça Júnior 18, T2234628. *Penta*, Av Mendonça Júnior 13D, T2235226. *Rio Norte*, at airport, T2220033. *TAM*, at airport, T2232688. *Varig*, R Cândido Mendes 1039, T2234612. *Vasp*, R Independência 146, T2241016. **Banks** *Banco do Brasil*, R Independência 250, and *Bradesco*, R Cândido Mendes 1316, have Plus ATMs for VISA withdrawals. *Câmbios* (cash only): *Casa Francesa*, R Independência 232. *Monopólio*, Av Isaac Alcoubre 80. Both US$ and French francs can be exchanged here. Best to buy francs in Belém if heading for Guyane as *câmbios* in Macapá are reluctant to sell them and they are more expensive and hard to obtain at the border. **Communications** Internet: *@llnet* in Macapá Shopping. Post office: Av Corialano Jucá. Telephone: R São José 2050. Open 0730-2200. **Embassies and consulates** *France*, at *Pousada Ekinox* (see above). Visas are not issued for non-Brazilians. **Medical services** *Geral*, Av FAB, T2126127. *Hospital São Camila & São Luiz*, R Marcelo Candia 742, T2231514. **Useful addresses** *Ibama*, R Hamilton Silva 1570, Santa Rita, CEP 68906-440, Macapá, T/F2141100.

North of Macapá

Only the first section of the road north to the Guyane border (BR-156) is paved. Although precarious in places, it is open throughout the year with buses and pick-ups operating even in the wet season. At all times, however, take food and water for the journey as services are scarce. Gasoline and diesel (not alcohol) are available along the road, but drivers should take extra fuel from Macapá.

North of Macapá the road divides at **Porto Grande**, and a branch heads northwest to Serra do Navio where manganese extraction has now ended (*Hotel Serra do Navio* and several bars and restaurants). The BR-156 continues north, passing the turn-offs for two jungle hotels, *Recanto Ecológico Sonho Meu*, Km 108, T2341298, and *Pontal das Pedras* (**B**), Km 109, T2512781, restaurant, fishing, boat trips, ecological trail, popular at weekends, recommended. The road goes to **Ferreira Gomes** on the shores of the Rio Araguari, where the pavement ends. Further on is **Amapá**, formerly the territorial capital and location of a Second World War American airbase. There are a few hotels, **C** *Hotel Amapá*, T4211108, and another, which is clean and comfortable, one block from the square towards docks, turn right, second house on the left. Beyond Amapá is **Calçoene**, with a government-owned hotel (**D**) by

Daniel Ludwig and the Jari Project

In the 1960s, the American billionaire and supertanker magnate, Daniel K Ludwig, investigated the possibilities of converting an area of Amazon rainforest into a large-scale, commercially viable plantation, producing wood for pulp and timber. His experts had convinced him that a tree called Gmelina arborea (originally from Burma and India) would grow in sufficient volume, and fast enough in an equatorial climate, to fulfil Ludwig's dream of supplying the world's wood pulp needs before the end of the 20th century. Politically and, apparently, agriculturally, conditions favoured Brazil, so Ludwig bought four million acres of land (at only US$1 per acre) on the northern shore of the Amazon and the east and west banks of the Rio Jari, which forms the border between Amapá and Pará. As two lengthy articles by Dr Jerry A Shields in the South American Explorer *magazine in January and April 1993 show, the project was beset with difficulties and delays, not least the failure of the Gmelina to grow quickly*

enough in the rainforest soil. Controversy surrounded every aspect of Jari, environmental, political/nationalistic, social and economic, and Ludwig had to sink an enormous amount of money into the land that he had cleared of jungle. Parallel with the forestry project were agricultural schemes (for example, huge rice paddies), kaolin production and bauxite mining. Ludwig himself ran out of enthusiasm in 1981, when he put Jari up for sale. The Brazilian government, which had initially encouraged the project, had to garner funds from a wide variety of public and private sources to buy Ludwig out and cover Jari's debts. By 1993 the pulp plant was operating profitably, but whether it could be called a success is a matter of debate. Loren McIntyre, in the June 1993 issue of the South American Explorer, *in which he updated Shields' report and questioned some of his conclusions, was not pessimistic about the future. Daniel Ludwig himself died in 1992, aged 95.*

the bus stop, which serves expensive food in an adjoining canteen; very cheap sleeping space is also advertized in a café on the Oiapoque road. North of Calçoene a road branches west to **Lourenço**, whose gold fields continue to produce even after various decades of prospecting. The main road continues north across the Rio Caciporé and on to the border with French Guyane at Oiapoque, on the river of the same name. About 7 km to the west is Clevelândia do Norte, a military outpost and the end of the road in Brazil.

Oiapoque
Colour map 1, grid A5
This is a remote place, 90 km inland from Cabo Orange, Brazil's northern-most point on the Atlantic coast, with its share of contraband, illegal migration and drug trafficking. It is also the gateway to gold fields in the interior of both Brazil and Guyane.

It is quite rough and the visitor should be cautious, especially late at night. Prices here are high but still lower than in neighbouring Guyane. The **Cachoeira Grande Roche** rapids can be visited, upstream along the Oiapoque River, where it is possible to swim, US$30 by motor boat. Mountain bikes can be rented at Jance de Aluguel in the street parallel to the riverfront for US$10 daily. The Associação dos Povos Indígenas de Oiapoque, in front of the *Banco do Brasil*, gives information about the indigenous peoples in the area, such as the Uaçá Indian Reserve.

Sleeping and eating C *Trânsito*, Av Joaquim Caetano da Silva, on the riverfront. Clean, with breakfast, fridge, TV, restaurant. **D** *Kayama*, on the same street, No 760, T5211448. A/c and bath, **E** with fan, good, international calls. Another, **F**, next door, basic. **D** *Pousada Central*, 1 street back from the river. A/c, bath, **E** with fan and shared

The Amazon

bath. Also **F** *Sonho Meu*, basic. Other cheap hotels along the waterfront are mainly used by Brazilians waiting to cross to Guyane. *Restaurant Paladar Drinks*, 1 block up from the river, expensive. *Pantanal Bar*, next to the monument at riverfront, has dancing at weekends.

Air Flights to **Macapá** 3 times a week. **Buses** *Estrela de Ouro* leaves for **Macapá** from **Transport** the waterfront, daily at 1000, 12 hrs (dry season), 14-24 hrs (wet season), US$35, also Cattani. Pick-up trucks depart from the same area when full, US$35 in cab, US$15 in the back. **Boats** Occasional cargo vessels to Belém or Macapá (Porto Santana).

Banks It is possible to exchange US dollars and reais to francs, but dollar rates are low **Directory** and TCs are not accepted anywhere. *Banco do Brasil*, Av Barão do Rio Branco, open 1000-1500, reais to francs and Visa facilities. Visa users can also withdraw reais at *Bradesco*, exchanging these to francs. Gold merchants, like *Casa Francesa* on the riverfront and a *câmbio* in the market, will sell reais for US$ or French francs. Rates are even worse in St-Georges. Best to buy francs in Belém, or abroad. **Communications** Post office: Av Barão do Rio Branco, open 0900-1200, 1400-1700. **Useful addresses** Immigration: Polícia Federal for Brazilian exit stamp is on the road to Calçoene, about 500 m from the river.

Motorized canoes cross to St-Georges de L'Oyapock, 10 minutes down- **Frontier with** stream, F20 per person, slightly cheaper in reais, bargain. A vehicle ferry will **Guyane** operate until a bridge is eventually built. *Catraias* (decrepit canoes) which carry illegal migrants for night landings, are expensive, dangerous and definitely not recommended.

   Into Guyane An unmade road from St-Georges to Cayenne has been cut through the jungle, but it is best to fly or take a boat. For more details, see the *South American Handbook*.

Pará

This northern state has many places of ecological interest, such as the fluvial island of Marajó in the Amazon Delta and the Amazônia National Park on the River Tapajós. There is excellent sport fishing and local cuisine based around the many varieties of local fish and fruits. The capital, Belém, is a good place to begin or end a journey on the River Amazon, while Santarém with its nearby river beaches is a quiet spot to spend a few days while changing boats. The more isolated parts of the state are linked by air as road travel can be difficult during the rainy season from December to May.

Established because of its strategic position in 1616, Belém soon became the centre for slaving expeditions into the Amazon Basin. The Portuguese of Pará, together with those of Maranhão, treated the Indians abominably. Being remote from the longer-established colonies, and having stronger links with distant Portugal itself, both places were relatively lawless. In 1655, the Jesuits, under Antônio Vieira, attempted to lessen the abuses, while enticing the Indians to 'descend' to the *aldeias* around Belém. This eventually led to further misery when smallpox spread from the south, striking the Pará *aldeias* in the 1660s.

   Soon after Brazil's Independence, the Revolta da Cabanagem, a rebellion by the poor blacks, Indians and mixed-race *cabanos* (who lived in *cabanas*), was led against the Portuguese-born class that dominated the economy. The

The Amazon

movement came to an end in 1840 when the *cabanos* finally surrendered, but the worst years of violence were 1835-36. Some estimates say 30,000 were killed. The state's strategic location once again became important during the Second World War, when Belém was used as an airbase by the Americans to hunt German submarines in the Atlantic.

Belém

Phone code: 091
Colour map 1, grid A6
Population: 1.3 million

Belém do Pará is the great port of the Amazon. The city has much of cultural interest, a fascinating market, and is the starting point for boat trips into the Amazon. With mean temperatures of 26°C, it is hot, but frequent showers freshen the streets.

Ins & outs
See also Transport, page 552

Getting there Val-de-Cans airport is 12 km from the city. Buses take 40 mins to the centre and charge US$0.50. Taxis charge US$10. Belém can be reached from Cayenne, Miami and Paramaribo as well as from Brasília, Rio de Janeiro and other cities in Brazil by air. There are road connections from São Luís and the northeastern coast as well as a 3-day bus link from São Paulo via Brasília. The rodoviária for interstate buses is 3 km from the centre; bus US$0.50, taxi US$5-7 to the centre. Boats arrive at the port from Macapá, Manaus and Santarém as well as other parts of the Amazon region and delta.

Getting around The city centre is easily explored on foot. City buses and taxis run to all the sites of interest and transport hubs away from the centre.

Tourist offices *Belemtur*, Av Gov José Malcher 592, T2420900, F2413194, belemtur@cinbesa.com.br, also at airport T2116151. *Paratur*, Praça Waldemar Henrique on the waterfront, T2232130, F2236198, by the handicraft shop, helpful,

Belém orientation

Detailed map
A Belém, page 549

0 metres 500
0 yards 500

■ Sleeping
1 Novotel

many languages spoken, has a good map of Belém in many languages (but some references are incorrect), town guidebook, US$2.75. *Ibama*, Av Conselheiro Furtado 1303, Batista Campos, CEP 66035-350, T2412621, F2231299.

History

The first settlement of Belém was based on the Forte do Presépio, now Forte do Castelo. Other than its importance as a slaving port, Belém was not a wealthy colonial possession until, in the mid-18th century, the Portuguese government encouraged the import of African slaves to work new agriculture ventures in which it was investing. The Revolta da Cabanagem (see above) brought disaster to the city; a memorial designed by Oscar Niemeyer stands at the eastern entrance to Belém. Further devastation came in 1850 in an epidemic of yellow fever.

The city's fortunes dramatically revived during the rubber boom (see below under Manaus), which accounts for the French belle-epoque appearance of much of the city centre. Decline followed the collapse of the rubber trade, with a brief revival during the Second World War. The city remains important as a port and gateway between the Atlantic and Amazon.

Sights

There are some fine squares and restored historic buildings set along broad avenues. Belém used to be called the 'City of Mango Trees' and there are still many such trees remaining. The largest square is the **Praça da República**, where there are free afternoon concerts; the main business and shopping area is along the wide Avenida Presidente Vargas, leading to the river and the narrow streets which parallel it.

The neoclassical, recently restored, **Teatro da Paz** (1874) is one of the largest theatres in the country and worth a visit. It stages performances by national and international stars and also gives free concert and theatre shows. ■ *0900-1800 Tue-Fri. Tours cost US$1.50.*

The **cathedral** (1748), on Praça Frei Caetano Brandão, is another neoclassical building which contains several remarkable paintings. ■ *1500-1800 Mon, 0800-1100, 1530-1800 Tue-Fri.* The cathedral stands directly opposite the restored 18th-century **Santo Aleixandre** church, which is noted for its wood carving.

The 17th-century **Mercês** church (1640), near the market, is the oldest church in Belém. It forms part of an architectural group known as the Mercedário, the rest of which was heavily damaged by fire in 1978 and has now been restored.

The **Basílica of Nossa Senhora de Nazaré** (1909), built from rubber wealth in romanesque style, is an absolute must for its beautiful marble and stained-glass windows. It is on Praça Justo Chermont, Avenida Magalhães Barata. ■ *0500-1130, 1400-2000 Mon-Sat, 0545-1130, 1430-2000 Sun.* A museum at the Basílica describes the Círio de Nazaré religious festival (see below).

The **Palácio Lauro Sodré** and **Museu do Estado do Pará**, on Praça Dom Pedro II, is a gracious 18th-century Italianate building. It contains Brazil's largest framed painting, 'The Conquest of Amazônia', by Domenico de Angelis. The building was the work of the Italian architect Antonio Landi who also designed the Cathedral and was the administrative seat of the colonial government. During the rubber boom many new decorative features were added. ■ *0900-1800 Mon-Fri, 1000-1800 Sat, T2253853.* Also on Praça Dom

Pedro II is the **Palácio Antônio Lemos**, which houses the **Museu de Arte de Belém** as well as the **Prefeitura**. It was originally built as the Palácio Municipal between 1868 and 1883, and is a fine example of the Imperial neoclassical style. In the downstairs rooms there are old views of Belém; upstairs the historic rooms, beautifully renovated, contain furniture, paintings, etc, which are all well explained. ■ *0900-1200, 1400-1800 Tue-Fri, 0900-1300 Sat-Sun.*

One of the most varied and colourful markets in South America

The Belém market, known as **Ver-o-Peso**, was the Portuguese Posto Fiscal, where goods were weighed to gauge taxes due, hence the name: 'see the weight'. It now has lots of gift shops selling charms for the local African-derived religion, *umbanda* and interesting medicinal herb and natural perfume stalls. You can see giant river fish being unloaded around 0530, with frenzied wholesale buying for the next hour; a new dock for the fishing boats was built just upriver from the market in 1997. The area around the market swarms with people, including many armed thieves and pickpockets.

In the old town, too, is the **Forte do Castelo**, Praça Frei Caetano Brandão 117, which was rebuilt in 1878. The fort overlooks the confluence of the Rio Guamá and the Baía do Guajara and was where the Portuguese first set up their defences. ■ *0800-2300 daily, T2230041.* Also on the site is a good restaurant, *Círculo Militar* (entry US$1; drinks and *salgadinhos* served on the ramparts from 1800 to watch the sunset). At the square on the waterfront below the fort, the *açaí* berries are landed nightly at 2300, after being picked in the jungle. *Açaí* berries, ground up with sugar and mixed with manioc, are a staple food in the region.

At the **Estação das Docas**, the abandoned warehouses of the port have been restored into a complex with an air-conditioned interior and restaurants outside. The Terminal Marítimo has an office of *Valverde Tours*, which offers sunset and nighttime boat trips. The Boulevard das Artes contains the *Cervejaria Amazon* brewery, with good beer and simple meals, an archaeological museum and arts and crafts shops. The Boulevard de Gastronomia has smart restaurants and the 5-star *Cairu* ice-cream parlour (try *açaí* or the *Pavê de Capuaçu*). In the Boulevard das Feiras there are trade fairs. Live music is transported between the pavilions on a moving stage. Also in the complex are ATMs, internet café, phones and good toilets.

The **Bosque Rodrigues Alves**, Avenida Almirante Barroso 2305, is a 16-ha public garden (really a preserved area of original flora), with a small animal collection. ■ *0800-1700 closed Mon. T2262308. Yellow bus marked 'Souza' or 'Cidade Nova' (any number) 30 mins from Ver-o-Peso market, also bus from Cathedral.* The **Museu Emílio Goeldi**, Avenida Magalhães Barata 376, takes up a city block and consists of the museum proper (with a fine collection of Marajó Indian pottery, an excellent exhibition of Mebengokre Indian lifestyle), a zoological garden (including manatees) and botanical exhibits including Victoria Régia lilies. ■ *0900-1200, 1400-1700 Tue-Thu, 0900-1200 Fri, 0900-1700 Sat and Sun. US$1, additional charges for specialist areas. Take a bus from the Cathedral.* The **Murucutu** ruins, an old Jesuit foundation, are reached by the Ceará bus from Praça da República, through an unmarked door on the right of the Ceará bus station.

Excursions

A passenger ferry (*foca*) to the small town of **Barcarena** makes an interesting half-day trip, departures from Ver-o-Peso, US$1. A return trip on the ferry from Ver-o-Peso to **Icaoraci** provides a good view of the river. Several restaurants here serve excellent seafood; you can eat shrimp and drink coconut water and appreciate the breeze coming off the river. Icaoraci is 20 km east of the city and is well known as a centre of ceramic production. The pottery is in Marajoara and Tapajonica style. Take the bus from Avenida Presidente Vargas to Icoaraci (one hour). Artisans are friendly and helpful, will accept commissions and send purchases overseas. ■ *All week, but best on Tue-Fri.*

The nearest beach is at **Outeiro** (35 km) on an island near Icoaraci, about an hour by bus and ferry (the bus may be caught near the Maloca, an Indian-style hut near the docks which serves as a nightclub). A bus from Icoaraci to Outeiro takes 30 minutes. Further north is the island of **Mosqueiro** (86 km), accessible by bridge and an excellent highway, with many beautiful sandy beaches and jungle inland. It is popular at weekends when traffic can be heavy (also July) and the beaches can get crowded and polluted. Buses Belém-Mosqueiro every hour from rodoviária, US$1.50, 80 minutes. There is also a ferry from Porto do Sal, on the street between Forte de Castelo and the cathedral. It takes about two hours. There are many hotels and weekend villas at the villages of Mosqueiro and Vila, which are recommended, but these may be full weekends and July. **B** *Farol*, on Praia Farol, T7711219, 1920s architecture in good repair, small restaurant, rooms face beach, good views. Restaurants at Mosqueiro include *Hotel Ilha Bela*, Avenida 16 de Novembro 409, recommended for fish, no evening meals. Highly recommended at Praia Chapeu Virado is *Marésia*. *Sorveteria Delícia*, Avenida 16 de Novembro, serves good local fruit ice-creams and the owner buys dollars. Camping is easy.

Belém

	Sleeping		5 Palacio das Musas	10 Zoghbi Park	3 Casa Portuguesa
1	Central	6	Regente		4 Círculo Militar
2	Itaoca	7	Sete-Sete	**Eating**	5 Lá em Casa
3	Le Massilia	8	Ver-o-Peso	1 Cantina Italiana	
4	Novo Avenida	9	Vitória Régia	2 Casa dos Sucos	

Related map
Belém orientation,
page 546

Essentials

Sleeping
■ *on map, page 549*
Price codes:
see inside front cover

Hotels in the city are
not up to much.
All hotels are fully
booked during Círio
(see box opposite)

A *Itaoca*, Av Pres Vargas 132, T2413434, F2410891. New, charming, but some rooms are noisy. **A** *Novotel*, Av Bernardo Sayão 4808, T2497111, F2497808. Pool, unprepossessing neighbourhood, far from centre (take Universidade bus). **A** *Regente*, Av Gov José Malcher 485, T2411222, F2420343, hregente@libnet.com.br Modest but comfortable, good breakfast, some English-speaking staff. **B** *Le Massilia*, R Henrique Gurjão 236, T2247147. Also has French restaurant. **C** *Novo Avenida*, Av Pres Vargas 404,T/F2238893, avenida@hotelnovoavenida.com.br central, on busy street, a/c, fridge, cheaper with fan. Very well looked after. Recommended. **C** *Vidonho's*, R Ó de Almeida 476, T2421444, F2247499. A/c, fridge, good breakfast, in a side street. **C** *Zoghbi Park*, R Padre Prudêncio 220, T/F2411800, zoghbi@zoghbi.com.br smart if dated, spacious, good value, small pool, restaurant, caters to business clients. Recommended.

There are many
cheap hotels close to
waterfront (none
too safe) and several
others near
the rodoviária
(generally OK)

D *Central*, Av Pres Vargas 290, T2424800, with a/c (**E** without bath), on busy street, some rooms noisy, but comfortable, good meals, a must for art-deco fans. **D** *Sete-Sete*, Trav 1 de Março 673, T2227730, F2242346. Clean, comfortable, safe, in quiet street, with breakfast. Recommended. **D** *Ver-o-Peso*, Av Castilho França 308, T2412022, Functional, rooftop restaurant, TV and fridge, not too clean, but good position near port and Ver-o-Peso market. **D** *Vitória Rêgia*, Trav Frutuoso Guimarães 260, T/F2122077. With breakfast, more with a/c, bath, fridge (**E** without), safe. **E** *Fortaleza*, Trav Frutuoso Guimarães 276, T2121055. Very basic but OK for price. **E** *Palacio das Musas*, Trav Frutuoso Guimarães 275, T2128422. Big rooms, clean, shared bath. **Camping** Nearest campsite is at Mosqueiro, 86 km away.

Eating
The many street
and market vendors
often sell delicious
local food, but view
them with care

Expensive All the major hotels have upmarket restaurants. The *Açaí* at the *Hilton*, Av Pres Vargas 882, T2426500. Recommended for regional dishes, daily lunch, dinner with live music and Sun brunch. *Círculo Militar*, Praça Ferreira Cantão, situated in the grounds of Forte do Castelo, T2234374. Belém's best Brazilian food and view over river (wide selection, try *filetena brasa*). *Lá em Casa*, Av Gov José Malcher 247, T2231212. Try *menu paraense*, good cooking, fashionable.

 Mid-range *Cantina Italiana*, Trav Benjamin Constant 1401, T2252033. Very good Italian, also delivers. *Casa Portuguesa*, R Sen Manoel Barata 897, T2424871. Good, Portuguese dishes. *Churrascaria Rodeio*, Rodovia Augusto Montenegro Km 4, T2483223. Excellent meat, salad bar, reasonable prices. *Churrascaria Tucuruvi*, Trav Benjamin Constant 1843, Nazaré. Good value, generous portions. *Germania*, R Aristides Lobo 604. Munich-style. *Miako*, Trav 1 de Março 766, behind Praça de República, T2422355. Very good Japanese, oriental and international food. *Okada*, R Boaventura da Silva 1522, past R Alcindo Cacela, T2463242. Japanese, excellent, try 'Steak House', various types of meat, rice and sauces, vegetables, all you can eat, also try *camarão à milanesa com salada*. *Pizzeria Napolitano*, Praça Justo Chermont 12, T2225177. Pizzas and Italian dishes.

 Cheap *Casa dos Sucos*, Av Pres Vargas, Praça da República. 41 types of juice (including Amazonian fruits) and delicious chocolate cake (vegetarian restaurant upstairs, recommended for lunches). *Nectar*, Av Gentil Bittencourt, Trav Padre Eutíquio 248, pedestrian zone. Good vegetarian, lunch only. *Tempero*, R Ó de Almeida, 348, self-service, some middle-eastern dishes, real bargain. Warmly recommended.

 Seriously cheap Specially recommended are some very good snack-bars, mostly outdoors, where you can buy anything up to a full meal, much cheaper than restaurants: *Charlotte*, Av Gentil Bittencourt 730, at Trav Quintino Bocaiúva. Best *salgadinhos* in the city, also good desserts, very popular. Many buffet-style restaurants along R Santo Antônio pedestrian mall and elsewhere in the *Comércio* district, including *Doce Vida Salgado*, Trav 1 de Março 217. Good food and prices, generally lunch only, good variety, pay by weight. *Sabor Paranse*, R 13 de Maio, 450. food by weight, lunch only.

The Festival of Candles

Círio, the Festival of Candles in October, is based on the legend of the Nossa Senhora de Nazaré, whose image was found on the site of her Basílica around 1700. On the second Sunday in October, a procession carries a copy of the Virgin's image from the Basílica to the cathedral. On the Monday, two weeks later, the image is returned to its usual resting place. There is a Círio museum in the crypt of the Basílica, enter at the right side of the church; free

entry. The festival, which is 'cheio de coração' (full of heart), has attracted many major Brazilian artists and musicians. It has developed into a massive national festival and is highly recommended. The biggest carnival performers attend, along with important rock groups and an increasing contingent of international artists. The non-religious element of the festival is known as Carnabelém. For dates check with Paratur, T2233130.

Bars & nightclubs

Many venues around Av Doca de Souza Franco, often just called 'Doca', especially popular Thu. *African Bar*, Praça Waldemar Henrique 2. Rock or Samba, weekends only. *Baixo Reduto*, R Quintino Bocaiúva, Reduto, T2426282. Blues on Wed; Brazilian pop, Thu; rock, Fri and Jazz, Sat. The Reduto district has recently become the place to go at night. *Bar Teatro Bora Bora*, R Bernal do Couto 38, T2415848, restaurant, bar and nightclub, MPB and Pagode open from 2100 until late Thu-Sun. *Colarinho Branco Chopperia*, Av Visconde de Souza Franco, 80, near the river. Open Tue-Sun, 1800 to last customer. Excellent draught beer and nightly perfomers of Brazilian popular music. Popular. *Escapóle*, Rodovia Augusto Montenegro 400. Huge dance hall with various types of music, live and recorded, frequented by all age groups, open Wed-Sat from 2200 (take a radio taxi for safety), no a/c, dress informally. *Olê Olá*, Av Tavares Bastos, 1234, T2432340. Disco, live music and dance floor. Thu-Sun only, 2230 to last customer.

Entertainment

Art galleries *Debret*, R Arcipreste Manoel Theodoro 630, Batista Campos, T2224046. Contemporary painting and sculpture, also has library specializing in art and philosophy. **Cinema** *Olímpia*, Av Pres Vargas 918, T2231882. In existence for over 80 years and was the first cinema in Belém. **Theatre** *Margarida Schiwwazappa*, Av Gentil Bittencourt 650, T2222923.

Festivals

Maundy Thu, half-day; *Good Fri*, all shops closed, all churches open and there are processions; **9 Jun**, *Corpus Christi*; **15 Aug**, accession of Pará to Independent Brazil; **7 Sep**, *Independence Day*, commemorated on the day with a military parade, and with a students' parade on the preceding Sun (morning); *Círio* through **Oct** (see box); **30 Oct**, half-day; **2 Nov**, *All Souls' Day*; **8 Dec**, *Immaculate Conception*; *Christmas Eve*, half-day.

Sport

Amazônia Sport & Ação, Av 25 de Setembro, 2345, T226 8442. Extreme sports, diving, rock-climbing. *Iate Clube do Pará*, Av Bernardo Sayão, 3324, T2297599. Swimming pools, gym and sports courts.

Shopping

Shopping Iguatemi, Trav Padre Eutique 1078. *Parfumaria Orion*, Trav Frutuoso Guimarães 268. Has a wide variety of perfumes and essences from Amazonian plants, much cheaper than tourist shops. The *Complexo São Brás* on Praça Lauro Sodré. Has a handicraft market and folkloric shows in a building dating from 1911. Belém is a good place to buy hammocks, look in the street parallel to the river, 1 block inland from Ver-o-Peso. Bookshop with English titles in the arcade on Av Pres Vargas.

Tour operators

City tours (3 hrs) and river tours are offered by most companies. *Amazon Star*, R Henrique Gurjão 236, T/F2126244, T9827911 (mob), amazstar@interconect.com.br French run, good

The Amazon

half-day boat tour with jungle walk, as well as tours to Marajó. *Angel*, in *Hilton Hotel*, T2242111, F2242030, angel@datanetbbs.com.br, tours and events, issues ISIC and IYHA cards. *Gran-Para*, Av Pres Vargas 676, T2123233, F2415531, good for airline bookings.

Transport
See also Ins and outs, page 546

Air International flights to Cayenne, Miami and Paramaribo. Domestic flights to Altamira, Brasília, Breves, Carajás, Fortaleza, Imperatriz, Macapá, Manaus, Marabá, Monte Dourado, Rio de Janeiro, Santarém, São Luís and São Paulo. Bus 'Perpétuo Socorro-Telégrafo' or 'Icoaraci', every 15 mins from the Prefeitura, Praça Felipe Patroni, to the airport, 40 mins, US$0.50. Taxi to airport, US$10 (ordinary taxis are cheaper than Coop taxis, buy ticket in advance in Departures side of airport). ATMs in the terminal.

Bus The rodoviária is at the end of Av Gov José Malcher, 3 km from the centre, take Aeroclube, Cidade Novo, No 20 bus, or Arsenal or Canudos buses, US$0.50, or taxi, US$5 (day), US$7 (night) (at rodoviária you are given a ticket with the taxi's number on it, threaten to go to the authorities if the driver tries to overcharge). It has a good snack bar and showers (US$0.10) and 2 agencies with information and tickets for riverboats. Regular bus services to all major cities. Transbrasiliana go direct to **Marabá**, US$20 (16 hrs). To **Santarém**, via Marabá once a week (US$45, more expensive than by boat and can take longer, goes only in dry season). To **São Luís**, 2 a day, US$20, 13 hrs, interesting journey through marshlands. To **Fortaleza**, US$35-40 (24 hrs), several companies. To **Salvador**, US$50.

Boat River services to Santarém, Manaus, and intermediate ports (see River transport, page 536). The larger ships berth at Portobrás/Docas do Pará (the main commercial port), either at Armazém (warehouse) No 3 at the foot of Av Pres Vargas, or at Armazém No 10, a few blocks further north (entrance on Av Marechal Hermes, corner of Av Visconde de Souza Franco). The guards will sometimes ask to see your ticket before letting you into the port area, but tell them you are going to speak with a ship's captain. Ignore the touts who approach you. Smaller vessels (sometimes cheaper, usually not as clean, comfortable or safe) sail from small docks along the Estrada Nova (not a safe part of town). Take a Cremação bus from Ver-o-Peso.

To **Macapá** (Porto Santana) daily service. *Silja e Souza* of *Souzamar*, Trav Dom Romualdo Seixas, corner of R Jerônimo Pimentel, T2220719, and *Comandante Solon* of *Sanave* (Serviço Amapaense de Navegação, Av Castilho Franca 234, opposite Ver-o-Peso, T2227810). Via Breves, *ENAL*, T2245210. There are 2 desks selling tickets for private boats in the rodoviária; some hotels (eg *Fortaleza*) recommend agents for tickets. Purchase tickets from offices 2 days in advance. Smaller boats to Macapá also sail from Estrada Nova.

Car hire *Avis*, R Antonio Barreto, 1653, T2302000, also at airport, freephone 0800 558066. *Localiza*, Av Pedro Álvares Cabral, 200, T2122700, and at airport, T2571541.

Hitchhiking Going south, take bus to Capanema, 3½ hrs, US$2.30, walk 500 m from the rodoviária to BR-316 where trucks stop at the gas station.

Directory

Airline offices *Penta*, Av Sen Lemos 4700, T2447777. *Surinam Airways*, R Gaspar Viana 488, T2127144, F2247879. English spoken, helpful with information and documentation. *Taba*, Av Dr Freitas 1191, international airport, T2574000. *Varig*, Av Pres Vargas 768, T2243344, airport T2570481. *Vasp*, Av Pres Vargas 345, T2122496, airport T2570944.

Banks open 0900-1630, but foreign exchange only until 1300

Banks *Banco do Brasil*, Av Pres Vargas, near *Hotel Central*, good rates, ATMs and other Brazilian banks (open 0900-1630, but foreign exchange only until 1300). *HSBC*, Av Pres Vargas near Praça da República has MasterCard Cirrus and Amex ATMs. *Banco de Amazônia* (Basa), on Pres Vargas, gives good rates for TCs (Amex or Citicorp only), but does not change cash. *Itaú*, R Boaventura 580, good TCs and cash rates. In early 2002 the local authorities closed all **Casas de câmbio**, so money could only be changed at banks during the week. At weekends hotels will only exchange for their guests, while restaurants may change money, but at poor rates.

Communications Internet: *Amazon*, 2nd floor of Estação das Docas. *InterBelém*, Av Jose Malcher 189, US$1 per hr, helpful South African owner, English spoken. *Convert*, Shopping Iguatemi, 3rd floor, US$1.40 per hr. **Post office**: Av Pres Vargas 498. Also handles telegrams and fax. **Telephone**: *Telemar*, Av Pres Vargas.

Embassies and consulates *Denmark* (Consul Arne Hvidbo), R Senador Barata 704, sala 1503, T2235888 (PO Box 826). *Finland*, Rodovia Arthur Bernardes 1393, Bairro Telégrafo, T2330333. *France*, R Pres Pernambuco 269, T2246818 (also for French Guiana, South Africans must apply in South Africa). *Germany*, Edif Comendador Pinho, Trav Campos Sales 63, room 404, T2225666. *Italy*, R Gaspar Viana 253, 1st floor, T2416489. *Netherlands*, Av Cláudio Saunder 1694, T2245811. *Sweden*, R Santo Antônio 316, mailing address Caixa Postal 111, T2224788, open 1600-1800. *UK*, Robin Burnett, Edif Palladium Centre, room 410, Av Gov José Malcher 811, T2225074. *USA*, Trav Padre Eutíquio 1309, T2230800. *Venezuela*, opposite French Consulate, R Pres Pernambuco 270, T2226396 (Venezuelan visa takes 3 hrs, costs US$30 for most nationalities, but we are told that it is better to get a visa at Manaus; latest reports indicate that a yellow fever vaccination certificate is not required but it is best to check in advance – see also Health, next paragraph).

Language schools *Unipop*, Av Sen Lemos 557, T2249074. Portuguese course for foreigners.

Laundry *Lav e Lev*, R Dr Moraes 576. *Lavanderia Paraense*, Trav. Dom Pedro, 1104, T2220057, dry and steam cleaning.

Libraries *UFPA*, Av Augusto Correa 1, T2111140, university library with many titles on Amazônia.

Medical services Health: a yellow fever certificate or inoculation is mandatory. It is best to get a yellow fever vaccination at home (always have your certificate handy) and avoid the risk of recycled needles. Medications for malaria prophylaxis are not sold in Belém pharmacies. You can theoretically get them through the public health service, but this is hopelessly complicated. Such drugs are sometimes available at pharmacies in smaller centres, eg Santarém and Macapá. Bring an adequate supply from home. *Clínica de Medicina Preventativa*, Av Bras de Aguiar 410 (T2221434), will give injections, English spoken, open 0730-1200, 1430-1900 (Sat 0800-1100). *Hospital da Ordem Terceira*, Trav Frei Gil de Vila Nova 59, T2122777, doctors speak some English, free consultation. Surgery open Mon 1300-1900, Tue-Thu 0700-1100, 24 hrs for emergencies. The British consul has a list of English-speaking doctors.

Security Police: for reporting crimes, R Santo Antônio and Trav Frei Gil de Vila Nova. Belém has its share of crime and is prone to gang violence. Take sensible precautions especially at night.

Voltage 110 AC, 60 cycles.

The Amazon

Around Belém

Marajó

Colour map 1, grid A5 This is the world's largest river island, a claim disputed by the Bananal, which is partly flooded in the rainy season January-June. It provides a suitable habitat for large numbers of water buffalo, which are said to have swum ashore after a shipwreck; many are now farmed; try the cheese and milk. Marajó is also home to numerous bird species, caiman and other wildlife, and has several good beaches. It is crowded in the July holiday season. The island was the site of the pre-Columbian Marajoaras culture.

Ponta de Pedras Boats leave Belém, near Porto do Sal, most days for the five-hour crossing to Ponta de Pedras. Seats are US$3.60, two-berth cabins US$38. In Ponta de Pedras is **D** *Hotel Ponta de Pedras*, which serves good meals. Bicycles can be hired at US$1 per hour to explore beaches and the interior of the island. Fishing boats make the eight-hour trip to Cachoeira do Arari (one hotel, **D**), where there is a fascinating Marajó museum. A 10-hour boat trip from Ponta de Pedras goes to the Arari lake where there are two villages: Jenipapo and Santa Cruz, which is less primitive, but less interesting; a hammock and a mosquito net are essential. There is a direct boat service to Belém twice a week.

Soure
Take plenty of insect repellent
The capital of the island is Soure. There are fine beaches: **Araruna**, 2 km away; take supplies and supplement with coconuts and crabs, beautiful walks along the shore; **do Pesqueiro** (bus from Praça da Matriz, 1030, returns 1600, eat at *Maloca*, good, cheap, big, deserted beach, 13 km away); and **Caju-Una** (15 km). A ferry from Belém sails weekends (four hours, US$5). Small craft await passengers from the Enasa boats, for Salvaterra village (good beaches and bars: seafood), US$12, 10 minutes. There is a ferry to Porto do Cámara (three hours). Then take a bus to Salvaterra and a ferry to Soure. There is a taxi-plane service to Soure.

Banco do Brasil has an ATM. Changing money is only possible at very poor rates
Sleeping and eating **A** *Pousada dos Guarãs*, Av Beira Mar, Salvaterra, T/F7651133, www.pousadadosguaras.com.br Well-equipped, tour programme, on beach. **B** *Hotel Ilha do Marajó*, 8a Rua 10, Matinha, T7411315 (Belém 2245966). **D** *Pousada Parque Floresta*, good meals. **C** *Soure* R 3 Centro, A/c, basic. **C** *Waldeck*, Trav 12, T7411414. Only 4 rooms. **E** *Pensão* at 2a R 575 (*Bar Guaraní*). Simple. Recommended. *Canecão*, Praça da Matriz. Sandwiches, meals. Recommended.

East and south of Belém

Salinópolis
Map 1, grid A6
Some 223 km away, at the extreme end of the eastern part of the Amazon Delta, this seaside resort has many small places where you can eat and drink at night by the waterfront and a fine sandy beach nearby (buses and cars drive on to the beach). It is a peaceful place mid-week and is best during the holiday month of July. Atalaia, an island opposite Salinópolis, is pleasant and can be reached by taxi (US$6) or with a fisherman. Salinópolis is four hours from Belém by bus on a good road, US$6.

Sleeping and eating **A** *Atalaia*, on Atalaia island, 15 km from Salinópolis, T/F8241122. Simple, beautiful setting, reserve in advance, take a taxi. **A** *Solar*, Av Beira Mar, T8231823. With bath, best in town, good restaurant. **A** *Jeanne d'Arc*, Av João

Pessoa 555, T/F8231422. With breakfast. *Bife de Ouro*, Av Dr Miguel Santa Brígida, opposite filling station. Simple, but excellent fish and shrimp, always crowded for lunch. *Gringo Louco*, further out than Atalaia, 15 km (take taxi or hitch), at Cuiarana beach, follow signs. Gringo owner serves good, unusual dishes, and some 'wild' drinks known as 'bombs', popular.

This agreeable town is a good place to stop if you prefer not to stay in Belém en route to São Luís. **Capanema**

Sleeping B *Diolindina*, Av Pres Médici 424, T8211667, has small clean rooms with fridge and bath, a/c, breakfast buffet and safe parking. Recommended. There are good restaurants and supermarket a opposite. Not as good is **D** *São Luís*.

Tomé-Açu, south of Belém on the Rio Acará-Mirim, affords a view of life on a smaller river than the Amazon; three buses a day from Belém, US$8. *Hotel Las Vegas*, owner Fernando is very friendly. Boat back to Belém on Sunday at 1100, arriving 1800, US$5.

Along the Transamazônica

The Transamazônica, about 5,000 km in length, represents the greater part of a direct road connection between Brazil's furthest east and furthest west points. It skirts the southern edge of the Amazonian plain, linking Estreito (junction with the Belém-Brasília highway, north of Araguaína), Marabá (on the Tocantins river), Altamira (on the Xingu), São Luís do Tapajós, near Itaituba (on the Tapajós), Jacarèacanga, Humaitá (on the Madeira), Rio Branco and Japim, in the far west of the State of Acre.

Officially opened in December 1973, only parts of the road have been paved and the harsh climate and inadequate maintenance have caused much deterioration. Some sections are often totally impassable throughout the rainy season (for example, Santarém to the Belém-Brasília Highway). Others may require a four-wheel drive and winch. There are stretches with regular truck traffic and scheduled bus services, but as conditions are constantly changing, detailed local inquiry is essential before heading out. The journey along the Transamazônica can be dangerous and it is essential to know some Portuguese. Also ensure that you have sufficient *reais*.

The Amazon

Marabá

Near Marabá are beaches on the Tocantins and Itacaiúnas rivers, which are best visited June-October. With the filling of the Tucuruí dam, the town has been moved; even so, it suffers from flooding. There is a bridge across the Tocantins at Marabá. There are essentially three parts of Marabá: Marabá Velha (also called Marabá Pioneira), Marabá Nova and Cidade Nova. The distance between Marabá Nova and Velha is about 2½ km. A good travel agent is *IBR Travel* on the main street of Marabá Velha. *Banco do Brasil* will not cash travellers' cheques; the parallel market operates in larger stores; for example, *Supermercado Bato Logo*.

Colour map 1, grid B5
Population: 150,000
Altitude: 84 m

The **Serra Pelada** gold mines are now worked by heavy machinery. This massive excavation was the scene of much human misery and also some fabulous fortunes. To get there, take a bus to Km 6 and change for the Serra Pelada bus, **Excursions**

US$6, three hours, last bus back 1400. About 11 km before the town is a police post: search for weapons and alcohol (forbidden); second search at the airport 2 km from the mine.

Sleeping **A** *Vale do Tocantins*, Folha 29, Cidade Nova, 7 km, T3222321, F3221841. Modern, restaurant, travel agency. **A** *Del Príncipe*, Av Marechal Rondon 95, Cidade Nova, T3241175. A/c, TV, fridge, restaurant, games room. **B** *Bahia*, Nova Marabá, next to the rodoviária. **B** *Dallas*, Nova Marabá, next to rodoviária. Recommended. **B** *Plaza*, Folha 32, Quadra 10, Lote 06, T3221610. Fan, quiet, helpful, very good breakfast, some English spoken. Recommended. **D** *Serra de Ouro*, all of wood, shower. Others near rodoviária.

Eating *Kome Aki no Chikão*, Av Antônio Maia 997, central. A/c, modest, 1200-1500, 1800-2300 (in theory). *Bambu*, Pedro Cameiro 111, Cidade Nova, 3 km. Mainly fish, clean, good value, 1100-1500, 1800-2300. Good *churrascaria* in the main square near the public TV set, juice bars and *DiscoTony* discotheque. *Lanchonete Domino*, opposite the rodoviária. Recommended.

Transport **Air** Airport in Cidade Nova, 3 km. There are no direct flights to Altamira or Santarém, only via Belém with *Brasil Central* or *Varig*. *Brasil Central* flies to several local destinations, eg São Luís, Imperatriz.

Boats Trips to **Belém** (24 hrs) and **Santarém** (18 hrs).

Buses Rodoviária in Nova Marabá, 4 km on PA-150, T3211892. Buses leave daily for **Belém** (654 km, paved, US$20), for **Santarém** (34 hrs) and many daily for **Imperatriz** (7-10 hrs, US$10, there is also a pick-up to the bank of the Tocantins opposite Imperatriz, 5 hrs, but more expensive); buses can be caught going south at Tocantinópolis, opposite Porto Franco on the Belém-Brasília road. Also a bus can be taken to **Araguaína**, 12½ hrs, US$20; bus Marabá-Goiânia (change at Araguaína). Bus to **Santa Inês** (Maranhão, on the Belém-Teresina road), 19 hrs, US$55. *Transbrasiliana* bus to **Altamira** daily, 1300 (if road is passable), 15 hrs, US$30. There are direct buses to **Rio** and **São Paulo**. On these bus trips take plenty of food and drink as local supplies are expensive. From the rodoviária to the railway station for trains on the São Luís-Parauapebas line (see below), take a colectivo bus US$0.75 from opposite the rodoviária to Km 6 (a kind of suburb of Marabá), then another colectivo bus, US$0.75, to the Estação Ferrovia. The colectivos are not frequent but are crowded. Alternatively taxis, which can be shared, cost US$15 from the railway station to town.

Directory **Airline offices** *TAM*, T3243644. *Varig*, T3221965. **Banks** *Banco do Brasil*, Praça Duque de Caxias 966. **Medical services** *Celina Gonçalves*, T3221031.

Carajás

The largest mineral development in Brazil Companhia Vale Rio Doce (CVRD) operates the very impressive iron mine at Carajás, which looks like a giant red hole in a green jungle. The ore is almost pure iron oxide and is therefore extremely profitable. It is ground, washed and shipped to São Luís by trains up to 2 km long, without further treatment or chemical processing. Apart from iron, other metals like manganese are also mined by the CRVD in the area. A city has built up around Carajás, but most of it is within CVRD bounds. To get into Carajás (the Núcleo and to visit the mine) and to pass the checkpoint 35 km from the project, you must have a permit, available from CVRD, phone locally T0XX91-3275300, or enquire in Marabá, São Luís, São Paulo or Rio: Avenida Graça Aranha 26, 16° andar, Centro, Rio 20030000 – attention Dr Hugo Mourão (hotel bookings handled here too). You need to apply in advance and have a good reason for visiting.

Roads to nowhere

In the early 1970s, Brazil's military rulers became increasingly unnerved by what they saw as foreign designs upon the resources of the Amazon basin. This real or imaginary fear of invasion was not only directed against the rich, developed countries, but also Brazil's neighbours who the Brazilians felt were slowly encroaching upon the country's borders. In the early 1960s, Peru's President Fernando Belaunde Terry had proposed the construction of the Carretera Marginal in order to link Peru's jungle with the rest of the country. Under the slogan of 'Integrar para não entregar' (takeover not handover), the Brazilian military announced the construction of the Transamazônica Highway. The road was originally designed to link João Pessoa, Paraíba, with Acre, thence to link up with the Peruvian road system to complete a road route across South America to the Pacific and open up Brazilian products to Asian markets. The Transamazônica itself would be 5,400 km, and would integrate Amazônia from east to west and unify it with the rest of the nation. In addition, it would give opportunities for people from the northeast to resettle in areas not affected by drought and to become economically active in small agricultural schemes. In the often-quoted words of President Emílio Garrastazu Médici, it would move 'Homens sem terra para terras sem homens' (men without land to land without men). All along the highway, purpose-built 'agrovilas' would offer Brazil's poor a new life. The project was proposed in 1970; huge financial investment failed to make the project work. Not only did fewer than anticipated northeasterners take up the offer, but those that did found that the Amazonian soils did not permit the type of rewards that they had been led to expect. The colonizers also found that social infrastructure did not meet their needs and the road itself began to deteriorate as the whole project wound down. By the late 1980s, a Movement for Survival along the Transamazônica had been set up by the farmers.

Another road which was intended to promote development in the Amazon region was the BR-364, from Cuiabá to Acre state. The government in the mid-1970s hoped that it would reinvigorate settlement in the Amazon, in a way that the Transamazônica had failed to do. Like the latter, the BR-364 was supposed to encourage small landholders to follow the building of the main highway and its feeder roads, but in Rondônia the main colonizers were cattle ranchers and land speculators who speeded up the process of deforestation and land conflicts with the traditional cultivators, forest farmers and indigenous people.

A third road in the Amazon which has come to grief, even more so than the other two, is the BR-319 from Manaus to Humaitá on the Transamazônica. Planned in 1960 and opened to traffic in 1975, the road has become a route from nothing to nowhere. The people living along it have been deserted, the only maintenance being the occasional team from Embratel who come to look at the telephone lines which follow the road. Initially there were farms, hotels, petrol stations and restaurants along the BR-319. Most have now gone. Access to health clinics and schools is all but impossible and the only public transport on the southern part of the road is a once-weekly truck. The only people to benefit are the shipping owners who take the traffic, which would have used the road, on barges along the Rio Madeira. The journalist Giuliano Cedroni tried to take the BR-319 in the late-1990s. He and his companions made it through, but not without a tow from the weekly truck after their jeep broke down. One inhabitant of the region pleaded with him, "Tell the people down there [in the south] what is happening in the north. This here is not a life."

Parque Zoo-Botânico is a pleasant zoo with local animals, and like everything else in the region is run by CVRD. The animals have very spacious, quasi-natural cages. There is a lot to see, including a small shop with Funai articles from the local Indians.

Some 37 km before the mine is **Parauapebas**. Originally intended as a temporary settlement for the Carajás construction workers, it is now a big city and still growing. Both Parauapebas and Núcleo Carajás are expensive, especially Carajás. In the dry season, summer, there are frequent bush fires in the region, ignited mainly by *fazendeiros*. The old part of Parauapebas is where the colourful fruit market, shops and banks are situated and is very busy.

Sleeping & eating   **Parauapebas** A *Almaribe*, T3461048. Very pleasant, manager Alipio speaks excellent English, some French and German, safe, a/c, fridge, TV, good breakfast, restaurant, gym machines, good atmosphere. Recommended. **C** *Ouro Verde*, Rio Verde district near market. Basic. *Florida Bar*, T3461038. Good cocktails and food, the friendly owner Neuma speaks good Austrian/German, opens from 2000, closed Mon and Tue. *Pit Dog*, on main street. Fast food and live music.

Transport   **Air** There are flights to Carajás from Belém, Marabá and Tucuruí. **Trains** Parauapebas is the final station of the Carajás railway line. To **Marabá**, departs 1930, 2 hrs, US$4. To **São Luís**, see page 525. **Buses** There are 8 daily buses to Marabá between 0545 and 1900. There is a daily bus to **Conceição de Araguaia**. Direct buses from **Rio**, **São Paulo** and **Vitória** to Parauapebas with *Aguia Branca*. Plenty of *Transbrasiliana* buses daily Marabá-Carajás, 4-5 hrs, US$6. Military police check for weapons and drugs at Curianópolis.

Altamira
Population: 120,000

The Transamazônica crosses the Rio Xingu at Favânia, 41 km east of Altamira, a busy, booming Amazônian town with many gold dealers. A road is being paved 46 km north to the fishing village of Vitória on the lower Xingu, from which boats go to Belém; a good place to watch the *garimpeiros* working below the last rapids. There are no organized trips but a boat can be hired, US$25 per day, for a trip up the Xingu, which is highly recommended. Many animals can be seen. The area is an Assurine Indian reservation and it is not allowed to enter villages; buy food in Altamira.

Sleeping and eating B *Alta Palace*, Av Tancredo Neves 3093. Bar/restaurant, a/c, good, T5152057. **C** *Pãe e Filho*, Trav. Pedro Gomes 840, T5152719, simple. **C** *Requinte*. Recommended. **C** *Lisboa*, Lindolfo Aranha 405, T5151825. A/c, TV, good value, slightly better than **C** *Imperatriz*, R Beto Somez near market. Bath, a/c.

Good *churrascos* and shopping in the market. *Restaurante Casa Grande*, R Anchieta, centre. Good *churrascos*, cheap, 1130-1430, 1930-2330. *Restaurante Esquina*, next to hotel *Lisboa*. Good *sucos*, closed Sun. Recommended.

Itaituba
Malaria is present in Itaituba

This *garimpeiro town* is the jumping-off place for the **Amazônia National Park**. See Father Paul Zoderer, who may help to arrange a visit, at the church on the waterfront – nearest Ibama information, Avenida Marechal Rondon, CEP 681811-970, Itaituba, T5181530.

Sleeping B *Hotel Central Plaza*, and **D** *Hotel 3 Poderes, clean, friendly*. **Transport** *Transbrasiliana* has a rodoviária on the Rio Tapajós, near the ferry docks. Bus to **Marabá**, about 34 hours, US$45. Bus to **Santarém** via Rurópolis, 11 hours, US$20. The road continues to Jacarèacanga, crosses the border with Amazonas and finally reaches **Humaitá** on the Rio Madeira (see page 586).

Southern Pará

South of Marabá are many ranches and new townships such as **Xinguara** (**D** *Hotel Rio Vermelho*, OK) and Redenção, where timber as well as ranching is important. There are several hotels on Av Santa Tereza: **A** *Inácio's*, T4241334, F4241168, restaurant, and **B** *Magnum*, T4241540, with air conditioning. The airport is 5 km from the centre. Air taxi with *Carajás*, T4241390. The bus station is on Av Alceu Veroneze, T4241231.

Directory Airline offices: *BRC*, T4241157. **Banks**: *Banco do Brasil*, Av Santa Tereza. *Bradesco*, Av Alacid Nunes 525. **Medical services**: *São Vicente*, Av Pedro Paulo Barcui, T4240818.

Redenção
Population: 60,000
These places are raw, dusty and not very safe for tourists, especially at night

These fast-developing frontier regions between the lower Araguaia and Xingu rivers are connected to the Brasília-Belém road. A soaring concrete bridge now spans the Araguaia just south of Conceição do Araguaia, which is the only bridge across the Araguaia between Barra dos Garças and Marabá.

Conceição do Araguaia

The town, once a centre for rubber extraction, still has a frontier atmosphere, although mudhuts are being replaced by brick houses, cowboy hats, battered Chevrolet pick-ups, skinny mules and a red light district.

Phone code: 091
Colour map 1, grid B5
Population: 52,000

B *Taruma Tropical*, Av Brasília 2120, T/F4211205. Pool, conference centre, garage, sauna, frigobars, expanded restaurant, clean and functioning bathrooms, a/c – when it works, the hotel is well patronized by ranchers and absentee landowners from Brasília. **B** *Pousada do Sol*, R Couto de Magalhães 2942, T4211483. A/c, bar, pool. Also *Marajoara*, Av JK 1587, T4211220. Some a/c, safe parking, breakfast. *Araguaia*, R Couto de Magalhães 2605. Breakfast, both small. *Café Taboquinha*, Av Francisco Vitor. Well-prepared fish, open 1200-1500, 1800-2300.

Sleeping & eating

Airport, 14 km southwest on the road to Guaraí. Bus station, Av Araguaia, T4211322.

Transport

Airline offices *BRC*, T4211467. **Banks** *Banco do Brasil*, Av 7 de Setembro 626. **Medical services** *Modelo*, R D Sebastião Tomás 32, T4211599.

Directory

The Amazon River

The mighty Amazon system is a staggering 6,577 km long, around half of which (3,165 km) are in Brazilian territory. Ships of up to 5,000 tons regularly negotiate the waterway as far as Iquitos in Peru, 3,646 km away.

Distances upstream from the river mouth to Manaus in nautical miles are: Belém 80, Narrows (entrance) 225, Narrows (exit) 330, Gurupá 334, Prainha 452, Santarém 538, Óbidos 605, Parintins 694, Itacoatiara 824, Manaus 930.

Travel a few hours up the broad river and you reach the region of the thousand islands. The passage through this maze of islets is known as 'The Narrows', and is perhaps the most scenic part of the journey. The ship winds through 150 km of lanes of yellow flood, with equatorial forest as close as 20 or 30 m on both sides. Here local children paddle toward the passing riverboats in their small dugout canoes, hoping for a handout. Passengers will often throw used clothing (in plastic bags), plastic utensils, containers and similar items overboard for them. If you want to do the same, make sure that your gift is useful and that it will float.

On one of the curious flat-topped hills after the Narrows stands the little stucco town of **Monte Alegre**, an oasis in mid-forest. There are lagoon cruises to see lilies, birds and pink dolphins, as well as visits to villages (US$25-40 per day). The town has an airport and some simple hotels, **E**.

Santarém

Phone code: 091
Colour map 1, grid B4
Population: 249,000

The third largest city on the Brazilian Amazon is small enough to walk around. It was founded in 1661 as the Jesuit mission of Tapajós; the name was changed to Santarém in 1758. There was once a fort here, and attractive colonial squares overlooking the waterfront still remain. Standing at the confluence of the Rio Tapajós with the Amazon, on the southern bank, Santarém is halfway (2 or 3 days by boat) between Belém and Manaus and most visitors breeze in and out on a stopover by boat or air.

Sights The yellow Amazon water swirls alongside the green-blue Tapajós at the **meeting of the waters** in front of the market square, which is nearly as impressive as that of the Negro and Solimões near Manaus. A small **Museu dos Tapajós** in the old city hall on the waterfront, now the **Centro Cultural João Fora**, downriver from where the boats dock, has a collection of ancient Tapajós ceramics, as well as various 19th-century artefacts and publications. The unloading of the fish catch between 0500 and 0700 on the waterfront is interesting. There are good beaches nearby on the Rio Tapajós. **Prainha**, a small beach, is between town and the port, by a park with many mango trees (Floresta-Prainha bus from centre). On the outskirts of town is Maracanã, with sandy bays (when the Tapajos is low) and some trees for shade (Maracanã bus from centre, 20 minutes). The **tourist**

Around Santarém

Monte Alegre

◀◀

Monte Alegre is the site of archaeological discoveries, which have threatened to alter radically views of the spread of civilization in South America. Dr Anna C Roosevelt, of the Field Museum of Natural History, Chicago, found in the early 1990s pottery fragments in a cave which, according to radio-carbon dating, appear to be from 7000 to 8000 BC. This predates by some 3,000 years what was thought to be the earliest ceramic ware in South America (from Colombia and Ecuador). Subsequent artefacts discovered here, however, have radio-carbon dates of 15000 BC, which calls for a significant rethink of the original idea that people moved from the Andes into the Amazon Basin. If nothing else, these finds suggest that the story of the people of the Americas is more diverse than hitherto understood. The cave which Dr Roosevelt excavated is called Caverna da Pedra Pintada. Also in the area are pictographs, with large designs of human and animal figures and geometrical shapes. Trips can be arranged.

We are grateful to Philip W Hummer, who sent us a description of a tour to the region, led by Dr Anna Roosevelt.

---

office, *Comtur*, Rua Floriano Peixoto 343, T/F5232434, has good information available in English.

Alter do Chão is a friendly village on the Rio Tapajós, at the outlet of Lago Verde, 34 km west. Of particular interest is the **Centro do Preservação da Arte Indígena**, R Dom Macedo Costa, which has a substantial collection of artefacts from tribes of Amazônia and Mato Grosso (T5271110). There is good swimming in the Tapajós from the beautiful, clean beach. Close to Alter do Chão (30 minutes by boat), the conjunction of the Rio Tapajós with the Aruã and the Arapiuns creates an island surrounded by clean rivers of differing colours, each teeming with life. The forested island, already popular, is being developed as an ecopark, **Parque Ecoturístico Arapiuns**, with accommodation for visitors. Monkeys and birds inhabit the woodlands, which are protected more for commercial reasons than any other. For information, contact Paratur in Belém, T2232130.

Excursions

Sleeping and eating **B** *Pousada Tupaiulândia*, R Pedro Teixera 300, T5271157, a/c, unimpressive but OK, very friendly and helpful, good breakfast for US$5, next to telephone office opposite bus stop. **D** *Alter do Chão*, R Lauro Sodré 74, T5271215, restaurant and orchid garden. **D** *Tia Marilda*, Trav Agostinho Lobato, T5271144, a/c, cheaper with fan. *Lago Verde*, Praça 7 de Setembro, good fresh fish, try *calderada de tucunaré*.

Transport Tickets and information from the bus company kiosk opposite *Pousada Tupaiulândia*. From Santarém: bus stop on Av São Sebastião, in front of Colégio Santa Clara, US$1, about 1 hr.

A *Amazon Park*, Av Mendonça Furtado 4120, T5232800, F5222631, amazon@stm.interconect.com.br Large, swimming pool, friendly, 4 km from centre, taxi US$4. **C** *Brasil Grande Hotel*, Trav 15 de Agosto 213, T5225660. Family-run with restaurant. **C** *New City*, Trav Francisco Corrêa 200,T5233149. A/c, frigobar, will collect from airport. **C** *Santarém Palace*, Rui Barbosa 726, T5232820, F5221779. A/c, TV, fridge, comfortable. **D** *Mirante*, Trav. Francisco Correa, 115, T5233054, freephone 08007073054, www.mirantehotel.com New, clean, homely. A/c, fridge, TV, some rooms with balcony, individual safes, Internet, good value. Recommended. **D** *Brasil*, Trav dos Mártires 30, T5235177. Nice, family-run, includes breakfast, communal bath,

Sleeping
All hotels, except Amazon Park, are in the compact grid of streets in the heart of the city near the waterfront

good food, good service. **D** *Horizonte*, Trav Senador Lemos, 737, T5225437, horizontehotel@bol.com.br With a/c, **F** with fan, modern, clean. **D** *Rios*, R Floriano Peixoto, 720, T5225701. New, large rooms, comfortable. In upper end of price category. A/c, fridge and TV. Recommended.

Eating **Mid-range** *Mascote*, Praça do Pescador 10, T5232844. Open 1000-2330. Restaurant, bar and ice-cream parlour. *Santa Antonio*, Av Tapajós 2061, T5232356. *Churrasco* and fish. *Mascotinho*, Praça Manoel de Jesus Moraes, on riverfront. Bar/pizzeria, popular, outside seating, good view. **Cheap** *Lucy*, Praça do Pescador. Good juices and pastries. Recommended.

Entertainment **Cinema** Av Rui Barbosa 183.

Festivals 22 Jun, *Foundation of the city*; 29 Jun, *São Pedro*, with processions of boats on the river and boi-bumbá dance dramas; 8 Dec, *Nossa Senhora da Conceição* (the city's patron saint). In *Alter do Chão*: second week in Jul, *Festa do Sairé*, religious processions and folkloric events. Recommended.

Shopping *Muiraquitã*, R Lameira Bittencourt 131. Good for ceramics, wood carvings and baskets.

Tour operators *Amazon Tours*, Trav Turiano Meira 1084, T5221928, T9751981 (mob), F5221098, www.amazonriver.com, owner Steve Alexander is very friendly and helpful who has lots of tips on what to do, he also organizes excursions for groups to Bosque Santa Lúcia with ecological trails, recommended. *Coruá-Una Turismo*, R Dr Hugo Mendonça, 600, T5181014, F5232670, offers various tours, Pierre d'Arcy speaks French, recommended. *Gil Serique*, Praça do Pescador 131, T5225174, English-speaking guide, recommended. *Santarém Tur*, R Adriano Pimental 44, T5224847, F5223141, branch in

Santarém

Encontro das Aguas Amazonas/Tapajós

The Amazon

■ Sleeping	4 Mirante	● Eating
1 Brasil	5 New City	1 Lucy
2 Brasil Grande	6 Rios	2 Mascote
3 Horizonte	7 Santarém Palace	3 Mascotinho

Not to scale

Santarém: the Confederates and other newcomers

In 1978, the American poet, Elizabeth Bishop, described the city thus:

"Two rivers full of crazy shipping – people
all apparently changing their minds,
embarking,

disembarking, rowing clumsy dories.
(After the Civil War some Southern families
came here; here they could still own slaves.

They left occasional blue eyes, English names,
and oars. No other place, no one
on all the Amazon's four thousand miles
does anything but paddle.)"

('Santarém' from New Poems, *1979;*
Complete Poems – London: Chatto and Windus, 1991)

She was referring to the Confederates who came in 1867, but the immigration had nothing like the impact of that of other people who came to Brazil in the 19th century and later. More successful, though, was another foreign resident in the 19th century, Henry Wickham, the Englishman who smuggled the first rubber seeds out of Brazil. Santarém shared in the rubber boom, first in the late 19th and early 20th centuries, then again during the Second World War. It was just south of here that Henry Ford set up his company's plantations; see Belterra and Fordlândia, below. The discovery of gold on the Upper Tapajós in 1959 sparked a gold rush which still continues. The city has become the jumping off point for the prospectors in the Mato Grosso territories to the south.

Amazon Park Hotel (above), friendly, helpful, also group tours (US$50 per person per day for a group of 5), recommended. **Tapam Turismo**, Trav 15 de Agosto, 127 A, T5232422, F5232055, recommended.

Transport

Local The port is in right in the centre of town; a taxi to any of the hotels in this area is around $US2.

Long distance Air: 15 km from town, T5231021. Internal flights only, to Alta Floresta, Almerim, Altamira, Belém, Boavista, Breves, Cuiabá, Imperatriz, Itaituba, Macapá, Manaus, Marabá, Monte Dourado, Óbidos, Oiapoque, Oriximiná, Parantins, Porto de Moz, Porto Trombetas, Rurópolis, Sinop and Urucu. Buses run to the centre or waterfront. From the centre the bus leaves in front of the cinema in Rui Barbosa every 80 mins from 0550 to 1910, or taxis (US$8 to waterfront). The hotels *Amazon Park*, *New City* and *Rio Dourado* have free buses for guests; you may be able to take these.

Buses: rodoviária, T5223392, is on the outskirts, take 'Rodagem' bus from the waterfront near the market, US$0.35. Santarém to **Itaituba**, US$11, 11 hrs, 2 a day. To **Marabá** on the Rio Tocantins (via Rurópolis US$7.50, 6 hrs, and **Altamira** US$23, 28 hrs), 36 hrs (if lucky; can be up to 6 days), US$41, with *Transbrasiliana*. Also to **Imperatriz**, via Marabá; office on Av Getúlio Vargas and at the rodoviária. Enquire at the rodoviária for other destinations. (Beware of vehicles that offer a lift, which frequently turn out to be taxis.) Road travel during the rainy season is always difficult, often impossible.

Boats: shipping services to **Manaus**, **Belém**, **Macapá**, **Itaituba**, and intermediate ports (see River transport, page 536). Boats to Belém and Manaus dock at the Cais do Porto, 1 km west, take 'Floresta-Prainha', 'Circular' or 'Circular Externo' bus; taxi US$4. Boats to other destinations, including Macapá, dock by the waterfront by the centre of town. Local service to **Óbidos**, US$10, 4 hrs, **Oriximiná** US$12.50, **Alenquer**, and **Monte Alegre** (US$10, 5-8 hrs).

The Amazon

Directory **Airline offices** *Fly*, Av Monsenhor Tabosa, 1069, T2197171. *META*, R Siquiera Campos 162, T5226222. *Penta*, Trav 15 de Novembro 183, T5232532. *TAVAJ*, R Floriano Peixoto, 95, T5237666. *Varig/Nordeste*, Av Rui Barbosa, 790, T5232488. *Vasp*, freephone 0800 998277. **Banks** *Banco do Brasil*, Av Rui Barbosa 794, exchanges TCs and cash, also withdrawals on Visa. It is very difficult to change dollars and impossible to change TCs. **Communications** Internet: *Tapajos On Line*, Mendonça Furtado 2454, US$3.50 per hr. **Post office**: Praça da Bandeira 81. **Telephone**: *Posto Trin*, R Siquiera Campos 511. Open 0700-1900 Mon-Sat, 0700-2100 Sun. **Laundry** *Storil*, Trav Turiano Meira 167, 1st floor. **Medical services** *Hospital São Raimundo Nonato*, Av Mendonça Furtado 1993, T5231176.

Floresta Nacional do Tapajós At Km 123, south of Santarém on BR 163, there is a section of the Floresta Nacional do Tapajós which has a vehicle track running due west through it. It is beautiful rainforest which can be entered with permission from Ibama, T0XX91-2245899, or Avenida Tapajos 2267, Aldeia CEP 68010-000, Santarém, T5223032, F5223476, if accompanied by one of their guides. It is well worth a visit if only to see the butterflies.

Belterra & Fordlândia Fordlândia, 300 km south of Santarém, was Henry Ford's first rubber plantation. He founded it in 1926 in an attempt to provide a cheaper source of rubber for his Ford Motor Company than the British and Dutch controlled plantations in Malaya. There is *Hotel Zebu*, in old Vila Americana (turn right from the dock, then left up the hill), one restaurant, two bars and three shops on the town square. A little pebble beach is north of the town.

Closer to Santarém, 37 km south on a dirt road, is Belterra, where Henry Ford established his second rubber plantation. In the highlands overlooking the Rio Tapajós, it is much closer to Santarém than his first project, which was turned into a research station. At Belterra, Ford built a well laid-out new town, where the houses resemble the cottages of Michigan summer resorts, many with white paint and green trim. The town centre has a large central plaza that includes a bandstand, the church of Santo Antônio (c1951), a Baptist church and a large educational and sports complex. A major hospital, which at one time was staffed by physicians from North America, is now closed.

Ford's project, the first modern attempt to invest in the Amazon, was unsuccessful. It was difficult to grow the hevea rubber tree, where it was unprotected from the heavy rains and harsh sun in plantation conditions. Boats could only come this far upriver in the rainy season and there were a series of disputes between the American bosses and the local employees. Ford sold up in 1945 and the rubber plantation is now run down.

Sleeping E *Hotel Seringueira*, in Belterra, has around 8 rooms and a pleasant restaurant.

Transport There is a 1 hr time difference between Santarém and Belterra, so if you take the 1230 bus you'll miss the 1530 return bus. Bus from **Santarém** to Belterra (from Trav Silvino Pinto between Rui Barbosa and São Sebastião), 1000 and 1230, Mon-Sat, return 1300 and 1530, US$4, about 2 hrs. Boats from Santarém to Itaituba stop at Fordlândia if you ask (leave Santarém 1800, arrive 0500-0600, US$12 for 1st class hammock space); ask the captain to stop for you on return journey, about 2300. The alternative is to take a tour with a Santarém travel agent.

Óbidos
Phone code: 091
Population: 42,500

Óbidos is located at the narrowest and deepest point on the river, where millions of years ago the Amazon squeezed through the gap in the Guyana and Brazilian Highlands to meet the Atlantic. It was a strategic point in the Portuguese expansion of the Amazon. The **Forte Pauxi** (1697) is a reminder of this fact (Praça Coracy Nunes). Today, Óbidos is a picturesque and clean city with many beautiful, tiled buildings and some pleasant parks. Worth seeing are the **Prefeitura Municipal**, T5471194, the cuartel and the **Museu Integrado de Óbidus**, Rua Justo Chermont 607. ■ *0700-1100, 1330-1730 Mon-Fri*. There is also a **Museu Contextual**, a system of plaques with detailed explanations of historical buildings througout town. Boating and fishing trips can be made and there is a popular beach at **Igarapé de Curuçambá** (buses go there). It is five hours by boat upriver from Santarém (110 km). A poor road runs east to Alenquer, Monte Alegre and Prainha and west to Oriximiná, impassable in the wet season. The small airport has flights to Manaus, Santarém and Parintins.

Sleeping and eating *C Braz Bello*, R Corrêia Pinto, on top of the hill. Shared bath, clean, full board available. *C Pousada Brasil*, R Correia Pinto. Basic with bath, cheaper without. *Pousada Curiô*, R Antônio Brito de Souza, in the upper town. *Pousada Casa Grande*, R Raimundo Chaves, near Prefeitura. *Restaurante Tucuruvi*, Praça Santana, fish.

Oriximiná
Population: 13,000

On the lower Rio Trombetas, a tributary on the north shore, Oriximiná is the regional centre for an area dedicated to ranching, timber extraction and brazil nut cultivation; on the upper Trombetas is a large bauxite mine. It has daily boat service to Santarém (8-10 hours) and regular service to Manaus (24 hours) and Belém. An excursion can be taken to Porteira on the upper Trombetas, 15 hours upriver; the Prefeitura runs a boat on Tuesday, returning Sunday; alternatively, it is four hours by speedboat (Sr Bonina, returning the same day or staying overnight, US$250 return). There is a small village without an infrastructure, visitors can hang their hammocks at the Electronorte camp or camp on the beach, take food and all supplies; nearby is the scenic Porteira waterfall. The area is malarial, take all necessary precautions.

Sleeping and eating *C Tropicão*, R 24 de Dezembro by the waterfront. With a/c and bath, cheaper shared bath and fan. *C Tapuyu*, with bath, fan, cheaper with shared bath, fan, basic. *Restaurante Jositara* and a few other simple restaurants.

Directory Banks: neither *Banco do Brasil* nor *BASA* change money.

Amazonas

This is the main centre for experiencing jungle lodges, riverboat trips and treks in the rainforest, all of which can be easily arranged in Manaus. The world's largest river archipelagos are located on the Rio Negro and are havens for wildlife. The region's Indian influence manifests itself in the Festa da Boi held on Parintins Island and in many other folklore festivals throughout the year.

Amazonas is the largest state in Brazil (1.6 million sq km), but with a population of only about 2.8 million. Half of the inhabitants live in the capital, Manaus, with the rest spread out amongst remote communities mainly linked by air and river only. Bordering Venezuela, Colombia and Peru, Amazonas has the longest frontier in the union.

Manaus

Colour map 1, grid B3
Phone code: 092
Population: 1.4 million

Manaus, was at one time an isolated urban island in the jungle, before becoming one of the wealthiest cities in South America during the rubber boom. It is now the most important port of entry for visiting the Amazon, with river islands and tranquil waterways less than a day away. Most people come to arrange a jungle trip, but, thanks to a major restoration programme, there is much of architectural and cultural interest, so try to spend a day or two in the Manaus itself.

The city sprawls over a series of eroded and gently sloping hills divided by numerous creeks (igarapés). It is the collecting point for the produce of a vast area which includes parts of Peru, Bolivia and Colombia. Though 1,600 km from the sea, Manaus is only 32 m above sea level.

Manaus orientation

Detailed map
A Manaus centre,
page 568

24 hours in Manaus

Start the day with an energy bomb of fresh juice and *guarana* from one of the many *suco* stalls in the Zona Franca. Wander down to the buzzing waterfront (not safe at night) and watch the boats at the huge floating dock. This is a great area for street food; try the delicious fried banana.

Take time to admire the 100-year-old Customs House before buying Amazonian handicrafts and magic potions for anything from happiness to fertility from Mercado Municipal Adolfo Lisboa. Lots of shops around the market offer bargain-priced goods. (Morning is the best time to come, as after lunch traders start to pack up.) This is also a good area for a bargain lunch, but if you want to splurge, tuck into the all-you-can-eat Brazilian buffet at the *churrascaria Búfalo*, a local institution.

After lunch, take a bus or taxi to the Botanic Gardens, Instituto Nacional de Pesquisas Amazonas. At this centre for Amazonian scientific research in the Amazon, you can see local wildlife and a large number of birds. From here, it's a short taxi ride to the Museu de Ciências Naturais da Amazônia (Natural Science Museum).

Soak up some early evening (starts 1800) culture at the Teatro da Instalação. This funky performance space hosts music and dance, both traditional and modern. If that leaves you wanting more, make your way to the Teatro Amazonas where there are ballet, theatre and opera performances several times a week, and Brazilian music on Monday nights between June and December.

For serious nightlife, you need to make a trip to Ponta Negra beach. This is where the city's best restaurants are found. Tuck into one of the local fish specialities such as *tambaqui* and then take your pick from everything from old-school samba to heavy techno. Look at listings magazines as nights change frequently. Most of the clubs here stay open all night, so you may as well continue until morning (taxis back to town are expensive) and have a swim in the river when the sun comes up.

The road from Porto Velho is very difficult and often impassable, making river or air travel essential. The road north to Boa Vista has been paved, bringing the frontiers of Venezuela and Guyana within easy reach.

Ins and outs

From the airport, which is 9 km from the city, a taxi to the centre costs US$16, fixed rate. Local buses to the city cost US$0.60, but there are none between 2330 and 0500. Manaus rodoviária is 5 km from the centre at the intersection of Av Constantino Nery and R Recife. The only long-distance route arriving here is that from Boa Vista and the Venezuelan border. Boat passengers arrive at the floating dock in the centre, with direct access to the main artery of Av Ed Ribeiro, a couple of blocks south from the Praça da Matriz.

Getting there
See also Transport, page 574

The city centre is easily explored on foot. Buses serve the entire urban area and there are taxis. Other towns in the state are best visited by air or boat, especially during the Dec-Jun wet season when road travel is almost impossible.

Getting around

Tourist offices Av Eduardo Ribeiro, 666, near *Teatro Amazonas*, T2311998, Mon-Fri 0800-1800, Sat 0800-1300. Limited English and information. *Secretaria de Estado da Cultura e Turismo*, Av 7 de Setembro 1546, Vila Ninita, behind *Centro Cultural Pálacio Rio Negro*, T6332850, F2339973, Mon-Fri 0730-1700. There is a tourist office at the airport, open daily 0700-2300, T6521120. Town map from *Amazon Explorers*, or from news kiosks. *Guide Book of Manaus*, US$3, in English, useful, available from *Selvatur*. Weekend editions of *A Crítica*, newspaper, list local entertainments and events.

Manaus time is one hour behind Brazilian standard time (two hours during October-March when the rest of Brazil is on summer time)

The Amazon

Security Manaus is a friendly, if busy city and a good deal safer than the big cities of southern Brazil. As in any city, the usual precautions against opportunist crime should be taken (see Essentials chapter). Bars along R Joaquim Nabuco are reported particularly unsafe due to drugging of drinks. This and the port area are not places to hang around after dark. A tourist police force, *Politur*, has been created in an effort to assist visitors.

Sights

Today, Manaus is building fast, with 20-storey modern buildings rising above the traditional flat, red-tiled roofs. It is an important base for scientific research in the Amazon, carried out by **Insitituto Nacional de Pesquisas Amazonas** (INPA). Under recent municipal administrations the city, including the Zona Franca, old commercial district, port area and nearby markets, has been kept relatively clean and orderly and new markets have been built. An impressive initiative in 2001 saw the start of a significant restoration programme in which historic buildings have been given a new lease of life and theatres, cultural spaces and libraries have been created.

Manaus centre

The Amazon

Sleeping	6 Ideal	14 Rio Branco	6 Himawari
1 Ana Cássia Palace	7 Jangada		7 Pizzeria Scarola
2 Best Western Lord	8 Manaós	● Eating	8 Senac
Manaus	9 Mônaco	1 Alemã	9 Skina dos Sucos
3 Brasil	10 Nacional	2 Bob's	10 Sorveteria Glacial
4 Dona Joana	11 Palace	3 Búfalo	11 Super Guaraná
5 Holiday Inn	12 Pensão Sulista	4 Fiorentina	12 Temperos D'Ouro
Taj Mahal	13 Rei Salomão	5 Gruta do Peixe	13 Xamêgo

Related map
Manaus orientation,
page 566

N

0 metres   200
0 yards   200

Dominating the centre is a **cathedral** on Praça Osvaldo Cruz, built in simple Jesuit style and very plain inside and out. Originally constructed in 1695 in wood and straw, it was burnt down in 1850 and rebuilt in neoclassical style. Nearby is the main shopping and business area, the tree-lined Avenida Eduardo Ribeiro, crossed by Avenida 7 de Setembro and bordered by ficus trees.

The star attraction is the opera house, **Teatro Amazonas**, on Praça São Sebastião, and not to be missed. Extraordinarily opulent, it was completed in 1896 during the great rubber boom and has been restored 4 times since then. It took 15 years to build because most of the materials were imported from Europe according to the fashion of the time. The driveway was paved in rubber to prevent the sound of carriage wheels spoiling performances and there is a wonderfully over-the-top ballroom. The designs on the backdrop inside the theatre and the black and white paving in the praça (copied throughout Brazil) at the front of the building represent the meeting of the waters. There are ballet, theatre and opera performances several times a week and popular Brazilian music on Monday nights, June-December, which is free. ■ *0900-1600 Mon-Sat. 20-min guided tour US$7, students US$2.50, recommended (around same price to attend a concert). Information on programmes, T6222420.* **Igreja São Sebastião**, on the same square, is worth a look inside to see its unusual altar of two giant ivory hands holding a water lily of Brazil wood.

On the waterfront, the **Mercado Adolfo Lisboa**, Rua dos Barés, 46 was built in 1882 as a miniature copy of the now-demolished Parisian Les Halles. The wrought ironwork, which forms much of the structure, was imported from Europe and is said to have been designed by Eiffel.

The remarkable **harbour installations**, completed in 1902, were designed and built by a Scottish engineer to cope with the Rio Negro's annual rise and fall of up to 14 m. The large passenger ship floating dock is connected to street level by a 150 m-long floating ramp, at the end of which, on the harbour wall, can be seen the high water mark for each year since it was built. When the water is high, the roadway floats on a series of large iron tanks measuring 2½ m in diameter. The large yellow **Alfândega** (Customs House) on Rua Marquês de Santa Cruz stands at the entrance to the city when arriving by boat. It was entirely prefabricated in England, and the tower once acted as lighthouse. ■ *0800-1300 Mon-Fri.*

The **Biblioteca Pública** (Public Library) at Rua Barroso 57, inaugurated in 1871, is part of the city's architectural heritage. Featuring an ornate European cast-iron staircase, it is well stocked with 19th-century newspapers, rare books and old photographs, and worth a visit. ■ *0730-1730 Mon-Fri. T2340588.*

The very small **Museu Tiradentes**, on Praça da Polícia, is run by the military police and holds selected historical items and old photographs. ■ *1400-1800 Mon, 0800-1200 and 1400-1800 Tue-Fri. T2347422.*

There is a curious little church, **Igreja do Pobre Diabo**, at the corner of Avenidas Borba and Ipixuna in the suburb of Cachoeirinha. It is only 4 m wide by 5 m long, and was built by a local trader, the 'poor devil' of the name. ■ *Take Circular 7 de Setembro Cachoeirinha bus from the cathedral to Hospital Militar.*

Instituto Geográfico e Histórico do Amazonas, Rua Bernardo Ramos 117 (near Prefeitura), is located in a fascinating older district of central Manaus. It houses a museum and library of over 10,000 books, which thoroughly document Amazonian life through the ages. ■ *Mon-Fri 0800-1200, T2327077, US$0.20.*

The Amazon

The **Centro Cultural Pálacio Rio Negro** on Avenida 7 de Setembro was the residence of a German rubber merchant until 1917 and later the state government palace. It now holds various cultural events, including exhibitions, shows and films; there is also a café. ■ *1000-1700 Tue-Fri, 1600-2100 Sat and Sun. T2324450.*

Museu do Índio, Rua Duque de Caxias (near Avenida 7 Setembro), is managed by the Salesian missionaries, but is rather run down. It has an interesting collection that includes handicrafts, ceramics, clothing, utensils and ritual objects from the various Indian tribes of the upper Rio Negro and an excellent craft shop. ■ *0830-1200 and 1400-1700 Mon-Fri, 0800-1130 Sat, closed Sun. T2341422. US$3.*

Museu do Homem do Norte, Avenida 7 de Setembro 1385 (near Avenida Joaquim Nabuco), is an interesting review of the way of life of the Amazonian population, or 'men of the north', although it has deteriorated in recent years. Social, cultural and economic aspects are displayed with photographs, models and other pieces, ■ *0900-1200, 1300-1700 Mon-Thu, 1300-1700 Fri. T2325373. US$1.*

Botanic Gardens, Instituto Nacional de Pesquisas Amazonas (INPA), Estrada do Aleixo at Km 3, not far from the Natural Science Museum (see below), is worth a visit. This is the centre for scientific research in the Amazon; labs here (not open to the public) investigate farming, medicines and tropical diseases in the area. There is a small museum and restaurant, lots of birds, named trees and manatees (best seen Wednesday and Friday mornings when the water is changed), caimans and giant otters. ■ *0900-1100, 1400-1630 Mon-Fri, 0900-1600 Sat-Sun. US$2. T6433377. Take any bus to Aleixo.*

The Natural Science Museum, **Museu de Ciências Naturais da Amazônia** has a pavilion with insects and fish of the region and is located at Al Cosme Ferreira, Colonia Cachoeira Grande, 15 km away. ■ *0900-1700 Mon-Sat. US$4. T6442799. Difficult to get to, take 'São José-Acoariquarape/Tropolis' bus 519 to Conjunto Petro, then 2-km walk. Best to combine with a visit to INPA, and take a taxi from there (see above).*

Jardim Botânico 'Chico Mendes' (Horto Municipal), Avenida André Araujo, contains a collection of plants from the Amazon region. ■ *0800-1200 and 1400-1700 daily. Take 'Aleixo' or 'Coroado' bus.*

The **Zoo**, Estrada Ponta Negra 750 (no sign), is run by CIGS, the Brazilian Army Unit specializing in jungle survival. It has been recently been expanded and improved. About 300 Amazonian animals are kept in the gardens, including anacondas in a huge pit. ■ *0900-1630 Tue-Sun. Foreigners, US$3, free on Sun. T6252044. Take bus 120 or 207 (marked 'Ponta Negra'), US$0.70, every 30 mins from R Tamandaré, opposite the cathedral in the centre, get off 400 m past the first Jungle Infantry Barracks (a big white building), look for the sentries.* There is also a small zoo at the *Hotel Tropical,* see below.

Excursions

Meeting of the waters

See also Amazon tours, page 577

About 15 km from Manaus is the confluence of the yellow-brown Solimões (Amazon) and the blue-black Rio Negro, which is itself some 8 km wide. The two rivers run side by side for about 6 km without their waters mingling, which is caused by differences in the temperature, density and velocity of the two rivers. Tourist agencies run boat trips to this spot (US$60-160). The simplest route is to take a taxi or No 713 'Vila

Buriti' bus to the Careiro ferry dock, and take the car ferry across. The ferry, which is very basic with no shelter on deck and no cabins, departs at 0700 returning 1000, and 1500 returning 1800 (approximately). Small private launches cross, a 40-minute journey costing about US$10-15 per seat, ask for the engine to be shut off at the confluence. You should see dolphins especially in the early morning. Alternatively, hire a motorized canoe from near the market (US$15 approximately; allow 3-4 hours to experience the meeting properly). A 2-km walk along the Porto Velho road from the Careiro ferry terminal will lead to a point from which Victoria Regia water lilies can be seen in April-September in ponds, some way from the road.

Manacapuru

This typical Amazon small market town is situated on the Solimões west of Manaus. It has three basic hotels and *Il Maccarone* pizzeria, Avenida Eduardo Ribeiro 1000. It is 84 km on AM-070 by bus, four daily, US$5, two hours including ferry crossing.

Araça

This village on the Rio Mamori has plenty of wildlife close at hand. Canoes can be hired. It is three hours by No 11 bus from the rodoviária in the direction of Castanho; the journey includes the ferry at the confluence of the Negro and Solimões (fare to Araça US$1.50, bus leaves 0600 and 1100). Three buses a day return to Manaus.

Arquipélago de Anavilhanas

This is the second largest river archipelago in the world. It is located in the Rio Negro, some 100 km upstream from Manaus, near the town of Novo Airão. There are hundreds of islands, covered in thick vegetation. When the river is low, white sand beaches are revealed, as well as the roots and trunks of the trees. Tour companies arrange visits to the archipelago (US$195-285, one day).

Bird-watching

Many kinds of birds can be seen in and around the grounds of the *Hotel Tropical* such as fly catchers – kingbirds and kiskadees – swallows, yellow-browed sparrows, aracaris – member of the toucan family – woodpeckers, woodcreepers, thrushes, anis, three species of tanager, two of parrots – the dusky and blue headed. Sloths and monkeys may also be seen. For further information, contact Moacir Fortes or Andrew Whittaker, birding@internext.com.br

Essentials

L *Tropical*, Estr da Ponta Negra 9015, T6585000, F6585026. Lavish 5-star hotel 20 km outside city (taxi to centre, US$20), 12% service tax, discount when arriving on *Varig* flights. Parkland setting, wave pools, beach with new dock, departure point for many river cruises, tennis courts. *Churrascaria*, pool and 24-hr coffee shop open to well-dressed non-residents. Take minibus from R José Paranaguá in front of Petrobras building at corner of Dr Moreira, US$5 return, 0830, 0930, 1130 to hotel, 1200, 1400, 1500, 1800 to town, or take Ponta Negra bus, US$0.70, then walk.

Centre L *Holiday Inn Taj Mahal* Av Getúlio Vargas 741, T6331010, F2330068, tajmahal@internext.com.br, near to centre. Large and impressive, one of best hotels in city, popular with airline and boat crew. Tour agency, revolving restaurant, massage and high level of service.

Sleeping
■ *on map, page 568*
Price codes:
see inside front cover

Hotel booking service at the airport. When taking a taxi from the airport, insist on being taken to the hotel of your choice, and not to the one which pays the driver commission

The Amazon

Although the area around Av Joaquim Nabuco and Rua dos Andradas has lots of cheap (pretty grubby) hotels, this is a low-key red-light district and not particularly safe at night. A much better option is the nearby Zona Franca, which is convenient for shops, banks, restaurants and the port area

A *Ana Cássia Palace*, R dos Andradas 14, T6223637, F2344163. Gloriously faded, large rooms, some with great views of port, restaurant, pool. **A** *Best Western Lord Manaus*, R Marcílio Dias 217, T6227700, F6222576, bwmanaus@internext.com.br Conveniently located in heart of Zona Franca, comfortable, bar. **A** *Manaós*, Av Eduardo Ribeiro, 881, T6335744, F2324443, manaos@argo.com.br Good option near *Teatro Amazonas*. **A** *Mônaco*, R Silva Ramos 20, T6223446, F6223637. Rooms have good view, pleasant (some rooms noisy), rooftop restaurant/bar, delicious breakfast.

B *Brasil*, Av Getúlio Vargas, 657, T2336575, F2339220, hotel-brasil@internext.com.br Friendly, mid-market option close to centre.

D *Nacional*, R Dr Moreira 59, T2329206. Fine for price. **D** *Palace*, Av 7 de Septembro, 593, T6224522, F9233623, palace@argo.com.br Recently restored, simple, traditional rooms with high ceilings; some with wrought-iron balconies. Excellent location on square overlooking cathedral. Highly recommended. **D** *Paradise*, R 10 de Julho 685, T2324840. A/c. **D** *Rei Salomão*, R Dr Moreira 119, T2347374. In commercial centre, very clean, modern, quiet, a/c, restaurant. Excellent value. Recommended.

E *Ideal*, R dos Andradas 491, T/F2339423. A/c, **F** with fan. **E** *Pensão Sulista*, Av Joaquim Nabuco 347, T2345814. Run-down, a/c, **F** with fan and shared bathroom. **E** *Rio Branco*, R dos Andradas 484, T/F2334019. Basic, laundry facilities, a/c.

F *Dona Joana*, R dos Andradas 553, T2337553. A/c, fridge, TV. Newly decorated, homely, good value, the hotel is safe although the area is not. **F** *Jangada*, R dos Andradas 473, T6220264. Basic, clean, a bargain. A/c and TV. Recommended.

Camping There are no campsites in or near Manaus; it is difficult to find a good, safe place to camp wild.

Eating

Many restaurants close on Sunday nights and Monday

Expensive *La Barca*, R Recife 684, T2367090. Wide variety of fish dishes, very swanky, popular, often has live music. *Himawari*, R 10 de Julho 618, T233 2208. Swish, sushi and Japanese food, attentive service, opposite *Teatro Amazonas*, open Sun night, when many restaurants close. Recommended. Japanese at *Miako*, R São Luís 230. *Restaurant Tarumã* in *Hotel Tropical* (see above). Dinner only.

Mid-range *Búfalo*, churrascaria, Av Joaquim Nabuco 628. Best in town, US$7, all you can eat Brazilian barbecue. *Canto da Peixada*, R Emílio Moreira 1677 (Praça 14 de Janeiro), T2343021. Superb fish dishes, lively atmosphere, unpretentious, close to centre, take a taxi. *Fiorentina*, R José Paranaguá 44, Praça da Polícia. Fan-cooled, traditional Italian, including vegetarian dishes, piped music. Average food but one of best options in centre, watch out for the mugs of wine! Great *feijoada* on Sat, half-price on Sun. *Pizzeria Scarola*, R 10 de Julho, corner with Av Getúlio Vargas, T2326503. Standard Brazilian menu, pizza delivery, popular. *Restaurante Natalia*, Av Epaminondas, downtown. With garden, has Pagode music and dancing on Fri nights. *São Francisco*, Blvd Rio Negro 195, 30 mins walk from centre (or bus 705), in Educandos suburb. Good fish, huge portions. *Suzuran*, R Teresina, 155, Adrianópolis, Japanese cuisine, closed Tue, take taxi.

Cheap *Alemã*, R José Paranaguá, Praça da Polícia. Food by weight, great pastries, hamburgers, juices, sandwiches. *Brasil*, next to hotel of same name, see above. Food by weight, juice and sandwich kiosk outside hotel. *Casa do Guaraná*, R Marcílio Dias. Marvellous juices mixed with *guaraná*. *Gruta do Peixe*, R Saldanha Marinho 609, T2348508. Self-service and *pratos* in attractive basement, lunch only. Recommended. *La Veneza*, Av Getúlio Vargas 257. Food by weight, lunch only. *Senac*, R Saldanha Marinho 644, T6332277. Cookery school, self-service. Open daily, lunch only. Highly recommended. *Sorveteria Glacial*, Av Getúlio Vargas 161, and other locations. Recommended for ice-cream.

Seriously cheap *Skina dos Sucos*, Eduardo Ribeiro e 24 de Maio. Juices and snacks. *Super Guaraná*, R Guilherme Moreira 395. *Guarana* with juice, hamburgers, pies.

Temperos D'Ouro, G Moreira. Self-service, lunch only. *Xamêgo*, Av Getúlio Vargas, corner with R 10 de Julio. Basic self-service, popular with locals.

Boiart's, R José Clemente 500, next to *Teatro Amazonas*, T6376807, touristy, popular disco with jungle theme and shows. Cachoeirinha has a number of bars offering music and dancing, liveliest at weekends. *Tucano* nightclub in the *Hotel Tropical*, T6595000, attracts Manaus's wealthy citizens on Thu-Sat, as does its bingo club. Nearby Ponta Negra beach becomes extremely lively late on weekend nights and during holidays, with outdoor concerts and samba in the summer season. *Studio 5*, R Contorno, Distrito Industrial, T2378333, disco, part of leisure complex with several cinema screens.

Bars & nightclubs

Performing Arts For *Teatro Amazonas* and *Centro Cultural Pálacio Rio Negro*, see above. *Teatro da Instala*ção, R Frei José dos Inocentes, T/F2344096. Performance space in recently restored historic buildings with free music and dance (everything from ballet to jazz), Mon-Fri May-Dec at 1800. Charge for performances Sat and Sun. Recommended. **Cinema** In R 10 de Julho and 8 screens at Amazonas shopping centre, bus Cidade Nova 5, or 204, 207, 208, 307. Most foreign films are shown with original soundtrack and Portuguese sub-titles. Afternoon performances are recommended as long queues often form in the evenings.

Entertainment

In Praça da Saudade, R Ramos Ferreira, there is a Sun **funfair** from 1700; try prawns and *calaloo* dipped in *tacaca* sauce. A 'train' circling the old town with loud music and cartoon characters is good fun for children.

6 Jan: *Epiphany*; *Ash Wed*, half-day; *Maundy Thu*; 24 Jun: *São João*; 14 Jul; 5 Sep; 30 Oct; 1 Nov, *All Saints Day*, half-day; *Christmas Eve*; *New Year's Eve*, half-day. **Feb**: *Carnival* in Manaus has spectacular parades in a sambadrome modelled on Rio's, but with 3 times the capacity. Tourists may purchase grandstand seats, but admission at ground level is free (don't take valuables), with every samba school member guaranteed entrance. Carnival dates vary – 5 days of Carnival, culminating in the parade of the Samba Schools. Third week in **Apr**: *Week of the Indians*, Indian handicraft. In **Jun**: *Festival do Amazonas*; a celebration of all the cultural aspects of Amazonas life, indigenous, Portuguese and from the northeast, especially dancing; *Festival Marquesiano* also in Jun; mostly typical dances from those regions of the world which have sent immigrants to Amazonas, performed by the students of the Colégio Marquês de Santa Cruz; **29 Jun**: *São Pedro*, boat processions on the Rio Negro. In **Sep**: *Festival de Verão do Parque Dez*, 2nd fortnight, festival with music, fashion shows, beauty contests, local foods, etc, Centro Social Urbano do Parque Dez; *Festival da Bondade*, last week, stalls from neighbouring states and countries offering food, handicrafts, music and dancing, SESI, Estr do Aleixo, Km 5. **Oct**: *Festival Universitário de Música* (FUM), the most traditional festival of music in Amazonas, organized by the university students, on the University Campus. **8 Dec**: *Processão de Nossa Senhora da Conceicão*, from the Igreja Matriz through the city centre and returning to Igreja Matriz for a solemn mass.

Festivals

Since Manaus is a free port, the whole area a few blocks off the river front is full of electronics shops. This area, known as the **Zona Franca**, is the commercial centre, where the shops, banks and hotels are concentrated.

Bookshops *Livraria Nacional*, R 24 de Maio, 415. Stocks some French books. *Usados CDs e Livros*, Av Getúlio Vargas 766. Selection of used books, English, German, French and Spanish. *Valer*, R Ramos Ferreira 1195. A few English classics stocked, best bookshop in city. **Markets and souvenirs** Go to the *Mercado Adolfo Lisboa* (see above) early in the morning when it is full of good quality regional produce, food and handicrafts, look out for *guaraná* powder or sticks, scales of *pirarucu* fish (used for

Shopping
All shops close at 1400 on Saturday and all day Sunday

The Amazon

manicure), and its tongue used for rasping *guaraná* (open Mon-Sat 0500-1800, Sun and holidays 0500-1200). See the 2 markets near the docks, best in the early morning. In the Praça do Congresso, Av E Ribeiro, there is a very good Sun craftmarket. Ponta Negra beach boasts a small 'hippy' market, very lively at weekends. There is a good supermarket at the corner of Av Joaquim Nabuco and R Sete de Setembro. *Artesanato da Amazônia*, R José Clemente, 500, loja A, opposite *Teatro Amazonas*, has a good, reasonably priced, selection of regional products. The *Central Artesanato*, R Recife, near Detran, has local craft work. The souvenir shop at the INPA has some interesting Amazonian products on sale. *Selva Amazônica*, Mercado Municipal. For wood carvings and bark fabric. For hammocks, try the shops in R dos Andradas.

Photographic *Photo Nacimento*, Av 7 de Setembro, repairs, slide and black and white film. 1-hr film processing at *Studio Universal*, R 24 de Maio 146, cheap, good quality.

Sport **Swimming** At Ponta Negra beach, 13 km from the centre (Soltur bus, US$0.70), though the beach virtually disappears beneath the water in Apr-Aug. Good swimming at waterfalls on the Rio Tarumã, where lunch is available, shade, crowded at weekends; take Tarumã bus from R Tamandaré or R Frei J dos Inocentes, 30 mins, US$0.70 (very few on weekdays), getting off at the police checkpoint on the road to Itacoatiara. There is also superb swimming in the natural pools and under falls of clear water in the little streams which rush through the woods, but take locals' advice on swimming in the river; electric eels and various other kinds of unpleasant fish, apart from the notorious *piranhas*, abound, and industrial pollution of the river is growing. Every Sun, boats leave from the port in front of the market to beaches along Rio Negro, US$2, leaving when full and returning at the end of the day. This is a real locals' day out, with loud music and food stalls on the sand.

Tour operators *Espaço Verde Turismo*, R Costa Azevedo, 240, T6334522, F6333304, rogerio-evtur@ internext.com.br opposite *Teatro Amazonas*. River boat tours, one day US$30, including lunch; flights; trips to lodges. English spoken, helpful. *Swallows and Amazons*, R Quintino Bocaiuva 189, Suite 13, T/F6221246, www.swallowsandamazonstours.com For flights, car hire, etc, tour agencies attached to 2 of largest hotels in city: *Best Western Lord Manaus* and *Holiday Inn Taj Mahal*. See below for advice on choosing a jungle tour.

Transport **Local Bus** all city bus routes start below the cathedral in front of the port entrance;
See also Ins and outs, just ask someone for the destination you want.
page 567

Check in time is
2 hrs in advance **Long distance Air**: Modern Eduardo Gomes airport is 9 km from the city, T6521120. There are international flights to Guayaquil, La Paz, Mexico City, Miami, Orlando, Santa

Cruz and Quito. To the Guyanas, a connection must be made in Belém. Domestic flights to Belém, Boa Vista, Brasília, Cruzeiro do Sul, Macapá, Parantins, Porto Velho, Rio Branco, Rio de Janeiro, Santarém, São Paulo, Tabatinga, Tefé and Trombetas.

Make reservations as early as possible, flights may be full. Do not rely on travel agency waiting lists; go to the airport 15 hrs early and get on the airport waiting list. Domestic airport tax US$7.

Taxi fare to airport US$7.25, fixed rate, or take bus marked 'Aeroporto Internacional' from Marquês de Santa Cruz at Praça Adalberto Vale, near the cathedral, US$0.70, or from Ed Garagem on Av Getúlio Vargas every 30 mins. No buses 2200-0700. Taxi drivers often tell arrivals that no bus to town is available, be warned! It is sometimes possible to use the more regular, faster service run by the *Hotel Tropical*; many tour agencies offer free transfers without obligation. Check all connections on arrival. Allow plenty of time at Manaus airport, formalities are very slow especially if you have purchased duty-free goods. The restaurant serves good à la carte and buffet food throughout the day. Many flights depart in the middle of the night and while there are many snack bars there is nowhere to rest. Local flights leave from Terminal 2. Check in advance which terminal you leave from.

Boats to Santarém, Belém, Porto Velho, Tefé, Tabatinga (for Colombia and Peru), São Gabriel da Cachoeira, and intermediate ports. Almost all vessels now berth at the first (downstream) of the floating docks, which is open to the public 24 hrs a day. Bookings can be made up to 2 weeks in advance at the ticket sales area by the port's pedestrian entrance (bear left on entry). The names and itineraries of departing vessels are displayed here as well as on the docked boats themselves. Touts will engulf you when you arrive at the pedestrian entry; be calm, patient and friendly. Travellers still recommend buying tickets from the captain on the boat itself. The port is relatively clean, well organized, and has a pleasant atmosphere.

See also River transport, page 536

ENASA (the state shipping company) sells tickets for private boats at its office in town (prices tend to be high here), T6333280. Local boats and some cargo barges still berth by the concrete retaining wall between the market and Montecristi. Boats for São Gabriel da Cachoeira, Novo Airão, and Caracaraí go from São Raimundo, up river from the main port. Take bus 101 'São Raimundo', 112 'Santo Antônio' or 110, 40 mins; there are 2 docking areas separated by a hill, the São Raimundo *balsa*, where the ferry to Novo Airão, on the Rio Negro, leaves every afternoon (US$10); and the Porto Beira Mar de São Raimundo, where the São Gabriel da Cachoeira boats dock (most departures Fri).

From **Manaus-São Paulo** it is cheaper to go by boat Manaus-Porto Velho, then bus to São Paulo, than to fly direct or go by boat to Belém then bus. Departures to the less important destinations are not always known at the Capitânia do Porto, Av Santa Cruz 265, Manaus. Be careful of people who wander around boats after they've arrived at a port; they are almost certainly looking for something to steal.

Immigration For those arriving by boat who have not already had their passports stamped (eg from Leticia), the immigration office is on the first of the floating docks next to the tourist office. Take the dock entrance opposite the cathedral, bear right, after 50 m left, pass through a warehouse to a group of buildings on a T section.

Bus rodoviária is 5 km out of town at the intersection of Av Constantino Nery and R Recife; take a local bus from centre, US$0.70, marked 'Aeroporto Internacional' or 'Cidade Nova' (or taxi, US$5).

Road The road north from Manaus to Boa Vista (770 km) is described on page 590.

   Car hire *Localiza*, R Major Gabriel 1558, T2334141, and airport, T6521176.

   Hitchhiking with truckers is common, but not recommended for women travelling alone. To hitch, take a Tarumã bus to the customs building and hitch from there, or try at 'posta 5', 2 km beyond the rodoviária.

The Amazon

The Catire Highway (BR-319), from Manaus to Porto Velho (868 km), has been officially closed since 1990. Several bridges are out and there is no repair in sight. The alternative for drivers is to ship a car down river on a barge, others have to travel by boat (see below).

To **Itacoatiara**, 285 km east on the Amazon, with Brazil-nut and jute processing plants (bus service 8 a day, 4 hrs); now paved route AM-010, 266 km, through Rio Preto da Eva.

Directory **Airline offices** *American Airlines*, Av Eduardo Ribeiro 664, T6333363. *Lloyd Aéreo Boliviano*, Av 7 de Setembro 993, 1st floor, T6334200. *TAM*, Av Tarumã, 433, T2331828. *TAVAJ*, R Rui Barbosa, 200B, freephone 0800 927070. *Transbrasil*, R Guilherme Moreira 150, T6221705. *Varig*, R Marcílio Dias 284, T6214500. *Vasp*, Av 7 de Setembro 993, T6223470.

Banks *Banco do Brasil*, Guia Moreira, and airport changes US$ cash, 8% commission, both with ATMs for Visa, Cirrus, MasterCard and Plus. Most offices shut at 1500; foreign exchange operations 0900-1200 only, or even as early as 1100. *Bradesco*, Av 7 de Setembro 895/293, for Visa ATM. *Credicard*, Av Getúlio Vargas 222 for Diner's cash advances. Cash at main hotels; *Câmbio Cortez*, 7 de Setembro 1199, converts TCs into US$ cash, good rates, no commission. Do not change money on the streets. *HSBC*, R Dr Moreira, 226. ATM for Visa, Cirrus, MasterCard and Plus.

Communications **Internet**: Free internet access available from all public libraries in city, eg. recently created *Biblioteca Arthur Reis*, Av 7 de Setembro, 444, open 0800-1200 and 1400-1700, with virtual Amazon library and English books. *Amazon Cyber Cafe*, Av Getúlio Vargas, 626, corner with R 10 de Julho, US$1.50 per hr. *Discover Internet*, R Marcílio Dias, 304, next to Praça da Polícia, cabins in back of shop with Internet 'phones and scanners, US$1.50 per hr. **Post office**: Main office including poste restante on Mcal Deodoro. On the 1st floor is the philatelic counter where stamps are sold, avoiding the long queues downstairs. Staff don't speak English but are used to dealing with tourists. For airfreight and shipping, Alfândega, Av Marquês Santa Cruz (corner of Marechal Deodoro), Sala 106. For airfreight and seamail, Correio Internacional, R Monsenhor Coutinho e Av Eduardo Ribeiro (bring your own packaging). *UPS* office, T2329849 (Custódio). **Telephone**: International calls can be made from local calikioiiioiil boxes with an international card. Also at *Telemar*, Av Getúlio Vargas 950.

Embassies and consulates Most open in the morning only. *Austria*, R 5, Qd E No 4, Jardim Primeravera II, T6421939, F6421582. *Belgium*, Conj Murici, Qd D No 13, Parque 10, T2361452. *Bolivia*, Av Efigênio Sales 2226, Qd B No 20, T2369988. *Colombia*, R 24 de Maio 220, Rio Negro Center, T2346777, check whether a Colombian tourist card can be obtained at the border. *Denmark*, Estr da Refinaria, T6151555, also handles Norway. *France*, Av Joaquim Nabuco 1846, T2336583. *Germany*, R 24 Maio 220, Edif Rio Negro Centre, sala 812, T2349045, 1000-1200. *Italy*, R Belo Horizonte 240, Adrianópolis, T6114877. *Japan*, R Fortaleza 460, T2348825. *Netherlands*, R Miranda Leão 41, T6221366. *Peru*, R A, Casa 1, Conj Aristocrático, Chapada, T6563267. *Portugal*, R Terezina 193, T6331577. *Spain*, Al Cosme Ferreira 1225, Aleixo, T6443800. *UK*, R Paraquê 240, T2377869. *USA*, R Recife 1010, Adrianópolis, T6334907, will supply letters of introduction for US citizens. *Venezuela*, R Ferreira Pena 179, T2336004, F2330481, 0800-1200, everyone entering Venezuela overland needs a visa. The requirements are 1 passport photo, an onward ticket and the fee, usually US$30 (check in advance for changes to these regulations – it is reported that a yellow fever certificate is not needed). Takes 24 hrs.

Laundry *Lavanderia Amazonas*, Costa Azevedo 63, near *Teatro Amazonas*. US$0.40 per item, closed Sat afternoon and Sun. *Lavanderia Central*, R Quintino Bocaiúva 602.

Lavalux, R Mundurucus 77, fast service washes. *Lavlev*, Av Sen A Maia 1108. One of few self-service laundries is opposite the cemetery, open Sun, but a taxi ride away.

Medical services *Clinica Sao Lucas*, R Alexandre Amorin 470, T6223678, reasonably priced, some English spoken, good service, take a taxi. *Hospital Tropical*, Av Pedro Teixeira (D Pedro I) 25, T6561441. Centre for tropical medicine, not for general complaints, treatment free, some doctors speak a little English. Take buses 201 or 214 from Av 7 de Setembro in the city centre. *Pronto Soccoro 28 de Agosto*, R Recife, free for emergencies.

Useful addresses Visas: To extend or replace a Brazilian visa, take bus from Praça Adalberto Vale to Kissia Dom Pedro for Polícia Federal post, people in shorts not admitted.

Voltage 110 volts AC; some hotels 220 volts AC, 60 cycles.

Amazon tours

There are two types of tours: those based at jungle lodges and river boat trips. Whatever you choose, bear in mind that the Amazon is a broad experience and not about one particular aspect. Most tours, whether luxury or budget, combine river outings on motorized canoes with piranha fishing, caiman spotting, visiting local families and short treks in the jungle. Specialist tours include fishing trips and those aimed specifically at seeing how the people in the jungle, *caboclos*, live.

Choosing a tour
If using a camera, do remember to bring a fast film as light is dim

Make sure to ascertain in advance the exact itinerary and that the price includes everything (even drinks and tips). Check that guides are knowledgeable, speak a language you understand, and will accompany you themselves. Insist that there will be no killing of anything rare, or even disruption of wildlife (many guides drag caimans out of the water which has negative long term effects). Ensure that others in your party share your expectations and are going for the same length of time. A shorter tour may be better than a long, poor one. Advance booking on the internet is likely to secure you a good guide (who usually work for several companies and may get booked up). Packaged tours, booked overseas, are usually of the same price and quality as those negotiated locally.

There are many hustlers at the airport and on the street (particularly around the hotels and bars on Joaquim Nabuco and Miranda Leão), and even at hotel receptions. It is not wise to go on a tour with the first friendly face you meet; all go-betweens earn a commission so recommendations cannot be taken at face value and employing freelance guides not attached to a company is potentially dangerous. Make enquiries and check credentials personally. *Secretaria de Estado da Cultura e Turismo* (see Directory above) are not allowed by law to recommend guides, but can provide you with a list of legally registered companies. Unfortunately, disreputable operations are rarely dealt with in any satisfactory manner, and most continue to operate. Book direct with the company itself and ask for a detailed, written contract if you have any doubts.

Bill Potter, resident in Manaus, writes: "opposite Manaus, near the junction of the Rio Negro and the Rio Solimões, lies the **Lago de Janauri**, a small nature reserve. This is where all the day or half-day trippers are taken, usually combined with a visit to the 'meeting of the waters'. Although many people express disappointment with this area because so little is seen and/or there are so many 'tourist-trash' shops, for those with only a short time it is worth a

Tour duration & itinerary

The Amazon

visit. You will see some birds and, with luck, dolphins. In the shops and bars there are often captive parrots and snakes. The area is set up to receive large numbers of tourists, which ecologists agree relieves pressure on other parts of the river. Boats for day trippers leave the harbour constantly throughout the day, but are best booked at one of the larger operators such as *Amazon Explorers* or *Selvatur*. Remember that in the dry season, one-day tours may not offer much to see if the river is low."

Those with more time can take the longer cruises and will see various ecological environments. To see virgin rainforest, a five-day trip by boat is needed. Most tour operators run trips on both the Rio Solimões and the Rio Negro. The Rio Negro is considered easier to navigate, more pristine, generally calmer and with fewer biting insects. This area has more visible upland rainforest and you are more likely to see animals such as sloths because there are fewer people. On the Rio Solimões there are more birds, piranha and alligators, but you're likely to be constantly fighting the mosquitoes and sandflies and the river is flooded for six months of the year. The Amazon has more monkeys and birds and it is generally easier to catch piranha, but there is less rainforest.

Another alternative is to go upriver to one of the jungle hotels. From the base, you can then take short trips into the forest or along the river channels. Flights over the jungle give a spectacular impression of the extent of the forest.

Taking a transport boat from Manaus is not a substitute for a tour as they rarely get near to the banks and are only interested in getting from A to B as quickly as possible.

Generally, between April and September excursions are only by boat; in the period October-March, the Victoria Regia lilies virtually disappear. Fishing is best between September and March (no flooding).

Prices vary but usually include lodging, guide, transport, meals (but not drinks) and activities. The recommended companies charge within the

Around Manaus

following ranges (per person): one day, US$60-95; three days, for example to Anavilhanas Archipelago, US$195-285. Longer, specialized (eg fishing tours), or more luxurious excursions will cost significantly more. Most river trips incorporate the meeting of the waters on the first day, so there is no need to make a separate excursion.

Leave luggage with your tour operator or hotel in Manaus and only take what is necessary for your trip. Long sleeves, long trousers, shoes and insect repellent are advisable for treks in the jungle where insects are voracious. A hat offers protection from the sun on boat trips. Bottled water and other drinks are expensive in the jungle, so you may want to take your own supplies. **What to take**

Essentials

There are several lodges within a few hours' boat or car journey from Manaus. Most **Lodges** emphasize comfort (although electricity and hot water is limited) rather than a real jungle experience, and you are more likely to enjoy a nice buffet in pleasant company than come face to face with rare fauna. Nevertheless the lodges are good if your time is limited and you want to have a brief taste of the Amazon rainforest. Two days is enough to experience the highlights (one day of this will be taken up with travel). Tour operators for reservations are also listed below. **L** *Acajatuba Jungle Lodge*, Lago Acajatuba, 4 hrs up the Rio Negro from Manaus. 40 apartments with shower, bar, restaurant, contact office at R Dr Almino 36, Centro, T/F2337642, www.acajatuba.com.br **L** *Ariaú Amazon Towers*, Rio Ariaú, 2 km from Archipélago de Anavilhanas, 60 km and 2 hrs by boat from Manaus on a side channel of the Rio Negro. 134 rooms in complex of towers connected by walkways, beach (Sep-Mar) trips to the Anavilhanas islands in groups of 10-20. Rates per person: US$280 for 2-days/1-night, US$400, 3 nights/4 days. Highly recommended. Contact *River Jungle Hotel*, R Silva Ramos 20, Centro, T6225000, F2335615, www.ariautowers.com.br, in Rio T/F021-2348779, in USA, Jill A Siegel, 17 Schenck Av 2C, Great Neck, NY 11021, T/F718-5230041, 1-800-4707636 (access 21), jsananda@aol.com **L** *Amazon Ecopark Lodge*, Igarapé do Tarumã, 20 km from Manaus, 15 mins by boat, jungle trails. 60 apartments with shower, bar, restaurant, contact T2332559, F2340027. Nearby is the **Amazon Monkey Jungle**, an ecological park where many monkey species are treated and rehabilitated in natural surroundings. The *Living Rainforest Foundation*, which administers the *Ecopark*, also offers educational jungle trips and overnight camps (bring your own food), entrance US$15. **L** *Amazon Village*, Lago do Puraquequara, 60 km, 2 hrs by boat, from Manaus. A comfortable lodge on dry land, with nice cabins, 32 apartments with cold shower, restaurant. Recommended. Contact T6331444, F6333217. **A** *Amazon Lodge*, a floating lodge on Lago do Juma, 80 km from Manaus, 30 mins by Careiro ferry, then 1½

To Itacoatiara & Boa Vista

To Parintins

Rio Puraquequara

4

Rio Amazonas

Encontro das Águas
Meeting of the Waters

Ilha do Careiro

Lago do Rei

Careiro

Ilha Xiborema

Ilha Machantaria

Rio Mamori

Lago Comprido

3

Lago Alvares

BR 319

To Castanho

The Amazon

hrs by bus, then 2 hrs by boat. 12 basic apartments with cold shower, restaurant, good excursions. Highly recommended. Contact T6563878, F6566101. **A** *Boa Vida Jungle Resort*, 53 km from Manaus by route AM-10, direction Itacoatiara. Seven apartments and 6 chalets, shower, fridge, bar, restaurant, fishing, boating, contact T2345722, F2322482. *Pousada dos Guanavenas* on Ilha de Silves, 300 km from Manaus on the road to Itacoatiara, then by boat along the Rio Urubu. Views of Lago Canacari, 33 rooms, a/c, fridge, electric showers, contact *Guanavenas Turismo*, Av Constantino Nery 2486, Flores, T6561500, F2381211, aristides@internext.com.br, www.guanavenas.com.br **A** *Lago Salvador Lodge*, Lago Salvador, 30 km from Manaus, 40 mins by boat from the *Hotel Tropical*. 12 apartments, cold shower, bar, restaurant, contact T6595119, F6584221. **A** *Rainforest Lodge*, on the banks of Lago Januacá, 4 hrs from Manaus. 14 bungalows with fans, pool, restaurant, snack bar, contact T2339182.

Tour operators   *Amazon Explorers*, R Nhamundá 21, Praça NS Auxiliadora, T6333319, F2345753, www.amazonexplorers.com.br, day tour including 'meeting of the waters', Lago do Janauari, rubber collecting and lunch has been highly recommended by most users (US$60), boat *Amazon Explorer* available for hire at about US$230 per day. *Amazonas Indian Turismo*, R dos Andradas, offers a different, authentic experience, staying with local river people, for around US$60 per day. *Amazon Travel Service*, Av Joaquim Nabuco 1626, sala 201/203, Centro, T6222788, F6222715, atstur@amazonet.com.br *Fontur*, in *Tropical Hotel*, Estr da Ponta Negra, Km 18, T6583052, F6583512, www.fontur.com.br *Heliconia*, R Col Salgado 63, Aparecida, T2345915, F6337094, alternatur@internext.com.br, run by French researcher Thérèse Aubreton. *Selvatur*, Praça Adalberto Vale 17, T6222577, F6222177, selvatur@manaus.br, Rio Negro trip, 0800-1500, with lunch at *Janaurylândia* floating hotel. *Swallows and Amazons*, R Quintino Bocaiúva 189, andar 1, Sala 13, opposite *Best Western Lord Manaus* hotel, T/F6221246, www.swallowsandamazonstours.com, Mark and Tania Aitchison offer a wide range of riverboat, adventure and speciality tours, with accommodation (up to 14 days). They have their own houseboat with 6 a/c cabins, covered motorized canoe and 8-bed private jungle lodge just before the Anavilhanas islands. Very comprehensive service, English, French and Spanish speaking guides.

Guides: Guides sometimes work individually as well as for various tour agencies, and the best ones will normally be booked up well in advance. Some will only accompany longer expeditions and often subcontract shorter trips. It is generally safer to book guides through agencies.

Down the Amazon River

Parintins   Just before the Amazonas-Pará border, between Manaus and Santarém, is
Phone code: 092   Parintins, a town on the Ilha Tupinambana. Boat trips can be taken to river
Population: 72,000   beaches in the dry season and to nearby lakes.

Here, on the last three days of June each year, the *Festa do Boi* draws thousands of visitors. Since the town has only two small hotels, everyone sleeps in hammocks on the boats that bring them to the festival from Manaus and Santarém (a large vessel will charge about US$130 per person, including breakfast, for the duration). The *Festa do Boi de Parintins* consists of lots of folkloric dancing, but its main element is the competition between two rival groups, the Caprichoso (whose colour is blue) and the Garantido (red), in the *bumbódromo*, built in 1988 to hold 35,000 spectators. There are about 2,500 competitors, but many more participants. During the festival, Mãe Catirina, Pai Francisco and Cunhãporanga (the beautiful woman) are major characters in this particular *boi-bumbá* drama. A preview of the festival is held in the *Hotel Tropical* in Manaus in the middle of June. Parintins' other main festival is the *Pastorinhas*, from 24 December-6 January.

Transport Boats call on the Belém-Manaus route: 60 hrs from Belém, minimum 10, maximum 26 from Manaus (depending on boat and if going up or down river). There are irregular sailings from Óbidos (ask at the port), 12-15 hrs. A boat from Santarém takes 20 hrs. There is also a small airport with flights to Manaus (1¼ hrs), Óbidos and Santarém (1 hr 20 mins).

Up the Rio Solimões

The river route from Manaus to Colombia and Peru can take as much as a week upriver. This journey will let you experience life on one of the world's great waterways.

Tefé is approximately halfway between Manaus and the Colombian border. **Tefé** The waterfront has a light sand beach and a market on Monday mornings. The nuns at the Franciscan convent sell handicrafts and embroidery.

Sleeping and eating D *Anilce*, Praça Santa Teresa 294. Clean, a/c, do not leave valuables in your room, very helpful. *Hotel Panorama*, recommended, good restaurant. Restaurant *Au Bec d'Or* by the port, French/Amazonian cuisine.

Transport Airport has a connection to Manaus. If travelling on to Tabatinga, note that Manaus-Tabatinga boats do not usually stop at Tefé. You must hire a canoe to take you out to the main channel and try to flag down the approaching ship.

Situated on the frontier with Peru, Benjamin Constant is served by boat services from Manaus, seven days or more; to Manaus, four days or more. Colombian territory is on the opposite bank of the river.

Benjamin Constant
Population: 15,000

Sleeping and eating B *Benjamin Constant*, beside ferry. All rooms a/c, some with hot water and TV, good restaurant, arranges tours, postal address Apdo Aéreo 219, Leticia, Colombia. *Mar Azur*, a/c, friendly. D *Benjamin*, very basic. D *Márcia Maria*, bath, a/c, fridge, clean, friendly. Recommended. E *São Jorge*, meals available. Recommended. E *Hotel Lanchonete Peruana*, good food. *Pensão Cecília*. *Bar-21 de Abril*, cheaper.

About 4 km from Leticia in Colombia is Tabatinga. The Port Captain here is reported as very helpful and speaking good English. The port area is called Marco. A good hammock will cost US$15 in Tabatinga (try Esplanada Teocides) or Benjamin Constant. A mosquito net for a hammock is essential if sailing upstream from Tabatinga; much less so downstream.

Tabatinga
Population: 38,000

Sleeping and eating *Hotel Martins*, good but expensive. D *Residencial Aluguel Pajé*, with bath, fan, clean. D *Solimões*, run by the military – close to the airport – with breakfast, other meals available if ordered in advance, excellent value. VW colectivo minibus from the barracks to town centre, harbour and Leticia. *Três Fronteiras*, excellent restaurant. *Canto do Peixado*, on main street. Highly recommended.

Transport Airport to Tabatinga by minibus, US$1. Flights to Manaus (3 times a week with *Varig*) and Tefé. Regular minibus to Leticia, US$0.60.

Directory Banks: it is difficult to change TCs in Tabatinga (try *Casa Branca*, *Casa Verde* or *Casa Amarela* on the main road, or the general manager of the main shopping centre), and far harder to purchase Peruvian soles than in Leticia. Good rates at *Câmbio Cortez*, Av da Amizade 2205 (near *Banco do Brasil*).

The Amazon

Border with Colombia and Peru

There are no customs formalities for everyday travel between Leticia and Tabatinga

It is advisable to check all requirements and procedures before arriving at this multiple border. As no foreign boat is allowed to dock at the Brazilian, Colombian and Peruvian ports, travellers should enquire carefully about embarkation/disembarkation points and where to go through immigration formalities. If waiting for transport, the best place for accommodation, exchange and other facilities is Leticia, Colombia. Travel between Colombia and Brazil and Peru is given below. Travel from/into Colombia is given under Leticia (see below).

Brazil **Brazilian immigration** Entry and exit stamps are given at the Polícia Federal, 10 minutes' walk from the Tabatinga docks, opposite *Café dos Navegantes* (walk through the docks and follow the road to its end, turn right at this T-junction for one block to a white building). ■ *0800-1200, 1400-1800 Mon-Fri; also at the airport, Wed and Sat only. Proof of US$500 or an onward ticket may be asked for.* There are no facilities in Benjamin Constant, although it is possible to buy supplies for boat journeys. One-week transit in Tabatinga is permitted. In this frontier area, carry your passport at all times. If coming from Peru, you must have a Peruvian exit stamp and a yellow fever certificate.

The **Colombian consulate** is near the border on the road from Tabatinga to Leticia, opposite *Restaurant El Canto de las Peixadas* (0800-1400). Tourist cards are issued on presentation of two passport photos.

Transport Taxis: travel between Tabatinga and Leticia is very informal. Taxis between the 2 towns charge US$5 (more if you want to stop at immigration offices,

Amazon border area with Colombia & Peru

exchange houses etc. Beware of taxi drivers who want to rush you expensively over the border before it 'closes'), or US$0.80 in a colectivo (more after 1800). It is not advisable to walk the muddy path between Tabatinga and Leticia; robbery occurs here.

Boats: from Manaus-Benjamin Constant, boats normally go on to Tabatinga and start from there when going to Manaus. They usually wait 1-2 days in both Tabatinga and Benjamin Constant before returning to Manaus; you can stay on board. Tabatinga and Leticia are 1½-2 hrs from Benjamin Constant (ferry/ *recreio* US$2; 25 mins by speedboat, US$4 per person, cheaper if more passengers).

For boats to/from Manaus, see Boats, page 575, and River transport, page 536

Colombian immigration *DAS*, C 9, No 8-32, T27189, Leticia, and at the airport. Exit stamps to leave Colombia by air or overland are given only at the airport. If flying into Leticia prior to leaving for Brazil or Peru, get an exit stamp while at the airport. Check both offices for entry stamps before flying into Colombia.

Colombia

Entering Colombia To enter Colombia you must have a tourist card to obtain an entry stamp, even if you are passing through Leticia en route between Brazil and Peru (the Colombian consul in Manaus may tell you otherwise; try to get a tourist card elsewhere). The Colombian Consular Office in Tabatinga issues tourist cards; 24-hour transit stamps can be obtained at the DAS office. If visiting Leticia without intending to go anywhere else in Colombia, you may be allowed to enter without immigration or customs formalities (but travellers' cheques cannot be changed without an entry stamp).

Consulates *Brazilian*, C 11, No 10-70, T27531, 1000-1600. Open Mon-Fri, efficient, helpful; onward ticket and 2 black-and-white photos needed for visa (photographer nearby); allow 36 hrs. *Peruvian*, Cra 11, No 6-80, T27204, F27825. Open 0830-1430; no entry or exit permits are given here.

Peruvian immigration Entry/exit formalities take place at Santa Rosa. Every boat leaving Peru stops here. There is also an immigration office in Iquitos (Malecón Tarapacá 382), where procedures for leaving can be checked. **Exchange** is available at Islandia (see below).

Peru

Consulates In Iquitos there are consulates for Brazil (C Sargento Lores 363, T005194-232081) and Colombia (C Putumayo 247, T231461).

Transport Boats sail from Iquitos to a mud bank called Islandia, on the Peruvian side of a narrow creek, a few metres from the Brazilian port of Benjamin Constant. The journey time is a minimum of 2 days upstream, 8-36 hrs downstream, depending on the speed of the boat. In ordinary boats, fares range from US$30-40 per person, depending on standard of accommodation, food extra. Speedboats charge US$75 per person, 3 a week run by *Amazon Tours and Cruises*. Passengers leaving Peru must visit immigration at Santa Rosa when the boat stops there. For entry into Brazil,

The Amazon

formalities are done in Tabatinga; for Colombia, in Leticia. Boats to Peru leave from Islandia, calling at Santa Rosa (2-3 days upstream to Iquitos). *Amazon Tours and Cruises* also operate a luxury service between Iquitos and Tabatinga leaving Sun, returning from Tabatinga on Wed, US$695 per person in the *Río Amazonas*. Also M/V *Arca* US$495 per person, return journey Wed-Sat.

Leticia

Phone code: 9819
Colour map 1, grid B1
Population: 27,000

This riverside city is clean and modern, though run-down, and is rapidly merging into one town with neighbouring Marco in Brazil. Leticia is a good place to buy typical Amazon Indian products and tourist services are better than in Tabatinga or Benjamin Constant. The best time to visit the area is in July or August, the early months of the dry season. At weekends, accommodation may be difficult to find. There is a **tourist office** at C 10, No 9-86. *MA* (Ministerio del Medio Ambiente), Cra 11, No 12-05, for general information on national parks.

The **museum**, at Cra 11 y Calle 9, set up by *Banco de la República*, covers local ethnography and archaeology, in a beautiful building with a library and a terrace overlooking the Amazon. There is a small **Amazonian zoo** and botanical garden on the road to the airport, within walking distance of town (20 minutes). ■ *US$1.*

Sleeping **AL** *Anaconda*, Cra 11, No 7-34, T5927119. Large a/c rooms, hot water, restaurant, good terrace and swimming pool. **B** *Colonial*, Cra 10, No 7-08, T5927164. A/c or fans, swimming pool, cafetería, noisy. **C-D** *Residencias Fernando*, Cra 9, No 8-80, T5927362. Well equipped, clean. Recommended. **D** *Residencias Marina*, Cra 9 No 9-29, T5926014. TV, some a/c, cold water, good breakfast and meals at attached restaurant, clean. **D** *Residencias La Manigua*, C 8, No 9-22, T5927121. Bath, fan, clean, friendly. **E** *Residencia Internacional*, Av Internacional, between centre and Brazilian border. Basic, bath, fan, friendly, hard beds, clean. **E** *Primavera*, C 8 between Cras 9 and 10. Bath and fan, noisy. **F** *Residencias Colombia*, Cra 10 y C 8. Good value, shared bath.

Eating **Mid-range** *Sancho Panza*, Cra 10, No 8-72. Good value meat dishes, big portions, Brazilian beer. Several small sidewalk restaurants downtown, good value *plato del día*. **Cheap** *Señora Mercedes*, C 8 near Cra 11. Meals until 1930. **Seriously cheap** Fried banana and meat, also fish and fruit is sold at the market near the harbour. Many café/bars overlook the market on the river bank. Take your own drinking water and anything stronger that you desire.

Transport **Air** The airport is 1½ km from town, taxi US$1.60; small terminal, few facilities. Expect to be searched before leaving Leticia airport, and on arrival in Bogotá from Leticia. To Bogotá, Mon and Fri, SAM (Tabatinga airport if Leticia's is closed).

Directory **Banks** *Banco de Bogotá*, will cash TCs, has ATM on Cirrus network, good rates for Brazilian *reais*. Apart from at this bank, TCs are hard to change, impossibe at weekends. There are street money changers, plenty of *cambios*, and banks for exchange. Shop around. **Communications** Post office: Avianca office, Cra 11, No 7-58. **Telephone**: Cra 11/C 9, near Parque Santander.

Up the Rio Negro

It is possible to get a public passenger boat (from Sao Raimundo port on the outskirts of Manaus) up the Rio Negro; see River transport, page 536. There

Are you sure you want to climb this mountain?

If you are tempted to climb Pico da Neblina, you will face plenty of discouraging factors before you set out. It is in an area of national strategic importance, with lots of minerals, including radioactive elements – in the surrounding soils. There is also gold in the neighbourhood, so garimpeiros are thick on the ground and they may not be too welcoming. The peak is in a Yanomami reserve and a permit is needed from Funai to enter. Similarly, a permit is required from Ibama to enter the national park. This can be a long-winded procedure in Manaus, where it is supposed to be done, although it may be a lot easier in São Gabriel da Cachoeira. Next, you have to get there, an expedition in itself, unless you go by helicopter like the Brazilian scientific and military teams (even then, choppers can't land on the top because of cross winds). Finally, there is the small matter of the climate. Almost 100 percent humidity, fierce heat until you get to the summit and, as Kevin Haight so delicately put it in South American Explorer, No 47, Spring 1997 (pages 9-15), a "four-letter word. Rain". The rain is torrential and can turn the rock faces into 'mini-Niagaras' in a matter of minutes. If you are happy to put up with all that, don't forget the insects – on Pico da Neblina itself there are countless species that haven't been catalogued yet.

are hardly any villages of more than a few houses, but these places are important in terms of communications and food resources. It is vital to be self-sufficient in food and cash and to be able to speak Portuguese or have a Brazilian guide. **Nova Airão**, on the west bank of the Negro, is an overnight, eight-hour boat trip upstream. It has a large boat-building centre at the south end, and a fish and vegetable market at the north end. Ice and bread can also be purchased here. It has a telephone, from which international calls can usually be made. There is road access and a bus service from Manaus.

It's two days from Nova Airão to the **Parque Nacional Jaú**. The only way to get here is with a tour; there is no transport or facilities. Permits are necessary; contact the Ibama office in Manaus, Rua Ministro João Gonçalves de Souza, BR-319, Km 01, Distrito Industrial, Caixa Postal 185, CEP 69900, T2373718/3710, F2375177.

Moura is about five days upstream from Manaus. It has basic medical facilities and the military base has an airstrip (only usable September to December) and telecommunications. About a day further upstream is **Carvoeira**, almost opposite the mouth of the Rio Branco. There is a vibrant festival in the first week of August. More than a day beyond is **Barcelos**, with a daily air service, except Sundays (Hotel *Oasis*, German spoken; *Macedo*), the centre for bass fishing on the Amazon.

A great distance further upstream is São Gabriel da Cachoeira, from where you can continue to Venezuela. It is a nice place, with beautiful white beaches and, in the river, rapids for 112 km. There is a daily air service, except Sundays. São Gabriel is near the **Pico da Neblina National Park**. Pico da Neblina is the highest mountain in Brazil (3,014 m). Contact the *Ibama* office in Manaus for more information and details of guides and trips to indigenous villages (not very traditional any more), see above. In São Gabriel there are two banks but no exchange facilities and **E** *Vaupes* hotel.

Cargo boats ply **Cucuí** at the border between Brazil, Colombia and Venezuela. Also twice-weekly bus, US$5 (one hotel, ask for Elias, no restaurants). From Cucuí there are daily boats to Guadalupe (Colombia) and infrequent boats to Santa Lucía (Venezuela).

São Gabriel da Cachoeira
The upper Rio Negro can be a rough area due to gold prospecting and drug running. Obtain local information and exercise caution when travelling in this region

South on the Rio Madeira

Humaitá
Phone code: 092
Population: 25,000

Humaitá is situated at the crossroads of the Rio Madeira with the Transamazônica highway and the BR-319 north to Manaus. Cattle ranching has begun in the area around the town. There are several basic hotels on the eastern edge of town (**C-D**) and the Soltur rodoviária in the centre.

There is very little traffic on the Transamazônica from Humaitá east to Itaituba (1,025 km); local drivers may give lifts. A ferry crosses the Rio Aripuanã at Vila do Carmo. The road is good for about 350 km from Humaitá, then it deteriorates badly. It is hilly, narrow, and the jungle usually grows over the side of the road. Bus to **Apuí** (**E** *Hotel Goaino*, basic), 458 km, about 12 hours, US$36, bus to Jacarèacanga erratic service, another 222 km (the town is 8 km off the highway). You need to stay overnight and catch the Transbrasiliana bus to Itaituba (24 hours, schedule erratic, the bus is replaced occasionally by a truck). **D** *Hotel São Cristóvão*, has a good restaurant, or try the filling station, on the Transamazônica near the Jacarèacanga turn-off, for hammock space. Travel times depend on the weather conditions, the condition of the bus, and whether the driver decides to stop somewhere for the night. There are flights Jacarèacanga-Itaituba (see page 558). Boat, not daily, ticket from filling station, US$25, 1½ days, very basic, hammock space only. About 70 km before Itaituba there are rapids; the rest of the journey is done by pick-up, US$10.

Roraima

This extreme northern state is little visited by travellers, except those making the journey between Manaus and the frontiers with Venezuela and Guyana. Mount Roraima, after which the territory is named, is possibly the original of Sir Arthur Conan Doyle's 'Lost World'.

The state's population is now only 325,000 in an area nearly twice the size of England. Land grants in the 1970s to encourage agricultural development caused the population to grow quickly from only 25,000 in 1960. Then, in the late 1980s a gold rush in the northwest of Roraima drew prospectors from all over the country. The mining took place on the Yanomami Indian Reserve, causing much disruption to their traditional way of life. Further tragedy came in January 1998 when forest fires spread across the state, causing massive destruction until extinguished by rains in March.

The forest cover gives way to grasslands in the northeast and there is a pronounced dry season. The Várzea (flood plain) along the main rivers irrigates the southeast of the state. Cattle ranching is important as is rice cultivation on the flood plain of the Rio Branco. Other crops are maize, beans, manioc and banana. Some gold mining still continues but at a reduced level.

Boa Vista

The capital of the extreme northern State of Roraima, 759 km north of
Manaus, has a modern functional plan, which often means long hot treks
from one place to another. It has an interesting modern **cathedral** and a badly
kept **museum** of local Indian culture. There is swimming in the Rio Branco,
15 minutes from the town centre (too polluted in Boa Vista), reachable by bus
only when the river is low. Under heavy international pressure, the Brazilian
government expelled some 40,000 gold prospectors (*garimpeiros*) from the
Yanomami Indian Reserve in the west of the state in the early 1990s. The economic consequences were very severe for Boa Vista, which went from boom
to bust. An increase in cattle ranching in the area has not taken up the slack.
The **tourist office** is at Rua Col Pinto 241, Centro, T6231230, F6231831. Also
at rodoviária, T6231238 and the airport. Travellers can seek information (and
free hammock space) from Klaus, T9963 7915/9111, or ask for Lula at *Guri
Auto Elétrica*, Rua das Mil Flores 738, near rodoviária.

Colour map 1, grid A3
Phone code: 095
Population: 200,000

*Economic hardship
has caused an
increase in crime,
sometimes violent*

Fortaleza and the North Coast

Boa Vista

To Airport

To Venezuela

Parque Anauá

9 de Julho

Av Ene Garcês

M Correia

Prof A Bitencourt

L Tiradentes

Av Major Williams

Gal Penha Brasil

Brig Eduardo Gomes

Mário Homem de Melo

N Moristsman

Av Terêncio Lima

Cap F Ferreira

3

2

Av Glycon Paiva

Palácio do
Governo

Cathedral

Expedicionário

R Coronel Pinto

Amatari

Castelo Branco

Paracaima

Ceará

Jaime Brasil

To Caracaraí & Manaus

Prof Diomedes

Av Ville Roy

Surumu

Cecília Brasil

Aluricaba

Amazonas

1

Mau

N S da Consolata

Av Getúlio Vargas

Sebastião Diniz

Bento Brasil

Benjamin Constant

Centro de
Artesanato

Rio Branco

N

To Bonfim & Guyana

Not to scale

■ **Sleeping**
1 Aipana Plaza

2 Eusêbio's
3 Uiramutam

Essentials

Sleeping
Accommodation is generally expensive

B *Aipana Plaza*, Praça Centro Cívico 53, T224 4800, aipana@technet.com.br Modern, a/c, good service, best food in town, buffet US$7.20-8. **C** *Eusébio's*, R Cecília Brasil 1107, T224 0300, F623 8690. Run-down in 2001, a/c, good restaurant, swimming pool, free transport to rodoviária or airport. **C** *Itamaraty*, Av NS da Consolata 1957, T/F2249757, itamaraty@osite.com.br A/c, parking, good. **C** *Roraima*, Av Cecília Brasil e Benjamin Constant, T224 9843. Recommended. The restaurant opposite is also recommended. **C** *Uiramutam Palace*, Av Capt Ene Garcez 427, T/F2249912. Good service, a/c, restaurant, pool. **D** *Três Nações*, Av Ville Roy 1885, T/F2243439. Close to the rodoviária, some rooms a/c, refurbished, basic. Often recommended. **E** *Imperial*, Av Benjamin Constant 433, T2245592. A/c, cheaper with fan, welcoming, safe motorcycle parking. Recommended.

Camping Rio Caaumé, 3 km north of town. Unofficial, pleasant site with small bar and clean river.

Eating
Most restaurants close at night, except for pizza, including delivery

Ver O Rio, R Floriano Peixoto 116. For best fish dishes. In same area are *Makuchic*, also for fish, and *Black and White*, fixed price lunch and more expensive by weight. *Café Pigalle*, R Cecília Brasil, just off central praça, next to *Eusébio's*. Good food, drinks and atmosphere, open till all hrs. *Churrascaria La Carreta*, R Pedro Rodrigues 185, 500 m from *Eusébio's*. Good, US$3 buffet, nice atmosphere. Recommended. *La Góndola*, Benjamin Constant e Av Amazonas. Good. *Vila Rica*, R Ville Roy, near the rodoviária. Good cheap lunch. *Catequeiro*, Araújo Filho e Benjamin Constant, recommended *prato feito*. *Café com Leite Suíço*, at Santa Cecilia, 15 mins by car on road to Bom Fim. Open 0630-1300 for regional food, US$4, good.

Transport

Local Buses: The local bus terminal is on Av Amazonas, by R Cecília Brasil, near the central praça. **Taxis**: radio taxis with *Tupã*, R Monte Castelo 318, T2249150.

Long distance Air: international airport is 4 km from the centre. Taxi to rodoviária, US$9, to centre US$12, Bus 'Aeroporto' to/from the centre is US$0.40, 45 mins' walk. No left luggage, information or exchange facilities at the airport. Flights to Belém, Brasília, Macapá, Manaus, Santarém and São Paulo. Confirm flights before reaching Boa Vista as they are often fully booked. Aircraft maintenance, baggage checking and handling are unreliable. Air taxis with *Rondônia*, Praça Santos Dumond, T2245068.

See also Border crossings below

Buses: rodoviária, Av das Guianas, 3 km out of town at the end of Av Ville Roy, T2240606. Taxi to centre, US$5, bus US$0.45, 10 mins. Note that it is difficult to get a taxi or bus to the rodoviária in time for early morning departures; as it's a 25-min walk, book a taxi the previous evening.

To **Manaus**, with *União Cascavel*, US$32.50, 18 hrs, 4 a day each way, can be very crowded, advisable to book. To **Caracaraí** US$9, 3 hrs. *Amatur* to **Bonfim**, daily 0730, 1430, 1700, 2 hrs, US$3.70.

Car hire: *Localiza*, Av Benjamin Constant 291E, T/F2245222 and *Yes*, Av Maj Williams 538, T/F2243723.

Hitchhiking: to **Santa Elena**, Venezuela is not easy; either wait at the bridge and police checkpoint on the road to the border, or try to find a Venezuelan driver on the square. Hitching from Boa Vista to **Manaus** is fairly easy on the many trucks travelling south; try from the service station near the rodoviária. You may have to change trucks at Caracaraí. At the ferry crossing over the Rio Branco there is usually a long queue of waiting hikers; try to arrange a lift on the ferry. Truck drivers ask for approximately half the bus fare to take passengers in the cab, which is a bargain; it's much cheaper or free in the back. The view from the truck is usually better than from the bus and you can see the virgin forest of the Indian Reserve in daylight. Take some food and water.

Airline offices *Penta*, T2246849. *META*, Praça Santos Dumond 100, T2247677. *Varig*, T2242269. **Banks** US$ and Guyanese notes can be changed in Boa Vista. TCs and cash in *Banco do Brasil*, Av Glycon Paiva 56, 1000-1300 (minimum US$200). There is no official exchange agency and the local rates for bolívares are low: the *Banco do Brasil* will not change bolívares. *Bradesco*, Jaime Brasil e Getúliol Vargas. Visa ATM. Best rate for dollars, *Casa Pedro José*, R Araújo Filho 287, T2244277, also changes TCs and bolívares. *Timbo's* (gold and jewellery shop), on the corner of R Cecília Brasil e Av Getúlio Vargas, will change money. **Embassies and consulates** *Venezuela*, Av Benjamin Constant 525E, Boa Vista, T2242182, Mon-Fri 0830-1300, but may close earlier. **Medical services** *Geral*, Av Brig Eduardo Gomes, T6232068. Yellow fever inoculations are free at a clinic near the hospital. **Guides** Boat trips on Rio Branco and surrounding waterways (jungle, beaches, Indian reservations), *Acqua*, R Floriano Peixoto 505, T2246576, guide Elieser Rufino is recommended.

Directory

The Rio Branco

The Rio Branco

The yellow Rio Branco is better for fishing than the Rio Negro and there is more wildlife to see. However, biting insects and their associated diseases are more prevalent outside the wet season. About two days up the Rio Branco from Manaus, on the way to Caracaraí, is **Santa Maria de Boiaçu**, a village with a military airstrip (in use in July and August), very basic medical facilities and an indirect radio link with Manaus. Three small shops sell basic necessities (frequently closed), and there are several tiny, but lively, churches.

Caracaraí

A paved road connects this busy port, with modern installations, to Manaus. A new bridge crosses the river for traffic on the Manaus-Boa Vista road (see below). The river banks are closer, so there is more to see than on the Amazon and stops in the tiny riverside settlements are fascinating.

The Amazon

Sleeping & eating	**D** *Maroca*, opposite fuel tanks, 1 street back from the river. Clean and friendly. **E** *Caracaraí*, down the street from the rodoviária. Friendly but dirty. *Sorveteria Pizzeria Lidiany*. Recommended.
Transport	**Buses** From Caracaraí to Boa Vista costs US$9, 3 hrs. The Perimetral Norte road marked on some maps from Caracaraí east to Macapá and west to the Colombian frontier does not yet exist; it runs only about 240 km west and 125 km east from Caracaraí, acting at present as a penetration road. **Boats** Passengers are rarely allowed on boats now that the Manaus-Boa Vista has been paved.
Directory	**Banks** Silas in the *drogaria* (pharmacy) on the south side of town will change US$.

To Venezuela and Guyana

The road which connects Manaus and Boa Vista (ferry crosses the Rio Branco at Caracaraí as long as there is traffic) is fully paved and regularly maintained. There are service stations with toilets, camping, etc, every 150-180 km (all petrol is low octane). At Km 100 is Presidente Figueiredo, with many waterfalls and a famous cave with bats, as well as shops and a restaurant. About 100 km further on is a service station at the entrance to the **Uaimiri Atroari Indian Reserve**, which straddles the road for about 120 km. Private cars and trucks are not allowed to enter the Indian Reserve between sunset and sunrise, but buses are exempt from this regulation. However, nobody is allowed to stop within the reserve at any time. At the northern entrance to the reserve there are toilets and a spot to hang your hammock (usually crowded with truckers overnight). At Km 327 is the village of **Vila Colina** where *Restaurante Paulista* is clean with good food, and you can use the shower and hang your hammock. At Km 359 there is a monument to mark the **equator**. At Km 434 is the clean and pleasant *Restaurant Goaio*. Just south of Km 500 is *Bar Restaurante D'Jonas*, a good place to eat; you can also camp or sling a hammock. Beyond here, large tracts of forest have been destroyed for settlement, but already many homes have been abandoned.

Boa Vista has road connections with the Venezuelan frontier at **Santa Elena de Uairén**, 237 km away. The road is paved, but the only gasoline available is 110 km south of Santa Elena. Boa Vista is also linked to Bonfim for the Guyanese border at **Lethem**. Both roads are open all year.

Border with Venezuela

Immigration & customs	Border searches are thorough and frequent at this border crossing. Ensure in advance that you have the right papers, including a yellow fever certificate, for entering Brazil before arriving at this frontier. Officials may give only 2 months' stay and car drivers may be asked to purchase an unnecessary permit. Ask to see the legal documentation. Everyone who crosses the border must have a visa for Venezuela. Current procedure is to take filled out visa form, onward ticket, a passport photo and deposit slip from *Banco do Brasil* (US$30) to the Venezuelan consulate in Boa Vista. Be prepared to wait an hour, but it may be possible to get a visa at the border; check requirements in advance. There is also a Venezuelan consulate in Manaus which issues 1-year, multiple entry visas (see page 576).
Sleeping	On the Brazilian side there are a basic hotel, *Pacaraima Palace*, a guesthouse, camping possibilities and a bank.

Buses leave Boa Vista rodoviária at 0730, 1000 and 1400 for Santa Elena de Uairén, stopping at all checkpoints, US$7.50, 3½-6 hrs, take water. Buses from Santa Elena to Boa Vista leave at 0830, 1200, 1500 and 1600. It is possible to share a taxi. **Transport**

Santa Elena de Uairén is the gateway to the Venezuelan Guiana Highlands for those entering the country from Brazil. It is a growing, pleasant frontier town, 10-12 hours by bus from Ciudad Bolívar, itself nine hours from Caracas. The road is paved all the way and there are also flights. The landscape is beautiful, an ancient land of flat-topped mountains and waterfalls. The road skirts the Parque Nacional Canaima, in which is the highest fall in the world, Salto Angel (Angel Falls). Not far north of Santa Elena is the route to Mount Roraima. **Santa Elena de Uairén**

In Santa Elena are plenty of hotels and places to eat, money changing facilities, a phone office with international connections and tour companies for trips into the Gran Sabana – as the region is known. The bus station is on Calle Mcal Sucre. Buses south to Ciudad Bolívar are run by several companies throughout the day, earliest at 0700, last at 1930 (10-12 hours). The Brazilian consulate is near the bus terminal opposite the Corpoven gas station; open 0800-1200, 1400-1800. Full details on this region, and the rest of the country, can be found in the *Venezuela Handbook*.

Border with Guyana

The main border crossing between Brazil and Guyana is from Bonfim, 125 km (all paved) northeast of Boa Vista, to Lethem. The towns are separated by the Rio Tacutu, which is crossed by small boats for foot passengers. Vehicles cross by ferrry on demand, US$4, or drive across in the dry season. The river crossing is 2½ km from Bonfim, about 1½ km north of Lethem. A bridge is under construction. Formalities are generally lax on both sides of the border, but it is important to observe them as people not having the correct papers may have problems further into either country.

There is another border crossing at Laramonta from where it is a hard, but rewarding, walk to the Guyanese town of Orinduik.

At Polícia Federal (closed for lunch): from the rodoviária in Bonfim take a taxi, otherwise it's a long, dusty walk to the police checkpoint. Obtain an exit stamp at the Polícia Federal, then take the path to the river which leads to the right (going straight on also leads to the river, but not to the crossing point). After 10-15 mins you reach the canoes which go to Guyana. Once across, keep to the right, on the road to the airport. For immigration formalities, do not go to the Guyanese police, but to a building on the road to *Cacique* guesthouse. Ask directions. The office is someone's front room. **Brazilian immigration**

At Ministério da Fazenda checkpoint, before entering Bonfim; jeeps from here charge US$1 to immigration. **Brazilian customs**

D *Bonfim*, owned by Mr Myers, who speaks English and is very helpful, fan, shower. There is a café at the rodoviária, opposite the church, whose owner speaks English and gives information. *Restaurante Internacional*, opposite the rodoviária, on other side from church. Another restaurant, a bit further from the rodoviária, serves good food. English-speaking teacher, Tricia Watson, has been helpful to bewildered travellers. **Sleeping & eating** *Electricity is officially turned off between 2200 and 0700; take a torch or candles*

Buses Boa Vista-Bonfim 3 a day, US$3.70. Weekly jeep Boa Vista-Laramonta US$30. **Boats** To cross the river, take a canoe (see above) US$0.25 (no boats at night). **Transport**

The Amazon

Directory   **Banks** Reais can be changed into Guyanese dollars in Boa Vista. There are no exchange facilities in Lethem, but reais are accepted in town. **Embassies and consulates** *Guyana*, there is no consul in Boa Vista, so if you need a visa for Guyana, you must get it in São Paulo or Brasília.

Rondônia

Rondônia is a state peopled by immigrants from other parts of Brazil. Foreigners are welcomed without question or curiosity and there is no regional accent. A local academic described the state as "a land where nobody has a name and everyone can have a dream". Most visitors tend to arrive via the BR-364 from Cuiabá or the Rio Madeira from Manaus.

Background   When the Portuguese first arrived they thought the land they had found was an enormous island. The Madeira, Guaporé and Amazon rivers do almost form a circle, but the Guaporé was thought, erroneously, to link with the Rio Paraguay on the southwestern side. A group of Tupinambá Indians, who fled from the Portuguese colonists on the Atlantic coast, migrated up the Rio São Francisco to the Madeira, settling eventually on the Ilha de Tupinambaranas near the river's mouth. It was probably their accounts of the rivers in this region which encouraged the idea that the Amazon and Río de la Plata systems were linked, making Brazil an island.

Slave and gold hunters in the 18th century used the Guaporé and Madeira rivers for their expeditions. As a frontier area between Portuguese and Spanish colonization, the rivers were scenes of tension between the opposing powers, as well as of conflicts between Indians and slave-traders, and *bandeirantes* and Jesuits.

Rondônia became a state in 1981 after the central government's push to open up the unpopulated, undeveloped far west brought roads and settlers to the region. The destructive effects of this are well-documented. The BR-364 highway, one of those roads prompted by plans for exaggerated growth, led to widespread deforestation and erosion of the way of life of many indigenous groups. Ironically, the name given to the state was that of the founder of the **Indian Protection Service (SPI)** in 1910, **Colonel Cândido Mariano da Silva Rondon**. Rondon was part Indian and the policies which he incorporated into the SPI included respect for the Indians' institutions, guarantee of permanent ownership by the Indians of their land, the right to exclusive use of natural resources on their land, and protection of the Indians against rapid change once contact between indigenous and 'civilized' worlds had been made. The pressures of contact between Indians and the people who subsequently encroached on their world – ranchers, gold-prospectors, rubber-tappers, Brazil-nut gatherers and so on – made the SPI's task very difficult.

Rondônia falls within the same climatic zone as the rest of western Amazônia, with average temperatures of 24-26°C and between 2,000 and 3,000 mm of rain a year. The wettest months are November-April, the driest June-August. Acre is slightly drier, with 1,500-2,000 mm of rain a year. Rondônia can be subject to the phenomenon known as the *friagem*, a sudden drop in temperature, to about 6°C, as a result of low pressure over the Amazon Basin attracting polar air from the South Atlantic. The cold weather can last for a week or more and occurs in the winter months. It is said to be an effect of El Niño, the changing patterns in ocean currents in the Pacific at Christmas time.

The River of Doubt

◀◀

In 1913, Colonel Rondon invited the former US president Theodore Roosevelt to accompany him on one of his surveys. Together they explored the Rio da Dúvida – the River of Doubt – in 1914, following it to the Rio Aripuanã, thence to the Madeira. On the expedition they suffered great difficulties on the river itself, and Roosevelt contracted a fever which incapacitated him on the voyage and from which he never fully recovered. Rondon rechristened the Rio da Dúvida the Rio Roosevelt. The former president's account is told in Through the Brazilian Wilderness (London: John Murray, 1914), which contains photographs of the expedition; Missão Rondon, notes on the project of the Mato Grosso ao Amazonas telegraph by Coronel Cândido Mariano da Silva Rondon, 1907-15, with photos, includes an account of the Roosevelt-Rondon expedition, pages 377 ff; Sam Moses, 'Down the River of Doubt' (Travelers' Tales Brazil, pages 351-9), gives an account, written in 1993, of an expedition in Roosevelt's footsteps, highlighting the effects of the late 20th-century mahogany trade on the Cinta Larga tribe who live on the Rio Roosevelt.

Porto Velho

Porto Velho stands on a high bluff overlooking a curve of the Rio Madeira, one of the Amazon's main tributaries. The city has seen the rubber, gold and timber booms come and go. Service and IT industries are now major employers. Today the city is a large sprawl of streets, laid out in blocks stretching 8 km into the interior. The lack of town planning means that many of the best shops, hotels and banks are now a fair distance from the old centre near the river.

Phone code: 069
Colour map 1, grid B2
Population: 330,000

Getting there Domestic flights arrive at the airport, 8 km west of town. Taxi to downtown US$15. Interstate buses from Rio Branco and Cuiabá arrive at the rodoviária on Jorge Teixeira.

Ins & outs
See also Transport, page 596

   Getting around Urban bus services are good. Consider hiring a car if you're going to stay for some time. Be patient as local residents get confused themselves by directions. Taxis in town are cheap and plentiful, *Radio Taxi Marmoré*, T2247070. Find your favourite driver and stick with him, all have mobile phones and work with partners to give prompt 24-hr service.

Malaria is common. The drinking water is contaminated with mercury from gold panning

   Security The city is relatively safe for tourists despite rising crime and unemployment. Caution is recommended in the evenings and at all times near the railway station and port.

   Tourist offices *Funcetur*, Av 7 de Setembro, above Museu Estadual, T2211881, F2211831, seplan@ronet.com.br, very helpful, publishes free annual events list *Calendario do Porto Velho*. *Departamento de Turismo*, R Padre Chiquinho 670, Esplanada das Secretarias, CEP 78904-060, T2211499, F2252827/2232276. *Fundação Cultural do Estado de Rondônia (Funcer)* is at the same address. Street maps are hard to find. For a free map go to the *Teleron* Office, Av Pres Dutra 3023, between 0600 and 2300, and ask for the *Guia de Porto Velho* which includes a map and city services listings.

At the top of the hill on Praça João Nicoletti is the **Cathedral**, built in 1930, with beautiful stained-glass windows; the **Prefeitura** (town hall) is across the street. The principal commercial street is Avenida 7 de Setembro, which runs from the railway station and market hall to the upper level of the city, near the rodoviária. The centre is hot and noisy, but not without its charm, and the port and old railway installations are interesting. As well as the **Museu Ferroviário**, there is a **Museu Geológico** at the old railway yards, known as

Sights

The Amazon

Praça Madeira-Mamoré. ■ *Both are open 0800-1800.* Also in the Praça Madeira-Mamoré is the **Casa do Artesão** (see Shopping below) and a promenade with bars by the river, a wonderful place to watch the sunset.

A neoclassical **Casa do Governo** faces Praça Getúlio Vargas, while Praça Marechal Rondon is spacious and modern. There are several popular viewpoints overlooking the river and railway yards. **Mirante I** (with restaurant) is at the end of Rua Carlos Gomes; **Mirante II** (with a bar and ice-cream parlour) is at the end of Rua Dom Pedro II and **Mirante III** (with restaurant) is at the end of Benjamin Constant.

It is possible to visit the **cemetery**, where many people who died during the construction of the railway are buried. It's about 2 or 3 km from the railway station, but it is best to go with a local guide, as the cemetery is located in a poorer part of town and can be difficult to find. It is an eerie place, with many of the tombstones overgrown, some of which have been tampered with by practitioners of 'macumba', and there are rumoured to be ghosts.

Parque National Municipal de Porto Velho is a small zoo with 12 km of marked trails. ■ *Thu-Sun with volunteer guides, Av Rio Madeira s/n, 10 km, T221 2769.*

Excursions The **Cachoeira de Santo Antônio**, rapids on the Rio Madeira 7 km upriver from Porto Velho, is a popular destination for a swim during the dry season. In the rainy season the rapids may be underwater and swimming is dangerous. Access is by boat, taking a tour from Porto Cai N'Água, one hour; or by city bus No 102, *Triângulo* (every 50 minutes from the city bus terminus or from the bus stop on Rua Rogério Weber, across from Praça Marechal Rondon). Gold dredges may be seen working near Porto Velho, ask around if interested.

The **Banho do Souza** is a bar, restaurant and swimming area, 36 km out of town on the BR-364. A coolbox of beers and soft drinks is left by your table and you pay for what you've drunk at the end of the afternoon, swimming is free.

Sleeping **AL** *Vila Rica*, Av Carlos Gomes 1616, T/F2243433. Tower block, restaurant, pool, sauna, flashy but efficient. **A** *Rondon Palace*, Av Gov Jorge Teixeira, corner R Jacy Paraná, away from the centre, T/F2246160. Restaurant, pool, travel agency. **B** *Central*, R Tenreiro Aranha 2472, T2242099, F2245114, www.enter-net.com.br/hcentral A/c, TV, fridge, good breakfast, clean and friendly. Highly recommended. **C** *Vitória Palace*, R Duque de Caxias 745, T219232. A/c, cheaper with fan, basic, clean and friendly. **D** *Líder*, Av Carlos Gomes near rodoviária. Honest, welcoming, reasonably clean, fan, coffee. Recommended. **E** *Tía Carmen*, Av Campos Sales 2995, T2217910. Very good, honest, good cakes in *lanche* in front of hotel. Highly recommended.

From the rodoviária, take bus No 301 'Presidente Roosevelt' which goes to the railway station at the riverside, then along Av 7 de Setembro as far as Av Marechal Deodoro, passing: **C** *Pousada da Sete*, No 894, T2218344. A/c, cheaper with fan, **D** with shared bath. **D** *Guaporé Palace*, Av G Vargas 1553, T2212495. A/c, restaurant. **D** *Cuiabano*, Av 7 de Setembo 1180, T2214084. Good, a/c, cheaper with fan, **E** with shared bath, no breakfast. Recommended. **E** *Laira*, Joaquim Nabuco, just off 7 de Setembro, good, cheap.

Arabic *Almanara*, R José de Alencar 2624. Good authentic Lebanese food, popular, not cheap. Recommended. **Churrascarias** *Assados na Brasa*, Av Carlos Gomes 2208. Similar. *Natal*, Av Carlos Gomes 2783. Good meat and chicken. *Ponto Certo*, Av Rio Madeira 45. Excellent view of river, best in town, closed Mon. **Italian/pizzas** *Bella Italia*, Av Joaquim Nabuco 2205. Italian, pizza and *comida caseira*. *Mister Pizza II*, Av Carlos Gomes and José de Alencar. Good. *Pizza & Cia* (known as Lady Pizza), Av Joaquim Araújo Lima 1625, T2219953. Delivery available, best in town, some English spoken. *Tutti Frutti Pizza*, Tenreiro Aranha I, Apt 201. Pizzas not recommended but rest of menu is excellent, no talking encouraged during evening soap operas! **Oriental** *Gengis Kan*, Av Pinheiro Machado 590. Reasonably priced Japanese. There is a good Chinese at Av Joaquim Nabuco 2264, oriental food. **Other** *Bar do Dico*, Av Joaquim Nabuco 955. Best fish in town, lively in evenings. *Carovela do Madeira*, R Jos Camache 104. Expensive, popular with businessmen. There are a number of good restaurants around the intersection of Dom Pedro II and Av Joaquim Nabuco, such as *Champagne*. Recommended for pizzas. **Fast food** Many *lanches* in town: recommended are *Petiskão*, Av 7 de Setembro and Joaquim Nabuco. Excellent juices. *Caffé*, Av Carlos Gomes 1097. Excellent and cheap pay-by-kg buffet with vegetarian choice, friendly service. Highly recommended. *Chá*, Av Pres Dutra 3024. By kg buffet, pricey. *Panificadora Popular*, Av Mcal Deodoro between 7 de Setembro and Dom Pedro II. Good juices and soups. *Xalezinho*, opposite, for an even bigger bowl of soup. *Banana Split*, Av 7 de Setembro. Popular, good pay-by-kg meals. Also *Sorvette Pinguim* for ice-creams.

Eating
Avoid eating too much fish because of mercury contamination

Tom Brasil club at *Peixe Noturnos*, near airport (Taxi US$15 essential to book return fare). Every Sun night from 2200, US$3 entry for men. *Maria Fumaça* collective, T2244385. Organizes regular raves, concerts and festas around town. Check radio and newspapers for details. *Mirantes I* (see above), lively bar and a popular meeting place, excellent bar snacks and live acoustic music.

Bars & nightclubs

Indian handicrafts at *Casa do Índio*, R Rui Barbosa 1407 and *Casa do Artesão*, Praça Madeira-Mamoré, behind the railway station. Open Thu-Sun 0800-1800. Hammocks are more expensive than in Manaus.

Markets There is a clean fruit and vegetable market at the corner of R

Shopping

The Amazon

Henrique Dias and Av Farquhar and a dry goods market 3 blocks to the south, near the port. On Sun there is a general market off Av Rogério Weber near port, excellent bargains but no souvenirs. Watch out for pickpockets. **Rocha e Costa**, Av Brasília 2235. Out of town hypermarket, selling everything from fruit to outboard motors.

Bookshop *Livraria da Rose*, Av Rogério Weber 1967, opposite Praça Marechal Rondon. Exchanges English paperbacks, Rose, the proprietor, speaks English, friendly. Other bookshops nearby.

Supermercado Maru, 7 de Setembro and Joaquim Nabuco. **Camping** supplies and gas at *Casa do Pescador*, Joaquim Nabuco and Pinheiro Machado.

Photography *Casa do Fotógrafo*, Av Mcal Deodoro 2361, T2246696, and *Fotógrafo Elmir* sell and develop film, expensive but quick and reliable. Film developing also at 7 de Setembro and José de Alencar.

Tour operators *Ecoporé*, R Rafael Vaz e Silva 3335, Bairro Liberdade, T221 5021, carol@ronet.com.br For ecotourism projects in rubber tappers' communities on the Brazil/Bolivia border, US$50 per person per day, full details from Carol Doria, who speaks English. **Voltage** 110 volts AC, Guajará-Mirim also, elsewhere in Rondônia 220 volts.

Transport **Air** Airport, 8 km west of town, T2251755. Flights to Brasília, Manaus and Rio Branco.
See also Ins and outs, Take bus marked 'Aeroporto' (last one between 2400 and 0100).
page 593

Buses Rodoviária is on Jorge Teixeira between Carlos Gomes and Dom Pedro II. From town take 'Presidente Roosevelt' bus No 301 (if on Av 7 de Setembro, the bus turns at Av Mcal Deodoro); 'Aeroporto' and 'Hospital Base' (No 400) also go to rodoviária. Health and other controls at the Rondônia-Mato Grosso border are strict. To break up a long trip is much more expensive than doing it all in one stretch.

Bus to Humaitá, US$5, 3 hrs. To **São Paulo**, 60-plus hrs, US$75. To **Cuiabá**, 23 hrs, US$45, expensive food and drink is available en route. To **Guajará-Mirim**, see below. To **Rio Branco**, *Viação Rondônia*, 5 daily, 8 hrs, US$12.50. Daily bus with *Eucatur* from **Cascavel** (Paraná, connections for Foz do Iguaçu) via Maringá, Presidente Prudente, Campo Grande and Cuiabá to Porto Velho (Porto Velho-Campo Grande 36 hrs, US$60). To **Cáceres** for the Pantanal, 18 hrs, US$30.

Roads Cuiabá (BR-364 – Marechal Rondon Highway) is 1,550 km, fully paved; see below and page 649; Rio Branco, 554 km, BR-364, poorly paved; north to Humaitá (205 km) on the Madeira river, BR-319, paved, connecting with the Transamazônica, BR-230 (frequently closed, ascertain conditions before travelling). The BR-319 north from Humaitá to Manaus is closed indefinitely. Road journeys are best done in the dry season, the 2nd half of the year.

Car hire *LeMans*, Av Nações Unidas 1200, T2242012. *Silva Car*, R Almte Barroso 1528, T2211423/6040. *Ximenes*, Av Carlos Gomes 1055, T2245766.

Hitchhiking This is difficult, try the gas/petrol stations on the edge of town.

Boat See River transport, page 536. Passenger service from *Porto Cai N'Água* (which means 'fall in the water', watch out or you might!), for best prices buy directly at the boat, avoid touts on the shore. The Rio Madeira is fairly narrow, so the banks can be seen and there are several 'meetings of waters'. **Shipping a car**: *São Matheus Ltda*, Av Terminal dos Milagros 400, Balsa, takes vehicles on pontoons, meals, showers, toilets, cooking and sleeping in your car is permitted.

6 days a week a boat leaves at 1800 for Manaus from Manicoré, at the confluence of the Rios Madeira and Manicoré, 2 nights and 1 day's journey, food included; boats from

Porto Velho to Manicoré on Mon, Wed and Sat (1800, arrives 0200, but you can sleep on the boat), connecting with Manicoré-Manaus boats (a recommended boat is *Orlandina*).

Airline offices *TAM*, R J Castilho 530, T2242180. *Tavaj*, T2252999. *Varig*, Av Campos Sales 2666, T2242262, F2242278, English spoken. *Vasp*, R Tenheiro Aranha 2326, T2244566. **Banks** Open in the morning only. *Banco do Brasil*, Dom Pedro II 607 and Av José de Alencar, cash and TCs with 2 commission, minimum commission US$10, minimum amount exchanged US$200. *Marco Aurélio Câmbio*, R José de Alencar 3353, T2232551, very quick, efficient, good rates for US$ cash, Mon-Fri 0900-1500. *Parmetal* (gold merchants), R Joaquim Nabuco 2265, T2211566, cash only, good rates, open Mon-Fri 0730-1800, Sat 0730-1300. Local radio news and papers publish exchange rates. Exchange is difficult elsewhere in Rondônia. **Communications** Post office: Av Pres Dutra 2701, corner of Av 7 de Setembro. Telephones: Av Pres Dutra 3023 and Dom Pedro II, 0600-2300 daily. **Laundry** *Lavanderia Marmoré*, Pinheiro Machado 1455B. **Medical services** *Hospital Central*, R Júlio de Castilho 149, T/F2244389, 24 hr emergencies. Dentist at Carlos Gomes 2577; 24-hr clinic opposite.

Directory

Along the BR-364

The Marechal Rondon Highway, BR-364, runs 1,550 km from Porto Velho to Cuiabá in Mato Grosso. The paving of this road has meant the development of farms and towns along it. Cattle ranches can be seen all along the road, with least population density in the south between Pimenta Bueno and Vilhena.

In Ariquemes, 202 km from Porto Velho, you can stay at *Ariquemes*, Av Capt Sílvio 1141, T5352200, F5353602, with air conditioning, fridge and parking, or **D** *Valérius Palace*, Av Tancredo Neves 3113, T5353311. There are buses to/from Porto Velho hourly from 0600, 3-4 hours. There is a *Banco do Brasil*. Further south are Nova Vida (200 km), Jaru (257 km) and Ouro Preto d'Oeste (297 km).

Ariquemes
Phone code: 069
Population: 75,000

About 250 km south of Porto Velho, it is possible to stay on a working *fazenda*, **A** *Pousada Ecológica Rancho Grande*, at Caixa Postal 361, Ariquemes, Rondônia 78914, T/F5354301, pousada@ariquemes.com.br About 450 bird species and numerous mammals can be seen on the 20 km of trails, Harald Schmitz speaks English, German and Spanish, highly recommended, especially for butterfly lovers. Reservations and tours can be arranged through *Focus Tours*, see Tours operators, page 23.

On the shores of the Rio Machado, 376 km from Porto Velho, is this pleasant town with a small riverside promenade, and several bars which are lively at night. There is swimming in the river, beware of the current, and a telegraph museum on Avenida Marechal Rondon.

Ji Paraná
Phone code: 069
Population: 95,500

Sleeping **A** *Transcontinental*, R Júlio Guerra 258, centre, T4221212, F4222064. Restaurant, pool, overlooking the river. Recommended. **B** *Vitória Regia*, R Júlio Guerra 172, centre, T4221432, F4221767. A/c, fridge, TV, parking, view of the river. **B** *Plaza*, R Martins Costa 336, across the bridge from the centre, T4222524. A/c, fridge, TV, parking. **C** *Nova Era*, Av Marechal Rondon 1845, 2 blocks from the rodoviária. With bath, a/c, TV, cheaper with fan, parking, good value. Recommended. **D** *Sol Nascente*, R Dr Osvaldo 101, across the bridge from the centre, T4211997, with *churrascaria*. *Casablanca*, R Padre Rohl 465, centre, T4215894. With bath, a/c, fridge, TV, cheaper with fan. Cheap hotels in front of the rodoviária are filthy – not recommended.

Tour operators *Transcontinental*, R Júlio Guerra 258, T4221433, F4222064.

Transport Air: airport, 12 km from centre on Av Brasil. Air taxi with *Eucatur*, T4222030. **Buses**: bus station, R dos Mineiros, T4222233. To **Porto Velho**, US$16.25, 16 hrs. To **Cuiabá**, 15 hrs, US$28. **Car hire**: *Localiza*, airport and R Dr Osvaldo 38, T4223221.

Directory Airline offices: *TAM*, T4221373. **Banks**: *Bradesco*, Av Mcal Rondon 385. **Medical services** *Pró-Saúde*, R Almte Barroso 99, T4221545.

Cacoal Further southeast is Cacoal, 481 km from Porto Velho, which is a coffee, cacau and timber exporting centre. The bus station is at Av Sergipe 396, T4412233.

Sleeping and eating B *Estoril Palace*, R São Luís 1065, T/F4414810. A/c, parking, pool. **B** *Cacoal Palace*, R Gen Osório 937, T4415011. A/c, parking. *Zeppelin*, Av 2 de Junho 2518. Fish restaurant.

Directory Banks: *Bradesco*, Av Porto Velho 2091. **Medical services**: *Cristo Rei*, Av Guaporé 2270, T4412483.

Vilhena The next town, 530 km from Porto Velho, is **Pimenta Bueno**, which has a gaso-
Population: 43,000 line station, rodoviária and hotels. On the Rondônia-Mato Grosso border **Vilhena**, 704 km from Porto Velho (bus US$40, 11 hours), 752 km from Cuiabá (bus US$21, 11 hours), is a good place to break the Cuiabá-Porto Velho trip.

Sleeping and eating A *Mirage*, Av Maj Amarantes 3536, on the main commercial street, T/F3222166. Parking, pool. **A** *Diplomata*, R Francisco Tildre 63, T3213173, F3213233. Parking, pool. **B** *Santa Rosa Palace*, R Dal Toé 191, T3213900. A/c, fridge, TV, parking, **C** with fan. **C** *Comodoro*, Av Capt Castro 3663, in the centre, T/F3221244. A/c, parking. In Nova Vilhena ('Circular' bus to the centre), near the rodoviária, are: **D** *Vitória*, at No 117, T3213918. With fan, cheaper with shared bath, parking.
On **Av Sabino Bezerra de Queiroz** are: **B** *Campinense*, No 5227, T/F3213156. Fan, park-ing, **D** with shared bath, good value. Recommended. **B** *Nacional*, No 5363, T3213952. A/c, TV, fridge, **C** with fan, parking. **C** *Rover Pálace*, No 5423, T/F3212253. With fan, TV, parking, simpler rooms **D**. **D** *Luz*, No 5341, T/F3211825. With fan, parking, good value. **D** *Rodoviário*, No 5537, T3213785. With fan, **E** with shared bath, basic, run down.
By the rodoviária are *Tókio*, Av Sabino Bezerra de Queiroz 5489, oriental, and *Bom Papão II*, Av Sabino Bezerra de Queiroz, 5261. Good *comida caseira*.

Transport Air: airport, 8 km from centre. **Buses**: bus station, BR-346 Km 690, T3222233. **Car hire**: *Interlocadura*, T3211050.

Directory Airline offices: *Pantanal*, T3212051. *TAM*, T3213823. **Medical ser-vices** *Santa Helena*, Av Liberdade 2832, T3213259. At the Mato Grosso state border, proof of yellow-fever inoculation is required: if no proof is presented, a new shot is given.

Pacaás Novos This park of 765,800 ha lies west of the BR-364 in a transitional zone, between
National Park open plain and Amazonian forest. The majority of its surface is covered with *cerrado* vegetation and the fauna includes jaguar, brocket deer, puma, tapir and peccary. The average annual temperature is 23°C, but this can fall as low as 5°C when the cold front known as the *friagem* blows up from the South Pole. Details from Ibama, Avenida Jorge Teixeira 3477, CEP 78904-320, T2232599/3597, Porto Velho, T2233607/3598, F2218021, or Rua João Batista Rios, CEP 78958-000 Pacaás Novas-RO. Also enquire here about the Jaru Biological Reserve in the east of the state.

The Amazon

On the Rio Guaporé is the Guaporé Biological Reserve, Avenida Limoeira, CEP 78971, Guaporé-RO, T6512239, in which is the Forte Príncipe da Beira, begun in 1777 as a defence of the border with Bolivia. The fort, which is being restored, can be reached from Costa Marques (20 km by road), which is some 345 km by unpaved road west of **Rolim de Moura**. This unplanned town, 40 km west of Pimenta Bueno, relies on agriculture, livestock and a small furniture industry.

Sleeping and eating Rolim de Moura: B *Transcontinental*, R Jaguaribe 5104, T4421722, F4421729 and C *Iguaçu Palace*, Av 25 de Agosto 4430, T/F4421414. *Restaurant Caribe*, Av João Pessoa 4925.

Transport Bus station, Av São Paulo, T4422397.

Directory Medical services: *Bom Jesus*, Av Macapá 5040, T4422463.

Guajará Mirim

From Porto Velho, the paved BR-364 continues 220 km southwest to Abunã (with a few hotels, **E**), where the BR-425 branches south to Guajará Mirim. About 9 km east of Abunã is a ferry crossing over the Rio Madeira, where it receives the waters of the Rio Abunã. The BR-425 is a fair road, partly paved, which uses the former rail bridges in poor condition. It is sometimes closed March-May. Across the Mamoré from Guajará Mirim is the Bolivian town of **Guayaramerín**, which is connected by road to Riberalta, from where there are air services to other Bolivian cities.

Phone code: 069
Colour map 1, grid C2
Population: 39,000

Guajará Mirim is a charming town. The **Museu Municipal** at the old Guajará Mirim railway station beside the ferry landing is interesting and diverse, and recommended. ■ *0500-1200, 1400-1800, T5413362.* An ancient stern wheeler plies on the Guaporé; 26-day, 1,250-km trips (return) can be made on the Guaporé from Guajará Mirim to Vila Bela in Mato Grosso, the fare includes food.

C *Jamaica*, Av Leopoldo de Matos 755, T/F5413721. A/c, fridge, parking, the best hotel in town. C *Lima Palace*, Av 15 de Novembro 1613, T5413421, F5412122. A/c, fridge, parking. C *Mini-Estrela*, Av 15 de Novembro 460, T5412399. A/c, parking. D *Chile*, Av Q Bocaiúva. Includes breakfast, good value. D *Fénix Palace*, Av 15 de Novembro 459, T5412326. D *Mamoré*, R Mascarenhas de Moraes 1105, T5413753. Clean, friendly. **Youth hostel** *Centro Deportivo Afonso Rodrigues*, Av 15 de Novembro, T5413732. There is a basic *dormitório*, **E**, opposite the rodoviária. Best restaurant is *Oásis*, Av 15 de Novembro 464. *Lanchonates*, self-service, good value. Recommended.

Sleeping & eating

The Amazon

Alfatur, Av 15 de Novembro 106, T/F5412853.

Tour operators

Buses from **Porto Velho**, 5½ hrs or more depending on season, 8 a day with *Viação Rondônia*, US$18. Taxi from Porto Velho rodoviária, US$25 per person for 4-5, 3 hrs, leaves when full.

Transport

Banks *Banco do Brasil*, foreign exchange in the morning only. *Loja Nogueira*, Av Pres Dutra, corner Leopoldo de Matos, cash only. There is no market in Brazil for bolivianos. **Communications** Post office: Av Pres Dutra. **Telephone**: Av B Ménzies 751. **Embassies and consulates** *Bolivia*, Av C Marquês 495, T5412862, visas are given here. **Medical services** *Regional*, Av Mcal Deodoro, T5412651.

Directory

Border with **Immigration** Brazilian exit/entry stamps from Polícia Federal, Av Pres Dutra 70, cor-
Bolivia ner of Av Quintino Bocaiúva, T5414021.

Transport Speedboat across the Rio Mamoré (border), US$1.65, 5-min crossing,
operates all day, tickets at the waterside; ferry crossing for vehicles, T5413811, Mon-Sat
0800-1200, Mon-Fri 1400-1600, 20-min crossing.

Guayaramerín The Bolivian town of Guayaramerín is a cheerful, prosperous little town, on
the bank of the Río Mamoré. It has an important *Zona Libre*. There are flights
to Trinidad, La Paz, Cobija, Cochabamba and Santa Cruz, as well as buses to
La Paz, Santa Cruz, Trinidad, Cobija and other destinations, but the roads are
in poor shape and appalling in the wet season. Boats sail to Trinidad. For more
details, see the *Bolivia Handbook* or *South American Handbook*.

Acre

*This intriguing state, rich in natural beauty, history and the seringueiro culture,
is still very much off the beaten track. The area is beginning to develop its considerable tourist potential for adventure tourism and historians, as links are opened
up with neighbouring Peru and Bolivia.*

In the mid-19th century, what is now Acre was disputed land between Brazil
and Bolivia. The Treaty of Ayacucho, 1866, gave the territory to Bolivia but
allowed the Bolivians to use the Brazilian Amazon river system to transport
their goods, rather than traverse the Andes to the Pacific Ocean. The onset of
the rubber boom in the 1880s upset this arrangement because many of the
landowners who were exporting rubber from Acre and down the Rio Madeira
were Brazilian. They resented the fact that the Bolivian government had nominal control, exacting duties, but had signed economic rights over to North
American interests. Many *Nordestinos* also migrated to this western frontier at
the time in search of fortune. In 1899 the Brazilians rebelled. Four years later
the Bolivian government yielded the territory to Brazil under the Treaty of
Petrópolis and the American company received US$2 mn compensation.
The other concession which the Brazilians made was the construction of the
Madeira-Mamoré railway to allow Bolivian goods to be transported east. In
1913, Rio Branco became capital of the new Território Federal do Acre, which
attained statehood in 1962.

Acre has a population of only 500,000, but as its land is much more productive than its neighbour, Rondônio, there was a flood of immigrants in the
1990s. The future of Acre's forests depend largely on whether any effort is
made to improve the lot of the landless of the south, who constitute the majority of the migrants into the far northwest.

The Amazon

Rio Branco

The Rio Acre is navigable upstream as far as the borders with Peru and Bolivia. It divides Rio Branco, the state capital, into two districts called Primeiro (west) and Segundo (east), on either side of the river. In the central, Primeiro district, are **Praça Plácido de Castro**, the shady main square; the **cathedral**, Nossa Senhora de Nazaré, along Avenida Brasil; the neoclassical **Palácio Rio Branco** on Rua Benjamin Constant, across from Praça Eurico Gaspar Dutra. Two bridges link the districts. In the Segundo district is the **Calçadão da Gameleira**, a pleasant promenade along the shore, with plaques and an old tree marking the location of the original settlement. The airport and rodoviária are in the Segundo district. The **tourist office**, *Secretaria de Indústria e Comércio*, is at Av Getúlio Vargas 659, Centro, or *Departamento de Turismo*, BR-364, Km 05, Distrito Industrial; T2243997 for either office.

Phone code: 068
Colour map 1, grid B2
Population: 253,000
544 km from
Porto Velho

Rio Branco time is
one hour behind
Porto Velho and
Manaus time
(therefore two hours
behind Brazilian
Standard Time)

There are several large parks in the city: the **Horto Forestal**, popular with joggers, in Vila Ivonete (Primeiro), 3 km north of the centre ('Conjunto Procon' or 'Vila Ivonete' city-buses), has native Amazonian trees, a small lake, walking paths and picnic areas; the **Parque Zoo-Botânico**, on the UFAC campus (Primeiro), is 5 km from the centre, along BR-364.

Museu da Borracha (Rubber Museum), Avenida Ceará 1177, is in a lovely old house with a tiled façade. It has information about the rubber boom, archaeological artefacts, a section about Acreano Indians, documents and memorabilia from the annexation and a display about the Santo Daime doctrine (see Excursions below), recommended. ■ *0900-1700 Mon-Fri.* **Casa do Seringueiro**, Avenida Brasil 216, on the corner of Avenida Getúlio Vargas, has a good exhibit on rubber tappers and on **Chico Mendes** in particular; the

The Amazon

Rio Branco

| 0 metres | 100 |
| 0 yards | 100 |

■ Sleeping
1 Albemar   3 Pinheiro Palace
2 Inácio Palace   4 Rio Branco

Chico Mendes – the first eco-martyr

The most famous seringueiro *(rubber-tapper) was Francisco (Chico) Alves Mendes, born in 1944. Chico's father had come to Acre from northeast Brazil as a* soldado da borracha, *engaged in providing rubber for the Allies during the Second World War. Chico learnt the trade of his father, became a leader of the Xapuri Rural Workers' Union and was a founder member of the CNS. He was instrumental in setting up a number of 'extractive reserves', parcels of land preserved for sustainable exploitation by those that lived there. He was shot dead on 22 December 1988 by cattle ranchers, to whose land-grabbing Mendes was in open opposition. He was by no means the only* seringueiro *who had been killed in such circumstances (he was the 90th rubber-tapper to be killed in 1988 alone), but his murder was the culmination of a decade of* fazendeiro-seringueiro *confrontation. Over 4,000 people attended his funeral; the world's media latched onto the story and Chico Mendes* became the first globally-recognized eco-martyr. He was honoured by the United Nations for his efforts in stopping the destruction of the rainforest. The universal outcry at his assassination led to the arrest, trial and imprisonment of his killers, members of the family of Darly Alves da Silva, a rare event in the history of Amazon land disputes. His death inspired changes in government policy over environmental protection, greater involvement of rubber-tappers and other forest workers in local organizations and the development of extractive reserves, first promoted in 1985 as protected areas for the seringueiros. Father Andre Ficarelli, assistant to the Bishop of Acre, said that Mendes' murder was like "the lancing of a tumour, exposing all the corruption and problems which the government [chose] to ignore". To others it was an opportunity to portray the whole affair in Hollywood-style melodrama; there was fierce competition for the film rights of Mendes' life story.*

Sala Hélio Melo has a display of Melo's paintings, mainly on the theme of the forest. ■ *0700-1200, 1400-1700 Mon-Fri.*

Security Despite improved air and road links, Rio Branco remains at the 'end of the line', a frontier outpost whose depressed economy, high unemployment and prevalent drug-running make the city unsafe at night, and some caution is advised at all hours.

Excursions About 8 km southeast of town, upriver along the Rio Acre, is **Lago do Amapá**, a U-shaped lake good for boating and watersports; access is by river or by land via route AC-40. About 2 km beyond along the AC-40 is **Praia do Amapá**, a bathing beach on the Rio Acre; an annual arts festival is held here in September. Excursions can be made to **rubber plantations** and rubber extraction areas in native forest (*seringais nativos*).

Some 13 km from Rio Branco is **Colônia Cinco Mil** (access along AC-10), a religious centre of the followers of the Santo Daime doctrine: its members, many originally from outside Acre and Brazil, live a communal life, working in agriculture and producing crafts made of latex. The religion centers around the use of *Ayahuasca*, a hallucinogenic potion adopted from local Indians. Visitors are usually welcome, but enquire beforehand.

The Amazon

1° distrito (west bank) **A** *Pinheiro Palace*, R Rui Barbosa 91, T2247191, F2245726, pinheiro@mdnet.com.br Pool. Recommended. **B** *Rio Branco*, R Rui Barbosa 193, by Praça Plácido de Castro, T2241785, F2242681. A/c, fridge, TV, nice but simple. **C** *Inácio Palace*, R Rui Barbosa 72, T2246397 (same fax and email address as Pinheiro Palace above). A/c, fair restaurant. **C** *Triângulo*, R Floriano Peixoto 727, T2249265, F2244117. A/c, TV, fridge, restaurant (see below). **C** *Albemar*, R Franco Ribeiro 99, T2241938. A/c, fridge, TV, good breakfast, good value. Recommended. **D** *Xapuri*, Nações Unidas 187, T2257268. Shared bath, fan, basic, 15 mins' walk from the centre.

2° distrito (east bank), in Cidade Nova by the rodoviária **B** *Rodoviária*, R Palmeiral 268, T2244434. A/c, fridge TV, **D** with shared bath, fan, good value. **C** *Skina*, Uirapuru 533, T2240087. A/c, fridge, TV, fan. **D** *Nacional*, R Palmeiral 496, T2244822. Fan, both cheaper with shared bath.

Youth hostel *Fronteira Verde*, Trav Natanael de Albuquerque, 2° distrito, T2257128.

Sleeping
There are few economical hotels in the centre, but a reasonable selection by the rodoviária

Kaxinawa, Av Brasil at the corner of Praça Plácido de Castro. The best in town for Acreano regional food. *Pizzeria Tutti Frutti*, Av Ceará 1132, across from the Museu da Borracha. Pizzas, ice-cream, not cheap. *Casarão*, Av Brasil 310, next to the telephone office. Good food and drink. *Churrascaria Triângulo*, R Floriano Peixoto 727. As much charcoal-grilled meat as you can eat. Recommended. *Remanso do Tucunaré*, R José de Melo 481, Bairro Bosque. Fish specialities. *Anexos*, R Franco Ribeiro 99, next door to *Albemar Hotel*. Popular for meals and drinks.

A local delicacy is tacacá: a soup served piping hot in a gourd (*cuia*), it combines manioc starch (*goma*), cooked *jambu* leaves which numb the mouth and tongue, shrimp, spices and hot pepper sauce. Recommendation from Sra Diamor, Blvd Augusto Monteiro 1046, Bairro 15 in the 2° distrito (bus Norte-Sul from the centre), other kiosks in town, ask around.

For ice-cream *Sorveteria Arte Sabor*, Trav Santa Inés 28, corner Aviario, 1° distrito, 15 mins' walk from the centre. Excellent home-made ice-cream, many jungle fruit flavours. Highly recommended.

Eating
There are boats on the river serving cheap but good local food

Arts and crafts fair in Praça do Seringueiro on Sun evenings. Market in 1° distrito, off R Epaminondas Jácome.

Shopping

Nilce's Tour, R Quintino Bocaiúva 20, T/F2232611, for airline tickets, helpful, 15 mins' walk from the centre. *Serra's Tur*, R Silvestre Coelho 372, T2244629. *Inácio's Tur*, R Rui Barbosa 91, at *Hotel Pinheiro*, T2249626.

Tour operators

Air The airport is on AC-40, Km 1.2, in the 2° distrito, T2246833. Taxi from the airport to the centre US$20 flat rate, but going to the airport the meter is used, which usually comes to less. By bus, take 'Norte-Sul' or 'Vila Acre'.

Flights to Porto Velho, Manaus, Brasília, São Paulo, Cuiabá and Campo Grande; once a week to Cruzeiro do Sul.

Transport
Car rentals with nationwide agencies are higher in Acre than other states

Buses Rodoviária on Av Uirapuru, Cidade Nova, 2° distrito (east bank), T2241182. City bus 'Norte-Sul' to the centre. To **Porto Velho**, *Viação Rondônia*, 5 daily, 8 hrs, US$12.50. To **Guajará Mirim**, daily with Rondônia at 1130 and 2200, 5-6 hrs, US$10; or take *Inácio's Tur* shopping trip, 3 per week.

Car hire *Locabem*, Rodovia AC-40, Km 0, 2° distrito, T2233000, F2245222. *Localiza*, R Rio Grande do Sul 310, T2247746, airport T2248478. *Unidas*, T2245044.

Airline offices *Varig*, T2242719. **Communications** Post office: On the corner of R Epaminondas Jácome and Av Getúlio Vargas. **Telephone**: Av Brasil between Mcal

Directory

The Amazon

The legend of the rubber tree

Once upon a time, an Amazonian Indian called Maitá was unfairly accused of theft. As a punishment, the chief of his tribe condemned him to a very peculiar and cruel task: to empty a small lake by using a wicker basket. The work was of course extremely unproductive, as the water always flowed through the holes of the basket. Maitá soon realized that he would have to work for the rest of his life and still never empty the lake.

Knowing that Maitá was innocent, a forest fairy approached the poor Indian and asked him to follow her. They walked in the jungle until they reached a very large tree. There, she showed Maitá how to make some cuts in the tree and as he did, he noticed that a milk-like liquid started to flow. The

tree was a rubber tree and the liquid was natural latex. Then the fairy told him to spread the sticky liquid over the basket and wait for a while. As the liquid started to dry, he realized that a thin layer of a water resistant material (rubber) was covering all the holes. On returning to the lake, he was very pleased to see that he had no problem in scooping out large amounts of the lake's water. He gratefully thanked the fairy and finished his task in a few days.

As in all good fairy tales, there was a happy ending. The chief discovered he had made a mistake and apologized to Maitá on his return to the tribe. A big party was held to celebrate Maitá's return and, most of all, an important secret had been revealed: the secret of the rubber tree.

Deodoro and Av Getúlio Vargas, long delays for international calls. **Medical services** *Santa Casa*, R Alvorada 178, T2246297.

From Rio Branco, the BR-364 continues west (in principle) to Cruzeiro do Sul and Japim, with a view to reaching the Peruvian frontier further west when completed. It is very difficult to get from Rio Branco to Cruzeiro do Sul by road because there is no bus service, but the occasional truck goes mainly in the dry season. The road is frequently impassable; it is open, on average, 20 days a year.

Cruzeiro do Sul
Population: 65,000

This is an isolated Amazonian town on the Rio Juruá in western Acre. Cheap excursions can be made on the river, for example to the village of Rodrigues Alves, 2-3 hours, return by boat or by road, 15 km. In the jungle one can see rubber-tapping, and collecting the latex into *borrachas*. Money changing is very difficult in Cruzeiro do Sul.

Sleeping and eating D *Savonne*, Av Col Mncio Lima 248, next to the cathedral, T3222481. Recommended. **E** *Novo do Acre*. A/c. Recommended. **E** *Flor de Maio*, facing river. Showers, full board available. Several other hotels and restaurants.

Transport Air: besides the scheduled *Varig* flight to **Rio Branco**, air taxis go to Rio Branco (Tavaj) and Pucallpa (Tasa). **Boats**: in the rainy season, river transport to **Manaus** is possible.

Border with Bolivia and Peru

The BR-317 from Rio Branco heads south and later southwest, parallel to the Rio Acre; it is paved as far as **Xapuri**. Here is the Fundação Chico Mendes, one very basic lodging and two restaurants. The road continues to **Brasiléia** opposite the Bolivian town of Cobija on the Rio Acre. In Brasiléia are a handful of hotels and restaurants; Polícia Federal give entry/exit stamps. There are three buses daily to/from Rio Branco, five hours in the wet, US$10. It is possible to stay in

The Amazon

Epitaciolândia (**D** *Hotel Kanda*, five minutes' walk from the police post) and cross the border into Bolivia early in the morning. There are two official crossings between Cobija and Brasiléia. One is by ferry to Cobija's boat wharf, just off Calle Bolívar, at the west end of town. The other is via the international bridge, east of the ferry. The former is often quicker, and certainly cheaper (US$0.35), as taxis are expensive (US$12). All visitors must carry a yellow fever certificate.

The road ends at Assis Brasil, where the Peruvian, Bolivian and Brazilian frontiers meet. Across the Rio Acre are Iñapari (Peru), where the border crossing is difficult, even out of the wet season, and Bolpebra, Bolivia. A bus service operates only in the dry season beyond Brasiléia to Assis Brasil, access in the wet season is by river. In **Assis Brasil** there is one basic but clean hotel, **E**, t**Security** Despite improved air and road links, Rio Branco remains at the 'end of the line', a frontier outpost whose depressed economy, high unemployment and prevalent drug-running make the city unsafe at night, and some caution is advised at all hours.

Rio Brancowo restaurants, some shops, a bank which does not change US dollars. The hotel owner may be persuaded to oblige. You get between Iñapari and Assis Brasil by wading across the river. **NB** There is no Polícia Federal in the village, get entry/exit stamps in Brasiléia. Take small denomination bills or Peruvian soles as there is nowhere to change money on the Peruvian side.

Cobija is roughly 500 km northwest of La Paz and there are air and road connections. The town is popular with both Brazilians and Peruvians for duty-free shopping. For more details, see the *Bolivia Handbook* or the *South American Handbook*.

Tocantins

Tocantins is not yet on the tourist track, other than for its share in the fishing bonanza around the Ilha do Bananal, one of the largest river islands in the world. There are some opportunities for ecotourism in the Parque Nacional do Araguaia (park entrance is at Santa Terezinha in Mato Grosso, see page 659). However, most visitors to this state are likely to be only passing through on the long road journey between Brasília and Belém.

Palmas

Brazil's newest city is an interesting detour on the highway between Belém (1,282 km away) and Brasília (973 km). There are waterfalls in the surrounding mountains and beaches on the River Tocantins, which make for a relaxing stop on an otherwise long drive. The BR-153 is close to the city and provides a good road connection, both north to Maranhão, Pará, and south to Goiás.

Phone code: 063
Colour map 1, grid B5
Population: 130,000

The new capital is a planned city, with wide, long avenues and modern public buildings. Construction began in 1989 and the state government was transferred a year later. The choice of name was partly influenced by the large numbers of palm trees in the area. The city is divided into four sectors: Noroeste (NO), Nordeste (NE), Sudoeste (SO) and Sudeste (SE). Like Brasília, the different blocks are named by use and location. Some address abbreviations are Área Central (AC), Área de Comércio and Serviço Urbano (ACSU) and Área Administrativa (AA).

The Amazon

The **Palácio Araguaia**, in Praça dos Girassóis, is an impressive modern building. The **Catedral de Nossa Senhora das Mercês** was built by the Dominicans from rocks from the Rio Tocantins. The **Parque da Cidade** is south of the city centre. See also **Praça do Bosque**, ARSE 51. The **Cachoeira de Taquarussu**, located near the city in the Serra do Carmos, is worth visiting. The tourist office is at: ACSE 1, Conj 4, Lt 10, Edif Jamir Resende, 2nd floor, CEP 77100-100, T2151481, F2151494.

Excursions About 8 km away at Canelas is **Praia da Graciosa**, a river beach on the Rio Tocantins. Popular at weekends, there are floating bars, sports courts, shows, and camping is possible. Along the Estrada do Rio Negro at Km 18 is the **Reserva Ecológica do Lajeado**, 1,500 sq km of caatinga, cerrado and humid forest. The Morro do Governador, near the entrance, offers good views. Further along the road at Km 36 there are trails along the river **Brejo da Lagoa**, until the 60 m-high **Cachoeira do Roncador** and other waterfalls are reached.

Essentials

Sleeping & eating **A** *Dos Buritis*, Av JK (ACNO 1), Conj 1, Lt 4/6, T/F2151936. Restaurant, pool. **A** *Rio do Sono*, Av Teotônio Segurado (ACSUSO 10), Conj 1, Lt 10, T/F2151733. Restaurant, pool, convention centre. **B** *Eldorado Plaza*, Av JK (ACSO 1), Conj 1, Lt 11A, T/F2152808. A/c, pool. **B** *Pousada dos Girassóis*, ACSO 1, Conj 3, Lt 43, T2151187, F2152321. A/c, restaurant, pool, sauna. **B** *Turim Palace*, ACNO 1, Conj 2, Lt 37/40, T2151484, F2152890. A/c, restaurant, sauna, pool, convention centre. **C** *Casa Grande*, Av Joaquim Teotônio Segurado (ACSUSO 20), Conj 1, Lt 1, T/F2151813. A/c, restaurant, pool.

Bela Palma, ACSUSO 40, Conj 1, Lt 19. Pizzas. *Estrela do Sul*, ACNO II, Conj 4, Lt 38/42. Churrasco, lunchtime only. *Minuano*, ACSUSE, Conj 9, Lt11/12.

Bars & nightclubs *Boulevard*, Av JK. *Carangueijos Bar*, Av Joaquim Teotônio Segurado (ACSUSE 40). *Consulado*, ACSO 1. *Phaeton Club*, ACSE 1, Conj 3, Lt 19.

Entertainment **Cinema** *Cine Blue*, *Palmas Shopping*, ACSU 10. **Theatre** *Espaço Cultural*, Av Teotônio Segurado, also has a library.

Palmas

Sleeping
1 Casa Grande
2 Dos Buritis
3 Eldorado Plaza
4 Pousada dos Girassóis
5 Turim Palace

Eating
1 Estrela do Sul

Gym *Academia Corpus*, ACNO 1 Conj 2, Lt 11.   **Sport**

Free Shopping, Av JK. *Palm Blue Shopping*, ACSUSO 10, Conj 2, Lt 10.   **Shopping**

Batista Pereira Turismo, ACSO 1, Conj 1, Lt 41, T2151228, F2151414.   **Tour operators**

Local City buses are plentiful and cheap. **Taxis** with *Rádio Táxi Palmas*, T2132001.   **Transport**

Long distance Air: airport, Av NS 5, 2 km from centre, T2161237. Air taxi with *Nobre*, T2161500, and *Aeropalmas*, T2161716. Flights to Belém and Brasília, Goiânia, São Paulo. **Buses**: bus station, ACSUSO 40, T2161603. **Boat**: port is 9 km from the city. Ferries to Miracema do Tocantins and Paraíso do Tocantins. **Car hire** *Hertz*, Av Nossa Senhora, T9781900, F2151900, and *Localiza*, ACSO 11-CL02, lote 41, Setor comercial, T2161104, and airport. *Rentauto*, Av Joaquim Teotônio Segurado (ASUSE10), Conj 1, Lt 6, T/F2151900.

Airline offices *Passeredo*, T2161515. *TAM*, T2161969. **Communications** Post   **Directory** office: Av Joaquim Teotônio Segurado. **Telephone**: Av JK. **Medical services** *Hospital Regional*, Praça ARSE, Qd 51, Setor Serrano, T2141424. **Dentist**: Dra Adriana Helena Toledo, ACNO 11, Conj 3, Lt 38, T2153201.

Brasília and the Pantanal

Introducing Brasilia and the Pantanal

The Centre West is where the Amazon meets the Central Plateau, forming the border with the country's South American neighbours of Bolivia, Paraguay and Peru. Brasília is the purpose-built 20th-century capital, which lies on undulating ground in the unpopulated uplands of Goiás, in the heart of the undeveloped Sertão. Symbol of the nation's commitment to its empty centre, it is now a **UNESCO World Heritage Site**. The state of Goiás has many historic mining towns such as **Pirenópolis** and **Goiás Velho**. Its capital, **Goiânia**, is famous for its outdoor cafés and bars with live music. The **Chapada dos Veadeiros** and **Emas** national parks are excellent for trekking and viewing wildlife.

Further west, in the heart of the Brazilian interior, is the Pantanal, one of Brazil's premier wildlife destinations. This enormous area of wetland offers the chance to fish for piranha, ride horses through clear rivers, bird-watch and relax in remote farmhouse accommodation. Three gateways to this unique region offer different experiences. To the north is **Cuiabá** and the ancient, mysterious landscapes of the **Chapada dos Guimarães**. South is **Campo Grande** and the lovely area around **Bonito** near the Paraguayan border. To the west **Corumbá** is a popular stop-off on the way to or from Bolivia.

Things to do in Brasilia and the Pantanal

① Ride horseback through the rivers that criss-cross the savannah-like Pantanal to see ridiculous giant guinea pigs, birds the size of humans and maybe even jaguars.

② Join a traditional Sunday barbecue at one of the *fazendas* in 'cowboy country'.

③ Take a sunset or sunrise safari by boat or jeep to see exotic birdlife.

④ See semi-precious stones being mined and panned at Cristalina and then indulge in a shopping spree at the local gem shops.

⑤ Shoot the rapids at Rio Formoso in Bonito, or snorkel in its crystal clear waters.

⑥ Spot maned wolf in the grasses of Emas National Park while brightly coloured macaws squawk overhead.

Brasília

Although not generally viewed as a tourist attraction, Brasília is interesting as a city of pure invention along the lines of Australia's Canberra and Washington in the United States. Its central position makes it a natural crossroads for visiting the north and interior of Brazil and, when passing through, it is well worth undertaking a city tour to view its innovative modern design. The climate is mild and the humidity refreshingly low, but trying in dry weather. The noonday sun beats hard, but summer brings heavy rains and the air is usually cool by night.

Ins and outs

Getting there
Phone code: 061
Colour map 4, grid A2
Population: 2.1 million

Flights arrive at the international airport, T3649000. Taxi to centre US$10, meter rate two is used to or from the airport. Left luggage facilities at airport (locker tokens, US$0.50). Interstate buses arrive at the rodoferroviária, T3632281 beside the railway station. Bus 131 between rodoviária, the municipal terminal, and rodoferroviária, US$1.25. Both bus stations have large luggage lockers.

Getting around
See also Transport, page 620

There is some gang violence in the city, so caution is advised at night

A good and cheap way of seeing Brasília is by taking bus rides from the municipal rodoviária at the centre: the destinations are clearly marked. The circular bus routes 106, 108 and 131 go round the city's perimeter. If you go around the lake by bus, you must change at the Paranoá dam; to or from Paranoá Norte take bus 101, 'Rodoviária', and to and from Sul, bus 100, bypassing the airport. It is worth telephoning addresses away from the centre to ask how to get there. An urban railway, Metrô, to the southwest suburbs, should have recently been completed.

Brasília orientation

At the Centro de Convenções, 3rd floor (*Adetur*, helpful, good map of Brasília, open to public 0800-1200 and 1300-1800 some English spoken, T3255700, F2255706); small stand at rodoferroviária (open daily 0800-2000), friendly but not very knowledgeable (open 24 hrs, daily). Airport tourist office, T3255730, open daily 0800-2000, will book hotels, limited English and information, no maps of the city. Adetur publishes a book called *Brasília, Coração Brasileiro*, which is full of practical information. *Embratur*, head office, Setor Comercial Norte, Quadra 02, bloco G, CEP 70710-500, T2249100, F3238936, webmaster@embratur.gov.br, office at airport. *Touring Club do Brasil*, on Eixo, has maps (members only). The information office in the centre of Praça dos Tres Poderes has a colourful map and lots of useful text information. The staff are friendly and have interesting information about Brasília and other places in Goias – only Portuguese spoken. **Maps:** 'Comapa', Venâncio 200 business complex, 2nd floor, have expensive maps.

Background

Plans for the capital have a long history. In 1810, Chancelor Veloso de Oliveira, suggested moving the capital inland to protect against potential invasions. The city was finally created from scratch after President Juscelino Kubitschek came to power in 1956 and personally oversaw the project. Sixty thousand workers known as *candangos* were recruited to transform the savanna into an enormous construction site. Work was completed in just three years, and the capital was moved here from Rio in 1960.

A competition for the best general plan was won by Professor Lúcio Costa, who laid out the city in the shape of a bent bow and arrow. It is also described as a bird or aeroplane in flight. The official name for central Brasília is the **Plano Piloto**.

The Eixo Monumental divides the city into Asa Norte and Asa Sul (north and south wings) and the Eixo Rodoviário divides it east and west. Buildings are numbered according to their relation to them. For example, 116 Sul and 116 Norte are at the extreme opposite ends of the city. The 100s and 300s lie west of the Eixo and the 200s and 400s to the east; Quadras 302, 102, 202 and 402 are nearest the centre, and 316, 116, 216 and 416 mark the end of the Plano Piloto.

Residential areas made up of large six-storey apartment blocks, called the 'Super-Quadras'. Each Super-Quadra houses 3,000 people and has a primary school and playgroup. Each group of four Super-Quadras should have a library, police station, club, supermarket and secondary school. All Quadras are separated by feeder roads, along which are the local shops. There are also a number of schools, parks and cinemas in the spaces between the Quadras (especially in Asa Sul), though not as systematically as was originally envisaged. On the outer side of the

▶▶ Oscar Niemeyer and Brasília

Oscar Niemeyer Soares Filho (born 1907 in Rio de Janeiro) was educated at the Escola Nacional de Belas Artes and in 1936 joined the group of architects charged with developing Le Corbusier's project for the Ministry of Education and Health building in Rio de Janeiro. His first international project was the Brazilian pavilion at the New York International Fair in 1939 in partnership with Lúcio Costa. In the 1940s he was one of the main designers of Pampulha (see under Belo Horizonte) and in 1947 he worked on the United Nations headquarters in New York. This was the period in which he affirmed his style, integrating architecture with painting and sculpture. He transformed utilitarian constructions with the lightness of his designs, his freedom of invention and the use of complex, curved surfaces. Throughout the 1950s he was commissioned to design a wide variety of national and international projects, but it was the years 1956-59 which stamped his signature on the architectural world. This was when he worked on Brasília, specifically the Palácio da Alvorada, the Ministries, the Praça dos Três Poderes, the Cathedral, University and, in 1967, the Palácio dos Arcos e da Justiça. After Brasília Niemeyer continued to work at home and abroad; among his more famous later projects were the Sambódromo in Rio (1984) and the Memorial da América Latina in São Paulo (1989). The Royal Institute of British Architects awarded him the prestigious Royal Gold Medal for Architecture in March 1998.

Many of Brazil's most famous architects, sculptors and designers were involved in Brasília. The city was built during Juscelino Kubitschek's term as president, 1955-1960, and was unparalleled in scale and architectural importance in Latin America at that time. A description of the city, and its effect on the economy at the time of its construction are dealt with elsewhere in the book. Niemeyer was appointed chief architecture and technical adviser to Novacap, the government authority which oversaw the new capital. But while it is common knowledge who the famous names were, it is also worth noting that 30,000 workers were involved in bringing the plan to reality. Most of them came from the Northeast. The city has been honoured not just for its architecture, but also for being the first purpose-built capital of the 20th century. In 1987 it was named a Unesco World Cultural Heritage Site, the first contemporary city to gain such protection from the United Nations.

Niemeyer himself has said "The modern city lacks harmony and a sense of occasion. Brasília will never lack these". And it is true that the principal buildings, and the overall plan itself, are strikingly powerful. The whole enterprise is deeply rooted in the 20th century, not just in its design, but also in the idea that it is a city you jet into and out of. If you arrive by road (which most people do not), the experience is even more fantastic. After hours and hours in the bus, travelling across the unpopulated central plateau, you come to this collection of remarkable buildings and sculptures in the middle of nowhere. The vastness of the landscape demands a grand city and yet, for all its harmony, it is almost as if not even Brasília can compete with the sky and the horizon.

300s and extending the length of the city is the Avenida W3, and on the outer side of the 400s is the Avenida L2, both of these being similarly divided into north and south according to the part of the city they are in.

Asa Norte is growing very fast, with standards of architecture and urbanization that promise to make it more attractive than Asa Sul in the near future. The main shopping areas, with more cinemas, restaurants and other facilities, are situated on either side of the old bus station (rodoviária). There are now several parks, or at least green areas. The private residential areas are west of the Super-Quadras, and on the other side of the lake.

At right angles to these residential areas is the 'arrow', the 8-km long, 250 m wide **Eixo Monumental**. The main north-south road (Eixo Rodoviário), in which fast-moving traffic is segregated, follows the curve of the bow; the radial road is along the line of the arrow – intersections are avoided by means of underpasses and cloverleaves. Motor and pedestrian traffic is segregated in the residential areas.

Sights

A good initial view of the city may be had from the **television tower**, West Eixo Monumental. It has a free observation platform 75 m up; also bar and souvenir shop. ■ *1400-2000 Mon, 0800-2000 Tue-Sun (closes for maintenance Mon mornings).* If the TV tower is closed, the nearby *Alvorada* hotel has a panoramic terrace on the 12th floor (lift to 11th only); ask at reception. Tours, from 1300-1700, start from the downtown hotel area and municipal rodoviária (US$12-20). Many hotels arrange city tours (see also Tour operators, page 620). Weekends have little to occupy the tourist except sightseeing (car needed) or visiting the market at the base of the TV tower.

Some buildings are open 1000-1400 Saturday and Sunday, with guided tours in English; well worth going

At the 'tip of the arrow' is the **Praça dos Três Poderes** (Three Powers Square), with the Congress buildings, the Palácio do Planalto (the President's office), the Palácio da Justiça and the Panteão Tancredo Neves. Nineteen tall Ministry buildings line the Esplanada dos Ministérios, west of the Praça, culminating in two towers linked by a walkway to form the letter H, representing Humanity. They are 28 storeys high: no taller buildings are allowed in Brasília. Where the bow and arrow intersect is the city bus terminal (rodoviária), with the cultural and recreational centres and commercial and financial areas on either side. There is a sequence of zones westward along the shaft of the arrow; a hotel centre, a radio city, an area for fairs and circuses, a centre for sports, the **Praça Municipal** (with the municipal offices in the Palácio do Buriti) and, lastly (where the nock of the arrow would be), the combined new bus and railway station (rodoferroviária) with the industrial area nearby. The most impressive buildings are all by Oscar Niemeyer (see box opposite).

The **Palácio da Alvorada**, the President's official residence (not very palatial and not open to visitors), is on the lakeshore. The 80-km drive along the road, round the lake to the dam, is attractive and there are spectacular falls below the dam in the rainy season. Between the Praça dos Três Poderes and the lake are sites for various recreations, including golf, fishing and yacht clubs, and an acoustic shell for shows in the open air. Some 395 ha between the lake and the northern residential area (Asa Norte) are reserved for the Universidade de Brasília, founded in 1961. South of the university area, the Avenida das Nações runs from the Palácio da Alvorada along the lake to join the road from the airport to the centre. Along it are found all the principal embassies. Also in this scenic area is the attractive vice-presidential residence, the **Palácio do Jaburu**, not open to visitors.

Congresso Nacional, Praça dos Três Poderes Visitors may attend debates when Congress is in session (Friday morning). The building also has excellent city views from the 10th floor in Annex 3. *0930-1200 and 1430-1630 Mon-Fri (take your passport). Guides free of charge (in English 1400-1600).* The **Palácio do Planalto**, Praça dos Três Poderes The guard is changed ceremonially at the Palácio do Planalto on Fridays at 1730. The President attends if he is available. ■ *Half-hour tours Sun only 0930-1330.* **Museu Histórico de Brasília**, Praça dos Três Poderes, is really a hollow monument, with tablets, photos and videos

Official buildings
Town clothes (not shorts) should be worn when visiting these buildings

telling the story of the city. ■ *Tue-Sun and holidays 0900-1800*. The sculpture *Os Candangos* (P of 3) in front of the Planalto is something of a symbol of the city. By Bruno Giorgi, it pays homage to the *candangos*, or pioneer workers who built Brasília on empty ground. Opposite the Planalto is the **Supremo Tribunal Federal** (Supreme Court). The marvellous building of the Ministry of Foreign Affairs, the **Itamarati**, has modern paintings and furniture and beautiful water gardens. ■ *Guided visits Mon, Wed, Fri 1500-1700, free*. Opposite the Itamarati is the **Palácio da Justiça**, with artificial cascades between its concrete columns. ■ *0900-1200*, 1500-1700 Mon-Fri.

Churches The **Catedral Metropolitana**, on the Esplanada dos Ministérios, is a spectacular circular building in the shape of the crown of thorns, designed by Oscar Niemeyer. Three aluminium angels, suspended from the airy, domed, stained-glass ceiling, are by the sculptor Alfredo Ceschiatti, who also made the four life-sized bronze apostles outside. The baptistry, a concrete representation of the Host beside the cathedral, is connected to the main building by a tunnel, open Sundays only. The outdoor carillon was a gift from the Spanish government: the bells are named after Columbus's ships. ■ *0800-1930, T2244073*.

South of the TV tower on Avenida W3 Sul, at Quadra 702, is the **Santuário Dom Bosco**, a Gothic-style building with narrow windows filled with blue glass mosaics, purple at the four corners, giving a wonderful effect when inside. ■ *0800-1800, T2236542*.

The **Templo da Boa Vontade**, Setor Garagem Sul 915, lotes 75/76, is a seven-faced pyramid topped one of the world's largest crystals, a peaceful place dedicated to all philosophies and religions. ■ *Open 24 hrs.*

Brasília: Plano Piloto

T2451070. Take bus 151 from outside the Centro do Convenções or on Eixo Sul to Centro Médico.

About 15 km out along the Belo Horizonte road is the small wooden house, known as **O Catetinho**, in which President Kubitschek stayed in the late 1950s during his visits to the city when it was under construction; it is open to visitors and is very interesting. A permanent memorial to Juscelino Kubitschek, the **Memorial JK**, contains his tomb and his car, together with a lecture hall and exhibits. ■ *0900-1800 Tue-Sun. US$0.50, with toilets and lanchonete.* The **Quartel-General do Exército**, Brazilian Army headquarters designed by Oscar Niemeyer, is interesting. The **Panteão Tancredo Neves** is a 'temple of freedom and democracy', built 1985-86 by Niemeyer. It includes an impressive homage to Tiradentes (see box, page 242). **Espaço Lúcio Costa** contains a model of Plano Piloto, sketches and autographs of the designer's concepts and gives the ideological background to the planning of Brasília. The **Monumental Parade Stand** has unique and mysterious acoustic characteristics (the complex is north of the Eixo Monumental, between the 'Memorial JK' and the rodoferroviária). There are remarkable stained-glass panels, each representing a state of the Federation, on the ground floor of the Caixa Econômica Federal.

Memorials & military buildings

Brasília is famous for its wealth of modern sculpture. Examples are: 'Cultura' (on the University campus), 'Meteoro' (above the Itamarati water-mirror), both by Bruno Giorgi; 'A Justiça' (in front of Supremo Tribunal Federal), the four evangelists in front of the Cathedral and 'As Banhistas' (The Water- Nymphs, above the Alvorada water-mirror) – all by Alfredo Scesciatte; 'Rito dos Ritmos' (Alvorada gardens), by Maria Martins; and the beautiful 'Sereia' (Mermaid), in front of the Navy Ministry on the Esplanada dos Ministérios. A statue of Juscelino Kubitschek stands above the 'Memorial JK'. A short distance west of here is a huge wooden cross marking the site of the first Mass said in Brasília (3 May 1957), at the city's highest point.

Sculptures

Lago Do Paranoá

Palácio da Alvorada

Palácio do Jabaru

Palácio do Planalto

Praça dos Três Poderes

Avenida das Nações

N

Not to scale

Brasília and the Pantanal

Essentials

Sleeping

Prices include breakfast, but 10% will be added. Weekend discounts of 30% are often available but must be requested. The tourist office has a list of pensões

Southern Hotel Sector L *Nacional*, Qd 1 bloco A, T3217575, F2239213, hotelnacional@hotelnacional.com.br Cavernous, old-fashioned and a city landmark with many tour agencies located outside. **A** *Alvorada*, Qd 4 bloco A, T3321122, F2253130, alvoradahotel@zaz.com.br Comfortable high rise with good view from roof terrace. **A** *Bristol*, Qd 4 bloco F, T3216162, F3212690, bristolh@tba.com.br Very traditional, piano bar, 24-hr room service. **D** *Pousada da Nilza*, W3 Sul, quadra 703, bloco A, casa 54, T2265786, F2255902. Family-run, range of rooms, functional, but one of few cheaper options in area.

Moderately priced hotels are mostly found in this sector only

Northern Hotel Sector AL *Eron Brasília*, Qd 5 bloco A, T3294000, F3292698. 5-star. **AL** *Aracoara*, Qd 5 bloco C, T3289222, F3289067, www.aracoara.com.br 4-star, 24-hr room service and international restaurant. The same road gives access to: **A** *Aristus*, Qd 2 bloco O, T3288675, F3265415. Good, TV, phone, money exchange, small restaurant. **A** *Casablanca*, Qd 3 bloco A, T3288586, F3288273, casablance@brasilia.com.br More intimate than most of hotels in this area. Some rooms noisy. **A** *Diplomat*, Qd 2 bloco L, T/F3262010. Good value. **B** *El Pilar*, Qd 3 bloco F, T3285915, F3289088. A/c or fan, TV. **C** *Mirage*, Qd 2 lote N, T2257150. Fan, good value. **D** *Cury's Solar*, Av W3 Sul, HIGS 707, bloco I, casa 15, T1136252, www.conectanet.com.br/curyssolar Cramped but helpful, safe, around 30 mins from the centre (Eixo Monumental) along W3 Sul. Recommended. **D** *Pensão da Zenilda*, W3 Sul Qd 704, bloco Q, casa 29, T2247532, safe. Teresa Tasso, SQN312-'K'-505, T2734844, tasso@tba.com.br, offers accommodation in an apartment in the Asa Sul at US$20 per person (sleeps 5, kitchen, bath, laundry facilities). Excellent value, Teresa gives city tours for US$15-20 per person for 3-4 hrs, and will collect you at the airport if you phone in advance (bus to flat from centre, 5 mins). Rooms to let (**D-C**) from: Getúlio Valente. Warmly recommended. Av W3 Sul, HIGS 703, Bl I, casa 73, near the TV tower, good, cheap meals available, Portuguese speakers, T2268507/9639 and Getúlio will pick you up; otherwise, turn right off Av W3 Sul between 703 and 702, then take first left (an unpaved driveway). Nearby is J Araújo, HIGS 703, Bl G, C35, T2264059.

The hotels outside the city in **Taguatinga** (take 102 or 106 bus, EIXO, 304 or 306 from rodoferroviária, taxi from airport US$33) and **Núcleo Bandeirante**, though fairly basic, are more economical, but it is difficult to get single rooms. Taguatinga is more pleasant than the Núcleo, which is full of *favelas*. There are many cheap hotels and restaurants of a reasonable standard, eg: **A** *Colorado*, Setor Hoteleira, Projeção B, T/F5613500. Price includes breakfast and taxes, with bath, fridge, TV, good, friendly, no English spoken, no credit cards, good food, huge portions enough for 2, in the centre. **C** *Pousada Brasília*, next door at Projeção L, T5625055. **C** *Globo*, CNB4, lote 1, T5611716. Without breakfast, basic. **D** *Solar*, C 7, lote 13, sobreloja, T5635660, near Pão de Açúcar Supermarket, basic and clean. Bus 'Estrutural' from Brasília rodoferroviária to Taguatinga Rodoviária where you change, without extra charge, to 700 bus which passes, in order: **C** *Camará*, QNE 16, lt 8, T5612597 (hourly rentals also). **C** *Palace*, CNB 11, basic, hot water. Bus 700 or 800 (marked 'Eixo') goes from opposite *Pão de Açúcar* supermarket in Taguatinga to old rodoviária in Brasília. Very cheap accommodation in Formosa (see page 484).

Camping The city's main site is 2 km out of the centre, by the Centro Esportivo, near the motor-racing track, with room for 3,100 campers, mixed reports. Take bus 109 (infrequent) from municipal rodoviária. *Água Mineral Parque*, 6 km northwest of city, direct buses only at weekend; mineral pool, showers. *Associação Brasileira de Camping* (Edif Márcia, 12th floor, Setor Comercial Sul, T2258768) has 2 sites: 1 at Km 19 on the Belo Horizonte Rd and 125 km northeast of Brasília at Sobradinho. *Camping Clube do Brasil* has a site at Itiquira waterfall, 100 km northeast of the city, near Formosa; information from Edif Maristela, room 1214, Setor Comercial Sul, T2236561.

Asa Norte Expensive: All of the large hotels in this area have upmarket restaurants, most catering to business visitors. **Mid-range**: *Boa Saúde*, Av W3 Norte Quadra 702, Edif Brasília Rádio Center. Vegetarian open Sun-Fri 0800-2000. *Bom Demais*, Av W3 Norte, Qd 706. Comfortable, serving fish, beef and rice etc, live music at weekends (cover charge US$0.50). *Churrascaria do Lago*, SHTN, Conj 1-A, by Palácio da Alvorada, a number of Brazilian restaurants and some serving Amazonian food. *El Hadj*, in Hotel Torre Palace, Setor Hoteleiro Norte, Qd 4 bloco A. Very good Arabic food. **Cheap**: *Conjunto Nacional*, SDN, Cj A, enormous mall and food court with 50 restaurants. **Seriously cheap**: *Habib's*, SCN Quadra 4, T3274400, Arabic food and pizzas at bargain prices at this upmarket chain restaurant. Recommended. The municipal rodoviária provides the best coffee and *pasteis* in town (bottom departure level).

Asa Sul Expensive: *Restaurant Gaf*, Centro Gilberto Salomão, Lago Sul, excellent international food, especially meat dishes. *Le Français*, Av W3 Sul, Qd 404, bloco B. French food served in bistro atmosphere, classic and modern dishes. *La Chaumière*, Av W3 Sul, quadra 408, bloco A. Traditional French cuisine in suitable surroundings, established 1966, no smoking. *Porcão*, Sector de Clubes Sul, Trecho 2, cj 35, lt 2B, T2332002. Upmarket chain restaurant specializing in *churrasco*, piano bar, large veranda. **Mid-range**: *China in Box*, Comércio local Sul 402, bloco C, loja 13, T3236500. Reliable Chinese, delivers. *Kazebre 13*, Av W3 Sul, Qd 504, loja 2. Traditional Italian. *O Espanhol*, Av W3 Sul, Qd 404, bloco C, loja 07. Spanish paella and seafood, open daily. *Roma*, Av W3 Sul, Qds 501 and 511. Good value Italian. **Cheap**: *Cedro do Líbano*, SCS, Qd 6, bloco A, loja 218. Self-service, some Arabic dishes, friendly, closes 2200. Recommended. *Centro Venâncio 2000* at the beginning of Av W3 Sul, has several budget options, including Salada Mista, lunch only. *Coisas da Terra*, SCS, Qd 5, bloco B, loja 41. Comfortable self-service, lunch only. Recommended. **Seriously cheap**: There are many cheap places on Avenida W3 Sul, eg at Blocos 502 and 506.

    Snack bars (ie those serving *prato feito* or *comercial*, cheap set meals) can be found all over the city, especially on Av W3 and in the Setor Comercial Sul. Other good bets are the Conjunto Nacional and the Conjunto Venâncio, 2 shopping/office complexes on either side of the municipal rodoviária. Tropical fruit flavour ice-cream can be found in various parlours, eg Av W3 Norte 302. Freshly made fruit juices in all bars.

There are 2 English-style bars: *Gates Pub*, Av W3 Sul 403, T2254576, with disco; and *London Tavern*, Av W3 Sul 409. The *Grenada* bar near the *Hotel Nacional* has good pavement atmosphere in early evening. Nightclubs in Conjunto Venâncio, Centro Gilberto Salomão and in the main hotels. *Bier Fass*, SHS Q 5, bloco E, loja 52/53, cavernous restaurant/bar with wine cellar, live music Tue-Sun, open to 0200. *Dom Quichopp Choparia*, SLCS 110, bloco A, loja 17, open Tue-Sun 1630-0300, sports theme bar.

Information about entertainment etc is available in 2 daily papers, *Jornal de Brasília* and *Correio Brasiliense*. Any student card (provided it has a photograph) will get you into the cinema/theatre/concert hall for half price. Ask for 'uma meia' at the box office. *Pier 21*, SCSS, Trecho 2, Cj 32/33 is an enormous complex with 13 cinema screens, nightclubs, restaurants, video bars and children's theme park.

    Cinema There are 15 cinemas in the Plano Piloto; for programme details, T139, entrance is half price on Wed.

    Theatre There are 3 auditoria of the *Teatro Nacional*, Setor Cultural Norte, Via N 2, next to the bus station, T3256109, foyer open 0900-2000, box office open at 1400: the

Eating
The Southern Hotel Sector tends to have more restaurants than the north. At weekends, few restaurants in central Brasília are open

Bars & nightclubs

Entertainment

Brasília and the Pantanal

Sala Villa-Lobos (1,300 seats), the Sala Martins Pena (450), and the Sala Padre José Maurício (120); the building is in the shape of an Aztec pyramid. The Federal District authorities have 2 theatres, the *Galpão* and *Galpãozinho*, between Quadra 308 Sul and Av W3 Sul. Concerts are given at the *Escola Parque* (Quadras 507-508 Sul), the *Ginásio Presidente Médici* (Eixo Monumental, near TV tower), the *Escola de Música* (Av L2 Sul, Quadra 602) and the outdoor *Concha Acústica* (edge of lake in the Setor Hoteleiro Norte). *Planetarium*, Setor de Divulgaoção Cultural, T3256245. West Eixo Monumental next to the TV tower, being restored at time of writing.

Festivals *Ash Wed; Maundy Thu, half-day; 8 Dec, Immaculate Conception; Christmas Eve*.

Shopping Shopping complexes include the vast *Conjunto Nacional* on the north side of the rodoviária, the *Conjunto Venâncio* on the south side, the *Centro Venâncio 2000* at the beginning of Av W3 Sul, the *Centro Venâncio 3000* in the Setor Comercial Norte, *Parkshopping* and the *Carrefour* hypermarket just off the exit to Guará, 12 km from the centre. For fine jewellery, *H Stern* has branches in the *Nacional* and *Carlton* Hotels and at the Conjunto Nacional and Parkshopping. The embassy sector is good for low-priced, high quality men's wear. For handicrafts from all the Brazilian states try *Galeria dos Estados* (which runs underneath the *eixo* from Setor Comercial Sul to Setor Bancário Sul, 10 mins walk from municipal rodoviária, south along Eixo Rodoviário Sul); for Amerindian handicrafts, *Artíndia* SRTVS, Qd 702, also in the rodoviária and at the airport. There is a *feira hippy* at the base of the TV tower Sat, Sun and holidays: leather goods, wood carvings, jewellery, bronzes. English books (good selection) at *Livraria Sodiler* in Conjunto Nacional and at the airport.

Tour operators Many tour operators have their offices in the shopping arcade of the *Hotel Nacional*: *Buriti Turismo*, SCLS 402, bloco A, lojas 27/33, Asa Sul, T2252686, American Express representative. *Toscana* SCLS 413, Bloco D, loja 22/24, T2429233, has been recommended as cheap and good. *Presmic Turismo*, SHS Q 1 Bloco A, loja, 35, T2255515. Full, half-day and night-time city tours (0845, 1400 and 1930 respectively). 3-4 hr city tours with English commentary can also be booked at the airport by arriving air passengers – a convenient way of getting to your hotel if you have heavy baggage. Some tours have been criticized as too short, others that the guides speak poor English, and for night-time tours, the flood lighting is inadequate on many buildings.

Transport
See also Ins and outs, page 612

Air Airport, 12 km from centre, T3549000. Flights to Araguaína, Barreiras, Belém, Belo Horizonte, Carajás, Cuiabá, Fortaleza, Goiânia, Ilhéus, Imperatriz, Macapá, Manaus, Marabá, Palmas, Porto Velho, Recife, Rio Branco, Rio de Janeiro, Salvador, São Paulo, Teresina and Uberaba. Airline offices are in the *Hotel Nacional* building. Bus 102 or 118 to airport, regular, US$0.65, 30 mins. Taxi is US$10 after bargaining, worth it. Left luggage facilities at airport (tokens for lockers, US$0.50).

Buses The bus terminal (rodoviária), T3274631(rodoferroviária, bus and train station T3632281, next door), from which long-distance buses leave, has post office (0800-1700, Sat 0800-1200), telephone and telegram facilities and showers (US$0.50). Taxi to Setor Hoteleiro Norte, US$9. Bus 131 between rodoviária, the municipal terminal, and rodoferroviária, US$1.25.

To **Rio**, 17 hrs, 6 *comuns* (US$32) and 3 *leitos* (about US$64) daily. To **São Paulo**, 16 hrs, 7 *comuns* (about US$30) and 2 *leitos* (about US$60) daily (*Rápido Federal* recommended). To **Belo Horizonte**, 12 hrs, 9 *comuns* (US$20) and 2 *leitos* (US$40) daily. To **Belém**, 36 hrs, 4 daily (US$55, *Trans Brasília*, T2337589, buses poorly maintained, but no alternative). To **Recife**, 40 hrs, US$49-60. To **Salvador**, 24 hrs, 3 daily (US$27). To **Campo Grande**, São Luís, 15 hrs, 1915, US$30, or **Viação Motta** via São Paulo 0930,

1930, or 1820 direct. To **Corumbá**, US$46. To **Cuiabá**, 17½ hrs (US$30) daily at 1200 with *São Luís*. **Mato Grosso**, generally Goiânia seems to be the better place for Mato Grosso destinations. **Barra do Garças**, 0830 and 2000, takes 9 hrs with *Araguarina*, T2337598, US$13.20 return. All major destinations served. Bus tickets for major companies are sold in a subsidiary office in Taguatinga, Centro Oeste, C8, Lotes 1 and 2, Loja 1; and at the city rodoviária.

Car hire All large companies are represented at the airport and the Car Rental Sector. *Avis*, airport, T/F3652780. *Interlocadora*, airport, T3652511 and *Localiza*, Setor Locadoras, T3651616, also at airport, T0800-992000. *Unidas*, T3653343, and at airport, T3651412.

Airline offices *BRA*, SHS Quadra 1, bloco A, loja 71/72, in front of *Hotel Nacional*, T3217070. *GOL*, airport, T3649370, premium rate number, T0300-7892121. *Rio-Sul/Nordeste*, SCLN 306, bloco B, loja 24, T2422590; airport T3659020. *TAM/Brasil Central*, SHN *Hotel Nacional*, Gallery Store, 36/37, T3251300; airport, T3651000. *Transbrasil*, SCLN 202, bloco A, loja 03, T3261101; airport, T3649303. *Varig*, SCN Qd 4, bloco B, T3291240; airport, T3649219. *Vasp*, SCLN 304, bloco E, lojas 80/100, T3290404; airport, T3653037.

Directory

Banks Foreign currency (but not always Amex cheques) can be exchanged at these banks and at the branches of: *Banco Regional de Brasília* and *Banco do Brasil*, Setor Bancário Sul, latter also at airport (ATM, bank open weekends and holidays), charge US$20 commission for TCs. *American Express*, Buriti Turismo, CLS 402 Bloco A, Lojas 27/33, T2252686. *Diners Club*, Av W3 Norte 502. *MasterCard*, for cash against a card, SCRN 502, Bl B, lojas 30 e 31, Asa Norte. Good exchange rates at *Hotel Nacional* and from hotels with 'exchange-turismo' sign. *HSBC*, SCRS 502, bloco A, lojas 7/12, ATM.

Communications Internet: *Café.Com.Tato*, CLS 505, bloco C, loja 17, Asa Sul, open daily. *Liverpool Coffee Shop*, CLS 108, R da Igreijinha. **Post office**: Poste restante, Central Correio, 70001; SBN-Cj 03, BL-A, Edif Sede da ECT, the central office is in the Setor Hoteleiro Sul, between *Hotels Nacional* and *St Paul*. Another post office is in Ed Brasília Rádio, Av 3 Norte.

Cultural centres *British Council*, Setor C Sul, quadra 01, Bloco H, 8th floor, Morro Vermelho Building, T3236080. *Cultura Inglesa*, SEPS 709/908 Conj B, T2433065. *American Library*, Casa Thomas Jefferson, Av W4 Sul, quadra 706, T2436588. *Aliança Francesa*, Sul Entrequadra 707-907, Bloco A, T2427500. *Instituto Cultural Goethe*, Edif Dom Bosco, Setor Garagem Sul 902, lote 73, Bloco C, T2246773. Mon-Fri, 0800-1200, also 1600-2000, Mon, Wed, Thu.

Embassies and consulates *Australia*, Caixa Postal 11-1256, SHIS QI-09, Conj 16, Casa 1, T2485569. *Austria*, SES, Av das Nações 40, T2433111. *Canada*, SES, Av das Nações 16, T3212171. *Denmark*, Av das Nações 26, T4438188. Open 0900-1200, 1400-1700. *Germany*, SES, Av das Nações 25, T4437330. *Guyana*, SDS, Edif Venâncio III, 4th floor, sala 410/404, T2249229. *Netherlands*, SES, Av das Nações 5, T3214769. *South Africa*, SES, Av das Nações, lote 06, T3129503. *Sweden*, Av das Nações 29, Caixa Postal 07-0419, T2431444. *Switzerland*, SES, Av das Nações 41, T4435500. *UK*, SES, Quadra 801, Conjunto K (with British Commonwealth Chamber of Commerce), or Av das Nações, Caixa Postal 070586, T2252710. *USA*, SES, Av das Nações 3, T3217272. *Venezuela*, SES, Av das Nações 13, T2239325.

Laundry *Lavanderia Laundromat*, CLN 104, bloco C, loja 106, Asa Norte. Self-service.

Voltage 220 volts, 60 cycles.

Brasília and the Pantanal

Around Brasília

Planaltina
Population: 50,000

Some 40 km northeast of the Plano Piloto via Saída Norte is Planaltina, originally a settlement on the colonial pack route from the mines of Goiás and Cuiabá to the coast. The old part still contains many colonial buildings. There are two good *churrascarias* on the main street and it is a good place for a rural Sunday lunch. About 5 km outside Planaltina is the Pedra Fundamental, the foundation stone laid by President Epitácio Pessoa in 1922 to mark the site originally chosen for the new capital.

Also outside Planaltina, at Km 30 on the BR-020, lies **Águas Emendadas**: from the same point spring two streams that flow in opposite directions to form part of the two great river systems, the Amazon and the Plate. Permission from the biological institute in Brasília is required to visit. At Km 70 is Formosa (see above). Some 20 km north of the town is the Itiquira waterfall (158 m high). From the top are spectacular views and the pools at the bottom offer good bathing, but it gets crowded at weekends. There are four smaller falls in the area and camping is possible. To get there from the centre of Formosa, follow the signs or ask. The only bus from Formosa to Itiquira leaves at 0730 and returns at 1700.

Parque Nacional de Brasília

Northwest of Brasília, but only 15 minutes by car from the centre, is this park of some 28,000 ha, founded in 1961 to conserve the flora and fauna of the Federal Capital. Only a portion of the park is open to the public without a permit. There is a swimming pool fed by clear riverwater, a snack bar and a series of trails through gallery forest, which is popular with joggers in the early morning and at weekends. The rest of the park is rolling grassland, gallery forest and *cerrado* vegetation. Large mammals include tapir, maned wolf and pampas deer; bird-watching is good (especially Brasília tapaculo, horned sungem, yellow-faced parrot and least nighthawk). ■ *Contact Ibama, SAIN, Av L/4 Lote 04/08, Ed Sede do Ibama, T3161080, or the park's office, Via Epia SMU, T2333251, F2335543.*

Goiás

Goiás is quite a mixture: colonial mining towns, a modern, planned state capital and centres which owe their existence to rapidly expanding agriculture. There is hydrotherapy tourism, a serious amount of fishing and two fine national parks, Emas and Chapada dos Veadeiros. An interesting festival, with processions on horseback, is held in Pirenópolis during May.

With an area of 364,714 sq km and some four million inhabitants, Goiás is one of Brazil's most rapidly developing frontier agricultural areas, producing coffee, soya and rice, most of Brazil's tin and tungsten, and raising beef on the country's largest cattle ranches.

Goiânia

Phone code: 062
Colour map 4, grid A1
Population: 1.1 million

The state capital is famous for its street cafés and is a good place to stop between Brasília and the rest of the Centro-Oeste. Tourism is not as developed as other parts of the country, but the city is pleasant and there are some interesting sights within easy reach.

Just off the BR-060, 209 km southwest of Brasília, is the second of Brazil's planned state capitals, after Belo Horizonte. Goiânia was founded in 1933 and replaced Goiás Velho as capital four years later.

Sights

It is a spacious city, with many green spaces and well-lit main avenues, ornamented with plants, radiating out from the central **Praça Cívica**, on which stand the Government Palace and main Post office.

The unremarkable **Metropolitan Cathedral**, corner Ruas 14 e 19, stands two blocks east of the Praça Cívica. Walk due north of the Praça Cívica on broad Avenida Goiás to see the painted walls of the **Projeto Galeria Aberta**; many city buses are also painted with eye-catching designs.

About 1½ km out along the Avenida Araguaia (which runs diagonally northeast from the Praça) is the shady **Parque Mutirama**, with recreational and entertainment facilities and a planetarium. ■ *Sessions at 1530 and 1630 on Sun*. There is also a pleasant **Parque Zoólogico**, Avenida Anhangüera, some distance west of the main square, with a good zoo, zoological museum, playground, lake and sports fields. ■ *0700-1800 Tue-Sun*.

Museums Just off the Praça Cívica is the **Museu Estadual 'Zoroastro Artiaga'**, Praça Dr PL Teixeira 13, with a collection of local handicrafts,

Goiânia

■ **Sleeping**	**4** Karajás
2 Castro's Park	**5** Príncipe
1 Augustus	**6** Umuarama
3 del Rey	**7** Vila Rica

0 metres 200
0 yards 200

Brasília and the Pantanal

religious objects, animals and Indian artefacts. **Museu Antropológico do UFG** on the Praça Universitária, 1 km east of Praça Cívica, houses wide-ranging ethnographic displays on the Indians of the Centre West. ■ *0900-1700 Mon-Fri*. **Museu de Ornitologia**, Avenida Pará 395, Sétor Campinas, has more than 8,000 stuffed birds and animals from many countries. ■ *0900-1900, except Mon.*

Tourist information *Sictur*, Centro Administrativo, Praça Cívica, 7th floor, CEP 74319-000, T2230669, F2233911. *Dirtur*, R 30 corner of R 4, Centro de Convenções, CEP 74025-020, T2171121, F2172256. Extensive information, maps and bus routes in *Novo Guia Turístico de Goiás*, readily available at news stands, US$2.25.

Excursions   The thermal springs at Cachoeira Dourada, 240 km south on the Rio Paranaíba, are worth a visit, as are the fantastic rock formations of the Serra das Galés at **Paraúna**, 160 km south-southwest off BR-060, and a host of delightful, colonial mining villages within two hours' drive on good (often paved) roads. Travel agents in town can arrange day tours, for example *Turisplan Turismo*, Rua 8 No 388, T2241941, which also sells regular bus tickets.

Sleeping   **L** *Castro's Park*, Av República do Líbano 1520, Setor Oeste, T2237766, F2257070.
Av Anhangüera,   Warmly recommended. **AL** *Augustus*, Praça Antônio Lisita 702, T2241022,
on which many   F2241410. Good. **AL** *Umuarama*, R 4 No 492, T2241555, F2241673. Good. **A** *Karajás*,
hotels are located,   Av Goiás and R 3 No 860, T2249666, F2291153, 3 blocks north of Praça. Convenient
runs east-west four   and comfortable. **A** *Vila Rica*, Av Anhangüera 5308, T2232733, F2232625. 2-star
blocks north of the   *Embratur* hotel, convenient. **C** *Príncipe*, Av Anhangüera 2936 and Av Araguaia,
Centro Cívico; it is   T2240085. Fan, good value. *Paissandú*, Av Goiás 1290 e R 55, T2244925. Fan, 8 long
busy and noisy   blocks north of Praça. *Hotel del Rey*, R 8 No 321, T2256306. Good location on pedestrian mall, fan, good value. Several cheap hotels (**C-D**) near the rodoviária: eg *Star*, R 68 No 537. Basic, interesting clientele. *Itaipú*, R 29A No 178 at the old rodoviária (Setor Aeroporto), T2124055. *Rodoviária*, opposite bus station. Safe, cheap, good. Northwest of the rodoviária are many cheap *dormitórios*.

Camping *Itanhangá* municipal site, Av Princesa Carolina, 13 km, T2921145. Attractive wooded location, reasonable facilities.

Eating   **Expensive** Varied menu at *Cliff Piano Bar e Restaurante*, R 23 No 72, corner Av
Goiânia is much   República do Líbano. Expensive, nice atmosphere. Recommended. *Lancaster Grill*, R
cheaper for eating.   89 No 117, T2420311. *Churrascaria*, A/c, live music. *Le Steak*, Av 85 No 352. Excellent
Good range of bars   *churrascaria*, a/c, good atmosphere.
and restaurants   **Mid-range** *Boi na Brasa*, *Churrascaria* on Praça Germano Roriz (the first large
around the Praça   square due south of Praça Cívica on R 84), open 1100-0100. *Fim de Tarde*, Av 85 No
Tamandaré   301. Good meat dishes (including *picanha* and *kibe*, Arabic appetizer) and beer, open
than Brasília   from 1700. *Costeleria do Marcão*, Av 31 de Março, past Praça do Cruzeiro. Best ribs in Goiás. Recommended. Open from 1700. *Bom Gourmet*, Av 85 No 1676. For meat and chicken dishes, very good, seats on street or in a/c room. *Piquiras*, Av República do Líbano 1758 (near *Castro's Hotel*) and R 139/R 146 No 464, T2814344, Setor Marista, serves regional food – try the appetizer *pastelzinho de piquí* (a regional fruit used in many traditional Goiás dishes).

Cheap Many small eating places near the rodoviária with good food at low prices. *Arroz Integral*, R 93 No 326 (1100-1400, 1800-2100, self-service) vegetarian.

Seriously cheap Street stands (*pamonharías*) sell *pamonha* snacks, tasty pastries made with green corn, sweet, savoury, or *picante*/spicy; all are served hot and have cheese in the middle, some include sausage. Recommended are: *Pomonharia 100*, R 101 corner R Dr Olinto Manso Pereira, behind the Forum, Setor Sul. *Frutos da Terra*, Av

Perimetral 669, for home delivery T2331507/2814049. *Pura*, Av 83 No 193, Setor Sul. Local meat pies (*empadões de Goiás*) are also delicious.

People Club and *Académia da Birita*, R 7 No 1000, Sector Oeste. Dance club, bar and restaurant, very popular, Thu, Fri, Sat afternoon. *Cave Bar*, Av 85, Caravelo Center, entrance through back of Center, access by narrow R 85C, on left. Small pub, nice drinks and decor, foreign owner Gisela, good soft music. *Café Madrid*, R 101, No 353, Setor Sul, behind the Forum. A/c, bar and restaurant, best *paella* in Goiânia, famous for *margaritas*, live music (MPB, saxophone groups), open daily from 2100. Av Ricardo Paranhos, Setor Sul, is full of bars and crowds of young people after 2000.

Bars & nightclubs
Goiânia is famous for its street bars, some with live music

Many sporting facilities throughout Goiânia, visitors welcome. For sunbathing, swimming and waterskiing go to the *Jaó Club*, T2612122, on reservoir near the city.

Sport

Ceramic, sisal and wooden handicrafts from *Centro Estadual do Artesanato*, Praça do Trabalhador (0800-1800); Sun handicrafts markets at the Praça Cívica (morning) and Praça do Sol (afternoon). The latter starts after 1530, until 2100, known as the Honey Fair as all types of honey are sold; also good for a Sun snack, with many sweets and tarts sold along the street.

Shopping

Air Santa Genoveva, 6 km northeast off Rua 57, T2071288. Flights to Brasília, Campinas, São Paulo, Uberaba and Uberlândia. Several car hire firms at the airport. Taxi from centre US$6.

Transport

Buses Rodoviária on Rua 44 No 399 in the Norte Ferroviário sector, about a 40-min walk to downtown (T2248466). Buses 'Rodoviária-Centro' (No 404) and 'Vila União-Centro' (No 163) leave from stop on city side of terminal, US$0.80; No 163 goes on to the Praça Tamandaré.
   To **Brasília**, 207 km, at least 15 departures a day, 2½ hrs, US$5, and **São Paulo**, 900 km via Barretos, US$25, 14½ hrs, *leito* services at night. To **Goiás Velho**, 136 km, hourly from 0500, 2½ hrs, US$5. **Pirenópolis** 0700 and 1700, 2 hrs, US$5. **Campo Grande**, 935 km, 4 services daily, 18 hrs, US$30. To **Cuiabá** (Mato Grosso), 916 km on BR-158/070 via Barra do Garças, or 928 km on BR-060/364 via Jataí (both routes paved, most buses use the latter route), 4 buses a day, US$25, 15-16 hrs, continuing to Porto Velho (Rondônia) and Rio Branco (Acre) – a very trying journey indeed.

Airline offices *Varig*, Av Goiás 285, T2245059. *Vasp*, R 3 No 569, T2246389. **Banks** National banks. Travel agents will exchange cash, poor rates for TCs. **Useful addresses** Immigration office: R 235, Setor Universitário.

Directory

This busy trading centre, 57 km nearer Brasília, has cheaper accommodation than the capital and is more convenient than Goiânia. The **Centro de Gemologia de Goiás**, Quadra 2, Módulo 13, Daia, about 10 km out on the Brasília highway (near the Embratel tower), has a fine collection of gemstones, library, sales and lapidary courses, and will show visitors how real and synthetic gemstones are distinguished. ■ *0730-1630 Mon-Fri*.

Anápolis
Phone code: 062
Population: 265,000

Sleeping and eating **AL** *Estância Park*, in parkland setting 6 km northeast, T3181200, F3181300. Pool, tennis, minizoo, etc, best in town. **A** *Príncipe*, R Eng Portela 165, T3111611, F3240936, and **A** *Itamaraty*, R Manoel d'Abadia 209, T3111444, F3111244, both comfortable. Many cheap ones around the rodoviária (Av Brasil-Norte), eg **D** *Serra Dourada*, Av Brasil 375, T3240051. Restaurant, parking, fans, good value. *Restaurante Caiçara*, 14 de Julho 905, T3243740. Good *churrasco*.

Transport At Anápolis, the BR-153 (Brasília-Belém) turns north and begins the long haul (1964 km) through Tocantins, Maranhão and Pará to Belém, a bumpy, monotonous trip of 35 hrs or more, US$55. There are regular bus services to Pirenópolis (66 km north).

Cristalina

Phone code: 062
Altitude: 1,189 m
Population: 28,500

This town is famous for its semi-precious stones, which can be bought cheaply in local shops. An interesting excursion is to the panning and mining sites amid magnificent rock formations, about 6 km away. Take the BR-040 (Brasília-Belo Horizonte road) and at Km 104 take a left turn along a dirt road, just after the highway police post, to the Cristalina waterfall (11 km along this road). There is a small **municipal museum** at Rua 21 de Abril 156 (■ *0800-1100, 1300-1700, daily except Tue*) and a **C** *Hotel Goyás*, at Rua da Saudade 41, with fan and fridge.

Goiás Velho

Phone code: 062
Colour map 1, grid C5
Population: 30,000

The former state capital, 144 km northwest of Goiânia, is a picturesque old gold mining town with narrow streets, seven baroque churches and many well-preserved 18th-century colonial mansions and government buildings. It was founded in 1727 as Vila Boa.

Most churches and museums are closed on Monday

The oldest church, **São Francisco de Paula** (1761), Praça Alves de Castro, faces the market. There is a good view of the town from **Santa Bárbara** church (1780), on the Rua Passo da Pátria. Also worth visiting is the **Museu da Boa Morte**, in the colonial church of the same name (a small, but interesting collection of old images, paintings, etc). The **Museu das Bandeiras** is in the Casa da Câmara e Cadeia (old town hall and prison), by the colonial fountain. The old **Government Palace** is next to the red-brick cathedral in the main praça. The **Palácio Conde dos Arcos**, Praça Castelo Branco (across from the cathedral), still has its original 1755 furniture on display. ■ *0800-1700 Tue-Sat, 0800-1200 Sun.* The 18th-century **Mercado Municipal** is next to the rodoviária, 500 m west of the central Praça do Coreto.

Sleeping & eating
AL *Vila Boa*, Av Dr Deusdete Ferreira de Moura, 1 km southeast on the Morro do Chapéu do Padre, T3711000. Pool, bar, restaurant, good views. Recommended. **D** *Araguaia*, Av Ferreira de Moura (the road into town from the south), T3711462. Best budget place, fan, comfortable. Recommended. Similar is the nearby *Serrano* (no phone), parking, bar. **D** *Pousada do Ipê*, R Boa Vista 32. Breakfast included, friendly, great lunch, garden. **Camping** Attractive, well-run *Cachoeira Grande* campground, 7 km along the BR-070 to Jussara (near the tiny airport), with bathing place and snack bar. More basic site (*Chafariz da Carioca*) in town by the river. *Dona Maninha*, R Dom Cândido, regional food, good value.

Festivals The streets of Goiás Velho blaze with torches during the solemn Fogaréu processions of Holy Week, when hooded figures re-enact Christ's descent from the cross and burial.

Shopping *Centro de Tradições Goianas*, in *Hotel Vila Boa*, and (cheaper) *Associação dos Artesãos de Goiás*, at the Rosário Church and in the Municipal Market, for local crafts; many types of sugary sweets can be purchased direct from the bakeries.

Transport The rodoviária is 2 km out of town. Regular bus services to Goiânia (2½ hrs), Aruanã, Barra do Garças and Jussara.

Pirenópolis

This lovely colonial silver mining town in the red hills of Goiás, 165 km due west of Brasília, was founded in the same year as Goiás Velho and declared a National Heritage Site in 1989. As the nation's unofficial silver capital, shopping for jewellery and related items here is unsurpassed. *Festa do Divino Espírito Santo*, held 45 days after Easter (Pentecost), is one of Brazil's most famous and extraordinary folkloric/religious celebrations. It lasts three days, with medieval costumes, tournaments, dances and mock battles between Moors and Christians, a tradition held annually since 1819.

Colour map 1, grid C5
Phone Code: 062
Population: 23,000
Altitude: 770 m

The **Igreja Matriz Nossa Senhora do Rosário** is the oldest church in the state (1728), but that of **Nosso Senhor de Bonfim** (1750-54), with three impressive altars and an image of the Virgin brought from Portugal, is the most beautiful. A museum of religious art is housed in the church of **Nossa Senhora do Carmo.** ■ *1300-1700 daily*. Another displays regional historical items, the **Museu Família Pompeu,** Rua Nova 33. ■ *1300-1700 Tue-Fri, 1300-1500 Sat, 0900-1200 Sun*. Pirenópolis was the birthplace of José Joaquim da Veiga Valle, the 'Aleijadinho of Goiás', many of whose works are in the Boa Morte museum in Goiás Velho. **Fazenda Babilônia**, 25 km southwest by paved road, is a fine example of an 18th-century sugar *fazenda*, now a small museum, original mill, no public transport.

All accommodation is filled during Festa (see above) and even the downtown municipal campsite beside the Rio das Alvas overflows; it's better to visit from Brasília at this time. **A** *Hotel Fazenda Quinta da Santa Bárbara*, in garden setting at R do Bonfim 1, T/F3311304. All facilities including *Restaurante Brasília*. **B** *Pousada das Cavalhadas*, Praça da Matriz, T3311261. Central, fan, fridge, best of the budget choices. *Pousada Tavares*, *Pensão Central* and *Dormitório da Geny* are all **D** and mostly for the desperate.

Sleeping & eating

This thermal resort, 167 km southeast of Goiânia, has good hotels and campsites with hot swimming pools. There are three groups of springs within this area: Caldas Novas, Fontes de Pirapetinga (7 km from the town) and Rio Quente (29 km from the town, bus from Caldas Novas); water temperatures are 37-51°C. There are many buses from Goiânia; best reached from Morrinhos on BR-153 (Goiânia-São Paulo). The daily bus from Morrinhos costs US$2, 30 minutes.

Caldas Novas
Phone code: 062
Population: 40,000

Sleeping and eating Very fashionable is **L** *Hotel Turismo-*AL *Pousada do Rio Quente* (4-star) complex at Rio Quente, T4521122, F4521177, São Paulo, T011-8525733, F2825281, Brasília, T061-2247166. Breakfast and lunch, transportation to main pools and recreation facilities included in price, other extras paid for with hotel's own currency, good hotel, accommodation in main buildings or chalets (the *Turismo* has a private airstrip). **AL** *Parque das Primaveras*, R do Balneário 1, T4531355, F4531294. Recommended. **B** *Serra Dourada*, Av Correia Neto 574, T4531300. Recommended. **D** *Imperial*, near rodoviária. Clean, friendly. **Camping** At *Esplanada*, and *Camping Clube do Brasil* site on the Ipameri Rd, 5 km from the centre. Many other *Clubes e Campings*, all with snack bars, eg *Tropical*, 2 sites in town, and *Berro d'Água*, Bairro do Turista. Recommended. *Caminho do Natural*, R José Borges 550, is a vegetarian restaurant; good, but expensive.

National parks

Goiás has two major national parks. In the elevated region 200 km north of Brasília is the popular Chapada dos Veadeiros, which was designated a World

Chapada dos Veadeiros

Brasília and the Pantanal

Heritage Site by UNESCO in 2001. The main attractions are a number of high waterfalls, with palm-shaded oases and natural swimming pools, and the varied wildlife: capibara, rhea, tapir, wolf, toucan, etc. ■ *US$0.50, contact Ibama R 219 No 95, Setor Universitário, 74605-800 Goiânia, T062-2242488.*

Sleeping There is a small hotel (**D**) by the rodoviária in **Alto Paraíso** and a very basic *dormitório* in São Jorge (take sleeping bag or hammock). The best season to visit is May-Oct.

Transport The park is reached by paved state highway 118 to Alto Paraíso de Goiás, then gravel road west towards Colinas for 30 km where a sign marks the turn-off (just before the village of São Jorge). Buses Brasília-Alto Paraíso 1000 and 2200, US$3.60; occasional local buses Alto Paraíso-São Jorge, includes 1600 departure, then 5 km walk to park entrance.

Emas National Park In the far southwest of the state, covering the watershed of the Araguaia, Taquari and Formoso rivers, is the small Emas National Park, 98 km south of **Mineiros**, just off the main BR-364 route between Brasília and Cuiabá (112 km beyond Jataí). The National Park was recently named as one of UNESCO's World Heritage Sites.

Douglas Trent of *Focus Tours* writes: "The near 132,868 ha of undulating grasslands and 'campo sujo' *cerrado* forests host the world's largest concentration of termite mounds. They provide a surreal setting for large numbers of pampas deer, giant anteater and greater rhea, or *ema* in Portuguese. Maned wolf are frequently seen roaming the grasses in search of tinamou and other prey. The park holds the greatest concentration of blue-and-yellow macaws outside Amazônia, and blue-winged, red-shouldered and red-bellied macaws can also be seen. There are many other animals and birds. A pair of bare-faced currasow, white-woodpeckers, streamer-tailed tyrants and other showy birds visit the park headquarters daily.

"Along with the grasslands, the park supports a vast marsh on one side and rich gallery forests on the other. The crystal clear waters of the Rio Formosa pass right by the headquarters and wander through the park. Many have compared this park with the African savannas. As many of the interesting mammals are nocturnal, a spotlight is a must."

Sleeping and eating Mineiros: **A** *Pilões Palace*, Praça Alves de Assis, T6611547. Restaurant, comfortable, and **C** *Boi na Brasa*, R Onze 11, T6611532. Fan, good *churrasco* restaurant attached. Next door **D** *Mineiros Hotel*, with bath and huge breakfast, good lunch. Recommended. Dormitory accommodation at the park headquarters; kitchen and cook available, but bring own food.

Transport The park is 6 hrs by car from Campo Grande, about 20 hrs from Goiânia, paved road poor. The road to the park is now paved; there is no regular transport, but tour operators can organize 4WD trips. The São José monastery, Mineiros, can arrange the necessary permission to visit, turn left out of the rodoviária and walk 500 m along dirt road (or from Ibama, as above, also from Secretaria de Turismo, Praça Col Carrijo 1, T6611551). Day trips are not recommended, but 4-day, 3-night visits to the park can be arranged through agencies (for example, *Focus Tours*, see Tours and tour operators, page 23).

Rio Araguaia

Brazilians are firmly convinced that the 2,630-km-long Rio Araguaia is richer in fish than any other in the world, and a visit to the 220-km stretch between

Aruanã and the Ilha do Bananal during the fishing season is quite an experience. As the receding waters in May reveal sparkling white beaches, thousands of Brazilian and international enthusiasts pour into the area, intent on getting the best camping spots. As many as 400 tent cities spring up, and vast quantities of fish are hauled in before the phenomenon winds down in September, when the rivers begin to rise again and flood the surrounding plains. Without Brazilian contacts, the best way of experiencing this annual event is with one of the specialist tour operators.

Porto Luís Alves AL *Pousada do Jaburu*, including meals. **A** *Pousada do Pescador*, access to boats and guides.

Sleeping
& eating

Recommended are *Transworld*, R 3 No 546, Goiânia, T2244340, F2121047 (1-week group trips in a 'botel' out of Aruanã to Bananal), and *KR International Travel*, R Mexico 8th floor, S 801, Rio de Janeiro, T021-2101238, ex-Peace Corps manager, good for info on the Centre-West region. Boats (US$25 per hr) and guides can also be hired in **Aruanã**, **Britânia**, **Barra do Garças** or **Porto Luís Alves**, guide Vandeir will arrange boat trips to see wildlife, take food and water. Interesting walks in surrounding jungle with Joel, ask at the hotel.

Tour operators

Health Yellow-fever vaccination is recommended for the region. *Borrachudas*, tiny biting insects, are an unavoidable fact of life in Central Brazil in Jun and Jul; repellent helps a little.

The Araguaia is most readily accessible from Aruanã, a port 180 km northwest of Goiás Velho by paved highway, which sees little excitement outside the winter fishing season when its comfortable hotels are booked up for months. Boats can be rented to visit some of the beautiful lakes and beaches nearby. Buses from the rodoviária serve Araguapaz, Britânia and Goiânia. Brazilian Canoeing Championships are also held along the river.

Aruanã
Population: 7,000

Sleeping and eating A *Recanto Sonhado*, on the river at the end of Av Altamiro Caio Pacheco (2 km), T3761230, self-service restaurant, boutique, includes lunch (reservations can be made through T062-2417913 in Goiânia). **A** *Araguaia*, Praça Couto Magalhães 53 (opposite the docks), T3761251. Both have pools and meals available. **Camping** The official campground is a 20-min boat ride away on Ilha Redonda, but open (and full) only in Jul. Restaurants in town rather poor, but try *Columbia*, R João Artiaga 221, T3761298 (opposite Municipal Stadium), clean, good menu.

Mato Grosso do Sul

The state is half covered with forest and the enormous wetland area the size of Portugal (230,000 sq km), called the Pantanal, *which is a mecca for bird and wildlife tourism. This is cowboy country, where over 20 million head of beef cattle graze on 16 million ha of free-range pasture.*

The state of Mato Grosso do Sul was only formed in 1977 when it was separated from Mato Grosso. It has a population of about two million. The Noroeste Railway (passenger service indefinitely suspended) and a road run across Mato Grosso do Sul via Campo Grande to Porto Esperança and Corumbá, both on the Rio Paraguai. Much of the road is across the wetland, offering many sights of birds and other wildlife.

Campo Grande

Phone code: 067
Colour map 3, grid C3
Population: 665,000

A major gateway to the Pantanal, Campo Grande is a pleasant, modern city on a grid system, with wide avenues. It was founded in 1899 and became the state capital in 1979. It Because of the terra roxa (red earth), it is called the 'Cidade Morena'.

In the centre is a shady park, the **Praça República**, commonly called the Praça do Rádio after the Rádio Clube on one of its corners. Three blocks west is **Praça Ari Coelho**. Linking the two squares, and running through the city east to west, is the broad Avenida Afonso Pena; much of its central reservation is planted with yellow ypé trees. Their blossom covers the avenue, and much of the city besides, in spring. City tours are generally expensive and there are few obvious sights.

The **Parque dos Poderes**, a long way from the centre, covers several hectares. As well as the Palácio do Governo and state secretariats, there is a small zoo for the rehabilitating animals from the Pantanal (phone the Secretaria do Meio Ambiente to visit), lovely trees and cycling and jogging tracks.

Tourist offices Maps and books are for sale at the municipal *Centro de Informação Turística e Cultural*, Av Noroeste 5140, corner of Afonso Pena, T3245830 ■ *Tue-Sat 0800-1900 and Sun 0900-1200*. Housed in Pensão Pimentel, a beautiful mansion built in 1913, also has a database about services in the city and cultural information. Kiosk at airport, open 24 hours, T3633116.

Campo Grande

■ Sleeping
1 Advanced
2 Americano
3 Cosmos
4 Iguaçu
5 Pousada LM
6 Village Palace
7 Youth Hostel

● Eating
1 Dom Leon

Not to scale

Museu Dom Bosco (Indian Museum), R Barão do Rio Branco, 1843, is | **Museums**
superb. Its exhibits from the five Indian groups with which the Salesian missionaries have had contact since the 20th century all have explanatory texts. There are also collections of shells, stuffed birds, butterflies and mammals from the Pantanal, as well as a 'monstrous' display showing two-headed calves, etc. Each collection is highly recommended. ■ *0800-1700 Mon-Sat, 1200-1700 Sun. US$0.50. T3833994.*

Museu do Arte Contemporâneo, Marechal Rondón and Avenida Calógeras, displays modern art from the region. ■ *1300-1800 Mon-Fri. Free.*

A *Exceler Plaza*, Av Afonso Pena 444, T3210102, F3215666. Very comfortable, traditional hotel that caters to tourists and businesss visitors. Small pool, tennis. **A** *Buriti*, Av A M Coelho 2301, T/F3212211. Large, and a little past its best. Pool, sauna, parking, restaurant. **A** *Vale Verde*, Av Afonso Pena 106, T3213355. Pleasant and well maintained, small pool. Recommended. **B** *Advanced*, Av Calógeras 1909, T3215000, F3257744, **C** with fan, a little dowdy, very small pool. **B** *Paris*, Av Costa e Silva 4175, T3871795, F3257744. A/c, mini bar, **C** with fan. **C** *Central*, R 15 de Novembro 472, T3846442. Fan, basic, cheaper with shared bath. **C** *Concord*, Av Calógeras 1624, T3843081, F3824987. Very good, swimming pool, mini bar. **E** *Americano*, R 14 de Julho 2311 and Mcal Rondón, T3211454. A/c, fridge, cheaper with fan, a bit run down, friendly, in main shopping area. By Praça Ari Coelho are **E** *Pousada LM*, R 15 de Novembro 201, T3215207, lmhotel@enersulnet.com.br Nice rooms motel-style around coutyard, TV, fridge, terrace, on busy road. **F** with fan, **G** single room, also rents by the month. Good value. Recommended.

Sleeping
Large, mid-market hotels, many with small pools and restaurants, and all very traditional, are found along Av Calógeras, away from the bus station and its budget options

Near the rodoviária There is a wide variety of hotels in the streets around the rodoviária so it is easy to leave bags in the *guarda volumes* and shop around. **A** *Internacional*, Allan Kardec 223, T3844677, F3212729, **B** with fan. Modern, comfortable, small pool. **B** *Palace*, R Dom Aquino 1501, T3844741. A/c, fridge, **C** with fan, some rooms small. **B** *Saigali*, Barão do Rio Branco 356, T3845775. A/c, mini bar, parking, cheaper with fan, comfortable. Recommended. **D** *Iguaçu*, R Dom Aquino 761, T3844621, F3213215. A/c, fridge, bar **E** with fan, modern, pleasant. Internet US$4 per hr. Recommended. **D** *Nacional*, R Dom Aquino, 610, T3832461. A/c, **E** with fan, shared bath, or single. Busy, includes breakfast, real bargain. **D** *Village Palace*, R Dom Aquino, 802, T/F3241954. **C** with a/c, laundry. **F** *Cosmos*, R Dom Aquino 771, T3844270. Nice, quieter than others in area, good value. Recommended.

This area is not safe at night

Youth hostel Campo Grande **E** Large block opposite rodoviária. Laundry, kitchen, reception open 24 hrs. Recommended. Offers Pantanal trips from office next door.

Mid-range *Cantina Romana*, R da Paz, 237. Established over 20 years, Italian and traditional cuisine, good atmosphere. *Casa Colonial*, Av Afonso Pena, 3997, on corner with R Paraíba. Traditional, regional and Italian cuisine, with large desert menu. *Dom Leon*, Av Afonso Pena, 1907. Large *churrascaria*, pizzeria and restaurant, self-service lunch. Live music evenings. *Largo de Ouro*, R 14 de Julho, 1345. No-frills, large pizzeria and restaurant that does a brisk trade. *Morada dos Bais*, Av Noroeste, 5140, corner with Afonso Pena, behind tourist office. Pretty courtyard, Brazilian and Italian dishes.

Eating

Cheap *Shopping Campo Grande* has a wide selection of restaurants in this category, including *Pão de Queijo Express*. There are also lots of good, cheap options around the bus station and Praça Ari Coelho, and several self-service restaurants on R Candido Mariano, Nos 1660-2512.

Seriously cheap *Morada dos Bais*, US$2 lunch Tue-Sat, see above.

Local specialities *Caldo de piranha* (soup), *chipa* (Paraguayan cheese bread), sold on the streets, delicious when hot, and the local liqueur, *pequi com caju*, which contains *cachaça*.

Entertainment *Morada dos Bais* , see above, restaurant and choperia, live music in courtyard nightly from 2030, free. *Opera Rock Cafe*, R Candido Mariano, corner with Joao Crippa. *Stones Blues Bar*, Av Ceara, 2124, T3264957. Large venue with Rock and Roll, Fri is main night. *Tango* , R Candido Mariano, 2181. Techno club, US$7. *Topogigio*, Alfonso, corner with Julho. Lanchonete/bar, popular, basic, local hang-out, open 24 hrs.

Shopping Local native crafts, including ceramics, tapestry and jewellery, are of good quality. A local speciality is Os Bugres da Conceição, squat wooden statues covered in moulded wax. Very good selections are found at *Casa do Artesão*, Av Calógeras 2050, on corner with Av Afonso Pena, housed in an historic building. Open Mon-Fri 0800-2000, Sat 0800-1200 and *Barroarte*, Av Afonso Pena, 4329. Also *Arte do Pantanal*, Av Afonso Pena 1743. There is a market (Feira Livre) on Wed and Sat. *Shopping Campo Grande*, Av Afonso Pena, is the largest shopping mall in the city, on its eastern edge.

Tour operators *Ecological Expeditions*, R Joaquim Nabuco, 185, T3210505, www.pantanaltrekking.com Attached to youth hostel at bus station, see above. Budget camping trips (sleeping bag needed) for 3/4/5 days ending in Corumba. First day travel by public bus free. Recommended. *Vox Tour*, R Cândido Mariano 1777, T3843335, F37258663, English and Spanish spoken, very helpful. *Impacto*, R Padre João Crippa 1065, sala 101, T3251333, Helpful Pantanal and Bonito tour operators established nearly 10 years. Prices vary according to standard of accommodation; a wide range is offered. 2-day packages for 2 people from US$190-600. Transfers and insurance included. *Asteco Turismo*, R 13 de Maio, 3192, T3210077, www.ecotur-ms.com.br/com/as 2-day (1-night) trips from US$60-US$75, depending on activities and hotel. *Time Tour*, R Joaquim Murtinho 386, T3122500, F37212879, American Express representative. *Stella Barros* (Thomas Cook), R Euchlides da Cunha 479, T3211040, F37216020.

Transport **Air** Airport, Av Duque de Caxias, 7 km, T37632444. Flights to Cuiabá, Londrina and São Paulo. City bus No 158, 'Popular' stops outside airport. Taxi to airport, US$6. It is safe to spend the night at the airport. *Banco do Brasil* at airport exchanges dollars. Post office, fax and phones in same office.

Buses The rodoviária is in the block bounded by R Barão do Rio Branco, R Vasconcelos Fernandes, R Dom Aquino and R Joaquim Nabuco, T3831678, all offices on 2nd floor. At the R Vasconcelos Fernandes end are town buses, at the R Joaquim Nabuco and state and interstate buses. 8 blocks' walk from Praça República. Taxi to rodoviária, US$3.60. There are shops, *lanchonetes* and a cinema, US$1.25.

Campo Grande has good connections throughout the country: To **São Paulo**, US$32, 14 hrs, 9 buses daily, first at 0800, last at 2400, 3 *leito* buses US$40. To **Cuiabá**, US$20, 10 hrs, 12 buses daily, *leito* at 2100 and 2200, US$50. To **Brasília**, US$32, 23 hrs at 1000 and 2000. To **Goiânia**, *São Luís* company 1100, 2000, 15 hrs on 1900 service, US$32, others 24 hrs, US$1 cheaper. **Rio de Janeiro**, US$54, 21 hrs, 4 buses daily, *leito* at 1540, US$64. To **Belo Horizonte**, 22 hrs, US$35. To **Corumbá**, with *Andorinha*, 8 daily from 0600, 6 hrs, US$12. Campo Grande-Corumbá buses connect with those from Rio and São Paulo, similarly those from Corumbá through to Rio and São Paulo. Good connections to all major cities. **Ponta Porã**, 5 hrs, 9 buses daily, US$10. **Dourados**, 4 hrs, 14 daily (Queiroz), US$7. Beyond Dourados is Mundo Novo, from where buses go to Ponta Porã (0530) and to Porto Frajelli (very frequent). From Mundo Novo, ferries for cars and passengers go to Guaíra for US$1. Twice daily direct service to **Foz do Iguaçu** (17 hrs) with *Integração*, 1600, US$27; same company goes to Cascavel, US$20. To **Pedro Juan Caballero** (Paraguay), del *Amambay* company, 0600, US$8.50. *Amambay* goes every Sun morning to **Asunción**.

Car hire On Av Afonso Pena are: *Localiza*, No 318, T3828786, at airport, T0800-992000. *Hertz*, No 2620, T3835331. *Locagrande*, No 466, T37213282, F37213282. *Unidas*, No 829, T3845626, F3846115, at airport, T3632145.

Airline offices *TAM*, airport, T3630000. *Varig*, R Barão do Rio Branco 1356, Centro, T3254070, at airport, T3634870. *Vasp*, R Cândido Mariano, 1837, T3218277. **Banks** ATMs at *Banco do Brasil*, 13 de Maio and Av Afonso Pena, open 1100-1600, commission US$10 for cash, US$20 for TCs, regardless of amount exchanged. and *Bradesco*, 13 de Maio and Av Afonso Pena. *HSBC*, R 13 de Maio, 2837, ATM. *Banco 24 horas*, R Maracaju, on corner with 13 de Junho. Also at R Dom Aquino and Joaquim Nabuco. *Overcash Câmbio*, RRui Barbosa, 2750, open Mon-Fri 1000-1600. **Communications** Internet: *Cyber Café Iris*, Av Alfonso Pena 1975. **Post office**: on corner of R Dom Aquino and Av Calógeras 2309, and Barão do Rio Branco on corner of Ernesto Geisel, both locations offer fax service, US$2.10 per page within Brazil. **Telephone**: *Telems*, R 13 de Maio e R 15 de Novembro, open 0600-2200 daily. **Embassies and consulates** *Bolivia*,R João Pedro de Souza 798, T3822190. *Paraguay*, R 26 Agosto 384, T3244934. **Medical services** Yellow and dengue fevers are both present in Mato Grosso do Sul. There is a clinic at the railway station, but it's not very hygienic, best to get your immunizations at home.

Directory

Campo Grande to São Paulo

The Campo Grande-São Paulo journey can be broken at **Três Lagoas**, 9½ hours from São Paulo (motorway) and six hours from Campo Grande by paved highway BR-262. About 16 km east of Três Lagoas is the massive **Jupiá Dam** on the Rio Paraná, which can be visited with prior permission. ■ *0800-1800 weekends and holidays only. T5212753.* Further north are other hydroelectric dams, most impressive of which is at **Ilha Solteira** (50 km, several hotels and good fish restaurants on São Paulo state side); guided tours at 1000 and 1500 weekends and holidays. Excellent swimming is to be had at **Praia Catarina**, with bars, playground and kiosks (6 km). Overlooking the river 35 km south of Ilha Solteira is restored **Fort Itapura**, built during the War of the Triple Alliance, with beach and restaurants nearby.

A *Três Lagoas*, Av Rosário Congro 629, T5212500. Best. **B** *Regente Palace*, R Parnaíba 580. A/c, good value. **D** *Novo*, Av Antônio de Souza Queiroz, near rodoviária. *Restaurant Casarão*, R Munir Tomé 30. Good selection. *Boi na Brasa*, Av Antônio Trajano 487. Recommended for *churrascos*.

Sleeping & eating

Buses Campo Grande-Três Lagoas 0800, 1200, 2230, US$12.50.

Transport

Campo Grande to the Paraguayan border

Ponta Porã is only separated from Pedro Juan Caballero in Paraguay by a broad avenue. With paved streets, good public transport and smart shops, Ponta Porã is decidedly more prosperous than its neighbour, although Brazilian visitors flock across the border to play the casino and buy cheaper 'foreign' goods. At the **Parque das Exposições**, by the rodoviária, an animal show is held each October.

Ponta Porã
Phone code: 067
Population: 54,000

Sleeping and eating **B** *Porta do Sol Palace*, R Paraguai 2688, T4313341, F4311193. A/c, pool, very nice. **B** *Guarujá*, R Guia Lopes 63, T4311619. Recommended. Opposite is **C** *Barcelona*, maze-like building, a/c, restaurant, pool. **C** *Alvorada*, Av Brasil 2977, T4315866. Good café, close to post office, good value but often full. **C** *Internacional*,

Brazilian hotels include breakfast in tariff; Paraguayan ones do not

R Internacional 1267, T4311243, **D** without a/c. Hot water, good breakfast. Recommended. **E** *Dos Viajantes*, across park opposite railway station. Very basic.

Top Lunches, beside Hotel Barcelona. Cheap and friendly. *Chopão*, R Marechal Floriano 1877. Good food at reasonable prices. *Comabem*, R 7 de Setembro, near Casas Pernambucanas on Av Mcal Floriano. For burgers and pizzas.

Transport Air: services to São Paulo, Dourados, Marília and Presidente Prudente.
Buses: to **Campo Grande**, 9 a day from 0100-2130, 4 hrs, US$5. The rodoviária is 3 km out on the Dourados road ('São Domingos' bus, taxi US$3).

Directory Banks: *Banco do Brasil* changes TCs. Many in the centre of town (but on Sun change money in hotels). **Voltage**: 220 volts AC.

Border with Paraguay There are no border posts between the two towns and people pass freely for local visits. The Brazilian Federal Police office (for entry/exit visas) is on the second floor of the white engineering supply company building at Rua Marechal Floriano 1483. ■ *0730-1130, 1400-1700 weekdays. T4311428.*

The two nations' consulates face each other on Rua Internacional (border street), a block west of Ponta Porã's local bus terminal; some nationalities require a visa from the Paraguayan consul (next to *Hotel Internacional*). ■ *0800-1200 Mon-Fri.* **Check requirements carefully**, and ensure your documents are in order: without the proper stamps you will inevitably be sent back somewhere later on in your travels. Taking a taxi between offices can speed things up if pressed for time, drivers know border crossing requirements, US$4.25.

Into Paraguay There are frequent buses and flights from Pedro Juan Caballero to Asunción. A road also runs to Concepción on the Rio Paraguay, where boat connections can be made. For more details, see the *South American Handbook*.

Bonito

Phone code: 067
Colour map 3, grid C2
Population: 17,000

A beautiful area of plunging waterfalls and deep caves makes up the municipality of Bonito, in the Serra do Bodoquena, which yields granite and marble and is clad in forest. There are spectacular walks through mountains and forest; rafting and snorkelling in clear rivers and wildlife such as birds, rheas, monkeys, alligators and anaconda. Bonito's attractions are nearly all on private land and require authorization. As there is no public transport, it is advisable to go on an organized tour. Owners also enforce limits on the number of daily visitors so, at busy times, pre-booking is essential. Bonito is very popular with Brazilian holidaymakers, especially during December-January, Carnival, Easter, and July (at these times advance booking is essential) and prices are high. The wet season is January-February; December-February is hottest, July-August coolest. The **tourist office**, *Setuma*, is at Rua Col Pilad Rebuá 1780, T2551351 ext 215.

Caves **Lagoa Azul**, 26 km from Bonito, is a cave with a lake 50 m long and 110 m wide, 75 m below ground level. The water, 20°C, is a jewel-like blue as light from the opening is refracted through limestone and magnesium. Prehistoric animal bones have been found in the lake. The light is at its best January-February, 0700-0900, but is fine at other times. A 25-ha park surrounds the cave. ■ *You must pay a municipal tax, US$5; if not using your own transport, a car for 4 costs US$20.* **Nossa Senhora Aparecida cave** has superb stalactites and stalagmites and can be visited, although there is no tourism infrastructure.

The **Balneário Municipal** on the Rio Formoso (7 km on road to Jardim) has River excursions
changing rooms, toilets, camping, swimming in clear water and plenty of colourful fish to see. Strenuous efforts are made to keep the water and shore clean.
■ *US$5*. **Horminio** waterfalls, 13 km, consist of eight falls on the Rio Formoso,
suitable for swimming; bar and camping. ■ *US$0.20*. You can go **rafting** on the
Rio Formoso. The 2½-hour trip is a mixture of floating peacefully downriver,
swimming and shooting four waterfalls (lifejackets available). ■ *US$15 per person, min. 4 people, arranged by* Hapakany Tour *and many other agencies, see below.*

The **Aquário Natural** is one of the springs of the Rio Formoso; to visit you
must have authorization from *Hapakany Tour*. Here you can swim and snorkel with five types of fish (remove suntan oil before swimming). ■ *US$25*.
Bird-watching and swimming or snorkelling in crystal-clear water from the
springs of the **Rio Sucuri** to its meeting with the Formoso imakes for a peaceful tour (permission from *Hapakany* or *TapeTur*). Other tours include
Aquidaban, a series of limestone/marble waterfalls in dense forest and **Rio da
Prata**, a beautiful spring with underground snorkelling for 2 km. Parrots and
animals can be seen on the trip. ■ *US$24*. There are also plenty of opportunities for walking trips along ecological trails, horseriding and fishing trips. The
fishing season is from 1 March to 31 October. In late October/early November is the *piracema* (fish run). The fish return to their spawning grounds and
hundreds can be seen jumping the falls.

A *Canaã*, R Col Pilad Rebuá 1376, T2551255, F2551282. Parking, restaurant and **Sleeping**
churrascaria. **A-B** *Pousada Olho d'Água*, Rod Três Morros, Km 1, T2551430, F2551741,
olhodagua@vip2000.net 3 km from town, accommodation in cabins, fan, showers with
solar-heated water, fruit trees, fresh vegetables, small lake, own water supply, horse riding, bicycles. Recommended. **A** *Tapera*, Estrada Ilha do Padre, Km 10, on hill above Shell
station on road to Jardim, T/F2551700. Peaceful location with fine views and cool
breezes. Very comfortable, but own transport an advantage. **B** *Bonanza*, R Col Pilad
Rebuá (main street) 628, T2551315, F2551235. Suites and family rooms available, a/c.
Recommended. Opposite is parking lot, with bar from 1800, darts and *churrascaria* on Fri.
C *Pousadinha da Praça*, R Col Pilad Rebuá 2097, T2551135. Rooms with 2-4 beds (latter
cramped), fan, hot water. **D** per person *Pousada Muito Bonito*, R Col Pilad Rebuá 1448,
T/F2551645. With bath, or rooms with bunk beds, nice patio, clean, excellent, helpful
owners, including breakfast, also with tour company (Mario Doblack speaks English,
French and Spanish). Warmly recommended. Also on Rebuá, at 1800, is a hostal **E**,
owned by the *Paraíso* tour agency, T2551477. Shared bath. Recommended.

Youth hostel E per person *Bonito*, R Lúcio Borralho 716, Vila Donária, T/F2551462,
www.ajbonito.com.br, IYHA. Pool, kitchen and laundry facilities. English spoken, very
friendly. Recommended.

Camping *Ilha do Padre*, 12 km north of Bonito, T/F2551430. On island with natural pools very pleasant, no regular transport, although Hapakany's raft trip ends here.
Four rustic cabins with either 4 bunk beds, or 2 bunks and a double, US$10 per person.
Youth hostel with dorms, US$6 per person, same price for camping. Toilets, showers,
clothes washing, meals available, bar, electricity, lots of trees. You can swim anywhere,
to enter the island for a day US$3. Camping also at *Poliana* on Rio Formosa, 100 m past
Ilha do Padre, very nice, T2551267.

Mid-range/cheap *Tapera*, Pilad Rebuá 480, T2551110. Good, home-grown vegeta- **Eating**
bles, breakfast, lunch, pizzas, meat and fish dishes, opens 1900 for evening meal.
Comida Caseira, Luís da Costa Leite and Santana do Paraíso. Good local food, lunch
and dinner, not open Sun afternoon. *Verdo-Frutos e Sucos Naturais*, Pilad Rebuá 1853,
next to *Bonanza* car park. Good juices and fruits.

Brasília and the Pantanal

Tour operators Sérgio Ferreira Gonzales, R Col Pilad Rebuá 628, T2551315 (opposite *Bonanza*), is an authority on the caves. Recommended. *Hapakany Tour*, Pilad Rebuá 628, T/F2551315. Jason and Murilo, for all local tours. Diving trips US$40 per day. Recommended. *TapeTur*, next to *Tapera* restaurant. Guides, information, tours, clothes shop. Also recommended. For information in English and French, contact Henrique Ruas, T/F2551430, see *Ilha do Padre* or *Pousada Olho d'Água* above.

Transport **Buses** Rodoviária is on the edge of town. From **Campo Grande**, US$11, 5½-6 hrs, 1500, returns at 0530. Bus uses MS-345, with a stop at Autoposto Santa Cruz, Km 60, all types of fuel, food and drinks available. For **Aquidauana**, take Campo Grande bus. Bus Corumbá-Miranda-Bonito-Jardim-Ponta Porã, Mon-Sat, leaves either end at 0600, arriving Bonito 1230 for Ponta Porã, 1300 for Miranda; can change in Jardim (1400 for 1700 bus) or Miranda (better connections) for Campo Grande; fare Corumbá-Bonito US$12.50. Also connections on 1230 route in Bela Vista at 2000 for **Asunción** and **Col Oviedo**. Ticket office opens at 1200.

Car hire *Yes Rent a Car*, R Senador Filinto Muller 656, T2551702. *Unidas*, R das Flores s/n, T2551066.

Directory **Banks** *Banco do Brasil*, R Luís da Costa Leite, 2279 for Visa. There are no *Banco 24 Horas*. Some hoteliers and taxi drivers may change money. **Communications** Post office: R Col Pilad Rebuá. **Telephone**: Santana do Paraíso.

Jardim Jardim, reached by paved road, has a wide, tree-lined main street. A few blocks uphill is *Panificadora Massa Pura*, clean and bright, and other eating places. There is a rodoviária for *Cruzeiro do Sul* buses. From Bonito a road leads to **Porto Murtinho**, where a boat crosses to Isla Margarita in Paraguay (entry stamp available on the island).

Sleeping and eating **E** *Eldorado*, friendly, clean, good food. **E** *Beira Rio*, basic. There are others; 2 *lanchonetes*, *Churrascaria Gaspão*.

Transport **Buses**: to Campo Grande 0530, 1200, 1600 and 2 in middle of night, US$10, 5 hrs. To **Aquidauana** 0730 and 1700. To **Bonito** (US$3.50), **Miranda** and **Corumbá** at 1130. To **Dourados** 0600. **Bela Vista** (Paraguayan border) 0200, 1030, 1500, 1930. To **Porto Murtinho** 0010 and 1530 (bus from Bonito connects). To **Ponta Porã** 0600, 1500; Sun only at 1400 to **São Paulo**.

Directory **Banks**: Elia, a taxi driver, will change money.

Campo Grande to Corumbá

The BR-262 is paved most of the way from Campo Grande to Corumbá and the Bolivian border; rail service along this route has been suspended indefinitely. It is best to make this journey during the day to take advantage of the marvellous scenery.

Aquidauana
Population: 41,000

Some 131 km west of Campo Grande, Aquidauana has several daily buses from Campo Grande. The BR-412 heads south from here to Jardim, with connections to Paraguay (see above). The Ibama-controlled *jacaré* farm, *Olhos d'Água*, is not open to visitors. Aquidauana is one of the smaller gateways to the Pantanal (see below), excursions in fishing boats negotiable, around US$50 per person a day, or via *Chalanatur*, T2413396; six-day trips recommended.

Sleeping and eating *Fazenda Toca da Onça*, see page 644; take taxi, owner also has a campsite. In town, several hotels around the railway station, including **D** *Fluminense*, with fan and breakfast, a/c more expensive. **D** *Lord*, R Manoel Paes de Barros 739, T2411857. Shared bathroom in single room, private bath in double room. Recommended. *O Casarão (grill)*, R Manoel Paes de Barros 533, T2412219. Recommended.

Tour operators All recommended *Buriti Viagens e Turismo*, R Manoel Paes de Barros 720, 79200, T2412718, F2412719. *Lucarelli Turismo*, R Manoel Paes de Barros 552, T2413410. *Cordon Turismo*, R Búzios, CEP 79003-101, T3841483. Organizes fishing trips into the Pantanal. *Panbratur*, R Estevão Alves Correa 586, T/F2413494. Tour operator in southern Pantanal.

Some 77 km further west is Miranda, another entrance to the Pantanal (see below). Here too is a *jacaré* farm, *Granja Caimã*, which is open to visitors. ■ *US$1*. A road heads south to Bodoquena and on to Bonito. Bus Campo Grande-Miranda, seven a day with Expresso Mato Grosso, US$8.50, and others. The Campo Grande-Corumbá road crosses the Rio Miranda bridge (two service stations before it), then carries on, mostly paved, to cross the Rio Paraguai.

Miranda
Population: 23,000

Corumbá

Corumbá is the best starting point for the southern part of the Pantanal, with boat and jeep trips and access to the major hotel and farm accommodation. Situated on the south bank by a broad bend in the Rio Paraguai, just 15 minutes from the Bolivian border, the city offers beautiful views of the river, especially at sunset. Corumbá is hot (particularly between September and January), with 70% humidity; June and July are cooler. Mosquitoes can be a real problem from December to February.

Phone code: 067
Colour map 3, grid B1
Population: 95,000

Corumbá was one of South America's most important river ports in the 19th century and the **port area** is worth a visit. The compact grid of streets includes spacious shady **Praça da Independência** and Avenida General Rondon,

Sights

Corumbá

Rio Paraguai

Docks

Bus to Frontier

Av Gral Rondon

Rua Delamaré

Rua 13 de Junho   Praça da Independência

Rua Dom Aquino

Rua Cuiabá

Rua América

Rua Colombo

Rua Cabral

Rua Joaquim Murtinho

Rua Porto Carreiro

Av Santa Cruz

Rua Mal Deodoro

Rua José Fragelli

Rua Cinaco de Toledo

Rua Edu Rocha

Rua 12 de Setembro

Rua Operária

Rua Firmo de Matos

Rua Major Gama

Rua 7 de Setembro

Rua 15 de Novembro

Rua Frei Mariano

Rua Antônio Maria

Rua Antônio João

Rua Tiradentes

Rua Ladário

Rua 1 de Abril

Rua Oriental

Rua Cáceres

Rua Junqueira

Forte Junqueira

Natureza Tours

Rua Melgaço

N

0 metres 100
0 yards 100

■ **Sleeping**
1 Nacional Palace

Brasília and the Pantanal

between Frei Mariano and 7 de Septembro, which has a pleasant palm-lined promenade which comes to life in the evenings. The **Forte Junqueira**, the city's most historic building which may be visited, was built in 1772. In the hills to the south is the world's greatest reserve of manganese, now being worked.

Emcotur, Rua América 969, T2316996, the municipal **tourist office**, for general information and city maps. The combination of economic hard times since 1994 and drug-running make the city unsafe late at night.

Sleeping
B *Internacional Palace*, R Dom Aquino Corrêa 1457, T2316247, F2316852. Pool, sauna, parking, café. **B** *Nacional Palace*, R América 936, T2316868, F2310202. Good pool, parking. **B** *Carandá*, R Dom Aquino 47, T2312023. Pool, restaurant, good, helpful. **B** *Laura Vicuña*, R Cuiabá 775, T2315874, F2312663. **C** for simpler room, parking, modern. Recommended.

C *Premier*, R Antônio Maria Coelho 389, T2314937. Small rooms, a/c. **C** *Salette*, R Delamaré 893, T2313768, F2314948. A/c, safe, **D** with bath and fan, **E** with shared bath and fan. Recommended. **C** *Santa Rita*, Dom Aquino 860 (unsigned), T2315453. A/c, **D** with fan, noisy, overpriced, good meals in restaurant.

D *Angola*, R Antônio Maria 124, T2317233. A/c, **E** with fan, restaurant. **D** *Beira Rio*, R Manoel Cavassa 109, by the port, T2312554. A/c, cheaper with fan, popular with fishermen. **D** *Lincoln*, R 15 de Novembro 205, T2314483. A/c, parking. **D** *Nelly*, Delamaré 902, T2316001, F2317396. A/c, **E** with shared bath and fan, good breakfast. **D** *Timoneiro*, R Cabral 879, between rodoviária and centre, T2315530. A/c, **E** with fan, cheaper with shared bath. **D** *Pensão do Tato*, R 13 de Junho 720, T2317727. A/c, cheaper with fan, small rooms.

E *Campus*, R Antônio João 1333. Fan, cheaper with shared bath, good value. **E-F** *City*, R Cabral 1031, between rodoviária and centre, T2314187. A/c or fan, private or shared bath, parking.

Near the rodoviária **D** *Internacional*, R Porto Carreiro 714, T2314654. Shared bath, fan, basic, simple breakfast, owner organizes fishing trips. **E** *Beatriz*, R Porto Carreiro 896, T2317441. Fan, cheaper with shared bath, small rooms, simple, friendly, clean. **E** *Esplanada*, opposite railway station. Cold shower, basic. **E** *Irure*, R 13 de Junho 776. Small and clean.

Outside town **B** *Gold Fish*, Av Rio Branco 2799, on riverfront, 4 km on the road to Ladário, T2315106, F2315433. Pool. **B** per person full board *Porto Vitória Régia*, 12 km from Corumbá past Ladário, on the riverfront. A/c, pool, restaurant, boats, camping area. **B** *Pousada do Cachimbo*, R Allan Kardec 4, on the way to the Bolivian border, T2313910. A/c, fridge, country setting by the river, gardens, pool. **B** *Paraíso do Pantanal*, Cunha Couto 1532, Ladário, T/F2315394. A/c, fridge, pool, restaurant, tours organized.

Youth hostel **E** per person *Pantanal*, R Antônio Maria Coelho 677, T2312305, F2317740, IYHA. Recommended. The owner, Sr Pontis, organizes jungle trips, cheaper for a group, negotiate price.

Eating
Local specialities include peixadas corumbaenses, a variety of fish dishes prepared with the catch of the day; as well as ice-cream, liquor and sweets made of bocaiúva, a small yellow palm fruit, in season September-February

Expensive *Peixaria do Lulú*, R Antônio João 410. Good fish and local dishes. *Viva Bella*, R Arthur Mangabeira 1, behind Clube Corumbaense, 1 block from Gen Rondon. Fish, meat, pizza, home made pastas, drinks, magnificent views over the river especially at sunset, live music Wed-Sat, opens at 1700, good food and atmosphere. Recommended.

Mid-range Several recommended restaurants in R Frei Mariano: *Churrascaria Gauchão*, No 879. Good value. *Tarantella*, No 780. Italian. *Barril de Ouro*, No 556. *Churrascaria Rodéio*, 13 de Junho 760. Excellent, lunchtime buffet. Recommended. *Restaurante Peixaria Galpão*, R 13 de Junho 797. Meat and fish. *Soba-Yá*, R Delamaré 1181. Chinese, opens at 1900. *Trivial*, R 15 de Novembro 148, Centro. Good, reasonably-priced buffet. Recommended. *Almanara*, R America 964, next to *Hotel Nacional* has good Arabic food. On the waterfront you can eat good fish at *Portal do Pantanal*. Lots of open-air bars on the riverfront.

Cheap *Drink's*, R Frei Mariano, 564. Economical set meals. Lanchonetes tend to overcharge – check prices. Many good ice-cream parlours: *Cristal*, R 7 de Setembro and Delamaré. Recommended.

Seriously cheap Bolivian snacks in *'Sslato*, R Dom Aquino.

2 Feb, *Festa de Nossa Senhora da Candelária*, Corumbá's patron saint, all offices and shops are closed. 24 Jun, *Festa do Arraial do Banho de São João*, fireworks, parades, traditional food stands, processions and the main event, the bathing of the image of the saint in the Rio Paraguai. 21 Sep, Corumbá's anniversary, includes a Pantanal fishing festival held on the eve. **Festivals**

Casa do Artesão, R Dom Aquino 405, in a converted prison. Open Mon-Fri 0800-1200 and 1400-1800, Sat 0800-1200, good selection of handicrafts and a small bookshop, friendly staff but high prices. *CorumbArte*, Av Gen. Rondon 1011, for good silk-screen T shirts with Pantanal motifs. *Livraria Corumbaense*, R Delamaré 1080, for state maps. **Supermarkets** *Ohara*, Dom Aquino 621, corner Antônio João. *Frutal*, R 13 de Junho 538. Open 0800-2000. **Shopping** *Shops tend to open early and close by 1700*

Corumbá has many travel agencies selling tours to the Pantanal. For more information see page 645: *Mutum Turismo*, R Frei Mariano 17, T2311818, F2313027. For airline tickets, tours, helpful. *Pantanal Tours/Sairú Turismo*, RM Cavassa 61A, T2315410, F2313130, fishing trips, agents for *Cabexy I* and *II*, luxurious floating hotels, day trips on land, US$55 per person, river trips US$15 per person per 3 hrs. Happily recommended. *Pantanal Service*, R Dom Aquino 700, T/F2315998, fishing and photo trips by boat, agents for *Hotel Porto Vitória Régia*. *Corumbatur*, Antônio M Coelho 852, T/F2311532, combined Pantanal/Bonito tours. *JMS Turismo*, RM Cavassa 215, T2315235. Small fishing boats for rent US$60 per day for 3 persons, minivans for trips to Bolivia US$10 per person. *Pérola do Pantanal*, RM Cavassa 255, T2311470, F2316585, river and land tours, good 1-day river tour with *Lancha Pérola*. *Taimã*, R Antônio M Coelho 786, T/F2312179, river trips, flights over Pantanal, airline tickets. *Pantur*, R América 969, T2312000, F2316006, tours, agents for *Hotel Fazenda Xaraés* in Nhecolândia. *Receptivo Pantanal*, R Frei Mariano 502, T2315795, helpful (1-day tour US$50, 3-day US$100, 4-day US$130). **Tour operators**

Air Airport, R Santos Dumont, 3 km, T2313322. Flights to Campo Grande, Cuiabá, Londrina and São Paulo (via Campo Grande). Check whether flights between Corumbá and Santa Cruz, Bolivia, are still operating. If in doubt, fly from Puerto Suárez in Bolivia. No public transport from airport to town, you have to take a taxi. **Transport**

Buses The rodoviária is on R Porto Carreiro at the south end of R Tiradentes, next to the railway station. City bus to rodoviária from Praça da República, US$0.80. Taxis are extortionate, but moto-taxis charge only US$0.65.

Andorinha services to all points east. To **Campo Grande**, 7 hrs, US$22, 13 buses daily, between 0630 and midnight, interesting journey ('an excursion in itself') – take an early bus to see plentiful wildlife, connections from Campo Grande to all parts of Brazil. To **São Paulo** direct, 22 hrs, US$50, 1100 and 1500, confirm bus times in advance as these change (T2312033). To **Rio de Janeiro** direct, 30 hrs, US$55, daily 1100. Cruzeiro do Sul operates the route south to the Paraguayan border. To **Ponta Porã**, 12 hrs, US$20, via Bonito (6 hrs, US$12.50) and Jardim (9 hrs, US$15), Mon-Sat at 0600; ticket office open 0500-0600 only, at other times call T2312383.

Boats The *Acurí*, a luxury vessel, sails between **Cáceres** and Corumbá, once a week, US$600 including return by air. (See page 657, under Cáceres.)

Car hire *Localiza*, airport and R Cabral 2064, T2316000. *Unidas*, R Frei Mariano 633, T/F2313124.

Directory **Airline offices** *TAM*, T2317299. *Visa*, T2311745.

Banks *Banco do Brasil*, R 13 de Junho 914, ATM. *HSBC*, R Delamare 1068, ATM. *HSBC*, R Delamare 1068, ATM. *Câmbio Mattos*, R 15 de Novembro 140, Mon-Fri 0800-1700, good rates for US$ cash, 5 commission on TCs. *Câmbio Rau*, R 15 de Novembro 212, Mon-Fri 0800-1700, Sat 0900-1200, cash only, good rates.

Communications Internet: *Pantanalnet*, R América 430, Centro, US$2.50 per hr. **Post office**: main at R Delamaré 708, fax service. Branch at R 15 de Novembro 229. **Telephone**: R Dom Aquino 951, near Praça da Independência, 0700-2200 daily. To phone Quijarro/Puerto Suárez, Bolivia, it costs slightly more than a local call, dial 214 + the Bolivian number.

Embassies and consulates *Bolivia*, R Antônio Maria Coelho 881, T2315605, Mon-Fri, 0700-1100, 1500-1730, closed Sat-Sun. A fee is charged to citizens of those countries which require a visa. A yellow fever vaccination certificate is required.

Laundry *Apae*, R 13 de Junho 1377, same day service.

Border with Bolivia
If you arrive in Brazil without a yellow fever vaccination certificate, you may have to go to Rua 7 de Setembro, Corumbá, for an inoculation

Immigration Immigration formalities are constantly changing, so check procedures in advance. You need not have your passport stamped to visit Quijarro or Puerto Suárez only for the day. Otherwise, get your passport stamped by Brazilian Polícia Federal at Praça da Republica 37. The visa must be obtained on the day of departure. If exiting Brazil merely to obtain a new visa, remember that exit and entry must not be on the same day.

Transport Leaving Brazil, take Canarinho city bus marked Fronteira from the port end of Rua Antônio Maria Coelho to the Bolivian border (15 mins, US$0.35), walk over the bridge to Bolivian immigration (blue building), then take a *colectivo* to Quijarro or Puerto Suárez.

When travelling from Quijarro, take a taxi or walk to the Bolivian border to go through formalities. Just past the bridge, on a small side street to the right, is the bus stop for Corumbá, take bus marked Fronteira or Tamengo to Praça da República, US$0.80, every 45 mins between 0630 and 1915, don't believe taxi drivers who say there is no bus. Taxi to centre US$6. Find a hotel then take care of Brazilian formalities at Polícia Federal, address above.

Into Bolivia Over the border from Corumbá are Arroyo Concepción, Puerto Quijarro and Puerto Suárez. From Puerto Quijarro a 650-km railway runs to Santa Cruz de la Sierra. There is a road of sorts. A better road route is from Cáceres to San Matías, thence to San Ignacio (see page 656). There are internal flights from Puerto Suárez. For more details, see the *Bolivia Handbook* or the *South American Handbook*.

Directory **Bank** Money changers at the border and in Quijarro offer the same rates as in Corumbá.

Pantanal

This vast wetland – well over half the size of France – between Cuiabá, Campo Grande and the Bolivian border, is one of the world's great wildlife preserves. Parts spill over into neighbouring Bolivia and Paraguay, and the entire area has been opened up to tourism. The water in the Pantanal is not stagnant, since a gentle gradient (1-3 cm per km) keeps it flowing from north to south. The region is drained by the São Lourenço, Cuiabá, Piquiri, Taquari, Aquidauana, Miranda and Apa rivers, all of which are tributaries of the Rio Paraguai.

Wildlife

The animals and birds found here are similar in many ways to the Amazon basin, but because of the more open land, they are easier to see than in the dense jungle growth. You are pretty much guaranteed to see lots of birds, many of them very large. The enormous jabiru stork (*tuiuíu*) is the height of a child at around 1.2 m, and the symbol of the Pantanal. The 300 or so species of bird include the hyacinth macaw, plumbeous ibis, both blue-throated and red-throated piping guans and roseate spoonbill.

Easy to see on the river-banks are the ubiquitous and bizarre *capivara*, a kind of giant aquatic guinea-pig, and the caiman (*jacaré*). You may also come across otters, anteaters, opossums, armadillos, bare-eared marmosets, black-and-gold howler monkeys and marsh deer. Harder to spot are the maned wolf, South American coati, ocelot, margay, jaguarundi and even the puma, jaguar and yellow anaconda. There are also around 230 varieties of fish, from the giant *pintado*, weighing up to 80 kg, to the tiny, voracious *piranha*. Fishing here is exceptionally good (best May-October). The extraordinary thing is that man and his domesticated cattle thrive, together with the wildlife, with seemingly little friction, and local farmers protect the area jealously.

Access

The Pantanal is not easy or cheap to visit. The best starting points are Corumbá, Cuiabá, and to a lesser extent Campo Grande, from where there is public transport all around the perimeter, but none at all within. Wild camping is possible if you have some experience and your own transport. Remember that the longer you stay and the further you go from the edges (where most of the hotels are located), the more likely you are to see rare wildlife.

From Corumbá there is access to the Pantanal by both road and river, offering a variety of day trips, luxury house boat excursions, and connections to many surrounding *fazendas*. Along the road from Corumbá to Campo Grande (BR-262) are Miranda and Aquidauana, both gateways to various fishing and tourist lodges. The BR-163, which connects Campo Grande and Cuiabá, skirts the east edge of the Pantanal; Coxim, 242 km north of Campo Grande, offers access via the Rio Taquari but few facilities. From Cuiabá there is year-round road access to Barão de Melgaço and Poconé, both of which can be starting points for excursions. The Transpantaneira Highway runs south from Poconé to Porto Jofre, through the heart of the Pantanal, providing access to many different lodges, but does not have any bus service. During the rainy season, access is restricted between Pixiam and Porto Jofre. Finally, Cáceres, 215 km west of Cuiabá at the northwest corner of the Pantanal, offers access along the Rio Paraguai to one of the least developed parts of the region.

Tourist facilities in the Pantanal cater to four main categories of visitor. **Tourist facilities** **Sports fishermen** usually stay at one of the numerous speciality lodges scattered throughout the region, which provide guides, boats, bait, ice and other related amenities. Bookings can be made locally or in any of Brazil's major cities. **All-inclusive tours**, combining air and ground transportation, accommodations at the most elaborate *fazendas*, meals, guided river and land tours, can be arranged from abroad or through travel agencies in Brazil's gateway cities. This is the most expensive option. **Moderately priced tours**, using private guides, camping or staying at more modest *fazendas*, can be arranged locally in Cuiabá (where guides await arrivals at the airport) or through the more reputable agencies in Corumbá. **The lowest priced tours** are offered by independent guides in Corumbá, some of whom are unreliable; some travellers have reported serious problems here (see below). For those with the barest minimum of funds, a glimpse of the Pantanal and its wildlife can be had on the bus ride from Campo Grande to Corumbá, by lodging or camping near the ferry crossing over the Rio Paraguai (Porto Esperança), and by staying in Poconé and day-walking or hitching south along the Transpantaneira.

Choosing a tour

Most tours combine 'safari' jeep trips, river-boat trips, piranha fishing and horse riding with accommodation in lodges. Excursions often take place at sunset and sunrise as these are the best times for spotting bird and wildlife. A two-day trip, with a full day taken up with travel each way, allows you to experience most of what is on offer. Longer tours tend to have the same activities spread out over a longer period of time. The best way to enjoy a tour is not to have fixed expectations about what you will see, but to take in the whole experience that is the Pantanal.

Many budget travellers en route to or from Bolivia make Corumbá their base for visiting the Pantanal. They are often approached, in the streets and at the cheaper hotels, by salesmen who speak foreign languages and promise complete tours for low prices; they then hand their clients over to agencies and/or guides, who often speak only Portuguese, and may deliver something quite different. Similarly, guides at the airport may give the impression that they will lead the tour, but they won't. Always ask who will lead the party and how big it will be. Less than four is not economic and a guide will make cuts in boats or guides. Some travellers have reported very unpleasant experiences and it is important to select a guide with great care. By far the best way is to speak with other travellers who have just returned from a Pantanal tour. Most guides also have a book containing comments from their former clients. Do not rush to sign up when first approached, always compare several available alternatives. Discuss the planned itinerary carefully and try to get it in writing (although this is seldom possible – threaten to go to someone else if necessary). Do not pay everything in advance of departure, and try to deal directly with agencies or guides, not salesmen (it can be difficult to tell who is who). Always get an itemized receipt. Bear in mind that a well-organized three-day tour can be more rewarding than four days with an ill-prepared guide. There is fierce competition between guides who provide similar services, but with very different styles. Although we list a few of the most reputable guides below, there are other good ones and most economy travellers enjoy a pleasant if spartan experience. (Once guides are recommended by a guidebook, they often cease to guide themselves and set up their own businesses using other guides to work under their names.) Travellers share part of the responsibility for the current chaotic guiding situation in Corumbá. Act responsibly and don't expect to get something for nothing. (See also Corumbá guides section.)

When to go

The Pantanal is good for seeing wildlife year-round. However, the dry season between July and October is the ideal time as animals and birds congregate at the few remaining areas of water. During these months you are very likely to see jaguars. This is the nesting and breeding season, when birds form vast nesting areas, with thousands crowding the trees, creating an almost unbearable cacophony of sounds. The white-sand river beaches are exposed, *jacarés* bask in the sun, and *capybaras* frolic in the grass. July sees lots of Brazilian visitors and the increased noise decreases the chances of sightings. From the end of November to the end of March (wettest in February), most of the area, which is crossed by many rivers, floods. At this time mosquitoes abound and cattle crowd on to the few islands remaining above water. In the southern part, many wild animals leave the area, but in the north, which is slightly higher, the animals do not leave.

What to take

Most tours arrange for you to leave your baggage in town, so you need only bring what is necessary for the duration of the tour with you. In winter (June-August), temperatures fall to 10°C, warm clothing and covers or sleeping bag are needed at night. It's very hot and humid during summer and a hat and sun protection is vital. Wear long sleeves and long trousers and spray clothes as well as skin with insect repellent. Insects are less of a problem July-August. Take insect repellent from home as mosquitoes, especially in the North Pantanal, are becoming immune to local brands. Drinks are not included in the price of packages and tend to be over-priced, so if you are on a tight budget bring your own. Most importantly, make sure you take a pair of binoculars.

Ecology and conservation

Only one area is officially a national park, the **Parque Nacional do Pantanal Matogrossense** in the municipality of Poconé, 135,000 ha of land and water, only accessible by air or river. You can obtain permission to visit at Ibama, Rua Rubens de Mendonça, Cuiabá, CEP 78008, T6441511/1581. Hunting in any form is strictly forbidden throughout the Pantanal and is punishable by four years imprisonment. Fishing is allowed with a licence, currently US$25. Application forms from Banco Brasil or Ibama Campo, T37822966, wwwsema.ms.gov.br, or ask travel agents for latest details; see Fishing, page 63). It is not permitted in the spawning season or *piracema* (1 October to 1 February in Mato Grosso do Sul, 1 November to 1 March in Mato Grosso). There are also restrictions on sizes of fish species that can legally be caught. Catch and release is the only kind of fishing allowed on rivers Abobral, Negro, Perdido and Vermelho. Like other wilderness areas, the Pantanal faces important threats to its integrity. Agro-chemicals and *garimpo* mercury, washed down from the neighbouring *planalto*, are a hazard to wildlife.

Visitors need to share the responsibility of protecting the Pantanal. You can make an important contribution by acting responsibly and choosing your guides accordingly. Take out your rubbish, don't fish out of season, don't let guides kill or disturb fauna, don't buy products made from endangered species, don't buy live birds or monkeys, and report any violation of these norms to the authorities. The practice of catching caimans, even though they are then released, is traumatizing for the animals and has potentially disruptive long-term effects.

The International Union for the Conservation of Nature is concerned at the amount of poaching, particularly of jacaré skins, birds and capybaras. The Forestry Police have built control points on all major access roads to the Pantanal. Biologists interested in research projects in the area should contact the Coordenador de Estudos do Pantanal, Departamento de Biologia, Universidade Federal do Mato Grosso do Sul, Caixa Postal 649, Campo Grande, CEP 79070-900, T067-7873311 ext 2113, F067-7875317.

Brasília and the Pantanal

Further reading *The Pantanal: Brazil's Forgotten Wilderness*, Vic Banks (Sierra Club Books, 1991, 730 Polk Street, San Francisco, CA 94100).

Essentials

Sleeping   The inexperienced are cautioned not to strike out on their own. There are many lodges with fair to good accommodation, some only approachable by air or river; most are relatively expensive. One option is to hire a car and check accommodation for yourself: in Jun-Sep, especially Jul, it is necessary to book accommodation in advance. An ordinary vehicle should be able to manage the Transpantaneira out of Cuiabá throughout most of the year, but in the wet season you should be prepared to get stuck, and muddy, pushing your car from time to time. Camping away from areas of human activity can allow you to see more wildlife, but is potentially dangerous. Protection against mosquitoes is essential. Care should also be taken to avoid dangerous animals: snakes (especially in the rainy season), piranhas (especially in the dry season), killer bees and the larger *jacarés*.

From Campo Grande LL full board *Pousada São Francisco*, 135 km from Aquidauana in the Rio Negro area of Nhecolândia, T2413494. Accessible only by air during the wet, with bath, fan, screening, horseback riding, price including transport, meals, tours, bookings through *Impacto Turismo*, Campo Grande, T/F067-7243167/7243616. **LL** full board *Refúgio Ecológico Caiman*, 36 km from Miranda, 236 km from Campo Grande. First class, full board, excursions, T0XX67-6872102, F6872103, or São Paulo T0XX11-8836622, member of the *Roteiros de Charme* group (see page 47). **L** full board *Pousada Aguapé*, Fazenda São José, 59 km north of Aquidauana, 202 km from Campo Grande, T6861036. Farmhouse hotel, screened rooms, some with a/c, pool, horse riding, boat trips, trekking, meals and tours included, bookings through *Impacto Turismo*, as above, or T2412889, F2413494. **L** *Cabana do Pescador*, 65 km from Aquidauana on the Rio Miranda, T067-2413697, F2412406, access by Bonito bus from Campo Grande (see page 634). Fishing lodge, includes breakfast. **AL** *Fazenda Salobra*, T067-2421162, 6 km from Miranda, 209 km from Corumbá, 198 from Campo Grande. Recommended. With bath, including all meals, tours, boat rentals and horses are extra, it is by the Rio Salobra (clear water) and Rio Miranda, with birds and animals easily seen. Take bus from Campo Grande to Miranda, and alight 50 m from the bridge over Rio Miranda, turn left for 1,200 m to the *Fazenda*. *Fazenda Rio Negro*, 13,000-ha farm on the shores of the Rio Negro, farmhouse dating to 1920, tours, horses, fishing, T37257853, F37249345, or São Paulo T011-2142777. *Pousada Mangabal*, in Nhecolândia, T2413494, farm setting, horses, tours, walks, bookings through *Panbratur*, Aquidauana, T/F as above, page 637. **A** *Toca da Onça*, 10 km from Aquidauana on the shores of the Rio Aquidauana, cabins, a/c, restaurant, boats, bookings through *Panbratur*, Aquidauana, T/F as above. **B** *Pousada Águas do Pantanal*, Av Afonso Pena 367, Miranda, T/F067-2421242, contact Fátima or Luís Cordelli, very good, good food, restaurant serves *jacaré* legally. There is a good campsite 30 km past Miranda. Alternatively, hire a car in Corumbá and drive to Miranda, but note that the dirt road is bad after rain (consequently not much traffic and more wildlife can be seen). Car with driver can be hired at Salobra for US$25. There are several camping possibilities along the shores of the Rio Aquidauana, including *Camping Baía*, 50 km from Aquidauana, on a bay on the river, trees for shade, boats; *Pequi Camping*, 48 km from Aquidauana, with toilets, electricity; *Camping Itajú*, sandy beach, cabins, lanchonete, shower, electricity, boat rental.

From Corumbá One-day river trips are available on river boats with a capacity of 80 passengers, US$25 half-day; US$50 full day, including transfers and hot fish meal.

Smaller boats US$15 per person for 3 hrs. Tickets at travel agents and by port. Boats may be hired, with fishing tackle and guide, at the port (US$100 per day, up to 3 people, in season only). Cattle boats will on occasion take passengers on their round trips to farms in the Pantanal, but take your own food – it is not always possible to disembark. Ask at Bacia da Prata, 10 mins out of Corumbá on the Ladário bus.

Lodges LL full board *Pousada do Pantanal*, T067-7255267, 125 km from Corumbá near the Campo Grande Rd at *Fazenda Santa Clara*. Working cattle ranch, very comfortable, easy access by bus. Reservations from all agencies in Corumbá; US$190 per person for 3 days/2 nights, minimum 2 persons, good food, drinks not included. Excursions on horse (US$8), car (US$20) and boat (US$20), guides included, canoes, simple fishing gear, motor boats for rent. Try bargaining for reduced rates in the off-season. **LL** full board *Hotel Fazenda Xaraes*, T067-2316777, T011-8704600, Rio Abobral, 130 km from Corumbá. Luxurious, pool, restaurant, horses, boats. **L** *Pousada Do Castelo*, 3 hrs by boat from Corumbá, T067-2313736, F2315040. **A** *Fazenda Santa Blanca*, on the Rio Paraguai, 15 mins by boat south of Porto Esperança (where the BR-262 crosses the Rio Paraguai). Full board, good kayak excursions, horse riding, information from R 15 de Novembro 659, Corumbá, T2311460, or *Flins Travel* (Walter Zoss), R do Acre 92, 6th floor, 602, CEP 20081, Rio de Janeiro, T021-2538588/0195 or *Safari Fotográfico*, R Frei Mariano 502, Corumbá, T2315797. *Fazenda Leque*, Roberto Kassan (contact through Rua América 262, Corumbá, T2311598). Take mosquito coils, unlimited use of horses and boats, on small lake behind the farm, good food, plenty of wildlife to be seen.

The going rate for a 3-day camping photo safari by jeep is US$100 per person for 4-6 people; US$110-120 per person for 4 days. Fishing trips in luxurious floating hotels for 8 (eg *Tuiuiú* T/F2312052 and *Cabexy II* T2314683, from *Pantanal Tours*, Corumbá – must be booked in advance), US$1,200-2,000 per day, minimum 5 days.

Hotels specializing in fishing, all reached from Corumbá by road: **LL** full board *Pesqueiro da Odila*, on the Rio Paraguai, reservations T067-2315623, from Belo Horizonte T031-2214003. Restaurant. **LL** full board *Porto Morrinho*, on the Rio Paraguai, T2311360. Pool. **LL** full board *Pesqueiro Paraiso dos Dourados*, 72 km from Corumbá, Rios Paraguai and Miranda, Corumbá office at R Antônio João, T/F2313021. Tours. **L** *Pantanal Park*, 20 mins by boat from Porto Esperança (where the BR-262 crosses the Rio Paraguai), T0182-215332. Restaurant. **L** *Pesqueiro Cabana do Lontra*, including meals, T067-3834532, 180 km from Aquidauana on the Corumbá Rd. **L** full board *Pesqueiro Tarumã*, Rio Paraguai, 65 km from Corumbá, Corumbá office at RM Cavassa 109, T/F2314771.

Tours out of Corumbá are of 3-4 days, costing up to US$100 (includes all food, accommodation and transport). Travel is in the back of a pick-up (good for seeing animals), up to a maximum of 6. Accommodation is in a hammock under a palm thatch on a *fazenda*. Food can be good and guides provide bottled mineral water (make sure enough is carried). If you want flushing toilets, showers or luxury cabins, approach an agency. Some guides go to *fazendas* without permission, have unreliable vehicles, or are inadequately equipped, so try to check their credentials. Agencies sometimes subcontract to guides over whom they have no control. If you are asked to pay half the money directly to the guide, check him out as if he were independent and ask to see his equipment. Guides will generally not make the trip with fewer than 5 people, so if you have not already formed a group, stay in touch with several guides (most important during Mar-Oct, when fewer tourists are around). We list below those guides who have received positive reports from most travellers: *Green Track*, R Delamaré s/n, between Tiradentes e Antônio João, T2312258, greentk@brasinet.com.br, recommended for those who like excursions that do not involve game fishing. *Katu*, R Dom

Tour operators
Some of Corumbá's many agencies are listed on page 639

Aquino 220, T2311987. Recommended. *Tucan Tours*, R Delamaré 576, T2313569, guide William Chaparro speaks English, Hebrew and Spanish, contact him at w_chaparro@hotmail.com *Saldanha Tour*, R Porto Carreiro 896B, T23116891, saldanha_v@hotmail.com or aguia@brasinete.com.br, owner Eliane is very helpful to travellers. *Colibri Pantanal Safari*, in *Hotel City*, R Cabral 1031, T2313934, Swiss owner Claudine. There are many other guides not listed here, some have similar names, lots have received criticisms (some repeatedly) from correspondents.

Coxim
Phone code: 067
Population: 28,500

Another access to the Pantanal from the east is Coxim, 242 km north of Campo Grande on the BR-163 and halfway between Campo Grande and Rondonópolis; it sits in a green bowl, on the shores of the Rio Taquari. The area has great potential for tourism, but there are no official tours to the Pantanal; it is a great place if you charter your own boat.

Sleeping and eating A *Coxim*, 4 km south of town, T/F2911479. Restaurant. **A** *Santa Ana*, R Miranda Reis on the riverbank, T2911602. Cabins for 4, pool. **C** *Santa Teresa*, 5 km south of town, T2912215, F2911289. With bath, fan. *Piracêma*, by the bridge over the Rio Taquari, restaurant. *Sinhazino*, north of the Taquari bridge. There are several simpler hotels in town.

Cuiabá to Pantanal

For tour operators in
Cuiabá see page 653

The Transpantaneira Highway, built in 1976, was originally projected to connect Cuiabá with Corumbá, but currently goes only as far as Porto Jofre on the Rio Cuiabá. Work has been suspended indefinitely because of difficulties, costs and ecological considerations.

Poconé
Phone code: 065
Population: 31,500

A paved road turns south off the main Cuiabá-Cáceres road to Poconé, founded in 1781 and known as the Cidade Rosa. Until 1995 there was much *garimpo* activity north of town and many slag heaps can be seen from the road.

Sleeping and eating E *Hotel Joá*, with bath, basic, acceptable, car parking. Also on the Transpantaneira just south of town are *Aurora do Pantanal*, T37211339, and **A** *Hotel Santa Cruz*, Km 1, T37211439. *Three Poderes Restaurant*, R Beri. Cheap good food. *Doce e Mel*, Praça Matriz. Pleasant café serving good sweets and coffee.

Transport Buses: from **Cuiabá** US$7.50 by *TUT*, T3224985, 6 a day between 0600 and 1900. Poconé has a 24-hr gas station with all types of fuel, but closed on Sun.

Porto Jofre

From Poconé the Transpantaneira runs 146 km south to Porto Jofre, where there is just a gas station, gasoline and diesel, but no alcohol fuel is available. At the entrance to the Pantanal there is a gate across the road where drivers are given a list of rules of conduct. The road is of earth, in poor condition, with ruts, holes and many bridges that need care in crossing. The easiest access is in the dry season (July-September), which is also the best time for seeing birds, and, in September, the trees are in bloom. In the wet, especially January-February, there is no guarantee that the Transpantaneira will be passable. The wet season, however, is a good time to see many of the more shy animals because more fruit, new growth and other high calorie foods are available, and there are fewer people.

Campos de Jofre

Campos de Jofre, about 20 km north of Porto Jofre, is magnificent between August and October, with very large concentrations of birds and animals. In

Poconé you can hitch (not much traffic, bumpy, especially in a truck) to Porto Jofre, or hire a vehicle in Cuiabá. You will get more out of this part of the Pantanal by going with a guide; a lot can be seen from the Transpantaneira in a hired car, but guides can take you into *fazendas* and will point out wildlife. Recommended guides in Cuiabá are listed below. Although there are gas stations in Pixaim and Porto Jofre, they are not always well stocked, so it is best to carry extra fuel.

Pixaim is 63 km south of Poconé, a journey of two hours in the dry season and up to five in the wet. It is the only easily accessible settlement in the Pantanal with any tourist infrastructure. It is located where a bridge crosses the Rio Pixaim and has two hotels, a fuel station (all types available, check that the pump is set to zero) and a tyre-repair shop (*borracheria*). Next to the *Pousada Pantaneira* (see below) is a private Jaguar Ecological Reserve, owned by *pantaneiros*, funded by donation. Further details, donations and reservations can be made through *Focus Tours* (see page 24), who helped to set up the reserve.

Pixaim
Colour map 3, grid B2

Sleeping and eating in Pixaim and on the Transpantaneira L *Pantanal Mato Grosso*, T/F065- 3219445, modern cabins, 35 rooms for 3-6 people, with full board, fan, clean, hot water (also family-size apartments with a/c), good home-grown food, in radio contact with office on R Barão de Melgaço in Cuiabá, camping possible, boat rental with driver US$30 per hr. On the opposite bank of the Rio Pixaim is **A** *Pousada Pixaim*, T37211899. Full board (meals also available separately), built on stilts, rooms with a/c or fan, mosquito-netted windows, hot water, electricity 24 hrs, pleasant setting, boat trips – US$30 per hr with driver, camping possible, US$10 per tent or free if you eat in the restaurant. Recommended. Bookings through *Faunatur* in Cuiabá (reservations through *Focus Tours*, see page 23).

AL *Hotel-Fazenda Cabanas do Pantanal*, 142 km from Cuiabá, 50 km from Poconé by the Rio Pixaim, on the northern edge of the Pantanal. 10 chalet bedrooms with bath, restaurant, boat trips (few in dry season), horse-riding, fishing, helpful proprietor and staff, everything except boat trips and bar drinks included in price (booking: *Confiança*, Cuiabá). **A** *Pousada Araras*, Km 32 on Transpantaneira. 14 rooms with bath. Recommended. Pool, good food, home-made *cachaça*, T6822800, F6821260, or book through *Expeditours* in Cuiabá. **A** *Pousada Pantaneira*, full board, 7 rooms with 2-3 bunk beds each, bath, simple, owned and operated by *pantaneiros* (reservations through *Faunatur* in Cuiabá, or through *Focus Tours*, see page 24), about 45 km from Pixaim.

L *Sapé Pantanal Lodge*, Caixa Postal 2241 – CEP 78020-970, Cuiabá, T3911442, www.sapehotel.com.br Rustic wooden accommodation on stilts aimed at luxury market. A complete programme includes road transport from Cuiabá airport to Barão de Melgaço (wet season) or Porto Cercado (dry season), with onward river transportation (around 1½ hrs). Specializes in sport fishing. Outboard powered boats with experienced guides at guests' disposal; optional trekking and horse riding in dry season, paddling in wet. English, French, Spanish spoken. Closed 20 Dec-31 Jan.

Situated on Rio Cuiabá, 130 km from Cuiabá (*TUT* bus leaves Cuiabá at 0730 and 1500, US$6.50), Barão de Melgaço is reached by two roads. The shorter, via Santo Antônio de Leverger, is unpaved from Santo Antônio to Barão (closed in the wet season), via São Vicente is longer, but has more pavement. The way to see the Pantanal from here is by boat down the Rio Cuiabá. Boat hire, for example from *Restaurant Peixe Vivo* on waterfront, costs up to

Barão de Melgaço
Colour map 3, grid A2

US$85 for a full day; or enquire with travel agencies in Cuiabá. The best time of day is sunset, but it would need some organizing to be in the best part at the best time without too much boating in the dark. Remember to protect against the sun when on the water.

Initially farms and small habitations line the river banks, but they become more forested, with lovely combinations of flowering trees (best seen September-October). After a while, a small river to the left leads to the Baia and Lakes Chacororé and Sia Mariana, which join each other. Boats can continue beyond the lakes to the Rio Mutum, but a guide is essential because there are many dead ends. The area is rich in birdlife and the waterscapes are beautiful.

Sleeping and eating In the town are *Barão Tour Hotel*, apartments with a/c, restaurant, boat trips and excursions (Cuiabá T3221568, or *Melgatur*), and, much humbler, *Nossa Senhora do Carmo Hotel* on the waterfront and *Pousada e Lanchonete Francisco de Asis* on the main road down to the waterfront. *Mercadinho do Povo* minimarket sells provisions, including cheap hats. **Around Barão de Melgaço** On Sia Mariana are *Pousada do Barão*, 6 chalets with bath, swimming pool, first class, boat and trekking expeditions (book through *Melgatur*). *Restaurant Flamingo*, simple food, rooms, camping with permission, popular with fishermen; 1 other restaurant. Barão de Melgaço is also the starting point for the **L** *Pousada Passárgada*, programmes from 3 days up, full board, boat, car and trekking expeditions, transport from Barão de Melgaço, owner speaks English, French and German, food excellent. Highly recommended, closed Dec-Feb; reservations T37131128, in Barão de Melgaço on riverside, through *Nature Safaris*, Av Marechal Rondon, Barão de Melgaço, or São Paulo T011-2845434, or Rio de Janeiro T021-2873390. Much cheaper if booked direct with the owner, Maré Sigaud, Mato Grosso, CEP 786807, *Pousada Passárgada*, Barão de Melgaço.

Mato Grosso

The state, with a population of about 2.5 million, is cattle ranching country. The vast flat marshland of the Pantanal in the southeast of the state changes to rolling hills and low plateaus north of the capital Cuiabá.

Although the area that is now Mato Grosso and Mato Grosso do Sul was demarcated as Spanish territory, it was the Portuguese Aleixo Garcia who was the first to explore it in 1525. Jesuits and then *bandeirantes* entered the Mato Grosso for their different ends during the 17th and early 18th centuries, and when gold was discovered near Cuiabá a new influx of explorers began. Mato Grosso became a captaincy in 1748 and the borders between Portuguese and Spanish territories were resolved in the following years. Throughout the 19th century, after the decline in gold extraction, the province's economy stagnated and its population dwindled. This trend was reversed when the rubber boom brought immigrants in the early 20th century to the north of the region. Getúlio Vargas' 'March to the West' in the 1940s brought added development, accompanied first by the splitting off of Rondônia and, some 80 years later, by the formation of Mato Grosso do Sul in 1977.

Cuiabá

An important starting point for trips into the Pantanal, Cuiabá is the state capital and a visibly wealthy city. It has a number of leafy praças and is known as the Cidade Verde (green city). Situated on the Rio Cuiabá, an upper tributary of the Rio Paraguai, it is in fact two cities: Cuiabá on the east bank of the river and Várzea Grande, where the airport is located, on the west. It is very hot; coolest months for a visit are June, July and August in the dry season.

Phone code: 065
Colour map 3, grid A2
Population: 470,000

Getting there Flights arrive at the airport in Várzea Grande. There are buses and taxis to the centre. Take any white Tuiuiú bus, name written on the side, in front of the airport to Av Tte Col Duarte. Interstate buses arrive at the rodoviária north of the centre. Town buses (see below) stop at the entrance.

Ins & outs
See also Transport,
page 653

  Getting around Many bus routes have stops in the vicinity of Praça Ipiranga. Bus 501 or 505 (Universidade) to University museums and zoo (ask for 'Teatro') from Av Tte Col Duarte by Praça Bispo Dom José, a triangular park just east of Praça Ipiranga. To rodoviária, No 202 from R Joaquim Murtinho behind the cathedral, about 20 mins.

  Tourist offices Secretaria de Desenvolvimento do Turismo, *Sedtur*, Praça da República 131, next to the post office building, T/F6249060, Mon-Fri, 0700-1800. Good maps, friendly, helpful regarding general information, hotels and car hire, some English and Spanish spoken. Also very helpful in settling disputes with local tour companies. *Ramis Bucair*, R Pedro Celestino 280, is good for detailed maps of the region.

  Security The port area is best avoided, even in daylight.

Cuiabá

Sleeping
1 Áurea Palace
2 Best Western Mato Grosso Pálace
3 Jaguar Palace
4 Mato Grosso
5 Pousada Ecoverde
6 Presidente
7 Samara

Eating
1 Hong Kong

Brasília and the Pantanal

Sights

Cuiabá has an imposing government palace and other fine buildings round the green **Praça da República**. On the square is the **cathedral**, with a plain, imposing exterior, two clock towers and, inside, coloured glass mosaic windows and doors. Behind the altar is a huge mosaic of Christ in majesty, with smaller mosaics in side chapels. Beside the cathedral is another leafy square, **Praça Alencastro**.

On **Praça Ipiranga**, at the junction of Avenidas Isaac Póvoas and Tenente Coronel Duarte, a few blocks southwest of the central squares, there are market stalls and an iron bandstand from Huddersfield in the UK, or Hamburg in Germany, depending on which story you believe.

On a hill beyond the square is the extraordinary church of **Bom Despacho**, built in the style of Notre Dame. It is best viewed from afar as it is sadly run down and not open to visitors. In front of the Assembléia Legislativa, Praça Moreira Cabral, is a point marking the **Geogedesic Centre of South America** (see also under Chapada dos Guimarães, below).

Museums   The rather dusty **Museus de Antropologia, História Natural e Cultura Popular**, in the Fundação Cultural de Mato Grosso, Praça da República 151, are worth a look. There are interesting historical photos, a contemporary art gallery, Indian weapons, archaeological finds and pottery. The section of stuffed wildlife from the Pantanal is disturbingly compelling. ■ *0800-1730 Mon-Fri, US$0.50.*

At the entrance to Universidade de Mato Grosso by the swimming pool, 10 minutes by bus from the centre, is the small **Museu do Índio/Museu Rondon** with well-displayed exhibits. Carrying on along the road through the campus, signed on the left before a right turn in the road, is the **Zoológico**. The jacaré, capybara, tortoise and tapir pen can be seen at any time, but are best in the early morning or late afternoon. It also has coatis, otters, emu, monkeys, peccaries, birds, etc. ■ *0800-1100, 1330-1700 (closed Mon), free.* Opposite the zoo is the theatre.

Excursions   The **Águas Quentes** hot springs, 86 km (9 km south of the BR-163, 77 km east of Cuiabá), can be visited. **L** *Hotel Águas Quentes* at the springs, all meals included, reservations through *Hotel Mato Grosso Palace*, address below, T6246637. The waters fill pools of 42°C and 36°C; no buses go there, arrange transport through *Hotel Mato Grosso Palace*.

Essentials

Sleeping   **L** *Áurea Palace*, Gen Mello 63, T/F3223377. Pleasant rooms, restaurant, swimming pool, good. **L** *Best Western Mato Grosso Palace*, Joaquim Murtinho 170, T6247747, F3212386. Central, sedate and very popular, restaurant but no pool. **A** *Almanara*, Av Col Escolástico 510, T3231244, F3232049. **A** *Skala Palace*, R Jules Rimet 26, T3224347. Restaurant, smart lobby, front rooms noisy.

B *Brazil*, R Jules Rimet 20, T6212703. A/c, fridge, parking, **D** with fan, cheaper with shared bath, ground floor rooms are best. **B** *Jaguar Palace*, Av G Vargas 600, T6244404, jaguarph@zaz.com.br New extension with rooms around large pool. Older rooms are large with sofas and wonderfully old-fashioned. Once used by prospectors who paid for their room in gold nuggets. Very comfortable and good value. Recommended. **B** *Real Palace*, 13 de Junho 102, Praça Ipiranga, T3215375, F6111141. Large rooms, some with a/c, good breakfast. **C** *Grande*, R Jules Rimet 30, T6213852. A/c, **D**

Monsoons

Although the Brazilian Monsoons (monções) were given their name in association with the weather, they were not, in fact, rainy seasons. They were, like their predecessors, the bandeirantes, another breed of pioneer who expanded Brazil's frontiers. In Portuguese, the monções were winds which determined the seasons which were best for sailing. When the term reached Brazil it was applied to the rainy seasons, rather than the winds, because the rain determined whether journeys into the interior could be made. From about the second decade of the 18th century, the expeditions which penetrated into the far west of Brazil took to the rivers, rather than going on foot. The people who made these trips acquired the name Monsoons.

Taking the Rio Tietê out of São Paulo, the Monsoons sailed to the heart of the continent. Their main destination was the gold mines of Senhor Bom Jesus do Cuiabá and the alluvial deposits on the Rio Coxipó-Mirim. Various routes were tried until the best way was found of getting from the Tietê to Mato Grosso. When this route had been established convoys would set out once a year to trade with the miners and bring the gold back to São Paulo. It was not an easy journey. Everything, including animals, had to be taken to Cuiabá on boats which were modelled on the Indian pirogue, using navigation which was also borrowed from the indigenous people. The remoteness of Cuiabá was only matched by the legends of vast wealth which drew the Monsoons to the area. It took longer to get from São Paulo to Cuiabá than it did from Rio de Janeiro to Lisbon; the journey time was about five months, as long as it took to get from Lisbon to India. Many lives and a great deal of merchandise was lost on the rivers, but this remained the only form of communication between São Paulo and Mato Grosso until the third decade of the 19th century. In the same way that the bandeirantes extended Brazil's boundaries and established Portuguese rule over the south and southwest, so the Monsoons brought the far west into Portuguese possession.

Taken from Sérgio Buarque de Holanda, The Monsoons, chapter 10 of Richard M Morse (ed), The Bandeirantes.

---

with fan, cheaper with shared bath, basic. **C** *Ipanema*, R Jules Rimet, T6213069. A/c, **D** with fan, cheaper with shared bath, good value, good breakfast. Recommended. **C** *Mato Grosso*, R Comandante Costa 2522, T6147777, F6147053, bwmt@zaz.com.br Excellent value, friendly, central, a/c, **D** with fan. Good restaurant. Recommended. **C** *Samara*, R Joaquim Murtinho 270, T3226001. Central, with bath, hot shower, fan, basic but good, cheaper with shared bath.

E *Pousada Ecoverde*, R Pedro Celestino 391, T6241386. 5 rooms with shared bath around a courtyard in colonial family house. **F**, single. Kitchen, laundry facilities and lovely walled garden with hammocks. Highly recommended. **E** *Presidente*, Barão de Melgaço and Av G Vargas 155A, T6241386, on a busy central corner with lots of traffic outside, a/c. Popular and cheap but very badly run down. **F** with fan, fridge, cheaper with shared bath.

Youth hostel F per person *Portal do Pantanal*, Av Isaac Póvoas 655, T/F6248999, www.portaldopantanal.com.br Breakfast included, Internet access (US$2.50 per hr), laundry, kitchen.

Lots of restaurants in the very centre are only open for lunch. On Av CPA are many good restaurants and small snack bars. **Eating**

Expensive *Getúlio*, Av Getúlio Vargas 1147. Somewhat pretentious a/c restaurant with pavement tables, dance floor and sushi bar. Excellent food, with meat specialities and pizza.

Brasília and the Pantanal

►► Guaraná

"In order to obtain guaraná, their favourite stimulant, the inhabitants of Cuiabá organized canoe expeditions lasting more than six months along the Tapajoz. The paste is compressed into a sausage shape and grated on the horny tongue of a pirarucu fish, which is kept in a deerskin pouch. These details are significant, because it is believed that the use of a metal grater or a different kind of leather pouch would cause the precious substance to lose its peculiar properties."

Thus Claude Levi-Strauss described the harvesting of guaraná in the 1930's. Today you can still buy the pirarucu tongues in markets in the Amazon region.

Guaraná is prepared into a paste from the fruit of the creeper Paullinia sorbilis. The Maué Indians of Cuiabá used to be the only ones to appreciate it as a stimulant but it is now world renowned. Guaraná is everywhere, consumed as a soft drink in such quantities that it rivals Coca-Cola in popularity, with massive advertising campaigns and sponsorship deals to boost sales. Taken in its powder form and made into an infusion, it as a natural pick-me-up with similar properties to coffee. It is even available now as a sports drink, consumed by fitness-crazy Brazilians after a long game of futevolei on the beach or a session in the gym. You can also buy it in chewing-gum form in Europe, where it is popular as an energiser after a hard night's clubbing.

Whether or not it really works is another matter; but it remains a popular drink today and some people combine it with alcohol to make cocktails with a distinctly Brazilian flavour. But to enjoy the real effects, perhaps you need to use the same method as the Cuiabans did in the 1930s.

Mid-range *Cedros*, Praça 8 de Abril 750, Goiabeiras. Fan-cooled, friendly and very popular place offering wide selection of Arabic food, including *tabule* salad and 'pizza' made with pitta bread. Delivery service, T6249134. Recommended. *China in Box*, Av Lavapés 70, T6238400. Chinese food with a Brazilian twist, also fish dishes and deserts. Open daily for lunch and dinner; delivery service. *Choppão*, Praça 8 de Abril. Established 30 years, this local institution buzzes at any time of the day or night. Go for huge portions of delicious food or just for *chopp* served by fatherly waiters. The house dish of chicken soup promises to give diners drinking strength in the early hours and is a meal in itself. Warmly recommended. *Lig-China*, R Presidente Marques 960. Sophisticated, air-conditioned restaurant with standard Chinese and Japanese menu. Open daily for lunch and dinner til 2400, also delivers.

Cheap There are several restaurants and lanchonetes on R Jules Rimet across from the rodoviária. *Hong Kong*, Av G Vargas 647, opposite *Jaguar Hotel*. Self-service Chinese, good quality for price.

Seriously cheap *Lanchonete Presidente*, Hamburgers and sandwiches, next to hotel of same name, open late for eating, drinking and TV watching.

Entertainment Cuiabá is quite lively at night, bars with live music and dance on Av CPA. *Bierhaus*, Isaac Póvoas 1200. Large, sophisticated, semi open-air bar/restaurant with music. *Choppão*, see eating above. *Tucano* Av CPA, bar/restaurant specializing in pizza with beautiful view, open daily 1800-2300. 4 cinemas in town.

Shopping Handicrafts in wood, straw, netting, leather, skins, Pequi liquor, crystallized *caju* fruit, compressed *guaraná* fruit, Indian objects on sale at the airport, rodoviária, craft shops in centre, and daily market, Praça da República, interesting. The *Casa de Artesão*, Praça do Expedicionário 315, T3210603, sells all types of local crafts in a restored building. Recommended. Fish and vegetable market, picturesque, at the riverside.

In **Cuiabá**: *Confiança*, R Cândido Mariano 434, T6234141, very helpful travel agency, tours to PantanalUS$75 per day. Also recommended *Pantanal Explorers*, Av Gov Ponce de Arruda 670, T6822800, sightseeing, fishing trips for 4-5 days by boat. *Anaconda*, R Mal Deodoro 2142, T6244142, F6246242, anaconda@ anacondapantanal.com.br Upmarket agency providing airport transfers, all meals and high standard of accommodation both in Cuiaba before departure and on trips. Pantanal 1-, 2- and 3-day tours to Pantanal, day tour to Chapada dos Guimarães or Águas Quentes, Amazon trips to Alta Floresta/Rio Cristalino region (price does not include airfare). Recommended. *Ametur*, R Joaquim Murtinho 242, T/F6241000, very helpful, good for air tickets. Adriana Coningham of *Ararauna Turismo Ecológica*, Av Lavapes 500, loja 07, T/F6261067. Highly recommended. All these agencies arrange trips to the Pantanal, for longer or special programmes, book in advance. *Focus Tours* (see page 24) specializes in tours in this part of the Pantanal and, starting from Cuiabá, to the southern Amazon, with bases at Alta Floresta and on the Rio Cristalino (see page 658).

Tour operators
You should expect to pay US$60-90 per person per day for tours in the Pantanal

Recommended guides (in alphabetical order): All guides work freelance for other companies as well as employing other guides for trips when busy. Most guides await incoming flights at the airport; compare prices and services in town if you don't wish to commit yourself at the airport. The tourist office recommends guides; this is not normal practice and their advice is not necessarily impartial. *Sérgio Alves*, F6235258, speaks English, bird-watching and other tours. *Paulo Boute*, R Getúlio Vargas 64, Várzea Grande, near airport, T6862231, speaks Portuguese, English, French, also sells Pantanal publications. *Marcus W Kramm*, R Franklin Cassiano da Silva 63, Cuiabá, T/F3218982, speaks Portuguese, English, German. *Djalma dos Santos Moraes*, R Arnaldo Addor 15, Coophamil, 78080 Cuiabá, T/F6251457, US$100 per person per day. *Laércio Sá*, *FaunaTour*, T6820101, T99837475 (mob; 24 hrs), faunatur@zaz.com.br Very well-informed, helpful and knowledgable about environmental issues. Speaks English, Spanish and Italian, 2 and 3-day Pantanal tours (including transport, accommodation in farmhouses rather than hotels, meals, trekking, horse riding, boat trips, fishing), Has own car, can arrange longer tours and camping (Aug-Oct) on request, also excursions to Chapada dos Guimarães. Warmly recommended. *Joel Souza*, owner of *Pousada Ecoverde*, see above. Can be contacted at Av Getúlio Vargas 155A, next to *Hotel Presidente*, T6461852, T99567229 (mob; 24 hrs). Speaks English, German and Italian, enthusiastic, very helpful, checklists for flora and fauna provided. Tends to employ other guides, rather than take trips himself.

Air Airport in Várzea Grande, T6822213. Flights to Alta Floresta, Brasília, Campo Grande, Itaituba, Rio Branco, Santarém, São Paulo and Sinop. Taxi from centre US$15, 'Aeroporto' bus from Praça Ipiranga, US$0.50. ATMs outside include Banco do Brasil for Visa, MasterCard, Cirrus and Maestro. There is a post office and a Sedtur office (not always open).

Transport
See also Ins and outs, page 649

Buses Rodoviária, R Jules Rimet, Bairro Alvorada, north of the centre. Comfortable buses (toilets) to **Campo Grande**, 10 hrs, US$20, 12 buses daily, *leito* at 2000 and 2100, US$50. To **Goiânia**, 14 hrs, US$25. Direct to **Brasília**, 24 hrs, US$30, *leito* US$60. To **Porto Velho**, 6 *União Cascavel* buses a day, US$45, 21 hrs. *Andorinha* 1700 bus São Paulo-Cuiabá connects with Porto Velho service. Several to **São Paulo**, eg Motta, US$42. To **Rio de Janeiro**, US$57. To **Barra do Garças**, *Xavante* 0800, 1300 and 2030, US$15, also *Barattur*. Connections to all major cities.

Car hire *Unidas*, airport, T6824062. *Localiza*, Av Dom Bosco 965, T6247979, and at airport, T6827900. *Atlântida*, Av Isaac Póvoas, T6230700. Cheapest at *Vitória*, R Comandante Costa 1350, T3227122.

Brasília and the Pantanal

Directory   **Airline offices** *Varig*, R 15 de Novembro 230, Bairro Porto, T6246498, at airport T6821140. **Banks** *Banco do Brasil*, Av Getúlio Vargas and R Barão de Melgaço, commission US$10 for cash, US$20 per transaction for TCs, very slow for TCs, but best rates. *Incomep Câmbio*, R Gen Neves 155, good rates. The following travel agents or gold dealers change cash only at poor rates (generally open Mon-Fri): *Mattos-Tur*, R Cândido Mariano 465. *Goldmine*, R Cândido Mariano 400, 0800-1600. *Ourominas*, R Cândido Mariano 401, 0800-1700, may change on Sat 0800-1200 if cash is available, enquire first, T6249400. *Portobello*, R Comandante Costa 555, 0900-1600. It is difficult to get cash advances on credit cards especially MasterCard, for Visa try *Banco do Brasil* or *Bradesco*. **Communications** Internet: *Copy Grafic*, Praça Alencastro 32, fax and email, English spoken, friendly. **Post office**: main branch at Praça da República, fax service. **Telephone**: R Barão de Melgaço 3209, 0700-2200, also at rodoviária, 0600-2130, international service. **Embassies and consulates** *Bolivia*, Av Isaac Póvoas 117, T6235094, open Mon-Fri. **Voltage** 110 Volts AC, 60 cycles.

Chapada dos Guimarães

Phone code: 065
Colour map 3, grid A2
Population: 13,500

Chapada dos Guimarães is one of the oldest plateaus on earth and one of the most scenic areas of Brazil. It retains much of the mystery attributed to it for centuries; and is still often described as as a mystical, energizing place. In the 1920s, Colonel Fawcett was told of many strange things hidden in its depths, and an unusual local magnetic force which reduces the speed of cars has been documented. The whole area is studded with waterfalls and caves, the bird-watching is very good and mammals, such as puma, giant river otter and black-tailed marmoset, live here.

The pleasant town of Chapada dos Guimarães, 68 km northeast of Cuiabá, is a base for many beautiful excursions in this area. It has the oldest church in the Mato Grosso, **Nossa Senhora de Santana** (1779), a bizarre blending of Portuguese and French baroque styles, and a huge springwater public swimming pool (on Rua Dr Pem Gomes, behind the town). Formerly the centre of an important diamond-prospecting region, today Chapada is a very popular destination for Cuiabanos to escape the heat of the city on weekends and holidays. It is a full day excursion from Cuiabá through lovely scenery, with many birds, butterflies and flora. The **Festival de Inverno** is held in the last week of July, and **Carnival** is very busy. Accommodation is scarce and expensive at these times. The **tourist office**, Rua Quinco Caldas 100 near the praça, provides a useful map of the region and organizes tours.

The Chapada is an immense geological formation rising to 700 m, with rich forests, curiously eroded rocks and many lovely grottoes, peaks and waterfalls. A **national park** has been established in the area just west of the town, where the Salgadeira tourist centre offers bathing, camping and a restaurant close to the **Salgadeira waterfall**. The beautiful 85-m **Véu da Noiva** waterfall (Bridal Veil), 12 km before the town near Buriti (well signposted, ask bus from Cuiabá to let you off), is reached either by a short route, or a long route through forest. Other sights include the **Mutuca** beauty spot, **Rio Claro**, the viewpoint over the breathtaking 80-m-deep **Portão do Inferno** (Hell's Gate), and the falls of **Cachoeirinha** (small restaurant), and **Andorinhas**.

About 8 km east of town is the **Mirante do Ponto Geodésico**, a monument officially marking the Geodesic Centre of South America. It overlooks a great canyon with views of the surrounding plains, the Pantanal and Cuiabá's skyline on the horizon.

Some 45 km east of Chapada is the access for **Caverna do Francês** or Caverna Aroe Jari ('dwelling of the souls' in the Bororo language), a sandstone cave over 1 km long, the second largest in Brazil. It is a 2-km walk to the cave which contains Lagoa Azul, a lake with crystalline blue water. Latest reports say visitors are not allowed to go to the lake. Take your own torch/flashlight (guides' lamps are sometimes weak). A guide is only really necessary to get through *fazenda* property to the cave.

Other excursions are to the **Cidade de Pedra** rock formations, 25 km from town along the road to the diamond prospecting town of Água Fria. Nearby is a 300 m wall formed by the Rio Claro. About 60 km from town are the **Pingador** and **Bom Jardim** archaeological sites, which are caverns with petroglyphs dating back some 4,000 years.

Hiring a car in Cuiabá is the most convenient way to see many of the scattered attractions, although access to several of them is via rough dirt roads which may deteriorate in the rainy season; drive carefully as the area is prone to dense fog. Hitchhiking from Chapada town to the national park is feasible on weekends and holidays, but expect crowds at the swimming holes.

Essentials

Sleeping

AL *Pousada da Chapada*, 2 km out on Cuiabá Rd, T37911171, F37911299. Cheaper with fan, very comfortable, restaurant, bar, pool, sports facilities, parking. **A** *Estância San Francisco*, at the entrance to town from Cuiabá (MT-251, Km 61), T37911102, F37911537. On 42 ha farm with 2 lakes, said to have the best breakfast in town fresh from the farm. **A** *Solar do Inglês*, R Cipriano Curvo, 142 Centro, T3011389, wwwchapadados guimaraes In an old converted house near town centre with 6 rooms each with private bathroom, TV and frigobar. Garden, swimming pool and sauna. Breakfast and afternoon tea included. **B** *Rio's Hotel*, R Tiradentes 333, T37911126. A/c, fridge, **C** with fan, cheaper with shared bath, good breakfast. Recommended. **B** *Chapadense*, R Vereador José de Souza 535, T/F37911410. A/c, fridge, **C** with fan, restaurant serves *comida caseira*. **B** *Turismo*, R Fernando Corrêa 1065, a block from rodoviária, T37911176, F37911383. A/c, fridge, cheaper with fan, restaurant, breakfast and lunch excellent, very popular, German-run; Ralf Goebel, the owner, is very helpful in arranging excursions. **C** *Pousada Bom Jardim*, Praça Bispo Dom Wunibaldo, T37911244. Fan, comfortable, parking, good breakfast. Recommended. **D** *São José*, R Vereador José de Souza 50, T37911152. Fan, cheaper with shared bath and no fan, hot showers, basic, good, owner Mário sometimes runs excursions. **D** *Dormitório*, R Tiradentes. Basic, no fan, cheaper with shared bath. **Camping E** per person *Aldeia Velha*, in

Pousada
Solar do Inglês

Rooms with private bathrooms
TV
Telephone
Swimming pool
Sauna
Rate includes breakfast and afternoon tea
Located 300 metres from the village of Chapada

Rua Cipriano Curvo
142-Centro
Chapada dos Guimarães - MT
CEP 78195-000

T 55 (65) 301 1389
Email solardoingles@vsp.com.br
www.chapadadosguimaraes.com.br

Brasília and the Pantanal

the Aldeia Velha neighbourhood at the entrance to town from Cuiabá, T3227178 (Cuiabá). Fenced area with bath, hot shower, some shade, guard. *Salgadeira*, unorganized camping 16 km from town at the tourist centre, watch your belongings.

Eating

Pequi is a regional palm fruit used to season many foods; arroz com pequi is a popular local rice and chicken dish

Nivios, Praça Dom Wunibaldo 631, for good regional food. *Fogão da Roça*, Praça Dom Wunibaldo 488, *comida mineira*. Generous portions, good quality. Recommended. *O Mestrinho*, R Quinco Caldas 119. Meat, regional dishes, *rodízio* at weekends. *Choppada* (*O Chopp da Chapada*), R Cipriano Curvo near praça. Drinks and meals, regional dishes, live music at weekends. *Trapiche*, R Cipriano Curvo 580. Pizza, drinks, regional dishes. *O Mestrinho*, *Peixaria Serrano*, R Dr Pem Gomes 505 (near pool). Fish specialities and *comida caseira*, cheaper than those near the praça. *Veu da Noiva*, R Dr Pem Gomes 524. Regional dishes, fish in season (*piracema* fishing ban 1 Oct-1 Mar).

Shopping

Crafts, indigenous artefacts, sweets and locally-made honey from *Casa de Artes e Artesanato Mato Grossense* (Praça Dom Wunibaldo). Regional sweets from *Doceria Olho de Sogra*, Praça Dom Wunibaldo 21. João Eloy de Souza Neves is a local artist, his paintings, music and history about Chapada (*Chapada dos Guimarães da descoberta aos dias atuais*) are on sale at *Pousada Bom Jardim*.

Tour operators

Travel agencies in Chapada and Cuiabá offer expensive tours to all the sights. José Paulino dos Santos is a guide working with the tourist office (weekdays 0800-1100, 1300-1800, T37911245). Recommended tours with Jorge Belfort Mattos from *Ecoturismo Cultural*, Praça Dom Wunibaldo 464, T/F37911393; he speaks English and knows the area well; several 4-6 hour itineraries from US$20-50 per person (minimum 4 people or prices increase). Cássio Martins of *AC Tour*, R Tiradentes 28, T37911122, often waits at the rodoviária. 4 hour tours are about US$20 per person, minimum 5 persons; 7-8-hr tours, US$25 per person, minimum 5; horseback day tour, US$25 per person, minimum 2; an 8-10-km hike with a guide, US$20 per person, minimum 2; bicycle tour with guide, US$20 per person, minimum 2. Tours from Cuiabá cost US$35-40 per person.

Transport

Bus 7 departures daily to and from Cuiabá (Rubi, 0700-1900, last back to Cuiabá 1800), 1½ hrs, US$.75.

Directory

Communications Post office: R Fernando Corrêa 848.

Cáceres

Phone code: 065
Colour map 3, grid A1
Population: 86,000

Cáceres is a very hot but clean and hospitable town on the banks of the Rio Paraguai, 200 km west of Cuiabá. It has many well-maintained 19th-century buildings painted in pastel colours and is known for its many bicycles. Until 1960, Cáceres had regular boat traffic, today it is limited to a few tour boats and pleasure craft. River trips from Cuiabá to Corumbá are very difficult since boats on the Cuiabá river are few and irregular, but to you can sometimes get to Corumbá by river from here.

The **Museu de Cáceres** on Rua Antônio Maria by Praça Major João Carlos is a small local history museum. Exhibits include funerary urns used by native Indians. The main square, **Praça Barão de Rio Branco**, has one of the original border markers from the Treaty of Tordesillas, which divided South America between Spain and Portugal; it is pleasant and shady during the day. In the evenings between November and March the trees are packed with thousands of chirping swallows (*andorinhas*), beware of droppings. The square is surrounded by bars, restaurants and ice-cream parlours and comes to life at night.

The beautiful **Serra da Mangabeira** is about 15 km east crossed by the road from Cuiabá; the town is also at the edge of the Pantanal. Vitória Regia lilies can be seen north of town, just across the bridge over the Rio Paraguai along the BR-174. There are archaeological sites on the river's edge north of the city. **Excursions**

A *Caiçaras*, R dos Operários 745 corner R Gen Osório, T2233187, F2232692. **B** without fridge and TV, pleasant, modern, parking. **A** *Ipanema*, R Gen Osório 540, T2231177, F2231743. Garage, good restaurant. **A** *Turbo*, Av São Luiz 1399 by BR 070, T2231984. Luxurious, restaurant, pool. **B** *Fênix*, R dos Operários 600, T2231027, F2212243. Fridge, a/c, comfortable. **B** *Rio*, Praça Major João Carlos 61, T2233387, F2233084. A/c, **C** without fridge, TV, **D** with shared bath, fan. **C** *Charm*, Col José Dulce 405, T/F2234949. A/c, **D** with shared bath, friendly. Near the rodoviária are: **C** *Capri*, R Getúlio Vargas 99, T2231711. A/c, comfortable. **C** *Gasparin*, Av Sangradouro 162, T2234579. A/c, fridge, cheaper with fan. **D** *União*, R 7 de Setembro 340. Fan, **E** with shared bath, basic, good value. **D** *Rio Doce*, R 7 de Setembro. A/c, cheaper with shared bath, good value. **Sleeping**

Expensive *Corimbá*, R 15 de Novembro s/n, on river front. Fish specialities, good. **Mid-range** *Bistecão*, R Costa Marques, 997. Meat specialities, opens erratically. **Cheap** *Gulla's*, R Cel José Dulce 250. Buffet by kg, good quality and variety. Recommended. *Hispano*, Praça Barão de Rio Branco 64. Buffet by kg. *Panela de Barro*, R Frei Ambrósio 34, near rodoviária, *comida caseira*. **Eating**

Piranha Festival, mid-Mar; *International Fishing Festival* in mid-Sep; annual cattle fair. **Festivals**

Traditional folkloric dance groups:*Chalana*, T2233317, and *Tradição*, T2234505, perform shows at different locations. **Entertainment**

Náutica Turismo, R Bom Jardim 119A, by the waterfront, for fishing/camping supplies and boat repairs. **Shopping**

Cáceres, Av Getúlio Vargas 408, T2231428, F2232440, fishing and photo tours to Pantanal, boat rentals, Cláudio Duarte helpful guide. *Pantanal Tour*, R Col Fária 180, T2231200, boat rentals, fishing trips, tickets. *Vereda Turismo*, R Padre Cassemiro 1121, T2234360, tours, boat rentals, fishing. **Tour operators**

Air *Aeroporto de Nível Internacional*, Av Tancredo Neves, T2236474. **Buses** *Colibrí/União Cascavel* buses Cuiabá-Cáceres, US\$9, many daily between 0630-2400 from rodoviária, Terminal da Japonesa, T2241261 (book in advance, very crowded), 3½ hrs. Cáceres-Porto Velho, US\$32.
Boats The *Acuri*, a luxury tourist vessel, sails to Corumbá, 1-week cruise including return by air from Corumbá to Cuiabá, US\$600 per person. For information on other boat sailings, ask at the Capitânia dos Portos, on the corner of the main square at the waterfront. If possible phone in advance to Cáceres, Posto Arrunda, T2211707, to find out if any boats are going. Also Portobrás on the outskirts at the waterfront (T2211728). In the dry season there are practically no boats to Corumbá. At the waterfront you can hire a boat for a day trip, US\$5 per person per hr, minimum 3 people; on holidays and some weekends there are organized day trips on the river.
Car hire *Localiza*, R Padre Cassimoro 630, T2231330, and at airport. *Locavel*, Av São Luiz, 300, T2231212. **Transport**

Directory **Banks** *Banco do Brasil*, R Cel Jose Dulcé, 234. *HSBC*, R Cel Jose Dulcé, 145. *Casa de Câmbio Mattos*, Comte Bauduino 180, next to main praça, changes cash and TCs at good rates. **Communications** **Telephone**: Praça Barão de Rio Branco.

Border An unpaved road runs from Cáceres to the Bolivian border at San Matías. Brazilian
with Bolivia immigration is at R Col Farías, Cáceres, for exit and entry formalities; when closed (for example Sun), go to Polícia Federal, Av Rubens de Medarca 909.

Leaving Bolivia, get your passport stamped at Bolivian immigration (1000-1200, 1500-1700), then get your passport stamped at Cáceres, nowhere in between, but there are 3 luggage checks for drugs.

Transport **Buses**: the bus fare from Cáceres to **San Matías** is US$9 with *Transical-Velásquez*, Mon-Sat at 0630 and 1500, Sun 1500 only (return at same times). *Trans Bolivia* to San Matías, Sun, Mon, Fri at 1500, Tue, Wed, Thu and Sat at 0700.

Into Bolivia San Matías is a busy little town with hotels, restaurants and a bank. The next major town in Bolivia is San Ignacio de Velasco, which is on the road route to Santa Cruz de la Sierra. There are buses San Matías-San Ignacio and San Ignacio-Santa Cruz; also flights. For more details, see the *Bolivia Handbook* or the *South American Handbook*.

North of Cuiabá

Alta Floresta The road due north from Cuiabá to Santarém (1,777 km) has been completed
Phone code: 065 and is all-weather, through **Sinop**, with a branch west to Colíder and Alta
Population: 71,500 Floresta (daily bus from Cuiabá with *São Luís* at 2000, 12 hours, US$45). Out-
When travelling north side Alta Floresta, the *Cristalino Jungle Lodge* on the Cristalino river is a basic
of Cuiabá, yellow lodge, with shared baths, in a very rich and well-preserved section of southern
fever vaccination is Amazônia. Many rare mammals are found here (including the short-eared
obligatory; if you do dog), as well as five species of macaw, harpy eagle and a few hundred other
not have a certificate, bird species. *Anaconda Operators* in Cuiabá run tours to *Cristalino Jungle*
you will be *Lodge*, US$100 per person per day plus airfare (US$200 return).
(re)vaccinated

Sleeping **Sinop**: **C** *Italian Palace*, Av das Figueras 493, T5312109. Restaurant, bar, sauna. **Alta Floresta**: **B** *Floresta Amazônica*, Av Perimetral Oeste 2001, T5213601, F5213801. In park, lovely views, pool, sports, all facilities. **C** *Pirâmide Palace*, Av do Aeroporto 445, T5212400. A/c, fridge, restaurant. **D** *Grande Hotel Coroados*, R F 1 118, T5213022. Not too well kept but has a/c, pool and bar.

East of Cuiabá

São Félix do This is a large town with a high population of Carajás Indians; a depot of their
Araguaia handicrafts is between the pizzeria and *Mini Hotel* (good view but not recom-
Population: 14,500 mended) on Avenida Araguaia. There is some infrastructure for fishing. Mos-
quito nets are highly recommended since there is a high incidence of malaria.

Many river trips are available for fishing or to see wildlife. Juracy Lopes, a very experienced guide, can be contacted through *Hotel Xavante*; he has many friends, including the chief and council, in Santa Isabela (see below). Morning or afternoon trips to the village or to see wildlife, cost US$15 for two; longer trips can be made to the meeting of the waters with the Rio das Mortes, or spending a night in the jungle sleeping in hammocks. *Icuryala* is recommended, T0XX62-2239518 (Goiâna), excellent food, drink, and service, US$100 per day, independent visitors also welcomed. *Fazenda* owners may invite you as their guest – do not abuse this privilege, and remember to take a gift.

Sleeping and eating **C** *Xavante*, Av Severiano Neves 391, T5221305. A/c, frigobar, excellent breakfast, delicious *cajá* juice, Sr e Sra Carvalho are very hospitable. Recommended. A good restaurant is the **Pizzeria Cantinho da Peixada** on Av Araguaia, next to the Texaco station, overlooking the river. The owner, Klaus, rents rooms, **E**, better than hotels, T5221320, he also arranges fishing trips. Recommended.

Transport **Air**: access to both São Félix and Santa Teresinha (see below) is by *Brasil Central/TAM* flights, unreliable and, as the planes hold just 15 passengers, it is common to get delayed up to several days. There is a daily *Votec* flight from São Felix to Belém, stopping at Redenção, Tucumã and many other places.

   Buses: rodoviária is 3 km from the centre and waterfront, taxi US$5. To **Barra do Garças** at 0500, arrive 2300, or 1730, arrive 1100 next day. Also to **Tucumã**, 6-8 hrs, and to **São José do Xingu**, 10 hrs. No buses to Marabá.

Bananal is the world's largest river island, located in the state of Tocantins on the northeastern border of Mato Grosso. The island is formed by a division in the south of the Rio Araguaia and is approximately 320 km long. The entire island was originally a national park (called **Parque Nacional Araguaia**), which was then cut in half and later further reduced to its current size of 562,312 ha. The island and park are subject to seasonal flooding and contain several permanent lakes. The island, and especially the park, form one of the more spectacular wildlife areas on the continent, in many ways similar to the Pantanal. The vegetation is a transition zone between the *cerrado* (woody savanna) and Amazon forests, with gallery forests along the many waterways. There are several marshlands throughout the island.

   The fauna is also transitional. More than 300 bird species are found here, including the hoatzin, hyacinthine macaw, harpy eagle and black-fronted piping guan. The giant anteater, maned wolf, bush dog, giant otter, jaguar, puma, marsh deer, pampas deer, American tapir, yellow anaconda and South American river turtle also occur here. The island is flooded most of the year, with the prime visiting (dry) season being from June to early October, when the beaches are exposed. Unfortunately, the infrastructure for tourism aside from fishing expeditions (the island is a premier spot for big fish) is very limited. ■ *Permission to visit the park should be obtained in advance from Ibama, Rua 219, No 95, Setor Universitário, 74605-800 Goiânia.*

   Access to the park is through the small but pleasant town of **Santa Teresinha**, which is north of São Félix (see above) and is the gateway to the park.

Ilha do Bananal

Sleeping A charming hotel is **A** *Bananal*, Praça Tarcila Braga 106, CEP 78395 (Mato Grosso), with full board. There is only room for 10; reserve well in advance, either by mail, allowing several months for the mail to get through, or by phoning the town's telephone operator, asking the hotel to call you back and hoping that you hear from them.

   There is some simple accommodation for scientists at the park, which can sometimes be reserved at the address above or from the national parks department in Brasília. Bring your own food and bedding, and the severely underpaid but dedicated staff would appreciate any extra food or financial help, although it will not be solicited. A boat to the park can be lined up at the *Hotel Bananal*.

Tour operators *Focus Tours*, see Specialist tour operators page 24, will arrange tours.

Brasília and the Pantanal

Bananal can be visited from São Félix do Araguaia – see above (with permission from Funai in the town) by crossing the river to the Carajá village of **Santa Isabela de Morra** and asking to see the chief, who can tell you the history of the tribe. The island can be crossed from São Félix to **São Miguel de Araguaia** by taking an eight-hour trip (contact the *Bar Beira*). From São Miguel, a five-hour bus trip brings you to **Porangatu** (**D** *Hotel Mauriti*, shower, restaurant) on the Belém-Brasília highway.

Background

History

Indigenous peoples

Origins Some 50,000 years ago the very first peoples crossed the temporary land bridge spanning Asia and America at the Bering Straits, and began a long migration southwards. They were hunters and foragers, following in the path of huge herds of now extinct animals, such as mammoth, giant ground sloth and antecedents of the camel and horse. The first signs that these people had reached South America date from around 10,000 BC, if not earlier.

Archaeological evidence The major handicap to archaeological study of tropical cultures is that most material remains deteriorate rapidly in the warm, humid climate. Since the majority of cultural output from Brazil was in perishable materials such as feathers, wood, baskets, and woven textiles, little has survived for modern analysis. Nevertheless various artefacts have been discovered from all around the country, showing considerable artistic and technical skill. The pottery produced by the early peoples was of a high standard, admired by the European newcomers. Early ceramics have been found on Marajó island at the mouth of the Amazon. The Annatuba culture lived here in small villages by the river. Most of their ceramics found are round bowls and jars, including huge funeral urns, which have been dated with increasing antiquity; the earliest to date from around 980 BC. Textile production was done mainly with hand-twisted fibres, using both cotton and bast. Objects found in Rio Grande do Sul, dating from 550 AD or earlier, included twined bags, nets and ropes. Most of the textiles found throughout Brazil were simple everyday items, such as hammocks and straps, with little decoration.

    It was assumed that the first humans in Brazil came down to the lowlands from the Andean chain, following the east-facing river valleys. Some very early human remains have been found in central and northeastern Brazil. In Pedra Furada, in northeast Brazil, a rock-shelter named Toca do Boquirão has yielded evidence of human presence from as early as 47,000 years ago. The cave, in a region well-known for its prehistoric rock paintings, is known to have been occupied by hunters about 8,000 years ago. However, French archaeologist Nède Guidon made deeper probings into the ground and claims to have found evidence of much earlier human presence. Guidon's claims sparked hot debate among other experts, many of whom argued that what she described as ash from fireplaces was in fact the remains of naturally caused forest fires. In Monte Alegre, opposite Santarém on the Rio Solimões, recent studies have been made of human remains, dating from around 15,000 BC, also predating previous estimates. These, and other controversial claims from sites in the mid-Amazon region, have led some experts to raise the theory of original human migration from across the Pacific Ocean. In general, however, the most authoritative studies of the first humans in Brazil point to a much later date, between 10,000-5,000 BC.

Amazon lifestyles The earliest people soon learnt to make the most of the rich food sources provided by the rivers of the Amazon basin. They lived on the flood plain and caught fish and manatee (large sea mammals, related to dugongs and sea cows) using spears thrown from the shore, or from dugout canoes. Besides fishing, these people also cultivated manioc and other plants found on the forest floor. They kept turtles in corrals at the river's edge, for eating and also for making tools and other artefacts from their shells.

    Their nomadic lifestyle was carefully planned, and they followed planting and harvesting seasons in accordance with the periodic rising and falling river levels. Worship of multiple deities, of the weather and agriculture for instance, was very important. The gods had to be appeased to prevent excessive fluctuations in the level of the river. At first, as hunters and gatherers, they built simple, temporary houses out of tree trunks and palm leaves, and slept in hammocks made from plant fibres. Clothing was equally simple; a large, ankle-length tunic called a *kushma* was the main garment worn. Although this may sound impractical wear for people living in a warm, humid climate, the *kushma* provided much-needed protection against biting insects. Compensating for their plain clothing, the people painted their bodies and wore colourful jewellery, such as feather head-dresses. Little has remained of the perishable adornments, but cylindrical and flat ceramic stamps have been found throughout Amazônia, which may have been used to apply ink designs onto the face and other parts of the body, still common today among ethnic groups.

Around 7000-4000 BC a climatic change increased the temperature throughout the south of Brazil, drawing people down from the inland *planalto* region to the coasts, and leading to an upsurge in population here. These coastal inhabitants lived on shellfish collected from the water's edge, as evidenced by *sambaquis* (huge shell mounds), discovered on the coast. In rare cases they also fed on whales that had probably been beached, but they did not go far out to sea to fish. Some of the *sambaquis* found measure up to 25 m high; many of them also served as dwellings, with floors and fireplaces, and as burial sites, with graves often underneath the houses. The dead were buried with personal adornments and some domestic artefacts.

Migration to the coast

By about 100-200 BC, people throughout Brazil were settled in structured, fixed communities by the coasts and rivers, living increasingly by farming instead of nomadic hunting and gathering. The subsequent population growth spread communities further along river courses and into seasonally flooded savanna lands.

Settlement & political structure

Unlike the great empires of the Andes, the lowland peoples did not form political groupings much larger than a few villages. By the 16th century AD, however, there was a very large population of different peoples spread throughout Brazil, some of them settled in chiefdoms. These structured groups contained several hundred individuals. One chieftain led a province composed of several villages, each of which was led by a lower-ranking chieftain. The first European explorers reported that there was at least one case of the title or name of one chief being the same as the local word for god, and as such the chief was revered far from his people's territory. One such chiefdom was at the village of Teso dos Bichos on Marajó island at the mouth of the Amazon. The oval-shaped village was built on a mound some 7 m high and covering 2½ ha. It is thought that the site was inhabited continuously for about 900 years, by 500-1,000 people living in houses made of earth, wooden poles and thatch. The village appeared to have been kept very clean and tidy and communal life was well organized, with duties divided between men and women.

The most widespread linguistic grouping in Brazil at the time of the European conquest was the **Tupi-Guarani**. These people originated from the Atlantic coast and rivers around 500-700 AD. They lived off slash and burn farming, cultivating tropical plants, but when they began moving inland and south they took over from resident hunters and gatherers. By the 1500s the Tupi-Guarani, who often moved from place to place, following a prophet, could be found from north of the Amazon south to Rio de la Plata, and west into Paraguay and Bolivia.

Linguistic groups

Another large, organized group of people were the **Tupinambá**. They lived on the coast, from the mouth of the Amazon south to São Paulo state. The Tupinambá lived by cultivating crops, such as manioc, sweet potato, yams, as well as cotton, gourds and tobacco. They lived in villages of four to eight large, rectangular, thatched houses, each containing up to 30 families. They usually built their villages on an elevation to catch the breeze, and moved to new sites every five years or so. A chief, the patrilineal head, enforced various social customs, such as marriages and puberty rites. Burial ceremonies were elaborate, with the body wrapped in a hammock and squeezed into a huge ceramic urn. The head of a family was usually buried under his house, others elsewhere within the village. Sometimes a hut was built over the grave, and a fire lit nearby to ward off evil spirits.

Cannibalism was also an important custom for the Tupinambá, as it had been for many other peoples throughout South America for thousands of years. The practice was highly ritualized, using prisoners of war. The victims were kept as slaves, often for long periods, being well fed and looked after; in some cases even marrying the owner's daughter or sister, who had their children. But all such slaves were eventually eaten, after an elaborate ceremony with much singing and dancing. An appointed executioner would kill them with a club and they were then cooked and different parts of the body divided up among various participants in the ritual. There have been many theories as to why people practised cannibalism; since they tended to eat victims of war it was thought that it gave them power over the spirits of their dead enemies. It is most commonly argued that human flesh supplemented the diet for large populations who had scarce resources. But this was not the case for the Tupinambá, who had ample food supplies. When the Tupinambá themselves were asked why they ate human meat they simply said they liked the taste of it.

European colonization

Arrival of the Portuguese

Pedro Álvares Cabral is believed to be the first Portuguese explorer to land on the Brazilian coast, having been blown off his course to India and making landfall on 22 April 1500. He claimed the territory for Portugal as a result of agreements with Spain under the papal bull of 1493 and the Treaty of Tordesillas (1494), but it was some years before the Portuguese realized that this was not just another island as the Spanish had found in the Caribbean, and that in reality they had stumbled across a huge new continent. Further expeditions were sent out in 1501 and 1503-04 and a few trading stations were set up to export the only commodity they felt was of commercial interest: a species of dyewood known as 'pau do brasil'. Little attention was paid to the new colony, as the Portuguese concentrated on the more lucrative trade with Africa, India and the Far East. Some settlers, often banished criminals as well as merchants, gained acceptance with the local Indian tribes and intermarried, fathering the first hybrid cultural Brazilians.

Colonization

The coastal trading stations at Salvador da Bahia, Pernambuco, São Vicente and Cabo Frio soon attracted the attention of French and British traders, who seized Portuguese ships and started to trade directly with the Indians. The French even proclaimed the right to trade in any part of Brazil not occupied by the Portuguese. This forced the Portuguese Crown to set up a colony and in 1530, Martim Afonso de Sousa was sent out with about 400 men. Faced with the impossibly huge task of colonizing the Brazilian coastline, the Crown turned to private enterprise to stake its claim. In 1534 the coast was divided into 15 captaincies, each of which was donated to an individual captain and governor to develop on behalf of the Crown. Although successful settlements were established in Pernambuco in the north and São Vicente in the south, the problems faced in most captaincies, Indian resistance, lack of capital and the difficulty of attracting settlers, led to the reassertion of Crown control in 1549. The Indians had been happy to barter brazil wood with the Portuguese and had helped in the logging and transporting of timber, but the introduction of sugar plantations was a different matter and the hunter-gatherers had no experience of such exhausting work. When they refused to co-operate in this profitable enterprise, the Portuguese took Indians as slaves on a massive scale, which destroyed the good relations previously enjoyed and led to attacks on Portuguese settlements.

Tomé de Sousa was sent out as Governor-General to the vacant captaincy of Bahia in **The Jesuits**
1549. He established his seat at Salvador, which became the first capital of Brazil.
With him travelled six Jesuit priests, the first of what was to become a hugely powerful missionary and educational order in Brazil. Their role was to smooth the path
between Indians and Europeans, convert and educate the Indians in Christian ways
and organize them into special villages, or *aldeias* (see box, page 354). This last move
brought them into conflict with the settlers, however, for their control over the
labour market, and with the clergy, who regarded the Indians as savages who could
be enslaved. As a result of disagreements with the first Bishop of Brazil, Fernandes
Sardanha, the Jesuits moved in 1554 from Bahia to the captaincy of São Vicente,
where they set up an *aldeia* at Piratininga, which later became the city of São Paulo.
In 1557 a new governor was appointed, Mem de Sá, who was more sympathetic to
the Jesuits and their aims and the *aldeias* began to spread.

The Crown still had difficulties in consolidating its hold on Brazil and other European **French &**
powers continued to encroach on its territory. A Protestant French expedition found **Dutch**
an area which had not been settled by the Portuguese and stayed there from the **incursions**
mid-1550s until they were finally ousted in 1567. Their colony was replaced by a new
royal captaincy and a town was founded: Rio de Janeiro. São Luís was also occupied
by the French in 1612-15, but it was the Dutch who posed the greatest threat on
both sides of the Atlantic (see The Dutch in Brazil, see page 436). They seized
Pernambuco in 1630, Portuguese Angola in 1641 and dominated the Atlantic

Exploration & settlement

Sources: John Hemming, *Red Gold* (London 1978)
Kevin Healey, *Exploration & Early Settlement* (1981)
Celso Antunes, *Geografia e Participação 2* (São Paulo, 1996)

Portugese settlement
  Occupied 1500-1600
  Occupied 1600-1700
  Occupied 1700-1760

→ Routes of bandeirantes
  & monções

†† Main Jesuit mission areas

ILHÉUS Captaincies in 16th century

Background

Portrait of a sugar engenho

Sugar cultivation began in Brazil in the 1550s and by early 17th century the colony had become the biggest sugar producer in the world. The fertile soil, warm climate and adequate rainfall of the Northeast meant that the land could produce two crops a year. Since the cane juices went sour within a day of being cut, it was essential that the processing plant was close to the fields; the resulting combination of plantation and factory was known as an engenho. The typical engenho was more than this, however: it also included a chapel, workshops, casa grande (the owner's house), senzala (slave quarters) and fields for growing maize, beans, manioc and rice to feed the slaves. The need for labour was met by importing African slaves but engenhos did not just consist of a white master and black slaves. While the latter did the backbreaking work of planting, weeding and cutting the cane, skilled workers were required to keep the machinery working, repair the buildings and keep the accounts.

One of the most famous of engenhos was Sergipe in Bahia, which was the subject of a long legal dispute over ownership in the 17th century involving the rival claims of two Jesuit colleges. Apart from providing work for lawyers, this dispute created masses of documents

which have given historians a vivid picture of life in Sergipe in the late 16th century.

At Sergipe the harvest (safra) continued from the beginning of August to early May, while planting took place between June and August and again in March and April. Because of the daytime heat work began at 1600 and continued to 1000 in the morning, after which the machinery was cleaned. Some of the entries in the Sergipe accounts are particularly intriguing. The biggest expense in 1707 was firewood, used for boiling the cane-juice. Firewood was obviously crucial; lack of it in 1651 led to the loss of 14 days work, while there was no work on another five days owing to repairs. As a Jesuit engenho it is not surprising that there were many religious holidays; 25 to 30 were observed each year, though these differed. Easter, for some reason, was not observed in 1612-13. Over 20 percent of expenses were in salaries, the best paid workers being the sugar master, the banker and the overseers, but there were other costs: in 1707 a slave catcher was paid 9 milreis for catching "the slave Caetano" while another two milreis went to pay for "three shrouds for diseased slaves". Interestingly the accounts indicate that Sergipe made a loss in most years between 1611 and 1754.

trading routes until the Portuguese managed to regain Angola in 1648-49 and Pernambuco in 1654.

Sugar & slaves Throughout the colonial period Brazil produced raw materials for Portugal. The colonial economy experienced a succession of booms and recessions, the first of these based on sugar: during the 17th century the northeastern provinces of Pernambuco, Bahia and Paraíba were the world's main producers of sugar. As European settlement had led to the death of much of the native population (over a third of the Indians in coastal areas died in epidemics in 1562-63 alone) and Indian slavery was unsuccessful, the Portuguese imported African slaves to meet the demand for labour on the sugar plantations (*engenhos*). "The most solid properties in Brazil are slaves", wrote the Governor in 1729, "for there are lands enough, but only he who has slaves can be master of them." As many as 10 million African slaves may have survived the dreadful conditions of the Atlantic crossing before the trade was abolished in 1854.

The gold rush As the sugar industry declined in the late 17th century in the face of competition from British, French and Dutch Caribbean colonies, gold was discovered inland in 1695 in Minas Gerais, Mato Grosso and other areas. Despite the lack of communications,

The Gold Rush

⏪

Although there was no shortage of rumours of gold and silver throughout the 16th and 17th centuries, it was only in the 1690s that large gold strikes were made inland from São Paulo in what became known as the area of the 'general mines' (minas gerais). Later there would be finds further west in Goiás and Mato Grosso, but these would be on a much smaller scale. What all these areas shared was their virtual inaccessibility: in 1755 it took one traveller, Marcos de Noronha, 11 weeks to travel from Goiás to Salvador. Even Minas Gerais, much nearer to the coast than Goiás, could be reached only by a long and dangerous journey across the coastal mountains. There were no roads and the rivers were of little use for transport. Yet early prospectors had to rely almost entirely on equipment and food brought in from the coast.

Despite the problems, reports of gold attracted the usual rush of prospectors and speculators, not only from elsewhere in the colony and from Portugal, but from other European countries. Towns grew up within months; between 1726 and 1729 the population of Cuiabá rose from 7,000 to 40,000. These new settlements were very different, however, from the cities of the coast; largely male, this was a violent, restless society, with little respect for traditional social mores or for the government.

The Portuguese Crown was, not surprisingly, eager to obtain its share, calculated as one fifth (quinto) of the gold produced; it also imposed special taxes and duties such as the special levy charged to help rebuild Lisbon after the earthquake of 1755. Tax collection, was, however, anything but simple. The Crown established royal foundries where the quinto would be subtracted from the gold returned to miners and traders. Faced with widespread evasion, illegal foundries and smuggling, the Crown established controls on the roads and searches in the main ports. The problems involved led to a different approach, with the quinto being collected by a per capita tax on everyone in the gold areas, an unpopular move which was not particularly effective owing to the lack of reliable records. In all 12 different methods were tried by the Crown to get its hands on the quinto; though the level of violent resistance varied, all were unpopular.

Although much of the gold left for Europe, by the late 18th century when production dropped off, the Gold Rush had transformed many aspects of the colony. For the first time large numbers of people settled in the interior. As they spent their newly acquired wealth, skilled building workers were in great demand to work on the beautiful churches and private mansions of Minas Gerais. Fortunes were made elsewhere, particularly in Rio de Janeiro and São Paulo, supplying the mining areas with meat and cereals and other goods. The reliance on African slaves to perform the hardest work in the mining areas pushed up the price of slaves, much to the discontent of the sugar planters of the northeast, and gave increased momentum to the slave trade. These changes were symbolized, perhaps above all, by the decision in 1763 to move the capital from Salvador to Rio de Janeiro, mirroring the decline in the wealth and power of the sugar planter elite and its partial replacement by Rio and São Paulo.

Background

prospectors rushed in from all over Europe. Shortly afterwards, diamonds were found in the Serra do Frio. The economy was largely driven by gold until the 1760s and a revival of world demand for sugar in the second half of the 18th century. Thereafter, there was diversification into other crops such as cacao, rice, cotton and coffee, all of which were produced for export by large numbers of slaves.

The gold rush shifted the power centre of Brazil from the northeast to the centre, in recognition of which new captaincies were created in Minas Gerais in 1720, Goiás in 1744 and Mato Grosso in 1748, and the capital was moved from Salvador to Rio de Janeiro in

Slavery

For over three centuries African slavery was a central feature of the economy and society of Brazil. Slave labour was a key part of the production of agricultural exports from the mid-16th century through to the abolition of slavery in 1888; slaves also provided much of the labour needed in the Gold Rush of the 18th century. In the 19th century, at a time when slavery was being abolished in the rest of South America, the demand for slaves increased in Brazil as they became the labour force on the new coffee fazendas of the south.

Although the first African slaves arrived in Brazil around 1550, it was only after 1580 with the expansion of sugar engenhos in the northeast that slave labour became common. Faced with a shortage of labour and the resistance of the indigenous population who tended to die of diseases, as well as the attitude of the Church, which opposed indigenous slavery, engenho owners soon resorted to African slave labour. The Church had few moral qualms about African slavery. By the

18th century, when slavery was introduced on a large scale in the mining areas of Minas Gerais, Goiás and Mato Grosso, slave ownership was common in most strata of white society and had spread north to Amazônia and south to Río Grande do Sul. The importance of slaves in this society was noted by local people and visitors alike: in 1729 Governor Luís Vahia Monteiro commented "the most solid properties in Brazil are slaves and a man's wealth is measured by having more or fewer for there are lands enough, but only he who has slaves can be masters of them".

While no one knows how many Africans survived the terrible 'middle passage' between Africa and the Brazilian ports, let alone how many died, estimates of three to four million are common. Most came from two areas of West Africa, corresponding roughly to the modern states of Ghana and Angola. Slaves were employed in a surprising range of roles: they were often the cowboys who drove herds of cattle to the coastal towns for slaughter, the sailors who navigated the rivers and coast, the

1763. Legacies of the period can be seen today in the colonial towns of Mariana, Congonhas, São João del Rei, Diamantina and, above all, in the exceptionally beautiful city of Ouro Preto, a national monument full of glorious buildings, paintings and sculpture.

Marquês de Pombal The decline of gold in the mid-18th century made economic reform necessary and the Marquês de Pombal was the minister responsible for a new programme for Portugal and her empire. Imbalances had arisen particularly in trade with Britain. Portugal imported manufactured goods and wheat but her exports of oil and wine left her in deficit, which for a while was covered by Brazilian gold. Pombal was a despotic ruler from 1750 to 1777, modernizing and reforming society, education, politics and the economy. In order to revive Portugal he concentrated on expanding the economy of Brazil, increasing and diversifying exports to cover the deficit with Britain. Cacao, cotton and rice were introduced by the new monopoly company of Grão Pará e Maranhão in the north and a similar company for Paraíba and Pernambuco revitalized the sugar industry in the northeast. The monopoly companies led to high prices and were not entirely successful so were closed in 1778-79, but the effects of Pombal's reforms were felt in the latter part of the 18th century and Portugal's trade with Britain turned into a surplus. From 1776 when the American colonies revolted, Britain was constantly at war and Portugal was able to supply rising British demand.

Rebellion Pombal's influence on society enabled the Portuguese Empire to last much longer than the Spanish Empire. He deliberately offered posts in the militia and the bureaucracy to Brazilians and was careful not to alienate the Brazilian élites. White Brazilians stevedores who loaded ships bound for Europe and they were frequently domestic workers, midwives and retailers. Despite this, the vast majority were labourers who worked under such poor conditions that there was a continual demand for more imported slaves.

Regardless of the overwhelming odds, slave resistance was continual: whites constantly complained about the reluctance of slaves to work hard and slaves often escaped and formed quilombos or mocambos, communities of escaped slaves. Though these were usually in impenetrable parts of the interior, they were sometimes on the outskirts of town or near plantations, from where they could launch raids for supplies. Though many quilombos were small and short-lived, the most famous, known as Palmares, survived from around 1630 until its final defeat in 1694. Though slave rebellions took place throughout the period of slavery, they were more common in certain parts of the country and occurred with greater frequency in the 19th century. There were over 20 rebellions around Bahia between 1809 and 1835, some of them led by slaves who were Muslim preachers.

By the late 19th century the days of slavery were clearly numbered; the slave trade to Brazil was finally ended by British pressure 1850. The defeat of the South in the Civil War put a finish to slavery in the USA, leaving Brazil as one of only two states in the Americas where slavery was legal (the other was Cuba). Though there had been an abolitionist movement since the 1830s, it made little headway until the 1860s. In 1871 the children of slaves were freed, a move which, when combined with the abolition of the slave trade, meant slavery would eventually end. Though plantation owners complained of labour shortages and bought slaves from the towns, they were forced to consider new sources of labour and from about 1880 they began to encourage European immigration, especially from Portugal and Italy. Thus, in 1888, when Congress finally debated the issue, there were only nine votes against abolition.

were on the same standing as the Portuguese and identified strongly with the mother country. Rebellion was therefore rare but did occur, influenced partly by the turmoil that was going on in Europe with the French Revolution. In 1788-89 a famous plot was uncovered in Minas Gerais called the *inconfidência mineira* (see page 242), which aimed to establish an independent republic in protest at the decline of the gold industry and high taxes. The rebels, who included many of the local hierarchy, were punished and the most prominent leader, Tiradentes (the teeth-puller), was hanged. Other plots were discovered in Rio de Janeiro in 1794, Pernambuco in 1801 and Bahia in 1807, but they were all repressed.

At the beginning of the 19th century, **Napoleon Bonaparte** caused a major upheaval in the monarchies of Europe. His expansion into the Iberian peninsula caused panic in both Spain and Portugal. In August 1807 he demanded that Portugal close its ports to British ships but the British sent a fleet to Lisbon and threatened to attack Brazil if that happened. In November of the same year the French invaded and occupied Portugal. The Prince Regent decided to evacuate the court to Brazil and under British escort sailed to Rio de Janeiro, which became the capital of the empire in 1808. The court stayed there even after 1814 when Napoleon was defeated and Portugal was ruled by a Regency Council, but King João VI was forced to return to Portugal in 1820 after a series of liberal revolts in the mother country, leaving his son Dom Pedro as Prince Regent in Brazil.

The Brazilian Empire

Background

Independence from Portugal

Dom Pedro oversaw a growing rift between Portugal and Brazil as the liberals in Lisbon tried to return Brazil to its former colonial status, cancelling political equality and the freedom of trade granted when the King left Portugal in the hands of the French. In October 1821 the government in Lisbon recalled the Prince Regent but Brazilians urged him not to go. Encouraged by his chief minister, José Bonifácio de Andrada e Silva, a conservative monarchist, Dom Pedro announced on 9 January 1822 that he would stay in Brazil, thereby asserting his autonomy. After another attempt to recall the Prince Regent, Dom Pedro made the final break with Portugal, proclaiming Brazil's independence on 7 September 1822. He was crowned emperor and Brazil became a constitutional monarchy in its own right. There was resistance in the north and north-east, particularly from the militia, but by 1824 violence had subsided. In 1825, under pressure from Britain, Portugal recognized the independent state of Brazil.

The first years of independence were unsettled, partly because of the Emperor's perceived favouritism for the Portuguese faction at court and lack of attendance to the needs of the local oligarchy. De Andrada e Silva resigned as opposition grew. In 1823 Dom Pedro dissolved the constituent assembly amidst fears that he had absolutist designs. However, he set up a royal commission to draft a new constitution which lasted from 1824 until the fall of the monarchy in 1889. This gave the emperor the right to appoint and dismiss cabinet ministers, veto legislation and dissolve parliament and call for elections. The parliamentary government consisted of two houses, a senate appointed by the monarch and a legislature indirectly elected by a limited male suffrage. A Council of State advised the monarch and ensured the separation of the executive, the legislature and the judiciary. Catholicism remained the official religion and the monarchy was supported by the Church.

Abdication Dom Pedro still failed to gain the trust of all his people. A **republican rebellion** broke out in Pernambuco in 1824, where the élite were suffering from the declining sugar industry, and there was further resentment from all the planter oligarchy as a result of the Anglo-Brazilian Treaty of 1826. This treaty granted British recognition of the independent Brazil in return for certain trading privileges, but, almost more importantly, stipulated that the Atlantic slave trade should come to an end in three years. There was also a **territorial dispute** in 1825 with the Argentine provinces over the left bank of the Río de la Plata, called the Banda Oriental, which flared up into war and was only settled in 1828 with the creation of Uruguay as a buffer state. The mistrust between the Portuguese and the Brazilians became even more pronounced. Portuguese merchants were blamed for the rising cost of living and in 1831 rioting broke out in Rio de Janeiro. Dom Pedro shuffled and reshuffled his cabinet to appease different factions but nothing worked and on 7 April he abdicated in favour of his five-year-old son, **Dom Pedro II**, choosing to leave Brazil a week later on a British warship.

Regency & During the 10 years of the young prince's boyhood, there were many separatist
rebellion movements and uprisings by the oppressed lower classes. In 1832-35 there was the **War of the Cabanos**, in Pernambuco, a guerrilla war against the slave-owning plantocracy of the northeast; in 1835 the **Cabanagem rebellion** of free Indians and mestizos took place in Pará after a white secessionist revolt and sporadic fighting continued until 1840 (see page 545); in 1837-38 in Bahia there was a federalist rebellion; in 1835 Rio Grande do Sul proclaimed itself a republic, remaining independent for nearly 10 years, with the movement spreading into Santa Catarina, which also declared itself a republic. By 1840 there was a general consensus that although he had not come of age, it was imperative that the 14-year old, Pedro, should ascend

the throne. He was duly crowned. Administration of the country was centralized again, the powers of provincial assemblies were curtailed, a national police force set up and the Council of State restored.

The second empire

It took a couple of years for the balance of power to be worked out between the conservative élites of Rio de Janeiro and the liberal élites of São Paulo and Minas Gerais, but once the interests of different groups had been catered for, the constitutional monarchy worked smoothly for 20 years. **Coffee** was now the major crop in São Paulo and Minas Gerais and it was important that the wealthy oligarchy who produced it shared in the power structure of the nation to prevent secessionist movements.

Abolition of slavery

Despite the Anglo-Brazilian Treaty of 1826, the slave trade continued until the British Royal Navy put pressure on Brazilian ships carrying slaves in 1850 and the trade was halted soon afterwards. As slaves in Brazil did not reproduce at a natural rate because of the appalling conditions in which they lived and worked, it was clear that an alternative source of labour would eventually have to be found. Anti-slavery movements gathered strength and in 1871 the first steps towards abolition were taken. A new law gave freedom to all children born to slaves from that date and compensation was offered to masters who freed their slaves. During the 1870s large numbers of European immigrants, mostly from Italy and Portugal, came to work on the coffee plantations, and as technology and transport improved, so the benefits of slavery declined. During the 1880s the abolition movement became unstoppable and, after attempts to introduce compensation for slave owners failed, a law abolishing slavery immediately was passed on 13 May 1888. Some plantation owners went bankrupt, but the large majority survived by paying immigrant workers and newly freed slaves a pittance. Those freed slaves who left the plantations to find employment in the cities were equally exploited and lived in poverty.

Proclamation of the Republic

The first Republic: 1889-1930

The monarchy did not long survive the end of slavery. The São Paulo coffee producers resented abolition and resented their under-representation in the structures of power nationwide, while being called upon to provide the lion's share of the Treasury's revenues. The republican movement started in the early 1870s in cities all over Brazil, but grew strongest in São Paulo. It gradually attracted the support of the military, who also felt under-represented in government, and on 15 November 1889 a bloodless **military *coup d'état*** deposed the monarchy and instituted a federal system. The constitution of the new republic established 20 states with wide powers of self-government, a directly elected president of a national government with a senate and a chamber of deputies. Suffrage was introduced for literate adult males (about 3% of the population) and the Church and state were separated. Although the birth of the Republic was bloodless, there were pockets of resistance in rural areas such as the northeast, where the sugar estates were in recession. In the 1890s O Conselheiro led tens of thousands of followers against the secular republic at Canudos, nearly all of whom were eventually killed by government troops. In 1911 there was another rebellion in the southern states of Paraná and Santa Catarina, led by a Catholic visionary in defence of the monarchy. The **Contestado movement** lasted until 1915, when it too was destroyed by the military.

Brazilian politics were now dominated by an alliance known as *café com leite* (coffee with milk), of the coffee growers of São Paulo and the cattle ranchers of Minas Gerais, occasionally challenged by Rio Grande do Sul, with periodic involvement of the military. The first two presidents of the republic were military: Marshal Deodoro da Fonseca (1889-91) and Marshal Floriano Peixoto (1891-94). In some ways the military took the place of the Crown in mediating between the states' oligarchies, but its interventions were always unconstitutional and therefore gave rise to political instability. By the 1920s tensions between São Paulo and Minas Gerais had come out into the open with the cattle ranchers resenting the way in which the coffee growers used their position to keep the price of coffee artificially high at a time when there was an oversupply. Other social groups also became restive and unsuccessful coup attempts were launched by junior army officers in 1922, 1924 and 1926.

The end of the First World War saw the **rise of the USA** as an industrial power and the decline of Britain's traditional supremacy in trade with Latin America. Although Brazil was still exporting its raw materials to Europe at ever lower prices, it now imported its manufactured goods from the USA, leading to difficulties with finance and fluctuating exchange rates. Brazil's terms of trade had therefore deteriorated and the profitability of its export-led economy was declining before the crash of Wall Street in 1929. The cost of stockpiling excess coffee had led to a rise in debt and by 1930 the government was spending a third of its budget on debt servicing. The growth of nationalism was a key feature of this period as well as the emergence of new political factions and parties such as fascists and communists.

Vargas & the Estado Nôvo: 1930-45

The **Wall Street crash** led to a sudden decline in demand for coffee and the São Paulo élite saw its hegemony wiped out. The elections of 1930 saw another win for the São Paulo candidate but the results were disputed by a coalition of opposition forces. After several months of tension and violence, the army intervened, deposed the outgoing president and installed the alternative candidate of Rio Grande do Sul, Getúlio Vargas, a wealthy rancher, as provisional president. Vargas in fact held office until 1954, with only one break in 1945-50. Vargas' main aim when he took office was to redress the balance of power away from São Paulo and in favour of his own state. However, the effects of his reforms were more far-reaching. He governed by decree, replacing all state governors with 'interventors' who reduced the state militias, and reorganized the system of patronage within the states in favour of Vargas. São Paulo naturally resisted and there was a rebellion in 1932, but it was soon put down by federal troops, effectively wiping out the threat to Vargas' authority. In 1934 a constituent assembly drew up a new constitution which reduced the power of the states and gave more power to the president. The assembly then elected Vargas as president for a four-year term.

With the decline of traditional oligarchic blocs came the rise of political parties. The first to fill the vacuum were the **fascists** and the **communists**, which frequently took to street violence against each other. The fascists, called Integralists, were founded by Plínio Salgado in 1932. The Aliança Libertadora Nacional (ALN), a popular front including socialists and radical liberals, was founded by the Brazilian Communist Party in 1935. The ALN attempted to gain power by infiltrating the junior ranks of the army and encouraging rebellions, but Vargas clamped down on the movement, imprisoning its leaders. The fascists aimed to take power in 1938, the year elections were due, at which Vargas was not eligible to stand. However, in October 1937, Vargas declared a state of siege against an alleged communist plot and suspended the constitution which had prevented him being re-elected. Instead, he proclaimed a new constitution and a new state, *Estado Nôvo*. The fascists tried to oust him but failed, leaving Vargas with no effective opposition whatsoever.

The *Estado Nôvo* was also a response to an **economic crisis**, brought on by a fall in coffee prices, rising imports, a resulting deficit in the balance of payments, a high level of debt and soaring inflation. Vargas assumed dictatorial powers to deal with the economic crisis, censoring the press, banning political parties, emasculating trade unions and allowing the police unfettered powers. There followed a transition from export-led growth to import substitution and industrialization with heavy state intervention. Agricultural resources were channeled into industry and the government became involved in mining, oil, steel, electricity, chemicals, motor vehicles and light aircraft. The military were allowed free rein to develop their own armaments industry. As **war** approached in Europe, Vargas hedged his bets with both Nazi Germany and the USA, to see who would provide the greatest assistance for Brazil's industrialization. It turned out to be the USA, and in return for allowing US military bases to be built in northern Brazil he secured loans, technical assistance and other investments for a massive steel mill at Volta Redonda and infrastructure projects. Brazil did not declare war on Germany until 1944, but it was the only Latin American country to send troops to join the allies, with a force of 25,000 men going to Italy.

The elections of 1943 had been postponed during the War, but Vargas scheduled a vote for December 1945 in an attempt to dispel his fascist image. He allowed the formation of political parties, which included two formed by himself: the Social Democratic Party (PSD), supported by industrialists and large farmers, and a Labour Party (PTB), supported by pro-Vargas trade unions. There was also the National Democratic Union (UDN), opposed to Vargas, and the newly legalized Communist Party. However, there were growing fears that Vargas would not relinquish power, and when he appointed his brother as chief of police in Rio de Janeiro, the military intervened. Faced with the prospect of being deposed, Vargas chose to resign in October 1945, allowing the elections to take place as planned in the December. They were won by the PSD, led by General Eurico Dutra, a former supporter of the *Estado Nôvo*, who had encouraged Vargas to resign.

Yet another constitution was drafted by a constituent assembly in 1946, this one based on the liberal principles of the 1891 constitution but including the labour code and the social legislation of the *Estado Nôvo*. Industrialization through state planning was retained, the foreign-owned railways were nationalized, hydroelectric power was developed, but deflation was necessary to bring down spiralling prices. The Communist Party was banned again in 1947. Meanwhile Vargas was elected Senator for Rio Grande do Sul, his home state, and kept active in politics, eventually being elected as candidate for the PSD and PTB alliance in the 1950 presidential elections. Although it was his third presidency, it was only his first by direct elections.

The Second Republic: 1946-64

The third Vargas presidency was beset by the problems of fulfilling populist election promises while grappling with **debt** and **inflation**. Rapid industrialization required levels of investment which could only be raised abroad, but the nationalists were opposed to foreign investment. He failed to reconcile the demands of the USA and the nationalists, particularly with regards to oil and energy, and he failed to control inflation and stabilize the economy. There were rumours of corruption, and after the president's bodyguard was implicated in a plot to kill a journalist which went wrong and another man was shot, the army issued him with another ultimatum to resign or be ousted. Instead, on 24 August 1954, Vargas shot himself, leaving a suicide note denouncing traitors at home and capitalists abroad.

The next president was **Juscelino Kubitschek**, who took office in January 1956 with the aim of achieving economic growth at any cost, regardless of inflation and debt. He is best known for building the new capital of Brazil, Brasília, nearly 1,000 km northwest of Rio de Janeiro in the state of Goiás. This massive modernist project served in the short term to expand the debt and in 1961, the next president, Jânio Quadros, inherited huge economic problems which brought his government down after only seven months and Congress unexpectedly accepted his resignation. Power passed to his vice-president, João Goulart, a populist and former labour minister under Vargas, who was mistrusted by the armed forces and the right wing. His powers were curtailed with the appointment of a prime minister and cabinet who would be jointly answerable to Congress. The 1960s were a turbulent time in Brazil as

Political parties in Brazil

The history of Brazil's modern political parties dates from December 1979 when the law was passed to end the two party system which had been in force since the military government which took power in 1964 outlawed political parties. The military approved two parties, its own supporters in the Aliança Renovadora Nacional (ARENA) and the Movimento Democrático Brasileiro (MDB), the tolerated opposition. (See the Military rule: 1964-85, below, for details of this period and the political movements which preceded it.) Between 1982 and 1994, a total of 68 parties put up candidates for some or all the elections held in this period. Only 23 of them obtained final registration, which suggests that the majority were transitory affairs. The fact that a political party can field a candidate while still only provisionally registered explains why there have been so many since the creation of the New Republic, but since 1994 there seems to have been a stabilization within the multiparty system.

There are two large parties, the PMDB and the PFL. There are also six medium-sized parties: Partido do Movimento Democrático Brasileiro *(PMDB – Democratic Movement Party);* Partido da Frente Liberal *(PFL – Liberal Front Party);* Partido da Social Democracia Brasileira *(PSDB – Brazilian Social Democracy Party);* Partido Progressista Reformador *(PPR – Progressive Reform Party);* Partido dos

Trabalhadores *(PT – Workers' Party);* Partido do Povo *(PP – Popular Party);* Partido Democrático Trabalhista *(PDT – Democratic Labour Party);* Partido Trabalhista Brasileiro *(PTB – Brazilian Labour Party). The PPR was an amalgamation of two earlier parties, the* Partido Democrático Social *(PDS – Social Democrat Party) and the* Partido Democrata Cristão *(PDC – Christian Democrat Party), while the PP was formed by former members of the* Partido Social Trabalhista *(PST – Social Labour Party) and the* Partido Trabalhista Renovador *(PTR – Labour Party for Renewal). A number of small parties usually hold under 10 seats. Even if the proportion of seats held by different-sized parties is beginning to adhere to a pattern, it does not prevent shifting alliances, the migration of deputies from one party to another or the fusion of parties. The style of government, therefore, is one of concensus, rather than government by majority.*

There is no space here to go into all the ramifications of the individual parties' histories, but perhaps a brief overview will help the reader understand some of the names which appear daily in the press. The PMDB was, basically, the successor to the MDB in 1980; at that time, the PDS was the party formed by a large number of ARENA's members. In the former, PMDB camp were such well known names as Itamar Franco, Orestes Quércia, Ulisses Guimarães and Mário Covas, and in the

elsewhere, with the universities a hotbed of revolutionary socialism after the Cuban Revolution, Trotskyist and Communist agitators encouraging land occupations, strikes in industry and a move to secure trade union rights for the armed forces. A nationalist Congress passed legislation cutting foreign companies' annual profit remittances to 10% of profits, which sparked a massive outflow in foreign capital and a halving of US aid. Goulart was forced to print money to keep the economy going, which naturally put further pressure on an already soaring inflation rate. When Goulart clashed with Congress over approval of an economic adjustment programme and tried to strengthen his position by appealing for popular support outside Congress, he alarmed the middle classes, who unexpectedly supported a military coup in March 1964. Goulart took refuge in Uruguay.

latter (PDS) José Sarney, Paulo Maluf and Antônio Carlos Magalhães. Two politicians, Ivete Vargas and Leonel Brizola, wished to register the PTB, a labour party that predated the military regime. The electoral tribunal gave the name to Vargas, so Brizola set up the PDT which became the vehicle for Brizola's own brand of left-wing populism (especially during his terms as governor of Rio de Janeiro). After the peaceful transition to the New Republic, the old-style labour movement fragmented into the PTB, PDT and PMDB, while a new party, the PT grew out of the union movement of the São Paulo metal workers in the late 1970s. The urban trades unionists of the PT were joined by members of other urban grass roots movements, rural unions and progressive Catholics. The union movement is represented by two confederations, the Central Única de Trabalhadores (CUT) and the Confederação Geral de Trabalhadores (CGT), which have certain ideological differences. Likewise Brazil's communist parties followed different paths: the Partido Comunista Brasileiro (PCB), founded in 1922 on the principles of the Russian revolution, and the Partido Comunista do Brasil (PC do B), which broke away from the PCB in 1962 to adopt a line in keeping with the Albanian model.

The PFL was founded in 1985 with the full return to democracy. Several of its leaders, among them José Sarney, were formerly in the PDS and they supported Tancredo Neves in the electoral college in

his bid for the presidency. Antônio Carlos Magalhães, also of the PDS, joined in 1986. The PSDB was one of the parties formed during the period of the National Constituent Assembly and the 1989 presidential campaign. PSDB was created by parliamentarians unhappy with the position taken by the PMDB on issues such as the length of the presidential term and the system of government to be laid down in the new constitution. Among its founders were the current president, Fernando Henrique Cardoso, and Mário Covas. At this time, Fernando Collor de Mello's election campaign took off and the Partido da Reconstrução Nacional (PRN – National Party of Reconstruction) was created, drawing in several unaffiliated politicians, such as Itamar Franco. Collor's demise led to the collapse of the PRN. One other party that deserves mention is the Partido Verde (PV – Green Party) which was started in 1985 in Rio de Janeiro, first associated with the PT, then becoming a party in its own right in 1988. It was registered in 1993.

Sources: Jairo Marconi Nicolau, Multipartidarismo e Democracia (Rio de Janeiro: Fundação Getúlio Vargas, 1996), pages 9-28; Leôncio Martins Rodrigues, 'As Eleições de 1994: Uma Apreciação Geral,' Dados, 38 (1995), pages 71-92; Michael M Hall and Marco Aurélio Garcia, 'Urban Labour,' Modern Brazil, edited by Michael L Conniff and Frank D McCann, pages 161-191. With thanks to Eduardo Noronha in São Paulo.

Military rule: 1964-85

Background

The 1964 coup was a turning point in Brazilian political history. This time the armed forces did not return to barracks as they had before. Opposition leaders were arrested, the press censored, labour unions purged of anyone seen as left wing, and the secret police were given wide powers. The political parties were outlawed and replaced by two officially approved parties: the government Aliança Renovadora Nacional (ARENA) and the opposition Movimento Democrático Brasileiro (MDB). Congress, consisting only of members of these two parties, approved a succession of military presidents nominated by the armed forces. A new constitution, introduced in 1967, gave the president broad powers over the states and over Congress. The worst period of repression occurred between 1968 and 1973 with a wave of urban **guerrilla warfare**. Around this time, the military government's economic adjustment programme paid dividends and the economy began to grow, making life

The Landless

The acclaimed Brazilian photographer, Sebastião Salgado, published a book in 1997 entitled Terra – Struggle for the Landless *(Phaidon Press) which documents the plight of a portion of Brazilian society which calls itself the* Movimento Sem Terra, *the Landless Movement. In one of the pictures, the horizon between half-tilled land and the sky is obliterated by an army of people raising flags, hoes and machetes to the clouds. It looks like an unstoppable force and yet conjures up images of the futile peasant revolts of bygone eras. In view of the many unkept promises by successive politicians to speed up the redistribution of unused land, 'unstoppable force' may be wishful thinking. Yet for the thousands who marched on Brasília in 1997, for the squatters who have reclaimed empty property, and for those who have been killed in disputes with landowners, the fight for somewhere to settle and grow crops is a reality. It is one of Brazil's biggest contradictions that so much potentially productive farmland is owned by a tiny proportion of the population and yet 42% of privately owned land is unused. For the millions of families who have little or no land to work, such inequality has been the spur for Sem Terra. The demand for land also encompasses the desire no longer to be at the outer margins of the economic and social progress that is taking place elsewhere in the country.*

The trek of over 1,000 km that the Movement made from São Paulo to Brasília in 1997 took two months and, as a sign of the popular support for the marchers, they were greeted like heroes by 120,000 people. Top politicians attended, announcements were made of new credit lines for settlements and of land confiscations, even a US$400 mn World Bank loan for land reform. But would the landowners who have set up private armies to keep Sem Terra out be convinced? Would the political system be radically altered?

In late 1999 the government said that it had acquired unused farmland for 370,000 families since 1994. Critics claimed, though, that the number of landless was still growing. History has not been on their side and another part of their reality is not to believe in anything until the land rights are in their hands. Even when a landowner is found not to have valid title to a property, the legal process to reallocate the land is lengthy and slows the progress of land reform. Such delays have led to the radicalization of Sem Terra, with some loss of its romantic appeal in Brazil.

easier for the middle classes and reducing any potential support for guerrilla groups. In 1968-74 the economy grew at over 10% a year, which became known as the Brazilian **'economic miracle'**. This spectacular growth, achieved because of the authoritarian nature of the regime, masked a widening gulf between the rich and poor, with the blacks and mulattos, always at the bottom in Brazilian society, suffering the most. Edwin Williamson (*The Penguin History of Latin America*) quotes statistics showing that in 1960 the richest 10% of the population received 40% of the national income; by 1980 they received 51%, while the poorest 50% received only 13%. In the shanty towns, or *favelas*, which had mushroomed around all the large cities, but especially São Paulo, disease, malnutrition and high mortality rates were prevalent and their citizens battled constantly in appalling housing lacking sewerage, running water and electricity.

By 1973 some military officers and their civilian advisors had become alarmed at the rising level of opposition. Arguing that repression alone would merely lead to further opposition and even to attempted revolution, they pressed for 'decompression': policies to relax the repression while remaining in power. The attempt to carry out this policy by legalizing political parties, permitting freer trade unions and strikes and reducing censorship, gave greater space for the opposition to demand an end to military rule. Attempts to introduce elections to Congress which were less controlled faced the same obstacle: they tended to result in victories for candidates who favoured civilian rule.

One of the main reasons for the military deciding to return to their barracks was the dire state of the economy. The armed forces had taken over in 1964 when the economy had hit rock bottom, their authoritarian regime had allowed rapid expansion and change which brought about the 'economic miracle', yet by 1980 the economy had gone full circle. Inflation was running at 100% a year and was set to go through the roof, foreign debt was the highest in Latin America, estimated at over US$87 bn, and unemployment was soaring. When international interest rates rose sharply in 1982, Brazil was no longer able to service its debt and it suspended interest payments. Unwilling to go through another round of authoritarianism and repression, the military decided to let the civilians have a go. Elections in 1982 produced a majority for the pro-government Social Democratic Party (PDS) in the electoral college which was to elect the next president, but splits in the PDS led to the election in January 1985 of the opposition candidate, Tancredo Neves (see under São João del Rei, page 254).

The return to democracy

In 1985 Tancredo Neves was elected as the first civilian president for 21 years. Before he could take office he fell ill and died. His vice-president José Sarney became president at a time of economic crisis, with inflation at 300%. Sarney introduced the Cruzado Plan in 1986, freezing prices and wages, but inflation exploded when the freeze was lifted. **Corruption & impeachment**

A new constitution brought direct presidential elections in November 1989. After two rounds of voting Fernando Collor de Melo, of the small Partido da Reconstrução Nacional, won 53% of the vote to narrowly defeat his left-wing rival, Luís Inácio da Silva (popularly known as Lula). Collor launched controversial economic reforms, including opening the economy to imports, privatisation and a freeze on savings and bank accounts. The policies failed; by 1991 inflation reached 1,500% and foreign debt payments were suspended.

Just over half way through his term, Collor was suspended from office after Congress voted overwhelmingly to impeach him for corruption. He avoided impeachment by resigning on 29 December 1992. Vice-president Itamar Franco took over, but had scant success in tackling poverty and inflation until the introduction of an anti-inflation package that introduced the *real* as the new currency.

The architect of the *Real* plan was finance minister **Fernando Henrique Cardoso**. Three decades earlier he had been a high-profile leftist and opponent of military rule, forced into exile after the 1964 military coup. The success of the *Real* plan led to his election as president in October 1994. After trailing Lula (see above) of the Workers Party (PT), Cardoso gained such popularity that he won the election in the first round of voting. However, his alliance of the Brazilian Social Democrat Party (PSDB), the Liberal Front (PFL) and the Labour Party (PTB) failed to gain a majority in either house of Congress. This severely hampered plans to reform the tax and social security systems and the civil service. The government was also criticized for its slowness in addressing social problems. Such problems ranged from the need for land reform and violence associated with landlessness, to the slave-like working conditions in some agricultural areas and the human rights of Indians and of street children in large cities. **The Plano Real** **Background**

Towards the end of 1997 the financial crisis in Asia sapped investor confidence throughout the world, and threatened Brazil's currency and economic stability. The failure to cut public spending had swollen the budget deficit and the *real* was exposed to speculation. Cardoso was obliged to take actions to prevent an upsurge in inflation and devaluation of the currency, but at the cost of slowing down economic growth. Crisis was avoided and inflation remained in single figures, in contrast to the hyperinflation of earlier periods.

The government still faced the serious social imbalances that it had failed to redress. However, Cardoso managed to beat Lula again in October 1998 without the need for a second poll. In doing so he became the first Brazilian president to be elected for a second term.

Cardoso's second term Cardoso and his PSDB party emerged victorious from the 1998 elections with 99 Deputies, but they needed allies both in the 513 seat Chamber of Deputies and in the Senate. Political opponents had also won many powerful state governorships. The PSDB's relations with its major ally the PFL came under increasing strain. Unlike the PSDB, the PFL is a conservative group dominated by old-style politicians, typified by its leader Antônio Carlos Magalhães, who increasingly controlled Congress. There were rumours of corruption in Cardoso's government, with not even the president himself above implication. Another financial crisis threatened, which was averted by an IMF loan of US$18 bn at the end of 1998, but the long delayed social security reforms had still not been passed. Finally when ex-president Itamar Franco, governor of Minas Gerais, refused to pay his state's debts to the Federal Government in January 1999, foreign investors lost confidence. The pressures on the *real* became too great and the central bank was forced to let it float freely against the dollar. It lost 50% of its value in the process. Two rather more stable years followed, but with its economic credibility eroded and shifting alliances in Congress the Cardoso government made little progress with its policies.

The 2002 elections As in the USA, Brazilian presidents cannot run for a third term. Four front-runners emerged in the 2002 elections. Taking an early commanding lead in the opinion polls was Luiz Inácio Lula da Silva, best known as Lula, who was making his fourth bid for the presidency. With a refurbished image, a new suit, moderated policies and a millionaire running mate, the veteran firebrand, gained support from all classes.

Against a backdrop of global crises, the *real* again lost some 50% of its value in less than a year. Foreign investors were concerned about repeated budget deficits, and the prospect that a more left-wing government might default on debts. In August 2002 the IMF again came to the rescue, this time with a record US$30 bn loan, subject to tough conditions. On 27 October Lula won a convincing victory in the run-off against government-backed José Serra. The new president – once shoe-shine boy, ex-leader of the Metal Workers' Union and head of the Workers' Party – is set to lead the first left-wing government in Brazil for 40 years. As this book goes to press and thousands of Brazilians celebrate his victory in the streets, Lula faces the onerous task of reconciling economics with the expectations of the nation.

Economy

Brazil's economy is the largest in Latin America and the 10th in the world, but its gdp per capita has grown little since 1980 and is less than the average for the whole of Latin America and the Caribbean. It has abundant and varied natural resources, not all of which are fully explored or exploited. The 40 years after 1945 were a period of massive state intervention and industrialization with public sector investment in energy, heavy industry, transport equipment and capital goods, but in the 1990s the country has moved towards a market economy with a smaller role for the state.

Background

Brazil remains a large farming country; processed and unprocessed agricultural products account for about a third of exports and agriculture, forestry and fishing account for 12% of gdp. Brazil is the world's largest producer and exporter of **coffee** and maintains a dominant position in international markets for **soya** and **orange juice**, mostly grown in the state of São Paulo. São Paulo state also produces over half Brazil's harvest of **sugar cane**, most of which is distilled into fuel alcohol for cars or electricity generating power plants. Although Brazil used to be the world's largest **cocoa** grower, with Ilhéus the main area of production, the industry has declined because of underinvestment, fungus and low prices. Most of Brazil's agricultural land is held by large landowners, with 10% of the farmers owning 80% of the land. Land reform is contentious and has proceeded very slowly with much conflict and violence.

Agriculture

The country is richly endowed with metals and other minerals. Brazil has up to a third of the world's **iron ore** reserves, found mainly in Minas Gerais and certain parts of the Amazon basin, especially the Serra dos Carajás region (Pará). Brazil also exports **manganese** and produces increasing amounts of **tin** and **copper**. In 1996, the state mining company (now 73.5% sold to the private sector), Companhia Vale do Rio Doce (CVRD), announced a 150-tonne **gold** find near Carajás, which would make it the largest gold mine in Latin America. It is expected to produce 10 tonnes a year, about 20% of Brazil's present output. The mine is also near Serra Pelada, an open mine which in the 1980s attracted a gold rush of 80,000 *garimpeiros*, wildcat goldminers, but the new one is much deeper and not suitable for being dug by hand. CVRD is one of the world's largest natural resources groups and owns mining and exploration rights worth an estimated US$40 bn, including Carajás, where reserves of iron ore are sufficient for 500 years.

Mining

Industrial production accounts for 22% of gdp and sales of mechanical equipment, cars, chemicals, textiles and other manufactures account for the majority of exports. The car industry fluctuates in line with domestic demand but produces on average some two million vehicles a year. The steel and vehicle industries are among the top 10 in the world. The Mercosur free trade area has encouraged exporters to look for markets in neighbouring countries instead of concentrating on the USA and Europe. Privatization, the abolition of price controls and falling tariffs have forced increased efficiency and productivity on to Brazilian companies, which have had to invest in modernization and gear their strategy to coping with competition rather than hyperinflation.

Manufacturing

Energy sector development was aimed at substituting local for imported energy. The **oil** industry was nationalized in 1953 and the state monopoly, Petrobrás, controlled exploration, production, refining and distribution of oil and gas. That monopoly ended in 1998, allowing private sector companies to compete, or form joint ventures with Petrobrás. Large investments have been made in **hydroelectricity**, **alcohol** and **nuclear power**. The system's total capacity in 1995 was 52,700MW, but investment was not keeping pace with demand of about 5% a year, so shortages and power cuts periodically affect parts of the country. It is estimated that 10% of homes are not connected to the electricity grid (47% in 1970), and some 16% of energy distributed is not paid for because of illegal connections. Privatization in the electricity sector has been taking place piecemeal, with various states selling off utilities.

Energy

Culture

People

Indigenous peoples How many indigenous Indians were living in Brazil when the Portuguese arrived? The probable figure is somewhere between three and five million. Today there are between 200,000 and 300,000. Whatever the exact numbers, the effects of European colonization have been devastating. Present-day tribal groups number about 220; each has a unique dialect, but most languages belong to four main linguistic families, Tupi-Guarani, Ge, Carib and Arawak. A few tribes remain uncontacted, others are exclusively nomadic, others are semi-nomadic hunter-gatherers and farmers, while some are settled groups in close contact with non-Indian society. There is no agreement on precisely how many tribes are extant, but the Centro Ecumênico da Documentação e Informação (CEDI) of São Paulo said that of the 200 or so groups it documented, 40% have populations of less than 200 people and 77% have populations of less than 1,000. Hemming underlines this depressing statistic when he reports that tribes contacted in recent decades have, as have others in previous centuries, suffered catastrophic reductions in numbers as soon as they encounter diseases which are common to non-indigenous people, but to which their bodies have no immunity.

The struggle of groups such as the Yanomami to have their land demarcated in order to secure title is well-documented. The goal of the Statute of the Indian (Law 6.001/73), for demarcation of all Indian land by 1978, is largely unmet. It was feared that a new law introduced in January 1996 would slow the process even more. Funai, the National Foundation for the Support of the Indian, a part of the Interior Ministry, is charged with representing the Indians' interests, but lacks resources and support. There is no nationwide, representative body for indigenous people. Most of Brazil's indigenous people live in the Amazon region; they are affected by deforestation, encroachment from colonizers, small- and large-scale mining, and the construction of hydroelectric dams. Besides the Yanomami, other groups include the Xavante, Tukano, Kreen-Akrore, Kaiapó, Bororo and Arara.

Mestiços At first the Portuguese colony grew slowly. From 1580 to 1640 the population was only about 50,000 apart from the million or so indigenous Indians. In 1700 there were some 750,000 non-indigenous people in Brazil. Early in the 19th century Humboldt computed there were about 920,000 whites, 1.96 million Africans, and 1.12 million Indians and people of mixed Portuguese and Indian origin (*mestiços*): after three centuries of occupation a total of only four million, and over twice as many Africans as there were whites.

The arid wastes of the Sertão remain largely uncultivated. Its inhabitants are *mestiço*; most live off a primitive but effective method of cultivation known as 'slash and burn', which involves cutting down and burning the brushwood for a small patch of ground which is cultivated for a few years and then allowed to grow back.

Afro-Brazilians Though there is no legal discrimination against black people, the economic and educational disparity – by default rather than intent of the Government – is such that successful Afro-Brazilians are active almost exclusively in the worlds of sport, entertainment and the arts.

Brazilian culture is rich in African influences. Those interested in the development of Afro-Brazilian music, dance, religion, arts and cuisine will find the whole country north of São Paulo fascinating, and especially the cities of Bahia and São Luís which retain the greatest African influences. Black Pride movements are particularly strong in Bahia.

Background

Modern immigration did not begin effectively until after 1850. Of the 4.6 million immigrants from Europe between 1884 and 1954, 32% were Italians, 30% Portuguese, 14% Spanish, 4% German, and the rest of various nationalities. Since 1954 immigrants have averaged 50,000 a year.

Europeans

Most of the German immigrants settled in Santa Catarina, Rio Grande do Sul, and Paraná. The Germans (and the Italians and Poles and other Slavs who followed them) did not in the main go as wage earners on the big estates, but as cultivators of their own small farms. Here there is a settled agricultural population cultivating the soil intensively.

There are some one million Japanese-descended Brazilians; they grow a fifth of the coffee, 30% of the cotton, all the tea, and are very active in market gardening. Today the whites and near-whites are about 53% of the population, people of mixed race about 34%, and Afro Brazilians 11%; the rest are either Indians or Asians. There are large regional variations in the distribution of the races: the whites predominate greatly in the south, which received the largest flood of European immigrants, and decrease more or less progressively towards the north.

Asians

Religion

In order to discuss religion in Brazil, it is necessary to consider the three main cultures from which the Brazilian people originated, the Indians, the Portuguese and the Blacks. Each has contributed its own religious traditions and in many cases they have intermingled and influenced each other.

Before the arrival of the Portuguese colonizers, Brazil was inhabited by many tribes of Indians. They had their own animist cults and a very rich, poetic mythology. The most important of their divinities was **Tupan**, the spirit of tempests, fire, lightning and thunder. It was he who had taught their ancestors the secrets of agriculture and hunting. The three other important gods were **Jaci**, the moon, **Guaraci**, the sun, and **Rudá**, love. There were also minor divinities such as Guirapuru, the lord of the birds, Caapora, the guardian of the animals, and Anhanga, the protector of hunters. There were also devils and one of the most feared was the **Jurupari**, an evil spirit which came in the night to bring nightmares to men. The designations of Tupan and Jurupari as the most important divinities in relation to Good and Evil were made by the Catholic missionaries in colonial times. The Europeans could not deal with the

Brazilian Indians

Indians dancing for the spirit of a Jaguar, Fábio Sombra, 1992

Indians' polytheistic religion, so they condensed the attributes of these spirits into concepts they could comprehend and educate against.

The priests, or shamans, were called **Pagés** and they knew the secrets of plants and magic potions. They would cure people in rituals in which they would invoke the spirits of the forest, their ancestors and certain animals. When faced with the diseases brought by the colonizers, however, the Pagés were almost helpless.

The Indians' religious system was based on many aspects of nature and on situations they had to face in their daily life. Today, the traditional cults of the Brazilian Indians have practically disappeared, not only because of the decrease in the numbers of the Indians themselves, but also because of the persistent work of missionaries, Catholic and Protestant, to convert them to Christianity, from the very first moments of European colonization.

Colonizers & the Catholic church A sword in one hand and a cross in the other: one of the principal, official motives for the European colonization of the 'New World' was the necessity to convert the indigenous people to Christianity. Most of the great Catholic religious orders, such as the Benedictines, Carmelites, Franciscans and Jesuits, went to Brazil precisely with this aim. At the beginning of the colonial period, mainly in the 16th and 17th centuries, the religious orders were practically the only institutions providing public education, artistic and academic studies. The Jesuits specifically were dedicated to converting the Indians and they created many missions (*aldeias*).

In the colonial period there was absolutely no tolerance of other religions and many Jewish and Muslim immigrants understood the convenience of converting to the Catholic faith. This practice was also common in Portugal and many of these 'cristãos novos', or newly-converted Christians, acquired Portuguese surnames related to trees and natural elements, such as Pereira (peach tree), Carvalho (oak tree), or Oliveira (olive tree).

At the beginning of the 19th century, when Napoleon invaded Portugal and forced the Portuguese royal family and nobility to move to Brazil, a stronger commercial and diplomatic relationship with the British Empire made the king, Dom João VI, more tolerant of the Protestants. After 1808, many English families and tradesmen emigrated to Rio de Janeiro. Even so, they were only allowed to build a Protestant cemetery in 1811 and their first church in 1819, "as long as it did not have the appearance of a religious temple", according to Dom João VI's decree.

During the Brazilian Empire and up to the creation of the Republic in 1889, Catholicism was the official state religion. After that, as stated in all Brazilian republican constitutions, there is total freedom of religion and no one may suffer any kind of religious persecution, under protection of the law. Nevertheless, the influence of the Catholic church remained very important, both economically and politically. At present, the majority of the Brazilian population is still Roman Catholic, although in the last 10 to 15 years many Brazilians, especially in the very poor areas, have converted to Protestantism. Among the traditional Protestant churches, the most important ones in Brazil are the Baptists, the Presbyterians and the Lutherans, particularly in the south, which was mostly colonized by Germans. In many cases, though, the nonconformists are represented by new evangelical sects, such as the Universal Church of God's Kingdom, directed by its 'bishop', Edir Macedo. These new Christian sects, generally called 'evangélicas', have been very successful in attracting new converts for their flocks. They use modern marketing techniques and electronic media, including their own TV channels, radio stations and newspapers. Their pastors use very dramatic speeches, full of examples of miracles, cures and solutions for all possible material and spiritual problems. In some cases, scandals have been widely reported in the press and the financial operations of certain churches have been subject to investigation.

When the Portuguese colonizers started to plant sugar cane on the northeast coast of Brazil, they soon realized that they would need a large, strong workforce to carry out the labour. The first option was to use the local indigenous population as slaves, but the Indians (those who did not die of European diseases) regarded that kind of work as demeaning, they soon became exhausted, frequently escaped, or simply refused to co-operate. Portugal, therefore, had to bring in black slaves. These people came from different regions of Africa and belonged to many different tribes, such as the Bantu, the Sudanese, the Angolans and the Hotentots. After the rigours of transatlantic shipment, they suffered further trauma on arrival at the Brazilian ports. They were often sold in groups which were segregated to avoid slaves from the same family or speaking the same language being together. By breaking all cultural and sentimental ties, the Portuguese hoped to eradicate ethnic pride and rebellions on the estates. Of course, these people brought their own religions, but the point is that none of their cults remained pure in Brazil. Taking, for example, the region of what is now Nigeria, there were different groups of people, each with its own divinity or Orixá (pronounced 'Orisha'). These Orixás were normally the spirit of a distinguished ancestor or a legendary hero and they were worshipped only in a particular region. As the slaves went to Brazilian estates in groups made up of people from different African regions, they soon started to worship all the Orixás, instead of just one. This was the origin of Candomblé and Umbanda, Afro-Brazilian religions, different from their African antecedents and therefore original.

Afro-Brazilian religions

Naturally, the Catholic Portuguese did not allow the slaves to maintain their own beliefs. So the Africans ingeniously began to associate their own gods with the Catholic saints who had more or less the same characteristics. For example, when the masters thought the slaves were praying to Saint George, the warrior saint, they were, in fact, praying to Ogun, the Orixá representing war and battles. This association is called religious syncretism and is one of the defining characteristics of the Afro-Brazilian religions.

Religious syncretism

In Candomblé, the figure of God, the Creator is called Olorum. But this figure is almost never mentioned. To some degree, this is because Olorum is too busy to care about mankind's small problems. These are taken care of by the Orixás, the spiritual guides responsible for all sorts of matters concerning our lives. According to Candomblé, from the moment of birth, every person has one or two Orixás to act as protector and tutor. The personality and the temperament of everyone is directly influenced by his or her Orixá. For example, a son or daughter of Ogun (the Orixá of war) is likely to be an impulsive and combative person, while the sons and daughters of Oxun (the Orixá of waterfalls and love) tend to be charming and coquettish.

The cult of the Orixás

To discover who your protector Orixá is, you must go to a Pai de Santo (male priest) or a Mãe de Santo (woman priest) and ask him or her to use the *Jogo de Buzios*. This is an oracle using 16 sea shells by which the priests can predict the future and answer questions related to material or spiritual matters. It is also very common to make offerings to the Orixás, consisting of special foods (every Orixá has his or her own preferences), alcoholic beverages, cigars, flowers, pop-corn, candles, toys and even ritually sacrificed animals such as cockerels, goats and pigeons. These offerings are delivered in different places, according to the Orixá. For example, offerings to

Mãe de Santo and the Buzios Oracle

Oxossi, the hunter, are delivered in a forest or a bush, and so on. The offerings are always associated with a wish being made, or by way of thanks to the Orixá for a favour received.

The religious ceremonies take place in *terreiros*, with much singing and drumming. The Pais de Santo and Mães de Santo enter into a trance and each is possessed by his or her protector Orixá, being able to communicate with humans, answer questions, give advice and predict the future.

It is very difficult to estimate the exact number of Brazilians who follow Candomblé and Umbanda. One of the main reasons is that many of their followers also profess themselves to be Catholics, which may be perfectly true. For many years the Afro-Brazilian religions were officially forbidden and only recently are people becoming more open in admitting their beliefs in public. The greatest influence of Candomblé and Umbanda is found in the cities of Salvador da Bahia and Rio de Janeiro. Many writers, academic and otherwise, have written on the subject, notably the novelist Jorge Amado, who was a member of the Candomblé cult until he died in 2001 (see his book, *The War of the Saints*, 1993).

Some of the most important Orixás

Exu (pronounced Eshoo) is considered the messenger between people and the Orixás. Sometimes associated with the Christian Devil, Exu is always represented with a trident and his colours are black and red. Offerings to this Orixá are always made at crossroads and normally consist of cigars, cachaça and red and black candles. His day is Monday.

Ogum the Orixá of war, thunder, lightning and iron. His colour is deep blue and he is always represented with an iron sword. The sons and daughters of Ogum are very combative and impulsive. His day is Tuesday.

Oxossi (pronounced Oshossee) is the hunter and protector of wild animals. This Orixá lives in the forest and is represented with a bow, arrows and a leather hat. His colour is green and sometimes blue. His day is Thursday and all his offerings, including raw tobacco and fruits, must be made in wooded places. People protected by this Orixá are normally very independent and solitary.

Xangô (pronounced Shango) is the Orixá of truth and justice. His colours are red and white and his day is Wednesday. He is represented with a double-headed axe, the African symbol of justice.

Oxum (pronounced Oshoon) is a feminine Orixá, associated with love and the family, found in waterfalls and whitewater. Pretty and extremely coquettish, she is sometimes represented as a siren with a golden mirror. Her colour is yellow and offerings to her should be delivered close to a waterfall. Her sons and daughters are very dedicated to the family. Her day is Saturday.

Yemanjá, the mother of the seas and saltwater. Her principal day is 31 December, New Year's Eve, and on this day people offer her white flowers, champagne and small boats full of candles and gifts placed in the sea. Her colour is light blue.

Iansã (pronounced Iansan) is a female Orixá related to tempests and storms. Very impulsive, Iansã is the only Orixá who can command the **Eguns**, the spirits of the dead. She wears red and her day is Wednesday.

Omolu, a strange Orixá who never shows his face (severely disfigured by smallpox), is always invoked in cases of disease and illness as he has the power

An offering to Exu

to cure. Often referred as the 'doctor of the poor', he is represented as a strong man covered by a straw coat and holding a straw box full of herbs and medicines.

Two other terms are sometimes used in relation to Afro-Brazilian religions: **Macumba** used to be employed, mainly in Rio de Janeiro, as a generic term to describe all Afro-Brazilian cults. It was a popular expression at the beginning of the 20th century, but has become a derogatory term, not very politically correct. To call someone a 'macumbeiro/a' is offensive. The other term is **Quimbanda**. This is the dark side of Afro-Brazilian religion. It is associated with black magic and sorcery. A 'trabalho de quimbanda' is a ritual designed to hurt someone through offerings or sacrifices. Perhaps performed in cemeteries or at crossroads, these 'trabalhos' may use wax models of the intended victim (like in voodoo), or may involve imaginative and weird practices such as writing the enemy's name on a piece of paper, putting it in a frog's mouth, then sewing up the mouth. The victim is supposed to die a death as slow and painful as the frog's. Quimbanda is a taboo subject and no one will profess to being involved with it.

Spiritism (*espiritismo*) is a philosophical and religious doctrine founded by the French scientist Allan Kardec (1804-69), in his famous *The Book of the Spirits*. Spiritists believe in reincarnation and in the possibility of contact between men and spirits. Life is a necessary experience for spiritual progress and death is just the beginning of another stage in the spirit's evolution. Brazil is said to be the country with the greatest number of spiritists in the world and many spiritist mediums have become internationally famous. A good example is Rubens Faria in Rio de Janeiro who performs thousands of mediumistic surgeries every day. Many influential people and artists have been operated on by him. Sadly, his mystique was called into question in 1999 when police investigated him for murder, charlatanism, tax evasion and money laundering.

Although it does not have an impressive number of followers, the sect called **Santo Daime** deserves mention. It has its origins in the Amazon region and is based in the visions produced by a hallucinogenic beverage called Ayahuasca. This is made from the roots of two plants known to Brazilian Indians for centuries (see Colônia Cinco Mil, page 602).

Other important religions in Brazil

Oxum   Omolu

Arts and crafts

Woodcarving   Woodworking has two principal origins, the African and the Jesuit. In northeastern Brazil, many woodcarving and sculpting techniques are inherited from the African slaves who were brought across the Atlantic to work the sugar plantations. One of the most prominent examples is the *carranca*, the grotesque figurehead that was placed on a boat's prow to ward off evil spirits. *Carrancas* are an adaptation of the African mask-making tradition and other carved and sculpted masks can be found in the northeast. The Jesuits passed on skills in the carving and painting of religious figures in wood. Originally they encouraged their Indian converts in the techniques, but today others practice the art. Woodcarving is widespread in Pernambuco and Bahia in the northeast. In Rio de Janeiro many contemporary artists work in wood and Embu, near São Paulo (see page 180), is an important centre for wooden sculptures and furniture making.

Ceramics   In northeastern Brazil, religious figures are also made in clay, for instance the unglazed, life-sized saints made from red clay in Tracunhaém, near Recife. Another centre for similar work is Goiana, also in Pernambuco. A third place from which the ceramics are even more famous is Alto da Moura, near Caruaru (Pernambuco – see page 454). Here Mestre Vitalino began modelling scraps of clay into little figures depicting everyday life (work, festivals, dancing, political events). He died in 1963, but the tradition that he started has continued and is known throughout Brazil.

   The pots that are made in the Amazon region come in various styles, some of them quite strange. Bahian and other northeastern pottery shows African influence.

Textiles, clothing & leather   Ceará, in the north, is famous for its lace-making, and beautiful pieces are sold all over Brazil. In other parts of the north hammocks and other woven items are found. The hammock is, of course, an essential household item and you may well need to buy one if you are travelling up the Amazon on a boat. Other utilitarian articles which have become craft items are the rugs and capes made in the highlands further south, such as Minas Gerais, to keep out the night-time cold.

   In the northeast, traditional costumes have their roots in the rituals of the African religions that came to Brazil with the slave trade. In southern areas where European immigration was heaviest, many traditional costumes can be seen, usually at the festivals and dances that have survived. Another type of clothing from the south is that associated with the *gaúchos*, the Brazilian cowboys of Rio Grande do Sul. As well as the clothes, which normally use hide in their manufacture, you may also buy saddlery, stirrups, silverware and the gourds used for drinking maté.

   Leatherwork is not confined to the south, but can be found in any region where cattle are raised.

Musical instruments   The most popular instruments that tourists like to buy are those connected with African music, espcially the drums, shakers and the *berimbau*, the one-stringed bow that is twanged in accompaniment to Capoeira. Here again, the best places to look are in the northeast where the African heritage is strongest. You can also purchase guitars and other stringed instruments.

Basketware   In Amazônia, a huge variety of raw materials are available for making baskets, nets, hammocks, slings for carrying babies, masks and body adornments. In the northeast, too, baskets come in all shapes and sizes, especially in Bahia, Pernambuco and Paraíba. Another northeastern craft, which does not fit into the above categories, is pictures made in bottles with coloured sands (Lençóis, Bahia, and Natal, Rio Grande do Norte, are good places to buy them – see pages 397 and 474). In Minas Gerais, two very common things to see and buy are soapstone carvings (for instance birds and animals) and the cooking pots used in *mineira* kitchens.

Legends of rich deposits, even mountains of precious stones preceded their discovery in the interior of the country. Prospectors looked for diamonds and emeralds as well as gold and silver to make them wealthy. The existence of gems was known about almost from the earliest days of the Portuguese colony, from the reports given to the new arrivals by the Indians and from scattered discoveries of different stones. But there was nothing to bring riches on the scale of the silver and gold found in the Spanish colonies. Gold was found in Minas Gerais in the 17th century and diamonds in 1725 at Diamantina (Minas Gerais) and thus Brazil's mineral wealth began to appreciate. The search for new deposits has never flagged.

Some of the commercially mined stones are: **diamonds**, found in Minas Gerais, Roraima, Bahia, Tocantins, Mato Grosso and Mato Grosso do Sul. Brazil was the world's largest producer of diamonds until South Africa entered the market in the 19th century. **Emeralds** were not discovered in Brazil until 1963 (many green beryls had been mined before then, but were known not to be true emeralds); they are now mined in Bahia, Minas Gerais and Goiás. **Aquamarine** is a clear blue beryl from Rio Grande do Norte, Paraíba, Bahia, Minas Gerais and Espírito Santo. **Ruby** and **sapphire** are two shades of the same mineral, corundum, the former rich red, the latter a deep blue. Rubies are found in Santa Catarina, sapphires in Minas Gerais. The two most valued forms of **topaz** found are the rare Imperial Topaz from Ouro Preto (Minas Gerais), which comes in a range of colours from honey-coloured through shades of red to pink, and Blue Topaz from Minas Gerais and Rondônia.

Tourmalines come from Minas Gerais, Ceará and Goiás; they have the widest range of colours of any gemstone, from colourless (white) to red, yellow, greens, blues, lilac and black. They even come in bi- and tricoloured varieties. **Opals**, unique for their rainbow flecks, are mined in Piauí and Rio Grande do Sul. **Amethyst**, a quartz which ranges in colour from pale lilac to deep purple, is mined in Tocantins, Pará, Bahia, Mato Grosso do Sul and Rio Grande do Sul. From the last three states, plus Minas Gerais, comes **citrine**, another quartz which is predominantly yellow. Less well-known, but equally beautiful are **kunzite**, a rare pinkish-violet stone, and **chrysoberyl**, both found in Minas Gerais. Chrysoberyl is found in a variety of forms, a golden-yellow-brown, 'cat's eye' chrysoberyl which has an luminous thread running through it, and the very rare **alexandrite**, which changes colour according to the light. Its most spectacular form changes from green in daylight to red in artificial light.

Music and dance

Perhaps because of its sheer size, Brazil has a greater musical inventory than any other Latin American country, not only reflected in the immense regional spread of folk music but also in its successive waves of urban popular music. Brazilians express themselves through music and dance to an extraordinary degree and the music covers the whole spectrum from the utmost rural simplicity to the ultimate state-of-the-art commercial sophistication. The far north of the country is virtually in the Caribbean, while the extreme south shares its culture with the Rio de la Plata countries.

In Paraná, Santa Catarina and Rio Grande do Sul, the music is strictly European in origin, rhythm and instrumentation. Rio Grande do Sul shares Gaúcho dances such as the Pericom and song styles such as the Milonga, Trova and Pajada with neighbouring Uruguay and Argentina. The Chula is a competitive dance for men to show off with (comparable to the Argentine Malambo), while the Pexinho is for men and

Capoeira and berimbau

One of the most exciting sounds to be heard in the streets of Salvador, Bahia, is that of the berimbau, the instrument that accompanies the dance-cum-martial arts form called Capoeira. The berimbau is a vertical wooden bow with a resonator at the lower end and a single steel string played with a thin stick. The player also holds a caxixi, a small rattle, in the stick hand and coin held against the string to modulate the pitch in the other. The berimbau is accompanied by one of a number of 'toques' or chants, such as the São Bento Grande, Angola, Benguela or

Cavalaria. Although the objective of the Capoeirista is to knock his opponent off his hands or feet, what the bystander will most appreciate is the wonderful grace with which the two bodies of the opponents whirl and cartwheel around one another, as though participating in some physically powerful ballet, never actually touching until a 'fall' is engineered by one of them. Undeniably of African origin, the Capoeira was practised much more violently in the past and did not acquire respectability until the celebrated Mestre Bimba opened the first Academy in 1932.

women. The guitar and the accordion are the favourite instruments, also true for Santa Catarina and Paraná, where the names of the dances denote their European origins: Mazurkas, Valsas, Chotes, Polquinhas and Rancheiras. The Chimarrita is a song style that came straight from the Azores. If you are feeling sentimental, you sing a Toada, if energetic, you stamp your feet to a Fandango. Except for the Batuque de Rio Grande do Sul in Porto Alegre, closely related to the Candombe of nearby Montevideo, there is no African influence in the music of this region and none of that classic Brazilian syncopation.

São Paulo, Rio de Janeiro & Minas Gerais Moving north into São Paulo, we enter an area rich in traditional folk dances and music, with the African admixture beginning to show up. At many religious festivals will be found the Congadas (European 'Moors & Christians', but danced by blacks) and Moçambique (a stick dance for men), while the Samba de Lenço, Fandango and Batuque are recreational dances for one or more couples. The instrumental accompaniment branches out into shakers (the *ganzá*), drums (*caixas* and *tambores*) and above all the guitar (*viola*). Try the great pilgrimage church at Aparecida do Norte on a Sunday. You might well see a group of religious dances. In the hinterland of Rio de Janeiro the Folias de Reis are out on the street from Christmas to Epiphany, singing from house to house, accompanying themselves on the *caixa* and *adufe* drums and the guitar, while in the old coastal towns of Paraty and Angra dos Reis are to be found the Dança de Velhos (the old men), performed to the accordion. The Jongo is a dance of African origin for men and women, naturally with a drum accompaniment. And there is hardly need to mention Rio de Janeiro at carnival and its samba schools. Further north again, we come to the states of Espírito Santo, Minas Gerais and Goiás. In colonial Ouro Preto, in Minas, you can hear the old Modinha sung to the Portuguese guitar as a serenade and be transported into the past. Espírito Santo is home to the Ticumbi, a kind of Congada, danced to the guitar and shakers (*chocalhos*). Goiás shares with Minas Gerais a very rich heritage of Portuguese derived religious folk song and dance, centred on Folias, Modas and Calangos.

Bahia Bahia is the heart of African Brazil and a very musical heart it is, born of the Yoruba religion that came with the slaves from what is now Nigeria. The resulting syncretic religion is known as Candomblé in Bahia and the gods or 'Orixás' are worshipped through song, dance and possession in the 'Terreiros', directed by the priests (Pais-de-Santo) and priestesses (Mães-de-Santo). The mainly female adepts, dressed entirely in white, circle

Dorival Caymmi, Minstrel from Bahia

Dorival Caymmi, born in Salvador in 1914, is not well known outside Brazil, but to most Brazilians he is rated as fine a singer and composer as even this outstandingly musical country has produced. His influence as a precursor of Bossa Nova is acknowledged by such as Tom Jobim, who was at the cutting edge of the movement. The ultimate exponent of what might be termed the 'laid back' as opposed to 'energetic' or even 'frenzied' style of Brazilian music, Dorival Caymmi arrived in Rio de Janeiro in 1938, aged 24, and has lived there ever since, leaving only his heart in Salvador. Within a year he was singing

his own compositions 'O que é que a Bahiana Tem?' and 'A Preta do Acarajé' with Carmen Miranda and over succeeding decades has become both a national icon and a living symbol of his native Bahia. Above all, he is famous for his songs about the fishermen of Salvador, who face the dangers of the ocean in their flimsy jangadas, of which he himself remains by far the best interpreter. Look for a record containing 'O Mar', 'O Vento', 'Promessa de Pescador', 'A Lenda do Abaeté' and the intensely moving 'A Jangada Voltou Só'. You won't be disappointed!

gracefully to the background chant of 'Pontos' and the thunderous pounding of the *atabaques*, the tall drums. The two most revered priestesses are Mãe Olga de Alakêto and Mãe Menininha de Gantois. Similar syncretic African religions are found elsewhere in Brazil (see Religion, page 681). Another vital African element in Bahian folk music is the spectacular dance-cum-martial arts form of Capoeira (see box, page 688). Bodies whirl and cartwheel around each other to the sound of the *berimbau* (a one-stringed bow with resonator) and the accompanying chant. Related to the Capoeira is the stick dance Maculelê. Two of the best *berimbau* groups on record are Camaféu de Oxóssi and the Cordão de Ouro. Bahia has a carnival almost as celebrated as that of Rio and here you can see the Afoxé, a serious religious dance, performed to drums alone.

North of Bahia is the Nordeste, with music that runs the whole gamut from black African to mediaeval Portuguese. In colonial times the church directed the peoples' musical energies into religious plays, songs and dances and a large number of these are still performed. The Bumba-Meu-Boi is a folk drama in the course of which a bull is killed and then brought back to life. Particularly popular in Piauí and Maranhão, its variants are found as far afield as Amazônia, where it is called the Boi-Bumbá, and Paraná in the far south, where it is known as Boi-Mamão. Also popular along the coast from Ceará to Paraíba is a nautical drama of Portuguese origin called Marujada or Nau Catarineta, a version of Moors and Christians, accompanied by Portuguese guitar (*violão*), drums and the *ganzá* scraper. In Alagoas, Sergipe and Pernambuco we find the sword dance called Reisado, danced after Christmas, the Caboclinhos, who are dressed like Indians and dance with bows and arrows, and the Guerreiros Alagoanos, a mixture of both. The last named are accompanied by the classical northeastern musical group called Terno de Pífanos, with the *pífano* vertical flute, accompanied by *maracas* and *ganzá*. The Banda de Pífanos of Caruaru in Pernambuco can be found on record. Recreational dance music in the Nordeste goes under the generic name of 'Forró', said to be derived from the expression 'For All', because the English companies operating at the turn of the century organized week-end dances for their workmen to which all comers were invited. Four very popular recreational folk dances of this region are the Ciranda (a round dance), the Coco, the Bate-Coxa (where the dancers bump bellies) and the Bambelô. Carnival in Recife, the largest city, is when and where to see the energetic and gymnastic Frevo, danced by young men with an umbrella in their hands, and the very stately and superbly

The Northeast

Repentistas and cordel

A fascinating experience in the Nordeste is to come across a pair of 'Violeiros' or 'Repentistas', troubadours who accompany themselves on the melodious Viola Nordestina, developed from the Portuguese seven-string guitar, generally to be found in markets. They will sing, jokingly but flatteringly, about individual members of the audience, expecting a tip in return. They also have a large repertoire of the ballads that deal with regional themes and personalities which are to be

found in the 'Folhetos', or pamphlets known under the generic title of 'Literatura de Cordel' (String Literature), because they are traditionally displayed for sale hung from a string. Both the ballads and the pamphlets are of archaic Portuguese origin. The ballads are made up of innumerable verse forms, such as the Mourão, Galope, Martelo, Sextilha and Quadrão. The celebrated bandit, Lampião, is a favourite subject and the compiling of long lists of words or names is popular too.

costumed Maracatu dancers, with their queen and king. The Nordeste is equally rich in song styles, notably the Desafios, Emboladas, Cocos and Aboios. The Desafios are performed by so-called Repentistas (see box) or Violeiros, who accompany themselves on the Portuguese guitar and whose repertoire includes a large inventory of verse styles. They will sing about individual spectators, who then pay willingly for the compliment. The Emboladas and Cocos are similar, but faster and accompanied solely by tambourines, while the Aboios are haunting songs related to cattle and cattlemen. Repentistas and Emboladores can normally be found at work in markets throughout the region. The premier Repentista is Otacílio Batista do Pajeú, who sang to Pope John Paul II during the latter's first visit to Brazil.

The music of the Nordeste has also been well propagated by more sophisticated groups that have based themselves on folk roots, such as the Quinteto Violado, Ariano Suassuna's Orchestra Armorial and Cussy de Almeida's Quinteto Armorial, not forgetting the veteran accordionist Luiz Gonzaga and the popular Alceu Valença. As a result of the huge migration of *nordestinos* to the urban south, moreover, it is just as easy to hear this regional music in São Paulo as it is in Recife.

Pará & the Amazon   Finally to Pará and the Amazon in the far north, where the music has been heavily influenced from the Caribbean. The most popular musical genre here is the Carimbó, danced to a Merengue-type rhythm and played on drums, wind or brass (usually the clarinet) and strings, particularly the banjo. Notable performers are Pinduca ('O Rei do Carimbó'), Veriquete and Vieira. It is the last-named who thought up the term 'Lambada' for his particular version of the Carimbó and the spectacular, thigh-entwining dance form introduced to the world in Paris by Karakos and Lorsac in 1988 had already been popular among young people at 'Forrós' throughout the region for some years. The song 'Bate Forte o Tambor' by the group Carapicho, originally from Parintins, has become an international hit, the English title being 'Tic, Tic, Tac'. The very traditional island of Marajó in the mouth of the Amazon has preserved versions of 18th-century dances, such as the Lundú and Chula.

Urban popular music   The vast range of Brazilian regional folk music is only equalled by the chronological depth of its urban popular music, which surges like endless waves on a beach. For the origins we have to go back to Jesuit missions and Portuguese folk music, influenced and blended by African slaves, from which emerged the 19th-century Lundús, Polcas and Maxixes that in turn gave way to the romantic and sentimental Choro song genre (from *chorar*, to weep), accompanied by guitar, flute and *cavaquinho* (small guitar), which became all the rage and indeed still has its adepts in Brazil today.

A key figure in urban music was Ernesto Nazaré, composer and pianist, who occupied a special niche somewhere between popular and light classical, composing between 1880 and 1930 a vast number of Tangos Brasileiros (not to be confused with the Argentine variety), Mazurkas, Polcas, Waltzes and other popular songs.

Around the turn of the century the instrumentation turned to brass and Rio's urban Samba was born, a birth that was announced by the recording in 1917 of Donga's 'Pelo Telefone'. Names from this early period are Pixinguinha, Sinhô, Heitor dos Prazeres, Ary Barroso, Noel Rosa and of course Carmen Miranda, who took the Samba to Hollywood and the rest of the world. It also became intimately connected with the carnival in the form of Marcha Ranchos and Sambas de Enredo as the first samba schools were formed, of which Salgueiro, Mangueira, Partido Alto, Portela, Mocidade Independente and Beija-Flor are some of the most famous. With the Escolas de Samba came the Batucada or percussion groups playing the *pandeiro* (tambourine), *atabaque* and *tamborim* (drum), *agogô* (cowbell), *reco-reco*, *chocalho*, *afoxê* and *cuíca*. This is the real engine room of Samba. Listen to Lúcio Perrone or Mocidade Independente de Padre Miguel. A new phase was ushered in with an invasion from Bahia and the Nordeste in the early 1950s. From Bahia came Dorival Caymmi (see box page 689), who dropped his fishermen's songs in favour of the Samba, and Luiz Gonzaga, who brought his accordion, *zabumba* drum and *triangulo*, with which to play his Baiões (his 'Asa Branca' is a classic) and almost put the Samba itself into eclipse for several years. Almost, but not quite, for out of the ashes there soon arose Bossa Nova – white, middle class and silky smooth. Vinícius de Moraes and Tom Jobim were its heroes; 1958 to 1964 the years; Copacabana, Ipanema and Leblon the scene; 'Samba de uma Nota Só', 'A Garota de Ipanema' and 'Desafinado' the songs and Nara Leão, Baden Powell, Toquinho, João Gilberto, Luís Bonfá and Astrud Gilberto the main performers. Stan Getz, the American jazz saxophonist, helped export it to the world. What was now being called MPB (Música Popular Brasileira) then took off in several directions. Chico Buarque, Edu Lobo and Milton Nascimento were protest singers. Out of Bahia emerged 'Tropicalismo' in the persons of Gilberto Gil, Caetano Veloso and his sister Maria Bethânia, Gal Costa, João Gilberto and 'Som Livre'. The words were important, but the rhythm was still there. Brazilian rock also now appeared, with such stars as Roberto Carlos, Elis Regina, Rita Lee, and Ney Mattogrosso. Heavy metal is a popular genre that continues to evolve, as exemplified by the band Sepultura. Another band which has achieved cult status is Legião Urbana from Brasília (its vocalist, Renato Russo, died of Aids in 1996). Recently, in turning towards international black consciousness, the Bahianos have mixed Reggae and Samba to produce 'axê'. Still, Samba has survived, either in its more commercialized form 'Pagode', or in the Roda de Samba, an informal meeting of musicians in a 'barzinho'. Amazingly, 40% of all Brazilian records sold are of Música Sertaneja, in its more traditional rural style known as Música Caipira, or a newer, highly commercialized pseudo-folk genre which is closer to American Country and Western than to most other Brazilian music. Listen to the 'Duplas' of Tonico & Tinoco, Jacó e Jacozinho, Vieira & Vieirinha or Leonardo & Leandro and you'll see. In the meantime a series of brilliant Brazilian instrumentalists have become international names and often live abroad – Sérgio Mendes, the guitarist Sebastião Tapajós, flautist Hermêto Paschoal, saxophonist Paulo Moura, accordionist Sivuca, percussionists Airto Moreira and Nana Vasconcelos, singer Flora Purim and all-rounder Egberto Gismonti are but a few. On the top of a huge recording industry, we're now a long way from the grassroots and the haunting flute music of the forest Indians.

Ever since the Catholic church and its missionaries arrived in all parts of present-day Latin America, appropriate religious music was being composed locally, particularly by the Jesuits, and this led on to Baroque and other classical music. Brazil was no

Brazilian classical composers

Brazilian cinema

My first encounter with Brazil came through the medium of its cinema when in the early 1980s I saw Hector Babenco's controversial drama Pixote, a Lei do Mais Fraco. *This left a lasting impression and curiosity that I was never to satisfy until my first visit to São Paulo nearly 15 years later. Hopefully the current resurgence of Oscar nominated films such as Walter Salles's* Central do Brasil *(Central Station) will inspire more people to explore the country where they were filmed rather sooner than I did!*

No one knows for sure when the first film was made in Brazil but a travelling Italian showman, Vittorio di Maio, was to claim this when he exhibited four films in Petrópolis in 1897. The industry developed steadily at the beginning of the century with often-repeated adaptations of literary texts such as O Guaraní *before later specializing in light entertainment musicals known as* chanchadas *during the 1930s and 1940s. A national star, Carmen Miranda, grew out of these before moving to Hollywood where she quickly became America's stereotype of the exotic Latin woman.*

During the 1950s more serious films such as Nelson Perreira dos Santos's Rio 40 Graus *began to appear before Anselmo Duarte's* O Pagador de Promessas *won best film at Cannes. This golden age continued in the 1960s with the birth of Cinema Novo. Glauber Rocha's* Deus e o Diabo no Terra do Sol *reinterpreted the popular theme of Lampião and the bandits of the northeast previously used in Lima Barreto's 1953 epic* O Cangaçeiro.

Other films such as O Barravento *also by Glauber Rocha challenged the previously passive role of the viewing public.*

In the 1970s and 1980s under the military dictatorship the national film industry led by the state run Embrafilme lost its way as pornochanchadas *and comedies like* Os Trapalhões *dominated the box office. There were however some films such as Bruno Barreto's* Dona Flor e Seus Dois Maridos *that combined both commercial and critical success and helped to push actress Sonia Braga to international fame. Cult horror film director, José Mojica Marins, better known as Zé do Caixão (Coffin Joe), also flourished during this period and is possibly better know outside his home country than his more artistic colleagues!*

The return came in the 1990s with Fabio Barreto's O Quatrilho, *showing the life of Brazil's Italian immigrants and Bruno Barreto's* O Que é Isso Companheiro *based on the 1969 kidnap of the American ambassador. Both were nominated for the Academy Awards best foreign film. Other good recent films, including* Anahy de las Missiones *based on a Gaúcho legend and* Terra Estrangeira *exploring the life of a Brazilian immigrant in Portugal, have displayed both excellent photography and innovative plots. Although the hotly-tipped* Central do Brasil *failed to win the coveted Oscar, it can surely only be a matter of time before Brazilian films gain the international recognition they so richly deserve.*

exception and Carlos Gomes' opera 'Il Guarany' achieved great popularity after its first performance in 1870. During the present century, Brazilian composers (together with those of Mexico and Argentina) are at the forefront of Latin American classical music and have produced many works based on folk and popular themes. The figure of Heitor Villa-Lobos (1857-1959) towers above all others and achieved world renown well within his lifetime. Largely self-taught, his prodigious output included the celebrated nine 'Bachianas Brasileiras' and six 'Choros'. Given to bold experimentation, he composed two pieces of which the melodic line was based on the skyline of New York and that of the Serra da Piedade mountains near Belo Horizonte, respectively. Other major names among the so-called 'nationalist' composers are Francisco Mignone, Camargo Guarnieri, Radames Gnatalli and Cesar Guerra Peixe (who found inspiration in the regional music of the Northeast).

Festivals

Brazilians love a party and the mixing of different ethnic groups has resulted in some particularly colourful and varied celebrations. The difficulties of daily life are often relieved by the fantasy and release of *carnaval* as well as the many other popular festivals held through the year. Wherever you go you will find street vendors selling ice cold beer and the smell of *churrasco* coming from improvised barbecues accompanied by loud vibrant music and dancing in the streets.

Carnaval

Almost all Brazilian towns have some form of carnival festivities. Although the most famous is Rio de Janeiro, there are equally spectacular and different traditions in Bahia and Pernambuco as well as a number of other good locations for those who wish only to party. The colonial mining towns of Diamantina and Ouro Preto in the interior of Minas Gerais are good locations to spend carnival in atmospheric surroundings. Florianópolis and Laguna on the coast of Santa Catarina have less traditional but still very popular and lively carnivals.

Out of season carnivals

Street carnivals with *trios eléctricos* in the style of Bahia are held throughout Brazil at various times of the year. Some of the most popular are *Micareta* in Feira de Santana (April), *Fortal* in Fortaleza (July) and *Carnatal* in Natal (December). Although by no means traditional they are nonetheless exuberant and enjoyable.

Other popular festivities

There are several other festivals which are almost as important to Brazilians as Carnaval. *Reveillon* (New Year's Eve) is a significant event and is generally celebrated on beaches. This can be either a hedonistic party as at Copacabana and Arraial D'Ajuda with the revellers dressed in white for luck, or as a respectful Candomblé ceremony in which flowers are launched into the sea at midnight as an offering to Yemanjá.

The Festas Juninhas (*São João*) are extremely popular especially in the northeast and are held around 24 June (St John's day). Fires are built and Forró is the music of choice with the festivities lasting for over a week at times. Fireworks and the co-ordinated dancing of groups called *quadrilhas* are also part of the celebrations.

In the north the African and Indian cultures have mixed to form the *Boi-Bumba* tradition. In Amazonas the Festa do Boi has become more commercialized but is still very impressive and popular. In Maranhão where it is known as *Bumba-meu-boi* the festivities are more traditional but equally as popular.

There are many Catholic saints' days that are sometimes celebrated in conjunction with African deities (especially in Bahia). Every town has a patron saint and his or her day will be an excuse for civic festivities, in addition to those of the foundation day of the town.

Immigrants from Europe to the south of Brazil and elsewhere have brought festivals from their own cultures such as the Oktoberfest held in Blumenau, believed to be second only to Munich.

Literature

The colonial period

Some of the major differences between Brazil and Spanish America spring from the history of colonization in the two areas. There were no great empires with large cities like those of the Incas or the Aztecs, and Portuguese exploitation concentrated first on extractive, then on cultivated export products (brazil-wood, then sugar). Although cities like Recife, Bahia and Rio de Janeiro did finally develop, there was, incredible as it may seem, no printing press in Brazil until the flight of the Regent, later King João VI to Rio in 1808. This is not to say that there was no colonial literature, though scholars can still quarrel about how 'Brazilian' it was. When the

Background

Portuguese set foot in Brazil in 1500, the letter sent back to King Manuel by Pero Vaz de Caminha, already wondering at the tropical magnificence of the country and the nakedness of the inhabitants, set themes which would recur in many later works. The first plays to be put on in Brazil were religious dramas, staged in three languages, Portuguese, Spanish, and Tupi, by the Jesuit **José de Anchieta** (1543-97). The most notable 17th-century poet is **Gregório de Matos** (1636-96), famous for his sharp satires on the corrupt life of the city of Salvador, and its tempting black and mulatta women. In the late 18th century, a group of poets from the gold-mining area of Minas, foremost among them **Tomás Antônio Gonzaga** (1744-1810), were at the centre of the early, abortive move for independence, the Inconfidência (1789 – see page 242). Although best known as a lyric poet, Gonzaga has been proved to be the author of the anonymous satirical poem *Cartas chilenas*, which gives a vivid portrait of colonial society.

The 19th century

It is helpful to understand Brazilian literature, even long after political independence, as a gradual and to some extent contradictory process of emancipation from foreign models. Every European literary movement – Romanticism, Realism, Symbolism, etc – had its Brazilian followers, but in each there was an attempt to adjust the model to local reality. A good example is the first of these, Indianism, which flourished in the mid-19th century, and produced two central figures, the poet **Antônio Gonçalves Dias** (1823-64) (himself partly of Indian descent) and the novelist **José de Alencar** (1829-77). It is a form of Romanticism, idealizing the noble savage, and with plots adapted from Walter Scott, and it happily ignored what was happening to real Indians at the time. However, it does express national aspirations and feelings, if in nothing else in the nostalgia for a kind of tropical Eden expressed in perhaps the most famous Brazilian poem, Gonçalves Dias 'Canção do exílio': "My land has palm-trees/ where the sabiá sings./ The birds that sing here/ don't sing like those back home." Alencar's novels, not all of them about Indians, are a systematic attempt to portray Brazil in its various settings, including the city. *O guarani* (1857), turned into a famous opera by Carlos Gomes, and *Iracema* (1865) are his most popular, the latter perhaps the most complete mythical version of the Portuguese conquest, allegorized as a love affair between a native woman and an early colonist, Martim Soares: Iracema, "the virgin with the honeyed lips" dies in childbirth at the end, but the future lies with their mixed-blood son, Moacir.

After his death, Alencar was succeeded as the chief figure in Brazilian letters by **Joaquim Maria Machado de Assis** (1839-1908). Perhaps Brazil's best writer, and certainly the greatest to appear in Latin America until well into the 20th century, he had to fight against formidable obstacles: he was of relatively poor origins, was mulatto, stammered and in later life was subject to epileptic fits. He wrote nine novels and more than 200 short stories as well as poetry and journalism. He ended his life as an establishment figure, founder of the Brazilian Academy of Letters, but his novels, especially those written after 1880, when he published *Memórias póstumas de Brás Cubas*, and the best of his stories are surprisingly subversive, covert attacks on slavery and on male power, for instance. He avoided detection by not using his own voice, hiding behind quirky, digressive narrators who are not always trustworthy. All the novels and most of the stories are set in Rio, which he hardly left, and give a remarkably varied account of the city and its different social levels. His most famous novel, *Dom Casmurro* (1900) is one of the best-disguised cases of an unreliable narrator in the history of the novel, and still arouses critical polemics.

Machado's atmosphere is predominantly that of the empire, which fell in 1889, a year after the abolition of slavery. In the Republic, a younger generation, more overtly rebellious in their aims, and affected by new scientific ideas from Europe, came to the fore. If Machado is the most famous Brazilian author, perhaps *Os sertões*, by **Euclides da Cunha** (1866-1909) is the most famous book. It is an account of the Canudos campaign in the interior the state of Bahia in 1896-97. The campaign was a horrific failure, victory being won only at a huge cost in casualties, and Euclides, sent to cover it as a journalist, turned this failure into an indictment of a social system which excluded huge groups of people. Written in a dramatic, somewhat self-indulgent style, with extensive use of scientific words, it has been excellently translated as *Rebellion in the Backlands*.

The other important prose writer of this period, the novelist **Afonso Lima Barreto** (1881-1922), was mulatto like Machado, but there resemblances end. Much more openly rebellious and less of a conscious artist than Machado, his novels, the most notable of which is *Triste fim de Policarpo Quaresma*, are overt attacks on intellectual mediocrity, and the corruption and despotism into which the Republic soon fell. A passing mention ought to be made, too, of one of the 'unclassifiable' books in which Brazilian literature abounds: **Helena Morley's** *Minha vida de menina* (translated by Elizabeth Bishop as *The Diary of Helena Morley*), and only published in 1942, it is the precocious, funny, and remarkably perceptive teenager's diary, written in Diamantina, Minas Gerais, at the end of the 19th century.

In general, the poetry of the turn of the century was imitative and stuffy: renewal did not come until the early 1920s, when a group of intellectuals from São Paulo, led by **Mário de Andrade** (1893-1945) and **Oswald de Andrade** (1890-1954) (unrelated) began the movement known as modernism. This is conveniently supposed to have begun in 1922, the centenary of political independence, with a Week of Modern Art in São Paulo: in fact it began earlier, and took until the mid-1920s to spread to the provinces. In great part, modernism's ideology was nationalist, and though the word spanned the political spectrum, at its best it simply meant the discovery of a real Brazil behind stereotypes: Mário travelled throughout the country, attempting to understand its variety, which he embodied in his major prose-work, the comic 'rhapsody' *Macunaíma* (1928), which in its plot and language attempts to construct a unity out of a complex racial and regional mix. Also in 1928, Oswald launched the 'anthropophagist', or cannibalist programme, which proclaimed that Brazilian writers should imitate their native predecessors, and fully digest European culture: a new kind of Indianism, perhaps ...

The most enduring artistic works to have emerged from modernism, however, are poetic: two of Brazil's major modern poets, **Manuel Bandeira** (1886-1968) and **Carlos Drummond de Andrade** (1902-87) were early enthusiasts of modernism, and corresponded at length with Mário. Bandeira, the older man, made a slow transition to the new, freer style: his poems, often short and based on everyday events or images, nevertheless have a power and rhythmic accuracy which are deceptively simple. Drummond's poetry is more self-conscious, and went through a complex intellectual development, including a period of political enthusiasm during the Second World War, followed by disillusionment with the beginning of the Cold War. His themes, including some remarkable love-poetry addressed by a 50-year old to a younger woman, and a lifelong attachment to Itabira, the small town in Minas Gerais where he was born, are very varied. Readers without Portuguese can best approach Drummond, widely regarded as Brazil's greatest poet, through an excellent anthology, *Traveling in the Family*.

The 1930s were a crucial decade. With increasing political mobilization, the growth of cities, and of an aspiring middle class, literature began to look to a wider audience: at first, however, it still reflected the dominance of rural life. The realism of this period, which often had a strong regionalist bias, had its *raison d'être* in a society still divided by huge social and/or geographical differences, and indeed played its part in diminishing those differences. Many of the first group came from the

The 20th century

Background

economically and socially backward northeast. **José Lins do Rego** (1901-57) is perhaps the most characteristic figure. He was highly influenced by the ideas of **Gilberto Freyre** (1900-87), whose *Casa grande e senzala* (*The Masters and the Slaves*), published in 1933, one of the most important and readable of Brazilian books. It is a study of the slave-based, sugar-plantation society, and one of the first works to appreciate the contribution made by Blacks to Brazil's culture. It remains, however, very paternalist, and Lins do Rego's fiction, beginning with the semi-autobiographical *Menino de engenho*, reflects that, commenting on the poverty and filth of the (ex-)slave-quarters as if they were totally natural. His 'Sugar-cane cycle' sold in large editions, in part because of its unaffected, simple style.

A greater novelist belonging to the same group is **Graciliano Ramos** (1892-1953). His fiction is much more aggressive, and in later life he became a communist. His masterpiece, turned into an excellent film in the 1960s, is *Vidas secas*, which returns to the impoverished interior of *Os sertões*, but concentrates on an illiterate cowhand and his family, forced from place to place by drought and social injustice: it is a courageous attempt to enter the mental world of such people. *Memórias do cárcere*, published after Ramos's death, is his unflinching account of his imprisonment for a year during the Vargas regime.

The essential novelist to read for anyone visiting the South of Brazil is **Érico Veríssimo** (1905-75), especially his epic trilogy collectively entitled *O tempo e o vento* (*O continente* [1949], *O retrato* [1951], and *O arquipélago* [1961]) spread over two centuries of the turbulent history of Rio Grande do Sul.

Gradually, in the 1940s and 1950s, a subtler and more adventurous fiction began to be published alongside the regionalist realism that was the major heritage of the 1930s. Three writers stand out: **João Guimarães Rosa** (1908-67) published his major novel, *Grande sertão: veredas* in 1956. Almost Joycean in its aspirations and linguistic innovations, it is a kind of mixture of a cowboy story and a modern version of Faustian pact with the devil. For those without stamina (and excellent Portuguese), the translation (*The Devil to Pay in the Backlands*) is unfortunately not an adequate alternative. Rosa is best approached through his stories, those of *Sagarana* (particularly "A hora e vez de Augusto Matraga") being perhaps the best.

The stories and novels of **Clarice Lispector** (1920-77) now have a considerable audience outside Brazil, as well as a huge one inside it. Her stories, especially those of *Laços de família* (1960), are in general set in middle-class Rio, and usually have women as their central characters: the turbulence, family hatreds, and near-madness hidden beneath routine lives are conveyed in unforgettable ways, with a language and symbolism that is poetic and adventurous without being exactly difficult (she said she fought with the Portuguese language daily). Some of her novels have over-ambitious metaphysical superstructures, and may not be to some readers' tastes – *A paixão segundo G H*, for instance, concerns a housewife's confrontation with a dead cockroach in her maid's room, and her final decision to eat it, seen as a kind of "communion". At her best, in some of her journalism, in her late, deliberately semi-pornographic stories, and above all in the posthumous novel, *A hora da estrela*, which approaches the poor in an utterly unsentimental way, Lispector can stimulate and move like no one else.

The greatest poet of this generation is **João Cabral de Melo Neto** (born 1920 in Pernambuco, died 1999), whose best poetry concerns his home state. The drought-ridden interior, the lush but oppressive landscape of the sugar-plantations, and the city slums are all present in the verse-play *Morte e vida severina* (1956), and his tight, spare poetry often returns to the same places, or analogous ones in the several countries (most importantly, in Spain) in which he has resided as a diplomat.

The 1964 military coup, and the increasing use of torture and censorship in the late 1960s and early 1970s, had profound effects on literature, especially as they were accompanied by vast economic changes (industrialization, a building boom, huge internal migration, the opening up of the Amazon). At first, censorship was haphazard, and the 1960s liberation movements had their – increasingly desperate – Brazilian equivalents. Protest theatre had a brief boom, with *Arena conta Zumbi*, about a 17th-century rebel slave leader, produced by **Augusto Boal** (born 1931), being one of the most important. The best fictional account of those years can be find in two novels by **Antônio Callado** (born 1917), *Quarup* (1967), set in the northeast and centred on a left-wing priest, and *Bar Don Juan* (1971), whose focus is on the contradictions of a group of middle-class guerrillas; and in **Ivan Ângelo's** *A festa* (1976), set in Belo Horizonte, a funny and hard-hitting account of a varied set of people, which chronicles the impact of the 'sex and drugs' revolution alongside its political concerns. A remarkable documentary account of the period is ex- guerrilla (now leader of the Green Party) **Fernando Gabeira's** *O que é isso companheiro?* (1982), which chronicles his involvement in the kidnapping of the American ambassador in 1969. Poetry at this time went through a crisis of self-confidence, and it was widely thought that it had emigrated into the (marvellous) lyrics of such popular composers as Chico Buarque de Holanda and Caetano Veloso, who were also the foremost standard-bearers of political protest in the 1970s.

It is impossible in the space available to give more than a few suggestions of some of the best work published in recent decades, concentrating on books which have been translated. A brilliant satirical novel by **Paulo Emílio Salles Gomes** (1916-77) about the São Paulo upper middle class is *Três mulheres e três pppês* (1977); **Darcy Ribeiro** (born 1922), an anthropologist and politician, took time off to write *Maíra* (1978), an updating of Indianism, but with real Indians and a threatened Amazon environment; **Rubem Fonseca** (born 1925), whose story 'Feliz ano novo' (1973) created a scandal because of its brutal treatment of class differences, has dedicated himself to the writing of hardnosed thrillers like *A grande arte* (1983); **Caio Fernando Abreu** (1948-96) is a short-story writer of considerable talent, dealing with the alienated urban young in such books as *Morangos mofados* and *Os dragões não conhecem o paraíso*; finally, **Milton Hatoum's** *Relato de um certo oriente* (1989) is a vivid novel set in Manaus, amongst the Lebanese immigrant community.

Essays and books which can be wholeheartedly recommended for those who want more information are: Ray Keenoy, David Treece and Paul Hyland, *The Babel Guide to the Fiction of Portugal, Brazil and Africa in English Translation* (London: Boulevard Books, 1995). Irwin Stern (ed) *Dictionary of Brazilian Literature* (New York: Greenwood Press, 1988). Mike González and David Treece, *The Gathering of Voices* (Verso, 1992) (on 20th-century poetry). Elizabeth Bishop and Emanuel Brasil (eds) *An Anthology of Twentieth-Century Brazilian Poetry* (Wesleyan University Press, 1972). John Gledson, 'Brazilian Fiction: Machado de Assis to the Present', in John King (ed), *Modern Latin American Fiction: A Survey* (Faber, 1987). Many of the essays in Roberto Schwarz, *Misplaced Ideas: Essays on Brazilian Culture* (Verso, 1992), especially those on Machado de Assis, and 'Culture and Politics in Brazil, 1964-69' are very stimulating.

Books

Machado de Assis, Joaquim Maria (1839-1908), the classical satirical novelist of the Brazilian 19th century, is one of the most original writers to have emerged from Latin America. *Epitaph of a Small Winner* (London: Hogarth Press, 1985). *Posthumous Memoirs of Bras Cubas* (New York: Oxford University Press, 1997). (The same novel.) *The Heritage of Quincas Borba* (London: WH Allen, 1954). *Philosopher or Dog?* (New York: Avon Books, 1985, also London: Bloomsbury, 1997). (The same novel.) *Dom Casmurro* (New York: Oxford University Press, 1997, also in Penguin Modern Classics, Harmondsworth, 1994). Abreu, João Capistrano de (1853-1929) A fascinating account of the first three centuries of Brazilian history. *Chapters of Colonia History*

Brazilian literature in English

▶▶ Jorge Amado

Amado is, both among Brazilians and foreigners reading Brazilian fiction, by far the most popular writer of the 20th century. Born in 1912 on a cocoa plantation outside Ilhéus, in the South of the State of Bahia, he had a very adventurous youth, and had direct experience of the endemic violence surrounding land claims that he was later to dramatize in such novels as Terras do sem-fim (The Violent Land) (1943). He was always committed to the left, though his position has softened somewhat in later years, accompanying changes in his fiction. In the early period (1931-1952), it showed first in an interest in the rural and urban poor: in such novels as Jubiabá (1935), about the self-education of a black man, and Capitães da areia (1937), one of his best, centred on a gang of street children, he began to show interest in the power of candomblé (Afro-Brazilian religion) as a political consciousness-raiser. He became, a Federal deputy for the Communist Party in 1946: in 1948, after the party was banned, he went into exile in Europe, and was something of a propagandist for Soviet Communism, receiving the Stalin Peace Prize in 1951. The fiction he wrote at this time (for example Seara vermelha [Red Harvest]) is by common consent his worst.

In 1953 he returned to Brazil, and in 1958 published the novel which gave his career a new lease of life, Gabriela, cravo e canela (Gabriela, Clove and Cinnamon). To achieve this, he abandoned politics for comedy and myth: Ilhéus in the 1920s, its harbour about to be opened so that it can export its cocoa, is presented to us in a colourful array of characters, at the centre of whom are Nacib, an Arab immigrant and shopkeeper, and spicy Gabriela, a girl from the interior whose cooking and sexual prowess keep him in her thrall. It is a modern, optimistic version of Alencar's Iracema (see page 694): immigrant meets native girl, and has to adjust to her culture,

while in the background, the (export) economy is opening up. Gabriela was a phenomenal success, selling 100,000 copies in just over a year. In part, Amado had tuned into the optimism of the years of the Kubitschek presidency which led to the foundation of Brasília.

Sex, comedy and cookery proved a potent combination. Other novels since Gabriela have been equally successful with the public: Dona Flor e seus dois maridos (1966), about a cookery teacher whose respectable second marriage is haunted by the ghost of her bohemian first husband (it actually provides the reader with recipes); Tenda dos milagres (The Tent of Miracles) (1969) about racial discrimination, and others there is no space to deal with here, many of them set in the city of Salvador (Bahia). Amado has been attacked by critics as being unconsciously anti-feminist and even racist (his Blacks do tend to be stereotypically good-hearted, with a perpetual smile on their faces). Perhaps this is to miss the point: essentially, he is a popular novelist in the tradition of Scott, Dumas and hundreds of others, predecessors of television soap operas, and he has often been successfully adapted to that medium.

Jorge Armando

(New York: Oxford University Press, 1997). Cunha, Euclides da (1866-1909) The 'epic' story of the military campaign to crush the rebellion centred in Canudos in the interior of the State of Bahia. One of the great books about the Brazilian national make-up. *Rebellion in the Backlands (Os sertões)* (Chicago: University of Chicago Press, 1944-) Often reprinted, including London: Picador, 1995. Lima Barreto, Afonso Henriques de (1881-1922) A sharp attack on some of the failings of the Brazilian political and social system, set in the 1890s. *The Patriot* (London: Rex Collings, 1978). Morley, Helena (1882-1970) The diary of a girl's life in Diamantina, in Minas Gerais: translated by the great American poet Elizabeth Bishop, who lived in Brazil for many years. A delightfully intimate and frank portrait of small-town life. *The Diary of Helena Morley* (London: Bloomsbury, 1997). Bandeira, Manuel (1886-1968) The oldest member of the Modernist movement, and one of Brazil's greatest poets, master of the short, intense lyric. *This Earth, that Sky: Poems by Manuel Bandeira* (Berkeley: University of California Press, 1988). Ramos, Graciliano (1892-1953) The greatest of the novelists of the 1930s and 1940s: a harsh realist. *São Bernardo* (London: Peter Owen, 1975). *Anguish* (New York: Knopf, 1972). *Barren Lives* (Austin: University of Texas Press, 1965). Andrade, Mário de (1893-1945) Written in the 1920s: a comic statement in picaresque form about Brazilian nationality, by the leader of Modernism.

Macunaíma* (London: Quartet, 1988). Freyre, Gilberto (1900-87) A central figure, still controversial: this account of racial mixture, and of sugar-plantation society in the northeast of Brazil in colonial times, is very readable. *The Masters and the Slaves* (Berkeley: University of California Press, 1986). Lins do Rego, José (1909-57) Highly influenced by Gilberto Freyre, this is an evocative account of childhood on a northeastern sugar plantation. *Plantation Boy* (New York: Knopf, 1966). Drummond de Andrade, Carlos (1902-87) Perhaps Brazil's greatest poet, with a varied, lyrical, somewhat downbeat style. *Travelling in the Family: Selected Poems* (New York: Random House, 1986). Veríssimo, Érico (1905-) A very popular and important novelist from Rio Grande do Sul, the southernmost State of Brazil. *Time and the Wind* (London: Arco, 1954). Guimareães Rosa, João (1908-67) The most poetic of modern prose-writers, who sets his work in the rural interior: very difficult to translate. *Sagarana* (Austin: University of Texas Press, 1990). Amado, Jorge (1912-2001) Over a long career Amado published many best-sellers: he is often criticized for producing an overly optimistic, sexily tropical view of the country, and of Bahia, his home State. The following is only a selection of his most important and popular novels. *The Violent Land* (London: Collins Harvill, 1989). *Captains of the Sands* (New York: Avon Books, 1988). *Gabriela, Clove and Cinnamon* (London: Abacus, 1984). *Dona Flor and her Two Husbands* (London: Serpent's Tail, 1987; New York: Avon Books, 1988). *Tent of Miracles* (London: Collins, 1989; New York: Avon Books, 1988). Lispector, Clarice (1920-77) Brazil's greatest woman writer, with a considerable following abroad. *Family Ties* (Manchester: Carcanet, 1986; Austin: University of Texas Press, 1990). *The Foreign Legion* (Manchester: Carcanet, 1986; New York: New Directions, 1992). *The Hour of the Star* (Manchester: Carcanet, 1986; New York: New Directions, 1982). Fonseca, Rubem (1925-) A thriller, set in Rio.

High Art* (London: Collins, 1987). *The Lost Manuscript* (London: Bloomsbury, 1997). Ribeiro, João Ubaldo (1940-) A panoramic historical novel, entitled *Long Live the Brazilian People* in the original. *An Invincible Memory* (London: Faber and Faber, 1989; New York: Harper and Row, 1989). Buarque de Holanda, Chico (1944-) Most famous as a pop singer and composer, Chico Buarque has written a short, fast-moving allegory of modern Brazil. *Turbulence* (London: Bloomsbury, 1992). *Benjamin* (London: Bloomsbury, 1997). Ângelo, Ivan (1936-) Much the best novel and about the political, social and economic crisis at the end of the 1960s, the worst period of the military regime. *The Celebration* (New York: Avon Books, 1992). Abreu, Caio Fernando (1948-1996) Short stories: one of the writers most effective in dealing with life in the

Latin American megalopolis. *Dragons...* (London: Boulevard Books, 1990). Weishort, Daniel (ed), *Modern Poetry in Translation*, No 6, Brazil (London: King's College, 1994) contains 19 poets, including Mário de Andrade, Oswald de Andrade, Carlos Drummond de Andrade, Manuel Bandeira, João Cabral de Melo Neto.

Fine art and sculpture

The colonial era: 16th & 17th centuries

No visitor to Brazil should miss visiting a colonial church. During the colonial period in Brazil the Church dominated artistic patronage, with the religious orders vying with each other to produce ever more lavish interiors. In the 17th century the Benedictines included several notable sculptors among their ranks. Much of the magnificent gilded interior of the monastery of São Bento in Rio de Janeiro is by Frei Domingos da Conceição (circa 1643-1718), who worked there during the 1660s. His *Crucifixion* of 1688 in the monastery of São Bento in Olinda sets up a deliberately shocking contrast between the sinuous elegance of Christ's body and the terrible lacerations of his flesh. Frei Agostinho de Piedade (died 1661) of the Benedictine community in Salvador produced some old-fashioned terracotta reliquary busts during the 1630s and 1640s (Museu de Arte Sacra, Salvador) but the powerful *Penitent Peter* in Salvador's Nossa Senhora do Monte (circa 1636), also attributed to him, prefigures the emotional intensity of subsequent generations.

A distinctive feature of colonial interiors is the incorporation of decorative scenes in blue and white painted tiles, *azulejos*, around the walls. These were imported from Portugal from the earlier 17th century onwards, with subject matter as often secular as religious. Good examples include the Franciscan foundations in Olinda, Salvador and Recife, and the church of Nossa Senhora da Glória in Rio de Janeiro, which has hunting scenes in the sacristy, Old Testament figures in the choir, and in the nave, astonishingly, scenes of pastoral love loosely based on the Song of Songs.

The 18th century

Although 17th-century church decoration is often lavish there is little warning of the extraordinary theatricality which characterizes the work of the 18th century. Behind their sober façades churches open out like theatres, with the equivalent of balconies and boxes for the privileged, and a stage for the high altar with a proscenium arch and wings of carved and gilded wood. Cherubs whisper to each other or gesticulate from their perches amongst the architectural scrolls; angels, older and more decorous, recline along a cornice or flutter in two dimensions across an illusionistic ceiling. The object of devotion is usually placed high above the altar on a tiered dais, surrounded by a Bernini-esque sunburst of gilded rays. A skilled exponent of this type of design was the sculptor Francisco Xavier de Brito (died 1751), as in Nossa Senhora do Pilar, Ouro Preto and São Francisco de Penitência, Rio.

This theatricality reaches its climax in the work of Aleijadinho, the 'Little Cripple' (1738-1814) a mulatto artist who worked in the province of Minas Gerais (see also page 251). As by far the most famous artist in the colonial period in the whole of Latin America it is perhaps not surprising to find his name attached to an impossible number of projects, but a consideration even of the securely documented reveals a man of extraordinary passion and energy who worked as a painter, architect and above all sculptor. The church at Congonhas do Campo offers the most dramatic example of Aleijadinho's art. Pilgrims paying homage to the miracle-working Bom Jesus do Matozinhos approach the church along a penitential road winding up the hill between six small chapels, each housing scenes from Christ's Passion represented by lifesize expressive statues of polychrome wood. The final ascent is up an imposing double staircase under the stony gaze of 12 judgmental prophets who variously lament, threaten or cajole, addressing the heavens, the distant horizon, each other, or the faithful on the stone steps below them. In a building beside the church a fascinating display of drawings and photographs of the many accidents and emergencies from which the Good Jesus has saved people testifies to the continuing popularity of this shrine.

The painterly equivalent to Aleijadinho's sculptures can be found in the work of his contemporary, Manuel da Costa Ataíde (1762-1830) from Mariana, whose vividly colourful narrative scenes decorate numerous churches in Minas Gerais. Ataíde's rococo settings are populated with solidly-built saints and angels whose rolling eyes and exaggerated gestures give them an earthy vigour sometimes at odds with the spirituality of the subject matter, as in the illusionistic ceiling of São Francisco de Assis, Ouro Preto, a church whose design is traditionally attributed to Aleijadinho.

In Bahia José Joaquim da Rocha (1737-1807) (see page 369) was one of the most successful artists of his day and his slightly Italianate ceiling paintings survive in many churches in Salvador. The best sculptor of the late colonial period in Bahia was Manuel Inácio da Costa (1763-1857) whose figures, often dramatically gaunt with protruding veins and large eyes, are reminiscent of Aleijadinho's work (see, for example, his *Christ at the Column* in the Museu de Arte Sacra in Salvador). It is in Rio that sculpture first begins to sober up again, as for example in the work of the sculptor Valentim de Fonseca e Silva, known as Mestre Valentim (circa 1750-1813) which can be seen in several churches including São Francisco de Paula and Nossa Senhora da Glória. Valentim also designed the first public gardens in Rio: the Passeio Público was inaugurated in 1783 and included walks, seats decorated with *azulejos* and pavilions. A unique series of six painted views of Rio and Guanabara Bay by Leandro Joaquim (1738?-1798?), originally made for one of the pavilions, are now in the Museu Histórico Nacional in Rio.

After the transfer of the Imperial court to Rio in 1808 João VI made a determined effort to renovate Brazilian culture, and in 1816 the French Artistic Mission – a boatload of painters, sculptors, architects, musicians and craftsmen – arrived from France to found what was to become the Imperial Academy. Two artists were particularly influential: Nicolas-Antoine Taunay (1755-1830) and Jean-Baptiste Debret (1768-1848). Taunay's luminous landscapes of the area around Rio and Debret's lively street scenes helped to open up new areas of secular Brazilian subject matter, and inspired artists throughout the 19th century. The Academy provided scholarships to send promising young artists to Paris, so reinforcing the French influence, and there are echoes of Delacroix in the work of Vítor Meireles (1832-1903) as for example, in his *Battle of the Guararapes* of 1879 in the Museu Nacional de Belas Artes, Rio, and of Ingres in *La Carioca* (1882) of Pedro Américo (1843-1905) in the same museum. The influence of Courbet can be seen in the so-called *belle époque* of the first republican years (1889-1922), in particular in the work of Meireles' pupil, José Ferraz de Almeida Júnior (1850-1899).

French influence in Imperial Brazil

Brazil moved from this essentially academic tradition straight into the radicalism of the early 20th century, and movements such as Cubism, Futurism, Fauvism and Constructivism were quickly translated into distinctively Brazilian idioms. Lasar Segall (1891-1957), Anita Malfatti (1896-1964) and the sculptor Vitor Brecheret (1894-1955) were pioneers of modernism, working in relative isolation before the Semana da Arte Moderna (Modern Art Week) in São Paulo in 1922 drew together a group of artists and intellectuals whose influence on Brazilian culture can still be felt today. They sought to challenge established bourgeois attitudes, to shake off the traditional cultural subservience to Europe, and to draw attention to the cultural diversity and social inequality of contemporary Brazil. Emilio di Cavalcanti (1897-1976) mocked the artificiality of middle class socialites (examples in the Museu de Arte Contemporânea, São Paulo). Tarsila do Amaral (1886-1973) borrowed her loud

The 20th century, towards a Brazilian vision

Background

colours from popular art while her imagery includes ironic reworkings of European myths about the savage cannabilistic Indians supposed to inhabit the Brazilian jungle. Cândido Portinari (1903-62) used murals to expose the exploitation and injustice suffered by workers and peasants while Osvaldo Goeldi (1895-1961) explored similar themes in his powerful wood engravings. Portinari, in an interesting revival of the colonial use of *azulejos*, created murals in blue and white painted tiles for modern building such as the MES building by Costa and Niemeyer of Rio, begun in 1937, and Niemeyer's church of São Francisco in Pampulha, Belo Horizonte (1943).

The economic strength of the middle years of the century encouraged state patronage of the arts. President Getúlio Vargas recognized that art and architecture could be used to present an image of Brazil as a modern industrialized nation, with Brasília being the culmination of this vision. Museums of Modern Art were founded in São Paulo and Rio, and in 1951 São Paulo hosted its first Bienal Internacional which attracted abstract artists from Europe and the US and confirmed Abstraction – symbol of progress and technological modernization – as the dominant mode in Brazil during the 1950s. Rivalry between the artistic communities of Rio and São Paulo helped to produce some outstanding avantgarde art. In the 1950s Waldemar Cordeiro (1925-73), leader of the São Paulo Grupo Ruptura, painted what at first sight appear to be rather simple geometric patterns in bright, contrasting colours, but on closer attention the flat surface seems to break up, suggesting recession, space and restless movement, in some ways prefiguring the British Op Art movement of the 1960s. The Neo-Concrete group of artists of Rio argued for the integration of art into daily life, and experimented with art which makes sensory and emotional demands on the 'spectator' whose participation leads in turn to creation. During the early 1960s Lygia Clark (1920-88) made *Bichos (Animals)* out of hinged pieces of metal which, as the name implies, are like creatures with a life of their own: they can be rearranged indefinitely but because of their complexity it is impossible to predetermine what shape will result from moving a particular section. Nowadays, unfortunately, they are displayed in museums where touching is not encouraged (as in the Pinacoteca do Estado, São Paulo). Hélio Oiticica (1937-80) took the idea further, working with people (poor and often black) from the samba schools in the Rio *favelas* to create artistic 'happenings' involving dance, music and flamboyant costumes called *Parangolés (Capes)*. The notion that a key function of art should be to shock the bourgeisie was first voiced by in the 1922 Week of Modern Art. Oiticica often succeeded, and he and other artists of the 1960s also realized another of the aims of the first modernists: to create a Brazilian modern art that was not the poor relation of developments in Europe or the US. A museum of his work has recently opened in Rio. Other important figures of this generation include the neo-concretist painter Ivan Serpa (1923-73), Sérgio Camargo (1930-90), who produced textured rhythmic constructions of white on white but because they are made with off-cuts of wood they suggest the tensions between form and material, geometry and nature, and Amílcar de Castro (born 1920) whose deceptively simple sculptures are often cut from one large panel of cast iron.

The military coup of 1964 marked the beginning of a period of political repression and of renewed artistic energy, with figurative tendencies re-emerging. In 1970 Antônio Enrique Amaral (born 1935) took as his theme the banana, so often used in dismissive references to Latin America, and in an extended series of paintings monumentalized it into an extraordinary symbol of power and fruitfulness. In an ironic neo-colonial altarpiece (circa 1966) installed in the Museu de Arte de São Paulo, Nelson Leirner (born 1932) makes the object of devotion the neon-lit head of pop star Robert Carlos. Conceptual art offers different ways of confronting the dominant ideology. Both Cildo Meireles (born 1948) and Jac Lierner (born 1961) have used, misused or forged banknotes, for example, and both they and Waltercio Caldas (born 1946) and Tunga (born 1952) have created installations which draw attention, directly and indirectly to environmental issues. The painter Siron Franco (born 1947) also often addresses the issue of the destruction of the Amazon rainforest, but his disturbing surreal images explore many other areas – industrial pollution, sexual fantasy, political corruption, national identity – making him one of the most exciting artists in Brazil today.

Architecture

Before the arrival of the Portuguese in 1500, Brazil was inhabited by the Tupi-Guarani Indians, who had developed forms of art and architecture which appeared very primitive in comparison with that of other precolumbian cultures such as the Incas, the Maya and the Aztecs. In fact, the first colonizers were disappointed with what they found. Instead of rich cities, impressive palaces, temples and massive stone walls, they faced relatively small groups of semi-naked Indians living in houses covered mostly with palm leaves.

Indian architecture

The tropical climate and their nomadic way of life did not allow these tribes to develop permanent cities or solid, lasting constructions. They lived in *tabas*, temporary sites formed by a group of *ocas* (collective buildings, made of branches, leaves and vegetable fibres), placed around a main square. After a year or two, they would abandon the *taba* and move to another place, in search of better hunting grounds and new fields for their subsistence agriculture. A few examples of these interesting building techniques can be seen in museums, such as the **Museu do Índio** in Rio de Janeiro, or other specific institutions in Brazil.

The earliest Portuguese colonizers to arrive in Brazil in the 16th century faced many problems in building their houses, forts, churches and other necessary structures. First of all there was a lack of building materials, such as bricks, roof tiles and mortar. Second, there were few trained craftsmen, such as carpenters and bricklayers, in the colony. They therefore had to improvise by developing unusual building techniques and trying different materials. In the hinterland, in places like São Paulo, Goiás and Minas Gerais the majority of the houses were built with *taipa de pilão*. This technique consisted in using a wooden form to build thick walls. These forms were filled with a mixture of clay, vegetable fibres, horsehair, ox blood and dung. This paste was then compacted with a pestle and allowed to dry for two to three days before the next layer was added. The roof tiles were often moulded on a female slave's thigh and dried in the sun.

Brazilian colonial style: houses & civic buildings

It is quite easy to identify a house in Brazilian colonial style. Their shapes, colours and building techniques remained virtually unchanged for almost three centuries.

A Brazilian colonial house

Firstly, they always had large, visible roofs, made with red clay tiles, finishing in eaves extending beyond the walls. All the buildings were painted in a white wash, with bright colours used only on window and door frames. These were made of wood and had, mostly, elegant arches at the top. In the 19th century, sash windows with squared 10 cm by 10 cm pieces of glass were added in many houses, as can be seen in cities like Paraty, Ouro Preto and Salvador.

Urban colonial houses had doors and windows opening directly onto the street. Courtyards were never placed in front of the house, but internally, forming airy patios which protected the privacy of the family. The furniture was extremely simple and rough. Often, the only pieces of furniture in a bedroom would be the bed itself and a leather box to store clothes and personal belongings. In the colonial period, the highest status symbol was to live in a *sobrado* (a house with more than one floor, usually two). The ground floor was normally a commercial business and above it the residence of the owner's family.

Churches, convents & religious buildings: the Baroque in Brazil

Houses, public buildings and other colonial civic edifices were generally unelaborate. All the refinement, style and sophistication in art, architecture and decoration was lavished on churches, convents and monasteries. The great religious orders, such as the Jesuits, Franciscans, Carmelites and Benedictines brought to Brazil the latest artistic trends from Europe, mainly the Baroque and Rococo.

Two separate strands in Brazilian religious architecture evolved. In the most important cities, close to the seaboard and more influenced by European culture, the churches and convents were built according to designs brought from Portugal, Italy and Spain. Some were merely copies of Jesuit or Benedictine temples in Europe. Examples of this can be found in Salvador (the main cathedral, the São Francisco church), Rio de Janeiro (the Mosteiro de São Bento, the Convento de Santo Antônio) and Olinda (church and convent of Nossa Senhora das Neves).

Brazilian Baroque

At the end of the 17th century gold was found in the region of Minas Gerais (see the Ouro Preto section, page 239). One of the first administrative acts of the Portuguese crown in response to this discovery was to banish the traditional European orders from the mining region. The royal administration wanted to control the mining itself, taxation and traffic in gold and, as the friars were regarded as among the most shameless of smugglers of the metal, the orders in this instance were denied the

A Jesuit-style church

f.s.

Background

support they were given elsewhere in
the Portuguese colonies. Therefore the
majority of the churches in cities like
Ouro Preto, Mariana, Congonhas and
Sabará were built by local associations,
the so-called 'third orders'. These lay
orders had the gold and the will to
build magnificent temples but,
although they wanted their projects to
be as European as possible, the original
designs were hard to obtain in such
out-of-the-way places. So the local artists had to find their own way. Inspired
by descriptions and second-hand information, they created their own interpretation of the Baroque, thoroughly
infused with regional influences and
culture. This is the reason why the
'Barroco Mineiro' is so original.

*Curved church: São
Francisco de Assis,
Ouro Preto*

**Curved
churches & the
decline of the
Gold Era**

At the beginning of the 18th century, when gold was easily found in Minas Gerais,
the main attraction was the inside of the church, richly and heavily decorated in
carved wood and gold. Many of the churches built in this period will be a total surprise for the visitor. Their façades and exteriors are so simple and yet the naves and
altars are so highly and artistically decorated. As the mines started to decline, the
outside of the buildings became more sophisticated, with curves, round towers and
sinuous walls, such as the churches of São Francisco de Assis and Rosário, in Ouro
Preto. As the gold for covering walls ran out, it was replaced by paintings and murals.

**The 19th
century &
the Neoclassic
style**

The beginning of 19th century brought a major change in the history of Brazilian
architecture. When Napoleon invaded Portugal in 1808, the Portuguese royal family
and some 15,000 nobles and wealthy families fled to Rio de Janeiro, bringing with
them their own view of what was sophisticated in the arts. In 1816 the king, Dom
João VI, invited a group of French artists (The French Artistic Mission) to Brazil to
introduce the most recent European trends in painting, sculpture, decoration and
architecture. This was the beginning of the Neoclassic style in Brazil. An Imperial
Academy of Fine Arts was created and all the new government buildings were built
in Neoclassic style. The great name of this period as the French architect Grandjean
de Montigny , who planned and built many houses and public buildings throughout
the city of Rio de Janeiro.

The rich and famous also wanted their houses in this newly fashionable style,
which revolutionized the Brazilian way of building. The large roofs were now hidden

Background

The Neoclassic style

*A coffee farmhouse
with Neoclassic
influences*

by a small wall, the plat band. Windows and doors acquired round arches and walls were painted in ochres and light tones of pink. Public buildings and churches started to look like ancient Greek temples, with triangular pediments and columns. This new style was not best suited Brazil's climate. The earlier, large colonial roofs were much more efficient in dealing with heavy tropical rains and, in consequence, the Neoclassic style never became popular in the countryside.

Even when the coffee planters, in the second half of 19th century, started to become extremely rich and fond of imported fashions, they would build their urban mansions in the Neoclassic style, but still keep their farm houses with large roofs, sometimes adding small Neoclassic details in windows, doors and internal decoration. Good examples of this 19th-century rural architecture can be found very close to Rio de Janeiro, in cities like Vassouras, Valença, Barra do Piraí and Bananal, where some of the old farm houses are open to visitors.

There are many examples of urban Neoclassic building in Rio de Janeiro, such as the Museu Nacional, the Santa Casa da Misericórdia, the Casa de Rui Barbosa and the Instituto Benjamin Constant. Also very close to Rio, in Petrópolis, the Museu Imperial (formerly the Emperor's summer palace) is also a perfect example of the style. This Neoclassic remained popular in Brazil until the end of the 19th century, being also the 'official' style of the First and the Second Brazilian Empires.

The early 20th century & the Eclectic style

After the Republic, in 1889, the Neoclassic style lost favour since it had been serving the king and the emperors for such a long time. A new style, or better, a new harmony of different styles started to gain popularity, also under the influence of Paris and the Belle Époque. There were elements of neoclassic architecture, but also an excess of decoration and adornment on the façades. A broad 'boulevard' was constructed in Rio de Janeiro in 1906, the Avenida Central (today Avenida Rio Branco), with the idea of creating 'a Paris in the Tropics'. There are many examples of buildings in the Eclectic style on this avenue: the Biblioteca Nacional, the Teatro Municipal (Opera House) and the Museu Nacional de Belas Artes, all of them built in the first decade of 20th century. Also in Manaus, during the rubber boom, many buildings adopted this style, such as the Teatro Amazonas (the Opera House). During the first two decades of this century, the Eclectic style remained very popular.

Ecletic style in Rio de Janeiro

In 1922 a group of artists, painters, poets and architects organized in São Paulo 'A Semana da Arte Moderna' or the Modern Art Week, during which they exhibited their distaste at the influence of foreign standards in Brazilian art. They considered their role to be a quest for a genuine Brazilian form of expression. This resulted in the rejection of all imported standards and, as far as architecture was concerned, two main currents emerged.

The 'Modern Art Week' of 1922 & national pride

The first movement sought its true Brazilian style in the past, in the colonial period. Architects like Lúcio Costa, studied the techniques, materials and designs of the 16th, 17th and 18th centuries, soon producing houses with a colonial look, but also combining elements which were only previously found in Baroque churches. These included pediments and decorated door frames. The style was called Neocolonial and remained popular until the 1940s, especially in Rio de Janeiro and São Paulo.

The Neocolonial

In search of greater authenticity, many architects employed original materials brought from demolished old houses. A good example of this can be found in Rio de Janeiro, in the Largo do Boticário (very close to the train station for Corcovado, in Cosme Velho), a small square surrounded by Neocolonial houses painted in fancy, bright colours.

The other current generated by the Semana da Arte Moderna looked to the future for its inspiration for Brazilian-ness. Architects such as Oscar Niemeyer, Lúcio Costa, Affonso Eduardo Reidy, the landscape designer Roberto Burle Marx and many others started to design functional and spacious buildings, with large open areas and *pilotis* (pillars carrying a building, leaving the ground floor open). The use of concrete and glass was intense and the masterpiece of the Brazilian architectural Modernism is Brasília, the capital, planned from scratch in the 1950 by Lúcio Costa and Oscar Niemeyer.

Modernism

Many examples of Modernist building can be found all over Brazil: in Brasília, the Cathedral, the National Congress, the Palácio do Planalto (the presidential palace), in fact the whole city, with its broad freeways and spacious urban blocks, called *quadras*; in Belo Horizonte, the church of São Francisco de Assis, in Pampulha; in São Paulo, the MASP (Museum of Art of São Paulo), the Memorial da América Latina, and many commercial buildings along the Avenida Paulista; in Rio de Janeiro, the Ministério da Educação e Saúde, the Museu de Arte Moderna, the Catedral Metropolitana, the Petrobrás building (Brazilian State Petrol Company), the BNDES building (National Bank of Social and Economic Development), all in the central area of the city.

The most recent trend is the post-modern. Many business centres, shopping malls and residential buildings are being designed in a style which uses coloured mirror glass, granite and stylized structures reminiscent of classical temples.

Brazilian contemporary architecture

Brazilian architects are also famous worldwide for their techniques in designing houses for construction on steeply-inclined hills. In Rio de Janeiro, if you are driving along the coastal road in the neighbourhoods of Barra and São Conrado you can see many of these astonishing projects, homes of the very wealthy.

Background

Neocolonial house with a Baroque influence

Land and environment

Geography

Brazil is the largest country in South America and the fifth largest in the world, almost as large as the USA. It is over 4,300 km from north to south and the same from east to west, with land borders of 15,700 km and an Atlantic coastline of 7,400 km. It has a common frontier with all the other South American countries except Chile and Ecuador and occupies almost half the total area of the continent. Its population of 162 million is now, after the recent break-up of the USSR, also the fifth largest in the world, and over half that of South America.

Geology   Although Brazil is dominated by the vast river basins of the Amazon and the Paraná which account for about three-fifths of the country, not much of it is 'lowlands'. Ancient rock structures, some of the oldest in the world, underlie much of the area creating resistant plateaux and a rounded hilly landscape. These ancient Pre-Cambrian rocks culminate in the Guiana highlands to the north and the crystalline ranges which run close to the coastline all the way from near the Amazon to the Uruguayan frontier.

It is believed that South America and Africa were joined in the geologic past, and there is a tolerable fit between the easterly bulge of Brazil and the Gulf of Guinea. Persuasive evidence has been found of identical ostracod fossils (freshwater fish) in corresponding Cretaceous rocks in both Brazil and Gabon, overlain by salt deposits that could have been the first appearance of the South Atlantic Ocean. This suggests that the split began some 125 million years ago. What is now accepted is that the South American Plate continues to move westwards with the consequent elevation of the Andes on the other side of the continent where it meets the Pacific Plates.

The Amazon   The Amazon River is the greatest in the world in area of drainage, about 7,000,000 sq
Basin   km, and in volume of discharge into the sea averaging 180,000 cu m per second (or 170 billion gallons per hour), 10 times that of the Mississippi, and more than all the rivers of Europe put together. Such is the flow that the salinity of the Atlantic Ocean is affected for 250 km out from the river delta. It is 6,400 km long (marginally shorter than the Nile) from its sources in the Andes of Peru, and still has over 3,000 km to go through Brazil when it leaves Leticia on the Colombia/Brazil border, yet with only a fall of 80 m to sea level. Unlike most major world rivers, the basin is reduced in width near its mouth, indeed hills come down to the river near Monte Alegre only 200 km from the delta. Some 200 km above this at Óbidos, the river is over 75 m deep, that is the bottom is well below sea level. This reflects the more recent geological history of the basin which until the latter part of the Tertiary Period (say 25 million years ago) was connected to the Pacific and drained through what is now Ecuador. With the uplift of the Andes, this route was closed off, and a huge inland sea was formed, helped by a downward folding of the older rocks (some geologists believe there was also significant rifting of the strata) to create a huge geosyncline. Eventually the water broke through the crystalline rocks to the east and made the new connection to the Atlantic. Deep layers of sediment were laid down and have been added to ever since, with today's heavy tropical rains continuing to erode the surrounding mountains. This gives the largest more or less level area in Brazil, but it is so heavily forested and the soils so continually leached by the climate, with vast expanses frequently under floodwaters, that the potential for agriculture is strictly limited.

A characteristic of virtually all the tributaries which join the Amazon from the south is that upstream navigation ends where the rivers tumble off the plateaux of central Brazil creating dramatic waterfalls and in many cases now providing hydroelectric power.

Cerrado

The cerrado, covering 25 percent of the national territory, is one of Brazil's most common ecosystems. Or perhaps one should say 'was one of the most common'. A study by Ibama suggests that all its cultivable surface will be occupied by the year 2000. Scientists are becoming aware that the cerrado has the richest biodiversity of any savanna on the planet. It has outcrops (chapadas) and valleys, vegetation that ranges from humid grassland to gallery forest to dry forest to scrub. 429 species of tree and bush have been catalogued as endemic. There are many orchids. Several animals that live in the cerrado are threatened with extinction, such as the maned wolf, the great anteater and some bird species. It extends over much of the central plateau and yet, in official documents which stress the importance of protecting various types of forest and coastal vegetation, it is not mentioned at all. It has been seen as a good alternative to the Amazon for the relocation of urban overpopulation. Agricultural development, claims Ibama, has been managed poorly, forcing colonizers to abandon uneconomic farms in favour of new lands in the cerrado. Even the wild plants' adaptation to fire, which occurs naturally every five-seven years, has been misunderstood, leading to intensive burning by cattle ranchers to clear land which never recovers.

The World Wide Fund for Nature is working with Ibama on a project in the Parque Nacional da Chapada dos Veadeiros in Goiás state to try to encourage sustainable development in the cerrado. This is an example of how the consciousness raised by the pressure to conserve Brazil's northern rainforests has prompted conservationists to look more closely at all Brazil's ecosystems.

Source: "Cerrado, o Bioma Esquecido", Ibama On Line.

The Centre West

South of the Amazon basin is a large area of undulating highlands, a dissected plateau mostly between 200 m and 800 m. These are ancient rocks, back as far as Pre-Cambrian crystallines. They produce poor soils but sufficient to provide the grasslands or *cerrado* (see box) of the Mato Grosso, Goiás, western Paraná and adjacent areas, widely used for ranching, though now increasingly found suitable for soya bean production, one of Brazil's foremost exports.

From Minas Gerais southwards, the rivers drain into the second largest basin of Brazil, the Paraná, which eventually reaches the Atlantic by way of the River Plate of Argentina/Uruguay. This is another large river system, 4,000 km long, of which about half is in Brazil. A principal tributary of the Paraná is the Rio Paraguay which, in its early stages, flows into a wide depression now filled with many thousands of metres of sediments and known in Brazil as the Pantanal. Further south, the swamps continue into the Chaco of Paraguay and Argentina. To the east of this, again the rivers fall off the old highland strata to form rapids and waterfalls, the largest of which was the former Sete Quedas falls (Salto de Guaíra) on the Paraná, sadly drowned by the Itaipu dam lake in 1982. Nearby however are the Iguaçu falls, the most impressive of South America, created by very resistant layers of basalt.

The coast & escarpment

Highlands follow the coastline, only a short distance inland, for 3,000 km. The ancient crystalline/granite ridges, known as *serras*, stretch from Porto Alegre in the south to near Belém in the north, just short of the Amazon estuary. Long stretches are in the form of a single or stepped escarpment, abrupt in the east and sloping more gently inland to the west. They are not high in South American terms – the highest point, Pico da Bandeira is only 2,890 m – but it is no more than 120 km from the ocean near Vitória. The narrowness of the coastal strip has had a profound effect on the history of settlement. Until comparatively recent times, the lack of natural access to the

The Sertão

The sertão (plural sertões) covers almost three-quarters of northeastern Brazil, extending into the north of Minas Gerais. Of the states in the northeast, only Maranhão lacks this geographic zone. It is hot, semi-arid and subject to frequent droughts. The soil is stony and the trees and bushes are twisted, covered in thorns. There is also a great variety of cacti. The vegetation is typical of the caatinga, adapted to land which can be parched, sometimes for years at a time. In the drought, the plants appear to die, the inhabitants and their animals face hunger and misery, and all life awaits the return of the rain.

The caatinga is "not an impenetrable barrier. Its unique vegetation makes it more like a labyrinth, with a multitude of paths and clearings, always alike, and transformed as if by magic, to revive for a day, only when a chance rain fills the merciless sky. If the peril of virgin forest is solitude without trails or egress, the terror of the caatinga is the bewilderment which their multiplicity never fails to cause. The beast, led by instinct, can range to the uttermost parts and reach his destination without straying; but once a man enters the caatinga and his memory falters in choosing a trail, he is a victim whom only a miracle will save." (Quoted from The Bandeirantes, edited by Richard M Morse, page 42.)

To the Portuguese colonists, the sertão was a region of legends. Unlike the routes along the Amazon in the north and the routes taken by the bandeirantes along the Tietê in the south, the trackless northeast was full of mystery because settlers were not tempted into it. The source of the only major river to run through it, the São Francisco, was a cause for speculation; the indigenous people were described as giants, or dwarves, or deformed in a bewildering variety of ways and all were believed to be savage fighters. And, of course, in this dangerous interior there were said to be great riches awaiting the intrepid explorer: silver mines, gold and mountains of emeralds.

In the 20th century the sertão has inspired some of the greatest Brazilian literature, but the geographical and human landscape portrayed is not the mythical sertão of the 16th and 17th centuries. Graciliano Ramos in Vidas secas (Barren Lives, 1938), João Guimarães Rosa in Grande sertão: veredas (The Devil to Pay in the Backlands, 1956) and Antônio Torres in Essa terra (The Land, 1976), among others, have all presented the region in memorable ways (see the Literature, page 693, for notes on Ramos and Guimarães Rosa). The direct realism of Ramos' Vidas secas emphasizes the harshness of the sertão, the family driven from their land by drought, by the "enemy vegetation". Yet there is an ambiguity to the flight. They head for the city, where the children will learn "difficult, necessary things", but that too is an alien world, unknown, civilized and it, like the climate they have left, will imprison them.

hinterland confined virtually all economic activity to this area, and today most of the major cities of Brazil and 80% of the population are on or near the coast.

Because of varying erosion over many millions of years, there are a number of interesting natural features in these highlands. The many granite 'peaks' in and around Rio de Janeiro are the resistant remnants of very hard rocks providing spectacular viewpoints, Pico da Tijuca (the highest, 1,012 m), Corcovado (710 m) and Pão de Açúcar (396 m) the best known. There are others in the neighbouring state of Espírito Santo. Near Curitiba are the eroded sandstones of Vila Velha and the wild scenery through the Serra do Mar towards the coast. In the state of Bahía, there are remarkable caves and waterfalls in the Chapada da Diamantina National Park. In many places, what rivers there are flowing eastwards necessarily have to lose height quickly so that gorges and waterfalls abound. There are also many kilometres of spectacular coastline and fine beaches. South of Porto Alegre, eroded material moved down the coast by the southerly ocean currents added to alluvials brought north from the River Plate by subsidiary currents, have created long sand bars to form several large freshwater lagoons. The longest, Lagoa dos Patos, is over 250 km long.

The escarpment forces most of the rain run-off to flow west into the interior to feed the Amazon and Paraná river systems. However, one major river breaks through the barrier to flow into the Atlantic. The São Francisco rises south of Belo Horizonte – one important tributary starts only 250 km from the sea – but flows, north then east, for 2,900 km before it gets there. Almost 500 km of rapids through the escarpment culminate in the 75 m Paulo Afonso falls, before completing the final 240 km to the sea. Where it turns east is one of the driest areas of the country, known as the *sertão*. The river is therefore of great significance particularly as the rains here are so unreliable. Together with the link it provides to so much of the interior and its course wholly within the country (unlike the Amazon and the Paraná), the São Francisco is revered by the Brazilians as the 'river of national unity'. Its value for irrigation, hydroelectric power, fish and navigation above the rapids is inestimable, but because of sand bars at its mouth and close proximity to the fall line, the river has not proved useful for shipping or access generally to the ocean in spite of being the third largest river system on the continent.

The Rio São Francisco

After sinking below the Amazon estuary, the Brazilian Highlands reappear to the north and sweep round to the west to form the border with the Guianas and Venezuela. The highest tabular uplands are near where Guyana, Venezuela and Brazil meet at Monte Roraima (2,810 m) and further west along the border where a national park has been set up focused on Pico de Neblina, 3,014 m, the highest point in Brazil.

The Northern Highlands

Climate

The climate of Brazil is a function of latitude and altitude. The average annual temperature exceeds 26°C along the northeast coast and in the central Amazon with little variation throughout the year. The highlands are cooler and further south there are seasonal variations: Brazil extends to 34° south which is equivalent to the latitude of North Carolina. High summer temperatures can occur almost anywhere here, yet frosts are not uncommon in July and August as coffee producers know only too well. Rainfall is more complicated. The northeast Trades bring moist air to the coast north of the Amazon, where there is heavy precipitation all year round. The same winds push saturated air into the Amazon basin where rainfall is progressively greater from east to west throughout the year and virtually on a daily basis. The abrupt rise of the Andes beyond the borders of Brazil increases the precipitation and so feeds the many tributaries of the river.

During the period December-May, the northeast Trades move north and Brazil between Belém and Recife receives less rain-bearing winds. From Salvador, the southeast Trades bring moisture from the South Atlantic and it is the gap between these two systems, known as the 'doldrums', that explains the dry areas of northeast Brazil. On average there is a significant rainfall here, but sometimes it fails to arrive causing prolonged periods of drought. Precipitation in the southern states of Brazil is concentrated in the escarpment thus feeding the Paraná system and is well distributed throughout the year.

Although there are occasional storms causing local damage, for example in the *favelas* (shanties) of Rio, Brazil is not subject to hurricanes or indeed to other natural disasters common elsewhere in Latin America such as earthquakes, volcanic eruptions or unexpected widespread and catastrophic floods.

Background

Flora and fauna

The neotropical realm is a land of superlatives, it contains the most extensive tropical rainforest in the world; drained by the Amazon which has by far the largest volume of any river. The fauna and flora are to a large extent determined by the influence of the great rivers and mountains – the Andes, which are the longest uninterrupted mountain chain in the world. Although not part of Brazil they dramatically affect the climate and hence the animals and plants that can inhabit the country. There are also huge expanses of open terrain, the Pantanal – a huge wet wilderness, vast mountain grasslands and tree-covered savannahs. It is this wide range of habitats which makes Brazil one of the greatest regions of biological diversity.

This diversity arises not only from the wide range of habitats available, but also from the history of the continent. South America has essentially been an island for some 70 million years joined only by a narrow isthmus to Central and North America. Land passage played a significant role in the gradual colonization of South America by species from the north. When the land-link closed these colonists evolved to a wide variety of forms free from the competitive pressures that prevailed elsewhere. When the land-bridge was re-established some four million years ago a new invasion of species took place from North America, adding to the diversity but also leading to numerous extinctions. Comparative stability has ensued since then and has guaranteed the survival of many primitive groups including a group of pouched mammals, the opossums.

Brazil can be divided into a number of biogeographical zones; two immense river basins comprising the River Amazon and the River Plate, mountains – the Guiana highlands to the north and the Brazilian highlands to the south, and a coastal strip of Atlantic rainforest.

Rainfall

The Atlantic rainforest used to cover 2,600,000 sq km in a coastal strip 160 km wide and 4,200 km long. The coastal rainforest is bounded inland by a series of mountain ranges which contribute to the varied landscape and hence species diversity. It is one of the Earth's biological hotspots. Now critically fragmented and reduced to less than 5% of its original extent, it remains home to a very high proportion of unique species. For example 17 of the 21 primate species found there are unique to that region, and of those, 13 species, including the golden lion tamarin (see box, page 139), are endangered. Populations of South America's largest primate, the woolly spider monkey, locally known as *muriqui*, were decimated by European colonists who first settled along this coastal zone.

Atlantic rain forest

Along the coast, mangroves provide a breeding ground for numerous species of fish including many that are commercially important. Further inland is the *restinga*, a zone of shrub forest, coastal sand dunes, ponds and wetlands. The lush coastal rainforest itself extends to 800 m in elevation and grades into cloud forest between 800 m and 1,700 m. Drenching by mist, fog and rain leads to a profusion of plant growth, trees and shrubs which are covered with a great variety of epiphytes – orchids, mosses lichens and bromeliads. At the highest elevations, the forest gives way to mountain grasslands or *campos de altitude*. In the southern zone of the Atlantic forest there are large stands of monkey puzzle tree, *araucária*, which is characterized by its own parrot community, many of which are also endemic.

The Amazon basin contains the largest area of tropical rainforest in the world, 6,000,000 sq km, 60% of which is located in Brazil. It is home to 20% of the world's plant and bird species; perhaps 10% of mammal species; an inestimable number of insects and perhaps some 2,000 species of fish inhabiting the 1,000 tributaries of the Amazon. When in flood the great river inundates the forest for a short period in its upper reaches to create a unique habitat called *várzea*; in the lower reaches this flooding may last for four to seven months forming *igapó* swamp forest.

The Amazon River & rainforest

The rivers of the Amazon are either classified as blackwater or whitewater rivers. The former are highly coloured due to the brown humic acids derived from the decomposing materials on the forest floor but contain little suspended material. The whitewaters owe their colour to the suspended soil particles which originate in the run-off from the Andes. Each has its characteristic fish. Within a 30 km radius of Manaus, there are estimated to be over 700 species of fish. The largest of these species is the *arapaima* reaching over 3 m and weighing in at over 150 kg. It gulps air at

Climate & vegetation

Equator

Transitional zones

0 km 500
0 miles 500

N

1 Equatorial, hot & humid; dense forest; rivers carrying large volumes of water
2 Tropical, with humid summers; *cerrado*: savanna with isolated bushes or stunted trees, sometimes in clumps; rivers that may dry up in winter
3 Semi-arid; *caatinga*: dry tropical scrub & thorn forest, typical of the so-called Polígono das Secas; intermittent rivers which dry up after the rainy season
4 Tropical; *caatinga*
5 Tropical, humid; forest covering seashore & the banks of the river
6 As 5 but at higher altitudes
7 Subtropical; forest
8 Subtropical with cooler summers & cold winters; tropical forest; rivers with a uniform flow of water the year round
9 Subtropical, as 8; pine forest (*araucárias*)
10 Subtropical with cold winters; *Gaúcho* lowlands, meadows gallery forest; rivers as 8 & 9

the surface and is harpooned by fishermen. The *pacu* or silver-dollar fish feeds on fruit falling from trees of the flooded forest. The voracious *piranha* normally feeds on other fishes although they are quite capable of removing the flesh from larger animals. They probably benefit the ecosystem by removing diseased and dying individuals as well as disposing of carrion. A greater risk is posed by the electric eels and sting rays found in turbid waters. An electrical shock of 650 volts has been recorded from a captive electric eel; these electric fields are used to locate and kill prey. The ray does not inject poison but its 10 cm long spine can puncture and lacerate flesh.

Várzea & Igapó   *Várzea* is a highly productive seasonally inundated forest found along the banks of the whitewater rivers; it is very rich as a consequence of the huge amount of silt and nutrients washed out of the mountains and trapped by the massive buttress-rooted trees. This lakeland swamp forest is flooded for relatively short periods of time. One of the commonest trees of the *várzea*, the Pará rubber tree, is the source of latex. The Brazilian rubber industry foundered in the 19th century when seeds of this tree were illegally taken to Asia to form the basis of huge rubber plantations and flourished in the absence of pest species.

In contrast the *igapó* forests are characteristic of the blackwater rivers with little silt deposition leading to sandy beaches fringing the forest. Despite being flooded for up to seven months of the year to a possible depth of 15 m, palms dominate this swampy habitat, although massive kapok trees are also typical. During the wet season, these flooded forests are inhabited by turtles and small fish, and the predators that feed upon them – otters and caiman.

Flooded meadows are frequently found in the still-flowing reaches of the *várzea*. These vast carpets of floating waterlilies, waterlettuce and waterhyacinth are home to the Amazonian manatee, a large herbivorous aquatic mammal which is the freshwater relative of the dugong of the Caribbean. Vast numbers of spectacled caiman populate the lakes feeding on the highly productive fish community.

The river corridors are often the best places to observe wildlife. Caiman and turtles are commonly seen basking on the riverbanks. Neotropical cormorants, roseate spoonbills and jabiru storks are commonly observed fishing in the shallow waters. The hoatzin is generally found along waterways where it feeds on leaves, and fruit. The newly hatched chicks of this primitive bird have claws at the tip of each wing which enable them to crawl around in the foliage.

Cross section of Amazonian forest

dry land forest; caaetê

várzea forest

igapó forest

land which does not flood;
crystalline deposits

silt deposits

recent silt deposits

source: Celso Antunes,
Geografia e Participação 2

The Macaw

One of Brazil's beautiful birds, "called arat [macaw], has wing and tail feathers about a foot and a half long, one half of each feather as red as fine scarlet, and the other half a sparkling sky-blue (the colours are divided from each other along the quill), with all the rest of the body the color of lapis lazuli; when this bird is in the sunlight, where it is ordinarily to be seen, no eye can weary of gazing upon it."

Jean de Léry, History of a Voyage to The Land of Brazil, Otherwise called America, *translated by Janet Whately (Berkeley and Oxford: University of California Press, 1990), page 87. De Léry was a French Protestant cleric who visited Brazil in the mid-16th century.*

In the relatively constant climatic conditions, animal and plant life has evolved to an amazing diversity over the millennia. It has been estimated that 4 sq km of forest can harbour some 1,200 vascular plants, 600 species of tree, and 120 woody plants. Here in these relatively flat lands a soaring canopy some 45 m overhead is the power-house of the forest. It is a habitat choked with strangling vines and philodendrons amongst which mixed troupes of squirrel monkeys and capuchins forage. In the high canopy small groups of spider monkeys perform their lazy aerial acrobatics, whilst lower down, clinging to epiphyte-clad trunks and branches, groups of tamarins and marmosets forage for gums, blossom, fruit and the occasional insect prey.

Caiman are South American alligators. They are relatively small, usually growing to no more than 2½ m in length. They are found in areas of relatively still water, ranging form marshland to lakes and slow-flowing rivers. Youngsters feed mainly on aquatic invertebrates while adults also take larger prey, including wild pigs and small travellers. During the dry season when pools dry up caimans can stop feeding altogether and burrow into the mud at the bottom of a pool waiting for the return of the rains.

The **giant otter** is found along the tributaries of the Amazon. It can measure up to 2 m in length. They are active by day when they hunt for food, often in small groups. They are not rare but are rarely seen as they are shy and submerge quickly at the slightest hint of danger. They feed on fish, molluscs and crustaceans, also small mammals and birds. They can be tamed easily and are often raised as pets by some tribes.

Pantanal

This ecologically diverse zone includes the largest area of wetlands in the world when flooded between December to March. In addition it includes dry savannahs or *cerrado*, chaco scrublands as well as gallery rainforest. The area is very flat and flooded by the rising rivers leaving isolated islands (*cordilheiras*) between vast lakes (*bahias*) which become saline as the waters evaporate. This mixed ecosystem supports a highly diverse fauna characteristic of the constituent habitat types which includes 200 species of mammal. Capybara (see below), tapir and peccaries are common along the waters edge as are marsh deer. Jaguar, more commonly associated with the forest, prey on these herbivores and the cattle and feral pigs which graze here. Spectacular assemblages of wading birds – egrets, jabiru storks, ibises, spoonbills and herons prey on the abundant invertebrate and fish fauna. Anacondas and caiman are still common, although the black caiman has been hunted out.

Jaguars are the largest of the New World cats. Jaguars are great wanderers, roaming even further than pumas. Usually they haunt forests where they hunt for deer, agoutis and especially peccaries. They follow the herds of these South American

▶▶ The beak of beaks

"The beak of this bird the toucan, which is longer than the whole body and proportionately thick (I will not compare or contrast it with that of the crane, which is nothing by comparison), must be regarded not only as the beak of beaks, but also as the most prodigious and monstrous that can be found among all the birds in the universe."

Jean de Léry, History of a Voyage to The Land of Brazil, Otherwise called America, *translated by Janet Whately (Berkeley and Oxford: University of California Press, 1990), page 90.*

swine and pounce on the stragglers. They also attack capybara. Unlike most cats, jaguars are often found beside rivers and frequently enter the water. It attacks the tapir as it comes down to drink and will even scoop fish from the water with its paws.

The **tapir** is a shy, nocturnal animal which confines itself to an intricate network of trails in the forests of the marshy lowlands of Bolivia, Brazil, Colombia, Venezuela, Ecuador, Peru and the north of Argentina.

Water is essential for its survival; it drinks a great deal and is an excellent swimmer. It is herbivorous, eating waterplants and the leaves and twigs of trees. Its only enemies are jaguars and alligators against which its only defence is to use its teeth.

The **capybara** is a large aquatic rodent that looks like a cross between a guinea pig and a hippopotamus. It is the largest of all the rodents at over 1 m long and weighing over 50 kg. They live in large groups along the riverbanks, where they graze on the lush grasses. It comes out onto dry land to rest and bask in the sun, but at the first hint of danger the whole troop dashes into the water. Its greatest enemy is the jaguar. They are rather vocal for rodents often emitting a series of strange clicks, squeaks and grunts.

National parks

Ecotourism is the international passion of this decade, but it is also a question of survival. It is modern and urgent to be a conservationist, to respect flora and fauna, not to pollute the beaches or the forests, to respect local populations, to value our cultural heritage, customs and traditions. *Guia do Turismo*, 10, 1997, page 25.

Different countries have different approaches to the relationship between national parks and tourism. In Brazil, the system which protects areas of outstanding beauty and unique flora and fauna has the dual role of providing centres of scientific research and places which are open to the public as an alternative form of recreation and education. Ibama (Instituto Brasileiro do Meio Ambiente e dos Recursos Naturais Renováveis – the Brazilian Institute for the Environment and Renewable Natural Resources) has in its care 35 national parks (Parques Nacionais, or PARNA). They are by no means the whole picture, though. They form part of a system of protected areas which go under different titles and which have varying degrees of public access. The network comprises, in addition to the national parks: Estações Ecológicas (ecological stations), Reservas Biológicas (biological reserves), Reservas Ecológicas (ecological reserves), Áreas de Relevante Interesse Ecológico (areas of relevant ecological interest), Reservas Particulares do Patrimônio Nacional (private national heritage reserves) and Áreas sob Proteção Especial (areas of special protection). In all these entities, the exploitation of natural resources is completely forbidden. They are for research, education and recreation only. Three other types of entity are designed to allow the sustainable use of natural resources, while still preserving their biodiversity: Florestas Nacionais (national forests), Áreas de Proteção Ambiental (areas of environmental protection) and Reservas Extrativas (extractive reserves – such as the rubber tapping zones in Acre state). A new initiative is the Projeto Corredores Ecológicos (Ecological Corridors Project), which aims to create avenues of forest between isolated protected areas so that fauna may move over a greater area to breed, thus strengthening the stock of endangered animals which might otherwise suffer the ills of inbreeding. An example of this is project to link the Mata Atlântica of Poço das Antas (see page 138) with other pockets of coastal forest to help the survival of the golden lion tamarin.

Ibama was created in 1989, under Law No 7.735 of the 5 October 1988 Constitution. The Institute was formed by uniting four separate bodies, the environmental secretariat (SEMA), the Brazilian Institute of Forest Development (IBDF), and the superintendencies for the development of fishing and rubber (SUDEPE and SUDHEVEA). Brazil has a long history of passing laws to protect natural resources, such as that of 1808 which excluded from international trade the export of *pau-brasil* and other woods. At the same time, though, enforcement of such laws has not been easy. Today, the achievement of Ibama's goals is determined by resources, but funds are insufficient to commit either enough money or staff to the job of protecting the areas that have been designated for preservation. Sad though this is, there are still a large number of parks open to the visitor which can give a good idea of the variety of Brazil's natural resources and the value that they hold for the country.

This Handbook does not describe all Brazil's national parks or other conservation entities, only those which have easy access. Nor does the book list all the offices of Ibama or its related departments throughout the country, but those nearest to the parks described are given and it is to these that readers should apply if a permit is needed to visit a specific park.

For more information, contact Ibama at its local addresses, its national headquarters, SAIN, Avenida L-4, bloco "B", Térreo, Edifiço Sede do Ibama, CEP 70.800-200, Brasília DF, T061-2268221/9014, F061-3221058, or at its website, www.ibama.gov.br

Information can also be obtained from the Ministério do Meio Ambiente (MMA – the environment ministry), Esplanada dos Ministérios, bloco "B", 5-9 andar (5th to 9th floors), CEP 70068-900, Brasília DF, or at its website www.mma.gov.br See also the book *Parque Nacionais Brasil*, Guias Philips (1999), with a good map, beautiful photographs, sections on history, flora and fauna and tourist services, US$15.

Footnotes

Useful words and phrases

Greetings and courtesies

hello	*oi*	How are you?	*Como vai você*
good morning	*bom dia*		*tudo bem?/tudo bom?*
good afternoon	*boa tarde*	I am fine	*vou bem/tudo bem*
good evening/night	*boa noite*	pleased to meet you	*um prazer*
goodbye	*adeus/tchau*	no	*não*
see you later	*até logo*	excuse me/	*com licença*
please	*por favor/faz favor*	I beg your pardon	
thank you	*obrigado (if a man is*	I do not understand	*não entendo*
	speaking)/obrigada	Please speak slowly	*fale devagar por favor*
	(if a woman is speaking)	What is your name?	*Qual é seu nome?*
thank you very much	*muito obrigado/*	my name is_	*O meu nome é_*
	muito obrigada	Go away!	*Vai embora!*

In conversation, most people refer to **you** as *você*, although in the south and in Pará *tu* is more common.
To be more polite, use *O Senhor/A Senhora*. For **us**, *gente* (people, folks) is very common when it includes
you too.

Basic questions

Where is_?	*Onde está/onde fica?*	Why?	*Por que?*
How much does it cost?	*Quanto custa?*	What for?	*Para que?*
How much is it?	*Quanto é?*	How do I get to_?	*Para chegar a_?*
When?	*Quando?*	I want to go to?	*Quero ir para_*
When does the bus	*A que hor sai/chega*	Is this the way to the	*Aquí é o caminho para*
leave?/arrive?	*o ônibus?*	church?	*a igreja?*

Basics

bathroom/toilet	*banheiro*	notes/coins	*notas/moedas*
police (policeman)	*a polícia (o polícia)*	travellers' cheques	*os travelers/os cheques*
hotel	*o hotel (a pensão,*		*de viagem*
	a hospedaria)	cash	*dinheiro*
restaurant	*o restaurante*	breakfast	*o café de manh*
	(o lanchonete)	lunch	*o almoço*
post office	*o correio*	dinner/supper	*o jantar*
telephone office	*(central) telefônica*	meal	*a refeição*
supermarket	*o supermercado*	drink	*a bebida*
market	*o mercado*	mineral water	*a água mineral*
green grocery shop	*a sacolão*	soft fizzy drink	*o refrigerante*
bank	*o banco*	beer	*a cerveja*
bureau de change	*a casa de câmbio*	without sugar	*sem açúcar*
exchange rate	*a taxa de câmbio*	without meat	*sem carne*

Getting around

on the left/right	*à esquerda/à direita*	bus	*o ônibus*
straight on	*direto*	train	*a trem*
second street on the right	*a segunda rua à direita*	airport	*o aeroport*
right		aeroplane/airplane	*o avião*
to walk	*caminhar*	flight	*o vôa*
bus station	*a rodoviária*	first/second class	*primeira/segunda clase*

train station	*a ferroviária*	ticket	*o passagem/o bilhete*
combined bus &	*a rodoferroviária*	ticket office	*a bilheteria*
train station		bus stop	*a parada*

Accommodation

room	*quarto*	hot/cold water	*água quente/fria*
noisy	*barulhento*	to make up/clean	*limpar*
single/double room	*(quarto de) solteiro/*	sheet(s)	*o lençol (os lençóis)*
	(quarto para) casal	blankets	*as mantas*
room with two beds	*quarto com duas*	pillow	*o travesseiro*
	camas	clean/dirty towels	*as toalhas limpas/sujas*
with private bathroom	*quarto com banheiro*	toilet paper	*o papel higiêico*
bathroom	*privado*		

Health

chemist	*a farmacia*	contraceptive (pill)	*anticonceptional*
(for) pain	*(para) dor*		*(a pílula)*
stomach	*o esômago (a barriga)*	period	*a menstruação/a regra*
head	*a cabeça*	sanitary towels	*toalhas absorventes/*
fever/sweat	*a febre/o suor*		*higiênicas*
diarrhoea	*a diarréia*	tampons	*absorventes internos*
blood	*o sangue*	contact lenses	*lentes de contacto*
doctor	*o coutor/a doutora*	aspirin	*a aspirina*
condoms	*as camisinhas/*		
	os preservativos		

Time

at one o'clock	*a uma hota*	it's twenty past six/	*são seis e vinte*
	(da manhã/da tarde)	six twenty	
at half past two/	*as dois e meia*	it's five to nine	*são cinco para*
two thirty			*as nove*
at a quarter to three	*quinze para as três*	in ten minutes	*em dez minutos*
it's one o'clock	*é uma*	five hours	*cinco horas*
it's seven o'clock	*são sete horas*	Does it take long?	*Dura muito?*

Days

Monday	*segunda feiro*	Thursday	*quinta feira*	Sunday	*domingo*
Tuesday	*terça feira*	Friday	*sexta feira*		
Wednesday	*quarta feira*	Saturday	*sábado*		

Months

January	*janeiro*	May	*maio*	September	*setembro*
February	*fevereiro*	June	*junho*	October	*outubro*
March	*março*	July	*julho*	November	*novembro*
April	*abril*	August	*agosto*	December	*dezembro*

Numbers

1	*um/uma*	9	*nove*	21	*vente e um*
2	*dois/duas*	10	*dez*	30	*trinta*
3	*três*	11	*onze*	40	*cuarenta*
4	*quatro*	12	*doze*	50	*cinqüe*
5	*cinco*	13	*treze*	60	*sessenta*
6	*seis* (note also that	14	*catorze*	70	*setenta*
	"*meia*" – half – is	15	*quinze*	80	*oitenta*
	frequently used	16	*dezesseis*	90	*noventa*
	for number 6,	17	*dezessete*	100	*cem, cento*
	ie half-dozen).	18	*dezoito*	1000	*mil*
7	*sete*	19	*dezenove*		
8	*oito*	20	*vinte*		

See also Language in Essentials, page 28

General pronunciation

Within Brazil itself, there are variations in pronunciation, intonation, phraseology and slang. This makes for great richness and for the possibility of great enjoyment in the language. A couple of points which the newcomer to the language will spot immediately are the use of the tilde (~) over 'a' and 'o'. This makes the vowel nasal, as does a word ending in 'm' or 'ns', or a vowel followed by 'm' + consonant, or by 'n' + consonant. Another important point of spelling is that for words ending in 'i' and 'u' the emphasis is on the last syllable, though (unlike Spanish) no accent is used. This is especially relevant in place names like Buriti, Guarapari, Caxambu, Iguaçu. Note also the use of 'ç', which changes the pronunciation of c from hard [k] to soft [s].

Index

Shorts index

Advertisers' index

Map index

Map symbols

Administration
- - - - International border
- - - State border
□ Capital city
○ Other city/town

Roads and travel
—— Main road
—— Other road
- - - - 4Wd track
······· Footpath
 Railway with station
Ⓜ Metro station

Water features
River
Lake, reservoir, tank
Seasonal marshland
Beach, dry river bed
Ocean
Waterfall
Reef
Ferry

Cities and towns
▫ Sight
Sleeping
Eating
Building
Main through route
Main street
Minor street
Pedestrianized street

→ One way street
⇌ Bridge
Park, garden, stadium
✈ Airport
Ⓢ Bank
Bus station
Hospital
Market
Museum
Police
Post office
Tourist office
Cathedral, church
Petrol
@ Internet
Golf
Parking
A Detail map
A Related map

Topographical features
Contours (approx), rock outcrop
Mountain
Mountain pass
Escarpment
Gorge
Palm tree

Other symbols
Archaeological Site
National park/wildlife reserve
Viewing point

Credits

Footprint credits

Text editor: Felicity Laughton
Map editor: Sarah Sorensen

Publishers: James Dawson and
Patrick Dawson
Editorial Director: Rachel Fielding
Editorial: Claire Boobbyer,
Caroline Lascom, Stephanie Lambe,
Alan Murphy, Sarah Thorowgood
Production: Emma Bryers, Mark Thomas,
Jo Morgan, Davina Rungasamy
Cartography: Claire Benison,
Kevin Feeney, Robert Lunn
Proofreading: Emma Bryers
Design: Mytton Williams
Marketing and publicity:
Rosemary Dawson, La-Ree Miners
Sales: Ed Aves
Advertising: Debbie Wylde,
Lorraine Horler
Finance and administration:
Sharon Hughes, Elizabeth Taylor,
Leona Bailey
Distribution: Pam Cobb, Mike Noel

Photography credits

Front cover: Brazilian Government
Back cover: James Davies Worldwide
Inside colour section: Marcela Haddad,
James Davies Worldwide, Gettyimages,
Eye Ubiquitous, Imagestate, TRIP,
Robert Harding Picture Library,
South American Pictures

Print

Manufactured in Italy by LegoPrint

Publishing information

Brazil Handbook
3rd edition
© Footprint Handbooks Ltd
December 2002

ISBN 1 903471 44 3
CIP DATA: A catalogue record for this
book is available from the British Library

® Footprint Handbooks and the Footprint
mark are a registered trademark of
Footprint Handbooks Ltd

Published by Footprint Handbooks

6 Riverside Court
Lower Bristol Road
Bath BA2 3DZ, UK
T +44 (0)1225 469141
F +44 (0)1225 469461
E discover@footprintbooks.com
W www.footprintbooks.com

Distributed in the USA by

Publishers Group West

Every effort has been made to ensure that
the facts in the Handbook are accurate.
However, travellers should still obtain
advice from consulates, airlines etc about
travel and visa requirements before
travelling. The authors and publishers
cannot accept responsibility for
any loss, injury or inconvenience
however caused.

Acknowledgements

A big thank you to the following people for their help with this handbook:

Fabio Sombra for showing me Rio; Antonio Cavallari of *Coopetur Agency* and Maylin Falconi for a memorable tour of Petropolis; Bah and José 'Bene' Benedides Joniir for their wisdom; all the staff at *Taberna do Leme* in Copacabana; Paulo Tarso for being a 'friend in Rio'; Alice and Kevan Prior at the *Hibiscus* hotel in Búzios for their help and hospitality; Paulo Celani from *Justfly* and *Rio Jeep Adventures*; David Maswary for his insights; Rodrigo Cunha from *Pousada do Principe* in Paraty for his advice; Marcelo Niemeyer Armstrong from *Favela Tours* in Rio.

Giovanna, my good friend, and Matt in Salvador; Emelia from *Pousada Praia Hotel* in Recife for her invaluable assistance; Mark and Tania Aitchison of *Swallows and Amazon Tours* in Manaus for all their advice; Carini Krieger from *Acquatur* for all her hard work; Adriano Augusto Campos in Sao Paulo for helping so much with the maps. A very warm thank you to Vicente and Francisco from *Anaconda Tours* for a highly enjoyable trip in the Pantanal.

A very big thank you to the staff of the many tourist offices: Vera Sanches and Isabela Serpa from *Brasilia Convention* who helped me not just in Brasilia but all around Brazil; Miriam Cutz of international relations at *TurisRio* for all her assistance throughout the state of Rio; all the staff at *Riotur*; Regina Athayde from *Bahia Tursa* for help during Carnival in Salvador; Igor Dantas from *Natal and Rio Grande do Norte Tourism*; Lilia Silveira and Pedro Lyra from *Fortaleza and Ceara Tourism*; Renan Wanderley from the tourist office in Paraty; Sever Rodrigues from *Recife Tourism*; Tom Falcão and Christopher Pickard from the Brazilian tourist office in London for their help with planning my trip.

Also thanks to Alan Murphy, Ben Box, Felicity Laughton, Debbie Wylde and everyone at Footprint. Sally Shirras and Kathy Kiddle are very much appreciated, as is Rebecca Compton and Fatima Carva for teaching me Portuguese. A special thank you to Michael Platt and also to Robin Eveleigh; Naomi Peirce; Conor O'Sullivan; Mick Day; Marc Starr; Robert and Daisy Kunstaetter and Cherry Austin for their special interest pieces throughout the book.

And finally thanks to the readers who have sent in letters: Ariane Janér for her comments about Rodonia; Cecilia in Campo Grande; Beatrix Boscardin in Curitiba; Olivia van Eegham from Pousada Ventania; Jeroen Hilak; Christopher Brown; Beatrice Stefan; Val Williams; Roberto Neuburger; Dr Marc Kerry; Judith Schnyder; Massimo Passera; David Paul; Christopher Reed; Ned Hopkins; Jeff Rothman; Christoph Wille; Sam Eyde; Roman Leone; David Levy; Evert Vink. Sa Engenharia.

Complete title listing

Footprint publish travel guides to over 120 countries worldwide. Each guide is packed with practical, concise and colourful information for everybody from first-time travellers to travel aficionados. The list is growing fast and current titles are noted below.

Available from all good bookshops

www.footprintbooks.com

(P) denotes pocket Handbook

Latin America & Caribbean

Argentina Handbook
Barbados (P)
Bolivia Handbook
Brazil Handbook
Caribbean Islands Handbook
Central America & Mexico
  Handbook
Chile Handbook
Colombia Handbook
Costa Rica Handbook
Cuba Handbook
Cusco & the Inca Trail Handbook
Dominican Republic Handbook
Ecuador & Galápagos Handbook
Guatemala Handbook
Havana (P)
Mexico Handbook
Nicaragua Handbook
Peru Handbook
Rio de Janeiro Handbook
South American Handbook
Venezuela Handbook

North America

Vancouver (P)
Western Canada Handbook

Africa

Cape Town (P)
East Africa Handbook
Libya Handbook
Marrakech & the High Atlas
  Handbook
Morocco Handbook
Namibia Handbook
South Africa Handbook
Tunisia Handbook
Uganda Handbook

Middle East
Egypt Handbook
Israel Handbook
Jordan Handbook
Syria & Lebanon Handbook

Australasia
Australia Handbook
New Zealand Handbook
Sydney (P)
West Coast Australia Handbook

Asia
Bali Handbook
Bangkok & the Beaches
  Handbook
Cambodia Handbook
Goa Handbook
India Handbook
Indian Himalaya Handbook
Indonesia Handbook
Laos Handbook
Malaysia Handbook
Myanmar (Burma) Handbook
Nepal Handbook
Pakistan Handbook
Rajasthan & Gujarat Handbook
Singapore Handbook
South India Handbook
Sri Lanka Handbook
Sumatra Handbook
Thailand Handbook
Tibet Handbook
Vietnam Handbook

Europe
Andalucía Handbook
Barcelona Handbook
Berlin (P)
Bilbao (P)
Bologna (P)
Copenhagen (P)
Croatia Handbook
Dublin Handbook
Dublin (P)
Edinburgh Handbook
Edinburgh (P)
England Handbook
Glasgow Handbook
Ireland Handbook
London Handbook
Madrid (P)
Naples (P)
Northern Spain Handbook
Paris (P)
Reykjavik (P)
Scotland Handbook
Scotland Highlands & Islands
  Handbook
Spain Handbook
Turkey Handbook

Also available
Traveller's Handbook (WEXAS)
Traveller's Healthbook (WEXAS)
Traveller's Internet Guide (WEXAS)

Footnotes

Keep in touch

Footprint feedback

We try as hard as we can to make each Footprint Handbook as up-to-date and accurate as possible but, of course, things always change. Many people write to us - with corrections, new information, or simply comments.

If you want to let us know about an experience or adventure - hair-raising or mundane, good or bad, exciting or boring or simply something rather special - we would be delighted to hear from you. Please give us as precise information as possible, quoting the edition number (you'll find it on the front cover) and page number of the Handbook you are using.

Your help will be greatly appreciated, especially by other travellers. In return we will send you details about our special guidebook offer. Email Footprint at:
bra3_online@footprintbooks.com

or write to:
Elizabeth Taylor
Footprint Handbooks
6 Riverside Court, Lower Bristol Road
Bath BA2 3DZ UK

www.footprintbooks.com

Dip in and keep on the pulse with what Footprint are up to online.

- Latest Footprint releases
- Entertaining travel articles and news updates
- Extensive destination information for inspiration and trip planning
- Monthly competitions
- Easy ways to buy Footprint guides

What the papers say...

"I carried the South American Handbook from Cape Horn to Cartagena and consulted it every night for two and a half months. I wouldn't do that for anything else except my hip flask."
Michael Palin, BBC Full Circle

My favourite series is the Handbook series published by Footprint and I especially recommend the Mexico, Central and South America Handbooks."
Boston Globe

"If 'the essence of real travel' is what you have been secretly yearning for all these years, then Footprint are the guides for you."
Under 26 magazine

"Who should pack Footprint-readers who want to escape the crowd."
The Observer

"Footprint can be depended on for accurate travel information and for imparting a deep sense of respect for the lands and people they cover."
World News

"The guides for intelligent, independently-minded souls of any age or budget."
Indie Traveller

Mail order
Available worldwide in bookshops and on-line. Footprint travel guides can also be ordered directly from us in Bath, via our website www.footprintbooks.com or from the address on the imprint page of this book.

BRAZILIAN MUSIC IS SO BEAUTIFUL BECAUSE COMPOSERS HAVE THE PERFECT SETTING FOR INSPIRATION.

Coming to Brazil, you can easily understand where all the joy and creativity of its music comes from: all you have to do is open any window. The scenery is soothing to the eyes and a treasure to any photo album.

The best way to discover all these wonders is by boarding a VARIG Boeing 777 flight direct from London Heathrow.

Choose one of VARIG's daily overnight flights and enjoy the unequaled service of 75 years experience and the renowned Brazilian warmth and friendliness

For further information or to make a reservation call your travel agent or VARIG: 0845 603 7601.
www.varig.co.uk

BRAZIL, 500 YEARS OF RHYTHM.

Brazil

	Altitude in metres			Primary Routes
	1000			Main Roads
	500			Minor Roads
	200		BR285	Route Number
	0		◆	National Park
	Neighbouring Country			International Border
				State Border

VENEZUELA

GUYANA

SURI-NAME

GUYANE

COLOMBIA

ECUADOR

Shown at smaller scale

Macapá○

○Belém

Manaus○

○São Luís

Fortaleza○

PERU

Rio Branco○ ○Porto Velho

Natal○
João Pessoa○
Recife○

Maceió○

Aracaju○

Lake Titicaca

BOLIVIA

○Cuiabá

□BRASÍLIA

Goiânia○

Salvador○

PARAGUAY

○Campo Grande

○Belo Horizonte
○Vitória

Rio de Janeiro○

Pacific Ocean

CHILE

○São Paulo

Curitiba○

Florianópolis○

Porto Alegre○

ARGENTINA

URUGUAY

Atlantic Ocean

N

0 km   300
0 miles   300

Map 3

MATO GROSSO

Piúva

Nova Mutum

Arenápolis

Tangará
da Serra

Parque
Nacional
da Chapada
dos Guimarães

*Planalto do
Mato Grosso*

Pontas e
Lacerda

Jangada

Chapada dos
Guimarães

Rio Mortes

Primavera
do este

BR070

Várzea Grande

Cuiabá

Cel Ponce

Alto Coité

Sto Antônio
do Leverger

São Vicente

Cáceres

Poconé

Barão de
Melgaço

Jaciara

Guaratinga

San Matías

Rondonópolis

Diama

Rio Claro

Pixaim

Rio Cuiabá

Rio São Lourenço

BR163

Alto Garças

Itiquíra

Porto Jofre

Pantanal do São Lourenço

Sonora

A

BOLIVIA

B

C

L. Uberaba

ParqueNacional
do Pantanal
Mato Grossense

L. Gaíba

Rio Negro

B. de Castelo

Pantanal do Taquari

Coxim

Silvolândia

Costa

Pl
M

Ar

Pantanal do Rio Negro

Rio Verde de
Mato Grosso

Puerto Suárez

Corumbá

Rio Paraguay

Map 1

MATO GROSSO DO SUL

Morrinho

Porto
Esperança

Guaicurus

Camapuã

Capim Verde

Miranda

Rochedo

Bonfim

Campo
Grande

Bodoquena

Aquidauana

N

0 km   50
0 miles   50

Bonito

Nioaque

Sidrolândia

PN Serra da
Bodoquena

Serra de Bodoquena

Porto
Murtinho

Jardim

Guia Lopes
da Laguna

Serra de Maracaju

Maracaju

Novo
Alvorada

Boqueirão

Cabeceira
do Apá

Itaum

Itaporã

Rio Apá

Bela Vista

Antônio
João

Dourados

BR376

Ivinhema

PARAGUAY

Pedro Juan
Caballero

Ponta Porã

Caarapó

Amambaí   Map 5

1

2

3

Map 5

PARAGUAY

ARGENTINA

URUGUAY

PARANÁ

RIO GRANDE DO SUL

Map 3

Eldorado
Parque Nacional
da Ilha Grande
Mundo Novo
Guaíra
Palotina
Umuarama
Cianorte
Mari
Campo
Mourão
Tern
Jur
Iretama

Toledo
Campina
Represa de
Itaipu
Cascavel
Pitanga

Medeaneira
Parque Nacional
do Iguaçu
Foz do
Iguaçu
Rio Iguaçu
Catanduvas

Laranjeiras
do Sul
Represa de
Salto
Santiago
Guarap

Campo
Eré
Pato
Branco
São Lourenço
d'Oeste
Ho

São Miguel
d'Oeste
Bom Jesus
Xanxeré
SA

Itapiranga
Chapecó
Treze

Federico
Westphalen
Iraí
Concórdia
Joaçaba

Barragem
Passo Fundo
Ereghim
Tupitang

Santa Rosa

Porto Xavier

RIO GRANDE DO SUL

São Luís
Gonzaga
Santo
Ângelo
Carazinho
Passo Fundo
La
Verr

Santo Tomé
Ijuí
BR285

São Borja
São Miguel
das Missões
Cruz Alta

Encruzilhada
Soledade

Itaqui
Santiago

Bento Gonçalves
Far
Garibaldi

Manuel
Viana
Lajeado
Novo Petr

Paso de
las Letras
Alegrete
Santa
María
Candelária
Santa Cruz
do Sul
Novo Hamb
Sapucaia do
São Leopol
Es

Uruguaiana

Barra do
Quaraí
Rio Jacuí
Porto Al

Bella
Unión
Rosário
do Sul
São Gabriel
BR290
Barra d
Ribeiro
BR290

Caçapava
do Sul
Encruzilhada
do Sul
Aguas Brancas
Ta
Le

Santana Do
Livramento
Camaquã

Rivera
Arambaré
Santa Rita
Mosta

Bagé
Canguçu
São
Lourenço
do Sul
Tava
Pa
Nac
Lagod

BR293
Pelotas
Dunas
Boj

Aceguá
Estreito

S José do Norte
Rio Grande

Cassino

Jaguarão
Estação
Ecológica
do Taim
Rio Branco
Laguna
Mirim

Curral Alto
Laguna
Mangabeira

Santa Vitória
do Palmar
Chuí

Ⓐ Ⓑ Ⓒ

① ② ③

For a different view of Europe, take a Footprint